What's What and Who's Who in Europe

What's What and Who's Who in Europe

Harry Drost

CASSELL

Cassell
Wellington House
125 Strand
London WC2R 0BB

387 Park Avenue
New York
NY 10016-8810

First published 1995

British Library Cataloguing-in-Publication Data

A catalogue record for this book is available from
the British Library.

ISBN: 0–304–34117–7 (hardback)
      0–304–34115–0 (paperback)

Typeset by Archetype

Printed and bound in Great Britain by
Mackays of Chatham plc.

What's What and Who's Who in Europe aims to provide concise information on
current affairs in Europe. The information is presented in the form of alphabetically
arranged entries which give basic definitions and background on people, places,
organizations, terms and events in the news. The book is intended to be of use to
students, researchers, journalists and businesspeople, in fact anyone who is interested
in European affairs and needs to get their facts straight. Topicality and accuracy are the
main considerations. There is extensive cross-referencing to ensure accessibility and
ease of use.

The project started from two simple premises: first, that in an increasingly
interdependent world a grasp of international affairs is essential; and second, that too
much discussion of European affairs is based on myths and misunderstandings and not
enough on facts. The starting point was coverage in newspapers, magazines, radio and
television broadcasts and so on. The final selection of items is to some extent a matter
of editorial judgement and inevitably reflects personal interests and preconceptions. I
make no apologies for that, but I do, of course, for any errors that have crept in.

In the course of researching and writing, two patterns emerged that were in constant
tension: on the one hand the great diversity within European society, politics and
culture, based on or derived from the multitude of historical experiences and traditions
that have come to make up Europe; and on the other the sense of a common heritage
passed down from the Roman Empire through Christendom and the Holy Roman
Empire to today's European Union and the notion of a 'common European home'.

The challenge for Europeans, it seems to me, is to respect and preserve this diversity,
channel the creative energies it generates, develop ways of resolving by peaceful
means the conflicts it undeniably also entails, and find a means of embedding it into
Europe-wide structures. I do not have any prescriptions on how this vision is to be
achieved. But I am convinced that awareness and recognition of the diversity of
Europe – in essence, the facts about Europe – is the first, and an essential, step towards
realizing the loftier goals.

What's What and Who's Who in Europe deals with the substratum of facts – dates,
biographical details, institutional structures, economic indicators etc – without which
no understanding of the contemporary world is possible. Interpretation of facts is of
course the stuff of political and historical controversy, but unless the facts are accurate
and agreed, such controversy amounts to no more than a dialogue of the deaf. I am

reminded here of Mark Twain's injunction to 'get the facts first' and his acknowledgement that 'you can always distort them later'. In providing the facts I hope through this
book to contribute to reducing fear of the unknown, breaking down barriers and
broadening understanding.

I would like to thank all the people who have helped in the compilation and
production of *What's What and Who's Who in Europe*. In particular, I am grateful to
Steve Cook for his confidence in the project and his support throughout its realization;
his colleagues at Cassell; Pandora Kerr Frost, who edited and proofread the
manuscript; Ron Clarke and Michael Phillips, who were responsible for design and
layout; Martin Woodroffe and Claire Baldwin, who made many helpful suggestions;
and, for their assistance in gathering information, Roger East, Frances Nicholson and
their colleagues at CIRCA Research and Reference Information, Chris Lailey,
embassies, and the press and information offices of governments, parties and
organizations. I would also like to thank my mother and late father, without whose
assistance and support I could not have undertaken this project.

Details on the book's scope, organization and format are provided on the following
pages.

Harry Drost
London
November 1994

NOTES

Scope

The 'Europe' of this factbook stretches from the Atlantic to the borders of the former Soviet Union, or from Portugal to Poland, Brest to Brest or Dublin to Lublin. It includes the Baltic countries, but not the Commonwealth of Independent States (CIS). The exclusion of the CIS states – most obviously Belorussia, Moldavia, Ukraine and, not least, Russia itself – should not be taken to imply rejection of their claims to be part of a 'common European home'. The reason for the demarcation is largely practical, in that coverage of Russia and the other CIS states would require a book to itself.

Entries broadly fall into the following categories:

(a) people (heads of state, government ministers, party leaders, trade union leaders, heads of international organizations etc);

(b) ethnic, linguistic, religious and other groups;

(c) countries and territories (including official data and information on geography, demography, sociography, infrastructure and communications, economic structure, political structure, security and international affiliations, history);

(d) regions (subdivisions of federal countries, other regions with autonomous status, historical and geographical regions etc);

(e) political organizations (parties, alliances etc);

(f) institutions and agencies (parliaments, government bodies, intelligence agencies etc);

(g) international organizations;

(h) economic and social organizations (central banks, employers' associations, trade-union federations etc);

(i) other non-governmental organizations, bodies and groups with an impact on current affairs;

(j) agreements, treaties, conventions and proposals;

(k) conflicts, disputes, controversies, affairs and scandals;

(l) concepts and terms (technical terms, general terms used in specific contexts or with specific meanings, administrative divisions etc);

(m) titles;

(n) miscellaneous (currencies, flags, anthems, symbols, labels etc).

The primary focus is political in a wide sense. Economic, social, environmental, scientific and cultural affairs are covered only insofar as they have a clear political dimension. In certain categories where coverage needs to be comprehensive (such as countries), entries are effectively self-selecting; but in others, topicality and relevance, in national and/or international terms, has been the decisive criterion for inclusion.

While coverage of people and events in the 'big four' countries – France, Germany, Italy, United Kingdom – is naturally more extensive because they have a greater impact on European affairs, the smaller countries are also given proper weight, not least because they contribute to the continent's diversity. Since coverage is largely news-driven, areas of conflict or turmoil, such as former Yugoslavia, Northern Ireland and the Basque Country, receive extensive coverage.

Two categories of items have been specifically excluded: derogatory terms and labels, which would no doubt make very interesting, and revealing, reading, but which would double the book's size; and terms, items and events which no longer have any relevance today, in particular many related to the communist period in Eastern Europe and the Cold War.

Organization

Each headword, including, where appropriate, the local-language equivalent and abbreviation, is followed by a short general identifier, such as 'Spanish trade-union federation' or 'European Union programme'.

As a rule, substantive information is provided under full English names, not under abbreviations, shorthands or foreign-language equivalents. Extensive cross-referencing has been provided to take account of variations of usage (e.g. translation of party names), spelling, abbreviations etc.

The aim has been to provide consistent and comparable information in the various categories. Thus, all entries on federal states of Germany provide information on demography, economic structure, political situation and history; and all entries on intergovernmental organizations provide information on aims and objectives, membership, structure, history and activities.

Longer entries are usually structured to move from the general to the specific. Thus, entries on major treaties (e.g. Treaty on European Union) provide a general description and background, followed by specific details on contents; and entries on major events (e.g. Bosnian civil war) provide general information followed by a detailed chronology of events.

A key organizational principle has been a 'pyramid' structure, in which the information becomes more detailed as entries become more specific. Thus, information becomes more detailed in a sequence of entries such as European Union – economic and monetary union – convergence criteria.

At the top of the pyramid are, broadly speaking, the entries on the countries and major intergovernmental organizations, which provide overviews, background information, specific references (key institutions, leading trade unions, names of ministers etc), with more detailed information provided under the specific head-words. The country entries can thus be used as starting points for further reading within the book or elsewhere. In reverse, readers may wish to turn from specific entries to the more general country entries, to provide a historical background to a border dispute or political scandal, for instance.

The major country and territory entries are: Albania, Andorra, Austria, Belgium, Bosnia-Herzegovina, Bulgaria, Croatia, Cyprus, Czech Republic, Denmark, Estonia, Faroe Islands, Finland, France, Germany, Gibraltar, Great Britain and Northern Ireland, Greece, Guernsey, Hungary, Iceland, Ireland, Italy, Jersey, Latvia, Liechtenstein, Lithuania, Luxemburg, Macedonia, Malta, Man, Monaco, Netherlands, Northern Cyprus, Norway, Poland, Portugal, Romania, San Marino, Slovakia, Slovenia, Spain, Sweden, Switzerland, Turkey, Vatican City and Yugoslavia. The major intergovernmental organizations are: Conference on Security and Cooperation in Europe (CSCE), Council of Europe, European Economic Area (EEA), European Free Trade Association (EFTA), European Union, Nordic Council of Ministers, North Atlantic Treaty Organization (NATO) and Western European Union (WEU).

Alphabetization

Entries are arranged in alphabetical order on the following basis:
(a) the order follows the English alphabet and ignores capital letters, accents and diacritics;

(b) the ordering is word-by-word and then letter-by-letter;
(c) hyphens and apostrophes are treated as word breaks (e.g. 'D-mark' and 'O'Malley' precede 'Dalli' and 'Occhetto' respectively);
(d) numbers (as in 'B'90', 'M-4') are treated as if written out, except in sequences of entries (e.g. 'UN Security Council Resolution 757' precedes '… 781');
(e) particles in personal names (af, de, von etc) are treated as part of the surname, regardless of national styles (e.g. Hans van den Broek is entered as 'van den Broek, Hans' and Jean-Marie Le Pen as 'Le Pen, Jean-Marie');
(f) articles, prepositions and other particles are treated as part of the entry (e.g. 'European Charter for Regional or Minority Languages' precedes 'European Charter of Local Self-Government');
(g) phrasal names are entered in their full form (e.g. 'Council of Europe', not 'Europe, Council of');
(h) monarchs are listed under their common name (e.g. Harald V, Margrethe II);
(i) when headwords have the same spelling, the order is (i) general topics, (ii) country-related entries, and (iii) international organization entries (e.g. 'Senate' in France 'Senate' in Italy).

Cross-references

Cross-references appear in SMALL CAPITALS. They are provided when the entry referred to expands on or provides specific background to the entry in question. Cross-references are not indicated in the text of the country and other major entries (e.g. 'Italian corruption scandals', 'single internal market') – most of these entries would have to be in small capitals – but specific and general cross-references are provided at the end of the entry. To avoid confusion, country or organization 'flags' are provided where appropriate (e.g. **PS** (Portugal) See SOCIALIST PARTY). Cross-references are also provided in cases where there may be some doubt about where the main entry is located; thus 'TREATY ON EUROPEAN UNION or Maastricht Treaty' means that the item is covered in detail under the 'Treaty on European Union' entry. In some cases an ellipsis (…) is used to save space or when words are repeated.

Style

Bold type is used for headwords (e.g. **Abruzzi**). Italic is used for general foreign words written out in the text (e.g. *fylke*) but not for proper names (e.g. Eduskunta). Small capitals are used for cross-references (e.g. **SV** *See* SOCIALIST LEFT PARTY). Square brackets are used for foreign-language equivalents of English terms and names (e.g. National Assembly [Assemblée Nationale]).

Spelling and transliteration

Modern British spellings are used throughout. In some cases cross-references are given where alternative spellings are common. Capitals have been used sparingly, primarily for institutions (e.g. Federal Chancellery) but not for functions and personal titles (e.g. federal chancellor).

All appropriate letters, accents and diacritics are indicated in non-English words.

Plurals of foreign-language terms are -s unless otherwise indicated.

Transliterations of non-Latin alphabets (i.e. Bulgarian, Greek, Macedonian and Serb) follow generally agreed conventions. In some cases cross-references are given where alternative spellings are common.

Abbreviations

The following abbreviations are used:

AD	anno Domini
BC	before Christ
CIS	Commonwealth of Independent States
EC	European Community
e.g.	for example
esp.	especially
etc	and so on
EU	European Union
excl.	excluding
GDP	gross domestic product
GNP	gross national product
i.e.	that is
incl.	including
km	kilometres
n.a.	not applicable or not available
NATO	North Atlantic Treaty Organization
pl.	plural
sing.	singular
sq km	square kilometres
UN	United Nations
US	United States
US$	US dollar

Two symbols have been used, % and =; the latter defines or gives a broad equivalent for a particular term, as in 'Swiss Federal Council (= government)'.

Currencies

Money amounts are generally expressed in national currencies, with an equivalent in ecus provided in brackets. GNP per head and other international indicators are expressed in US dollars, their usual format.

As at 31 October 1994 the following exchange rates applied:

1 ecu = US$ 1.27	US$ 1	= 0.79 ecus
1 ecu = £ 0.78	£ 1	= 1.28 ecus = $ 1.63
1 ecu = DM 1.92	DM 1	= 0.52 ecus = $ 0.66
1 ecu = FF 6.56	FF 1	= 0.15 ecus = $ 0.19
1 ecu = L 1971	L 1,000	= 0.51 ecus = $ 0.64
1 ecu = Ptas 160	Ptas 100	= 0.63 ecus = $ 0.80
1 ecu = *f* 2.15	*f* 1	= 0.47 ecus = $ 0.59
1 ecu = Bfr 39.4	Bfr 100	= 0.25 ecus = $ 0.32
1 ecu = Skr 9.16	Skr 1	= 0.11 ecus = $ 0.14
1 ecu = Sfr 1.59	Sfr 1	= 0.63 ecus = $ 0.80
1 ecu = ¥ 123	¥ 100	= 0.81 ecus = $ 1.03

Terms

As always, terminology is a minefield. Political labels such as *centre-right*, *right-wing* and *far-right* are of course a matter of interpretation, and may even be a source of confusion when used in the context of post-communist Eastern Europe. Broadly speaking, the *right/left* scale has been used to identify a party's economic policies, ranging from a commitment to free-market policies to state intervention, and the *conservative/ liberal* scale has been used to indicate views on social issues such as abortion and law and order. Terms such as christian democratic (= centre-right), social democratic and socialist (= centre-left or left-wing) are assumed to be understood, unless a party's outlook diverges from this pattern (e.g. the centre-right Social Democratic Party of Portugal). *Ethnic* is used in a wide sense to refer to common ties based on language, religion, culture, nationality, 'race' etc; such ties are often a matter of self-identification, which has been recognized in this factbook. *European Union* and *EU* have been used throughout to refer to the organization as a whole, even when, in certain circumstances, it is technically correct to use 'European Community' or 'EC' (as in 'EU law', which should formally be 'EC law' since the EU does not have legal personality). It was felt that to distinguish between EC/EU along these lines would only add to the already widespread confusion on nomenclature. (For the precise relationship between the two organizations, see the entry on the European Union.) Unless otherwise indicated, *Ireland* means the Republic of Ireland and *British* refers to the United Kingdom. *Billion* means 1,000 million and *trillion* means 1,000 billion. The United Nations Development Programme's *human development index* (referred to in the country entries) aims to measure a country's standard of living on the basis of real income per head, life expectancy and educational attainment. *Gross national product* means gross domestic product plus international transfers.

Terms of abuse and ambivalent terms such as 'fascist', 'racist' and 'terrorist' have been avoided in this book.

When headwords are described as a *shorthand* or a *common name* for another term (e.g. 'European Convention of Human Rights' as a shorthand for the 'European Convention for the Protection of ... '), their use is widely accepted and acceptable in formal writing or speaking. Those defined as an *informal name* (e.g. 'Eastern Europe Bank' as an informal name for the 'European Bank for Reconstruction and Development', EBRD) should not be used in formal contexts.

Sources
A wide range of source material has been used in the compilation of this factbook. This includes the *Europa World Yearbook* (1993 and 1994), *Keesing's Record of World Events* (a monthly news digest prepared by CIRCA Research and Reference Information for Cartermill), the *Britannica World Data* (1993 and 1994), the *International Who's Who* (1993/94 and 1994/95) and other reference works on European and world affairs; information from the Reuters and Associated Press newswires, the *Neue Zürcher Zeitung*, *Le Monde*, *The Guardian*, *The Economist*, *Der Spiegel*, the BBC's Summary of World Broadcasts and other newspapers, magazines etc; and information from embassies, government press offices, parties and organizations.

The information in the country entries (on infrastructure, economic structure etc) has been compiled from the above sources. No specific date references are given to save space and because the data are intended primarily to indicate the general situation in a country and to allow international comparisons. Broadly speaking, population figures are from 1993, economic performance figures (GDP growth, inflation, unemployment) cover the period up to the end of 1993; foreign-trade figures are from 1992 and 1993 and in some cases 1991; sociography, infrastructure and communications figures are from 1991, 1992 or 1993; the human development index ratings are from 1992. The use of 'around', as in 'there are around 1.5 million television sets', indicates that the figure is an estimate. In some cases (e.g. student enrolment in Albania), official statistics may not be a true reflection of the present situation.

Cut-off date
Every effort has been made to ensure that material is up-to-date to the end of August 1994. It has also been possible to cover some events in September and October.

A Abbreviation for Austria, used for international vehicle registrations, postal addresses etc.

A (Iceland) *See* SOCIAL DEMOCRATIC PARTY.

A *See* NORWEGIAN LABOUR PARTY.

A *See* SOCIAL DEMOCRATIC LABOUR PARTY OF SWEDEN.

A Cuncolta *See* NATIONALIST COUNCIL.

AA Abbreviation for Auswärtiges Amt ('Foreign Office'), the German foreign ministry.

AAC *See* ATLANTIC ARC COMMISSION.

Aaland Islands *See* ÅLAND ISLANDS.

Ab *See* PEOPLE'S ALLIANCE.

abatement In the European Union (EU), the mechanism whereby a member state receives back a proportion of its budget contribution to correct a situation in which it pays in far more than it receives in grants etc. It is usually referred to as a 'budgetary compensation' or 'budget rebate'. The United Kingdom has received an annual rebate of around two-fifths to compensate it for the fact that, with a relatively small and efficient agricultural industry, it does not greatly benefit from the Common Agricultural Policy (CAP), traditionally the largest single budget item. The amount of the rebate is calculated by a set formula.

Abdić, Fikret (1940–) Bosnian businessman and politician. He built up the Agrokomerc company, based in the Bihać region of Bosnia, into Yugoslavia's largest food-processing concern in the 1980s. He held senior posts in the League of Communists at this time, but was expelled from the party after being accused of corruption in 1987. He was detained for nearly two years but eventually acquitted. In 1990 he was elected to parliament for the Muslim Democratic Action Party (SDA) and to Bosnia's collective State Presidency. After the outbreak of the civil war in March 1992 he established himself as the political leader of the Muslim-majority Bihać region, which was surrounded by Serb-held areas. Increasingly critical of what he saw as the central government's intransigence in the face of the 'new situation' created by the civil war, he proclaimed the Autonomous Province of Western Bosnia in September 1993 and was elected its president and leader of the new Muslim Democratic Party (MDS). He was then dismissed from the State Presidency. When the rebellion collapsed in August 1994, he fled to Serb-held territory.

Abete, Luigi (1947–) Italian businessman and employers' representative. He is president of the family printing and publishing concern ABETE. He has been on the board of the General Confederation of Italian Industry (CONFINDUSTRIA) since 1978. He became its director of research in 1985 and was elected vice-president in 1988 and president in May 1992.

Abgeordnetenhaus ('House of Representatives') Parliament of Berlin, a federal state of Germany.

Abrene question Border dispute between Latvia and Russia. The Abrene district in the northeast was ceded to Russia in 1944, four years after Latvia's annexation by the Soviet Union. It is now part of Pytalovo district.

Abruzzi Autonomous region of Italy. Situated in the east along the Adriatic Sea, Abruzzi has an area of 10,794 sq km and a population of 1,249,000. The capital is L'Aquila, and the other main city is Pescara. The economy is based on agriculture (livestock farming, cereals), tourism and light industry. Part of the MEZZOGIORNO, Abruzzi is one of the country's poorer regions. It became part of the Kingdom of Naples in the 12th century and was incorporated into unified Italy in 1860.

ABVV *See* GENERAL LABOUR FEDERATION OF BELGIUM.

ACE *See* ALLIED COMMAND EUROPE.

ACE Rapid Reaction Corps *See* ALLIED COMMAND EUROPE RAPID ....

Açores *See* AZORES.

acquis communautaire ('Community patrimony' in French) or **Community acquis** In the European Community (EC) and now the European Union (EU), the body of existing laws, regulations etc. It comprises all the decisions of the Council of Ministers and the Commission under

1

the Treaty of Rome and its amendments and all relevant case law of the Court of Justice. Countries joining the EU are expected to accept the *acquis communautaire* – the French term is normally used – and to amend national legislation to accord with it.

acquis politique ('political patrimony' in French) or **political acquis** In the European Union (EU), the body of decisions, resolutions and views adopted by the member states in the field of foreign policy. Such issues were discussed initially within the framework of European Political Cooperation (EPC) and now the Common Foreign and Security Policy (CFSP). As with '*acquis communautaire*', the French term is normally used.

Act of Stockholm *See* STOCKHOLM DOCUMENT.

Action Committee for Democracy and Pension Justice [Aktiounskomitee fir Demokratie a Rentegerechtegkeet (Letzeburgish), Comité d'Action pour la Démocratie et la Réforme des Pensions (French)] (ADR) Luxemburg political organization. Founded in 1989 as the Five-Sixths Action Committee, this was originally a single-issue pressure group calling for the extension of pensions worth five-sixths of final salary to all citizens of retirement age. (This benefit is currently available only to civil servants.) It now seeks to defend the interests of the elderly in general. At the June 1994 election it gained 7.0% of the vote and 5/60 seats. The leader is Robert Mehlen.

ACV *See* CONFEDERATION OF CHRISTIAN TRADE UNIONS.

AD *See* DEMOCRATIC ALLIANCE.

Adams, Gerry (1948–) British and Irish politician. He was active in the civil-rights movement in Northern Ireland, aimed at securing equal rights for Catholics, in the late 1960s. An advocate of the province's reunification with Ireland and suspected of being a member of the Irish Republican Army (IRA), he was detained by the British authorities on several occasions in the 1970s. He was elected leader of the left-wing nationalist Sinn Féin in November 1983. He has been a member of the Northern Ireland Assembly (1982

until its abolition in 1986) and the British House of Commons (1983–92), but in line with party policy he did not take his seat in either body.

additionality In the European Union (EU), the principle that EU grants and other financial assistance to regions and projects in the member states should be in addition to, rather than as a substitute for, funding normally provided by national governments.

AdI *See* ALLIANCE OF INDEPENDENTS.

ADLV *See* ASSOCIATION OF VATICAN LAY WORKERS.

ADR *See* ACTION COMMITTEE FOR DEMOCRACY AND PENSION JUSTICE.

Adunarea Deputaţilor *See* ASSEMBLY OF DEPUTIES.

Aegean Sea question Border dispute between Greece and Turkey concerning the delimitation of territorial waters and, by extension, airspace jurisdiction. The Aegean Sea is a branch of the Mediterranean Sea. Most of its numerous islands have been part of Greece since the 1910s, and sovereignty over them is not in question. Under arrangements in force since the 1923 Treaty of Lausanne, based on a six-mile territorial sea limit, Greece controls just over a third of the Aegean Sea and Turkey just under a tenth, with the remainder considered international waters. Since the early 1970s Greece, citing changes in international law, has claimed the right to extend its territorial waters from six to 12 miles. In essence Turkey disputes the Greek definition of the continental shelf surrounding the islands – some of which lie within sight of the Turkish coast – on which the claim is based. (International rulings and conventions on continental-shelf rights are highly complex and open to varying interpretations.) Turkey has said that unilateral action by Greece would constitute a cause for war. In March 1987 both countries declared a state of military alert during a dispute over oil-drilling rights in the northern Aegean. The Aegean dispute is one of several sources of friction between the two countries, which are nominally allies within the North Atlantic Treaty Organization (NATO) but whose relations have been strained since Greece gained its independence from the Ottoman Empire in the 1820s. Progress on its resolution has been hampered by the long-standing problem of Cyprus, home to Greek Cypriot and Turkish Cypriot communities and effectively divided since 1974.

AER *See* ASSEMBLY OF EUROPEAN REGIONS.

af Ugglas, Margaretha (Baroness af Ugglas) (1939–) Swedish journalist and politician. From 1968–74 she worked as a leader writer on the *Svenska Dagbladet*, a leading daily newspaper, and then became publisher of a major periodical. She was elected to parliament for the centre-right Moderate Coalition Party (MS) in 1973 and became the party's foreign-affairs spokeswoman. She was appointed foreign minister in the centre-right coalition formed in October 1991.

AFD *See* ALLIANCE OF FREE DEMOCRATS.

AG Alp *See* ASSOCIATION OF THE CENTRAL ALPS.

AGALEV *See* LIVE DIFFERENTLY.

Ágion Óros *See* HOLY MOUNTAIN.

Agrarian Democratic Party of Romania [Partidul Democrat Agrar din România] (PDAR) Romanian political party. Founded in 1990, the PDAR is a right-wing party supportive of farmers' interests and committed to modernization of the agricultural sector. Many of its leading members belonged to the Communist Party during the Ceauşescu period (1965–89). At the September 1992 election it narrowly failed to secure the 3% of the vote required for representation in the Assembly of Deputies, but gained 3.3% and 5/128 seats in the vote for the Senate. The leader is Victor Surdu.

Agrarian Party [Zemědělská Strana] (ZS) Czech political party. Founded in 1990, the ZS is a centrist party which acts primarily as a voice for farming interests. It gained 3.8% of the vote in the June 1990 election and contested the June 1992 election within the LIBERAL SOCIAL UNION (LSU) alliance. The leader is Jiří Vackár.

Agreement on Social Policy or Social Agreement International agreement adopted within the framework of the European Union (EU). The Social Agreement – also known informally as the Social Chapter or Social Protocol – provides the framework for implementing specific measures under the CHARTER OF THE FUNDAMENTAL SOCIAL RIGHTS OF WORKERS or Social Charter, approved by all member states except the United Kingdom in December 1989. Since the British government was also opposed to including similar social provisions in the Treaty on European Union, it was agreed, in an unprecedented move, to remove the entire chapter on social policy and turn it into a separate intergovernmental agreement among the other 11 member states. It is thus formally an annex to the Maastricht Treaty, concluded in December 1991 and in force since November 1993. Under another annex to the Treaty, the Protocol on Social Policy, it was also agreed that the 11 states would use the institutions, procedures and mechanisms of the European Union to implement the Agreement. (Decisions on social policy thus effectively remain within the EU's supranational framework, except that the United Kingdom does not take part in the deliberations and is not bound by any decisions.) Article 1 of the Agreement defines the objective of social policy as 'the promotion of employment, improved living and working conditions, proper social protection, dialogue between management and labour, and the development of human resources with a view to lasting high employment and the combating of exclusion'. It establishes a set of basic rights in the fields of health and safety, working conditions, information and consultation of workers, equality between men and women, and integration of persons excluded from the labour market. Decisions are generally by qualified majority (i.e. broadly two-thirds); unanimity is required in the areas of social security, social protection of workers, protection of redundant workers, representation and the collective defence of the interests of workers and employers (including co-determination), conditions of employment for third-country nationals, and financial contributions for job creation. Issues related to pay, the right of association, the right to strike and the right to impose lockouts are specifically excluded from the Agreement.

Agreement on the European Economic Area or **EEA Agreement** International agreement adopted by the member states of the European Union (EU) and the European Free Trade Association (EFTA) establishing a single market, the EUROPEAN ECONOMIC AREA (EEA). Signed on 2 May 1992 and effective from 1 January 1994, it essentially provides for the extension of the EU's single market, inaugurated at the start of 1993, to the EFTA states. The latter undertake to incorporate the EU's accumulated legislation on the free movement of goods, services, people and capital – some 1,700 separate decisions and regulations – into their national laws. There are several exceptions and transitional arrangements to the so-called 'four freedoms', particularly regarding agriculture and fisheries. The Agreement also provides for cooperation in spheres of importance to the operation of the single market, such as social policy, consumer protection and the environment, as well as other spheres, including research and education. It sets up various joint institutions, in particular the Joint Committee of government representatives, which deals with any disputes concerning its interpretation and application.

Agreement on the Protection of the Alps or **Alps Convention** International agreement. The Convention was signed by Austria, France, Germany, Italy, Liechtenstein and Switzerland in November 1991 and subsequently by Slovenia, the seven states with territory in the Alps, Europe's most extensive mountain system. It provides a framework for the adoption of protocols on minimum standards in the spheres of environmental protection, physical planning, tourism, transport, economic development and exploitation of natural resources. The specific agreements will be binding but must be adopted by unanimity.

Agriculture Council Institution of the European Union (EU), a specialist meeting of the agriculture ministers within the framework of the COUNCIL OF THE EUROPEAN UNION or Council of Ministers, the organization's main decision-making body.

Agusta affair Controversy in Belgium concerning allegations that senior members of the Walloon Socialist Party (PS) accepted kickbacks from an Italian aircraft manufacturer, Agusta, after it won a government arms contract in 1988 worth 12 billion francs (304 million ecus) for 46 military helicopters. Evidence of bribery was uncovered by the magistrate investigating the murder of André Cools, another senior PS figure, in 1991 (*see* COOLS CASE). Her report, leaked to the media in January 1994, said that the awarding of the contract was 'tainted with illegal acts and forgery'. Although it contained no specific evidence of payments, it implicated Guy Coëme, federal deputy prime minister and defence minister in 1988; Guy Spitaels, head of the Wallonian regional government and party leader in 1988; and Guy Mathot, interior minister in Wallonia. (The affair was subsequently dubbed the 'three Guys affair'.) All three denied any wrongdoing but resigned from their respective offices. Parliament then lifted their immunity from prosecution so that they could be questioned by a specially appointed magistrate.

Ahern, Bertie (1951–) Irish accountant and politician. He worked at a Dublin hospital until his election to parliament for the centre-right Fianna Fáil in 1977. Briefly a junior minister in 1982, he was appointed labour minister when the party returned to power in 1987 and became finance minister in November 1991.

Aho, Esko (1954–) Finnish politician. Leader of the youth wing of the Centre Party (KESK) from 1974–80, he was elected to parliament in 1983. He was elected party leader in July 1990 and became prime minister of a centre-right coalition in April 1991.

Ahtisaari, Martti (1937–) Finnish teacher, diplomat and politician. A specialist on development issues and Africa, he held senior posts in the foreign ministry from 1965–73, 1984–86 and 1991–93 and was Finland's ambassador to Tanzania from 1973–77. He served as

4

the United Nations commissioner for Namibia from 1977–81, was the UN secretary-general's special representative for Namibia from 1978–86 and oversaw the country's transition to independence from South Africa in 1989–90. He was also a UN undersecretary-general from 1987–91, responsible for administration and management. Nominated by the Finnish Social Democratic Party (SDP), he was elected president of Finland in January/February 1994 and was sworn in for a six-year term in March.

Ahvenanmaa *See* ÅLAND ISLANDS.

AIC *See* FEDERATION OF CANARY ISLANDS INDEPENDENT GROUPS.

air-exclusion zone or **no-fly zone** In Bosnia-Herzegovina, the ban on military flights in the country's airspace imposed by the United Nations as part of its efforts to end the civil war between Muslims, Serbs and Croats. It was adopted by the Security Council in October 1992 (under Resolution 781), but not implemented until April 1993, when the Council asked the North Atlantic Treaty Organization (NATO) to provide forces to conduct air patrols and deal with violations of the ban. It was enforced for the first time in February 1994, when four Serb planes were shot down over Novi Travnik. (This was also NATO's first combat action in its 45-year history.) *See also* BOSNIAN CIVIL WAR.

Aitken, Jonathan (1942–) British journalist, businessman and politician. He was a foreign correspondent for the London *Evening Standard* from 1966–71 and director of TV-am, a major television franchise, from 1981–88. Elected to Parliament for the Conservative Party in 1974, he became a junior defence minister in 1992. In July 1994 he was appointed chief secretary to the Treasury, a post with Cabinet rank with responsibility for public spending.

Ajuria Enea Pact [Pacto de Ajuria Enea] Agreement in Spain among all but one of the main parties in the Basque Country on the principles of political activity. Signed in January 1988, it rejects the use of violence as a means of determining the region's future and accepts the Statute of Guernica, which established the Basque Country as an autonomous community in 1979, as the basis for 'realizing Basque aspirations'. The party outside the consensus is People's Unity (Herri Batasuna, HB), which advocates full independence for the region and has close links with Basque Homeland and Liberty (ETA), the main separatist guerrilla group. The agreement takes its name from the seat of the Basque government.

Akashi, Yasushi (1931–) Japanese diplomat. He has worked for or at the United Nations (UN) since 1957. Initially a political affairs officer, he was a member of the Japanese mission to the UN from 1974–79 and was appointed a UN undersecretary-general in 1979, responsible for information until 1987 and for disarmament affairs until 1992. He then headed the UN Transitional Authority in Cambodia (UNTAC), set up to supervise an agreement to end the civil war in that country. In December 1993 he was made the UN secretary-general's special representative for former Yugoslavia. As such he has been closely involved in the international effort to end the civil war in Bosnia-Herzegovina and provide humanitarian relief.

AKEL *See* PROGRESSIVE PARTY OF WORKING PEOPLE.

Akrotiri and Dhekelia British military bases in Cyprus. They were retained by the United Kingdom as 'sovereign base areas' under the 1959 London Agreement granting independence to Cyprus. Their total area is 256 sq km and 4,100 troops are stationed there. They are used as training and staging areas and have extensive information-gathering facilities. They also provide support to the United Nations Peace-Keeping Force in Cyprus (UNFICYP).

AL Abbreviation for Albania, used for international vehicle registrations, postal addresses etc.

Åland Islands [Åland (Swedish), Ahvenanmaa (Finnish)] Autonomous province of Finland. Situated in the Gulf of Bothnia between mainland Finland and Sweden, the Åland Islands consist of around 6,500 islands, of which around 80 are inhabited.

5

The province has an area of 1,527 sq km and a population of 25,000. Nearly all the people are ethnic Swedes, and Swedish is the official language. The capital is Mariehamn [Maarianhamina (Finnish)]. The economy is based on tourism, agriculture and fishing. The islands have extensive autonomy over local affairs, including education and economic policy. Political power is exercised by the 30-member Provincial Assembly [Landsting], an executive council, and a provincial governor appointed by the Finnish government. The Åland Islands formed part of Sweden until 1809, when along with Finland they were ceded to Russia. When Finland became independent in 1917 the islanders demanded reunification with Sweden. After mediation by the League of Nations, Finnish sovereignty was confirmed in 1921 and the islands were granted wide-ranging autonomy. This was further extended in 1951 and 1991.

Albania [Shqipëria] Country in southeastern Europe.

Official data. Name: Republic of Albania [Republika e Shqipërisë]; capital: Tirana [Tiranë]; form of government: parliamentary republic; head of state: president; head of government: prime minister; flag: red with the state emblem (a black double-headed eagle) in the centre; national holiday: 28 November (Independence Day); language: Albanian; religion: none; currency: lek (L) (pl. -ë) = 100 qindarka; abbreviation: AL.

Geography. The smallest of the Balkan countries, Albania has an area of 28,748 sq km. It is bordered by Yugoslavia in the north and east, Macedonia in the east, Greece in the south, and the Adriatic Sea and Ionian Sea in the west; a neighbouring country across the sea is Italy. The terrain is largely mountainous, with a narrow coastal plain and hills in the centre. Some 25% of the land is arable, another 15% is covered by pastures and 38% is forested. The climate is mediterranean, with hot summers and cool winters; rainfall is heavy; temperatures are generally lower and rainfall heavier in the mountains.

Demography. Albania has a population of 3,422,000. The birth rate (25 births per 1,000 people per year) and the population growth rate (2.0% per year) are the highest in Europe. Population density is 126 per sq km (land area). With 35% of the people living in urban areas, Albania is the least urbanized country in Europe. The main city is Tirana; other centres are Durrës, Elbasan, Shkodër and Vlorë. The 1989 census, which showed that 98.0% of the population was ethnically Albanian, significantly underrepresented the size of the ethnic minorities, the largest of which is the Greek community in the south, estimated to number around 125,000 (5% of the total population). There are also small numbers of Gipsies, Vlachs, Macedonians and Montenegrins. There are large Albanian communities in neighbouring Yugoslavia (around 1.5 million in the Kosovo region) and Macedonia (400–600,000) as well as smaller groups in Greece and Italy. Since 1991 there has been substantial emigration, primarily to the United States, Germany and Greece. The main language is Albanian, spoken in two distinct dialects, Geg in the north and Tosk in the south. In religious terms around 65% of the people are nominally Sunni Muslim, 20% Greek Orthodox and 13% Roman Catholic.

Sociography. Albania scores 0.714 on the United Nations human development index (HDI), ranking 76th in the world and last among 32 European countries. Education is compulsory between the ages of seven and 15. There is one teacher for every 19 students. Enrolment is around 30% at the secondary level and around 5% at the tertiary level. The literacy rate is 85%, the lowest in Eastern Europe. Real annual income per head (in terms of purchasing power) is around US$ 3,500, the lowest in Europe.

Infrastructure and communications. Albania's transport and communications network is by far the least developed in Europe; especially the road and telecommunications systems in the rural areas are more limited than in many developing countries. There are 6,680 km of paved roads and 16,000 passenger cars (1 per

210 people); private car ownership was banned during communist rule. There are 680 km of railways and 43 km of navigable waterways. The main port is Durrës. The main airport is at Tirana (Rinas). There are two daily newspapers, with a combined circulation of 135,000 (42 per 1,000 people). There are 525,000 radio receivers, 325,000 television sets and 52,600 telephones in use (respectively 159, 102 and 16 per 1,000 people).

Economic structure. The Albanian economy is largely based on agriculture and food processing, with mining and manufacturing of secondary importance. The least developed in Europe, it is in need of major investment and restructuring and has a highly inefficient distribution system. The collapse of communist rule in 1990 and the transition from a command to a market-based economy initiated subsequently is causing severe dislocation and has led to steep falls in industrial and agricultural production as well as food and energy shortages. The economy virtually collapsed in 1990, when GDP fell by 42%. Since then growth has resumed, inflation has been very high but falling (to 20% by the end of 1993), the currency has lost seven-eighths of its value, the current account has remained in deficit, and unemployment has risen to around 50% (unofficial estimate).

Services contribute 16% of GDP, industry 48% (manufacturing around 35%, mining around 5%), and agriculture and forestry 36%. Some 47% of the labour force is employed in farming, 23% in manufacturing and 7% in construction. The main crops grown are cereals (wheat, maize), sugarbeets, tobacco and potatoes; horticulture (fruit and vegetables, esp. olives and grapes), livestock raising (sheep, goats, cattle, poultry) and dairy farming are other important agricultural activities. Forestry is also important. The main mineral resources are chromium, oil, lignite, copper and nickel; Albania is the world's seventh-largest producer of chromium ore; minerals are the major source of foreign exchange. The main industry is food processing; other branches are textiles, metalworking, building materials, wood processing and oil refining. The main energy sources are hydroelectric power and fossil fuels; Albania is a net exporter of fuels. The main exports are chromium, oil and other minerals and metals (47% of the total) and foodstuffs (esp. fruit) (20%). The main imports are machinery and transport equipment, foodstuffs and miscellaneous manufactures. The main trading partners are: exports: Italy (22%), Germany (17%), Greece (9%), Japan (6%); imports: Italy (21%), Germany (13%), France (11%); half of all trade is with European Union (EU) countries. Net invisible earnings (remittances from Albanians living and working abroad, development assistance) account for around a fifth of GNP.

The Albanian State Bank [Bankë e Shtëtit Shqiptar] is the central bank. There are as yet no employers' associations of note; the main labour organizations are the Union of Independent Trade Unions of Albania (BSPSh) and the Trade Union Confederation of Albania (KSSh).

Political structure. Albania is a republic on the basis of an interim constitution adopted in 1991, replacing the communist constitution of 1976. Executive power is shared by the president, the head of state, and the government. The president is elected for a five-year term by a two-thirds majority of the legislature; barred from holding party office, s/he is commander of the armed forces, appoints the prime minister and has several other powers. Legislative power is vested in the People's Assembly [Kuvend Popullor], whose 140 members are elected for a four-year term by a mixed system of majority voting and proportional representation (with a 3% threshold for gaining seats). All citizens over the age of 18 are entitled to vote. Judicial power is ultimately vested in the Supreme Court [Gyikata e Lartë], whose 15 members are appointed for a four-year term by the legislature. Administratively the country is divided into 26 districts [rreth, pl. -ët], including the district-level city of Tirana; the districts are subdivided into 3,315 towns and villages.

The main political parties are the Democratic Party of Albania (PDSh), Socialist Party of Albania (PSSh, the successor to the communist Party of Labour, PPSh), Democratic Alliance Party of Albania (PADSh, a breakaway from the PDSh), Social Democratic Party of Albania (PSDSh), Party for the Protection of Human Rights (PMDN) or Human Rights Union (EAD) and Republican Party of Albania (PRSh). At the general election in March 1992 the PDSh gained 62.1% of the vote and 92/140 seats, the PSSh 25.7% and 38 seats, the PSDSh 4.4% and seven seats, the EAD 2.9% and two seats, and the PRSh 1.8% and one seat. The government is formed by a centre-right coalition of the PDSh, PSDSh and PRSh, with Aleksandër Meksi as prime minister. Other senior ministers are Bashkim Kopliku (deputy prime minister), Alfred Serreqi (foreign affairs), Pirro Dishnica (finance), Kudret Çela (justice) and Safet Zhulali (defence). The head of state is President Sali Berisha, who was elected in April 1992.

Security and international affiliations. The Albanian armed forces number 73,000 (army 60,000, navy 2,000, airforce 11,000). There are also several paramilitary forces, with a combined strength of 16,000. Military service is compulsory and consists of 18 months' basic training.

Albania is a member of the Black Sea Economic Cooperation Organization (BSECO) and the Conference on Security and Cooperation in Europe (CSCE), as well as the Islamic Conference Organization and the United Nations and its specialized agencies.

History. Settled by Illyrians, the area of modern Albania was conquered by the Romans in the 2nd and 1st centuries BC. It was allocated to the Eastern Roman or Byzantine Empire in AD 395. Between the 4th and the 7th centuries successive invasions of the Balkan region by Visigoths, Ostrogoths, Huns and Slavic peoples triggered major population movements and depleted the Illyrians. Many sought refuge in the relatively inaccessible mountains of Albania. Between the 8th and the 14th centuries the country was divided into many small principalities, with foreign powers – Byzantium, Bulgaria, Serbia, Epirus, Naples/Sicily and Venice – competing for control over the strategic coastline in particular. From the late 14th century the Ottoman Turks gradually subjected the principalities. The Albanians launched a rebellion against Turkish rule in 1443 under the leadership of Gjergj Kastrioti (also called Skanderbeg). It collapsed after his death in 1468, and by 1501 the Turks had reasserted control. During the five centuries of Ottoman rule the country declined economically and a majority of the population converted to Islam. Central authority was generally weak in the later period, so that local governors had considerable powers, which they frequently exercised arbitrarily.

The 19th century saw the emergence of an Albanian national consciousness. After forty years of agitation, Albania declared its independence from Turkey in 1912. It was occupied by various foreign armies, however, and full sovereignty was not achieved until the major European powers and all its neighbours recognized Albania in 1921. After a brief period of democratic government Ahmet Zogu took power in 1924 and proclaimed himself King Zog I in 1928. In 1939 the Italian army invaded Albania and forced Zog to abdicate in favour of the Italian king. After Italy's surrender in the Second World War (1939–45) German troops occupied Albania in 1943 but were soon pushed into retreat by various resistance groups. The communist-dominated guerrillas emerged the victors in a civil war being waged at the same time.

Albania was proclaimed a 'people's republic' in 1946 under what became the Party of Labour (PPSh). Led by Enver Hoxha, the regime suppressed all dissent and, stressing 'self-reliance', pursued rigidly orthodox marxist-leninist economic policies and an increasingly isolationist foreign policy (giving rise to the term 'albanianization'). It broke off all relations with the Soviet Union in 1961 and with China, its only remaining ally, in 1978, and did not participate in any

Europe-wide organizations. Hoxha died in April 1985 and was succeeded by Ramiz Alia. Although strongly opposed to the demands for reform that led to the collapse of communist rule in the other Eastern European countries in 1989, the government was forced to concede reforms as popular unrest grew in 1990. It implemented economic changes, committed itself to respect for human rights, abandoned its isolationist foreign policy (establishing diplomatic relations with all its neighbours), lifted travel restrictions and legalized opposition parties. The renamed Socialist Party (PSSh) won the multiparty election in March/April 1991, the first since the 1920s. An interim constitution adopted in April guaranteed fundamental rights and established a pluralist system of government. An all-party coalition was formed in June 1991, but collapsed in December in the face of industrial unrest and calls for more extensive reforms. The economy, already the least developed in Europe, went into steep decline. Albania joined the Conference on Security and Cooperation in Europe (CSCE) in June 1991. The centre-right Democratic Party (PDSh) led by Sali Berisha won the early election in March 1992. The new government committed itself to radical economic reform, including price liberalization, land reform and comprehensive privatization, and the restoration of law and order. The economy showed some signs of recovery in 1993. Relations with Greece, Macedonia and Yugoslavia deteriorated over the treatment of the Greek minority in southern Albania, the Albanian minority, and the Albanians in Kosovo province respectively.

See also entries on specific institutions, organizations, parties, people, terms etc.

albanianization The voluntary political and economic self-isolation by a country. The term derives from the 'self-reliance' pursued by the orthodox communist regime in power in Albania from 1944–91. The policy led to the country's growing isolation, initially from non-communist countries, then from its Eastern European communist allies in the 1960s, and finally from its last remaining ally, China, in the late 1970s.

Alberdi, Cristina (1946–) Spanish lawyer and politician. She practised law from 1975 and was also appointed by parliament to the supervisory General Council of Judicial Power (CGPJ) in 1985. In July 1993 she was appointed minister of social affairs in the minority government formed by the Spanish Socialist Workers' Party (PSOE). She is not a member of the party.

Albero, Vicente (1944–) Spanish businessman, civil servant and politician. Before entering politics he was director of the Aznar textile company. Elected to parliament for the Spanish Socialist Workers' Party (PSOE) in 1986, he has held several senior administrative and political posts in the ministry of agriculture, food and fisheries and was appointed its minister in July 1993. He resigned in May 1994 after admitting he had failed to pay tax on investment income.

Albert II (1934–) King of Belgium. He became king in August 1993 after the death the previous month of his brother, Baudouin, who had no children. He is married to an Italian princess, now Queen Paola. They have three children.

alcalde Spanish local government official, usually translated as 'mayor'. Elected by the municipal council [ayuntamiento], the *alcalde* is its head and has considerable executive powers. In the past the office also comprised judicial functions, but these have largely been removed.

Alderdice, John (1955–) British doctor and politician. He worked in several hospitals in his native Northern Ireland from 1978–87. He is also a qualified psychiatrist. In October 1987 he was elected leader of the Alliance Party, the only party in the province attracting support from both the Protestant and Catholic communities.

Alderney Dependency of Guernsey, which in turn is a dependency of the United Kingdom. The third-largest of the Channel Islands, Alderney has an area of 7.9 sq km and a population of 2,000. The main town is Saint Anne's. The economy is based on dairy farming and tourism. The island has considerable autonomy over local affairs. Political power is exercised by the 12-member States of Alderney elected for a three-year term, a president and a chief executive officer. Guernsey is responsible for internal security, health and education matters.

Aleksandar (Yugoslavia) *See* KARADJOR-DJEVIĆ, ...

Aleksandrov, Stoyan (1949–) Bulgarian economist and politician. He has worked for a local branch of the Bulgarian National Bank (= central bank), at the Higher Financial and Economics Institute and as head of the taxation department in the finance ministry. He was appointed finance minister in the non-party government formed in December 1992.

Aleksandrov, Valentin (1946–) Bulgarian journalist and politician. A graduate in law and international relations, he has worked as a researcher, journalist and writer on current affairs. He became an adviser to the defence minister in 1991. He was appointed minister of defence in the non-party government formed in December 1992.

Alexander (Yugoslavia) *See* KARADJORDJE-VIĆ, ALEKSANDAR.

Alfa *See* ALPHA CARTEL.

Alia, Ramiz (1925–) Albanian politician. Leader of the youth wing of the ruling communist Party of Labour (PPSh) for many years, he was elected to the politburo in 1961 and, having held a number of senior posts, became head of state in 1982 and party leader in 1985. Succeeding the hard-line Enver Hoxha, he initiated some cautious reforms. Although the party won the multiparty election in March 1991, he failed to win a seat in parliament. In line with new constitutional provisions debarring the president from holding other offices, he resigned as party leader in May. He resigned as president in April 1992 after the renamed Socialist Party (PSSh) lost an early election to the Democratic Party (PDSh). In July 1994 he was convicted of abuse of power and misappropriation of state funds and sentenced to nine years' imprisonment.

ALL Abbreviation for the LEK, the Albanian currency, used in banking etc.

All-Cyprus Federation of Labour [Pan-kípria Ergatikí Omospondía] (PEO) Cypriot trade-union federation. Founded in 1941 as the All-Cyprus Trade Union Committee and reorganized in 1946, the PEO has 10 affiliated unions with a total membership of 75,000 (nearly a third of the labour force). The president is Avraam Antoniou.

All-Poland Trade Unions Alliance [Ogólnopolskie Porozumienie Związków Zawodowych] (OPZZ) Polish trade-union federation. The OPZZ was founded by the communist regime in 1984, three years after all unions had been banned under martial law, a move that had been aimed primarily at the Solidarity reform movement. The OPZZ was relatively independent of the ruling communist Polish United Workers' Party (PZPR). Since the party's dissolution in 1989 it has developed close links with its successor, the Social Democratic Party (SdRP), cooperating with it in the DEMOCRATIC LEFT ALLIANCE (SLD). It represents around 4.5 million workers (a quarter of the labour force). The leader is Ewa Spychalska.

Alleanza Nazionale *See* NATIONAL ALLIANCE.

Alleanza Progressista *See* PROGRESSIVE ALLIANCE.

Alliance (Greece) *See* PROGRESSIVE LEFT ALLIANCE.

Alliance for Poland [Przymierze dla Polski] (PdP) Polish political organization. The PdP was formed in May 1994 as an alliance of five right-wing parties with a strongly conservative stance on social issues: the Christian National Union (ZChN), Centre Alliance (POC), Peasant Alliance (PL), Conservative Coalition (KK, a breakaway from the Conservative Party, PK) and a wing of the Movement for the Republic (RdR). Between them they had polled around 15% in the September 1993 general election, but none had passed the 5% threshold required for parliamentary representation. The leadership rotates among the party leaders. *See also individual party entries and* ELEVENTH OF NOVEMBER ALLIANCE.

Alliance 90 [Bündnis 90] (B'90) Former German political party. B'90 had its roots in three left-alternative and environmentalist groups – Democracy Now, the Peace and Human Rights Initiative and parts of New Forum – which emerged in the late 1980s as 'citizens' movements' opposed to communist rule in East Germany and were in the forefront of the 1989 revolution. It contested the all-German election in December 1990 in alliance with the (East German) Greens and gained 6.0% of the vote in eastern Germany (equivalent to 1.2% nationally) and 8/662 seats. In September 1991 the three groups merged to form B'90. In May 1993 it merged with the GREENS of former West Germany, but continued to operate under the name 'Bündnis 90' in the eastern states.

Alliance of 11 November *See* ELEVENTH OF NOVEMBER ALLIANCE.

Alliance of Free Democrats [Szabad Demokraták Szövetsége] (SzDSz) Hungarian political party. Founded in 1988, the centrist SzDSz advocates a rapid transition to a market economy and has liberal views on social issues. At the March/April 1990 election it became the second largest group in parliament, gaining 21.4% of the vote and 92/386 seats. After the May 1994 election, when it gained 19.8% and 70 seats, it became the junior coalition partner of the Hungarian Socialist Party (MSzP). The leader is Iván Pető.

Alliance of Independents [Landesring der Unabhängigen (German), Alliance des Indépendants (French)] (LdU or AdI) Swiss political party. A centrist party founded in 1936, the Alliance of Independents champion consumers' interests and environmental concerns in particular. At the October 1991 election the party gained 2.7% of the vote and 9/200 seats. The party president is Monika Weber, the parliamentary leader is Verena Grendelmeier.

Alliance of Young Democrats [Fiatal Demokraták Szövetsége] (FIDESz) Hungarian political party. Founded in 1988 as a student movement opposed to communist rule, the FIDESz is a centrist party with a strong commitment to environmental issues and social reform. Its target group was originally young people, and until May 1993 party membership was restricted to those aged between 16 and 35. At the May 1994 election it gained 7.0% of the vote and 20/386 seats. The leader is Viktor Orbán.

Alliance Party (AP) British political party. Founded in 1970, the centrist Alliance Party is the only major party in Northern Ireland which attracts support from both the Protestant and Catholic communities, primarily among the middle classes. It advocates a decentralized and 'power-sharing' form of government for the province within the United Kingdom. At the May 1993 local elections in Northern Ireland it gained 7.7% of the vote. The leader is John Alderdice, the party president is Philip McGarry.

Allied Command Europe (ACE) Military arm of the North Atlantic Treaty Organization (NATO). The more important of NATO's two major military commands (the other covers the North Atlantic Ocean area), ACE is responsible for the operational aspects of the territorial defence of most of the Western European member states. The commander of ACE, called the Supreme Allied Commander Europe (SACEUR), is directly answerable to the NATO Military Committee, which is composed of the national chiefs-of-staff. The headquarters of ACE, called the Supreme Headquarters Allied Powers Europe (SHAPE), is located in Casteau, near Mons in Belgium. The structure of ACE is currently under review.

Allied Command Europe Rapid Reaction Corps, ACE Rapid Reaction Corps or **Allied Rapid Reaction Corps** (ARRC) Military arm of the North Atlantic Treaty Organization (NATO). The ARRC forms the core of NATO's new defence structure developed to cope with the new situation that has arisen in Europe since the end of the Cold War and the collapse of the Warsaw Pact. It was agreed in May 1991 and inaugurated in October 1992, and is due to be fully operational by 1995. It will eventually have a total strength of between 70–100,000 soldiers, organized in mobile multinational units. They will be drawn from the European members of

NATO (except for France, which is not part of the organization's integrated military structure, and Iceland, which has no armed forces), with additional air support provided by the United States. The Corps is based in Bielefeld, Germany. It is sometimes also referred to as the Allied Rapid Reaction Force (ARRF).

Allied Progressive Group [Gruppo Progressista-Federativo] Italian political organization. This is a centre-left parliamentary group comprising the Democratic Left Party (PDS), Greens (Verdi), Network (La Rete) and Social Christian Party (PCS), four of the eight parties which contested the March 1994 election within the Progressive Alliance. It is the main opposition group and has 143/630 seats. The leader is Luigi Berlinguer, a PDS deputy.

allocation (Italy) *See* LOTTIZZAZIONE.

Almunia, Joaquín (1948–) Spanish politician. A graduate in law and economics, he worked as an adviser to the General Workers' Union (UGT) from 1976 until his election to parliament for the Spanish Socialist Workers' Party (PSOE) in 1979. He was minister of labour and social security from 1982–86 and minister of public administration from 1986–91. In May 1994 he was elected leader of the PSOE parliamentary group.

Alpe-Adria and **Alpen-Adria** *See* ASSOCIATION OF THE EASTERN ALPS.

Alpha Cartel [Cartelul Alfa] (Alfa) Romanian trade-union federation. Founded in 1990 as one of the successors to the official communist organization, Alfa represents a total of around 1.1 million workers (a tenth of the labour force). It generally works closely with the National Confederation of Free Trade Unions of Romania - Brotherhood (CNSLR-Frăţia) and the National Trade Union Bloc (BNS), two other major federations. The leader is Bogdan Hossu.

Alphandéry, Edmond (1943–) French economist, academic and politician. He lectured in political economy at the University of Paris II and several other universities from 1969–92. Elected to parliament for the centre-right Union for French Democracy (UDF) in 1978, he

was appointed minister of the economy in March 1993.

Alps Convention Shorthand for the AGREEMENT ON THE PROTECTION OF THE ALPS.

Alsace Region of France. Situated in the northeast and bordering on Germany and Switzerland, Alsace has an area of 8,280 sq km and a population of 1,640,000. German is widely spoken in the rural areas; it has no official status but is allowed to be taught in schools. The capital is Strasbourg, and the other main city is Mulhouse. The economy is based on manufacturing (engineering, textiles, chemicals) and agriculture (wine, cereals). It is one of France's most prosperous regions. Historically part of the Holy Roman or German Empire, most of Alsace became part of France in the late 17th century. It was ceded to Germany in 1871 after the Franco-Prussian War, returned to France in 1919 after the First World War, annexed by Germany during the Second World War, and again returned to France in 1945. Alsace was established as a region in 1982 as part of a decentralization programme.

alternate minister or **deputy minister** [anaplirotís ipourgós] In Greece, a junior member of the government who is allocated special tasks within a department or ministry and deputizes for the minister when required.

Alternative Europe *See* ANOTHER EUROPE.

Althing [Alþing] Parliament of Iceland. It has 63 members elected for a four-year term by proportional representation in eight multi-member constituencies. First convened in 930, the Althing lays claim to being the world's oldest parliament.

Altissimo, Renato (1940–) Italian businessman and politician. He worked as a manager and commercial director before his election to parliament for the Italian Liberal Party (PLI) in 1972. He was vice-president of the General Confederation of Italian Industry (CONFINDUSTRIA), the national employers' association, from 1970–74. He has been minister of health (1979–80 and 1981–83) and industry (1983–86). Elected PLI party leader in May 1986, he resigned in March 1993 when he was accused of accepting bribes from several state-owned utility companies.

Alto Adige *See* SOUTH TYROL.

AM Abbreviation for Aeronautica Militare ('Military Airforce'), the Italian airforce.

Amador, Maria Angeles (1949–) Spanish lawyer, civil servant and politician. She held a senior post in the ministry of public transport from 1986–91. Appointed a junior minister of health and consumer affairs in 1991, she was given the ministerial portfolio in the minority government formed by the Spanish Socialist Workers' Party (PSOE) in July 1993. She is not a member of the party.

Amato, Giuliano (1938–) Italian lawyer, academic and politician. A professor of constitutional law, he was elected to parliament for the Italian Socialist Party (PSI) in 1983. He was treasury minister from 1987–89. In June 1992 he became prime minister at the head of a four-party coalition. His administration became engulfed by the party-financing and other corruption scandals involving all the governing parties (*see* ITALIAN CORRUPTION SCANDALS). (He was not personally implicated.) He resigned in April 1993 after the passage of referendums on electoral and other reforms. In September 1994 he founded a centre-left political movement, Italy Tomorrow (Italia Domani).

Ambonese *See* SOUTH MOLUCCANS.

Ampelkoalition *See* TRAFFIC-LIGHT COALITION.

AMS *See* LABOUR MARKET BOARD.

Amsterdam Capital of the Netherlands. The city is the country's largest and its financial and cultural centre, but not the seat of government, which is The Hague.

amtskommune (pl. -r) or **amt** (pl. -er) Danish administrative division, usually translated as 'county'. Each of the 15 *amter* has a council [amtsråd] elected for a four-year term and headed by an elected mayor. The councils are supervised by the interior ministry. Copenhagen, the national capital and considered a county for administrative purposes, has a slightly different structure.

ANAP *See* MOTHERLAND PARTY.

Ančev, Eftim (1945–) Macedonian agronomist, academic and politician. A specialist in entomology, he was appointed minister of agriculture, forestry and water resources in September 1992. He is a member of the Social Democratic Alliance (SDSM).

Anciaux, Bert (1959–) Belgian lawyer and politician. He has been a member of the executive of the centrist People's Union (VU) of Flanders since 1976 and a member of the Brussels city council since 1987. He was elected party leader in June 1992.

AND Abbreviation for Andorra, used for international vehicle registrations, postal addresses etc.

AND (Andorra) *See* NATIONAL DEMOCRATIC ASSOCIATION.

Andalucía *See* ANDALUSIA.

Andalusia [Andalucía] Autonomous community or region of Spain. Situated in the south, Andalusia is the country's largest region, with an area of 87,268 sq km and a population of 6,984,000. The capital is Seville [Sevilla], and the other main cities are Málaga, Córdoba, Granada, Almería and Cádiz. The economy is based on agriculture (fruit and vegetables, cotton, wine, sheep farming), tourism, manufacturing and mining (coal, iron, copper). Traditionally one of Spain's least developed and poorest regions, Andalusia has experienced considerable economic development since the 1970s. Political power is exercised by a 109-member assembly elected for a four-year term and an executive council headed by a president. The dominant party is the Spanish Socialist Workers' Party (PSOE), which held an absolute majority of seats from the first regional election in 1982 until 1994; the other main parties are the centre-right People's Party (PP), the United Left (IU) and Andalusian Power (PA). At the election in June 1994 the PSOE gained 38.6% of the vote and 45 seats, the PP 34.5% and 41 seats, the IU 19.2% and 20 seats, and the PA 5.8% and three seats. The president is Manuel Chaves. Andalusia was under Muslim rule for longer than any other region of Spain. The north and west were conquered by Castile in the

14th century, and the Kingdom of Granada, the last Muslim state, was annexed in 1492. Andalusia has a strong regional identity, and in 1981 it became the fourth historical region of Spain to be granted extensive autonomy.

Andalusian Power [Poder Andaluz] (PA) Spanish political party. Founded in 1976 as the Socialist Party of Andalusia (PSA) and renamed in 1984, the PA advocates greater autonomy for Andalusia within a federal Spain. It is centre-left in its economic policies and has liberal views on social issues. At the June 1990 regional election it gained 10.8% of the vote and 10/109 seats, but in June 1994 its support fell to 5.8% and three seats. The president is Alejandro Rojas-Marcos, the general secretary Miguel Angel Arredonda.

Andersen, Jytte (1942–) Danish politician. She was active in local government until her election to parliament for the Social Democratic Party (SD) in 1979. She was secretary of the parliamentary party from 1981–86. A specialist on labour and training issues, she was appointed minister of labour in the centre-left coalition formed in January 1993.

Andersson, Claes (1937–) Finnish doctor, writer and politician. A specialist in psychiatry, he worked at several medical institutions from 1963. Elected to parliament in 1987, he was elected leader of the new Left-Wing Alliance (VL), formed by the merger of the main communist and left-socialist groups, in April 1990. He has published a number of plays, novels and collections of poetry.

Andorra Country in southwestern Europe.
Official data. Name: Principality of Andorra [Principat d'Andorra]; capital: Andorra la Vella; form of government: parliamentary monarchy; heads of state: two co-princes, ex officio the president of France and the Roman Catholic bishop of Urgell (Spain); head of government: head of government; flag: three vertical stripes, blue, yellow and red, with the state emblem in the centre; national holiday: 8 September (National Day); language: Catalan; religion: Roman Catholicism; currencies: French franc and Spanish peseta; abbreviation: AND.

Geography. Situated in the eastern Pyrenees [Pirineus], Andorra has an area of 468 sq km. It is bordered by France in the north and Spain in the south. The terrain is mountainous. Some 2% of the land is arable, another 56% is covered by pastures and 22% is forested. The climate is alpine, with mild summers and cold winters; rainfall is heavy.

Demography. Andorra has a population of 61,900. Annual population growth has been high since the 1980s as a result of immigration. Population density is 132 per sq km. The main town is Andorra la Vella, home to just under a third of the population. Only 28.6% of the people are Andorran citizens. Foreign nationals account for the remaining 71.4%, and include citizens of Spain (49.7% of the total, mainly from Catalonia), France (7.6%) and Portugal (7.2%). The main languages are Spanish, Catalan and French. In religious terms nearly all the people are nominally Roman Catholic.

Sociography. The standard of living in Andorra is high. There are 20 doctors and 23 hospital beds for every 10,000 people. Education is provided under the French and Spanish systems at the primary and secondary levels. There is one teacher for every 25 students. Enrolment is 95% at the secondary level and 33% at the tertiary level (mostly abroad). The literacy rate is virtually 100%. GNP per head (unadjusted for purchasing power) is US$ 13,550.

Infrastructure and communications. Andorra has a developed but limited transport and communications network. There are 980 km of paved roads and 34,200 passenger cars (617 per 1,000 people). There are no railways or navigable waterways. The nearest major ports are Barcelona in Spain and Bordeaux in France. The nearest major international airports are at Barcelona and Toulouse (France). There are no local daily newspapers; Spanish and French papers are widely read. There are around 15,000 radio receivers, 6,000 television sets and around 25,000 telephones in use (respectively 271, 108 and 451 per 1,000 people).

Economic structure. The Andorran economy is highly developed but heavily dependent on tourism. Andorra forms a customs union with the European Union (EU). Taxation is very low. Since the late 1980s economic performance has been marked by steady growth, relatively high inflation (averaging around 6% per year) and negligible unemployment (detailed figures n.a.).

Services contribute 68% of GDP, industry contributes 31%, and agriculture and forestry 1% (detailed figures n.a.). Some 43% of the labour force is employed in trade, 12% in construction and 11% in manufacturing. The main agricultural activity is livestock raising (sheep, cattle); the main crops grown are cereals (wheat, barley), tobacco and potatoes. Forestry is also important. The main mineral resource is marble. The main industries are textiles (clothing, leather) and tobacco (cigarettes, cigars); other branches are electrical goods, furniture and printing (stamps). The tourism industry (winter and summer) is the mainstay of the economy and provides nearly all the country's foreign exchange. Banking and other financial services are also important. The main energy sources are hydroelectricity and imported fossil fuels. The main exports are clothing (52% of the total), foodstuffs (around 30%, incl. mineral water 16% and cattle 8%) and electrical equipment (7%). The main imports are machinery and transport equipment, foodstuffs and miscellaneous manufactures; most imports are consumer goods intended for sale to tourists. The main trading partners are: exports: France (56%) and Spain (30%); imports: France (36%), Spain (32%), Germany (7%) and Japan (6%). Net invisible earnings (tourism receipts, income from financial services) account for the majority of GNP.

There is no central bank. There are no employers' associations or labour organizations of note.

Political structure. Under the constitution in force since May 1993, Andorra is a parliamentary monarchy. The joint heads of state or co-princes [copríncep, pl. -s] are the president of France and the Roman Catholic bishop of Urgell (in Spain), represented in Andorra by the French magistrate [veguer de França] and episcopal magistrate [veguer episcopal] respectively. Executive power is vested in the prime minister [cap de govern], who is elected by the legislature, and the council of ministers. Legislative power is vested in the General Council [Consell General], whose 28 members are elected for a four-year term, half by majority voting and half by a system of proportional representation. All citizens over the age of 18 are entitled to vote. Judicial power is ultimately vested in the five-member Higher Court of Justice [Tribunal Superior de la Justícia] appointed for a six-year term; the Constitutional Tribunal [Tribunal Constitucional], with four members appointed for an eight-year term, adjudicates on constitutional matters. Administratively the country is divided into seven parishes [parròquia, pl. -s].

The main political parties are the National Democratic Association (AND), Liberal Union (UL), New Democratic Party (ND), Andorran National Coalition (CNA) and National Democratic Initiative (IDN). At the general election in December 1993 the AND gained 26.4% of vote and 8/28 seats, the UL 22.0% and five seats, the ND 19.1% and five seats, the CNA 17.2% and four seats, the IDN 15.3% and two seats, and independents four seats. The government is formed by the centre-right AND and is supported by the ND and IDN, with Oscar Ribas Reig as prime minister. Other senior ministers are Josep Casal (finance), Jaume Serra (economy) and Marc Vila Amigo (foreign affairs). The joint heads of state are François Mitterrand, president of France, and Joan Martí Alanis, bishop of Urgell.

Security and international affiliations. Andorra has no standing army. Responsibility for defence is delegated to France and Spain. Andorra forms a customs union with the European Union (EU) but is not a member of the organization itself. It is a member of the United Nations and several of its specialized agencies. It has applied for membership of the Council of Europe.

History. A long-running dispute over control of Andorra between the county of Foix in France and the Roman Catholic bishopric of Urgel in Catalonia (now Spain) was resolved in 1278 with an agreement under which the territory was made a principality under the joint suzerainty of the two feudal lords. (*For earlier developments, see* SPAIN: HISTORY.) The rights of the count of Foix passed to the king of France by marriage in 1589 and to his successors as heads of state. The co-princes retained virtually absolute powers until 1866, when a measure of constitutional government was introduced.

From the 1950s tourism rapidly developed into the main industry. The electoral franchise, highly selective until the 1960s, was gradually extended and was granted to all citizens by 1976. Popular pressure for the introduction of representative government and other political reforms persuaded the co-princes to separate the legislative and executive branches and set up an executive council. In January 1982 Oscar Ribas Reig became the country's first prime minister. The 1980s were dominated by the issue of political reform. Liberal and conservative forces alternately held majorities in the General Council (= parliament). In July 1991 Andorra joined the European Community (EC) customs union (but not the organization itself). In March 1993 voters approved the country's first constitution by a margin of 74.2% to 25.8%. Promulgated in May, it established Andorra as a fully sovereign state, removed the co-princes' executive powers, established an independent judiciary and legalized political parties and trade unions. In July 1993 Andorra became a member of the United Nations. In a general election in December five newly formed parties secured seats. In February 1994 Ribas Reig formed a government composed of members of his centre-right National Democratic Association (AND) and independents.

See also entries on specific institutions, organizations, parties, people, terms etc.

Andov, Stojan (1935–) Macedonian economist, diplomat and politician. From the 1970s he held a series of senior posts in the League of Communists and in the republican Macedonian and federal Yugoslav governments and was also a member of parliament at both levels. In December 1990 he became leader of the Macedonian branch of the Alliance of Reform Forces of Yugoslavia (SRSJ), subsequently renamed the Reform Forces of Macedonia - Liberal Party (RSM-LP). He was also elected president of the Sobranie (= parliament) in January 1991.

Andreatta, Beniamino or **Nino** (1928–) Italian lawyer, economist, academic and politician. He was appointed professor of economics at the University of Bologna in 1963 and was rector of the University of Calabria from 1971–75. He was elected to parliament for the Christian Democratic Party (DC), now the Italian People's Party (PPI), in 1976. He has been budget minister (1979–80), minister without portfolio (1980) and treasury minister (1980–82). He returned to government as budget minister in February 1993 and was foreign minister in the transitional Ciampi administration in office from April 1993 until May 1994. He then became the PPI's parliamentary leader.

Andrejčák, Imrich (1941–) Slovakian soldier and politician. A career army officer, now with the rank of general, he was a member of the Communist Party until the regime's collapse in 1989. He was Czechoslovakia's deputy defence minister from 1990–92 and defence minister until the federation's dissolution at the end of 1992. Nominated defence minister of independent Slovakia in January 1993, he was not confirmed in the post until March because of controversy over his role in the suppression of anti-communist demonstrations in November 1989. He held the post until the Mečiar government lost a vote of confidence in March 1994.

Andrējevs, Georgs (1932–) Latvian doctor and politician. Elected to parliament for the pro-independence People's Front (LTF) in 1990, when Latvia was still part of the Soviet Union, he became foreign minister in November 1992. He was elected to parliament for the centre-right Latvian Way (LC) in June 1993. He

16

was suspended by parliament in April 1994 following allegations that he had been an informer for the State Security Committee (KGB) during the Soviet period. He admitted he had passed medical information to the KGB from 1963, but claimed he had also used his knowledge of KGB activities to warn potential victims that they were under suspicion. He resigned from parliament and the government in June, but was asked to carry on as foreign minister in the caretaker government in office from July–September 1994. He is an ethnic Russian.

Andreotti, Giulio (1919–) Italian lawyer and politician. He was first elected to parliament for the Christian Democratic Party (DC) in 1947. He gained his first ministerial post in 1954 and remained a member of the government without interruption until 1992. During this time he held 33 ministerial portfolios, including all the major offices of state – minister of the interior, finance, treasury, defence, foreign affairs and prime minister – and established himself as the country's most influential politician. He headed seven centrist coalitions from 1972–73, 1976–79 and 1989 until May 1992 and was foreign minister from 1983–87. In April 1993 he was first accused of violating the laws on party financing and then of association with the Mafia crime syndicate. Citing evidence from Mafia informers, magistrates alleged that he had acted as the organization's 'protector' from 'at least 1978 … certainly until 1992'. He was also alleged to have been involved in the murder of a journalist, Mino Pecorelli, in 1979 and a senior Mafia investigator, Carlo Dalla Chiesa, in 1982. Both were said to have been in possession of information damaging to him in connection with, among other matters, the kidnapping and murder in 1978 of former prime minister Aldo Moro. It was also claimed that he had met Mafia leaders on several occasions between 1979 and 1988. Andreotti initially denied all the allegations, but in December 1993 magistrates published a photograph showing him with leading Mafia figures. In July 1994 he was charged not just with association

with the Mafia but with actual membership of the organization. *See also* ITALIAN CORRUPTION SCANDALS.

Andrews, David (1935–) Irish lawyer and politician. Elected to parliament for the centre-right Fianna Fáil in 1965, he was a junior foreign minister from 1977–79. He was appointed foreign minister in 1992 and minister of defence and the marine in January 1993.

Andreyev, Georgi *See* ANDREJEVS, GEORGS.

Anglo-Irish Agreement Bilateral agreement between the United Kingdom and Ireland providing a framework for cooperation on political, security and legal matters related to Northern Ireland, a component of the United Kingdom. Northern Ireland is riven by conflict between the Protestant or unionist majority, which wants the territory to remain part of the United Kingdom, and the Catholic or nationalist minority, which supports the reunification of Ireland (*see* NORTHERN IRELAND QUESTION). Signed on 15 November 1985, the Anglo-Irish Agreement (i) reaffirms the rights of the province's two 'traditions', Protestant and Catholic, (ii) recognizes the right of each to pursue its aspiration by peaceful constitutional means, (iii) establishes an intergovernmental conference to discuss matters of common interest and to enable the Irish government to put forward its views in all areas of policy affecting Northern Ireland and the Catholic community, and (iv) affirms that any change in the status of Northern Ireland can only come about 'with the consent of a majority of [its] people'. The two main unionist parties reject the accord, primarily because it gives the Irish government a consultative role in Northern Ireland affairs.

Anglo-Irish Declaration *See* DOWNING STREET DECLARATION.

Anglo-Irish Intergovernmental Conference or **Anglo-Irish Conference** Intergovernmental body set up under the ANGLO-IRISH AGREEMENT on Northern Ireland, signed by the British and Irish governments in 1985. Made up of ministers and officials from both governments, the Conference meets at regular intervals to discuss all aspects of policy related to

Northern Ireland. It provides a framework for practical cooperation on a range of issues, such as cross-border security, and serves as a forum for developing initiatives for a political solution to the conflict between the province's Protestant unionist and Catholic nationalist communities. The Conference is assisted by a permanent secretariat based in Belfast, the Northern Ireland capital.

Anguita, Julio (1941–) Spanish teacher and politician. Mayor of Córdoba from 1983–87 and leader of the Andalusian branch of the Communist Party of Spain (PCE), he was elected the party's general secretary in February 1988. He also leads the United Left (IU) alliance, of which the PCE is the main component.

ANISS *See* NATIONAL AGENCY FOR INFORMATION AND STATE SECURITY.

Ankara Shorthand for the Turkish government. Ankara is the capital of Turkey.

Another Europe [L'Autre Europe] French political organization. L'Autre Europe was formed to contest the June 1994 election to the European Parliament, the parliament of the European Union (EU), on a platform of opposition to the perceived centralizing or 'federalist' tendencies within the EU. It also supported a range of populist policies aimed at attracting votes from the main right-wing parties. Headed by Philippe de Villiers, a member of the centre-right Republican Party (PR), and James Goldsmith, a prominent Anglo-French businessman, the list gained 12.3% of the vote and 13/87 seats. Together with four Danish and two Dutch deputies it formed the Europe of Nations (EN) parliamentary group.

Anselme, Bernard (1945–) Belgian politician. He worked briefly as a civil servant and then for the Walloon Regional Economic Council (CERW) from 1972–77. He was elected to parliament for the Socialist Party (PS) in 1977. From 1988–92 he was chief minister of the Wallonian regional government and then became chief minister of the French Community, the body in Belgium's federal structure responsible for French-language education, culture and other matters. He was appointed national minister of social

affairs in May 1993 and became Wallonia's interior minister in January 1994.

Antall, József (1932–93) Hungarian teacher, historian and politician. Having supported the 1956 uprising against the communist regime, he was banned from working as a teacher and instead became a librarian and archivist. A founding member of the centre-right Hungarian Democratic Forum (MDF) in 1987, he was elected its leader in October 1989. After the party had become the largest in parliament in the multiparty election in March/April 1990, he became prime minister of a centre-right coalition in May. He died of cancer in December 1993.

anti-federalism In the European Union (EU), criticism or rejection of further integration, specifically the plans for economic, monetary and political union contained in the Maastricht Treaty (in force since November 1993) and other 'centralizing' or 'federalist' measures in foreign affairs, defence and other spheres. *See also* BRUGES GROUP *and* EUROPE OF NATIONS.

Anti-Mafia Investigation Directorate [Direzione Investigativa Anti-Mafia] (DIA) Italian government agency. The DIA was established in December 1992 as the successor to the High Commission for the Fight Against the Mafia, which had been set up in the early 1980s but had had little success in combating organized crime (*see* MAFIA). Answerable to the interior ministry, it is modelled on the American Federal Bureau of Investigation (FBI) and consists of a relatively small team of experts drawn from the main law-enforcement agencies and judiciary bodies. It was given additional powers and resources after the assassination of two senior judges who had been tipped to head the new agency, Giovanni Falcone and Paolo Borsellino, by the Sicilian Mafia in May and July 1992 respectively. It is allowed to use undercover operations and tap telephones during its investigations. The main focus of its work has been to persuade former Mafia members, known as *pentiti* ('repenters'), to give evidence in camera in exchange for protection.

Anti-Terrorist Liberation Groups
[Grupos Antiterroristas de Liberación]
(GAL) Spanish guerrilla group. Since the
GAL emerged in 1983 it has been implicated in the killings of more than 25
alleged members and supporters of Basque
Homeland and Liberty (ETA), the separatist guerrilla group. The assassinations
were usually carried out across the border
in southwestern France, in some cases by
foreign mercenaries. In 1991 a judicial
investigation into the undercover operations confirmed allegations that police
officers and perhaps higher-ranking officials had been involved in the recruitment
of mercenaries and other GAL-related
activities. Several police officers have been
convicted of association with the GAL.

Aosta Valley [Val d'Aoste (French), Valle
d'Aosta (Italian)] Special autonomous
region of Italy. Situated in the northwest
in the Alps and bordering on France and
Switzerland, the Aosta Valley is Italy's
smallest region, with an area of 3,262 sq
km and a population of 117,000. The
capital is Aosta. Most Aostans speak
dialects of Franco-Provençal or French,
and French is an official language. The
economy is based on tourism and agriculture (dairy farming). Political power is
exercised by the Regional Assembly
[Conseil Régional / Consiglio Regionale],
with 35 members elected for a five-year
term, and an executive council headed by
a president. The main parties are the
Aosta Valley Union (UV), Italian People's
Party (PPI, the successor to the Christian
Democratic Party, DC), Democratic Left
Party (PDS), Northern League (Lega
Nord) and the Greens (Verdi). At the
regional election in May 1993 the UV
gained 37.3% of the vote and 13 seats,
the DC 14.9% and five seats, and the
PDS, Lega Nord and Greens respectively
9.6%, 7.6% and 7.1% and three seats
each. Aosta became part of Savoy in the
11th century. When Savoy was ceded to
France in 1860, it remained part of what
was then the Kingdom of Sardinia, the
nucleus of unified Italy. In recognition of
its distinctive linguistic and cultural character, Aosta Valley was made an autonomous region with special statute in 1945.

Aosta Valley Union [Union Valdôtaine
(French)] (UV) Italian political party.
Founded in 1945, the UV is the main
representative of the majority French-
speaking community in the Aosta Valley
region. It advocates full autonomy for the
region within a federal Italy, is centrist in
its economic policies and takes a conservative view on social issues. The largest
party in the regional assembly since 1978,
it gained 37.3% of the vote and 13/35
seats at the May 1993 regional election.
At the April 1992 and March 1994 general
elections it gained one seat (out of 630).
The leader is Carlo Perrin.

AOV *See* GENERAL ELDERLY PEOPLE'S
UNION.

AP *See* ALLIANCE PARTY.

apparentement ('alliance') In France, an
electoral alliance between two or more
parties aimed at maximizing their chances
of gaining seats in parliament. Under the
arrangement, parties may agree on a single
candidate to contest the first round of
voting in the single-member constituencies or agree to back one of their candidates who has come first or second in the
first round and thus qualifies for the
second round.

approximation In the European Union
(EU), the adaptation of member states'
laws, rules and regulations to the extent
required for the smooth functioning of the
single internal market and other common
policies and programmes. Approximation
is similar to 'harmonization' but not as far-
reaching, since it does not require legislation to be identical across the member
states. *See also* MUTUAL RECOGNITION.

APS *See* FREEDOM PARTY OF SWITZERLAND.

Apsītis, Romāns (1939–) Latvian academic
and politician. He lectured in law at the
University of Latvia from 1965. He was
elected to parliament for the pro-independence People's Front (LTF) in 1990, when
Latvia was still part of the Soviet Union,
and for the centre-right Latvian Way (LC)
in 1993. He was appointed a junior justice
minister in September 1993 and became
the minister in September 1994.

Apulia [Puglia] Autonomous region of
Italy. Situated in the southeast, in the
'heel' of the Italian peninsula, Apulia has

19

an area of 19,348 sq km and a population of 3,971,000. The capital is Bari, and other main cities are Taranto, Foggia, Lecce and Brindisi. The economy is based on agriculture (cereals, fruit and vegetables, tobacco, sheep farming), manufacturing (food processing, chemicals, petrochemicals, metalworking) and fishing. Part of the MEZZOGIORNO, the region is traditionally one of the country's poorest; there has been substantial emigration since the 19th century. Apulia formed part of the Kingdom of Naples from the 11th century until it was incorporated into unified Italy in 1860.

Apulian Mafia *See* SACRA CORONA.

Aquitaine Region of France. Situated in the southwest and bordering on the Atlantic Ocean and Spain, Aquitaine has an area of 41,308 sq km and a population of 2,827,000. Perhaps a tenth of the population considers itself Basque (detailed figures n.a.). Basque is spoken by around 130,000 people in the southwest; it has no official status but is allowed to be taught in schools. The capital is Bordeaux, and the other main cities are Pau and Bayonne. The economy is based on agriculture (wine, fruit), forestry, manufacturing (food processing, petrochemicals) and tourism.

Aragón Autonomous community or region of Spain. Situated in the northeast, Aragón has an area of 47,650 sq km and a population of 1,207,000. The capital is Zaragoza. The economy is based on agriculture (cereals, sugarbeets, olives, cotton), manufacturing (engineering, motor vehicles, metalworking) and mining (lignite). The main political parties are the Spanish Socialist Workers' Party (PSOE), the Aragonese Party (PAR), the centre-right People's Party (PP) and the United Left (IU). At the May 1991 election the PSOE gained 30 seats in the 67-member legislature, the PAR and PP 17 each and the IU three. The government is formed by a PAR-PP coalition. In the Middle Ages Aragón was the core of an independent kingdom that eventually also included Catalonia, Valencia and the Balearic Islands. Aragón and Castile were united in 1479 to form Spain. Aragón proper, coextensive with the current region, retained a degree of autonomy until the 18th century. It was established as an autonomous community in 1982.

Aragonese Party [Partido Aragonés] (PAR) Spanish political party. Founded in 1978 as the Aragonese Regionalist Party, the PAR advocates greater autonomy for Aragón within a federal Spain. It is centre-right in its economic policies and has conservative views on social issues. It became the largest party in the regional assembly in 1987 and has led a centre-right coalition since then. It gained 17/67 seats at the May 1991 regional election, and one seat (out of 350) at the June 1993 general election. The leader is José María Mur.

Ardanza, José Antonio (1941–) Spanish lawyer and politician. He was head of the legal department of a savings bank from 1969–83. A member of the Basque Nationalist Party (EAJ/PNV), he became president of the Basque regional government in February 1985.

ARE *See* EUROPEAN RADICAL ALLIANCE.

area state [Flächenland, pl. -länder] In Germany, one of the 13 federal states that are not 'city states'. The latter (Berlin, Bremen and Hamburg) have somewhat different administrative structures and are sometimes treated separately because of their distinctive economic and social characteristics.

Arge-Alp *See* ASSOCIATION OF THE CENTRAL ALPS.

Arike, Heiki (1965–) Estonian policeman, civil servant and politician. A graduate in economics and business administration, he joined the Tartu police department as deputy chief constable in 1991. The following year he took up a senior post in the interior ministry, and in December 1993 he was appointed interior minister. He is not a member of a political party, but is close to the centre-right Estonian National Independence Party (ERSP).

Arkan *See* RAZNJATOVIĆ, ZELJKO.

Armed Communist Nuclei *See* RED BRIGADES.

Armed Phalange [Falange Armata] (FA) Italian guerrilla group. Since it emerged in 1990 the Armed Phalange has claimed responsibility for a spate of bombings, assassinations, fires and other attacks, including the murder of a senior judge, Giovanni Falcone, in May 1992 and bomb attacks in Rome, Florence and Milan in 1993. It has threatened to murder politicians, industrialists, judges and journalists. It has revealed little about its motivations and aims, but is widely thought to be operating on behalf of a coalition of forces – widely known as the 'HIDDEN GOVERNMENT' [sottogoverno] – aimed at destabilizing the state, including far-right elements in the intelligence agencies, the army and the police, right-wing groups and politicians intent on preserving the old order, and the Sicilian Mafia and other crime syndicates. *See also* ITALIAN CORRUPTION SCANDALS.

Armija BiH and **BiH** Abbreviations for Armija Bosna i Hercegovina ('Army of Bosnia-Herzegovina'), the Bosnian army. Initially multiethnic, it has become increasingly Muslim-dominated since the start of the civil war in March 1992 and the resultant polarization between the Muslim, Serb and Croat communities. Its soldiers are known informally as the 'green berets' [zeleni bereti].

arms embargo In former Yugoslavia, a complete ban on arms sales and shipments to the region imposed by the United Nations Security Council. It was adopted (under Resolution 713) in September 1991, at the height of the civil war precipitated by the Croatian and Slovenian declarations of independence. It now applies to the successor states, Bosnia-Herzegovina, Croatia, Macedonia, Slovenia and rump Yugoslavia. The protagonists in the Bosnian and Croatian civil wars have nevertheless been able to secure arms supplies through a range of official and unofficial channels.

arms-smuggling affair (Slovenia) *See* MARIBOR ....

arms-to-Iraq affair Controversy in the United Kingdom surrounding allegations that the government broke its own guidelines, misled Parliament and sought to suppress documents related to arms exports to Iraq during the 1980s. A public inquiry into the affair provided an insight into the working of the government machinery and revealed evidence, critics claimed, of secrecy, duplicity, disregard for constitutional conventions, conflicting legal advice, personal rivalries and a cover-up. In October 1992 three senior executives of the engineering firm Matrix Churchill went on trial for breaching the ban on arms sales to Iraq (which had been imposed in 1984, four years after it had launched a war against Iran, which was also covered by the ban). The prosecution claimed that between 1988 and Iraq's invasion of Kuwait in August 1990 they had fraudulently obtained export licences for machine tools and computer software with a potential military capability, including components for a so-called 'supergun', by pretending the equipment was for civilian use. The defence in turn claimed that government officials had encouraged the pretence in order to maintain intelligence contacts and promote British exports. When, in November, a former junior defence minister, Alan Clark, admitted as much in court, the case collapsed. It also emerged that government ministers had refused to disclose certain documents relevant to the case for reasons of national security. The government agreed to set up a wide-ranging public inquiry into the affair. Chaired by a senior judge, Richard Scott (Lord Justice Scott), it heard testimony from senior current and former ministers and civil servants. The key evidence to emerge was that: (i) the government had effectively allowed the resumption of arms sales to Iraq in December 1988, four months after the (Iran-Iraq) Gulf War ceasefire, but had not informed Parliament of the policy change; and (ii) ministers had in effect been willing to accept the possible conviction and imprisonment of the Matrix Churchill executives by withholding key documents from the court that would have cleared them. In May 1993 the attorney-general, Patrick Mayhew, was accused by a fellow Conservative member of Parliament of trying to suppress important documents. In October the December 1988 document came to light, in which the then prime minister, Margaret

21

Thatcher, agreed that licences already granted to Matrix Churchill should not be revoked even though they related to equipment believed destined for military use. In December Thatcher testified she had not been told of the policy change. The later hearings focused on the circumstances in which four senior ministers had signed 'public interest immunity' certificates (PIIs), which are used to prevent the disclosure of official information in court. In this instance they related not only to the identity of intelligence sources but also to the change of criteria for allowing arms-related sales to Iraq. In March 1994 the attorney-general, Nicholas Lyell, appeared to indicate that in some cases ministers were in effect obliged to sign PIIs. The trade and industry minister, Michael Heseltine, had earlier testified that Lyell had given him conflicting advice. The Scott inquiry completed its work in March 1994. Its report was expected to be published towards the end of 1994.

Aromanians and **Aromuns** *See* VLACHS.

ARRC *See* ALLIED COMMAND EUROPE RAPID REACTION CORPS.

arrêt ('judgement' in French) In the European Union (EU), a decision by the Court of Justice. The French legal term is widely used.

ARRF *See* ALLIED COMMAND EUROPE RAPID REACTION CORPS.

arrondissement French administrative division. Intermediate units between the department and commune, the 322 *arrondissements* have few functions and no elected bodies or officials. They form the basis of the electoral districts for the National Assembly, the lower house of parliament. The administrative divisions of Paris, Lyon and Marseille, the country's three largest cities, are also called *arrondissements*.

Arsenis, Gerasimos (1931–) Greek economist and politician. He worked for the Organization for Economic Cooperation and Development (OECD) and the United Nations from 1960, serving as director of the UN Conference on Trade and Development (UNCTAD) from 1973–81. A member of the Pan-Hellenic Socialist Movement (PASOK), he was governor of the Bank of Greece (= central bank) from 1981–82 and then became minister of finance. He briefly held the merchant marine portfolio in 1985 before being dismissed for criticizing the government's austerity policies. He formed a left-socialist party in 1986 but returned to PASOK three years later. When the party regained power in October 1993, he was appointed minister of defence.

article 2 and **article 3** (Ireland) *See* ARTICLES 2 AND 3.

Article 10 Provision of the EUROPEAN CONVENTION FOR THE PROTECTION OF HUMAN RIGHTS AND FUNDAMENTAL FREEDOMS dealing with freedom of expression. One of the Convention's key sections, it guarantees freedom of expression but makes it subject to specific restrictions. Paragraph 1 states: 'Everyone has the right to freedom of expression. This right shall include freedom to hold opinions and to receive and impart information and ideas without interference regardless of frontiers'. Paragraph 2 states: 'The exercise of these freedoms, since it carries with it duties and responsibilities, may be subject to such formalities, conditions, restrictions or penalties as are prescribed by law and are necessary in a democratic society, in the interests of national security, territorial integrity or public safety, for the prevention of disorder or crime, for the protection of health or morals, for the protection of the reputation or rights of others, for preventing the disclosure of information received in confidence, or for maintaining the authority and impartiality of the judiciary'.

article 16 In Germany, the provision of the constitution which deals with the right of political asylum. The 1949 Basic Law declared that 'persons persecuted on political grounds shall enjoy the right to asylum'. This clause – drafted in response to the nazi regime's record of persecution – was not circumscribed in any way, so that in practice any immigrant could claim asylum and would enjoy the right of residence while the application was being considered (a process which often took many years). The influx of mainly economic migrants following the collapse of communist rule in Eastern Europe in 1989, which reached a peak of 456,000 in 1992, created strong pressures for tightening the liberal asylum regulations. In May 1993 parliament adopted an amendment to the constitution that restricted the right of asylum to exclude those arriving from 'safe countries' and those deemed to be economic migrants. This brought Germany's immigration and asylum policies broadly in line with practice in other Western European countries.

article 24 and **article 26** (Germany) *See* ARTICLES 24, 26 ....

article 40.3.3 In Ireland, the provision of the constitution guaranteeing the 'equal right to life' of mother and foetus and thus effectively banning abortion under any circumstances. This amendment to the constitution – replacing an existing legal ban on abortion – was adopted after gaining voters' approval in a referendum in September 1983. Like other constitutional provisions based on Roman Catholic moral precepts, such as the ban on divorce, it arouses intense controversy. (Article 44, granting the Catholic Church a 'special position' in the state, was repealed in 1973 but other provisions reflecting its doctrine were left in place.) Following a highly charged case in February 1992, when a court sought to bar a 14-year-old rape victim from travelling to Britain to have an abortion, the government called three referendums in November. Two, on the right to receive information about abortion services and the right to travel to other European Union (EU) states to have abortions, were approved; the third, providing for the availability of abortion to save the life of the mother, was rejected (with many pro-choice groups also urging a no vote because of its ambiguous wording). The centrist government which took office in January 1993 committed itself to relaxing the ban on abortion.

article 49 In Macedonia, the provision of the constitution dealing with obligations to ethnic Macedonians in neighbouring countries and Macedonian citizens resident abroad. (There are substantial Macedonian communities in Bulgaria and Greece.) Paragraph 1 states that 'The Republic cares for the status and rights of those persons belonging to the Macedonian people in neighbouring countries, as well as Macedonian expatriates, assists their cultural development and promotes links with them'; paragraph 3 states that 'The Republic shall not interfere in the sovereign rights of other states and their internal affairs'. The latter was an amendment adopted in January 1992 in response to concerns raised by the European Community (EC) that the wording of the first paragraph could be construed to imply territorial claims. At the same time another clause was added to the constitution stating that 'The Republic of Macedonia has no territorial claims against neighbouring states' (article 3, paragraph 4). The changes did not satisfy Greece, however, which insisted that article 49 implied a territorial claim on the northern Greek region of Macedonia and an appeal to the 'Slav Macedonians' living there. *See also* MACEDONIA NAME QUESTION.

article 87a (Germany) *See* ARTICLES 24, 26 AND 87A.

article 189b procedure In the European Union (EU), an alternative name for the CO-DECISION PROCEDURE, a method of enacting legislation. It refers to the relevant section in the Maastricht Treaty establishing the EU.

article 189c procedure In the European Union (EU), an alternative name for the COOPERATION PROCEDURE, a method of enacting legislation. It refers to the relevant sections in the Single European Act and the Maastricht Treaty.

articles 2 and 3 In Ireland, the provisions of the constitution which establish a claim to Northern Ireland, a part of the United Kingdom. They state that the constitution applies to 'the whole island of Ireland', but that 'pending the reintegration of the national territory' the laws enacted by Parliament will apply only to the Irish Free State and (since 1949) the Republic of Ireland. The constitution was adopted in 1937, sixteen years after the partition of Ireland into the independent Free State and Northern Ireland, whose majority Protestant or unionist community wanted to remain within the United Kingdom.

Repeal of the two articles has been a long-standing demand of unionists.

articles 24, 26 and 87a In Germany, provisions of the constitution governing defence and deployment of the armed forces. Article 24 permits the country to 'enter a system of mutual collective security'; article 26 prohibits acts intended to 'disturb the peaceful relations between nations, especially to prepare for war of aggression'; and article 87b states that 'Apart from defence, the armed forces may only be used insofar as explicitly permitted' by the constitution. These articles – drafted in the aftermath of the Second World War, caused by Germany – were traditionally interpreted as meaning that German troops could only be used within the context of the North Atlantic Treaty Organization (NATO), of which Germany became a member in 1955, and within NATO's area of operation, i.e. the member states and the North Atlantic region. They became highly controversial at the time of the 1991 Gulf War, when it was suggested that Germany should contribute troops to the United Nations force assembled to end the Iraqi occupation of Kuwait. There is now a broad consensus that German troops should be allowed to participate in UN humanitarian and peacekeeping operations. But there is no agreement among the major parties whether combat troops can be deployed in a UN or other multilateral context outside the NATO area. In a preliminary ruling in April 1992 the Federal Constitutional Court approved German participation in monitoring the UN-sponsored air-exclusion zone over Bosnia-Herzegovina. The same month 1,600 troops were sent to Somalia to assist the UN relief effort in that country. In July 1994 the Court ruled that German troops could be sent on operations anywhere abroad within the context of a system of collective security or defence (e.g. UN, NATO) provided each deployment was approved by parliament on a case-by-case basis.

Arumäe, Urmas (1957–) Estonian lawyer, businessman and politician. He has practised as a lawyer and worked for several industrial companies, including two distilleries. A member of the right-wing Fatherland (Isamaa) party, he was appointed minister of justice in June 1994.

Arzallus, Xabier (1932–) Spanish clergyman, lawyer, academic and politician. A Basque, he worked in other parts of Spain and Germany in the 1950s and 60s. He joined the then illegal Basque Nationalist Party (EAJ/PNV) in 1964. After leaving the Catholic priesthood in 1967, he taught law in Madrid and the Basque Country and defended political prisoners. After the restoration of democracy he was briefly a member of parliament (1977–79). He was elected party leader in February 1985.

AS Abbreviation for the SCHILLING, the Austrian currency.

Ashdown, Paddy (1941–) British soldier, diplomat and politician. He pursued careers in the Royal Marines, the diplomatic service, industry and local government before entering politics. Elected to Parliament for the Liberal Party in 1983, he became trade and then education spokesman for the Liberal and Social Democratic alliance. He was elected leader of the newly merged Liberal Democrats in July 1988.

ASÍ *See* LABOUR FEDERATION OF ICELAND.

Assemblée and **Assemblée Nationale** *See* NATIONAL ASSEMBLY (France).

Assembly (Bosnia-Herzegovina) *See* SKUPŠTINA.

Assembly (Greece) *See* VOULÍ.

Assembly (Latvia) *See* SAEIMA.

Assembly (Lithuania) *See* SEIMAS.

Assembly Shorthand for ASSEMBLY OF THE REPUBLIC, the parliaments of Macedonia, Northern Cyprus and Portugal.

Assembly (Poland) *See* SEJM.

Assembly of Deputies [Adunarea Deputaţilor] Lower house of the Romanian parliament. Of its 341 members, 328 are elected for a four-year term by a system of proportional representation. Parties must obtain at least 3% of the popular vote to qualify for seats. The remaining 13 members are appointed by the president of the republic to represent ethnic minorities. *See also* SENATE.

Assembly of Europe *See* PARLIAMENTARY ASSEMBLY (Conference on Security and Cooperation in Europe).

Assembly of European Regions (AER) Intergovernmental organization at regional level. Founded as the Council of the European Regions (CER) in 1985, the AER brings together regions from 18 European Union (EU) and Council of Europe member states. It is a forum for discussion, research and joint action. Its structure includes a general assembly, which meets annually, an executive bureau of 22 regional presidents, and a general secretariat (based in Strasbourg, France). It has a number of working groups, which focus on regional development, job creation, culture and cross-border cooperation and other issues.

Assembly of the Republic [Sobranie na Republika] Parliament of Macedonia. It has 120 members elected for a four-year term by absolute majority in single-member constituencies; if no candidate wins a majority, a second round is held.

Assembly of the Republic [Cumhuriyet Meclisi] Parliament of Northern Cyprus. It has 50 members elected for a five-year term. The voting system is based on proportional representation in three multi-member constituencies, with additional seats for parties gaining more than 36% of the vote in a constituency. Parties must secure a minimum of 5% of the popular vote nationwide to qualify for representation.

Assembly of the Republic [Assembleia da República] Parliament of Portugal. It has 230 members elected for a four-year term by proportional representation in 24 multi-member constituencies. Four seats are reserved for Portuguese citizens living abroad.

Assembly of the Western European Union or **WEU Assembly** Interparliamentary assembly, a consultative body of the Western European Union (WEU). The 115-member Assembly is composed of the member states' delegates to the Parliamentary Assembly of the Council of Europe and meets at least twice a year in Paris (France). It makes recommendations to the Council, the WEU's decision-making body composed of foreign and defence ministers, and to national parliaments and governments.

assent procedure In the European Union (EU), a method of decision making in which certain decisions taken by one institution require the approval of another. Thus, for instance, the European Parliament must give its assent to the accession of new member states and to cooperation and association agreements concluded with other states, which are negotiated by the Council of Ministers and the European Commission respectively; and the Council must give its assent to Commission decisions that adapt rules laid down in the founding treaties and on other important matters.

Assizes Informal name for the CONFERENCE OF THE PARLIAMENTS, an advisory body of the European Union (EU).

Associated List *See* ASSOCIATED LIST OF SOCIAL DEMOCRATS.

Associated List of Social Democrats [Združena Lista Socialdemokratov] (ZLSD) Slovenian political party. The ZLSD was formed in May 1993 from the merger of the Social Democratic Reform Party (SDP) and two smaller parties, the Social Democratic Union (SDUS) and Workers' Party (DSS). The SDP had been founded as the successor to the League of Communists (ZKS) in 1990 and had adopted a mainstream left-wing programme committed to a market-based economy and social justice. (The ZKS had been supportive of limited reforms since the mid 1980s.) The three parties and the small Democratic Party of Pensioners (DeSUS) had contested the December 1992 election as the Associated List (ZL), gaining 13.6% of the vote and 14/90 seats. The leader is Janez Koncijančič. Milan Kučan, who led the ZKS in the 1980s and is now president of the republic, retains considerable influence.

association agreement In the European Community (EC) and now the European Union (EU), a treaty with a non-member state covering economic and political cooperation. More comprehensive than cooperation or trade agreements, which have been signed with many countries, an 'association agreement' offers the associate free access to the EU market for most industrial products, reduced tariffs on agricultural products, and financial and technical assistance. The EC signed association agreements with Greece in 1961 (it became a full member in 1981), Turkey in 1963, Malta in 1970 and Cyprus in 1972. Some 70 developing countries, called the African, Caribbean and Pacific Group of States (ACP Group), nearly all former colonies of EU member states, also have associated status under the LOMÉ CONVENTION. In recent years association agreements known as 'EUROPE AGREEMENTS' have been signed with several Eastern European countries.

Association for the Republic - Republican Party of Czechoslovakia [Sdružení pro Republiku - Republikánská Strana Československa] (SPR-RSČ) or **Republicans** [Republikány] Czech political party. Founded in 1990, the Republicans are a far-right nationalist and populist group which has attracted disaffected youth and protest voters. At the June 1992 election the party gained 5.9% of the vote and 14/200 seats in the Czech parliament. The leader is Miroslav Sládek.

Association of Austrian Industrialists [Vereinigung Österreichischer Industrieller] (VÖI) Austrian employers' association. Founded in 1946, the VÖI's main function is to offer advice to its members and lobby for their interests. Formally it does not deal with industrial-relations matters, which are the responsibility of the statutory Federal Economic Chamber (BWK), but it generally works closely with the BWK. The president is Heinz Kessler, the general secretary Franz Ceska.

Association of Estonian Trade Unions [Eesti Ametiühingute Keskliit] (EAK) Estonian trade-union federation. Founded in 1990, when Estonia was still part of the Soviet Union, the EAK has 27 affiliated unions with a total membership of 340,000 (around two-fifths of the labour force). The leader is Raivo Paavo.

Association of Free Trade Unions of Latvia [Latvijas Brīvo Arodbiedrību Savienība] (LBAS) Latvian trade-union federation. The LBAS was founded in 1990, when Latvia was still part of the Soviet Union, after most of the republic's unions had withdrawn from the Soviet structure. It has 34 affiliated unions with a total membership of 608,000 (just under half the labour force). The leader is Andris Siliņš.

Association of the Central Alps (Arge-Alp or AG Alp) Intergovernmental organization at regional level. Established in 1972, the Arge-Alp group is composed of 10 Alpine regions: the Austrian provinces of Salzburg, Tyrol and Vorarlberg, the German state of Bavaria, the Italian region of Lombardy and provinces of South Tyrol and Trento, and the Swiss cantons of Grisons, Sankt Gallen and Ticino. It aims to promote regional cooperation in the economic, social, environmental and cultural fields. The secretariat is based in Innsbruck, Austria.

Association of the Eastern Alps (Alpe-Adria or Alpen-Adria) Intergovernmental organization at regional level. Established in 1978, the Alpen-Adria group is composed of countries and regions in Central Europe. They include five Austrian provinces, Croatia, the German state of Bavaria, three Hungarian counties, four Italian regions, and Slovenia. The organization aims to promote regional cooperation in the areas of tourism, energy, environment, transport, agriculture, forestry, sport and culture. It has close links with the CENTRAL EUROPEAN INITIATIVE (CEI). The secretariat is based in Venice, Italy.

Association of the Expelled [Bund der Vertriebenen] (BdV) German political and cultural organization. Formed in West Germany by the merger in 1958 of two federations comprising 31 regional associations, the BdV represents Germans who fled or were expelled from German and German-occupied territories at the end of the Second World War in 1945. The most populous of these regions were Silesia and Pomerania in what is now Poland and Sudetenland in what is now the Czech Republic. The BdV had around 2.5 million members in the 1960s, but its membership and influence declined in the 1970s and 80s. After the collapse of the Eastern European communist regimes in 1989 it reaffirmed long-standing demands for compensation, restitution of property and/or the right to resettle for its members and their descendants.

Association of Vatican Lay Workers [Associazione Dipendenti Laici Vaticani] (ADLV) Vatican trade union. The ADLV was founded in 1979 primarily to secure the introduction of labour regulations that conform to international norms. It represents 1,000 employees of the Vatican City State (two-fifths of the labour force). The leader is Valerio Arringoli.

Asturias Autonomous community or region of Spain. Situated in the north between the Bay of Biscay and the Cantabrian Mountains, Asturias has an area of 10,565 sq km and a population of 1,119,000. The capital is Oviedo, and the other main city is Gijón. The economy is based on manufacturing (metalworking), mining (coal, zinc, iron) and agriculture (dairy farming). Asturias is Spain's main coal-mining region; its economic base is not greatly diversified, and the restructuring of the mining and heavy industries has led to widespread unemployment. The dominant political party is the Spanish Socialist Workers' Party (PSOE), which has been in power since the first regional election in 1983; the other main parties are the centre-right People's Party (PP) and the United Left (IU). At the May 1991 election the PSOE gained 21 seats in the 45-member legislature, the PP 15 and the IU six. An independent kingdom from the 8th century, Asturias later formed the core of the Kingdom of León, which merged with Castile in 1230. Its traditionally strong regional identity was strengthened by the development of coal mining and related heavy industries in the mid 19th century. It was established as an autonomous community in 1981.

Asunción, Antoni (1951–) Spanish mechanical engineer, civil servant and politician. He was active in local government for the Spanish Socialist Workers' Party (PSOE) in his native Valencia region in the 1970s and 80s. In 1988 he was appointed director-general of prisons, a post within the justice ministry. From 1991–93 he was secretary-general and then secretary of state (= junior minister) for prison affairs, both posts within the interior ministry. He was appointed interior minister in November 1993.

Atanasov, Georgi (1933–) Bulgarian historian and politician. Elected to the central committee of the Bulgarian Communist Party (BKP) in 1968, he served as deputy director of the State Planning Commission and director of the Control Commission in the 1970s and 80s. He was prime minister from 1986 until his replacement in February 1990 by a reformist. In November 1992 he was convicted of embezzling public funds while in office and sentenced to 10 years' imprisonment. He was pardoned on health grounds in August 1994.

Athens Shorthand for the Greek government. Athens is the capital of Greece.

Áthos *See* HOLY MOUNTAIN.

Atienza, Luis (1957–) Spanish economist, academic and politician. He lectured in economics from 1981–86 and then worked briefly at the European Parliament. A member of the Spanish Socialist Workers' Party (PSOE), he served in the Basque regional government as junior minister for planning from 1987–89 and as economy minister from 1989–91. He then took up a senior position in the national agriculture ministry. He was appointed minister of agriculture, food and fisheries in May 1994.

Atilla, İsmet (1940–) Turkish administrator and politician. A graduate of the Social Services Academy, he has been director of an insurance company and an adviser to the labour and social security ministry. Elected to parliament for the centre-right True Path Party (DYP) in 1991, he was appointed finance and customs minister in June 1993.

Atlantic alliance Shorthand for the military and political alliance between the United States, Canada and 14 European countries, formalized in the NORTH ATLANTIC TREATY ORGANIZATION (NATO).

Atlantic Arc Commission (AAC) Intergovernmental organization at regional level. Founded in 1989, the Atlantic Arc brings together 23 Irish, British, French, Spanish and Portuguese counties and regions bordering on the Atlantic Ocean. Representing relatively poor peripheral regions within the European Union (EU), the Commission's main aim is to secure more EU development funding. It has drawn up a work plan focusing on cooperation in infrastructure, training, financial services, aquaculture, environmental issues and tourism.

atlanticism Close cooperation in international affairs, in particular at military and political level, between the countries of Western Europe and the United States. First outlined in the Atlantic Charter adopted by the United Kingdom and the United States in 1941, during the Second World War, it was formalized in the North Atlantic Treaty Organization (NATO) set up in 1949. Within the alliance, the British, Dutch and Portuguese governments are traditionally the strongest 'atlanticists'.

atraso ('backwardness') In Spain, a term used to describe the country's relative underdevelopment, in economic, political and social terms, compared to other Western European countries. The perceived gap has narrowed sharply since the acceleration of economic development in the 1960s and the restoration of democratic rule in the late 1970s.

ATS Abbreviation for the SCHILLING, the Austrian currency, used in banking etc.

Attali, Jacques (1943–) French mining engineer, economist and banker. He worked briefly in the mining industry and then lectured in economics and held senior posts in the civil service. From the mid 1970s he was a close adviser of François Mitterrand, leader of the Socialist Party (PS) and from 1981 president of the republic. In May 1990 he became president of the new European Bank for Reconstruction and Development (EBRD), set up to support economic development in the former communist countries of Eastern Europe. He resigned in July 1993 following allegations of overspending. He has written extensively on political and economic issues.

Attila Line Alternative name for the Green Line, the neutral buffer zone separating Greek Cypriot and Turkish Cypriot forces in Cyprus. 'Attila Line' was the name given to the ceasefire line accepted by

Turkey following its invasion of the island in 1974 (*see* CYPRUS QUESTION).

attorney-general (United Kingdom) *See* LAW OFFICERS.

Atun, Hakkı (1935–) Northern Cypriot architect, civil servant and politician. He worked for the planning and public works department of the Turkish Cypriot administration from 1963–75, serving as its director from 1967. Elected to the Northern Cypriot parliament for the National Unity Party (UBP) in 1975, he has been minister of housing (1976–79 and 1983–85), economy and finance (1979–81) and youth and culture (1981–82). He was speaker of parliament from 1985–93. In July 1992 he was elected leader of the new Democratic Party (DP), a breakaway from the UBP. After the December 1993 election he was appointed prime minister, and in January 1994 he formed a centrist coalition with the Republican Turkish Party (CTP).

Auken, Svend (1943–) Danish politician. He lectured in political science until his election to parliament for the Social Democratic Party (SD) in 1971. He was minister of labour from 1977–82. He became the party's deputy leader in 1985 and was its leader from 1987–92. He was appointed environment minister in the centre-left coalition which took office in January 1993.

Aussiedler (sing. -/in) ('emigrants' or 'resettlers') In Germany, a collective name for ethnic Germans from Eastern Europe and the former Soviet Union who have settled in Germany. They are the descendants of German colonists who migrated eastwards from the late Middle Ages onwards. Since 1950 a total of 2.4 million, mainly from the Soviet Union, Poland and Romania, have moved to Germany. Arrivals rose rapidly in the late 1980s, reaching a peak of 397,000 in 1990. They have fallen sharply since then, largely because eligibility rules were tightened and applicants must now submit requests for resettlement in their country of residence. As a group *Aussiedler* should be distinguished from asylum seekers and economic migrants who entered Germany in large numbers between 1989 and 1993.

Austria [Österreich] Country in central Europe.

Official data. Name: Republic of Austria [Republik Österreich]; capital: Vienna [Wien]; form of government: federal republic; head of state: federal president; head of government: federal chancellor; flag: three horizontal stripes, red, white and red; national holiday: 26 October (National Day); language: German; religion: none; currency: Schilling (S) (pl. -e) = 100 Groschen; abbreviation: A.

Geography. Austria has an area of 83,856 sq km. Land-locked, it is bordered by Germany and the Czech Republic in the north, Slovakia and Hungary in the east, Slovenia and Italy in the south, and Switzerland and Liechtenstein in the west. The Austrian Alps and other mountain ranges cover nearly two-thirds of the country. Most of the north and far east consists of hill lands and low mountains, and the northeast is a low-lying river plain. Some 18% of the land is arable, another 24% is covered by pastures and 39% is forested. The climate is alpine in the mountains (with mild summers and cold winters, warmer in the southern regions) and humid continental in the northeast (hot summers and cold winters); rainfall is moderate; temperatures and rainfall vary considerably with relief and altitude.

Demography. Austria has a population of 7,938,000. Population density is 96 per sq km (land area). Most of the people live in the eastern lowlands. Some 54% live in urban areas, and around a quarter lives in Vienna and its suburbs (population 1.9 million, city 1.5 million). Other major cities are Graz, Linz, Salzburg, Innsbruck and Klagenfurt. In ethnic and linguistic terms Austria is very homogeneous. Some 93.4% of the population is Austrian and German-speaking. Ethnic minorities include 22,000 Croats and 12,000 Hungarians in the east and 16,000 Slovenes in the southeast. Foreign nationals account for 6.6% of the population, and include citizens of Croatia, Slovenia, Turkey and Germany. Austria has also taken in around 60,000 refugees from former Yugoslavia.

In religious terms 80.6% of the population is nominally Roman Catholic, 4.9% Protestant and 1.5% Muslim; there are also around 7,000 Jews; most of the remainder is not religious.

Sociography. Austria scores 0.917 on the United Nations human development index (HDI), ranking 12th in the world and 8th among 32 European countries. There are 30 doctors and 103 hospital beds for every 10,000 people. Education is compulsory between the ages of six and 15. There is one teacher for every nine students, among the best ratios in Europe. Enrolment is 79% at the secondary level and 33% at the tertiary level. The literacy rate is virtually 100%. Real annual income per head (in terms of purchasing power) is US$ 17,690.

Infrastructure and communications. Austria has a highly developed transport and communications network, including several key north-south transit routes across the Alps and Vienna as a major centre for links with the neighbouring formerly communist countries. There are 107,180 km of paved roads and 2.99 million passenger cars (383 per 1,000 people), 6,660 km of railways and 446 km of navigable waterways. The main (inland) ports are Vienna and Linz. The main airport is at Vienna (Schwechat), and there are five other airports with scheduled services. There are 30 daily newspapers, with a combined circulation of around 2.8 million (around 350 per 1,000 people). There are 4.70 million radio receivers, 2.69 million television sets and 4.54 million telephones in use (respectively 601, 344 and 581 per 1,000 people).

Economic structure. The Austrian economy is highly developed, diversified and trade-oriented (exports account for two-fifths of national income), with close links to the German economy and traditionally a substantial state-owned sector. It is based on manufacturing, tourism and forestry. After a period of steady and rising growth in the 1980s (averaging 2.0% per year and reaching 4.6% in 1990), growth has declined in the 1990s. The 1990s have also been marked by balanced current accounts and relatively low inflation (averaging 3.6%) and unemployment (around 5%).

Services contribute 61% of GDP, industry contributes 36% (manufacturing 27%), and agriculture and forestry 3%. Some 27% of the labour force is employed in manufacturing, 19% in trade, 9% in construction and 8% in farming and forestry. The main crops grown are cereals (wheat, barley, maize), sugarbeets and potatoes; livestock raising (cattle, pigs, poultry), dairy farming and horticulture (fruit and vegetables) are also important agricultural activities. Forestry is also important. The main mineral resources are iron and tungsten. The main industries are engineering and food processing; other important branches are electrical goods, chemicals, metalworking and textiles. Tourism is a very important source of foreign exchange, contributing 9% of GNP (4% net). The main energy sources are imported fossil fuels and domestic hydroelectric power; 7% of export earnings are required to cover net fuel imports. The main exports are industrial machinery (18% of the total), electrical equipment (11%), wood and wood products (9%), textiles and clothing (8%) and motor vehicles (7%); machinery and transport equipment account for 37% of the total, basic manufactures for 31%. The main imports are machinery and transport equipment, basic manufactures, chemicals and fuels. The main trading partners are: exports: Germany (38%), Italy (10%), Switzerland (6%), France, United Kingdom, Hungary; imports: Germany (43%), Italy (9%), Japan (5%), Switzerland, France, United States; two-thirds of all trade is with European Union (EU) countries.

The Austrian National Bank [Österreichische Nationalbank] is the central bank. The main employers' associations are the Association of Austrian Industrialists (VÖI) and the Federal Economic Chamber (BWK); the main labour organizations are the Austrian Trade Union Federation (ÖGB) and the Federal Chamber of Labour (BAK or ÖAKT); there is a high degree of formal and informal cooperation among these organizations.

Political structure. Austria is a federal republic composed of nine provinces [Land, pl. Länder] on the basis of a constitution adopted in 1920. The head of state is the federal president [Bundespräsident], who is directly elected for a six-year term; s/he appoints the head of government and has certain emergency powers, but normally acts on the advice of the government. Executive power is vested in the federal chancellor [Bundeskanzler] and council of ministers. Legislative power is vested in the bicameral Parliament [Parlament], composed of the 183-member National Council [Nationalrat] elected for a four-year term by a system of proportional representation, and the 63-member Federal Council [Bundesrat] indirectly elected by the provincial assemblies for varying terms. On certain matters of special importance the two chambers sit together as the Federal Assembly [Bundesversammlung]. All citizens over the age of 19 are entitled to vote; voting is compulsory for presidential elections and in some provinces. Judicial power is ultimately vested in the Supreme Court [Oberster Gerichtshof] for civil and criminal cases, the Administrative Court [Verwaltungsgerichtshof] for administrative cases and the Constitutional Court [Verfassungsgerichtshof] on constitutional matters. The provinces have their own assemblies and governments and have extensive autonomy. They are Burgenland, Carinthia [Kärnten], Lower Austria [Niederösterreich], Salzburg, Styria [Steiermark], Tyrol [Tirol], Upper Austria [Oberösterreich], Vorarlberg and Vienna [Wien]. The provinces are divided administratively into districts and then communes, except in Vienna, where the functions of province and commune are combined.

The main political parties are the Social Democratic Party of Austria (SPÖ), Austrian People's Party (ÖVP), Freedom Party of Austria (FPÖ), Green Alternative or Greens (GA or Grüne) and Liberal Forum (LF, a breakaway from the FPÖ). At the general election in October 1990 the SPÖ gained 42.8% of the vote and 80/183 seats, the ÖVP 32.1% and 60 seats, the FPÖ 16.6% and 33 seats, and the Greens 4.8% and 10 seats. The government is formed by a centrist coalition of the SPÖ and ÖVP, with Franz Vranitzky as federal chancellor. Other senior ministers are Erhard Busek (deputy chancellor, science and research), Alois Mock (foreign affairs), Wolfgang Schüssel (economic affairs), Ferdinand Lacina (finance), Franz Löschnak (internal affairs), Nikolaus Michalek (justice) and Werner Fasslabend (defence). The head of state is President Thomas Klestil, who was elected in April/May 1992.

Security and international affiliations. The Austrian armed forces number 52,000 (army 46,000, airforce 6,000). Military service is compulsory and consists of six months' basic training and annual refresher training for 15 years.

Austria is a member of the Central European Initiative (CEI), Conference on Security and Cooperation in Europe (CSCE), Council of Europe, European Economic Area (EEA) and European Free Trade Association (EFTA), as well as the Organization for Economic Cooperation and Development (OECD) and the United Nations and its specialized agencies. It is due to join the European Union (EU) at the start of 1995.

History. The Celtic kingdom of Noricum, established in the 4th century BC, included most of modern Austria south of the Danube river. It was conquered by the Romans by 14 BC. During the Europewide migrations of the 5th–7th centuries the region was overrun by various Germanic tribes as well as the Huns, Avars and Slavs and was finally settled by the Germanic Bavarians. It was incorporated into the Frankish Kingdom in 790 and divided into several border provinces or marches. These included the Eastern March [Ostmark] – from which Austria [Österreich] derives its name – broadly corresponding to the modern provinces of Lower and Upper Austria, Styria and Carinthia. Christianity became the dominant religion around this time. Under the East Frankish Kingdom, later the Holy Roman or German Empire, the marches became autonomous duchies. The Baben-

berg family was invested with Austria proper in 976 and acquired Styria by inheritance in 1192. After the last Babenberg died childless in 1246 the two duchies were disputed between neighbouring Bohemia and Hungary and Rudolf of Habsburg, who had been elected emperor in 1273. Austria and Styria were confirmed as Habsburg possessions in 1282, and Carinthia, Carniola and Tyrol were acquired by inheritance in 1335. Over the next two centuries a combination of conquest, diplomacy, marriage and inheritance secured a great expansion of Habsburg domains from their Austrian base. (The Habsburgs' ancestral lands in Switzerland were lost in the 14th and 15th centuries.) When Charles V became emperor in 1519 he was already king of Spain and ruler of much of the Low Countries and Italy and would soon rule over a colonial empire in the Americas. He entrusted the Austrian possessions to his younger brother Ferdinand in 1521. In 1526 Ferdinand was elected king of Hungary and Bohemia (including Moravia and Silesia) after their ruler, King Louis II, had died in battle against the Ottoman Turks. Together with the Austrian crown lands these territories formed the core of the future Austrian Empire. The division of the Habsburg domains between the Austrian and Spanish branches of the family became permanent on Charles's abdication in 1555/56. In the 16th and 17th centuries the Habsburgs were able to counter the Protestant Reformation in their own possessions but not in the Holy Roman Empire as a whole. At the end of the Thirty Years' War (1618–48) the German states secured full sovereignty and the Holy Roman Empire disappeared as an effective political unit (although it continued in name until 1806). From the 16th century Austria was involved in a prolonged struggle with the Ottoman Empire for control of Hungary and the Balkan region. The Turks laid siege to Vienna in 1529 and 1683. In 1699 Austria gained control of historical Hungary (including Transylvania and Croatia), which had been in Turkish hands since 1526. At the end of the War of the Spanish Succession (1701–13/14) Austria acquired extensive territories in Italy and the Southern Netherlands (modern Belgium). In the second half of the 18th century the administration was centralized and a number of social and economic reforms were introduced. At the same time the Empire's stability was undermined by resentment among Hungarians, Czechs and others at Austrian dominance and at two costly wars, the War of the Austrian Succession (1740–48) and the Seven Years' War (1756–63). During the French Revolutionary and Napoleonic Wars (1792–1815) Austria was a leading member of the anti-French alliances. The chief minister, Klemens Metternich, played the key role in the post-Napoleonic reorganization of Europe carried out by the Congress of Vienna (1814–15).

After 1815 domestic policy became increasingly conservative and autocratic, and many of the 18th-century reforms were reversed. Democratic and nationalist uprisings in Austria, Hungary and elsewhere in 1848–49 were suppressed but forced some political reforms, the resignation of Metternich and the abdication of Emperor Ferdinand II. The latter was succeeded by his nephew, Francis Joseph II (1848–1916). Austria's defeat by Prussia in the Seven Weeks' War (1866) ended its ambition to dominate what became a united Germany. It also sparked renewed agitation for self-determination among the Empire's many component nations. In 1867 a 'dual monarchy' was established, with separate parliaments and administrations for Austria and Hungary. While going some way towards meeting Hungarian demands, it merely strengthened nationalist agitation among Czechs and Slovenes (within Austria) and Croats, Slovaks, Serbs and Romanians (within Hungary). The assassination of Archduke Francis Ferdinand by a Bosnian Serb nationalist in Sarajevo in 1914 provided the spark for the First World War (1914–18). Although relatively successful in military terms, the Habsburg Empire disintegrated politically. The various nations declared their independence and the monarchy was abolished in 1918. The

1919 Treaty of Saint-Germain reduced Austria to a rump state comprising the German-speaking areas. A federal constitution was adopted in 1920. The following years saw widespread economic and social dislocation and political instability. The government under Engelbert Dollfuss suspended parliament in 1933 and established a far-right dictatorship. Dollfuss was assassinated the following year during an abortive German-inspired coup. In 1938 German troops occupied Austria and the country was annexed to Germany – in what was called the *Anschluss* ('union') – as part of the National Socialist (Nazi) policy of uniting all German-speaking lands.

Like Germany, Austria was occupied by the victorious allies at the end of the Second World War (1939–45). The republic and constitution were restored. The occupation by American, British, French and Soviet troops ended in 1955. Austria regained full sovereignty and committed itself to 'permanent neutrality' and a non-aligned foreign policy. This allowed the country to act as a bridge between East and West during the Cold War. Austria became a founding member of the European Free Trade Association (EFTA) in 1960. From 1945–66 the two main parties, the Austrian People's Party (ÖVP) and Socialist Party (SPÖ, now the Social Democratic Party, SPÖ), held power in a series of grand coalitions. This period saw the development of the 'social partnership', i.e. close cooperation between government, employers and trade unions with the aim of ensuring full employment and steady economic growth. The ÖVP gained an absolute majority in the 1966 election but was defeated by the SPÖ four years later. The SPÖ ruled alone for 13 years until May 1983, in coalition with the then centre-right Freedom Party (FPÖ) until September 1986, and again with the ÖVP from January 1987. Bruno Kreisky was federal chancellor (= prime minister) from 1970–83 and Franz Vranitzky assumed the office in June 1986. In July 1989 Austria applied for membership of the European Community (EC), now the European Union (EU); accession negotiations were concluded in March 1994; membership was approved in a referendum in June (by 66.6% to 33.4%); and the country was due to join the EU at the start of 1995.

See also entries on specific institutions, organizations, parties, people, terms etc.

Austrian People's Party [Österreichische Volkspartei] (ÖVP) Austrian political party. Founded in 1945, the ÖVP is a christian democratic party. It was the senior partner in a grand coalition with the Socialist Party (SPÖ, now the Social Democratic Party, SPÖ) until 1966. It returned to government, this time as the SPÖ's junior partner, in January 1987. In recent years it has been losing support to the now far-right Freedom Party (FPÖ). At the October 1990 election it gained 32.1% of the vote and 60/183 seats. The leader is Erhard Busek.

Austrian Trade Union Federation [Österreichischer Gewerkschaftsbund] (ÖGB) Austrian trade-union federation. Founded in 1945, the ÖGB has 15 affiliated unions with a total membership of around 1.7 million (half the labour force and two-thirds of all employees). It cooperates with employers and the government on a range of macroeconomic issues, particularly through the Joint Commission on Wages and Prices. Although traditionally close to the Social Democratic Party (SPÖ), it has no formal links with it. The president is Friedrich Verzetnitsch.

autogestion ('self-management') In France, the devolution of power or the decentralization of political structures. The term was originally applied to arrangements for joint management-worker control in industry. An extensive programme of decentralization aimed at bringing decision making closer to those directly affected was introduced in 1982.

Automobile Party of Switzerland *See* FREEDOM PARTY OF ....

Autonome Gruppe *See* AUTONOMOUS GROUP.

autonomism [autonomismo] In Italy, a term used by the Northern League (Lega Nord) and other regional groupings advocating the country's conversion into a federal state. They call for wide-ranging autonomy for the existing 20 regions or for the creation of larger semi-independent states, in particular a 'Republic of the North' or 'Padania'.

autonomismo *See* AUTONOMISM.

autonomous community [comunidad autónoma, pl. -es -s] Semi-federal division of Spain. Each of the 17 communities or regions has a statute of autonomy (outlining its structure and the powers delegated to it), a legislature, and a government headed by a president. Most regions have considerable powers in matters such as economic development, transport, health, culture and police. In recognition of their distinctive identities, Andalusia, the Basque Country, Catalonia and Galicia have more extensive autonomy. The communities were set up in the early 1980s as part of a new system of decentralized government.

autonomous group [Autonome Gruppe, pl. -n] In Germany, a group of people who reject the existing economic, social and political system and have adopted an alternative lifestyle. They usually live communally and support far-left and/or radical environmentalist policies.

autonomous province (Yugoslavia) *See* POKRAJINA.

Autonomous Province of Western Bosnia [Pokrajina Zapadna Bosna] State proclaimed within Bosnia-Herzegovina by Muslims in the far northwest. Soon after the start of civil war in March 1992 (*see* BOSNIAN CIVIL WAR) the Bihać region, home to around 250,000 people, nearly all Slav Muslims, was surrounded by Serb-controlled areas, the self-proclaimed Serbian Republic to the south and Republic of Serbian Krajina across the border in Croatia. The Bihać 'pocket' was thus cut off from the Sarajevo-based central government and army. Exploiting the region's strategic position as a road and rail crossroads, local leaders were able to come to informal accommodations with the rebel Serb states and the government of Croatia. This and their criticism of the government's perceived intransigence in the face of the 'new situation' in the country led to growing tensions. Led by Fikret Abdić, a prominent businessman and member of the State Presidency, dissident members of the ruling Democratic Action Party (SDA) proclaimed the 'autonomous province' in September 1993. A government and assembly were set up in Velika Kladuša, Abdić was elected president, and the Muslim Democratic Party (MDS) was formed. The following month fighting erupted between forces loyal to the central government and those supporting the Abdić faction. The rebel forces initially controlled most of the Bihać region, but they were gradually pushed northwards and were finally defeated in August 1994.

autonomous region or **region** [regione autonoma, pl. regioni autonome] Italian administrative division. Each of the 20 autonomous regions has a statute (setting out its structure and the powers delegated to it), an assembly [consiglio regionale] elected for a five-year term, and an executive council [giunta regionale] headed by a president. The regions have wide-ranging powers in matters such as administrative organization, economic development, public services and environment. Five regions have greater autonomy and are called AUTONOMOUS REGIONS WITH SPECIAL STATUTE.

autonomous region with special statute or **special autonomous region** [regione autonoma con statuto speciale, pl. regioni autonome con ...] Italian administrative division. In recognition of their distinct identities, five of the country's twenty AUTONOMOUS REGIONS (Aosta Valley, Friuli - Venezia Giulia, Sardinia, Sicily, Trentino - Alto Adige) have been granted a 'special statute', which gives them extensive powers in matters of particular concern to them, such as language, education, culture and economic development.

Autonomous Trade Union Federation of Yugoslavia [Savez Samostalnih Sindikata Jugoslavije] (SSSJ) Yugoslav trade-union federation. The SSSJ was founded in 1945 and renamed in 1948. It has 15 affiliated unions with a total membership of 1.9 million (just under half of the labour force). Although 'autonomous' was added to the name in 1993, it maintains close links with the ruling Socialist Party of Serbia (SPS) and Democratic Socialist Party of Montenegro (DPSCG), the successors to the League of Communists. The president is Grožḍana Miljanović.

Autopartei See FREEDOM PARTY OF SWITZERLAND.

Autre Europe See ANOTHER EUROPE.

Auvergne Region of France. Situated in the centre, Auvergne has an area of 26,013 sq km and a population of 1,317,000. Dialects of Occitan are widely spoken in the region, but the language has no official status. The capital is Clermont-Ferrand. The economy is based on agriculture (dairy farming), manufacturing and tourism. It is one of the country's poorer regions. Like the other regions of southern France, Auvergne has a strong regional identity.

ÁVH and **ÁVO** Abbreviations for Államvédelmi Hatóság ('State Security Office') and Államvédelmi Osztály ('State Security Department') respectively, the two main Hungarian government agencies responsible at various times for internal security and the surveillance of dissidents during communist rule. Both were departments of the interior ministry.

avis ('opinion' in French) In the European Union (EU), an opinion expressed by one of the institutions on a specific issue. The European Commission, European Parliament, Economic and Social Committee (ECOSOC) etc may issue opinions as part of a formal consultation procedure or on their own initiative. The French term is widely used.

ÁVO See ÁVH.

avviso di garanzia ('cautionary warrant') In Italy, a document issued by magistrates informing a person that s/he is under investigation in connection with a specific crime. Issuing this warrant marks the start of an inquiry and may or may not lead to the pressing of formal charges.

Ayaz, Nevzat (1930–) Turkish lawyer, civil servant and politician. He served as governor of the provinces of Zonguldak, İstanbul and İzmir before entering politics. Elected to parliament for the centre-right True Path Party (DYP) in October 1991, he was appointed defence minister

34

in the centrist coalition which took office the following month. Held responsible for setbacks in the army's efforts to contain the Kurdish insurgency in the southeast, he was moved to education in October 1993.

Ayion Oros *See* HOLY MOUNTAIN.

Aznar, José María (1953–) Spanish civil servant and politician. He worked as a tax inspector before entering politics. He was president of the regional government of Castile-León from 1987–89 and was then elected to the national parliament for the centre-right People's Party (PP). He was elected party leader in April 1990.

Azores [Açores] Autonomous region of Portugal. Situated in the North Atlantic Ocean between 1,400 and 1,800 km west of the mainland, the Azores archipelago consists of nine main islands and several islets, with a total area of 2,247 sq km and a population of 237,000. The capital is Ponta Delgada. The economy is based on agriculture (dairy farming, fruit and vegetables) and fishing. The main political parties are the centre-right Social Democratic Party (PSD) and the Socialist Party (PS). At the election in October 1992 the PSD gained 28/51 seats in the regional legislature. The Azores were uninhabited when they were discovered in 1427. They have been a Portuguese possession since then, and the first settlements date from around 1432. The archipelago was granted extensive autonomy in 1976. There is a separatist movement, but it has little electoral support.

35

B Abbreviation for Belgium, used for international vehicle registrations, postal addresses etc.

B'90 *See* ALLIANCE 90.

Baader-Meinhof Group *See* RED ARMY FACTION.

Babić, Milan (1956–) Croatian dentist and politician. He was active in the League of Communists until the party's disintegration in 1990, when he joined the new Serbian Democratic Party (SDS, subsequently renamed the SDS of Krajina, SDSK), the main representative of the Serb community in Croatia. He was elected mayor of his native Knin in June 1990. A strong supporter of the Serbs' rebellion against Croatia's secession from Yugoslavia, he was elected president of the breakaway Republic of Serbian Krajina (RSK) in December 1991, at the height of the civil war. He was ousted the following February after rejecting the ceasefire plan sponsored by the United Nations, but regained a power base when he became leader of the SDSK in April. In January 1994 he narrowly lost the RSK presidential election to Milan Martić.

backbencher In the United Kingdom, a member of Parliament who does not hold a government office or is not a senior member of the opposition. Backbenchers are called thus because they sit on the benches behind the front benches reserved for government ministers and members of the shadow cabinet.

Baden-Württemberg Federal state [Land] of Germany. Situated in the southwest and bordering on France and Switzerland, Baden-Württemberg is the third-largest state, with an area of 35,751 sq km and a population of 10,149,000. The capital is Stuttgart, and the other main cities are Mannheim, Karlsruhe, Freiburg and Heidelberg. The economy is based on manufacturing (motor vehicles, machinery, electronics, chemicals), agriculture (wine, fruit and vegetables), forestry and tourism. The state is one of Germany's most productive and affluent. Political power is exercised by the State Assembly [Landtag], with 146 members elected for a four-year term, and a government headed by a minister-president. The dominant party is the Christian Democratic Union (CDU), which has been in power since 1952; the other main parties are the Social Democratic Party (SPD), the far-right Republicans, the Greens and the centrist Free Democratic Party (FDP). At the election in April 1992 the CDU gained 39.6% of the vote and 64 seats, the SPD 29.4% and 46 seats, the Republicans 10.9% and 15 seats, the Greens 9.5% and 13 seats, and the FDP 5.9% and eight seats. The government is formed by a CDU-SPD coalition headed by Erwin Teufel. Historically divided into Baden, Württemberg and a number of smaller states within the Holy Roman Empire, Baden-Württemberg was formed in 1952 from the merger of three states constituted after the Second World War.

Baile Átha Cliath Irish name for Dublin, the capital of Ireland.

bailiff Head of government, speaker of parliament and head of the judiciary in Guernsey and Jersey. The bailiffs are appointed by the British crown, i.e. the government, the sovereign power in both territories. In addition to being the chief executives, they also preside over the States (= parliament) and the Royal Court in the two territories. The dual nature of the office has evolved from the bailiffs' role since the Middle Ages as the crown's representatives in the islands.

Bailiwick of Guernsey and **Bailiwick of Jersey** Official names of Guernsey and Jersey respectively. 'Bailiwick' is a legal term denoting the area over which a bailiff has jurisdiction. During the Middle Ages the bailiffs were the representatives of the sovereign (i.e. the English, later British, monarch) in Guernsey and Jersey. They are now the senior civil officers in each territory.

Baja, Ferenc (1955–) Hungarian teacher, administrator and politician. He has taught in primary schools and worked for various public institutions and local authorities, becoming director of the Nyíregyháza city art gallery in 1990. Elected to parliament for the Hungarian Socialist Party (MSzP) in May 1994, he was appointed minister of the environment and regional policy in the MSzP-led centre-left coalition which took office two months later.

BAK *See* FEDERAL CHAMBER OF LABOUR.

Balcerowicz plan *See* CONTROLLED SHOCK.

Baleares Shorthand for Islas Baleares, the Spanish name for the BALEARIC ISLANDS.

Balearic Islands [Illes Balears (Catalan), Islas Baleares (Spanish)] Autonomous community or region of Spain. An archipelago in the Mediterranean Sea to the east of the mainland and consisting of Mallorca, Menorca, Ibiza [Eivissa in Catalan] and several smaller islands, the Balearic Islands have an area of 5,014 sq km and a population of 688,000. Around three-quarters of the population is Catalan, and Catalan is the first official language. The capital is Palma de Mallorca. The economy is based on tourism, agriculture (cereals, cattle farming) and some fishing, forestry and manufacturing. The dominant political parties are the centre-right People's Party (PP) and its ally the Mallorcan Union (UM), which have been in power since the first regional election in 1983. At the May 1991 election the PP and UM gained 31 seats in the 59-member legislature, and the Spanish Socialist Workers' Party (PSOE) 21. The Balearic Islands were conquered by Aragón in the 12th century after three centuries of Muslim rule. They formed an autonomous kingdom under the Aragonese crown until 1349. Menorca was a British possession from 1713–1802. The province of the Balearic Islands was established as an autonomous region in 1983.

Balears Shorthand for Illes Balears, the Catalan name for the BALEARIC ISLANDS.

Balkan civil wars *See* BOSNIAN CIVIL WAR *and* CROATIAN CIVIL WAR.

Balkan countries or **the Balkans** Collective name for Albania, Bosnia-Herzegovina, Bulgaria, Croatia, Greece, Macedonia, Romania, Slovenia and Yugoslavia. Geographically, the Balkan Peninsula covers the whole of southeastern Europe, including part of Turkey. The name was coined in the early 19th century – *balkan* means 'forested mountains' in Turkish – to denote the European territories of the Ottoman Empire.

Balkan wars *See* BOSNIAN CIVIL WAR *and* CROATIAN CIVIL WAR.

Balkanization The fragmentation of a region into antagonistic states. The term is taken from the Balkan region, where the break-up of the Ottoman Empire in the late 19th and early 20th centuries created tension and sparked a series of wars between the newly independent states. In recent years it has been used particularly in the context of Yugoslavia and the former Soviet Union.

Balkans, the Shorthand for the BALKAN COUNTRIES.

Balladur, Édouard (1929–) French civil servant and politician. Trained as a lawyer and administrator, he initially worked for the Council of State, a government advisory body. In the 1960s and early 70s he was a senior adviser to Georges Pompidou, who was prime minister from 1964–68 and president from 1969–74. He then became chairman of two subsidiaries of the state electricity company. Elected to parliament for the right-wing Rally for the Republic (RPR) in 1986, he was minister for the economy, finance and privatization during the Chirac administration (1986–88). When the right returned to power at the March 1993 election, he was appointed prime minister and formed a centre-right government.

Balladur plan Proposal for improving security in Eastern Europe put forward by the French prime minister, Édouard Balladur. The main aim of the initiative, formally presented at a European Union (EU) summit in June 1993, is to prevent tensions in and between Eastern European countries from erupting into violent conflicts (as happened in Yugoslavia in 1991). It seeks specifically to encourage the region's states to improve relations among themselves, resolve border disputes and guarantee the rights of ethnic minorities. The initiative was adopted by the EU, which sponsored the Conference on Stability in Europe in Paris (France) in May 1994. Attended by foreign ministers from 40 countries, it set up a framework for the negotiation of bilateral goodneighbourliness agreements among Eastern

European countries and called for their eventual inclusion in a general 'stability pact' within the framework of the Conference on Security and Cooperation in Europe (CSCE).

Ballhausplatz Shorthand for the Austrian government. The Ballhausplatz is a square in Vienna which contains the Federal Chancellery (= prime minister's office) and the foreign ministry.

Baltic Assembly Interparliamentary assembly, a consultative body of the Baltic Council. The Assembly brings together parliamentarians from Estonia, Latvia and Lithuania. It first met in January 1992.

Baltic Council Intergovernmental organization. Comprising Estonia, Latvia and Lithuania, the Baltic Council – not to be confused with the Council of Baltic Sea States (CBSS) or Baltic Sea Council – is the successor to the Baltic Entente established in 1934 and abolished when the three countries were annexed by the Soviet Union in 1940. The Council was established in May 1990, when the republics were still part of the Soviet Union, to coordinate policy in all areas of common interest. Its aims are to further cooperation in economic, defence and other political fields and to adopt common positions on such matters as the three countries' integration into pan-European structures and relations with Russia and other members of the Commonwealth of Independent States (CIS). The three countries concluded a free-trade agreement abolishing virtually all trade restrictions in September 1993, and have signed treaties covering cooperation on visa requirements, criminal investigations, environmental problems and other matters. The Council's main organs are: (i) the Council of Baltic States, comprising the presidents, heads of government and/or foreign ministers; (ii) a permanent working group for the exchange of information and coordination of foreign policy; and (iii) specialist committees. The secretariat is based in Rīga, the Latvian capital. The Baltic Assembly is a consultative assembly of parliamentarians from the three countries.

Baltic countries or **the Baltics** Collective name for Estonia, Latvia and Lithuania. Situated on the eastern shores of the Baltic Sea, the Baltic region became part of the Russian Empire in the 18th century. The three countries became independent at the end of the First World War, were annexed by the Soviet Union in 1940, and regained their independence after the abortive Soviet coup in August 1991. Although the three countries are often treated as a unit by outsiders and they do cooperate in many fields, particularly foreign affairs, they have little in common in historical, linguistic and religious terms. *See also* BALTIC COUNCIL.

Baltic Marine Environment Protection Commission or **Helsinki Commission** (HELCOM) Intergovernmental organization. HELCOM was set up in 1980 to implement the CONVENTION ON THE PROTECTION OF THE MARINE ENVIRONMENT OF THE BALTIC SEA AREA or Helsinki Convention, signed that year in the Finnish capital. All nine littoral states are members: Denmark, Estonia, Finland, Germany, Latvia, Lithuania, Poland, Russia and Sweden. The Commission meets annually at ministerial level, and its secretariat is based in Helsinki.

Baltic republics *See* BALTIC COUNTRIES.

Baltic Sea Council *See* COUNCIL OF BALTIC SEA STATES.

Baltics, the Shorthand for the BALTIC COUNTRIES, republics or states, i.e. Estonia, Latvia and Lithuania.

Balts Informal name for the peoples of the Baltic countries, i.e. Estonians, Latvians and Lithuanians. The name is purely conventional and does not indicate any close ethnic, linguistic, cultural or historical links.

Banca d'Italia *See* BANK OF ITALY.

Banco Ambrosiano affair Financial and political scandal in Italy surrounding the affairs of a major bank and its collapse. The president of the Milan-based Banco Ambrosiano, Roberto Calvi, was found hanged under a London bridge in June 1982. His death – initially thought to be suicide but eventually ruled a case of murder – precipitated the bank's collapse in August with worldwide debts estimated at US$ 1.3 billion. It emerged that the bank had had close links with the Vatican's Institute of Religious Works (IOR), the bank of the Roman Catholic Church, which had issued dubious letters of patronage and had cooperated in questionable share dealings. The allegations of impropriety strained relations between Italy and the Vatican. In May 1984 the IOR agreed to pay Banco Ambrosiano's 109 creditor banks US$ 468 million (around two-thirds of the total claims) in final settlement 'in recognition of moral involvement' but without admitting liability in the collapse. Over the following years a number of senior businesspeople and politicians were tried on charges relating to the bank's operations and collapse. In March 1985 three former directors were convicted of illegal share dealings and contraventions of foreign-exchange regulations; they were given suspended prison sentences and heavy fines, reduced on appeal in June 1986. In May 1990 35 people went on trial for complicity in fraudulent bankruptcy and other offences. Among them was Licio Gelli, head of the Propaganda Two secret society (*see* P-2 AFFAIR), of which Calvi had also been a member. In April 1992 all but three of the accused were found guilty, with Gelli and a close associate receiving sentences of 18½ and 19 years respectively; most cases went to appeal. In November 1993 one of the country's most prominent businessmen, Carlo De Benedetti, who had briefly been a major shareholder and a vice-president of Banco Ambrosiano before ceding control to Calvi in January 1982, was acquitted, on appeal, of fraud in connection with the sale of his stake. The Banco Ambrosiano affair was tied directly into the party-funding scandals that broke in 1992 and 1993 (*see* ITALIAN CORRUPTION SCANDALS) when the former leader of the Italian Socialist Party (PSI), Bettino Craxi, and his deputy, Claudio Martelli, were charged with accepting funds from Calvi and the bank. They were convicted of corruption and sentenced to 8½ years' imprisonment in July 1994. (At the time both were also on trial in two other major

corruption cases.) *See also* HIDDEN GOVERNMENT.

Bangemann, Martin (1934–) German lawyer and politician. He was elected to parliament for the centrist Free Democratic Party (FDP) in 1973. He became minister of economic affairs in 1984 and party chairman in 1985. In January 1989 he became a commissioner of the European Community (EC). He was responsible for overseeing the completion of the single market and for industrial policy until January 1993, and has been in charge of industrial policy, technology and telecommunications since then.

Bank for International Settlements (BIS) International financial organization. Founded in 1930, the BIS aims to promote cooperation among national central banks and to provide facilities for international financial operations. Its 33 members are the central banks or comparable financial institutions of all major European countries, Japan, the United States and several other industrialized countries. In legal terms it is a limited company, not an intergovernmental organization, but it is governed by international law. Its structure comprises the annual General Meeting, the Board of Directors, and a chief executive officer who is responsible for administrative matters. Sometimes referred to as the 'central banks' bank', the BIS acts as a trustee or agent with regard to international financial settlements. In this context it provided several services to the European Community (EC) until the establishment of the European Monetary Institute (EMI) in January 1994: it functioned as the secretariat for the Committee of Governors of the EC states' central banks and for the Board of Governors of the European Monetary Cooperation Fund (EMCF), managed the EMCF and the European Monetary System (EMS), and organized meetings of experts on a range of subjects. The secretariat is based in Basel, Switzerland. The president is Wim Duisenberg (Netherlands), the general manager is Andrew Crockett (United Kingdom).

Bank of Crete affair Financial and political scandal in Greece involving several leading members of the Pan-Hellenic Socialist Movement (PASOK). In November 1988 the owner of the Bank of Crete [Trápeza Krítis], Giorgos Koskotas, under investigation for fraud and embezzlement estimated at 19.6 billion drachmas (67 million ecus), claimed that PASOK ministers had taken bribes to cover up the bank's dealings. The following March he also claimed that Andreas Papandreou, prime minister at the time, had initiated a scheme to divert public funds to the bank and cream off most of the interest for party purposes. The allegations contributed to the party's defeat in the November 1989 general election. The trial of Papandreou and three former ministers, Dimitris Tsovolas, Agamemnon Koutsogiorgas and Georgios Petsos (responsible for finance, justice and public order respectively), opened in March 1991. Koskotas failed to substantiate most of his claims, however, and was later found guilty of forging a key document allegedly signed by Papandreou. In January 1992 Papandreou was cleared of all charges; Tsovolas and Petsos were convicted of corruption; Koutsogiorgas had died during the trial.

Bank of England Central bank of the United Kingdom. Founded in 1694 as a joint-stock company, the Bank of England was nationalized in 1946. It issues banknotes, implements the government's monetary and credit policies, and supervises and regulates the banking and financial sector. It is headed by a governor appointed by the government. The governor is Eddie George.

Bank of France [Banque de France] Central bank of France. Founded in 1800, the Banque de France was nationalized in 1946. It is the sole issuer of banknotes and has primary responsibility for monetary and credit policies. It was made independent from the government and charged with defining and implementing monetary policy in January 1994. It is headed by a governor and two deputy governors, who are appointed by the president of the republic. The governor is Jean-Claude Trichet.

Bank of Italy [Banca d'Italia] Central bank of Italy. Founded in 1893, the Banca d'Italia has had the sole right to issue banknotes since 1926 and plays a key role in the formulation of monetary and credit policies and the regulation of the financial sector. It was given greater autonomy from the treasury ministry in 1981, and has been allowed to set interest rates since 1992. The governor is Antonio Fazio.

Banque de France *See* BANK OF FRANCE.

Banski Dvori Shorthand for the Croatian presidency. The Banski Dvori ('Presidential Palace') in Zagreb is the president's official residence.

Barcelona Convention Shorthand for the CONVENTION FOR THE PROTECTION OF THE MEDITERRANEAN SEA AGAINST POLLUTION.

Barents Euro-Arctic Council *See* COUNCIL OF THE EURO-ARCTIC REGION.

Barents Sea question Border dispute between Norway and the Soviet Union and now Russia. The Barents Sea is an outlying portion of the Arctic Ocean to the north of Norway and Russia between the Spitsbergen and Novaya Zemlya archipelagos. It includes the access routes to the strategically important Russian ports of Murmansk and Arkhangelsk and contains rich fishing grounds and extensive oil and gas reserves. During the Cold War the area had added strategic significance as a point of contact between North Atlantic Treaty Organization (NATO) and Warsaw Pact forces. The dispute over the demarcation of the border between Norway and the Soviet Union arose in 1976 after both countries had declared 200-mile exclusive economic zones which overlapped. Agreement on the status of three-quarters of the disputed area of 175,000 sq km was reached in principle in June 1991. *See also* COUNCIL OF THE EURO-ARCTIC REGION.

Barnier, Michel (1951–) French politician. A graduate in business studies, he was an adviser to various ministers from 1973 and was elected to parliament for the right-wing Rally for the Republic (RPR) in 1978. He was appointed minister of the environment in the centre-right administration which took office in March 1993.

Basic Law [Grundgesetz] Formal name of the German constitution. It came into force in West Germany in 1949, and was extended to East Germany on reunification in October 1990.

Basilicata Autonomous region of Italy. Situated in the south, Basilicata has an area of 9,992 sq km and a population of 592,000. The capital is Potenza. The economy is based on agriculture (livestock farming, cereals, fruit and vegetables). Part of the MEZZOGIORNO, the region is one of the country's poorest; there has been substantial emigration since the 19th century. Basilicata became part of the Kingdom of Naples in the 12th century and was incorporated into unified Italy in 1860.

basket In the Conference on Security and Cooperation in Europe (CSCE), one of the four main sections of the HELSINKI FINAL ACT.

Basque Country [País Vasco (Spanish), Euskadi (Basque)] Autonomous community or region of Spain. Situated in the north along the Bay of Biscay and bordering on France, the Basque Country has an area of 7,261 sq km and a population of 2,130,000. The majority of the people consider themselves ethnic Basques (detailed figures n.a.). Basque or Euskara, a language isolate (i.e. not related to any other known language), is spoken by around a third of the population; it has equal official status with Spanish. There are also substantial numbers of Basques and Basque speakers in neighbouring Navarra and across the border in France. The capital is Vitoria [Gasteiz in Basque], but the largest cities are Bilbao [Bilbo] and San Sebastián [Donostia]; Guernica [Guernika], the traditional Basque capital, has no official status. The economy is based on manufacturing (metalworking, food processing, chemicals, paper), agriculture (cereals, fruit, sheep farming), services and forestry. The Basque Country is one of Spain's most industrialized and affluent regions, although the decline of the traditional heavy industries has led to considerable structural unemployment. Political power is exercised by the 75-member Legislature [Parlamento/Lege-

biltzarre] elected for a four-year term and the Government [Gobierno/Jaurlaritza] headed by a president [lendakari]. The main parties are the centre-right Basque Nationalist Party (PNV/EAJ); the Basque Socialist Party - Basque Left (PSE-EE), the regional branch of the Spanish Socialist Workers' Party (PSOE); People's Unity (Herri Batasuna, HB), which advocates full independence for the region and supports violent action to that end; Basque Solidarity (EA), which advocates independence but rejects violence; and the centre-right People's Party (PP). At the October 1990 election the PNV/EAJ gained 28.9% of the vote and 22 seats, the PSE 20.8% and 16 seats, HB 17.3% and 13 seats, EA 10.4% and nine seats, the PP 8.7% and six seats, and the EE 7.9% and six seats. Since October 1991 government has been formed by a coalition of the PNV/EAJ and PSE-EE, with José Antonio Ardanza as president. Roman authors first recorded the presence of 'Vascones' in the region in the 2nd century BC. Relative geographical isolation has enabled the Basques to retain their identity ever since. Part of Navarre in the early Middle Ages and later of Castile and Spain, the Basque Country enjoyed a large measure of autonomy under a system of traditional charters or *fueros*. These were gradually withdrawn by Spain's central government in the 19th century. Wide-ranging autonomy was granted during the Second Republic in 1936. Under the Franco regime (1939–75) all manifestations of Basque culture, including the use of the Basque language, were banned. Basque Homeland and Liberty (ETA), founded by radical nationalists, launched a guerrilla campaign for independence in the 1960s which at the time enjoyed considerable latent support. In the 1970s the counter-insurgency activities of the security forces further strengthened Basque opposition to the central government. In 1979, after the restoration of democratic rule, the Basque Country was granted autonomy under the Statute of Guernica. Powers of self-government were extended during the 1980s.

Basque Country or **Basque Lands** [Euskal Herri (Basque)] Collective name for the historical homeland of the Basque people and language. It comprises the BASQUE COUNTRY [Euskadi] proper and Navarre, two autonomous communities of Spain, and the Pyrénées-Atlantiques department of France. The Basque language, which has official status in Spain but not in France, is spoken by around 1 million people, around a quarter of the total population of the three regions. Many more people consider themselves Basque.

Basque Homeland and Liberty [Euskadi ta Askatasuna (Basque)] (ETA) Spanish guerrilla group. ETA was founded in 1959 by radical members of the Basque Nationalist Party (PNV/EAJ) who considered violent action against the Spanish state the only means of securing independence for the Basque Country. It has carried on a guerrilla campaign since the late 1960s and has been responsible for more than 700 deaths since then. Its activities include assassinations of military personnel, police officers and government officials, and bombings of government buildings and economic targets. To finance its operations it has robbed banks, kidnapped industrialists for ransom, and extorts or collects a 'revolutionary tax' from businesses. Its most devastating attacks were the assassination of the prime minister, Admiral Luis Carrero Blanco, in 1973; the bombing campaigns in resorts (known as 'tourist wars') carried out regularly since 1979; and the bombing of a Barcelona supermarket in 1987, which killed 21 shoppers. In 1974 the organization split into a 'political-military' and a 'military' wing, ETA-Militar (ETA-M). The former has been largely inactive since the granting of autonomy to the region in 1980. ETA had considerable support among the Basque people in the 1960s and 70s, during the Franco regime and the transition to democracy (from 1975). Since then People's Unity (Herri Batasuna, HB), the party which generally supports its campaign of violence, has gained about a sixth of the vote in successive regional elections. In the late 1980s ETA's impact and influ-ence were reduced by a combination of more effective police operations and the declining appeal of its radical nationalist message in an increasingly federal Spain. In the most serious blow to the organization since its foundation, French police in March 1992 captured three top leaders, including Francisco Múgica Garmendia, known as 'Artapalo'. ETA leaders and Spanish officials have held several rounds of informal talks since the late 1980s.

Basque Left [Euskadiko Ezkerra (Basque)] (EE) Former Spanish political party. Founded in 1975, the EE gained 7.9% of the vote and 6/75 seats in the regional election in the Basque Country in October 1990. In March 1993 it merged with the Basque Socialist Party (PSE), the regional branch of the Spanish Socialist Workers' Party (PSOE). A minority wing, led by Xabier Gurrutxaga, broke away to form the Basque Left [Euskal Ezkerra] (EUE).

Basque Nation and Liberty See BASQUE HOMELAND AND LIBERTY.

Basque Nationalist Party [Partido Nacionalista Vasco (Spanish), Eusko Alderdi Jeltzalea (Basque)] (PNV or EAJ) Spanish political party. The oldest of the Basque parties, founded in 1895, the PNV/EAJ advocates internal autonomy for the Basque Country within a federal Spain. It is centre-right in its economic policies and has conservative views on social issues. It has been the region's largest party since the first regional election in 1980 and has led successive coalitions. It gained 28.9% of the vote and 22/75 seats at the October 1990 regional election, and the equivalent of 1.2% nationally and 5/350 seats at the June 1993 general election. The party leader is Xabier Arzallus, while José Antonio Ardanza heads the government.

Basque Socialist Party - Basque Left [Partido Socialista de Euskadi - Euskadiko Ezkerra] (PSE-EE) Spanish political party, the Basque branch of the SPANISH SOCIALIST WORKERS' PARTY (PSOE). The PSE-EE was formed in March 1993 by the merger of the Basque Socialist Party (PSE), the PSOE's regional branch, and the independent Basque Left (EE). It is the second-largest party in the Basque

Country. At the October 1990 regional election the PSE had gained 20.8% of the vote and 16/75 seats and the EE 7.9% and six seats. The president is Txiki Benegas, the general secretary is Ramón Jauregui.

Basque Solidarity [Eusko Alkartasuna (Basque)] (EA) Spanish political party. Founded in 1986 as a breakaway from the Basque Nationalist Party (PNV/EAJ), EA advocates independence for the Basque Country, is centre-left in its economic policies, and has liberal views on social issues. It gained 10.4% of the vote and 9/75 seats at the October 1990 regional election, and one seat (out of 350) at the June 1993 general election. The leader is Carlos Garaikoetxea.

Basque Workers' Solidarity [Eusko Langilleen Alkartasuna (Basque), Solidaridad de Trabajadores Vascos (Spanish)] (ELA or STV) Spanish trade-union federation. Founded in 1911, the ELA/STV is the main labour organization in the Basque Country, an autonomous community or region of Spain. It has around 110,000 members (a sixth of the region's labour force), concentrated in the manufacturing sector. It supports greater autonomy for the Basque Country, but has no formal links with any political parties. The president is José Miguel Leunda Etxeberria.

Basse-Normandie *See* LOWER NORMANDY.

Bastille Day Common name for France's national holiday. Celebrated on 14 July, it commemorates the storming of the Bastille prison in Paris in the early days of the French Revolution in 1789.

Baudis, Dominique (1947–) French journalist and politician. In the 1970s he worked in television, as a foreign correspondent and newscaster. He was active in local government in Paris and the Midi-Pyrénées region from the early 1970s and was elected mayor of Toulouse in March 1983 (succeeding his father, Pierre). A member of the centre-right Social Democratic Centre (CDS), he was also elected to the European Parliament in 1984 but gave up his seat after becoming a National Assembly deputy in 1988. He was again elected to the European Parliament in June 1994.

Baudouin I (French) or **Boudewijn I** (Dutch) (1930–93) King of Belgium. He succeeded to the throne in 1951 on the abdication of his father, Leopold III. He married a Spanish princess, Fabiola of Aragón, in 1960. He died of heart failure in July 1993. As he had no children, he was succeeded by his brother, now King Albert II.

Baudyš, Antonín (1946–) Czech mechanical engineer, academic and politician. He lectured in precision mechanics and optics from 1970–89. A member of the Christian Democratic Union - Czechoslovak People's Party (KDU-ČSL), he was deputy prime minister and minister of transport and communications in the Czechoslovak federal government from June 1992 until the federation's dissolution at the end of the year. In January 1993 he was appointed minister of defence of the newly independent Czech Republic.

Bavaria [Bayern] Federal state [Land] of Germany. Situated in the southeast and bordering on the Czech Republic and Austria, Bavaria has an area of 70,554 sq km and a population of 11,770,000. It is the largest state in terms of area and the second-largest in terms of population. The capital is Munich [München], and the other main cities are Nuremberg [Nürnberg], Augsburg and Würzburg. The economy is based on manufacturing (motor vehicles, machinery, electronics, chemicals), agriculture and tourism. Traditionally agricultural, Bavaria has become highly industrialized and is one of Germany's most prosperous states. Political power is exercised by a bicameral parliament, composed of a 204-member State Assembly [Landtag] elected for a four-year term and a 60-member Senate [Senat] elected for a six-year term, and a government headed by a minister-president. The dominant party is the right-wing Christian Social Union (CSU), the Bavarian counterpart of the Christian Democratic Union (CDU), which has been in power since 1957; the other main parties are the Social Democratic Party (SPD), the Greens, the far-right Republicans (REP) and the centrist

43

Free Democratic Party (FDP). At the election in September 1994 the CSU gained 52.8% of the vote and 120 seats, the SPD 30.1% and 70 seats, the Greens 6.1% and 14 seats, the Republicans 3.9% and no seats, and the FDP 2.8% and no seats. The minister-president is Edmund Stoiber. Unlike most German states, Bavaria has existed as a distinct political and cultural entity since the early Middle Ages and has a strong regional identity. Under the house of Wittelsbach, which held the ducal throne from 1181, it became one of the dominant states within the Holy Roman Empire. It became a kingdom in 1806 and a state of the German Empire in 1871.

Bavčar, Igor (1955–) Slovenian administrator and politician. In the 1980s he worked for the communist youth federation, the communist-dominated Socialist Alliance of Working People (SZDL) and a computer firm. In 1988 he became leader of the Council for the Protection of Human Rights, one of the first high-profile opposition groups in Slovenia. After the multiparty election in April 1990 (when Slovenia was still part of Yugoslavia), he was appointed interior minister, a post he held until January 1993. He was leader of the centrist Democratic Party (DSS) from October 1991 until it joined the new Liberal Democratic Party (LDS) in March 1994.

Bayern *See* BAVARIA.

Bayrou, François (1951–) French teacher and politician. He was national secretary of the Social Democratic Centre (CDS) from 1980–86 and deputy general secretary from 1986–93. He has also held several senior posts in the centre-right Union for French Democracy (UDF) alliance. Elected to parliament in 1986, he was appointed minister of education in the centre-right administration which took office in March 1993.

BBWR *See* NON-PARTY BLOC IN SUPPORT OF REFORMS.

BDA *See* CONFEDERATION OF GERMAN EMPLOYERS' ASSOCIATIONS.

BDI *See* CONFEDERATION OF GERMAN INDUSTRY.

BdV *See* ASSOCIATION OF THE EXPELLED.

Beatrix (1938–) Queen of the Netherlands. She succeeded to the throne on the abdication of her mother, now Princess Juliana, in 1980. She married the German diplomat Claus von Amsberg, now Prince Claus, in 1966. They have three children.

Beckett, Margaret (1943–) British researcher and politician. She has worked as a technician in a university metallurgical department and as a researcher for the Granada television company and the Labour Party. She has been a Labour member of Parliament from 1974–79 and since 1983. She became a senior spokeswoman on financial affairs in 1989 and was elected deputy party leader in 1992. She became acting leader on the death of John Smith in May 1994. In the ensuing party elections in July she stood unsuccessfully for the leadership and deputy leadership.

beef industry affair Business scandal in Ireland involving fraud and malpractice in the beef-processing industry and, specifically, political controversy surrounding the use of government funds to underwrite beef exports by Goodman International, Europe's largest meat-processing concern. In May 1991 a British television programme and the then opposition Labour Party alleged widespread irregularities in the beef industry, in particular the misuse of European Community (EC) 'intervention funds' (i.e. subsidies) in the granting of 'export credit insurance' (ECI) for beef exports to Iraq and other countries by Goodman in the late 1980s. An inquiry was set up in June under a senior judge, Liam Hamilton, which began hearing evidence in October. The 21-month public inquiry revealed evidence of extensive breaches of EC rules, widespread tax evasion by Goodman and other meat-processing companies, and collusion between company managers and officials of the agriculture ministry (responsible for operating the EC's intervention system in Ireland). Specifically, it emerged that much of the beef covered by Irish government guarantees came not from Ireland but from Britain and even from EC 'intervention stocks' (the 'beef mountain'). Public interest centred on the involvement of Albert Reynolds, industry and commerce minister in the Fianna Fáil government in 1987–88 and thus responsible for approving ECI at the time of the alleged irregularities, who had become prime minister in February 1992. In October 1992 Des O'Malley, the industry and commerce minister and leader of the Progressive Democrats (PDs), the junior coalition partner, described Reynolds's handling of export credits as 'imprudent' and 'very seriously wrong', and Reynolds in turn accused O'Malley of 'dishonest' testimony. The recriminations led to the break-up of the coalition and an early election in November. In January 1993 Fianna Fáil formed a coalition with Labour. The inquiry report, published in August 1994, (i) confirmed 'flagrant abuse' of EC intervention schemes and widespread tax evasion, (ii) criticized weaknesses in public administration, and (iii) highlighted the ineffectiveness of the industry's regulatory bodies. However, it found no evidence that senior managers or ministers had known of the irregularities. It described Reynolds's decisions to grant ECI to Iraq, against the advice of his own officials and the regulatory bodies, as ill-considered, but accepted that he had acted in the national interest as he saw it. The report thus broadly vindicated both Reynolds and Dick Spring, the Labour leader and deputy prime minister, who while in opposition had accused the government of incompetence and corruption. This meant that the coalition was not under threat. The affair did raise issues of the relationship between government and business in Irish public life, and specifically the close links between Goodman International and Fianna Fáil. In this context the concern's rescue from liquidation by the government in 1990/91 was also controversial. (Its financial problems were in large part due to the Iraqi government defaulting on payments after Iraq's invasion of Kuwait in August 1990 and the imposition of United Nations sanctions.)

beef mountain (European Union) *See* FOOD MOUNTAINS.

BEF Abbreviation for the FRANC, the Belgian currency, used in banking etc.

Békesi, László (1942–) Hungarian economist and politician. He worked as a full-time official of the communist Hungarian Socialist Workers' Party (MSzMP) from 1968–85. He then became deputy finance minister and was finance minister from 1989 until the reconstituted Hungarian Socialist Party (MSzP) lost power in the 1990 multiparty election. In July 1994 he was appointed finance minister in the new MSzP-led coalition.

Belém Palace [Palácio de Belém] Shorthand for the Portuguese presidency. The Palácio de Belém in Lisbon is the official residence of the president.

Belgian Business Federation [Verbond van Belgische Ondernemingen (Dutch), Fédération des Entreprises de Belgique (French)] (VBO or FEB) Belgian employers' association. Founded in 1895, it comprises 46 trade associations representing most of the country's employers. The president is Urbain Devoldere, the managing director Tony Vandeputte.

Belgian language question Controversy in Belgium over language, education and other rights for Dutch and French speakers. The northern half of what is now Belgium has been Dutch-speaking since the early Middle Ages, while the south has been French-speaking. (The language 'border' ultimately has its roots in the dividing line between Germanic and Celtic areas of settlement during the Roman period.) The two regions are now called Flanders and Wallonia respectively. When Belgium became independent in 1830 French was made the sole official language. After decades of agitation by the Flemish, Dutch became the second official language in 1898. The language issue has been the defining feature of national politics ever since, with disputes concerning Brussels (the bilingual capital) and the rights of minorities on either side of the 'border' particularly frequent. Since the 1950s the divisions have been exacerbated by economic factors, with Flanders enjoying sustained growth while Wallonia's heavy industries have been in decline. Proposals for the establishment of a federal structure based on regions and language-based cultural communities were agreed in principle in the 1970s. The constitutional changes were implemented over a 15-year period from 1978. *See also* COMMUNITY (Belgium) *and* VOEREN QUESTION.

Belgium [België (Dutch), Belgique (French)] Country in western Europe.

Official data. Name: Kingdom of Belgium [Koninkrijk België / Royaume de Belgique]; capital: Brussels [Brussel/ Bruxelles]; form of government: federal monarchy; head of state: king/queen; head of government: prime minister; flag: three vertical stripes, black, yellow and red; national holiday: 21 July (Independence Day); languages: Dutch and French; religion: none; currency: frank/franc (F) (pl. -, -s) = 100 centiemen/centimes; abbreviation: B.

Geography. One of the three Low Countries or Benelux countries, Belgium has an area of 30,518 sq km. It is bordered by the Netherlands in the north, Germany and Luxemburg in the east, France in the south, and the North Sea in the west. The north is a low-lying fertile plain with some hill lands in the east and centre, the south consists of a plateau and low mountains (Ardennes). Some 25% of the land is arable, another 20% is covered by pastures and 21% is forested. The main rivers are the Scheldt [Schelde/ Escaut], Meuse [Maas/Meuse] and Sambre. The climate is temperate marine, with mild summers and cool winters; continental influences (hotter summers, colder winters) are evident in the southeast; rainfall is moderate.

Demography. Belgium has a population of 10,072,000. Population density is 333 per sq km (land area), one of the highest in Europe. Only the Ardennes region in the southeast is relatively sparsely populated. Some 97% of the people live in urban areas. The main cities are Brussels (metropolitan population 1.5 million), Antwerp [Antwerpen] (1.1 million), Ghent [Gent], Charleroi and Liège; Bruges [Brugge], Namur and Mons are important regional centres. In ethnic and linguistic terms Belgium is sharply

divided: the Flemings in the north, who speak a range of dialects of Dutch usually referred to collectively as Flemish, account for 57.7% of the total population, French-speaking Walloons in the south for 32.7%, and German speakers in the far east for 0.6%. Foreign nationals account for 9.0%, and include citizens of Italy (2.4% of the total), Morocco (1.4%), France (0.9%), Turkey and the Netherlands. The main languages are Dutch and French; French is the dominant language in Brussels, which is officially a bilingual region. In religious terms 89.5% of the population is nominally Roman Catholic and 1.5% Muslim; there are also 50,000 Protestants and 35,000 Jews.

Sociography. Belgium scores 0.916 on the United Nations human development index (HDI), ranking 13th in the world and ninth among 32 European countries. There are 33 doctors and 93 hospital beds for every 10,000 people. Education is compulsory full-time between the ages of six and 16 and part-time until 18; it is the responsibility of the cultural communities. There is one teacher for every nine students, among the best ratios in Europe. Enrolment is 89% at the secondary level and 37% at the tertiary level. The literacy rate is virtually 100%. Real annual income per head (in terms of purchasing power) is US$ 17,510.

Infrastructure and communications. Belgium has a highly developed transport and communications network, with the road and rail networks among the densest in the world and with excellent links with neighbouring countries. There are 123,210 km of paved roads and 3.83 million passenger cars (384 per 1,000 people), 5,590 km of railways, and 2,043 km of navigable waterways; the latter are particularly important for freight transport. The main port is Antwerp, the second-busiest in Europe; other ports are Ghent, Zeebrugge and Ostend. The main airport is at Brussels, and there are three other airports with scheduled services. There are 35 daily newspapers, with a combined circulation of 2.12 million (213 per 1,000 people). There are 4.52 million radio receivers, 4.20 million television sets and 5.43 million telephones in use (respectively 453, 421 and 544 per 1,000 people).

Economic structure. The Belgian economy is highly developed, and diversified, one of the most trade-oriented in the world (exports account for three-quarters of national income), and closely linked to its neighbours. It is based on manufacturing, trade and transport. Since the late 1980s economic performance has been characterized by steady growth (averaging 3.6% per year) until 1991 and negligible growth since then, current-account surpluses (over 2% of GDP), low inflation (averaging 2.7%) and persistent high unemployment (around 11%); the national debt stands at around 140% of GDP, the highest level in the European Union (EU). Growth has been concentrated in Flanders and unemployment is considerably higher in Wallonia, with its declining heavy industries.

Services contribute 68% of GDP, industry contributes 30% (manufacturing 22%), and agriculture and fisheries 2%. Some 19% of the labour force is employed in manufacturing, 17% in trade, 8% in finance and 5% in construction. The main crops grown are sugarbeets, potatoes and cereals (wheat, barley); livestock raising (cattle, pigs), dairy farming (milk, butter) and horticulture (fruit and vegetables) are also important agricultural activities. Forestry and fishing are of regional importance. There are no significant mineral resources. The main industries are engineering and food processing; other important branches are chemicals, textiles, metalworking, electrical goods and petrochemicals. The main energy sources are nuclear power and imported fossil fuels; 5% of export earnings are required to cover net fuel imports. The main exports are chemicals (14% of the total), motor vehicles (12%), foodstuffs (9%), iron and steel (8%), textiles and clothing (7%), precious stones (esp. diamonds) (6%), industrial machinery (5%), non-ferrous metals and oil products; basic manufactures account for 31% of the total, machinery and transport equipment for 27%. The main imports are machinery and transport equipment, basic manufactures, chemicals, fuels and foodstuffs. The main trading partners are: exports: Germany (23%), France (19%), Netherlands (14%), United Kingdom (8%), Italy (6%), United States; imports: Germany (24%), Netherlands (17%), France (16%), United Kingdom (8%), United States, Italy; three-quarters of all trade is with other European Union (EU) countries. Belgium and Luxemburg, which form an economic and monetary union, are the world's ninth-largest trading power. (All above trade figures include Luxemburg.)

The National Bank of Belgium [Nationale Bank van België / Banque Nationale de Belgique] is the central bank. The main employers' association is the Belgian Business Federation (VBO/FEB); the main labour organizations are the General Labour Federation of Belgium (ABVV/ FGTB) and the Confederation of Christian Trade Unions (ACV/CSC).

Political structure. Belgium is a parliamentary monarchy on the basis of a constitution adopted in 1831 and amended on several occasions between 1970 and 1993 to introduce a federal structure consisting of overlapping geographical regions [gewest/région, pl. -en, -s] and language-based cultural communities [gemeenschap/communauté/Gemeinschaft, pl. -pen, -s, -en]. Executive power is formally vested in the king/queen but is exercised by the prime minister and the cabinet. The monarch's limited powers include the appointment of a *formateur* to negotiate the formation of a new government. Legislative power is vested in the bicameral Legislative Chambers [Wetgevende Kamers / Chambres Législatives], composed of a 212-member Chamber of Representatives [Kamer van Volksvertegenwoordigers / Chambre des Représentants] elected for a four-year term by a system of proportional representation, and a Senate [Senaat/Sénat] of 182 members who are either directly or indirectly elected; the size of the two chambers is due to be reduced to 150 and 72 members respectively. Voting is compulsory for all citizens over the age of 18. Judicial power is vested in the 25-member Supreme

Court [Hof van Cassatie / Cour de Cassation] appointed by the monarch on the advice of the government. Under the new federal structure the central government retains control of defence, foreign policy, finance, social security and justice; the regions are responsible for all other areas except language issues, education, culture, health and social policy, which are devolved to the communities. The three regions are Flanders [Vlaanderen], Wallonia [Wallonie] and Brussels-Capital [Bruxelles-Capitale/Brussel-Hoofdstad], the three communities are the Flemish Community [Vlaamse Gemeenschap], French Community [Communauté Française] and German-Speaking Community [Deutschsprachige Gemeinschaft]. Administratively the country is also divided into 10 provinces [provincie/province, pl. -s] and 589 municipalities.

The main political parties are, in Flanders, the Christian People's Party (CVP), Socialist Party (SP), Flemish Liberals and Democrats (VLD, the successor to the Party for Freedom and Progress, PVV), Flemish Bloc (Vlaams Blok, VB), People's Union (Volksunie, VU) and Live Differently (AGALEV); in Wallonia, the Socialist Party (PS), Liberal Reform Party (PRL), Christian People's Party (CVP), Ecology Party (ÉCOLO) and Francophone Democratic Front (FDF). At the general election in November 1991 the CVP gained 16.7% of the vote and 39/212 seats, the PS 13.6% and 35 seats, the SP 12.0% and 28 seats, the PVV 11.9% and 26 seats, the PRL 8.2% and 20 seats, the PSC 7.8% and 18 seats, the VB 6.6% and 12 seats, the VU 5.9% and 10 seats, ÉCOLO 5.1% and 10 seats, and AGALEV 4.9% and seven seats. The government is formed by a centrist coalition of the CVP, PS, SP and PSC, with Jean-Luc Dehaene as prime minister. Other senior ministers are Elio Di Rupo (deputy prime minister, communications and public enterprises), Willy Claes (deputy prime minister, foreign affairs), Melchior Wathelet (deputy prime minister, justice, economic affairs), Herman van Rompuy (deputy prime minister, budget), Philippe Maystadt (finance) and Leo Delcroix (defence). The head of state is King Albert II, who succeeded to the throne in August 1993; the heir is Prince Philippe.

Security and international affiliations. The Belgian armed forces number 80,700 (army 54,000, navy 4,400, airforce 17,300, medical service 5,000); they are due to be reduced to 66,000. Military service was abolished in January 1994.

Belgium is a member of the Benelux Economic Union, Conference on Security and Cooperation in Europe (CSCE), Council of Europe, European Economic Area (EEA), European Union (EU), North Atlantic Treaty Organization (NATO) and Western European Union (WEU), as well as the Francophone Community and Organization for Economic Cooperation and Development (OECD) and the United Nations and its specialized agencies.

History. The Romans completed the conquest of the Celtic and Germanic tribes inhabiting the area of modern Belgium – among them the Belgae – in 51 BC. After the collapse of Roman control in the late 4th century the region became a core territory of the Germanic Franks. They adopted Christianity in the late 5th century. Over the next three centuries the Frankish Kingdom expanded to cover most of Western Europe, reaching its apogee under Charlemagne (768–814), who was crowned 'Roman emperor' in 800. The various partitions after his death left the core Frankish districts divided between the West Frankish Kingdom, later France, and the East Frankish Kingdom, later the Holy Roman or German Empire. Feudal fragmentation from the 10th century onwards led to the emergence of a number of autonomous states in the region, the most important of which were Flanders (formally part of France) in the west, Brabant in the centre, Hainault in the southwest, Liège (a bishopric) in the east, and Luxemburg in the southeast. In the 14th and 15th centuries the towns of Flanders and Brabant – Bruges, Ghent, Antwerp, Brussels etc – were among the most important industrial, commercial and cultural centres of Europe. The French dukes of Burgundy inherited Flanders in 1384. Over the next half century Burgundy gained control over most of the Low Countries (i.e. including the Netherlands) through inheritance, marriage or purchase and thus briefly became a major European power. The Burgundian possessions passed to the Habsburgs in 1482. After the abdication of Emperor Charles V in 1555/56 the Habsburg Empire was divided into Austrian and Spanish branches, with the Low Countries allocated to the latter. A rebellion against Spanish rule, led by the powerful merchant class and sections of the nobility and fuelled in part by the rise of Protestantism, broke out in the 1560s. In 1579 several southern provinces formed the Union of Arras and reaffirmed their loyalty to the Spanish king and Roman Catholicism. Over the next six years the Spanish reasserted control in all the southern provinces, an area broadly coextensive with modern Belgium. (The seven northern provinces declared their independence from Spain in 1581 and established the Dutch Republic.) The exodus of wealthy Protestant merchants from the south to the north and the imposition of a blockade on Antwerp, one of Europe's busiest ports, by the Dutch in 1585 inaugurated a prolonged economic decline for the southern provinces. In 1713 the Southern Netherlands was transferred to Austrian Habsburg rule. There was a rebellion against Austrian rule in 1789–90. The region was occupied by French troops in 1792, at the start of the French Revolutionary Wars, and was annexed by France in 1795 despite widespread demands for independence.

As part of the post-Napoleonic reorganization of Europe in 1814/15 the Congress of Vienna allocated the region to the new Kingdom of the Netherlands. The union was short-lived, however, and the southern provinces, overwhelmingly Catholic and dominated by French speakers, declared their independence from the Netherlands in 1830. Leopold of Saxe-Coburg-Gotha, a German prince, was elected king of the Belgians in 1831.

Belgium's independence and neutrality were internationally recognized in 1831 and 1839. From the 1850s the coal and steel industries in French-speaking Wallonia formed the basis for rapid industrialization in that region. From the 1880s Belgium acquired a colonial empire in the Congo region of Africa. Universal suffrage for men was introduced in 1893 and extended to women in 1948; in 1899 Belgium became the first European country to introduce an electoral system based on proportional representation. Coalition governments have been the norm ever since. In 1898, after decades of agitation by a growing Flemish national and cultural movement, Dutch was made an official language alongside French. The language issue has been a defining feature of national politics ever since. German troops invaded Belgium at the start of the First World War (1914–18) and occupied most of the country. The front line in Flanders was the scene of some of the War's bloodiest battles. Belgium and Luxemburg formed a customs and monetary union in 1922. Belgium was hard-hit by the worldwide economic depression of the 1930s. During the Second World War (1939–45) the country was again occupied by Germany from 1940–44.

Belgium joined the Netherlands and Luxemburg in the Benelux Economic Union in 1948, became a founding member of the North Atlantic Treaty Organization (NATO) in 1949 and of the European Economic Community (EEC), now the European Union (EU), in 1958. Independence was granted to the Congo, now Zaire, in 1960. Tensions between Flemings and Walloons grew from the 1950s. They were exacerbated by divergent economic developments in the two regions, with Wallonia's heavy industries going into decline and Flanders enjoying sustained growth. Proposals for the establishment of a federal structure based on overlapping geographical regions and language-based cultural communities were agreed in principle in the 1970s, but implementation was delayed because of disagreements over the status of bilingual Brussels and over practical aspects. The constitutional reforms were completed in 1993. Since 1945 Belgian politics has been dominated by three ideological blocs, Christian Democrats, Socialists and right-wing Liberals, each divided into Flemish and Walloon parties. A Socialist-led centre-left coalition was in power from 1945–47. Since then the Christian Democrats have led all coalitions with the exception of the period 1954–58, and they governed alone from 1950–54. They led centre-right coalitions from 1947–50, 1958–61, 1966–68 and 1981–88. A Socialist-led left-right coalition held power from 1954–58. Four broad-based coalitions comprising the three ideological blocs and several regional parties were in office from 1973–78, when the plans for constitutional reform were being drawn up. Centre-left coalitions dominated by the Christian Democrats and Socialists have held power in 1947–50, 1961–66, 1968–72, 1979–81 and since May 1988. Wilfried Martens of the Flemish Christian People's Party (CVP) became prime minister in April 1979; he was succeeded by his party colleague Jean-Luc Dehaene in March 1992. Reducing budget deficits and the national debt have been the main economic priority for all coalitions since the early 1980s.

See also entries on specific institutions, organizations, parties, people, terms etc.

Belgium-Luxemburg Economic Union (BLEU or UEBL) Intergovernmental organization. The BLEU was established to administer the customs union between Belgium and Luxemburg agreed in 1921 and in force from 1922. Amended on several occasions since, the union comprises a common market in goods and services, a common external tariff and a common currency. As such it provided a model for the Benelux Economic Union and the European Economic Community (EEC). The values of the Belgian and Luxemburg francs have been at parity since 1940.

Belgrade Shorthand for the Yugoslav or the Serbian government. Belgrade is the capital of Yugoslavia as well as Serbia, the larger of its two constituent republics.

Beli Orlovi *See* WHITE EAGLES.

Belloch, Juan Alberto (1950–) Spanish lawyer and politician. He worked as a magistrate from 1981 and was elected by parliament to the supervisory General Council of Judicial Power (CGPJ) in 1990. He was appointed justice minister in the minority Spanish Socialist Workers' Party (PSOE) government formed in July 1993 and also became interior minister in May 1994. He is a not a party member.

Belvedere Palace or **Belweder Palace** [Pałac Belweder] Shorthand for the Polish presidency. The Belweder in Warsaw is the official residence of the president.

Benda, František (1944–) Czech glassworker, chemist and politician. He worked as a researcher in organic chemistry in the 1970s and 80s and joined the Institute of Landscape Ecology of the Czechoslovak Academy of Sciences in 1989. Elected to parliament for the Christian Democratic Party (KDS) in June 1992, he was appointed minister of the environment the following month.

Benelux countries or **Benelux** Collective name for Belgium, Luxemburg and the Netherlands. Taken from the initial letters of the three countries, it has been in use since the establishment of the Benelux Economic Union in the late 1940s.

Benelux Economic Union (Benelux) Intergovernmental organization. The Benelux was established by Belgium, the Netherlands and Luxemburg as a customs union in 1948 and expanded into a full economic union by 1960. This provided for free mutual movement of persons, goods, services and capital among the three countries, coordination of national economic policies, and a common trade policy towards other countries. As Europe's first wholly free international market the Benelux played a major role in the formation and subsequent development of the European Economic Community (EEC) from 1958. The Benelux countries were founding members of the EEC. As economic integration proceeded at Community level, culminating in the completion of the internal market in 1993, the role of the Benelux diminished. Policies on a wide range of issues continue to be coordinated through the Committee of Ministers, which includes at least three ministers from each country and meets quarterly. Other organs include the Inter-parliamentary Consultative Council, College of Arbitration, Court of Justice and a range of supervisory and advisory councils. The secretariat is based in Brussels, the Belgian capital.

Benvenuto, Giorgio (1937–) Italian trade-union official, civil servant and politician. A law graduate, he began working for the Italian Union of Labour (UIL) in 1955 as a researcher. He later held several senior posts in the federation and became its leader in 1976. In 1992 he was appointed director-general of the finance ministry. He was elected leader of the Italian Socialist Party (PSI) in February 1993, after Bettino Craxi had been forced to resign over his and the party's involvement in political corruption. Claiming that attempts at internal reform were being thwarted by Craxi and his supporters, he resigned the following May. He later became leader of the new Socialist Renewal (RS).

BERD French abbreviation for the EURO-PEAN BANK FOR RECONSTRUCTION AND DEVELOPMENT (EBRD).

Bérégovoy, Pierre (1924–93) French lawyer and politician. A qualified lathe operator who went on to study labour law, he was a leading member of several socialist groups in the 1950s and 60s and then of the Socialist Party (PS). An adviser to François Mitterrand in the first two years of his presidency (1981–82) and then minister of social affairs (1982–84), he held the ministry of economy, finance and budget from 1984–92 except for the two years of right-wing government from 1986–88. In April 1992 he was appointed prime minister and formed a centre-left government. He resigned after the PS's heavy election defeat in March 1993. Said to be depressed by the result and by criticism over an interest-free loan he had received while in office (to buy his flat), he committed suicide two months later.

Berge, Gunnar (1940–) Norwegian metalworker, trade-union official and politician. He was elected to parliament for the Norwegian Labour Party (DNA) in 1969. He was appointed finance minister in 1986 and became the leader of the DNA parliamentary party in 1989. In September 1992 he was appointed minister of local government and labour.

Berisha, Sali (1941–) Albanian doctor, academic and politician. A leading cardiologist and surgeon, he also lectured at Tirana University from 1967. He was a founding member of the Democratic Party (PDSh), the first opposition party allowed under communist rule in 1990. He was formally elected its leader in September 1991. He led the party to victory in the March 1992 election, and was elected president of the republic by parliament the following month. As required by the constitution, he then resigned all other political offices.

Berķis, Aivars (1936–) Latvian forestry engineer, journalist and politician. He worked for the forestry service from 1959–69 and as a correspondent and editor for Latvian radio from 1969–91. In the 1980s, when Latvia was still part of the Soviet Union, he was a prominent activist in the reform and later pro-independence movement. He was elected leader of the relaunched right-wing Farmers' Union (LZS) in September 1989. He has been a member of parliament since 1990.

Berlaymont, the Shorthand for the EURO-PEAN COMMISSION, the administrative and executive arm of the European Union (EU). The Berlaymont building in Brussels was the Commission's headquarters until the end of 1991, when it was closed down for extensive refurbishment (due to be completed by 1998). Most offices were moved to the nearby Breydel building.

Berlin Federal state [Land] of Germany. Situated in the east and surrounded by Brandenburg, Berlin has an area of 883 sq km and a population of 3,466,000. The state is coextensive with the city of Berlin, the national capital. It was formed on German reunification in 1990 by the merger of West Berlin, a West German enclave in former East Germany, and East Berlin, the former East German capital. The economy is based on manufacturing (engineering, electronics, food processing) and services. There is a considerable gap in prosperity between the west and east. Political power is exercised by the House of Representatives [Abgeordnetenhaus], with 241 members elected for a four-year term, and the executive Senate [Senat] headed by a governing mayor. The administration combines the functions of a municipality and a state. The main parties are the Christian Democratic Union (CDU), the Social Democratic Party (SPD), the Democratic Socialist Party (PDS, the successor to the communist Socialist Unity Party, SED), the centrist Free Democratic Party (FDP) and the Greens (now merged with the left-alternative Alliance 90, B'90). At the all-Berlin election in December 1990 the CDU gained 40.4% of the vote and 101 seats, the SPD 30.4% and 76 seats, the PDS 9.2% and 23 seats, the FDP 7.1% and 18 seats, the Greens 5.0% and 12 seats, and B'90 4.4% and 11 seats. The government is formed by a CDU-SPD coalition headed by Eberhard Diepgen. From the Middle Ages Berlin was successively the capital of Brandenburg, Prussia and united Germany (from 1871). At the end of the Second World War the victorious powers divided the city into American, British, French and Soviet sectors. The first three became West Berlin, which was effectively but not formally incorporated into West Germany; the Soviet sector became East Berlin. The city was a flashpoint of East-West tension throughout the Cold War. The East German communist regime erected the Berlin Wall in 1961 to stop people fleeing to the West. The city's division came to an end in November 1989 when the Wall was opened and travel restrictions were lifted by the new reformist regime in East Germany. The two halves were formally reunited on German reunification in October 1990. In June 1991 the federal parliament decided in principle to transfer the seat of the federal government from Bonn to Berlin.

Berlin Wall Former barrier around West Berlin, separating it from East Berlin and the surrounding territory of East Germany (*see* BERLIN). The Wall was built by the East German authorities in 1961 – the first barbed-wire fences were put up on 13 August, followed by the construction of a concrete wall eventually 160 km long – to stem the outflow of mostly young and skilled people to the western half of the city and West Germany. Heavily guarded, it became a symbol of communist repression. In the 28 years of its existence around 200 people were shot trying to escape over it. The opening of the Wall by the new reformist communist regime on 9 November 1989 marked the first step in the reunification of Berlin and Germany over the following year. This event is now widely regarded as the symbolic end of communist domination in Eastern Europe and of the 'cold war' between East and West. The Wall was demolished in 1990. Several small sections remain as memorials and tourist attractions.

Berlinguer, Luigi (1932–) Italian historian, academic and politician. He has lectured in the history of Italian law and political institutions at the universities of Sassari and Siena (1969–85), and served as the latter's rector from 1985–94. He was active in local politics for the Italian Communist Party (PCI) in his native Sardinia in the 1960s and was a member of the Tuscany regional council from 1975–85. Elected to parliament for the Democratic Left Party (PDS), the PCI's successor, in March 1994, he became leader of the Allied Progressives parliamentary group the following month. He is the cousin of the late Enrico Berlinguer, PCI leader from 1972–84.

Berlusconi, Silvio (1936–) Italian businessman and politician. In the 1960s and 70s he built up a construction and property group centred on his native Milan. In the late 1970s he began to expand his media interests. His Fininvest group, one of Italy's largest conglomerates, has extensive interests in the broadcasting, publishing, advertising, retailing, property, insurance, construction, sports and entertainment sectors; the group's media interests include three national television channels, the daily *Il Giornale*, several news magazines and the Mondadori publishing house. He was a member of the elite masonic lodge Propaganda Two (P-2) in the late 1970s and was closely associated with the Italian Socialist Party (PSI) until it was discredited by the party-funding scandal in 1992/93. In October 1993 he founded the Come On Italy (Forza Italia) movement. In January 1994 he announced his formal entry into politics and forged an alliance with other right-wing groups. The Freedom Alliance won the March election and he became prime minister in May.

Bern Shorthand for the Swiss government. Bern is the capital of Switzerland.

Bernadotte Royal dynasty of Sweden. The name is taken from the French marshal Jean-Baptiste Bernadotte, who was proclaimed crown prince by parliament in 1810 and ruled as King Carl XIV Johan from 1818–44.

Bernini, Giorgio (1928–) Italian lawyer, academic and politician. A specialist in international law and arbitration issues, he has lectured in commercial law since the 1950s. He entered politics with the new Come On Italy (Forza Italia) movement in January 1994, was elected to parliament in March and appointed minister of foreign trade in the right-wing coalition which took office in May.

Berntsen, Thorbjørn (1935–) Norwegian plumber, trade-union official and politician. He worked at the Nylands shipyard until 1966, held several posts in the Norwegian Union of Iron and Metalworkers, and was a leading member of the Oslo branch of the Norwegian Labour Party (DNA) in the 1960s and 70s. Elected to parliament in 1977, he was appointed environment minister in September 1992.

Berov, Lyuben (1925–) Bulgarian economist, academic and politician. He has lectured in economic history and was a senior researcher at the Institute of Balkan Studies from 1985–90. From 1990–92 he was President Zhelev's chief economic adviser. He was appointed prime minister in December 1992 and formed a non-party 'government of experts'.

Berufsverbot ('employment ban') In Germany, a ban on exercising one's profession imposed under certain circumstances, specifically the exclusion of those deemed to be political radicals from posts in the public services. Under the criminal code the *Berufsverbot* is a general measure 'to protect society against those who have committed an offence involving a gross violation of their professional duties'. After the Federal Constitutional Court ruled in 1972 that public servants might be breaking their oath of loyalty to the constitution by belonging to an 'anti-constitutional' party or engaging in 'anti-constitutional' activities, it was used in West Germany in particular against civil servants, teachers and others belonging to or sympathizing with far-left organizations. This specific use of the *Berufsverbot* legislation, based on the so-called Radicals' Decree [Radikalenerlass] adopted by the state governments (the competent authority in this field in Germany's federal system), was highly controversial. After an attempt to enshrine the Decree in law failed in 1976, it fell into disuse at federal level and in many states. Since reunification in 1990 it has been used in former East Germany as a means of removing members of the old communist elite from the civil service.

Bessarabia question Controversy over formerly Romanian territory now divided between Moldavia and Ukraine. Bessarabia, the eastern half of the medieval principality of Moldavia, was ceded to Russia in 1812. (The western half joined Wallachia to form Romania in 1859.) It became part of Romania after the First World War, but was ceded to the Soviet Union in 1940. Most of the territory was constituted as the Moldavian Soviet Socialist Republic, but a strategically important area along the Black Sea coast together with Serpent's Island, an uninhabited islet to the east of the Danube delta, were allocated to Ukraine. Some nationalist groups in Romania are calling for reunification of Moldavia or Moldova, now an independent country, with Romania and for the return of the other territories. The majority of Moldavia's population is ethnically Romanian, but there is only limited support for reunification. Romania

BF — BIRKAVS

formally disputes Ukrainian sovereignty over Serpent's Island.

BF and **BFr** Abbreviations for the FRANC, the Belgian currency.

BfV *See* FEDERAL OFFICE FOR THE PROTECTION OF THE CONSTITUTION.

BG Abbreviation for Bulgaria, used for international vehicle registrations, postal addresses etc.

BGL Abbreviation for the LEV, the Bulgarian currency, used in banking etc.

BGS *See* FEDERAL BORDER GUARD.

BH Abbreviation for Bosnia-Herzegovina.

bicommunal and bizonal federation *See* CYPRUS QUESTION *and* RESOLUTION 716.

Biedenkopf, Kurt (1930–) German academic, businessman and politician. He lectured in commercial law and then became managing director of the Henkel chemical concern before being appointed general secretary of the Christian Democratic Union (CDU) in 1973. He was a CDU deputy chairman from 1977–83 and a member of parliament from 1987–90. In October 1990 he led the CDU to victory in the state election in Saxony, formerly part of East Germany, and became its prime minister.

Bielecki, Jan Krzysztof (1951–) Polish economist and politician. He taught at the University of Gdańsk and then became an economic adviser to the anti-communist Solidarity trade union in 1980. He was barred from his previous job following the declaration of martial law in 1981 and started a timber-haulage company and economic consultancy. He entered parliament on the Solidarity ticket in the partially free elections of 1989. A founding member of the right-wing Liberal Democratic Congress (KLD, now part of the Freedom Union, UW), he was appointed prime minister in January 1991. He resigned in October after his policies of rapid economic reform failed to gain voters' support at the general election. From July 1992 until October 1993 he was minister with responsibility for relations with the European Community (EC).

big bang (Poland) *See* CONTROLLED SHOCK.

BIH or **BiH** Abbreviation for Armija Bosna i Hercegovina ('Army of Bosnia-Herzegovina'), the Bosnian army. Initially

multiethnic, it became increasingly Muslim-dominated after the outbreak of the civil war in March 1992 and the resultant polarization between Muslims, Serbs and Croats. Its soldiers are also known informally as 'green berets' [zeleni bereti].

BIH or **BiH** Abbreviation for Bosnia-Herzegovina, used for international vehicle registrations, postal addresses etc.

Bihać region *See* AUTONOMOUS PROVINCE OF WESTERN BOSNIA.

Bildt, Carl (1949–) Swedish politician. Having worked for the centre-right Moderate Coalition Party (MS) as a full-time official and as a policy adviser, he was elected to parliament in 1979 and was a junior minister from 1979–81. He was elected party leader in August 1986. He became prime minister of a centre-right coalition in October 1991.

Binnenhof Shorthand for the Dutch parliament or the government more generally. The Binnenhof is a square in The Hague which contains the parliament building, the prime minister's office and several other government departments.

Biondi, Alfredo (1928–) Italian lawyer and politician. He was elected to parliament for the Italian Liberal Party (PLI) in 1968. He was a minister without portfolio responsible for European Community (EC) affairs in 1982–83 and environment minister in 1985–86. In 1993, with the PLI discredited because of its involvement in political corruption, he joined the new Centre Union (UDC). He was appointed justice minister in the right-wing coalition formed in May 1994.

Birkavs, Valdis (1942–) Latvian lawyer, civil servant, academic and politician. He worked for the Latvian justice ministry from 1969–86 and then lectured in law and criminology at the University of Latvia. He was elected to parliament for the Latvian Communist Party (LKP) in 1990, when the republic was still part of the Soviet Union, and for the centre-right Latvian Way (LC) at the June 1993 election. He was appointed prime minister the following month and formed a coalition with the Farmers' Union (LZS). In September 1994 he became a deputy prime

54

minister and foreign minister in a new LC government.

Birmingham Six and Guildford Four cases Judicial scandals and political controversy in the United Kingdom involving the false conviction of nine Irishmen and one Englishwoman for terrorist offences. They were arrested in 1974 shortly after the bombing of public houses in Birmingham and Guildford by the Irish Republican Army (IRA), the guerrilla group fighting for the withdrawal of British troops from Northern Ireland and the reunification of Ireland. They were convicted of murder and sentenced to life imprisonment on the basis of uncorroborated confessions which they claimed had been obtained under duress. Subsequently evidence emerged that the police had tampered with case notes, forensic and alibi details had been withheld from the defence, and forensic tests had been unreliable; and IRA members arrested in 1975 admitted they had carried out the Guildford bombings. An appeal in the Birmingham Six case was rejected in January 1988. An appeal in the Guildford Four case overturned the convictions in October 1989, and the four were released. The convictions of the Birmingham Six were overturned in March 1991. At the same time the government announced the establishment of a royal commission to consider reform of the criminal justice system. These and other miscarriages of justice, such as the MAGUIRE SEVEN CASE, cast doubt on the system's integrity and also soured relations between Ireland and the United Kingdom. In July 1994 an independent inquiry concluded that the Guildford Four had been the victims of individual failings by police officers, prosecutors and lawyers and not of any inherent fault in the police or legal system.

BIS Abbreviation for Bezpečnostní a Informační Služba ('Security and Information Service'), the Czech intelligence agency.

BIS *See* BANK FOR INTERNATIONAL SETTLEMENTS.

Bisky, Lothar (1941–) German sociologist, academic and politician. He was a researcher at the Institute of Youth Research in Leipzig from 1967–80. He then joined the Academy of Social Sciences in East Berlin and lectured in cultural and media issues at the Humboldt University. In 1986 he was appointed a lecturer at the Babelsberg film and television college and later became its director. In 1990 he was elected to the state assembly of Brandenburg for the Democratic Socialist Party (PDS), the successor to the communist Socialist Unity Party (SED). He was elected party leader at federal level in January 1993.

bizonal and bicommunal federation *See* CYPRUS QUESTION *and* RESOLUTION 716.

Björck, Anders (1948–) Swedish politician. He was elected to parliament for the centre-right Moderate Coalition Party (MS) in 1968. He was president of the Parliament Assembly of the Council of Europe from 1989–91. He was appointed defence minister in the centre-right coalition formed in October 1991.

BKA *See* FEDERAL CRIMINAL INVESTIGATION OFFICE.

black In some countries, the colour associated with Roman Catholicism and thus with christian democratic parties and organizations. Examples are the Austrian People's Party (ÖVP), the Christian People's Party (CVP) and Christian Social Party (PSC) in Belgium, the Christian Democratic Union (CDU) in Germany and the Christian National Union (ZChN) in Poland.

black In Italy, the colour associated with far-right parties and organizations. It was originally associated with the National Fascist Party (PNF), which held power under Benito Mussolini from 1922–43.

Black Legion [Crna Legija] Croatian and Bosnian paramilitary group. Established in 1991, the Black Legion is a volunteer force nominally under the command of the national police but in effect autonomous. It is strongly nationalistic and models itself on the far-right Ustasha [Ustaša] movement of the 1930s and 40s. It is active 'in the defence of Croat interests' in Croatia – nearly a third of which is controlled by the self-proclaimed Republic of Serbian Krajina – and Bosnia-Herzegovina.

black-red coalition [schwarzrote Koalition] In Germany, a coalition between the Christian Democratic Union (CDU) and Social Democratic Party (SPD), the country's two main parties. Such a coalition held power at federal level from 1966–69 and others have been formed at state level on several occasions. It is also called a 'grand coalition'.

Black Sea Economic Cooperation Organization (BSECO) Intergovernmental organization. The proposal for the creation of a 'zone of economic cooperation' in the Black Sea region was first made by the Turkish government in 1989 and revived after the collapse of the Soviet Union in 1991. A treaty outlining the principles of cooperation and establishing the BSECO as the basis for a 'Eurasian economic community' modelled on the European Community was signed in February 1992. A more specific treaty signed in June 1992 covered cooperation in the fields of energy, transport, communications, environment and information and provided for the establishment of a trade and development bank. The BSECO's 11 members are: Albania, Armenia, Azerbaijan, Bulgaria, Georgia, Greece, Moldavia, Romania, Russia, Turkey and Ukraine. The main decision-making bodies are summit meetings of heads of state and government and the Council of Foreign Ministers, which meets every six months; there are also ministerial committees and a consultative parliamentary assembly. The presidency rotates among the members. The secretariat is based in İstanbul (Turkey).

Blagojević, Djordje (1933–) Yugoslav policeman and politician. A lawyer by training, he has worked in the police force of the Serbian town of Niš, eventually becoming chief of police. He was appointed interior minister in March 1993. He is a member of the Socialist Party of Serbia (SPS), the successor to the League of Communists.

Blair, Tony (1953–) British lawyer and politician. A specialist in labour law, he practised until his election to Parliament for the Labour Party in 1983. From 1988 he was successively the party's spokes-man on energy, employment and home affairs (1992–94). He was elected party leader in July 1994.

BLEU *See* BELGIUM-LUXEMBURG ECONOMIC UNION.

blizheye zarubezhe *See* NEAR ABROAD.

bloc party [Blockpartei, pl. -en] In former East Germany, one of the four nominally independent political parties that were allowed to function during communist rule (1945–89). They were the Christian Democratic Union (CDU), Democratic Peasants' Party (DBP), Liberal Democratic Party (LDPD) and National Democratic Party (NDPD). On German reunification in October 1990, the first two merged with West Germany's Christian Democratic Union (CDU) and the last two with the Free Democratic Party (FDP).

block vote In the United Kingdom, the traditional system of voting within the Labour Party and the Trades' Union Congress (TUC) whereby a delegation from an affiliated trade union is allocated a block of votes in accordance with the union's total membership. Within the Labour Party the system has been diluted in recent years by reducing the unions' overall share of the vote at annual conferences (in favour of individual members) and by introducing a system of 'one-member-one-vote' at leadership elections.

blocking minority (European Union) *See* QUALIFIED MAJORITY VOTING.

Blondel, Marc (1938–) French administrator and trade-union official. From 1959–70 he worked for the agency managing the construction industry's unemployment-insurance scheme. He was also a secretary of the Federation of Employees and Managerial Staff (FEC) from 1965, became a permanent secretary in 1971 and the organization's general secretary in 1974. He was elected leader of Workers' Power (Force Ouvrière, FO), one of the main trade-union federations, in February 1989.

blue In some countries, the colour associated with right-wing political parties. Examples are the Liberal Reform Party (PRL) in Belgium, the National Coalition Party (KOK) in Finland, the British Conservative Party, the People's Party for Freedom and Democracy (VVD) in the Netherlands and the People's Party (PP) in Spain.

blue berets, blue hats and **blue helmets** Informal names for the multinational military forces of the United Nations engaged in humanitarian and peace-keeping operations. Two such forces are currently deployed in Europe: the United Nations Peace-Keeping Force in Cyprus (UNFICYP) and the United Nations Protection Force (UNPROFOR) in Bosnia-Herzegovina, Croatia and Macedonia. The names are taken from the distinctive light blue headgear worn by the soldiers. *See also individual force entries.*

Blue Europe Informal name for the COMMON FISHERIES POLICY (CFP), a common policy of the European Union (EU), and related issues.

blue hats and **blue helmets** *See* BLUE BERETS ....

blue zone In Croatia, a demilitarized buffer zone between territory controlled by Croatian government forces and rebel Serb forces, patrolled by the United Nations Protection Force I (UNPROFOR I). A number of 'blue zones' were established as part of a ceasefire agreement signed in March 1994. *See also* CROATIAN CIVIL WAR.

Blüm, Norbert (1935–) German politician. He started work as a toolmaker and later studied philosophy. He was first elected to parliament for the Christian Democratic Union (CDU) in 1972. After a brief spell as a minister in the West Berlin government (1981–82), he was appointed minister of labour and social policy when the CDU returned to power at federal level in October 1982. He is a prominent member of the party's trade-union wing.

BND *See* FEDERAL INTELLIGENCE SERVICE.

BNG *See* GALICIAN NATIONALIST BLOC.

BNS *See* NATIONAL TRADE UNION BLOC.

BOB Abbreviation for Bijzondere Opsporingsbrigade ('Special Investigations Unit'), the Dutch name of the Belgian intelligence agency. It is called the Brigade Spéciale de Recherche (BSR) in French.

Boban, Mate (1940–) Bosnian economist and politician. He established himself as the dominant leader of the country's Croats soon after the outbreak of the civil war in March 1992. In November he was elected leader of the Croatian Democratic Union (HDZ), and in August 1993 he was elected president of the breakaway Croatian Republic of Herzeg-Bosnia. A strong advocate of Bosnia's partition and the incorporation of Croat districts into Croatia, he lost support after international pressure and military setbacks made this increasingly unlikely. He was effectively replaced in February 1994, when a new 'presidential council' was set up under Kresimir Zubak. He lost the HDZ leadership in July 1994.

Bohemia [Čechy] Historical region of the Czech Republic. Centred on Prague, the national capital, Bohemia comprises the western half of the country. It was an independent kingdom in the Middle Ages and came under Austrian rule in 1526. It became a province of Czechoslovakia in 1918, and was divided into several regions in 1949. *See also* CZECH REPUBLIC: HISTORY.

Bohl, Friedrich (1945–) German lawyer and politician. He was a member of the Hesse regional parliament for the Christian Democratic Union (CDU) from 1970–80 and has been a member of the federal parliament since 1980. He held several senior posts within the CDU parliamentary party until he became head of the Federal Chancellery (= prime minister's office) and minister for special projects in November 1991.

Bokmål ('written language') Form of the Norwegian language, formerly also called Riksmål. It is used by around four-fifths of the population and is the dominant written form. *See also* NYNORSK.

Bolkestein, Frits (1933–) Dutch businessman and politician. Trained as a lawyer, he worked as a senior manager for the Shell petrochemical concern in several countries from 1960–76. Elected to parliament for the right-wing People's Party for Freedom and Democracy (VVD) in 1977, he was a junior economy minister from 1982–86 and minister of defence from 1988 until the party went into opposition the following year. He was elected party leader in May 1990. (The VVD returned to government in August 1994.)

Bologna bombing case Judicial and political scandal surrounding the bombing of the railway station at Bologna, Italy, by far-right extremists in 1980. The bomb was planted in a crowded waiting room during a holiday weekend in August and killed 85 people and injured 200. It was Italy's worst atrocity during a period of political violence in the late 1970s and early 80s known as the 'years of tension' or 'years of lead'. In 1988 13 people were convicted of involvement in the bombing. They included four young far-right sympathizers (given life sentences for planting the bomb), two senior members of the Information and Military Security Service (SISMI, one of the intelligence agencies), and Licio Gelli, grandmaster of the banned Propaganda Two (P-2) masonic lodge (convicted in his absence). All but the two secret-service agents were controversially acquitted on appeal in 1990. Subsequently further evidence emerged that the bombing had been part of a strategy of destabilization sponsored by far-right groups and elements in the secret services, part of what has been dubbed Italy's 'HIDDEN GOVERNMENT' [sottogoverno]. (Bologna is a traditional stronghold of the Italian Communist Party, PCI, now the Democratic Left Party, PDS.) The case was reopened in 1992 and a new trial with the same defendants was convened in October 1993. The judges at the original trials have also come under investigation for corruption.

Bolzano See SOUTH TYROL.

Bondevik, Kjell Magne (1947–) Norwegian clergyman and politician. He was elected to parliament for the Christian People's Party (KrF) in 1973 and was ordained a Lutheran Protestant pastor in 1977. He was elected party leader in April 1983. He has served as minister of education and religious affairs (1983–86) and foreign minister (1989–90) in two centre-right coalitions.

Bonello du Puis, George (1928–) Maltese notary and politician. Elected to parlia-

ment for the centre-right Nationalist Party in 1971, he was appointed minister of finance in 1987 and minister of economic affairs in February 1992.

Bonino, Emma (1948–) Italian politician. A prominent campaigner on civil-rights and international-development issues, she was coordinator of the Centre for Information on Sterilization and Abortion (CISA) in the 1970s. First elected to parliament for the Radical Party (PR) in 1976, she became its secretary (= leader) in February 1993.

Bonn Shorthand for the German government. Bonn became the provisional capital of West Germany in 1949. Following the reunification of Germany in 1990 it was decided to transfer the seat of government to Berlin, which had always remained the national capital in name. Under the current plans most ministries and the Bundestag, the lower house of parliament, will go to Berlin, while several ministries and the Bundesrat, the upper house, will remain in Bonn.

bonus seats In Malta, the additional parliamentary seats allocated to a party that gains a majority of the popular vote in a general election but not a majority of seats. In this event, which may arise due to anomalies in the electoral system, the party is allocated a sufficient number of additional seats to give it an overall majority of one in the House of Representatives, which normally has 65 members.

Borbón or **Bourbon** Royal dynasty of Spain. See HOUSE OF BOURBON.

Borchert, Jochen (1940–) German agronomist, farmer and politician. Elected to parliament for the Christian Democratic Union (CDU) in 1980, he was appointed minister for food, agriculture and forestry in January 1993.

Border Guard Group Nine [Grenzschutzgruppe Neun] (GSG-9) German paramilitary police force. GSG-9 is a specialist unit of the FEDERAL BORDER GUARD (BGS) charged with anti-terrorist operations.

Bordon, Willer (1949–) Italian politician. In the 1970s and 80s he was active in local and regional government for the Italian Communist Party (PCI, now the Democratic Left Party, PDS) in his native

Friuli - Venezia Giulia. He was elected to parliament in 1987. He joined the new centre-left Democratic Alliance (AD) in 1993 and became its coordinator (= leader) in April 1994.

borgerliga parti and **borgerlige parti** *See* BOURGEOIS PARTY.

Borman, Onur (1941–) Northern Cypriot civil servant and politician. She worked in the finance section and later the prime minister's office of the Turkish Cypriot administration from 1965 until her election to parliament for the centre-right Democratic Party (DP) in 1993. She was appointed minister of economy and finance in the DP-led coalition which took office in January 1994.

Boross, Péter (1928–) Hungarian lawyer, businessman and politician. Because of his involvement in the anti-communist uprising in 1956 he was dismissed from his job with the Budapest city council the following year. He eventually found work with a catering company, running it from 1971–89. He became a leading human-rights activist. Politically unaffiliated, he was appointed minister without portfolio in the centre-right coalition led by the Hungarian Democratic Forum (MDF) which took office after the multiparty election in April/May 1990. He became interior minister the following December. He joined the MDF in October 1992. He took over as prime minister on the death of József Antall in December 1993. He resigned after the party's heavy defeat in the May 1994 election, remaining in office in a caretaker capacity until July.

borough Shorthand for either a London or a metropolitan borough, two British administrative divisions. Historically, 'boroughs' were towns which had been granted special privileges by royal charter. *See* LONDON BOROUGH *and* METRO-POLITAN DISTRICT.

Borowski, Marek (1946–) Polish economist, civil servant and politician. A specialist in foreign-trade issues, he was banned from working in his field and expelled from the communist Polish United Workers' Party (PZPR) for seven years after organizing a student rally in

1968. He then worked for a major chain of department stores. In 1982 he was appointed to a senior post in the ministry for internal trade, and from 1989–91 he was a junior minister at the department. Elected to parliament for the Social Democratic Party (SdRP), the PZPR's successor and main component of the Democratic Left Alliance (SLD), in 1991, he was appointed deputy prime minister in charge of the economy and finance minister in the left-wing government which took office in October 1993. He resigned in February 1994 claiming that his economic-reform policies were being undermined by the prime minister, Waldemar Pawlak (the leader of the SLD's coalition partner, the Polish Peasant Party, PSL).

Borsellino case *See* FALCONE AND ....

Borst-Eilers, Els (1932–) Dutch doctor and politician. A specialist in hematology, she was attached to the Academic Hospital at Utrecht University from 1966–86, serving as its medical director from 1976. She became deputy director of the Health Council, a government advisory body, in 1986. She also lectured at Amsterdam University from 1992. A member of the centre-left Democrats 66 (D'66), she was appointed minister of health, welfare and sport in the left-right coalition formed in August 1994.

Bosevski, Valentin (1940–) Bulgarian doctor and politician. He has worked in several medical and research establishments, including the Centre for Radiation Protection and the Higher Institute of Military Medicine. He was appointed a junior environment minister in 1990 and became minister of the environment in the non-party government formed in December 1992.

Bosnia Shorthand for Bosnia-Herzegovina. It properly refers to the northern two-thirds of the country.

Bosnia-Herzegovina [Bosna i Hercegovina] Country in southeastern Europe, formerly part of Yugoslavia, also commonly referred to as Bosnia.

Note: The information below in part reflects the situation in Bosnia-Herzegovina before the disintegration of the old

Yugoslav federation and the outbreak of civil war in 1992 and in part takes account of the dislocation and disruption that has occurred since then; date references are given as appropriate.

Official data. Name: Republic of Bosnia and Herzegovina [Republika Bosna i Hercegovina]; capital: Sarajevo; form of government: parliamentary republic; head of state: president of the State Presidency; head of government: prime minister; flag: white, with the state emblem in the centre; national holiday: 27 July; language: Serbocroat; religion: none; currency: none: the old Yugoslav dinar (Din, divided into 100 para), the new Yugoslav dinar and the Croatian kuna are all in use in various parts of the country; abbreviations: BH and BIH or BiH.

Geography. Bosnia-Herzegovina has an area of 51,129 sq km. Land-locked except for a 20-km stretch along the Adriatic Sea, it is bordered by Croatia in the west and north, and Yugoslavia in the east and south. The terrain is largely mountainous (Dinaric Alps and other ranges); the north consists of hill lands and the fertile plain of the Sava river along the border with Croatia. Other important rivers are the Drina and Bosna. Some 22% of the land is arable, another 25% is covered by pastures and 36% is forested. The climate is humid continental (with hot summers and cold winters) in most of the country, and mediterranean (with hot summers and mild winters) in the southwest; rainfall is moderate in the north, heavier in the south.

Demography. In ethnic and religious terms Bosnia-Herzegovina is one of the most diverse countries in Europe. The three main groups are the Slav Muslims (considered an ethnic group in former Yugoslavia, now also referred to as 'Bosnians'), Serbs and Croats, who are nominally Sunni Muslim, Serbian Orthodox and Roman Catholic respectively. The main language is Serbocroat, or Serb and Croat, written in the cyrillic and latin script respectively. At the time of the 1991 census Bosnia-Herzegovina had a population of 4,366,000. Population density was 85 per sq km. Around half the people lived in urban areas. The largest city was Sarajevo; other major centres were Banja Luka, Zenica, Mostar and Tuzla. Some 43.7% of the people were Slav Muslims, 31.3% Serbs, 17.3% Croats and 5.5% Yugoslavs (self-description); there were also small numbers of Gipsies, Montenegrins and others; Gipsies were considerably underestimated in the figures and were thought to number around 175,000 (4% of the total population). Broadly speaking, the Muslims formed the majority in the centre, far northwest and parts of the south and east; the Serbs in the northwest, far south and parts of the northeast and east; the Croats in the southwest and parts of the northeast and centre; and the main cities were very mixed. Since the start of the civil war around 250,000 people have been killed, around 2.75 million have been displaced within the country and another 400,000 have fled abroad.

Sociography. Bosnia was one of the less developed republics in former Yugoslavia, which scored 0.857 on the UN's human development index (HDI) in 1990, ranking 37th in the world and 23rd among 27 European countries. Before the war there were 16 doctors and 46 hospital beds for every 10,000 people. Education is compulsory between the ages of seven and 15, but the system has largely broken down. Before the war there was one teacher for every 22 students, enrolment was 32% at the secondary level and 7% at the tertiary level. The literacy rate is 86%. GNP per head (unadjusted for purchasing power) was around US$ 2,450 in 1990.

Infrastructure and communications. Bosnia's transport and communications network has been extensively damaged in the course of the civil war. Before 1992 it was relatively developed but in need of modernization. There were 11,440 km of paved roads and 438,000 passenger cars (100 per 1,000 people), 1,040 km of railways and around 300 km of navigable waterways. The main (inland) port was Bosanski Brod. (The nearest major seaports are Split and Rijeka in Croatia.) The main airport was at Sarajevo (Butmir), and there were three other airports with scheduled services. There were four daily newspapers, with a combined circulation of 161,000 (34 per 1,000 people); other Yugoslav papers were also widely read. There were 904,000 radio receivers, 844,000 television sets and 727,000 telephones in use (respectively 210, 196 and 169 per 1,000 people).

Economic structure. The Bosnian economy is traditionally based on agriculture, manufacturing and mining. Like the other Yugoslav republics in the late 1980s and early 90s, it was essentially developed and diversified but in need of major investment and restructuring. The transition from a command to a market-based economy initiated at this time caused severe dislocation and led to sharp falls in industrial and agricultural production. In 1991 GDP contracted by 37%, inflation averaged around 80% per month, and unemployment rose to around 25%. Since then the financial system has collapsed and economic activity has been concentrated on raising food crops and producing military equipment.

Before the war, services contributed 46% of GDP, industry 45% (manufacturing around 40%), and agriculture, forestry and fisheries 9%. Some 48% of the labour force was employed in manufacturing and mining, 13% in trade and 7% in construction. The main crops grown were cereals (wheat, maize), potatoes, sugarbeets, tobacco and flax. Horticulture (fruit and vegetables, esp. plums, grapes), livestock raising (sheep) and forestry were other important agricultural activities. The main mineral resources were coal, iron, copper, bauxite, lead and zinc. The main industries were textiles (incl. footwear) and metalworking (esp. iron, steel and aluminium); other important branches were engineering, wood processing, chemicals, food processing and armaments. The main energy sources were domestic and imported fossil fuels and hydroelectric power; 28% of export earnings were required to cover net fuel imports. The main exports were textiles and clothing, cars, iron and steel, electrical goods, minerals and chemicals; basic manufactures accounted for 31% of the total, and machinery and transport

equipment for 21%. The main imports were fuels, machinery and transport equipment and miscellaneous manufactures. The main trading partners were the other Yugoslav republics, Germany, Italy and the Soviet Union.

The National Bank of Bosnia-Herzegovina [Narodna Banka Bosne i Hercegovine] is the central bank. There are no functioning employers' and labour organizations at national level.

Political structure. Under the 1990 constitution, Bosnia-Herzegovina is a parliamentary republic. Executive power is vested in the seven-member State Presidency [Državno Predsjedništvo]. It is elected for a four-year term by the legislature and should reflect the country's ethnic diversity; it elects one of its members as president, who acts as head of state and appoints the prime minister. The prime minister and council of ministers are responsible for the administration of the country. Legislative power is vested in the bicameral Assembly [Skupština], composed of the 130-member Chamber of Citizens [Vijeće Gradjanstvo] and the 110-member Chamber of Municipalities [Vijeće Općina], both elected for four-year terms by a system of proportional representation. All citizens over the age of 18 are entitled to vote. Judicial power is ultimately vested in the Supreme Court [Vrhovni Sud]; the Constitutional Court [Savezni Sud] adjudicates on constitutional matters. Administratively the country is divided into 100 districts [općina, pl. općine]. The two historical regions of Bosnia and Herzegovina have no administrative or political functions.

The main political parties are the Democratic Action Party (SDA), Serbian Democratic Party (SDS), Croatian Democratic Union of Bosnia-Herzegovina (HDZ-BiH or HDZ) and Democratic Socialist Party of Bosnia-Herzegovina (DSS-BiH or DSS). At the November 1990 election the SDA gained 86/240 seats, the SDS 72 seats, the HDZ 44 seats and the DSS 20 seats. The SDS and HDZ subsequently withdrew from the government structures and set up separate assemblies, which proclaimed the breakaway Serbian Republic and the Croatian Republic of Herzeg-Bosnia respectively. The members of the State Presidency are Alija Izetbegović (president), Ejup Ganić (vice-president), Nijaz Duraković, Stjepan Kljuić, Ivo Komsić, Tatjana Ljuić-Mijatović and Mirko Pejanović. The government includes members of the SDA, HDZ and SDS. The prime minister is Haris Silajdžić, and other senior ministers are Jadranko Prlić (deputy prime minister, defence), Irfan Ljubijankić (foreign affairs), Bakir Alispahić (internal affairs), Neven Tomić (finance) and Mate Tadić (justice). The head of state is Alija Izetbegović, who was elected in December 1990. The president of the Serbian Republic is Radovan Karadžic; the president of Herzeg-Bosnia is Kresimir Zubak. The president of the Federation of Bosnia-Herzegovina, established by the Bosnian government and Herzeg-Bosnia, is Kresimir Zubak, and the vice-president is Ejup Ganić.

Security and international affiliations. The Bosnian armed forces number 60,000 (all army). The Serbian Republic forces number around 80,000 and those of Herzeg-Bosnia around 50,000. Some 14,400 United Nations troops of the UN Protection Force II (UNPROFOR II) are stationed in the country.

Bosnia-Herzegovina is a member of the Central European Initiative (CEI) and Conference on Security and Cooperation in Europe (CSCE), as well as the United Nations and some of its specialized agencies. It has applied for membership of the Council of Europe.

History. Settled by Illyrians, the area of modern Bosnia-Herzegovina was conquered by the Romans in the 1st century BC. During the Europe-wide migrations that helped trigger the collapse of the Roman Empire in the 5th century, it was ruled by the Germanic Ostrogoths until the 550s. In the 7th century the Slavic Croats and Serbs, migrating from the northeast, began to settle in the wider region. Over the following centuries control of the region was disputed by the Eastern Roman or Byzantine Empire, Croatia (from the 1060s until its incorporation into Hungary in the 1090s), Hungary and local rulers. Under the Kotromanić dynasty (1254–1463) Bosnia asserted its independence from Hungary and Serbia (1322) and briefly became a major regional power under Stefan Tvrtko (1353–91). The Ottoman Turks first attacked Bosnia in 1386 and finally conquered it in 1463. In 1483 Herzegovina was also incorporated into the Ottoman Empire. (In the Middle Ages Bosnia and Herzegovina were separate territories, the former largely Catholic/Croat and the latter largely Orthodox/Serb. The distinction was rendered meaningless after the Ottoman conquest as populations became increasingly mixed and administrative borders were redrawn.) Throughout the Middle Ages the region had been a flashpoint of religious conflict, with Roman Catholics, Eastern Orthodox and Bogomils (followers of a heterodox Christian faith similar to Catharism that had originated in Bulgaria and been modified in Bosnia) vying for supremacy. During the Ottoman period most of the Bogomils converted to Islam, as did many others who sought to advance themselves.

With the rise of nationalism in the 19th century, Orthodox and Catholics increasingly identified themselves in national terms as Serbs and Croats respectively. There were uprisings against Ottoman rule in 1821, 1828, 1831, 1837, 1862 and 1875. Against local opposition Bosnia and Herzegovina were put under Austrian administration after the Russo-Turkish War of 1877–78. Opposition to Austrian rule intensified after the annexation of the two provinces in 1908. The assassination of Archduke Francis Ferdinand of Austria by a Serb nationalist in Sarajevo provided the spark for the outbreak of the First World War (1914–18). In 1918 Bosnia and Herzegovina joined the new Kingdom of Serbs, Croats and Slovenes. The new state was destabilized from the outset by dissatisfaction with the centralized administration and rivalry between Serbs and Croats in particular. In 1929 King Alexander II imposed a personal dictatorship. The name Yugoslavia – meaning 'country of the South Slavs' – was adopted at this time to symbolize the common heritage of the main ethnic groups. During the Second World War (1939–45) the German and Italian armies overran Yugoslavia in 1941, and Bosnia-Herzegovina was incorporated into the Independent State of Croatia (NDH). Modelled on the fascist regimes of Italy and Germany, the NDH implemented a policy of croatianization culminating in numerous atrocities and genocide against Serbs, Gipsies and Jews, hundreds of thousands of whom were killed. Many others died in the armed resistance to the NDH and the occupying forces and in fighting between the two main resistance movements, the monarchist Chetniks and the communist-dominated Partisans. The latter were victorious in the civil war. (Around 1.5 million people, most of them civilians, were killed throughout Yugoslavia in the four war years.)

On liberation in 1945 the Communists, led by Josip Broz Tito, took power throughout Yugoslavia. The monarchy was abolished and Bosnia-Herzegovina became a constituent republic of the new federation. The regime suppressed political opposition and implemented orthodox communist economic policies. After breaking with the Soviet Union in 1948, it pursued more pragmatic and liberal policies. The Slav Muslims, the largest ethnoreligious group in Bosnia-Herzegovina, were recognized as a 'nation' alongside the Serbs and Croats in 1967. Like the other republics, Bosnia-Herzegovina was given greater autonomy under a new federal constitution adopted in 1974. As Communist authority crumbled in the late 1980s, new, largely ethnically based, parties emerged. In the November 1990 multiparty election the Muslim Democratic Action Party (SDA), Serbian Democratic Party (SDS) and Croatian Democratic Union (HDZ) secured more than five-sixths of the vote between them. The three parties agreed to share power, and SDA leader Alija Izetbegović was elected head of the collective presidency. Ethnic tensions mounted as the Yugoslav federation disintegrated in 1991. A referendum on independence held in Febru-

ary/March 1992 was boycotted by the SDS. Independence was declared in March and internationally recognized in April, and Bosnia-Herzegovina was admitted to the United Nations in May. The decision to secede from Yugoslavia triggered the three-cornered civil war between the Muslim-led government and Serb and Croat breakaway states, the Serbian Republic and the Croatian Republic of Herzeg-Bosnia. More than 200,000 people have been killed and up to two-thirds of the population has been uprooted in the course of the conflict – by far the most violent in Europe since the Second World War. The United Nations launched a humanitarian aid effort soon after the outbreak of hostilities in March 1992 and later deployed peace-keeping troops in some parts of the country. International mediation efforts have been aimed at securing agreement on some form of partition along ethnic lines. The Muslim-led government and the break-away Croat state agreed a ceasefire in February 1994 and formed a federation the following month.

See also BOSNIAN CIVIL WAR *and entries on specific institutions, organizations, parties, people, terms etc.*

Bosniak-Croat Federation *See* FEDERATION OF BOSNIA-HERZEGOVINA.

Bosniaks Alternative name for BOSNIANS, taken from the Serbocroat equivalent, Bosniaki.

Bosnian civil war Armed conflict in Bosnia-Herzegovina between the established government and breakaway Serb and Croat states. The three-sided conflict, which broke out in March 1992, has its roots in Bosnia's heterogeneity. Around two-fifths of the people are Slav Muslims, a third Eastern Orthodox Serbs and a sixth Roman Catholic Croats. Before the war the three communities were highly intermingled: broadly speaking, Muslims formed a majority in the centre and far northwest and parts of the south and east, the Serbs in the northwest and far south and parts of the northeast and east, and Croats in the southwest and parts of northeast and centre, while the main towns and cities and much of eastern

Bosnia were very mixed. As the old Yugoslav federation disintegrated in 1990/91, most Bosnian Serbs favoured continuation of the federation in one form or other, while Muslims and Croats were reluctant to remain part of what became a Serb-dominated smaller Yugoslavia after Croatia and Slovenia had declared their independence in June 1991 and Macedonia in November. Growing tensions in Bosnia were accentuated by the uprising of Serbs across the border in Croatia (*see* CROATIAN CIVIL WAR). Most Serb deputies withdrew from parliament in October and set up their own assembly. Their call for a boycott of the referendum on independence held in February/March 1992 was widely heeded by Serbs. Fighting broke out throughout the country after independence was declared in March. Within three months the forces of the self-proclaimed Serbian Republic, assisted by the Yugoslav/Serb army and Serb paramilitary groups, controlled around two-thirds of the country's total area, including all Serb-majority districts and some mixed areas in the east. The Croat Defence Council (HVO) forces, assisted by the Croatian army and Croat paramilitary groups, established control in the Croat-majority southwest. The Serb and Croat insurgents had appropriated most of the old Yugoslav federal army's supplies and equipment deployed in Bosnia-Herzegovina, while the government forces were hampered by a lack of heavy equipment and the United Nations arms embargo (imposed on all of old Yugoslavia in September 1991). In their initial offensive the Serbs resorted to what was called 'ethnic cleansing', forced expulsions of Muslims and Croats in order to create ethnically homogeneous areas. Eventually all three sides took up this practice. In consequence hundreds of thousands of people were uprooted from their homes. The United Nations organized humanitarian aid and deployed peace-keeping troops in some parts of the country. International efforts to end the fighting and find a political settlement, coordinated by the United Nations (UN) and the European Union (EU), but also involving the United States

and Russia, produced a series of peace plans providing for some sort of partition along ethnic lines. None was accepted by all three sides, however, with the principle of partition and subsequently the exact division of territory the main points of contention. In the first 2½ years of fighting around 250,000 people have been killed, 2.75 million people have been displaced and around 400,000 have fled abroad (out of a total pre-war population of 4.37 million). Throughout the war some Croats and Serbs, particularly from Sarajevo and other cities, have remained committed to the concept of a multiethnic unitary state, and Croats and Serbs continue to be represented in the Bosnian presidency and government.

Chronologically, in February/March 1992 Muslims and Croats voted overwhelmingly for independence from Yugoslavia in a referendum boycotted by most Serbs. In March independence was declared, fighting broke out across the country, and the Serbian Republic was proclaimed. In April Serb forces laid siege to Sarajevo. In June the first United Nations Protection Force (UNPROFOR) troops were deployed. In July the UN launched a humanitarian relief operation, flying supplies in to Sarajevo and later delivering them by road to other locations as well; the Croatian Community (later Republic) of Herzeg-Bosnia was proclaimed; and media reports revealed evidence of 'ethnic cleansing' by Serb forces and the operation of detention camps. In August the International Conference on Former Yugoslavia was opened, marking the start of joint UN-EC mediation efforts. In September the UN Security Council approved the deployment of another 6,000 UNPROFOR troops; and the Serbian Republic assembly formally declared its support for eventual unification with Serbia. In October the UN Security Council called for an 'air-exclusion zone' for military aircraft over Bosnian airspace; fighting broke out between government and Croat forces in central Bosnia, with the latter taking Mostar, the historical capital of Herzegovina; and the international mediators tabled a peace plan providing for the country's division into ten provinces. In March 1993 the government and the Croats accepted the Vance-Owen plan, but the Serbs rejected it. In April Serb forces, yielding to international pressure, lifted the year-long siege of the Muslim town of Srebrenica, which had gained worldwide attention. In May the UN Security Council declared Srebrenica, Sarajevo and four other mainly Muslim cities and towns to be 'safe areas' and approved additional UNPROFOR deployments to protect them. In July the international mediators tabled a peace plan providing for a three-way division of the country. In August three Croat members of the collective state presidency, including the prime minister, resigned in protest at Muslim-Croat fighting in central Bosnia; and the Owen-Stoltenberg plan was accepted by the Serbs and Croats, but the Bosnian parliament made acceptance conditional on changes to its territorial provisions. In September dissident Muslims proclaimed the Autonomous Province of Western Bosnia in the Bihać region in the far northwest. In October the new administration headed by Haris Silajdžić still included Croats and Serbs but had a stronger Muslim component. In November the Bosnian army made significant advances against the Croats in central districts. In December the Owen-Stoltenberg plan was effectively abandoned. In February 1994 Serb forces lifted their 22-month siege of Sarajevo in response to a United Nations threat of military action issued after 68 civilians had been killed in a mortar attack on a crowded marketplace; the Bosnian army and Croat forces signed a general ceasefire; and the flight ban was enforced for the first time when North Atlantic Treaty Organization (NATO) forces acting on behalf of the United Nations shot down four Serb planes. In March the government and Herzeg-Bosnia agreed to set up the Federation of Bosnia-Herzegovina. In April NATO forces launched air strikes on Serb positions around Goražde, one of the UN-declared 'safe areas', which had come under attack. In June the United

Nations brokered a ceasefire across the country; after initial observance it was widely violated. In July the Contact Group, a more broadly based international mediation effort, tabled a new peace plan; this was accepted in principle by the Muslim-Croat federation but rejected by the Serbs. In August the Yugoslav government, which supported the Contact Group plan, closed the country's border with Serb-held Bosnia-Herzegovina and imposed several other sanctions on the Bosnian Serbs; and the rebellion in the Bihać region was defeated by government forces.

See also BOSNIA-HERZEGOVINA: HISTORY *and entries on specific plans, states, terms etc.*

Bosnian Federation and **Bosnian-Croat Federation** *See* FEDERATION OF BOSNIA-HERZEGOVINA.

Bosnians Shorthand for citizens of Bosnia-Herzegovina and more specifically for SLAV MUSLIMS, the country's largest ethnic group. In recent years, especially after the outbreak of civil war in March 1992 and the resultant polarization between Muslims, Serbs and Croats, many Muslims began to call themselves 'Bosnians' or 'Bosniaks' [Bosniaki]. In September 1993 an informal but representative convention of Muslims decided to adopt the name 'Bosniaks' for themselves. Their appropriation of the name anticipated the country's eventual partition.

Bossano, Joe (1939–) Gibraltarian trade-union official and politician. Having worked in various jobs in industry and qualified as an economist, he was elected leader of the Gibraltar branch of the Transport and General Workers' Union (TGWU), the territory's only industrial union, in 1974. He became leader of the Gibraltar Socialist Labour Party (GSLP) in January 1984. He became chief minister after the party won the March 1988 election.

Bossi, Umberto (1941–) Italian civil servant and politician. He studied medicine for some time and worked in local government in the 1960s and 70s. An advocate of autonomy for his native Lombardy region, he co-founded and became leader of the Lombard League (Lega Lombarda) in April 1979. He was elected to parliament in 1987. In February 1991 he also became leader of the Northern League (Lega Nord), which brought together the Lega Lombarda and other regional parties based in northern and central Italy.

Bosson, Bernard (1948–) French lawyer and politician. He has held elected office in his native Annecy, Haute-Savoie department and Rhône-Alpes region for the Social Democratic Centre (CDS), part of the centre-right Union for French Democracy (UDF) alliance, since 1977. He became mayor of Annecy in March 1983. Elected to parliament in 1986, he served as a junior minister with responsibility for European affairs until 1988. He was appointed minister of public works, transport and tourism in the centre-right government formed in March 1993.

Bottomley, Virginia (1948–) British social worker and politician. She worked as a researcher on child poverty and as a psychiatric social worker until her election to Parliament for the Conservative Party in 1984. She became a junior health minister in 1989 and was appointed secretary of state for health in April 1992.

Boucheron affair Political and business scandal in France surrounding Jean-Michel Boucheron, a prominent left-wing politician. Boucheron was mayor of Angoulême from 1977–89 and a member of parliament for the Socialist Party (PS) from 1978–90. After he left office it emerged that huge sums had gone missing from the city's funds. In October 1990 he was suspended from the PS at his own request. In February 1991 he was accused of extorting kickbacks from industrial companies in exchange for public-works contracts and of diverting public funds to himself, associates and the party, leaving the city with creditors claiming 1.2 billion francs (183 million ecus). He fled to Argentina – which has no extradition agreement with France – and set up a restaurant business. In July 1994 he was convicted in absentia of corruption, forgery and fraud and sentenced to four years' imprisonment. A close associate,

Michel Gabaudé, also a PS member, was sentenced to 2¹/₂ years' imprisonment on similar charges.

Boudewijn *See* BAUDOUIN.

Bourbon [Borbón] Royal dynasty of Spain. *See* HOUSE OF BOURBON.

Bourbon Palace [Palais Bourbon] Shorthand for the NATIONAL ASSEMBLY, the lower house of the French parliament. The Palais Bourbon in Paris is the seat of the Assembly.

Bourgeois, André (1928–) Belgian lawyer and politician. He was active in local government for the Flemish Christian People's Party (CVP) from the 1950s and was elected to parliament in 1971. He was appointed minister of agriculture and small and medium-sized enterprises in March 1992.

bourgeois party [borgerlige parti (Norwegian), borgerliga parti (Swedish), pl. - -er] In Norway and Sweden, a traditional non-socialist party on the centre and right. In Norway the main 'bourgeois parties' are the Centre Party (Sp), Conservative Party (Høyre, H) and Christian People's Party (KrF); and in Sweden the Moderate Coalition Party (MS), People's Party - The Liberals (Fp) and Centre Party (Cp).

Bourgogne *See* BURGUNDY.

Bozen *See* SOUTH TYROL.

Bozkurt and **-lar** *See* GREY WOLVES.

Brandenburg Federal state [Land] of Germany, formerly part of East Germany. Situated in the east, surrounding Berlin but not including it, Brandenburg has an area of 29,060 sq km and a population of 2,549,000. There is a small Sorb-speaking minority of 30,000 people in the southeast. The capital is Potsdam, and the other main cities are Cottbus and Frankfurt an der Oder. The economy is based on agriculture (cereals, fruit and vegetables), manufacturing (engineering, chemicals) and mining (coal). Like the other eastern states, Brandenburg is experiencing extensive economic restructuring and high unemployment. Political power is vested in the State Assembly [Landtag], with 88 members elected for a four-year term, and a government headed by a minister-president. The dominant party is the Social Democratic Party (SPD); other major parties are the Christian Democratic Union (CDU), the Democratic Socialist Party (PDS, the successor to the communist Socialist Unity Party, SED), the left-alternative Alliance 90 / Greens (B'90) and the centrist Free Democratic Party (FDP). At the election in September 1994 the SPD gained 54.1% of the vote and 52 seats, the CDU 18.7% and 18 seats, the PDS 18.7% and 18 seats, B'90 2.9% and no seats, and the FDP 2.1% and no seats. The minister-president is Manfred Stolpe. A state within the Holy Roman Empire since the 12th century, Brandenburg formed the core of what became the Kingdom of Prussia in 1701. A province of Prussia within the German Empire from 1871, it was made a separate state on the dissolution of Prussia in 1947 but was divided into three districts by the East German authorities in 1952. It was reconstituted as a state in 1990 prior to German reunification.

Brandt, Willy (1913–92) German politician. A member of the Social Democratic Party (SPD), he fled Germany for Norway when the nazis came to power in 1933, returning in 1945. He was governing mayor of West Berlin from 1957–66, during the period of East-West tension caused by the building of the Berlin Wall. He was elected leader of the SPD in 1964. He was foreign minister from 1966–69 and became federal chancellor in an SPD-led centre-left coalition in 1969. His government normalized relations and concluded treaties of reconciliation with the Soviet Union, East Germany and other Eastern European countries. For this work he was awarded the Nobel Peace Prize in 1971. He resigned the chancellorship in 1974 when a senior member of his staff was exposed as an East German spy. He remained the SPD's chairman until 1987, when he became its honorary chairman. One of the world's most respected politicians, he chaired the Independent Commission on International Development Issues (later known as the Brandt Commission) which published *North-South: A Programme for Survival* in 1980 and *Common Crisis* in 1983. From 1976–92 he was also president of

the Socialist International (SI), the umbrella organization of the world's democratic socialist parties. He died of cancer in October 1992.

Bratislava Shorthand for the Slovakian government. Bratislava is the capital of Slovakia.

Brazauskas, Algirdas Mykolas (1932–) Lithuanian hydraulic engineer, economist and politician. He held senior posts in the state planning office, the Lithuanian Communist Party (LKP) and the republic's government from the 1960s onwards. A member of the party's politburo from 1977, he was elected leader in 1988. Under his leadership the party declared its independence from the Communist Party of the Soviet Union a year later. In December 1990 he was elected leader of the relaunched Democratic Labour Party (LDDP). He led the party to victory in the first election since Lithuania regained its independence in October/November 1992. He was elected president of the Seimas (= parliament) and became acting head of state. In February 1993 he was elected president of the republic.

BRD Abbreviation for Bundesrepublik Deutschland ('Federal Republic of Germany'), the official name of Germany.

Breatnach, Niamh (1945–) Irish teacher and politician. A specialist in remedial teaching, she was elected to parliament for the Labour Party in 1992 and appointed education minister in January 1993.

Breizh Breton name for BRITTANY, a region of France.

Bremen Federal state [Land] of Germany. Situated in the north and consisting of the cities and ports of Bremen and Bremerhaven, Bremen is Germany's smallest state, with a total area of 404 sq km and a population of 686,000. Bremen is the country's second largest port and a major industrial centre. Political power is exercised by the Citizens' Assembly [Bürgerschaft], with 100 members elected for a four-year term, and the executive Senate [Senat] headed by a president. The administration combines the functions of a municipality and a state. The dominant party is the Social Democratic Party (SPD), which has been in power for most years since 1949 and without interruption since 1971; the other main parties are the Christian Democratic Union (CDU), the Greens, the centrist Free Democratic Party (FDP) and the far-right German People's Union (DVU). At the election in September 1991 the SPD gained 38.8% of the vote and 41 seats, the CDU 30.7% and 32 seats, the Greens 11.4% and 11 seats, the FDP 9.5% and 10 seats, and the DVU 6.2% and six seats. The government is formed by the SPD, Greens and FDP, headed by Klaus Wedemeier. A leading member of the Hanseatic League in the Middle Ages, Bremen became a free city of the Holy Roman Empire in 1646 – its official name is still the Free Hanse City of Bremen – and a state within the unified German Empire in 1871.

Bretagne *See* BRITTANY.

Breton Democratic Union [Union Démocratique Brétonne (French), Unvaniezh Demokratel Breizh (Breton)] (UDB) French political party. Founded in 1964, the UDB advocates 'self-determination' for Brittany but rejects violence in pursuit of this aim. (Several separatist guerrilla groups have been active in Brittany over the years.) Its economic policies are broadly left-wing, and it has liberal views on social issues. The party has gained local-council seats and some mayorships in the region since 1977. The leader is Jean-Jacques Monnier.

Breuel, Birgit (1937–) German politician and civil servant. Trained in commerce, she was elected to the Hamburg state assembly for the Christian Democratic Union (CDU) in 1966. She became economy minister in the Lower Saxony government in 1978 and finance minister in 1986. In 1990 she was appointed to the board of the Treuhandanstalt, the government agency set up to sell off the state-owned enterprises of former East Germany. She became its director in April 1991.

Breydel, the Shorthand for the EUROPEAN COMMISSION, the administrative and executive arm of the European Union (EU). The Breydel building in Brussels is the Commission's temporary headquarters while repairs are being carried out on the

nearby Berlaymont building. 'Berlaymont' is still used to refer to the Commission.

bribery scandals (Italy) and **Bribesville scandals** *See* ITALIAN CORRUPTION SCANDALS.

Brigate Rosse *See* RED BRIGADES.

Brinkman, Elco (1948–) Dutch civil servant and politician. He has worked in public administration and planning and held several senior posts in the interior ministry from 1975–82, serving as its director-general from 1980–82. A member of the Christian Democratic Appeal (CDA), he was minister of welfare, health and culture from 1982–89, became a member of parliament in 1986, and was elected leader of the CDA parliamentary party in November 1989. He was the CDA's candidate for prime minister in the May 1994 election, but resigned as leader after the party lost a third of its support and was forced into opposition in August.

Britain Shorthand for GREAT BRITAIN and an informal name for the United Kingdom of Great Britain and Northern Ireland.

Britannia Personification of Great Britain or the United Kingdom. As used on coins and in caricatures, she is usually represented in ancient Roman dress and with a shield, helmet and trident. Britannia is the Latin name for Britain.

BRITE, in full **Basic Research in Industrial Technologies for Europe** Programme of the European Union (EU). Launched in 1985, it is aimed at promoting research, development and application of new technologies in the manufacturing, chemical, textile and other industries. It gives financial support to projects undertaken by industrial companies and research institutes.

British or **Britons** People of Great Britain (i.e. England, Scotland and Wales), or, more generally, citizens of the United Kingdom as a whole (i.e. including Northern Ireland).

British Isles Collective name for Great Britain, Ireland, Man, the Channel Islands and the smaller islands off the northwest coast of the European continent. It is used in a geographical, not a political, sense.

Britons *See* BRITISH.

Brittan, Leon (1939–) British lawyer and politician. Elected to Parliament for the Conservative Party in 1974, he held several junior ministerial posts from 1979 and became home secretary in 1983 and trade and industry secretary in 1985. The following year he was forced to resign after being implicated in the leak of a confidential letter by government officials. In January 1989 he was appointed a commissioner of the European Community (EC), responsible for competition policy and financial institutions until January 1993, and subsequently for external economic affairs and trade.

Brittannia *See* BRITANNIA.

Brittany [Bretagne] Region of France. Situated in the west and surrounded by the Atlantic Ocean and the Channel on three sides, Brittany has an area of 27,208 sq km and a population of 2,816,000. Breton, a Celtic language, is the first language of perhaps 570,000 people, mainly in the western rural areas; it has no official status but is allowed to be taught in schools. Perhaps two-thirds of the people consider themselves Breton (detailed figures n.a.). The region's capital is Rennes, and the other main city is Brest. The economy is based on agriculture (cattle and pig farming), manufacturing (engineering, electronics), tourism and fishing. Relative geographical isolation and the distinctive language and culture have fostered a strong sense of identity in Brittany. The region enjoyed a large measure of independence during the Middle Ages and was not formally incorporated into France until 1547. In the late 19th century several movements and parties emerged with the aim of reviving the Breton language and attaining some form of self-government. Several small separatist guerrilla groups were also active in the 1960s and 70s. Brittany was established as a region in 1982 as part of a decentralization programme.

Brno Shorthand for the Supreme Court of the Czech Republic. The Court sits in Brno, the country's second city.

broad band (European Union) *See* EXCHANGE RATE MECHANISM.

broadcasting ban In Ireland and the United Kingdom, the prohibition on transmitting on radio or television statements by or interviews with representatives of banned organizations or those deemed to support terrorist activities. Introduced in Ireland in 1972 and in the United Kingdom in 1988, it was primarily aimed at denying a platform to the Irish Republican Army (IRA), the guerrilla group fighting for the reunification of Ireland, and Sinn Féin, the party widely regarded as its political wing. The ban was highly controversial, not least because Sinn Féin is a legal political party in both countries, with sizeable electoral support in Northern Ireland. It was lifted in Ireland in January 1994, and in the United Kingdom the following September, after the IRA had declared a ceasefire.

broadening or **widening** In the European Union (EU), a term associated with those who argue that the EU should concentrate on forging closer links with other European countries, by concluding cooperation agreements with them and paving the way for their eventual accession to the organization. It is contrasted with 'DEEPENING', i.e. concentrating on strengthening the existing EU's internal cohesion and on further integration.

Brooke initiative Proposal for negotiations on the future of Northern Ireland, a component of the United Kingdom, riven by tension and conflict between Protestants and Catholics (*see* NORTHERN IRELAND QUESTION). The initiative was launched in 1991 by Peter Brooke, secretary of state for Northern Ireland from 1989–92. It envisaged three rounds or 'strands' of negotiations. Strand one would involve the 'constitutional parties' (i.e. those who reject violence); strand two would bring in the Irish government; and strand three would involve the Irish and British governments. Any agreed outcome would be put to a referendum in both Northern Ireland and the Republic of Ireland. The first phase of the process began in June 1991 with a meeting of the leaders of the Ulster Unionist Party (UUP), Democratic Unionist Party (DUP), Social Democratic and Labour Party (SDLP) and Alliance

Party, the first since 1975. The talks broke down the following month over procedural issues and were shelved in January 1992. They were revived in July, with a meeting of representatives of the Northern Ireland parties and the Irish government and a meeting of British and Irish government ministers. The talks broke down again in November, although the four Northern Irish parties agreed to continue informal consultations. The British and Irish governments continued their cooperation within the ANGLO-IRISH AGREEMENT and launched another initiative, the DOWNING STREET DECLARATION, in December 1993.

Brotherhood *See* NATIONAL CONFEDERATION OF FREE TRADE UNIONS ....

brown In Germany and other countries, the colour associated with far-right parties and organizations. It was originally associated with the National Socialist (Nazi) Party, which held power under Adolf Hitler from 1933–45.

Brown, Gordon (1951–) British lecturer and politician. An economics and history graduate, he taught at a tertiary college and worked in television in his native Scotland until his election to parliament for the Labour Party in 1983. He has been the party's spokesman on trade and industry and, since July 1992, finance and economic affairs.

Bruges Group International political organization. The Bruges Group is an informal grouping of parliamentarians, academics, businesspeople and others from the United Kingdom and other European Union (EU) member states who oppose what they see as the centralizing or 'federalist' tendencies within the EU. It was set up in 1989 to promote the views on European integration of Margaret Thatcher, then the British prime minister. In a speech at the College of Europe in Bruges (Belgium) in September 1988 she had rejected the idea of political union and had warned against the emergence of a European 'superstate'. *See also* EUROPE OF NATIONS.

Brundtland, Gro Harlem (1939–) Norwegian doctor and politician. She was appointed minister of the environment in

1974, became deputy leader of the Norwegian Labour Party (DNA) in 1975, and was elected to parliament in 1977. In 1981 she succeeded Odvar Nordli as party leader and prime minister. Labour lost power after the election later that year, but she returned as prime minister in 1986, heading a minority government until 1989 and again from November 1990. She chaired the independent World Commission on Environment and Development, which published *Our Common Future* (also known as the 'Brundtland Report') in 1987. In November 1992 she resigned the party leadership for personal reasons, but remained as prime minister.

Brussels Shorthand for the Belgian government. Brussels is the capital of Belgium. It is also the political centre of the European Union (EU) and the headquarters of the Western European Union (WEU), the North Atlantic Treaty Organization (NATO) and many other intergovernmental organizations and institutions.

Brussels Shorthand for BRUSSELS-CAPITAL, a region of Belgium. The longer name is increasingly used to distinguish the region from the city of Brussels proper and from the Brussels metropolitan area, which extends beyond the region.

Brussels Shorthand for the European Union (EU) and its institutions. The European Commission, the administrative and executive arm, and many other EU bodies are based in Brussels, the Belgian capital. The Council of Ministers usually meets there, as do the committees of the European Parliament. (The Parliament's plenary sessions are held in Strasbourg, France.)

Brussels-Capital [Bruxelles-Capitale (French), Brussel-Hoofdstad (Dutch)] Region of Belgium, widely referred to as Brussels. Situated in the centre and surrounded by Flanders, Brussels-Capital has an area of 162 sq km and a population of 977,000. It is composed of the city of Brussels proper and 18 suburban communes. French and Dutch are the official languages; French is the first language of around 85% of the population. The economy is based on services and manufacturing. The service sector is buoyed by Brussels's status as the national capital and headquarters of several major international organizations, in particular the European Union (EU) and the North Atlantic Treaty Organization (NATO). Political power is exercised by the 75-member Council [Conseil/Raad], elected for a five-year term, and an executive headed by a president. The Council divides into a 64-member French Community Commission and an 11-member Flemish Community Commission to deal separately with health, education, social security, social services, culture and language issues. The main parties are the Walloon Socialist Party (PS), the right-wing Walloon Liberal Reform Party (PRL), the Francophone Democratic Front (FDF), the Walloon Christian Social Party (PSC), the Ecology Party (ÉCOLO) and the Flemish Christian People's Party (CVP). At the election in June 1989 the PS gained 18 seats, the PRL 15, the FDF 12, the PSC nine and the CVP four. The government is a six-party coalition headed by Charles Piqué of the PS. Historically a Flemish city, Brussels has had a French-speaking majority since the 19th century. It has been a flashpoint for linguistic and other disputes between Flemings and Walloons ever since. The establishment of a bilingual Brussels region was agreed in principle in 1970 but held up for many years because of disagreements over its exact structure and powers. The region was constituted in January 1989, and the first election to the regional legislature was held in June of that year.

Bruton, John (1947–) Irish politician. A lawyer by training and a farmer, he was elected to parliament for the centre-right Fine Gael in 1969. A junior minister from 1973–77, he has been minister of finance (1981–82 and 1986–87), industry, commerce and tourism (1982–86) and public service (1987). He became Fine Gael's deputy leader in 1987 and was elected party leader in November 1990.

BSDP *See* BULGARIAN SOCIAL DEMOCRATIC PARTY.

BSEC and **BSECO** *See* BLACK SEA ECONOMIC COOPERATION ORGANIZATION.

BSP *See* BULGARIAN SOCIALIST PARTY.

BSPSh *See* UNION OF INDEPENDENT TRADE UNIONS OF ALBANIA.

BSR Abbreviation for Brigade Spéciale de Recherche ('Special Investigations Unit'), the French name of the Belgian intelligence agency. It is called the Bijzondere Opsporingsbrigade (BOB) in Dutch.

BUBA or **Buba** Abbreviation for Deutsche Bundesbank ('GERMAN FEDERAL BANK'), the German central bank.

Bucharest Shorthand for the Romanian government. Bucharest is the capital of Romania.

Büchel, Markus (1959–) Liechtenstein lawyer and politician. He is a specialist in European law. A member of the right-wing Progressive Citizens' Party (FBP), he was appointed prime minister in May 1993. He lost power the following September after his own party had criticized his style of leadership and tabled a motion of no confidence in his government.

Büchel, Thomas (1952–) Liechtenstein chemist and politician. Elected to parliament for the right-wing Progressive Citizens' Party (FBP) in 1993, he was appointed deputy prime minister (also responsible for internal affairs, education and agriculture, forestry and environment) in December that year.

Budapest Shorthand for the Hungarian government. Budapest is the capital of Hungary.

budget rebate and **budgetary compensation** (European Union) *See* ABATEMENT.

Budiša, Dražen (1948–) Croatian politician. After leading student protests in 1971, he was imprisoned by the communist authorities for four years and subsequently banned from political activity. He graduated in philosophy and sociology in 1976 and from 1977–90 worked in the finance department of the National University library in Zagreb. In May 1989 he became leader of the new Croatian Social Liberal Party (HSLS).

Bugaj, Ryszard (1944–) Polish economist, civil servant and politician. He was dismissed from university and from the communist youth movement in 1968 for his opposition to the regime. He then completed his studies extramurally. He joined the Construction Institute in 1970, worked as a planner in several government agencies from 1973 and at the Economic Institute of the Academy of Sciences from 1982. Active in the opposition Solidarity movement from 1980, he was elected to parliament on its ticket in 1989. He became leader of the left-wing Labour Solidarity (SP) in August 1990 and of the more broadly based Labour Union (UP) in January 1993.

Bugár, Béla (1958–) Slovakian mechanical engineer and politician. An ethnic Hungarian, he was elected leader of the Hungarian Christian Democratic Movement (MKDM) in March 1991. He also represented the party in the Czechoslovak parliament from 1990 until the federation's dissolution at the end of 1992.

Bukovina question *See* NORTHERN BUKOVINA QUESTION.

Bulatović, Momir (1955–) Yugoslav economist, academic and politician. In the mid 1980s he lectured in economics and was active on the reformist wing of the League of Communists in his native Montenegro. He became leader of the party, since renamed the Democratic Socialist Party (DPSCG), in April 1989. He was elected president of Montenegro in December 1990 and reelected in January 1993.

Bulatović, Pavle (1948–) Yugoslav economist and politician. He was appointed interior minister of Montenegro in April 1989 and also became interior minister at federal level in July 1992. He was made defence minister in March 1993. He is a member of the Democratic Socialist Party (DPSCG), the successor to the League of Communists in Montenegro.

Bulgaria [Bŭlgariya] Country in southeastern Europe.

Official data. Name: Republic of Bulgaria [Republika Bŭlgariya]; capital: Sofia [Sofiya]; form of government: parliamentary republic; head of state: president; head of government: prime minister; flag: three horizontal stripes, white, green and red, with the state emblem in the canton; national holiday: 3 March (Liberation Day); language: Bulgarian; religion: none; currency: lev (Lv) (pl. -a) = 100 stotinki; abbreviation: BG.

Geography. One of the Balkan countries, Bulgaria has an area of 110,994 sq km. It is bordered by Romania in the north, the Black Sea in the east, Turkey and Greece in the south, and Macedonia and Yugoslavia in the west. The Balkan Mountains [Stara Planina] run east-west across the country; to the north are the low-lying river plain of the Danube [Dunav] and other lowlands, to the south the Thracian Plain, hill lands and the Rhodope Mountains [Rodopi Planina] along the border with Greece. Some 37% of the land is arable, another 18% is covered by pastures and 35% is forested. The main rivers are the Maritsa, Tundzha and Danube, which forms the border with Romania. The climate is generally humid continental, with hot summers and cold winters; temperatures are lower in the mountains, higher in the south; rainfall is moderate.

Demography. Bulgaria has a population of 8,465,000. Population density is 77 per sq km. Some 68% of the people live in urban areas. The main city is Sofia (population 1.1 million), and other major cities are Plovdiv, Varna and Burgas; Ruse and Stara Zagora are important regional centres. In ethnic terms 85.3% of the people are Bulgarians, 8.5% Turks, 2.6% Gipsies and 2.5% Macedonians; there are also small groups of Armenians, Russians, Greeks and Romanians. Most Turks live in the northeast and the southern mountains; since 1989 around 250,000 of them have emigrated, mainly to Turkey. Gipsies are considerably underrepresented in official figures; they are thought to number around 450,000 (5.2% of the total population). The main languages are Bulgarian and Turkish. In religious terms around 80% of the population is nominally Bulgarian Orthodox; Muslims account for around 12%, and include nearly all Turks and around 300,000 ethnic Bulgarians, known as Pomaks; there are also small groups of Protestant, Roman Catholic and Armenian Christians.

Sociography. Bulgaria scores 0.815 on the United Nations human development index (HDI), ranking 48th in the world and 29th among 32 European countries.

There are 32 doctors and 98 hospital beds for every 10,000 people. Education is compulsory between the ages of six and 16. There is one teacher for every 15 students. Enrolment is 62% at the secondary level and 31% at the tertiary level. The literacy rate is 93%. Real annual income per head (in terms of purchasing power) is US$ 4,810.

Infrastructure and communications. Bulgaria's transport and communications network is relatively well developed but in need of modernization and extension; the telecommunications system is limited especially in the rural areas. There are 33,970 km of paved roads and 1.28 million passenger cars (142 per 1,000 people), 4,290 km of railways and 470 km of navigable waterways. The main ports are Burgas and Varna. The main airport is at Sofia, and there are two other airports with scheduled services. There are 17 daily newspapers, with a combined circulation of 2.40 million (267 per 1,000 people). There are 1.91 million radio receivers, 2.30 million television sets and 2.52 million telephones in use (respectively 212, 255 and 279 per 1,000 people).

Economic structure. The Bulgarian economy is based on manufacturing, agriculture and food processing. Although essentially developed, diversified and trade-oriented, it is in need of major investment and restructuring. The transition from a command to a market-based economy initiated in 1990 is causing severe dislocation and has led to steep falls in industrial and agricultural production as well as energy shortages. Between 1990 and 1993 GDP contracted by 27%, inflation averaged 91% per year, the currency lost five-sixths of its value, the current-account deficit averaged 10% of GDP per year, and unemployment rose to 16%. Inflation fell sharply and growth resumed in 1993. The foreign debt stands at around US$ 13 billion (90% of GDP).

Services contribute 37% of GDP, industry contributes 50% (manufacturing around 30%), and agriculture, forestry and fisheries 13%. Some 33% of the labour force is employed in manufacturing, 19% in public service, 19% in farming, 9% in trade and 8% in construction. The main crops grown are cereals (maize, wheat, barley), sugarbeets, oilseeds and tobacco; horticulture (fruit and vegetables, esp. grapes and tomatoes), livestock raising (sheep, pigs, cattle, poultry) and dairy farming are also important agricultural activities. Forestry is of regional importance. The main mineral resources are lignite, iron, lead, zinc and oil. The main industries are food processing, engineering and textiles; other important branches are electrical goods, chemicals, wood processing, metalworking, building materials and tobacco processing. Tourism is of regional importance (Black Sea coast). The main energy sources are domestic and imported fossil fuels and nuclear power; 15% of export earnings are required to cover net fuel imports. The main exports are cigarettes and other tobacco products (9% of the total), chemicals (8%), industrial machinery (5%) and iron and steel (5%); Bulgaria is the world's fourth-largest exporter of tobacco products; foodstuffs account for 23% of total exports, machinery and transport equipment for 18%. The main imports are fuels, machinery and transport equipment and basic manufactures. The main trading partners are: exports: Russia, Ukraine and other members of the Commonwealth of Independent States (CIS) (20%), Germany (9%), Italy (6%), Greece (5%), France; imports: Russia, Ukraine and other CIS members (28%), Germany (13%), Greece (7%), Italy (5%), Austria, France; a third of all trade is with European Union (EU) countries.

The Bulgarian National Bank [Bŭlgarska Narodna Banka] (BNB) is the central bank. There are several employers' associations, including the Bulgarian Industrial Association (BISA) and the National Employers' Association (NAR); the main labour organizations are the Confederation of Independent Trade Unions of Bulgaria (KNSB), Support (Podkrepa) and Unity (Edinstvo).

Political structure. Bulgaria is a parliamentary republic on the basis of a constitution adopted in 1991, replacing the communist constitution of 1971. The head of state is the president, who is directly elected for a four-year term; s/he is commander of the armed forces, appoints the prime minister and has certain emergency powers, but normally acts on the advice of the government. Executive power is vested in the prime minister and the council of ministers. Legislative power is vested in the National Assembly [Narodno Sobranie], whose 240 members are elected for a four-year term by a system of proportional representation (with a 4% threshold for gaining seats); parliament has the power to dismiss ministers. Major constitutional changes must be adopted by a specially elected 400-member Grand National Assembly [Veliko Narodno Sobranie]. Voting is compulsory for all citizens over the age of 18. Judicial power is ultimately vested in the Supreme Court [Vŭrkhoven Sŭd], whose members are elected by a council elected by the legislature and representatives of the judiciary; constitutional matters are adjudicated by the Constitutional Court [Konstitutionen Sŭd]. Administratively the country is divided into nine regions [oblast, pl. -i], including the region-level city of Sofia; the regions are subdivided into 282 municipalities and around 4,000 towns and villages.

The main political parties are the Bulgarian Socialist Party (BSP, the successor to the Bulgarian Communist Party), Democratic Party (DP), Radical Democratic Party (RDP), Movement for Rights and Freedoms (DPS) and Bulgarian Agrarian National Union (BZNS); the Union of Democratic Forces (SDS) is an alliance of the DP, RDP and other parties and social movements. At the general election in October 1991 the SDS gained 34.4% of the vote and 110/240 seats, the BSP 33.1% and 106 seats, and the DPS 7.6% and 24 seats. The government is formed by nominally non-party technocrats supported by the BSP and DPS, with Lyuben Berov as prime minister. Other senior ministers are Kiril Tsochev (deputy prime minister, trade), Evgeni Matinchev (deputy prime minister, labour and social welfare), Stoyan Aleksandrov (finance), Stanislav Daskalov (foreign affairs), Viktor Mikhailov (interior), Petŭr Kornazhev (justice) and Valentin Aleksandrov (defence). The head of state is President Zhelyu Zhelev, who was first elected in August 1990.

Security and international affiliations. The Bulgarian armed forces number 99,400 (army 52,000, navy 3,000, airforce 21,800, central staff 22,600). There is also a 12,000-strong paramilitary border guard. Military service is compulsory and consists of 18 months' basic training.

Bulgaria is a member of the Black Sea Economic Cooperation Organization (BSECO), Conference on Security and Cooperation in Europe (CSCE) and Council of Europe, and works closely with the Visegrad Group; it is also a member of the United Nations and its specialized agencies.

History. The Thracians inhabiting the southeastern corner of Europe became subject to the Persian Empire in the early 6th century BC. The region was conquered by neighbouring Macedonia in 343. (Alexander the Great conquered the Persian Empire in the 330s.) The Thracians regained their independence in the 2nd century, but remained internally divided. The districts north of the Balkan Mountains were conquered by the Romans in 29 BC (becoming the province of Moesia) and those of Thrace to the south were annexed in AD 46. The whole region was allocated to the Eastern Roman Empire, later Byzantium, in 395. During the Europe-wide migrations that began in the 4th century it was invaded by Goths and other Germanic tribes and then by Slavic tribes. By the 7th century the Slavs formed the majority of the population. The Bulgars, a nomadic Turkic people from the Eurasian steppes, invaded the region in the late 7th century. After defeating a Byzantine army in 681 they established an independent state comprising the territory between the Danube and the Balkan Mountains and much of modern Serbia, Macedonia and northern Greece to the west. During the 8th and 9th centuries the Bulgars were assimilated by the Slav population, a process facilitated by the spread of Chris-

tianity. The independent Bulgarian Orthodox Church was established in 870. Under
Simeon I (893–927) Bulgaria became the
dominant regional power. Internal rivalries among his successors paved the way
for defeat and subjugation by Byzantium
in 1018. Bulgaria regained its independence in 1185 and again became a leading power in the 13th century. Internal
divisions, incursions by nomadic Tatars
in 1285 and defeat by Serbia in 1330
(after which the western territories were
lost) led to the disintegration of the kingdom into feudal states. The Ottoman Turks
first attacked Bulgaria in the 1350s and
by the end of the century they controlled
the whole country. During the five centuries of Ottoman rule (1396–1878) the
peasants were reduced to serfs of Turkish
landowners, there was some Turkish immigration and conversion to Islam, but
there were no attempts to turkify or islamicize the population. Central authority
was generally weak in the later period, so
that local Turkish, Greek or Slav governors had considerable powers, which they
frequently exercised arbitrarily. There
were uprisings against Ottoman rule in
1598, 1686 and 1688.

The 19th century saw a revival of Bulgarian national consciousness, the movement being initially aimed at eliminating
Greek influence in religious and cultural
matters. The Bulgarian Orthodox Church
was restored in 1870. Increasing demands
for political independence led to an uprising in 1876. After military intervention
by Russia, Turkey was obliged to grant
independence to Bulgaria (including
Macedonia) in 1878 under the Treaty of
San Stefano. At the Congress of Berlin
later in the year the other major powers,
fearful of growing Russian influence in
the Balkan region, forced the new principality to relinquish Eastern Rumelia (the
region south of the Balkan Mountains)
and Macedonia and accept nominal Turkish suzerainty. A parliamentary form of
government was established under the
1879 Tŭrnovo Constitution, but the fragmentation of political parties induced
Prince Ferdinand to establish a 'personal
regime' in 1894. Bulgaria annexed East-

ern Rumelia in 1885 and gained full independence as a kingdom in 1908. Democratic rule was restored in 1918, but the
ensuing period was marred by unstable
coalitions and political violence. The
constitution was suspended after a coup
in 1934, and the following year King
Boris III (1918–43) established a personal
dictatorship with army support. In 1912
Bulgaria briefly acquired Macedonia, the
overriding foreign-policy aim since independence, but at the end of the Second
Balkan War (1913) it was left with only
the Pirin region. Regaining all of Slav-
speaking Macedonia was the major factor
determining Bulgaria's participation in
the First World War (1914–18) and the
Second World War (1939–45) and the
alliance with Germany in 1941.

Soviet troops invaded the country in
1944, and a coalition dominated by the
Bulgarian Communist Party (BKP) took
power. The monarchy was abolished in
1946 and a 'people's republic' was proclaimed in 1947. The regime suppressed
political dissent, nationalized the economy and introduced central planning.
Bulgaria was a close ally of the Soviet
Union throughout the communist period.
The dominant political leader was Todor
Zhivkov, BKP leader from 1954–89. An
extensive industrialization programme
was initiated in the 1950s. In November
1989 Zhivkov was replaced by reformists
committed to a pluralist system. The relaunched Bulgarian Socialist Party (BSP)
won the multiparty election of June 1990.
Demonstrations and a general strike
forced the government's resignation in
November and replacement by an all-
party coalition. A new democratic constitution came into effect in July 1991. The
Union of Democratic Forces (SDS), a
broad-based anti-BKP/BSP alliance,
became the largest party at the early election in September. Bulgaria was admitted
to the Council of Europe in May 1992.
The SDS administration of Filip Dimitrov
lost a vote of confidence in October and
was replaced by a non-party 'government
of experts' in December. The transition to
a market-based economy, initiated in
1990 and accepted by all major political

parties, has been accompanied by widespread economic and social dislocation.

See also entries on specific institutions, organizations, parties, people, terms etc.

Bulgarian Agrarian National Union [Bŭlgarski Zemedelski Naroden Sŭyuz] (BZNS) Bulgarian political party. Founded in 1899, the BZNS was a major political force in the 1920s and 30s. From 1946 until 1989 it formed part of the ruling communist-dominated Fatherland Front. It was reconstituted after the end of communist rule but split into several factions in 1990. At the October 1991 election the two largest groups each just failed to gain the 4% needed for representation in parliament. They merged in November 1992. The leader is Anastasiya Moser.

Bulgarian Social Democratic Party [Bŭlgarska Sotsial-Demokraticheska Partiya] (BSDP) Bulgarian political party. Founded in 1891, the BSDP was one of the country's main parties in the 1920s and 30s. It was suppressed by the communists in 1948, although never actually banned. Relaunched in 1990, it split the following year over participation in the centre-right Union of Democratic Forces (SDS) alliance; the SDS wing later became the Social Democratic Party (SDP). At the October 1991 election the BSDP gained 3.2% of the vote but, having failed to reach the 4% required for representation, no seats. The leader is Petŭr Dertliev.

Bulgarian Socialist Party [Bŭlgarska Sotsialisticheska Partiya] (BSP) Bulgarian political party. The BSP was founded as the Bulgarian Communist Party (BKP) in 1919. It was the dominant party in the Fatherland Front, which ruled from 1944 until 1989. The party adopted a left-socialist programme and was renamed in April 1990. It won the election in the following June, but narrowly lost to the Union of Democratic Forces (SDS) in an election under the new constitution in October 1991, gaining 33.1% of the vote and 106/240 seats. The party leader is Zhan Videnov, the parliamentary leader Nana Ananieva.

Bundesbank Shorthand for Deutsche Bundesbank ('GERMAN FEDERAL BANK'), the German central bank.

Bundeskanzler or **Kanzler** ('federal chancellor') Head of government or prime minister of either Austria or Germany.

Bundeskriminalamt *See* FEDERAL CRIMINAL INVESTIGATION OFFICE.

Bundesland or **Land** (pl. Bundesländer, Länder) Federal division of Austria, usually translated as 'federal province' or 'province'. Each province has a Provincial Assembly [Landtag] elected for a four-year term, and a government headed by a provincial governor [Landeshaupt]. The assemblies elect the members of the Federal Council [Bundesrat], the upper house of parliament. The provinces have wide-ranging powers and are also responsible for the administration of federal law.

Bundesland or **Land** (pl. Bundesländer, Länder) Federal division of Germany, usually translated as 'federal state' or 'state'. The 16 *Länder* have their own constitutions, legislatures, governments and judiciaries. They have considerable autonomy and extensive legislative powers in all matters except those expressly reserved for the federal government (such as finance, posts and telecommunications, defence and foreign affairs). They have exclusive powers in matters of education, culture and police.

Bundesländer Plural of *Bundesland* ('federal province' or 'federal state'), the federal division of Austria and Germany respectively.

Bundesrat *See* FEDERAL COUNCIL.

Bundesrepublik Deutschland (BRD) ('Federal Republic of Germany') Official name of Germany.

Bundestag *See* FEDERAL ASSEMBLY (Germany).

Bundesverfassungsgericht *See* FEDERAL CONSTITUTIONAL COURT (Germany).

Bundesversammlung (Germany) *See* FEDERAL CONVENTION.

Bundeswehr ('Federal Defence Forces') German name for the German armed forces. It is sometimes used informally to refer just to the army.

burden sharing In the North Atlantic Treaty Organization (NATO), member states' equitable contribution to their collective defence in terms of costs and responsibilities. In the 1970s and 80s the

US Congress, concerned at the cost of maintaining US forces in Western Europe, repeatedly called for greater financial commitments from NATO's European members. The issue caused some tension between the US and European governments in the late 1980s. This was largely resolved when the collapse of the Warsaw Pact, the signing of the Treaty on Conventional Forces in Europe (CFE) and changes in NATO's defence strategy enabled the United States to draw up plans to withdraw around two-thirds of its forces stationed in Western Europe.

Burgenland Federal province [Land] of Austria. Situated in the east and bordering on Hungary, Burgenland has an area of 3,965 sq km and a population of 271,000. There are two ethnic minorities, 22,000 Hungarians and 12,000 Croats. The capital is Eisenstadt. The economy is based on agriculture (cereals, vegetables, wine) and some manufacturing (food processing). The Provincial Assembly [Landtag] has 36 members elected for a five-year term. The main political parties are the Social Democratic Party (SPÖ), the centre-right Austrian People's Party (ÖVP) and the far-right Freedom Party (FPÖ). At the election in June 1991 the SPÖ gained 17 seats, the ÖVP 15 and the FPÖ four. The chief minister is Karl Stix. Historically part of Hungary, Burgenland was formed from the German-speaking border areas transferred to Austria in 1921.

Bürgermeister (pl. -) German local government official, usually translated as 'mayor' or 'burgomaster'. The *Bürgermeister* is the elected head and chief executive officer of a municipality [Gemeinde]. In large cities the mayor is called the *Oberbürgermeister* ('senior mayor'). The head of government in the city state of Berlin is called the *Regierender Bürgermeister* ('governing mayor').

Bürgerschaft ('Citizens' Assembly') Parliaments of Bremen and Hamburg, two federal states of Germany.

burgh Scottish English spelling of borough, a unit of local government. *See* DISTRICT.

Burgundy [Bourgogne] Region of France. Situated in the centre, Burgundy has an area of 31,582 sq km and a population of 1,612,000. The capital is Dijon. The economy is based on agriculture (wine, dairy farming), manufacturing (metalworking, engineering, food processing, chemicals) and tourism. During the late Middle Ages Burgundy was a virtually independent duchy and, with extensive holdings in Germany and the Low Countries, a major European power in its own right. It fell to the French crown in 1477.

Busek, Erhard (1941–) Austrian politician. He has held a range of posts in the centre-right Austrian People's Party (ÖVP) and affiliated organizations since 1964. He was the party's general secretary from 1975–76, a member of parliament from 1975–78 and deputy mayor of Vienna from 1978–87. He was appointed minister of science and research in April 1989 and also became ÖVP party leader and vice-chancellor (= deputy prime minister) in June 1991.

Busquin, Philippe (1941–) Belgian teacher and politician. Elected to parliament for the Walloon Socialist Party (PS) in 1978, he held a series of ministerial posts from 1980, including education (1980–81), budget and energy (1982–85) and social affairs (1988–92). He was elected PS party president in January 1992.

Butkevičius, Audrius (1960–) Lithuanian doctor and politician. He is a qualified psychotherapist. A prominent opponent of Soviet communist rule, he was made head of the republic's defence department in 1990 (when Lithuania was still part of the Soviet Union) and became minister of defence when the country regained its independence in August 1991. He resigned in September 1993 after a mutiny in the Volunteer Home Guard. He does not belong to a political party.

butter mountain (European Union) *See* FOOD MOUNTAINS.

Buttiglione, Rocco (1948–) Italian philosopher, academic and politician. A lecturer at the University of Urbino, he has written several books on social theory. In the mid 1980s he became a close adviser to Pope John Paul II, the head of the Roman Catholic Church, on issues of morality. He entered politics in early 1994 as an adviser to Mino Martinazzoli, the leader of the centre-right Italian Popular Party (PPI, the successor to the Christian Democratic Party, DC). He was elected party leader in July 1994. (Martinazzoli had resigned after the March general election.)

BVD Abbreviation for Binnenlandse Veiligheidsdienst ('Internal Security Service'), the Dutch intelligence agency.

BVG *See* FEDERAL CONSTITUTIONAL COURT.

BWK *See* FEDERAL ECONOMIC CHAMBER.

BZNS *See* BULGARIAN AGRARIAN NATIONAL UNION.

C *See* CENTRE PARTY (Sweden).

Cabinet Government of the United Kingdom. The term is also used informally in many other countries to denote the government or council of ministers.

cabinet In the European Union (EU), the private office of a commissioner, i.e. a member of the European Commission, the organization's administrative and executive arm.

CAEC *See* COURT OF AUDITORS OF THE EUROPEAN COMMUNITIES.

Calabria Autonomous region of Italy. Situated in the south, in the 'toe' of the Italian peninsula, Calabria has an area of 15,080 sq km and a population of 2,010,000. The capital is Catanzaro; Reggio di Calabria is the largest city and Cosenza the other main city. The economy is based on agriculture (livestock farming, cereals, fruit and vegetables) and light industry. Part of the MEZZOGIORNO, the region is one of the country's poorest; there has been substantial emigration since the 19th century. Calabria formed part of the Kingdom of Naples from the 11th century until it became part of unified Italy in 1860.

Calabrian Mafia *See* 'NDRANGHETA.

Camera and **Camera dei Deputati** *See* CHAMBER OF DEPUTIES (Italy).

Camorra Italian crime syndicate. Based in Naples and the surrounding Campania region, the Camorra has its roots in the 18th century but did not develop into a structured organization until the 1970s. At this time it was involved in extortion (mainly in the construction sector) and cigarette and drug smuggling. It was transformed in the 1980s by a new generation of leaders, known as the 'New Family' [Nuova Famiglia], who were able to divert most of the public funds that flowed into the region after a major earthquake in 1980 to extend their influence locally and build up an international cocaine-smuggling and money-laundering network. They generally did so in alliance with the MAFIA, the Camorra's longer-established counterpart based in neighbouring Sicily. The syndicate's supposed supreme boss, Michele Zaza, was arrested in May 1993. The nationwide corruption scandals which broke in 1993 exposed close links between the Camorra and leading members of the then ruling Christian Democratic Party (DC).

camorrista (pl. camorristi) Member of the Camorra, the criminal organization based in the Italian city of Naples, comparable to the Sicilian Mafia.

Campania Autonomous region of Italy. Situated in the south along the Tyrrhenian Sea, Campania has an area of 13,595 sq km and a population of 5,626,000. The region is dominated by Naples [Napoli], the capital; the other major city is Salerno. The economy is based on agriculture (cereals, fruit and vegetables, wine) in the fertile plain, and on manufacturing in the Naples conurbation (metalworking, chemicals, food processing). Campania is the only region in southern Italy, the MEZZOGIORNO, with a major concentration of industry. The region is nevertheless one of the country's poorest, and levels of structural under- and unemployment are high. Campania was the heartland of the Kingdom of Naples established in the 12th century. It became part of unified Italy in 1860.

Câmpeanu, Radu (1922–) Romanian lawyer, economist and politician. Leader of the students' organization of the National Liberal Party (PNL), he was imprisoned when the communists took power in 1947. He was released in 1956 and eventually went into exile in France. He returned to Romania after the collapse of communist rule and was elected the PNL's leader in January 1990. He lost the leadership to Mircea Ionescu-Quintus in February 1993, but was reinstated by a minority faction in February 1994.

Campora List [Liste Campora] Monaco political organization. Headed by Anne-Marie Campora, the mayor of Monaco-Ville, this alliance won 15/18 seats at the election in January 1993. Its members are broadly right-wing in outlook and support the policies of Prince Rainier and the government appointed by him. (There are no formal political parties in Monaco.)

Canarias and **Canaries** Shorthands for Islas Canarias and CANARY ISLANDS respectively, an autonomous community or region of Spain.

Canary Coalition [Coalición Canaria] (CC) Spanish political organization. The CC was formed in 1992 as a loose alliance of the left-wing Canary Initiative [Iniciativa Canaria] (ICAN) and two other regional parties in the Canary Islands (which between them hold 8/60 seats in the regional parliament). They were joined by the centre-right Federation of Canary Islands Independent Groups (FAIC or AIC), the main regional alliance, for the June 1993 general election. The more broadly based CC gained 4/350 seats.

Canary Islands [Islas Canarias] Autonomous community or region of Spain. A group of seven inhabited islands (including Gran Canaria and Tenerife) and six uninhabited islets situated 100 km off the northwest coast of Africa and around 1,000 km southwest of Spain, the Canary Islands have an area of 7,242 sq km and a population of 1,502,000. The people are ethnically Spanish. The two capitals and main cities are Las Palmas de Gran Canaria and Santa Cruz de Tenerife. The economy is based on agriculture (fruit and vegetables), tourism, manufacturing (food processing, textiles, leather goods, chemicals) and fishing. The main political parties are the Spanish Socialist Workers' Party (PSOE), the Federation of Canary Island Independent Groups (FAIC or AIC), which advocates greater autonomy for the islands, the Democratic and Social Centre (CDS), the centre-right People's Party (PP) and the left-wing Canary Initiative (ICAN). There are also several groups advocating the creation of an independent 'Guanche Republic'. At the May 1991 election the PSOE gained 23 seats in the 60-member legislature, the AIC 16, the CDS seven, the PP six and ICAN five. The government is formed by the AIC, with external support from the CDS, ICAN and several other parties. The Canary Islands were conquered by Spain between 1404 and 1496. The native inhabitants, known as Guanches and Canarios, have disappeared as an identifiable ethnic group. The autonomous region was established in 1982.

Canary Islands Independent Groups *See* FEDERATION OF ....

Cantabria Autonomous community or region of Spain. Situated in the north between the Bay of Biscay and the Cantabrian Mountains, Cantabria is one of Spain's smallest regions, with an area of 5,289 sq km and a population of 526,000. The region is dominated by Santander, the capital. The economy is based on manufacturing (metalworking, petrochemicals, chemicals), mining (zinc, pyrites, iron) and some agriculture. Cantabria is one of Spain's major industrial regions. The restructuring of the heavy industries in the 1980s has caused widespread structural unemployment. The dominant political party is the centre-right People's Party (PP), which has been in power since the first regional election in 1983; the other main parties are the Spanish Socialist Workers' Party (PSOE) and the Regionalist Party of Cantabria (PRC). At the May 1991 election the PP gained 21 seats in the 39-member legislature, the PSOE 16 and the PRC two. Historically part of Old Castile, the province of Cantabria became a separate autonomous region in 1981 in recognition of its geographical separation from the Castilian heartland and its distinctive economic and social structure.

canton (Bosnia-Herzegovina) *See* CANTONIZATION.

canton French administrative division. An intermediate unit between the department and commune, the 3,208 cantons have few administrative functions and no elected bodies or officials. They form the basis of the electoral districts for the departmental councils.

canton [Kanton (German), canton (French), cantone (Italian), pl. -e, -s, cantoni] Federal division of Switzerland. The cantons have their own constitutions, legislatures, governments and judiciaries, and have extensive autonomy in virtually all matters except finance, posts and communications, defence and foreign policy. The cantonal legislatures elect two representatives to the Council of States, the upper house of parliament. Three of the 23 cantons are divided into HALF-CANTONS.

Since these effectively function as full cantons, there are in practice 26 federal states.

cantonization In Bosnia-Herzegovina, the proposed division of the country along ethnic lines into Muslim, Serb and Croat regions or 'cantons'. Cantonization was first proposed by the European Community (EC) in March 1992 as a means of defusing tensions and minimizing the possibility of civil war. It was eventually rejected by the government on the grounds that it would lead to the dissolution of Bosnia (with the Serb and Croat cantons seeking to merge with Serbia and Croatia respectively) and was in any case impracticable because many districts were ethnically mixed. Fighting broke out in March, and the armies of all three communities eventually resorted to 'ethnic cleansing' or forced expulsions to create more homogeneous regions. The July 1993 Owen-Stoltenberg plan effectively revived the cantonization concept, although it did not use the term but spoke instead of a loose 'union of three republics'. The Muslim-Croat federation established in March 1994 provided for the creation of eight cantons.

CAP *See* COMMON AGRICULTURAL POLICY.

cap de govern ('head of government') Head of government or prime minister of Andorra.

capitano reggento *See* CAPTAIN-REGENT.

captain-regent [capitano reggento, pl. capitani reggenti] Head of state and government of San Marino. There are two captains-regent, who jointly serve as senior officers of state. They are elected for a six-month term by and from the members of the Grand and General Council, the national parliament.

Car Party of Switzerland *See* FREEDOM PARTY OF ....

carabiniere (pl. carabinieri) Member of the CORPS OF CARABINIERI or Carabinieri, an Italian paramilitary police force.

Carabinieri *See* CORPS OF CARABINIERI.

Carignon, Alain (1949–) French politician. He worked for the Economic and Social Council (CÉS), a government advisory body, from 1976–78. Active in local government for the right-wing Rally for the Republic (RPR) from the early 1970s, he was elected mayor of Grenoble in 1983. He was an RPR secretary, responsible for environmental affairs, from 1984–86. First elected to parliament in 1986, he was a junior minister in the Chirac government (1986–88) and was appointed communications minister when the right returned to power in March 1993. He resigned in July 1994 following allegations of financial improprieties in connection with the sale of Dauphiné News, a newspaper set up to back his campaign for reelection as mayor in 1989. He was subsequently placed under investigation on suspicion of fraud.

Carinthia [Kärnten] Federal province [Land] of Austria. Situated in the south and bordering on Slovenia and Italy, Carinthia has an area of 9,533 sq km and a population of 556,000. There is an ethnic minority of 16,000 Slovenes in the southeast. The capital is Klagenfurt, and the other main city is Villach. The economy is based on agriculture, forestry, manufacturing, tourism and mining. The Provincial Assembly [Landtag] has 36 members elected for a five-year term. The main political parties are the Social Democratic Party (SPÖ), the far-right Freedom Party (FPÖ) and the centre-right Austrian People's Party (ÖVP). At the March 1994 provincial election the SPÖ gained 14 seats, the FPÖ 13 and the ÖVP nine. The government is an all-party coalition headed by Christof Zernatto (ÖVP) as chief minister.

Caritas affair Controversy in Romania surrounding a pyramid-selling scheme and its backing by political parties. Caritas – not to be confused with the international aid organization of the same name – was set up by a businessman, Ion Stoica, in March 1992. Relying on chain-letter practices familiar and discredited in Western Europe and elsewhere but previously unknown in Romania, it quickly gained strong support from several political parties, in particular the far-right Romanian National Unity Party (PUNR). With initial investors (including the PUNR) making large profits, the scheme mushroomed and spawned others

81

across the country. By late 1993 Caritas was no longer able to pay off investors, and it collapsed in May 1994, leaving hundreds of thousands of people out of pocket. Up to 4 million Romanians had invested an estimated 1.5 trillion lei (700 million ecus) in Caritas. Stoica was charged with fraud and forgery in August 1994.

Carl XVI Gustaf (1946–) King of Sweden. He succeeded to the throne on the death of his grandfather, Gustaf VI Adolf, in September 1973. He married the German interpreter Silvia Sommerlath, now Queen Silvia, in 1976. They have three children.

Carlsson, Ingvar (1934–) Swedish politician. He has held senior positions within the Social Democratic Labour Party (SAP) since 1958. He was leader of the youth wing from 1961–67 and the party's deputy leader from 1982–86. He has been minister of education and culture (1969–73), housing and planning (1973–76) and deputy prime minister (1982–86). He became party leader and prime minister in March 1986 after the assassination of Olof Palme. He resigned as prime minister in October 1991 after the party suffered heavy losses in the election held the previous month.

Carniti, Pierre (1936–) Italian printer, trade-union official and politician. He joined the Italian Metalworkers' Union (FIM) as an organizer in 1962 and rose up the ranks to become its general secretary in 1970. In 1974 he became a federal secretary of the Italian Confederation of Workers' Unions (CISL). He was its general secretary from 1979–85. Elected to parliament for the Christian Democratic Party (DC) in 1987, he was elected leader of the breakaway Social Christian Party (PCS) in October 1993.

Čarnugorský, Ján (1944–) Slovakian lawyer and politician. He defended dissidents in the 1970s and 80s and was himself arrested in 1989 and charged with incitement. He was released after the collapse of communist rule and appointed deputy prime minister in the national-unity government of 1989–90. He became leader of the new Christian Democratic Movement (KDH) in March 1990. After

the June 1990 election he became deputy prime minister in the Slovakian government and was prime minister in 1991–92.

Carpathian Euroregion Intergovernmental organization. Established in February 1993 by Hungary, Poland and Ukraine, the Carpathian Euroregion aims to promote cooperation in economic, cultural and environmental matters in the border areas of the three countries. The intention is to set up a council of local authorities to develop links and coordinate long-term regional planning. Slovakia and Romania, which were involved in the overlapping Carpathia-Tisza Community established in January 1992, did not sign the new organization's founding agreement.

Carpatho-Ruthenia and **-Ukraine question** *See* SUBCARPATHIA QUESTION.

Carvalhas, Carlos (1941–) Portuguese economist, journalist, civil servant and politician. He has written for and edited several publications on economic issues and has worked for the National Planning Council. Elected to parliament for the Portuguese Communist Party (PCP) in 1976, he held a range of senior posts for the party at national and European level in the 1980s. He was elected party leader in December 1992.

Carvalho da Silva, Manuel (1947–) Portuguese electrician and trade-union official. First elected as a workers' representative in 1974, he became head of the organization department of the General Confederation of Portuguese Workers - National Union Federation (CGTP-IN) in 1977. He was elected the federation's leader in May 1986.

Casal, Josep (1952–) Andorran economist, banker and politician. He was appointed minister of public services in 1991 and minister of finance in May 1992. The previous month he had been elected to parliament for the centre-right National Democratic Association (AND).

Casini, Pierferdinando (1955–) Italian politician. A law graduate, he was elected to parliament for the Christian Democratic Party (DC) in 1983. He rejected the need for the party's relaunch after it had been discredited by the corruption scandals which broke in 1993. When this did happen in January 1994, he was elected leader of the breakaway Christian Democratic Centre (CCD).

Castegnaro, John (1944–) Luxemburg machine fitter and trade-union official. He became a full-time organizer for the Luxemburg Workers' Association (LAV) in 1963. He was elected its general secretary in May 1976, and the following November he was elected president of the General Confederation of Labour (CGT-L), the main trade-union federation. In January 1979 he also became leader of the newly founded Independent Trade Union Confederation (OGB-L).

Castellano Alternative Spanish native name for the Spanish language. *See* CASTILIAN.

Castile - La Mancha [Castilla - La Mancha] Autonomous community or region of Spain. Situated in the centre, to the south of the Sierra de Guadarrama range and Madrid, Castilla - La Mancha has an area of 79,230 sq km and a population of 1,717,000. The capital is Toledo, and the other main cities are Albacete, Ciudad Real and Guadalajara. The economy is based on agriculture (cereals, wine, olives, sheep farming) and some manufacturing (food processing, petrochemicals). Castile - La Mancha is one of Spain's poorer regions, with emigration high throughout the 20th century. The main political parties are the Spanish Socialist Workers' Party (PSOE), the centre-right People's Party (PP) and the left-wing United Left (IU). At the May 1991 election the PSOE gained 27 seats in the 47-member legislature, the PP 19 and the IU one. Broadly coextensive with the historical region of New Castile, Castile - La Mancha was established as an autonomous region in 1982. The province of Madrid was made a region in its own right the following year.

Castile-León [Castilla-León] Autonomous community or region of Spain. Situated in the centre, to the north of the Sierra de Guadarrama range and Madrid, Castile-León has an area of 94,193 sq km and a population of 2,618,000. It is the country's largest region in terms of area. The capital is Valladolid, and the other main cities are Salamanca, Burgos and León. The economy is based on agriculture (cereals, sheep and cattle farming) and some manufacturing and forestry. Castile-León is one of Spain's poorer regions, with emigration from the rural areas high throughout the 20th century. The main political parties are the Spanish Socialist Workers' Party (PSOE) and the centre-right People's Party (PP). At the May 1991 election the PSOE gained 43 seats in the 84-member legislature and the PP 35. Composed of the historically closely linked regions of León and Old Castile, Castile-León was established as an autonomous region in 1983.

Castilian [Castellano] Alternative name for the Spanish language. The term – taken from the medieval Kingdom of Castile, the core of unified Spain – has been in common use in Latin America for many years. It is now increasingly used in Spain itself, in recognition of the fact that around a quarter of the country's population does not speak Spanish as a first language.

Castilian Spaniards People of Spain whose first language is Spanish or CASTILIAN.

Castilla - La Mancha *See* CASTILE - LA MANCHA.

Castilla-León *See* CASTILE-LEON.

Catalan Lands [Paisos Catalans] Collective name for the regions where Catalan is spoken. They include the autonomous communities of Catalonia, Balearic Islands and Valencia in Spain, the Pyrénées-Orientales department in France (the historical region of Roussillon) and Andorra. Catalan is a Romance language related to Occitan and Spanish. It was the official language of the Kingdom of Aragón during the Middle Ages, but its use was discouraged in Spain after the 18th century and prohibited under the Franco regime (1939–75). Since the early 1980s it has been strongly promoted in its heartland of Catalonia. It is spoken by around 7.5 million people.

Catalonia [Catalunya (Catalan), Cataluña (Spanish)] Autonomous community or region of Spain. Situated in the northeast along the Mediterranean Sea and bordering on France, Catalonia has an area of

31,930 sq km and a population of 6,018,000. Around two-thirds of the population is Catalan, and Catalan is the first official language. There are large numbers of Catalan speakers in the neighbouring regions of the Balearic Islands and Valencia and across the border in France and Andorra. The region is dominated by Barcelona, the capital and Spain's second city. Other main cities outside the Barcelona conurbation are Tarragona, Lleida/Lérida and Girona/Gerona. The economy is based on manufacturing (engineering, motor vehicles, petrochemicals, chemicals, textiles), services, agriculture (fruit and vegetables) and tourism. Catalonia is Spain's most industrialized and wealthiest region. Political power is exercised by the Parliament [Parlament], whose 135 members are elected for a four-year term, and the Government [Generalitat] headed by a president. The dominant party is the centre-right Convergence and Union (CiU), which has been in power since the first regional election in 1980; the other main parties are the Socialist Party of Catalonia (PSC, the regional branch of the Spanish Socialist Workers' Party, PSOE), the Republican Left (ERC), which advocates full independence for the region, the left-wing Initiative for Catalonia (IC), and the centre-right People's Party (PP). At the March 1992 election the CiU gained 46.4% of the vote and 71 seats, the PSC 27.3% and 39 seats, the ERC 8.0% and 11 seats, the IC 6.4% and seven seats, and the PP 6.0% and seven seats. The County of Barcelona, which had been virtually independent since the 9th century, was united with Aragón in 1137. Catalonia retained considerable autonomy until the 15th century and was the economic centre of Aragón's expansion prior to the unification of Spain in 1479. The centralizing policies of successive Spanish governments since the 17th century were strongly resisted in Catalonia. Nationalist parties won municipal elections from the 1900s onwards. The region enjoyed extensive autonomy during the Second Republic (1931–39). Under the Franco regime (1939–75) all manifestations of Catalan culture, including the use of the language, were banned. In 1979, after the restoration of democratic rule, Catalonia was established as an 'autonomous community'.

Cataluña and **Catalunya** *See* CATALONIA.

Catholic Election Committee *See* HOMELAND.

Catholics or **Roman Catholics** Religious and ethnic group in NORTHERN IRELAND, a component of the United Kingdom. The religious label is often used interchangeably with 'nationalists' and 'republicans'.

Catroga, Eduardo (1942–) Portuguese economist, businessman, academic and politician. He has worked for several companies in the chemicals and other sectors and from 1981–93 was managing director of the SAPEC group, which deals mainly in agricultural supplies. He also lectured in economics and business studies at the Higher Institute of Economics and Management (ISEG). A member of the centre-right Social Democratic Party (PSD), he was appointed finance minister in December 1993.

cautionary warrant [avviso di garanzia] In Italy, a document issued by magistrates informing a person that s/he is under investigation in connection with a specific crime. Under Italian law suspects must be informed that they are under investigation. Issuing the warrant thus marks the start of an inquiry and may or may not lead to the pressing of formal charges.

Cavaco Silva, Aníbal (1939–) Portuguese economist and politician. He worked for the Bank of Portugal, the central bank, before serving as minister of finance (1980–81) and president of the National Planning Council (1981–84). He was elected leader of the centre-right Social Democratic Party (PSD) in May 1985. He became prime minister of a minority government the following November. He has remained in office ever since, with the PSD gaining absolute majorities in the 1987 and 1991 elections. He has written extensively on economic issues.

CBI *See* CONFEDERATION OF BRITISH INDUSTRY.

CBSS *See* COUNCIL OF BALTIC SEA STATES.

CC (Italy) *See* CORPS OF CARABINIERI.

CC (Spain) *See* CANARY COALITION.

CCD *See* CHRISTIAN DEMOCRATIC CENTRE.

CCEET *See* CENTRE FOR COOPERATION WITH EUROPEAN ECONOMIES IN TRANSITION.

CCOO *See* TRADE UNION CONFEDERATION OF WORKERS' COMMISSIONS.

CCP *See* COMMON COMMERCIAL POLICY.

CCRE *See* COUNCIL OF EUROPEAN MUNICIPALITIES AND REGIONS.

CD (Denmark) *See* CENTRE DEMOCRATS.

CD (Netherlands) *See* CENTRE DEMOCRATS.

CDA *See* CHRISTIAN DEMOCRATIC APPEAL.

CDC *See* CONVERGENCE AND UNION.

CDR *See* DEMOCRATIC CONVENTION OF ROMANIA.

CDS (France) *See* SOCIAL DEMOCRATIC CENTRE.

CDS (Portugal) *See* DEMOCRATIC SOCIAL CENTRE - PEOPLE'S PARTY.

CDS (Spain) *See* DEMOCRATIC AND SOCIAL CENTRE.

CDS-PP *See* DEMOCRATIC SOCIAL CENTRE - PEOPLE'S PARTY.

CDU (Germany) *See* CHRISTIAN DEMOCRATIC UNION.

CDU (Portugal) *See* UNITED DEMOCRATIC COALITION.

CE Abbreviation for the Council of Europe. It is not often used, since it may cause confusion with the European Community (EC), the core of the European Union (EU), whose abbreviation in French and other languages is also CE. An alternative abbreviation is CoE.

CE French, Irish, Italian, Portuguese and Spanish abbreviation for the European Community (EC), the core of the EUROPEAN UNION (EU).

ceann comhairle ('head of the assembly') Speaker or president of the Dáil Éireann, the lower house of the Irish parliament. The title is also used by English speakers.

CEC Abbreviation for Commission of the European Communities, the former name of the EUROPEAN COMMISSION, the administrative and executive arm of the European Union (EU). It was in use from 1967 until the entry into force of the Maastricht Treaty in November 1993.

Čechy *See* BOHEMIA.

CEECs Abbreviation for Central and Eastern European Countries, a collective name for the region's former communist countries, used in particular in the context of economic development and the transition to market-based economies.

CEFTA *See* CENTRAL EUROPEAN FREE TRADE AGREEMENT.

CEI *See* CENTRAL EUROPEAN INITIATIVE.

ceinture rouge *See* RED BELT (France).

Çela, Kudret (1945–) Albanian lawyer, academic and politician. He lectured in law and politics at Tirana University from 1970. He was appointed justice minister in December 1991. He does not belong to a political party.

Celtic League International political and cultural organization. The League was founded in 1961 to foster cooperation between the six 'Celtic nations' in Western Europe – Bretons, Cornish, Irish, Manx, Scots and Welsh. It supports nonviolent movements for political autonomy in these countries and regions as well as cultural organizations promoting their Celtic languages and traditions.

CEMR *See* COUNCIL OF EUROPEAN MUNICIPALITIES AND REGIONS.

centime French monetary unit, equivalent to 1/100th of a franc. Common abbreviations are c and cent.

Central and Eastern European countries Collective name for the former communist countries and their successor states, i.e. Albania, Bosnia-Herzegovina, Bulgaria, Croatia, Czech Republic, Estonia, Hungary, Latvia, Lithuania, Macedonia, Poland, Romania, Slovakia, Slovenia and Yugoslavia. It may also include the former Soviet republics, in particular Belorussia, Moldavia and Ukraine. The term 'Central Europe' is generally preferred in the Czech Republic, Hungary, Poland and Slovakia to stress their countries' historical links with Austria and Germany (*see* MITTELEUROPA).

Central European countries Collective name for the Czech Republic, Hungary, Poland and Slovakia. They are also called the VISEGRAD COUNTRIES, after the informal grouping the (then three) governments established in 1991. *See also* MITTELEUROPA.

Central European Free Trade Agreement (CEFTA) International agreement by the member states of the Visegrad Group (i.e. Czech Republic, Hungary, Poland and Slovakia). Signed in December 1992 and in force since March 1993, the CEFTA aims to eliminate most tariff barriers between the four countries by the year 2001. It provides for the staged removal of tariffs on raw materials, imports that do not compete with locally produced goods, agricultural products and most industrial goods.

Central European Initiative (CEI) Intergovernmental organization. The CEI has developed from an informal grouping set up in November 1989 by Austria, Hungary, Italy and Yugoslavia; this became known as the Pentagonal Group when Czechoslovakia joined in 1990 and the Hexagonal Group after Poland joined in 1991; it was renamed the Central European Initiative in January 1992. Proposed by the Italian government, the group's original intention had been to develop economic and cultural cooperation across the East-West divide, but the collapse of the communist regimes in Eastern Europe added new dimensions. The CEI's main aim is to facilitate both the integration of the region's economies and infrastructures and the transformation of the former communist command economies into market-based economies. Cooperation has concentrated on environmental issues, transport, small businesses, information, telecommunications, science, culture, tourism and energy. Recent activities have been overshadowed by the crisis caused by the wars in former Yugoslavia, in particular the influx of refugees into the member states. The CEI's 10 members are: Austria, Bosnia-Herzegovina, Croatia, Czech Republic, Hungary, Italy, Macedonia, Poland, Slovakia and Slovenia; Yugoslavia's membership was suspended in 1992 because of its involvement in the Bosnian civil war. The organization's structure is deliberately informal: the main decision-making bodies are summit meetings of heads of government and foreign ministers, ministerial-level committees and other working groups.

Central Organization of Finnish Trade Unions [Suomen Ammattiliittojen Keskusjärjestö] (SAK) Finnish trade-union federation. Founded in 1907, the SAK has 24 affiliated unions with a total membership of around 1.1 million (two-fifths of the labour force). It has close, but not formal, links with the Finnish Social Democratic Party (SDP). The president is Lauri Ihalainen.

Central Organization of Salaried Employees [Tjänstemännens Centralorganisation] (TCO) Swedish trade-union federation. Founded in 1937, the TCO has 19 affiliated unions with a total membership of around 1.3 million (over a quarter of the labour force). It is the dominant labour organization in the service sectors and in managerial grades. The president is Björn Rosengren.

Centre [Keskus] (K) Estonian political organization. The Centre is the parliamentary group formed by the centre-left ESTONIAN PEOPLE'S CENTRE PARTY (ERKE) and two other groups which had contested the September 1992 election as the People's Front (Rahvarinne). It holds 15/101 seats. The parliamentary leader is Arvo Junti.

Centre (Finland) *See* CENTRE PARTY.

Centre Region of France. Situated in the centre, the region has an area of 39,151 sq km and a population of 2,400,000. The capital is Orléans, and the other main city is Tours. The economy is based on agriculture (cereals) and manufacturing (engineering, electronics).

Centre Alliance [Porozumienie Centrum] (POC or PC) Polish political party. Founded by members of the Solidarity movement in 1990, the POC is a right-leaning christian democratic party. It was originally strongly supportive of Lech Wałęsa, then Solidarity leader and now president of the republic, but relations became strained in 1992. At the September 1993 election the party gained 4.4% of the vote but no seats, having failed to reach the 5% required for representation. It joined the Alliance for Poland (PdP) in May 1994. The leader is Jarosław Kaczyński.

Centre Democrats [Centrum-Demokraterne] (CD) Danish political party. Founded in 1973 as a breakaway from the Social Democratic Party (SD), the Centre Democrats are one of the country's three main centrist parties. The party participated in a centre-right coalition from 1982–88 and joined a centre-left coalition in January 1993. At the December 1990 election it had gained 4.7% of the vote and 9/175 seats. The leader is Mimi Jakobsen.

Centre Democrats [Centrum-Democraten] (CD) Dutch political party. Founded in 1980, this far-right party campaigns almost exclusively on an anti-foreigner platform, calling specifically for an end to financial support and other assistance for minorities, immigrants and refugees. It entered parliament in 1989 and trebled its support in the May 1994 election, gaining 2.5% of the vote and 3/150 seats. The leader is Hans Janmaat.

Centre for Cooperation with European Economies in Transition (CCEET) Institution of the Organization for Economic Cooperation and Development (OECD). The CCEET was founded in 1990 to act as the point of contact between the OECD, which brings together the world's industrialized countries, and the former communist countries of Central and Eastern Europe intending to establish market-based economies and pluralist political systems. It channels advice and technical assistance in a range of economic and related fields, including development, structural adjustment, competition, labour market, social aspects, banking and financial systems, taxation, trade, investment, industry, agriculture, energy, education, environment, and statistics. It operates a range of training programmes, such as Partners in Transition, and conducts seminars, workshops etc for economists, civil servants and politicians from the countries concerned. The secretariat is based in Paris (France). *See also* GROUP OF TWENTY-FOUR *and* PHARE PROGRAMME.

Centre for the Prevention of Conflict *See* CONFLICT PREVENTION CENTRE.

Centre Party [Keskustapuolue] (KESK) Finnish political party. Founded in 1906 as the Agrarian League (ML) and last renamed in 1988, the Centre Party has led or participated in most coalition governments since 1945. Traditionally based in the rural areas, it has broadened its support in recent years. At the March 1991 election it became the largest party in parliament, gaining 24.8% of the vote and 55/200 seats. The party leader is Esko Aho, the parliamentary leader is Kalevi Mattila.

Centre Party [Senterpartiet] (Sp) Norwegian political party. Founded in 1920 as the Farmers' Party and renamed in 1959, the Centre Party retains strong roots in the rural areas. It is committed to agricultural interests and environmental protection in particular and is conservative in its social views. The party has participated in several centre-right coalitions since 1945, most recently in 1989–90. Largely because of its long-standing opposition to Norwegian membership of the European Community (EC), it virtually trebled its support at the September 1993 election, gaining 16.8% of the vote and 32/165 seats and becoming the second-largest party in parliament. The leader is Anne Enger Lahnstein.

Centre Party [Centerpartiet] (Cp or C) Swedish political party. Founded in 1910 as the Farmers' Union Party and renamed in 1957, the Centre Party retains strong roots in the rural areas and is committed to agricultural interests and environmental protection in particular. It was part of a centre-right coalition from 1976–82 and joined another such coalition in October 1991. At the previous month's election it had gained 8.4% of the vote and 31/349 seats. The leader is Olof Johansson.

Centre Union [Unione di Centro] (UDC) Italian political organization. The UDC was founded in August 1993 by reformist members of the Italian Liberal Party (PLI), Italian Republican Party (PRI) and Italian Democratic Socialist Party (PSDI). These parties had been discredited by the nationwide corruption scandals which had broken earlier in the year. The UDC contested the March 1994 election within the right-wing Freedom Alliance, gaining 4/630 seats. The four deputies joined the Come On Italy (Forza Italia) parliamentary group. The leader is Raffaele Costa, who is also leader of the PLI.

CEOE *See* SPANISH CONFEDERATION OF EMPLOYERS' ORGANIZATIONS.

CERN *See* EUROPEAN ORGANIZATION FOR NUCLEAR RESEARCH.

Černák, L'udovít (1951–) Slovakian electrical engineer and politician. He worked for the Závody engineering company from 1972–92, as managing director from 1989. Elected to parliament for the right-wing Slovak National Party (SNS) in June 1992, he was appointed minister of the economy, also in charge of industry, trade and tourism. He was also elected SNS party leader in October 1992. He resigned from the government in March 1993 following the appointment of a former communist as defence minister. Objecting to the SNS's rightward drift, he left the party in February 1994 and founded the centre-right National Democratic Party (NDS).

CÉS *See* ECONOMIC AND SOCIAL COUNCIL.

CESID Abbreviation for Centro Superior para la Información de la Defensa ('Defence Information Agency'), the Spanish intelligence agency.

Česká Republika Czech name for the Czech Republic.

Českomorava *See* CZECHOMORAVIA.

Československo Czech and Slovak names for former CZECHOSLOVAKIA.

Çetin, Hikmet (1937–) Turkish economist and politician. He worked for the State Planning Organization from 1960–77. He was a member of parliament for the centre-left Republican People's Party (CHP) from 1977 until the military coup in 1980, also serving as deputy prime minister in 1978–79. In 1987 he returned to parliament for the Social Democratic People's Party (SHP), a successor to the disbanded CHP. He was appointed foreign minister in November 1991. He was replaced in a government reshuffle in July 1994.

Četnici *See* CHETNIKS *and* SERBIAN CHETNIK MOVEMENT.

CEU *See* COUNCIL OF THE EUROPEAN UNION.

Ceuta Dependency of Spain. Situated on the coast of Morocco and separated from Spain by the Strait of Gibraltar, the town of Ceuta has an area of 19.5 sq km and a population of 70,700. It is one of the 'sovereign territories' [plazas de soberanía] known collectively as Spanish North Africa. Most of the people are Spanish, but just over a sixth are Arabs from Morocco. The economy is based on the duty-free port and the military base; fishing, light manufacturing and tourism are also important. Ceuta is administered as an integral part of Spain, as part of Cádiz province, but its special status is recognized in certain provisions of the local government structure. There is considerable support for greater autonomy. Ceuta came under Portuguese control in 1415 and under Spanish control in 1580. Its hinterland was transferred to Morocco when that country became independent in 1956, but Spain retained control of the town and its strategic port. Morocco disputes Spanish sovereignty over Ceuta and neighbouring Melilla.

CFDT *See* DEMOCRATIC FRENCH CONFEDERATION OF LABOUR.

CFE Treaty Shorthand for the TREATY ON CONVENTIONAL FORCES IN EUROPE.

CFE-1A Concluding Act Shorthand for the amendment to the TREATY ON CONVENTIONAL FORCES IN EUROPE or CFE Treaty dealing with troop levels.

CFI *See* COURT OF FIRST INSTANCE.

CFM *See* COUNCIL OF FOREIGN MINISTERS (Conference on Security and Cooperation in Europe).

CFP *See* COMMON FISHERIES POLICY.

CFSP *See* COMMON FOREIGN AND SECURITY POLICY.

CGIL *See* ITALIAN GENERAL CONFEDERATION OF LABOUR.

CGT *See* GENERAL CONFEDERATION OF LABOUR.

CGT-FO *See* GENERAL CONFEDERATION OF LABOUR - WORKERS' POWER.

CGT-L *See* GENERAL CONFEDERATION OF LABOUR - LUXEMBURG.

CGTP-IN *See* GENERAL CONFEDERATION OF PORTUGUESE WORKERS - NATIONAL UNION FEDERATION.

CH Abbreviation for Switzerland, used for international vehicle registrations, postal addresses etc. It is taken from Confœderatio Helvetica ('Swiss Confederation'), the country's official name in Latin.

Chamber of Citizens [Veće Gradjana] Lower house of the Yugoslav parliament, the Federal Assembly. The Chamber has 138 members, 108 from Serbia and 30 from Montenegro, elected for a four-year term by a system of proportional representation. It has equal powers with the upper house, the Chamber of Republics.

Chamber of Deputies or **Chamber of Representatives** [Kamer van Volksvertegenwoordigers (Dutch), Chambre des Députés (French)] Lower house of the Belgian parliament, the Legislative Chambers. The Chamber currently has 212 members elected for a four-year term by proportional representation. Under the constitutional changes transforming Belgium into a federal state, adopted in July 1993, its membership will be reduced to 150. *See also* SENATE.

Chamber of Deputies (Croatia) *See* HOUSE OF REPRESENTATIVES.

Chamber of Deputies [Poslanecká Směnovna] Lower house of the Czech parliament. The Chamber has 200 members elected for a four-year term by proportional representation in multi-member constituencies. Parties must obtain at least 5% of the popular vote to qualify for representation. It elects the president of the republic. *See also* SENATE.

Chamber of Deputies [Camera dei Deputati] Lower house of the Italian parliament. The Chamber has 630 members elected for a five-year term. Under reforms adopted in 1993, 475 members are elected by simple majority in single-member constituencies and the remaining 155 seats are allocated on a proportional basis among parties which have gained at least 4% of the popular vote. Previously the Chamber was elected by proportional representation in 47 multi-member constituencies.

Chamber of Deputies [Chambre des Députés] Parliament of Luxemburg. It has 60 members elected for a five-year term by proportional representation in four multi-member constituencies. *See also* COUNCIL OF STATE.

Chamber of Deputies (Romania) *See* ASSEMBLY OF DEPUTIES.

Chamber of Representatives (Belgium) *See* CHAMBER OF DEPUTIES.

Chamber of Republics [Republičko Veće] Upper house of the Yugoslav parliament, the Federal Assembly. The Chamber has 40 members, 20 each for Serbia and Montenegro, elected for a four-year term by the republican assemblies on the basis of party representation in those bodies. It has equal powers with the lower house, the Chamber of Citizens.

Champagne-Ardenne Region of France. Situated in the northeast, Champagne-Ardenne has an area of 25,606 sq km and a population of 1,346,000. The capital is Châlons-sur-Marne, but the main cities are Reims and Troyes. The economy is based on agriculture (cereals, wine) and manufacturing (electronics, food processing).

Chancellery (Germany) *See* FEDERAL CHANCELLOR'S OFFICE.

chancellor Shorthand for federal chancellor [Bundeskanzler], the head of government or prime minister of either Austria or Germany.

chancellor Shorthand for chancellor of the exchequer, the British finance minister.

chancellor [kancleris] President or speaker of the Seimas, the Lithuanian parliament.

chancellor candidate [Kanzlerkandidat] In Germany, the person chosen by a party to lead it in a general election and to become federal chancellor or prime minister if it is victorious.

chancellor of the Duchy of Lancaster British government minister. This office, which goes back to 1389, carries certain ceremonial duties and is usually combined with responsibility for a specific department or with non-departmental work. It has also been used to give a senior official of the party in power a seat in the Cabinet.

chancellor of the exchequer or **chancellor** British government minister. The chancellor is the senior minister in charge of finance and economic affairs.

Chancery (Germany) *See* FEDERAL CHANCELLOR'S OFFICE.

Channel Islands Collective name for
Guernsey and Jersey and their dependencies. The Channel Islands are situated off
the coast of France and include Jersey,
Guernsey, Alderney, Sark and a number
of islets. Historically and culturally they
have much in common, and they are often
considered as a unit. But politically they
consist of two separate entities, the bailiwicks of Guernsey and Jersey. Both are
dependencies of the British crown, with
considerable internal autonomy (including tax sovereignty). They are not part
of the United Kingdom.

Charlemagne, the Shorthand for the Council of Ministers, the main decision-making
body of the European Union (EU). The
Charlemagne building in Brussels is the
Council's headquarters. Its secretariat is
based there and most of its meetings are
held there. *See* COUNCIL OF THE EURO-
PEAN UNION.

Charles (1948–) Prince of Wales, heir to
the British throne. He studied history and
then attended several military colleges
and served with the Royal Navy from
1971–76. In 1969 he was invested as
prince of Wales, the traditional title for
the heir to the throne. He married Diana
Spencer, the daughter of an English
aristocrat, in 1981. They separated in
December 1992. They have two children.

Charter 88 British political organization.
Founded in 1988 as a 'citizens' movement', Charter 88 campaigns for an extensive overhaul of what it regards as the
United Kingdom's antiquated political
system. It calls for the adoption of a written constitution, a 'bill of rights' (setting
out the rights of the individual), a system
of proportional representation for elections, devolution of power to the regions,
and open and accountable decision making
at all levels of government.

Charter of Paris for a New Europe or
Paris Charter International agreement
adopted by the states participating in the
Conference on Security and Cooperation
in Europe (CSCE). Signed on 21 November 1990, the Paris Charter is a non-binding set of declarations and commitments
widely seen as marking the formal end of
the 'cold war' between East and West and

the division of Europe. It declared that
the 'era of confrontation and division of
Europe has ended' and that henceforth the
signatories would conduct their bilateral
and multilateral relations on the basis of
'respect and cooperation'. It also established new CSCE structures aimed at
settling disputes by peaceful means. The
Charter is divided into three sections. The
first outlines 10 principles of the 'new era
of democracy, peace and unity' in Europe.
Broadly based on the 1975 HELSINKI
FINAL ACT, the first major CSCE agreement, they commit the signatories to,
among other things, (i) building and
strengthening democracy as the 'only
system of government', (ii) recognizing
human rights as 'the birthright of all
human beings', (iii) holding 'free and fair
elections', (iv) affirming the right of all
individuals to freedom of thought and
ownership of property, (v) protecting the
'ethnic, cultural, linguistic and religious
identity of national minorities', and (vi)
developing 'market economies'. The
second section gives guidelines for future
activities. The third section provides for
new structures and institutions, transforming the CSCE from a 'process' into a fully
fledged intergovernmental organization.

**Charter of the Fundamental Social
Rights of Workers** or **Social Charter**
International agreement adopted within
the framework of the European Community (EC), now the European Union (EU).
Not to be confused with the European
Social Charter adopted within the framework of the Council of Europe, the Social
Charter was approved in December 1989
by all member states except the United
Kingdom. It was intended to provide a
basis for developing the 'social dimension'
(i.e. the non-economic side) of the projected single internal market by granting
citizens and working people in particular
certain rights regarding freedom of movement, equal pay, working conditions,
health and safety, sexual equality etc.
The British Conservative government
rejected the proposals because they ran
counter to its policy of deregulating the
labour market and would lead, it argued,
to higher unemployment by raising non-

wage labour costs. The Charter establishes 12 basic principles: (i) the right to work in the EU country of one's choice; (ii) the right to a fair wage; (iii) the right to improved living and working conditions; (iv) the right to social protection under prevailing national systems; (v) the right to freedom of association and collective bargaining; (vi) the right to vocational training; (vii) the right of men and women to equal treatment; (viii) the right of employees to information, consultation and participation; (ix) the right to health protection and safety at work; (x) the right of children and adolescents to protection; (xi) the right of the elderly to guaranteed minimum living standards; and (xii) the right of the disabled to improved social and professional integration. The Charter has no legal force itself but provides the framework for formulating laws under the AGREEMENT ON SOCIAL POLICY, often called the Social Chapter or Social Protocol, adopted in December 1991 by all member states except the United Kingdom.

Chaves, Manuel (1945–) Spanish lawyer, academic and politician. A lecturer in labour law, he joined the Spanish Socialist Workers' Party (PSOE) when it was still illegal in 1968. Elected to parliament in 1977, he was minister of labour and social security from 1986–90. He was elected head of the regional government of Andalusia in July 1990.

Chernobyl accident Environmental disaster caused by an explosion at a nuclear power station in Chernobyl, Ukraine, in April 1986. The world's worst acknowledged nuclear accident, it produced a radioactive cloud which spread rapidly across Ukraine, Belorussia, Eastern Europe, the Nordic countries and the rest of Europe and raised background radiation levels worldwide. At least 250 people died as a direct result of the accident, around 130,000 people had to be evacuated, and an area of around 1,000 sq km in northern Ukraine and southern Belorussia was heavily contaminated. The accident has had longer-term environmental and other effects in these regions but also further afield, such as in Lapland

in the Nordic region. Chernobyl sparked a debate on the safety of nuclear power, particularly in the European countries most directly affected by the radioactive fall-out, and prompted many governments to review their nuclear development plans. In June 1994 the European Union (EU) signed a cooperation agreement with Ukraine which provided for financial and technical assistance to close down the remaining reactors at Chernobyl and construct three western-style reactors elsewhere.

Chetniks [Četnici] Shorthand for the SERBIAN CHETNIK MOVEMENT (SČP), a Serb paramilitary group active in Yugoslavia, Bosnia-Herzegovina and Croatia. The term 'chetniks' is also used generically for all Serb paramilitary groups active in the region. The Chetniks fought a guerrilla war variously against the Germans, Croats and communist resistance fighters during the Second World War.

Chevènement, Jean-Pierre (1939–) French politician. He worked as a commercial attaché for the government from 1965–68 and also headed the Centre for Research Studies and Socialist Education (CERES). Elected to parliament for the Socialist Party (PS) in 1973, he became one of its most influential members as leader of a small left-wing faction. While the party was in power during the 1980s he was minister for research, technology and industry (1981–84), education (1984–86) and defence (1988–91). He resigned from the government in January 1991 over its support for military action to end the Iraqi occupation of Kuwait. He left the PS in April 1993 and founded a new left-wing organization, the Citizens' Movement (MdC).

CHF Abbreviation for the FRANC, the Swiss currency, used in banking etc.

chief administrator (Faroe Islands) *See* HIGH COMMISSIONER.

chief minister Head of government in Gibraltar and Man, both internally self-governing British dependencies.

chief secretary to the Treasury British government minister. Junior to the chancellor of the exchequer, who has overall responsibility for financial and economic policy, the chief secretary is nevertheless usually a minister of Cabinet rank. S/he is primarily responsible for the control of public expenditure.

Chigi Palace [Palazzo Chigi] Shorthand for the Italian prime minister's office. The Palazzo Chigi in Rome is the official residence of the prime minister.

Chirac, Jacques (1932–) French civil servant and politician. He held a range of public and political offices until his election to parliament as a supporter of President de Gaulle in 1967. He was minister of agriculture (1972–74) and the interior (1974) before being appointed prime minister by President Giscard d'Estaing in 1974, a post he held until 1976. In December of that year he became leader of the right-wing Rally for the Republic (RPR), the relaunched gaullist party. In March 1977 he was elected mayor of Paris. After the victory of the right in the 1986 general election he was again appointed prime minister, this time by President Mitterrand. (The following two years became known as the period of 'cohabitation' of a left-wing president and a right-wing prime minister.) He was dismissed after the left won the 1988 election. One of France's leading politicians, he stood for the presidency in 1981 and 1988. He reportedly did not wish to be considered for the premiership or a senior ministerial post when the right returned to power in March 1993.

Chiuzbaian, Iosif Gavril (1945–) Romanian lawyer and politician. He worked at the Bucharest law courts from 1967–84, eventually serving as a judge. He then became a legal adviser to the culture ministry and was appointed inspector-general of the justice ministry in 1987. He was appointed minister of justice in March 1994. He is a member of the far-right Romanian National Unity Party (PUNR).

CHP *See* REPUBLICAN PEOPLE'S PARTY.

Christian Democratic Appeal [Christen-Democratisch Appel] (CDA) Dutch political party. The CDA was formed in 1975 as an electoral alliance of the three main denominational parties, the centrist Catholic People's Party (KVP), the centre-right Protestant Anti-Revolutionary Party (ARP) and the Christian Historical Union (CHU). It was constituted as a unified party in 1980. The CDA and its predecessors have led or participated in all coalition governments from 1918–94, most recently with the right-wing People's Party for Freedom and Democracy (VVD) from 1982–89 and then with the Labour Party (PvdA). In the 1989 election the party gained 35.3% of the vote and 54/150 seats. In May 1994 its support fell to 22.2% and its representation to 34 seats, and it went into opposition for the first time. Ruud Lubbers, party leader and prime minister since 1982, did not stand in the 1994 election; his successor as party leader, Elco Brinkman, resigned in August (after a left-right administration had been formed) and was succeeded by Enneüs Heerma.

Christian Democratic Centre [Centro Cristiano Democratico] (CCD) Italian political party. The CCD was founded in January 1994 by a traditionalist right-wing minority within the Christian Democratic Party (DC) which opposed its relaunch as the ITALIAN PEOPLE'S PARTY (PPI). It contested the March 1994 election within the right-wing Freedom Alliance and gained 27/630 seats. The leader is Pierferdinando Casini.

Christian Democratic Community Party [Kristdemokratiska Samhällspartiet] (KdS) Swedish political party. Founded in 1964, the KdS is a right-leaning christian democratic party. It failed to pass the 4% threshold for representation in parliament until the September 1991 election, when it more than doubled its vote and gained 7.2% and 26/349 seats. It subsequently joined a centre-right coalition. The leader is Alf Svensson.

Christian Democratic Group (European Union) *See* EUROPEAN PEOPLE'S PARTY.

Christian Democratic Movement [Kresťanskodemokratické Hnutie] (KDH) Slovakian political party. Founded in 1990, the KDH came second in the June 1990 election and was a leading member of the coalition government formed subsequently. It lost ground at the June 1992 election, gaining 8.8% of the vote and

18/150 seats in the Slovakian parliament. The leader is Ján Čarnugorský.

Christian Democratic National Peasants' Party [Partidul Naţional Ţărănesc - Creştin şi Democrat] (PNT-CD) Romanian political party. The PNT-CD was formed in 1990 from the merger of the National Peasants' Party (PNT), founded in 1869 and banned during the communist regime from 1947–89, and the new Christian Democratic Party (PCD). Its policies are broadly centre-right and particularly supportive of farmers' interests. It contested the September 1992 election within the opposition DEMOCRATIC CONVENTION (CDR) alliance and gained 42/341 seats. The leader is Corneliu Coposu.

Christian Democratic Party [Křesťansko-Demokratická Strana] (KDS) Czech political party. Founded in 1989, the KDS has a free-market economic programme and broadly christian democratic social policies. It contested the June 1992 election in an alliance with the victorious Civic Democratic Party (ODS) and gained 10/200 seats. The leader is Ivan Pilip.

Christian Democratic Party [Partito della Democrazia Cristiana] (DC) Former Italian political party. The DC was the country's dominant political force until it was discredited by a series of corruption and other scandals that broke in 1993. It was relaunched in January 1994 as the ITALIAN PEOPLE'S PARTY (PPI), with a minority wing forming the CHRISTIAN DEMOCRATIC CENTRE (CCD).

Christian Democratic Party [Krikščionių Demokratų Partija] (KDP) Lithuanian political party. Founded in 1904, the KDP has been proscribed for most of its existence. Relaunched in 1989, it is generally more conservative than its European counterparts. It contested the October/November 1992 election in an alliance with two other parties, which gained 11.6% of the vote. The party has 10/141 seats in parliament. The leader is Povilas Katilius.

Christian Democratic People's Party [Kereszténydemokrata Néppárt] (KDNP) Hungarian political party. Founded in 1989, the KDNP is a continuation of the centre-right Democratic People's Party (DNP) disbanded by the communists in 1949. Its policies are now right-leaning christian democratic. The party gained 6.5% of the vote and 21/386 seats in the March/April 1990 election and then joined the centre-right coalition which held power until the May 1994 election, when it gained 7.1% and 22 seats. The leader is László Surján.

Christian Democratic People's Party of Switzerland [Christlichdemokratische Volkspartei der Schweiz (German), Parti Démocrate Chrétien Suisse (French)] (CVP or PDC) Swiss political party. Founded in 1912 as the Swiss Conservative Party and last renamed in 1970, this right-wing party has been one of the country's leading political forces for many years and is a member of the four-party coalition which has been in power since 1959. Its support is strongest in the central Catholic cantons. At the October 1991 election it gained 17.8% of the vote and 37/200 seats. The party president is Anton Cottier, the parliamentary leader is Peter Hess.

Christian Democratic Union [Christlich Demokratische Union] (CDU) German political party. Founded in 1945, the CDU has formed the government at federal level in West Germany, either alone or as the senior coalition partner, from 1949–69 and since October 1982. The party's dominant figure until his retirement in 1963 was Konrad Adenauer. The CDU also held power for many years in several federal states, in particular Baden-Württemberg and Rhineland-Palatinate in the south and Schleswig-Holstein in the north. Its counterpart in Bavaria, the CHRISTIAN SOCIAL UNION (CSU), is the dominant political force in that state. In October 1990 the Christian Democrats in former East Germany, who had been part of the ruling communist-dominated bloc, merged with the CDU in the west. At the all-German election in December 1990 the CDU gained 36.7% of the vote (35.5% in the west and 41.8% in the east) and 268/662 seats. Helmut Kohl has been party leader since 1973. The deputy leader is Angela Merkel, the parliamentary leader Wolfgang Schäuble, and the general secretary Peter Hintze.

Christian Democratic Union - Czechoslovak People's Party [Křesťansko-Demokratická Unie - Československá Strana Lidová] (KDU-ČSL) Czech political party. The KDU-ČSL has its roots in the Czechoslovak People's Party (ČSL), a right-wing Catholic party founded in 1919 which was allowed to function within the communist-dominated National Front from 1948–89. It was relaunched under a new leadership after the collapse of communist rule. Its policies are now broadly on the right of the christian democratic mainstream. At the June 1992 election it gained 6.3% of the vote and 15/200 seats in the Czech parliament. The leader is Josef Lux.

Christian Democratic Union of Latvia [Latvijas Kristīgo Demokrātu Savienība] (LKDS) Latvian political party. Founded in 1991, the LKDS is generally more right-leaning and conservative on social issues than its European counterparts. At the June 1993 election it gained 5.0% of the vote and 6/100 seats. The party president is Paulis Kļaviņš, the parliamentary leader is Aida Prēdele.

Christian National Trade Union Federation [Christelijk Nationaal Vakverbond] (CNV) Dutch trade-union federation. Founded in 1909, the CNV has 17 affiliated unions with a total membership of 330,000 (around 5% of the labour force). The president is Anton Westerlaken, the general secretary Peter Cammaert.

Christian National Union [Zjednoczenie Chrześcijańsko-Narodowe] (ZChN) Polish political party. Founded in 1989, the ZChN advocates centre-right economic policies and very conservative social policies, basing both on Roman Catholic principles. It became the third-largest party at the October 1991 election (which it contested within the Catholic Election Action, WAK) and participated in successive coalition governments over the following two years. At the September 1993 election it was the dominant partner in the Homeland (Ojczyzna) alliance, which gained 6.4% of the vote but no seats, having failed to reach the

8% alliances need to secure for representation. It joined the Alliance for Poland (PdP) in May 1994. The leader is Wiesław Chrzanowski.

Christian People's Party [Christelijke Volkspartij] (CVP) Belgian political party. Founded in 1945 as the Flemish wing of the Christian Social Party, the CVP became a separate organization in 1971. Generally more right-leaning than its Walloon counterpart, the Christian Social Party (PSC), it has led or participated in all coalitions since 1945. It is the largest party in Flanders. At the November 1991 election it gained 16.7% of the vote and 29/212 seats. The party president is Herman van Rompuy; other influential leaders are Jean-Luc Dehaene (prime minister since 1992) and Wilfried Martens (prime minister from 1979–92).

Christian People's Party [Kristeligt Folkeparti] (KrF) Danish political party. Founded in 1970, the KrF gained 2.3% of the vote and 4/175 seats at the December 1990 election. It joined the centre-left coalition formed in January 1993. The president is Jann Sjursen.

Christian People's Party [Kristelig Folkeparti] (KrF) Norwegian political party. Founded in 1933, the KrF has participated in several centre-right coalitions since 1945. At the September 1993 election it gained 7.9% of the vote and 13/165 seats. The leader is Kjell Magne Bondevik.

Christian Social Party [Parti Social Chrétien] (PSC) Belgian political party. Founded in 1945 as the Walloon wing of the national party of the same name, the PSC became a separate organization in 1971. Like its larger Flemish counterpart, the Christian People's Party (CVP), it has participated in all coalitions since 1945. It is the third-largest party in Wallonia. At the November 1991 election it gained 7.8% of the vote and 18/212 seats. The leader is Melchior Wathelet.

Christian Social Party (Italy) *See* SOCIAL CHRISTIAN PARTY.

Christian Social People's Party [Chrëschtlech-Sozial Vollekspartei (Letzeburgish), Parti Chrétien-Social (French)] (CSV or PCS) Luxemburg political party. Founded in 1914, the CSV has been the country's largest party since 1919 and has been in power as the senior partner in every coalition since then with the exception of 1974–79. At the June 1994 election it gained 31.5% of the vote and 21/60 seats. The leader is Jacques Santer, the party president is Jean-Claude Juncker.

Christian Social Union [Christlich Soziale Union] (CSU) German political party. Founded in 1946, the CSU is the dominant party in Bavaria, where it has held power since 1957. At federal level it forms a joint parliamentary group with the CHRISTIAN DEMOCRATIC UNION (CDU) – which is not active in Bavaria – and has participated in all CDU-led coalitions. Right-wing and more conservative on social issues than the CDU, the party was dominated for years by Franz-Josef Strauss, leader from 1961 until his death in 1988. The CSU gained 52.8% of the vote and 120/204 seats in the September 1994 state election, and the equivalent of 7.1% nationally and 51/662 seats at the December 1990 federal election. Theo Waigel is the leader at federal level, and Edmund Stoiber is the leader in Bavaria; the general secretary is Erwin Huber.

Christiansborg Shorthand for the Danish parliament or the government more generally. The Christiansborg Palace in Copenhagen is the seat of the Folketing (= parliament), the prime minister's office and the supreme court. Many other government departments are housed nearby.

Christofias, Dimitrios (1946–) Cypriot politician. Leader of the youth wing of the left-wing Progressive Party of Working People (AKEL) from 1977, he was elected party leader in April 1988.

Christophersen, Henning (1939–) Danish economist, journalist and politician. Elected to parliament for the Liberals (Venstre) in 1971, he became party leader in 1978 and was foreign minister in 1978–79. He was appointed a commissioner of the European Community (EC) in January 1985, with responsibility for the budget until January 1989 and for economic, financial and monetary affairs since then. He is also one of the Commission's two vice-presidents.

Chrzanowski, Wiesław (1923–) Polish lawyer, academic and politician. He was imprisoned by the communist regime from 1948–54 for sedition. He subsequently practised law and worked as a researcher, and acted as an adviser to the opposition Solidarity movement in the early 1980s. From 1982 he taught at the Catholic University of Lublin. In October 1989 he was elected leader of the new right-wing Christian National Union (ZChN). He was justice minister from January 1991 until his election to the Sejm (= parliament) in October. He was elected its marshal (= speaker) the following month, a post he held until the September 1993 election, when the ZChN failed to pass the threshold for representation.

Churkin, Vitaly (1952–) Russian diplomat. He joined the Soviet foreign ministry in 1974, initially as a translator and interpreter. He worked in the Soviet embassy in the United States from 1982–87 and in the Soviet Communist Party's international department from 1987–89. He then returned to the foreign ministry as a special adviser and became its spokesman in 1990. In June 1992 (nine months after the disintegration of the Soviet Union) he was appointed a deputy foreign minister of the Russian Federation, with special responsibility for European affairs. As such he has become closely involved in the international effort to end the civil war in Bosnia-Herzegovina.

CI Abbreviation for the Channel Islands, an archipelago comprising the bailiwicks of Guernsey and Jersey and their dependencies.

Ciampi, Carlo Azeglio (1920–) Italian banker and politician. He has been with the Bank of Italy, the central bank, for most of his working life. He joined it in 1946 and was appointed deputy director-general in 1976, director-general in 1978 and governor in 1979. A member of the Christian Democratic Party (DC) but not politically active, he was asked to form a government in April 1993, after the established political leaders and parties had been discredited by a series of corruption scandals. He became prime minister of a transitional five-party coalition committed to reform. He submitted his government's resignation after the early election in March 1994 and remained in office in a caretaker capacity until May.

Cigani (sing. Ciganin/Ciganka), **Cigány** (sing. Cigán/ka), **Cigányok** (sing. Cigány) Serbocroat, Slovak and Hungarian names respectively for GIPSIES or Romanies.

CII *See* IRISH BUSINESS AND EMPLOYERS' CONFEDERATION.

Cikány (sing. Cikán/ka) Czech name for GIPSIES or Romanies.

Çiller, Tansu (1946–) Turkish economist, academic and politician. She lectured in economics at various universities until she entered politics. In 1991 she was elected to parliament for the centre-right True Path Party (DYP) and appointed a state minister (= without portfolio) with responsibility for economic affairs. In June 1993 she was elected party leader and prime minister in succession to Süleyman Demirel, who had been elected president of the republic the previous month.

Cimoszewicz, Włodzimierz (1950–) Polish lawyer, academic, farmer and politician. He taught at the Institute of International Law at Warsaw University from 1972–85 and then worked as a cattle and pig farmer in the Białystok region. Elected to parliament for the communist Polish United Workers' Party (PZPR) in 1989, he was parliamentary leader of its successor, the Social Democratic Party (SdRP), in 1990–91. He was its candidate in the 1990 presidential election. He left the party in 1991 but was reelected to parliament for the SdRP-dominated Democratic Left Alliance (SLD). He was appointed deputy prime minister in charge of social policy and justice minister in the left-wing government which took office in October 1993.

Cinquième République *See* FIFTH REPUBLIC.

cintura rossa *See* RED BELT (Italy).

CIP *See* CONFEDERATION OF PORTUGUESE INDUSTRY.

Cirino Pomicino, Paolo (1939–) Italian doctor and politician. He is a specialist in neuropsychiatry. Elected to parliament for the Christian Democratic Party (DC) in 1976, he was minister for public adminis-

tration from 1988–89 and budget minister from 1989–92. In November 1993 he became one of the first senior DC leaders to acknowledge his involvement in political corruption. He admitted receiving 5 billion lire (2.5 million ecus) in connection with the ENIMONT AFFAIR and passing it to party colleagues with links to organized crime to spend during the 1992 election campaign.

CIS *See* COMMONWEALTH OF INDEPENDENT STATES.

CISL *See* ITALIAN CONFEDERATION OF WORKERS' UNIONS.

Citizens' Assembly [Bürgerschaft] Parliament in Bremen and Hamburg, two federal states of Germany.

Citizen's Charter British government programme. Proposed in July 1991 and implemented from April 1992 onwards, the Citizen's Charter aims to improve the quality of public services by defining standards of service to which customers are entitled. To this end public-sector bodies are obliged to publish information that allows comparison between service-level targets and actual performance, their performance is monitored by independent experts and regulators, and bodies within a service are ranked in 'league tables'. Within this framework specific charters have been drawn up for central government departments, local government authorities, the health, education and postal services etc. The concept has also been extended to the privatized public utilities (water, electricity, gas). The Conservative government has also proposed a 'European citizen's charter' to improve the accountability of the European Commission and other European Union (EU) institutions.

Citizens' Charter [Piliečių Chartija] (PCh) Lithuanian political party. Founded in 1991, the PCh is a centre-right party committed to strengthening 'civil society' in Lithuania. Contesting the October/November 1992 election in alliance with the Reform Movement (Sąjūdis), it gained 9/141 seats. It subsequently joined the opposition Homeland Accord (Tėvynės Santara). The leader is Vytautas Kubilius.

Citizens' Europe Programme of the European Union (EU), also known as People's Europe. Citizens' Europe is an umbrella title for the measures aimed at strengthening the Union's identity and improving its image among the citizens of the member states. Among the measures taken since the mid 1980s, when the need to bring the then European Community closer to the people was first identified, have been the adoption of a European flag and anthem, the introduction of a common passport and driving licence, the establishment of exchange programmes for students (ERASMUS, LINGUA etc), the reduction and in some cases abolition of border controls, the sponsoring of sports events and the annual selection of a major city as the 'European city of culture'. The Maastricht Treaty, which came into force in November 1993, provides for a common EUROPEAN UNION CITIZENSHIP with additional rights for national citizens, the right of individuals to petition the European Parliament, and the appointment of an OMBUDSPERSON to investigate complaints of maladministration within the EU.

Citizens' Movement [Mouvement des Citoyens] (MdC) French political party. The MdC was founded in April 1993 by Jean-Pierre Chevènement, a leading member of the left wing of the Socialist Party (PS), which had been heavily defeated at the general election the previous month. It sees itself as a new force on the left untainted by dishonesty and corruption.

Città del Vaticano Italian name for the Vatican City.

CITUB *See* CONFEDERATION OF INDEPENDENT TRADE UNIONS IN BULGARIA.

City, the Shorthand for the financial district of London. The City is Europe's largest financial centre by far and one of the world's three major centres along with New York and Tokyo. The institutions based there include the Stock Exchange, foreign-exchange and commodity markets, the Lloyds insurance company, the Bank of England and many commercial and merchant banks. The City of London proper comprises the historical centre of Greater London and is a separate corporation or unit of local government.

city state [Stadtstaat, pl. -en] In Germany, a city which has the status of a federal state [Land]. The three 'city states' – Berlin, Bremen and Hamburg – have somewhat different administrative structures than the 'area states', combining the functions of a municipality and a state. They are sometimes treated separately because of their distinctive economic and social characteristics.

CiU *See* CONVERGENCE AND UNION.

Civic Alliance Party [Partidul Alianței Civice] (PAC) Romanian political party. The PAC has its roots in the Civic Alliance (AC), a movement formed in 1990 to campaign for the introduction of more extensive political and economic reforms. In July 1991 the AC decided to turn itself into a political party. The centrist PAC contested the September 1992 election within the DEMOCRATIC CONVENTION (CDR) alliance and gained 13/341 seats. The leader is Nicolae Manolescu.

Civic Democratic Alliance [Občanská Demokratická Aliance] (ODA) Czech political party. The ODA has its roots in the Civic Forum, the broad-based movement which spearheaded the opposition to communist rule in 1989 and won the multiparty election in June the following year. When the Forum split in early 1991, the ODA was set up as a free-market, right-wing party. At the June 1992 election it gained 5.9% of the vote and 14/200 seats in the Czech parliament. It is part of the right-wing coalition led by the Civic Democratic Party (ODS). The leader is Jan Kalvoda.

Civic Democratic Party [Občanská Demokratická Strana] (ODS) Czech political party. The ODS has its roots in the Civic Forum, the broad-based movement which spearheaded the opposition to communist rule in 1989 and won the multiparty election in June the following year. After the Forum split into rival factions in early 1991, one of its wings, the Democratic Right Club, founded the ODS. The party advocates a rapid transition to a market economy, wholesale privatization of state assets, and restrictions on social benefits. At the June 1992 elections it became the largest party in the Czech parliament, gaining 29.7% of the vote and 76/200 seats in alliance with the Christian Democratic Party (KDS). Party leader Václav Klaus then formed a four-party right-wing coalition. The ODS now holds 65 seats.

Civic Movement *See* FREE DEMOCRATS (Czech Republic).

Civil Guard [Guardia Civil] Spanish paramilitary police force. Formed in 1844, the Civil Guard was orginally a rural police force. During the Franco regime (1939–75) it spearheaded the drive against left-wing and separatist opposition groups. Today it is mainly responsible for general police duties and guarding the national frontiers. It has a strength of 66,000 and is headed by an army general, who is answerable to the interior minister.

civil guard [guardia civil, pl. -s -es] In Spain, a member of the Civil Guard, the paramilitary police force.

Civitas Vaticanae Latin name for the Vatican City.

CJEC *See* COURT OF JUSTICE OF THE EUROPEAN COMMUNITIES.

CJHA *See* COOPERATION ON JUSTICE AND HOME AFFAIRS.

Čk Abbreviation for the KORUNA, the Czech currency.

C£ Abbreviation for the LÍRA or pound, the Cypriot currency.

Claes, Willy (1938–) Belgian politician. Elected to parliament for the Flemish Socialist Party (SP) in 1968, he has been minister of education (1972–73 and 1988–89) and economic affairs (1973–74, 1977–81 and 1989–92). He has been foreign minister since March 1992. One of the party's senior leaders, he has also been a deputy prime minister in the centre-left coalition since May 1988. In July 1992 he was also elected president of the Confederation of Socialist Parties of the European Community (CSPEC), which was relaunched as the Party of European Socialists (PES) three months later.

Clarke, Kenneth (1940–) British lawyer and politician. Elected to parliament for the Conservative Party in 1970, he held several junior ministerial posts from 1979–85. Since then he has held the portfolios of employment (1985–87), trade and industry (1987–88), health (1988–90), education (1990–92) and home affairs (1992–93). In May 1993 he was made chancellor of the exchequer (= finance minister).

Clean Hands [Mani Pulite] Codename for the investigations into illegal party funding by a Milan-based team of magistrates, which in 1992 first exposed the web of political corruption in Italian public life. *See* ITALIAN CORRUPTION SCANDALS.

cleansing (former communist countries) *See* DECOMMUNIZATION *and* SCREENING.

Clerides, Glafcos *See* KLERIDES, GLAVKOS.

clientelismo *See* CLIENTISM.

clientism [clientelismo] In Italy, a system of patronage whereby people in positions of power dispense financial and other favours and protection in exchange for loyalty, and specifically a system whereby political parties and party members provide contracts, jobs, pensions etc in exchange for votes and other political support. Clientism has its roots in the Middle Ages and ultimately in the ancient Roman practice of plebeians placing themselves under the protection of a patrician. In the modern political context it formed the basis of the 'PARTYOCRACY' [partito-crazia] and the system of LOTTIZZAZIONE, by which the Christian Democratic Party (DC) and the other ruling parties exercised political control from the 1950s onwards through political appointments, personal recommendation and bribery. Although widely criticized, especially after the exposure in 1992 and 1993 of the nationwide web of political corruption (*see* ITALIAN CORRUPTION SCANDALS), the *clientelismo* was implicitly condoned for many years as a necessary lubricant of economic and social life and operated with the consent of the millions of people who benefited from it. The Sicilian Mafia, Neapolitan Camorra and other criminal organizations also rely on *clientelismo* relationships, specifically in the context of the extortion of protection money etc.

CLRAE *See* STANDING CONFERENCE OF LOCAL AND REGIONAL AUTHORITIES OF EUROPE.

CMEA *See* COUNCIL FOR MUTUAL ECONOMIC ASSISTANCE.

ČMKOS *See* CZECHOMORAVIAN TRADE UNION CONFEDERATION.

ČMSS *See* CZECHOMORAVIAN CENTRE PARTY.

CMTU *See* CONFEDERATION OF MALTA TRADE UNIONS.

CN *See* CORSICA NATION.

CNPF *See* NATIONAL COUNCIL OF FRENCH EMPLOYERS.

CNSLR and **CNSLR-Frăţia** *See* NATIONAL CONFEDERATION OF FREE TRADE UNIONS OF ROMANIA - BROTHERHOOD.

CNT *See* NATIONAL LABOUR COUNCIL.

CNV *See* CHRISTIAN NATIONAL TRADE UNION FEDERATION.

co-decision procedure In the European Union (EU), a method of decision making in which the EUROPEAN PARLIAMENT has equal rights with the Council of Ministers, the organization's main legislative body. It applies in a number of policy areas, including health, education, training, science and technology, culture, health, consumer affairs, trans-European networks (energy, transport and telecommunications), environmental issues, regional policy and development cooperation. These are areas in which the Council generally takes decisions by qualified majority (i.e. broadly two-thirds) rather than unanimity. Introduced under the Maastricht Treaty, which came into force in November 1993, and also known as the 'article 189b procedure' after the relevant section of the treaty, the co-decision procedure gives the Parliament the right to amend or reject legislative proposals put to it by the Council. If the two bodies are unable to agree on a piece of legislation, a bipartisan conciliation committee is convened to work out a compromise. If this cannot be found, the proposal falls. *See also* COOPERATION PROCEDURE *and* DEMOCRATIC DEFICIT.

co-prince [copríncep] Head of state of Andorra. There are two co-princes, ex officio the bishop of Urgell in Spain and the president of France. Until the adoption of the country's first constitution in May 1993, they had extensive legislative and judicial powers, generally exercised through their personal representatives [veguers]. The constitution transferred sovereignty to the people, so that the co-princes' powers are now largely nominal, similar to constitutional monarchs in other countries.

Coalition for the Republic *See* MOVEMENT FOR ....

COCOM *See* COORDINATING COMMITTEE ON EXPORT CONTROLS.

COE (Slovakia) *See* COEXISTENCE.

CoE *See* COUNCIL OF EUROPE.

Coëme, Guy (1946–) Belgian politician. A member of the Walloon Socialist Party (PS), he held a range of posts at local, provincial and regional level from 1974–88. He was briefly chief minister of the Wallonian regional government in 1988 before being appointed defence minister. In the centre-left coalition formed in March 1992 he became a deputy prime minister and minister of communications and public enterprises. He resigned in January 1994 after being implicated in the AGUSTA AFFAIR.

Coexistence [Együttélés (Hungarian), Spolužitie (Slovak), Wspólnota (Polish), Soužití (Czech)] (ESWS or COE) Slovakian political party. Founded in 1990, Coexistence calls for equal treatment of all ethnic groups and aims to advance the interests of the Hungarian and Gipsy minorities as well as the small communities of Poles, Ruthenians and Ukrainians. It contested the June 1992 election jointly with the Hungarian Christian Democratic Movement: the alliance gained 7.4% of the vote and the party 9/150 seats. The leader is Miklós Duray.

cohabitation In France, the situation where the president of the republic (who has extensive executive powers in some spheres) and the prime minister are from different political parties. The term was coined in 1986, when a centre-right alliance won the general election during the first term of President Mitterrand, a socialist. The uneasy coexistence – it raised issues of competences, prerogatives and responsibilities – came to an end two years later when Mitterrand was reelected and an early general election returned the left to power. A second period of cohabitation began with the victory of the centre-right in March 1993. The term has also been used for similar situations in other countries, as in Portugal (since 1986) and Poland (briefly in 1989–90).

cohesion (European Union) Shorthand for ECONOMIC AND SOCIAL COHESION.

cohesion countries In the European Union (EU), a collective name for Greece, Ireland, Portugal and Spain, the four member states eligible for support from the COHESION FUND.

Cohesion Fund Programme of the European Union (EU). Set up under the Maastricht Treaty provisionally in April 1993 and formally in May 1994, the Cohesion Fund is intended to help the four poorest member states – Greece, Ireland, Portugal and Spain – with the cost of adapting to the planned economic and monetary union (EMU). It finances projects in the fields of transport infrastructure and environmental protection. It forms a key plank in strengthening 'economic and social cohesion' within the EU by helping these states, which have an income per head at least 10% below the EU average, to catch up economically with the more prosperous members. As such it is similar in scope to the European Regional Development Fund and other 'structural' funds. A total of 15.15 billion ecus has been committed to the Cohesion Fund for the period 1994–99.

Cold War The ideological, political and economic conflict between the North Atlantic Treaty Organization (NATO) led by the United States and the Warsaw Pact led by the Soviet Union from the end of the Second World War (1945) until the late 1980s. The Cold War – the term was first used in the United States in 1947 – was marked by periods of extreme tension (particularly during the 1950s and early 1980s), arms proliferation, mutual suspicion (fuelled by propaganda and subversion) and involvement on opposing sides in Third World conflicts, but no direct military confrontation between the two blocs. The impact of the Cold War was most evident in Europe: the continent was divided between the communist East and capitalist West, with both the Warsaw Pact and NATO maintaining huge armies and arsenals of nuclear and conventional weapons on their side of what was often called the 'Iron Curtain'. After several efforts to reduce tension in the 1970s and 80s, it was the Soviet Union's new commitment to detente under President Gorbachev and the collapse of the communist regimes in Eastern Europe in 1989 and the Warsaw Pact in 1990 that brought the Cold War to an end.

collective (state) presidency (Bosnia-Herzegovina) *See* STATE PRESIDENCY.

collectivité territoriale *See* TERRITORIAL COLLECTIVITY.

Collignon, Robert (1943–) Belgian lawyer and politician. He was first elected to parliament for the Walloon Socialist Party (PS) in 1971 and has been mayor of Amay since 1987. He has held a range of senior posts in the PS since the late 1980s, including leader of the parliamentary groups in the Senate and the Wallonia regional council. In January 1994 he became chief minister of the Wallonian government.

Colombo, Emilio (1920–) Italian politician. He was first elected to parliament for the Christian Democratic Party (DC) in 1946. He was given his first junior ministerial post in 1948 and from 1955 was successively minister of agriculture, industry, foreign trade and the treasury. He was prime minister from 1970–72, and then minister of justice (1972–73), finance (1973–75) and the treasury (1975–77). From 1977–79 he was president of the European Parliament. He then returned to domestic politics and was foreign minister from 1980–83 and from June 1992 – April 1993. In March 1993 he was elected president of the Christian Democratic International.

COM Abbreviation for Council of Ministers, the common name for the COUNCIL OF THE EUROPEAN UNION, the EU's main decision-making body.

Combined Loyalist Military Command British guerrilla group. The Command is an umbrella organization for the main unionist or loyalist guerrilla groups claiming to defend the interests of the majority Protestant community in Northern Ireland. It comprises the Ulster Freedom Fighters (UFF), Ulster Volunteer Force (UVF) and Red Hand Commando. They declared a ceasefire in October 1994. *See also individual group entries.*

Come On Italy [Forza Italia] (FI) Italian political party. Forza Italia – the name is taken from a popular football slogan – was formed as a network of around 14,000 locally based 'supporters' clubs' in October 1993 by Silvio Berlusconi, a prominent businessman and owner of Italy's largest media empire. He announced his entry into politics in January 1994 at the head of a right-wing 'freedom crusade' to counter the left. Forza Italia stresses free-market economic policies and institutional reform, calling in particular for deregulation of economic activity, privatization of state-owned industries, reductions in taxation, public spending and the national debt, and decentralization of revenue-raising and -spending powers to the regions. It claims to be a force of renewal in Italy, which has been thrown into crisis by a series of corruption and other scandals. It was instrumental in the formation of the Freedom Alliance, including the Northern League (Lega Nord) in the north and the National Alliance (AN) in the south, which won the March 1994 election. Attracting support from the right and centre of the political spectrum, Forza Italia gained 21.0% of the vote and 102/630 seats. The Freedom Alliance formed a government in May, with Berlusconi as prime minister. The Forza Italia parliamentary group also includes the Pannella List and Centre Union (UDC) and has 112 seats.

COMECON *See* COUNCIL FOR MUTUAL ECONOMIC ASSISTANCE.

Comino, Domenico (1955–) Italian agronomist, teacher and politician. He taught agricultural sciences in vocational schools before entering politics. Elected to parliament for the federalist Northern League (Lega Nord) in 1992, he was appointed minister for European affairs in the right-wing coalition which took office in May 1994.

Comisiones Obreras *See* TRADE UNION CONFEDERATION OF WORKERS' COMMISSIONS.

comitology procedure In the European Union (EU), a method of implementing legislation. Comitology – taken from *comité*, French for 'committee' – describes the practice of delegating the implementation of decisions reached by the European Commission, the EU's administrative and executive arm, to committees composed of officials from the member states. (Broadly speaking, the Commission is responsible for carrying out decisions adopted by the Council of Ministers, the EU's main legislative body, and has some legislative powers of its own.)

Commission, the In the European Union (EU), shorthand for the EUROPEAN COMMISSION, the organization's administrative and executive arm.

Commission of Human Rights *See* EUROPEAN ....

Commission of Inquiry Assessing East German History or **Eppelmann Commission** [Enquete-Kommission zur Aufarbeitung der DDR Vergangenheit] German parliamentary commission. This commission was set up by the Bundestag, the lower house of parliament, in March 1992. It has 27 members, 16 members of parliament and 11 private citizens, and is headed by Rainer Eppelmann, a leading opposition figure in former East Germany. Its brief is to assess the methods and legacy of the communist regime which was in power in East Germany from 1945–89.

Commission of the European Communities Former name of the EUROPEAN COMMISSION, the administrative and executive arm of the European Union (EU). The title was in use from 1967 until the entry into force of the Maastricht Treaty in November 1993.

commissioner In the European Union (EU), a member of the European Commission, the organization's administrative and executive arm.

commissioner of the republic or **commissioner** [commissaire de la république] French local government official, widely referred to as 'prefect' [préfet]. Appointed by the interior minister as the representative of central government at local level, the commissioner is charged with supervising the institutions of the departments and the lower-level communes. The office and title were introduced as part of the programme of decentralization adopted in 1982. Previously the prefect had held more extensive powers, acting as the department's chief executive officer.

commitology procedure *See* COMITOLOGY....

Committee of Ministers Institution of the Council of Europe. Composed of the foreign ministers of the member states, the Committee of Ministers is the organization's decision-making body. It normally meets twice a year; the ministers' deputies, accredited as permanent representatives to the Council, meet every month. It (i) considers proposals submitted by conferences of specialist ministers, committees of government experts and the consultative Parliamentary Assembly, (ii) makes recommendations to governments, and (iii) discusses political aspects of European cooperation. Decisions on all major issues require unanimity. The Committee is assisted by 11 permanent steering committees and around 90 committees of experts.

Committee of Permanent Representatives (COREPER) Institution of the European Union (EU). Composed of the member states' ambassadors to the Community, COREPER – the French abbreviation is commonly used – is responsible for preparing meetings of the Council (composed of ministers from the national governments) and following up its decisions. It liaises closely with the European Commission, the organization's administrative and executive arm, and is assisted by a large number of working parties. The ambassadors are assisted by committees of national civil servants.

Committee of Senior Officials (CSO) Institution of the Conference on Security and Cooperation in Europe (CSCE). The CSO is composed of the member states' permanent representatives. It prepares meetings of the Council of Foreign Ministers, the organization's senior decision-

making body, makes recommendations to it and implements its decisions. Emergency meetings of the CSO may be convened to discuss alleged violations of the Helsinki Final Act – the CSCE's basic document, concerned mainly with security and human-rights issues – in a member state or if events in a member state are thought to constitute a 'major disruption' to peace, security and stability. Such a meeting must be requested a quarter of the member states.

Committee of the Regions (COR) Advisory body of the European Union (EU). Established under the Maastricht Treaty, which came into force in November 1993, the Committee of the Regions brings together representatives of the regional and local authorities from the 12 member states. Its 189 members, between six and 24 per country, are nominated by the national governments for a four-year term; the actual selection process differs from country to country. The Committee must be consulted by the Council and the Commission, the EU's main decision-making bodies, on legislation in a wide range of fields, including regional development ('economic and social cohesion'), health, education, culture, training and transport. It may also express a view on any other matter which it believes to have regional implications. The COR has a joint organizational structure with the Economic and Social Committee (ECOSOC). The president is Jacques Blanc, president of the Languedoc-Roussillon region (France); the vice-president is Pasqual Maragall, mayor of Barcelona (Spain).

committee of wise people *See* GROUP OF....

committology procedure *See* COMITOLOGY....

Common Agricultural Policy (CAP) Common policy of the European Union (EU). In 1962 the CAP became the first major common policy to be implemented by the European Economic Community (EEC, now the European Community, EC) established four years earlier. Its objectives are set out in the Treaty of Rome: to increase agricultural productivity, ensure a fair standard of living for farmers and their staff, stabilize markets, guarantee supplies, and ensure reasonable prices for consumers. It was organized on the principles of free movement of agricultural products within the EC; preference for domestic production and control of imports from outside the EC (by setting 'threshold prices'); and common financing through the European Agricultural Guidance and Guarantee Fund (EAGGF). The latter's workings were undermined by the breakdown of the international system of fixed exchange rates in the late 1960s, which led to the introduction in 1969 of notional 'green currencies' and the payment of 'monetary compensation amounts' (MCAs). In creating a highly protected market, introducing extensive price-support mechanisms (such as 'target prices' for products) and giving priority to farmers' incomes, the CAP encouraged overproduction and pushed up prices for consumers. By the mid 1980s agricultural subsidies accounted for two-thirds of EC expenditure and massive surpluses or 'food mountains' had been accumulated in many foodstuffs. Attempts to correct the system had little effect until a major reform of the CAP was agreed in May 1992. Essentially replacing price guarantees with direct income support, the package included significant cuts in intervention prices (to reduce overproduction), compensation payments for farmers provided they took out of production or 'set aside' 15% of their arable land, and measures to protect the environment. At the start of 1993 the 'green money' system was reformed to conform with the principles of the new single market.

common citizenship Shorthand for EUROPEAN UNION CITIZENSHIP.

Common Commercial Policy (CCP) Common policy of the European Union (EU). The objective of a common commercial or foreign-trade policy was set out in the Treaty of Rome establishing the European Economic Community (EEC) in 1958. It was one of the first common policies to be implemented. Between 1959 and 1968 customs duties on goods traded between member states were removed and a common external tariff was introduced on imports from non-

Community states. The policy also covers the conclusion of tariff or trade agreements with third parties and measures relating to liberalization, export policy and protection (such as subsidies and dumping). The European Commission, the EU's administrative and executive arm, represents the member states in this sphere and conducts negotiations on their behalf with third countries and in the context of the worldwide General Agreement on Tariffs and Trade (GATT) on the basis of previously agreed positions.

common currency (European Union) *See* HARD ECU PLAN.

common European home Concept used by advocates of a Europe-wide security system. It was coined in 1967 by representatives of the North Atlantic Treaty Organization (NATO) to popularize proposals for reducing tension between the Cold War adversaries, NATO and the Warsaw Pact. It gained wide currency in 1987 after the then Soviet leader, Mikhail Gorbachev, used it to describe a new security system for Europe. In an address to the Council of Europe in July 1989 he defined it as 'a restructuring of the international order in Europe that would put common European values in the forefront and make it possible to replace the traditional balance of forces with a balance of interests'. Since the collapse of communist rule in Eastern Europe later that year and the dissolution of the Warsaw Pact in 1991, the notion of the 'common European home' has been used in the context of developing new security arrangements for the continent as a whole.

Common Fisheries Policy (CFP) Common policy of the European Union (EU). The terms of a common fisheries policy were agreed by the original six members of the European Community (EC) in 1970, but its implementation had to be postponed following the accession of Denmark, Ireland and the United Kingdom in 1973, all of which had large fishing fleets and had negotiated 10-year transitional arrangements. The CFP came into effect at the beginning of 1983. It divides the EU's 200-mile maritime claim into a 6-mile zone with exclusive rights for national fishing fleets, a 6- to 12-mile zone with limited access for other EU fleets, and a zone of un-restricted access beyond that. EU and national quotas, known as 'total allow-able catches' (TACs), are set annually for species threatened by overfishing. The policy also comprises various sur-veillance and conservation measures, marketing standards, restructuring programmes and agreements with third countries. The CFP applies only in part to Spain and Portugal. Its fishing fleets are larger than the others combined and were made subject to 10-year transitional arrangements when the two countries joined the EC in 1986.

Common Foreign and Security Policy (CFSP) Common policy of the 12 mem-ber states of the European Union (EU), known as European Political Cooperation (EPC or PoCo) until the Maastricht Treaty took effect in November 1993. The CFSP is one of the EU's two intergovernmental 'pillars' (the other being Cooperation on Justice and Home Affairs, CJHA). This means that it formally operates outside the supranational structures of the Euro-pean Community (EC), such as the Com-mission and Parliament, although the former in particular is closely involved in its work. The CFSP is implemented through the Council of Ministers, the EU's main decision-making body. The Maastricht Treaty defines its objectives as (i) to safeguard the common values, fundamental interests and independence of the Union, (ii) to strengthen the secu-rity of the Union and its member states in all ways, (iii) to preserve peace and strengthen international security, (iv) to promote international cooperation, and (v) to develop and consolidate democracy and the rule of law. These objectives are to be pursued by establishing 'systematic cooperation' between the member states and by 'gradually implementing joint action in areas in which the member states have important interests in common'. The Council defines areas for 'joint action' on the basis of an agreed 'common position'. Decisions must be unanimous and are binding on the member states. When the

Council has not taken a position on a foreign-policy issue, a member state is free to act as it sees fit but should inform and consult the Council as appropriate. While the CFSP in principle covers the security of the EU, issues with defence and security implications are specifically excluded from these procedures. The Maastricht Treaty talks of the 'eventual framing of a common defence policy' and commits the EU to developing the West-ern European Union (WEU), an indepen-dent intergovernmental organization, as its 'defence component'. Pending a revision of the security and defence provi-sions (due by 1998 and possibly leading to the WEU's full integration into the EU framework), the WEU has been asked 'to elaborate and implement decisions and actions of the Union which have defence implications'. EPC or PoCo, the CFSP's forerunner, was set up in 1970 and given a formal basis in the 1987 Single Euro-pean Act.

Common Foreign Policy *See* COMMON FOREIGN AND SECURITY POLICY.

Common Market Informal name for the European Community (EC) or the Euro-pean Union (EU). The creation of a common market was laid down in the Treaty of Rome establishing the European Economic Community (EEC, now the EC). Customs duties and similar barriers were eliminated by 1968 and the SINGLE INTERNAL MARKET was broadly completed by the end of 1992. By this time the acti-vities of the Community had extended well beyond these narrow confines. The term 'Common Market' is now used mainly in Britain and Denmark, in parti-cular by those opposed to any further European integration.

common market (European Union) *See* SINGLE INTERNAL MARKET.

Common Security Policy *See* COMMON FOREIGN AND SECURITY POLICY.

Commons, the Shorthand for the HOUSE OF COMMONS, the lower house of the British Parliament.

Commonwealth of Independent States [Sodruzhestvo Nezavisimykh Gosudarstv (Russian)] (SNG or CIS) Intergovernmen-tal organization. The CIS was formed in

December 1991, after the disintegration of the Soviet Union, to promote coordination of policies in the fields of trade, security etc. Twelve of the 15 former Soviet republics eventually joined the organization. They include, to the west of Russia, Belorussia, Moldava and Ukraine. The three Baltic republics – Estonia, Latvia and Lithuania – did not join.

Communal Liberation Party [Toplumcu Kurtuluş Partisi] (TKP) Northern Cypriot political party. Founded in 1976, the TKP has a centre-left orientation and advocates a confederal solution to the division of Cyprus between the Greek and Turkish communities (*see* CYPRUS QUESTION). It gained 13.3% of the vote and 5/50 seats at the December 1993 election. The leader is Mustafa Akıncı.

communautaire (European Union) *See* COMMUNITARIAN.

communauté *See* COMMUNITY (Belgium).

Communauté Française *See* FRENCH COMMUNITY.

commune French administrative division. The smallest unit of local government, each commune has a council [conseil municipal] elected for a six-year term and a number of executive deputies and a mayor [maire] elected by the council. They are responsible for most local services, including schools and hospitals. There are around 31,000 communes, most of them with less than 1,000 inhabitants. Small rural communes as well as those within large conurbations often form unions for the purpose of providing certain services jointly. Paris, the national capital, combines the functions of a commune and a higher-tier department.

commune [comune, pl. comuni] Italian administrative division. The smallest unit of local government, each commune has a council [consiglio comunale] elected for a five-year term, an executive council [giunta comunale] and a mayor [sindaco]. They have extensive responsibilities and some autonomous powers in matters of local concern.

Communist Party (Cyprus) *See* PROGRESSIVE PARTY OF WORKING PEOPLE.

Communist Party of Bohemia and Moravia [Kommunistická Strana Čech a Moravy] (KSČM) Czech political party. Founded in 1921, the Communist Party of Czechoslovakia (KSČS) became the country's largest party in 1946 (with 38% of the vote) and seized power in 1948. Reforms introduced during the brief 'Prague Spring' of 1968 were reversed after a Soviet-led invasion. After the regime's collapse in 1989, the party was relaunched the following year in the Czech Republic as the KSČM. It defines itself as a left-socialist party and bases its policies on Marx's humanism and methodology. At the June 1992 election it was the dominant partner in the Left Bloc (LB) alliance, which gained 14.1% of the vote and 35/200 seats and became the second-largest group in the Czech parliament. The party split in July 1993, when a reformist wing left to form the Democratic Left Party (SDL). The rump KSČM holds 10 seats. The leader is Miroslav Grebeníček.

Communist Party of Greece [Kommounistikó Kómma Elládos] (KKE) Greek political party. Founded in 1918, the KKE was banned from 1947–74 and operated mostly in exile (which is why in the past it was often referred to as the 'exterior' Communist Party). From 1974 it led several left-wing alliances which enjoyed the support of around a tenth of the electorate. The party split in 1991 when a reformist wing joined the Progressive Left Alliance (Sinaspismós). Campaigning on an orthodox marxist-leninist platform, the KKE gained 4.5% of the vote and 9/300 seats at the October 1993 election. The leader is Aleka Papariga.

Communist Party of Spain [Partido Comunista de España] (PCE) Spanish political party. The PCE was formed from the merger of several communist and left-socialist groups in 1922. It was forced underground later in the 1920s and during the Franco dictatorship (1939–75). The PCE was one of the prime movers in the development of the reformist 'eurocommunist' movement in the 1970s. Relegalized in 1977, it initially gained around a tenth of the vote but its support declined in the 1980s. It has been the dominant partner in the UNITED LEFT (IU) alliance since its formation in 1986. The leader is Julio Anguita.

Communist Refoundation Party [Partito della Rifondazione Comunista] (PRC or RC) Italian political party. The RC was founded in 1991 by a minority wing of the former Italian Communist Party (PCI) which opposed its conversion into the Democratic Left Party (PDS). It upholds the traditional positions of the PCI as an independent communist party, but has also attracted various far-left groups. At the April 1992 election it gained 5.6% of the vote and 35/630 seats. It contested the early election in March 1994 within the Progressive Alliance and gained 6.0% and 39/630 seats. The leader is Fausto Bertinotti.

communitarian In the European Union (EU), a term for matters pertaining to the European Community (EC), the supra-national core of the Union. It is contrasted with 'intergovernmental'. Depending on the issue and policy area, cooperation and decision making within the EU may be on a 'communitarian' basis, i.e. within the EC structures and in the form of EC directives and other measures, or on an 'inter-governmental' basis, i.e. outside the EC structures and in the form of agreements among the member states. The French term *communautaire* is widely used. *See also* SUPRANATIONAL COOPERATION *and* ACQUIS COMMUNAUTAIRE.

Communities, the Shorthand for the EURO-PEAN COMMUNITIES, the formal name of the main 'pillar' of the European Union (EU).

community [gemeenschap (Dutch), communauté (French), Gemeinschaft (German), pl. -pen, -s, -en] One of the two federal divisions of Belgium. Under the constitutional reforms agreed in prin-ciple in 1970 and finalized in July 1993, the country's new federal structure is based on overlapping geographical regions and language-based cultural communities. The three communities – Flemish, French and German-Speaking – are responsible for health, social security, social services, education, culture and language issues, all regarded as 'person-related' matters. The communities are defined in social

and cultural, not geographical, terms: the French Community, for instance, is responsible for French-speaking Wallonia as well as French speakers in the Brussels region and in the German-Speaking Community. The structures of the three communities differ in some respects.

community British administrative division. A subdivision of the district, the commu-nity is the smallest unit of local govern-ment in Scotland and Wales outside the major cities. Around four-fifths of the around 1,000 communities in Wales have councils elected for four-year terms. The counterpart to the English parishes, they have limited powers in some matters of local concern. The around 1,000 commu-nities in Scotland have even more limited powers.

community Shorthand for AUTONOMOUS COMMUNITY, the semi-federal division of Spain.

Community, the Shorthand for the Euro-pean Community (EC), the core of the EUROPEAN UNION (EU), or for the Union as a whole.

Community acquis *See* ACQUIS COMMU-NAUTAIRE.

comune *See* COMMUNE (Italy).

comunidad autónoma *See* AUTONOMOUS COMMUNITY.

Comunidad de Madrid *See* MADRID COMMUNITY.

Comunidad Valenciana *See* VALENCIAN COMMUNITY.

concentric circles *See* EUROPE OF ....

Concha affair *See* IBERCORP AFFAIR.

Concord [Omónoia] Albanian cultural and political organization. Omónoia was founded underground in 1989, while the communist regime was still in power, to represent the interests of the ethnic Greek community in the south. Its political arm, the Democratic Union of the Greek Minority (BKMG), participated in the multiparty election of March/April 1991, and the BKMG's successor, the PARTY FOR THE DEFENCE OF HUMAN RIGHTS or Human Rights Union, participated in the March 1992 election. The leader is Thomas Kyriakou.

Concord for Latvia - Economic Rebirth *See* NATIONAL HARMONY PARTY.

Concordat between the Italian Republic and the Holy See or **Concordat** Bilateral agreement between Italy and the Roman Catholic Church regulating their mutual relations. Signed on 18 February 1984 and in force from 3 June 1985, the Concordat – the name for a treaty concluded between the pope as head of the Catholic Church and a secular government – rescinded key provisions of its precursor, the 1929 Lateran Treaty. It no longer specified Roman Catholicism as Italy's 'state religion', made religious instruction in schools optional, and reduced the number of religious institutions eligible for tax exemptions and financial contributions. The Italian government continued to give automatic recognition to church marriages, grant full freedom to Catholic schools and pay the salaries of some members of the clergy. The agreement did not affect the status of the Vatican City, the Church's headquarters in Rome, which Italy had recognized as a sovereign state in the 1929 treaty.

Confederal Group of the European United Left Formal name of the EUROPEAN UNITED LEFT (EUL or GUE), a political group of the European Parliament.

Confederation, the Shorthand for Switzerland. Swiss Confederation is the country's official name.

Confederation for an Independent Poland [Konfederacja Polski Niepodległej] (KPN) Polish political party. Founded in 1979, the KPN is strongly nationalist and right-wing. It came fifth in the September 1993 election, gaining 5.8% of the vote and 22/460 seats. The leader is Leszek Moczulski.

Confederation of British Industry (CBI) British employers' association. The CBI was formed in 1965 by the merger of the Federation of British Industries, the British Employers' Confederation and the National Association of British Manufacturers. It has a membership of around 250,000 companies, affiliated directly or indirectly through branch associations. It has close, but not formal, links with the Conservative Party. The president is Bryan Nicholson, the director-general Howard Davies.

Confederation of Business and Industry [Næringslivets Hovedorganisasjon] (NHO) Norwegian employers' association. The NHO was formed in 1989 when the Norwegian Federation of Industry (NIF) and Norwegian Crafts Federation (NHF) merged with the Norwegian Employers' Federation (NAF). It has around 12,000 member companies. The president is Sven Aaser, the director-general is Karl Glad.

Confederation of Christian Trade Unions [Algemeen Christelijk Vakverbond (Dutch), Confédération des Syndicats Chrétiens (French)] (ACV or CSC) Belgian trade-union federation. Founded in 1904, it has 18 affiliated unions with a total membership of around 1.3 million (nearly a third of the labour force). It has close links with the Flemish Christian People's Party (CVP) and the Walloon Christian Social Party (PSC). The president is Willy Peirens.

Confederation of Employers' Associations of Turkey [Türkiye İşveren Sendikaları Konfederasyonu] (TİSK) Turkish employers' association. Founded in 1962, the TİSK has 17 affiliated associations representing 1,600 member companies from all sectors of the economy. The president is Refik Baydur, the secretary-general Kubilay Atasayar.

Confederation of Free Trade Unions of Slovenia [Zveza Svobodnih Sindikatov Slovenije] (ZSSS) Slovenian trade-union federation. The ZSSS was founded in 1990 as the successor to the Association of Trade Unions (ZSS), which had been an arm of the ruling communists. It has 14 affiliated unions with a total membership of around 425,000 (half the labour force). The president is Dušan Semolič.

Confederation of German Employers' Associations [Bundesvereinigung der Deutschen Arbeitgeberverbände] (BDA) German employers' association. Founded in 1950 and based in Cologne, the BDA is an umbrella organization for 46 branch associations and 12 regional associations, which include most of the country's business enterprises. It works closely with the

Confederation of German Industry (BDI), which is primarily concerned with general economic issues. The president is Klaus Murmann, the director-general is Fritz-Heinz Himmelreich.

Confederation of German Industry [Bundesverband der Deutschen Industrie] (BDI) German employers' association. Founded in 1949, the BDI is the largest organization of its kind in Europe, bringing together 40 industrial associations representing around 100,000 businesses. It works closely with the Confederation of German Employers' Associations (BDA), which is primarily concerned with industrial relations and social-policy issues. The president is Tyll Necker, the director-general is Ludolf von Wartenberg.

Confederation of Independent Trade Unions in Bulgaria [Konfederatsiya na Nezavisimite Sindikati v Bŭlgariya] (KNSB) Bulgarian trade-union federation. The KNSB was founded in 1990 as the successor to the Central Council of Trade Unions (TsSPS), which had been an arm of the communist-dominated Fatherland Front. The new federation has declared its independence from all political parties and government. It remains the country's largest labour organization, comprising 75 affiliates with a total membership of around 1.5 million (a third of the labour force). The leader is Krŭstyo Petkov.

Confederation of Industry and Employers [Teollisuuden ja Työnantajain Keskusliitto] (TT) Finnish employers' association. Founded in 1907 as the Finnish Employers' Confederation (STK) and renamed in 1993, the TT brings together around 7,000 enterprises in all major industrial and service branches. The president is Tauno Matomäki, the director-general Johannes Koroma.

Confederation of Irish Industry *See* IRISH BUSINESS AND EMPLOYERS' CONFEDERATION.

Confederation of Malta Trade Unions [Konfederazzjoni ta' Trade Unions Maltin] (KTUM or CMTU) Maltese trade-union federation. Founded in 1958, the CMTU has six affiliated unions with a total membership of 28,000 (a fifth of the labour

force). The president is Salvino Spiteri, the general secretary is Charles Naudi.

Confederation of New Trade Unions of Slovenia *See* INDEPENDENCE.

Confederation of Portuguese Industry [Confederação da Indústria Portuguesa] (CIP) Portuguese employers' association. Founded in 1974, the CIP has around 35,000 members from all branches of the economy. The president is Pedro Ferraz da Costa.

Confederation of Salaried Employees [Toimihenkilö- ja Virkamiesjärjestöjen Keskusliitto] (TVK) Former Finnish trade-union federation. Founded in 1952, the TVK had 20 affiliated unions with a total membership of 400,000 workers (a sixth of the labour force), mainly health- and shopworkers and banking, insurance and clerical staff. The country's second-largest federation, it filed for bankruptcy in September 1992 after incurring huge losses on investments.

Confederation of Socialist Parties of the European Community *See* PARTY OF EUROPEAN SOCIALISTS.

Confédération Suisse and **Confederazione Svizzera** ('Swiss Confederation') Official names of Switzerland in French and Italian.

Conference of the Parliaments Advisory body of the European Union (EU), also known informally as the Parliamentary Assizes or Assizes. Set up under the Maastricht Treaty, which came into force in November 1993, the Conference brings together representatives of the European Parliament and the member states' national parliaments. It is to be consulted by the Council and the European Commission, the EU's main decision-making bodies, on all the 'main features' of the Union. The first informal joint conference of parliamentarians was held in 1990 to discuss the plans for establishing the Union.

Conference on Security and Cooperation in Europe (CSCE) Intergovernmental organization. The CSCE has its roots in the East-West 'detente' of the late 1960s, which sought to reduce tension and build confidence between the two military blocs confronting each other on the continent, the North Atlantic Treaty Organization (NATO) and the Warsaw Pact. Launched in 1972 as a 'process', it brought together all the states of Europe and the Soviet Union – the first major forum to do so – as well as the United States and Canada (both NATO members). The negotiations resulted in the signing of the Helsinki Final Act in 1975, which set out the principles governing relations among signatory states and contained commitments on respect for human rights and on cooperation in a range of fields. Various follow-up conferences were held under the aegis of the CSCE, but the deterioration in East-West relations in the early 1980s entrenched divisions and stalled the 'Helsinki process'. The end of the Cold War and the collapse of communist rule in Eastern Europe and the Soviet Union which transformed the political situation in Europe also prompted a recasting of the CSCE. It was relaunched in 1990 as a fully fledged intergovernmental organization rather than a vague 'process', with the aim of establishing, in due course, a pan-European security system. Since then several institutions have been established and several mechanisms for managing crises and settling disputes have been developed. But the efforts to enhance and expand the CSCE's role have been hampered by several factors, not least that membership carries no legally binding commitments, that all substantive decisions require unanimity, and that new tasks arising from the changes in Europe have been allocated to or taken on by the long-established NATO and, to some extent, the European Union (EU) and Western European Union (WEU).

Aims and objectives. The Helsinki Final Act, signed on 1 August 1975, defines the dual purpose of the CSCE as: (i) consolidating respect for human rights, democracy and the rule of law; and (ii) strengthening peace and promoting unity in Europe. The Charter of Paris for a New Europe (Paris Charter), signed on 21 November 1990, elaborates on this by stressing the commitment to (i) strength-

ening pluralist democracy and observance of human rights and (ii) settling disputes between member states by peaceful means. These objectives are to be achieved on the basis of certain principles guiding relations among the member states, including respect for sovereignty, inviolability of frontiers, respect for human rights etc. The Helsinki Document, signed on 10 July 1992, declares the CSCE a 'regional arrangement' under Chapter VIII of the United Nations Charter, which states that such groupings 'shall make every attempt to achieve peaceful settlement of local disputes ... before referring them to the Security Council'.

Membership. All sovereign states in Europe, the successor states to the Soviet Union as well as Canada and the United States are members of the CSCE, in total 54 states. There were 35 founding members: Austria, Belgium, Bulgaria, Canada, Cyprus, Czechoslovakia, Denmark, East Germany, Finland, France, Greece, Hungary, Iceland, Ireland, Italy, Liechtenstein, Luxemburg, Malta, Monaco, Netherlands, Norway, Poland, Portugal, Romania, San Marino, Soviet Union, Spain, Sweden, Switzerland, Turkey, United Kingdom, United States, Vatican (Holy See), West Germany and Yugoslavia. The reunification of Germany in October 1990 reduced this number to 34. Albania was admitted in June 1991, and Estonia, Latvia and Lithuania in September. Russia assumed the seat of the former Soviet Union and the former Soviet republics of Armenia, Azerbaijan, Belorussia, Kazakhstan, Kirgizistan, Moldavia, Tajikistan, Turkmenistan, Ukraine and Uzbekistan were admitted in January 1992, Croatia, Georgia and Slovenia in March, and Bosnia-Herzegovina in April. The Czech Republic and Slovakia, the successor states to the Czechoslovak federation, were admitted in January 1993, and Macedonia was admitted as an observer in July. Yugoslavia was suspended from CSCE activities in July 1992 because of its involvement in the Bosnian and Croatian civil wars.

Structure and activities. The CSCE's highest body is the biennial summit of heads of state and government. The key decision-making body is the Council of Foreign Ministers (CFM), which meets at least once a year. Its presidency rotates annually among the foreign ministers of the member states. The Council is assisted by the Committee of Senior Officials (CSO), composed of the member states' permanent representatives, which is empowered to implement CFM decisions. Under a procedure for crisis management, an emergency meeting of the CSO must be convened if requested by a quarter of the member states. All substantive decisions must be unanimous.

Other CSCE bodies dealing with aspects of conciliation and problem solving are: the Forum for Security and Cooperation (FSC), which holds continuous negotiations on confidence- and security-building measures and arms-control and disarmament issues; the Conflict Prevention Centre (CPC), based in Vienna (Austria); the Office for Democratic Institutions and Human Rights (ODIHR, the successor to the Office of Free Elections, OFE), based in Warsaw (Poland); and the Office of the High Commissioner on National Minorities, which is primarily responsible for monitoring ethnic conflicts. The CSCE also organizes conferences, seminars and other meetings on specific issues, such as human rights, arms conversion, the role of the armed forces in democratic societies, environmental protection, migration etc. There is also a consultative Parliamentary Assembly, composed of 312 parliamentarians from the member states.

The Office of the Secretary-General, responsible for coordinating activities, is based in Vienna (Austria), and the CSCE secretariat is based in Prague (Czech Republic). The official languages are English, French, German, Italian, Russian and Spanish. The CSCE secretary-general is Wilhelm Höynck (Germany), the director of the secretariat is Nils Eliasson (Sweden); the high commissioner on national minorities is Max van der Stoel (Netherlands).

History. Following on from a Soviet proposal to reduce East-West tensions and agree a series of 'confidence- and security-building measures', the original Conference on Security and Cooperation in Europe was held in three stages between 1973 and 1975 and culminated in the signing of the Helsinki Final Act in August 1975. The first two 'follow-up conferences', held in Belgrade (Yugoslavia) from 1977–78 and Madrid (Spain) from 1980–83, failed to produce any tangible results, largely because of renewed tension between East and West arising from the deployment of new generations of nuclear missiles in Europe (SS-20s, Pershing-IIs, cruise missiles etc). A measure of practical cooperation was achieved at several low-level conferences dealing with mechanisms for the peaceful settlement of disputes, exchange of scientific information (especially in the medical and environmental fields) and security in the Mediterranean region. The Conference on Confidence- and Security-Building Measures and Disarmament in Europe (CDE), aimed at reducing the risk of military confrontation, was held in Stockholm (Sweden) from 1984–86. The Stockholm Document, approved in September 1986, set out procedures for the notification, observation and inspection of military manoeuvres. This marked a significant improvement in East-West relations, made possible by the overhaul of Soviet foreign policy initiated under Mikhail Gorbachev (who had come to power in March 1985). The main result of the third follow-up conference, held in Vienna (Austria) from 1986–89, was the convening of a new negotiating forum on reducing conventional land-based forces. The first section of the Treaty on Conventional Forces in Europe (CFE Treaty), dealing with weapons systems, was signed in November 1990. Three conferences on the so-called 'human dimension' were held between May 1989 and September 1991. The Copenhagen Document approved at the second conference in June 1990 – months after the collapse of communist rule in Eastern Europe – guaranteed the rights of citizens and committed governments to multiparty democracy and the rule of law.

The Paris Charter adopted in November 1990 was widely seen as marking the symbolic end of the Cold War, the period of military and political confrontation that had divided Europe since the late 1940s. It also provided for the transformation of the CSCE into an intergovernmental organization and the establishment of pan-European mechanisms for settling disputes. The CSCE's first permanent institution, a secretariat, was opened in Prague (Czech Republic) in February 1991, and the Office of Free Elections (OFE, later renamed the Office for Democratic Institutions and Human Rights, ODIHR) and Conflict Prevention Centre (CPC) were established later in the year. A conference on the rights of ethnic minorities was held in July 1991. In the same month the first-ever emergency meeting of the Committee of Senior Officials (CSO) was convened to discuss the Yugoslav civil war. The first meeting of the consultative Parliamentary Assembly was held in July 1992. Meeting in Helsinki (Finland) later that month, the heads of state and government adopted the Helsinki Document, which strengthened the existing institutions and established new instruments of conflict prevention and crisis management, including the post of high commissioner on national minorities. The section of the CFE Treaty dealing with troop levels was also signed at this time. (This had been held up primarily by the collapse of the Soviet Union in 1991 and consequent disagreements among the successor states.) In December 1992 a majority of member states agreed to set up a voluntary tribunal to arbitrate and mediate disputes. The CSCE has sought to mediate in a number of regional conflicts, such as that in Nagorno-Karabakh involving Armenia and Azerbaijan in the former Soviet Union, and has initiated a number of missions for fact-finding and monitoring purposes to former Yugoslavia, the Baltic countries, Georgia and elsewhere.

See also entries on specific institutions, organizations, agreements, terms etc.

Conference on Stability in Europe *See* BALLADUR PLAN.

confidence- and security-building measures (CSBMs) *See* CONFERENCE ON SECURITY AND COOPERATION IN EUROPE.

confidence-building measures (Cyprus) *See* CYPRUS QUESTION.

CONFINDUSTRIA *See* GENERAL CONFEDERATION OF ITALIAN INDUSTRY.

Conflict Prevention Centre (CPC) Institution of the Conference on Security and Cooperation in Europe (CSCE). The Centre was set up in 1991 under the Charter of Paris signed the previous year. Conceived as part of a system of 'confidence- and security-building measures' in Europe, its main purpose is to collect and disseminate information on the military forces and weapons systems deployed by CSCE member states. It is based in Vienna (Austria).

Confœderatio Helvetica Latin name for the Swiss Confederation, the official name of Switzerland. It is used on coins, notes, postage stamps etc in place of the equivalents in the country's three official languages, i.e. German, French and Italian. 'Helvetia', Latin for 'Switzerland', is used in the same way.

Congreso and **Congreso de los Diputados** *See* CONGRESS OF DEPUTIES.

Congress [Congrès] French legislative body. The Congress is a joint session of both houses of parliament, the National Assembly and the Senate, convened to amend the constitution. Such amendments can be submitted to a popular referendum or to the Congress, in which case a three-fifths majority is required for approval. The Congress has been convened on five occasions since the adoption of the 1958 constitution, twice in 1993.

Congress of Deputies [Congreso de los Diputados] Lower house of the Spanish parliament, the Cortes. It has 350 members elected for a four-year term by proportional representation in multi-member constituencies based on the 52 provinces. *See also* SENATE.

Congress of State [Congresso dello Stato] Government of San Marino. The Congress is composed of 10 members: three secretaries of state and seven ministers of state. It is elected by the Great and General Council (= parliament) for the duration of its five-year term.

Conseil Constitutionnel *See* CONSTITU-
TIONAL COUNCIL (France).

Conseil d'État *See* COUNCIL OF STATE
(France).

Conseil des États *See* COUNCIL OF STATES.

Conseil National *See* NATIONAL COUNCIL
(Switzerland).

consejero ('councillor') In Spain, a member
of the government in an autonomous
community or region.

Consell General *See* GENERAL COUNCIL.

conselleiro ('councillor' in Galician) In
Galicia (Spain), a member of the regional
government.

conseller ('councillor' in Catalan) In Catalonia (Spain), a member of the regional
government.

Conservative Party British political party.
The Conservatives trace their roots to
the Tories, a political grouping which
emerged in the late 17th century and held
power on several occasions in the 18th
and early 19th centuries. ('Tory Party'
and 'Tories' are still widely used nick-
names for the party.) The name 'Conservative Party' was first used in the early
1830s and the first Conservative government was established in 1834. The party
has been the dominant force in British
politics ever since. Its main rivals were
the Liberals in the 19th century and
Labour since the 1920s. It held power for
31 of the 71 years between 1834 and
1905 and for most of the 1920s and 30s,
either alone or in coalition. Since 1945 it
has been in power from 1951–64, 1970–
74 and since 1979. Broadly centre-right
since the 1940s, the party swung sharply
to the right under the leadership of
Margaret Thatcher (1975–90). Since 1979
it has pursued radical reforms of the
country's economic structure and social-
welfare system by reducing the role of
the state and increasing individual choice.
The party's main bases of support are the
professional and middle classes, but since
1979 it has also secured significant
support among working-class voters in
the south of England. At the April 1992
election it gained 41.9% and 336/651
seats, achieving an unprecedented fourth
consecutive election victory after 1979,
1983 and 1987. The leader is John Major,
the chairman (in charge of organization
and campaigning) is Jeremy Hanley. (The
party's official name, Conservative and
Unionist Party, was adopted in 1912 after
Liberals opposed to autonomy for Ireland
joined the party. The full name fell into
disuse in the 1970s as the links with
Northern Ireland's unionists were severed
because of policy differences.)

Conservative Party [Høyre] (H) Norwegian political party. Founded in 1884,
Høyre ('Right') is the main right-wing
party and has led several centre-right
coalition governments since 1945, most
recently in 1981–86 and 1989–90. It
gained 16.9% of the vote and 28/165
seats at the September 1993 election.
The leader is Kaci Kullmann Five.

Conservative Party [Partia Konserwatywa]
(PK) Polish political party. The PK was
founded in December 1992 by the Forum
of the Democratic Right (FPD), a faction
of the Democratic Union (UD), and two
smaller right-wing parties. It contested
the September 1993 election within the
HOMELAND (Ojczyzna) alliance. It joined
the Eleventh of November Alliance in
December 1993. A right-leaning section
of the party broke away in February 1994
to form the Conservative Coalition (KK).
The leader is Aleksander Hall.

Conservative Party (Sweden) *See* MODER-
ATE COALITION PARTY.

Conservative People's Party [Det Konser-
vative Folkeparti] (KF) Danish political
party. Founded in 1916, the KF became
the country's second largest party in 1981.
It led successive centre-right minority
coalitions from September 1982 until
January 1993 under Poul Schlüter, the
party leader from 1974 until September
1993. At the December 1990 election it
gained 16.0% of the vote and 30/175
seats. The leader is Hans Engell, the party
president is Torben Rechendorf.

Consiglio dei Dodici ('Council of Twelve')
Supreme court of San Marino.

Consiglio dei Stati *See* COUNCIL OF STATES.

Consiglio di Stato *See* COUNCIL OF STATE
(Italy).

Consiglio Nazionale *See* NATIONAL COUN-
CIL (Switzerland).

Constantine of Glücksburg *See* KONSTANTINOS ....

Constantinescu, Emil (1939–) Romanian geologist, academic and politician. He studied law and geology and then lectured in the latter at Bucharest University. After the overthrow of the Ceauşescu regime in 1989 he was elected deputy rector and then rector of the university. A deputy leader of the centrist Civic Alliance Party (PAC), he was the candidate of the opposition Democratic Convention (CDR) alliance in the presidential election of September/October 1992, losing to Ion Iliescu in the second round. In November 1992 he was elected president of the CDR. He has since left the PAC.

Constitutional Council [Conseil Constitutionnel] French judicial body. The Constitutional Council rules on the constitutionality of all draft bills, laws and organic laws (i.e. those elaborating an element of the constitution). The latter must be submitted to it for a ruling. It also supervises arrangements for presidential elections and referendums and oversees the rules of procedure for the National Assembly and the Senate, the two houses of parliament. The Council has nine members serving non-renewable nine-year terms, with a third renewed every three years: three are appointed by the president of the republic, three by the president of the National Assembly and three by the president of the Senate. In addition, former presidents are life members by right.

Constitutional Court (Germany) *See* FEDERAL ....

Constitutional Court [Corte Costituzionale] Italian judicial body. Standing apart from the judicial system, the Constitutional Court rules on the constitutionality of laws (including ones passed prior to the adoption of the current constitution), rules on disputes between state authorities, and sits in judgement on charges brought against the president of the republic and government ministers. It has 15 members serving non-renewable nine-year terms: five are nominated by the president, five are elected in joint session by both houses of parliament, and five are elected by and from senior judiciary bodies.

constitutional party In Northern Ireland (United Kingdom), a political party which works within the electoral process and rejects violence as a means of resolving the province's problems (*see* NORTHERN IRELAND QUESTION). The main ones are the Ulster Unionist Party (UUP) or Official Unionist Party (OUP), Ulster Democratic Unionist Party (DUP), Social Democratic and Labour Party (SDLP) and Alliance Party (AP). These have excluded Sinn Féin, Northern Ireland's other major party, from inter-party talks on the grounds that it condones the violent campaign for the reunification of Ireland waged by the Irish Republican Army (IRA). (The IRA declared a ceasefire in September 1994.)

Contact Group Intergovernmental organization. This informal group was set up by France, Germany, Russia, the United Kingdom and the United States in April 1994 to coordinate their approach to finding a settlement to the civil war in Bosnia-Herzegovina. It provided a broader basis for the international mediation process, hitherto carried on by the European Union (EU) and United Nations (UN), by directly involving Russia and the United States for the first time. The twin aims were to obtain a ceasefire as soon as practicable and to draw up a map dividing the country broadly along ethnic lines. The five foreign ministers, senior officials, the EU and UN mediators, David Owen and Thorvald Stoltenberg, and the Russian and US special envoys, Vitaly Churkin and Charles Redman, were all involved in meetings of the Contact Group. A ceasefire was negotiated in June but crumbled soon afterwards, and a peace plan was tabled in July (*see* CONTACT GROUP PLAN).

Contact Group plan Proposal for a settlement of the civil war in Bosnia-Herzegovina, unveiled by the five-nation CONTACT GROUP in July 1994. The successor to the OWEN-STOLTENBERG PLAN, it provided for the country's division along ethnic lines between the Muslim-Croat Federation (established in March by the Muslim-dominated government and the break-away Croatian Republic of Herzeg-Bosnia) and the breakaway Serbian Republic. Since previous peace plans had foundered on the issue of territory, the Contact Group decided to focus its efforts on this aspect. The core of the plan was a map allocating 51% of the country to the Muslims and Croats and 49% to the Serbs. The latter would thus have to give up about a third of the territory they controlled (around 70% of the total area). Some disputed strategic areas would be placed under United Nations (UN) or European Union (EU) protection and administration: the city of Sarajevo and the towns of Brčko, Doboj, Rogatica and Višegrad under the UN, and the city of Mostar and a corridor linking Sarajevo and the Muslim enclaves of Goražde, Srebrenica and Žepa in eastern Bosnia under the EU. The plan incorporated elements from previous plans concerning demilitarization and the deployment of international armed forces to enforce the settlement. It also reaffirmed certain constitutional principles, but left detailed arrangements for future negotiation. It explicitly provided for the right of secession – a key issue for the Serbian Republic – after a two-year period during which Bosnia-Herzegovina would nominally remain a single state. The Contact Group plan was accepted by the Muslim-Croat Federation, but the Serbs raised a number of objections and effectively rejected the map.

contae *See* COUNTY (Ireland).

contaminated blood affair (France) *See* HIV-INFECTED BLOOD AFFAIR.

contaminated cooking-oil affair Commercial scandal in Spain concerning the sale of industrial oil as cooking oil, and political controversy over the payment of compensation to the thousands of victims. In 1981 around 600 people died in central Spain and up to 25,000 were paralysed or suffered other permanent injuries after consuming adulterated rapeseed oil meant for industrial use which had been sold as olive oil by door-to-door salespeople. Thirteen people, including the men who had imported the oil from France and

arranged for its treatment (to remove a dye) and distribution, were convicted of professional irresponsibility, offences against public health and fraud in May 1989 after a 26-month trial. Their sentences were increased on appeal in April 1992 from a total of 72 years' imprisonment to 260 years'. At this point, 11 years after the events in question, virtually no compensation had been paid to the victims. In August 1994 an examining magistrate indicted seven former government officials, including the chief laboratory technician of the Customs Service, for negligence. They were specifically accused of authorizing the use of the dye-removing agent, flouting rules on the granting of import licences, and failing to spot that the oil was being sold to cooking-oil dealers. If any or all of those charged are convicted, the government may become liable for compensation payments to the victims or surviving relatives. On past precedents for such payments, the total amount may reach 600 billion pesetas (3.8 billion ecus).

conto Portuguese monetary unit, equal to 1,000 escudos.

controlled shock [szok kontrolowany] In Poland, the implementation of radical economic reforms after the end of communist rule aimed at laying the foundations of a market-based economy. The programme was formulated in May 1989 by a team of economists led by Leszek Balcerowicz and advised by several American academics. Also referred to as 'shock therapy', 'big bang' and the Balcerowicz plan, it was adopted by parliament in December and implemented at the start of 1990. Government spending and subsidies were slashed, price controls were removed, money-supply growth was reined in, the currency was devalued to real market levels, import tariffs were reduced, and wages became subject to strict controls. As a result, consumer-goods shortages disappeared, inflation came down sharply, the złoty's exchange rate stabilized, the government budget moved into surplus (temporarily), and the private sector boomed. At the same time, however, output and real incomes plummeted and unemployment soared. By the end of 1991 inflation had come down to 70% (from 586% in 1990), output had fallen by 18%, and unemployment had risen from virtually nil to 12%. The negative consequences had been predicted, although the full impact of the 'shock' and the time lag until the economy would pick up were underestimated. The social and economic cost of the reforms led to popular discontent and political tension. Balcerowicz, who had been appointed finance minister in September 1989, resigned in October 1991. The 'controlled shock' was the first comprehensive economic-reform programme implemented in the former communist countries. Poland thus became the first to be plunged into deep recession, but also the first to record the beginnings of recovery in 1992 and 1993. Although the other countries introduced similar measures in the early 1990s, none opted for virtually overnight marketization.

convener British local government official. 'Convener' is a title used for several offices in Scotland, in particular the leader of a regional or island council (the first tier of local government) and, in many cases, the leader of a district council. S/he is usually the leader of the largest party on the council.

Convention for the Prevention of Marine Pollution by Dumping from Ships and Aircraft or **Oslo Convention** International agreement. Adopted in Oslo (Norway) in 1972 and in force since 1974, this treaty aims to prevent the dumping of waste into the northeast Atlantic Ocean. It has been signed by the 13 littoral states: Belgium, Denmark, France, Germany, Iceland, Ireland, Luxemburg, Netherlands, Norway, Portugal, Spain, Sweden and the United Kingdom. The Convention prohibits the dumping of specified hazardous substances and regulates dumping and incineration operations through specific codes of practice. It is administered by the Oslo Commission (OSCOM), which operates a joint secretariat with the Paris Commission (PARCOM) responsible for a companion treaty, the CONVENTION FOR THE PREVENTION OF MARINE POLLUTION FROM LAND-BASED SOURCES. The secretariat is based in London (United Kingdom).

Convention for the Prevention of Marine Pollution from Land-Based Sources or **Paris Convention** International agreement. Adopted in Paris (France) in 1974 and in force since 1978, this treaty aims to prevent the dumping of waste into the northeast Atlantic Ocean. It has been signed by the 13 littoral states: Belgium, Denmark, France, Germany, Iceland, Ireland, Luxemburg, Netherlands, Norway, Portugal, Spain, Sweden and the United Kingdom. Under a more specific agreement concluded in September 1992, the signatories are obliged to adopt the best available techniques for controlling marine pollution, reduce discharges of toxic waste to harmless levels by the year 2000, and observe a 15-year moratorium on the dumping of radioactive waste. The Convention is administered by the Paris Commission (PARCOM). It operates a joint secretariat with the Oslo Commission (OSCOM), which is responsible for a companion treaty, the CONVENTION FOR THE PREVENTION OF MARINE POLLUTION BY DUMPING FROM SHIPS AND AIRCRAFT. The secretariat is based in London (United Kingdom).

Convention for the Protection of the Mediterranean Sea against Pollution or **Barcelona Convention** International agreement. Adopted in Barcelona (Spain) in 1976 by the European, North African and Middle Eastern states bordering on the Mediterranean, the Convention obliges the signatories to take all necessary measures to prevent pollution of the Mediterranean through dumping, economic activities and discharging waste water. Its first protocol includes a ban on dumping heavy metals, plastic, oil and other toxic substances; the second protocol provides for coordinated action in cases of oil spills and other environmental disasters; the third protocol, adopted in 1980, deals with pollution from land-based sources; the fourth protocol, adopted in 1982, provides for the establishment of protected marine areas. The Convention is administered by the MEDITERRANEAN ACTION PLAN (MAP).

Convention on Long-Range Transboundary Air Pollution or **Geneva Convention** International agreement. Negotiated under the auspices of the United Nations Economic Commission for Europe (ECE), this Convention was signed by 29 European countries, Canada and the United States in November 1979 in Geneva (Switzerland) and came into force in March 1983. It obliges the signatories to limit, reduce and prevent air pollution, to exchange information and research findings, and to give advance warning to others of air-pollution risks. In September 1985 most of the signatories adopted a protocol which committed them to reducing emissions of sulphur dioxide – a major cause of acid rain – from industrial plants and power stations by 30% by 1993 (based on 1980 levels). Called the Helsinki Protocol, this was the first binding international agreement to cut air pollution. A similar protocol on nitrogen oxide emissions was adopted in November 1988. In June 1994 25 European countries and Canada signed a protocol under which they agreed to set stricter targets for cutting sulphur emissions (with Germany pledging a reduction of 87% by 2000, and Britain one of 80% by 2010).

Convention on the Protection of the Marine Environment of the Baltic Sea Area or **Helsinki Convention** International agreement. Adopted in Helsinki (Finland) in 1974 and in force since 1980, this was the first international treaty on the protection of the marine environment against pollution from all sources. It has been signed by all nine littoral states (Denmark, Estonia, Finland, Germany, Latvia, Lithuania, Poland, Russia and Sweden). It obliges the contracting parties to take all appropriate legislative, administrative and other relevant measures to prevent and abate pollution and to protect and enhance the marine environment of the Baltic Sea area. The Baltic Marine Environment Protection Commission or Helsinki Commission (HELCOM) was established to implement the agreement. A second convention, providing for more wide-ranging measures to protect the Baltic, was adopted in April 1992.

Convention on the Right to Asylum or **Dublin Convention** International agreement adopted by the member states of the European Union (EU). The Dublin Convention was signed in June 1990 by 11 of the 12 members of the then European Community (EC) and by Denmark a year later. Providing a framework for cooperation on asylum policy and immigration, it is intended (i) to prevent asylum seekers from applying for asylum in more than one EU member state, (ii) to stop them being sent from country to country, and (iii) to give them a guarantee that their application will be examined by a member state. (The practice whereby asylum seekers lodged applications in several EU member states in turn, thereby achieving a short stay in each, is known as 'orbiting'.) The Convention stipulates that, generally speaking, the country where the refugee arrives is responsible for dealing with his/her request for asylum.

Conventional Forces in Europe Treaty *See* TREATY ON ....

convergence (European Union) *See* ECONOMIC CONVERGENCE.

Convergence and Union [Convergència i Unió] (CiU) Spanish political organization. CiU was formed in 1979 as an alliance of the Democratic Convergence of Catalonia [Convergència Democrática de Catalunya] (CDC) and the Democratic Union of Catalonia [Unió Democrática de Catalunya] (UDC). It advocates full autonomy for Catalonia within a federal Spain, is centre-right in its economic policies, and has conservative views on social issues. It has been in power in Catalonia since regional autonomy was granted in 1980. As the country's largest regional party, it is also influential at national level. It gained 46.4% of the vote and 71/135 seats at the March 1992 regional election, and the equivalent of 5.0% nationally and 17/350 seats at the June 1993 general election. The leader is Jordi Pujol; the leader of the CDC is Miquel Roca and the leader of the UDC is Josep Durán.

convergence criteria (European Union) *See* ECONOMIC CONVERGENCE.

cooking-oil affair (Spain) *See* CONTAMINATED ....

Cools case Murder of André Cools, a leading Belgian politician, in 1991. A senior member of the Walloon Socialist Party (PS), Cools had held a series of ministerial posts since the 1960s, including that of deputy prime minister in 1969–73. He was shot dead in his native Liège in July 1991. The assassin escaped. The murder has been linked to personal jealousy, local party rivalry, right-wing extremists (critical of Cools's role in Belgium's transformation into a federal state), and bribes paid by an Italian firm to secure a government defence contract (*see* AGUSTA AFFAIR).

Cooperation Group to Combat Drug Abuse and Illicit Trafficking in Drugs or **Pompidou Group** Intergovernmental organization. This group was set up in 1971 on the initiative of President Pompidou of France to coordinate a Europe-wide response to the growth in illicit drug trafficking and drug abuse. Its work has been carried out under the aegis of the Council of Europe since 1980. All the Council's members (now nearly all European countries) participate in its activities. Ministerial conferences are generally held every two years. In 1987 a plan of action was agreed which called for the introduction of legislation on the seizure of profits from drugs, improved border controls and increased exchange of information.

Cooperation on Justice and Home Affairs (CJHA) Common policy of the 12 member states of the European Union (EU), conducted by the Trevi Group until the entry into force of the Maastricht Treaty in November 1993. The CJHA is one of the EU's two intergovernmental 'pillars' (the other being the Common Foreign and Security Policy, CFSP). This means that it formally operates outside the supranational structures of the European Community (EC), such as the Commission and the Parliament, although the former in particular is closely involved in its work. It is implemented through the Council of Ministers, the EU's main decision-making body. The Maastricht Treaty defines the following areas as 'matters of common interest' to be covered by the CJHA: asylum policy, rules governing the crossing of the EU's external borders, immigration policy, combating drug addiction, combating fraud on an international scale, judicial cooperation in civil and criminal matters, customs cooperation and police cooperation. The Council may adopt 'joint positions' and take 'joint action' in any of these areas on the basis of unanimity. It is assisted by a coordinating committee of senior officials from the member states. The CJHA's forerunner, the Trevi Group (the name was taken from the French acronym for Terrorism, Radicalism and International Violence), was set up as an informal grouping in 1976 by the interior and justice ministers of the member states to coordinate information gathering on extremist groups and responses to terrorist violence. In the 1980s the scope of its activities was gradually widened to cover other policy areas within the justice and interior spheres, such as drug trafficking, organized crime, public order, political asylum and immigration.

cooperation procedure In the European Union (EU), a method of decision making in which the EUROPEAN PARLIAMENT has limited rights to amend legislative proposals put to it by the Council of Ministers, the organization's main decision-making body. Introduced under the 1987 Single European Act and also known as the 'article 189c procedure' after the relevant section of the treaty, it is used in particular for measures related to the completion of the single internal market. Some spheres, such as fiscal measures and free movement of persons, are specifically excluded. Under the procedure the Parliament may amend or reject, by an absolute majority of its members, a draft piece of legislation or 'common position' agreed by the Council. The Parliament's decisions may ultimately be overridden by the Council by a unanimous vote. *See also* CO-DECISION PROCEDURE *and* DEMOCRATIC DEFICIT.

Coordinating Committee on Export Controls (COCOM) Former intergovernmental organization. COCOM was an informal – and highly secretive – agency set up in 1949 by the member states of the North Atlantic Treaty Organization (NATO), Australia and Japan. Its aim was to prevent the transfer of military technology to communist countries by controlling western exports of strategically important goods such as computers and other electronic equipment. After the collapse of communist rule in Eastern Europe in 1989 and the Soviet Union in 1991 the list of embargoed products was significantly reduced. In November 1993 it was decided to disband the organization and replace it with a new scheme open to the former communist countries and aimed at restricting technology exports to areas of regional conflict. COCOM was formally wound up in March 1994.

Coordination Rurale *See* RURAL COORDI-NATION.

Copenhagen Shorthand for the Danish government. Copenhagen is the capital of Denmark.

Copenhagen Charter of Human Rights *See* COPENHAGEN DOCUMENT.

Copenhagen Document International agreement adopted by the states participating in the Conference on Security and Cooperation in Europe (CSCE). The Copenhagen Document, also called the Copenhagen Charter of Human Rights, was adopted on 29 June 1990 at the end of the second Conference on the Human Dimension. Elaborating aspects of the 1975 Helsinki Final Act, the CSCE's founding document, it guarantees the rights of citizens and commits governments to pluralist democracy and the rule of law. These principles are described as 'essential' for ensuring respect for human rights and fundamental freedoms. They are deemed to encompass regular free elections, the separation of party and state, an independent judiciary, and the right of free expression, organization and assembly. The development of societies along these lines is a 'prerequisite for progress in setting up a lasting order of peace, security, justice and cooperation in Europe', it declares. The Copenhagen Document was considered particularly significant at the time of its adoption, less than a year after the collapse of Eastern Europe's communist regimes (in late

1989) and during a period of accelerating political and economic reforms in the Soviet Union.

Coposu, Corneliu (1915–) Romanian lawyer and politician. A leading member of the National Peasants' Party (PNT), he was arrested by the communist authorities in 1948 and imprisoned for a total of 17 years. When the party was reestablished after the overthrow of the Ceauşescu regime in December 1989, he was elected its leader. He became leader of the more broadly based Christian Democratic National Peasants' Party (PNT-CD) in March 1990 and was elected to parliament two months later. He was also leader of the opposition Democratic Convention (CDR) from 1990–92.

copríncep *See* CO-PRINCE.

COR *See* COMMITTEE OF THE REGIONS.

Corcuera, José Luis (1945–) Spanish electrician, trade-union official and politician. He joined the Spanish Socialist Workers' Party (PSOE) in 1973, when the party was still illegal. He was a leading union organizer during the transition to democratic rule in the late 1970s, and was general secretary of the metalworkers' union affiliated to the General Workers' Union (UGT) from 1977–88. He was elected to parliament in 1979 and appointed minister of the interior in July 1988. He resigned his government post in November 1993 after an anti-terrorist measure he supported was ruled unconstitutional. He resigned his parliamentary seat in May 1994 in connection with the ROLDAN AFFAIR.

COREPER *See* COMMITTEE OF PERMANENT REPRESENTATIVES.

Corps of Carabinieri or **Carabinieri** [Corpo dei Carabinieri] (CC) Italian paramilitary police force. The Carabinieri were formed in 1814 in Savoy and incorporated into the armed forces of unified Italy in 1861. Numbering 111,800, they mainly carry out general police duties, including maintaining public order and investigating crimes. They are answerable to the defence minister in certain matters but to the interior minister regarding their police duties. Their activities overlap with those of national police forces, such as the Public Security Guard (PS) and the Revenue Guard (GdF).

corruption scandals (Italy) *See* ITALIAN....

Corse *See* CORSICA.

Corsica [Corse] Region of France. An island situated in the Mediterranean Sea off the French and Italian coasts, Corsica has an area of 8,680 sq km and a population of 251,000. Around two-fifths of the people are native Corsicans, who speak a form of Italian. The capital is Ajaccio, and the other main city is Bastia. The economy is based on agriculture (fruit and vegetables, wine, sheep farming) and tourism. It is one of France's poorest regions, and there is substantial emigration. In recognition of the island's geographical, economic and social distinctiveness, Corsica has the status of a territorial collectivity [collectivité territoriale], with more extensive powers for the 51-member Assembly [Assemblée] and the executive council than in the other regions. At the regional election in March 1992 the centre-right Corsican Republican Union (URC) gained 16 seats, the autonomist Corsican Nation (Corsica Nazione, CN) nine seats, the centre-right Concerted Action (Agir Ensemble) eight seats, the left-wing Republican Rally (RR) five seats, and the separatist Movement for Self-Determination (MPA) four seats; the URC and RR are allies respectively of the Union for France (UPF) and the Socialist Party (PS) at national level. Corsica was part of the Genoese Republic from the 14th century until 1768, when it was sold to France. Regional identity is very strong. Several separatist guerrilla groups, including the Corsican National Liberation Front (FLNC), have been active since the early 1970s. As part of a programme of decentralization, the island was designated a 'territorial collectivity' in 1982, with a directly elected regional assembly and somewhat wider powers than the other regions. Greater autonomy in the spheres of education, training, transport and tourism was granted in 1991, but a government proposal to recognize a distinct 'Corsican people' was declared unconstitutional.

Corsica Nation [Corsica Nazione (Corsican] (CN) French political organization. Formed in 1991, Corsica Nation is a broad alliance of five parties calling for wide-ranging autonomy for the island within France but rejecting violent action to achieve this end. (Separatist guerrilla groups have been active in Corsica since the early 1970s.) Its main component is the Corsican People's Union (UPC), founded in 1977 by the Association of Corsican Patriots (APC). At the regional election in March 1992 it gained 13.7% of the vote and 9/51 seats. The leader is Edmond Siméoni, a former leader of the UPC.

Corsica Nazione *See* CORSICA NATION.

Corsican National Liberation Front [Front de Libération Nationale de la Corse] (FLNC) French guerrilla group. Formed in 1976 to secure 'recognition of Corsica's national rights', the FLNC was banned as a terrorist organization in 1983. It considers Corsica a 'colony' of France in danger of losing its identity owing to immigration from the mainland and uncontrolled tourist development. It concentrates its violent actions on holiday homes and other property and public buildings. It has denied responsibility for killings of local mayors and other officials, attributing these instead to corrupt property speculators or right-wing groups. Factions within the FLNC announced ceasefires on several occasions in the late 1980s to facilitate dialogue on government plans for autonomy. One faction abandoned violence in 1991 on the grounds that it was counterproductive, but a 'historical' faction and several others remain active. In 1992 FLNC declared its intention to impose a 'revolutionary tax' on companies and wealthy individuals and also declared that it would 'intervene militarily' to counter drug-trafficking-related activities by the Mafia and other criminal organizations.

Corte Costituzionale *See* CONSTITUTIONAL COURT (Italy).

Cortes Generales or **Cortes** Parliament of Spain, composed of the CONGRESS OF DEPUTIES and the SENATE.

Cosa Nostra ('Our Affair') Alternative name for the MAFIA, the Italian crime syndicate based in Sicily. Cosa Nostra was the name adopted by Mafia members who emigrated to the United States in the late 19th century and set up a similar organization there.

Coşea, Mircea (1942–) Romanian economist, academic, civil servant and politician. He began lecturing at the Academy of Economic Studies in Bucharest in 1966. He also held a senior post at the United Nations Economic Commission for Europe (ECE) from 1973–80. A strong supporter of economic reform, he was appointed director of the National Economic Forecasting Agency in 1990. He was brought into the government in August 1993 as a minister of state (= deputy prime minister) and president of the key Council for Economic Strategy and Reform. He does not belong to a political party.

Ćosić, Dobrica (1921–) Yugoslav writer and politician. He was a leading member of the League of Communists until 1968, when he was criticized for his Serb nationalist views. One of the country's best-known novelists, he was elected federal president (a largely non-executive post) in June 1992. In June 1993 parliament removed him from office for exceeding his constitutional powers by pursuing an independent foreign policy. He had previously repeatedly clashed with the federal government and President Milošević of Serbia over Yugoslavia's involvement in the Bosnian civil war.

Cossiga, Francesco (1928–) Italian lawyer, academic and politician. A specialist in constitutional law, he was elected to parliament for the Christian Democratic Party (DC) in 1958. He held several junior ministerial posts from 1966 and became minister of public administration in 1974 and minister of the interior in 1976. He resigned in 1978 after the kidnapping and murder of Aldo Moro, a former prime minister. He was briefly prime minister in 1979–80. He was elected to the Senate in 1983 and also became its president. He was elected president of the republic (a largely non-executive post) in July 1985. He resigned in April 1992, three months before the expiry of his term, in protest at what he called the 'paralysis' caused by the established political parties.

Costa, Raffaele (1936–) Italian lawyer, journalist and politician. He was elected to parliament for the Italian Liberal Party (PLI) in 1976. He held several junior ministerial posts from 1979, and became minister without portfolio with responsibility for European Community and regional affairs in 1992, health minister in February 1993 and transport minister in April. In May 1993 he was also elected PLI leader in succession to Renato Altissimo, who had been accused of breaking the party-funding laws. In August 1993 he also became leader of the new Centre Union (UDC). He was also appointed minister of health in the right-wing coalition formed in May 1994.

Cotroceni Palace [Palatul Cotroceni] Shorthand for the Romanian presidency. The Cotroceni Palace in Bucharest is the official residence of the president and also houses several government departments.

Cotti, Flavio (1939–) Swiss politician. An Italian Swiss, he was chief minister of Ticino canton from 1977–81 and president of the Christian Democratic Party nationally from 1984–86. In December 1986 he was elected to the Federal Council (= government). He was responsible for internal affairs, which includes social affairs and the environment, until March 1993 and has held the foreign-affairs portfolio since then.

Council Institution of the Western European Union (WEU). The Council is the organization's decision-making body, responsible for formulating policy and issuing directives to the subsidiary bodies. It is composed of the member states' foreign and defence ministers. It generally meets twice a year; separate meetings of foreign and defence ministers are also held to deal with specific issues. Substantive decisions must be unanimous. The presidency of the Council is held by each member state for a one-year term. The Council is assisted by the Permanent Council and a secretariat.

Council, the In the European Union (EU), shorthand for the COUNCIL OF THE EUROPEAN UNION or Council of Ministers, the organization's main decision-making body. It is also used sometimes for the EUROPEAN COUNCIL, the summit meeting of the heads of government.

Council for Mutual Economic Assistance (CMEA or COMECON) Former intergovernmental organization. COMECON was founded in 1949 with the aim of facilitating and coordinating economic development on orthodox communist principles. Its original members were the seven communist countries of Eastern Europe: Bulgaria, Czechoslovakia, East Germany, Hungary, Poland, Romania and the Soviet Union. They were later joined by Cuba, Mongolia and Vietnam. In March 1990, in the wake of the collapse of communist rule in Eastern Europe and the new governments' declared intention to develop trade and other economic links with Western Europe, the members agreed to abolish multilateral cooperation and coordination of economic planning, two of COMECON's most important functions. After an attempt to remodel the organization along market-oriented lines failed, it was formally dissolved in June 1991.

council leader (United Kingdom) *See* LEADER OF THE COUNCIL.

Council of Austrian Chambers of Labour *See* FEDERAL CHAMBER OF LABOUR.

Council of Baltic Sea States (CBSS) Intergovernmental organization. The CBSS or Baltic Sea Council – not to be confused with the Baltic Council – was set up in March 1992 following a joint Danish-German initiative. Its aims are to create an economic growth zone in the Baltic Sea region through cooperation in the fields of environment, energy, transport, communications, health, tourism, culture and education. The Council's 10 members are Denmark, Estonia, Finland, Germany, Latvia, Lithuania, Norway, Poland, Russia and Sweden; the European Commission is an observer (on behalf of the European Union, EU). Its main organs are (i) the Council of Foreign Ministers, which meets annually, and (ii) ministerial-level committees. Since its formation the Council's activities have centred on developing ways of reducing pollution in the Baltic Sea and rehabilitating the marine environment, assisting economic reconstruction in the former communist members (Estonia, Latvia, Lithuania, Poland and Russia), and establishing new regional infrastructure links.

Council of Baltic States *See* BALTIC COUNCIL.

Council of Economy and Finance Ministers (ECOFIN) Institution of the European Union (EU), a specialist meeting of the COUNCIL OF THE EUROPEAN UNION or Council of Ministers, the main decision-making body.

Council of Europe (CoE or CE) Intergovernmental organization. Founded in 1949 to protect and strengthen pluralist democracy and human rights and promote awareness of a European cultural identity, the Council of Europe – not to be confused with the European Council, an institution of the European Union (EU) – is the oldest major institution of pan-European cooperation. Originally solely a Western European organization, it has admitted most of the former communist countries in the 1990s. The Council has become a key institutional link between Eastern and Western Europe.

Aims and objectives. Article 1 of the Statute of the Council of Europe, adopted on 5 May 1949 and in force from 3 August 1949, defines the Council's aim as: 'to achieve a greater unity between its members for the purpose of safeguarding and realizing the ideals and principles which are their common heritage and facilitating their economic and social progress' (paragraph a); this aim is to be pursued 'by discussion of questions of common concern and by agreements and common action in economic, social, cultural, scientific, legal and administrative matters' (paragraph b). Article 3 affirms that every member 'must accept the principles of the rule of law and the enjoyment by all persons within its jurisdiction of human rights and fundamental freedoms'.

Membership. The Council has 32 members: Austria, Belgium, Bulgaria, Cyprus, Czech Republic, Denmark, Estonia, Finland, France, Germany, Greece, Hungary, Iceland, Ireland, Italy, Liechtenstein, Lithuania, Luxemburg, Malta, Netherlands, Norway, Poland, Portugal, Romania, San Marino, Slovakia, Slovenia, Spain, Sweden, Switzerland, Turkey and the United Kingdom. The following countries have been admitted since 1989: Hungary in October 1990, Czechoslovakia in February 1991, Poland in November 1991, Bulgaria in May 1992, Estonia, Lithuania and Slovenia in May 1993, the Czech Republic and Slovakia (the successor states to Czechoslovakia) in June 1993, and Romania in November 1993. Albania, Bosnia-Herzegovina, Belorussia, Croatia, Latvia, Macedonia, Moldavia, Russia and Ukraine have 'special guest' status. Yugoslavia's special guest status was withdrawn in June 1992.

Structure and activities. The Council's senior decision-making body is the Committee of Ministers, which brings together the member states' foreign ministers and meets twice yearly. Most of the detailed work is carried out by member states' permanent representatives, who meet monthly. Conferences of specialist ministers are also held regularly. Decisions on all major issues must be unanimous. The Committee is assisted by 11 permanent steering committees and around 90 committees of experts. There are a number of consultative bodies, the most important of which are the Parliamentary Assembly, whose members are drawn from national parliaments, and the Standing Conference of Local and Regional Authorities of Europe (CLRAE). The Council secretariat provides services to all the ministerial, governmental and parliamentary bodies and coordinates activities.

The Council has adopted over 145 conventions and other agreements covering human rights, health, social welfare, education, culture, media issues, legal issues and other areas. The most important conventions are, in chronological order of their adoption: the European Convention for the Protection of Human Rights and Fundamental Freedoms (European Convention of Human Rights), the European Cultural Convention, the European Social Charter, the European Convention on the Suppression of Terrorism, the European Charter of Local Self-Government, the European Convention for the Prevention of Torture and Inhumane and Degrading Treatment or Punishment, and the European Charter for Regional and Minority Languages. Other major conventions deal with social security issues, the legal status of migrant workers, standards for medicinal substances, protection of the architectural heritage, trans-frontier television broadcasting, conservation of wildlife and natural habitats, and trans-frontier cooperation between local authorities. Many conventions deal with more specific issues, such as data protection, money laundering, insider trading, spectator violence at sports events ('hooliganism'), recognition of university degrees, classification of patents, adoption and custody of children, au-pair placement, and protection of pet animals. With the exception of the European Convention of Human Rights (adoption of which is a condition of membership), member states are not obliged to sign up to the conventions, but if they do they are legally bound by them.

Many of the Council's activities are organized through many institutions and programmes. These include the Social Development Fund, which contributes to education, training and development programmes; the European Youth Foundation (EYF) and European Youth Centre (EYC), which support activities for young people; and the Demosthenes programme, which assists the former communist countries of Eastern Europe in carrying out constitutional, legislative and administrative reforms. The Council also organizes a wide range of other educational, cultural and other activities.

Two key bodies attached to the Council are the European Commission of Human Rights and the European Court of Human Rights, which examine and adjudicate cases brought under the European Convention of Human Rights. The Cooperation Group to Combat Drug Abuse and Illicit Trafficking in Drugs (Pompidou Group) is an intergovernmental organization whose work has been carried out under the aegis of the Council of Europe since 1980.

The Council secretariat is based in Strasbourg (France). The official languages are English and French. The secretary-general is Daniel Tarschys (Sweden).

History. The Council of Europe has its roots in the desire for reconciliation in the aftermath of the Second World War (1939–45), which had resulted in millions of deaths and the physical and economic destruction of much of Europe. It was founded in 1949 by 10 Western European countries to promote discussion and, where appropriate, common action and coordination of legislation in the economic, social, cultural, scientific, legal and administrative spheres and in the protection of human rights. Matters related to defence were specifically excluded from its scope. The commitment to the principles of the rule of law, human rights and fundamental freedoms enshrined in the founding statute meant that only the parliamentary democracies were eligible for Council membership. The Eastern European communist states were thus excluded (they did not apply for membership in any case). Portugal and Spain were only admitted after their far-right dictatorships had been replaced by democratic systems in the mid 1970s. Greece was forced to withdraw after the military took power in 1967; it was readmitted after the restoration of democratic rule in 1974. Turkey's membership was suspended for the same reason from 1981–85.

In 1950 the Council adopted its first – and most important – convention, the European Convention of Human Rights. Modelled on the Universal Declaration of Human Rights adopted by the United Nations two years earlier, it went beyond it in that it was binding on its signatories and established legal procedures to ensure compliance. The Convention came into force and the European Court of Human Rights was established in 1953. Other major conventions adopted since then are the European Cultural Convention (adopted in 1954, in force from 1955), the European Social Charter (1961, 1965), the European Convention on the Suppression of Terrorism (1977, 1978), the European Charter of Local Self-Government (1985, 1989), the European Convention for the Prevention of Torture and Inhumane and Degrading Treatment or Punishment (1987, 1989), and the European Charter for Regional and Minority Languages (1992).

In May 1989 the Committee of Ministers adopted a declaration on the future role of the Council which stressed closer cooperation with the European Community (EC, now the European Union, EU) and the Eastern European countries. Since then much of the Council's work has been directed towards helping the former communist countries reform their institutions and legislation. In November 1990 Hungary became the first former communist country to be admitted to the Council. Others were admitted as they were deemed to have introduced multiparty political systems and held free elections. In October 1993 the Council held its first summit meeting of heads of state and government in Vienna (Austria). Its main decision was to streamline and speed up the handling of cases brought under the European Convention of Human Rights. Measures to this end were implemented in April 1994.

See also entries on specific institutions, agreements etc.

Council of Europe Human Rights Prize
Award made every three years by the Committee of Ministers of the Council of Europe to an individual, group or organization in recognition of an outstanding contribution to the cause of human rights as enshrined in the European Convention of Human Rights. The prize was instituted in 1980. Winners have included the Polish trade-union leader and politician Lech Wałęsa and the International Helsinki Federation for Human Rights (IHF) (both in 1989).

Council of European Municipalities and Regions (CEMR or CCRE) Intergovernmental organization at local and regional level, the European arm of the International Union of Local Authorities (IULA). The CEMR was founded as the Council of European Municipalities (CEM) in 1951 and was reorganized as the European section of the IULA in 1991. It is the representative body for the national associations of local and regional authorities of 24 countries. Its primary aim is to further the interests of its members in a range of Europe-wide institutions, in particular the Council of Europe and the European Union (EU). Its structure includes the Assembly of Delegates, which meets every two years, the executive European Policy Committee, and a secretariat. The latter is based in Paris.

Council of Foreign Ministers (CFM) Institution of the Conference on Security and Cooperation in Europe (CSCE). Established under the Paris Charter adopted in 1990, the Council is the organization's central forum for political consultation and decision making. It meets at least once a year and is assisted by the Committee of Senior Officials (CSO). The presidency rotates annually among the foreign ministers of the member states.

Council of Government [Conseil de Gouvernement] Government of Monaco. The four-member Council is headed by the minister of state [ministre d'état].

Council of Ministers Common name for the COUNCIL OF THE EUROPEAN UNION, the EU's main decision-making body.

Council of State (Denmark) *See* STATE COUNCIL.

Council of State (Finland) *See* STATE COUNCIL.

Council of State [Conseil d'État] French advisory and judicial body. Composed of around 200 experts and presided over by the prime minister, the Council is the primary consultative body of the government. It advises ministers on the administrative and legal aspects of proposed legislation in internal, financial and other matters. It also acts as the highest court of administrative law, judging cases of alleged arbitrary government action against citizens and appeals against judgements by administrative tribunals and the Audit Court [Cour des Comptes].

Council of State [Simvoúlio tis Epikráteias] Greek advisory body. The Council advises the president of the republic in the exercise of his/her powers to dissolve parliament and appoint or dismiss a prime minister. It is composed of all former democratically elected presidents, the prime minister, the leader of the opposition and former democratically elected prime ministers.

Council of State [Consiglio di Stato] Italian judicial and advisory body. Composed of senior judges, the Council of State is the ultimate arbiter in administrative disputes and also has various consultative functions. It also elects one member of the Constitutional Court.

Council of State [Staatsrôt (Letzeburgish), Conseil d'État (French)] Luxemburg advisory, legislative and judicial body. Composed of 21 members appointed for life by the grand duke/duchess (generally acting on the advice of the legislature or the Council itself), the Council gives advice on all draft laws, which must be submitted to it, acts as the ultimate arbiter in administrative disputes, and may express an opinion on any question submitted to it by the monarch. Its decisions can be overruled by the Chamber of Deputies.

Council of State [Raad van State] Dutch advisory and judicial body. Composed of up to 28 members appointed for life by the monarch (generally acting on the advice of the prime minister), the Council of State must be consulted on all draft legislation, acts as ultimate arbiter in administrative disputes, and issues advice to the monarch and the government on any question put to it. The monarch is president of the Council but its day-to-day running is in the hands of the vice-president. Members are usually retired politicians, academics, judges or businesspeople.

Council of State (Norway) *See* STATE COUNCIL.

Council of State [Conselho de Estado] Portuguese advisory body. The Council advises the president of the republic, who has considerable powers under the constitution. Its 17 members include the president of the Assembly of the Republic

(= parliament), the prime minister, the president of the Constitutional Tribunal, the superintendent of justice (= senior law officer), the presidents of the regional governments and former presidents of the republic (currently only one); the president and the Assembly nominate five members each.

Council of States [Ständerat (German), Conseil des États (French), Consiglio dei Stati (Italian)] Upper house of the Swiss parliament, the Federal Assembly. The Council has 46 members, two each from the 20 cantons and one each from the six half-cantons. They are elected by means which differ from canton to canton: a simple majority system is used in all except in Appenzell, Glarus and Unterwalden, where councillors are chosen by the Landsgemeinde, the annual open-air citizens' assembly. The Council of States has equal powers with the lower house, the National Council. The two houses elect the members of the Federal Council (= government) in joint session.

Council of the Baltic States *See* BALTIC COUNCIL.

Council of the Euro-Arctic Region Intergovernmental organization. Also known as the Barents Euro-Arctic Council, the Council was set up in January 1993 by Denmark, Finland, Iceland, Norway and Russia to promote regional trade and co-operation in the Barents Sea area. This had been largely disrupted after the 1917 Russian Revolution and during the post-1945 Cold War, when the region was part of the northern front between the Soviet Union and the North Atlantic Treaty Organization (NATO). The intention is to renew ties between local authorities, institutions and industry in trade, technology and education. Specific concerns are (i) protection of the vulnerable Arctic environment and the pollution caused by the dumping at sea of radioactive waste by the former Soviet authorities, and (ii) the welfare of the Lapps, the indigenous people of the region, whose traditional homeland stretches from Norway to the Kola Peninsula in Russia. The Barents region is defined as the Finnish province of Lapland [Lappi], the Norwegian counties of Finnmark, Nordland and Troms, the Russian regions of Arkhangelsk and Murmansk (including the Kola Peninsula) and the Swedish province of Norrbotten. The Council presidency rotates annually among the member states.

Council of the European Communities Former name of the COUNCIL OF THE EUROPEAN UNION, the EU's main decision-making body. It was in use from 1967 until the entry into force of the Maastricht Treaty in November 1993.

Council of the European Economic Area or **EEA Council** Institution of the European Economic Area (EEA), the intergovernmental organization of the European Union (EU) states and six of the seven members of the European Free Trade Association (EFTA) established to create a single market across the 18 countries. Composed of government ministers and a member of the European Commission, the EU's administrative and executive arm, the Council is the EEA's most senior body. Its primary role is to lay down general guidelines for the Joint Committee, which deals with all practical matters. Decisions must be by consensus.

Council of the European Free Trade Association or **EFTA Council** Institution of the European Free Trade Association (EFTA). The Council is the organization's governing body. It meets regularly at ministerial or ambassadorial level; the chair rotates among the member states every six months. The Council's decisions are binding on member states and must be unanimous when they involve new obligations. Each member state has one vote. The Council is assisted by six standing committees, including the Committee of Trade Experts, Committee on Technical Barriers to Trade, Economic Committee and Consultative Committee (which seeks the views of employers, trade unions and others in the member states).

Council of the European Union (CEU) Institution of the European Union (EU), formerly the Council of the European Communities and commonly known as the Council of Ministers. The Council is the major decision-making body of the

Union's three 'pillars', the European Community (EC), Common Foreign and Security Policy (CFSP) and Cooperation on Justice and Home Affairs (CJHA), the latter two being intergovernmental forms of cooperation, i.e. formally outside the EC's supranational structures. Not to be confused with the European Council, the more informal summit meetings of heads of government, the Council of Ministers' role is often summarized in the phrase 'the Commission proposes, the Council disposes'. It consists of representatives of the 12 member states, normally the minister responsible for the subject under discussion. Its membership varies, in other words. A pivotal role is played by the foreign ministers, who are regarded as the member states' main representative in the Council. They meet roughly every month as the General Affairs Council. Ministers of agriculture, economic and financial affairs, justice and home affairs, environment, social affairs, employment, transport etc also meet regularly in specialist councils known as the Council of Agriculture Ministers, the Council of Economy and Finance Ministers (ECOFIN) etc. On occasion the 'specialist' ministers meet jointly with the foreign ministers. The responsible member of the Commission usually also attends meetings. Each member state holds the presidency of the Council for six months, and its foreign minister serves as president. The presidency rotates in two cycles based on the alphabetical order of members in their respective official languages: Belgium, Denmark, Germany, Greece, Spain, France, Ireland, Italy, Luxemburg, Netherlands, Portugal and United Kingdom, and then (reversing the order of pairs of countries to create a variation in the sequence) Denmark, Belgium, Greece, Germany, France, Spain, Italy, Ireland, Netherlands, Luxemburg, United Kingdom and Portugal. (Greece held the presidency from January–June 1994 and Germany from July–December 1994.) The presidency (i) chairs all meetings held within the framework of the Council and the Union as a whole (such as the European Council summits), (ii) coordinates the work of the Council, drafts agendas and timetables meetings, (iii) facilitates policy making by preparing proposals and working out compromises, and (iv) represents the Council at the European Parliament and the EU internationally. Council decisions are taken either by simple majority, qualified majority or unanimity. Simple majority is confined to minor procedural matters. Unanimous voting has traditionally been used for all important decisions. Qualified majority voting (QMV), under which member states have votes broadly weighted according to their populations, was very limited until the 1980s, but it has gradually been extended to include budget decisions, matters relating to the single market and other spheres. The Council is assisted by the Committee of Permanent Representatives (COREPER), composed of the member states' ambassadors. They prepare the ministerial meetings, which are generally held in Brussels. The Council also has its own secretariat. The Council was established in its current form and renamed in November 1993, when the Maastricht Treaty on European Union came into force.

Council of the Republic *See* COUNCIL OF STATE (Greece).

Council of Twelve [Consiglio dei Dodici] Supreme court of San Marino.

councillor or **counsellor** [consejero (Spanish), conseller (Catalan), conselleiro (Galician)] In Spain, a member of the government in an autonomous community or region.

councillor of state (Norway) *See* STATE COUNCILLOR.

counsellor (Spain) *See* COUNCILLOR.

county British administrative division. In England outside the major conurbations and Wales, the 47 counties are the first tier of local government. Each has a council elected for a four-year term. It is formally headed by a chair; the executive leader is called the leader of the council. County councils are primarily responsible for land-use planning, transport, education and social services. In recent years many of their powers have been transferred to bodies appointed by central government. A reorganization of the structure of counties and the lower-level districts, under which single-tier or 'unitary' authorities would be established in some areas, is under consideration.

county [contae, pl. contha] Irish administrative division. Each of the 29 counties has a council [comhairle] elected for a five-year term and an appointed manager. They are responsible for physical planning and a range of local services. In many rural areas they also perform functions nominally the responsibility of lower-level urban districts and boards. The five main cities are administered separately as county boroughs. *See also* REGION (Ireland).

county borough [contaebuirg, pl. -f] Irish administrative division. Each of the five county boroughs (Cork, Dublin, Galway, Limerick and Waterford, the country's main cities) has a council elected for a five-year term and an appointed manager. They are responsible for most local services.

coupon [talonas] Former currency of Lithuania. *See* LITAS.

coupon privatization (former communist countries) *See* MASS PRIVATIZATION.

Court of Auditors of the European Communities or **European Court of Auditors** (CAEC or ECA) Institution of the European Union (EU). Established in 1977 as a successor to two less formal bodies, the Court of Auditors is one of the Union's five main institutions, the others being the Council of Ministers, European Commission, European Parliament and Court of Justice. Its main function is to audit the accounts of the three European Communities (EC), the central 'pillar' of the Union, and their institutions (it thus has no competence in the two intergovernmental pillars outside the EC structures, the Common Foreign and Security Policy, CFSP, and Cooperation on Justice and Home Affairs, CJHA). It examines whether revenue and expenditure have been properly and lawfully received and incurred, and whether financial management has been sound. It prepares an annual report, delivers opinions at the request of an EU institu-

tion and may also, at any time, submit observations on specific questions. It has 12 members, one from each member state, appointed by the Council of Ministers after consultation with the European Parliament. The members elect a president from among their number for a three-year term. The Court is based in Luxemburg. The president is André Middelhoek (Netherlands). (The Court of Auditors is technically an institution of the European Communities and has no competence in the EU's two intergovernmental 'pillars', the Common Foreign and Security Policy, CFSP, and Cooperation on Justice and Home Affairs, CJHA.)

Court of First Instance (CFI) Institution of the European Union (EU). Set up in 1989 to reduce the workload of the COURT OF JUSTICE OF THE EUROPEAN COMMUNITIES (CJEC), the Court of First Instance has jurisdiction over certain categories of cases, such as those arising under the competition rules and those brought by the Commission and other EU officials. Its rulings are subject to appeal to the Court of Justice. It is composed of 12 judges, one from each member state, appointed for a six-year term.

Court of Human Rights *See* EUROPEAN ....

Court of Justice of the European Communities or **European Court of Justice** (CJEC or ECJ) Institution of the European Union (EU). The Court of Justice – not to be confused with the European Court of Human Rights (an institution of the Council of Europe) or the International Court of Justice (part of the United Nations system) – is one of the EU's five main institutions, the others being the Council of Ministers, European Commission, European Parliament and Court of Auditors. It is the supreme judicial body of the three European Communities (EC), the central 'pillar' of the European Union; it has no competence in the two intergovernmental pillars outside the EC structures, the Common Foreign and Security Policy (CFSP) and Cooperation on Justice and Home Affairs (CJHA). The Court's main functions are: (i) to ensure that the laws enacted by the Council, the Commission and other institutions are compatible with the EU treaties; (ii) to interpret EU law and decide on the compatibility of EU and national law; (iii) to rule on disputes arising from EU law; (iv) to adjudicate on alleged breaches by member states of such law; and (v) to advise the Commission on the conclusion of external treaties. A matter may be brought before the Court by an EU institution (in most cases the Commission when a member state fails to implement EU legislation), a member state, or members of the public who consider their rights to have been violated by EU law. The Court's rulings are final on matters of EU law, which takes precedence over national law. The Court has 13 judges, one from each member state and one other, appointed for a six-year term by the Council of Ministers. The majority of cases are heard by a full bench of judges, others are heard by one of the six chambers of between two and four judges, and some are first heard by the subsidiary COURT OF FIRST INSTANCE. The judges are assisted by six advocates-general. Originally set up in 1952 within the framework of the European Coal and Steel Community (ECSC), the Court of Justice was renamed and its remit expanded with the foundation of the European Economic Community (EEC) in 1958. Under the Maastricht Treaty establishing the EU, in force since November 1993, it was given the power to fine states that do not comply with its rulings. The Court sits in Luxemburg. Its president is Ole Due (Denmark).

Court of Justice of the Republic [Cour de Justice de la République] French judicial body. The Court of Justice was set up in March 1994 under an amendment to the constitution approved the previous July. It is responsible for trying members or former members of the government for offences allegedly committed while in office. It is composed of three judges and twelve members of parliament, six each from the National Assembly and the Senate. The power to try government ministers was previously held by the High Court of Justice, composed solely of parliamentarians.

Court of the European Free Trade Association or **EFTA Court** Institution of the European Free Trade Association (EFTA). The Court was set up at the start of 1994 with the launch of the European Economic Area (EEA), the Western-Europe-wide internal market also covering the European Union (EU) countries. Composed of five judges, it is competent to (i) adjudicate actions brought by the SURVEILLANCE AUTHORITY against an EFTA state concerning the implementation, application and interpretation of EEA rules, (ii) settle disputes between EFTA states concerning the EEA, (iii) act as a court of appeal for decisions taken by the Surveillance Authority, and (iv) give advisory opinions to national courts on the interpretation of EEA rules.

Covenant for Poland See ALLIANCE FOR ....

Cp See CENTRE PARTY (Sweden).

CPC See CONFLICT PREVENTION CENTRE.

CR and **ČR** Abbreviations for the Czech Republic and Česká Republika, the country's official name in Czech.

CR (France) See RURAL COORDINATION.

Craxi, Bettino (1934–) Italian journalist and politician. Elected to parliament for the Italian Socialist Party (PSI) in 1968, he was elected party secretary (= leader) in 1976. In 1983 he formed a five-party coalition government in which the PSI was a junior partner to the Christian Democratic Party (DC). Although the party increased its share of the vote in the June 1987 election, the premiership passed back to the DC. In 1992 he was the first senior political leader to be implicated in the party-financing scandal which broke in his native Milan. In December he was formally accused of corruption, breaking the party-financing laws, embezzlement and receiving stolen property. He resigned as party leader in February 1993. He initially denied the allegations, but subsequently agreed to cooperate with magistrates and effectively admitted he had been a key player in the nationwide web of political corruption (*see* ITALIAN CORRUPTION SCANDALS). He did not stand in the March 1994 general election and thus lost his parliamentary immunity. In July 1994 he was convicted of corruption in connection with the BANCO AMBROSIANO AFFAIR and sentenced to 8½ years' imprisonment. In the same month he was also put on trial in two major cases of illegal party funding.

Cresson, Edith (1934–) French economist and politician. She has worked as a business consultant when not holding political office. She joined the Socialist Party (PS) secretariat in 1975 and was elected to the European Parliament in 1979. After the left came to power in 1981 she served as minister of agriculture (1981–83), foreign trade and tourism (1983–84), and foreign trade and industrial relocation (1984–86), and after its return to office in 1988 she became minister of European affairs. She resigned in 1990 and took up a senior post with the Schneider engineering group. She was appointed prime minister by President Mitterrand in May 1991, but was replaced in April 1992 after the PS's defeat in regional elections. In September 1994 she was nominated one of France's members of the European Commission, the administrative and executive arm of the European Union (EU), to serve from January 1995.

Crna Gora *See* MONTENEGRO.

Crna Legija *See* BLACK LEGION.

Croat [Hrvatski] Official language of Croatia. *See* SERBOCROAT.

Croat-Muslim war (Bosnia-Herzegovina) *See* BOSNIAN CIVIL WAR.

Croat-Serb war (Croatia) *See* CROATIAN CIVIL WAR.

Croatia [Hrvatska] Country in southeastern Europe, formerly part of Yugoslavia.

Note: Some of the information below does not reflect the dislocation and disruption caused by the disintegration of Yugoslavia and the civil war in Croatia in 1991/92.

Official data. Name: Republic of Croatia [Republika Hrvatska]; capital: Zagreb; form of government: presidential republic; head of state: president; head of government: prime minister; flag: three horizontal stripes, red, white and blue, with the state emblem in the centre; national holiday: 30 May (Republic Day); language: Croat; religion: none; currency:

kuna (K) (pl. kune) = 100 lipe; abbreviation: HR.

Geography. Croatia has an area of 56,538 sq km. Shaped like a crescent, it is bordered by Slovenia and Hungary in the north, Yugoslavia in the east and far south, Bosnia-Herzegovina in the south, and the Adriatic Sea in the west. The northwest consists of hill lands, Slavonia [Slavonija] in the north is part of the low-lying fertile Pannonian Basin, and Dalmatia [Dalmacija] in the southwest is dominated by the Dinaric Alps and other ranges. Off the coast there are around 1,200 islands and islets. Some 52% of the land is arable, another 18% is covered by pastures and 15% is forested. The main rivers are the Sava, Drava and Danube [Dunav], which in part form the borders with Bosnia-Herzegovina, Hungary and Yugoslavia respectively. The climate is mediterranean along the coast (with hot summers and mild winters) and humid continental in the rest of the country (with hot summers and cold winters); rainfall is heavy along the coast and moderate inland.

Demography. Croatia has a population of 4,821,000. Population density is 85 per sq km (land area). Around half the people live in urban areas, and a sixth in Zagreb. Other major cities are Split, Rijeka, Osijek and Zadar. In ethnic terms 77.9% of the people are Croats, 12.2% Serbs (concentrated in the Krajina region in the southwest, Banija in the centre and parts of Slavonia in the east), 2.2% Yugoslavs (self-description) and 1.0% Slav Muslims (considered an ethnic group in former Yugoslavia). The number of Gipsies is estimated at around 175,000 (3.7% of the total population). There are also small numbers of Hungarians, Italians, Slovaks, Germans and Ruthenians. Around 248,000 people have been displaced as a result of the civil war, and Croatia has also taken in around 281,000 refugees from Bosnia-Herzegovina and Serbia. There is a substantial ethnic Croat community in Bosnia-Herzegovina. The main languages are Croat and Serb, forms of Serbocroat written in the latin and cyrillic script respectively. In religious terms

129

76.5% of the population is nominally Roman Catholic, 11.1% Serbian Orthodox, 1.4% Protestant and 1.2% Muslim.

Sociography. Croatia was among the more developed republics in former Yugoslavia, which scored 0.857 on the United Nations human development index (HDI) in 1990, ranking 37th in the world and 23rd among 27 European countries. There are 21 doctors and 75 hospital beds for every 10,000 people. Education is compulsory between the ages of six and 15. There is one teacher for every 18 students. Enrolment is 43% at the secondary level and 14% at the tertiary level. The literacy rate is 94%. GNP per head (unadjusted for purchasing power) is around US$ 2,000.

Infrastructure and communications. Until 1991 Croatia's transport and communications network was relatively well developed but in need of modernization and extension. The road and rail networks in particular were severely damaged during the civil war. There are 23,310 km of paved roads and 736,000 passenger cars (155 per 1,000 people), 2,440 km of railways and 785 km of navigable waterways. The main ports are Rijeka and Split. The main airport is at Zagreb (Pleso); there are currently no other airports with scheduled services. There are nine daily newspapers, with a combined circulation of 636,000 (133 per 1,000 people). There are 1.11 million radio receivers, 1.03 million television sets and 1.14 million telephones in use (respectively 232, 216 and 235 per 1,000 people).

Economic structure. The Croatian economy is based on manufacturing, agriculture and tourism. Although essentially developed, diversified and trade-oriented, it is in need of major investment, restructuring and reconstruction. The transition from a command to a market-based economy initiated in the late 1980s, the disruption of traditional economic links following the disintegration of the Yugoslav federation in 1991/92 and the damage and disruption resulting from the civil war have led to severe dislocation, steep falls in industrial and agricultural production and the collapse of the tourism indus-

try in particular. Between 1990 and 1993 GDP contracted by around half, inflation averaged around 275% per year (peaking at 662% in 1992) and unemployment rose to around 25%. There were some signs of recovery in 1993.

Services contribute 41% of GDP, industry contributes 47% (manufacturing 37%), and agriculture, forestry and fisheries 12%. Some 32% of the labour force is employed in manufacturing, 13% in trade, 7% in transport and communications and 6% in construction. The main crops grown are cereals (wheat, maize), sugarbeets, oilseeds and potatoes; horticulture (fruit and vegetables, incl. grapes), livestock raising (cattle, pigs) and dairy farming are also important agricultural activities. Forestry and fishing are of regional importance. The main mineral resources are oil, natural gas, bauxite, barite and graphite. The main industries are textiles and clothing (incl. footwear), engineering (incl. shipbuilding) and food processing; other important branches are chemicals, iron and steel and other metalworking, wood processing (paper, furniture), electrical goods, petrochemicals and building materials. Tourism has traditionally been an important source of foreign exchange (contributing around 5% of GNP in 1990). The main energy sources are domestic oil, gas and hydroelectric power and imported fossil fuels; 13% of export earnings are required to cover net fuel imports. The main exports are textiles and clothing (18% of the total, incl. clothing 12%), foodstuffs (12%), transport equipment (10%), fuels (9%), chemicals (8%) and wood and wood products (incl. furniture) (6%); miscellaneous manufactures account for 23% of the total, machinery and transport equipment for 18%, basic manufactures for 18%. The main imports are machinery and transport equipment, chemicals and foodstuffs. The main trading partners are: exports: Slovenia (24%), Italy (20%), Germany (17%), Sweden (7%), Bosnia-Herzegovina; imports: Slovenia (20%), Germany (17%), Italy (17%), Iran (5%), Austria; around half of all trade is with European Union (EU) countries. Net invisible earnings (remittances from Croatians living and working abroad, tourism receipts) account for a significant share of GNP.

The National Bank of Croatia [Narodna Banka Hrvatske] (NBH) is the central bank. The main employers' association is the Association of Industrial Business-people (USP); the main labour organization is the Croatian Trade Union Centre (HUS).

Political structure. Croatia is a republic on the basis of a constitution adopted in December 1990, replacing one defining it as part of the Yugoslav federation. Executive power is shared between the president and the government. The president is directly elected for a five-year term; if no candidate gains an absolute majority of votes, a run-off is held between the top two candidates. The president is the head of state and commander of the armed forces, appoints the prime minister and has a range of other executive powers. The prime minister and council of ministers are responsible for the administration of the country. Legislative power is vested in the bicameral Parliament [Sabor] composed of the House of Representatives [Zastupnički Dom], whose 138 members are elected for a four-year term by a mixed system of proportional representation and majority voting (with a 3% threshold for gaining seats), and the House of Counties [Županijski Dom], whose 63 members are elected on a regional basis; 13 seats in the House of Representatives are reserved for ethnic Serbs and five for other minorities; the president may also appoint up to five members of the House of Counties. All citizens over the age of 18, including those living abroad, are entitled to vote. Judicial power is ultimately vested in the 15-member Supreme Court [Vrhovni Sud] and the 11-member Constitutional Court [Ustavni Sud], both elected for eight-year terms by the House of Representatives on the proposal of the House of Counties. Administratively the country is divided into 21 counties [županija, pl. županije], including the county-level city of Zagreb; the counties are subdivided into 102 districts [općina, pl. općine],

including two autonomous districts (with Serb majorities), and then towns and villages; the historical regions of Dalmatia, Istria and Slavonia have no administrative or political functions.

The main political parties are the Croatian Democratic Union (HDZ), Croatian Independent Democrats (HND, a break-away from the HDZ), Croatian Social Liberal Party (HSLS), Social Democratic Party of Croatia (SDPH, the successor to the Social Democratic Party - Party of Democratic Changes, SDP), Croatian People's Party (HNS), Croatian Party of Rights (HSP), Croatian Farmers' Party (HSS), Istrian Democratic Assembly (IDS) and Serb People's Party (SNS). The main party in the breakaway Republic of Serbian Krajina is the Serbian Democratic Party of Krajina (SDS Krajine or SDSK). At the general election in August 1992 the HDZ gained 44.7% of the vote and 85/138 seats, the HSLS 17.7% and 14 seats, SDP 5.5% and 11 seats, the HNS 6.7% and six seats, the HSP 7.1% and six seats, the HSS 4.3% and three seats, the IDS 3.2% (in alliance with two other parties) and three seats, and the SNS 1.1% and three seats. The government is formed by the right-wing HDZ, with Nikica Valentić as prime minister. Other senior ministers are Ivica Kostović (deputy prime minister, with responsibility for humanitarian affairs), Mate Granić (deputy prime minister, foreign affairs), Vladimir Šeks (deputy prime minister), Borislav Škegro (deputy prime minister), Gojko Šušak (defence), Ivan Jarnjak (internal affairs), Nadan Vidošević (economy) and Bozo Prka (finance). The head of state is President Franjo Tudjman, who was first elected in May 1990 and reelected in August 1992.

Security and international affiliations. The Croatian armed forces number 103,300 (army 95,000, navy 4,000, airforce 300, air defence 4,000). There are also two paramilitary forces, an 8,000-strong border police and a 16,000-strong interior police. Military service is compulsory and consists of 10 months' basic training. Defence spending as a proportion of GDP is among the highest in

Europe. The forces of the Republic of Serbian Krajina number around 50,000. Some 18,000 United Nations troops of the UN Protection Force I (UNPROFOR I) are stationed in the Serb-majority United Nations Protected Areas (UNPAs).

Croatia is a member of the Central European Initiative (CEI) and Conference on Security and Cooperation in Europe (CSCE), as well as the United Nations and its specialized agencies. It has applied for membership of the Council of Europe.

History. Settled by Illyrians, the coastal area of modern Croatia (Dalmatia) was conquered by the Romans in 155 BC, and they extended control over the inland areas in the 1st century BC. During the Europe-wide migrations that triggered the collapse of the Roman Empire in the 5th century, the Germanic Ostrogoths controlled the region until the 550s. In the 7th century the Slavic Croats, migrating from the northeast, settled in the wider region. They converted to Roman Catholicism (while the related Serbs to the east converted to Eastern Orthodoxy). Divided into Frankish and Byzantine spheres of influence in the early 9th century, Croatia became an independent kingdom in 880. Under Petar Kresimir (1058–74) it was an important regional power and included Bosnia and Herzegovina. Civil war broke out after the assassination of one of his successors in 1089, and two years later core Croatia was forced to recognize Hungarian suzerainty while Byzantium regained control over the Dalmatian coast. In 1102 the Croatian and Hungarian crowns were joined in personal union, a link that would be maintained for the next 816 years. During this period Croatia had its own Croat *ban* ('viceroy'), administration and parliament, and generally enjoyed extensive local autonomy. The Dalmatian islands came under Venetian control in the 11th century and the whole region became part of the Venetian Republic in 1420. After the Battle of Mohács in 1526 most of Croatia came under Ottoman Turkish rule, with the northwest falling to the Austrian Habsburgs. From 1578 Austria established 'military frontier' zones in the (largely depopulated) regions bordering the Ottoman Empire, which became subject directly to the emperor and were settled by Serbs fleeing from Turkish domination. The reconquest by Austria of historical Hungary, including Croatia, was completed in 1699. Some social and economic reforms were introduced in the second half of the 18th century. Following the dissolution of the Venetian Republic in 1797 Dalmatia became an Austrian possession. Western Croatia was incorporated into the Illyrian Provinces of the French Empire from 1809–14.

The Croat national movement grew in strength in the 19th century. New autonomy arrangements instituted in 1868, a year after the establishment of the 'dual monarchy' of Austria-Hungary, failed to meet Croat aspirations. The special status of the Serb-populated Military Frontier [Vojna Krajina] was abolished in 1881. As the Habsburg Empire disintegrated at the end of the First World War (1914–18) the Croatian parliament voted to join the other South Slav peoples in the Kingdom of Serbs, Croats, and Slovenes, renamed Yugoslavia in 1929. The new state was destabilized from the outset by dissatisfaction with the centralized administration – the Croatian parliament was dissolved in 1920 – and by rivalry between Serbs and Croats in particular. In 1929 King Alexander II imposed a personal dictatorship. He was assassinated in 1934 by the far-right Croat nationalist Ustasha [Ustaša] movement. During the Second World War (1939–45) the German and Italian armies overran Yugoslavia in 1941, and the Independent State of Croatia (NDH) was established in Croatia and Bosnia-Herzegovina. Modelled on the fascist regimes of Italy and Germany and headed by Ustasha leader Ante Pavelić, the NDH implemented a policy of croatianization culminating in numerous atrocities and genocide against Serbs, Gipsies and Jews, hundreds of thousands of whom were killed. Many others died in the armed resistance to the NDH and the occupying forces and in fighting between rival resistance movements. The communist-dominated Partisans were victorious in the civil war. (Around 1.5 million people, most of them civilians, were killed throughout Yugoslavia in the four war years.)

On liberation in 1945 the Communists, led by Josip Broz Tito, took power throughout Yugoslavia. The monarchy was abolished and Croatia became a constituent republic of the new federation. The regime suppressed political opposition and implemented orthodox communist economic policies. After breaking with the Soviet Union in 1948, it pursued more pragmatic and liberal policies. Croatia was Yugoslavia's second most prosperous republic during the communist period (after Slovenia). A short-lived reform experiment with nationalist overtones, the Croatian Spring, was suppressed in 1971. Like the other republics, Croatia was given greater autonomy under a new federal constitution adopted in 1974. Communist authority crumbled in the late 1980s amid calls for economic and political reforms and Croatian independence. The multiparty election in April/May 1990 was won by the right-wing Croatian Democratic Union (HDZ), and its leader Franjo Tudjman was elected president of the republic. Croatia declared its independence in June 1991. Serbs in the Krajina region thereupon rebelled and, assisted by elements of the Yugoslav federal army, established control over virtually all the Serb-majority areas, comprising nearly a third of Croatian territory. The Republic of Serbian Krajina (RSK) was proclaimed in December 1991. Up to 10,000 people were killed and 400,000 made homeless in six months of fighting. A ceasefire was agreed in January 1992, and the United Nations Protection Force I (UNPROFOR I) was deployed in the Serb-populated areas, designated United Nations Protection Areas (UNPAs). Croatia's independence was recognized internationally in January 1992. The country was admitted to the United Nations the following May and to the Council of Europe in May 1993. The transition to a market-based economy has been hampered by the disruption and dislocation caused by the civil war and the conflict in neighbouring Bosnia-Herzegovina.

See also CROATIAN CIVIL WAR *and entries on specific institutions, organizations, parties, people, terms etc.*

Croatian civil war Armed conflict in Croatia involving the established government and rebel Serbs. The conflict, which broke out in July 1991, has its roots in enmity between Serbs and Croats (*see* FORMER YUGOSLAVIA) and, specifically, Croatia's decision in June 1991 to declare its independence from Yugoslavia. Serbs account for around an eighth of the country's population and form the majority in a belt along the border with Bosnia-Herzegovina, the KRAJINA region. Tension mounted after the right-wing nationalist Croatian Democratic Union (HDZ) won the multiparty election in April/May 1990. Croatia's Serbs strongly favoured continuation of the Yugoslav federation in some form or other. After Croatia declared its independence, local Serb forces, backed by the Yugoslav federal army, took up arms and quickly established control over most Serb-majority areas, comprising nearly a third of Croatian territory. In December the Republic of Serbian Krajina (RSK) was proclaimed with the goal of eventual unification with Serbia. In January 1992 the United Nations brokered a ceasefire and the Serb-majority areas were declared United Nations Protected Areas (UNPAs). Some 14,000 United Nations Protection Force (UNPROFOR) troops were deployed to patrol the ceasefire. Up to 10,000 people were killed during the six months of fighting and 400,000 were made homeless (of whom 250,000 were displaced within Croatia and the remainder fled to Serbia and elsewhere). The town of Vukovar on the Danube river was destroyed during a three-month siege by Yugoslav/Serb forces; the latter also inflicted extensive damage on the historic city of Dubrovnik on the Adriatic Sea, outside the immediate war zone. There was intermittent fighting in 1993. A new ceasefire was agreed in March 1994. Under its provisions UNPROFOR I troops would patrol a buffer zone between the rival forces.

Croatian Community of Herzeg-Bosnia *See* CROATIAN REPUBLIC OF ....

Croatian Defence Association [Hrvatske Obrambeni Savez] (HOS) Croatian and Bosnian paramilitary group. The HOS is the armed wing of the far-right Croatian Party of Rights (HSP), which advocates the creation of a 'Greater Croatia' including Bosnia-Herzegovina and parts of Yugoslavia. Like similar groups, it takes its inspiration from the Ustasha [Ustaša], a Croat nationalist movement founded in 1929 to secure an independent state (realized with German support during the Second World War). The HOS fought alongside the Croatian army in the civil war against local Serb forces which broke out in July 1991. It was banned the following November after the HSP had become strongly critical of the government. It claims a strength of 10,000 and is now mainly active in Bosnia-Herzegovina.

Croatian Defence Council [Hrvatsko Vijeće Obrane] (HVO) Bosnian irregular military force. The HVO is the army of the breakaway Croatian Republic of Herzeg-Bosnia, which was set up in July 1992 in the Croat-populated areas in the southwest. It generally works closely with – but should not be confused with – the Croatian Army (HV), the army of neighbouring Croatia.

Croatian Democratic Community *See* CROATIAN DEMOCRATIC UNION.

Croatian Democratic Union [Hrvatska Demokratska Zajednica] (HDZ) Croatian political party. Founded in 1989, the HDZ is a right-wing nationalist party. It became the dominant force in the republic after the multiparty election in April/May 1990 and has since secured control of nearly all levers of power in the republic. In 1991 and 1992 it also achieved its initial objective, full independence and international recognition for Croatia. At the August 1992 election it gained 44.7% of the vote and 85/138 seats. Franjo Tudjman, now president of the republic, has been party leader since its foundation; the head of the executive committee is Slavko Degoricija. A more centrist wing,

including 16 deputies, left the party in April 1994 to form the Croatian Independent Democrats (HND).

Croatian Democratic Union of Bosnia-Herzegovina [Hrvatska Demokratska Zajednica Bosne i Hercegovine] (HDZ-BiH or HDZ) Bosnian political party. Founded in 1990 and closely linked to the party of the same name in Croatia, the HDZ is the main representative of the Croat community in Bosnia-Herzegovina. At the December 1990 election in the republic it gained 44/240 seats. It has been the moving force behind the self-proclaimed Croatian Republic of Herzeg-Bosnia. The leader is Kresimir Zubak, the party president is Dario Kordić.

Croatian Farmers' Party [Hrvatska Seljačka Stranka] (HSS) Croatian political party. Founded in 1904, the HSS was the main Croat nationalist party in Yugoslavia in the 1920s and 30s. It was suppressed by the right-wing dictatorship during the Second World War and operated from exile during communist rule. It was relaunched in Croatia in 1989. Its programme now combines commitments to private ownership, mutual cooperation, liberal social views and pacifism. At the August 1992 election it gained 4.3% of the vote and 3/138 seats. The leader is Drago Stipac.

Croatian Independent Democrats [Hrvatski Nezavisni Demokrati] (HND) Croatian political party. The centre-right HND was founded in April 1994 by members of the ruling Croatian Democratic Union (HDZ) who objected to its strong nationalism, in particular the government's policy – since abandoned – aimed at incorporating Croat districts of neighbouring Bosnia-Herzegovina into Croatia. They also criticized the 'dictatorial methods' employed by the party leader, President Tudjman. The HND holds 16/138 seats in parliament. The leader is Stipe Mesić.

Croatian National Party *See* CROATIAN PEOPLE'S PARTY.

Croatian Party of Rights [Hrvatska Stranka Prava] (HSP) Croatian political party. Founded in 1861, banned by the Yugoslav authorities in 1929 and relaunched in 1990, the HSP is a far-right nationalist party which advocates the establishment of a 'Greater Croatia' comprising Bosnia-Herzegovina (whose Slav Muslim community it considers Croats of Muslim faith) and parts of Yugoslavia. It has close links with the banned paramilitary Croatian Defence Association (HOS). At the August 1992 election it gained 7.1% of the vote and 5/138 seats. The party split in September 1993, with one wing supporting the original leader Dobroslav Paraga and another backing a new executive committee headed by Boris Kandare as leader and Vlado Jukić as secretary.

Croatian Peasant Party *See* CROATIAN FARMERS' PARTY.

Croatian People's Party [Hrvatska Narodna Stranka] (HNS) Croatian political party. Founded in 1991, the HNS has broadly centrist economic policies and has relatively liberal views on social issues. At the August 1992 election it gained 6.7% of the vote and 6/138 seats. The leader is Savka Dabčević-Kučar.

Croatian Republic of Herzeg-Bosnia or **Herzeg-Bosnia** [Hrvatska Republika Herceg-Bosne] State proclaimed within Bosnia-Herzegovina by representatives of local Croats. Set up as a 'community' in July 1992, four months after the outbreak of the civil war (*see* BOSNIAN CIVIL WAR), it was reconstituted as a 'republic' in August 1993. It is centred on the southwest of the country along the border with Croatia, a region of predominantly Croat settlement. Although Mostar is considered the capital, the assembly and government are based in Grude. The 50,000-strong Croatian Defence Council (HVO) controls around a sixth of Bosnian territory. The dominant political party is the Croatian Democratic Union of Bosnia-Herzegovina (HDZ-BiH or HDZ). Both the HVO and the HDZ work closely with their counterparts in Croatia. The president is Kresimir Zubak. In February 1994 the Bosnian army and HVO signed a ceasefire, and in March the Bosnian parliament and Herzeg-Bosnia assembly agreed to the formation of the FEDERATION OF BOSNIA-HERZEGOVINA.

Croatian Rights Party *See* CROATIAN PARTY OF RIGHTS.

Croatian Social Liberal Party [Hrvatska Socijalno Liberalna Stranka] (HSLS) Croatian political party. Founded in 1989, the HSLS is a centrist party committed to liberal values. At the August 1992 election it gained 17.7% of the vote and 14/138 seats, becoming the second-largest party in parliament and the main opposition force. The leader is Dražen Budiša.

Croatian Union of Herzeg-Bosnia *See* CROATIAN REPUBLIC OF ....

crossbencher In the United Kingdom, a member of the House of Lords, the upper house of Parliament, who is not affiliated to a political party. Crossbenchers sit on benches placed between the government and opposition benches.

crown Anglicized version of various currency names, e.g. the koruna (Czech Republic and Slovakia), króna (Faroe Islands and Iceland), krona (Sweden), krone (Denmark and Norway) and kroon (Estonia). *See individual currency entries.*

crown, the In the parliamentary monarchies (e.g. Belgium, Denmark, Luxemburg, Netherlands, Norway, Spain, Sweden and the United Kingdom), the monarch and the powers invested in him/her, now almost invariably exercised by the government. Actions and decisions taken by 'the crown' are thus taken by the government in the monarch's name.

crown prerogative (parliamentary monarchies) *See* ROYAL PREROGATIVE.

CRS *See* REPUBLICAN SECURITY COMPANIES.

Crvenkovski, Branko (1962–) Macedonian electronics engineer and politician. He joined the League of Communists in 1990 and was elected leader – at the age of 28 – of the relaunched Social Democratic Alliance (SDSM) in April 1991. He became prime minister in September 1992.

Crvenkovski, Stevo (1947–) Macedonian film maker and politician. He worked for the Vardar film studio from the mid 1970s and was its general manager from 1986–91. A member of the Reform Forces of Macedonia - Liberal Party (RSM-LP), he was appointed a deputy prime minister in

September 1992 and also became foreign minister in February 1993.

CS or **ČS** Abbreviation for former Czechoslovakia, used for international vehicle registrations, postal addresses etc. The equivalent abbreviations for the new Czech Republic and Slovakia are CZ and SK or SQ respectively.

CSBMs Abbreviation for 'confidence- and security-building measures'. *See* CONFERENCE ON SECURITY AND COOPERATION IN EUROPE.

CSC *See* CONFEDERATION OF CHRISTIAN TRADE UNIONS.

CSCE *See* CONFERENCE ON SECURITY AND COOPERATION IN EUROPE.

CSCE Final Act Informal name for the HELSINKI FINAL ACT, the first agreement within the Conference on Security and Cooperation in Europe (CSCE).

CSCE process or **Helsinki process** Shorthand for the Europe-wide negotiations on cooperation in security, economic, scientific, technological, environmental and human-rights matters initiated within the CONFERENCE ON SECURITY AND COOPERATION IN EUROPE (CSCE) in 1972. Intended to provide a framework for East-West relations and reduce tension between the two blocs, they initially resulted in the adoption of the Helsinki Final Act in August 1975. The process was continued with a series of follow-up conferences and agreements dealing with specific aspects. The Paris Charter adopted in November 1990 established the CSCE as a formal intergovernmental organization. The terms 'CSCE process' and 'Helsinki process' are still used informally to indicate the scope of its activities.

CSCE troika *See* TROIKA.

ČSFR Abbreviation for Czech and Slovak Federal Republic, the official name of former CZECHOSLOVAKIA. The common abbreviations for the new Czech Republic and Slovakia are CZ and SK or SQ respectively.

CSK Abbreviation, used in banking etc, for the koruna, the currency of the former Czechoslovakia. The equivalent abbreviations for the new Czech and Slovakian koruna are CZK and SKK respectively.

CSO *See* COMMITTEE OF SENIOR OFFICIALS.

CSPEC *See* PARTY OF EUROPEAN SOCIALISTS.

ČSSD *See* CZECH SOCIAL DEMOCRATIC PARTY.

CSU (Germany) *See* CHRISTIAN SOCIAL UNION.

CSU (San Marino) *See* UNITED TRADE UNION CENTRE.

Csurka, István (1934–) Hungarian writer and politician. A leading playwright and novelist, he was briefly banned from publishing after supporting the 1956 uprising against the communist regime. His works were also banned on several occasions between the 1960s and 80s. He was one of the founding members of the centre-right Hungarian Democratic Forum (MDF) in 1987 and was elected to parliament in 1990. The most prominent leader of the MDF's right wing, he founded the Hungarian Way (Magyar Ut) cultural movement in September 1992 and also joined the new Hungarian Justice and Life Party (MIÉP), becoming its joint leader in November 1993.

CSV *See* CHRISTIAN SOCIAL PEOPLE'S PARTY.

CTP *See* REPUBLICAN TURKISH PARTY.

cultural community (Belgium) *See* COMMUNITY.

Cuncolta and **Cuncolta Nazionalista** *See* NATIONALIST COUNCIL.

Cunha, Arlindo (1950–) Portuguese economist, academic and politician. He lectured in economics and agricultural policy from 1980–86. A member of the centre-right Social Democratic Party (PSD), he was appointed a junior agriculture minister in 1986 and became agriculture minister in January 1990.

Cunhal, Alvaro (1913–) Portuguese politician. He joined the then illegal Portuguese Communist Party (PCP) in the early 1930s and became a member of its central committee in 1936. He was repeatedly imprisoned for his political activities during the Salazar regime (1932–68), but escaped and fled into exile in Eastern Europe in 1960. He was elected the PCP's leader in 1961. He returned to Portugal after the overthrow of the dictatorship in 1974 and was briefly minister without portfolio in

1974–75. Under his leadership the PCP remained a strictly orthodox communist party. He resigned as leader in December 1992, but retains considerable influence as head of the party's national council.

CVP (Belgium) *See* CHRISTIAN PEOPLE'S PARTY.

CVP (Switzerland) *See* CHRISTIAN DEMOCRATIC PEOPLE'S PARTY OF SWITZERLAND.

CY Abbreviation for Cyprus, used for international vehicle registrations, postal addresses etc.

Cymru Welsh name for WALES, a constituent country of the United Kingdom.

CYP Abbreviation for the LÍRA or pound, the Cypriot currency, used in banking etc.

Cyprus [Kípros] Country in southeastern Europe or southwestern Asia.

Note: The information below relates to the territory controlled by the internationally recognized government of the Republic of Cyprus and does not cover the self-proclaimed Turkish Republic of Northern Cyprus (TRNC). Provision of separate entries and information for the two states does not imply recognition of the TRNC but reflects the de facto division of the island since 1974.

Official data. Name: Republic of Cyprus [Kipriakí Dimokratía]; capital: Nicosia [Levkosía]; form of government: presidential republic; head of state and government: president; flag: white, with a gold map of Cyprus garlanded with olive branches in the centre; national holiday: 1 October (Independence Day); languages: Greek and Turkish; religion: none; currency: líra (£) (pl. líres) = 100 sént; abbreviation: CY.

Geography. The third largest island in the Mediterranean Sea, Cyprus is situated 80 km south of Turkey, 100 km west of Syria and 350 km southeast of the Greek island of Rhodes. The area of the Republic of Cyprus is 5,896 sq km. The southwest consists of the Troodos Mountains, the southeast of a plateau, while the centre is dominated by the Mesaoria Plain which runs east-west across the island. Some 47% of the land is arable, another 10% is covered by pastures and 18% is forested. The climate is mediterranean, with hot summers and mild winters; rainfall is light.

Demography. Cyprus has a population of 586,000. Population density is 99 per sq km. Most of the people live in the central plain and on the coast, and 64% live in urban areas. The main city is Nicosia; other major centres are Limassol [Lemesós], Larnaca [Lárnax] and Paphos [Néa Páfos]. In ethnic, linguistic and religious terms Cyprus is very homogeneous: virtually all the people are Greek Cypriots and nominally Greek Orthodox Christians. There are small groups of Maronite, Armenian and other Christians. There is a substantial Greek Cypriot community in the United Kingdom. English is widely spoken as a second language.

Sociography. Cyprus scores 0.873 on the United Nations human development index (HDI), ranking 26th in the world and 18th among 32 European countries. There are 21 doctors and 60 hospital beds for every 10,000 people. Education is compulsory between the ages of five and 12. There is one teacher for every 16 students. Enrolment is 84% at the secondary level and 13% at the tertiary level. The literacy rate is 95%. Real annual income per head (in terms of purchasing power) is US$ 9,840.

Infrastructure and communications. Cyprus has a developed transport and communications network; it is a major centre for links with the countries of the Middle East. There are 4,220 km of paved roads and 165,000 passenger cars (288 per 1,000 people). There are no railways or navigable waterways. The main ports are Limassol, Larnaca and Paphos. The main airport is at Larnaca. There are 11 daily newspapers, with a combined circulation of 90,000 (162 per 1,000 people). There are 180,000 radio receivers, 234,000 television sets and 210,000 telephones in use (respectively 314, 408 and 366 per 1,000 people).

Economic structure. The Cypriot economy is developed, relatively diversified and strongly trade-oriented (exports account for more than half of national income). It is based on agriculture, tourism and light industry. Since the late

1980s economic performance has been marked by high growth (averaging 5.7% per year), relatively low inflation (averaging 4.7%) and low unemployment (around 2%), but current accounts moving from surplus into substantial deficit. The foreign debt stands at around US$ 3 billion (50% of GDP).

Services contribute 67% of GDP (trade 19%, finance 16%), industry contributes 27% (manufacturing 15%), and agriculture, forestry and fisheries 6%. Some 22% of the labour force is employed in trade, 17% in manufacturing, 12% in agriculture and 8% in construction. The main crops grown are potatoes and cereals (wheat and barley); horticulture (olives, grapes, fruit and vegetables, esp. citrus fruit) and livestock raising (sheep, goats, pigs) are other important agricultural activities. Forestry is important. The main mineral resources are asbestos, copper, pyrites and limestone. The main industries are food processing (incl. wine and other beverages and tobacco products) and textiles (incl. footwear); other important branches are building materials (esp. cement), wood processing (incl. furniture), metalworking, chemicals and petrochemicals. Tourism is a mainstay of the economy, contributing 22% of GNP (19% net). Shipping, insurance and financial services are also important. The main energy source is imported fossil fuels; 22% of export earnings are required to cover net fuel imports. The main exports, including reexports, are textiles and clothing (28% of the total), potatoes (8%), citrus fruit (7%), footwear (6%), chemicals (5%), fruit and vegetable juices, wine, cigarettes and cement; foodstuffs account for 34% of the total, basic manufactures for 33%. The main imports are machinery and transport equipment, basic manufactures and fuels. The main trading partners are: exports: United Kingdom (21%), Lebanon (13%), Greece (8%), Germany (5%); imports: United Kingdom (13%), Japan (11%), Italy (10%), Germany (10%), United States (8%); half of all trade is with European Union (EU) countries. Net invisible earnings (tourism receipts, shipping and other charges, income from financial services, development assistance) account for 25% of GNP, one of the highest shares in Europe.

The Central Bank of Cyprus [Kentrikí Trápeza Kíprou] is the central bank. The main employers' association is the Employers' and Industrialists' Federation (OEV); the main labour organizations are the All-Cyprus Federation of Labour (PEO) and the Cyprus Workers' Confederation (SEK).

Political structure. Cyprus is a presidential republic on the basis of a constitution adopted in 1960. Executive power is vested in the president, who is directly elected for a five-year term; s/he appoints the members of the government and chairs cabinet meetings. Legislative power is vested in the House of Representatives [Voulí Antiprósopon], whose 56 members are elected for a five-year term by a system of proportional representation. All citizens over the age of 18 are entitled to vote; voting is compulsory in presidential elections. Judicial power is ultimately vested in the 13-member Supreme Court [Anótato Dikastírio]. (The constitutional provisions for Turkish Cypriot participation in government, including the allocation of an additional 24 seats in the legislature and the right to the vice-presidency and a set number of ministerial posts, have been in abeyance since 1963.) Administratively the country is divided into five districts [eparchía, pl. eparchíes], which are subdivided into 27 municipalities.

The main political parties are the Democratic Rally (DISI), Progressive Party of Working People (AKEL), Democratic Party (DIKO), Unified Democratic Union of Cyprus - Socialist Party (EDEK-SK), Democratic Socialist Renewal Movement (ADISOK) and Liberal Party (KF). At the general election in May 1991 DISI and the KF gained 35.8% of the vote and 20/56 seats, AKEL 30.6% and 18 seats, DIKO 19.5% and 11 seats, and EDEK-SK 10.9% and seven seats. The head of state and government is President Glavkos Klerides, who was elected in February 1993. The centre-right government includes members of DISI, DIKO and independents. Senior ministers are Alekos Michaelides (foreign affairs), Faidros Oikonomides (finance), Dinos Michaelides (interior), Kostas Eliades (defence) and Alekos Evangelou (justice and public order).

Security and international affiliations. The Cypriot armed forces number 10,000 (all army). There is also a 3,700-strong paramilitary police force. Military service is compulsory and consists of 26 months' basic training. Some 1,000 Greek troops are stationed in Cyprus, as well as 1,400 United Nations troops of the UN Peace-Keeping Force in Cyprus (UNFICYP) and 4,100 British troops at two sovereign military bases (Akrotiri and Dhekelia).

Cyprus is a member of the Council of Europe and Conference on Security and Cooperation in Europe (CSCE), as well as the Commonwealth, the Non-Aligned Movement (NAM) and the United Nations and its specialized agencies. It has applied for membership of the European Union (EU).

History. During the Late Bronze Age (16th–11th centuries BC) Cyprus was an important link in a trade nexus that also included Egypt, Syria, Crete and other parts of the Eastern Mediterranean region. The island was settled by Greek-speaking peoples from the Peloponnese peninsula from the 11th century onwards. By the early 8th century they had established 11 kingdoms, which recognized Assyrian and later Egyptian suzerainty, although this was largely nominal. In 522 the states became part of the Persian Empire. With the rest of the Empire they fell to Alexander the Great in the 330s. After his death in 323 the strategically important and wealthy island was disputed among his successors, and eventually the Ptolemies of Egypt gained control. Cyprus was annexed by the Roman Republic in 58 BC. Christianity reached the island in the 1st century AD, and Christians may have constituted a majority of the population by the early 4th century. It was allocated to the Eastern Roman Empire in 395 and remained subject to the Byzantine Empire for the next eight centuries. Muslim Arab attacks began in the late 7th century, and from 688–965 the island was in effect a condominium of the Byzantine Empire and the Abbasid Caliphate. After the Third Crusade – one of the many Christian campaigns to wrest Palestine, the 'Holy Land', from Muslim control – a feudal kingdom along European lines was established in 1191. During this period the Genoese and Venetians vied for control of the island's valuable trade. The former held Famagusta, the main port, from 1369–1464, and the Venetian Republic annexed the whole island in 1489. Cyprus was conquered by the Ottoman Turks in 1571. In the following years many Turks and other Muslims settled on the island. There were several uprisings against Ottoman rule during the 18th and 19th centuries.

In 1878 the island's administration was transferred to the British government. The British established several strategically important military bases and formally annexed the island in 1914. At this time around four-fifths of the people were Greek-speaking Orthodox Christians and one-fifth were Turkish-speaking Muslims. Tension between the two communities intensified as support for *énosis* or union with Greece gained ground among Greek Cypriots, while many Turkish Cypriots favoured some form of partition. The British government also rejected union with Greece and was committed to a power-sharing solution. There followed years of negotiations on independence. These were complicated by intermittent intercommunal violence, in particular a guerrilla campaign in the 1950s by the anti-British and pro-*énosis* National Organization of Cypriot Struggle (EOKA). In 1959 the terms of a constitution were agreed, and the leaders of the Greek and Turkish communities, Archbishop Makarios III (the head of the Cypriot Orthodox Church) and Fazıl Küçük, were elected president and vice-president respectively.

Cyprus became an independent republic in 1960, its status guaranteed by the United Kingdom, Greece and Turkey. Intercommunal tension worsened, however, and the power-sharing arrangement collapsed after an outbreak of violence in

1963 in which thousands of Turkish Cypriots were killed. The following year the United Nations Peace-Keeping Force in Cyprus (UNFICYP) was deployed throughout the island. In 1974 *énosis* supporters, backed by the military regime in power in Greece at the time, staged a coup. Turkish troops thereupon invaded and occupied an area equivalent to 37% of its total area. More than 200,000 people, mainly Greek Cypriots, fled or were expelled from their homes during the four weeks of fighting. The Turkish Cypriots, who had already set up separate administrative structures in the mid 1960s, established a functioning government in the north and later proclaimed the Turkish Republic of Northern Cyprus. (This is recognized only by Turkey.) The first UN-sponsored talks on a constitutional settlement were held in April 1975. President Makarios died in office in August 1977. He was succeeded by Spyros Kyprianou of the Democratic Party (DIKO), who was elected in January 1978 and reelected in February 1983. In February 1988 he was defeated by Georgios Vassiliou, who was backed by the communist Progressive Party of Working People (AKEL). In the May 1991 general election the Democratic Rally (DISI) became the largest party, followed by DIKO and AKEL. In February 1993 DISI leader Glavkos Klerides defeated Vassiliou for the presidency. Since 1974, when the island's division deprived government-held Cyprus of a large share of its traditional resources, the economy has been extensively restructured and has enjoyed strong growth.

See also CYPRUS QUESTION *and entries on specific institutions, organizations, parties, people, terms etc.*

Cyprus Guarantee Treaty *See* TREATY OF GUARANTEE.

Cyprus question Controversy over the constitutional status of Cyprus, which has effectively been divided between Greek Cypriot and Turkish Cypriot states since 1974. Cyprus gained its independence from the United Kingdom in 1960 under a constitution which provided for power sharing between the Greek Cypriot majority and the Turkish Cypriot minority. (*For earlier developments, see* CYPRUS: HISTORY.) The Turkish Cypriots withdrew from the arrangements after an outbreak of intercommunal violence in December 1963 and eventually set up many separate administrative structures. In July 1974 Greek Cypriot supporters of *énosis* or union with Greece, backed by the military regime in power in Greece at the time, staged a coup. Turkey thereupon invoked the 1960 Treaty of Guarantee (signed by Cyprus, Greece, Turkey and the United Kingdom), which banned any change in Cyprus's status. Turkish troops invaded the island and occupied the north, an area equivalent to 37% of the island's total area. During the four weeks of fighting around 160,000 Greek Cypriots fled southwards and around 45,000 Turkish Cypriots fled northwards. (Both parts of the island thus became largely homogeneous.) The Turkish Cypriots established a functioning government in the north and unilaterally proclaimed the Turkish Republic of Northern Cyprus in November 1983. This has been recognized only by Turkey. The first negotiations on a constitutional settlement were held in April 1975. Over the years the United Nations has sponsored a series of indirect 'proximity talks' and direct talks between the two sides. Senior Greek and Turkish officials have also met on numerous occasions to discuss the issue, which is a major source of tension between the two countries. The focus of the negotiations has been a UN proposal for the establishment of a 'bicommunal' and 'bizonal' federal state (*see* RESOLUTION 716), supplemented since April 1992 with a 'set of ideas' put forward by the secretary-general, Boutros Boutros-Ghali. In June the UN tabled for the first time a map showing possible territorial allocations within a bizonal state. In July 1993 it proposed a package of 'confidence-building measures' to promote political, economic and cultural cooperation, in particular the reopening of Nicosia's international airport and the resort of Varosha (near Famagusta) under UN administration. The negotiations have effectively been deadlocked for years, largely because of mutual mistrust. The main points of disagreement concern: (i) self-determination, in particular whether the Turkish community should have the right to secede from the federal state; (ii) territory, in particular the allocation of the city of Famagusta and the district around Morphou [Güzelyurt (Turkish)], both under Turkish Cypriot control; (iii) displaced persons, in particular their entitlement to compensation for lost property and the right of return for Greek Cypriot refugees; (iv) government structures, in particular the division of powers between the federal and state levels; and (v) security, in particular the presence of Turkish forces in the north. The stalemate is also due to internal political changes and disagreements on both sides of the divide. In the past, for instance, many Greek Cypriots were opposed to a federal solution, while in recent years support for the establishment of two separate sovereign states has been growing among Turkish Cypriots.

Cyprus Workers' Confederation [Sinomospondía Ergatón Kíprou] (SEK) Cypriot trade-union federation. Founded in 1944, the SEK has seven affiliated federations with a total membership of 53,000 (over a fifth of the labour force). The general secretary is Michalis Ioannou.

CZ Abbreviation for the Czech Republic, used for international vehicle registrations, postal addresses etc.

Czech and Slovak Federal Republic (ČSFR) Official name of former CZECHO-SLOVAKIA.

Czech Republic [Česká Republika] Country in central Europe, formerly part of Czechoslovakia.

Official data. Name: Czech Republic [Česká Republika]; capital: Prague [Praha]; form of government: parliamentary republic; head of state: president; head of government: prime minister; flag: two horizontal stripes, white and red, with a blue triangle with its apex in the centre superimposed in the hoist; national holiday: 28 October (Independence Day); language: Czech; religion: none; currency:

koruna (k) (pl. koruny) = 100 haléřů; abbreviations: ČR and CZ.

Geography. The Czech Republic has an area of 78,864 sq km. Land-locked, it is bordered by Poland in the north, Slovakia in the east, Austria in the south, and Germany in the west. At the centre of the country are two low plateaus, the Bohemian and Moravian basins, which are ringed by the ranges of the Bohemian Massif [České Masív] and the foothills of the Carpathian Mountains in the east. The main rivers are the Moldau [Vltava], Elbe [Labe] and Morava. Some 43% of the land is arable, another 11 is covered by pastures and 33 is forested. The climate is humid continental, with mild summers and cold winters; rainfall is moderate.

Demography. The Czech Republic has a population of 10,339,000. Population density is 134 per sq km (land area). Central Bohemia and central and north-eastern Moravia are the most densely populated regions. Some 71% of the people live in urban areas. The main cities are Prague (population 1.2 million), Brno and Ostrava; other important cities are Olomouc, Zlín (formerly Gottwaldov), Pilsen [Plzeň], České Budějovice and Jihlava. In ethnic terms 81.3% of the people are Czechs, 13.2% Moravians and 3.1% Slovaks; these totals include around 400,000 Gipsies (around 4% of the total population). There are also small numbers of Poles, Germans and Hungarians. The main language is Czech. In religious terms 39.2% of the people are Roman Catholics and 18.5% Protestants, including Czech Brethren (2.0% of the total) and Hussites (1.7%); 39.9%, the highest percentage in Europe, describe themselves as unaffiliated or non-religious.

Sociography. Former Czechoslovakia scored 0.872 on the United Nations human development index (HDI) in 1992, ranking 27th in the world and 19th among 32 European countries. In the Czech Republic there are 38 doctors and 81 hospital beds for every 10,000 people. Education is compulsory between the ages of six and 16. There is one teacher for every 18 students. Enrolment is 45% at the secondary level and 17% at the tertiary level. The literacy rate is 98%. Real annual income per head in Czechoslovakia (in terms of purchasing power) was US$ 6,570 in 1992.

Infrastructure and communications. The Czech Republic has a developed transport and communications network, although it is in need of modernization. There are 49,950 km of paved roads and 2.52 million passenger cars (244 per 1,000 people), 9,451 km of railways and 480 km of navigable waterways. The main (inland) ports are Prague and Děčín. The main airport is at Prague (Ruzyně), and there are five other airports with scheduled services. There are 22 daily newspapers, with a combined circulation of 2.36 million (229 per 1,000 people). There are 4.14 million radio receivers, 4.11 million television sets and 3.24 million telephones in use (respectively 402, 399 and 314 per 1,000 people).

Economic structure. The Czech economy is based on manufacturing, agriculture and mining. Although essentially developed, diversified and trade-oriented (exports account for two-fifths of national income), it is in need of major investment and restructuring. The transition from a command to a market-based economy initiated in 1990 is causing dislocation and has led to falls in industrial and agricultural production, but less so than in neighbouring former communist countries. Between 1990 and 1993 GDP contracted by 21%, inflation averaged 24% per year, and unemployment rose to 4%. Growth resumed in 1993.

Services contribute 36% of GDP, industry contributes 56% (manufacturing around 45%), and agriculture and forestry 8%. Some 33% of the labour force is employed in manufacturing, 11% in trade, 10% in construction and 9% in farming. The main crops grown are cereals (wheat, barley), potatoes, sugarbeets, oilseeds and hops; horticulture (fruit and vegetables, esp. apples), livestock raising (pigs, cattle, poultry) and dairy farming are other important agricultural activities. Forestry is also important. The main mineral resources are lignite, coal, magnesite, lead and iron. The main industries are engineering (industrial machinery, cars etc) and metalworking (esp. iron and steel); other important branches are textiles, food processing, chemicals, wood processing, petrochemicals, building materials and ceramics (glass). Tourism is of regional importance (Prague). The main energy sources are domestic lignite and coal and nuclear power and imported fossil fuels; around 20% of export earnings are required to cover net fuel imports. The main exports are machinery (18% of the total), iron and steel (13%), textiles and clothing (incl. footwear) (12%), chemicals (11%), transport equipment (7%), foodstuffs (6%), electrical equipment, wood products and oil products; basic manufactures account for 32% of the total, machinery and transport equipment for 25%. The main imports are fuels and machinery and transport equipment. The main trading partners are: exports: Germany (33%), Russia, Ukraine and other members of the Commonwealth of Independent States (CIS) (9%), Austria (7%), Italy (6%), Poland (5%); imports: Germany (27%), Russia, Ukraine and other CIS members (18%), Austria (9%), France (6%), United States (5%), Italy (5%); half of all trade is with European Union (EU) countries. (Foreign-trade figures refer to 1992 and exclude trade with Slovakia.)

The Czech National Bank [Česká Národní Banka] is the central bank. The main employers' association is the Confederation of Industry of the Czech Republic (SPČR); the main labour organization is the Czechomoravian Trade Union Confederation (ČMKOS).

Political structure. The Czech Republic is a parliamentary republic on the basis of a constitution which took effect when it became an independent state on 1 January 1993. The head of state is the president, who is elected for a five-year term by a joint session of the legislature; s/he is commander-in-chief of the armed forces, appoints the prime minister and has some other powers. Executive power is vested in the prime minister and the council of ministers. Legislative power is vested in the bicameral Parliament of the

Czech Republic [Parlament České Republiky], composed of the 200-member Chamber of Deputies [Poslanecká Sněmovna] elected for a four-year term by a system of proportional representation, and the 81-member Senate [Senát] elected for a six-year term by a system of majority voting, with a third of seats renewed every two years; there is a 5% threshold for gaining seats in both houses. All citizens over the age of 18 are entitled to vote. Judicial power is ultimately vested in the Supreme Court [Nejvyšší Soud], the Supreme Administrative Court [Nejvyšší Spravní Soud] and the Constitutional Court [Ústavní Soud], all of whose members are appointed by the president for 10-year terms with the consent of the Senate. Administratively the country is divided into eight regions [kraj, pl. -e], including the region-level city of Prague; the regions are subdivided into 73 districts [okres, pl. -y] and communes. The historical regions of Bohemia, Moravia and Silesia have no administrative or political functions.

The main political parties are the Civic Democratic Party (ODS), Left Bloc (LB), Czech Social Democratic Party (ČSSD), Christian Democratic Union - Czechoslovak People's Party (KDU-ČSL), Liberal National Social Party (LSNS, the successor to the Czechoslovak Socialist Party, ČSS), Association for the Republic - Republican Party of Czechoslovakia (SPR-RSČ) or Republicans (Republikány), Civic Democratic Alliance (ODA), Christian Democratic Party (KDS), Communist Party of Bohemia and Moravia (KSČM), Czechomoravian Centre Party (ČMSS, the successor to the Movement for Self-Governing Democracy of Moravia and Silesia, HSDMS), Agrarian Party (ZS), Green Party (SZ) and Free Democrats (SD, the successor to the Civic Movement, OH); the Left Bloc (LB) and Liberal Social Union (LSU) were electoral alliances dominated by the KSČM and composed of the ČSS, ZS and SZ respectively. At the general election in June 1992 the ODS and KDS gained 29.7% of the vote and 76/200 seats, the

LB 14.1% and 35 seats, the ČSSD 6.5% and 16 seats, the LSU 6.5% and 16 seats, the KDU-ČSL 6.3% and 15 seats, the Republicans 6.0% and 14 seats, the ODA 6.0% and 14 seats, the HSDMS 5.9% and 14 seats, and the OH 4.6% and no seats. The government is a right-wing coalition formed by the ODS, KDU-ČSL, ODA and KDS, with Václav Klaus as prime minister. Other senior ministers are Josef Lux (deputy prime minister, agriculture), Ivan Kočárník (deputy prime minister, finance), Jan Kalvoda (deputy prime minister), Josef Zieleniec (foreign affairs), Karel Dyba (economy), Jan Ruml (interior), Jiří Novák (justice), Antonín Baudyš (defence) and Stanislav Bělehrádek (economic competition). The head of state is President Václav Havel, who was elected in January 1993.

Security and international affiliations. The Czech armed forces number 106,500 (army 41,900, airforce 35,600, general 29,000); they are due to be reduced to around 65,000. Military service is compulsory and consists of 12 months' basic training.

The Czech Republic is a member of the Central European Initiative (CEI), Conference on Security and Cooperation in Europe (CSCE), Council of Europe and Visegrad Group, as well as the United Nations and its specialized agencies.

History. The earliest known inhabitants of the modern Czech Republic were the Celtic Boii – from whom the name Bohemia is derived – and Cotini. They were supplanted by the Germanic Marcomanni and Quadi in the 1st century BC. Other Germanic tribes passed through the region during the Europe-wide migrations from the 4th century, and from the 6th century it was settled by Slavs migrating from the east. The Avars, a nomadic Asian people, held sway until their defeat by the Frankish Kingdom in the 790s. Several Slav states emerged in Bohemia and Moravia. Great Moravia was a major regional power in the 9th century, dominating Bohemia and parts of modern Poland, Slovakia and Hungary. It was destroyed by the Magyars or Hungarians in 906. Christianity became the dominant religion around this time. The Přemysl dynasty controlled all of Bohemia by 955 and acquired Moravia in 1029. Over the next two centuries Bohemia developed close political and economic links with the Holy Roman or German Empire. It became a kingdom within the Empire in 1086 and the king became one of the seven electors who chose the emperor. In the 12th and 13th centuries an influx of German merchants and farmers, officially encouraged, provided a major boost to the economy. Under Ottokar II (1253–78) Bohemia was briefly the dominant regional power. Four years after the death of the last Přemysl in 1306, the nobles elected John of Luxemburg as king. His son Charles became king in 1346 and Holy Roman emperor in 1355. He moved the imperial administration to Prague, capital of the Empire's most prosperous state and considered Europe's third city (after Constantinople and Paris). The Bohemian crown lands included, besides Moravia, Lusatia and Silesia (until 1618 and 1742 respectively). In 1402 the priest and scholar Jan Hus launched a mass religious and political reform movement. Its appeal to the Czech-speaking peasants and antipathy towards the German and germanized elite gave the movement nationalist overtones, strengthened after Hus's execution for heresy in 1415. The Hussites survived several imperial 'crusades' and secured a favourable peace in 1436. The civil and religious wars, which continued until 1485, weakened the crown, strengthened the nobility (which had acquired ecclesiastical estates) and devastated the countryside. Bohemia passed to the Habsburgs when Ferdinand of Austria was elected king in 1526. The Hussites and other Protestant groups rebelled against Catholic Habsburg rule in 1618 – the event that sparked the Europe-wide Thirty Years' War (1618–48) – but were defeated in 1620. The Habsburgs abolished traditional privileges and pro-scribed all non-Catholic faiths. In the second half of the 18th century some social and economic reforms were intro-duced and the state administration was centralized.

In the 19th century a Czech national movement emerged and relations between Czechs and local Germans worsened. At this time Bohemia and Moravia were the Empire's most industrialized regions. The Czechs proclaimed their independence at the end of the First World War (1914–18). They dominated the new state of Czecho-slovakia, which comprised the Slav-majority crown lands in the north of the old Habsburg Empire, i.e. the Czech lands of Bohemia and Moravia as well as Slovakia and Ruthenia, which had been part of Hungary since the 10th century. A democratic constitution was adopted in 1920. Coalition governments including the main Czech and Slovak parties were the norm. The dominant political leaders of the period were Tomáš Masaryk, presi-dent from 1918–35, and Edvard Beneš, foreign minister from 1918–35 and presi-dent from 1935–38. The German minority became increasingly disaffected, and after the National Socialists (Nazis) took power in Germany (1933) it began to agitate for incorporation into the Third Reich. Yielding to pressure from the major Euro-pean powers, Czechoslovakia in 1938 ceded Sudetenland, the German-majority areas on the rim of Bohemia and Moravia, to Germany under the Munich Agreement. In 1939 Slovakia declared its indepen-dence, and rump Bohemia-Moravia was occupied by German troops and declared a German 'protectorate'. At the end of the Second World War (1939–45) Czecho-slovakia was occupied by Soviet troops, the pre-1938 borders were restored (with the exception of Ruthenia, which was ceded to the Soviet Union), and the remaining Sudeten Germans were expelled.

The Czechoslovak Communist Party (KSČ) became the largest party in the 1946 election and formed a coalition government. In 1948 the KSČ took power and declared the country a 'people's republic'. The regime suppressed political dissent, nationalized the economy, intro-duced central planning and allied itself closely with the Soviet Union. In 1968 a new leadership headed by Alexander Dubček introduced far-reaching political and economic reforms. The Prague Spring was crushed after seven months when Soviet and other Warsaw Pact troops invaded the country. In the only surviving measure from the reform programme, the unitary state was reconstituted as a federation of the Czech and Slovak republics in 1969. Economic stagnation in the 1980s led to some liberalization measures. Growing calls for political reform in 1989 culminated in mass demonstrations and a general strike in November. In what was dubbed the 'velvet revolution', a majority non-communist government was appointed in December and Václav Havel, a leading writer and dissident, was elected president. The new government initiated a process of political and economic transformation. In February 1990 the Soviet Union agreed to withdraw its troops. The anti-communist Civic Forum (OF) and Public Against Violence (VPN), its counterpart in Slovakia, won the multiparty election in June. Czechoslovakia was admitted to the Council of Europe in January 1991. At a new election in June 1992 the Civic Democratic Party (ODS) under Václav Klaus became the largest party in the Czech Republic and formed a right-wing coalition committed to a rapid transition to a market-based economy. (The OF had fragmented in 1991.) With the new Slovak administration committed to self-determination for the republic, the two governments negotiated the federation's dissolution, and the Czech Republic became an independent state at the start of 1993.

See also entries on specific institutions, organizations, parties, people, terms etc.

Czech Social Democratic Party [Česká Strana Sociálně Demokratická] (ČSSD) Czech political party. One of Europe's oldest socialist parties, founded in 1878, the ČSSD was one of Czechoslovakia's leading parties in the 1920s and 30s. It was forced to merge with the Communist Party in 1948. Revived in 1990, it gained 6.5% of the vote and 26/200 seats in the Czech parliament at the June 1992 election. The leader is Miloš Zeman.

Czechia and **Czechland** Alternative names for the Czech Republic. Following the dissolution of the Czechoslovak federation at the end of 1992, the French, German and other language equivalents of 'Czechia' were readily accepted in many countries, but its use in the English-speaking world remains rare. 'Čechy' is the Czech name for Bohemia, the country's dominant historical region.

Czechomoravia [Českomorava] Slogan associated with those who advocate the conversion of the Czech Republic into a federation of Bohemia [Čechy] and Moravia or Moravia-Silesia, the country's main historical regions.

Czechomoravian Centre Party [Českomoravská Strana Středu] (ČMSS) Czech political party. The ČMSS was founded in 1990 as the Movement for Self-Governing Democracy of Moravia and Silesia (HSDMS) and launched as a party under the new name in January 1994. It advocates full autonomy for the Moravia-Silesia region and the country's reconstitution as the 'Czechomoravian republic'. At the June 1992 election the HSDMS gained 5.9% of the vote and 14/200 seats in the Czech parliament. The leader is Jan Kryčer.

Czechomoravian Trade Union Confederation [Českomoravská Konfederace Odborových Svazů] (ČMKOS) Czech trade-union federation. The ČMKOS was founded in 1990 as the successor of the Czech section of the Revolutionary Trade Union Movement (ROH) of Czechoslovakia, which had been an arm of the communist regime. Its affiliated unions represent around 2.1 million workers (just under two-fifths of the labour force). The president is Richard Falbr.

Czechoslovakia [Československo] Former country in central Europe, now the Czech Republic and Slovakia. Czechoslovakia was created in 1918 from the former Austro-Hungarian territories of Bohemia and Moravia, known collectively as the 'Czech lands', and Slovakia. Although Czechs and Slovaks speak closely related languages, their separate histories – the Czech lands had been part of the Holy Roman Empire and Austria, Slovakia part of Hungary – gave them distinct cultural, political and economic identities. This caused friction from the country's birth. It was dismembered during the Second World War, with Bohemia and Moravia becoming a 'protectorate' of Greater Germany and Slovakia a nominally independent state under German domination. The communists took control in 1948. The country was reconstituted as a federation in 1969 to meet Slovak demands for greater autonomy. After the collapse of the communist regime in 1989 calls for sovereignty and independence gained ground in Slovakia. When parties favouring independence won a majority in the republic's parliament at the 1992 elections, it was agreed to dissolve the federation by the end of the year. On 1 January 1993 the Czech Republic and Slovakia were constituted as Czechoslovakia's successor states. *See also* CZECH REPUBLIC: HISTORY *and* SLOVAKIA: HISTORY.

CZK Abbreviation for the KORUNA, the Czech currency, used in banking etc.

D Abbreviation for Germany, used for international vehicle registrations, postal addresses etc. It is taken from Deutschland, the country's name in German.

D Abbreviation for the DENAR, the Macedonian currency.

D Abbreviation for the DINAR, the Yugoslav currency.

D'Alema, Massimo (1949–) Italian politician. He was active in local and regional government for the Italian Communist Party (PCI), now the Democratic Left Party (PDS), until his election to parliament in 1987. He has held a range of senior posts in the PCI and PDS, including leader of the youth section, editor of the newspaper *L'Unità* (1988–90), coordinator of the parliamentary party and deputy leader. He was elected party leader in succession to Achille Occhetto in July 1994.

D'Antoni, Sergio (1946–) Italian trade-union official. A law graduate, he joined the Sicilian branch of the Italian Confederation of Workers' Unions (CISL), one of the country's main labour organizations, in 1970. He became regional secretary in 1976. He moved to the national secretariat in 1983. He was elected CISL's deputy general secretary in 1989 and general secretary in April 1991.

d'Estaing, Valéry Giscard *See* GISCARD D'ESTAING, ...

D-Mark or **D-mark** Abbreviation for Deutsche Mark and DEUTSCHMARK, the German currency.

D'Onofrio, Francesco (1939–) Italian lawyer, academic and politician. He has lectured in constitutional law, political institutions and public law at several universities. He was elected to parliament for the Christian Democratic Party (DC) in 1983. After the party was discredited because of its involvement in the corruption scandals which broke in 1993, he rejected the need for a relaunch. When this did happen, he joined the breakaway Christian Democratic Centre (CCD). He was appointed minister of education in the right-wing coalition formed in May 1994.

D'66 *See* DEMOCRATS 66.

Dabčević-Kučar, Savka (1923–) Croatian economist, academic and politician. She has lectured at the University of Zagreb since 1950. During the 1960s she held a range of senior government posts in Croatia (then part of Yugoslavia). She was a leading reformist within the League of Communists, but was barred from political activity after the suppression of the 'Croatian Spring' in 1971. In January 1991 she was elected leader of the new centrist Croatian People's Party (HNS).

DAF *See* DANISH EMPLOYERS' CONFEDERATION.

Dafiment and Jugoskandić affairs Financial and political scandal in Yugoslavia concerning the collapse of the country's two largest private banks. In 1991 the Dafiment and Jugoskandić banks began to offer very high rates of interest (eventually up to 15% per month) on hard-currency deposits. This attracted millions of small investors who sought to protect themselves against the rampant hyper-inflation caused above all by Yugoslavia's involvement in the Bosnian and Croatian civil wars and the consequent imposition of economic sanctions by the United Nations (in May 1992). The high interest payments were the sole source of income for many people. The scheme was of dubious legality and carried high financial risks, but had the strong backing of the Milošević government, since it helped to contain social unrest at a time of economic collapse. In March 1993 Jugoskandić's owner, Jezdimir Vasiljević, fled to Israel and all the bank's branches were closed. Its collapse put great strain on its larger rival, Dafiment. It immediately slashed its interest rates, thus abandoning the high-interest scheme, but it was also forced to close down the following month. In the political fallout from the affair, the Serbian trade and tourism minister and his predecessor were arrested on fraud charges, and the then president of the Federal Assembly (= parliament) and former Serbian prime minister, Radoman Božović, was also implicated. In May 1994 Dafiment's former owner, Dafina Milanović, claimed that leading politicians, judges and civil servants as well as paramilitary leaders had been involved in financial irregularities connected to the bank's collapse.

Dáil Éireann or **Dáil** ('Assembly of Ireland' or 'House of Representatives') Lower house of the Irish parliament. The Dáil – the English equivalents are hardly ever used – has 166 members elected for a five-year term by proportional representation (using the single-transferable-vote system) in 41 multi-member constituencies.

Dalli, John (1948–) Maltese accountant and politician. He worked for a management consultancy until his election to parliament for the centre-right Nationalist Party in 1987. He was appointed minister of economic affairs in 1990 and minister of finance in February 1992.

Danish Employers' Confederation [Dansk Arbejdsgiverforening] (DAF) Danish employers' association. Founded in 1896, the DAF has around 29,000 members in all branches of industry and the services. The chairman is Niels Laurits Thygesen, the director-general Poul Erik Pedersen.

Danish Trade Union Confederation [Landsorganisationen i Danmark ('National Organization in Denmark')] (LO) Danish trade-union federation. Founded in 1898, the LO has 32 affiliated unions with a total membership of 1.47 million (around two-fifths of the labour force). It has close links with the Social Democratic Party (SD). The president is Finn Thorgrimson.

Dankert, Piet (1934–) Dutch teacher and politician. He was elected to parliament for the Labour Party (PvdA) in 1968 and to the European Parliament in 1977. He was president of the latter from 1982–84. In November 1989 he was appointed a junior foreign minister, with special responsibility for European affairs. He was reelected to the European Parliament in June 1994.

Danmark Danish name for Denmark.

Dannebrog ('Danish Banner') National flag of Denmark. Adopted by King Valdemar II, who ruled from 1202–41, it consists of a white Scandinavian cross (with an elongated right arm) on a red background. The design served as a

model for the flags of all other Nordic countries.

Danube Commission (DC) Intergovernmental organization. The Commission was established in 1948 to supervise shipping regulations on the navigable stretches of the Danube, one of Europe's major waterways. The eight member states are Austria, Bulgaria, Hungary, Romania, Slovakia, Russia, Ukraine and Yugoslavia; Germany has guest status. The secretariat is based in Budapest (Hungary).

Danube Countries' Working Assembly or **Danube Group** Intergovernmental organization at regional and national level. Established in 1990, the Danube Group is an informal working group comprising 21 regions and countries through which the Danube flows: four Austrian provinces, seven Hungarian counties, Croatia, the Serbian republic of Yugoslavia, four Bulgarian regions, three Romanian counties, and Moldavia.

Danube Group *See* DANUBE COUNTRIES' WORKING ASSEMBLY.

Daskalov, Stanislav (1952–) Bulgarian economist, civil servant and politician. A specialist in international economic relations, he has worked for a state import company, in the diplomatic service (1988–91) and as a junior trade minister (1991–93). He was appointed foreign minister in the non-party government in June 1993.

Davies, Howard (1951–) British civil servant, management consultant and employers' representative. He worked in the diplomatic service from 1973–76, at the Treasury (= finance ministry) from 1976–82, for the McKinsey management consultancy from 1982–87, and as controller of the Audit Commission, an independent body set up to monitor local authorities, from 1987–92. In July 1992 he was appointed director-general of the Confederation of British Industry (CBI), the main employers' association.

DC *See* ITALIAN PEOPLE'S PARTY.

DC *See* DANUBE COMMISSION.

DDR Abbreviation for Deutsche Demokratische Republik ('German Democratic Republic'), the official name of former

EAST GERMANY. It was used for international vehicle registrations, postal addresses etc.

De Benedetti, Carlo (1934–) Italian businessman. He was managing director of the family engineering firm, CITBF, from 1959–72 and chairman of the Gilardini group from 1972–76. After a brief stint as managing director of the Fiat car concern he became president of the Compagnia Industriali Riunite (CIR) in September 1976. This conglomerate, now one of Italy's largest, has extensive interests in the engineering, electronics, financial and publishing sectors; it owns the Olivetti electronics concern (acquired in 1978) and the daily newspaper *La Repubblica.* In May 1993 he admitted paying bribes to politicians to obtain public-sector contracts over a 10-year period, and the following November he was specifically charged with authorizing bribes of up to 10 billion lire (5.1 million ecus) to obtain contracts for Olivetti equipment from the state postal service. In the same month he was cleared of any wrongdoing in the BANCO AMBROSIANO AFFAIR.

de Boer, Margreeth (1939–) Dutch social worker, administrator and politician. A member of the Labour Party (PvdA), she was active in local and provincial government in her native North Holland from 1970–92. From 1980–87 she worked for Amsterdam and then Zaanstad city council as director of sheltered workshops for handicapped people. In 1993 she was appointed royal commissioner (= senior executive officer) of Drente province. She became minister of housing, physical planning and environment in the left-right coalition formed in August 1994.

de Carvalho, Otelo Saraiva *See* SARAIVA DE CARVALHO, ...

De Galan, Magda (1946–) Belgian lawyer and politician. In the 1970s and 80s she worked in the private sector and for the National Labour Council, an advisory body bringing together employers and trade unions. A member of the Walloon Socialist Party (PS), she was elected mayor of Forest, a suburb of Brussels, in 1989 and was also elected to parliament in 1991. She was appointed minister for social affairs and health in the French Community (an element of Belgium's federal structure) in 1992 and minister of health, environment and social integration at national level the following year. She became minister of social affairs in January 1994.

de la Concha affair *See* IBERCORP AFFAIR.

de Larosière, Jacques (1929–) French economist, civil servant and banker. He held several senior positions in economic ministries from 1971–78. He was director of the International Monetary Fund (IMF) from 1978–86 and governor of the Bank of France, the central bank, from 1987 until August 1993, when he was appointed president of the European Bank for Reconstruction and Development (EBRD).

De Lorenzo, Francesco (1938–) Italian doctor and politician. He has worked as a surgeon and taught at medical school. Elected to parliament for the Italian Liberal Party (PLI) in 1983, he was environment minister from 1986–89 and health minister from 1989 until February 1993. He resigned when his father was arrested on corruption charges. He was later accused of vote buying and extorting payments from drug companies in exchange for government contracts. His trial opened in June 1994.

de Marco, Guido (1931–) Maltese lawyer and politician. A lecturer in criminal law and a human-rights specialist, he was elected to parliament for the centre-right Nationalist Party in 1966. He was its general secretary from 1972–77 and has been deputy leader since then. When the party returned to power in May 1987 he became deputy prime minister. He has also been minister of the interior and justice (1987–90), foreign affairs and justice (1990–92) and foreign affairs (since February 1992).

De Michelis, Gianni (1940–) Italian chemist, writer and politician. A lecturer and later professor of chemistry, he was elected to parliament for the Italian Socialist Party (PSI) in 1976. He has been minister of state-owned industries (1980–83), labour (1983–87), deputy prime minister (1988–89) and foreign minister (1989–92). Soon after he left office in June 1992 he was accused of violating the party-funding laws, embezzlement and misappropriation of public funds. In mid 1994 he was on trial in two major illegal party-funding cases.

De Mita, Ciriaco (1928–) Italian politician. He was elected to parliament for the Christian Democratic Party (DC) in 1963. In the 1970s he served as minister of trade and industry (1973–74) and foreign trade (1974–76) and as minister without portfolio with responsibility for southern Italy (1976–79). He was the party's general secretary from 1982–89 and its president, a largely honorary post, from 1989–92 (with a brief interruption in 1990 when he resigned over the party's media policy). He was also prime minister of a five-party coalition government in 1988–89. He was asked to head a new commission on constitutional reform in September 1992, but resigned the following March after his brother was charged with fraud. Two months later he was implicated in the same scandal, involving the embezzlement of funds allocated for reconstruction work after a major earthquake in his native Naples region in 1980. When the DC split in January 1994, he joined the reformist Italian Popular Party (PPI), staying on as its leader in the Senate (= upper house) until August.

de Villiers, Philippe (1949–) French civil servant and politician. He worked in the arts and the media in the 1970s and early 80s. He joined the interior ministry as a local-government administrator in 1978. A member of the centre-right Republican Party (PR), he became a junior minister of culture and communications in 1986 and was elected to parliament the following year. In the 1990s he became increasingly critical of his party's general policies and support for closer European integration in particular. He was a founding member of the Movement for Basic Values (Mouvement pour les Valeurs) and co-sponsor of Another Europe (L'Autre Europe). He was elected to the European Parliament in June 1994.

de Vries, Bert (1938–) Dutch economist, academic and politician. He has worked for the tax service and the Philips electronics company and has lectured at Rotterdam's Erasmus University. Elected to parliament for the Christian Democratic Appeal (CDA) in 1978, he became its parliamentary leader in 1982. In November 1989 he was appointed minister of social affairs and employment, a post he held until the party lost power in August 1994.

de Vries, Gijs (1956–) Dutch politician. He was leader of the youth wing of the right-wing People's Party for Freedom and Democracy (VVD) from 1976–78 and president of the European Young Liberals from 1978–80. He lectured in international relations from 1981 until his election to the European Parliament in 1984. He was elected leader of the Liberal, Democratic and Reformist Group (LDR) in July 1994.

decision In the European Union (EU), one of the three binding legal instruments for implementing policy or decisions (the others being the 'directive' and the 'regulation'). A 'decision' is a formal agreement or ruling adopted by the Council or the Commission addressed to one or more specifically named governments, organizations or individuals. It usually clarifies or elaborates a general piece of legislation in relation to a specific case.

decommunization In the former communist countries, the process of removing public officials and others closely associated with the communist regimes from positions of authority. Special targets were officers of the security agencies, which played a key role in suppressing dissent during the communist period (from the late 1940s until 1989) and operated extensive networks of informants to this end. They have generally been barred from holding public office and other senior posts in economic and social life, either for a certain period or for life. Some have been brought to trial for alleged crimes committed before 1989. In some countries (e.g. Albania and Bulgaria) former senior government leaders have been prosecuted on specimen charges of abuse of power, misappropriation of public funds and human-rights violations. In many countries the process has been given a formal basis through the adoption of legislation providing for the SCREENING or vetting of all senior public officials and others in sensitive positions. *See also* NOMENKLATURA.

deepening In the European Union (EU), a term associated with those who argue that the EU should concentrate on strengthening its internal cohesion rather than enlarging its membership. It is contrasted with 'broadening' or 'weakening'. In one sense the deepening/broadening argument is contrived, since in practice both strategies have been pursued since the early 1990s (through the adoption of the Maastricht Treaty on European Union and the opening of accession negotiations with Austria, Finland, Norway and Sweden). But it reflects a more profound argument about the EU's future between proponents and opponents of further integration. The latter assume that the Union's enlargement to 20 or more member states over the next decade will inevitably lead to a looser structure.

Defence Planning Committee (DPC) Institution of the North Atlantic Treaty Organization (NATO). The DPC deals with most defence matters, including collective defence planning, and also gives guidance to NATO's military authorities. In the defence field it has the same competence as the North Atlantic Council (NAC), the organization's senior decision-making body. It is composed of the defence ministers of the member states or their permanent representatives. Since France is not part of NATO's integrated military structure, it is not represented on the DPC.

Dehaene, Jean-Luc (1940–) Belgian lawyer and politician. A senior adviser in various ministries from 1972–81, he was appointed minister of social affairs and institutional reform (dealing with the devolution of power to the Flanders and Wallonia regions) in 1981. He was elected to parliament for the Flemish Christian People's Party (CVP) in 1987 and became a deputy prime minister and minister of communications and institutional reform in the centre-left coalition

formed in 1988. In March 1992 he took over as prime minister from his party colleague Wilfried Martens.

Déi Gréng *See* GREENS (Luxemburg).

Dekaeptá Noémvris *See* SEVENTEENTH OF NOVEMBER REVOLUTIONARY ORGANIZATION.

Dekélia *See* AKROTIRI AND DHEKELIA.

Delamuraz, Jean-Pascal (1936–) Swiss politician. A law graduate, he was mayor of Lausanne from 1974–81. He was a member of parliament for the centre-right Radical Democratic Party from 1975–83. He became a member of the Federal Council (= government) in 1984, with responsibility for defence until January 1987 and for economic affairs since then.

Delcroix, Leo (1949–) Belgian politician. He taught personnel policy and labour law and worked as a personnel manager before becoming national secretary of the Flemish Christian People's Party (CVP) in 1984. Elected to the Senate in 1991, he was appointed defence minister in March 1992.

Delors, Jacques (1925–) French economist, civil servant and politician. He worked at the Bank of France (= central bank) from 1945 and held a number of senior civil-service and advisory posts from 1962. In 1976 he became the Socialist Party (PS) spokesman on international economic affairs. When the left gained power in 1981 he was made minister of the economy and finance. In January 1985 he was appointed president of the European Commission, the administrative and executive arm of the European Community (EC), now the European Union (EU).

DEM Abbreviation for the DEUTSCHMARK or mark, the German currency, used in banking etc.

Demaci, Adem (1936–) Yugoslav writer. An ethnic Albanian from the Kosovo region, he has been a champion of the rights of his community and an opponent of Serb domination since the 1950s. He was imprisoned for a total of 28 out of 32 years between 1958 and 1990. His work has been banned since he published his first novel in 1958.

demi-canton *See* HALF-CANTON *and* CANTON (Switzerland).

Demirel, Süleyman (1924–) Turkish hydraulic engineer and politician. From 1949 until 1964 he worked on a range of major hydroelectric, irrigation and electrification projects. He was head of the Directorate-General of Hydraulic Works from 1955–60 and was attached to the Middle East Technical University as a consultant and lecturer from 1962–64. He was elected to parliament for the centre-right Justice Party (AP) in 1961 and became its leader in 1964. He was appointed deputy prime minister in 1965, and became prime minister after the AP gained an absolute majority at the election in October. Returned to office in 1969, he was forced to resign by the military in 1971. He headed coalition governments from 1975–77 and from 1979 until the military took power the following year. The AP was disbanded and Demirel, along with other senior politicians, was banned from political activity for 10 years. Following the lifting of the ban (which had been widely ignored) in 1987, he was elected leader of the new True Path Party (DYP) and elected to parliament. After the DYP came first in the October 1991 election he formed a coalition with the Social Democratic People's Party (SHP). In May 1993 he was elected president of the republic in succession to Turgut Özal and thereupon resigned as prime minister and DYP leader.

Democratic Action Party [Stranka Demokratske Akcije] (SDA) Bosnian political party. Founded in 1990, the SDA is the main representative of the Slav Muslim community in Bosnia-Herzegovina. It gained 86/240 seats at the election in December 1990 and then formed a coalition government. In the early stages of the civil war, which broke out in March 1992, it remained strongly in favour of maintaining Bosnia-Herzegovina as a unitary, multiethnic state. Since then it has had to shift its stance and now accepts the country's eventual partition. It supports economic reforms and takes a conservative line on social issues. The leader is Alija Izetbegović, president of the republic.

Democratic Alliance [Alleanza Democratica] (AD) Italian political party. The AD was founded as a loose grouping in October 1992 to offer voters 'honest' alternatives to the government parties (discredited by a series of corruption scandals) and to reform the country's political system. It was formally constituted as a party in May 1993. The AD includes many members of the old centrist parties, in particular the Italian Republican Party (PRI), Italian Socialist Party (PSI) and Italian Liberal Party (PLI). It is committed to free-market economic policies and has liberal views on social issues. It contested the March 1994 general election within the Progressive Alliance and gained 1.2% of the vote and 17/630 seats. The leader is Willer Bordon.

Democratic Alliance of Kosovo *See* DEMOCRATIC LEAGUE OF ....

Democratic Alliance Party of Albania [Partia Aliancë Demokratika e Shqipërisë] (PADSh) Albanian political party. The PADSh was founded in October 1992 as a breakaway from the ruling Democratic Party (PDSh), which it accuses of reneging on its programme of economic reforms. It has adopted broadly centre-right policies and holds 6/140 seats in parliament. The leader is Neritan Ceka.

Democratic and Social Centre [Centro Democrático y Social] (CDS) Spanish political party. The centrist CDS was founded in 1982 as the successor to the Union of the Democratic Centre (UDC), which had formed the government during the transition to democracy in the late 1970s. The CDS's support declined steadily in the 1980s and sharply after the resignation in 1991 of party leader Adolfo Suárez, who had been prime minister from 1976–81. At the October 1989 general election it gained 7.9% of the vote and 14/350 seats, but at the June 1993 election it gained only 1.8% and no seats. The leader is Rafael Calvo Ortega.

Democratic Community of Vojvodina Hungarians *See* DEMOCRATIC UNION OF ....

Democratic Confederation of San Marino Workers *See* UNITED TRADE UNION CENTRE.

Democratic Convention of Romania
[Convenție Democratic din România] (CDR) Romanian political organization. The CDR is an alliance of opposition parties advocating a more rapid transition to a market economy and more extensive political reforms. Its name and membership have changed repeatedly since its foundation in 1990. At the September 1992 election it comprised 18 parties, including the Christian Democratic National Peasants' Party (PNT-CD), the Civic Alliance Party (PAC), two wings of the National Liberal Party (PNL) which subsequently merged to form the Liberal Party 1993 (PL'93), the Romanian Social Democratic Party (PSDR) and the Romanian Ecology Party (PER). Gathering most of its support in the main cities, the CDR came second with a total of 20.0% of the vote and 82/341 seats. The alliance has since been joined by the Hungarian Democratic Union (RMDSz). The leader is Emil Constantinescu. *See also individual party entries.*

Democratic Convergence of Catalonia
See CONVERGENCE AND UNION.

democratic deficit In the European Union (EU), the perceived lack of democratic control over decision making in the organization, specifically the European Parliament's lack of legislative powers and the inability of national parliaments to hold decision makers to account. The problem arises from the EU's unique structure and evolution: decision-making powers are concentrated not in the Parliament, which was originally merely a consultative body, but in the Council of Ministers; and the Council's meetings, like those of a national government, are closed. In response to calls for reducing the 'democratic deficit' in the then European Community (EC) and strengthening its 'democratic legitimacy', the Parliament was given limited legislative powers under the 1986 Single European Act through the COOPERATION PROCEDURE, and equal powers in 14 policy areas under the Maastricht Treaty, which came into force in November 1993, through the CO-DECISION PROCEDURE. *See also* TRANSPARENCY.

Democratic French Confederation of Labour [Confédération Française Démocratique du Travail] (CFDT) French trade-union federation. The CFDT was founded in 1919 as the French Confederation of Christian Workers (CFTC) and reorganized along secular lines in 1964. It has around 2,300 affiliated unions, organized in 22 trade federations, 22 regional organizations and 102 departmental and overseas organizations. Their total membership has been falling steadily since the mid 1970s, and now stands at around 560,000 (2.5% of the labour force). The CFDT has traditionally had close links with the Socialist Party (PS). The general secretary is Nicole Notat.

Democratic Labour Party of Lithuania [Lietuvos Demokratinė Darbo Partija] (LDDP) Lithuanian political party. The LDDP was founded in 1990 by the majority reformist wing of the Lithuanian Communist Party (LKP), which had lost the multiparty election earlier in the year to the Reform Movement (Sąjūdis). Its programme is now mainstream left-wing: it supports the market economy but objects to a hasty dismantling of existing economic and social structures. The party returned to power at the October/November 1992 election, gaining 44.7% of the vote and 72/141 seats. The party leader is Adolfas Šleževičius. Algirdas Brazauskas, the former leader and now president of the republic, retains considerable influence.

Democratic League of Kosovo [Demokratski Savez Kosovo (Serb), Lidhja Demokratike e Kosovës (Albanian)] (DSK or LDK) Yugoslav political party. Founded in 1989, the LDK is the main representative of the majority Albanian community in the Kosovo region of Serbia. It initially called for full autonomy for the region within a federal Yugoslavia, but since the collapse of the old federation and the imposition of a policy of 'serbianization' by the Serbian authorities it has become radicalized and is now calling for 'self-determination' (implying eventual unification with Albania). In May 1992 the LDK gained 76.4% of the vote and 96/130 seats in the unofficial election for the assembly of the self-proclaimed Republic of Kosovo. It boycotted the Yugoslav and Serbian elections in December 1992 and the Serbian election in December 1993. The leader is Ibrahim Rugova.

Democratic Left (Ireland) *See* DEMOCRATIC LEFT PARTY.

Democratic Left Alliance [Sojusz Lewicy Demokratycznej] (SLD) Polish political organization. The SLD was founded in 1991 as an electoral alliance of the Social Democratic Party of the Republic of Poland (SdRP), the successor to the communist Polish United Workers' Party (PZPR), the All-Poland Trade Unions Alliance (OPZZ), the largest trade-union federation, and several other parties and unions. Campaigning on a mainstream left-wing programme committed to a market-based economy and social justice, it gained 20.4% of the vote and 171/460 seats at the September 1993 election, becoming the largest single group in parliament. It formed a coalition with the Polish Peasant Party (PSL) the following month. The leader is Aleksander Kwaśniewski.

Democratic Left Party [Strana Demokratické Levice] (SDL) Czech political party. The SDL has its roots in the Democratic Left (DL) movement, which contested the June 1992 election within the Left Bloc (LB), which also included the Communist Party of Bohemia and Moravia (KSČM) and several other left-wing groups. The party was set up in July 1993 by DL members and reformers within the KSČM. It forms part of the reconstituted Left Bloc (LB) alliance, which holds 25/200 seats in parliament. The leader is Josef Mecl.

Democratic Left Party (DLP or DL) Irish political party. The Democratic Left was founded in February 1992 as a left-socialist party by a large section of the Workers' Party (WP) after proposals to abandon the WP's orthodox communist programme had been rejected by the party conference. The new party is committed to the reunification of Ireland by peaceful means, and is active in Northern Ireland. At the November 1992 election it gained 2.8% of the vote and 4/166 seats (while the WP gained 0.7% and no seats). The leader is Proinsias de Rossa, who had also been leader of the WP before the split.

Democratic Left Party [Partito Democratico della Sinistra] (PDS) Italian political party. The PDS is the successor to the Italian Communist Party (PCI). Founded in 1921, the PCI was briefly part of a coalition government after the Second World War. From the 1950s it was the country's second-largest and main opposition party. From 1976–79 it gave external support to a centrist coalition. It achieved its best result in 1976, with 34.4% of the vote, but its support then declined steadily to 26.6% in 1987. The party had followed an increasingly independent line since the 1960s, and in the 1980s it redefined itself as a democratic left-wing party. The change was formalized by its conversion into the PDS in February 1991, which prompted a minority wing to break away to form the Communist Refoundation Party (RC). At the April 1992 election the PDS gained 16.1% of the vote and 107/630 seats. The party was largely untainted by the corruption scandals which broke in 1992 and 1993, certainly in comparison with the Christian Democratic Party (DC) and other coalition parties, although some lower-ranking PCI and PDS members were implicated. The PDS increased its support in local and regional elections in 1993, consolidating a position of dominance in the PCI's traditional powerbase, the central regions of Emilia-Romagna, Tuscany and Umbria (known as the 'red belt'), as well as making gains in the south. At the March 1994 election it gained 20.4% of the vote and 117 seats as the dominant partner in the Progressive Alliance. The leader is Massimo D'Alema, the party president is Stefano Rodota.

Democratic Left Party [Strana Demokratickej L'avice] (SDL') Slovakian political party. The SDL' was founded in 1991 as the successor to the Communist Party of Slovakia (KSS), which was founded in 1939 as a separate organization within the federal Communist Party of Czechoslovakia (KSČS). It defines itself as a left-socialist party, basing policy on

Marx's humanism and methodology, and is committed to market reforms but also to a mixed economy with a strategic role for the state. At the June 1992 election it became the second-largest party in the Slovakian parliament, gaining 14.7% of the vote and 29/150 seats. The leader is Peter Weiss.

Democratic Left Party [Demokratik Sol Parti] (DSP) Turkish political party. The DSP was founded in 1985 as one of the successors to the centre-left Republican People's Party (CHP), which had been disbanded after the 1980 military coup. At the October 1991 election it gained 10.8% of the vote and 7/450 seats. The party leader is Bülent Ecevit, who had been leader of the CHP.

democratic legitimacy (European Union) *See* DEMOCRATIC DEFICIT.

Democratic Movement [Movimento Democratico] (MD) San Marino political party. The MD has its roots in the San Marino Independent Democratic Socialist Party (PSDIS) and one of its successors, the San Marino Democratic Socialist Party (PSDS), which adopted the current name in 1988. Its policies are broadly centrist. At the May 1993 election it gained 5.3% of the vote and 3/60 seats. The leader is Emilio Della Balda.

Democratic Movement of Serbia [Demokratska Pokret Srbije] (DEPOS) Yugoslav political organization and party. DEPOS was formed in 1992 as a coalition of diverse groups opposed to the policies of President Milošević and his Socialist Party of Serbia (SPS) government. It includes parties and groups from the right to the centre-left of the political spectrum. Its membership shifted, but the dominant partner was the right-wing Serbian Renewal Movement (SPO). At the December 1992 elections it gained 18.0% of the vote and 50/250 seats in the Serbian parliament and 20/138 seats in the Federal Assembly; at the early election for the former in December 1993 it gained 17.4% and 45 seats. In June 1994 11 deputies not affiliated to the SPO established DEPOS as a party. Its leader is Slobodan Rakitić.

Democratic National Salvation Front *See* SOCIAL DEMOCRACY PARTY OF ROMANIA.

Democratic Party (Albania) *See* DEMOCRATIC PARTY OF ALBANIA.

Democratic Party [Demokraticheska Partiya] (DP) Bulgarian political party. Founded in 1886, the right-wing DP was one of the country's main parties in the 1920s and 30s, holding power on several occasions. It was suppressed by the communists in 1948. Relaunched in 1990, it is now a key member of the UNION OF DEMOCRATIC FORCES (SDS) alliance. The leader is Stefan Savov.

Democratic Party [Dimokratikó Kómma] (DIKO) Cypriot political party. Founded in 1976, DIKO advocates broadly centre-right economic policies and is conservative on social issues. It calls for a federal solution to the island's division, and has traditionally been more willing to take account of Turkish Cypriot concerns than its main rival on the right, the Democratic Rally (DISI) (*see* CYPRUS QUESTION). At the May 1991 election it gained 19.5% of the vote and 11/56 seats. The leader is Spyros Kyprianou, who was president of the republic from 1977–88.

Democratic Party [Demokrātiskā Partija] (DP) Latvian political party. Founded in October 1992, the Democratic Centre Party (DCP) gained 4.8% of the vote and 5/100 seats at the June 1993 election. The name was changed the following September. The leader is Aivars Kreituss.

Democratic Party [Demokratesch Partei (Letzeburgish), Parti Démocratique (French)] (DP or PD) Luxemburg political party. Founded in the 1840s, the DP is a right-leaning liberal party. Traditionally the country's third largest political force, it has participated in most coalition governments since 1945 but has been out of power since 1984. At the June 1994 election it gained 18.8% of the vote and 12/60 seats. The leader is Charles Goerens, the general secretary Kik Schneider.

Democratic Party [Demokrat Parti] (DP) Northern Cypriot political party. The DP was founded in July 1992 by members of the ruling centre-right National Unity Party (UBP) who disapproved of its increasing unwillingness to consider some form of federal or confederal solution to the island's division between the Greek and Turkish communities (*see* CYPRUS QUESTION). The move was backed by President Denktaş, a former UBP leader. The New Dawn Party (YDP) and Social Democratic Party (SDP) merged with the new party in May 1993. After gaining 29.2% of the vote and 15/50 seats at the December 1993 election, the DP formed a coalition with the Republican Turkish Party (CTP) and party leader Hakkı Atun became prime minister.

Democratic Party [Partidul Democrat] (PD) Romanian political party. The PD has its roots in the National Salvation Front (FSN), which emerged during the revolution which overthrew the communist regime of Nicolae Ceauşescu in December 1989. It formed a provisional government and assumed legislative authority. Having converted itself into a political party with a broadly centre-left orientation, it gained two-thirds of the vote at the May 1990 election. Growing tension between centre-left reformers and conservative former communists led to a split within the party in April 1992, with the latter founding the Democratic National Salvation Front (FSND, now the Social Democracy Party, PDSR). At the September 1992 election the FSN, campaigning on a free-market programme, gained 10.2% of the vote and 43/341 seats. The party was renamed in June 1993. The leader is Petre Roman, the party president is Ion Aurel Stoica.

Democratic Party [Demokrat Partisi] (DEP) Former Turkish political party. The DEP was the successor to the People's Labour Party (HEP), formed in 1990 by Kurdish members of the Social Democratic People's Party (SHP). The HEP nevertheless contested the October 1991 election in alliance with the SHP and gained 22/450 seats. The party had its electoral base in the Kurdish community and was strongly supportive of demands for Kurdish autonomy. Accused by opponents of maintaining links with the Kurdistan Workers' Party (PKK) guerrilla group, it was banned in July 1993 for advocating Kurdish separatism. The

DEP was set up the same month. In March 1994 parliament lifted the immunity of DEP leader Hatip Dicle, four other DEP members and an independent Kurdish member, and all six were immediately arrested. In June the DEP was declared unconstitutional and the party's remaining 13 deputies were expelled from parliament. The previous month a group of DEP members, anticipating the party's closure, had formed the People's Democratic Party (HADEP) and elected Murat Bözlak as leader. At the opening of their trial in August 1994 Dicle and the others were charged with treason.

Democratic Party [Demokratska Stranka] (DS) Yugoslav political party. Founded in 1990, the Democratic Party – not to be confused with the Democratic Party of Serbia (DSS), which broke away from it in 1991 – is a centrist party in Serbia calling for a proper implementation of a pluralist political system and protection of human rights. At the December 1992 elections it gained 4.4% of the vote and 6/250 seats in the Serbian parliament and 5/138 seats in the Federal Assembly; at the early election for the former in December 1993 it gained 12.1% and 29 seats. The leader is Zoran Djindjić.

Democratic Party of Albania [Partia Demokratike të Shqipërisë] (PDSh) Albanian political party. Founded in 1990 as the country's first independent party under communist rule, the PDSh became the spearhead of the opposition movement. It failed to dislodge the communists in the multiparty election of March 1991 but went on to win the election a year later, gaining 62.1% of the vote and 92/140 seats. The centre-right coalition government it formed with several smaller parties is committed to the rapid introduction of a market economy. The leader is Eduard Selami. Sali Berisha, the party's first leader and now president of the republic, retains considerable influence.

Democratic Party of Serbia [Demokratska Stranka Srbije] (DSS) Yugoslav political party. The DSS was founded in 1991 by right-wing members of the centrist Democratic Party (DS). It contested the December 1992 elections within the opposition DEMOCRATIC MOVEMENT (DEPOS), and gained 2.8% of the vote and 7/250 seats in the early election to the Serbian republican parliament in December 1993. The leader is Vojislav Kostunica.

Democratic Party of Slovenia [Demokratska Stranka Slovenije] (DSS or DS) Slovenian political party. The DSS was formed in 1991 by the minority centrist wing of the Social Democratic Alliance (SDZ). At the December 1992 election it gained 5.0% of the vote and 6/90 seats. In March 1994 the party voted to join the new Liberal Democratic Party (LDS), but a minority wing, including three deputies, opted to remain independent.

Democratic Party of Socialists of Montenegro *See* DEMOCRATIC SOCIALIST PARTY OF ....

Democratic Party of the Left *See* DEMOCRATIC LEFT PARTY (Italy).

Democratic Progressive Party [Partito Democratico Progressista] (PDP) San Marino political party. The PDP was founded in 1941 as the San Marino Communist Party (PCS). It redefined itself as party of the 'democratic left' in the 1980s and changed its name in 1990. It led a centre-left coalition from 1978–86 and participated in a left-right administration from 1986–92. At the May 1993 election it gained 18.6% of the vote and 11/60 seats. The leader is Stefano Macina.

Democratic Rally [Dimokratikós Sinagermós] (DISI) Cypriot political party. Founded in 1976, DISI advocates broadly free-market economic policies and has conservative views on social issues. It has traditionally been less willing to accept a federal solution to the division of Cyprus than its main rival on the right, the Democratic Party (DIKO) (*see* CYPRUS QUESTION). DISI has been the country's largest party since 1981. It gained 35.8% of the vote and 20/56 seats at the May 1991 election, which it contested in alliance with the small Liberal Party (KF). The leader is Yiannakis Matsis. Glavkos Klerides, who led the party from its foundation until his election as president of the republic in February 1993, remains its dominant figure.

Democratic Social Centre - People's Party [Centro Democrático Social - Partido Popular] (CDS-PP or CDS) Portuguese political party. Founded in 1974, the CDS is a christian democratic party which shifted from the centre-right to the right in the 1980s. After initial successes and participation in government, its support has declined steadily in recent years. At the October 1991 election it gained 4.4% of the vote and 5/230 seats. The leader is Manuel Monteiro.

Democratic Socialist Party [Partei des Demokratischen Sozialismus] (PDS) German political party. The PDS is the successor to the Socialist Unity Party (SED), the orthodox communist party which ruled East Germany from 1949–89. It was renamed and redefined itself as a democratic left-wing party after the fall of the Berlin Wall and the collapse of communist rule in November 1989. It retains considerable support in the eastern states. At the all-German election in December 1990 it gained 2.4% of the vote (0.3% in the west and 11.1% in the east) and 17/662 seats. The leader is Lothar Bisky. It is also referred to in English as the Party of Democratic Socialism.

Democratic Socialist Party of Bosnia-Herzegovina [Demokratska Stranka Socijalista Bosne i Hercegovine] (DSS-BiH or DSS) Bosnian political party. The DSS has its roots in the League of Communists (SK-BiH) and the more broadly based Socialist League of Working People (SSRNJ) in power until 1990. Both formations were relaunched as mainstream left-wing parties prior to the December 1990 election, at which they gained 24/240 seats between them. After several further name changes and reorganizations they merged in 1991. The DSS is the only major multiethnic party in Bosnia-Herzegovina. It has remained part of the government coalition throughout the civil war between Muslims, Serbs and Croats which broke out in March 1992. The leader is Nijaz Duraković.

Democratic Socialist Party of Montenegro [Demokratska Partija Socijalista Crne Gore] (DPSCG or DPS) Yugoslav political party. The DPS was founded in

1991 as the successor to the Montenegro League of Communists (SKCG). The party has adopted a mainstream left-wing programme, while its leadership is virtually identical with that of the old SKCG. Initially closely allied to the Socialist Party of Serbia (SPS), it has followed a more independent line since 1992 and calls for greater autonomy for the republic within the Yugoslav federation. At the December 1992 elections it gained 44.0% of the vote and 46/85 seats in the Montenegrin parliament and 17/138 seats in the Federal Assembly. The leader is Momir Bulatović, the president of the republic.

Democratic Union [Unia Demokratyczna] (UD) Former Polish political party. The UD was formed in 1991 by the merger of the centre-left Citizens' Movement - Democratic Action (ROAD) and Democratic Union (UD) and several other groups within the broadly based Citizens' Parliamentary Club (OKP), the political wing of the Solidarity movement, which had spearheaded the opposition to communist rule in the 1980s and won the partially free election of 1989. At the October 1991 election the UD became the largest party of a highly fragmented parliament. Having led several governments in the following two years, it came third in the September 1993 election, gaining 10.6% of the vote and 74/460 seats. In April 1994 it merged with the centre-right Liberal Democratic Congress (KLD), another post-Solidarity party, to form the FREEDOM UNION (UW).

Democratic Union of Catalonia *See* CONVERGENCE AND UNION.

Democratic Union of Cyprus - Socialist Party *See* UNIFIED ....

Democratic Union of Slovakia [Demokratická Únia Slovensky] (DEÚS or DÚ) Slovakian political party. The DÚ was founded in March 1994 by a wing of the then ruling MOVEMENT FOR A DEMOCRATIC SLOVAKIA (HZDS). The following month it merged with the Alliance of Democrats (ADSR), which had split from the HZDS in June 1993. It describes itself as a centre-right and liberal party. It holds 16/150 seats in parliament. The leader is Jozef Moravčík.

Democratic Union of Vojvodina Hungarians [Demokratska Zajednica Vojvodanskih Madžara (Serb), Vajdasádi Magyarok Demokratikus Közössége (Hungarian)] (DZVM or VMDK) Yugoslav political party. Founded in 1990, the VMDK is the main representative of the ethnic Hungarian community in the Vojvodina region of Serbia. It advocates autonomy for the region. At the December 1992 elections it gained 3.2% of the vote and 9/250 seats in the Serbian parliament and 3/138 seats in the Federal Assembly; at the early election for the former in December 1993 it gained 2.0% and five seats. The leader is András Agoston.

Democratic Unionist Party *See* ULSTER DEMOCRATIC UNIONIST PARTY.

Democrats 66 [Democraten 66] (D'66) Dutch political party. Founded in 1966, D'66 is a left-leaning liberal party which has established itself as the fourth-largest group in parliament. It participated in centre-left coalitions in 1973–77 and 1981–82. At the September 1989 election it gained 7.9% of the vote and 12/150 seats; in May 1994 it doubled its support, gaining 15.5% and 24 seats. In August it joined the Labour Party (PvdA) and the People's Party for Freedom and Democracy (VVD) in a left-right coalition. The party leader is Hans van Mierlo, the parliamentary leader is Gerrit Jan Wolffensperger.

Demosthenes Council of Europe programme. It was set up in 1990 to help the former communist countries of Eastern Europe carry out constitutional, legislative and administrative reforms. It puts the expertise acquired by the Council and its (Western European) member states regarding the structure and functioning of a democratic society at their disposal by organizing meetings of experts, workshops, training courses, scholarships and study visits for civil servants and politicians. The programme is named after an ancient Greek orator and political leader.

Demotic [Dimotikí] ('popular language') Form of the Greek language. Demotic is based on the standard spoken language. It replaced the more formal Katharevusa as the official language of the state in 1976.

Den Abbreviation for the DENAR, the Macedonian currency.

Den Haag Dutch name for The Hague, the Dutch seat of government. The formal name is 's-Gravenhage.

denar (pl. -i) Currency of Macedonia. Common abbreviations are D, Den, and MKD (the international standard in banking etc). It is divided into 100 deni. The simple plural form 'denar' and the anglicized 'denars' are also used. It was introduced in April 1992 in place of the Yugoslav dinar.

Denktaş, Rauf (1924–) Northern Cypriot lawyer and politician. He was elected president of the Turkish Cypriot communal parliament on Cyprus's independence in 1960. He lived in exile from 1963–68. Following the abortive military coup in 1974 and the subsequent Turkish intervention, he was elected president of the newly proclaimed Northern Cypriot state (recognized only by Turkey) in June 1976. He established himself as the undisputed leader of the Turkish Cypriot community and was reelected in 1981, 1985 and 1990. He remained the dominant figure in the National Unity Party (UBP) until 1992, when he declared his support for the breakaway Democratic Party (DP).

Denmark [Danmark] Country in northern Europe.

Official data. Name: Kingdom of Denmark [Kongeriget Danmark]; capital: Copenhagen [København]; form of government: parliamentary monarchy; head of state: king/queen; head of government: prime minister; flag: red with a white Scandinavian cross; national holiday: 16 April (Queen's Birthday); language: Danish; religion: Evangelical Lutheranism; currency: krone (kr) (pl. -r) = 100 øre; abbreviation: DK.

Geography. The southernmost of the Scandinavian or Nordic countries, Denmark consists of the Jutland [Jylland] peninsula, four main islands (Zealand [Sjælland], Funen [Fyn], Lolland, Falster), the island of Bornholm in the Baltic Sea, and around 480 smaller islands. The total area is 43,093 sq km. The country is bordered by the Skagerrak and Kattegat (arms of the North Sea) in the north, Sweden in the east (across the Sound Strait), Germany in the south, and the North Sea in the west. It consists almost entirely of low-lying rolling plains. Some 61% of the land is arable, another 6% is covered by pastures and 12% is forested. The climate is temperate marine, with mild summers and cold winters; rainfall is moderate.

Demography. Denmark has a population of 5,187,000. Population density is 122 per sq km (land area). Some 86% of the people live in urban areas, and around a quarter live in Copenhagen and its suburbs (population 1.3 million). Other major cities are Århus, Odense, Ålborg, Esbjerg and Randers. In ethnic, linguistic and religious terms Denmark is very homogeneous. Some 96.2% of the population is Danish and 90.6% nominally Lutheran Protestant. The only ethnic minority is the German-speaking community in southern Jutland, which numbers around 50,000. There are also small groups of other Protestants, Roman Catholics and Jews. Foreign nationals account for 2.8% of the population, and include citizens of Sweden, Norway, the United Kingdom, Croatia and Iran. Denmark has also taken in around 20,000 refugees from former Yugoslavia.

Sociography. Denmark scores 0.912 on the United Nations human development index (HDI), ranking 15th in the world and 11th among 32 European countries. There are 28 doctors and 64 hospital beds for every 10,000 people. Education is compulsory between the ages of seven and 15. There is one teacher for every 13 students. Enrolment is 86% at the secondary level and 32% at the tertiary level. The literacy rate is virtually 100%. Real annual income per head (in terms of purchasing power) is US$ 17,880.

Infrastructure and communications. Denmark has a highly developed transport and communications network, including a combination of bridges, ferries and local air services linking all the islands. There are 66,480 km of paved roads and 1.59 million passenger cars (309 per 1,000 people), 2,840 km of railways and 417 km of navigable waterways. The main ports are Copenhagen, Århus, Ålborg and Esbjerg. The main airport is at Copenhagen, and there are 11 other airports with scheduled services. There are 46 daily newspapers, with a combined circulation of 1.85 million (361 per 1,000 people). There are 2.24 million radio receivers, 2.51 million television sets and 4.51 million telephones in use (respectively 434, 488 and 876 per 1,000 people).

Economic structure. The Danish economy is highly developed, diversified and strongly trade-oriented. It is based on manufacturing, food processing, livestock raising and fishing. Since the late 1980s economic performance has been characterized by steady growth (averaging 1.1% per year), the current account moving from deficit to surplus, and low and falling inflation (from around 4.5% to around 2%), but also persistent high unemployment (around 11%).

Services contribute 68% of GDP, industry contributes 28% (manufacturing 19%), and agriculture and fishing 4%. Some 20% of the labour force is employed in manufacturing, 15% in trade, 9% in finance, 7% in construction, 7% in transport and communications and 5% in agriculture and fishing. Livestock raising (pigs) and dairy farming are the main agricultural activities; the main crops grown are sugarbeets, pulses, barley and wheat. The fishing industry is the second-largest in Europe. The only significant mineral resources are oil and natural gas (in the North Sea). The main manufacturing industries are food processing and engineering; other important branches are chemicals, metalworking and electrical goods. Tourism is an important source of revenue. The main energy sources are domestic and imported fossil fuels; only 2% of export earnings are required to cover net fuel imports. The main exports are industrial machinery (14% of the total), meat and meat products (10%), chemicals (6%), fish (6%), transport equipment (6%), electrical equipment (6%); machinery and transport equipment account for 27% of the total, foodstuffs for 25%; Denmark is Europe's largest

exporter of fish and fish products. The main imports are machinery and transport equipment, basic manufactures, chemicals and foodstuffs. The main trading partners are: exports: Germany (23%), Sweden (11%), United Kingdom (10%), France (6%), Norway (6%), United States, Italy, Netherlands, Japan; imports: Germany (23%), Sweden (11%), United Kingdom (8%), United States (6%), France (6%), Netherlands (6%), Norway, Italy, Japan; half of all trade is with other European Union (EU) countries.

The National Bank of Denmark [Danmarks Nationalbank] is the central bank. The main employers' associations are the Danish Employers' Confederation (DAF) and the Confederation of Danish Industry (DI); the main labour organizations are the Danish Trade Union Confederation (LO) and the Federation of Civil Servants and Salaried Employees (FTF).

Political structure. Denmark is a parliamentary monarchy on the basis of a constitution adopted in 1953. Executive power is formally vested in the king/queen but is exercised by the State Council [Statsråd] or council of ministers headed by the prime minister [statsminister]. Legislative authority is vested in the Legislature [Folketing], whose 179 members are elected for a four-year term by a system of proportional representation (with a 2% threshold for gaining seats); two seats each are reserved for the Faroe Islands and Greenland. Bills adopted by the Folketing must be submitted to a popular referendum if demanded by a third of its members. All citizens over the age of 18 are entitled to vote. Judicial power is ultimately vested in the Supreme Court [Højesteret], whose 15 members are appointed on the advice of the minister of justice. Administratively the country is divided into 15 counties [amtskommune, pl. -r], including the county-level city of Copenhagen; the counties are subdivided into 275 communes.

The main political parties are the Social Democratic Party (SD), Conservative People's Party (KF), Socialist People's Party (SF), Liberal Party (Venstre, V), Radical Liberal Party (RV), Centre

Democrats (CD), Progress Party (FP) and Christian People's Party (KrF). At the general election in December 1990 the SD gained 37.4% of the vote and 69/175 seats, the KF 16.0% and 30 seats, Venstre 15.8% and 29 seats, the SF 8.3% and 15 seats, the FP 6.4% and 12 seats, the CD 5.1% and nine seats, the RV 3.5% and seven seats, and the KrF 2.3% and four seats (results for metropolitan Denmark). The government is formed by a minority centre-left coalition of the SD, CD, RV and KrF, with Poul Nyrup Rasmussen as prime minister. Other senior ministers are Marianne Jelved (economic affairs), Mogens Lykketoft (finance), Niels Helveg Petersen (foreign affairs), Birte Weiss (internal affairs), Erling Olsen (justice), Hans Hækkerup (defence), Bjørn Westh (agriculture and fisheries) and Mimi Jakobsen (industry). The head of state is Queen Margrethe II, who succeeded to the throne in January 1972; the heir is Prince Frederik.

Denmark has two overseas dependencies, the Faroe Islands (*see separate entry*) and Greenland, both internally self-governing integral parts of the kingdom.

Security and international affiliations. The Danish armed forces number 27,700 (army 16,900, navy 4,500, airforce 6,300). Military service is compulsory and consists of 9–12 months' basic training.

Denmark is a member of the Council of Baltic Sea States (CBSS), Council of Europe, Conference on Security and Cooperation in Europe (CSCE), European Economic Area (EEA), European Union (EU), North Atlantic Treaty Organization (NATO), Nordic Council and Western European Union (WEU), as well as the Organization for Economic Cooperation and Development (OECD) and the United Nations and its specialized agencies.

History. During the Europe-wide migrations of the 5th century many Angles and Jutes left their ancestral lands in modern Denmark, mainly for Great Britain across the North Sea, and were replaced by the Dan or Danes from southern Sweden. These played a prominent role in the seaborne Viking raids, conquests and migrations across Europe from the 9th–11th

centuries. The Danish clans were united under King Gorm in the early 10th century. (Denmark is one of Europe's oldest monarchies.) Christianity was established by the late 11th century. King Knut (Canute) (1014–35) briefly united Denmark, Norway and England. Under Valdemar I (1157–82) and his successors Denmark gradually came to dominate the whole Nordic region, including Iceland and Greenland. In 1397 Denmark, Norway and Sweden (including Finland) were loosely united in the Union of Kalmar. The Danish towns and trade in particular prospered during the Kalmar period, which came to an end with the secession of Sweden in 1523. The Protestant Reformation sparked a three-year civil war, which had deeper economic and political roots, after which the Evangelical Lutheran Church was proclaimed the established church in 1536. A new constitution adopted in 1660 broke the power of the nobility and established an absolute monarchy, initially supported by the middle classes. During the 17th century Denmark fought a series of costly wars with Sweden. It lost its possessions in southern Sweden in 1660 and those further east in the Baltic region by the end of the Great Northern War (1700–21). This marked the end of Denmark as a regional power.

After allying itself with France during the Napoleonic period (1799–1815) Denmark was forced to cede Norway to Sweden in 1814. This period left Denmark impoverished but also paved the way for the emergence of a liberal reform movement and of farmers as a strong political force. A new constitution adopted in 1849 abolished the absolute monarchy, introduced parliamentary government and guaranteed basic freedoms. After a short war in 1864 Denmark was forced to cede Schleswig and Holstein to the German Confederation; northern Schleswig was returned after a plebiscite held in 1920 (under the terms of the Treaty of Versailles ending the First World War). Universal adult suffrage was introduced in 1915. In 1929 the Social Democratic Party (SD) and the Radical Liberals (RV) formed a coalition which during the 1930s laid the foundations of a comprehensive welfare state. Denmark was hard-hit by the world-wide economic depression of the 1930s. During the Second World War (1939–45) Denmark was invaded and occupied by Germany in 1940.

Abandoning its traditional policy of neutrality, Denmark became a founding member of the North Atlantic Treaty Organization (NATO) in 1949. In 1953 it set up the Nordic Council with its northern neighbours. The welfare state was extended under various SD-led governments during the 1950s and 60s. Under a major revision of the constitution adopted in 1953 the Faroe Islands and Greenland were recognized as integral and equal parts of the Kingdom of Denmark. (Internal self-government had been granted to the Faroes five years earlier and was granted to Greenland in 1979.) In 1960 Denmark became a founding member of the European Free Trade Association (EFTA). Following a swing to the right in the 1968 elections the Social Democrats went into opposition for the first time since 1929. Denmark joined the European Community (EC) in 1973, membership having been approved by 63.3% of voters in a referendum the previous year. A period of unstable minority and coalition governments ended in September 1982, when Poul Schlüter, leader of the Conservative People's Party (KF), formed a centre-right coalition with the Liberals and two smaller parties. KF-led coalitions under Schlüter held power until January 1993. In June 1992 voters rejected the Maastricht Treaty establishing the European Union (EU) by 50.7% to 49.3%; after the government negotiated several 'opt-outs', it was approved by 56.7% of voters in a second referendum in May 1993. Schlüter resigned as prime minister in January 1993 after being accused of misleading parliament. The Social Democrats then returned to power at the head of a centre-left coalition.

See also entries on specific institutions, organizations, parties, people, terms etc.

Deny Flight Codename for the military operation monitoring the AIR-EXCLUSION ZONE or no-fly zone over Bosnian airspace. Compliance with the ban, which was imposed by the United Nations in October 1992, is in the hands of North Atlantic Treaty Organization (NATO) forces.

Dép Abbreviation for Député ('Deputy'), a member of the National Assembly, the lower house of the French parliament.

Dep Abbreviation for Deputato ('Deputy'), a member of the Chamber of Deputies, the lower house of the Italian parliament.

DEP (Turkey) *See* DEMOCRATIC PARTY.

département *See* DEPARTMENT.

department [département] French administrative division. The department is the main intermediate tier of government between the region and the commune. Each of the 96 departments has a general council [conseil général] elected for a six-year term and is headed by a commissioner [commissaire] appointed by the central government. The councils are responsible for many spheres of local administration, while the commissioner is responsible for maintaining public order and ensuring that council decisions conform with existing legislation. Councillors elect the members of the Senate, the upper house of parliament. The departments are subdivided into arrondissements and cantons, neither of which have any significant functions. As part of a decentralization programme initiated in 1982, the commissioner replaced the traditionally powerful departmental prefect [préfet] and many of the latter's powers were transferred to the elected council. There are also four overseas departments.

Department of National Heritage British government department. Established in April 1992 by combining functions previously covered by six different departments, this ministry is responsible for historical buildings and monuments, tourism, sports, the media and the arts. It is thus broadly equivalent to the culture ministry in other countries.

Department of the Environment British government department. One of the largest ministries in terms of staff and budget, it is responsible for planning, local government, housing and urban development as well as environmental protection and conservation.

DEPOS *See* DEMOCRATIC MOVEMENT OF SERBIA.

deputy minister (Greece) *See* ALTERNATE MINISTER.

derogation In the European Union (EU), a special dispensation under which a member state is exempted from implementing all or part of a 'directive' or 'regulation', the organization's two main legal instruments. It is usually granted for a specific period, particularly to give a member state more time to adapt to EU legislation, but on occasion it has been open-ended. A special dispensation under which a member state is not bound by certain provisions of the founding treaties and their amendments is known as an 'opt-out'.

desalojados ('the displaced' or 'the expelled') In Portugal, an alternative name for 'RETORNADOS', settlers in Africa who returned when the colonies became independent in the mid 1970s.

desovietization In Estonia, Latvia and Lithuania, the process of removing public officials and others closely associated with Soviet rule (1940–91) from positions of authority. The main targets of 'desovietization' are agents of the State Security Committee (KGB) and, to a lesser extent, Communist Party officials. The former played a key role in suppressing dissent and operated an extensive network of informants to this end. *See also* DECOMMUNIZATION *and* SCREENING.

deterrent force (France) *See* FORCE DE DISSUASION.

DEÚS *See* DEMOCRATIC UNION OF SLOVAKIA.

Deutsche Bundesbank *See* GERMAN FEDERAL BANK.

Deutsche Demokratische Republik (DDR) ('German Democratic Republic') Official name of former EAST GERMANY.

Deutsche Mark *See* DEUTSCHMARK.

Deutschland German name for Germany.

Deutschlandlied ('Song of Germany') Common name for the national anthem of Germany. Written in 1848, at the height of the campaign for the unification of Germany, it was adopted as the national anthem in 1922. After the Second World War, the first verse, which begins 'Deutschland, Deutschland über alles' ('Germany, Germany above all'), was replaced with the third verse, which begins 'Einigkeit und Recht und Freiheit' ('Unity, justice and freedom'). This phrase is now the anthem's formal title.

deutschmark or **mark** [Deutsche Mark] Currency of Germany. Common abbreviations are DM, D-Mark and DEM (the international standard in banking etc). It is divided into 100 pfennigs [Pfennige].

Dev-Sol *See* REVOLUTIONARY LEFT.

devolution In the United Kingdom, the transfer of powers from central government to regional assemblies and governments in Scotland and Wales. Pressure for devolution began to grow in the early 1970s, but in referendums in March 1979 Welsh voters rejected proposals drawn up by the then Labour government, while in Scotland they did not gain the support of the required 40% of the total electorate. The opposition Labour and Liberal Democratic parties support devolution for Scotland and Wales as well as the English regions. The Scottish National Party (SNP) and Plaid Cymru in Wales call for 'independence within Europe' for their countries.

Dfl Abbreviation for the gulden or GUILDER, the Dutch currency. It is taken from 'florin' [florijn], an old name for the guilder.

DG and **DG-I … DG-XXIII** or **DG-1 … DG-23** *See* DIRECTORATE-GENERAL.

DGB *See* GERMAN TRADE UNION FEDERATION.

DGSE *See* DIRECTORATE-GENERAL OF EXTERNAL SECURITY.

Dhekelia *See* AKROTIRI AND ....

Di Pietro, Antonio (1950–) Italian policeman and public prosecutor. He joined the Bergamo police force in 1970. He became a detective inspector and later a commissioner and then, having studied law, a public prosecutor. In 1985 he was transferred to neighbouring Milan. In both cities he established a reputation for rigorous investigation of corruption. He came to national prominence in 1992 as one of the leading investigators involved in Operation Clean Hands [Mani Pulite], which exposed a web of political corruption initially in Milan and then nationwide (*see* ITALIAN CORRUPTION SCANDALS).

Di Rupo, Elio (1951–) Belgian chemist and politician. The son of Italian immigrants, he worked as a researcher and was active in local government in Mons during the 1980s. He was elected to parliament for the Walloon Socialist Party (PS) in 1988. In January 1992 he was appointed education minister of the French Community, the body in Belgium's federal structure responsible for French-language education, culture and related matters. In January 1994 he became deputy prime minister at national level and minister of communications and public enterprises.

DIA *See* ANTI-MAFIA INVESTIGATION DIRECTORATE.

diamerísma (pl. -ta) Greek administrative division, usually translated as 'region'. The *diamerísmata*, now 13 in number, were created in 1987 to facilitate planning and coordinate regional development at a higher level than the existing structure of 51 *nomói*. Currently neither tier has any elected bodies.

Dias Loureiro, Manuel (1951–) Portuguese lawyer and politician. He was active in local government until his election to parliament for the centre-right Social Democratic Party (PSD) in 1985. He was the party's general secretary from 1985–90. He was appointed minister for parliamentary affairs in 1989 and interior minister in November 1991.

Die Grünen (Austria) *See* GREEN ALTERNATIVE.

Die Grünen (Germany) *See* GREENS.

Die Republikaner *See* REPUBLICANS (Germany).

die Wende ('the change' or 'the turning point') In Germany, a shorthand for the period which began with the collapse of the communist regime in East Germany in November 1989 and culminated in the country's reunification the following October.

Dienstbier, Jiří (1937–) Czech journalist and politician. After he was dismissed from his job with Czechoslovak Radio in 1970 because of his political views, he worked as an archivist and boilerman. A founding member of the Charter 77 opposition group, he was imprisoned by the communist authorities from 1979–82. In 1989 he became a leading member of the new Civic Forum. After the collapse of communist rule later that year he was appointed foreign minister, a post he held until July 1992. When the Forum split in early 1991, he became leader of the centre-left Civic Movement (OH), now the Free Democrats (SD), in April.

Diepgen, Eberhard (1941–) German lawyer and politician. Elected to the parliament of his native West Berlin for the Christian Democratic Union (CDU) in 1971, he became leader of the parliamentary group in 1983. He was mayor from 1984–89. When, after the reunification of Germany, the CDU came first in the election for an all-Berlin parliament in December 1990, he returned as mayor the following month at the head of a coalition with the Social Democratic Party (SPD).

DIGOS *See* GENERAL INVESTIGATIONS AND SPECIAL OPERATIONS DIVISION.

Dijkstal, Hans (1943–) Dutch financial consultant and politician. He worked in insurance and investments from 1967 and was also a lecturer in management training from 1970–78. He was active in local government for the right-wing People's Party for Freedom and Democracy (VVD) from 1974–86. Elected to parliament in 1982, he was appointed first deputy prime minister and minister of internal affairs in the left-right coalition formed in August 1994.

DIKO *See* DEMOCRATIC PARTY (Cyprus).

Dillen, Karel (1925–) Belgian manager and politician. He worked for the Renault car company in Antwerp from 1947–85. A leading advocate of independence for Flanders from the 1960s, he founded the far-right Flemish National Party (VNP) in 1975. In May 1979 the VNP merged with a similar party to form the Flemish Bloc (VB), and he was elected leader of the new party. He was a member of parliament from 1978–89 and has been a member of the European Parliament since 1989.

Dimitrov, Filip (1955–) Bulgarian lawyer and politician. Politically unaffiliated until the collapse of communist rule in 1989, he gained prominence as a leader of the Ecoglasnost environmentalist movement. He was elected leader of the Union of Democratic Forces (SDS) alliance in December 1990. After it came first in the October 1991 election he also became prime minister of a minority government, but he resigned a year later after losing a vote of confidence.

Dimotikí *See* DEMOTIC.

Din Abbreviation for the DINAR, the Yugoslav currency.

dinar Former currency of Croatia. *See* KUNA.

dinar Currency of Yugoslavia. Common abbreviations are D, Din and YUD (the international standard in banking etc). It is divided into 100 para. The simple plural form 'dinar' and the anglicized 'dinars' are also used.

Dini, Lamberto (1931–) Italian economist, banker and politician. He has worked for and represented Italy in a number of international financial institutions, including the International Monetary Fund (IMF) (1976–80) and Bank for International Settlements (BIS). In 1979 he was appointed director-general of the Bank of Italy, the central bank. He was appointed treasury minister in the right-wing coalition formed in May 1994. He does not belong to a political party.

Diplock courts Common name for special courts in Northern Ireland (United Kingdom). Diplock courts were introduced in 1974 to try individuals accused of 'scheduled' offences related to the political violence between Protestants and Catholics in the province (*see* NORTHERN IRELAND QUESTION). They were a response to the perceived difficulty of obtaining convictions because of biased and/or intimidated juries and witnesses. Trials in Diplock courts differ from the ordinary judicial process in that they are heard by a single judge and not by juries, the defendants cannot claim the right to silence, and the rules on admissible evidence are less strict. They are highly controversial and have been criticized by human-rights organizations. The courts are named after Kenneth Diplock (Lord Diplock), a senior judge who chaired the commission which recommended their introduction.

directive In the European Union (EC), one of the three binding legal instruments for implementing policy or decisions (the others being the 'regulation' and the 'decision'). A 'directive' is an instruction adopted by the Council to one or more member states to legislate on a specific matter within a defined period of time. It gives an outline of the required legislation, but leaves the details of implementation to the member states. Directives are usually known either by the subject matter and order in which they appear (e.g. the Second Banking Directive), the name of the commissioner who proposed them (e.g. the Vredeling Directive on worker participation) or by a specific reference (e.g. the Seveso Directive, after a major chemical accident in an Italian town).

directorate-general (DG) In the European Union (EU), the main departments or 'ministries' of the EUROPEAN COMMISSION, the organization's administrative and executive arm. There are 23 directorates-general, each headed by one of the 17 commissioners. They are usually designated by the abbreviation 'DG' and a roman or arabic numeral: DG-I (external relations), DG-II (economic and financial affairs), DG-III (internal market and industrial affairs), DG-IV (competition), DG-V (employment, industrial relations and social affairs), DG-VI (agriculture), DG-VII (transport), DG-VIII (development), DG-IX (personnel and administration), DG-X (information, communication and culture), DG-XI (environment, consumer protection and nuclear safety), DG-XII (science, research and development), DG-XIII (telecommunications, information industries and innovation), DG-XIV (fisheries), DG-XV (financial institutions and company law), DG-XVI (regional policy), DG-XVII (energy), DG-XVIII (credit and investments), DG-XIX (budgets), DG-XX (financial control), DG-XXI (customs and indirect taxation), DG-XXII (coordination of structural policies) and DG-XXIII (enterprise policy, commerce and tourism).

Directorate-General of External Security [Direction Générale de la Sécurité Extérieure] (DGSE) French intelligence agency. A branch of the defence ministry, the DGSE is responsible for intelligence gathering abroad. It was called the External Documentation and Counter-espionage Service (SDECE) until 1982.

dirigisme In France, the policy of state direction, intervention and participation in the national economy. It has its roots in government economic policy of the 17th century and has informed policy making in some form or other ever since. Since the 1950s it has consisted of a system of indicative planning, in which government ministries work in close partnership with business organizations and broad multi-year national plans are framed to give guidance to the private sector.

Dishnica, Pjetër or **Pirro** (1957–) Albanian economist, civil servant and politician. Director of the Institute of Statistics from 1991, he was appointed minister of economic affairs in November 1993. He is a member of the centre-right Democratic Party (PDSh).

DISI *See* DEMOCRATIC RALLY.

DİSK *See* PROGRESSIVE TRADE UNION CONFEDERATION OF TURKEY.

district British administrative division. In England outside the major conurbations, Wales and Scotland, the districts are the second tier of local government below the counties (in England and Wales) or regions (Scotland). Most urban districts have the status of borough (burgh in Scotland) or city. Each has a council elected for a four-year term. A council is formally headed by a chair, mayor (in a borough) or lord mayor (city); the executive leader is called the 'leader of the council'. District councils are responsible for housing and a range of other local services. In recent years many of their powers have been transferred to bodies appointed by central government. A reorganization of the local government structure, under which single-tier or 'unitary' local authorities would be established in some areas, is under consideration. In Northern Ireland, the districts are the only tier of local government. Their councils are also elected for a four-year term, but these have very limited powers and responsibilities.

district [distrito] Portuguese administrative division. The 18 districts of mainland Portugal are administered by a governor [governador] appointed by the central government and an assembly [assembleia] composed of representatives of the lower-level *concelhos* or *municipios*, the main units of local government, and *freguesias*. The reorganization of the districts into regions, with directly elected councils, is under consideration. The Azores and Madeira are already constituted as autonomous regions.

distrito *See* DISTRICT (Portugal).

DISY *See* DEMOCRATIC RALLY.

divario Nord-Sud *See* NORTH-SOUTH DIVIDE (Italy).

DK Abbreviation for Denmark, used for international vehicle registrations, postal addresses etc.

DKK and **DKr** Abbreviations for the KRONE, the Danish currency. DKK is used in banking etc.

DL *See* DEMOCRATIC LEFT PARTY (Ireland).

Dlouhý, Vladimír (1953–) Czech economist and politician. A prominent member of the Czechoslovak Academy of Sciences, he was appointed deputy prime minister after the collapse of communist rule in 1989. He was elected to parliament for the Civic Forum (OF) in 1990 and became minister of economic affairs. When the Forum split in early 1991, he joined the right-wing Civic Democratic Alliance (ODA). In July 1992 he was appointed industry and trade minister in the government of the Czech Republic.

DLP (Ireland) *See* DEMOCRATIC LEFT PARTY.

DLP *See* DEMOCRATIC LABOUR PARTY OF LITHUANIA.

DM Abbreviation for Deutsche Mark or DEUTSCHMARK, the German currency.

DMF Abbreviation for Département Militaire Fédéral ('Federal Military Department'), the French name of the Swiss defence ministry.

DNA *See* NORWEGIAN LABOUR PARTY.

DNSF *See* SOCIAL DEMOCRACY PARTY OF ROMANIA.

Doğan, Ahmed (1954–) Bulgarian philosopher, academic and politician. An ethnic Turk, he was imprisoned by the communist regime for a total of three years during the 1980s for championing the rights of his community. In January 1990, after the collapse of communist rule, he was elected leader of the new Movement for Rights and Freedoms (DPS).

DOM Abbreviation for *département d'outre-mer* ('overseas department'), a French administrative division. The four overseas departments (French Guyana, Guadeloupe, Martinique and Reunion) are integral parts of the republic and hence of the European Union (EU). *See also* OUTERMOST REGIONS.

Dorrell, Stephen (1952–) British businessman and politician. He was director of the family industrial-clothing firm from 1975–87. Elected to Parliament for the Conservative Party in 1979, he became a junior health minister in 1990 and financial secretary at the Treasury (= finance ministry) in 1992. He was appointed secretary of state (= minister) for national heritage, which also carries responsibility for the arts and the media, in July 1994.

double majority In Switzerland, the requirement that amendments to the federal constitution and other legislative proposals put to a popular vote under the country's system of semi-direct democracy must secure the consent of a majority of voters as well as a majority of the 26 cantons and half-cantons. *See* REFERENDUM.

Downing Street Shorthand for the British prime minister's office or the government more generally. Number 10 Downing Street in London is the official residence of the prime minister, and Number 11 that of the chancellor of the exchequer (= finance minister). The Foreign and Commonwealth Office is also based Downing Street.

Downing Street Declaration Bilateral agreement between the British and Irish governments setting out general principles for a solution to the conflict between Protestants and Catholics in Northern Ireland, a component of the United Kingdom (*see* NORTHERN IRELAND QUESTION). Signed in December 1993 at 10 Downing Street, the British prime minister's residence, the Declaration largely restates joint positions on self-determination, consent and the rejection of violence, as set out comprehensively in the 1985 ANGLO-IRISH AGREEMENT. It contains what were widely seen as two new departures: in one passage the British government 'reiterates' that it has 'no strategic or economic interest' in Northern Ireland; and the two governments also state that 'parties which establish a commitment to exclusively peaceful methods and which have shown that they abide by the democratic process, are free ... to join in dialogue in due course between the governments and the political parties'. This implied that they would be willing to negotiate with Sinn Féin, hitherto excluded from negotiations on the grounds that it was the political wing of the Irish Republican Army (IRA), once it was deemed to have rejected violence as a means of achieving political ends. (In August 1994 the IRA declared a ceasefire from September.)

DP (Bulgaria) *See* DEMOCRATIC PARTY.

DP (Latvia) *See* DEMOCRATIC PARTY.

DP (Luxemburg) *See* DEMOCRATIC PARTY.

DP (Northern Cyprus) *See* DEMOCRATIC PARTY.

DPC *See* DEFENCE PLANNING COMMITTEE.

DPS (Bulgaria) *See* MOVEMENT FOR RIGHTS AND FREEDOMS.

DPS (Yugoslavia) and **DPSCG** *See* DEMOCRATIC SOCIALIST PARTY OF MONTENEGRO.

Dr Abbreviation for the drachmí or DRACHMA, the Greek currency.

drachma [drachmí, pl. drachmés] Currency of Greece. Common abbreviations are Dr, Drch and GRD (the international standard in banking etc). It is divided into 100 leptá.

drachmí *See* DRACHMA.

Drašković, Vuk (1946–) Yugoslav journalist, writer and politician. He worked for the state news agency Tanjug from 1968–81. Since then he has published several novels, including four on the ethnic conflicts in Yugoslavia during the Second World War. In January 1990 he founded and became leader of the right-wing Serbian Renewal Movement (SPO). One of the country's leading opposition figures, he was arrested and badly beaten in June 1993 and accused of 'seeking to overthrow the constitutional order'. He was released the following month and all charges were dropped.

Drch Abbreviation for the drachmí or DRACHMA, the Greek currency.

Dreifuss, Ruth (1940–) Swiss economist, civil servant, trade-union official and politician. Born in the German-speaking canton of Aargau, she grew up in French-speaking Geneva. She worked for the federal government department responsible for humanitarian aid from 1972–81. From 1981–93 she was general secretary of the Swiss Trade Union Federation. A member of the Social Democratic Party, she was elected to the Federal Council (= government) in March 1993, taking responsibility for internal affairs, which includes social affairs and environmental issues.

Drnovšek, Janez (1950–) Slovenian economist and politician. A specialist in international finance and trade relations, he has worked in industry, banking and the diplomatic service. Standing as an independent, he was elected Slovenia's representative on the Yugoslav collective presidency in 1989, a post he held until the republic withdrew from the federation in October 1991. He was elected leader of the centre-left Liberal Democratic Party (LDS) in March 1992 and became prime minister of a centrist coalition the following May.

Državni Svet See NATIONAL COUNCIL (Slovenia).

Državni Zbor See NATIONAL ASSEMBLY (Slovenia).

DS Abbreviation for Dŭrzhavna Sigurnost ('State Security'), the Bulgarian government agency responsible for internal security and surveillance of dissidents during communist rule.

DS See DEMOCRATIC PARTY OF SLOVENIA.

DS See SWISS DEMOCRATS.

DS (Yugoslavia) See DEMOCRATIC PARTY.

DSK See DEMOCRATIC LEAGUE OF KOSOVO.

DSP See DEMOCRATIC LEFT PARTY (Turkey).

DSS See DEMOCRATIC SOCIALIST PARTY OF BOSNIA-HERZEGOVINA.

DSS See DEMOCRATIC PARTY OF SLOVENIA.

DSS (Yugoslavia) See DEMOCRATIC PARTY OF SERBIA.

DSS-BiH See DEMOCRATIC SOCIALIST PARTY OF BOSNIA-HERZEGOVINA.

DST See TERRITORIAL SURVEILLANCE DIRECTORATE.

DSU See GERMAN SOCIAL UNION.

DÚ See DEMOCRATIC UNION OF SLOVAKIA.

Dubček, Alexander (1921–92) Czechoslovak politician. An official of the Communist Party of Czechoslovakia (KSČ) from the 1950s, he was elected party leader in 1968 by reformers embarking on what became known as the Prague Spring. This ended with the Soviet-led invasion later that year. He was forced to resign as party leader in 1969. After a brief spell as ambassador to Turkey he was expelled from the party and worked in the state forestry service. He returned to public life as the communist regime collapsed in 1989. He was elected chairman of the Federal Assembly (a post he held until June 1992). Briefly a member of the Movement for a Democratic Slovakia (HZDS), he left because of its separatist policies and joined the Social Democratic Party (SDSS), of which he was elected leader in March 1992. He died in November from injuries sustained in a car accident.

Dublin Shorthand for the Irish government. Dublin is the capital of Ireland.

Dublin Convention Shorthand for the CONVENTION ON THE RIGHT TO ASYLUM.

Duisenberg, Wim (1935–) Dutch economist, academic and politician. He worked for the International Monetary Fund (IMF) from 1966–69 and lectured at the University of Amsterdam from 1970. A member of the Labour Party (PvdA), he was minister of finance in the centre-left coalition that was in office from 1973–77. In January 1982 he was appointed governor of the Netherlands Bank, the central bank. In January 1994 he also became president of the Bank of International Settlements (BIS).

Dumas, Roland (1922–) French lawyer, journalist and politician. He was first elected to parliament in 1945 for a fore-runner of the Socialist Party (PS). A foreign-policy specialist, he was appointed minister of European affairs in the PS-led government in 1983 and foreign minister in 1984. He retained this post until 1986, when the party lost power, and again from 1988–93. He lost his parliamentary seat at the March 1993 election and became a foreign-policy adviser to President Mitterrand.

DUP *See* ULSTER DEMOCRATIC UNIONIST PARTY.

Dupont, Jacques (1929–) French diplomat and politician. He entered the diplomatic service in 1954, serving in several North African countries, the United States, Greece, Italy, South Vietnam and the Soviet Union. He was France's ambassador to Israel from 1982–86 and to South Africa from 1988–91. In April 1991 Prince Rainier of Monaco appointed him the principality's minister of state (= head of government).

Durão Barroso, José Manuel (1956–) Portuguese lawyer, academic and politician. He has lectured in political science and constitutional law in several countries. Elected to parliament for the centre-right Social Democratic Party (PSD) in 1985, he held several junior ministerial posts before being appointed foreign minister in November 1992.

Duray, Miklós (1945–) Slovakian geologist and politician. An ethnic Hungarian, he was a leading human-rights activist during communist rule in the 1970s and 80s. In March 1990 he became leader of Coexistence (ESWS), a political movement set up to advance the interests of the Hungarian community and other minorities. He was a member of the Czechoslovak parliament from 1990 until the federation's dissolution at the end of 1992.

Dušan Yugoslav, Bosnian and Croatian paramilitary group. Like similar groups, Dušan advocates the creation of a 'Greater Serbia'. It was founded in 1991 and is named after Stefan Dušan, king of Serbia from 1331–55 and the country's most revered ruler. It has fought alongside local Serb forces in the civil wars in Bosnia-Herzegovina and Croatia and has been linked to a number of massacres of Muslims and Croats. It is also said to be involved in organized crime in Serbia. The leader is Dragoslav Bokan.

Dushan *See* DUŠAN.

Dutch Citizens or people of the Netherlands.

Dutch Christian Employers' Federation [Nederlands Christelijk Werkgevers-verbond] (NCW) Dutch employers' association. Founded in 1970, the NCW has around 11,000 member companies from all industrial and service branches. It cooperates with the Federation of Dutch Industry (VNO), the other national employers' federation, in the Council of Dutch Industrial Federations (RNW). The president is Hans Blankert.

Dutch Trade Union Confederation [Federatie Nederlandse Vakbeweging] (FNV) Dutch trade-union federation. The FNV was formed in 1975 by the merger of the Dutch Trade Union Federation (NVV) and the Dutch Catholic Trade Union Federation (NKV). Its 19 affiliated unions have a total membership of around 1.1 million (a sixth of the labour force). The president is Johan Stekelenburg.

DVU *See* GERMAN PEOPLE'S UNION.

Dyba, Karel (1940–) Czech economist and politician. He has taught at the Prague School of Economics, researched at the Czechoslovak Academy of Sciences, and headed the Economic Institute within the Academy. He was appointed economy minister of the Czech Republic in June 1990. He was elected to parliament for the right-wing Civic Democratic Party (ODS) in 1992.

DYP *See* TRUE PATH PARTY.

DZVM *See* DEMOCRATIC UNION OF VOJVODINA HUNGARIANS.

E Abbreviation for Spain, used for international vehicle registrations, postal addresses etc. It is taken from España, the country's name in Spanish.

EA *See* BASQUE SOLIDARITY.

EAD *See* PARTY FOR THE DEFENCE OF HUMAN RIGHTS.

EAEC *See* EUROPEAN ATOMIC ENERGY COMMUNITY.

EAGGF *See* EUROPEAN AGRICULTURAL GUIDANCE AND GUARANTEE FUND.

EAJ *See* BASQUE NATIONALIST PARTY.

EAK *See* ASSOCIATION OF ESTONIAN TRADE UNIONS.

East, the Shorthand for the Soviet Union and its Eastern European allies during the Cold War, the military and political confrontation with the North Atlantic Treaty Organization (NATO) – the West – from the late 1940s until the late 1980s. They were organized in the Warsaw Pact, which was formally dissolved in July 1991.

East Anglia Standard region of the United Kingdom. Situated in eastern England, East Anglia comprises the counties of Cambridgeshire, Norfolk and Suffolk. It has an area of 12,574 sq km and a population of 2,091,000. The main cities are Norwich and Ipswich. The economy is based on agriculture (cereals) and manufacturing (food processing, engineering). East Anglia has a strong regional identity. It is considered a unit principally for statistical purposes and has no administrative or political functions.

East Germany Former country in central Europe, officially called the German Democratic Republic (GDR), now part of Germany. After its defeat in the Second World War (1939–45) Germany was divided into American, British, French and Soviet zones of occupation, and Berlin, the capital, situated within the Soviet zone, was also divided into four zones. The Soviet zone covered the eastern third of the country under its redrawn borders (i.e. after territories east of the Oder and Neisse rivers were allocated to Poland). The Soviet military authorities, whose main initial aim was to collect war reparations, promoted members of the Communist Party of Germany (KPD) into positions of power. In 1946 the Social Democratic Party (SPD) was forcibly merged with the KPD to create the Socialist Unity Party (SED). Disagreements over economic policy and Germany's future political structure exacerbated the latent distrust between the Soviet Union and its former allies and led to a growing rift with the western powers. A Soviet blockade of West Berlin in 1948–49 marked the start of a 'cold war' between the two sides. Preparations to set up a separate state in the Soviet zone began in 1948, and the German Democratic Republic (GDR) was proclaimed in 1949. (The Federal Republic of Germany was set up in the three western zones.) The new SED government introduced orthodox communist policies, nationalizing the economy, introducing central planning and suppressing all political opposition (although several 'bloc parties' were allowed to function). East Germany was fully integrated into the Soviet system, becoming a founding member of the Warsaw Pact in 1955. Up to 400,000 Soviet troops were stationed in the GDR, which was in the front line of the confrontation between East and West. Anti-government demonstrations in 1953 were suppressed with the help of Soviet troops. Between 1945 and 1961 economic development was hampered by the emigration of around 3.5 million mostly young and skilled people to the west. This exodus was stemmed in two stages, by the construction of extensive border fortifications from 1952 and by the construction of a concrete wall around West Berlin in 1961. As part of a new 'eastern policy' [Ostpolitik], West Germany recognized the GDR in 1972. Relations between the two states thereafter reflected the overall state of East-West relations. With communist authority crumbling across Eastern Europe, popular opposition to the regime increased in 1989. In September thousands of East Germans fled to West Germany via Czechoslovakia, Hungary and Austria after Hungary's reformist government opened the border with Austria. Confronted with mass demonstrations in East Berlin, Leipzig and other cities, Erich

Honecker, the country's leader since 1971, and other conservatives were forced to resign in October. In November the new government announced political reforms and opened the Berlin Wall – a potent symbol of communist repression and the division of Germany. The multiparty election held in March 1990 was won by the centre-right Alliance for Germany, which was dominated by allies of the West German Christian Democratic Union (CDU) and supported the rapid reunification of Germany. A monetary, economic and social union between the two states (with the West German mark as the common currency) took effect in July. Full reunification took place in October, when the five East German states (reconstituted earlier in the year) were absorbed into the Federal Republic under article 23 of the constitution, which provides for the readmission of former German territories. As in the other former communist countries, the transition to a market-based economy has been accompanied by severe economic disruption and social dislocation, with production collapsing and unemployment soaring. Living standards in the east are about half of those in the west, and the gap would be even wider were it not for massive government subsidies to the region. The east-west divide, exacerbated by widespread resentment in the east at the West German 'takeover' or 'colonization', has become a defining feature of the reunited Germany.

East Midlands Standard region of the United Kingdom. Situated in central England, the East Midlands comprises the counties of Derbyshire, Leicestershire, Lincolnshire, Northamptonshire and Nottinghamshire. It has an area of 15,630 sq km and a population of 4,026,000. The main cities are Nottingham and Derby. The economy is based on manufacturing (engineering, textiles, chemicals), agriculture and mining (coal). The region is considered a unit principally for statistical purposes and has no administrative or political functions.

east-west divide [Ost-West-Gefälle] In Germany, the perceived economic, social and cultural gap between the states [Länder] in former West Germany and those in former East Germany. Since reunification in October 1990 East Germany, like the other former communist countries, has experienced severe economic disruption and social dislocation during the transition to a market-based economy. Living standards in the east are about half of those in the west, and the difference would be even greater were it not for massive government subsidies to the region. The east-west divide in economic terms has been exacerbated by widespread resentment in the east at the West German 'takeover' or 'colonization', and resentment in the west at tax increases and the huge financial transfers to the east.

Eastern Europe Bank Informal name for the EUROPEAN BANK FOR RECONSTRUCTION AND DEVELOPMENT (EBRD).

Eastern European countries Collective name for the former communist countries and the successor states, i.e. Albania, Bosnia-Herzegovina, Bulgaria, Croatia, Czech Republic, Estonia, Hungary, Latvia, Lithuania, Macedonia, Poland, Romania, Slovakia, Slovenia and Yugoslavia. The Soviet successor states of Belorussia, Moldavia, Russia and Ukraine are often also included.

EBRD See EUROPEAN BANK FOR RECONSTRUCTION AND DEVELOPMENT.

Ebrei (sing. Ebreo/Ebrea) Italian name for JEWS.

EC Abbreviation for the European Community or the European Communities. The former is by far the most important of the three Communities, which in turn form the core of the EUROPEAN UNION (EU).

EC ... See EU ....

ECA See COURT OF AUDITORS OF THE EUROPEAN COMMUNITIES.

ECAS See EURO CITIZEN ACTION SERVICE.

ECDU See EUROPEAN CHRISTIAN DEMOCRATIC UNION.

ECE See UNITED NATIONS ECONOMIC COMMISSION FOR EUROPE.

Ecevit, Bülent (1925–) Turkish journalist and politician. From 1950–61 he worked as a senior editor for *Ulus*, the daily newspaper of the centre-left Republican

People's Party (CHP). He was elected to parliament for the CHP in 1957 and was minister of labour from 1961–65. He became general secretary of the party in 1966 and leader in May 1972. In the 1970s he was prime minister of three short-lived governments (1974, 1977 and 1978–79). After the military took power in 1980 the CHP was disbanded and Ecevit, along with other leading politicians, was banned from political activity for 10 years. Following the lifting of the ban (which had been widely ignored) in September 1987, he was elected leader of the Democratic Left Party (DSP), which had been founded by his wife, Rahşan, in 1985. He was again elected to parliament in 1991.

ECF *See* EUROPEAN CULTURAL FOUNDATION.

ECJ *See* COURT OF JUSTICE OF THE EUROPEAN COMMUNITIES.

ECOFIN Abbreviation for the Council of Economy and Finance Ministers, a specialist meeting of the COUNCIL OF THE EUROPEAN UNION, the EU's main decision-making body.

ÉCOLO *See* ECOLOGY PARTY.

Ecology Generation [Génération Écologie] (GE) French political party. GE was founded in 1990 as a more pragmatic alternative to the Greens (Les Verts). Its support base is in the cities and it has attracted many disenchanted Socialist Party (PS) activists and voters. Despite their differences, GE and the Greens contested the March 1993 election as an alliance, with the GE gaining 3.6% of the vote but no seats. The leader is Brice Lalonde.

Ecology Party [Parti Écologiste] (ÉCOLO) Belgian political party. Founded in 1978, the Walloon ÉCOLO gained 5.1% of the vote and 10/212 seats at the November 1991 election. This made it, together with its Flemish counterpart Live Differently (AGALEV), one of the most successful environmentalist movements in Europe. The leadership is collective.

Ecology Party - The Greens [Miljöpartiet de Gröna] (MpG) Swedish political party. Founded in 1981, the MpG gained 5.5% of the vote and 20/349 seats at the 1988 election. But with 3.4% at the September 1991 election it failed to pass the 4% threshold for parliamentary representation. The leadership is collective.

economia sommersa ('submerged economy') In Italy, the unofficial or black economy. It is thought to be equivalent to around a sixth of the official gross domestic product.

economic and monetary union (EMU) In the European Union (EU), a policy objective aimed at the full integration of the member states' economies. It was formally proclaimed in the Single European Act signed in February 1986 and set out in detail in the Maastricht Treaty agreed in December 1991. EMU is without doubt the most ambitious project undertaken thus far within the context of European integration. Its realization calls for far-reaching coordination of member states' economic, financial, monetary and social policies. Specifically, it is generally considered to require the following: (i) the free movement of goods, services, capital and people ('single internal market'); (ii) the progressive alignment of economic performance in terms of inflation rates, public finances, exchange rates and interest rates ('economic convergence'); (iii) the reduction of structural and regional disparities in economic and social development ('economic and social cohesion'); and (iv) the establishment of permanently fixed exchanges rates ('single currency'). The single internal market was completed at the end of 1992. Under proposals agreed in June 1989, progress towards EMU would be in three stages. Stage one began in July 1990 and provided for closer cooperation among governments and central banks, in particular through the European Monetary System (EMS) and its Exchange Rate Mechanism (ERM) and the European Monetary Cooperation Fund (EMCF). The Maastricht Treaty sets out the next two stages. Stage two provides for the establishment of the European Monetary Institute (EMI) to strengthen coordination of monetary policy, promote economic convergence and prepare the transition to a single currency. Stage three provides for the creation of an independent European central bank (replacing the EMI) at the apex of a system of national central banks and for the introduction of a single currency. Stage two was launched in January 1994. Stage three is to be launched by the end of 1996 if a qualified majority of member states (i.e. broadly two-thirds) agrees that a 'critical mass' among them has met the criteria for economic convergence; a single currency would then be introduced in 1997. If this has not happened, those states that do qualify can decide to move to stage three in 1998 and introduce a single currency by the beginning of 1999. Under 'opt-outs' negotiated by their governments, the United Kingdom and Denmark are not committed to moving to stage three. Economic and monetary union has been a long-standing aspiration of the European Community (EC) and now the EU.

Chronologically, in March 1971 the original six-member EC endorsed a plan calling for a single currency by 1980. This foundered primarily on the economic and monetary crisis of the mid 1970s. The EMS and ERM were established in March 1979 to coordinate monetary policy and reduce exchange-rate fluctuations. In June 1988 the heads of government charged a committee headed by the president of the European Commission, Jacques Delors, to draw up a new plan for EMU. Its proposals were approved in June 1989 and formed the basis for the section on EMU in the Maastricht Treaty, agreed in December 1991. The British government refused to commit itself to stage three of EMU without a separate decision by Parliament in due course, a stance accepted by the other states. Denmark negotiated a similar opt-out after a first referendum on the Maastricht Treaty was narrowly defeated in June 1992. Subsequent turmoil in the currency markets and economic problems called the timetable and the whole EMU project into question, but despite the setbacks stage two was launched on schedule in January 1994 with the establishment of the EMI. The French, German and some other governments are considering pursuing a 'fast track' to EMU,

which would involve introducing a single currency as soon as conditions permit and member states joining when they are able to do so.

See also ERM CRISES *and entries on specific institutions, terms etc.*

economic and social cohesion or **cohesion** In the European Union (EU), the reduction of structural and regional disparities in the economic and social development of member states. Strengthening cohesion – in effect a development programme to help less prosperous regions – became a major focus of activity in the then European Community (EC) in the 1970s and was proclaimed as an objective in the 1986 Single European Act and reaffirmed in the 1991 Maastricht Treaty. It is considered particularly important in the context of the SINGLE INTERNAL MARKET and ECONOMIC AND MONETARY UNION (EMU). It is pursued by coordinating national economic policies, by taking account of regional differences in formulating common policies, and above all by joint action through EU institutions and programmes. Funds for specific projects in a wide range of fields are allocated primarily through the European Regional Development Fund (ERDF), the European Social Fund (ESF), the Guidance Section of the European Agricultural Guidance and Guarantee Fund (EAGGF), the European Investment Bank (EIB) and the Cohesion Fund. *See also* STRUCTURAL FUND.

Economic and Social Committee (ECOSOC or ESC) Advisory body of the European Union (EU). ECOSOC – not to be confused with the United Nations committee of the same name – was set up under the 1957 Treaty of Rome establishing the European Economic Community (EEC), now the European Community (EC), the core of the EU. It must be consulted by the European Commission and the Council of Ministers during the preparation of legislation in the economic and social spheres. It may also issue opinions on its own initiative. The Committee has 189 members: 24 each from France, Germany, Italy and the United Kingdom, 21 from Spain, 12 each from Belgium, Greece, the Netherlands and Portugal, nine each from Denmark and Ireland, and six from Luxemburg. Drawn from trade unions and employers', industrial, agricultural and consumer organizations and other interest groups, they are appointed for a four-year term by the Council on the nomination of the national governments. ECOSOC has a joint organizational structure with the Committee of the Regions (COR). The president is Susanne Tiemann (Germany), the secretary-general Simon-Pierre Nothomb (Belgium). In recent years ECOSOC has been increasingly overshadowed by the European Parliament.

Economic and Social Council [Conseil Économique et Social] (CÉS) French advisory body. Set up under the 1958 constitution and composed of around 200 experts, the Economic and Social Council gives advice on bills, orders and decrees in the economic and social sphere and may express an opinion on any related matter submitted to it by the government. All draft legislation dealing with economic and social issues must be submitted to it for advice.

economic cohesion (European Union) *See* ECONOMIC AND SOCIAL COHESION.

Economic Commission for Europe *See* UNITED NATIONS ECONOMIC COMMISSION FOR EUROPE.

economic convergence or **convergence** In the European Union (EU), the progressive alignment of member states' economic performance as a prerequisite for ECONOMIC AND MONETARY UNION (EMU). Under the Maastricht Treaty, in force since November 1993, the member states commit themselves to pursuing policies which bring about greater convergence, especially in terms of inflation, budget deficits and public debt, exchange rates and interest rates. The Treaty sets out four targets which a member state has to meet before it can participate in the third and final stage of EMU, the introduction of a single currency and a European system of central banks in 1997 or 1999. These 'convergence criteria' are: (i) a high degree of price stability, indicated by a level of inflation no more than 1.5% above the average of the three best-performing member states, sustained over at least a

year; (ii) sound public finances, indicated by government budget deficits not exceeding 3% of GDP and a total public debt not exceeding 60% of GDP; (iii) a stable exchange rate, indicated by the currency staying within the 2.25% fluctuation margins of the Exchange Rate Mechanism (ERM) of the European Monetary System (EMS) for at least two years without devaluation against other ERM currencies; and (iv) a durable alignment of economic performance with other states, indicated by a level of long-term interest rates no more than 2% above the average of the three best-performing states on price stability, sustained over at least a year.

Economic Council [Økonomiske Råd] (ØR) Danish advisory body. Founded in 1962, the ØR monitors national economic development and seeks to coordinate the actions of economic interest groups. Its 27 members represent the trade unions, employers' associations and government and also include independent experts.

economic union (European Union) *See* ECONOMIC AND MONETARY UNION.

Economides, Phaedros *See* OIKONOMIDES, FAIDROS.

Economists' Political Association [Tautsaimnieku Politiskā Apvienība] (TPA) Latvian political party. The TPA was formed in February 1994 and formally constituted the following May, after a split in the Concord for Latvia - Economic Rebirth (SLAT) alliance, which had gained 12.0% of the vote and 13/100 seats at the June 1993 election. It favours a more rapid transition to a market economy than the SLAT's other successor, the National Harmony Party (TSP). The TPA holds four seats in parliament. The leader is Edvīns Kide.

ECOSOC *See* ECONOMIC AND SOCIAL COMMITTEE.

ECSC *See* EUROPEAN COAL AND STEEL COMMUNITY.

ecu Notional currency of the European Union (EU). The ecu is made up of the currencies of the member states, weighted according to their share of the EU's gross 'national' product and internal trade. The balance within the 'basket' of currencies

174

is normally reassessed every five years. The ecu's main function is as the accounting unit within the EU: budgets, grants, loans, fines etc have all been denominated in ecus since 1981. It is also used as the currency denominator in the Exchange Rate Mechanism (ERM) of the European Monetary System (EMS) and for payments between central banks, international bond issues and, increasingly, international commercial transactions. It is backed by a large reserve fund administered by the European Monetary Institute (EMI), into which member states are required to pay a fifth of their gold reserves and a fifth of their dollar reserves. 'ECU' formally stands for European Currency Unit, but 'ecu' also echoes the *écu*, a silver coin used in medieval France. *See also* ECON-OMIC AND MONETARY UNION.

EDA *See* EUROPEAN DEMOCRATIC ALLIANCE.

EDEK, EDEK-SK and **EDEK Socialist Party of Cyprus** *See* UNIFIED DEMOCRA-TIC UNION OF CYPRUS - SOCIALIST PARTY.

Edinstvo *See* UNITY.

EDU *See* EUROPEAN DEMOCRAT UNION.

Eduskunta Parliament of Finland. The Eduskunta has 200 members elected for a four-year term by proportional represen-tation in 15 multi-member constituencies. A feature of its law-making arrangements is that most bills effectively require a two-thirds majority, since the constitu-tion provides for the deferral of a bill until after the next election if it is opposed by more than a third of the members of parliament.

EE Abbreviation for Estonia, used for international vehicle registrations, postal addresses etc. It is taken from Eesti, the country's name in Estonian.

EE (Spain) *See* BASQUE LEFT *and* BASQUE SOCIALIST PARTY - BASQUE LEFT.

EE Greek abbreviation for the European Union (EU).

EEA *See* EUROPEAN ECONOMIC AREA.

EEA *See* EUROPEAN ENVIRONMENT AGENCY.

EEA Agreement Shorthand for the AGREE-MENT ON THE EUROPEAN ECONOMIC AREA establishing a single market covering the European Union (EU) and the European Free Trade Association (EFTA). *See also* EUROPEAN ECONOMIC AREA.

EEA Council Shorthand for the COUNCIL OF THE EUROPEAN ECONOMIC AREA.

EEA Joint Committee Shorthand for the JOINT COMMITTEE OF THE EUROPEAN ECONOMIC AREA.

EEC Abbreviation for the European Econ-omic Community, the former name of the European Community (EC), the main component of the EUROPEAN UNION (EU). It is also used informally to refer to the Union as a whole.

EÉE French abbreviation for the European Economic Area (EEA).

EEK Abbreviation for the KROON, the Esto-nian currency, used in banking etc.

Eerste Kamer *See* FIRST CHAMBER.

Eesti Estonian name for Estonia.

Eesti Vabariik ('Republic of Estonia') Official name of Estonia.

EF Danish abbreviation for the European Community (EC), the core of the Euro-pean Union (EU).

EFA *See* EUROFIGHTER 2000.

efficientism [efficienzismo] In Italy, a term associated with those who argue that the country's political system is excessively bureaucratic and corrupt and should be overhauled and infused with 'modern' values such as efficiency and transparency of decision making.

efficienzismo *See* EFFICIENTISM.

EFTA *See* EUROPEAN FREE TRADE ASSOCIATION.

EFTA Council Shorthand for the COUNCIL OF THE EUROPEAN FREE TRADE ASSOCIA-TION, the organization's governing body.

EFTA Court Shorthand for the COURT OF THE EUROPEAN FREE TRADE ASSOCIATION.

EFTA Surveillance Authority Shorthand for the SURVEILLANCE AUTHORITY OF THE EUROPEAN FREE TRADE ASSOCIATION.

EG Dutch and German abbreviation for the European Community (EC), the core of the EUROPEAN UNION (EU).

EGPGC *See* FREE GALICIAN PEOPLE'S GUERRILLA ARMY.

Eguigaray, Juan Manuel (1945–) Spanish economist, civil servant and politician. He held several senior posts at local and regional level for the Spanish Socialist Workers' Party (PSOE) in his native Basque Country in the 1980s. He has been the government's delegate to the autonomous community or region of Murcia (1988–89) and the Basque Country (1989–91). In 1991 he was appointed minister for public administration and in July 1993 he became industry minister.

Együttélés *See* COEXISTENCE.

EI Abbreviation for Esercito Italiano ('Italian Army'), the Italian army.

EIB *See* EUROPEAN INVESTMENT BANK.

EIF *See* EUROPEAN INVESTMENT FUND.

EIP Abbreviation for Ethnikí Ipiresía Plioforíon ('National Information Service'), the Greek intelligence agency.

EIR Abbreviation for Ireland. It is taken from Éire, the country's name in Irish.

Éire Irish name for Ireland. This was the country's official name, also in English, from 1937 until 1949, when it was renamed the Republic of Ireland. 'Éire' is still sometimes used in Britain to distinguish the Republic from Northern Ireland, which is part of the United Kingdom, and from the island of Ireland as a whole.

EK Abbreviation for the KROON, the Estonian currency.

EK Greek abbreviation for the European Community (EC), the core of the EUROPEAN UNION (EU).

EKE *See* ESTONIAN COALITION PARTY.

EKL *See* ESTONIAN CITIZENS' UNION.

ELA (Greece) *See* REVOLUTIONARY PEOPLE'S STRUGGLE.

ELA (Spain) and **ELA/STV** *See* BASQUE WORKERS' SOLIDARITY.

ELDR *See* FEDERATION OF LIBERAL, DEMOCRATIC AND REFORM PARTIES OF THE EUROPEAN UNION.

Eleven, the Shorthand for the European Union (EU) member states excluding the United Kingdom. The term was widely used in the 1980s, when the British government under Margaret Thatcher was often the sole dissenting voice on specific aspects of the integration process.

Eleventh of November Alliance [Porozumienie Jedenastego Listopada] Polish political organization. The Alliance was formed in December 1993 as an alliance of four right-wing parties, the Real Politics Union (UPR), Conservative Party (PK), Christian Democratic Party (PChD) and Peasant Christian Party (SLCh), later joined by the National Democratic Party (SND). The UPR had contested the September 1993 general election on its own and the other parties had done so within the Homeland (Ojczyzna) alliance, but none had passed the threshold required for representation in parliament. The leadership rotates among the five party leaders. The alliance is named after the day in 1918 that Polish independence was restored after 123 years of foreign rule. *See also* ALLIANCE FOR POLAND (PdP).

Eliades, Konstantinos or **Kostas** (1950–) Cypriot doctor and politician. Elected to parliament for the centre-right Democratic Party (DIKO) in 1991, he was appointed defence minister in February 1993.

Elizabeth II (1926–) Queen of the United Kingdom. She succeeded to the throne on the death of her father, George VI, in February 1952. She is also head of the Church of England, head of the Commonwealth (the intergovernmental organization comprising the United Kingdom and most of its former colonies), and head of state in a number of Commonwealth countries (including Australia, Canada and New Zealand). She married Philip Mountbatten, now Prince Philip, Duke of Edinburgh, in 1947. They have four children.

Elláda Greek name for Greece.

Ellan Vannín Manx name for the Isle of Man. It is used on coins, postage stamps and in other contexts. Manx, a Celtic language, is virtually extinct and has no official status.

Ellás Greek name for Greece.

Ellemann-Jensen, Uffe (1941–) Danish journalist and politician. He worked for a leading daily newspaper from 1967, for Danish television from 1970 and was editor of the business paper *Børsen* in 1975–76. A member of parliament for the Liberals (Venstre) since 1977, he was the party's parliamentary leader from 1978–82 and was elected party leader in September 1984. He was foreign minister in successive centre-right coalitions from 1982 until January 1993.

Ellinikí Dimokratía ('Hellenic Republic') Official name of Greece. Ellás and Elláda are the native names for the country.

Élysée Palace or **Élysée** [Palais de l'Élysée] Shorthand for the French presidency. Situated off the Avenue des Champs-Élysées in Paris, the Élysée is the official residence of the president.

Élysée telephone-tapping affair Controversy in France surrounding the activities of an anti-terrorist unit based at the Élysée Palace, the presidential residence, and nominally answerable to President Mitterrand. In March 1993 – shortly before the general election – newspapers reported that a surveillance unit based at the Élysée had illegally bugged the telephones of dozens of people between 1983 and 1986, including politicians, journalists, lawyers and actors. The operation was reportedly supervised by Gilles Ménage, at the time head of Mitterrand's private office and now head of Électricité de France (ÉdF), the state-owned utility company. The then prime minister, Pierre Bérégovoy, ordered the National Supervisory Commission on Security Interceptors (CNCIS) to investigate the allegations. Its report in December 1993 (i) confirmed that the unit had authorized at least 114 wiretaps for reasons ranging from suspected arms trade to terrorism links or presidential security and (ii) concluded that it had been guilty of 'serious abuses' of power. The unit was then disbanded. The CNCIS initially refused to release its report to the magistrate investigating the affair because it contained military secrets, but in March 1994 the prime minister, Édouard Balladur, authorized publication of parts of it. He also announced that Ménage and the other key figure in the affair, Christian Prouteau, the head of the unit, were not, as previously thought, protected by secrecy laws and could therefore be questioned by investigating magistrates.

EM *See* EUROPEAN MOVEMENT.

EMCF *See* EUROPEAN MONETARY COOPERATION FUND *and* EUROPEAN MONETARY INSTITUTE.

EMD Abbreviation for Eidgenössisches Militärdepartement ('Federal Military Department'), the German name of the Swiss defence ministry.

Emerald Isle Literary name for Ireland. It refers to the island's verdant countryside.

emerging democracies Informal name for the countries of Central and Eastern Europe, which abandoned communism between 1989 and 1991 and committed themselves to creating pluralist political systems and market-based economies.

EMI *See* EUROPEAN MONETARY INSTITUTE.

Emilia-Romagna Autonomous region of Italy. Situated in the north between the Apennine mountains and the Po river and bordering on the Adriatic Sea, it has an area of 22,123 sq km and a population of 3,984,000. The capital is Bologna, and the other main cities are Modena, Parma, Ferrara, Ravenna, Reggio nell'Emilia and Rimini. The economy is based on agriculture (livestock and dairy farming, fruit and vegetables, cereals), manufacturing (food processing, engineering, chemicals, textiles), tourism and fishing. The region is one of Italy's most productive agriculturally and among the most prosperous. The cities of Emilia-Romagna have a long history of autonomy. Many were nominally part of the Papal States from the 10th century, but papal control was not firmly established until the 16th century. The whole region, including the independent duchies of Modena and Parma, was incorporated into unified Italy in 1860.

EMKE *See* ESTONIAN RURAL CENTRE PARTY.

EML *See* ESTONIAN RURAL UNION.

Emmanuelli, Henri (1945–) French banker and politician. Elected to parliament for the Socialist Party (PS) in 1977, he held several junior ministerial posts from 1981–86. He was party treasurer from 1988–92 and president of the National Assembly, the lower house of parliament, from January 1992 until the PS lost power in March 1993. In September 1992 he was indicted on fraud charges in relation to illegal party funding (*see* URBA AFFAIR).

Employers' Federation of Iceland [Vinnuveitendasamband Íslands] (VSÍ) Icelandic employers' association. Most of the country's companies are affiliated to the VSÍ, which was founded in 1934. The president is Einar Oddur Kristjansson.

employment ban (Germany) *See* BERUFSVERBOT.

EMS *See* EUROPEAN MONETARY SYSTEM.

EMU *See* ECONOMIC AND MONETARY UNION.

EN *See* EUROPE OF NATIONS (political group).

énarque Common name for a student or graduate of the École Nationale d'Administration (ENA) in France. Established in 1945, the ENA is the elite school of higher education which trains senior civil servants and government officials. Many leading politicians have graduated from it.

Énergie Radicale *See* RADICAL ENERGY.

Engell, Hans (1948–) Danish journalist and politician. He was director of the Conservative People's Party (KF) press office from 1978–82. He was minister of defence from 1982–87 and justice from 1989 until the party lost power in January 1993. First elected to parliament in 1984, he led the KF parliamentary group from 1987–89. He was elected party leader in September 1993.

Engholm, Björn (1939–) German politician. A member of parliament for the Social Democratic Party (SPD) from 1969–82, he was appointed minister of education and science in 1981. After the SPD lost power in 1982, he was elected party leader in his home state of Schleswig-Holstein. He became the state's prime minister in May 1988. In May 1991 he was elected leader of the SPD at federal level. He resigned from both posts in May 1993 after admitting that he had lied to a parliamentary inquiry about his knowledge of a 'dirty tricks' campaign against him and the party at the time of the 1987 state election.

England Constituent country of the United Kingdom. Situated in the southern two-thirds of Great Britain and surrounded by the North Sea, the Channel and Irish Sea on three sides, England has an area of 130,439 sq km and a population of 48,068,000. The dominant country within the United Kingdom, it accounts for 53% of its area and 84% of its population. The capital is London, and the other main cities are Birmingham, Manchester, Leeds, Liverpool, Sheffield and Bristol.

The economy is based on services (trade, financial services), manufacturing and agriculture. In a sense England no longer exists in constitutional and political terms. This situation has arisen largely because in the course of the creation of the United Kingdom – through the incorporation of Wales, Scotland and Ireland (later Northern Ireland) – English institutions have evolved into those of the United Kingdom as a whole. A notable exception is the Church of England. Popular identification with England as a country is generally strong, as is regional identification in some of the regions. England was gradually united under the kings of Wessex in the 9th and 10th centuries. After its conquest by the Norman French in 1066 it became the dominant power in the British Isles. *See also* GREAT BRITAIN AND NORTHERN IRELAND.

England Informal name for the United Kingdom of Great Britain and Northern Ireland, widely used outside the country. It properly refers only to the United Kingdom's largest component country.

Engliš, Alojz (1947–) Slovakian metalworker, mechanical engineer and trade unionist. He worked for a steelworks in Košice from 1971–89. After the collapse of the communist regime in 1989 he was elected chairman of the local branch of the Slovakian metalworkers' union. From 1991–92 he was president of the Czechoslovak Metalworkers' Federation (OSKČS) and vice-president of the Czech and Slovak Trade Union Confederation (ČSKOS). In June 1992 he was elected president of the Trade Union Confederation of the Slovak Republic (KOZSR).

English People of England, a constituent country of the United Kingdom, or, informally, of the United Kingdom as a whole.

ENI Abbreviation for Ente Nazionale Idrocarburi ('National Hydrocarbons Agency'), one of Italy's major state-owned concerns. It dominates the energy sector.

Enimont affair Political and business scandal in Italy, the largest single case of bribery and illegal party funding in the web of corruption exposed since early

1992 (*see* ITALIAN CORRUPTION SCANDALS). Enimont was a short-lived joint venture between the Montedison chemical concern, part of the Ferruzzi conglomerate, and the state-owned energy concern Ente Nazionale Idrocarburi (ENI). It began trading in January 1989 but made heavy losses and was wound up in November 1990 under a deal that brought it wholly into state ownership. Bribes totalling 150 billion lire (77 million ecus) were paid to the governing parties, initially to gain approval for the setting up of Enimont (which would have had near-monopoly control of the country's petrochemical industry) and then to induce the government to buy Montedison out. The inflated price paid for Montedison's stake provided most of the funds for the pay-offs. They were distributed to the Christian Democratic Party (DC), Italian Socialist Party (PSI) and the other three coalition parties and directly involved all their leaders, including Giulio Andreotti and Arnaldo Forlani of the DC and Bettino Craxi of the PSI. Payments were also made to bankers and a judge. The transactions were brought to light in early 1993. Two of the senior industrialists implicated, Raul Gardini of Montedison and Gabriele Cagliari of ENI, committed suicide in July. The Enimont trial opened in October 1993. The only defendant was the financier Sergio Cusani, who was accused of false accounting, breaking the law on party funding and illegal appropriation of funds. But because many leading discredited politicians were called as witnesses, it was widely seen as a symbolic trial of the political elite which had ruled Italy since the early 1970s. Cusani was convicted and sentenced to eight years' imprisonment in April 1994.

énosis ('union' in Greek) In Cyprus, a term associated since the 1930s with those who advocate the country's unification with Greece. Strongly opposed by the Turkish Cypriot minority on the island, the *énosis* movement was particularly influential in the 1950s and 60s and in the attempted coup of 1974. Today none of the main Greek Cypriot political parties supports it. *See also* CYPRUS QUESTION.

enverism [enverizëm] Political outlook in Albania based on the values and policies of Enver Hoxha (1908–85), the country's leader from 1944 until his death. The Hoxha regime sought to build a 'socialist and communist society' in Albania based on 'self-reliance'. The means to achieve this goal were rigidly orthodox marxist-leninist economic policies and a monolithic single-party political structure. The system was underpinned by an extensive internal-security apparatus. In 1991 the Party of Labour (PPSh, now the Socialist Party, PSSh) effectively abandoned enverism – it had never used the term as such – and expelled its supporters.

Environment Council Institution of the European Union (EU), a specialist meeting of ministers responsible for environmental protection and related issues within the framework of the COUNCIL OF THE EUROPEAN UNION or Council of Ministers, the main decision-making body.

Environment Department (United Kingdom) *See* DEPARTMENT OF THE ENVIRONMENT.

EP *See* EUROPEAN PARLIAMENT.

EPC Abbreviation for European Political Cooperation, the former name of the COMMON FOREIGN AND SECURITY POLICY (CFSP), an intergovernmental 'pillar' of the European Union (EU).

EPP *See* EUROPEAN PEOPLE'S PARTY.

Eppelmann Commission *See* COMMISSION OF INQUIRY ASSESSING EAST GERMAN HISTORY.

Equal Rights [Līdztiesība (Latvian), Ravnopraviye (Russian)] Latvian political party. Equal Rights has its roots in the Communist Party (LKP), banned in 1991, and the Interfront movement, set up in 1988 (when Latvia was still part of the Soviet Union) to defend the rights of the large ethnic Russian minority. It draws its support from Russian speakers, many of whom have not been granted citizenship of independent Latvia, and from former LKP members. It has adopted a mainstream left-wing programme and advocates a major role for the state in the economy. At the June 1993 election it gained 5.8% of the vote and 7/100 seats. The leader is Sergeis Dimanis.

Equality Party *See* SOCIAL DEMOCRATIC PARTY (Faroe Islands).

ERA *See* EUROPEAN RADICAL ALLIANCE.

ERASMUS, in full **European Community Action Scheme for the Mobility of University Students** Programme of the European Union (EU). Set up in 1987, ERASMUS is aimed at developing a network of cooperation among EU universities. It provides financial support for students and lecturers to study and teach for a period (usually a term) in a university of another member state, and also includes an extensive range of measures to promote mutual recognition of qualifications.

Erbakan, Necmettin (1926–) Turkish mechanical engineer, academic and politician. He taught at the Technical University of Istanbul from 1954–66. The country's most prominent Islamic fundamentalist politician since the 1970s, he has been leader of the National Order Party (MHP) and the National Salvation Party (MSP), both of which were banned following military coups in 1971 and 1980, and the Welfare Party (RP) since July 1983. He was deputy prime minister in centre-right coalitions in 1974, 1975–77 and 1977.

ERC *See* REPUBLICAN LEFT OF CATALONIA.

ERDF *See* EUROPEAN REGIONAL DEVELOPMENT FUND.

ERKE *See* ESTONIAN PEOPLE'S CENTRE PARTY.

ERM *See* EXCHANGE RATE MECHANISM.

ERM crises Currency and political crises in 1992 and 1993 surrounding the EXCHANGE RATE MECHANISM (ERM), the system of semi-fixed exchange rates operated by member states of the European Community (EC), now the European Union (EU). The ERM was set up in 1979 to create greater monetary stability and thus promote economic growth. In the mid 1980s exchange rates became relatively stable largely because national authorities set interest rates at the same or higher levels than in Germany – Europe's largest economy – so that their respective currencies attracted sufficient investment capital to hold their own against the stronger deutschmark. The system came under strain in 1992 as the financial markets began to doubt the various authorities' commitment to maintaining existing parities by matching the high interest rates imposed in Germany for domestic reasons (an overheating economy following reunification in 1990), a policy which was having serious adverse consequences for economic growth and unemployment levels throughout Europe. When the German Bundesbank raised interest rates again in July 1992, speculation mounted against the weaker currencies, in particular the British pound and Italian lira. In an attempt to calm the markets, EC finance ministers and central-bank governors on 28 August and 5 September declared their opposition to an exchange-rate realignment and stressed their determination to support the weaker currencies. Speculative pressure on the lira nevertheless mounted in early September. After support in the form of interest-rate rises and massive intervention failed, it was devalued on 13 September. The following day the Bundesbank and other central banks announced interest-rate cuts of 0.25–0.5%. This failed to calm the markets, however, and pressure switched mainly to the pound. After it dropped through its permitted 'floor' despite support measures, the British government on 16 September announced the pound's suspension from the ERM. The following day the lira was also suspended 'temporarily' and the Spanish peseta was devalued. (The pound and lira were also sharply devalued over the following two weeks.) Despite several minor realignments and limited interest-rate cuts by the Bundesbank and other central banks, speculation against the French franc, the Spanish peseta and other currencies continued over the following months. The second ERM crisis was triggered on 29 July 1993 by the Bundesbank's decision, contrary to expectations, not to cut its main interest rate. The franc and peseta fell below their 'floors' the following day. On 2 August finance ministers agreed to let currencies fluctuate by up to 15% on either side of their central rates. The decision, effectively suspending the ERM, constituted a major setback in the process of economic and monetary integration and called into question the plans for the introduction of a single currency in the late 1990s.

Eroğlu, Derviş (1938–) Northern Cypriot doctor and politician. He was elected to parliament for the centre-right National Unity Party (UBP) in 1976 and was elected party leader in November 1983. He was prime minister from August 1985 until the UBP's defeat in the December 1993 election.

ERP *See* ESTONIAN ROYALIST PARTY.

Erse Informal name for the IRISH language, or for the Gaelic language spoken by around 65,000 people in northwest Scotland (United Kingdom).

ERSP *See* ESTONIAN NATIONAL INDEPENDENCE PARTY.

ertzain (pl. -ak) ('territorial guard' in Basque) Member of the Ertzaintza, the autonomous police force of the Basque Country, an autonomous community or region of Spain.

Ertzaintza ('Territorial Guard' in Basque) Spanish police force. The Ertzaintza is the autonomous police force of the Basque Country. It replaced the Civil Guard [Guardia Civil] in the region in 1988. The name is also used by Spanish speakers.

ESA *See* EUROPEAN SPACE AGENCY.

ESA *See* SURVEILLANCE AUTHORITY OF THE EUROPEAN FREE TRADE ASSOCIATION.

Esc Abbreviation for the ESCUDO, the Portuguese currency.

ESC *See* ECONOMIC AND SOCIAL COMMITTEE (European Union).

escudo Currency of Portugal. Common abbreviations are Esc, $ and PTE (the international standard in banking etc). It is divided into 100 centavos. A thousand escudos is called a conto.

ESDP *See* ESTONIAN SOCIAL DEMOCRATIC PARTY.

ESF *See* EUROPEAN SCIENCE FOUNDATION.

ESF *See* EUROPEAN SOCIAL FUND.

ESP Abbreviation for the PESETA, the Spanish currency, used in banking etc.

España Spanish name for Spain.

ESPRIT, in full **European Strategic Programme for Research and Development in Information Technology** Programme of the European Union (EU). Started in 1984, ESPRIT is aimed at promoting research and development in microelectronics, data-processing systems, office automation, information-exchange systems etc. It brings together representatives from government, industry, universities and research institutes to develop objectives and collaborate in transnational research projects.

Estonia [Eesti] Country in northeastern Europe, formerly part of the Soviet Union.

Official data. Name: Republic of Estonia [Eesti Vabariik]; capital: Tallinn; form of government: parliamentary republic; head of state: president; head of government: prime minister; flag: three horizontal stripes, blue, black and white; national holiday: 24 February (Independence Day); language: Estonian; religion: none; currency: kroon (K) = 100 sent; abbreviations: EE and EV.

Geography. The northernmost and smallest of the three Baltic countries, Estonia has an area of 45,226 sq km. It is bordered by the Gulf of Finland in the north, Russia in the east, Latvia in the south, and the Baltic Sea in the west; neighbouring countries across the sea are Finland and Sweden. It consists of low-lying plains in the west and low hills in the east and south. There are many lakes, the largest of which is Lake Peipus [Peipsi Järv] on the Russian border. Off the west coast there are around 1,500 islands, the largest of which are Saaremaa and Hiiumaa. Some 22% of the land is arable, another 11% is covered by pastures and 31% is forested. The main river is the Pärnu. The climate is humid continental, with mild summers and cold winters; rainfall is light to moderate.

Demography. Estonia has a population of 1,536,000. Population density is 35 per sq km (land area), among the lowest in Europe. Some 72% of the people live in urban areas, and around a third in Tallinn. Other cities are Tartu, Narva, Kohtla-Järve and Pärnu. In ethnic terms 61.5% of the people are Estonians, 30.3% Russians,

3.1% Ukrainians, 1.8% Belorussians and 1.1% Finns. Most Russians live in the northeast and around Tallinn. Under legislation adopted since independence in 1991, most non-Estonians are not eligible for citizenship. The main languages are Estonian and Russian. In religious terms most Estonians are nominally Lutheran Protestant and most Russians are nominally Russian Orthodox.

Sociography. Estonia scores 0.867 on the United Nations human development index (HDI), ranking 29th in the world and 21st among 32 European countries. There are 37 doctors and 120 hospital beds for every 10,000 people, among the highest figures in Europe. Education is compulsory between the ages of seven and 17. There is one teacher for every 11 students. Enrolment is around 90% at the secondary level and around 20% at the tertiary level. The literacy rate is 96%. Real annual income per head (in terms of purchasing power) is US$ 8,090.

Infrastructure and communications. Estonia's transport and communications network is relatively developed but in need of modernization and extension; the telecommunications system in particular is limited. There are 44,100 km of paved roads and 238,000 passenger cars (150 per 1,000 people). There are 1,030 km of railways and 500 km of navigable waterways. The main port is Tallinn. The main airport is at Tallinn (Ulemiste). There are six daily newspapers, with a combined circulation of 315,000 (198 per 1,000 people). There are 926,000 radio receivers, 605,000 television sets and 354,000 telephones in use (respectively 583, 381 and 223 per 1,000 people).

Economic structure. The Estonian economy is based on manufacturing and agriculture. Although essentially developed and diversified, it is in need of major investment and restructuring. The transition from a command to a market-based economy initiated in the late 1980s is causing severe dislocation and has led to steep falls in industrial and agricultural production. Between 1990 and 1993 GDP contracted by 43%, inflation averaged around 190% per year, and unemploy-

ment rose to around 10% (unofficial estimate). There were some signs of recovery in 1993 and 1994.

Services contribute 48% of GDP, industry contributes 40% (manufacturing 29%), and agriculture, forestry and fisheries 12%. Some 28% of the labour force is employed in manufacturing, 18% in farming, forestry and fishing, 10% in trade and 10% in transport and communications. The main agricultural activities are livestock raising (cattle, pigs, chickens) and dairy farming (milk, eggs); horticulture (vegetables) is also important; the main crops grown are potatoes, cereals (barley, rye), sugarbeets and animal fodder (hay). Forestry provides a major source of foreign exchange, and fishing is also important. The main mineral resources are oil shale, phosphorite, limestone and dolomite. The main industry is engineering (esp. farm and industrial machinery, electrical goods); other important branches are textiles, food processing, wood processing (paper, furniture), metalworking, chemicals and building materials (cement, glass). The main energy sources are domestic and imported fossil fuels; 4% of export earnings are required to cover net fuel imports. The main exports are foodstuffs (17% of the total, esp. meat, dairy and fish products), textiles and clothing (15%), metal products (11%), fuels (11%), wood and wood products (incl. paper) (10%), chemicals (7%), transport equipment (7%) and industrial machinery (5%); basic manufactures account for 33% of the total, foodstuffs for 17%, machinery and transport equipment for 13%. The main imports are machinery and transport equipment, fuels and chemicals. The main trading partners are: exports: Finland (21%), Russia (21%), Latvia (11%), Sweden (8%), Ukraine (7%); imports: Russia (28%), Finland (23%), Germany (8%), Belorussia (6%), Sweden (6%).

The Bank of Estonia [Eesti Pank] is the central bank. There are several employers' associations; the main labour organization is the Association of Estonian Trade Unions (EAKL).

Political structure. Estonia is a parliamentary republic on the basis of a constitution adopted in June 1992, which replaced the 1938 constitution and various resolutions and laws related to the severing of the country's links with the Soviet Union. The head of state is the president, who is elected for a five-year term by a two-thirds majority of the legislature. The president is commander of the armed forces, appoints the prime minister, and has several other major powers. Most executive power is vested in the prime minister and the council of ministers. Legislative power is vested in the National Assembly [Riigikogu], whose 101 members are elected for a four-year term by a system of proportional representation. All citizens over the age of 18, including those living abroad, are entitled to vote; citizenship is generally restricted to those who were Estonian citizens at the time of the Soviet annexation in 1940 and their descendants. Judicial power is ultimately vested in the National Court [Riigikohus], whose members are appointed for life by the legislature. Administratively the country is divided into 15 districts [maakond, pl. -ed] and six district-level towns [linn, pl. -ad]; the districts are subdivided into communes.

The main political parties are Fatherland (Isamaa), the Estonian People's Centre Party (ERKE), Estonian National Independence Party (ERSP), Estonian Coalition Party (EKE), Estonian Rural Union (EML), Estonian Rural Centre Party (EMKE), Estonian Social Democratic Party (ESDP), Estonian Citizens' Union (EKL), Estonian Royalist Party (ERP), Liberal Democratic Party (LDP), Free Democrats (VD), Greens (Rohelised, ER), Estonian Entrepreneurs' Party (EEE) and Russian Democratic Movement (VDL or RDD); Secure Home (Kindel Kogu) was an electoral alliance of the EKE and EML; the People's Front (Rahvarinne) was electoral alliance dominated by the ERKE which formed the Centre (Keskus, K) parliamentary group; the Moderates (Mõõdukad, M) is an electoral alliance and parliamentary group of the ESDP and EMKE. At the general

election in September 1992 Isamaa gained 23/101 seats, Kindel Kogu 17 seats, Rahvarinne 15 seats, the Mõõdukad 12 seats, the ERSP 10 seats, the EKL and ERP eight seats each, the LDP six seats and the Greens and EEE one seat each. The government is formed by a centre-right coalition of Isamaa, Mõõdukad and ERSP, with Mart Laar as prime minister. Other senior ministers are Jüri Luik (foreign affairs), Toivo Jürgenson (economy), Andres Lipstok (finance), Heiki Arike (interior), Enn Tupp (defence) and Urmas Arumäe (justice). The head of state is President Lennart Meri, who was elected in October 1992.

Security and international affiliations. The Estonian armed forces number 2,500; they are in the process of formation. There is also a 2,000-strong paramilitary border guard and a small coast guard. Military service is compulsory and consists of 12 months' basic training.

Estonia is a member of the Baltic Council, Conference on Security and Cooperation in Europe (CSCE), Council of Baltic Sea States (CBSS) and Council of Europe, as well as the United Nations and its specialized agencies.

History. Originating further east, the ancestors of the Estonians (closely related to the Finns) settled in modern Estonia during the 1st millennium BC. Vikings from across the Baltic Sea raided the coastal areas and established trading posts from the 8th century AD onwards. At this time the country consisted of 12 small states and was divided into Viking and Kievan (Russian) spheres of influence. Christian missionaries first arrived in the 12th century. Historical Estonia, i.e. the northern half of modern Estonia, was conquered by Denmark in 1219–22. Livonia to the south (also including northern Latvia) was conquered by the Brothers of the Sword, a German Christian military order that later merged with the Teutonic Knights. In 1346 Denmark sold the Duchy of Estonia to the Livonian Order, a branch of the Teutonic Knights. Society was organized along feudal lines, and there developed a sharp division between the German elite and the Estonian peasantry. Following a Russian invasion in 1558 the rulers sought protection from neighbouring powers. In 1561 Sweden took control of Estonia, and Poland-Lithuania of Livonia; in 1629 the latter also fell to Sweden. The Swedes introduced a number of reforms aimed at improving the condition of the peasantry. Russia occupied both territories during the Great Northern War (1700–21), fulfilling a long-standing ambition to acquire a 'window to the seas'. Tallinn, then called Reval, became an important Russian port.

An Estonian cultural and national movement emerged in the 19th century. The Russian authorities introduced reforms from the 1860s but reverted to a policy of russification in the 1880s. Estonia was granted autonomy after the overthrow of the tsar in 1917, and declared its independence in 1918. It was briefly occupied by German troops in the latter stages of the First World War (1914–18). Independence was recognized by the Soviet Union in 1920. A constitution establishing a parliamentary democracy was adopted the same year. Many economic and social reforms were implemented in the 1920s, including the division of the large German-owned agricultural estates among landless peasants. Government coalitions were short-lived. The introduction of a presidential system, advocated by the far-right Vap movement among others, was approved in a referendum in 1933. But the following year President Konstantin Päts, the dominant political leader of the period, took power and suspended parliament. He was reelected president under a new constitution in 1938. During the Second World War (1939–45) the country was invaded and annexed by the Soviet Union in 1940 and occupied by German troops from 1941–44.

During the Soviet period Estonia was integrated into the communist economic system and suffered political repression, most harshly in the 1940s and 50s. There was also substantial Russian immigration and extensive industrialization. Estonia was the most prosperous Soviet republic. The greater freedom of expression allowed under the policy of *glasnost* ('openness'), introduced after Mikhail Gorbachev became the Soviet leader in 1985, gave rise to an increasingly vociferous reform movement. Initially focused on human-rights, environmental and cultural issues, it became overtly economic and political with the establishment of the broad-based People's Front (Rahvarinne) in April 1988. The republican parliament declared Estonia 'sovereign' in November that year and assumed further autonomous powers, in name as well as in practice, after the victory of the Front and other pro-independence groups in the March 1990 multiparty election. Estonia proclaimed the restoration of its independence during the abortive Soviet coup by communist hardliners in August 1991. This was recognized by the Soviet Union the following month. The government initiated a range of market reforms in 1992. A new constitution came into force in July. A general election in September resulted in victory for the right. (Rahvarinne had fragmented after the restoration of independence.) The transformation of the economy has been accompanied by disruption and social dislocation. Estonia was admitted to the Council of Europe in May 1993. Relations with Russia have been tense since independence, largely because of related disputes over the citizenship status and treatment of the large ethnic Russian minority and the slow pace of the Russian troop withdrawal from Estonia. The latter was completed in August 1994.

See also entries on specific institutions, organizations, parties, people, terms etc.

Estonian Citizens' Union [Eesti Kodanike Liit] (EKL) Estonian political party. Founded in 1991, the right-wing EKL was the dominant partner in an alliance which gained 8/101 seats at the September 1992 election. The leader is Jüri Toomepuu.

Estonian Coalition Party [Eesti Koonderakond] (EKE) Estonian political party. Founded in 1991, the EKE has its roots in the reformist wing of the Estonian Communist Party (EKP). Its policies are now mainstream left-wing. It contested the

September 1992 election within the Secure Home (Kindel Kogu) alliance and gained 8/101 seats. The party leader is Tiit Vähi, the parliamentary leader Riivo Sinijärv.

Estonian National Independence Party [Eesti Rahvusliku Sõltumatuse Partei] (ERSP) Estonian political party. Founded in 1988, the ERSP is broadly centrist in its economic policies, conservative on social issues and strongly nationalistic concerning relations with Russia and the Russian minority in Estonia. It gained 10/101 seats at the election in September 1992 and joined the centre-right coalition formed the following month. The leader is Tunne Kelam.

Estonian People's Centre Party [Eesti Rahva-Keskerakond] (ERKE) Estonian political party. The ERKE has its roots in the reformist People's Front (Rahvarinne), set up in 1988, when Estonia was still part of the Soviet Union. Founded in 1991, the party is broadly centre-left in outlook. It contested the September 1992 election within the PEOPLE'S FRONT alliance, which gained 15/101 seats. The leader is Edgar Savisaar.

Estonian People's Front *See* PEOPLE'S FRONT.

Estonian Royalist Party [Eesti Rojalistlik Partei] (ERP) Estonian political party. Founded in 1988, the ERP is a right-wing party which advocates the transformation of Estonia into a constitutional monarchy. At the September 1992 election it gained 8/101 seats. The leader is Kalle Kulbok.

Estonian Rural Centre Party [Eesti Maa-Keskerakond] (EMKE) Estonian political party. It was founded in 1990 to represent the country's farming community, and is broadly centrist in its policies. It contested the September 1992 election within the Moderates (Mõõdukad, M) alliance, which gained 12/101 seats. The leader is Ivar Raig.

Estonian Rural Union [Eesti Maaliit] (EML) Estonian political party. Founded in 1990, the EML has its roots in the reformist wing of the Estonian Communist Party (EKP). Broadly centre-left and aimed at advancing the interests of the farming community, it contested the

September 1992 election within the Secure Home (Kindel Kogu) alliance and gained 8/101 seats. The party leader is Arvo Sirendi.

Estonian Social Democratic Party [Eesti Sotsiaaldemokraatlik Partei] (ESDP) Estonian political party. The ESDP was formed in 1990 by the merger of three parties. It is generally more right-leaning than other European social democratic parties. It contested the September 1992 election within the MODERATES (M) alliance, which gained 12/101 seats. The leader is Marju Lauristin.

ESWS *See* COEXISTENCE.

ETA *See* BASQUE HOMELAND AND LIBERTY.

ETA-M and **ETA-Militar** Abbreviation and shorthand for Basque Homeland and Liberty (ETA), the Spanish separatist guerrilla group. ETA-Militar was formed in the 1970s by radical members of ETA who advocated an intensification of the organization's violent campaign for Basque independence. The rival 'political' wing is now virtually inactive, so the distinction has become redundant.

etarra Member of Basque Homeland and Liberty (ETA), the Spanish guerrilla group fighting for Basque independence.

ethnic cleansing [etničko čišćenje] In Bosnia-Herzegovina, the forced expulsion by members of one ethnic group of other groups in order to create ethnically homogeneous areas. Involving systematic intimidation, detention, looting, rape and murder, it was practised by Serbs against Muslims in eastern Bosnia in the early stages of the civil war that broke out in March 1992. Since then it has also been practised in other parts of the country and by Muslims and Croats. More than 3 million people have been uprooted by the expulsions, precipitating the worst refugee crisis in Europe since the end of the Second World War. The term 'ethnic cleansing', coined by Croat nationalists in the 1940s, is now also used for similar practices in other parts of former Yugoslavia and elsewhere.

Etkin, Taner (1943–) Northern Cypriot politician. He worked in President Denktaş' office from 1974 until his election to parliament for the centre-right

Democratic Party (DP) in 1993. He was appointed interior minister in the DP-led centre-left coalition which took office in January 1994.

etničko čišćenje *See* ETHNIC CLEANSING.

ETUC *See* EUROPEAN TRADE UNION CONFEDERATION.

EU *See* EUROPEAN UNION.

EU Danish, Dutch and German abbreviation for the European Union (EU).

EU Commission Shorthand for the EUROPEAN COMMISSION, the administrative and executive arm of the European Union (EU).

EU Council Shorthand for either the EUROPEAN COUNCIL, the regular summit meetings of the heads of government of the European Union (EU) member states, or the COUNCIL OF THE EUROPEAN UNION or Council of Ministers, the EU's main decision-making body.

EU presidency Shorthand for the presidency of the COUNCIL OF THE EUROPEAN UNION or Council of Ministers, the EU's main decision-making body. It is held in turn by each member state for six months.

EU troika *See* TROIKA.

EUCD *See* EUROPEAN CHRISTIAN DEMOCRATIC UNION.

EUCLID, in full **European Cooperation for the Long Term in Defence** Programme of the Independent European Programme Group (IEPG), an informal group of the European members of the North Atlantic Treaty Organization (NATO). EUCLID was set up in 1989 to promote joint research and development among Western European arms manufacturers and thus to strengthen Europe's competitive position in the field of defence.

EUL *See* EUROPEAN UNITED LEFT.

EURATOM Shorthand for the EUROPEAN ATOMIC ENERGY COMMUNITY (EAEC), one of the three European Communities (EC) which form the core of the European Union (EU).

euregio In the European Union (EU), a form of cooperation between local, regional or national governments in border areas. The name is taken from the Euregio, the first such body set up in the 1950s in the Dutch-German border area centred on

the Rhine, Ems and IJssel rivers. Similar regional structures, also known as 'euro-regions', have been set up in other parts of the EU and, since the late 1980s, also in other parts of Europe. *See also* EUROREGION.

EUREKA Organization or **Eureka** Intergovernmental organization. Based on an initiative launched by President Mitterrand of France, EUREKA – a loose acronym of European Research Coordination Agency – was set up in 1985 to coordinate Europe-wide cooperation in non-military research and development in advanced technology in order to strengthen the competitive position of European industry. EUREKA projects generally involve cooperation among companies and research institutes from different participating countries. More than 500 have been approved in the fields of electronic optics, new materials, computers, high-power lasers, particle beams, ultra-rapid microelectronics, transport, robotics, biotechnology, energy and environmental protection. EUREKA has 21 members: Austria, Belgium, Denmark, Finland, France, Germany, Greece, Hungary, Iceland, Ireland, Italy, Luxemburg, Netherlands, Norway, Portugal, Spain, Sweden, Switzerland, Turkey, the United Kingdom and the European Commission (on behalf of the European Union, EU). The senior decision-making bodies are the Ministerial Conference, held annually, and the High Level Group, which meets regularly between conferences at ambassadorial level. The organization's secretariat is based in Brussels (Belgium). In 1990 members agreed to make EUREKA's project database available to Eastern European companies and research institutes.

Euro Citizen Action Service (ECAS) International social and political organization. Founded in 1990, ECAS is a representative body of voluntary organizations within the European Union (EU). Essentially a lobby group, it aims to strengthen their voice within the Union by providing them with information on institutions and activities, advising on contacts and fundraising, and helping them to defend the rights and interests of EU citizens. It has more than 400 affiliated organizations active in the fields of citizens' rights, health, social welfare, culture etc. The secretariat is based in Brussels (Belgium), the EU headquarters. The director is Tony Venables (United Kingdom).

Eurocities Intergovernmental organization at local level. The Eurocities movement was founded in 1986 following an initiative by the Dutch city of Rotterdam. The other founding members were Barcelona, Birmingham, Frankfurt, Lyon and Milan. By the end of 1993 it comprised most major cities in the European Union (EU) countries, 56 in all. Eurocities aims to stimulate cooperation on urban structural problems, particularly in the spheres of economic development, transport and environmental protection. It holds an annual general assembly, attended by the mayors of member cities. It operates a secretariat in Brussels (Belgium), the EU headquarters. The president is Jorge Sampaio, the mayor of Lisbon, the Portuguese capital.

Eurocorps Shorthand for the EUROPEAN CORPS.

eurocrat Informal name for an official attached to the European Commission, the administrative and executive arm of the European Union (EU), or more generally for any EU official.

eurocurrency Common name for foreign-currency deposits held by European banks. The term is used in specific variations with the prefix 'euro-', e.g. US dollars held by a French bank are called 'eurodollars' and German marks held by a British bank are called 'euromarks'.

eurodollar *See* EUROCURRENCY.

euroenthusiasm Support for the process of integration within the framework of the European Union (EU), specifically the plans for economic, monetary and political union contained in the Maastricht Treaty (in force since November 1993) and further measures. It is contrasted with 'euroscepticism'. *See also* FEDERALISM *and* FEDERAL EUROPE.

Eurofighter 2000 Intergovernmental programme. The Eurofighter 2000 is a scaled-down version of the European Fighter Aircraft (EFA), a project agreed in 1985 by Germany, Italy, Spain and the United Kingdom to replace the generation of combat aircraft that would become obsolete by the mid 1990s. It was the first major example of Western European collaboration in the arms-procurement field. Following the end of the 'cold war' between East and West and the collapse of the Warsaw Pact in 1991, the highly sophisticated and expensive EFA was increasingly criticized as anachronistic. Doubts expressed by the German government in June 1992 prompted a reconsideration of the project which resulted in an agreement in November to scale down the aircraft's specifications. This reduced the overall cost by nearly a third (to around 42 billion ecus). The renamed Eurofighter 2000 is due to become the four airforces' main combat aircraft shortly after the turn of the century.

Eurogroup Intergovernmental organization. The Eurogroup is an informal grouping of the European member states of the North Atlantic Treaty Organization (NATO) except France and Iceland. Established in 1968, it is primarily a forum of discussion on major political and security issues within the NATO framework, but also seeks to promote practical cooperation between the members' armed forces. It has been instrumental in the formation of the INDEPENDENT EUROPEAN PROGRAMME GROUP (IEPG) and the adoption of the EUCLID programme on long-term defence collaboration. Meetings are held twice a year at the level of defence minister, usually in conjunction with meetings of NATO's Defence Planning Committee (DPC).

EUROM *See* EUROPEAN ROMANY PARLIAMENT.

euromissiles Shorthand for EUROSTRATEGIC MISSILES, intermediate-range nuclear missiles deployed in Europe until the late 1980s.

Europe Shorthand for the European Union (EU). The identification of the EU with Europe as a whole has traditionally been resented in countries which are not members of the organization.

Europe à la carte In the European Union (EU), a concept associated with those who argue that the integration process should allow member states to participate in common policies and programmes according to their requirements or preferences. The phrase was coined by the German sociologist Ralf Dahrendorf in 1979 to express his view that the scope of European integration should remain flexible and that some common policies (e.g. the Common Agricultural Policy, CAP) should be abandoned when no longer required or appropriate. It was later extended to mean that each member state should be able to choose from a selection of common policies – hence 'à la carte'. A group of states could thus embark on cooperation in a specific field without compelling others and without being held back by them. The idea initially found little support within the then European Community (EC), which had always operated on the principle that members proceed at the same speed and in step. But it was picked up in the late 1980s by politicians increasingly sceptical of or opposed to further integration. Terms and phrases like 'two-speed Europe', 'MULTI-TRACK EUROPE' and 'variable geometry' broadly express the same sentiment. *See also* OPT-OUT *and* DEROGATION.

Europe agreement In the European Union (EU), a treaty with a non-member state in Eastern Europe covering economic and political cooperation. Like the ASSOCIA-TION AGREEMENTS, which have been signed with many countries, Europe agreements offer (i) free access to EU markets by removing tariffs and quotas for most manufactured goods (while retaining restrictions on textiles and agricultural products) and (ii) financial and technical assistance. In addition they provide for cooperation on foreign policy and security matters and, in effect, hold out the prospect of a free-trade agreement and eventual full membership of the Union. Europe agreements were signed with Czechoslovakia, Hungary and Poland in December 1991, Romania in February 1993, Bulgaria in March 1993, and the Czech Republic and Slovakia (modified to allow for the dissolution of the Czechoslovak federation) in October 1993.

Europe Day Official day of the Council of Europe. Celebrated on 5 May, the anniversary of the Council's foundation in 1949, its purpose is to involve Europe's citizens more closely in the process of European unification. It was instituted in 1964.

Europe des états, ... des nations and ... **des patries** *See* EUROPE OF NATIONS.

Europe des Nations *See* EUROPE OF NATIONS.

Europe of Citizens *See* CITIZENS' EUROPE.

Europe of concentric circles Concept used by advocates of a structure of graduated economic and political integration and cooperation among European states centred on the European Union (EU). Broadly speaking, the following 'circles' are identified: an 'inner core' of EU member states committed to a much closer integration, especially in the economic, monetary and political spheres; an 'outer core' of EU states, including some or all recent members; other members of the European Economic Area (EEA), i.e. those members of the European Free Trade Association (EFTA) not joining the EU; the Visegrad countries (Czech Republic, Hungary, Poland and Slovakia), which have signed association agreements, and other prospective members (Cyprus and Malta); other Eastern European states which have signed association agreements or are likely to do so in the coming years (Albania, Bulgaria, Romania, the Baltic states and Yugoslav successor states); peripheral states with which various forms of cooperation can be developed (Russia, Ukraine, Turkey etc). These 'concentric circles' are broadly reflected in the security and defence sphere through various forms of membership of and cooperation with the Western European Union (WEU), the EU's future 'defence component', and the North Atlantic Treaty Organization (NATO). *See also* MULTI-TRACK EUROPE.

Europe of nation states *See* EUROPE OF NATIONS.

Europe of Nations International political organization. This movement was founded in April 1994 by parliamentarians and others from European Union (EU) member states committed to a Europe based on 'sovereign nation states' and opposed to centralizing tendencies within the EU. Its founding document, the Declaration of Paris, repudiates the 'utopian dream of a single European people within a single European state' and calls for the reversal of the 'federalist process' exemplified by the Maastricht Treaty (in force since November 1993). Its aims are similar to those of the BRUGES GROUP.

Europe of Nations (EN) Political group in the European Parliament, the parliament of the European Union (EU). This group is opposed to the perceived centralizing or 'federalist' tendencies within the EU, in particular the Maastricht Treaty (in force since November 1993). It is dominated by Another Europe (L'Autre Europe), a French list, and also includes the Danish June Movement (JB) and People's Movement against the European Community (FB mod EF), and representatives of Dutch Christian fundamentalist parties. It has 19/567 seats. The leader is James Goldsmith.

Europe of nations In the European Union (EU), a concept associated with those who argue that the process of European integration should result in a relatively loose organization of sovereign states rather than a closely integrated, 'supranational' or 'federal' government structure. Most see the Maastricht Treaty (which came into force in November 1993) as the prime example of the prevailing centralizing tendency within the EU. The term 'Europe of nations' is taken from *Europe des patries* ('Europe of the fatherlands' in French), reportedly first used by President De Gaulle of France in 1961 to define his vision for the then European Economic Community (EEC). (He later claimed he had actually spoken of a *Europe des états*, a 'Europe of states'.) It is contrasted with a 'federal Europe' and a more recent variant, a 'Europe of the regions', in which some powers are transferred from national governments up to the Union and others down to regions.

Europe of states *See* EUROPE OF NATIONS.

Europe of the Citizen *See* CITIZENS' EUROPE.

Europe of the regions In the European Union (EU), a concept associated with those who advocate the devolution of a wide range of powers from national governments to regional authorities within the member states. This is often set within a vision of a 'federal' Europe in which other national powers are transferred up to a supranational union. Both notions are contrasted with a 'Europe of nations', in which the key powers remain with national governments.

Europe Prize Award made annually by the Parliamentary Assembly of the Council of Europe to a municipality in a member state for its contribution to European cooperation. It was instituted in 1955.

European Agricultural Fund Shorthand for the EUROPEAN AGRICULTURAL GUIDANCE AND GUARANTEE FUND (EAGGF), a programme of the European Union (EU).

European Agricultural Guidance and Guarantee Fund or **European Agricultural Fund** (EAGGF) Programme of the European Union (EU). Also widely known by its French acronym, FEOGA, the EAGGF provides the financial basis for administering the COMMON AGRICULTURAL POLICY (CAP). It was set up in 1962 and consists of two elements: (i) the guidance section, which funds measures to modernize the production and distribution of agricultural products; and (ii) the guarantee section, which funds the CAP's price-support and other mechanisms. All but around 3% of EAGGF funds are allocated to the guarantee section.

European Assembly Informal name for the EUROPEAN PARLIAMENT, the parliament of the European Union (EU), used in particular by opponents of its transformation into a body with full legislative powers. 'European Assembly' was the parliament's original name. 'European Parliament' came into use in the 1960s but did not become the formal name until 1987.

European Atomic Energy Community (EAEC or EURATOM) Intergovernmental organization, one of the three

European Communities which in turn form the core of the European Union (EU). EURATOM was established at the same time as the European Economic Community (EEC, now the European Community, EC): the treaty was signed on 25 March 1957 and it came into effect on 1 January 1958. Its aims are to coordinate research on the peaceful use of nuclear power and to promote the growth of the nuclear-energy industry. It is responsible for securing the requisite fuel supplies to nuclear power stations, establishing safety standards and ensuring they are met. It also offers financial assistance for investments and carries out research. The main project sponsored by EURATOM is the Joint European Torus (JET) project, based at Culham in the United Kingdom, which seeks to develop a safe form of nuclear power through nuclear fusion (rather than fission, the current method, which produces radioactive material). EURATOM's institutions were merged with those of the EEC and the European Coal and Steel Community (ECSC) in 1967 to form a single Council of Ministers and European Commission. Since then its activities have been integrated into the EC framework, although it retains a separate legal identity.

European Bank for Reconstruction and Development (EBRD) Intergovernmental organization, a subsidiary of the World Bank. First proposed by President Mitterrand of France in 1989 and founded in 1990, the EBRD began operations in April 1991 with a starting capital of 10 billion ecus. Its aim is to assist with the economic reconstruction of the countries of Central and Eastern Europe and the former Soviet Union, provided they put into practice the principles of pluralist democracy and a market economy. It does so by extending market-rate loans and making equity investments. Priorities include projects which improve infrastructure, reform the financial sector, promote the private sector and small business in particular, restructure industry, encourage foreign investment, clean up the environment and promote trade. The EBRD's 57 members or shareholders include all major European countries, Russia and the other members of the Commonwealth of Independent States (CIS), Australia, Canada, Egypt, Israel, Japan, Mexico, Morocco, New Zealand, South Korea and the United States; the European Commission and the European Investment Bank (EIB), institutions of the European Union (EU), are also shareholders in their own right. The EU countries hold a controlling share of 51%. The Bank's organs include: (i) the Council of Governors, representing all the shareholders; (ii) the 23-member Board of Directors, which is responsible for day-to-day operations; and (iii) a secretariat, based in London (United Kingdom). The president is Jacques de Larosière (France), the secretary-general is Bart Le Blanc (Netherlands).

European Charter for Regional or Minority Languages International agreement adopted within the framework of the Council of Europe. Signed in November 1992, the Charter aims to preserve minority languages in Europe and promote their use in education, government, administration, the courts, the media and cultural activities. Among the measures it calls for is the launch of at least one radio station and a television station broadcasting in the relevant language. There are around 50 minority languages in Europe as defined by the Charter (i.e. excluding dialects of official languages and languages of non-European immigrants), spoken by around 50 million people.

European Charter of Local Self-Government International agreement adopted within the framework of the Council of Europe. Signed in October 1985 and in force since September 1989, the Charter sets out (i) the constitutional and legal basis for local autonomy and the principles governing such matters as powers, controls and finance which should be respected by any democratic and accountable system of government, and (ii) guidelines for structures and resources adequate to the tasks local authorities have to undertake.

European Charter on Environment and Health International agreement. It was adopted by 29 states in December 1990 at the first-ever pan-European conference of environment and health ministers in Geneva (Switzerland). It establishes the principle of the primacy of human health over economic growth. A consultative committee to monitor observance of the Charter was set up under the auspices of the World Health Organization (WHO), a specialist agency of the United Nations.

European Christian Democratic Union [Union Européenne de Démocrates Chrétiens (French), Europäische Union Christlicher Demokraten (German)] (UEDC, EUCD or ECDU) International political organization. Founded in 1965 as the successor to a more informal grouping, the ECDU brings together 45 christian democratic parties (29 full members and 16 observers) from 31 countries. The full members include the Social Democratic Centre (CDS) in France, the Christian Democratic Union (CDU) in Germany, the Italian People's Party (PPI, the successor to the Christian Democratic Party, DC) and the People's Party (PP) in Spain. The member parties within the European Union (EU) are also members of the European People's Party (EPP). Wilfried Martens, a former Belgian prime minister, is president of both organizations. They operate a joint secretariat in Brussels (Belgium).

European Coal and Steel Community (ECSC) Intergovernmental organization, one of the three European Communities which in turn form the core of the European Union (EU). Based on a French proposal, the ECSC was set up under the Treaty of Paris signed by Belgium, France, Italy, Luxemburg, Netherlands and West Germany on 18 April 1951 and effective from 25 July 1952. The aim of the ECSC was to create a common market for coal and steel – two key industries at the time – administered by a supranational authority. As such it represented one of the first steps in the process of European integration and formed the model for the much more comprehensive European Economic Community (EEC, now the European Community, EC),

which was established by the same six countries six years later. Given the contraction of the coal sector in Western Europe from the early 1960s (due to competition from oil and natural gas) and the steel sector from the early 1980s (due to a general fall in demand and competition from outside the region), the activities of the ECSC have in practice concentrated on assisting with the extensive restructuring of the two industries in the member states. It provides financial assistance for investment and modernization projects and for retraining and job creation in the regions affected. The ECSC's institutions were merged with those of the EEC and the European Atomic Energy Community (EAEC or EURATOM) in 1967 to form a single Council of Ministers and European Commission. Since then its activities have been integrated into the EC framework, although it retains a separate legal identity.

European Commission Institution of the European Union (EU). The Commission is one of the EU's five main institutions, the others being the Council of Ministers, European Parliament, Court of Justice and Court of Auditors. Broadly speaking it acts as the executive civil service of the European Communities, the three supranational organizations which form the core of the Union and of which the European Community (EC) is by far the most important. It has no formal powers in the Union's two intergovernmental 'pillars', the Common Foreign and Security Policy (CFSP) and Cooperation on Justice and Home Affairs (CJHA), but in practice is closely involved in their work. It has the sole right of proposing legislation but – contrary to popular perception – very limited powers of enactment, only of implementing laws adopted by the Council of Ministers, the main decision-making body. (In practice it also acts on suggestions from the Council.) The Commission was established in its current form in 1967 by the merger of the commissions of the European Economic Community (EEC, now the EC) and the European Atomic Energy Community (EAEC or EURATOM) and the High

Authority of the European Coal and Steel Community (ECSC).

The Commission's main functions are: (i) to ensure compliance with the EU treaties and the decisions and regulations adopted under them, and if necessary to bring actions to the Court of Justice for alleged breaches; (ii) to propose and draft legislation and draft a preliminary budget; (iii) to implement the Council's decisions; (iv) to administer the 'structural funds' and other programmes; (v) to mediate between the Council and the Parliament and between the national governments as required; (vi) to defend the Community interest in the Council; (vii) to represent the Community, particularly in foreign-trade negotiations; and (viii) to legislate in certain spheres of Community activity, such as the Common Agricultural Policy (CAP), coal and steel policy, the completion of the internal market etc. The Commission has 17 members or commissioners, two each from France, Germany, Italy, Spain and the United Kingdom and one each from the seven smaller states. They are appointed for a four-year term by the national governments. The president and two vice-presidents are appointed for two-year terms. (From 1995 the commissioners' term of office will be five years and run concurrently with that of the European Parliament.) Decisions are taken by simple majority. Commissioners are obliged to act in the interests of the Community as a whole and are prohibited from representing the interests of their countries or national governments. The Commission is answerable to the Parliament, which may vote motions of censure and has the ultimate sanction of dismissing the Commission as a whole (a power it has never used). The Commission is supported by 23 DIRECTORATES-GENERAL (DGs), all based in Brussels, although some services are based in Luxemburg. Each commissioner is responsible for one or more DGs.

The Commission president is Jacques Delors, a former French finance minister, who has held the post since 1985. The other members are Henning Christophersen (Denmark) (vice-president, economic, financial and monetary affairs), Manuel Marín (Spain) (vice-president, cooperation and development), Leon Brittan (United Kingdom) (external economic affairs and trade), Hans van den Broek (Netherlands) (foreign and security affairs), Martin Bangemann (Germany) (industry, technology, telecommunications), Karel van Miert (Belgium) (competition policy, personnel), René Steichen (Luxemburg) (agriculture and rural development), Pádraig Flynn (Ireland) (social affairs), Bruce Millan (United Kingdom) (regional affairs), Ioannis Paleokrassas (Greece) (environment, fisheries), Marcelino Oreja (Spain) (energy, transport), Raniero Vanni d'Archirafi (Italy) (internal market, financial institutions, small and medium-sized enterprises), João de Deus Pinheiro (Portugal) (information, relations with European Parliament, culture), Peter Schmidhuber (Germany) (budget), Antonio Ruberti (Italy) (science, research, training) and Christiane Scrivener (France) (taxation, consumer affairs).

European Commission of Human Rights Institution of the Council of Europe. Composed of 22 independent jurists, the Commission – not to be confused with the United Nations Committee of Human Rights – makes an initial examination of cases brought by individuals, groups or governments alleging a violation of the European Convention of Human Rights. It decides whether an application should be admitted, ascertains the facts of the case, and offers its services to reach an amicable settlement. If no settlement is reached, it refers the case to the Committee of Ministers or to the EUROPEAN COURT OF HUMAN RIGHTS for adjudication. Reforms aimed at streamlining and speeding up the handling of cases brought under the Convention were adopted in April 1994. They included the eventual merger of the Commission and the Court.

European commissioner or **commissioner** Member of the European Commission, the administrative and executive arm of the European Union (EU).

European Communities (EC) Formal name of the three supranational organizations at the core of the European Union (EU), i.e. the European Community (EC, formerly the European Economic Community, EEC), European Coal and Steel Community (ECSC) and European Atomic Energy Community (EAEC or EURATOM). After the merger of their institutions in 1967, the singular 'European Community' gained wide currency to denote either the European Communities as a whole or the EEC, by far the most important of the three. *See also* EUROPEAN COMMUNITY.

European Community (EC) Component of the European Union (EU), formerly called the European Economic Community (EEC). The EC is by far the most important of the three European Communities which form the supranational core of the EU. The name 'European Community' has been widely used to denote the EEC or the European Communities since the 1960s. Since the establishment of the European Union in 1993 under the Maastricht Treaty it has also been used to denote the Union as a whole. The Treaty also formally changed the EEC's name to EC. *For full organization entry, see* EUROPEAN UNION.

European Convention for the Prevention of Torture and Inhumane and Degrading Treatment or Punishment International agreement adopted within the framework of the Council of Europe. The result of 10 years of negotiations, the Convention was signed in November 1987 and took effect in February 1989. It differs from the similar United Nations Convention on Torture adopted in 1984 in that it is binding on its signatories and not only provides a framework for dealing with accusations of torture and inhumane treatment but also establishes preventive mechanisms. This is done through an independent committee which carries out regular visits to prisons and other centres of detention and prepares confidential reports on conditions of imprisonment in the signatory states. However, the only sanction provided under the Convention is publication of the committee's reports.

European Convention for the Protection of Human Rights and Fundamental Freedoms or **European Convention of Human Rights** International agreement adopted within the framework of the Council of Europe. Signed on 4 November 1950 and in force since 3 September 1953, the European Convention of Human Rights provides the foundation for the Council's primary objective of protecting individual rights and freedoms. It largely reiterates the Universal Declaration of Human Rights adopted by the United Nations in 1948, but unlike this document it is binding on its signatories – signing the Convention is a condition of Council membership – and establishes a unique legal procedure by which an individual, organization or government can lodge a complaint against a signatory government for an alleged violation of the Convention. Cases brought under the Convention are dealt with in the first instance by the EUROPEAN COMMISSION OF HUMAN RIGHTS. If it believes there is a case to answer and is unable to resolve the matter, it refers it to the EUROPEAN COURT OF HUMAN RIGHTS.

Specifically, the Convention's principal provisions are as follows: 'Everyone's right to life shall be protected by law. No one shall be deprived of his life intentionally save in the execution of a sentence of a court following his conviction of a crime for which this penalty is provided by law' (article 2, paragraph 1); 'No one shall be subject to torture or to inhuman or degrading treatment or punishment' (article 3); 'No one shall be held in slavery or servitude' (article 4.1); 'No one shall be required to perform forced or compulsory labour' (article 4.2); 'Everyone has the right to liberty and security of person. No one shall be deprived of his liberty save ... in accordance with a procedure prescribed by law' (article 5.1); 'In the determination of his civil rights and obligations or of any criminal charge against him, everyone is entitled to a fair and public hearing within a reasonable time by an independent and impartial tribunal established by law' (article 6.1); 'No one shall be held guilty of any criminal offence ... which did not constitute a criminal offence under national or international law at the time when it was committed' (article 7.1); 'Everyone has the right to respect for his private and family life, his home and his correspondence' (article 8.1); 'Everyone has the right to freedom of thought, conscience and religion ...' (article 9.1); 'Everyone has the right to freedom of expression' (article 10.1); 'Everyone has the right to freedom of peaceful assembly and to freedom of association with others' (article 11.1); 'Men and women of marriageable age have the right to marry and to found a family' (article 12); and 'The enjoyment of the rights and freedoms set forth in this Convention shall be secured without discrimination on any ground such as sex, race, colour, language, religion, political or other opinion, national or social origin, association with a national minority, property, birth or other status' (article 14). The rights set out in articles 8, 9, 10 and 11 are restricted, in slightly varying formulations, as prescribed by law and as is necessary in a democratic society in the interests of national security, public safety, and the protection of health and morals and the rights of others. Most of the remaining 52 articles establish the mechanisms for dealing with complaints.

Nine protocols to the Convention have been adopted that extend existing rights or establish new ones. The most important additional provisions are: 'No person shall be denied the right to education' (first protocol, article 2); the signatories 'undertake to hold free elections at reasonable intervals by secret ballot' (first protocol, article 3); 'No one shall be deprived of his liberty merely on the grounds of inability to fulfil a contractual obligation' (fourth protocol, article 1); 'No one shall be expelled ... from the territory of the state of which he is a national' (fourth protocol, article 3.1) or 'deprived of the right to enter' it (article 3.2); 'Collective expulsion of aliens is prohibited (fourth protocol, article 4); 'The death penalty shall be abolished' (sixth protocol, article 1) except 'in respect of acts committed in time of war' (article 2); 'Everyone con-

victed of a criminal offence ... shall have the right to have his conviction or sentence reviewed by a higher tribunal' (seventh protocol, article 2.1); and 'spouses shall enjoy equality of rights and responsibilities of a private law character between them ...' (seventh protocol, article 5).

European Convention of Human Rights Shorthand for the EUROPEAN CONVENTION FOR THE PROTECTION OF HUMAN RIGHTS AND FUNDAMENTAL FREEDOMS.

European Convention on the Suppression of Terrorism International agreement adopted within the framework of the Council of Europe. Signed in January 1977 and in force since August 1978, the Convention aims to facilitate the extradition and prosecution of those suspected of having committed what are deemed terrorist acts inspired by political motives. It breaks with a tradition of international criminal law under which 'political offences' are excluded from extradition agreements. It lists a number of offences which will no longer be subject to special treatment for extradition purposes, including the seizure of aircraft, attacks against the life or liberty of diplomats, kidnappings, hostage taking, and the use of bombs, grenades, rockets and automatic firearms.

European Corps or **Eurocorps** International military force. The Eurocorps was set up by France, Germany and Belgium in November 1993, and Spain and Luxemburg have joined since then. The result of a Franco-German initiative of 1987 and an extension of a 5,000-strong joint army brigade created in 1990, it is intended as the nucleus of a united Western European military capability. It has been put at the disposal of the Western European Union (WEU), which under the Maastricht Treaty is to become the 'defence component' of the European Union (EU). In an emergency the force can also be placed under the command of the North Atlantic Treaty Organization (NATO). Based in Strasbourg (France), it is due to have a strength of 40–45,000 soldiers when it becomes fully operational in 1995.

European Council Institution of the European Union (EU). Not to be confused with Council of Ministers, the EU's main legislative body, or the Council of Europe (a separate intergovernmental organization), the European Council is the name given to the biannual summit meetings of the member states' heads of government. Relatively informal, these meetings are intended broadly to (i) give direction to and stimulate the EU's activities and (ii) provide a means of solving intractable policy problems at the highest level. Decisions are normally but not invariably taken by unanimity; they are subsequently worked out in detail and made official by the Council of Ministers. The meetings are hosted by the country holding the presidency of the Council of Ministers towards the end of its six-month term. Extraordinary meetings are usually held in Brussels, the EU's headquarters. The following participate in the European Council: the president of France (an executive head of state), the 12 heads of government and foreign ministers, the president and a vice-president of the European Commission, and the president of the European Parliament. The origins of the European Council lie in a series of summit meetings held in the late 1960s and early 70s. The first meeting of the Council proper was held in 1974 in Paris. The current format was formalized in the Single European Act adopted in 1986.

European Court of Auditors *See* COURT OF AUDITORS OF THE EUROPEAN COMMUNITIES.

European Court of Human Rights Institution of the Council of Europe. The Court – not to be confused with the European Court of Justice, an institution of the European Union (EU) – examines cases brought either by individuals, groups or governments alleging a violation of the European Convention of Human Rights. It only hears cases referred to it by the EUROPEAN COMMISSION OF HUMAN RIGHTS, the examining body in the first instance, when this has not been able to negotiate an amicable settlement. The Court's judgements are final, and it can award compensation to aggrieved parties. The Council of Europe's Committee of Ministers is responsible for the enforcement of the Court's decisions. Each of the Council's member states nominates a judge to the Court, which sits in chambers of seven judges. Reforms aimed at streamlining and speeding up the handling of cases brought under the Convention were adopted in April 1994. The president is Rolv Einar Ryssdal (Norway).

European Court of Justice *See* COURT OF JUSTICE OF THE EUROPEAN COMMUNITIES.

European Cultural Convention International agreement adopted within the framework of the COUNCIL OF EUROPE. Signed on 19 December 1954 and in force since 5 May 1955, this convention provides the framework for the Council's programmes on education, culture, heritage, sport and youth. It is designed 'to foster among the nationals of all members ... the study of the languages, history and civilization of the others and of the civilization which is common to them all'. It is implemented through the Council for Cultural Cooperation (CDCC) and the Cultural Fund. The programmes carried out under the Convention are concerned with teaching methods, the teaching and learning of languages, school links and exchanges, education research, national cultural policies, training schemes for arts administrators, Europe's film heritage etc.

European Cultural Foundation (ECF) International cultural and political organization. The ECF was set up in 1954 to promote cultural contacts and cooperation across the continent. To this end it administers an extensive grants programme and coordinates a network of 17 institutes and centres carrying out research in the fields of the arts, education, media, environment and social affairs. The ECF is administered by an international board of governors and funded primarily by proceeds from the Dutch state lottery. It is represented in 22 countries by national committees. The secretariat is based in Amsterdam (Netherlands). The president is Princess Margriet of the Netherlands.

European Currency Unit Formal name of the ECU, the notional currency of the European Union (EU).

European defence identity *See* EUROPEAN SECURITY IDENTITY.

European Democrat Union (EDU) International political organization. Founded in 1978, the EDU brings together 24 centre-right and right-wing parties from 18 countries. The full members include the Austrian People's Party (ÖVP), the Rally for the Republic (RPR) in France, the Christian Democratic Union (CDU) in Germany, the Conservative Party in Britain and the People's Party (PP) in Spain. It has close links with the International Democrat Union (IDU), and some member parties also belong to the European Christian Democratic Union (ECDU). Alois Mock, a former ÖVP leader, is president of both organizations. The secretariat is based in Vienna (Austria).

European Democratic Alliance (EDA or RDE) Political group in the European Parliament, the parliament of the European Union (EU). Originally called the European Progressive Democrats, the EDA is dominated by the right-wing Rally for the Republic (RPR) of France and the centre-right Fianna Fáil of Ireland, and also includes members from Portugal and Greece. It has 26/567 seats. The leader is Jean-Claude Pasty (France).

European Economic Area (EEA) Intergovernmental organization. The EEA administers the single market covering the 12 member states of the European Union (EU) and six of the seven members of the European Free Trade Association (EFTA) set up under the Agreement on the European Economic Area signed in May 1992. This is the largest multi-nation single market and free-trade zone in the world, with a combined population of 374 million, marginally smaller than that covered by the North American Free Trade Agreement (NAFTA). Conceived in the late 1980s as an alternative for the EFTA states to joining the then European Community (EC), the EEA is now seen as a transitional arrangement, since four of the six participating EFTA members (Austria, Finland, Norway and Sweden) have negotiated membership of the European Union.

Aims and objectives. Article 1 of the Agreement on the European Economic Area, signed on 5 May 1992 and in force since 1 January 1994, states that the aim of the EEA is 'to promote a continuous and balanced strengthening of trade and economic relations between the contracting parties with equal conditions of competition'. To attain this objective, the EEA will (i) establish a single market based on the freedom of movement of goods, persons, services and capital, and (ii) foster closer cooperation in other fields such as research and development, the environment, education and social policy.

Membership. The EEA has 18 members: Austria, Belgium, Denmark, Finland, France, Germany, Greece, Iceland, Ireland, Italy, Liechtenstein, Luxemburg, Netherlands, Norway, Portugal, Spain, Sweden and the United Kingdom. These are the 12 members of the European Union (EU) and six of the seven members of the European Free Trade Association (EFTA, i.e. Austria, Finland, Iceland, Liechtenstein, Norway and Sweden). Switzerland, which signed the original agreement but did not ratify it, has observer status.

Structure and activities. The EEA has two main joint EU-EFTA bodies to ensure the proper functioning of the single market and to deal with any disputes arising from its implementation. They are: (i) the Council, the senior political body, composed of ministers of the 18 governments and a member of the European Commission, the EU's administrative and executive arm; and (ii) the Joint Committee, composed of government representatives and responsible for day-to-day administration and resolving disputes. There are also two consultative committees: (i) the Joint Parliamentary Committee, composed of members of the European Parliament and the national parliaments of the EFTA states; and (ii) the Consultative Committee, composed of representatives of employers' associations and trade unions from the participating countries. The secretariat is based in Geneva (Switzerland).

History. The call for the creation of a 'European economic space' was first issued by EFTA leaders at a summit meeting in March 1989, which had been called to discuss the implications of the plans by the then European Community (EC) to establish a single internal market by the end of 1992. The EFTA countries would or could not consider full EC membership at this time because they were politically and militarily neutral, but they did desire closer economic cooperation so as not to lose out on the benefits expected from the single market. The two organizations began discussions in June 1990, despite the fact that the EFTA countries had not been able to agree a joint strategy. The collapse of communism in Eastern Europe and the end of the Cold War around this time created a new geopolitical situation in Europe, and closer political cooperation with the EC now became possible or attractive for the previously neutral countries. The decision by Austria and then Sweden, Finland and Switzerland to apply for full EC membership further complicated the negotiations. A draft agreement on the European Economic Area (EEA) was initialled in October 1991. The EC Court of Justice objected to the provision for a joint EC-EFTA court to adjudicate disputes, and the terms were modified to give it the sole power to interpret EEA laws. The agreement was signed in May 1992. The planned timetable for ratification by the end of the year, to allow the launch of the EEA to coincide with that of the single market in the EC, had to be abandoned when Swiss voters rejected the agreement in a referendum in December. Several technical aspects then had to be renegotiated, in particular the future links between Liechtenstein and Switzerland (which form a customs union) and the EFTA states' respective contributions to the Cohesion Fund due to be set up to help the EU's poorer members to cope with the costs of implementing the single market. The EEA was established at the start of 1994, initially without the participation of Liechtenstein.

See also entries on specific institutions, organizations, agreements, terms etc.

European Economic Community (EEC) Former name of the European Community (EC), the core of the EUROPEAN UNION (EU). It is still used informally to refer to the Union as a whole.

European Energy Charter International agreement. Originally proposed by the Dutch government, the Charter was signed in December 1991 by virtually all European countries, most Soviet successor states, Canada, Japan and the United States. In essence it seeks to provide a framework for Europe-wide cooperation in the energy sector. In practical terms it provides for the transfer of western finance and technology to Russia and the former Soviet republics to encourage the development, principally through private investment, of their vast energy resources in exchange for guarantees of secure oil and gas supplies from those countries. (Many European countries rely on these to a greater or smaller extent.) It also provides for cooperation in related fields, such as the integration of the Eastern and Western European electricity networks. Formal negotiations on the text of a legally binding treaty were finalized in June 1994, and the European Energy Charter Treaty was due to be signed later in the year.

European Environment Agency (EEA) Institution of the European Union (EU). Agreed in June 1990 and set up in December 1993, the EEA is intended to provide the EU and member states with objective and reliable comparable information on the environment. Its principal aims are to assess the quality of the environment and the pressures on it. An extension of its powers to monitor member states' compliance with EU environmental legislation and standards is under consideration. Non-EU countries have been invited to join the new agency. It is based in Copenhagen (Denmark).

European Fighter Aircraft *See* EURO-FIGHTER 2000.

European Foundation for the Improvement of Living and Working Conditions Institution of the European Union (EU). Established in 1975, the Foundation aims to promote improvements in the quality of life and the working environment, primarily by providing research and information to other EU institutions (in particular the European Commission, the EU's administrative and executive arm), trade unions, employers' associations and member-state governments. All of these are represented on its Administrative Board. The Foundation is based in Dublin (Ireland).

European Free Trade Association (EFTA) Intergovernmental organization. EFTA was established in 1960 in order to remove obstacles to free trade among its members and to contribute to the liberalization and expansion of European and world trade. In recent years the goal of closer cooperation with the European Community (EC), now the European Union (EU), and the creation of a single European market – one of its original aims – have been the focus of the organization's activities. The latter was achieved with the agreement on the European Economic Area (EEA) in 1991. Reflecting the move towards further integration in Western Europe, four of EFTA's seven members (Austria, Finland, Norway and Sweden) applied for membership of the EC between 1989 and 1992. Accession negotiations were completed in 1994, and the four countries were due to join the EU at the start of 1995 pending the outcome of national referendums.

Aims and objectives. The Treaty of Stockholm, signed on 4 January 1960 and in force from 3 May 1960, defines EFTA's objectives as: (i) to promote a sustained expansion of economic activity, full employment, increased productivity and the rational use of resources, financial stability, and a continuous improvement in living standards; (ii) to secure that trade between member states takes place under fair conditions; and (iii) to contribute to the harmonious development and expansion of world trade. Member states undertook to reduce tariffs on all goods according to various agreed timetables, cooperate on wider economic issues and adopt common positions where possible in the multilateral international organizations. They also affirmed their commitment to cooperation with the European Economic Community (EEC) in the pursuit of the common goals of trade liberalization and European integration.

Membership. EFTA has seven members: Austria, Finland, Iceland, Liechtenstein, Norway, Sweden and Switzerland. The seven founding members were Austria, Denmark, Norway, Portugal, Sweden, Switzerland and the United Kingdom. Iceland joined in March 1970. Denmark and the United Kingdom left at the end of 1972 to join the then European Community (EC), as did Portugal at the end of 1985. Finland, which had been an associate member since 1961 (under an agreement which had contained special provisions concerning its trade links with the Soviet Union), became a full member in January 1986. Liechtenstein, which had been an associate member through its customs union with Switzerland, became a full member in May 1991.

Structure and activities. EFTA's governing body is the Council, which meets regularly at ministerial or ambassadorial level. Its decisions are binding and must be unanimous when they involve new obligations. Each member state has one vote. The Council is assisted by six standing committees, including the Consultative Committee, which seeks the views of employers' representatives, trade-union leaders and others in the member states. There is also a consultative Committee of Members of Parliament from member states. EFTA's secretariat is based in Geneva (Switzerland) and has an office in Brussels (Belgium), the EU headquarters. The official language is English. The secretary-general is Georg Reisch (Austria). The independent Surveillance Authority and Court are responsible for supervising and enforcing implementation of the EEA Agreement respectively.

History. EFTA has its roots in the abortive attempt in the late 1950s to create a free-trade area embracing the then six-member European Economic Community (EEC, later the European Community, EC, and now the European Union, EU) and the other Western European countries. Austria, Denmark, Norway, Portugal, Sweden, Switzerland and the United Kingdom then negotiated the Treaty of Stockholm establishing EFTA. It was signed and came into force in 1960. The organization's first target, the elimination of tariffs on industrial goods, was achieved by the end of 1966. Free trade in fishery products came into effect in 1990. In line with its ultimate objective of creating a single market including all the countries of Western Europe, EFTA also sought to eliminate tariffs between its member states and the EC. When Denmark, Ireland and the United Kingdom withdrew from EFTA to join the EC in 1973, agreements were concluded bilaterally between each of the remaining EFTA members and the EC. The last restriction on free trade in industrial goods between the two blocs was removed in January 1984. In April of that year EFTA and the EC agreed on general guidelines for developing the relationship between them, including closer cooperation in transport, agriculture, fisheries, energy, economic and monetary policy, telecommunications, information technology and other fields. (Closer political cooperation was not possible because several EFTA members were committed to neutrality.) By this time trade with EC countries accounted for more than half of the EFTA countries' total trade. In the light of the EC's plans to introduce a single internal market by the end of 1992, EFTA leaders in March 1989 reaffirmed their commitment to a single market covering all EC and EFTA countries. The terms of the European Economic Area (EEA) were finalized in October 1991. The EEA Agreement, which removes virtually all restrictions on the movement of people, goods, services and capital, was signed in May 1992 and ratified by all member states except Switzerland (where it was rejected in a referendum) by the end of the year. It came into force at the start of 1994. The collapse of communist rule in

Eastern Europe and the establishment of the EEA – which in effect realized EFTA's original objective – accelerated member states' moves to seek full EC membership. Austria was the first to make an application in June 1989, with Sweden following suit in July 1991, Finland in March 1992 and Norway in November 1992. (Switzerland's application, lodged by the government in May 1992, was suspended following voters' rejection of the EEA Agreement.) Accession negotiations were opened in February 1993 and concluded in March 1994. Provided voters expressed their approval in national referendums, the four countries were due to join the EU at the start of 1995. Since 1989 EFTA has also established links with the former communist countries of Eastern Europe, in particular the Czech Republic, Hungary, Poland and Slovakia.

See also entries on specific institutions, organizations, agreements, terms etc.

European Greens International political organization. Founded in 1984, the European Greens is a loose grouping of 20 environmentalist parties from 13 countries, including the Greens in France and Germany, the Green List in Italy and the Green Party in the United Kingdom. *See also* GREEN GROUP.

European Investment Bank (EIB) Institution of the European Union (EU). The EIB was established in 1958 under the Treaty of Rome. Its aim is to provide loans or give guarantees for investment projects which contribute to the balanced development of the EU. These are generally projects which promote regional development, improve communications, strengthen industry, secure energy supplies or protect the environment. A particular priority is major projects which a member state cannot finance alone or ones of interest to several member states which create similar funding difficulties. Some loans also go to projects in non-EU Mediterranean and Eastern European countries and developing countries in Africa, the Caribbean and the Pacific. The EIB operates on a non-profit basis. Usually it lends no more than half the cost of an individual project. Loans are made from money borrowed on the capital markets or from capital subscribed by member states (currently 57.6 billion ecus). The EIB's organizational structure comprises: (i) the Board of Governors, normally the finance ministers of the 12 member states; (ii) the part-time Board of Directors appointed by the Board of Governors for a six-year term; and (iii) the Management Committee, similarly appointed, responsible for administration. The Management Committee is headed by a president, currently Brian Unwin (United Kingdom). The EIB was given legal personality under the Maastricht Treaty establishing the European Union, which came into force in November 1993.

European Investment Fund (EIF) Programme of the European Union (EU). Agreed in December 1992 and launched June 1994, the EIF is intended to promote economic growth and reduce unemployment by providing financial assistance for major infrastructure projects and for capital investments by small and medium-size enterprises. It does not lend money directly but extends loan guarantees. The EIF is administered by the European Investment Bank (EIB), which contributes 40% of its capital of 2.3 billion ecus, with 30% coming from the EU budget and 30% from private financial institutions. The aim is to support investment projects worth up to 20 billion ecus.

European Liberals, Democrats and Reformers (ELDR) Shorthand for the FEDERATION OF LIBERAL, DEMOCRATIC AND REFORM PARTIES OF THE EUROPEAN UNION.

European Monetary Cooperation Fund (EMCF) Former institution of the European Union (EU). The EMCF was set up in 1973 to coordinate the monetary policies of the member states and operate the 'snake', a mechanism for reducing exchange-rate fluctuations. This was the forerunner of the Exchange Rate Mechanism (ERM) set up six years later. The EMCF was dissolved at the end of 1993 and its tasks were transferred to the new EUROPEAN MONETARY INSTITUTE (EMI).

European Monetary Institute (EMI) Institution of the European Union (EU). The EMI was established in January 1994 under the Maastricht Treaty at the start of stage two of ECONOMIC AND MONETARY UNION (EMU). Its main tasks are: (i) to strengthen cooperation between the national central banks; (ii) to strengthen the coordination of monetary policies of the member states with the aim of ensuring price stability; (iii) to monitor the functioning of the European Monetary System (EMS), the common policy aimed at improving monetary stability; (iv) to take over the tasks of the European Monetary Cooperation Fund (EMCF), which operated the EMS and its Exchange Rate Mechanism (ERM); and (v) to facilitate the use of the ecu, the EU's notional currency, and oversee its development. It also takes over a range of functions previously carried out on the EU's behalf by the Bank of International Settlements (BIS). The EMI's overall objective is to prepare the transition to stage three of EMU, specifically the introduction of a single currency. The EMI is in effect the forerunner of an EU central bank: under the Maastricht Treaty it is to be replaced by the European Central Bank (ECB) and a system of (national) central banks at the start of stage three. It is governed by a council composed of a president (appointed by the member states) and the governors of the national central banks. It is based in Frankfurt, Germany's main financial centre. The president is Alexandre Lamfalussy (Belgium).

European Monetary System (EMS) Common policy of the member states of the European Union (EU). The aim of the EMS is to improve monetary stability by reducing fluctuations in the exchange rates of the member states' currencies. It was established in 1979 in response to the breakdown of the worldwide Bretton Woods system of fixed exchange rates in the early 1970s and the consequent disruption to the European economies caused by floating exchange rates. It was given a formal footing under the Single European Act, which came into force in 1987. By this time the EMS was also increasingly seen as the framework for closer financial cooperation and the forerunner of a full ECONOMIC AND MONETARY UNION (EMU). All EU member states formally participate in the EMS and its structures, including the European Monetary Institute (EMI, formerly the European Monetary Cooperation Fund, EMCF) and the key Monetary Committee (MC), composed of representatives of national governments, central banks and the European Commission (the EU's administrative and executive arm) and independent experts. But at no time since the EMS's foundation have all states participated in its key element, the EXCHANGE RATE MECHANISM (ERM). The effective collapse of the ERM in two stages in September 1992 and August 1993 (*see* ERM CRISES) threw into doubt the scope of future cooperation within the EMS. ('EMS' and 'ERM' are often used interchangeably, and 'EMS' is often used when referring to the ERM.)

European motor regions (European Union) *See* FOUR MOTORS.

European Movement (EM) International political organization. Founded in 1947 by a number of organizations committed to European integration, the European Movement's aims are to study and offer solutions to the political, economic and technical problems of creating a European union, and to promote the concept of integration to the people of Europe. Its membership includes national councils in 16 countries across the continent and 13 affiliated organizations. It is governed by a federal council, general conference and executive committee; the secretariat is based in Brussels, the headquarters of the European Union (EU). The president is Valéry Giscard d'Estaing, a former president of France.

European Organization for Nuclear Research (CERN) Founded in 1954 as the successor of the European Council for Nuclear Research established two years earlier, CERN – the original Council's abbreviation in French, which is still commonly used – provides for collaboration among European countries in the field of basic nuclear research. Its work is of a pure scientific and fundamental nature, and primarily concerns subatomic, high-energy and elementary-particle physics. Its laboratories in Meyrin, near Geneva (Switzerland), include the world's largest particle accelerator, the Large Electron-Positron Collider. CERN has 19 members: Austria, Belgium, Czech Republic, Denmark, Finland, France, Germany, Greece, Hungary, Italy, Netherlands, Norway, Poland, Portugal, Slovakia, Spain, Sweden, Switzerland and the United Kingdom. Its senior decision-making body is the Council, with two representatives from each member state.

European Parliament (EP) Institution of the European Union (EU). The Parliament – not to be confused with the Parliamentary Assembly of the Council of Europe – is one of the EU's five main institutions, the others being the Council of Ministers, European Commission, Court of Justice and Court of Auditors. Unlike a national parliament, it has only limited legislative powers; these are primarily vested in the Council of Ministers. Its formal powers are also restricted to the European Community (EC), the core of the Union, and do not extend to its two intergovernmental 'pillars', the Common Foreign and Security Policy (CFSP) and Cooperation on Justice and Home Affairs (CJHA). The Parliament's main tasks are to (i) scrutinize draft legislation and the budget, (ii) supervise the executive organs, the Commission and the Council, (iii) draw attention to the problems of constituents, and (iv) debate issues of immediate concern to the Union. It may question members of the Commission, which is formally answerable to it, and the president of the Council. It may amend aspects of the budget or reject it as a whole, dismiss the Commission by a vote of censure, and veto an application for membership of the Union. It participates in the legislative process in two principal ways: through the 'cooperation procedure', which gives it limited powers to amend proposals related to the creation of the single internal market, and through the 'co-decision procedure', which gives it powers equal to those of the Council in 14 policy areas. The Parliament has 567 members (99 from Germany, 87 each from France, Italy and the United Kingdom, 64 from Spain, 31 from the Netherlands, 25 each from Belgium, Greece and Portugal, 16 from Denmark, 15 from Ireland and six from Luxemburg) elected for a five-year term by various systems of proportional representation in 11 member states and by majority voting in the United Kingdom. Members sit in cross-national party groups, not national delegations. The work of the Parliament is organized by the 15-member Bureau, headed by the president, who is elected for a 2½ year term. There are 19 standing committees dealing with specific policy areas. The Parliament is based in three cities: plenary sessions are generally held in Strasbourg (France), committee meetings in Brussels, and the secretariat is based in Luxemburg.

After the June 1994 elections nine party groups were formed. The Party of European Socialists (PES) (Socialist Group) holds 198/567 seats, the European People's Party (EPP) (Christian Democratic Group) 157 seats, the European Liberal Democratic and Reformist Party (ELDR) (Liberal Group) 43 seats, the communist and left-wing European United Left (EUL) 28 seats, the Come on Europe Group or Forza Europa Group (FE) (comprising the right-wing Come On Italy, Forza Italia) 27 seats, the right-wing European Democratic Alliance (EDA) 26 seats, the Greens 23 seats, the centre-left European Radical Alliance (ERA) 19 seats and the Europe of Nations Group (EN) 19 seats; the remaining 27 seats are held by independents, primarily by two far-right parties, the National Alliance (AN) of Italy with 12 seats and the National Front (FN) of France with 11 seats. The president is Klaus Hänsch, a German social democrat.

Originally called the European Assembly, the Parliament's powers have gradually been extended from the purely consultative. It was directly elected for the first time in 1979. The Single European Act, which came into force in July 1987, gave it a significant role in the budget-setting process and introduced the 'cooperation procedure'. The Maastricht Treaty establishing the European Union, in force since November 1993, introduced the 'co-decision procedure'. Efforts to resolve the 'seat question', i.e. concentrating the Parliament's work in one city, have foundered on rivalries among national governments.

See also specific entries on party groups, parties, terms etc.

European People's Party (EPP or PPE) European Union (EU) political organization. A federation set up in 1976, the EPP brings together 14 christian democratic parties, including the Social Democratic Centre (CDS) in France, the Christian Democratic Union (CDU) in Germany, the Italian People's Party (PPI, the successor to the Christian Democratic Party, DC) and the People's Party (PP) in Spain. It has campaigned on a joint programme for European Parliament elections since 1979. The EPP group in the Parliament, also called the Christian Democratic Group, is the second-largest, with 157/567 seats, and includes representatives from all 12 EU member states. The British Conservative group joined the EPP group in April 1992 as individual members, but the Conservative Party as such is not a member of the EPP. The party president and parliamentary group leader is Wilfried Martens, a former prime minister of Belgium. *See also* EUROPEAN CHRISTIAN DEMOCRATIC UNION.

European pillar In the North Atlantic Treaty Organization (NATO), the common name for the European component of the alliance, which comprises 14 Western European countries and the United States and Canada. There have been attempts to strengthen the European 'pillar' since the late 1960s, mainly through collaboration on arms-procurement projects (not least to reduce their cost) and the development of parameters of a common defence policy. The EUROGROUP provided an initial impetus, but since the late 1980s the WESTERN EUROPEAN UNION (WEU) has become the main focus of the process.

European Police Office (EUROPOL)
Institution of the European Union (EU).
EUROPOL was set up under the Maastricht Treaty, which came into force
in November 1993, as part of the intergovernmental cooperation on justice and
home affairs. Based on a proposal by the
German government, its aim is to coordinate and enhance cooperation among
the national police forces in combating
major international criminal activities
such as drug trafficking, terrorism, money
laundering and toxic- and nuclear-waste
smuggling. Primarily concerned with
collecting and sharing information and
crime prevention, it is a criminal intelligence agency rather than an integrated
operational police force (as originally
proposed). Many details of its eventual
powers and procedures have yet to be
decided. EUROPOL's activities overlap
to some extent with those of the Schengen
Information System (SIS), set up by nine
of the 12 EU member states, and the
worldwide International Police Organization (INTERPOL). It is expected to
work closely with both agencies. It is
based in The Hague (Netherlands).

European Political Cooperation (EPC or
PoCo) Former name of the COMMON
FOREIGN AND SECURITY POLICY (CFSP),
an intergovernmental 'pillar' of the European Union (EU) established under the
Maastricht Treaty, which came into force
in November 1993. EPC was set up
informally as a forum for cooperation
on foreign-policy issues in 1970 and
given a formal basis under the 1986
Single European Act.

European Radical Alliance (ERA or ARE)
Political group in the European Parlia-
ment, the parliament of the European
Union (EU). The ERA is a broad left-
wing alliance including France's Radical
Energy list, Italy's Radical Party (PR)
and the Scottish National Party (SNP).
It holds 19/567 seats. The leader is Jean-
François Hory (France).

European Regional Development Fund
(ERDF) Programme of the European
Union (EU). One of the three STRUC-
TURAL FUNDS, the ERDF was established
in 1975 to reduce regional economic

disparities between and within the
member states. Its funding arrangements,
procedures and priorities have been
changed several times over the years.
Since 1989 its main priorities are: (i)
promotion of growth and structural
adjustment in regions whose economic
development is lagging behind, with the
emphasis on improving infrastructure; (ii)
conversion of regions affected by industrial decline, with the emphasis on creating and preserving jobs; and (iii) assistance for regions with severe problems
of rural development, with the emphasis
on creating jobs outside the agricultural
sector. Investments are also made in the
energy, technology and environmental
fields. The main beneficiaries are the
poorer regions of Greece, Ireland, Italy,
Portugal and Spain. The ERDF generally
provides up to half the total cost of a
project, the balance being contributed by
the member state concerned. Funding
decisions are taken by the Council of
Ministers. The ERDF's commitments
rose from 258 million ecus in 1975 to
3,920 million ecus in 1989, when it was
agreed to double its size and that of the
other structural funds by 1993. *See also*
EUROPEAN SOCIAL FUND.

European Regional Fund *See* EUROPEAN
REGIONAL DEVELOPMENT FUND.

**European Research Coordination
Agency** Formal name of the EUREKA
ORGANIZATION.

European Romany Parliament (EUROM)
Gipsy political organization. EUROM
was set up in August 1992 by 22 Gipsy or
Romany organizations from 10 European
countries. Its aim is to represent the legal,
social and cultural interests of the Gipsy
community in Europe – estimated at
around 5 million – and to work for an end
to discrimination of all kinds against it.
See also GIPSIES.

European Science Foundation (ESF)
International scientific and political organization. The ESF was founded in 1974
to serve as a coordinating body for major
European research institutes and councils,
promote cooperation among researchers,
identify areas of research in need of stim-
ulation, and represent the interests of the

scientific community in major European institutions such as the Council of Europe and the European Union (EU). Its activities are divided into five spheres, each supervised by a standing committee: natural sciences, biomedical sciences, space science, social sciences, and humanities. A series of 'scientific networks' has also been set up to coordinate activities in specific fields. The Foundation's membership includes 59 research academies and councils in 21 countries. Its governing bodies include a general assembly, which meets annually, a board and an executive council. The secretariat is based in Strasbourg (France).

European security identity or **European defence identity** In the European Union (EU), North Atlantic Treaty Organization (NATO) and Western European Union (WEU), a common name for the emerging Western-Europe-wide defence capability and security structure. The end of the Cold War and the collapse of communist rule in Eastern Europe in the late 1980s and the consequent withdrawal of US troops from Europe sparked a major rethink in Western Europe on defence and security issues. Some countries (e.g. France and Germany) broadly favoured strengthening the WEU and/or adding a defence dimension to the EU, while others (e.g. the United Kingdom and the Netherlands) favoured strengthening the European 'pillar' of NATO. The latter were particularly worried by a process that might lead to the marginalization of the United States in European security and defence matters. These opposing views initially caused some tensions, but a consensus view emerged by the early 1990s. Since then the WEU has become the main focus for the elaboration of a 'European security identity'; according to the Maastricht Treaty it is eventually to become the 'defence component' of the EU. On the practical side the main developments have been the establishment of NATO's Rapid Reaction Corps, the Franco-German army corps and the more broadly based European Corps, which is widely seen as the forerunner of a Western European army. Important

in this context was also the French government's decision in October 1992 to take a more active role in NATO (from whose integrated military command structure it had withdrawn in 1966).

European Social Charter International agreement adopted within the framework of the Council of Europe. Signed in October 1961 and in force since February 1965, the European Social Charter – not to be confused with the Social Charter, Chapter or Protocol, a European Union (EU) document – aims to protect individual social rights. It is considered the counterpart to the European Convention of Human Rights, which protects civil and political rights. It guarantees a wide range of rights, including the rights to just conditions of work, safe and healthy working conditions, fair remuneration, freedom of association, collective bargaining, appropriate facilities for vocational guidance and training, social security and social and medical assistance. It also provides protection for the young, the disabled, families and migrant workers. An additional protocol adopted in 1988 guarantees the rights to equal opportunities and treatment, information and consultation at one's place of work, and participation in the determination and improvement of working conditions at one's place of work; it also provides protection for elderly people. The Charter also establishes a system to monitor the effective application of guaranteed rights in the signatory countries.

European Social Fund (ESF) Programme of the European Union (EU). One of the three STRUCTURAL FUNDS, the ESF was set up in 1960 to improve employment opportunities by assisting training and mobility of workers. Its priorities have been redefined on several occasions over the years. Currently its two overriding priorities are (i) providing vocational training for young people and (ii) setting up training, retraining and job-creation programmes in regions and industries with high unemployment. Other beneficiaries are the long-term unemployed, disabled workers, migrant workers and women wanting to return to work. The

ESF generally provides up to half the total cost of a project, the balance being contributed by the member state concerned. Funding decisions are taken by the Council of Ministers. In 1989 it was agreed to double the size of the ESF and the other structural funds by 1993. *See also* EUROPEAN REGIONAL DEVELOPMENT FUND.

European Socialist Party *See* PARTY OF EUROPEAN SOCIALISTS.

European Space Agency (ESA) Intergovernmental organization. The ESA was formed in 1975 by the merger of the European Space Research Organization (ESRO) and the European Organization for the Development and Construction of Space Vehicle Launchers (ELDO). Its aims are to promote cooperation in space research and technology for peaceful purposes. The ESA's 13 members are Austria, Belgium, Denmark, France, Germany, Ireland, Italy, Netherlands, Norway, Spain, Sweden, Switzerland and the United Kingdom; Finland is an associate member, and Canada has signed various cooperation agreements. The ESA's main organ is the Council, in which each member state has one vote; decisions are normally taken by simple majority. The secretariat is based in Paris (France); the managing director is Jean-Marie Luton (France). The activities of the ESA and its predecessors, limited in comparison to the US and Soviet space programmes in the 1960s and 70s, expanded significantly in the 1980s. The ESA has carried out several joint projects with the US National Aeronautics and Space Administration (NASA), in particular the encounter between Halley's Comet and the space probe Giotto in 1985 and the launch of the Hubble space telescope in 1990. Current long-term projects include the upgrading of the Ariane launcher, the development of the Hermes space plane and the Columbus crewed space station (the latter in collaboration with NASA). Cooperation with Russia is also being explored. The three countries with the highest level of financial involvement in ESA projects are France, Germany and Italy.

European summit In the European Union (EU), an informal term for a meeting of the EUROPEAN COUNCIL, which brings together the heads of government of the member states.

European Trade Union Confederation (ETUC) International trade-union federation. The ETUC was formed in 1973 by a merger of the Confederation of Trade Unions in the European Communities and the Trade Union Committee of the European Free Trade Association (EFTA). It aims to represent and defend the economic, social and cultural interests of working people at the European level, particularly within the framework of European institutions. Its 46 members include most major national federations in 22 countries, representing around 45 million workers; it also has 10 observer organizations from six Eastern European countries. It cooperates closely with the International Confederation of Free Trade Unions (ICFTU). It is based in Brussels (Belgium). The general secretary is Emilio Gabaglio (Italy).

European Turks Collective name for the Turkish communities in Western Europe. Not to be confused with the people of the European part of Turkey (centred on İstanbul) or the long-established Turkish communities in Bulgaria, Macedonia and other Balkan countries, the European Turks left Turkey in the 1960s to take up work (mostly unskilled and low-paid) in factories and service industries in Western Europe, whose booming economies had an acute labour shortage at the time. Most of the immigrants put down roots in their adoptive countries. From the 1980s they and especially their descendants began to branch out into other sectors of the economy, setting up small businesses in retailing, catering etc. There are around 2.8 million European Turks: around two-thirds live in Germany and most of the remainder live in France, the Netherlands and Belgium. Nearly all, including the second and third generations, remain Turkish citizens, not least because the host countries have generally not allowed naturalization. In recent years racist attacks on European Turks have been rising.

European Union (EU) Intergovernmental organization. The origins of the EU lie in the desire for reconciliation among Western Europeans in the aftermath of the Second World War (1939–45). To many, cooperation and integration seemed to offer the best hope of overcoming the national enmities that had thrown Europe into two devastating wars in the first half of the 20th century. A French proposal in 1950 to pool coal and steel resources led to the establishment of the European Coal and Steel Community (ECSC) in 1952. This served as a model for the more comprehensive European Economic Community (EEC) established in 1958. Since then cooperation has expanded from the purely economic to encompass virtually all aspects of policy making, the most recent major developments being the introduction of the single internal or common market at the start of 1993 and the establishment of the European Union the following November. Membership has expanded from six countries to 12, and may reach 20 or so within the next decade. The scope of both actual and planned cooperation among the member states is without precedent in international relations. The progress of the integration process is reflected in the nomenclature: Common Market, European Economic Community, European Community, European Communities and European Union have all been or are in official or common use. The difficulties inherent in finding common ground among sovereign states with widely different traditions, institutions and interests are reflected in a complex structure, with various forms of cooperation and methods of decision making applicable in different spheres and contexts. Over the years both factors – the plethora of names and diffuse organization – have given rise to much confusion over the power, influence and operation of the EU and its forerunners.

The European Union has a population of around 349 million (6.3% of the world total), a combined gross domestic product of around US$ 6.3 trillion (28% of the world total), and a share of world trade of around 21% net (i.e. excluding intra-EU trade). (The equivalent figures for the United States are: 258 million or 4.7%, US$ 5.7 trillion or 26%, and 19%.)

Aims and objectives. The basic treaties governing the European Union are the Treaty of Rome establishing the European Economic Community (EEC), signed on 25 March 1957 and in force from 1 January 1958; its two comprehensive revisions, the Single European Act, signed on 17 February 1986 and in force from 1 July 1987, and the Treaty on the European Union (Maastricht Treaty) agreed on 11 December 1991, signed on 7 February 1992 and in force since 1 November 1993; and the Treaty Establishing a Single Council and a Single Commission of the European Communities (Merger Treaty), signed on 8 April 1965 and in force from 1 July 1967. The preamble of the Treaty of Rome states that its scope is to lay the foundations for 'an ever closer union among the peoples of Europe'. This phrase is reiterated in Article A of the Maastricht Treaty and amended with 'in which decisions are taken as closely as possible to the citizen', which expresses the essence of the principle of 'subsidiarity' as the basis for decision making. Article B defines the objectives of the Union as: (i) 'to promote economic and social progress which is balanced and sustainable, in particular through the creation of an area without internal frontiers, through the strengthening of economic and social cohesion and through the establishment of economic and monetary union, ultimately including a single currency'; (ii) 'to assert its identity on the international scene, in particular through the implementation of a common foreign and security policy including the eventual framing of a common defence policy, which might in time lead to a common defence'; (iii) 'to strengthen the protection of the rights and interests of the nationals of its member states through the introduction of a citizenship of the Union'; (iv) 'to develop close cooperation on justice and home affairs'; and (v) 'to maintain in full the *acquis communautaire* [= laws etc] and build on it'. It concludes by stating that 'These objectives shall be achieved ... while respecting the principle of subsidiarity'.

Membership. The EU has 12 members: Belgium, Denmark, France, Germany, Greece, Ireland, Italy, Luxemburg, Netherlands, Portugal, Spain and the United Kingdom. The six founding members were Belgium, France, Italy, Luxemburg, Netherlands and West Germany. Denmark, Ireland and the United Kingdom joined in January 1973, Greece in January 1981, Portugal and Spain in January 1986. The former East Germany was incorporated on German reunification in October 1990. The four French overseas departments (French Guyana, Guadeloupe, Martinique and Reunion) are among the 'outermost regions' (ORs), which are integral parts of the Union. The member states' dependencies outside Europe, known as the 'overseas countries and territories' (OCTs), are not part of the Union but have special links with it. Austria and Finland are due to join in January 1995, as will Norway and Sweden if their electorates approve membership in referendums in November 1994. Greenland was a member from 1973–85.

Structure and activities. The European Union consists of three 'pillars' with distinct competences and structures: (i) the European Communities, composed in turn of the European Community (EC, the original European Economic Community, EEC), the European Coal and Steel Community (ECSC) and the European Atomic Energy Community (EAEC or EURATOM), which have a joint institutional framework and are for all practical purposes a single unit – hence the common usage of 'European Community' and 'EC' to cover all three – but are separate legal entities; (ii) the Common Foreign and Security Policy (CFSP); and (iii) Cooperation on Justice and Home Affairs (CJHA). The core of the EU, the EC, is a 'supranational' organization, i.e. one to which the member states have transferred specified legislative and executive powers and whose decisions are binding on them and their citizens. The CFSP and CJHA are forms of intergovernmental cooperation, in which the member states retain

full sovereign rights, and hence decision making is by unanimity. All legislation is adopted within the supranational framework of the EC. Technically there is thus no such thing as 'EU legislation', only EC legislation.

Within the EU, the EC is competent to formulate and decide policy in 17 areas: free movement of goods (an aspect of the single market); agriculture and fisheries; free movement of persons, services and capital (an aspect of the single market); transport; competition, taxation and approximation of laws; economic and monetary policy; commercial policy (i.e. foreign-trade issues); social policy, education, vocational training and youth; culture; public health; consumer protection; trans-European networks (i.e. infrastructure and communications); industry; economic and social cohesion; research and technological development; environment; and development cooperation. The CFSP deals with foreign-policy matters and, to a limited extent, defence and security issues. And the CJHA deals with asylum policy, rules governing the crossing of the EU's external borders, immigration policy, drug trafficking and international fraud; it also oversees cooperation in judicial matters and among customs and police services.

The EU's five main institutions are: (i) the Council of the European Union or Council of Ministers, the main decision- and law-making body, composed of government representatives from the member states; (ii) the European Commission, the administrative and executive arm, composed of 17 commissioners appointed for a five-year term and headed by a president, and organized in 23 directorates-general; (iii) the European Parliament, composed of 567 members elected on a country-by-country basis for a five-year term, which has a consultative role and limited decision-making powers; (iv) the Court of Justice, which adjudicates all legal issues and disputes; and (v) the Court of Auditors, which audits the financial affairs of the organization and all its institutions. The last four are technically institutions of the European

Communities and have no competence in the two intergovernmental pillars (CFSP and CJHA), although the Commission in particular is closely involved in their work.

The key body is the Council of Ministers. Each member state holds the presidency of the Council for six months, and its foreign minister serves as president. Decisions are taken by unanimity, qualified majority (broadly two-thirds) and simple majority, depending on the importance of the subject matter and the policy area; simple majority voting is used only for procedural matters. The three binding legal instruments at the disposal of the Council, and the Commission on its behalf, to implement decisions are the 'directive', in essence an instruction to member states to legislate on a specific matter, the 'regulation', which has direct effect in the member states, and the 'decision', which deals with specific cases. On certain issues and in certain policy areas the Council shares legislative powers with the Parliament. This is regulated through various procedures, namely, in rising order of the latter's involvement, 'consultation', 'cooperation', 'co-decision' and 'assent'.

Other major EU institutions or bodies are: the European Council, the biannual summit meetings of the member states' heads of government, which are intended to give general guidance to the EU's activities; the Committee of Permanent Representatives (COREPER), composed of the member states' ambassadors, which assists the Council of Ministers; the European Monetary Institute (EMI), which is charged with preparing the transition to economic and monetary union; the Monetary Committee (MC), composed of government representatives and other experts, which is charged with coordinating the monetary policies of the member states; the European Investment Bank (EIB), which provides loans or gives guarantees for investment projects; the European Police Office (EUROPOL), which coordinates cooperation among member states' police forces; the European Environment Agency (EEA), which collects information on the quality of the environment; the European Foundation for the Improvement of Living and Working Conditions; and the Court of First Instance (CFI), which assists the Court of Justice and has jurisdiction over certain categories of cases.

There are also several major consultative bodies: the Economic and Social Committee (ECOSOC), which brings together representatives of trade unions, employers' associations, industrial, agricultural and consumer organizations and other interest groups; the Committee of the Regions (COR), which brings together representatives of regional and local authorities; and the Conference of the Parliaments, which brings together representatives of the European Parliament and the member states' national parliaments.

The EU's activities are carried out in a wide array of common policies, programmes, committees etc. Besides the Common Foreign and Security Policy (CFSP) and Cooperation on Justice and Home Affairs (CJHA), the key common policies are the Common Agricultural Policy (CAP), the Common Commercial Policy (CCP), which covers foreign-trade issues, the Common Fisheries Policy (CFP), and the European Monetary System (EMS) and its Exchange Rate Mechanism (ERM), aimed at improving monetary stability and operating a system of semi-fixed exchange rates. The three major EU programmes which account for a large share of expenditure are the European Social Fund (ESF), the European Regional Development Fund (ERDF) and the guidance section of the European Agricultural Guidance and Guarantee Fund (EAGGF). Known as the 'structural funds', these are aimed at eliminating economic, social and regional disparities in the member states. Other major programmes are: the Cohesion Fund, which helps the poorest member states with the costs of adapting to the planned economic and monetary union; the European Investment Fund (EIF), which extends loan guarantees for infrastructure projects and for capital investments by small and medium-size enterprises; the European Development Fund (EDF), which provides loans and grants for projects in developing countries; the PHARE programme, which provides assistance to the former communist countries of Eastern Europe; and Citizens' Europe, which aims to strengthen the Union's identity and improve its image among the citizens of the member states. Among the hundreds of specific programmes are Basic Research in Industrial Technologies for Europe (BRITE), Community Action Programme in Education and Training for Technology (COMETT), European Community Action Scheme for the Mobility of University Students (ERASMUS) and European Strategic Programme for Research and Development in Information Technology (ESPRIT).

On the international plane the EU is active in a number of ways. It maintains diplomatic relations in its own right with most of the world's countries, participates in many intergovernmental organizations and international conferences (including the Group of Seven, G-7, and the General Agreement on Tariffs and Trade, GATT) and is party to various international conventions. In some cases it acts on behalf of and/or to the exclusion of the member states. It has signed agreements with many states on cooperation on trade, development and other matters. The most wide-ranging forms of cooperation are the 'association agreements' and the 'Europe agreements', which have been signed with most European states. A special form of association is extended to the members of the African, Caribbean and Pacific Group of States (ACP Group), nearly all former colonies of the member states. Two major international agreements signed by the EU and its member states are the Agreement on the European Economic Area, which covers the Western-Europe-wide single internal market, and the Lomé Convention, which provides the framework for development assistance to the ACP countries. (Technically all the above international activities are carried out by the EC, not the EU, because the EU does not have legal personality and hence cannot sign treaties, conventions etc.)

There are two intergovernmental organizations in which all or most EU member states participate and which in practice deal with, or are intended to deal with, policy areas covered under the basic treaties. They are the Schengen Group, composed of nine EU member states, which deals with the removal of border controls between the participating states; and the Western European Union (WEU), composed of all EU states and three others, which is to be built up as the defence arm of the Union. (The anomalous status of these two organizations is due to the lack of consensus among the member states on the integration of the respective policy areas into the EU framework.)

The EU's activities are financed from four 'own resources', namely, in order of importance, a proportion of value-added tax receipts collected by the member states, a proportion of the gross domestic product of each member state, customs duties, and agricultural levies. The budget is drafted by the Commission and adopted by the Parliament.

The EU has ten official languages: Danish, Dutch, English, French, German, Greek, Irish, Italian, Portuguese and Spanish, the official languages of the member states. All are full working languages except Irish, which is used only for the basic treaties. In practice English, French and (to a lesser extent) German are the main languages.

The Council presidency is currently held by Germany and the president is Klaus Kinkel. (In 1995 and 1996 it will be held successively by France, Spain, Italy and Ireland.) The president of the Commission is Jacques Delors (France). The president of the Parliament is Klaus Hänsch (Germany). The president of the Court of Justice is Ole Due (Denmark). The president of the Court of Auditors is André Middelhoek (Netherlands).

History. Belief in the need for closer cooperation among European states or even some form of European unification gained currency in the aftermath of the

Second World War (1939–45), which had resulted in millions of deaths and the physical and economic destruction of much of Europe. Reconciliation, between France and Germany in particular, seemed to offer the best hope of avoiding another war. Fear of a resurgent Germany also convinced policy makers in other Western European countries that (West) Germany should be integrated or 'locked into' regional economic, military and political structures so that another war would become not only unthinkable but impossible. Among the other factors which influenced Western European policy makers in the late 1940s and early 50s were: (i) fear of Soviet aggression, which led to the signature of the Brussels Treaty, which provided for 'collective self-defence' as well as economic, social and cultural cooperation; (ii) the practical experience of economic cooperation gained during the implementation of the Marshall Plan (1948–52), the American-sponsored reconstruction programme organized through the Organization for European Economic Cooperation (OEEC, the forerunner of the Organization for Economic Cooperation and Development, OECD); and (iii) the precedent of the Benelux Economic Union, agreed by Belgium, Luxemburg and the Netherlands in 1944 and established in 1948, initially a customs union but intended to become a full economic union in due course. During a Franco-German dispute over the Saarland, an important coal- and steel-producing region, the French foreign minister, Robert Schuman, proposed in 1950 that all French and West German coal and steel industries be placed under a single 'high authority'. What became known as the Schuman Plan had originated with the French economist Jean Monnet, one of the most influential thinkers on European integration. The European Coal and Steel Community (ECSC) was set up by Belgium, France, Italy, Luxemburg, Netherlands and West Germany under the Treaty of Paris, signed in 1951 and effective from 1952. The new organization was unique in that the members transferred part of their

sovereignty to a 'supranational' authority with wide-ranging powers. The ECSC was always intended as a first step in a long-term integration process. In 1952 the six states signed a treaty providing for the creation of a European Defence Community (EDC), but this project was abandoned in 1954 after the French parliament refused to ratify it. The focus then shifted back to the economic sphere. In 1955 the Six set up a committee under the Belgian foreign minister, Paul-Henri Spaak, to investigate the possibility of establishing a common market. Its report, submitted in 1956, formed the basis for the Treaty of Rome establishing the European Economic Community (EEC) and another treaty establishing the European Atomic Energy Community (EAEC or EURATOM). Both treaties were signed in 1957 and came into force at the start of 1958. The EEC was essentially an extension of the ECSC, again with a strong supranational element. The widespread expectation that economic cooperation would lead eventually to political integration was expressed in the phrase that the Treaty of Rome laid the foundations for 'an ever closer union among the peoples of Europe'.

In its first decade the EEC both benefited from and stimulated rapid economic growth and political stability in the six member states. Intra-EEC trade increased by an average of 28% per year between 1958–67, and trade with third countries by 10% per year over the same period. A major barrier to the free movement of goods was removed in 1968 with the completion, ahead of schedule, of the customs union, which abolished internal tariffs and imposed a common external tariff. The Common Agricultural Policy (CAP), the first major common policy, inaugurated in 1962, gave a strong boost to food production and farmers' incomes. The economic success of the Community and the challenge it presented prompted the launch of the looser European Free Trade Association (EFTA) in 1960. Four EFTA members – Denmark, Ireland, Norway and the United Kingdom – applied for EEC membership in 1961/62, but the British application was vetoed by France in 1963, whereupon the other three withdrew theirs. The four countries applied again in 1967, but France again used its veto. (The French vetoes were based on President de Gaulle's contention that Britain would always give greater priority to its links with the United States and the Commonwealth than to any European commitment.) In 1961 the Six agreed in principle that the 'economic union' should be complemented by a 'political union', but for many years no practical steps were taken towards this goal because the smaller states feared domination by the larger ones. Growing tension between France and the other five states, not least over the enlargement issue and the financing of the CAP, came to a head in 1965–66 over another major point of contention, the decision-making process within the Council of Ministers and the more fundamental question of the extent of supranational cooperation with the Community. In protest at proposals to extend qualified majority voting (i.e. broadly two-thirds, as provided for under the Treaty of Rome) to a wide range of issues, France withdrew from the EEC institutions for six months. The crisis was resolved by the 'Luxemburg compromise', an informal agreement under which a member state could veto legislation subject to majority voting if it deemed a 'vital' national interest to be at stake. In practice most decisions over the next two decades continued to be taken by unanimity rather than majority. The president of the Commission, Walter Hallstein, a strong advocate of the 'federal' line, resigned over this issue in 1967; he had held the post since the EEC's foundation. (Like the division between large and small states and, since the 1980s, north and south, the supranational/intergovernmental argument, also expressed in the concepts 'federal Europe' and 'Europe of nations', has been one of the major faultlines within the integration process from the beginning.) The EEC, ECSC and EURATOM were merged under a single Council of Ministers and Commission in 1967. The

three organizations, which were effectively integrated but retained their separate legal identities, were collectively called the European Communities (EC). The term 'European Community' gained wide currency to denote either the European Communities as a whole or the EEC, which was – and is – by far the most important of its three components. (The name 'European Community' had no official status until 1993, when the EEC was renamed thus under the Maastricht Treaty.) In the late 1960s and mid 1970s a number of other measures were taken to rationalize the EC and put it on a sounder financial footing. It was given its own budgetary resources, the budgetary powers of the European Parliament were extended, and the Court of Auditors was established (1977). But despite these institutional changes, the integration process stagnated during the mid 1960s.

A summit meeting in The Hague (Netherlands) in 1969, shortly after de Gaulle's resignation as president of France, took several far-reaching decisions which contributed to the EC's revival: it approved proposals on the financing of the CAP (the single largest expenditure item by far), agreed in principle to establish an 'economic and monetary union' (EMU), commissioned a report on 'political cooperation', and laid down conditions for new members (with France in effect abandoning its objections to enlargement). Accession negotiations were concluded with the United Kingdom, Ireland, Denmark and Norway in 1972, and the first three countries joined the EC at the start of 1973; Norway did not join after membership was narrowly rejected in a referendum. European Political Cooperation (EPC or PoCo) was set up as a forum for cooperation on foreign-policy issues in 1970. In the same year the Council of Ministers approved a plan to complete the economic and monetary union in stages by 1980. The first stage was the establishment in 1972 of the 'snake', a system for managing exchange rates. Neither the snake nor the goal of EMU survived the convulsions of the international monetary system in the mid

1970s, and proposals to move to a second stage of EMU were abandoned. Another attempt at closer monetary cooperation was made in 1979 with the establishment of the European Monetary System (EMS) and its Exchange Rate Mechanism (ERM), a system of semi-fixed exchange rates. Until the mid 1980s there were frequent realignments, most of them involving devaluations of the French franc and other currencies against the German mark, but by the late 1980s exchange rates within the ERM had become very stable.

The European Council, the regular meetings of heads of government, was set up in 1974. The informal Trevi Group was set up by interior and justice ministers in 1976 to coordinate both information gathering on extremist groups and responses to terrorist violence; the scope of its activities was gradually widened in the 1980s to include drug trafficking, organized crime and other matters. The first direct elections to the European Parliament were held in June 1979. Greece joined the EC in January 1981, and Portugal and Spain joined in January 1986. The Common Fisheries Policy (CFP) came into effect in January 1983. A long-running dispute between the United Kingdom and the other member states over finance was resolved in June 1984, when it was agreed that the former should receive an annual rebate on its budget contribution.

The appointment of Jacques Delors, a former French economy and finance minister, as Commission president in January 1985 marked the beginning of a new phase in the EC's development. The Milan summit in June adopted a timetable for completing the 'single internal market' by the end of 1992. (Progress on removing the remaining barriers had been very slow since the establishment of the customs union in 1968.) It was also agreed to hold an intergovernmental conference to discuss amendments to the Treaty of Rome. The outcome was the Single European Act, signed in February 1986 and in force from July 1987. It formalized the status of several Community bodies and structures (such as the

European Council, EPC and EMS), streamlined decision making within the organization, and extended cooperation to several other policy areas. The single-market programme – dubbed '1992' in some countries, '1993' in others – renewed the momentum of European integration and led to many new initiatives. With pressures on the budget increasing, the EC's financing was put on a new basis in February 1988 with a package of measures that included a new source of revenue (based on member states' gross domestic products), a ceiling on overall expenditure, and a doubling of the 'structural funds', the programmes aimed at reducing structural and regional disparities in the member states. The implications of the single-market programme and the ERM's success in stabilizing exchange rates put the project of 'economic and monetary union' (EMU) back on the agenda in the late 1980s. The Hannover summit in June 1988 set up a committee, under the chairmanship of Delors, to study and propose concrete stages leading to EMU. Its report, approved in June 1989, identified three stages culminating in the introduction of a single currency but set no dates either for the stages or for the achievement of full EMU. In December 1989 all member states except the United Kingdom adopted the Charter of the Fundamental Social Rights of Workers (Social Charter), which was intended as a basis for developing the 'social dimension' (i.e. the non-economic side) of the single market.

The British government's opposition to EC involvement in social legislation was indicative of growing tensions among – and within – the member states about the depth and the pace of the integration process. These came to the fore during the two intergovernmental conferences on 'economic union' and 'political union' convened in December 1990, when the notion of 'subsidiarity', i.e. the appropriate level of decision making, emerged as a focus of debate. The outcome of the two conferences was the Treaty on European Union, agreed in Maastricht (Netherlands) in December 1991 and signed there in

February 1992. The Maastricht Treaty, a comprehensive revision of the Treaty of Rome, extended cooperation in a number of fields, including foreign affairs and (in principle) defence, and also set a timetable for economic and monetary union and the introduction of a single currency. The issue whether the EU would be too centralized or 'federalist' became highly controversial in Britain and Denmark, and the Treaty's ratification was delayed in both countries. Both governments had also negotiated 'opt-outs' on economic, social and other aspects of the Treaty. The plans for EMU were called into question after heavy speculation on the financial markets against the pound, lira and other ERM currencies led to a major financial crisis in September 1992 and to the ERM's effective suspension in July/August 1993. In the meantime a major reform of the Common Agricultural Policy (CAP) was agreed in May 1992; the single internal market was established on schedule at the start of 1993; and the Cohesion Fund, providing assistance to the poorest member states, was set up in April 1993. The Maastricht Treaty finally came into force in November 1993. The European Monetary Institute (EMI) was set up in January 1994 at the start of stage two of EMU. Since late 1992 measures to combat the economic recession and rising unemployment in the EU have become a major focus of attention. In December 1993 the Commission put forward a set of interlocking proposals on improving growth, competitiveness and employment. Opposition to further integration grew in some countries in 1993 and 1994, both among governments and the population at large, and ideas such as a 'multitrack Europe' and 'variable geometry' were given serious consideration.

The transformation sparked by the collapse of communist rule in Eastern Europe in the late 1980s and the end of the division of Europe also had a marked effect on the EC. After two years of negotiations, the EC and EFTA states in May 1992 agreed to establish a single market, the European Economic Area (EEA); the agreement came into force in January

1994. In the meantime four EFTA countries – Austria, Finland, Norway and Sweden – had applied for EU membership. Accession negotiations began in February 1993 and were completed in March 1994. The four countries were due to join the EU at the start of 1995 provided voters expressed their approval in national referendums (Austria's and Finland's did so in June and October 1994 respectively). The EU has also signed cooperation or association agreements with most of the former communist countries of Eastern Europe.

See also entries on specific institutions, policies, programmes, terms, people etc.

European Union citizenship, **Union citizenship** or **common citizenship** Common citizenship of the European Union (EU). Article 8 of the Maastricht Treaty on European Union, which came into force in November 1993, states that 'Every person holding the nationality of a member state shall be a citizen of the Union'. Union citizenship – a unique 'supranational' citizenship – does not replace but complements national citizenship and the rights derived from it. It guarantees the holders' rights to free movement and residence within the Union, gives them the right to vote and stand as candidates in municipal and European Parliament elections in the member state in which they are resident, and entitles them to assistance and protection from any EU member state embassy or consulate in third countries where their own country is not represented.

European United Left (EUL or GUE) Political group in the European Parliament, the parliament of the European Union (EU). The EUL is a broad-based group encompassing orthodox as well as reform communists. It includes the French Communist Party (PCF), the Communist Refoundation Party (RC) of Italy and the United Left (IU) of Spain. It has representatives from five of the 12 EU member states and holds 28/567 seats. The leader is Alonso Puerta (Spain).

European Youth Foundation (EYF) Institution of the Council of Europe. Set up in 1972, the EYF provides financial support to national and international youth organizations for a wide range of activities. These should have a multinational and multicultural dimension and should be organized by young people themselves. The EYF is governed by a board composed of an equal number of representatives of governments and youth organizations. It works closely with another Council institution, the European Youth Centre (EYC), an educational establishment and residential centre.

europhilia and **europhoria** Support and strong support respectively for the process of integration within the framework of the European Union (EU), specifically the plans for economic, monetary and political union contained in the Maastricht Treaty (in force since November 1993) and further measures. *See also* FEDERALISM *and* FEDERAL EUROPE.

europhobia Rejection of the process of integration within the framework of the European Union (EU), specifically the plans for economic, monetary and political union contained in the Maastricht Treaty (in force since November 1993). It is contrasted with 'europhoria' and 'europhilia'. *See also* EUROPE OF NATIONS.

europhoria *See* EUROPHILIA.

EUROPOL or **Europol** *See* EUROPEAN POLICE OFFICE.

euroregion Form of cooperation between local, regional or national governments in border areas. Many such bodies have been set up within what is now the European Union (EU) since the 1960s and in other parts of the continent since the late 1980s. Examples are the Euregio (covering parts of the Dutch-German border region), Meuse-Rhine Euroregion (covering adjoining regions in Belgium, Germany and the Netherlands), the Association of the Eastern Alps, the Association of the Central Alps and the Council of the Euro-Arctic Region. Within the EU 'euregio' is also used as a generic term.

euroscepticism Doubts concerning or criticism of the process of integration within the framework of the European Union (EU), specifically the plans for economic, monetary and political union contained in the Maastricht Treaty (in force since

November 1993). It is contrasted with 'europhilia' and 'euroenthusiasm'. *See also* EUROPE OF NATIONS.

eurostrategic missiles or **euromissiles** Shorthand for intermediate-range nuclear forces (i.e. those with a range of between 500 and 5,000 km) intended for deployment in Europe and aimed at targets in Europe, including western Russia. All missiles of this type deployed by the Soviet Pact and the Warsaw Pact on the one hand and the United States and North Atlantic Treaty Organization (NATO) on the other were removed from the continent under the Intermediate Nuclear Forces Treaty signed by the two countries in December 1987. (They included US Tomahawk cruise missiles and Pershing IIs and Soviet SS-20s.) The British and French independent nuclear forces are usually described as 'strategic', but on the basis of their range and purpose they are in effect 'eurostrategic'.

Euskadi Basque name for the BASQUE COUNTRY, an autonomous community or region of Spain. It is now also widely used by Spanish speakers in preference to the Spanish equivalent, País Vasco.

Euskal Herri *See* BASQUE COUNTRY.

Euskara or **Euskera** Native name for the Basque language, spoken in the Basque Country, an autonomous community of Spain, the neighbouring region of Navarre and across the border in France. In Spain the name is widely used in preference to its Spanish equivalent, Vascuence.

Eusko Jaurlaritza or **Jaurlaritza** ('Basque Government') Basque name for the government of the Basque Country, an autonomous community or region of Spain.

Eusko Legebiltzarre or **Legebiltzarre** ('Basque Legislature') Basque name for the parliament of the Basque Country, an autonomous community or region of Spain.

EV or **EW** Abbreviation for Estonia, used for international vehicle registrations etc. It is taken from Eesti Vabariik ('Republic of Estonia'), the country's official name in Estonian. 'EW' is an older form.

Evangelical Political Federation *See* REFORMATIONAL POLITICAL ....

Evangelou, Alexandros or **Alekos** (1939–)
Cypriot lawyer, civil servant and politician. He worked in local government
before joining the Legal Service in 1972.
He has been a counsel and attorney and
has also served as acting attorney-general.
In February 1993 President Klerides
appointed him minister of justice and
public order. He does not belong to a
political party.

**ever closer union among the peoples of
Europe** Phrase denoting the overriding
objective of the European Union (EU).
The preamble of the Treaty of Rome
establishing the then European Economic
Community (EEC) in 1958 states that its
scope is to 'lay the foundations for an
ever closer union among the peoples
of Europe'. Article A of the Maastricht
Treaty, agreed in December 1991,
describes it as a 'new stage in the process
of creating an ever closer union ...'. The
exact wording of this passage proved
highly controversial. An earlier draft
describing the Treaty as a 'new stage in
the gradual process leading to a union
with a federal goal' was removed at the
insistence of the British government,
which argued that in the United Kingdom
the word 'federal' implied centralization
of decision making.

Evert, Miltiades (1939–) Greek economist and politician. A member of
parliament for the centre-right New
Democratic Party (ND) from 1974–86
and since 1989, he held several junior
ministerial posts from 1976 and was
minister of finance from 1980 until the
party lost power in 1981. He was mayor
of Athens, the national capital, from 1986–
90. When the party returned to government in April 1990 he was appointed to
the key post of minister to the prime
minister. He was dismissed in October
1991 for criticizing the government's
free-market policies. He was elected ND
leader in November 1993, succeeding
Konstantinos Mitsotakis, who had
resigned after the party's defeat in the
general election the previous month.

EWR German abbreviation for the European Economic Area (EEA).

ex-Yugoslavia *See* FORMER YUGOSLAVIA.

excess seats [Überhangmandat, pl. -e] In
Germany, additional seats a party may
gain in the Bundestag, the lower house
of parliament, or state parliaments owing
to an anomaly in the country's 'alternative member' electoral system. Under this
system voters have two votes, one for a
candidate in their constituency and one
for a party. The number of single-member
constituencies is equivalent to half the
number of seats in a parliament. A party's
representation is made up of the constituency seats it has won and a proportion
of the other seats so that the total reflects
its share of the party vote. Excess seats
occur when a party gains more constituency seats than it would be entitled to on
the basis of the party vote. The Bundestag
elected in December 1990 had six such
seats, and so has a membership of 662
rather than 656.

Exchange Rate Mechanism (ERM) Common policy of member states of the European Union (EU), part of the EUROPEAN
MONETARY SYSTEM (EMS). The ERM is a
voluntary system of semi-fixed exchange
rates based on the ecu, the EU's notional
currency. The outcome of a Franco-
German initiative, the EMS and ERM
were established in March 1979 to limit
currency fluctuations and create greater
monetary stability within the then European Community (EC) and thus to promote economic growth. They replaced the
'snake', a similar but looser mechanism
set up following the collapse in the early
1970s of the worldwide Bretton Woods
system of fixed exchange rates. All the
then nine member states agreed on the
creation of the EMS, but the United
Kingdom refused to join the ERM. Of
the three new members admitted in the
1980s, Greece did not join the ERM,
Spain joined in June 1989 and Portugal
in April 1992. The United Kingdom
joined in October 1990 but suspended its
membership in September 1992, as did
Italy. Under the system each participating
state deposits a fifth of its gold and
currency reserves with the European
Monetary Institute (EMI, the successor
to the European Monetary Cooperation
Fund, EMCF). The finance ministers

decide by unanimity on a bilateral exchange rate for each participating currency against the ecu. Currencies are allowed to fluctuate around this 'central rate' by a certain margin, ideally plus or minus 2.25% ('narrow band') or 6% ('broad band'). When a currency crosses the 'threshold of divergence', usually referred to as its 'floor', set at 75% of the margin of fluctuation, the authorities of the country concerned are obliged to correct the situation by intervening in the currency markets, negotiating short- or medium-term loans from the EMI, changing domestic policy or, if the situation persists, requesting a currency 'realignment'. Until the mid 1980s there were frequent realignments, most of them involving devaluations of the French franc and other currencies against the German mark. By the late 1980s exchange rates with the ERM had become very stable. The Maastricht Treaty on European Union, agreed in December 1991, provided for ECONOMIC AND MONETARY UNION (EMU) by the late 1990s on the basis of the EMS and ERM. Persistent speculation on the financial markets against the pound and lira in particular forced the British and Italian governments to suspend their participation in the ERM in September 1992. After further speculation against the French franc, Spanish peseta and other currencies, it was agreed in August 1993 that all currencies except the German mark and the Dutch guilder could fluctuate by up to 15% on either side of their central rates (*see* ERM CRISES). This decision meant that the aim of progressively reducing exchange-rate fluctuations was effectively abandoned for the time being. (The terms 'ERM' and 'EMS' are often used interchangeably, and 'EMS' is often used when referring to the ERM.)

exclusion In the United Kingdom, an entry ban on people deemed to be connected with terrorist activities in or relating to Northern Ireland (*see* NORTHERN IRELAND QUESTION). Under the 1974 Prevention of Terrorism Act the home secretary may not only ban a suspected person from entering the United Kingdom, s/he may also ban British citizens from travelling from one part of the Kingdom to another, specifically from Northern Ireland to mainland Great Britain (i.e. England, Scotland and Wales). Exclusion orders have been issued primarily against members of Sinn Féin, a legal political party but regarded as the political wing of the Irish Republican Army (IRA), and against suspected IRA members and sympathizers.

exclusion zone (Bosnia-Herzegovina) *See* SAFE AREA.

Extremadura Autonomous community or region of Spain. Situated in the west and bordering on Portugal, Extremadura has an area of 41,602 sq km and a population of 1,131,000. The capital is Mérida, but the largest cities are Badajoz and Cáceres. The economy is based on agriculture (sheep and pig farming, cereals, fruit and vegetables), forestry and some light industry (food processing). Extremadura is one of Spain's least developed and poorest regions; emigration has been high throughout the 20th century. The main political parties are the Spanish Socialist Workers' Party (PSOE) and the centre-right People's Party (PP). At the May 1991 election the PSOE gained 39 seats in the 65-member legislature and the PP 19 seats. Extremadura was conquered by León and Castile in the 13th century after five centuries of Muslim rule. It was established as an autonomous region in 1983.

Eyskens, Mark (1933–) Belgian academic and politician. He lectured in economics from 1966 and was elected to parliament for the Flemish Christian People's Party (CVP) in 1977. He has been minister for development cooperation (1979–80), finance (1980–81 and 1985–89), economic affairs (1981–85) and foreign affairs from 1989 until March 1992. He was also briefly prime minister in 1981.

F Abbreviation for the FRANC, the currencies of Belgium, France, Luxemburg and Switzerland.

F Abbreviation for France, used for international vehicle registrations, postal addresses etc.

F (Iceland) *See* PROGRESSIVE PARTY.

f Abbreviation for the gulden or GUILDER, the Dutch currency. It is taken from 'florin' [florijn], an old name for the guilder.

F (Sweden) *See* PEOPLE'S PARTY - THE LIBERALS.

FA *See* ARMED PHALANGE.

Fabius, Laurent (1946–) French politician. He worked as an auditor for the Council of State, an advisory and judicial body, until his election to the National Assembly for the Socialist Party (PS) in 1978. When the party gained power in 1981 he became a junior minister. In 1984 he was appointed prime minister by President Mitterrand, a post he held until the left lost the 1986 election. He was president of the National Assembly from 1988–91. Elected first secretary (= leader) of the PS in January 1992, he resigned in April 1993 after the party's heavy election defeat. He was the most senior minister accused of negligence in the HIV-INFECTED BLOOD AFFAIR which broke in late 1992.

Faeroe Islands and **Faeroes** *See* FAROE ISLANDS.

Færøerne Danish name for the Faroe Islands.

FAIC *See* FEDERATION OF CANARY ISLANDS INDEPENDENT GROUPS.

Falange Armata *See* ARMED PHALANGE.

Falbr, Richard (1940–) Czech lawyer, civil servant and trade-union official. He taught Spanish and English at the Czechoslovak interior ministry in the 1960s. He worked for the Municipal Workers' Union (OSPMH) in the 1970s and 80s and for Prague Zoo in 1989–90. In 1990 he was elected leader of the Czechomoravian Union of Service Workers (ČMOSPS) and vice-president of the Czechomoravian Trade Union Confederation (ČMKOS) in 1990. He was elected the latter's president in April 1994.

Falcone and Borsellino cases Murders of two senior magistrates, Giovanni Falcone and Paolo Borsellino, by the Sicilian Mafia in May and July 1992. Falcone had been a senior prosecutor in the 'maxi-trial' of 473 members of the Mafia, Italy's most powerful crime syndicate, in 1986–87 and was widely expected to be appointed director of the Anti-Mafia Investigation Directorate (DIA), a new government agency. Borsellino was the chief public prosecutor in Palermo, the Sicilian capital. Both were killed by car bombs. The assassinations prompted parliament to introduce a range of special measures to combat organized crime, including additional powers for the police and the judiciary and the deployment of troops in Sicily and elsewhere. In November 1992 investigating magistrates revealed the names of 18 Mafia members they believed to be responsible for Falcone's murder.

Falcons *See* SERBIAN FALCONS.

fall of the Berlin Wall *See* BERLIN WALL.

Faremo, Grete (1955–) Norwegian lawyer, civil servant and politician. She worked for several ministries and government agencies in the 1980s, specializing in development issues. From 1986–90 she worked in private industry. A member of the Norwegian Labour Party (DNA), she was appointed minister for development cooperation in 1990 and became justice minister in September 1992.

Faria de Oliveira, Fernando (1941–) Portuguese mechanical engineer, civil servant and politician. He worked for several engineering firms from 1965 and was a deputy director of the State Investment and Participations (IPE) holding company on three occasions between 1983 and 1990. During this time he held several junior ministerial posts. A member of the centre-right Social Democratic Party (PSD), he was appointed minister for trade and tourism in April 1990.

Farmers' Union of Latvia [Latvijas Zemnieku Savienība] (LZS) Latvian political party. Founded in 1917, the LZS was one of the country's leading parties in the 1920s and 30s. It was relaunched in 1989 (when Latvia was still part of the

Soviet Union). It is generally right-wing and favours state support for the agricultural sector. At the June 1993 election it gained 10.6% of the vote and 12/100 seats. From August 1993 – July 1994 it was the junior partner in a centre-right coalition with the Latvian Way (LC). The leader is Aivars Berķis.

Farnesina Palace [Palazzo Farnesina] Shorthand for the Italian foreign ministry. The Palazzo Farnesina in Rome is the headquarters of the foreign ministry.

Faroe Islands [Føroyar (Faroese), Færøerne (Danish)] Territory in northwestern Europe, a dependency of Denmark, also referred to as the Faroes.

Official data. Name: Faroe Islands [Føroyar/Færøerne]; capital: Thorshavn [Tórshavn]; form of government: internally self-governing integral part of Denmark; head of state: Danish monarch, represented by a high commissioner; head of government: chief minister; flag: white with a red blue-edged Scandinavian cross; national holidays: 16 April (Queen's Birthday), 29 June (Saint Olaf's Day); languages: Faroese and Danish; religion: Evangelical Lutheranism; currencies: króna (kr) (pl. krónur) = 100 oyru, Danish krone; abbreviation: FR.

Geography. Situated in the Atlantic Ocean, 340 km north of Scotland, 590 km southeast of Iceland and 1,040 km northwest of Denmark, the Faroe Islands consists of 16 islands and a number of islets and reefs, with a total area of 1,399 sq km. The main islands are Streymoy [Strømø] and Eysturoy [Østerø]. The terrain is mountainous, with high cliffs and deep fjords. Some 2% of the land is arable and virtually none is covered by pastures or forested. The climate is temperate marine, with cool summers and slightly colder winters; rainfall is heavy.

Demography. The Faroe Islands has a population of 46,800. Population density is 33 per sq km, among the lowest in Europe. Around two-thirds of the people live on the two islands of Streymoy and Eysturoy, and just under a third live in Thorshavn. Nearly all the people are Faroese. In religious terms 74.4% of the people are Lutheran Protestants and

19.8% are Plymouth Brethren. The main languages are Faroese and Danish.

Sociography. The standard of living in the Faroe Islands is high. There are 17 doctors and 75 hospital beds for every 10,000 people. Education is compulsory between the ages of seven and 16. There is one teacher for every 14 students. Enrolment is around 95% at the secondary level; there is one college of higher education, but most students study abroad, in Denmark and other countries. The literacy rate is virtually 100%. GNP per head (unadjusted for purchasing power) is US$ 13,850. Income differentials are very small.

Infrastructure and communications. The Faroe Islands has a highly developed but limited transport and communications network. There are 430 km of paved roads and 14,200 passenger cars (296 per 1,000 people). There are no railways or navigable waterways. The main port is Thorshavn. There is an airport at Vágar. There is one daily newspaper and three biweeklies, with a combined circulation of 29,400 (372 per 1,000 people). There are 20,000 radio receivers, 14,000 television sets and 28,000 telephones in use (respectively 416, 291 and 580 per 1,000 people).

Economic structure. The Faroese economy is highly developed but heavily dependent on the fishing industry, which employs a quarter of the labour force, contributes a quarter of GDP and generates nine-tenths of export earnings; it is consequently highly vulnerable to changes in world prices and demand for fish. After a period of high growth in the 1980s (averaging over 4% per year), the economy has been thrown into deep recession in the 1990s, with GDP contracting by around 15%, large current-account deficits, low inflation (below 3%), and a sharp rise in unemployment (from virtually nil to around 20%); the national debt stands at around 130% of GDP, one of the highest levels in Europe.

Services contribute 50% of GDP, industry 33% (manufacturing 21%), and agriculture and fisheries 17% (fishing 16%). Some 22% of the labour force is employed in manufacturing, 17% in fishing, 17% in public services, 11% in transport and communications and 11% in construction. The main agricultural activity is livestock raising (sheep, wool); the main crops grown are potatoes and vegetables. The fishing industry (cod etc, whales) is the mainstay of the economy. There are no significant mineral resources. The main industry is fish processing; other branches are shipbuilding and ship repairing and handicrafts. The main energy sources are hydroelectric power and imported fossil fuels; 9% of exports are required to cover net fuel imports. The main exports are fish and fish products (94% of the total). The main imports are foodstuffs, machinery and transport equipment, basic manufactures and fuels. The main trading partners are: exports: Denmark (20%), Germany (18%), United Kingdom (12%), France (9%), Italy (8%), United States (7%), Spain (7%); imports: Denmark (45%), Norway (18%), United Kingdom, Iceland, Germany, Sweden; two-thirds of all trade is with European Union (EU) countries. Net invisible earnings (financial assistance from the Danish government) account for a significant share of GNP.

There is no central bank. The main employers' association is the Faroese Employers' Organization (FAgf), and there are also several organizations in the fishing industry; the main trade union is the Faroese Labour Organization (FAf).

Political structure. Under the Danish constitution adopted in 1953, the Faroe Islands is an internally self-governing integral part of the kingdom. The Danish government is responsible for foreign affairs, defence, justice and the monetary system. Executive power is formally vested in the Danish monarch, but is exercised by the high commissioner [ríkisumboðsmaður/rigsombudsmand] appointed by the Danish government and the chief minister [løgmaður/lagmand] and government [Landsstýri/Landsstyre]. Legislative power is vested in the Legislature [Løgting/Lagting], whose 32 members are elected for a four-year term by a system of proportional representation. Two repre-

sentatives are directly elected to sit in the Danish parliament. All citizens aged over 20 are entitled to vote. Administratively the territory is divided into 50 communes [kommuna, pl. kommunur]; they are organized into seven districts, which have no administrative or political functions.

The main political parties are the Union Party (Sb), People's Party (Fkfl), Equality Party or Social Democratic Party (Jvfl), Republican Party (Tvfl), Labour Front (Vf), Self-Government Party or Home Rule Party (Sjfl), Christian People's Party (KF) and Centre Party (Mfl). At the election in July 1994 the Sb gained 8/32 seats, the Fkfl six seats, the Jvfl five seats, the Tvfl four seats, the Vf three seats, and the Sjfl, KF and Mfl two seats each. The government is formed by a centre-left coalition of the Sb, Jvfl, Sjfl and Vf, with Edmund Joensen as chief minister (also responsible for foreign affairs and administration). Other senior ministers are Jóannes Eidesgaard (deputy chief minister, finance, economy) and Eilif Johannesen (fisheries, trade). The head of state is Queen Margrethe II, represented by Bent Kline as high commissioner; the heir is Prince Frederik.

Security and international affiliations. Defence and foreign affairs are the responsibility of the Danish government. Military service within the Danish armed forces is compulsory and consists of 9–12 months' basic training. Defence and foreign affairs are the responsibility of the Danish government. The Faroese government is generally allowed to act independently in matters of immediate concern to the islands (such as fisheries policy and related international agreements). The Faroe Islands plays a full role in the Nordic Council. The territory did not join the then European Community (EC) when Denmark joined in 1973, but it has signed a special trade agreement with the organization.

History. The Faroes' first inhabitants were Irish monks, who arrived in the 8th century but left soon afterwards following the arrival of Viking settlers. The islands became a Norwegian province in 1035 and, like Norway, came under Danish rule in 1380. In 1709 they were declared a royal trade monopoly, which inhibited economic development. When Norway was transferred to Sweden in 1814, the Faroes remained part of Denmark. The regional parliament, the Løgting, was abolished in 1816. A Faroes cultural and political movement emerged in the 19th century. The Løgting was restored in 1852, initially as a consultative body, and the trade monopoly was lifted in 1856. During the Second World War (1939–45) British troops occupied the islands in 1940, after metropolitan Denmark had been occupied by Germany.

Internal self-government was granted in 1948. Coalition governments have been the rule. Traditionally, the issue of relations with Denmark – whether to maintain the status quo, introduce greater autonomy or move to full independence – has shaped a party's outlook as much as ideological considerations. The Faroes joined the European Free Trade Association (EFTA) in 1968 but left the organization in 1972 because of the adverse effect of membership on the fishing industry, the mainstay of the economy. Membership of the European Community (EC) was rejected in a referendum for the same reason, and a special trade agreement was negotiated instead. (Metropolitan Denmark joined the EC in 1973.) Government coalitions were broadly centre-left from 1974–81 and 1985–89, centre-right from 1981–85 and centrist from 1989–91. A centre-left coalition was formed in January 1991, led by the Social Democratic Party (Jvfl) until September 1994 and by the Union Party (Sb) since then. The economy overheated in the 1980s and went into deep recession in the 1990s. Emigration, traditionally high, levelled off during the 1980s but has soared since then.

See also entries on specific institutions, organizations, parties, people, terms etc.

fascism [fascismo] Political outlook in Italy based on the values and policies of Benito Mussolini (1883–1945), who founded the far-right fascist movement in 1919 and held power from 1922 until the country's defeat and his execution during the Second World War. Fascism was essentially authoritarian, corporatist and nationalist. Its key tenet was the primacy of the state over the individual, from which followed the emphasis on charismatic and dictatorial leadership, government direction of the economy and an aggressive foreign policy on the one hand and the denigration of civil rights, pluralist democracy and cultural diversity on the other. Its perceived archenemies were liberalism, socialism and communism. Mussolini adopted the symbol of state authority in ancient Rome, the *fasces*, to underline his belief in the 'rebirth' of the Roman Empire and styled himself *Il Duce*, 'The Leader'. The National Fascist Party (PNF) was able to take power because of widespread economic dislocation and disillusionment with traditional political parties. After Italy's defeat in the Second World War – which it had fought in alliance with Germany – the PNF was banned. From 1953 the 'neo-fascist' Italian Social Movement (MSI) secured consistent electoral support (around 6%) but remained on the fringes of Italian political life until it launched the more broadly based but still far-right National Alliance (AN) in January 1994. Its leadership now describes the MSI as 'post-fascist'. In the 1930s the term 'fascist' was also applied to comparable movements in Germany, Spain and other countries (*see* NAZISM *and* FRANCOISM). Since then 'fascist' and 'neo-fascist' have also been used as generic terms for far-right parties or groups and as terms of abuse for right-wing formations with nationalist overtones or individuals with such views.

Fasslabend, Werner (1944–) Austrian lawyer, manager and politician. Active in local government in Lower Austria, he was elected to parliament for the centre-right Austrian People's Party (ÖVP) in 1987. He was appointed defence minister in December 1990.

fast track (European Union) *See* ECONOMIC AND MONETARY UNION *and* MULTI-TRACK EUROPE.

Fatherland [Isamaa], in full **National Coalition Party 'Fatherland'** [Rahvuslik

Koonderakond 'Isamaa'] (Isamaa) Estonian political party. Isamaa – also referred to as Pro Patria – was established as an electoral alliance in 1992 by the country's main right-wing parties, the Christian Democratic Party (KDP), Christian Democratic Union (KDL), Conservative People's Party (KRE), Liberal Democratic Party (LDP) and Republican Coalition Party (VKE). These had been formed between 1988 and 1990, when Estonia was still part of the Soviet Union but the authority of the Communist Party was crumbling. At the September 1992 election the alliance became the largest group in parliament, gaining 29/101 seats, and formed a centre-right coalition. The KDL, KDP, KRE and VKE formally merged in November that year, but the new party has been riven by internal disagreements and defections. The leader is Mart Laar, the parliamentary leader Tiit Sanisaar.

Fatherland and Freedom *See* FOR FATHERLAND ....

Fatherland Union [Vaterländische Union] (VU) Liechtenstein political party. Founded in 1918, the centre-right VU has ruled the country in coalition with the other main party, the right-wing Progressive Citizens' Party (FBP), since 1938. At the February 1993 election it gained 45.3% of the vote and 11/25 seats; at the early election in October (precipitated by internal divisions within the FBP) it again became the largest party, with 50.1% and 13 seats. The leader is Mario Frick, the party president is Oswald Kranz.

Fatherland Union (Lithuania) *See* HOMELAND UNION.

Fazio, Antonio (1936–) Italian economist and banker. He joined the research department of the Bank of Italy, the central bank, in 1963. He became its head of general research in 1973, head of economic research in 1980, deputy governor in 1982 and governor in May 1993.

FB Abbreviation for the FRANC, the Belgian currency.

FDE *See* GERMAN UNITY FUND.

FDF *See* FRANCOPHONE DEMOCRATIC FRONT.

FDP (Germany) *See* FREE DEMOCRATIC PARTY.

FDP (Switzerland) *See* RADICAL DEMOCRATIC PARTY.

FEB *See* BELGIAN BUSINESS FEDERATION.

Federal Agency for the Administration in Trust of State-Owned Companies [Bundesanstalt zur treuhänderischen Verwaltung des Volkseigentums] Formal name of the TRUST AGENCY or Treuhandanstalt, a German government agency.

Federal Assembly [Bundestag] Lower house of the German parliament. The Bundestag has 656 members elected for a four-year term. They are elected by a form of proportional representation known as the alternative member system, under which voters have two votes, one for a candidate in one of the 278 single-member constituencies and one for a party, which determines the overall distribution of seats. Parties must secure at least 5% of the popular vote to qualify for representation. An anomaly in the system, when a party gains more directly elected seats than it is entitled to on the basis of its overall share of the vote, produces 'excess seats'. The Bundestag elected in December 1990 had six such seats, and therefore has 662 members. *See also* FEDERAL COUNCIL.

Federal Assembly [Bundesversammlung (German), Assemblée Fédérale (French), Assemblea Federale (Italian)] Parliament of Switzerland, composed of the NATIONAL COUNCIL and the COUNCIL OF STATES. The Assembly elects in joint session the seven members of the Federal Council (= government) for a four-year term, and from among them the president and vice-president for a one-year term.

Federal Assembly [Savezna Skupština] Parliament of Yugoslavia, composed of the CHAMBER OF CITIZENS and CHAMBER OF REPUBLICS. The Assembly elects in joint session the federal president and the federal prime minister.

Federal Border Guard [Bundesgrenzschutz] (BGS) German paramilitary police force. The BGS is an elite corps of around 24,800 officers. Its commander is answerable to the interior minister. Its main functions are to police the borders and protect federal institutions (including the railways). A specialist unit of the

BGS, called GSG-9, is involved in anti-terrorist operations.

Federal Chamber of Commerce and Industry *See* FEDERAL ECONOMIC CHAMBER.

Federal Chamber of Labour [Bundesarbeiterkammer] (BAK), in full **Council of Austrian Chambers of Labour** [Österreichischer Arbeiterkammertag] (ÖAKT) Austrian labour organization. Founded in 1946, the Chamber is a statutory body to which all employees in private enterprises must belong. It represents their interests and provides advice and training. It works closely with the Austrian Trade Union Federation (ÖGB). Within Austria's system of 'social partnership' it cooperates with its employer counterpart, the Federal Economic Chamber (BWK), the Association of Austrian Industrialists (VÖI), the ÖGB and the government on a range of macro-economic issues, in particular through the Joint Commission on Wages and Prices. The president is Heinz Vogler.

Federal Chancellery and **Federal Chancery** *See* FEDERAL CHANCELLOR'S OFFICE.

federal chancellor or **chancellor** [Bundeskanzler, Kanzler] Head of government or prime minister of Austria or Germany.

Federal Chancellor's Office, **Federal Chancellery** or **Chancellery** [Bundeskanzleramt] German government department. Charged with assisting the federal chancellor (= prime minister) and coordinating the work of the government ministries, the Chancellery is broadly similar to the prime minister's office in other countries. Its head is a minister of cabinet rank who is usually also minister for special projects.

Federal Constitutional Court [Bundesverfassungsgericht] Supreme court of Germany. It adjudicates on the interpretation of the federal constitution, the constitutionality of federal and state laws and government decisions, disputes between federal and state authorities, and alleged breaches of the constitutional rights of citizens. Its 16 judges are elected for 12-year non-renewable terms by the two houses of parliament, half by the Federal Assembly (Bundestag) and half by the Federal Council (Bundesrat). The judges

are generally drawn from the federal and state judiciaries, university law departments and political parties. The Court sits in Karlsruhe.

Federal Convention [Bundesversammlung] German electoral body. The Federal Convention – not to be confused with the Federal Assembly (Bundestag), the lower house of parliament – is convened solely to elect the federal president, a non-executive post. It consists of 1,322 members, the 656 members of the Bundestag and an equal number of delegates nominated by the 16 state assemblies.

Federal Council [Bundesrat] Upper house of the Austrian parliament. The Bundesrat has 63 members elected by the nine provincial assemblies and reflecting their party strengths. Its decisions may be overridden by the lower house, the National Council (Nationalrat), by a simple majority.

Federal Council [Bundesrat] Upper house of the German parliament. The Bundesrat has 68 members appointed by and from among the members of the 16 state governments. Each state has between three and six representatives, depending on its population. Each delegation votes as a bloc. The Bundesrat has limited veto powers over legislation passed by the lower house, the Federal Assembly (Bundestag), which may in turn override its decisions by a simple majority. Amendments to the constitution require the Bundesrat's approval by a two-thirds majority. In July 1991 the Bundesrat voted to remain in Bonn, the seat of the West German government before reunification; the Bundestag had previously decided to move to Berlin in due course.

Federal Council [Bundesrat (German), Conseil Fédéral (French), Consiglio Federale (Italian)] Government of Switzerland. The Federal Council has seven members elected for a four-year term by the two houses of parliament, the Federal Assembly, in joint session. Two of its members are also elected federal president and vice-president for a one-year term. In effect the two offices rotate among the Council members.

Federal Criminal Investigation Office [Bundeskriminalamt] (BKA) German police force. The BKA is the only major police force at federal level. An agency of the interior ministry, it deals with political and anti-terrorist matters as well as general crime.

Federal Economic Chamber [Bundeswirtschaftskammer] (BWK), in full **Federal Chamber of Commerce and Industry** [Bundeskammer der gewerblichen Wirtschaft] Austrian employers' association. The BWK was founded in 1946 but has roots going back to the 1840s. It is a statutory body to which all 297,000 private enterprises must belong and which represents their interests to parliament and government and, most importantly, in collective bargaining. It works closely with the Association of Austrian Industrialists (VÖI). Within Austria's system of 'social partnership' it cooperates with its employee counterpart, the Federal Chamber of Labour (BAK or ÖAKT), the Austrian Trade Union Federation (ÖGB), the VÖI and the government on a range of macroeconomic issues, in particular through the Joint Commission on Wages and Prices. The president is Leopold Maderthaner, the general secretary is Günter Stummvoll.

federal Europe In the European Union (EU), a concept associated with those who argue that the process of integration should be aimed at the creation of a closely knit union in which many national powers are transferred to a supranational or federal level of government. In recent years it has become linked with calls for a 'Europe of the regions', in which many powers are devolved to the regional level. It is contrasted with a 'Europe of nations' or 'Europe of states', in which all key powers remain with national governments. *See also* FEDERALISM.

Federal Intelligence Service [Bundesnachrichtendienst] (BND) German intelligence agency. The BND is engaged in intelligence gathering and espionage abroad. It is answerable to the federal chancellor (= prime minister). It is based in Munich.

Federal Office for the Protection of the Constitution [Bundesamt für Verfassungsschutz] (BfV) German intelligence agency. Founded in 1950, the BfV is

responsible for internal security matters and is answerable to the interior minister. Its main function is to gather information on extremist groups and others deemed to be a threat to the constitution and the democratic order. It works closely with similar agencies in each of the federal states. It is based in Cologne.

Federal Republic, the Shorthand for Germany. Federal Republic of Germany has been the country's official name since 1949.

Federal Republic of Germany [Bundesrepublik Deutschland] (FRG) Official name of Germany. It was also the official name of West Germany from 1949 until reunification with East Germany in 1990.

Federal Republic of Yugoslavia [Federativna Republika Jugoslavija] (FRY) Official name of Yugoslavia since its reconstitution in April 1992 as a federation of two of the formerly six republics, Serbia and Montenegro.

federalism In the European Union (EU), support for the creation of a closely knit union in which many national powers are transferred to a supranational or federal level of government. The federal ideal has its roots in the desire for reconciliation among Western Europe's peoples in the aftermath of the Second World War. Unlike most other intergovernmental organizations, the EU has always had a strong federal dimension in the sense that national governments have transferred certain sovereign powers to it from the beginning, primarily in the economic field. Over the years other policy areas have been incorporated into the supranational framework. How far this process should go has become increasingly controversial. The issue came to a head in the negotiations and subsequent debate on the Maastricht Treaty (adopted in December 1991 and in force since November 1993). In particular, its provisions for economic and monetary union and cooperation in foreign affairs and defence are decried by critics as 'centralizing' or 'federalist'. In this context the concept of 'SUBSIDIARITY', i.e. the most appropriate level of government (local, regional, national or supranational) at which decisions should be taken, has become a major focus of debate. *See also* FEDERAL EUROPE.

federalismo fiscale *See* FISCAL FEDERALISM.

Federated Progressive Group *See* ALLIED PROGRESSIVE GROUP.

Federation of Bosnia-Herzegovina [Federacija Bosne i Hercegovine] State proclaimed by the parliaments of Bosnia-Herzegovina and the breakaway Croatian Republic of Herzeg-Bosnia, conceived as the eventual successor to the Republic of Bosnia-Herzegovina. The Federation was established in March 1994, a month after government and Croat forces agreed a ceasefire that ended 16 months of heavy fighting between the former allies in the BOSNIAN CIVIL WAR. The two sides agreed on a decentralized state composed of ethnically based 'cantons', power sharing at federal level, and economic and other links with Croatia within an eventual 'confederation' of the two countries. Many details were left to be worked out by the constituent assembly, composed of the two parliaments, and the federal government.

Specifically, the accords provide for: (i) the establishment of eight ethnically based cantons (four predominantly Muslim, two Croat, two mixed) with extensive powers; (ii) a strong federal government with responsibility for foreign affairs, defence, foreign trade and other aspects of economic policy; (iii) the division of senior government and other posts between Muslims and Croats broadly on a 2:1 basis, reflecting the two groups' numerical strengths; (iv) the annual rotation of the presidency and other senior posts between Muslims and Croats; (v) the establishment of a joint army; and (vi) the return of displaced people and refugees. The preliminary agreement with Croatia provides for the introduction of a common market and monetary union 'when conditions are ripe' and for cooperation in education, culture, defence and other fields. (Close economic links with its neighbour would give Bosnia an outlet to the sea.)

The informal alliance between Muslims and Croats at the outbreak of the civil war in March 1992 broke down in October,

and the two sides engaged in heavy fighting in central and southern Bosnia in 1993. The ceasefire became possible after a change of policy by the Croatian government, which had come under strong international pressure to end its support for hard-line Bosnian Croats and the partition of Bosnia-Herzegovina. In the weeks after the ceasefire, negotiations, sponsored by the United States, between representatives of the Bosnian government, the Bosnian Croats and the Croatian government resulted in a provisional agreement signed in Washington in early March. Agreements on a constitution and on practical issues such as the disengagement of rival forces and exchange of prisoners followed. They were approved by the Herzeg-Bosnian assembly and the Bosnian parliament later in the month. The final accord was 'confirmed' in May, but formal signature was delayed until the new Federation had reached agreement on the division of Bosnia-Herzegovina with the breakaway Serbian Republic, which controlled many areas claimed by the Federation. In May Kresimir Zubak, president of Herzeg-Bosnia, and Ejup Ganić, the Bosnian vice-president, were elected federal president and vice-president respectively, while Haris Silajdžić, the Bosnian prime minister, was elected federal prime minister. They were to hold their offices for a transitional period leading up to federal and local elections. (Alija Izetbegović, the Bosnian president, remained as head of its collective presidency.)

Federation of Canary Islands Independent Groups [Federación de Agrupaciones Independientes Canarias (FAIC or AIC)] Spanish political organization. The AIC was founded in 1985 as a loose alliance of centre-right parties and groups in the Canary Islands. It has participated in several coalitions and formed a minority administration in April 1993. It gained 16/60 seats at the May 1991 regional election and took part in the June 1993 general election within the Canary Coalition (CC), which gained 4/350 seats. The leader is Rafael Pedrero.

Federation of Civil Servants and Salaried Employees [Funktionærernes og Tjenestemændenes Fællesråd] (FTF) Danish trade-union federation. Founded in 1952, the FTF has 106 affiliated unions with a total membership of around 360,000 (an eighth of the labour force), primarily teachers, civil servants and finance- and insurance-sector workers. The chairman is Anker Christoffersen.

Federation of Dutch Industry [Verbond van Nederlandse Ondernemingen] (VNO) Dutch employers' association. Founded in 1968, the VNO has around 25,000 member companies from all industrial and service branches. It cooperates with the Dutch Christian Employers' Federation (NCW), the other national employers' association, in the Council of Dutch Industrial Federations (RNW). The president is Alexander Rinnooy Kan.

Federation of Free Democrats *See* ALLIANCE OF ....

Federation of Greek Industries [Síndesmos Ellinikón Viomichaníon] (SEV) Greek employers' association. Founded in 1907, the SEV has around 3,500 member companies. The president is Stelios Argyros.

Federation of Irish Employers *See* IRISH BUSINESS AND EMPLOYERS' CONFEDERATION.

Federation of Liberal, Democratic and Reform Parties of the European Union or **European Liberals, Democrats and Reformers** (ELDR) European Union (EU) political organization. Founded in 1976, the ELDR brings together 17 centrist, centre-right and right-wing liberal parties, including the Republican Party (PR) and Radical Party (Rad) in France, the Free Democratic Party (FDP) in Germany and the Liberal Democrats in Britain. The ELDR group in the European Parliament, also known as the Liberal, Democratic and Reformist Group (LDR) or Liberal Group, is the third-largest, with 43/567 seats. It includes representatives from all but two of the 12 EU member states. The ELDR president is Willy de Clerq (Belgium), and the leader of the parliamentary group is Gijs de Vries (Netherlands).

Federation of Luxemburg Industrialists [Fédération des Industriels Luxembourgeois] (FÉDIL) Luxemburg employers' association. Founded in 1918, FÉDIL has 350 members, representing most of the country's firms in the manufacturing sector and many in the services sector. The president is Marc Assa, the administrator Lucien Jung.

Federation of Monaco Trade Unions [Union des Syndicats de Monaco] (USM) Monaco trade-union federation. Founded in 1944, the USM has 35 affiliated unions with a total membership of 4,000 (around a third of the labour force). The president is Charles Soccal.

Federation of Muslims and Croats *See* FEDERATION OF BOSNIA-HERZEGOVINA.

Federation of Swiss Employers' Organizations [Zentralverband Schweizerischer Arbeitgeber-Organisationen (German), Fédération des Organisations Patronales Suisses (French)] (ZSAO or FOPS) Swiss employers' association. Founded in 1908, the federation has 71 affiliated associations from all industrial and service sectors. The president is Guido Richterich, the director Heinz Allenspach.

Federation of Young Democrats *See* ALLIANCE OF ....

FÉDIL *See* FEDERATION OF LUXEMBURG INDUSTRIALISTS.

Fenech-Adami, Edward or **Eddie** (1934–) Maltese lawyer, journalist and politician. He edited a weekly newspaper before being elected to parliament in 1969 for the centre-right Nationalist Party (PN). He was elected the party's leader in April 1977. He became prime minister after the PN won the May 1987 election. His administration was returned to office in February 1992.

FEOGA French abbreviation for the EUROPEAN AGRICULTURAL GUIDANCE AND GUARANTEE FUND (EAGGF), a major programme of the European Union (EU).

Ferrara, Giuliano (1952–) Italian journalist and politician. He worked as an organizer for the Italian Communist Party (PCI) in the 1970s. He left the party in 1980 and became a columnist on the *Corriere della Sera* newspaper. In 1987 he turned to television, hosting several current-affairs and later entertainment programmes. From 1989–94 he was also a member of the European Parliament for the Italian Socialist Party (PSI). Having joined the new Come On Italy (Forza Italia) movement in January 1994, he was appointed to the key post of government spokesman and minister in charge of relations with parliament in the right-wing coalition which took office in May.

Ferreira Leite, Manuela (1936–) Portuguese teacher and politician. She has taught in a primary school. Elected to parliament for the centre-right Social Democratic Party (PSD) in 1987, she served as a junior budget minister before being appointed education minister in December 1993.

FF Abbreviation for the FRANC, the French currency.

FF (Ireland) *See* FIANNA FÁIL.

FFAA Abbreviation for Forze Armate ('Armed Forces'), the Italian armed forces.

FFAA Abbreviation for Fuerzas Armadas ('Armed Forces'), the Spanish armed forces.

FFr Abbreviation for the FRANC, the French currency.

FG *See* FINE GAEL.

FGTB *See* GENERAL LABOUR FEDERATION OF BELGIUM.

FI *See* COME ON ITALY.

Fianna Fáil ('Soldiers of Destiny') or **Republican Party** (FF) Irish political party. Fianna Fáil – the English names are hardly ever used – has its roots in the struggle for Irish independence. It was founded in 1926 by opponents of the Anglo-Irish treaty which partitioned the country and established the Irish Free State in 1922. It became the country's largest party in 1932, and has been in power for most years since then, most recently since 1987. Its support is strongest in the countryside and among the less well off. Compared to its main rival, Fine Gael, it has traditionally been more interventionist in its economic policies, more conservative on social issues and more hard-line on the issue of Irish reunification. Although it recorded its worst result since the 1920s at the November 1992 election, gaining 39.1% of the vote and

68/166 seats, it remained the largest party by far and formed a coalition with the Labour Party. The leader is Albert Reynolds.

fiches affair (Switzerland) *See* SECRET FILES AFFAIR.

FIDESz *See* ALLIANCE OF YOUNG DEMOCRATS.

FIE *See* IRISH BUSINESS AND EMPLOYERS' CONFEDERATION.

Fifth Republic [Cinquième République] Common name for the current system of government in France. It was established in 1958 with the adoption of a new constitution, which granted extensive executive powers to the president. The preceding Fourth Republic (1946–58) had been a parliamentary system.

Fighting Communist Nuclei and **Fighting Communist Party** *See* RED BRIGADES.

files affair (Switzerland) *See* SECRET FILES AFFAIR.

Filesa, Malesa and Time Export affairs Political scandal in Spain concerning illegal funding of the ruling Spanish Socialist Workers' Party (PSOE). In April 1991 a former employee of the Time Export company claimed that it formed part of a network of front companies engaged in channelling illegal corporate donations to the PSOE and that two senior party officials, Guillermo Galeote, the treasurer, and Carlos Navarro, treasurer of the parliamentary group, had set up and run the operation. In June Galeote was suspended from his duties and Navarro resigned. In March 1993 an inquiry into the party's finances by government auditors confirmed that between 1989–91 the two officials had raised an estimated 997 million pesetas (6.3 million ecus) in illegal donations from major companies and banks by using Time Export and two other companies, Filesa and Malesa, to invoice them for fictional consultancy services. Several of the donors had subsequently been awarded government contracts. The affair became the most notorious in a number of illegal funding scandals involving the political parties, in particular the PSOE.

Filkus, Rudolf (1927–) Slovakian economist and politician. He was attached to the Economic Institute of the Slovak Academy of Sciences from 1953–90, specializing in research on prices and general economic issues. After the collapse of communist rule in 1989 he was appointed the Institute's chief scientist. Elected to the Czechoslovak federal parliament in 1990 for Public Against Violence (VPN), the Slovak arm of the broad-based anti-communist movement, he joined one of its successors, the Movement for a Democratic Slovakia (HZDS), the following year. He was Slovakia's minister of economic strategy in 1990–91 and a federal deputy prime minister and minister of control (= economic affairs) from June 1992 until the federation's dissolution at the end of the year. He left the HZDS for the new Democratic Union (DEÚS) in March 1994 and was appointed minister of finance in the centrist coalition which took office later that month.

FIM Abbreviation for the MARKKA, the Finnish currency, used in banking etc.

Final Act *See* HELSINKI ....

Finance Guard or **Finance Police** *See* REVENUE GUARD.

financial and development secretary Gibraltarian government official. The secretary is responsible for economic affairs. The post has become controversial in recent years because the incumbent is appointed by the British government, which means that the Gibraltar government's authority is restricted in a key area of domestic affairs. Strengthening the territory's economic autonomy is a priority of the Bossano government. (Under the 1969 constitution Gibraltar is an internally self-governing dependency of the United Kingdom.)

Fine Gael ('People of Ireland') or **United Ireland Party** (FG) Irish political party. Fine Gael – the English names are hardly ever used – has its roots in the struggle for Irish independence. It was formed in 1932 from the merger of Cumann na nGaedhael and several other parties which accepted the Anglo-Irish treaty under which the island had been divided and the Irish Free State established in 1922. Traditionally the second largest party, it has led several coalition governments since 1945, most recently from 1982–87. Most of its support comes from the middle classes. Compared to its main rival, Fianna Fáil, it has traditionally been more right-wing in economic policy, more liberal on social issues and more conciliatory on the issue of Irish reunification. At the November 1992 election it gained 24.5% of the vote and 45/166 seats. The leader is John Bruton.

Fini, Gianfranco (1952–) Italian journalist and politician. Elected to parliament for the far-right Italian Social Movement (MSI) in 1983, he was leader of its youth wing until his election as party leader in December 1987. He narrowly lost the leadership to Pino Rauti in January 1990 but regained it in July 1991. In January 1994 he also became leader of the National Alliance (AN), a new, more broadly based grouping.

Finland [Suomi (Finnish), Finland (Swedish)] Country in northeastern Europe.

Official data. Name: Republic of Finland [Suomen Tasavalta / Republiken Finland]; capital: Helsinki/Helsingfors; form of government: parliamentary republic; head of state: president; head of government: prime minister; flag: white with a light blue Scandinavian cross; national holiday: 6 December (Independence Day); languages: Finnish and Swedish; religions: Evangelical Lutheranism and Orthodox Christianity (Orthodox Church of Finland); currency: markka (Mk) (pl. -a) = 100 penniä; abbreviation: SF.

Geography. One of the Nordic countries, Finland has an area of 338,145 sq km. It is bordered by Norway in the north, Russia in the east, the Gulf of Finland in the south, and the Gulf of Bothnia and Sweden in the west; a neighbouring country across the sea is Estonia. With the exception of the far northwest, the country consists of low-lying rolling, heavily forested plains. There are around 50,000 lakes, covering over a tenth of the total area; the largest are Saimaa, Päijänne and Pielinen. One third of the country lies north of the Arctic Circle. Some 8% of the land is arable, virtually none is covered by pastures and 76% is forested. Finland is Europe's most heavily forested country. The climate is largely continental, with short, cool summers and very cold, long winters; rainfall is moderate.

Demography. Finland has a population of 5,058,000. Population density is 17 per sq km (land area), one of the lowest in Europe. Around half the people live in the southern third of the country, 62% live in urban areas, and around a fifth lives in Helsinki and its suburbs. Other major cities are Tampere, Turku [Åbo (Swedish)], Oulu, Lahti, Kuopio, Pori and Jyväskylä. In ethnic terms 93.6% of the people are Finns and 6.0% Swedes; Lapps or Sami in the far north number around 4,000. Most Swedes live in the western and southern coastal areas and the Åland Islands. The main languages are Finnish and Swedish. Foreign nationals account for 0.4% of the population. In religious terms 88.4% of the population is nominally Lutheran Protestant and 1.1% Finnish Orthodox; most of the remainder is not religious.

Sociography. Finland scores 0.911 on the United Nations human development index (HDI), ranking 16th in the world and 12th among 32 European countries. There are 20 doctors and 135 hospital beds for every 10,000 people. Education is compulsory between the ages of seven and 16. There is one teacher for every 13 students. Enrolment is 93% at the secondary level and 47% at the tertiary level. The literacy rate is virtually 100%. Real annual income per head (in terms of purchasing power) is US$ 16,130. Income differentials are small.

Infrastructure and communications. Finland has a highly developed transport and communications network. There are 46,610 km of paved roads and 1.93 million passenger cars (385 per 1,000 people), 5,870 km of railways and 6,675 km of navigable waterways. The main ports are Helsinki, Turku, Kotka, Hamina and Rauma. The main airport is at Helsinki (Vantaa), and there are 24 other airports with scheduled services. There are 54 daily newspapers, with a combined circulation of 2.60 million (521 per 1,000

people, one of the highest rates in the world). There are 4.94 million radio receivers, 1.89 million television sets and 3.70 million telephones in use (respectively 989, 379 and 740 per 1,000 people).

Economic structure. The Finnish economy is highly developed, diversified and trade-oriented. It is based on forestry and wood processing and engineering and other manufacturing industries. After a period of high growth in the 1980s (averaging 5% per year), the economy was thrown into deep recession in 1990 as a result of overheating and the collapse of traditional markets in the Soviet Union and other Eastern European countries (which used to account for around a quarter of exports). Between 1990 and 1993 GDP contracted by 13%, current-account deficits averaged around 5% of GDP per year, unemployment rose to 19%, and inflation fell from around 6% to 3%. Growth resumed in 1994.

Services contribute 60% of GDP, industry contributes 34% (manufacturing 22%), and agriculture and forestry 6%. Livestock raising and dairy farming (cattle) are the main agricultural activities; the main crops grown are cereals (barley, oats), sugarbeets and potatoes. The main mineral resources are gold and mercury. The extensive coniferous forests provide the main source of foreign exchange. The main industry is wood processing, ranging from the production of sawn wood and pulp to plywood, paper, newsprint, building materials and furniture; other important branches are engineering, food processing, chemicals, electrical goods, metalworking and shipbuilding. The main energy sources are imported fossil fuels and nuclear and hydroelectric power; some 10% of export earnings are required to cover net fuel imports. The main exports are wood products (29% of the total, incl. paper and newsprint 25%), industrial machinery (16%), wood and pulp (9%), electrical equipment (8%), chemicals (6%) and iron and steel (5%); Finland is the world's third-largest exporter of wood and wood products; basic manufactures account for 41% of the total, machinery and transport equipment for 31%. The main imports are machinery and transport equipment, basic manufactures, chemicals and foodstuffs. The main trading partners are: exports: Germany (16%), Sweden (13%), United Kingdom (11%), France (7%), United States (6%), Netherlands (5%), Norway (5%); Italy; imports: Germany (17%), Sweden (12%), United Kingdom (9%), Russia (7%), United States (6%), Japan (6%), France (5%), Norway; half of all trade is with European Union (EU) countries.

The Bank of Finland [Suomen Pankki / Finlands Bank] is the central bank. The main employers' associations are the Confederation of Industry and Employers (TT) and Confederation of Service Industries (LTK); the main labour organization is the Central Organization of Finnish Trade Unions (SAK).

Political structure. Finland is a parliamentary republic with a strong presidency on the basis of a constitution adopted in 1919. The head of state is the president, who is directly elected for a six-year term; if no candidate gains an absolute majority of the votes, a run-off is held between the top two candidates. The president is commander of the armed forces, appoints the prime minister, may veto legislation and override some cabinet decisions, and has considerable powers in the foreign-policy sphere. Most executive power is vested in the prime minister and the State Council [Valtioneuvusto/Statsråd] or council of ministers. Legislative power is vested in the Parliament [Eduskunta/Riksdag], whose 200 members are elected for a four-year term by a system of proportional representation. All citizens over the age of 18, including those living abroad, are entitled to vote. Judicial power is ultimately vested in the Supreme Court [Korkein Oikeus / Högsta Domstolen], whose 22 members are appointed by the president. Administratively the country is divided into 12 provinces [lääni, pl. -t / län, pl. -], which are subdivided into 439 communes. The Åland Islands have extensive autonomy.

The main political parties are the Centre Party (KESK), Finnish Social Democratic Party (SDP), National Coalition Party (Kokoomus, KOK), Left-Wing Alliance (VL or Vas), Green Alliance (Vihreät), Swedish People's Party (SFP), Finnish Rural Party (SMP), Finnish Christian Union (SKL) and Liberal People's Party (LKP). At the general election in March 1991 the KESK gained 24.8% of the vote and 55/200 seats, the SDP 22.1% and 48 seats, Kokoomus 19.3% and 40 seats, the VL 10.1% and 19 seats, the Vihreät 6.8% and 10 seats, the SFP 5.5% and 12 seats, the SMP 4.8% and seven seats, the SKL 3.1% and eight seats, and the LKP 1.2% and one seat. The government is formed by a coalition of the KESK, Kokoomus and SFP, with Esko Aho as prime minister. Other senior ministers are Heikki Haavisto (foreign affairs), Hannele Pokka (justice), Mauri Pekkarinen (internal affairs), Elisabeth Rehn (defence) and Iiro Viinanen (finance). The head of state is President Martti Ahtisaari, who was elected in February 1994 and took office in March.

Security and international affiliations. The Finnish armed forces number 32,800 (army 27,300, navy 2,500, airforce 3,000). There is also a 4,400-strong paramilitary border guard. Military service is compulsory and consists of 8–11 months' basic training.

Finland is a member of the Conference on Security and Cooperation in Europe (CSCE), Council of Baltic Sea States (CBSS), Council of Europe, European Economic Area (EEA), European Free Trade Association (EFTA) and Nordic Council, as well as the Organization for Economic Cooperation and Development (OECD) and the United Nations and its specialized agencies. It has negotiated membership of the European Union (EU), and is due to join the organization at the start of 1995 pending the outcome of a referendum in October 1994.

History. Originating further east and southeast, the ancestors of the Lapps and Finns arrived in modern Finland during the 1st millennium BC. The former were gradually pushed northwards by the latter. Hunting, fishing and gathering were the main economic activities until well into the 1st millennium AD. Vikings from across the Baltic Sea raided, traded and eventually settled in the coastal areas from the 8th century. Christian missionaries arrived in the 12th century. At this time the country was divided into a number of states, including Finland proper, Tavastia and Karelia. Swedes, Russians (from Novgorod) and Danes vied for commercial and political advantage in the region, with the Swedes gradually gaining the upper hand. Swedish control over all Finnish lands except for eastern Karelia was confirmed in a 1323 treaty. Finland became a grand duchy under the Swedish crown in 1581 and an integral part of the Kingdom of Sweden in 1634. Society became sharply divided between a Swedish and swedified elite and the Finnish peasantry. Finland's borders were pushed eastwards during the 17th century, when Sweden was the major regional power. Russian troops occupied the country in 1714, during the Great Northern War (1700–21), and in 1741. They withdrew both times in exchange for territorial concessions. In 1809, after another invasion, all of Finland was ceded to Russia under the Treaty of Hamina, and it became an autonomous grand duchy within the Russian Empire.

A Finnish national movement emerged in the 19th century. It was initially focused on the language issue, and in 1863 Finnish became an official language alongside Swedish. In 1899 the Russian authorities effectively abolished the country's autonomy but reversed their decision after seven years of nationalist agitation. A constitution providing for universal adult suffrage and parliamentary government was adopted in 1906. (Finland was the first European country to introduce universal adult suffrage.) With Russia in turmoil following the October Revolution, which brought the communists to power and established the Soviet Union, Finland declared itself independent in 1917 and became a republic in 1919. Independence was recognized by the Soviet Union in 1920. Finland's refusal to meet Soviet demands for certain territorial concessions led to the

Winter War in 1939–40 and the Continuation War in 1941–44. Under settlements in 1940 and 1947 Finland was forced to cede a tenth of its territory, in particular eastern Karelia and Petsamo in the north. In 1948 the two countries signed a treaty of 'friendship and cooperation', in which Finland agreed to come to the Soviet Union's defence in case of attack and adopt a non-aligned foreign policy in exchange for non-interference in domestic politics (an arrangement that has given rise to the term 'finlandization').

Since independence domestic politics has been dominated by four parties: the Agrarian League (ML) and its successor, the Centre Party (KESK); the Social Democratic Party (SDP); the right-wing National Coalition Party (Kokoomus); and the communist-dominated Finnish People's Democratic League (SKDL) and its successor, the Left-Wing Alliance (VL). None has ever gained more than 28% of the vote. Government coalitions have been dominated by the ML/KESK and/or the SDP. The dominant leader for many years was Urho Kekkonen, prime minister from 1950–56 and president from 1956–81. Since the 1950s the Finnish economy has been transformed from a largely agricultural to a highly industrialized one. Finland joined the Nordic Council in 1955, the European Free Trade Association (EFTA) as an associate member in 1961 and a full member in 1986, and the Council of Europe in 1989. (Membership of the latter was not requested until 1988 in deference to Soviet objections.) After the March 1987 election Kokoomus entered the government for the first time in 21 years, with its leader Harri Holkeri heading a left-right coalition excluding the KESK. At the March 1991 election the government parties suffered major losses. The SDP went into opposition for the first time in 25 years and KESK leader Esko Aho formed a centre-right coalition. By this time the economy had been thrown into a deep recession due to overheating in the 1980s and the collapse of traditional markets in the Soviet Union and Eastern Europe. In January 1992 Finland

and Russia signed a new friendship treaty which replaced the unequal 1948 agreement. Finland applied to join the European Community (EC), now the European Union (EU), in March 1992; accession negotiations were concluded in March 1994 and a referendum on the issue was due to be held in October.

See also entries on specific institutions, organizations, parties, people, terms etc.

Finlandization The accommodation by a small state of the strategic interests of a neighbouring large state in exchange for self-determination in internal matters. The term is taken from the relationship between Finland and the Soviet Union from 1945 until 1991, under which Finland adopted a neutral foreign policy and maintained friendly relations with the Soviet Union (formalized in a treaty of friendship, cooperation and, crucially, mutual assistance in the event of war), while the Soviet Union in effect agreed not to interfere in Finland's market-based economy and pluralist political system. In January 1992 a new treaty of good-neighbourliness between Finland and Russia, the successor state to the Soviet Union, formally put bilateral relations on an equal footing.

Finnbogadóttir, Vigdís (1930–) Icelandic linguist, teacher and politician. Before 1980 she taught French literature, directed the Reykjavík theatre company and presented a television series on French literature. Supported by the right-wing and centrist parties, she was elected president of the republic, a non-executive post, in June 1980. She thus became the world's first directly elected female head of state. She was overwhelmingly reelected in 1984, 1988 and 1992.

Finnish Centre Party *See* CENTRE PARTY (Finland).

Finnish Christian Union [Suomen Kristilliinen Liitto] (SKL) Finnish political party. A Christian fundamentalist party founded in 1958, it gained 3.0% of the vote and 8/200 seats at the March 1991 election. It joined the centre-right coalition, but withdrew in June 1994 over the issue of Finland's prospective membership of the European Union (EU), which

it opposes. The party leader is Toimi Kankaanniemi, the parliamentary leader C.P. Bjarne Kallis.

Finnish Employers' Confederation *See* CONFEDERATION OF INDUSTRY AND EMPLOYERS.

Finnish Rural Party [Suomen Maaseudun Puolue] (SMP) Finnish political party. Founded in 1959 as a breakaway from the Agrarian League (ML, later the Centre Party, KESK) to promote the interests of small farmers, the SMP participated in two coalition governments from 1983–90. At the March 1991 election it gained 4.8% of the vote and 7/200 seats. The party leader is Raimo Vistbacka, the parliamentary leader Sulo Aittoniemi.

Finnish Social Democratic Party [Suomen Sosialidemokraattinen Puolue] (SSDP or SDP) Finnish political party. Founded in 1899, the SDP has traditionally had the support of between a fifth and a quarter of the electorate and has led or participated in most coalition governments since independence in 1917, most recently from 1966–91. At the March 1991 election it gained 22.1% of the vote and 48/200 seats. The party leader is Paavo Lipponen, the parliamentary leader is Antti Kalliomäki, and the general secretary is Markku Hyvärinen.

finnmark Anglicized version of the Finnish currency, the MARKKA.

Fiori, Publio (1938–) Italian lawyer and politician. He was active in local and regional politics for the Christian Democratic Party (DC) in his native Rome and Lazio until his election to parliament in 1979. After the DC became discredited by the exposure of its involvement in corruption and other scandals in 1993, he joined the far-right National Alliance (AN). He was appointed minister of transport in the right-wing coalition formed in May 1994.

FIR *See* RAPID INTERVENTION FORCE.

First Chamber [Eerste Kamer] Upper house of the Dutch parliament, the States-General. It has 75 members elected for a four-year term by the 12 provincial legislatures. It may reject but cannot amend legislation passed by the lower house, the Second Chamber.

first lord of the Treasury Honorary title held ex officio by the prime minister of the United Kingdom. S/he is nominally head of the Treasury (= finance ministry) but takes no direct part in its work; its effective head is the chancellor of the exchequer.

First of October Anti-Fascist Resistance Group [Grupo de Resistencia Antifascista Primero de Octubre] (GRAPO) Spanish guerrilla group. The armed wing of an illegal far-left political group describing itself as 'maoist' and aiming to establish a revolutionary communist regime, GRAPO emerged in 1975. It carried out a series of small-scale bombings of Spanish and US military facilities as well as several assassinations, kidnappings and robberies in the late 1970s and early 1980s. Most of its leaders were arrested by 1985. But the organization resurfaced after GRAPO prisoners began a hunger strike in 1989, and it has been responsible for several assassinations and bombings since then.

first pillar In the European Union (EU), an informal name for the European Community (EC), the supranational core of the organization. The other two 'pillars' are the Common Foreign and Security Policy (CFSP) and Cooperation on Justice and Home Affairs (CJHA). *See also* TREATY ON EUROPEAN UNION.

First Republic [Prima Repubblica] Common name for the system of government in Italy from the abolition of the monarchy and the establishment of the republic in 1946 until the March 1994 election, which swept away a political elite discredited by revelations of endemic corruption and other scandals (*see* ITALIAN CORRUPTION SCANDALS).

first secretary [premier secrétaire] In France, the official title of the leader of the Socialist Party (PS).

fiscal federalism [federalismo fiscale] In Italy, a term used by the Northern League (Lega Nord) and others advocating the country's conversion into a federal state. They call for wide-ranging autonomy for the regions or for the creation of larger 'republics'. What matters to them is not so much political decentralization as control over tax revenue and public spending, i.e.

autonomy in fiscal matters. In this way the federalists hope to end what they see as 'wasteful' spending by central government and the transfer of resources from the rich north to the poor south.

Fischer, Joschka (1948–) German politician. He was a member of the federal parliament for the Greens from 1983–85. He became environment and energy minister in Hesse in 1985, the first time the Greens joined a coalition at state level (with the Social Democratic Party, SPD). He was the Greens' parliamentary group leader in the state legislature from 1987, and returned to his previous ministerial post in April 1991. He is regarded as a leading member of the party's 'realist' [realo] or more pragmatic wing.

Five, Kaci Kullmann (1951–) Norwegian politician. She was leader of the youth wing of the Conservative Party (Høyre) from 1977–79 and was elected to parliament in 1981. She held the key post of minister of trade and shipping in the centre-right coalition that held office in 1989–90. She was elected party leader in April 1991.

five new states [fünf neue Länder] In Germany, a collective term for the federal states on the territory of former East Germany. They are Brandenburg, Mecklenburg - West Pomerania, Saxony, Saxony-Anhalt and Thuringia. They were dissolved by the communist regime in 1952 but were reconstituted prior to German reunification in October 1990.

five wise people (Germany) *See* GROUP OF WISE PEOPLE.

Fkfl *See* PEOPLE'S PARTY (Faroe Islands).

FKgP *See* INDEPENDENT SMALLHOLDERS'... PARTY.

FKr Abbreviation for the KRÓNA, the Faroese currency.

FL *See* FREE LIST (Liechtenstein).

FL Abbreviation for Liechtenstein, used for international vehicle registrations, postal addresses etc. It is taken from Fürstentum Liechtenstein ('Principality of Liechtenstein'), the country's official name in German.

FL Abbreviation for the FRANC, the Luxemburg currency.

fl Abbreviation for the gulden or GUILDER, the Dutch currency. It is taken from 'florin' [florijn], an old name for the guilder.

Flächenland *See* AREA STATE.

Flanders [Vlaanderen] Region [gewest] of Belgium. Covering the northern half of the country, Flanders has an area of 13,512 sq km and a population of 5,769,000. It comprises the Dutch- or Flemish-speaking provinces of Belgium, namely West Flanders and East Flanders (i.e. Flanders proper), Antwerp, Flemish Brabant and Limburg. The main cities are Antwerp [Antwerpen], Ghent [Gent] and Bruges [Brugge]. Brussels [Brussel], the country's largest city and political centre and historically a Flemish city, lies within Flanders but is a region in its own right (with a predominantly French-speaking population). Government institutions are based in Ghent and Brussels. The economy is based on manufacturing (textiles, petrochemicals, engineering, food processing, electronics), agriculture (cereals, sugarbeets, potatoes) and services. Until the 1950s the economy was largely agricultural, but since then industrial development has been rapid and the region has become considerably more prosperous than Wallonia, its French-speaking counterpart. Under the constitutional reforms transforming Belgium into a federal state, finalized in July 1993, legislative power is exercised by the 118-member Flemish Parliament [Vlaams Parlement] elected for a five-year term, and by the Flemish Community Council [Vlaamse Gemeenschapsraad], formed by the Parliament and six members coopted from the Brussels-Capital regional council, which is responsible for education, culture, language issues and some other matters (*see* FLEMISH COMMUNITY); executive power is exercised by a government headed by a minister-president. Government institutions are based in Ghent and Brussels. The main parties are the Christian People's Party (CVP), the Socialist Party (SP), the right-wing Flemish Liberals and Democrats (VLD, the successor to the Party for Freedom and Progress, PVV), the far-right Flemish Bloc (Vlaams Blok, VB), the centre-right

People's Union (Volksunie, VU) and the environmentalist Live Differently (AGALEV). The government is formed by a CVP-SP coalition, headed by Luc van den Brande. During the Middle Ages the region, comprising the county of Flanders proper and the duchy of Brabant, was among the most prosperous in Europe. It was united under the dukes of Burgundy in the 14th and 15th centuries and, along with the rest of the Low Countries, became part of the Habsburg Empire and then Spain by inheritance. It became an Austrian possession in 1713, was annexed by France in 1795, became part of the Netherlands in 1815 and part of Belgium in 1830. The 19th century saw a revival of Flemish national consciousness and agitation for equal rights for the Dutch language with French. This was achieved in the 1920s and 30s. As Flanders became more prosperous, demands also grew for greater regional control of economic affairs. The creation of a federal structure was agreed in principle in 1970, and its final terms were adopted in July 1993. There is considerable popular support for greater autonomy and some support for full independence.

flanking measures In the European Union (EU), measures designed to support the aims and objectives of a particular common policy or programme but not integral to it. Thus, for instance, the single-market programme implemented between 1985 and 1992 was complemented by measures dealing with workers' rights, regional assistance, immigration, competition and tendering rules etc.

Flemings People of FLANDERS, a region of Belgium, or, more generally, the Dutch- or Flemish-speaking people of Belgium as a whole.

Flemish [Vlaams] Collective name for the dialects of Dutch spoken in Belgium, specifically the regions of Flanders and Brussels-Capital. The formal spoken and written language is virtually identical with Dutch, and Dutch is the official language of Flanders. *See also* BELGIAN LANGUAGE QUESTION.

Flemish Bloc [Vlaams Blok] (VB) Belgian political party. Formed in 1979 from the merger of two parties, the Bloc advocates full independence for Flanders, has very conservative views on social issues, and calls for compulsory repatriation of 'ethnic immigrants'. It more than trebled its share of the vote at the November 1991 election, gaining 6.6% and 12/212 seats. Karel Dillen has been the party's leader since its foundation.

Flemish Community [Vlaamse Gemeenschap] Community of Belgium. Under the constitutional reforms transforming Belgium into a federal state, finalized in July 1993, the Flemish Community is responsible for health, social security, social services, education, culture and language issues in FLANDERS and for the Dutch- or Flemish-speaking population of Brussels. The 124-member Flemish Community Council [Vlaamse Gemeenschapsraad] is composed of the 118 members of the Flemish Parliament and six coopted members from the Brussels regional council, both groups elected for a five-year term. Executive powers are exercised by the government of Flanders. *See also* COMMUNITY (Belgium).

Flemish Liberals and Democrats [Vlaamse Liberalen en Demokraten] (VLD) Belgian political party. The VLD was founded in December 1992 as a more broadly based successor to the Freedom and Progress Party (PVV). Rooted in the Liberal Party founded in 1846, the PVV became the Flemish wing of the renamed party in 1961 and a separate organization in 1974. It has participated in a number of coalitions since 1945. Like its Walloon counterpart, the Liberal Reform Party (PRL), the VLD has a right-wing economic programme and liberal views on social issues. At the November 1991 election it gained 11.9% of the vote and 26/212 seats. The leader is Guy Verhofstadt.

Flemish Socialist Party *See* SOCIALIST PARTY (SP) (Belgium).

FLNC *See* CORSICAN NATIONAL LIBERATION FRONT.

floor (European Union) *See* EXCHANGE RATE MECHANISM.

Flynn, Pádraig (1939–) Irish teacher, publican and politician. Elected to parliament for the centre-right Fianna Fáil in

1977, he was briefly minister for the Gaeltacht (= Irish-speaking areas) and minister of trade, commerce and tourism in 1982. He was environment minister from 1987–91 and justice minister from February 1992. In January 1993 he became a commissioner of the European Community (EC), with responsibility for social affairs, employment and immigration.

FM and **FMk** Abbreviations for the MARKKA, the Finnish currency.

FN *See* NATIONAL FRONT.

FNL Abbreviation for *fünf neue Länder* ('five new states'), a collective term for the federal states of Germany on the territory of former East Germany. *See* NEW FEDERAL STATE.

FNSEA *See* NATIONAL FEDERATION OF FARMERS' UNIONS.

FNV *See* DUTCH TRADE UNION CONFEDERATION.

FO *See* GENERAL CONFEDERATION OF LABOUR - WORKERS' POWER.

FO/E Abbreviation for Forsvarets Overkommando / Etterretningsstab ('Defence Supreme Command - Intelligence Section'), the Norwegian intelligence agency.

Fodor, Gábor (1962–) Hungarian lawyer and politician. He was a founding member in 1988 of the Alliance of Young Democrats (FIDESz), initially an anti-communist student movement and later a political party. Elected to parliament in 1990, he left the party and resigned his seat in November 1993 following disputes with the leadership. He returned to parliament in May 1994 as an independent, elected with the support of the centrist Alliance of Free Democrats (SzDSz). He was appointed minister of education and culture in the centre-left coalition which took office in July 1994.

FOK Abbreviation for the KRÓNA, the Faroese currency, used in banking etc.

Folketing Parliament of Denmark. The Folketing has 179 members, 175 from metropolitan Denmark and two each from the Faroe Islands and Greenland. They are elected for a four-year term. Of the metropolitan seats, 135 are elected by proportional representation in 17 multi-member constituencies and 40 are allocated to parties which did not gain seats in the constituencies. Parties require at least 2% of the popular vote to qualify for representation.

follow-up conference In the Conference on Security and Cooperation in Europe (CSCE), a major conference held at regular intervals to review the 1975 Helsinki Final Act, consider progress on its implementation and negotiate further agreements. There have been four follow-up conferences: Belgrade (1977–78), Madrid (1980–83), Vienna (1986–89) and Helsinki (March–July 1992).

Fonds Deutsche Einheit *See* GERMAN UNITY FUND.

food mountains In the European Union (EU), the common name for the 'intervention stocks' accumulated over the years within the context of the COMMON AGRICULTURAL POLICY (CAP). Because the CAP set 'target prices' for most foodstuffs and provided for their purchase by the authorities at relatively high 'intervention prices' if market prices fell below them, farmers were encouraged to produce regardless of demand. As a result huge stocks of cereals, beef, milk ('milk lake'), butter, olive oil, wine ('wine lake'), tobacco and other products had been built up by the mid 1980s. Since then a number of measures have been introduced to reduce the surpluses, including production quotas.

FOPS *See* FEDERATION OF SWISS EMPLOYERS' ORGANIZATIONS.

For Fatherland and Freedom [Tēvzemei un Brīvībai] (TUB or TB) Latvian political organization. The TUB was formed prior to the June 1993 election as an alliance of several far-right nationalist groups, including a wing of the National Independence Movement (LNNK). It gained 5.4% of the vote and 6/100 seats. The leader is Roberts Milbergs.

force de dissuasion ('deterrent force') and **force de frappe** ('strike force') Common names for France's strategic nuclear force. Constituted under President de Gaulle in the 1960s to signal France's determination to retain an independent defence capability, the *force de frappe*

has always been, in effect, a key component of the collective defence of Western Europe. Its mainstays are the M-4 submarine-launched missiles and the S-3D land-based missiles.

Force Ouvrière *See* GENERAL CONFEDERATION OF LABOUR - WORKERS' POWER.

forint (pl. -) Currency of Hungary. Common abbreviations are Ft and HUF (the international standard in banking etc). It is divided into 100 fillér.

Forlani, Arnaldo (1925–) Italian journalist and politician. He was elected to parliament for the Christian Democratic Party (DC) in 1958. One of the party's leading figures from the 1960s, he was its general secretary from 1969–73 and from 1989 until October 1992 and president from 1986–89. He has also held a number of senior government posts, including minister of state enterprises (1969–70), defence (1974–76), foreign affairs (1976–79), prime minister (1980–81) and deputy prime minister (1983–87). In April and July 1993 he was accused of breaking the party-financing laws. He went on trial in July 1994.

formateur In Belgium and the Netherlands, a senior politician asked by the king or queen to form a coalition government. The appointment – one of the monarch's few remaining powers – is usually conferred on the leader or a senior member of the largest party or, more rarely, of the party thought most likely to build a majority coalition. *See also* INFORMATEUR.

former communist countries, former Eastern bloc, former Eastern Europe and **former Soviet bloc** Collective names for the Eastern European countries where communist regimes held power from the late 1940s until the upheavals of 1989. These were Albania, Bulgaria, Czechoslovakia, East Germany, Hungary, Poland, Romania and Yugoslavia. All but Albania and Yugoslavia were closely linked to the Soviet Union through the now defunct Warsaw Treaty Organization and Council for Mutual Economic Assistance (CMEA or COMECON).

former Czechoslovakia *See* CZECHOSLOVAKIA.

former East Germany *See* EAST GERMANY.
former Eastern Europe and **former Soviet bloc** *See* FORMER COMMUNIST COUNTRIES ....
Former Yugoslav Republic of Macedonia (FYROM) Provisional name under which Macedonia, one of the Yugoslav successor states, was admitted to the United Nations in April 1993 and recognized by most European Union (EU) states the following December. It was adopted as a compromise to meet Greece's objection to 'Republic of Macedonia', the country's official name, which it said implied a territorial claim on the northern Greek region of the same name. *See also* MACEDONIA NAME QUESTION.
former Yugoslavia Shorthand for Yugoslavia as it existed from 1918 until its disintegration in 1991/92. Its territory is now divided between Bosnia-Herzegovina, Croatia, Macedonia, Slovenia and Yugoslavia or rump Yugoslavia. The multi-ethnic Kingdom of Serbs, Croats and Slovenes was established in 1918 as a unitary state comprising Serbia (which had gained its independence from the Ottoman Empire in 1878), Montenegro, and the former Austro-Hungarian territories of Bosnia-Herzegovina, Croatia and Slovenia. Although the new state was welcomed by its main constituent nations, it was soon destabilized by dissatisfaction with the Serb-dominated centralized administration and rivalry between Serbs and Croats in particular. More generally, the region was also heavily burdened by its past in that it straddled several major historical 'faultlines': the border between the Western and Eastern Roman empires which foreshadowed the split between the Roman Catholic and Orthodox churches in the early Middle Ages, and the border between the Austrian and Ottoman empires and, by extension, Christianity and Islam from the late Middle Ages. In 1929 King Alexander imposed a personal dictatorship. The name Yugoslavia – meaning 'country of the South Slavs' – was adopted at this time to symbolize the common heritage of the main ethnic groups. During the Second World War (1939–45) a separate Croatian state was

established with German support, and the rest of the country was partitioned and many regions were allocated to neighbouring states. Hundreds of thousands of people died in a fierce civil war between Serbs and Croats. In 1945 Yugoslavia was reconstituted as a federation of six republics – Bosnia-Herzegovina, Croatia, Macedonia, Montenegro, Serbia (including the autonomous provinces of Vojvodina and, from 1971, Kosovo-Metohija) and Slovenia – under the leadership of the League of Communists of Yugoslavia (SKJ) and the strong personal authority of Josip Broz Tito. After Tito's death in 1980 a collective presidency was established. In 1981 the ethnic composition of what was then Europe's most heterogeneous country was as follows: Serbs 36.3%, Croats 19.7%, Slav Muslims (mainly in Bosnia-Herzegovina) 8.9%, Slovenes 8.0%, Albanians (in Kosovo) 7.7%, Macedonians 6.0%, Yugoslavs (self-description) 5.4%, Montenegrins 2.6%, Hungarians (in Vojvodina) 1.9%, Gipsies, Turks, Slovaks, Romanians, Bulgarians, Ruthenians, Vlachs and others 3.7%. In the late 1980s, as communist authority crumbled throughout Eastern Europe, calls in Croatia and Slovenia for a looser federation which would give the two republics greater control over their economies gained widespread support, as did increasingly demands for full independence. These were strongly resisted by Serbia, which favoured the status quo and was also concerned for the fate of the substantial Serb minorities in Croatia and Bosnia-Herzegovina. Croatia and Slovenia declared their independence in June 1991, precipitating 10 days of fighting in Slovenia and the occupation of the Serb-majority areas in Croatia by the Yugoslav federal army and local Serb forces. Macedonia declared its independence in November 1991. Bosnia-Herzegovina declared its independence in March 1992, precipitating a civil war between Muslims, Serbs and Croats in which the latter two enjoyed strong support from Serbia and Croatia respectively. The collapse of the old Yugoslavia was effectively accepted by Serbia and its ally Montenegro in April 1992 when they formed the Federal Republic of Yugoslavia, often referred to as 'rump Yugoslavia'. *See also* YUGOSLAVIA *and entries on the other successor states.*

formule magique *See* MAGIC FORMULA.

Føroyar Faroese name for the Faroe Islands.

Fortress Europe Slogan used by those who detect tendencies within the European Union (EU) towards protectionism and isolationism. The term gained currency in the early 1990s in the context of the completion of the single internal market, achieved at the end of 1992, which it was feared might lead to the adoption of measures aimed at restricting outsiders' access to the EU market. It is also used in the context of the attempts to restrict immigration into the EU from Eastern Europe, North Africa and elsewhere. (The term 'Festung Europa' was coined in Germany during the Second World War to denote an impregnable and self-sufficient Europe.)

Forum for Security Cooperation (FSC) Institution of the Conference on Security and Cooperation in Europe (CSCE). Inaugurated in September 1992 in Vienna (Austria), the FSC is an intergovernmental conference which holds continuous negotiations on confidence- and security-building measures and arms-control and disarmament issues. It deals with such matters as exchange of information on defence planning, arms transfers, military cooperation, and stabilizing measures in conflict areas.

Forza Italia *See* COME ON ITALY.

four freedoms In the European Union (EU), the collective name for the free movement of goods, services, capital and labour or people, the basic principle of the SINGLE INTERNAL MARKET established at the end of 1992.

Four Motors Intergovernmental organization at regional level. The Four Motors project brings together four large and developed regions: Baden-Württemberg in Germany, Catalonia in Spain, Lombardy in Italy and Rhône-Alpes in France, centred on Stuttgart, Barcelona, Milan and Lyon respectively. Under an agree-

ment signed in 1988 – one of the first of its kind – they cooperate in such fields as research, technology, education and culture, concentrating on exchanges to promote new ideas and development.

Fourons question *See* VOEREN QUESTION.

fourth resource (European Union) *See* OWN RESOURCES.

FP (Denmark) *See* PROGRESS PARTY.

Fp (Sweden) *See* PEOPLE'S PARTY - THE LIBERALS.

FPÖ *See* FREEDOM PARTY OF AUSTRIA.

FPS *See* FREEDOM PARTY OF SWITZERLAND.

Fr Abbreviation for the FRANC, the currencies of Belgium, France, Luxemburg and Switzerland.

FR Abbreviation for the Faroe Islands, used for international vehicle registrations, postal addresses etc.

Fraga, Manuel (1922–) Spanish lawyer, civil servant and politician. He held several senior government and diplomatic posts under the Franco regime, including that of information minister from 1962–66 and interior minister from 1975–76. In 1976, during the transition to democracy, he founded and became leader of the People's Alliance (PA), later renamed the People's Party (PP). He became chief minister of his home region of Galicia in February 1990. The following April he resigned as the PP's leader at national level.

franc [frank (Dutch), franc (French), pl. -, -s] Currency of Belgium. Common abbreviations are F, BF, BFr, FB and BEF (the international standard in banking etc). It is divided into 100 centiemen or centimes. The Belgian franc is also legal tender in Luxemburg.

franc Currency of France. Common abbreviations are F, FF, FFr, Fr and FRF (the international standard in banking etc). It is divided into 100 centimes. The French franc is also legal tender in Andorra and Monaco.

franc Currency of Luxemburg. Common abbreviations are F, LF, LFr, FL and LUF (the international standard in banking etc). It is divided into 100 centimes. It has parity with the Belgian franc, which is also legal tender in Luxemburg.

franc [Franken (German), franc (French), franco (Italian), pl. -, -s, franchi] Currency of Switzerland. Common abbreviations are F, Fr, SF, SFr, FS and CHF (the international standard in banking etc). It is divided into 100 Rappen, centimes or centesimi. The Swiss franc is also legal tender in Liechtenstein.

franc fort (France) *See* STRONG FRANC.

France Country in western Europe.

Official data. Name: French Republic [République Française]; capital: Paris; form of government: republic; head of state: president; head of government: prime minister; flag: three vertical stripes, blue, white and red; national holiday: 14 July (National Day); language: French; religion: none; currency: franc (F) = 100 centimes; abbreviation: F.

Geography. With an area of 543,965 sq km, France is the largest country in Europe (excluding Russia and Ukraine). It is bordered by the Channel, Belgium and Luxemburg in the north, Germany, Switzerland and Italy in the east, the Mediterranean Sea, Monaco, Spain and Andorra in the south, and the Atlantic Ocean in the west. Broadly the country consists of low-lying and undulating plains in the northwest and southwest (including the Seine or Paris Basin), hills and low mountains in the northeast, centre and far west (including the Ardennes, Vosges and Jura mountains and the Massif Armoricain in Brittany), mountains in the southeast (Massif Central), and high mountains on the eastern and southern borders (Alps and Pyrenees). Some 34% of the land is arable, another 23% is covered by pastures and 27% is forested. The main rivers are the Seine, Rhône, Loire and Garonne. The climate is temperate marine in most of the country (with mild summers and cool winters), and mediterranean (with hot summers and mild winters) in the south; continental influences (colder winters) are evident in the east; rainfall is moderate, and generally heavier in the north and west than in the south.

Demography. France has a population of 57,690,000. Population density is 106 per sq km (land area). Some 74% of the people live in urban areas. The most densely populated region is the Île-de-France centred on Paris; the city itself has a population of 2.2 million, the metropolitan area 9.0 million. The other main centres are the metropolitan areas of Lyon (population 1.3 million), Marseille (1.1 million), Lille (1.0 million), Bordeaux, Toulouse, Nantes, Nice, Toulon, Grenoble, Strasbourg, Rouen, Valenciennes, Cannes, Lens, Saint-Étienne, Nancy, Tours, Béthune, Clermont-Ferrand, Le Havre, Dijon, Angers and Brest. Some 93.6% of the people are French citizens; this total includes around 3.0 million people with roots in the overseas dependencies (in particular Guadeloupe, Martinique and Réunion) or former colonies (including 1.0 million French settlers or *pied noirs* and 450,000 Harkis from Algeria). The number of Gipsies is estimated at around 275,000. The main language is French. A number of other languages are also spoken: Occitan or Provençal by at least 1.55 million people (2.7% of the total) in the south and southeast, German by 1.30 million (2.3%) in Alsace and Lorraine, Breton by 570,000 (1.0%) in Brittany, Catalan by 210,000 in Roussillon in the south, Corsican (a form of Italian) by 170,000 in Corsica, Basque by 130,000 in the southwest, Flemish (a form of Dutch) by 100,000 in the far north, and Italian by 50,000 in the southeast; Arabic is spoken by 1.5 million second-generation immigrants (2.6% of the total population). Substantially more people consider themselves Bretons or Basques than speak the respective languages. Foreign nationals account for 6.4% of the population, and include citizens of Portugal (1.4% of the total), Algeria (1.3%), Spain (0.9%), Italy (0.9%), Morocco, Tunisia, Croatia, Turkey, Senegal, Mali and other West Africans. In religious terms 76.4% of the population is nominally Roman Catholic, 4.5% Muslim, 1.4% Protestant and 1.2% Jewish; most of the remainder is not religious.

Sociography. France scores 0.927 on the United Nations human development index (HDI), ranking sixth in the world and fourth among 32 European countries. There are 26 doctors and 126 hospital beds for every 10,000 people. Education is compulsory between the ages of six and 16. There is one teacher for every 13 students. Enrolment is 83% at the secondary level and 43% at the tertiary level. The literacy rate is virtually 100%. Real annual income per head (in terms of purchasing power) is US$ 18,430.

Infrastructure and communications. France has a highly developed transport and communications network. There are 741,150 km of paved roads and 23.6 million passenger cars (414 per 1,000 people), 34,420 km of railways, and 14,930 km of navigable waterways. The main ports are Marseille, Le Havre, Dunkerque, Rouen, Nantes/Saint-Nazaire and Bordeaux. The main airports are at Paris (Orly and Charles de Gaulle), Marseille (Marseille-Provence), Nice (Côte d'Azur), Lyon (Satolas), Toulouse (Blagnac) and Bordeaux (Mérignac), and there are 59 other airports with scheduled services. There are 114 daily newspapers, with a combined circulation of around 10.3 million (around 180 per 1,000 people). There are 49.0 million radio receivers, 29.3 million television sets and around 37 million telephones in use (respectively 861, 515 and 650 per 1,000 people).

Economic structure. The French economy is highly developed, diversified, trade-oriented and closely linked to its neighbours. It is the second-largest economy in Europe and the fourth-largest in the world as well as the world's fourth-largest trading power. It is based on engineering and other manufacturing, agriculture and tourism. Since the late 1980s economic performance has been marked by steady growth (averaging 2.8% per year) until 1992 and negligible growth since then, current accounts moving from deficit into surplus, low inflation (averaging 2.9%), but also persistent high unemployment (around 11%).

Services contribute 68% of GDP, industry contributes 26% (manufacturing 18%), and agriculture, forestry and fisheries 6%. Some 17% of the labour force is employed in manufacturing, 16% in trade and 7% in farming. The main crops grown are cereals (wheat, barley, maize), potatoes, sugarbeets, oilseeds and pulses; other important agricultural activities are dairy farming (milk, cheese, butter, eggs), livestock raising (cattle, pigs, sheep, chickens) and horticulture (fruit and vegetables, esp. apples and grapes); the agricultural industry is by far the largest in Europe. Forestry and fishing are of regional importance. The main mineral resources are iron, coal, potash, uranium and oil. The main industries are engineering (esp. industrial machinery, cars, aircraft), electrical goods and electronics (incl. office machinery); other important branches are food processing (esp. wine and meat and dairy products), iron and steel and other metalworking, chemicals, petrochemicals, textiles, wood processing and armaments. Tourism is a major source of foreign exchange, contributing 1.8% of GNP (0.7% net); the tourism industry is the largest in Europe and the second-largest in the world. The main energy sources are nuclear and hydroelectric power and imported fossil fuels; 8% of export earnings are required to cover net fuel imports. The main exports are transport equipment (15% of the total, incl. cars 6%, aircraft), industrial machinery (13%), electrical equipment (9%), textiles and clothing (5%), iron and steel (5%), chemicals, cereals, beverages (esp. wine), oil products; machinery and transport equipment account for 36% of the total, basic manufactures for 18%, foodstuffs for 15% and chemicals for 14%; France is the world's second-largest exporter of agricultural products. The main imports are machinery and transport equipment, miscellaneous manufactures, basic manufactures and chemicals. The main trading partners are: exports: Germany (18%), Italy (11%), United Kingdom (9%), Belgium and Luxemburg (9%), Spain (6%), United States (6%), Netherlands (5%), Switzerland, Japan, Sweden, Portugal; imports: Germany (18%), Italy (11%), United States (9%), Belgium and Luxemburg (8%), United Kingdom (8%), Netherlands (5%), Spain (5%), Japan,

Switzerland, Sweden, Norway; three-fifths of all trade is with other European Union (EU) countries.

The Bank of France [Banque de France] is the central bank. The main employers' association is the National Council of French Employers (CNPF or Patronat); the main labour organizations are the General Confederation of Labour (CGT), General Confederation of Labour - Workers' Power (Force Ouvrière, FO), Democratic French Confederation of Labour (CFDT), National Federation of Farmers' Unions (FNSEA), French Confederation of Managers (CGC), French Confederation of Christian Workers (CFTC) and Confederation of Free Unions (CSL).

Political structure. France is a republic on the basis of a constitution adopted in 1958. Executive power is shared between the president and the government. The president is directly elected for a seven-year term; if no candidate gains an absolute majority of votes, a run-off is held between the top two candidates. S/he is head of state, appoints the prime minister, chairs cabinet meetings, has wide-ranging powers in foreign-affairs, defence and other spheres, and may call popular referendums. The prime minister and the government are responsible for the administration of the country. Legislative power is vested in the bicameral Parliament [Parlement], composed of the 577-member National Assembly [Assemblée Nationale] elected for a five-year term by a two-round system of majority voting, and the 321-member Senate [Sénat] indirectly elected by departmental and municipal councils for a nine-year term (with a third of seats renewed every three years). All citizens over the age of 18, including those living abroad, are entitled to vote. Judicial power is ultimately vested in the Court of Cassation [Cour de Cassation] for criminal and civil cases, the Constitutional Council [Conseil Constitutionnel] for constitutional matters and the Council of State [Conseil d'État] for administrative and other cases. Administratively the country is divided into 22 regions [région, pl. -s]: Alsace,

Aquitaine, Auvergne, Brittany [Bretagne], Burgundy [Bourgogne], Centre, Champagne-Ardenne, Corsica [Corse], Franche-Comté, Île-de-France, Languedoc-Roussillon, Limousin, Loire Country [Pays de la Loire], Lorraine, Lower Normandy [Basse-Normandie], Midi-Pyrénées, Nord-Pas-de-Calais, Picardy [Picardie], Poitou-Charentes, Provence-Alpes-Côte-d'Azur, Rhône-Alpes and Upper Normandy [Haute-Normandie]. These are divided into 96 departments [département, pl. -s], which are in turn subdivided into over 31,000 communes; the intermediate-level *arrondissements* and *cantons* have no administrative or political functions.

The main political parties are the Rally for the Republic (RPR), Republican Party (PR), Socialist Party (PS), National Front (FN), Social Democratic Centre (CDS), French Communist Party (PCF), Greens (Verts), Ecology Generation (GE), Left Radical Movement (MRG), Social Democratic Party (PSD) and Radical Party (Rad); the Union for French Democracy (UDF) is an alliance of the PR, CDS, PSD, Rad and several smaller groups. At the general election in March 1993 the RPR gained 20.4% of the vote and 247/577 seats, the UDF 19.1% and 213 seats, the PS 17.6% and 54 seats, the PCF 9.2% and 23 seats, the MRG 1.1% and six seats, right-wing independents 24 seats and left-wing independents 10 seats; the FN gained 12.4%, the Greens 4.0% and the GE 3.6%, but no seats. The government is formed by a centre-right coalition of the RPR and UDF, with Édouard Balladur as prime minister. Other senior ministers are Simone Veil (deputy prime minister, social affairs, health and urban affairs), Charles Pasqua (deputy prime minister, interior), Pierre Méhaignerie (deputy prime minister, justice), François Léotard (deputy prime minister, defence), Alain Juppé (foreign affairs), François Bayrou (education), Edmond Alphandéry (economy), Gérard Longuet (industry, postal services and telecommunications, foreign trade), Michel Giraud (labour), Jacques Toubon (culture), Nicolas Sarkozy (budget) and Jean Puech (agriculture and fisheries). The head of state is President François Mitterrand, who was first elected in May 1981 and re-elected in May 1988 with 54.0% of the vote in the second round.

France has a number of overseas dependencies: four departments (French Guyana, Guadeloupe, Martinique, Reunion), two territorial collectivities (Mayotte, Saint Pierre and Miquelon) and four territories (French Polynesia, French Southern and Antarctic Territories, New Caledonia, Wallis and Futuna). All are integral parts of the French Republic; they send representatives to the National Assembly and Senate and take part in presidential elections. France also lays claim to part of Antarctica.

Security and international affiliations. The French armed forces number 412,200 (strategic nuclear forces 17,000, army 239,700, navy 60,400, airforce 80,900, central staff etc 14,200); they are due to be reduced to around 370,000. There is also the 95,700-strong paramilitary Gendarmerie. Military service is compulsory and consists of 10 months' basic training. Defence spending is equivalent to 3.4% of GDP, among the highest rates in Europe. A substantial number of French troops are stationed abroad, including 20,200 in the overseas dependencies, 16,000 in Germany, 8,600 in seven African countries, and around 6,500 on United Nations assignments.

France is a member of the Conference on Security and Cooperation in Europe (CSCE), Council of Europe, European Economic Area (EEA), European Union (EU), North Atlantic Treaty Organization (NATO) and Western European Union (WEU), as well as the Francophone Community, Group of Seven (G-7), Organization for Economic Cooperation and Development (OECD) and the United Nations and its specialized agencies.

History. The Celtic peoples inhabiting the area of modern France (and northern Italy) were called Gauls by the Romans. After gaining a foothold along the Mediterranean coast in the late 2nd century BC, the Romans conquered the whole of Gaul, a process completed by the end of

the 50s. In 49 they annexed the city of Massilia (modern Marseille), a long-standing ally, which had been established by Greek colonists in the 7th century and had developed into a major commercial centre. Gaul became thoroughly romanized during five centuries of Roman rule. Christianity was introduced in the early 2nd century AD and became the dominant religion in the 5th century. Roman rule collapsed during the Europe-wide migrations in the 4th and 5th centuries. In 486, when the Germanic Franks overthrew the last Roman governor in the north, the south was held by the Visigoths and the east by the Burgundians. Under King Clovis (486–511) and his successors the Franks gained control of the whole of Gaul and parts of southern Germany in the 6th century. Effective power within the kingdom passed from the Merovingian kings to the regional governors, the 'mayors of the palace' or 'majordomos', in the 7th century. The last Merovingian was dethroned in 751 by Pepin III of Austrasia. Under his rule and that of his son Charlemagne (768–814) the Frankish Kingdom conquered the remaining Germanic kingdoms and northern Italy. Charlemagne was crowned 'Roman emperor' in 800. After his death the Empire was partitioned on several occasions, with the West Frankish Kingdom forming the core of what became France. (The East Frankish Kingdom became the Holy Roman or German Empire.)

From the late 9th century feudal fragmentation gave rise to a number of powerful regional duchies and counties – Flanders, Normandy, Brittany, Anjou, Burgundy, Guyenne/Aquitaine, Gascony, Toulouse etc – and weakened royal authority. When Hugo Capet succeeded the last Carolingian king in 987 the royal domain comprised only the region around Paris. Over the following three centuries the crown gradually asserted direct control over most of northern France. The Valois dynasty replaced the Capetians in 1328. In 1348–49 between a third and half the people died during the Europe-wide plague epidemic known as the 'black death'; the country's population did not recover to its pre-1348 level until the middle of the 16th century. French attempts to reassert control over extensive English possessions in the south and west (nominally fiefs held by the English king from the French king) led to the Hundred Years' War (1337–1453). At its conclusion the English had lost all their French holdings (except for Calais, which was returned in 1558) and France had been consolidated as a unified state. Western Europe's most populous country by far, it now became not only the focus of economic, commercial and cultural life on the continent but also a major political force. During the late 16th century the country was riven by religious wars between Catholics and Protestants (called Huguenots in France). Henry of Navarre, a Protestant, ascended the throne as King Henry IV in 1589. He agreed to become a Catholic in 1593. In 1598 he issued the Edict of Nantes, which granted freedom of worship to the Huguenots but left Roman Catholicism as the state religion. Henry was the first of the Bourbon kings. Under Louis XIII (1610–43) and the Catholic cardinal Armand-Jean Richelieu, his chief minister from 1624–42, a standing army and a streamlined system of regional administration were established. King Louis XIV (1643–1715) introduced further reforms strengthening central authority and thus consolidated the absolute monarchy as the system of government. Artois, parts of Flanders, Franche-Comté, Lorraine and Alsace were acquired in a series of wars. (This expansion north- and eastward broadly established France's current borders.) France replaced Spain as the dominant continental power after the 1659 Peace of the Pyrenees, which ended a protracted war between the two countries. The Edict of Nantes was revoked in 1685, and many Huguenots thereupon emigrated. French settlers established colonies in North America and elsewhere, and French commercial interests were particularly active in the Caribbean and India.

Defeat in a series of costly foreign wars during the 18th century lost France several overseas territories (most notably Canada at the end of the Seven Years' War in 1763) and contributed to a growing financial and economic crisis. Widespread discontent, for different reasons, among the nobility and the bourgeoisie undermined the government. In 1789 King Louis XVI summoned the advisory Estates-General in an attempt to secure additional revenue. The 'third estate' (i.e. commoners) demanded extensive political changes and proclaimed a separate National Assembly, marking the beginning of the French Revolution. The Assembly issued a Declaration of the Rights of Man, adopted new constitutions in 1790 and 1791 and abolished the monarchy in 1792. The demands raised during the Revolution and expressed in its major documents foreshadowed many of the democratic reforms (extension of the franchise, equality before the law, accountability of the executive to an elected parliament etc) introduced in the 19th and 20th centuries in France and worldwide. (Constitutional reforms in the United Kingdom and the American Revolution were the other formative influences on the democratic movement.) Factional disputes intensified from 1792, and all the prominent revolutionary leaders were executed in internecine rivalries over the next two years. The former king, Louis XVI, was executed in 1793. Internal order was restored by Napoleon Bonaparte, a successful general, who took power in 1799. Crowned emperor of France in 1804, he introduced a number of reforms (including a new legal code). Abroad he led a series of successful campaigns against Austria, Prussia, the United Kingdom, Russia and their allies, which had waged war against revolutionary France since 1792. At the height of Napoleon's power, in 1810/11, France controlled most of western and central Europe, either directly or indirectly through vassal states and alliances. The Napoleonic empire collapsed after a disastrous invasion of Russia in 1812, further military setbacks in 1813 and 1814 and defeat at the Battle of Waterloo in 1815. (Napoleon died in exile in 1821.) The Bourbon monarchy was restored in

France and the Congress of Vienna restored many of Europe's pre-1792 borders. However, many of the legal and administrative changes introduced during the revolutionary and Napoleonic periods, in France and elsewhere, were retained. Revolutions in 1830 and 1848 toppled the monarchy and introduced a range of reforms, including adult male suffrage in 1848. Louis Napoleon Bonaparte, a nephew of Emperor Napoleon, was elected 'prince-president' in 1848. He seized power in 1851 and proclaimed himself emperor the following year. During the Second Empire (1852–70) industrial development took off and the first workers' organizations emerged. Napoleon III was deposed during the disastrous Franco-Prussian War (1870–71). A left-wing uprising, the Paris Commune, was suppressed at considerable human cost in 1871. France was forced to cede Alsace-Lorraine to the newly unified Germany. The Third Republic (1870–1940) was marked by political instability, with governments in power for less than eight months on average, but also by rapid industrialization at home and colonial expansion in Africa and Indochina. The Dreyfus case, in which a Jewish army captain was convicted of treason on forged evidence in 1894, dominated public life for the next decade: it highlighted characteristic rifts in French society – between the Catholic Church and anti-clericalists, monarchists and republicans, right and left etc – and tarnished the reputation of the army and church in particular. (Dreyfus was eventually acquitted in 1906.) Growing tensions among the major powers led to the First World War (1914–18), which France fought principally in alliance with the United Kingdom, Russia, Italy (from 1915) and the United States (from 1917) against Germany, Austria-Hungary, the Ottoman Empire and others. The French and British armies were involved in inconclusive trench warfare with German forces in Belgium and northern France. An Allied offensive in 1918 brought the first major territorial gains for either side

in four years. With its army in retreat and unrest at home Germany accepted an armistice on terms that effectively meant surrender. Some 1.4 million French soldiers died in the fighting, and the infrastructure of northern France was largely destroyed. Alsace-Lorraine was returned to France under the 1919 Versailles Treaty. Social reforms were introduced by left-dominated 'popular front' governments in power from 1936–38, but political and social antagonisms intensified. During the Second World War (1939–45) German troops invaded France in 1940 and forced a surrender within six weeks. The nazi regime took direct control of most of the country, while a German-backed government under Philippe Pétain, a senior general and war hero, was installed at Vichy in the southeast. An internal resistance movement emerged dominated by the French Communist Party (PCF), and a government in exile was set up by Charles de Gaulle. In 1942 German troops also occupied the Vichy state.

After liberation in 1944 de Gaulle formed a provisional government, which introduced female suffrage (1945) and social-welfare measures and nationalized key industries. A new constitution, providing for a parliamentary form of government, was approved in 1946. The Fourth Republic (1946–58), like its predecessor, was marked by rapid changes of government. France was a founding member of the North Atlantic Treaty Organization (NATO) in 1949 and of the European Economic Community (EEC), now the European Union (EU), in 1958. The French economy grew by around 5% annually during the 1950s and 60s, and outperformed its main competitors during the 1970s. During the 1950s France was involved in two major colonial wars: in Indochina, which ended with defeat by Vietnamese forces in 1954, and in Algeria from 1954. Both were highly controversial and contributed to political instability at home. In 1958, at the height of the Algerian crisis and with civil war looming, de Gaulle returned to public life. A new constitution was adopted which provided for a strong presidency, and de Gaulle was elected the first president of the Fifth Republic. He oversaw the granting of independence to most of the African colonies in 1960, with Algeria following in 1962. France became the world's fourth nuclear power in 1960. Suspicious of US domination, it withdrew from NATO's integrated military command structure in 1966. In 1968 violent demonstrations by left-wing students and a general strike by workers precipitated a national crisis. Supporters of de Gaulle and other right-wing parties secured a landslide victory in an early election, but a number of reforms in education and other spheres were nevertheless adopted. De Gaulle resigned the following year after losing a referendum on decentralization. He was succeeded by Georges Pompidou, a close associate who had been prime minister from 1962–68. Pompidou died in office in 1974, and Valéry Giscard d'Estaing was elected president with the support of a centre-right alliance.

In May 1981 François Mitterrand, the Socialist Party (PS) leader, became president after narrowly defeating Giscard. In an early general election the following month the PS also gained a parliamentary majority. A wide-ranging decentralization programme, devolving powers to departments and newly created regions, was implemented from March 1982. Faced with mounting financial problems and crumbling business confidence, the new government abandoned its traditional left-wing economic programme of interventionism and nationalization in March 1983. The March 1986 election was won by a centre-right alliance of the Rally for the Republic (RPR) and the Union for French Democracy (UDF) gained a majority. RPR leader Jacques Chirac was appointed prime minister, initiating a two-year period of 'cohabitation' with Mitterrand. Mitterrand was elected for a second term in May 1988, defeating Chirac in the second round. An early election in June left the PS as the largest party, but without an overall majority. Michel Rocard became prime minister at

the head of a centre-left coalition. The far-right National Front (FN) led by Jean-Marie Le Pen made significant advances in national and local elections in the late 1980s and early 1990s. In an attempt to revitalize the administration, Mitterrand appointed Edith Cresson as France's first woman prime minister in May 1991. She was replaced by Pierre Bérégovoy in April 1992. In the March 1993 election the RPR-UDF alliance gained an overwhelming victory and Édouard Balladur was appointed prime minister. The new government committed itself to stimulating the economy, reducing unemployment (around 10% since the mid 1980s), implementing a wide-ranging privatization programme, and restricting immigration.

See also entries on specific institutions, organizations, parties, people, terms etc.

Franche-Comté Region of France. Situated in the east and bordering on Switzerland, Franche-Comté has an area of 16,202 sq km and a population of 1,104,000. The capital is Besançon. The economy is based on manufacturing (precision instruments, engineering), agriculture and forestry. Franche-Comté was part of the Kingdom of Arles in the early Middle Ages, a possession of Burgundy within the Holy Roman Empire from 1384, and part of the Spanish Habsburg Empire from 1477. It became part of France in 1678.

Franco-German Corps *See* EUROPEAN CORPS.

Franco-Swiss *See* FRENCH SWISS.

francoism [franquismo] Political outlook in Spain based on the values and policies of Francisco Franco (1892–1975), leader of a far-right military dictatorship from 1939 until his death. Franco was commander of the rebel nationalist forces which won the three-year civil war in 1939. His regime was strictly authoritarian in the political sphere, centrist in economic terms and strongly conservative on social issues. Today a number of small far-right groups and organizations take their inspiration from Franco, stressing in particular his commitment to strongly centralized political structures. (Wide-ranging devolution of powers to the regions has been a characteristic of the democratic system established since the late 1970s.) *See also* FASCISM.

Francophone Community (Belgium) *See* FRENCH COMMUNITY.

Francophone Democratic Front [Front Démocratique des Francophones] (FDF) Belgian political party. Founded in 1964, the FDF is active only in the Brussels-Capital region. It advocates the creation of a federal state with autonomy for Brussels – an aim now largely realized under the new constitution – and seeks to protect the interests of French-speakers in the city. At the election for the Brussels parliament in June 1989 it gained 12/75 seats, and at the November 1991 general election it gained the equivalent of 1.5% of the vote nationally and 3/212 seats. The leader is Georges Clerfayt.

Frankfurt Shorthand for the GERMAN FEDERAL BANK (Bundesbank), the central bank of Germany. The Bundesbank is based in Frankfurt, the country's main financial centre. In December 1993 the city was also designated the site of the European Monetary Institute (EMI), a new institution of the European Union (EU).

franquismo *See* FRANCOISM.

Fratelli d'Italia ('Brothers of Italy') National anthem of Italy. Soon after its composition in 1847 it was adopted by the Risorgimento movement campaigning for the unification of Italy. In 1946 it became the national anthem of the Italian Republic.

Frăţia *See* NATIONAL CONFEDERATION OF FREE TRADE UNIONS OF ROMANIA - BROTHERHOOD.

Frčkovski, Ljubomir (1957–) Macedonian academic and politician. A political scientist, he was a minister without portfolio from 1991–92 and was appointed interior minister in January 1992. He is a member of the Social Democratic Alliance (SDSM).

Free Democratic Party [Freie Demokratische Partei] (FDP) German political party. A centrist liberal party founded in 1948, the FDP has been in government for most years since, as the junior partner in centre-right coalitions with the Christian Democratic Union (CDU) from

1949–56, 1961–66 and since 1982, and in centre-left coalitions with the Social Democratic Party (SPD) from 1969–82. In August 1990 three liberal parties in East Germany merged with the FDP in the west. Traditionally polling 5–10% of the vote in West Germany, it gained 11.0% (10.6% in the west and 12.9% in the east) and 79/662 seats at the all-German election in December 1990. The party leader is Klaus Kinkel, the parliamentary leader Hermann-Otto Solms. Hans-Dietrich Genscher, party leader from 1974–85, remains influential.

Free Democrats [Svobodní Demokraty] (SD) Czech political party. The centre-left SD is the successor to the Civic Movement (OH), which in turn has its roots in the Civic Forum, the broad-based movement which spearheaded the opposition to communist rule in 1989 and won the multiparty election in June the following year. When the Forum split in early 1991, one of its wings, the Liberal Club, founded the OH. At the June 1992 election it gained 4.6% of the vote but, having failed to pass the 5% needed for representation, no seats in the Czech parliament. The leader is Jiří Dienstbier.

Free Democrats [Vabad Demokraadid] (VD) Estonian political organization. The VD is a parliamentary group established by six deputies (out of 101) in May 1994. Their views are broadly centrist. The leader is Jaan Kaplinski.

Free Democrats (Hungary) *See* ALLIANCE OF FREE DEMOCRATS.

Free Galician People's Guerrilla Army [Exército Guerrilheiro do Pobo Galego Ceibe (Galician)] (EGPGC) Spanish guerrilla group. The EGPGC calls for full independence for Galicia. Since its emergence in 1987 it has been responsible for a number of bomb attacks on government buildings and several attacks on security officers in the region.

Free List [Freie Liste] (FL) Liechtenstein political party. Founded in 1985, the Free List has a strong commitment to environmental and civil-rights issues. Its sees itself as the only real political alternative in Liechtenstein, which has been ruled by a centre-right coalition of the Progressive

Citizens' Party (FBP) and Fatherland Union (VU) since 1938. It entered parliament for the first time at the February 1993 election, gaining 10.4% of the vote and 2/25 seats. In the early election in September (precipitated by internal divisions within the FBP) it gained 8.5% and one seat. The leadership is collective.

Freedom Alliance [Polo della Libertà] Italian political organization. The Alliance was formed in February 1994 as an electoral alliance of five right-wing parties. The moving force behind it was the newly formed Come On Italy (Forza Italia), and the other key members were the federalist Northern League (Lega Nord) in the north and the far-right National Alliance (AN, based on the Italian Social Movement, MSI) in the south. The two other parties in the Alliance were the Christian Democratic Centre (CCD), formed by conservative members of the discredited Christian Democratic Party (DC), and the Centre Union (UDC). Several smaller groups also backed the Alliance. Campaigning on a general programme of economic and political reform, the Alliance won the March 1994 election, gaining 42.9% of the vote and 336/630 seats. The member parties then formed a government under Silvio Berlusconi, Forza Italia's leader. *See also individual party entries.*

Freedom Party of Austria [Freiheitliche Partei Österreichs] (FPÖ) Austrian political party. Founded in 1956 as a centrist liberal party, the FPÖ was a junior coalition partner of the Social Democratic Party (SPÖ) from 1983–86. Since then, under the leadership of Jörg Haider, it has shifted sharply rightwards, increasing its support at provincial and federal level on an anti-establishment and -immigration platform. At the October 1990 election it virtually doubled its share of the vote, gaining 16.6% and 33/183 seats. A wing left in February 1993 to form the LIBERAL FORUM (LF).

Freedom Party of Switzerland [Freiheitspartei der Schweiz (German), Parti Suisse de la Liberté (French)] (FPS or PSL) The Freedom Party was founded in 1985 as the Car Party [Autopartei der Schweiz / Parti Suisse des Automobilistes] (APS or PSA), a single-issue pressure group aimed at defending the interests of motorists. It has since broadened the scope of its concerns and advocates a range of right-wing populist policies, including restrictions on immigration. At the October 1991 election it doubled its share of the vote, gaining 5.1% and 8/200 seats. The party was renamed in May 1994. The leader is Jürg Scherrer.

Freedom Union [Unia Wolości] (UW) Polish political party. The UW was formed in April 1994 by the merger of the centrist DEMOCRATIC UNION (UD) and the centre-right LIBERAL DEMOCRATIC CONGRESS (KLD). The new party has 74/460 seats in parliament, all elected on the UD ticket in the September 1993 election. The leader is Tadeusz Mazowiecki, the parliamentary leader Bronisław Geremek.

French Communist Party [Parti Communiste Français] (PCF) French political party. Founded in 1920, the PCF gained around a quarter of the vote in elections in the late 1940s and 50s, but its support has declined steadily since then. It joined the government formed by the Socialist Party (PS) in 1981, but broke with it three years later over economic policy. The party's official positions remained soundly orthodox throughout the 1980s, although a reformist wing known as the *refondateurs* ('reformers') gained some ground. In January 1994 the party formally abandoned the principle of 'democratic centralism', but the formulation of policy remained the prerogative of the national bureau (formerly the politburo). At the March 1993 election the PCF gained 9.2% of the vote and 23/577 seats. Georges Marchais led the party from 1972 until January 1994, when he was succeeded by Robert Hue. The parliamentary leader is André Lajoinie.

French Community [Communauté Française] Community of Belgium. Under the constitutional reforms transforming Belgium into a federal state, finalized in July 1993, the French Community is responsible for health, social security, social services, education, culture and language issues in Wallonia (except for the German-speaking population in the east) and for the French-speaking population of Brussels. The 94-member French Community Council [Conseil de la Communauté Française] is composed of the 75 members of the Wallonian Parliament and 19 coopted members from the Brussels regional council, both elected for a five-year term. Executive power is exercised by a four-member government. It is formed by the Socialist Party (PS) and the Christian Social Party (PSC) and headed by Laurette Onkelinx. *See also* COMMUNITY (Belgium) *and* WALLONIA.

French-Speaking Community *See* FRENCH COMMUNITY.

French Swiss or **Swiss Romands** Collective name for the French-speaking people of Switzerland. Most live in the west of the country and they number around 1.2 million (20.1% of Swiss citizens and 17.2% of the total population).

FRF Abbreviation for the FRANC, the French currency, used in banking etc.

FRG Abbreviation for Federal Republic of Germany, the official name of Germany.

Friaul Friulian name for Friuli, part of the Italian autonomous region of FRIULI - VENEZIA GIULIA.

Frick, Mario (1965–) Liechtenstein lawyer, civil servant and politician. He worked in the government legal service until his election to parliament for the centre-right Fatherland Union (VU) in February 1993. In May he became deputy prime minister, with responsibility for internal affairs, justice, environment and agriculture. After the VU came first in an early election in October (precipitated by internal divisions within its coalition partner, the Progressive Citizens' Party, FBP), he became prime minister – Europe's youngest – and minister of finance and justice in December 1993.

Frisians Ethnic group in the Netherlands and Germany. The Frisians have retained a distinct cultural and linguistic identity since the early Middle Ages, when they controlled the North Sea coastal area from the tip of Holland to what is now the German-Danish border. Most of the 600,000 people of Friesland province in the northern Netherlands consider themselves Frisians. Around 400,000 of them speak Frisian, a language related to Dutch and English, which has official status in the province alongside Dutch. In Germany there are around 60,000 Frisians in the East Friesland region of Lower Saxony and 10,000 in western Schleswig-Holstein. They have no special position as a minority group and only a few still speak the language.

Friuli - Venezia Giulia Special autonomous region of Italy. Situated in the northeast and bordering on Austria and Slovenia, Friuli - Venezia Giulia has an area of 7,845 sq km and a population of 1,216,000. Around half the people speak Friulian, a language related to Italian and Romansh; it has semi-official status. There is also a 53,000-strong ethnic Slovene community. The capital is Trieste, and the other main city is Udine. The economy is based on agriculture (livestock and dairy farming, wine, fruit and vegetables), manufacturing, and tourism. Political power is exercised by the Regional Assembly [Consiglio Regionale], with 60 members elected for a five-year term, and an executive council headed by a president. The main parties are the federalist Northern League (Lega Nord), the Italian People's Party (PPI, the successor to the Christian Democratic Party, DC), the Democratic Left Party (PDS), the far-right National Alliance (AN, based on the Italian Social Movement, MSI) and the Communist Refoundation Party (RC); there are also several regionalist parties. At the election in June 1993 the Lega Nord gained 26.7% of the vote and 17 seats, the DC 22.3% and 15 seats, the PDS 9.9% and seven seats, the MSI 8.3% and five seats, and the RC 5.5% and four seats. Apart from Trieste and its hinterland, the region formed part of the Venetian Republic from 1421 until 1797. It came under Austrian control in 1815 and was incorporated into unified Italy in 1866. Trieste became an Austrian possession in the 14th century and developed into the main port of the Austrian Empire. After the First World War it was disputed between Italy and Yugoslavia. Under an agreement reached in 1954 the city of Trieste became part of Italy, while most of the surrounding district became part of Yugoslavia. In recognition of its distinctive character, Friuli - Venezia Giulia was made an autonomous region with special statute in 1963.

FRJ Abbreviation for Federativna Republika Jugoslavija ('Federal Republic of Yugoslavia'), the official name of Yugoslavia in Serb.

from Brest to Brest, from Dublin to Lublin and **from Portugal to Poland** Phrases denoting Europe excluding the former Soviet Union, now the Commonwealth of Independent States (CIS). They are used in many contexts. Brest is the name of a city on the western tip of France as well as a city (formerly Brest-Litovsk) on the Polish-Belorussian border; Dublin is the capital of Ireland and Lublin is a city in southeastern Poland. Portugal and Poland broadly mark the western and eastern extremes of the territory in question.

from the Atlantic to the Urals Phrase denoting Europe including western Russia, used in particular in the context of security policy and arms-control and disarmament agreements (such as the Treaty on Conventional Forces in Europe and the Intermediate Nuclear Forces Treaty). By convention the Ural Mountains in Russia are considered the eastern border of the continent of Europe.

from Vancouver to Vladivostok Phrase denoting North America, Europe and the former Soviet Union, used in particular in the context of security policy and the activities of the Conference on Security and Cooperation in Europe (CSCE). All the countries between Vancouver in Canada and Vladivostok in Russia participate in the CSCE.

Front National See NATIONAL FRONT.

Frp See PROGRESS PARTY (Norway).

FRY Abbreviation for Federal Republic of Yugoslavia, the official name of Yugoslavia.

FS Abbreviation for the FRANC, the Swiss currency.

FSC See FORUM FOR SECURITY COOPERATION.

FSND See SOCIAL DEMOCRACY PARTY OF ROMANIA.

Ft Abbreviation for the FORINT, the Hungarian currency.

FTF See FEDERATION OF CIVIL SERVANTS AND SALARIED EMPLOYEES.

Funar, Gheorghe (1949–) Romanian agronomist, academic and politician. Before entering politics he was a lecturer in agricultural science at Cluj University. In February 1992 he was elected mayor of Cluj-Napoca for the far-right nationalist Romanian National Unity Party (PUNR). He was its candidate in the September 1992 presidential election and was elected party leader the following month.

fünf Weisen (Germany) See GROUP OF WISE PEOPLE.

Für, Lajos (1938–) Hungarian historian and politician. He was briefly interned and then effectively barred from political activity for his involvement in the anti-communist uprising in 1956. He worked as a labourer and teacher until 1964, and then at the Museum of Agriculture. In 1987 he was given a professorship at the University of Budapest. A founding member of the centre-right Hungarian Democratic Forum (MDF) in 1987, he was elected its leader in February 1994. He also served as defence minister from May 1990 until July 1994.

Fürstentum Liechtenstein ('Principality of Liechtenstein') Official name of Liechtenstein in German.

fylke (pl. -r) Norwegian administrative division, usually translated as 'county'. Each of the 19 *fylker* has a council [fylkesting] elected for a four-year term, an executive committee [fylkesutvalg] generally composed of a quarter of the council members, and a governor [fylkesmann] appointed by the central government. Oslo, the national capital and considered a county for administrative purposes, has a slightly different structure.

FYRM and **FYROM** See FORMER YUGOSLAV REPUBLIC OF MACEDONIA.

G-24 *See* GROUP OF TWENTY-FOUR.

GA *See* GREEN ALTERNATIVE.

Gabaglio, Emilio (1937–) Italian teacher and trade-union official. He was president of the Italian Workers' Christian Association (ACLI) from 1969–72. He began working full-time for the Italian Confederation of Workers' Unions (CISL), one of the main trade-union federations, in 1974. He was head of its international department from 1977–83 and was then successively in charge of regional and environmental policy, administration, and European policy. He was elected general secretary of the European Trade Union Confederation (ETUC) in May 1991.

Gabčíkovo question Border dispute and environmental controversy between Hungary and Slovakia concerning the diversion of the Danube river, the border between the two countries, and the construction of a hydroelectric power station at Gabčíkovo on the Slovak side. Gabčíkovo-Nagymáros was conceived in the 1980s as a combined dam and power-station project. It was strongly criticized by environmentalists, who argued that it threatened the ecosystem of the Danube valley, in particular drinking water supplies. The Hungarian government eventually bowed to public pressure and withdrew from the project in July 1990, halting construction of the dam and reservoir at Nagymáros. In July 1991 the then Czechoslovak authorities announced their intention to resume work on the Gabčíkovo plant and to divert a 20-km stretch of the Danube to supply the water to operate it. Negotiations between the two countries and mediation by the European Community (EC) were inconclusive. In October 1992 the Slovak government authorized the final stage of construction work. The following month it agreed to a stoppage pending a report by an independent international panel of experts. On the basis of its recommendations the two countries agreed to operate a temporary water-management scheme which aims to reconcile the Slovakian need for energy with Hungarian fears for the environment. In April 1993 they agreed to submit the dispute to the International Court of Justice (ICJ).

GAC Abbreviation for General Affairs Council, the formal name of the meeting of foreign ministers within the COUNCIL OF THE EUROPEAN UNION or Council of Ministers, the EU's main decision-making body.

Gaelic Alternative name for IRISH, one of the official languages of Ireland. It is taken from Gaeilge, the native name for the language.

Gaelic and **Gaels** Language and ethnic group in Scotland (United Kingdom). A Celtic language, Gaelic is spoken by around 65,000 people in the northwest of the country.

Gaeltacht Collective name for the Irish-speaking areas of Ireland. Irish or Gaelic, the island's original Celtic language, was still the dominant spoken language in the western counties in the early 19th century, but has steadily lost ground to English since then. Today it is the first language of around 70,000 people. The Gaeltacht consists of several scattered rural districts along the western seaboard, the largest of which are in the counties of Donegal and Galway.

Gailis, Māris (1951–) Latvian mechanical engineer and politician. He was chief engineer in a furniture factory and a wood-processing plant and then worked in the communications sector. He joined the foreign ministry in 1991, was elected to parliament for the centre-right Latvian Way (LC) in June 1993, and was appointed a deputy prime minister and minister of state reform in August. In September 1994 he became prime minister of a new LC government.

Gajauskas, Balys (1926–) Lithuanian electrician and politician. He joined the guerrilla army which fought the Soviet occupation in the 1940s. Arrested in 1948, he was given a summary 25-year prison sentence for 'anti-Soviet activities' and served the full term in a labour camp in Kazakhstan. In 1977 he was again arrested and sentenced to 10 years' internal exile (he worked as a militiaman in eastern Siberia). He was released in 1987, having served a total of 35 years' imprisonment. In April 1989 he founded the Political Prisoners' and Exiles' Union (PKTLS). He was elected to parliament on the Sajūdis ticket in 1990, when Lithuania was still part of the Soviet Union, and for the PKTLS itself in 1992. He is chairman of a special parliamentary commission investigating the activities of the Soviet State Security Committee (KGB) in Lithuania.

GAL (Austria) *See* GREEN ALTERNATIVE.

GAL (Spain) *See* ANTI-TERRORIST LIBERATION GROUPS.

Galea, Louis (1948–) Maltese politician. A lawyer by training, he was general secretary of the centre-right Nationalist Party from 1977–87. He was appointed minister for social policy when the party returned to power in 1987, and has been minister for home affairs and social development since February 1992.

Galego Native name for Galician, the language spoken in GALICIA, an autonomous community or region of Spain.

Galicia [Galiza (Galician)] Autonomous community or region of Spain. Situated in the northwest, surrounded by the Atlantic Ocean and the Bay of Biscay on two sides and bordering on Portugal, Galicia has an area of 41,602 sq km and a population of 2,793,000. Around four-fifths of the people speak Galician, a language related to Portuguese, or a mixture of Galician and Spanish known as Castrapo; Galician is officially recognized, but Spanish remains the main language of public administration and education. The capital is Santiago de Compostela, but the largest cities are Vigo and La Coruña. The economy is based on agriculture (cereals, potatoes, pig farming), fishing, forestry, mining (wolfram) and manufacturing (food processing, shipbuilding). Although there has been considerable development since the 1960s, the region remains one of Spain's poorest; emigration has been high since the 18th century. Political power is exercised by the 75-member Parliament [Parlamento] elected for a four-year term, and by the executive Council [Xunta] headed by a president. The main parties are the centre-right People's Party (PP), the Socialist Party of Galicia (PSdG, the

regional branch of the Spanish Socialist Workers' Party, PSOE) and the left-wing Galician Nationalist Bloc (BNG). At the October 1993 election the PP gained 52.2% of the vote and 43 seats, the PSdG 23.5% and 19 seats, and the BNG 18.7% and 13 seats. The chief minister is Manuel Fraga. A distinct political and administrative entity since the early Middle Ages, Galicia was part successively of the kingdoms of Asturias, León and Castile. It lost much of its autonomy in the 16th century. In 1981 it became the third region of Spain to be granted autonomous status. There has been some activity by separatist guerrilla groups.

Galician Nationalist Bloc [Bloque Nacionalista Galego] (BNG) Spanish political party. Founded in 1983, the BNG advocates greater autonomy for Galicia and traditional left-wing economic policies. Its support has risen steadily in successive regional elections: it gained 8.0% of the vote and 5/75 seats in December 1989, and 18.7% and 13 seats in October 1993. The leader is Xosé Manuel Beiras.

Galiza Galician name for GALICIA, an autonomous community or region of Spain.

Galland, Yves (1941–) French businessman and politician. He has been managing director of several publishing and publicity companies, including the Jep Continentale advertising agency, since 1969. He was elected to parliament for the centrist Radical Party (Rad) in 1979, became party general secretary in 1983 and was elected party leader in December 1988. From 1986–88 he was also a junior minister for local affairs and decentralization in the centre-right Chirac government. He was elected to the European Parliament in 1989 and was leader of its Liberal Group from 1992 until July 1994.

Gallego Spanish name for Galician, the language spoken in GALICIA, an autonomous community or region of Spain.

Ganić, Ejup (1946–) Bosnian mechanical engineer, academic and politician. He studied in the United States and lectured in engineering at the University of Illinois from 1977–81. He then held several academic posts in Yugoslavia. Elected to the Bosnian parliament for the Muslim

Democratic Action Party (SDA) in 1990, he was elected vice-president of the collective state presidency in December 1992. In May 1994 he was also elected vice-president of the new Muslim-Croat Federation.

GAP *See* GREENS (Luxemburg).

Garaikoetxea, Carlos (1938–) Spanish lawyer, businessman and politician. He managed several companies in the Basque Country before entering politics. He was elected leader of the Basque Nationalist Party (PNV/EAJ) in 1979, and became chief minister of the autonomous Basque government when it was set up in 1980. His uncompromising line on Basque independence lost him support within the party, and he was forced to resign in 1984. He left in October 1986 to found Basque Solidarity (EA), of which he has been leader ever since.

García Vargas, Julián (1946–) Spanish economist, civil servant and politician. A specialist in civil administration and taxation matters, he was president of the Institute of Official Credit from 1982–86. A member of the Spanish Socialist Workers' Party (PSOE), he was appointed minister of health and consumer affairs in 1986 and minister of defence in March 1991.

garda (pl. -í) Member of the Garda Sióchána or Garda, the Irish police force. The Irish names are commonly used, also by English speakers.

Garda Sióchána or **Garda** ('Guard of the Peace') Irish police force. The Irish name is commonly used, also by English speakers.

Gąsienica-Makowski, Andrzej (1952–) Polish mechanical engineer and politician. He was elected to parliament for the Non-Party Bloc in Support of Reforms (BBWR), formed by supporters of President Wałęsa, in September 1993. He was elected its parliamentary leader the following month.

Gaspari, Mitja (1952–) Slovenian economist, banker and politician. He worked at the Slovenian central bank from 1975–88, was deputy governor at the National Bank of Yugoslavia from 1988–91, and worked at the World Bank from 1991–92.

A member of the Liberal Democratic Party (LDS), he was appointed finance minister in June 1992.

Gastarbeiter (sing. -/in) ('guest workers') In Germany, a collective name for foreign immigrant workers. *Gastarbeiter*, mainly from Turkey and former Yugoslavia, were invited into the country during the 1960s to alleviate an acute labour shortage in manufacturing industry and other sectors of the economy. The term is also used in other German-speaking countries. *See also* EUROPEAN TURKS.

gaullism [gaullisme] Political outlook in France based on the values and policies of Charles de Gaulle (1890–1970), prime minister from 1944–46 and president of the republic from 1958–69. De Gaulle was the leader of the French government in exile during the Second World War (1939–45). The main thrust of his political philosophy was nationalism, which expressed itself in the pursuit of an independent role for France on the international stage and support for significant state participation in the economy to strengthen the country's industrial base. The Rally for the Republic (RPR), the successor to the party founded by de Gaulle, has largely abandoned the statist economic thinking in favour of deregulation and privatization. For this reason it is now often called a 'neo-gaullist' party. De Gaulle saw European integration essentially in terms of a confederation of nation states, expressed in the notion of *Europe des patries* ('Europe of the fatherlands'). In this sense the term 'gaullist' is now also used outside France to denote support for such a vision of what is now the European Union (EU) and rejection of strong supranational structures. Gaullism also involved a suspicion of American influence in Europe in the economic, political, military and cultural spheres.

Gaullist Party and **Gaullists** Informal names for the French RALLY FOR THE REPUBLIC (RPR), which traces its roots to the party founded by Charles de Gaulle in 1947.

Gava, Antonio (1930–) Italian lawyer and politician. A member of the Christian Democratic Party (DC), he was active in local and regional government in his native Naples and Campania in the 1960s. He was elected to parliament in 1972 and has been minister of posts and communications (1983–87), finance (1987–88) and internal affairs (1989–92). In April 1993 he was charged with association with the Camorra, the Naples-based crime syndicate; investigating magistrates accused him of being 'not just an ally but part of its criminal structure'. As interior minister he had been in charge of combating organized crime.

GB Abbreviation for Great Britain and Northern Ireland or the United Kingdom, used for international vehicle registrations, postal addresses etc.

GBA Abbreviation for Alderney, one of the Channel Islands, a dependency of Guernsey, which in turn is a dependency of the United Kingdom.

GBG Abbreviation for Guernsey, used for international vehicle registrations etc. The GB refers to Great Britain or the United Kingdom, of which Guernsey is a dependency.

GBJ Abbreviation for Jersey, used for international vehicle registrations etc. The GB refers to Great Britain or the United Kingdom, of which Jersey is a dependency.

GBM Abbreviation for Man, used for international vehicle registrations etc. The GB refers to Great Britain or the United Kingdom, of which the Isle of Man is a dependency.

GBP Abbreviation for the POUND STERLING or pound, the British currency, used in banking etc.

GBZ Abbreviation for Gibraltar, used for international vehicle registrations. The GB refers to Great Britain or the United Kingdom, of which Gibraltar is a dependency; the Z was adopted because GBG was already allocated to Guernsey.

GdF See REVENUE GUARD.

GDR Abbreviation for German Democratic Republic, the official name of former EAST GERMANY.

GE See ECOLOGY GENERATION.

Geg [Gegë] Form of the Albanian language. Geg or Gheg is spoken in the north of the country and the adjoining regions of Yugoslavia and Macedonia. It provided the basis for the written language until the 1940s, when it was replaced by Tosk, the other main form of Albanian.

gemeenschap See COMMUNITY (Belgium).

Gemeinde (pl. -n) German administrative division, usually translated as 'municipality'. The smallest unit of local government, each municipality has a council [Gemeinderat] elected for a four-year term and an executive headed by a mayor [Bürgermeister]. (There are some variations in titles and structures.) The municipalities are primarily responsible for town planning, housing, public transport, education, social services and other local services. They have considerable powers in local matters. Most major cities also exercise the functions of the higher-level districts or counties (see LANDKREIS). The three city states of Berlin, Bremen and Hamburg combine the functions of a municipality, district and federal state.

Gemeinschaft See COMMUNITY (Belgium).

gendarme Member of the National Gendarmerie, the French paramilitary police force.

Gendarmerie Shorthand for the NATIONAL GENDARMERIE, the French paramilitary police force.

General Affairs Council (GAC) Institution of the European Union (EU), the specialist meeting of foreign ministers within the COUNCIL OF THE EUROPEAN UNION or Council of Ministers, the EU's main decision-making body.

General Confederation of Greek Workers [Genikí Sinomospondía Ergáton Elládos] (GSEE) Greek trade-union federation. Founded in 1918, the GSEE has 82 affiliated unions and 86 regional branches, with a total membership of around 700,000 (a sixth of the labour force). The president is Christos Protopapas.

General Confederation of Italian Industry [Confederazione Generale dell'Industria Italiana] (CONFINDUSTRIA) Italian employers' association. Founded in 1919 and reconstituted in 1944, it comprises 106 regional and 98 branch associations, with a total membership of around 130,000 enterprises of all sizes. The president is Luigi Abete, the director-general is Innocenzo Cipolletta.

General Confederation of Labour [Confédération Générale du Travail] (CGT) French trade-union federation. Founded in 1895, the CGT is the oldest and largest labour organization in France. It has a total membership of around 900,000 workers (4% of the labour force) organized in 33 affiliated federations. It has traditionally close links with the French Communist Party (PCF). The general secretary is Louis Viannet.

General Confederation of Labour - Luxemburg [Confédération Générale du Travail - Luxembourg] (CGT-L) Luxemburg trade-union federation. Founded in 1927, the CGT-L brings together the Independent Trade Union Confederation (OGB-L) and two smaller federations, with a total membership of 45,000 (a quarter of the labour force). It has close links with the Luxemburg Socialist Workers' Party (LSAP). John Castegnaro is president of both the CGT-L and the OGB-L.

General Confederation of Labour - Workers' Power or **Workers' Power** [Confédération Générale du Travail - Force Ouvrière] (CGT-FO or FO) French trade-union federation. Force Ouvrière was founded in 1947 by opponents of the growing communist domination of the General Confederation of Labour (CGT). It is the second-largest federation in France, with 27 affiliated unions and a total membership of around 1.2 million (6% of the labour force). It is most strongly represented among public servants. It has no links with any political parties or other organizations. The leader is Marc Blondel.

General Confederation of Portuguese Workers - National Union Federation [Confederação Geral dos Trabalhadores Portugueses - Intersindical Nacional] (CGTP-IN) Portuguese trade-union federation. The CGTP-IN was founded underground as the National Union Federation (IN) in 1970 and reorganized after the overthrow of the Caetano regime in 1974. The current name was adopted in 1977. The federation comprises 147 unions representing around 880,000 workers (just under a fifth of the labour force). It has traditionally been dominated by the Portuguese Communist Party (PCP), although only a minority of affiliated members vote for the party. The leader is Manuel Carvalho da Silva.

General Council [Consell General] Parliament of Andorra. It has 28 members elected for a four-year term, half by majority voting (two from each parish) and half by proportional representation on a national list. It acquired full legislative powers under the constitution adopted in May 1993.

General Elderly People's Union [Algemeen Ouderenverbond] (AOV) Dutch political party. The AOV was founded in November 1993 in protest at cuts in welfare provision, in particular a temporary freeze on state pensions. It also campaigns on other issues of interest to older people, such as healthcare and crime, and on populist policies such as immigration controls. It attracted support from across the political spectrum, not just from older people, at the May 1994 election: it gained 3.6% of the vote and 6/150 seats, thus becoming the fifth-largest party in parliament. The leader is Jet Nijpels.

General Information Branch [Renseignements Généraux] (RG) French police force and intelligence agency. A branch of the National Police [Police Nationale], the RG is involved in political and internal-security matters and also polices the national borders. Its work overlaps with that of the Territorial Surveillance Directorate (DST).

General Investigations and Special Operations Division [Divisione Investigazioni Generali e Operazioni Speciali] (DIGOS) Italian police force. DIGOS deals with specialist policing matters, such as surveillance of political extremists and anti-terrorist operations. Its activities overlap with those of the Corps of Carabinieri and other forces.

General Labour Federation of Belgium [Algemeen Belgisch Vakverbond (Dutch), Fédération Générale du Travail de Belgique (French)] (ABVV or FGTB) Belgian trade-union federation. Founded in 1899, the federation has 11 affiliated unions with a total membership of around 1.0 million (a quarter of the labour force). It has close links with the socialist parties. The president is François Janssens, the general secretary Mia de Vits.

General Workers' Union (GWU) Maltese trade union. Founded in 1946, the GWU comprises six branch sections representing a total of 39,000 workers (over a quarter of the labour force) in all sectors of the economy. It has close formal links with the Labour Party. The president is Lawrence Lautier, the general secretary Angelo Fenech.

General Workers' Union [Unión General de Trabajadores] (UGT) Spanish trade-union federation. Founded in 1888, the UGT was banned during the Franco dictatorship (1939–75). It has 15 affiliated federations with a total membership of 700,000 (5% of the labour force). It is most strongly represented in the manufacturing sector. It has traditionally had close links with the Spanish Socialist Workers' Party (PSOE), but in the 1980s relations became strained as the PSOE government pursued increasingly centrist economic policies; formal links with the party were cut in 1990. The UGT was led for many years by Nicolás Redondo. He retired in April 1994 and was succeeded by Cándido Méndez.

General Workers' Union of Portugal [União Geral dos Trabalhadores de Portugal] (UGTP) Portuguese trade-union federation. The UGTP was founded in 1978 to challenge the communist-dominated General Confederation of Portuguese Workers (CGTP-IN). Its 50 affiliated unions represent around 940,000 workers (a fifth of the labour force), although its real membership is thought to be far lower. The president is José Pereira Lopes, the general secretary is José Manuel Torres Couto.

Generalitat Catalan name for the government of Catalonia, an autonomous community or region of Spain. It is also widely used by Spanish speakers. It is also the name of the government of the Valencian Community.

Génération Écologie *See* ECOLOGY GENERATION.

Geneva Conference Shorthand for the INTERNATIONAL CONFERENCE ON FORMER YUGOSLAVIA. Many of its negotiating sessions are held in Geneva (Switzerland).

Geneva Convention Shorthand for the CONVENTION ON LONG-RANGE TRANS-BOUNDARY AIR POLLUTION. It is not linked in any way to the Geneva conventions on the treatment of prisoners of war, civilians in war zones etc.

Geneva process Shorthand for the negotiations held within the context of the INTERNATIONAL CONFERENCE ON FORMER YUGOSLAVIA. Many of its sessions are held in Geneva (Switzerland).

Gennimatas, Giorgos (1939–94) Greek civil engineer and politician. Elected to parliament for the Pan-Hellenic Socialist Movement (PASOK) in 1977, he served as minister of the interior (1981–83), health, welfare and social services (1983–87), labour (1988–89) and economy and finance (1989–90). After PASOK won the October 1993 election, he was reappointed to the double portfolio of economy and finance. He resigned from the latter for health reasons in February 1994. He died of cancer in April.

Genscher, Hans-Dietrich (1927–) German politician. He studied law and economics in East Germany in the 1940s and settled in West Germany in 1952. He worked for the parliamentary group of the centrist Free Democratic Party (FDP) from 1956 and was elected to parliament in 1965. He was appointed interior minister in the centre-left coalition in 1969. In 1974 he became both foreign minister and leader of the FDP. In 1982 he led the party into a centre-right coalition with the Christian Democratic Union (CDU). One of the world's longest-serving foreign ministers, he established himself as an influential politician both at home and on the European stage in the 1980s. He resigned as party leader in 1985 to concentrate on his government work. He resigned as foreign minister in May 1992.

GEO *See* SPECIAL OPERATIONS GROUPS.

Geoghegan-Quinn, Máire (1950–) Irish teacher and politician. Elected to parliament for the centre-right Fianna Fáil in 1975, she became the country's first woman minister in 1979, taking responsibility for the Gaeltacht (= Irish-speaking areas). She held the post until the party lost power in 1981. A junior minister from 1987–91, she was minister of transport from 1992–93 and became minister of justice in January 1993.

George, Edward or **Eddie** (1938–) British banker. An economics graduate, he joined the Bank of England, the central bank, in 1962. He specialized in international monetary questions. He became an executive director in 1982 and was appointed governor in July 1993.

Georgescu, Florin (1953–) Romanian economist, academic and politician. He worked for the finance ministry and also lectured at the Academy of Economic Studies from 1976. Politically unaffiliated, he was appointed a minister of state (= deputy prime minister) and finance minister in November 1992.

Georgievski, Ljupčo (1966–) Macedonian politician. A graduate in general and comparative literature, he was elected leader of the right-wing Internal Macedonian Revolutionary Organization - Democratic Party for Macedonian National Unity (VMRO-DPMNE) in June 1989. After the party became the largest group in parliament at the 1990 election, he was elected vice-president of the republic in February 1991. He resigned the following October over policy differences with the then government.

Geremek, Bronisław (1932–) Polish historian, academic and politician. He was a member of the Academy of Sciences from 1954–60, taught at the Sorbonne in Paris from 1960–65 and then returned to the Academy to head a research unit on medieval culture. A member of the ruling communist Polish United Workers' Party (PZPR) from 1950–68, he became an adviser to the Solidarity trade union in 1980 and was interned twice in the 1980s for his dissident views. After the partially free election in 1989 he was elected leader of the Solidarity parliamentary group. When it split in January 1991 he became parliamentary leader of the new centre-left Democratic Union (UD), now the Freedom Union (UW).

German Community *See* GERMAN-SPEAKING COMMUNITY.

German Democratic Republic (GDR) Official name of former East Germany.

German Federal Bank [Deutsche Bundesbank] (Bundesbank) Central bank of Germany. Formed in 1957 as the successor to the Bank of German States, the Bundesbank – not to be confused with the Deutsche Bank, a commercial bank – is the sole issuer of banknotes and determines monetary and credit policy. It is independent of the federal government, but is required to support its general economic policy. By law it is also responsible for ensuring the stability of the currency and prices. (This is a highly sensitive issue in Germany, which experienced two periods of hyperinflation in the early 1920s and late 1940s.) Over the years the Bundesbank has had several serious disagreements with the government, most recently over the terms of German economic and monetary union and over monetary policy. In recent years it has gained considerable influence beyond Germany's borders owing to the pivotal position of the German economy within the European Union (EU) and Europe as a whole. The Bundesbank's decision-making body is the 19-member Central Council, composed of a president, vice-president, eight directors and the nine directors of the states' central banks. The president is Hans Tietmeyer. The head office is in Frankfurt, Germany's main financial centre.

German People's Union [Deutsche Volksunion] (DVU) German political party. Founded in 1987, the DVU is a far-right party which makes little secret of its admiration for the Hitler regime (1933–45). Campaigning on a strongly anti-foreigner platform, it has not made an impression at federal level, but has gained seats in state elections in Bremen in 1987 and 1991 and in Schleswig-Holstein in 1992. Gerhard Frey has led the party since its foundation.

German Social Union [Deutsche Soziale Union] (DSU) German political party. The DSU was founded in East Germany in 1990 as an umbrella group for several right-wing and far-right parties. At the March 1990 election it gained 6.6% of the vote, but in the post-reunification all-German election in December it gained only 0.9% in the eastern states. In April 1993 it decided to extend its area of operation to the whole country. The leader is Roberto Rink.

German-Speaking Community [Deutschsprachige Gemeinschaft] Community of Belgium. Under the constitutional reforms transforming Belgium into a federal state, the German-Speaking Community is responsible for health, education, social security, social services, culture and language issues for the 67,000-strong German-speaking population of eastern Wallonia. Power is exercised by the 25-member Council of the German-Speaking Community [Rat der Deutschsprachigen Gemeinschaft] elected for a five-year term and by a three-member government. At the community election in October 1990 the Christian Social Party (CSP) gained eight seats, the Party for Freedom and Democracy (PFF) five, and the Party of German-Speaking Belgians (PDB), Socialist Party (SP) and Ecology Party four each. The government is headed by Joseph Maraite. Historically part of the duchies of Limburg and Luxemburg and part of Prussia from 1815 and united Germany from 1871, the region then referred to as Eupen-Malmédy was transferred to Belgium at the end of the First World War in 1919. It was granted autonomy on cultural matters in 1973 and acquired more powers in 1984. *See also* COMMUNITY (Belgium) *and* WALLONIA.

German Swiss or **Swiss Germans** Collective name for the German-speaking people of Switzerland. Most live in the north and east and they number around 4.2 million (73.5% of Swiss citizens and 61.3% of the total population). The Swiss German dialects are widely used in public life, but the written and official language is standard German.

German Trade Union Federation [Deutscher Gewerkschaftsbund] (DGB) German trade-union federation. Founded in 1949, the DGB is Europe's largest labour organization, with a total membership of around 10.3 million (nearly a third of the labour force). Among its 16 constituent federations, organized on a branch rather than a trade basis, are some of Europe's largest and most powerful unions, including the Metalworkers' Union (IG Metall) and the Public Services and Transport Union (ÖTV). The DGB has close, but no formal, links with the Social Democratic Party (SPD). The president is Dieter Schulte.

German Unity Fund [Fonds Deutsche Einheit] (FDE) German government programme. The Fund was set up after reunification in October 1990 to stimulate economic and other investment in former East Germany. It is jointly financed by the federal government and the western federal states. It was originally meant to disburse 95 billion marks (50 billion ecus) over a four-year period, but the amount was subsequently raised to 160 billion marks (83 billion ecus) to take account of the unexpected weakness of the East German economy and low tax receipts. *See also* SOLIDARITY PACT.

Germany [Deutschland] Country in central Europe.

Official data. Name: Federal Republic of Germany [Bundesrepublik Deutschland]; capital: Berlin; provisional seat of government: Bonn; form of government: federal republic; head of state: federal president; head of government: federal chancellor; flag: three horizontal stripes, black, red and gold; national holiday: 3 October (Unity Day); language: German; religion: none; currency: Deutsche Mark (DM) = 100 Pfennige; abbreviation: D.

Geography. Germany has a total area of 356,957 sq km. It is bordered by the North Sea, Denmark and the Baltic Sea in the north, Poland and the Czech Republic in the east, Austria and Switzerland in the south, and France, Luxemburg, Belgium and the Netherlands in the west. The northern third of the country consists of a low-lying plain (North German Plain); the centre of hills, plateaus and mountains (including the Hunsrück, Eifel, Taunus, Harz and Erz ranges); the south of plateaus and mountains (including the Black Forest [Schwarzwald] and the

Bavarian Forest [Bayerischer Wald]); the Alps in the far southeast form the border with Austria. Some 35% of the land is arable, another 16% is covered by pastures and 30% is forested. The main rivers are the Rhine [Rhein], Elbe, Danube [Donau], Moselle [Mosel], Weser, Neckar, Main and Oder. The climate is generally temperate marine in the north and west (with mild summers and cool to cold winters) and humid continental in the east and south (with hot summers and cold winters); rainfall is generally moderate, heavier in the mountains and heavy in the Alps.

Demography. With a population of 81,187,000, Germany is the most populous country in Europe (excluding Russia). Between 1990 and 1992 the population increased by around 1.8 million as a result of immigration, particularly of ethnic Germans from Russia, Poland and Romania and asylum seekers from many countries. Population density is 232 per sq km (land area). Only the northeast, parts of the northwest and north and the mountainous areas in the south are relatively sparsely populated. Some 84% of the people live in urban areas. The main centres of population are the Ruhr area in the west, a conurbation of 4.5 million people centred on the cities of Essen, Dortmund and Duisburg, and the adjoining metropolitan areas of Düsseldorf (population 1.2 million), Cologne [Köln] (1.8 million), Wuppertal, Bonn and Mönchengladbach; together they form the Rhine-Ruhr conurbation, with a total population of around 9.5 million. Other conurbations are Berlin (population 3.8 million, city 3.4 million), the Rhine-Main area, centred on Frankfurt, Wiesbaden and Mainz (2.9 million), Hamburg (2.2 million, city 1.7 million), Munich (2.0 million, city 1.2 million), the Neckar area, centred on Stuttgart (1.9 million), the Rhein-Neckar area, centred on Mannheim (1.4 million), Hannover (1.0 million), and the Saar area centred on Saarbrücken (1.0 million). Other major cities are Bremen, Leipzig, Dresden, Karlsruhe, Halle, Aachen, Chemnitz, Augsburg, Magdeburg, Kassel, Braunschweig, Kiel, Osnabrück, Münster, Lübeck, Rostock

and Erfurt. The overwhelming majority of the population is German. Ethnic minorities include 120,000 Sorbs in southeastern Brandenburg and northeastern Saxony, 90,000 Gipsies, 70,000 Frisians along the northwest coast, and 30,000 Danes in northern Schleswig. Foreign nationals account for 7.3% of the population, and include citizens of Turkey (1.85 million or 2.3% of the total, including 450,000 ethnic Kurds), former Yugoslavia (1.0%, mainly from Croatia and Macedonia), Italy (0.7%), Greece, Poland, Austria, Spain, Netherlands, United States, United Kingdom, Iran, Portugal and Romania. Germany has also taken in around 400,000 refugees from former Yugoslavia (around 600,000 according to unofficial estimates). There is a substantial ethnic German community in Poland and smaller ones in Hungary and the Czech Republic. In religious terms 36.3% of the population is Lutheran Protestant, 35.3% Roman Catholic, 2.2% Muslim and 0.6% Orthodox; most of the remainder is not religious. Broadly speaking the north is mainly Protestant and the south mainly Catholic, but many areas are mixed.

Sociography. Germany scores 0.918 on the United Nations human development index (HDI), ranking 11th in the world and seventh among 32 European countries. There are 29 doctors and 105 hospital beds for every 10,000 people. Education is compulsory full-time between the ages of six and 15 or 16 and part-time until 18; it is the responsibility of the federal states. There is one teacher for every 19 students. Enrolment is 84% at the secondary level and 33% at the tertiary level. The literacy rate is virtually 100%. Real annual income per head (in terms of purchasing power) is US$ 19,770. Income levels in the eastern states are roughly a third of those in the west (around $ 7,000 compared to $ 20,000).

Infrastructure and communications. The transport and communications network in the western states (former West Germany) is highly developed, while that of the eastern states (former East Germany) is developed but in need of modernization. Since reunification, investment has been concentrated on developing east-west transport routes and integrating the telecommunications system in particular. There are 550,000 km of paved roads and 35.5 million passenger cars (449 per 1,000 people, one of the highest rates in Europe), 44,330 km of railways and 7,541 km of navigable waterways. The main ports are Hamburg, Bremen, Rostock, Lübeck and (inland) Duisburg. The main airport is at Frankfurt, the second-busiest in Europe; other major airports are at Düsseldorf, Munich (Riem), Hamburg (Fuhlsbüttel) and Berlin (Tegel), and there are 33 other airports with scheduled services. There are 395 daily newspapers, with a combined circulation of 32.7 million (420 per 1,000 people). There are 32.2 million radio receivers, 45.2 million television sets and around 47 million telephones in use (respectively 408, 571 and 594 per 1,000 people).

Economic structure. The German economy is highly developed, diversified, trade-oriented (exports account for a third of national income) and closely linked to its neighbours. It is the largest economy in Europe and the third-largest in the world as well as the world's second-largest trading power. It is based on engineering and other manufacturing and trade and other services. The economy of the eastern states (former East Germany) is in need of major investment and restructuring; the transition from a command to a market-based economy is causing severe disruption and has led to a steep fall in industrial production and mass unemployment; there was a return to growth in 1993. During the second half of the 1980s West Germany's economic performance was marked by steady growth (averaging 2.6% per year), substantial current-account surpluses (4% of GDP), low inflation (1.3%) and relatively high unemployment (6.3%). In part because of the cost and disruption of reunification, growth declined from 5.1% in 1990 to -1.5% in 1993, the current account moved into deficit, inflation peaked at 4% in 1992 and 1993, and unemployment rose to 10% (9% in the west, 16% in the east). Growth resumed in 1994.

Services contribute 61% of GDP, industry contributes 37% (manufacturing 29%), and agriculture, forestry and fisheries 2%. Some 33% of the labour force is employed in manufacturing, 14% in trade, 7% in construction, 6% in finance and 6% in transport and communications. The main crops grown are cereals (wheat, barley, rye, oats), potatoes and sugarbeets; other important agricultural activities are dairy farming (milk, butter, cheese, eggs), livestock raising (cattle, pigs, poultry) and horticulture (fruit and vegetables); although very small in terms of GDP, Germany's agriculture industry is the fifth-largest in Europe. Forestry is also important; the industry is the largest in Europe. Fishing is of regional importance. The main mineral resources are coal, lignite, natural gas, potash, zinc, lead and uranium. The main industries are engineering (esp. industrial machinery, motor vehicles), electrical goods and electronics; other important branches are chemicals, iron and steel and other metalworking, food processing, petrochemicals, wood processing, textiles and building materials; the manufacturing industry is by far the largest in Europe. Transport, trade, tourism and financial services are important sources of foreign exchange. The main energy sources are domestic and imported fossil fuels and nuclear power; 7% of export earnings are required to cover net fuel imports. The main exports are transport equipment (18% of the total, incl. cars 11%), industrial machinery (15%), chemicals (13%), electrical and electronic equipment (12%), textiles and clothing (5%), foodstuffs (5%), iron and steel, wood and wood products and scientific instruments; machinery and transport equipment account for 49% of the total, basic manufactures for 17%, chemicals for 13%. The main imports are machinery and transport equipment, miscellaneous manufactures and basic manufactures. The main trading partners are: exports: France (13%), Italy (9%), Netherlands (8%), United Kingdom (8%), Belgium and Luxemburg (7%), United States (6%), Austria (6%), Switzerland (5%), Spain, Japan, Sweden, Denmark; imports:

France (12%), Netherlands (10%), Italy (9%), Belgium and Luxemburg (7%), United Kingdom (7%), United States (7%), Japan (6%), Austria, Switzerland, Spain, Sweden, Denmark, China; half of all trade is with other European Union (EU) countries.

The German Federal Bank [Deutsche Bundesbank] is the central bank. The main employers' associations are the Confederation of German Employers' Associations (BDA) and the Confederation of German Industry (BDI); the main labour organizations are the German Trade Union Federation (DGB), German Civil Servants' Association (DBB) and German Salaried Employees' Union (DAG).

Political structure. Under the 1949 constitution, Germany is a federal republic composed of 16 states [Land, pl. Länder]. The head of state is the federal president [Bundespräsident], who is elected for a five-year term by the Federal Convention [Bundesversammlung] composed of the members of the legislature and an equal number of delegates from the states. Executive power is vested in the federal chancellor [Bundeskanzler] and the federal government. Legislative power is vested in the bicameral Parliament [Parlament], composed of the 656-member Federal Assembly [Bundestag] elected for a four-year term by a system of proportional representation (with a 5% threshold for gaining seats), and the 68-member Federal Council [Bundesrat] indirectly elected for varying terms by the state legislatures; an anomaly in the electoral system may produce several excess seats in the Bundestag. All citizens over the age of 18 are entitled to vote. Judicial power is ultimately vested in the 12-member Federal Constitutional Court [Bundesverfassungsgericht], half elected by the Bundestag and half by the Bundesrat for 12-year non-renewable terms. The states have their own constitutions, legislatures and governments and have considerable autonomy, particularly in the areas of education, law and order and culture. They are Baden-Württemberg, Bavaria [Bayern], Berlin, Brandenburg, Bremen, Hamburg, Hesse [Hessen], Lower Saxony [Niedersachsen], Mecklenburg - West Pomerania [Mecklenburg-Vorpommern], North Rhine - Westphalia [Nordrhein-Westfalen], Rhineland-Palatinate [Rheinland-Pfalz], Saarland, Saxony [Sachsen], Saxony-Anhalt [Sachsen-Anhalt], Schleswig-Holstein and Thuringia [Thüringen]. Administratively most states are divided into districts [Landkreis, pl. -e], district-level cities and municipalities; the intermediate-level administrative districts [Regierungsbezirk, pl. -e] in some states have no political functions.

The main political parties are the Christian Democratic Union (CDU), Social Democratic Party of Germany (SPD), Christian Social Union (CSU), Free Democratic Party (FDP), Greens (Grünen, including Alliance 90, B'90), Democratic Socialist Party (PDS, the successor to the Socialist Unity Party, SED, of East Germany) and Republicans (REP). At the general election in December 1990 the CDU gained 36.7% of the vote and 268/662 seats, the SPD 33.5% and 239 seats, the FDP 11.0% and 79 seats, the CSU 7.1% and 51 seats, the Greens 3.9% and no seats, the PDS 2.4% and 17 seats, the Republicans 2.1% and no seats, and B'90 1.2% and eight seats. The government is formed by a centre-right coalition of the CDU, FDP and CSU, with Helmut Kohl as federal chancellor. Other senior ministers are Günter Rexrodt (deputy chancellor, economy), Klaus Kinkel (foreign affairs), Manfred Kanther (interior), Theo Waigel (finance), Sabine Leutheusser-Schnarrenberger (justice), Volker Rühe (defence), Norbert Blüm (labour and social affairs), Jochen Borchert (food, agriculture and forestry), Klaus Töpfer (environment) and Friedrich Bohl (head of the Federal Chancellery, special projects). The head of state is President Roman Herzog, who was elected in May 1994 and took office in July.

Security and international affiliations. The German armed forces number 408,200 (army 287,000, navy 31,200, airforce 90,000); they are due to be reduced to around 370,000. There is also a 24,800-strong paramilitary force, the Federal Border Guard [Bundesgrenz-schutz] (BGS), and a small coast guard. Military service is compulsory and consists of 12 months' basic training. Substantial numbers of foreign troops are stationed in Germany within the frame-work of the North Atlantic Treaty Organization (NATO), including US, British, French, Belgian and Dutch troops; their numbers are being reduced.

Germany is a member of the Council of Baltic Sea States (CBSS), Conference on Security and Cooperation in Europe (CSCE), Council of Europe, European Economic Area (EEA), European Union (EU), North Atlantic Treaty Organization (NATO) and Western European Union (WEU), as well as the Group of Seven (G-7), Organization for Economic Cooperation and Development (OECD) and United Nations and its specialized agencies.

History. Germanic tribes gradually migrated outward from their heartland in southern Scandinavia and the North German Plain from the 8th century BC. The Cimbri, Teutoni and Ambrones invaded the Roman Republic in the 110s and 100s. From 12 BC the Romans sought to subdue the tribes between the Rhine and Elbe rivers, but the attempt was abandoned after the Cherusci inflicted a heavy defeat in AD 9. The Rhine and Danube rivers effectively formed the northern borders of the Roman Empire for the next four centuries. Visigoths, Ostrogoths, Lombards, Allemans, Burgundians, Vandals, Franks and others crossed the border during the Europe-wide migrations of the 4th and 5th centuries which helped trigger the collapse of the Roman Empire. In 486 the Franks overthrew the last Roman governor in the west. Under King Clovis (486–511) and his successors they extended their control over the whole of Gaul (modern France) and several Germanic kingdoms in the 6th century. Christianity became the dominant religion around this time. With the defeat of the Saxon and Bavarian kingdoms during the reign of Charlemagne (768–814) the Frankish

Kingdom was extended to the Elbe river and the Bohemian border. (The lands to the east were inhabited by Slavic peoples.) Charlemagne's coronation as 'Roman emperor' on Christmas Day 800 was a largely symbolic attempt to restore the Western Roman Empire. After his death the Empire was partitioned on several occasions, with the East Frankish Kingdom forming the core of Germany. (The West Frankish Kingdom became France.)

In the late 9th and early 10th centuries royal authority was weak and the duchies of Bavaria, Franconia, Lower Lorraine, Saxony, Swabia and Upper Lorraine became increasingly powerful. After the death of the last descendant of Charlemagne in 905 the German throne was held by various powerful ducal or princely families with strong regional powerbases, such as the Saxon Liudolfings (919–1024), the Franconian Salians (1024–1125) and the Swabian Hohenstaufen (1138–1254). The title 'Roman emperor' was revived in 962, when King Otto I, emulating Charlemagne, was crowned in Rome. During the Middle Ages the core of the Holy Roman or German Empire comprised what is now Germany, Austria, Bohemia and Moravia (Czech Republic), and the Polish regions of Pomerania and Silesia; northern and central Italy, the Low Countries and Switzerland were also included until 1648, but effectively imperial authority was broken in these regions in the 13th, 14th and 15th centuries respectively. Feudalization set in train a process of fragmentation into hundreds of states, large and small, secular and ecclesiastic, that was to characterize German history until the 19th century. Besides the territorial states there were numerous 'imperial cities', some mere country towns but others large, wealthy and powerful (and politically generally supportive of the emperor against the princes). The 11th and 12th centuries were dominated by a power struggle between the Empire and the Papacy. In the 12th and 13th centuries the lands between the Elbe and Oder rivers were colonized (and the small Slav populations germanized). This migration was part of a broader eastward movement

260

that lasted until the late 14th century, during which German influence was extended through settlement and conquest to parts of Bohemia and Poland and beyond in the Baltic and Balkan regions. In the 13th and 14th centuries a number of northern cities formed the Hanseatic League, which held a near-monopoly of trade in the Baltic and North Sea regions and became an independent political power with its own armed forces. The principle of the elective imperial monarchy was firmly established in 1273, after a 19-year interregnum, and formalized in the Golden Bull of 1356, which also established a basic law for imperial government. Henceforward four lay and three ecclesiastical princes (the king of Bohemia, duke of Saxony, count palatine of the Rhine, markgrave of Brandenburg, and the archbishops of Cologne, Mainz and Trier) held the right to elect the emperor; they were joined by the duke of Bavaria in 1623 and the duke of Hannover in 1692. This marked a decisive erosion of central authority to the regional princes. The imperial title was held by Austrian Habsburgs (1273–91, 1298–1308), Luxemburgers (1308–13, 1346–1400, 1410–37) and Bavarian Wittelsbachs (1314–46, 1400–10); from 1438 it became in effect hereditary in the Habsburg line. In 1517 the theologian Martin Luther's challenge to the legitimacy of the Catholic and imperial system sparked the Protestant Reformation, which spread quickly throughout Germany and was embraced by several powerful princes. Economic and political aims overlaid with reformist religious fervour sparked the Peasants' Revolt, a major but diffuse uprising in southern and central Germany in 1524–25. The Schmalkaldic League formed by the Protestant states in 1531 was defeated by imperial forces in 1547. Nevertheless, under the Peace of Augsburg of 1555 Emperor Charles V (1519–56) in effect accepted the right of the princes to decide the recognized faith in their own territories. The Habsburg-inspired Catholic Counterreformation sparked further conflict, culminating in the Thirty Years' War (1618–48). This initially set the

German states against each other over religious and political issues, but became a complex Europe-wide struggle after Denmark, Sweden and (Catholic) France entered the war in 1625, 1630 and 1635, all on the Protestant side against the Austrian and Spanish Habsburgs. The War was fought mainly on German soil and had a devastating effect on the country's population (a sixth of whom were killed or died) and on the economy, primarily because the various mercenary-based armies plundered cities and the countryside for supplies on an unprecedented scale.

The 1648 Treaty of Westphalia marked a major break in German, and European, history. Most importantly for Germany, it recognized the political and religious sovereignty of the Empire's component states, thus formalizing a situation that had obtained for some time, ending any vestige of imperial authority and accentuating the country's fragmentation. At this time Germany consisted of around 300 states as well as 1,500 cities, towns and minor lordships whose nominal suzerain was the emperor and which were thus effectively also sovereign. In the late 17th and 18th centuries several states apart from Austria became regional or European powers in their own right, in particular Brandenburg-Prussia, Saxony, Bavaria and Hannover. In Brandenburg, the foundations of an efficient administration, professional army and interventionist economic policy characteristic of what became the Kingdom of Prussia in 1701 were laid under Frederick William I (byname 'the Great Elector') (1640–88). Under his successors, in particular King Frederick William I (1713–40) and King Frederick II (byname 'the Great') (1740–86), Prussia extended its territories through a combination of conquest, diplomacy, inheritance and purchase, and became the dominant state in northern Germany and the main counterweight to Austria. (Prussia and especially Austria also held extensive territories outside the Empire.) During the French Revolutionary and Napoleonic Wars (1792–1815) France annexed the lands to the west of the Rhine in 1793, dissolved the Holy Roman Empire in 1806 after inflicting heavy defeats on Prussia and Austria, and redrew the political map of Germany by merging the smaller states into 16 larger states, bound together in the Rhine Confederation. This new structure provided the basis for the German Confederation, set up under nominal Austrian leadership in 1815 by the Congress of Vienna (which carried out the post-Napoleonic reorganization of Europe). In territorial terms Prussia was the main beneficiary: it acquired the Rhineland, Germany's future industrial heartland. The dominant states in the Confederation, besides Austria and Prussia, were Bavaria, Saxony, Württemberg, Baden and Hannover (the latter was annexed by Prussia in 1866). Some southern states established constitutional forms of government, but liberal and nationalist demands for reform and German unification were suppressed in most states. The establishment of the Customs Union [Zollverein] in 1834, which eventually encompassed all the German states except Austria, marked the first effective step in the process of unification. Inspired by the Europe-wide uprisings of 1848, a directly elected confederal parliament demanded a united and democratic Germany and approved a constitution in 1849. The project collapsed after it was rejected, for different reasons, by Austria and Prussia. The 1850s marked the beginning of a process of industrialization which transformed Germany into a major economic power within a few decades. The unification of 'smaller' Germany (i.e. without Austria) was pursued by a combination of diplomacy and war by Otto von Bismarck, Prussian and then German chancellor (= prime minister) from 1862–90 and the dominant political leader of the period. The various stages were a successful war with Denmark over Schleswig and Holstein (1864), the Seven Weeks' War with Austria (1866), which ended Habsburg influence in German affairs, the establishment of the North German Confederation under Prussian leadership (1867), and the involvement of the southern states in the Franco-Prussian War (1870–71).

The German Empire was proclaimed in 1871 and King William I of Prussia became emperor. The Second Empire consisted of 25 states (four kingdoms, six grand duchies, five duchies, seven principalities and three free cities) which retained considerable autonomy, but it was completely dominated by Prussia, which accounted for 65% of its area and 62% of its population. Alsace-Lorraine was ceded by France in 1871. Unification and a massive indemnity paid by France gave a major boost to industrial development. The 1870s and 80s were dominated by a protracted struggle between the government and the Catholic Church (formally over powers of appointment and control of education, but in practice over the integration of the mostly Catholic south into the Prussian-dominated Empire) and by the emergence of working-class organizations, in particular the Social Democratic Party (SPD). In response to the latter, a wide-ranging scheme of social insurance (covering industrial injury, sickness etc) and other welfare provisions were enacted in the 1880s. Germany acquired colonies in Africa and the Pacific in the 1880s and 90s. Germany's massive economic expansion across the continent alarmed the other powers (France, Russia and Britain), as did the build-up of its military forces. The rivalry among the major powers led to the First World War (1914–18). The German army invaded Belgium and France and became involved in inconclusive trench warfare with French and British forces. A successful offensive on the eastern front in 1917 precipitated the collapse of the tsarist regime and the conclusion of an advantageous peace treaty with the new communist government in 1918. An offensive on the western front failed to make a breakthrough, however, and an Allied counteroffensive forced the German army into retreat. (The United States had entered the War on the side of the Allies in 1917.) Within days of the surrender of Germany's major ally, Austria-Hungary, a communist revolution broke out across the country, Emperor William II abdicated, a republic was proclaimed, a new SPD-led government was formed, and Germany accepted an armistice on terms that effectively meant surrender. Some 1.8 million German soldiers had been killed during the fighting. The government suppressed the revolutionary workers' and soldiers' councils set up in many cities and defeated the communist Spartacists in Berlin and a soviet republic in Bavaria in 1919. A general election was held in 1919. The new assembly, convened at Weimar, adopted a new constitution and elected SPD leader Friedrich Ebert as president of the republic. The main terms of the Treaty of Versailles, signed in 1919, were the cession of Alsace-Lorraine to France and extensive territories to Poland, the loss of all colonies, the demilitarization and occupation of the Rhineland and Saarland industrial areas, restrictions on military capacity, and the payment of huge reparations (in acknowledgement of 'war guilt'). The early years of the Weimar Republic (1919–33) were marked by short-lived governments, several coup attempts, economic dislocation and financial chaos and hyperinflation. The introduction of a new currency in 1923 provided the basis for an economic recovery and greater political stability. Both ended with the post-1929 worldwide depression, which in addition to causing mass unemployment undermined the fragile political structures of the Weimar Republic. The far-right National Socialist German Workers' Party (NSDAP) or Nazi Party under Adolf Hitler became a major political force after the 1930 election and replaced the SPD as the largest single party in 1932 (gaining 37.4% and 33.2% of the vote in the two elections held that year). The authorities were unable to control escalating street violence between nazis and communists. President Hindenburg (1925–34) appointed Hitler as chancellor at the head of a centre-right coalition in 1933. Hitler immediately called fresh elections, at which the NSDAP gained 43.9% of the vote. The party took power through an 'enabling act', passed with the support of the right-wing German

National People's Party (DNVP), which allowed the government to bypass parliament. This provided the constitutional basis of Hitler's dictatorship in what was proclaimed the Third Reich or Empire (after the Holy Roman Empire and the post-1871 Empire). The nazi regime reflated the economy through infrastructure projects and arms production. (The subsequent recovery also benefited from the worldwide economic upturn in the mid 1930s.) It also suppressed all opposition, stripped Jews of civic rights (an application of its racial principles), promoted a personality cult around Hitler, and pursued an expansionist foreign policy ostensibly aimed at bringing all ethnic Germans into the Reich and overturning the 'unjust' Treaty of Versailles. On Hindenburg's death in 1934 Hitler assumed the role of head of state and commander of the armed forces and was proclaimed 'leader' [Führer]. Saarland was returned to Germany in 1935, German troops entered the Rhineland (in violation of the Treaty of Versailles) in 1936, and Austria and the German-speaking Sudetenland region of Czechoslovakia were annexed in 1938. Bohemia and Moravia were declared a 'protectorate' in 1939. The invasion of Poland sparked the Second World War (1939–45). In 1940 the German army invaded and occupied Denmark, Norway, the Low Countries and France; and in 1941 it launched offensives against Yugoslavia, Greece and the Soviet Union. By 1942 Britain was the only major European country not occupied or controlled by or allied with Germany. The nazi regime committed innumerable atrocities across Europe, including the use of slave labour, summary executions and random acts of violence, and (from 1942) the systematic genocide of the Jewish people. Around 6 million Jews were killed in what became known as the Holocaust. In late 1942 the tide turned against Germany and its allies, primarily Italy. By late 1943 the Soviet army was advancing on the eastern front, the Allies had defeated Germany's North African army and Italy had surrendered. And by late 1944 France and Belgium had been liberated and the Soviet army had entered German territory. With Berlin about to fall, Hitler committed suicide in 1945. Germany surrendered a week later. Some 3.5 million German soldiers and 780,000 civilians were killed during the fighting, the cities and infrastructure were largely destroyed, and around 13.5 million ethnic Germans fled or were expelled from their homes after 1944.

Germany was divided into American, British, French and Soviet zones of occupation, and Berlin, situated within the Soviet zone, was also divided into four zones. German territory to the east of the Oder and Neisse rivers was allocated to Poland. The growing rift between the three western allies and the Soviet Union created special strains in occupied Germany. The Soviet blockade of West Berlin in 1948–49 marked the onset of a worldwide 'cold war' between East and West. This was reflected in the establishment of two states in Germany in 1949, the German Democratic Republic (GDR) or East Germany in the Soviet-occupied zone and the Federal Republic of Germany (FRG) or West Germany in the other zones. West Berlin effectively became part of West Germany, and East Berlin became the capital of the GDR. In East Germany the communist Socialist Unity Party (SED) regime suppressed all opposition, nationalized the economy, introduced central planning and allied itself closely with the Soviet Union. In West Germany, on the other hand, a free-market economy with extensive welfare provisions and a multiparty federal political system were established. The West German economy made a rapid recovery during 1950s and 60s – it grew by an average of 5% per year between 1948–73 – in what became known as the 'economic miracle' [Wirtschaftswunder]. The millions of refugees were also successfully integrated. The main political parties were the Christian Democratic Union (CDU) and its Bavarian counterpart the Christian Social Union (CSU), the Social Democratic Party (SPD), and the centrist Free Democratic Party (FDP), which was small but influential because it often held the balance of power at federal and state level. The CDU/CSU led coalition governments or ruled alone until 1966. The dominant political leaders of the period were Konrad Adenauer, federal chancellor (= prime minister) from 1949–63, and Ludwig Erhard, minister of economic affairs from 1949–63 and chancellor from 1963–66. From the 1950s Germany was the front line of the confrontation between East and West and the main prospective battleground for any 'hot' war between the two blocs. In parallel developments in 1954/55, the foreign occupations were formally ended in East and West Germany, the two states were given full sovereignty, and the huge numbers of troops stationed in each were now deployed as part of the respective military alliances, the Warsaw Pact and North Atlantic Treaty Organization (NATO). Berlin in particular was a flashpoint. The Berlin Wall, constructed by the East German authorities in 1961 around West Berlin to stop the exodus of East Germans to the west, became a symbol of communist oppression and of the division of Germany and Europe. West Germany's reconciliation with its western neighbours, above all France, was signalled by its participation in the European Coal and Steel Community (ECSC) in 1952 and in the more comprehensive European Economic Community (EEC), now the European Union (EU), in 1958, and by the signing of a Franco-German friendship treaty in 1963. The Saarland, which had been under French administration since 1945, joined West Germany as its 10th federal state in 1959. The CDU and SPD shared power in a 'grand coalition' from 1966–69, during a brief economic downturn. After the 1969 election the SPD and FDP formed a centre-left coalition, which remained in power until 1982, under Willy Brandt until 1974 and then under Helmut Schmidt. The Brandt government initiated a new 'eastern policy' [Ostpolitik], which led to the normalization of relations and the signing of treaties of reconciliation with the Soviet Union, Poland, East Germany and the other eastern neighbours. The treaty between the two Germanies was signed in

1972. Both states joined the United Nations in 1973. The late 1960s and early 70s was a period of widespread left-wing student agitation in West Germany. The Red Army Faction (RAF) or Baader-Meinhof Group, a far-left urban guerrilla group, also emerged at this time. The SPD-FDP coalition was returned with an increased majority in the October 1980 election, but disagreements over economic and defence policy prompted the FDP to withdraw from the coalition and thus bring down the Schmidt government. In October 1982 Helmut Kohl became chancellor at the head of a CDU-FDP coalition. The Greens entered parliament for the first time in March 1983 and became an influential force, not just in Germany. The 1980s saw the emergence of a mass 'peace movement', which sought to prevent the deployment of a new generation of nuclear missiles (cruise and Pershing-II) by NATO and called for general disarmament and the eventual dismantling of the military blocs. Between 1984 and 1989 the West German economy, by now the engine of the larger Western European economy, grew at an average of 3% per year.

As communist rule crumbled across Eastern Europe in 1989, opposition to the regime in East Germany became more open and thousands of East Germans fled to West Germany (via Czechoslovakia, Hungary and Austria). Erich Honecker, East Germany's leader since 1971, and other hard-line communists were forced to resign in October. The new reformist regime opened the Berlin Wall in November, marking the first step in the reunification of Berlin and Germany over the following year. (The opening of the Wall is now widely seen as marking the symbolic end of the Cold War, communist domination in Eastern Europe and the division of Europe.) A multiparty election in March 1990 brought victory for a centre-right alliance calling for rapid reunification. A monetary, economic and social union between the two states, with the West German mark as the common currency, came into effect in July. Full reunification took place in October. Kohl's CDU-FDP coalition was victorious in the all-German election in December. Reunification has had far-reaching consequences in both east and west. In the east, as in the other former communist countries, the transition to a market-based economy has been accompanied by economic disruption and social dislocation; in the west it has created problems unprecedented in the post-1945 period in terms of inflation (due to overheating in the immediate post-reunification boom), public-borrowing requirements (to finance the east's reconstruction) and, since 1991, recession and rising unemployment. The east-west economic divide has been exacerbated by eastern resentment at the 'takeover' by the west, and western resentment at tax increases and the huge financial transfers to the east. The eastern economy recorded strong growth in 1994, but living standards remain about half of those in the west. Growing social tension has also been reflected in attacks on immigrants, refugees and asylum seekers and the emergence of far-right groups. In March 1993 a national consensus was reached on a 'solidarity pact' to finance the reconstruction of eastern Germany. In order to end the large and increasingly controversial influx of economic migrants from the Eastern European countries since 1989, parliament in May 1993 amended the constitution to restrict the hitherto very liberal right to asylum.

See also entries on specific institutions, organizations, parties, people, terms etc.

gewest *See* REGION (Belgium).

Gheg *See* GEG.

Gheorghescu, Florin *See* GEORGESCU, ...

Gherman, Oliviu (1930–) Romanian physicist, academic and politician. He lectured in physics at the University of Cluj from 1955 and at the University of Craiova from 1966. He was elected to parliament for the National Salvation Front (FSN) in 1990. When the movement split he joined the Democratic National Salvation Front (FSND), now the Social Democracy Party (PDSR). He was elected party president in June 1992. He is also president of the Senate, the upper house of parliament.

Giannopoulos, Evangelos (1918–) Greek lawyer and politician. He fought in the resistance movement during the Second World War, first entered parliament for the Centre Union (EK) in 1960 and was imprisoned under the military dictatorship (1967–74). A founding member of the Pan-Hellenic Socialist Movement (PASOK) in 1974, he has been minister of labour (1982–86), merchant marine (1987–88) and Aegean affairs (1988–89). He was again given responsibility for labour when PASOK returned to power in October 1993. He was dismissed in July 1994 after criticizing the government's 'right-wing' economic policies.

Gibraltar Territory in southwestern Europe, a dependency of the United Kingdom.

Official data. Name: City of Gibraltar; capital: n.a.; form of government: internally self-governing dependency of the United Kingdom; head of state: British monarch, represented by a governor; head of government: chief minister; flag: two horizontal stripes, white and red, with a red castle in the white; national holidays: Queen's Official Birthday (second Saturday in June), 10 September; language: English; religion: none; currencies: pound (G£) = 100 pence, British pound; abbreviation: GBG.

Geography. Situated at the eastern end of the Strait of Gibraltar linking the Atlantic Ocean and the Mediterranean Sea on the south coast of Spain, Gibraltar consists of a rocky peninsula; across the sea is Morocco. The total area is 5.8 sq km. None of the land is arable, covered by pastures or forested. The climate is mediterranean, with hot summers and cool winters; rainfall is moderate.

Demography. Gibraltar has a population of 29,100. The whole territory is built up. Gibraltarians account for 66.5% of the population, other British citizens for 18.0%, and foreign nationals, mainly from Morocco, for 15.5%. The main languages are English and Spanish; most people are bilingual; the local dialect is known as Llanito or Yanito. In religious terms 74.5% of the population is nominally Roman Catholic, 8.5% Muslim, 8.0% Anglican and 2.5% Jewish.

Sociography. The standard of living in Gibraltar is relatively high. There are nine doctors and 82 hospital beds for every 10,000 people. Education is compulsory between the ages of five and 15. There is one teacher for every 20 students. Enrolment is 54% at the secondary level; there is one college of higher education, but most students study abroad, in Britain and other countries. The literacy rate is virtually 100%. GNP per head (unadjusted for purchasing power) is US$ 15,080.

Infrastructure and communications. Gibraltar has a highly developed but limited transport and communications network. There are 43 km of paved roads and 17,900 passenger cars (571 per 1,000 people). There are no railways or navigable waterways. Gibraltar is a port and there is an airport at North Front. There are two daily newspapers, with a combined circulation of 3,000 (107 per 1,000 people); British and Spanish papers are also widely read. There are 17,000 radio receivers, 7,000 television sets and 17,000 telephones in use (respectively 543, 224 and 543 per 1,000 people).

Economic structure. The Gibraltarian economy is developed but heavily dependent on tourism and trade, in particular transhipment of oil products. More than half the economy is state-owned. Since the late 1980s economic performance has been characterized by moderate growth, substantial current-account deficits, rising inflation (to around 7%) and rising unemployment (to around 9%).

The services sector contributes around four-fifths of GDP and industry around a fifth (detailed figures n.a.). Some 22% of the labour force is employed in trade, 15% in construction, 10% in finance and 8% in manufacturing. There are no agricultural activities or mineral resources. The main industries are shipbuilding and -repairing (primarily for the British navy), food processing (tobacco, beverages), ceramics and handicrafts. Tourism is the major source of foreign exchange, contributing 40% of GNP. Transport and commercial services (incl. ship provisioning) are also important, as are banking and other financial services. The main energy sources are imported fossil fuels; 14% of export earnings are required to cover net fuel imports. The main exports, including reexports, are oil and oil products (52% of the total), machinery and transport equipment (18%) and wines and spirits (8%). The main imports are foodstuffs, basic manufactures, machinery and transport equipment and fuels. The main trading partners are: exports: Morocco (28%), United Kingdom, Spain, Portugal; imports: United Kingdom (32%), Spain, Japan, Netherlands; three-fifths of all trade is with European Union (EU) countries. Net invisible earnings (tourism receipts, shipping charges, assistance from the British government) account for a substantial share of GNP.

There is no central bank. There are several employers' associations; the main labour organizations are the Transport and General Workers' Union (TGWU) and Gibraltar Trades Council (GTC).

Political structure. Under the constitution adopted in 1969, Gibraltar is an internally self-governing British crown colony. The British government is responsible for foreign affairs, defence and security. Executive power is formally vested in the British monarch, represented by a governor, but is exercised by the chief minister and the council of ministers. The governor usually acts on the advice of the nine-member Gibraltar Council, a consultative and executive body composed of senior officers of state and government ministers. Legislative power is vested in the 18-member House of Assembly, composed of 15 members elected for a four-year term by a system of proportional representation, and three non-voting members (the attorney-general and financial and development secretary, who are members ex-officio, and a speaker appointed by the governor). The largest party is allowed a maximum of eight seats regardless of its share of the popular vote. All citizens over the age of 18 are entitled to vote. Judicial power is vested in the three-member Supreme Court. There is no local government structure.

The main political parties are the Gibraltar Socialist Labour Party (GSLP),

Gibraltar Social Democrats (GSD) and Gibraltar National Party (GNP). At the general election in January 1992, the GSLP gained 73.1% of the vote and eight seats (out of 15), the GSD 20.2% and seven seats, and the GNP 4.7% and none. The government is formed by the GSLP, with Joe Bossano as chief minister. Other senior ministers are Joe Pilcher (deputy chief minister, tourism) and Michael Feetham (trade and industry). The head of state is Queen Elizabeth II, represented by John Chapple as governor.

Security and international affiliations. Defence and foreign affairs are the responsibility of the British government. The local armed forces number 250, and there is also a 900-strong British detachment. There is no conscription. The advisory Gibraltar Council plays an important role in formulating foreign policy in matters of immediate concern to the territory (such as relations with Spain). As a British dependency in Europe, Gibraltar forms part of the European Union (EU).

History. 'Gibraltar' is a corruption of Jabal Ṭāriq ('Mount Tariq' in Arabic), named after Ṭāriq ibn Ziyād, the general who led the Muslim conquest of Spain in 711. (*For earlier developments, see* SPAIN: HISTORY.) Gibraltar was held by successive Muslim dynasties until 1462, when it fell to the Spanish. A combined British and Dutch force occupied the strategically important site in 1704, during the War of the Spanish Succession (1701–13/14), and it was ceded to the United Kingdom under the 1713 Treaty of Utrecht. Spain has disputed British sovereignty over the territory ever since. It made several attempts to retake it, most notably through a four-year siege from 1779. Gibraltar was made a 'crown colony' in 1830. It became an important British naval base, especially after the opening of the Suez Canal in 1869, and the naval docks became the mainstay of the economy.

In the 1960s the Spanish government stepped up its demands for the 'decolonization' of Gibraltar. In a referendum in 1967 Gibraltarians voted overwhelmingly in favour of continued British sovereignty.

A new constitution adopted in 1969 gave the territory wide-ranging internal self-government. Spain responded by closing the border. Spain and the United Kingdom signed a cooperation agreement on Gibraltar in November 1984, and the border was reopened the following February. The closure of the naval dock-yards and the reduction of the British military presence in 1984 brought extensive economic disruption. (Revenue from British forces had accounted for around three-quarters of the territory's income.) The centre-right Gibraltar Labour Party - Association for the Advancement of Civil Rights (GLP-AACR) held power from 1969–88, under Joshua Hassan as chief minister until his retirement in December 1987. The Gibraltar Socialist Labour Party (GSLP), led by Joe Bossano, won the March 1988 and January 1992 elections on a platform of greater 'self-determination' for Gibraltar, particularly in the economic sphere.

See also GIBRALTAR QUESTION *and entries on specific institutions, organizations, parties, people, terms etc.*

Gibraltar Council Gibraltarian advisory body. The Council has nine members: the deputy governor, the commander of the armed forces, the financial and development secretary and the chief minister ex officio, and five elected members of the House of Assembly (= parliament). Its role is influential in matters relating to external affairs, defence and internal security, for which the governor, the representative of the head of state (the British sovereign), is nominally responsible. S/he usually acts on the Council's advice.

Gibraltar question Dispute between Spain and the United Kingdom over the status of Gibraltar, an internally self-governing British dependency. Strategically located on the southern tip of Spain, Gibraltar was occupied by a combined British and Dutch force in 1704 and ceded to the United Kingdom under the Treaty of Utrecht in 1713. Spain has disputed British sovereignty over the territory ever since. It raised the issue with the United Nations Committee on Decolonization in 1963. At the UN's behest the two governments held several rounds of negotiations between 1966 and 1968. In a referendum in 1967 Gibraltarians voted overwhelmingly to remain British subjects. After the adoption in 1969 of a new constitution granting full internal autonomy to the territory and reaffirming the link with the United Kingdom, the Spanish government closed the border. Formal negotiations between the Spanish and British governments resumed in 1974, but made little progress until the restoration of democratic rule in Spain in the late 1970s. At a meeting in April 1980 both sides stressed their determination to resolve the Gibraltar question in a spirit of friendship. An agreement concluded in Brussels in November 1984 provided in effect for the normalization of relations between Gibraltar and Spain at a practical level, e.g. by allowing free movement of goods and people. It also contained, for the first time, a British undertaking to discuss the issue of sovereignty. (The Brussels agreement removed a major obstacle to Spain's subsequent entry to the then European Community, EC.) Spain reopened the border in February 1985. Since then bilateral negotiations, with the intermittent involvement of the Gibraltar government, have led to several cooperation agreements on practical issues. But the positions on sovereignty remain unchanged. All political parties in Gibraltar reject the Spanish claim on the territory.

Gibraltar Social Democrats (GSD) Gibraltarian political party. Founded in 1989, the GSD became the main opposition party after the January 1992 election, when it gained 20.2% of the vote and 7/15 seats. It takes a more conciliatory line on relations with Spain than its main rival, the Gibraltar Socialist Labour Party (GSLP). The leader is Peter Caruana.

Gibraltar Socialist Labour Party (GSLP) Gibraltarian political party. Founded in 1976, the GSLP is a mainstream left-wing party. It advocates 'self-determination' for Gibraltar, i.e. greater autonomy from the United Kingdom and possibly eventual independence, and is strongly opposed to Spain's claim of sovereignty over the territory. It became the main opposition party in 1984 and was elected to power in 1988. At the January 1992 election it gained 73.1% of the vote and 8/15 seats. The leader is Joe Bossano.

GIGN *See* INTERVENTION GROUP OF THE NATIONAL GENDARMERIE.

GIP Abbreviation for the POUND, the Gibraltarian currency, used in banking etc.

Gipsies Ethnic group in Europe, also known as Roma or Romanies (their self-description, increasingly also used by outsiders), Sinti, Manush, Manouches, Gitanos, Gitans, Kalderash, Travellers etc. The Gipsies are traditionally a nomadic or itinerant people. Their ancestors left northern India in several migrations, probably from the 10th century but perhaps earlier, and reached Europe in the 14th century. (The English term 'Gipsy' reflects the mistaken medieval belief that they came from Egypt; in France they were originally called 'Bohemians'.) They had spread throughout the continent by the 16th century and some emigrated to the Americas and Australia in the 19th. Today the Gipsies number around 5 million in Europe, equivalent to around 1% of the continent's total population (excluding Russia and the other members of the Commonwealth of Independent States and Turkey). The largest communities are in Romania (750,000, 3.3% of the total population), Hungary (600,000, 5.8%), Spain (500,000, 1.3%), Bulgaria (450,000, 5.3%), Slovakia (400,000, 7.6%), Czech Republic (400,000, 3.9%), Yugoslavia (375,000, 3.7%), France (275,000, 0.5%), Bosnia-Herzegovina (175,000, 4.0%), Croatia (175,000, 3.7%), Portugal (100,000, 1.0%), Greece (90,000, 0.9%), Germany (90,000), Italy (80,000), Macedonia (80,000, 3.7%), Poland (70,000), Albania (60,000, 1.7%) and the United Kingdom (50,000). The majority thus lives in the southeastern quarter of the continent. (Special factors such as their migratory lifestyle, marginal social position, reluctance to declare themselves and official reluctance to recognize them as a distinct group make it very difficult to estimate Gipsy populations. The above figures seek to take account of these problems.)

Although Gipsies speak the languages and have nominally adopted the religions of the countries they live in, they have a strong identity and have to a large extent retained their customs, institutions and language, Romany. And although many are now settled, they remain largely outside established economic and social structures and earn a living as musicians, entertainers, car mechanics, scrap-metal dealers, horsedealers, coppersmiths, sievemakers etc (the latter three are traditional occupations). The Gipsies' standard of living is generally low. The distinctive way of life means that Gipsy society is highly atomized and centred on the extended family [vitsa] and bands headed by a chieftain [voivode], who is elected for life. The Gipsy 'kings' and 'emperors' may have large followings but their authority is not institutionalized. There are also larger divisions, in particular the three traditional tribal groups of Kalderash, Gitanos and Sinti or Manush, but they have little political significance. The Gipsies' main representative organizations are the International Romany Union, active worldwide, and the European Romany Parliament (EUROM), set up in 1992 by 22 organizations from 10 European countries.

Over the centuries the Gipsies, a marginal and distinctive minority everywhere they travelled, suffered widespread prejudice, harassment, discrimination and persecution. During the Second World War around 500,000 were killed as part of a programme of genocide perpetrated by Germany's nazi regime. In Eastern Europe the communist regimes sought to settle Gipsies and force their assimilation, while in Western Europe some attempts were made to reduce institutional discrimination (e.g. on the basis of recommendations by the Council of Europe). Unusually, in 1981 Gipsies were officially recognized as a 'nationality' in former Yugoslavia, at the time Europe's most ethnically diverse country with the largest Gipsy community. This gave them better access to educational facilities and the media in particular and sparked an international emancipation movement. Since the collapse of the communist regimes in 1989 Gipsies have encountered more open hostility, but they have also become more vociferous in demanding an end to discrimination and respect for their culture.

Giraud, Michel (1929–) French businessman and politician. He worked as a senior manager and director of several companies in the wood-processing industry from 1951. A member of the right-wing Rally for the Republic (RPR), he has been leader of the Île-de-France regional council since 1976, a senator from 1977–88 and a member of the National Assembly since 1988. He was appointed minister of labour, employment and vocational training in the centre-right administration which took office in March 1993.

GIS *See* SPECIAL INTERVENTION GROUP.

Giscard d'Estaing, Valéry (1926–) French politician. Elected to parliament in 1956, he was minister of economy and finance from 1962–66 and 1969–74 in various centre-right governments. In 1966 he co-founded and became leader of the centre-right National Federation of Independent Republicans (FNRI), now the Republican Party (PR). He was elected president of the republic in 1974, defeating François Mitterrand, but lost to him in 1981. He returned to prominence in the late 1980s. In July 1988 he became leader of the Union for French Democracy (UDF), a centre-right alliance including the PR. He was also elected president of the Auvergne regional council in April 1992 and was a member of the European Parliament from 1989–93.

Gitanos (sing. Gitano/Gitana) and **Gitans** (sing. Gitan/e) Alternative names for GIPSIES or Romanies, widely used in Spain and France respectively. The Gitanos are one of the traditional major regional and occupational subdivisions among Gipsies.

G£ Abbreviation for the POUND, the Gibraltarian currency.

G£ Abbreviation for the POUND, the Guernsey currency.

Gladio affair Political scandal in Italy surrounding the activities of a secret paramilitary force codenamed Gladio. Operated by the secret services and numbering up to 1,000 people, Gladio – from the Latin for 'sword' – was set up in 1956 with the aim of organizing internal armed resistance in the event of an invasion by Warsaw Pact forces or a communist takeover. It was part of a network of similar groups set up in all the member states of the North Atlantic Treaty Organization (NATO) around this time, the height of the 'cold war' between East and West. In July 1990 a magistrate accidentally discovered its records in the archives of the Information and Military Security Service (SISMI), one of the state intelligence agencies. A parliamentary report published in January 1992 described Gladio as an illegal 'armed band' and confirmed that it had overstepped its brief in the 1970s by becoming involved in campaigns to discredit left-wing politicians and, far more seriously, by teaming up with far-right extremists to carry out a series of bombings and other attacks as part of a 'strategy of tension' aimed at destabilizing the state. Gladio was formally disbanded in November 1990, but one offshoot, the Scorpion Group [Gruppo Scorpione], was uncovered in 1992. *See also* HIDDEN GOVERNMENT.

GLEI *See* GREENS (Luxemburg).

Gligorov, Kiro (1917–) Macedonian economist, academic and politician. He joined the League of Communists in 1944. He lectured at Belgrade University in the 1950s. He then held a range of party and government posts at federal Yugoslav level, notably minister of economic affairs (1955–62) and finance (1962–67), deputy prime minister (1967–69) and president of the Federal Assembly (1974–78). During the 1980s he concentrated on academic studies. In January 1991 he was elected president of Macedonia (then still part of Yugoslavia). Nominally above party politics, he remains close to the Social Democratic Alliance (SDSM), the successor to the League of Communists.

Glistrup, Mogens (1926–) Danish lawyer and politician. A specialist on income-tax law, he founded the right-wing populist Progress Party (FP) in 1972. Under his leadership its main platform was the abolition of income tax. He was convicted of tax fraud in 1983 and expelled from parliament. After his release in 1985 he was unable to retain the party leadership and was eventually expelled. He founded the Growth Party (TP) in November 1990.

GNA *See* GRAND NATIONAL ASSEMBLY OF TURKEY.

Gnutti, Vito (1939–) Italian chemical engineer, businessman and politician. He was managing director of a chemical company in his native Brescia until he entered politics. Elected to parliament for the federalist Northern League (Lega Nord) in 1992, he was appointed industry minister in the right-wing coalition formed in May 1994.

Go Italy *See* COME ON ITALY.

God Save The Queen National anthem of the United Kingdom. The tune is of uncertain origin, and the words were frequently altered after the song gained currency in the early 18th century. It was first used for a royal occasion in 1745.

Godal, Bjørn Tore (1945–) Norwegian politician. He was head of the Norwegian Labour Party (DNA) research department from 1973–80 and chairman of the Oslo Labour Party from 1982–90. Elected to parliament in 1989, he was appointed minister of trade and shipping in September 1992. He became foreign minister in January 1994.

Godmanis, Ivars (1951–) Latvian physicist, academic and politician. He worked at the Physics Institute of the Latvian Academy of Sciences from 1973–86 and lectured at the University of Latvia from 1986–90. He joined the reformist and eventually pro-independence People's Front (LTF) in 1988, when Latvia was still part of the Soviet Union. When the LTF won the multiparty election in March 1990, he was appointed prime minister in May. The movement fragmented in 1992. He led the rump LTF in the June 1993 election, but it failed to win any seats. He then resigned as prime minister.

Goebbels, Robert (1944–) Luxemburg journalist and politician. He was secretary of the Luxemburg Socialist Workers' Party (LSAP) parliamentary group from 1974–84 and also the party's general secretary from 1980–85. Elected to parliament in 1984, he became minister of the economy, foreign trade, transport and public works in June 1989, and minister of the economy, public works and energy in July 1994.

Gol, Jean (1941–) Belgian lawyer, lecturer and politician. He practised law and held several academic posts at Liège University until his election to parliament in 1971 for the right-wing Liberal Reform Party (PRL) of Wallonia. He was party leader from 1979–81 and a deputy prime minister and minister of justice and institutional reform from 1981–88. In January 1992 he was again elected party leader.

Goldsmith, James or **Jimmy** (1933–) British and French businessman and politician. Having built up a pharmaceuticals business in France, he acquired a wide range of industrial enterprises in France, the United Kingdom and the United States in the 1970s and 80s, in particular in the retailing, media and financial sectors. He sold most of these assets in 1987. Strongly opposed to centralizing or 'federalist' tendencies within the European Union (EU), in particular the Maastricht Treaty, he co-founded the Europe of Nations movement in April 1994. He was elected to the European Parliament in June on the Another Europe (L'Autre Europe) list in France. In July he was elected leader of the Europe of Nations (EN) parliamentary group.

Gölhan, Mehmet (1929–) Turkish civil engineer, civil servant and politician. He worked in the private sector and then served as director of the Road, Water and Electricity Authority (YSE) and the Turkish Petroleum Corporation (TPAO). He was elected to parliament for the centre-right True Path Party (DYP) in 1987 and was appointed defence minister in November 1993.

Gómez Navarro, Javier (1945–) Spanish businessman, civil servant and politician. He has worked in the tourism, sports, cultural and publishing sectors. From 1987–93 he was president of the Sports Council, a post of junior ministerial rank. In July 1993 he was appointed minister of trade and tourism in the minority government formed by the Spanish

Socialist Workers' Party (PSOE). He is not a member of the party.

Göncz, Árpád (1922–) Hungarian lawyer, writer, translator and politician. An opponent of communist rule, he was imprisoned from 1956–62 for his political views and then worked as a translator and playwright. Following political liberalization he was elected president of the Association of Hungarian Writers in 1989 and elected to parliament for the Alliance of Free Democrats (SzDSz) at the March/April 1990 election. With the support of other parties he was elected interim president in May and confirmed as president (a largely non-executive post) the following August.

González Márquez, Felipe (1942–) Spanish lawyer and politician. In the 1960s he worked as a labour lawyer in his native Andalusia. He joined the then illegal Spanish Socialist Workers' Party (PSOE) in 1964. The leading spokesman of a new generation of home-based activists, he was elected party leader in October 1974. When the PSOE was legalized in 1977 he effectively became the leader of the opposition. He became prime minister in December 1982 following the party's election victory two months earlier. Returned to office in 1986, 1989 and 1993, he has become the longest-serving prime minister in modern Spanish history and the country's dominant political figure.

Good Government Alliance [Polo del Buon Governo] Italian political organization. This is the name under which the right-wing Come On Italy (Forza Italia) and the far-right National Alliance (AN, based on the Italian Social Movement, MSI) have fought regional and local elections in southern Italy since the formation in January 1994 of the FREEDOM ALLIANCE, which also included the Northern League (Lega Nord).

Goodman International affair *See* BEEF INDUSTRY AFFAIR.

Gorbunov, Anatoly *See* GORBUNOVS, ANATOLIJS.

Gorbunovs, Anatolijs (1942–) Latvian politician. Trained as a construction engineer, he held a number of senior posts in

the Latvian Communist Party (LKP) from 1974. In 1988 he was elected chairman of the republic's parliament. He subsequently expressed support for Latvian independence while remaining a member of the LKP, and after the multiparty election in 1990 he was reelected president of parliament with the support of the pro-independence People's Front (LTF). When Latvia regained its independence following the abortive Soviet coup in August 1991, he effectively became head of state. In February 1993 he was elected leader of the Latvian Way (LC), a new centre-right party. After the party came first in the election in June, he was also elected president of the Saeima (= parliament) the following month.

Goria, Giovanni (1943–94) Italian economist, banker and politician. He was elected to parliament for the Christian Democratic Party (DC) in 1976. He was treasury minister in four governments from 1982–87. In 1987 President Cossiga asked him to form a government, and he became Italy's youngest ever prime minister. His five-party coalition fell the following March. He returned to the government as agriculture minister in 1991 and became finance minister in June 1992. He resigned in February 1993 after being accused of false accounting in connection with the collapse of a savings bank in his native Asti. He was cleared of this charge, but was put on trial on other bribery charges in February 1994. He died of a lung tumour in May.

Gošev, Tuše (1951–) Macedonian lawyer and politician. He worked for a trade organization in the 1980s. A member of the League of Communists and its successor, the Social Democratic Alliance (SDSM), he was appointed justice minister in September 1992.

governing mayor [Regierender Bürgermeister] Head of government in Berlin, a federal state of Germany. Since Berlin is a city state, its government structure combines the functions of a municipality and a state.

government councillor [Regierungsrat, pl. Regierungsräte] Member or minister of the Liechtenstein government.

governo istituzionale and **governo tecnico**
See INSTITUTIONAL GOVERNMENT.

governor Shorthand for provincial governor [Landeshaupt], the head of government in a federal province of Austria.

governor Senior officer of state in Gibraltar. Appointed by the British crown, i.e. the government, the governor is the personal representative of the sovereign and the official channel of communication between the legislature and the British government. Nominally responsible for defence, foreign affairs and other matters not delegated to the territory's government, s/he generally follows the recommendations of the advisory Gibraltar Council in these matters.

GPS *See* GREEN PARTY OF SWITZERLAND.

GPV *See* REFORMED POLITICAL ASSOCIATION.

GR Abbreviation for Greece, used for international vehicle registrations, postal addresses etc.

Grafschaft (pl. -en) German administrative division, usually translated as 'county'. In some parts of the country, *Grafschaft* is the name given to the intermediate-level tier between the state [Land] and the municipality known elsewhere as the LANDKREIS.

Grand and General Council [Consiglio Grande e Generale] Parliament of San Marino. The Council consists of 60 members elected for a five-year term by proportional representation. It elects the Congress of State (= government) and also elects two of its members as captains-regent, who jointly act as heads of state and government for a six-month term.

grand coalition [grosse Koalition] In Germany, a coalition of the Christian Democratic Union (CDU) and Social Democratic Party (SPD), the two largest parties at federal level and in all the states. Such a coalition held power at federal level from 1966–69, and others have been formed at state level. The term is also used in neighbouring Austria, where the Social Democratic Party (SPÖ) and the Austrian People's Party (ÖVP) have shared power from 1945–66 and since 1986.

Grand Duchy, the Shorthand for Luxemburg. The country has been a grand duchy since 1815.

Grand National Assembly [Veliko Narodno Sobranie] Bulgarian legislative body. The 400-member Grand National Assembly has the sole right to adopt a new constitution and amend key provisions of the existing constitution. It is elected specifically and only for these purposes. Decisions require a two-thirds majority. Less important constitutional amendments may be passed by a three-quarters majority of the legislature, the National Assembly, which also decides on the convening of a Grand National Assembly.

Grand National Assembly of Turkey [Türkiye Büyük Millet Meclisi] (TBMM) Parliament of Turkey. The TBMM – sometimes abbreviated in English as GNA or TGNA – has 450 members elected for a five-year term by proportional representation, with additional seats awarded to the party winning the largest number of votes. Parties must obtain 7% of the popular vote to qualify for representation.

grands corps In France, an informal collective name for high-ranking and influential civil servants who often play a key role in the formulation of government policy and administer major government agencies.

Granić, Mate (1947–) Croatian doctor and politician. A specialist in diabetes and endocrinology, he was attached to several medical institutions and the School of Medicine in Zagreb until he entered politics. A member of the right-wing Croatian Democratic Union (HDZ), he was appointed a deputy prime minister in August 1991 and was also given the foreign-affairs portfolio in June 1993.

GRAPO *See* FIRST OF OCTOBER ANTI-FASCIST RESISTANCE GROUP.

Gray/gray ... *See* GREY/GREY ....

GRD Abbreviation for the drachmí or DRACHMA, the Greek currency, used in banking etc.

Great Britain or **Britain** Shorthand for the United Kingdom of Great Britain and Northern Ireland. Geographically the name refers to the largest of the British Isles. It was adopted as a political name on the union of England and Scotland in 1707, and properly refers to the three countries on the island, England, Scotland and Wales, and does not include Northern Ireland. It is often used to refer to the whole of the United Kingdom. The short form 'Britain' is widely used in the English-speaking world but not elsewhere. *See also* UNITED KINGDOM.

Great Britain and Northern Ireland
Country in western Europe, often referred to as the United Kingdom (the official name used in diplomatic circles), Great Britain or Britain, and informally (especially elsewhere in Europe) as England.

Official data. Name: United Kingdom of Great Britain and Northern Ireland; capital: London; form of government: parliamentary monarchy; head of state: king/queen; head of government: prime minister; flag: blue with red, white diagonal and red diagonal crosses superimposed; national holiday: Queen's Official Birthday (second Saturday in June); language: English; religion: Anglicanism (Church of England) in England, Presbyterianism (Church of Scotland) in Scotland; currency: pound sterling (£) = 100 pence; abbreviations: GB or UK.

Geography. The United Kingdom consists of the island of Great Britain (comprising England, Wales and Scotland), the northeastern quarter of the island of Ireland (Northern Ireland) and around 4,000 smaller islands. It is bordered by the North Sea to the north and east, the Channel to the south, and the Atlantic Ocean and Irish Sea to the west. The only land border is with the Republic of Ireland. Much of the north, west and southwest is hilly or mountainous, and most of the east and southeast consists of level or rolling plains. The Scottish Highlands are mountains and uplands; central Scotland is low-lying; southern Scotland and northern England are also mostly uplands, dominated by the Pennine Mountains, which extend north-south down the upper 'spine' of England; Wales is mostly hilly or mountainous; central and southeastern England is predominantly low-lying with some hill ranges; the southwest has low mountains; Northern Ireland consists of several hill and low mountain ranges surrounding a wide basin centred on Lough Neagh, the country's largest lake. Some 29% of the land is arable, another 48% is covered by pastures and 9% is forested. The main rivers are the Severn, Trent, Thames and Clyde. The climate is temperate marine, with mild summers and cool winters; temperatures are lower in the north; rainfall is moderate in the east, heavy in the west and north.

Demography. The United Kingdom has a population of 58,080,000. Population density is 241 per sq km (land area). Only the Scottish Highlands, central Wales and the uplands of northern England and southern Scotland are relatively sparsely populated. Some 92% of the people live in urban areas, around two-fifths in the eight largest conurbations, and a fifth in Greater London. The main conurbations are: Greater London (population 11.1 million, city 6.4 million), West Midlands, centred on Birmingham and Coventry (3.2 million), Greater Manchester (2.8 million), Strathclyde, centred on Glasgow (1.8 million), West Yorkshire, centred on Leeds and Bradford (1.5 million), Merseyside, centred on Liverpool (1.5 million), Tyne and Wear, centred on Newcastle on Tyne and Sunderland (1.3 million), and South Yorkshire, centred on Sheffield (1.2 million). Other major cities are Nottingham, Edinburgh, Bristol, Belfast, Cardiff, Leicester, Kingston upon Hull (Hull), Stoke on Trent, Middlesbrough, Southampton, Portsmouth, Plymouth and Swansea. Some 97.8% of the population are British or Commonwealth citizens (the latter have broadly speaking the same political and social rights as British citizens). In ethnic terms 73.1% of the population is English, 9.1% Scottish, 4.8% Welsh, 3.2% Northern Irish (1.8% Protestant, 1.4% Catholic), 3.0% South Asian and 1.1% Caribbean; there are also substantial numbers of Greek and Turkish Cypriots, Africans and Chinese. In total around 3.2 million people have their roots in the overseas dependencies, former colonies or Commonwealth countries.

Foreign nationals from outside the Commonwealth account for 2.2% of the population, and include citizens of Ireland (1.0% of the total), Germany, the United States, Italy, Poland, South Africa and Turkey. The main language is English; Welsh is also spoken by around 520,000 people (around a fifth of the population in Wales) and Gaelic by 65,000 people in northwestern Scotland; there are also substantial numbers of Punjabi, Urdu, Hindi, Bengali and Chinese speakers. In religious terms 56.8% of the population is nominally Anglican, 17.0% Protestant (including 7.0% Presbyterian, 4.3% Methodist and 1.4% Baptist), 13.1% Roman Catholic, 1.5% Muslim, 0.7% Hindu, 0.7% Sikh and 0.6% Jewish; most of the remainder is not religious.

Sociography. The United Kingdom scores 0.919 on the United Nations human development index (HDI), ranking 10th in the world and sixth among 32 European countries. There are 16 doctors and 62 hospital beds for every 10,000 people. Education is compulsory between the ages of five and 16. There is one teacher for every 19 students. Enrolment is 79% at the secondary level and 24% at the tertiary level. The literacy rate is virtually 100%. Real annual income per head (in terms of purchasing power) is US$ 16,340.

Infrastructure and communications. The United Kingdom has a highly developed transport and communications network. There are 356,520 km of paved roads and 19.7 million passenger cars (343 per 1,000 people), 18,470 km of railways and 2,291 km of navigable waterways. The main ports are London, Hartlepool/Tees, Grimsby/Immingham, Newcastle/Tyne, Southampton, Liverpool, Medway, Felixstowe, Glasgow, Manchester, Dover and Belfast. The main airports are at London (Heathrow and Gatwick, the former the busiest in Europe), Manchester, Glasgow and Birmingham, and there are 51 other airports with scheduled services. There are 99 daily newspapers, with a combined circulation of 22.3 million (388 per 1,000 people). There are 57.5 million radio receivers, 24.8 million television sets and around 33 million telephones in use (respectively 999, 431 and 573 per 1,000 people).

Economic structure. The British economy is highly developed, diversified and trade-oriented. It is the fourth-largest economy in Europe and the sixth-largest in the world as well as the world's fifth-largest trading power. It is based on engineering and other manufacturing, trade, finance and other services, and mining (offshore oil and natural gas). After a period of sustained growth from 1982–89 (averaging 3.2% per year), economic performance in the 1990s has been marked by a 3% contraction of GDP in 1991–92 and a resumption of growth in 1993, substantial current-account deficits (averaging 2% per year), falling inflation (from around 9% to below 2%) and high unemployment (around 10%).

Services contribute 65% of GDP, industry contributes 33% (manufacturing 22%, mining 2%), and agriculture, forestry and fisheries 2%. Some 19% of the labour force is employed in trade, 18% in manufacturing, 11% in finance and 6% in construction. The main crops grown are cereals (wheat, barley), potatoes, sugarbeets and oilseeds; other important agricultural activities are dairy farming (milk, cheese, butter, eggs), livestock raising (cattle, sheep for meat and wool, pigs) and horticulture (fruit and vegetables). The main mineral resources are oil and natural gas (in the North Sea), coal, limestone and clay; the mining industry is by far the largest in Europe and the sixth-largest in the world. The main industries are engineering (esp. industrial machinery, cars), electrical goods and electronics; other important branches are food processing, textiles, chemicals, petrochemicals, ceramics, building materials, printing, iron and steel and other metalworking, textiles, wood processing and armaments. Banking, insurance and other financial services, trade and tourism are important sources of foreign exchange. The main energy sources are fossil fuels and nuclear power; in net terms the United Kingdom is virtually self-sufficient in energy. The main exports are industrial machinery (14% of the total), chemicals (13%), transport equipment 12% (cars etc 7%), oil and oil products (7%), foodstuffs (7%), office equipment (6%), electrical equipment (5%), textiles and clothing, iron and steel and scientific instruments; machinery and transport equipment account for 42% of the total, basic manufactures for 15% and chemicals for 13%. The main imports are machinery and transport equipment, basic manufactures, foodstuffs and fuels. The main trading partners are: exports: Germany (14%), France (11%), United States (11%), Netherlands (8%), Italy (6%), Belgium and Luxemburg (6%), Ireland (5%), Spain, Sweden, Japan, Switzerland; imports: Germany (15%), United States (11%), France (10%), Netherlands (8%), Japan (6%), Italy (5%), Belgium and Luxemburg (5%), Ireland, Norway, Switzerland, Sweden; over half of all trade is with other European Union (EU) countries. Net invisible earnings (income from financial and other services, tourism receipts) account for 0.9% of GNP.

The Bank of England is the central bank. The main employers' associations are the Confederation of British Industry (CBI) and the Institute of Directors (IoD); the main labour organization is the Trades' Union Congress (TUC).

Political structure. The United Kingdom is a parliamentary monarchy on the basis of constitutional practice, statute law and common law; there is no written constitution. It consists of England, Wales [Cymru in Welsh] and Scotland (collectively called Great Britain) and Northern Ireland. Executive power is formally vested in the king/queen but is exercised by the prime minister and the Cabinet. Legislative power is vested in the bicameral Parliament, composed of the 651-member House of Commons elected for a five-year term by a system of majority voting, and the House of Lords of around 1,200 hereditary, appointed and ex-officio members. All citizens over the age of 18 are entitled to vote; resident Commonwealth and Irish citizens normally also have voting rights. Judicial power is ultimately vested in the House of Lords, specifically its members who are lords of appeal in ordinary,

commonly known as law lords; Scotland and Northern Ireland have separate legal structures. Administratively England is divided into 39 counties, subdivided into districts, and seven metropolitan counties (which have no administrative or political functions), subdivided into metropolitan districts or boroughs; the eight standard regions have no political functions; Wales is divided into eight counties, subdivided into districts; Scotland is divided into nine regions, subdivided into districts, and three island areas; Northern Ireland is divided into 26 districts, the historical six counties having no administrative or political functions;

The main national political parties are the Conservative Party, Labour Party and Liberal Democrats. The main regional parties are the Scottish National Party (SNP), Plaid Cymru (PC) in Wales, and the Ulster Unionist Party (UUP), Social Democratic and Labour Party (SDLP), Ulster Democratic Unionist Party (DUP), Sinn Féin, Alliance Party and Ulster Popular Unionist Party (PUP) in Northern Ireland. At the general election in April 1992 the Conservatives gained 41.9% of the vote and 336/651 seats, Labour 34.4% and 271 seats, the Liberal Democrats 17.9% and 20 seats, the UUP nine seats, the SDLP and Plaid Cymru four seats each, the SNP and DUP three seats each, the PUP one seat, and Sinn Féin and Alliance Party no seats. The government is formed by the Conservatives, with John Major as prime minister. Other senior ministers are Douglas Hurd (foreign and Commonwealth affairs), Kenneth Clarke (chancellor of the exchequer = finance and economy), Michael Howard (home affairs), Michael Heseltine (trade and industry), Malcolm Rifkind (defence), James Mackay (Lord Mackay) (lord chancellor = justice), John Gummer (environment, incl. local government), Peter Lilley (social security) and Jonathan Aitken (chief secretary to the Treasury = finance). The head of state is Queen Elizabeth II, who succeeded to the throne in February 1952; the heir is Prince Charles.

The United Kingdom has a number of

overseas dependencies: Gibraltar, Guernsey, Jersey and Man in Europe (*see separate entries*); the British Indian Ocean Territory and Hongkong in Asia (the latter is due to be returned to Chinese sovereignty in 1997); the Pitcairn Islands in the Pacific; Anguilla, Bermuda, British Virgin Islands, Cayman Islands, Montserrat, and the Turks and Caicos Islands in the Caribbean; and the Falkland Islands, Saint Helena, and South Georgia and South Sandwich Islands in the South Atlantic. All but the smallest have a wide measure of internal self-government, with the British government taking responsibility for defence and foreign affairs. The United Kingdom also lays claim to part of Antarctica.

Security and international affiliations. The British armed forces number 274,800 (strategic nuclear forces 1,900, army 134,600, navy 57,400, airforce 80,900); they are due to be reduced to 241,000. There is no conscription. Defence spending is equivalent to 3.3% of GDP, among the highest rates in Europe. A substantial number of British troops are stationed abroad, including around 10,000 in the overseas dependencies, 53,600 in Germany (due to be reduced to around 25,000), 4,100 in Cyprus, 1,500 in Belize, and around 3,500 on United Nations assignments. Some 16,800 American troops are stationed in the United Kingdom.

The United Kingdom is a member of the Conference on Security and Cooperation in Europe (CSCE), Council of Europe, European Economic Area (EEA), European Union (EU), North Atlantic Treaty Organization (NATO) and Western European Union (WEU), as well the Commonwealth, Group of Seven (G-7), Organization for Economic Cooperation and Development (OECD) and United Nations and its specialized agencies.

History. When the Romans first invaded Great Britain in the 1st century BC, it was divided into a number of Celtic states. The Romans returned in AD 43 and conquered the whole island except the north (modern Scotland). Over the next four centuries the population in the southern districts of Britannia province became thoroughly romanized. Christianity became a significant force in the 4th century. Threats to Roman rule in Gaul (modern France) led to the gradual withdrawal of Roman troops between 383 and 410. As part of Europe-wide migrations, Germanic Saxons, Angles and Jutes from across the North Sea settled in large numbers from the mid 5th century onwards and drove the romanized Celtic Britons westward. (Many emigrated across the Channel to Brittany.) By the end of the 6th century all of Britain except Wales, Cornwall and Scotland was under Anglo-Saxon control. Five kingdoms became dominant in the 7th and 8th centuries: Northumbria, Mercia, Wessex, East Anglia and Kent. The Anglo-Saxons converted to Christianity around this time. In the 8th and 9th centuries the Vikings raided the coastal areas. Most of Scotland was united in 843 when Kenneth MacAlpin became king of the Scots and Picts. A Danish Viking army invaded England in 865 and conquered all the kingdoms except Wessex. Under King Alfred of Wessex (871–99) and his successors the country was divided into Wessex and Danish spheres of influence, with the former controlling the southwestern half. King Edward the Elder (899–924) was the first to call himself king of England. Under Canute (Knut) (1016–35) Danish rule was briefly accepted throughout England. All of Scotland was united under Malcolm II (1005–34). In 1066 an army led by William of Normandy invaded England and was victorious at the Battle of Hastings.

Under William I (1066–87) and his successors the Normans consolidated the feudal system and established a strong central government. Under Henry II (1154–89) the English crown gained control over vast areas of France through marriage and the first incursions into Ireland began. In 1215 King John was forced to sign the Magna Carta, which granted a number of privileges to the barons and also established several major principles of law (such as the right to a fair trial). The royal faction was victorious in a short civil war in 1264–65, but some of the reforms demanded by the baronial faction, including the regular summoning of parliaments, were nevertheless implemented. In 1267 the three Welsh kingdoms united under Llywelyn ap Gruffydd in an attempt to resist English encroachment, but they were decisively defeated in 1284. Scotland, which had come under English influence in the 11th century, regained its independence after the Battle of Bannockburn in 1314. During the Hundred Years' War (1337–1453) England's extensive possessions in France (nominally fiefs held by the English king from the French king) were eventually lost. In 1349–50 between a third and a half of the population died during the Europe-wide plague epidemic known as the 'black death'. A major peasants' revolt was suppressed in 1381. The 15th century was marked by dynastic struggles, culminating in the Wars of the Roses (named after the emblems of the rival houses). The Tudor period (1485–1603) saw major administrative, economic, social and cultural changes. A commercial wool-processing industry emerged at this time, laying the foundation for future economic expansion. King Henry VIII (1509–47) broke with the Roman Catholic Church and established the Church of England as the state church. Wales was formally incorporated into the kingdom in 1536. Around this time English rule was also consolidated in Ireland, although there were several major uprisings until the end of the 17th century. Under Elizabeth I (1558–1603) and her successors England became a major maritime, commercial and colonial power, successfully competing for influence with Spain and France in Europe and above all in North America and the Caribbean. On the death of Elizabeth (who had remained unmarried and childless) King James VI of Scotland ascended to the English throne as James I, thus uniting the two countries' crowns. An attempt by King Charles I (1625–49) in 1629 to rule without Parliament eventually led to a four-year civil war between royalists and parliamentarians. The latter were victorious in 1646, Charles was executed

in 1649, the monarchy was abolished and a 'commonwealth' or republic was proclaimed. Oliver Cromwell, the commander of the army and already the effective ruler, was appointed 'lord protector' in 1653. Two years after his death in 1658 the monarchy was restored but Parliament retained its powers. King James II (1685–88) tried to restore royal and Catholic domination, but was forced into exile. Parliament offered the crown to James's daughter Mary and her husband, William of Orange. The Bill of Rights adopted in 1689 confirmed the crown's subordination to Parliament. A major uprising against English rule in Ireland, led by James II, was defeated in 1690/91. Jacobite uprisings continued in Scotland until 1745. In 1707 the English and Scottish parliaments agreed to the union of the two countries as the United Kingdom of Great Britain. On the death of Queen Anne in 1714 the throne passed to a German prince, George Louis of Hannover, who became King George I. The ensuing period saw major constitutional and political developments which were to have a lasting impact not just on Britain but also, as its colonial empire expanded and the 'Westminster model' was eventually adopted in the post-colonial states, in many parts of the world. The limited monarchy, the institution of cabinet government and the notion of ministerial accountability to Parliament emerged at this time as important elements of constitutional government. The latter half of the 18th century was dominated by economic problems at home (principally due to the large national debt), the expansion of the colonial empire but the loss of most of the North American colonies, and a rebellion against British rule in Ireland (1798). In 1801 Ireland was formally incorporated into the United Kingdom. During the French Revolutionary and Napoleonic Wars (1792–1815) Britain was a leading member of the anti-French alliances.

From the 1730s until the 1860s the country experienced a revolution which transformed a largely agricultural economy into an industrial one – the world's first. The transformation began with improvements in agriculture that produced a food surplus large enough to support a substantial urban population, the partial mechanization of the textile industry, the development of mining technology and improvements in transport, and was accelerated by the development of the coal and iron industries, the use of the steam engine as a power source and (from the 1840s) the development of a railway network. The exploitation of new technological and entrepreneurial opportunities during the Industrial Revolution was made possible in large part through the rise of an urban merchant and manufacturing class and the willingness of the landowning class to invest in industrial and commercial ventures. Britain thus became the world's foremost technological, economic and commercial power, and the British Empire was hence the dominant world power, during the reign of Queen Victoria (1837–1901). Major reforms were implemented during this period. Electoral reform bills passed in 1832, 1867 and 1884 extended the franchise, the repeal in 1846 of the protectionist 'corn laws' reduced food prices, and new health and social laws sought to improve the condition of the working classes. Mass extra-parliamentary movements, such as 'chartism' in the 1840s, were important vehicles of radical and working-class political action throughout the 19th century. The main political parties were the Conservatives and Liberals, and the dominant leaders in the later Victorian period were Benjamin Disraeli and William Gladstone. The Liberals were in power from 1906–22, at the head of an all-party coalition after 1915. In part in response to the rise of organized labour and the Labour Party, a number of welfare measures (including state pensions and unemployment insurance) were introduced during this period. The powers of the (unelected) House of Lords were cut in 1911. Growing tension between the major powers, not least between Britain and Germany, led to the First World War (1914–18). Some 723,000 British and 200,000 Empire troops lost their lives during the fighting,

mainly in trench warfare in France and Belgium. The franchise was extended to all adult men in 1918 and to women in two stages in 1918 and 1928. In response to long-standing Irish demands for independence, growing political violence and determined opposition by most Irish Protestants to a change in the island's status, two separate Irish parliaments were established in 1920, one in the Protestant-majority north and one in the south. The south became independent as the Irish Free State in 1922, while Northern Ireland remained an internally self-governing part of the United Kingdom. In 1926 the British Commonwealth was established, in which Canada, Australia, New Zealand, South Africa and Newfoundland (which later joined Canada) became fully self-governing dominions equal in status to the United Kingdom. The 1920s and 30s were marked by relative political instability, with most elections failing to produce overall majorities for any of the major parties, Conservatives, Labour or Liberals. Britain was hard-hit by the worldwide economic depression of the 1930s. At the start of the Second World War (1939–45) an all-party coalition was formed and Winston Churchill became prime minister in 1940. Britain was the only major European country not to come under German occupation and played a key role in securing the eventual defeat of Germany and Japan. Some 375,000 British and Empire soldiers and around 90,000 civilians lost their lives during the fighting, and the country's cities suffered extensive bomb damage.

The Labour government elected in 1945 nationalized key industries and initiated a major programme of welfare legislation, creating in particular a 'national health service' in 1948 based on free treatment. In 1949 the United Kingdom became a founding member of the North Atlantic Treaty Organization (NATO). The dismantling of the country's worldwide colonial empire – a largely peaceful process – began with the independence of India and Pakistan in 1947 and continued into the 1970s. Nearly all the newly independent states joined the recast Commonwealth. In 1952 Britain became the world's third nuclear power (after the United States and the Soviet Union). The Conservatives held power for 13 years until 1964, under Harold Macmillan from 1956–63. The United Kingdom was a founding member of the European Free Trade Association (EFTA) in 1960. Applications for membership of the European Economic Community (EEC), now the European Union (EU), were vetoed by France in 1963 and 1967; another application was lodged in 1970 and the United Kingdom joined in 1973. Labour was in power from 1964–70 and 1974–79, with very small or no overall majorities except for 1966–70 and under Harold Wilson until 1976. The intervening Conservative administration was headed by Edward Heath. The 1960s Labour government introduced a number of social reforms. In 1969 troops were deployed in Northern Ireland to deal with intercommunal violence between Protestants and Catholics; direct rule from London was introduced in the province in 1972. The two elections in 1974 saw a revival of the Liberals' electoral fortunes. The economy grew steadily in the 1960s (albeit at a lower rate than its competitors), but low growth, inflation and balance-of-payments deficits became particular problems in the 1970s. In the 1980s Britain became a major producer of oil and natural gas, exploited from offshore fields in the North Sea.

The election of the Conservatives in May 1979 proved a watershed. Strongly committed to free-market policies, the new government under Margaret Thatcher embarked on a radical economic programme of privatization, deregulation, tax reform and trade-union reform (to curb the power of organized labour). Its policies caused a deep recession in 1980–81 and a trebling of unemployment, but also brought sharp rises in output and productivity later in the decade. The party was reelected with large majorities in June 1983 and June 1987, in part owing to a split within the Labour Party and to a military victory in the Falklands War (fought with Argentina over the Falkland Islands, a British dependency in the South Atlantic, in April–June 1982). Controversial reforms (of local taxation, healthcare etc) and above all the end of the economic boom eroded the government's support after 1988. Thatcher, the country's dominant politician of the 1980s, was replaced by John Major in November 1990. The Conservatives won the April 1992 election with a reduced majority; Labour made up more of the ground lost in 1983; and the Liberal Democrats, formed by the merger of the Liberals and the Social Democratic Party (SDP) in January 1988, confirmed their recovery after a collapse of support during the merger period. In September 1992 the government was forced to accept a sharp devaluation of the pound, which in turn allowed the economy to begin to pull out of recession. The Irish Republican Army (IRA), which since 1969 had waged a guerrilla war aimed at securing the withdrawal of British troops from Northern Ireland and the province's reunification with Ireland, declared a ceasefire in September 1994; the Protestant 'loyalist' paramilitary groups did so in October.

See also entries on specific institutions, organizations, parties, people, terms etc.

Greater Albania [Shqipëria e Madhë] Slogan used by those who advocate the incorporation of all territories with ethnic Albanian majorities into a single state. This would include, in addition to Albania itself, the neighbouring Kosovo region of Yugoslavia and the northwestern part of Macedonia.

Greater Croatia [Velika Hrvatska] Slogan used by those who advocate the restoration of the 'historical' borders of Croatia, i.e. as they existed when it was an independent state in the 11th century and in 1941–45. This would include, in addition to Croatia itself, all of Bosnia-Herzegovina, much of the Vojvodina province of Serbia and some parts of Slovenia. The claim is based on historical rather than ethnic criteria, since many of these territories, including parts of Croatia itself, have non-Croat majorities.

Greater Hungary [Nagy Magyarország] Slogan used by those who advocate the return to Hungary of all areas in neighbouring countries with ethnic Hungarian majorities. There are large Hungarian communities in the Transylvania region of Romania, southern Slovakia, the Vojvodina region of Yugoslavia and the Transcarpathia region of Ukraine. All were part of the Kingdom of Hungary until the end of the First World War.

Greater London *See* SOUTHEAST.

Greater Romania [România Măre] Slogan used by those who advocate the return to Romania of territories ceded to the Soviet Union in 1940. These comprise northern Bukovina and southern Bessarabia, now part of Ukraine, and Moldavia or Moldova, now an independent republic. The first two regions have substantial ethnic Romanian minorities and the majority of Moldavia's population is ethnically Romanian. None of the main parties in Moldavia supports reunification.

Greater Romania Party [România Măre] Romanian political party. Founded in 1990, România Măre is a far-right nationalist party. It calls for restrictions of the rights of ethnic minorities, in particular Hungarians, Gipsies and Jews, and controls on foreign investment. At the September 1992 election it gained 3.9% of the vote and 16/341 seats. The leader is Corneliu Vadim Tudor, formerly an official in the communist Ceauşescu regime.

Greater Serbia [Velika Srbija] Slogan used by those who advocate the unification of all 'Serb lands' within former Yugoslavia. This would include, in addition to Serbia itself: Montenegro, the second Yugoslav republic, whose inhabitants they consider ethnic Serbs; most of eastern and northern Bosnia-Herzegovina (principally the breakaway Serbian Republic); all parts of Croatia with a Serb majority (principally the breakaway Republic of Serbian Krajina); and Macedonia, whose inhabitants they consider 'South Serbs'. The putative borders of such a Greater Serbia are largely but not entirely based on ethnic criteria. They also hark back to the medieval Serbian state and include territories, in particular the Kosovo province of Serbia, with non-Serb majorities.

Grebeníček, Miroslav (1947–) Czech teacher, historian and politician. A specialist in marxist-leninist philosophy and a member of the Communist Party of Czechoslovakia since his youth, he was elected leader of the Communist Party of Bohemia and Moravia (KSČM) in June 1993.

Greece [Ellás, Elláda] Country in southeastern Europe.

Official data. Name: Hellenic Republic [Ellinikí Dimokratía]; capital: Athens [Athínai]; form of government: parliamentary republic; head of state: president; head of government: prime minister; flag: nine horizontal stripes, five blue and four white, with a white cross in a blue square canton; national holiday: 25 March (Independence Day); language: Greek; religion: Orthodox Christianity (Greek Orthodox Church); currency: drachmí (Dr) (pl. drachmés) = 100 leptá; abbreviation: GR.

Geography. The southernmost of the Balkan countries, Greece consists of a mainland peninsula covering around four fifths of the total area of 131,957 sq km and around 1,400 islands to the east, south and west. The main islands are Crete [Kríti], Rhodes [Ródos], Lesbos [Lésvos] and Chíos, the main island groups the Dodecanese [Dodekánisos] and Cyclades [Kikládes] in the Aegean Sea and the Ionian Islands [Iónioi Nísoi] in the Ionian Sea. The country is bordered by Albania, Macedonia and Bulgaria in the north, Turkey in the east, the Mediterranean Sea in the south and west. The terrain is mostly mountainous. The main ranges are the Pindus Mountains [Píndos Óros] in the west and the Rhodope Mountains [Orosirá Rodópis] in the northeast along the border with Bulgaria. The only low-lying areas are coastal strips and several river valleys and plains in the north. Some 31% of the land is arable, another 40% is covered by pastures and 20% is forested. The climate is mediterranean, with hot summers and mild winters; temperatures are lower in the mountains; rainfall is light to moderate.

Demography. Greece has a population of 10,310,000. Population density is 79 per sq km (land area). Some 63% of the people live in urban areas, and around a third in the central Attica region [Attikí] centred on Athens and Piraeus [Piraiévs] (metropolitan population 3.3 million). Other major cities are Thessalonika or Salonika [Thessaloníki], Patras [Pátrai], Lárisa, Iráklion and Vólos. In ethnic, linguistic and religious terms Greece is very homogeneous. Some 95.5% of the population is Greek and 97.6% nominally Greek Orthodox. The Greek language is used in two forms, Demotic and Katharevusa. Ethnic minorities include Macedonians (150,000 or 1.5% of the total population) in the north, Turks (90,000) in the northeast, Gipsies (90,000), Albanians (60,000) in the northwest, Vlachs in the centre and Bulgarians in the northeast. The Turkish and Albanian communities are overwhelmingly Muslim. There are thought to be around 500,000 illegal immigrants, mainly from Albania and other Balkan countries.

Sociography. Greece scores 0.874 on the United Nations human development index (HDI), ranking 25th in the world and 17th among 32 European countries. There are 32 doctors and 51 hospital beds for every 10,000 people. Education is compulsory between the ages of six and 15. There is one teacher for every 19 students. Enrolment is 85% at the secondary level and 28% at the tertiary level. The literacy rate is 93%. Real annual income per head (in terms of purchasing power) is US$ 7,680.

Infrastructure and communications. Greece has a developed transport and communications network, with shipping particularly important in freight transport and ferries linking the islands; the rail system is relatively small, and the road and telecommunications systems are limited in some mainland rural areas. There are 102,700 km of paved roads and 1.73 million passenger cars (168 per 1,000 people), 2,480 km of railways and 80 km of navigable waterways. The main ports are Piraeus and Salonika. The main airports are at Athens (Hellinikon) and Salonika, and there are 31 other airports with scheduled services. There are 145 daily newspapers, with a combined circu-

lation of around 1.5 million (around 150 per 1,000 people). There are 4.09 million radio receivers, 2.28 million television sets and 4.70 million telephones in use (respectively 398, 222 and 457 per 1,000 people).

Economic structure. The Greek economy is developed, diversified and trade-oriented, with a substantial state-owned sector. It is based on agriculture, tourism, shipping and manufacturing. Compared to other Western European countries it is far more dependent on agriculture and low-added-value manufacturing (esp. textiles); several regions are relatively undeveloped and highly dependent on agriculture. Since the late 1980s economic performance has been marked by fluctuating and falling growth (averaging 1.8% per year), substantial current-account deficits (up to 5% of GDP), high inflation (averaging around 16%), and high unemployment (around 10%); the national debt stands at around 110% of GDP, one of the highest levels in the European Union (EU). The unofficial economy is estimated to be equivalent to two-fifths of official GDP.

Services contribute 57% of GDP (trade 15%), industry contributes 27% (manufacturing 16%), and agriculture, forestry and fisheries 16%. Some 25% of the labour force is employed in farming and fishing, 18% in manufacturing, 15% in trade and 6% in construction. The main crops grown are cereals (wheat, maize), tobacco, cotton and potatoes; horticulture (olives, grapes, nuts, tomatoes and other fruit and vegetables), fishing and livestock raising (sheep, goats, cattle) are other important agricultural activities. The main mineral resources are lignite, bauxite, magnesite, marble and natural gas; mining contributes 2% of GDP. The main industries are food processing and textiles; other important branches are metalworking (iron and steel, aluminium), chemicals, shipbuilding, building materials, petrochemicals and tobacco processing. Tourism is an important source of foreign exchange, contributing 4% of GNP (2% net). Shipping is also a major service industry and source of foreign exchange; the Greek merchant fleet is the largest in Europe and the fourth-largest in the world. The main energy sources are imported and domestic fossil fuels; 12% of export earnings are required to cover net fuel imports. The main exports are textiles and clothing (22% of the total, clothing 19%), fruit and vegetables (14%), oil products (8%), iron and steel (6%), tobacco, olive oil, wheat and chemicals; foodstuffs account for 31% of the total, basic manufactures for 27% and miscellaneous manufactures for 27%. The main imports are machinery and transport equipment, basic manufactures, foodstuffs and fuels. The main trading partners are: exports: Germany (24%), Italy (17%), France (8%), United Kingdom (7%), United States (6%), Netherlands; imports: Germany (19%), Italy (14%), France (8%), Japan (7%), Netherlands (6%), United Kingdom (5%), United States, Belgium; two-thirds of all trade is with other European Union (EU) countries. Net invisible earnings (shipping charges, tourism receipts, funds from EU programmes, remittances from workers abroad) account for 10% of GNP, one of the highest shares in Europe.

The Bank of Greece [Trápeza tis Elládos] is the central bank. The main employers' association is the Federation of Greek Industries (SEV); the main labour organization is the General Confederation of Greek Workers (GSEE).

Political structure. Greece is a parliamentary republic on the basis of a constitution adopted in 1975 and amended in 1986. The head of state is the president, who is elected for a five-year term by a two-thirds majority of the legislature; s/he is commander of the armed forces and appoints the prime minister, but normally acts on the advice of the government and the Council State [Simvoúlio tis Epikráteias] composed of senior political leaders. Executive power is vested in the prime minister and the council of ministers. Legislative power is vested in the Parliament [Voulí], whose 300 members are elected for a four-year term by a system of proportional representation (with a 3% threshold for gaining seats). All citizens over the age of 18 are entitled to vote. Judicial power is ultimately vested in the Supreme Court [Áreos Págos]. Administratively the country is divided into 13 regions [diamerísma, pl. -ta], which are subdivided into 51 prefectures or departments [nomós, pl. nomói], which are subdivided into 276 cities and around 5,000 municipalities. The theocratic republic of Holy Mountain [Ágion Óros] or Mount Athos, sometimes considered the 52nd prefecture, has extensive autonomy.

The main political parties are the Pan-Hellenic Socialist Movement (PASOK), New Democratic Party (ND), Political Spring (POLA), Communist Party of Greece (KKE) and Progressive Left Alliance (Sinaspismós, SIN). At the general election in October 1993 PASOK gained 46.9% of the vote and 170/300 seats, the ND 39.3% and 111 seats, POLA 4.9% and 10 seats, the KKE 4.5% and nine seats, and Sinaspismós 2.9% and no seats. The government is formed by PASOK, with Andreas Papandreou as prime minister. Other senior ministers are Anastasios Peponis (minister to the Prime Minister's Office), Karolos Papoulias (foreign affairs), Kostas Skandalidis (internal affairs), Ioannis Papantoniou (economy), Alexandros Papadopoulos (finance), Giorgos Kouvelakis (justice) and Gerasimos Arsenis (defence).

Security and international affiliations. The Greek armed forces number 159,300 (army 113,000, navy 19,500, airforce 26,800). There are also two paramilitary forces, the 26,500-strong Gendarmerie [Chorofilakí] and a 4,000-strong coast guard. Military service is compulsory and consists of 19–23 months' basic training. Defence spending is equivalent to 5.6% of GDP, among the highest rates in Europe. Some 2,300 Greek troops are stationed in Cyprus to support the Greek Cypriot forces.

Greece is a member of the Black Sea Economic Cooperation Organization (BSECO), Conference on Security and Cooperation in Europe (CSCE), Council of Europe, European Economic Area (EEA), European Union (EU), North Atlantic Treaty Organization (NATO) and Western European Union (WEU), as well as the Organization for Economic Cooperation and Development (OECD) and the United Nations and its specialized agencies.

History. Europe's first advanced civilization flourished on the island of Crete from the 23rd–15th centuries BC. The Minoans were influenced by Egypt and maintained commercial contacts throughout the Eastern Mediterranean. From the 19th century Ionians, Achaeans and Aeolians, the ancestors of the Greeks, entered the region from the north. They dominated the mainland and the islands by the 15th century and, through migration and conquest, brought about the end of the Minoan kingdoms around 1450. The Mycenaean culture, centred on the Peloponnese peninsula, flourished until the 12th century, when a new wave of migrations from the north spearheaded by the Dorians disrupted settlement patterns. While the region was politically fragmented into many small states, cultural cohesion among the Greeks – they called themselves Hellenes – was maintained by their common language (and alphabet) and religion. From the 8th century Greek city states established trading posts and farming colonies in southern Italy and further afield. Miletus and the other Ionian cities on the Anatolian coast were dominant at this time. After the subjugation of the Ionian cities by Lydia in 560 and the Persian Empire in 546, the most powerful city states became Athens, Sparta, Thebes, Corinth and Argos on the Greek mainland and Syracuse in Greek Sicily. Between 499 and 478 the Greeks repulsed two invasions by the Persians and liberated the Ionian cities. This period marked the beginning of a remarkable flowering of the arts, literature, philosophy and scientific thought that laid the foundations for many European intellectual, political and aesthetic traditions. (The other formative influences on European culture, ancient Rome and Christianity, were also heavily influenced by Greek and hellenistic traditions.) Weakened by a series of wars, between Athens, Sparta and Thebes in particular, the city

states lost their political independence to the northern Greek kingdom of Macedonia in 338. The conquest of the Persian Empire under Alexander the Great (336–23) paved the way for the spread of Greek culture throughout the Eastern Mediterranean region. After Alexander's death his empire was partitioned. Rump Macedonia remained the dominant power in Greece, but the city states eventually regained a measure of independence with the help of the Romans. The Roman Republic annexed Macedonia in 148 and the rest of Greece in 146. Greek cultural influence became a dominant factor in the Roman Republic and the Empire thereafter. Christianity became the dominant religion in the 4th century AD.

In 395 Greece was allocated to the Eastern Roman Empire. What became the Byzantine Empire used Greek as its official language and preserved Greco-Roman culture and traditions. It was the strongest and most prestigious power in Europe until the 11th century, and its capital, Constantinople (modern İstanbul in Turkey), was the region's largest city and main cultural centre. After centuries of divergence and tension, the division of Christianity into (Eastern) Orthodox and (Roman) Catholic branches was sealed by the Great Schism of 1054. At this time the Byzantine Empire stretched from Bosnia in the west to Armenia in the east. Weakened by progressive feudalization, internal power struggles and attacks by Slav states in the west and Muslim states in the east, it was gradually reduced to a core area around Constantinople. In the 13th century Western European armies ostensibly engaged in the Crusades – the intermittent Christian attempts to wrest Palestine, the 'Holy Land', from Muslim control – occupied much of the Empire, including Greece, which was divided into a number of feudal states. The Ottoman Turks conquered most of northern Greece in the first half of the 15th century, and the rest of the mainland in the years following the fall of Constantinople in 1453 (which marked the demise of the Byzantine Empire). Some of the islands (Rhodes, Crete, Corfu etc) and parts of the Peloponnese peninsula did not come under Ottoman rule until later or were held by the Venetian Republic, the region's major maritime power. There were no systematic attempts to turkify or islamicize the population during the four centuries of Ottoman rule, and the extensive Greek trade network was left undisturbed. Central authority was generally weak in the later period, so that local Turkish or Greek governors had considerable powers, which they frequently exercised arbitrarily. The Greek Orthodox Church played a key role in the preservation of Greek culture and thus in the revival of Greek national consciousness in the late 18th century. There were localized uprisings against Ottoman rule in 1770 and 1786. Another uprising in 1821 spread across the country, but was soon hampered by internal divisions and languished until the major European powers (United Kingdom, Russia and France) intervened in 1827.

Greece's independence was internationally recognized in 1830 and confirmed in 1832, when a Bavarian prince was proclaimed King Otho I. Constitutional government was established in 1843. In 1862 parliament deposed Otho and the following year endorsed a Danish prince as King George I. The overriding aim of Greek foreign policy was to extend the borders of the state, which initially comprised only the southern half of the mainland and the Cyclades archipelago, to include all Greek-speaking areas within the Ottoman Empire. The Ionian Islands (a British protectorate since 1815) were acquired in 1863 and Thessaly in 1881. Southern Epirus, southern Macedonia, Crete and the eastern Aegean islands were acquired in the First Balkan War (1912–13). During the First World War (1914–18) disagreements over foreign policy between King Constantine I (1913–17 and 1920–22), supported by the army, and the government, led by Eleftherios Venizelos, the country's leading politician between 1910 and 1935, led to a rift between royalists and republicans that would be a defining feature of Greek politics until the 1970s. (In general policy

terms the former were broadly conservatives and the latter liberals.) At the insistence of the royalists Greece remained neutral until 1917, but then joined the Allies against Germany, Austria-Hungary and the Ottoman Empire. The 1920 Treaty of Sèvres provided for Greek occupation of what is now European Turkey (with the exception of İstanbul) and the region around Smyrna (now İzmir). But Turkish forces expelled the Greeks from these territories during a two-year war. The 1923 Treaty of Lausanne provided for the compulsory exchange of Turkish Muslim and Greek Christian populations between the two countries. As a result Greece had to assimilate around 1.4 million refugees. The power struggle between royalists and republicans created great political instability in the 1920s and 30s. The monarchy was abolished in 1924 but restored in 1935. In 1936 Ioannis Metaxas established a far-right dictatorship with the support of the king and the army. During the Second World War (1939–45) Greece successfully repelled an Italian invasion in 1940 but was overrun by the German army the following year. Of the resistance movements that emerged, the National People's Liberation Front (ELAS), the military arm of the communist-dominated National Liberation Front (EAM), was the most effective. By 1944 it controlled much of the country, but the government returning from exile was able to assert control with British help and the EAM-ELAS was disbanded.

A disputed right-wing election victory and plebiscite on the monarchy in 1946 and escalating violence against left-wingers induced the communists to take up arms again. They were defeated in a three-year civil war that cost an estimated 80,000 lives. Italy formally ceded the Dodecanese archipelago to Greece in 1947. Greece joined the North Atlantic Treaty Organization (NATO) in 1952. The right-wing Greek Rally (ES), later the National Radical Union (ERE), held power from 1952–63, with Konstantinos Karamanlis as prime minister from 1955. The centre-left Centre Union (EK), led by

Georgios Papandreou, formed a minority administration after the 1963 election and secured an overall majority the following year. Papandreou clashed with King Constantine II (1964–73) over control of the armed forces and was dismissed in 1965. A new election planned for 1967 was preempted by a military coup. The 'colonels' regime', led by Georgios Papadopoulos until 1973, suspended civil rights and banned left-wing organizations. Constantine went into exile after a failed countercoup. A republic was proclaimed in 1973. The regime collapsed in 1974 after supporting an abortive coup by Greek Cypriots that led to the island's invasion by Turkish troops. The New Democratic Party (ND, the ERE's successor) won the election held later in the year, and Karamanlis returned as prime minister. Restoration of the monarchy was rejected in a referendum and a new constitution was adopted in 1975. Greece joined the European Community (EC), now the European Union (EU), in January 1981. The Pan-Hellenic Socialist Movement (PASOK), led by Andreas Papandreou, son of Georgios, won the October 1981 and June 1985 elections. Criticized for economic mismanagement and discredited by corruption allegations, it lost its majority in June 1989. After another inconclusive election in November the ND, led by Konstantinos Mitsotakis, gained a narrow majority in April 1990. PASOK and Papandreou returned to power in October 1993 and committed themselves to fiscal discipline, economic deregulation and some privatization.

See also entries on specific institutions, organizations, parties, people, terms etc.

Greek Communist Party *See* COMMUNIST PARTY OF GREECE.

Greek Cypriots Ethnic group in Cyprus. They are the Greek-speaking and Greek Orthodox Christian people of Cyprus. Numbering around 575,000, they have been concentrated in the southern two-thirds of the island since its effective division in 1974. There is a large Greek Cypriot community in the United Kingdom.

Greek General Confederation of Labour *See* GENERAL CONFEDERATION OF GREEK WORKERS.

green In most countries, the colour associated with environmentalist parties.

green In Northern Ireland (United Kingdom), the colour associated with the nationalist or republican movement supporting the reunification of Ireland.

green In Turkey, the colour associated with Islamic fundamentalism.

Green, Pauline (1948–) British secretary, policewoman and politician. A graduate in social sciences and comparative government, she began working as a Cooperative Union lobbyist at the European Community (EC) in 1984. Elected to the European Parliament for the Labour Party in 1989, she was elected leader of the British Labour group in 1993 and became leader of the whole Socialist Group in July 1994.

Green Alliance or **Greens** [Vihreä Liitto] (Vihreät) Finnish political party. Formed as an electoral alliance of environmentalist groups in 1983 and constituted as a party in 1987, the Greens gained 6.8% of the vote and 10/200 seats at the March 1991 election. The leader is Pekka Sauri, the general secretary Katarina Poskiparta.

Green Alternative or **Greens** [Grüne Alternative, Die Grünen] (GA) Austrian political party. Founded in 1987 from the merger of the Alternative List of Austria (ALÖ) and two other environmentalist groups and initially called the Green Alternative List (GAL), the Greens gained 4.8% of the vote and 9/183 seats at the October 1990 election. The federal spokesman is Peter Pilz, the parliamentary leader Madeleine Petrovic.

Green Alternative Party *See* GREENS (Luxemburg).

green berets [zeleni bereti] In Bosnia-Herzegovina, an informal name for soldiers of the government-controlled army.

green currencies (pound, franc etc) (European Union) *See* COMMON AGRICULTURAL POLICY.

Green Europe Informal name for the COMMON AGRICULTURAL POLICY (CAP), a common policy of the European Union (EU), and related issues.

Green Federation or **Greens** [Federazione dei Verdi] (Verdi) Italian political organization. The Federation was formed in 1984 as an alliance of environmentalist, anti-nuclear and alternative groups. It is generally less radical and more practical in its policies than its counterparts in other Western European countries. At the April 1992 election it gained 2.8% of the vote and 16/630 seats; it contested the March 1994 election within the Progressive Alliance and gained 2.7% and 11/630 seats. The leader is Carlo Ripa di Meana.

Green Group or **Greens** Political group in the European Parliament, the parliament of the European Union (EU). The Green Group includes representatives from seven of the 12 member states, including Germany, Italy, Belgium and Ireland. It holds 23/567 seats. The joint leaders are Alexander Langer (Italy) and Claudia Roth (Germany). *See also* EUROPEAN GREENS.

Green Left [Groen Links] Dutch political party. Green Left was established as an electoral alliance of the Radical Political Party (PPR), Pacifist Socialist Party (PSP), Communist Party (CPN) and Evangelical People's Party (EVP) in 1989. The four parties merged in 1991. The Green Left's programme is broadly left-alternative and focuses on environmental and social issues. At the May 1994 election it gained 3.5% of the vote and 5/150 seats. The leader is Paul Rosenmöller.

Green Line Common name for the neutral buffer zone separating Greek Cypriot and Turkish Cypriot forces in Cyprus, in particular the Greek and Turkish quarters of Nicosia, the capital. It is patrolled by the United Nations Peace-Keeping Force in Cyprus (UNFICYP). The name was reputedly coined after a British general on UNFICYP duty used a green pen to mark on a map the ceasefire line ending the hostilities in 1974 which left the island divided (*see* CYPRUS QUESTION). It has also been used in other situations involving the separation of rival forces, e.g. in Beirut, the Lebanese capital, in the 1980s, and in Sarajevo, the Bosnian capital, in the context of a ceasefire between government troops and rebel Serb forces in February 1994.

Green List (Italy) *See* GREEN FEDERATION.

Green List Ecological Initiative *See* GREENS (Luxemburg).

green money system (European Union) *See* COMMON AGRICULTURAL POLICY.

green paper In the European Union (EU), a document published by the European Commission outlining and analysing policy options on a specific issue. It is intended as a basis for public discussion and consultation. The term 'green paper' or 'green book' is also used in many countries for a government consultative document.

Green Party [Strana Zelených] (SZ) Czech political party. Founded in 1989, the Greens are a mainstream environmentalist party. They gained 3.1% of the vote in the June 1990 election and contested the June 1992 election within the LIBERAL SOCIAL UNION (LSU) alliance. The leader is Jan Jecmínek.

Green Party British political party. Founded in 1973 as the Ecology Party and renamed in 1985, the Green Party has made little electoral impact, with the exception of the 1989 European Parliament elections, when it gained 14.9% of the vote but no seats because of the single-member constituency voting system. At the April 1992 election it stood in most of the 651 seats and gained 0.5% of the vote. The leadership is collective.

Green Party of Switzerland [Grüne Partei der Schweiz (German), Parti Écologiste Suisse (French)] (GPS or PÉS) Swiss political party. Formed in 1983 from the merger of several regional environmentalist movements and renamed in 1985, the Greens gained 6.4% of the vote and 14/200 seats at the October 1991 election. The party president is Verena Diener, the parliamentary leader Cécile Bühlmann.

green pound (European Union) *See* COMMON AGRICULTURAL POLICY.

Greens (Austria) *See* GREEN ALTERNATIVE.

Greens (Finland) *See* GREEN ALLIANCE.

Greens [Les Verts] French political party. Founded in 1984, the Greens follow an 'autonomist' line, i.e. they refuse to ally themselves with any of the traditional

parties of the left or right. They made
little electoral impression until their candidate in the 1988 presidential election,
Antoine Waechter, gained 3.8% of the
vote in the first round. At the March 1993
general election, which they contested in
alliance with the more pragmatic Ecology
Generation (GE), they gained 4.0% of
the vote but no seats. Since then the party
has been riven by internal divisions.
The main spokeswoman is Dominique
Voynet.

Greens [Die Grünen] German political
party. Founded in 1979, the Greens
became the most successful environmentalist party in Europe in the 1980s, increasing their share of the vote from 1.5% in
1980 to 8.3% in 1987. After 1985 they
also shared power with the Social Democratic Party (SPD) in several states. Unlike many other European environmentalist parties, it has always had a strong left-
alternative stance, expressed in opposition to military alliances and defence
spending and espousal of liberal policies
on immigration, social issues etc.
Tensions between a 'realist' [realo] wing
willing to take part in government and a
'fundamentalist' [fundi] wing rejecting
this on principle divided the party in the
late 1980s. Coupled with an equivocal
stance on German reunification, this led
to a sharp decline in electoral support at
the all-German election in December
1990: they gained 3.9% (4.8% in the west
and 0.1% in the east) and thus failed to
pass the 5% threshold required for parliamentary representation. In May 1993 the
Greens merged with Alliance 90 (B'90),
the main left-alternative and environmentalist party in eastern Germany. The
merged party inherited the 8/662 parliamentary seats held by B'90. The joint
spokespeople are Marianne Birthler and
Ludger Volmer.

Greens (Italy) *See* GREEN FEDERATION.

Greens [Déi Gréng] Luxemburg political
organization. The Greens are an electoral
alliance of two environmentalist groups,
the Green Alternative Party [Gréng Alter-
nativ Partei] (GAP) and the Green List
Ecological Initiative [Gréng Lëscht Eko-
logesch Initiativ] (GLEI), founded in 1983

and 1989 respectively. The alliance has
been among Europe's most successful
environmentalist groups, gaining 8.4% of
the vote and 4/60 seats at the June 1989
election and 10.9% and five seats at the
June 1994 election.

Greens (Sweden) *See* ECOLOGY PARTY -
THE GREENS.

Greens (European Union) *See* GREEN
GROUP.

Greens of Slovenia [Zeleni Slovenije] (ZS)
Slovenian political party. The Greens
were founded in 1989 from the merger of
several environmentalist groups which
had been active in Slovenia since the late
1960s. They gained 9.0% of the vote and
8/80 seats at the April 1990 multiparty
election, thus becoming one of Europe's
most successful environmentalist parties.
Their support fell to 3.7% and 5/90 seats
at the December 1992 election. In September 1993 a left-leaning wing, including the five deputies, left to form a new
party, the Greens of Slovenia - Eco-Social
Party (ZS-ESS), which joined the new
Liberal Democratic Party (LDS) in March
1994. The party leader is Vane Gošnik.

Gréng *See* GREENS (Luxemburg).

grey In several countries, the colour
associated with political parties or groups
seeking to defend the interests of older
people. These have come to the fore in
parts of Western Europe in recent years
as an ageing population and financial
constraints have forced governments to
reconsider expenditure on welfare provision, in particular state pensions and
health services. Examples are the General
Elderly People's Union (AOV) and Union
55+ (Unie 55+) in the Netherlands, the
Action Committee for Democracy and
Pension Justice (ADR) in Luxemburg and
the Grey Panthers or Greys in Germany.

grey economy [siva ekonomija] In Yugoslavia, the unofficial or black economy.
This has mushroomed since the collapse
of the communist command economy in
the late 1980s and above all since the imposition of United Nations sanctions in
May 1992 because of the country's involvement in the Bosnian civil war. The
'grey economy' operates largely on a
non-cash, barter or foreign-currency

basis, since hyperinflation has destroyed confidence in the dinar.

Grey Wolves [Bozkurtlar] or **Idealists** [Ülkücüler] Turkish guerrilla group. The Grey Wolves are members of the Hearths of the Ideal [Ülkü Ocakları] (ÜO) movement, which is closely linked to the far-right NATIONAL ACTION PARTY (MHP). During the 1970s they were responsible for a number of assassinations of left-wing activists, including human-rights campaigners, trade unionists, journalists and guerrillas. They were less active in the 1980s, when many were imprisoned and some were sentenced to death. In the 1990s they have concentrated their attacks on Kurdish activists.

grey zone In Bosnia-Herzegovina, a disputed area to be placed under temporary international administration within the framework of a settlement of the civil war. Under the Owen-Stoltenberg plan tabled in July 1993, Sarajevo, the capital, was to be placed under United Nations administration; and under the Contact Group plan tabled in July 1994 other strategic towns and corridors were to be placed under UN or European Union (EU) protection and administration. In July 1994 the city of Mostar, which had been the scene of heavy fighting between Muslims and Croats, became the first 'grey zone' to be put under international administration, namely of the EU for a two-year period.

Grimaldi Royal dynasty of Monaco. The Grimaldi family has reigned in the principality since 1297.

Grímsson, Ólafur Ragnar (1940–) Icelandic sociologist, academic and politician. He taught political science at the University of Iceland in the 1970s. Elected to parliament for the left-wing People's Alliance (Ab) in 1979, he was elected its leader in November 1987. He was minister of finance in a centre-left coalition from 1988–91.

Griñan, José Antonio (1946–) Spanish lawyer, civil servant and politician. He worked as a technical inspector of industry from 1970–82 and also lectured in industrial law from 1972–75. From 1982–87 he was a junior minister and from

1990–92 health minister in the Andalusian regional government. He held a senior post in the national ministry of labour and social security from 1987–90. He was appointed minister of health and consumer affairs in 1992 and minister of labour and social security in July 1993. He is a member of the Spanish Socialist Workers' Party (PSOE).

Groen Links *See* GREEN LEFT.

Grossherzogtum Luxemburg ('Grand Duchy of Luxemburg') Official name of Luxemburg in German.

Group of Twenty-Four (G-24) Intergovernmental organization. The G-24 – not to be confused with the G-24 of developing countries cooperating on monetary affairs – is a loose grouping of the member states of the Organization for Economic Cooperation and Development (OECD), which brings together most of the world's major industrialized countries. It was set up in 1989 to channel economic aid to the countries of Eastern Europe which were abandoning communism. Its activities are coordinated by the European Commission, the administrative and executive arm of the European Union (EU). The G-24's Assistance for Economic Restructuring in the Countries of Central and Eastern Europe programme is similar in scope to the EU's PHARE PROGRAMME. The OECD also set up the CENTRE FOR COOPERATION WITH EUROPEAN ECONOMIES IN TRANSITION (CCEET) in 1990.

group of wise people In several countries, a group of experts commissioned by the government to produce regular reports on the state of the economy and to advise it on economic policy. A group of 'five wise people' [fünf Weisen], the Expert Committee to Assess Overall Economic Development, has been doing so in Germany for many years, and a group of 'seven wise people' was set up in the United Kingdom in 1992. The term is also used in other contexts, for instance in the European Union (EU), for any informal group or committee asked to address a particular controversial problem. Thus an EU 'reflection group' has been set up to consider issues for the Maastricht Treaty review conference due in 1996.

Grousherzogdem Lëtzebuerg ('Grand Duchy of Luxemburg') Official name of Luxemburg in Letzeburgish.

Grude Shorthand for the government of the Croatian Republic of Herzeg-Bosnia, the state proclaimed by Croats in Bosnia-Herzegovina in July 1992. The town of Grude is the seat of the government and the assembly.

Grundgesetz ('Basic Law') Formal name of the German constitution. It came into force in West Germany in 1949, and was extended to East Germany on the country's reunification in October 1990.

Grünen (Austria) *See* GREEN ALTERNATIVE.

Grünen (Germany) *See* GREENS.

Grupo INI *See* NATIONAL INDUSTRY INSTITUTE.

Gruppo Misto *See* MIXED GROUP.

GSD *See* GIBRALTAR SOCIAL DEMOCRATS.

GSEE *See* GENERAL CONFEDERATION OF GREEK WORKERS.

GSG-9 Abbreviation for Grenzschutzgruppe Neun ('Border Guard Group Nine'), the specialist unit of the FEDERAL BORDER GUARD (BGS) charged with anti-terrorist operations.

GSLP *See* GIBRALTAR SOCIALIST LABOUR PARTY.

guarantee power In Cyprus, one of the signatories along with Cyprus of the TREATY OF GUARANTEE concerning the island's independence and territorial integrity. They are Greece, Turkey and the United Kingdom.

Guarantee Treaty (Cyprus) *See* TREATY OF GUARANTEE.

Guardia Civil *See* CIVIL GUARD.

guardia civil (pl. -s -es) Member of the Civil Guard, the Spanish paramilitary police force.

Guardia di Finanza *See* REVENUE GUARD.

GUE *See* EUROPEAN UNITED LEFT.

Guernsey Territory in western Europe, a dependency of the United Kingdom.

Official data. Name: Bailiwick of Guernsey; capital: Saint Peter Port; form of government: internally self-governing dependency of the British crown; head of state: British monarch, represented by a lieutenant-governor; head of government: bailiff; flag: white with a red cross; national holidays: Queen's Official Birthday (second Saturday in June), 9 May (Liberation Day); languages: French and English; religion: Anglicanism (Church of England in Guernsey); currencies: pound (£) = 100 pence, British pound; abbreviation: GBG.

Geography. Part of the Channel Islands archipelago situated between France and Britain, Guernsey has a total area of 78 sq km. It consists of Guernsey itself, the smaller islands of Alderney, Sark, Herm and Jethou and several islets. The terrain is generally low-lying, with hills rising to a low plateau in the southwest of Guernsey. Around a fifth of the land is arable and around three-fifths is covered by pastures. The climate is temperate marine, with mild summers and cool winters; rainfall is moderate.

Demography. Guernsey has a population of 63,500. Population density is 814 per sq km. The main town is Saint Peter Port. Most people are native Channel Islanders, but there is also a substantial number of immigrants from Britain. The main language is English; Norman French (a dialect of French) is also spoken in the rural areas; French is used for some official purposes. In religious terms most people are nominally Anglicans; there are also small groups of Roman Catholics and other Christians.

Sociography. The standard of living in Guernsey is very high. There are 13 doctors and 91 hospital beds for every 10,000 people. Education is compulsory between the ages of five and 16. There is one teacher for every 17 students. Enrolment is 78% at the secondary level; there is one college of higher education, but most students study in Britain. The literacy rate is virtually 100%. GNP per head (unadjusted for purchasing power) is US$ 25,250, among the highest in Europe.

Infrastructure and communications. Guernsey has a highly developed but limited transport and communications network closely integrated with that of Britain; ferry and air links are particularly important. There are around 270 km of paved roads and 34,900 passenger cars (574 per 1,000 people). There are no railways or navigable waterways. The main

port is Saint Peter Port. There is an
airport at La Villaize (Guernsey). There
is one daily newspaper, with a circulation
of 16,000 (277 per 1,000 people); British
papers are also widely read. There are
around 75,000 radio receivers, around
35,000 television sets and 60,000 telephones in use (respectively around 1,200,
around 600 and 987 per 1,000 people).

Economic structure. The Guernsey
economy is highly developed, relatively
diversified and closely linked to the
British economy. Guernsey maintains a
customs and monetary union with the
United Kingdom and Jersey. Taxation is
low. The economy is based on tourism,
agriculture and financial services. Since
the late 1980s economic performance has
been marked by relatively high growth,
relatively low inflation and very low
unemployment (detailed figures n.a.).

Services contribute around 75% of
GDP, industry contributes around 15%,
and agriculture and fisheries around 10%
(detailed figures n.a.). Some 25% of the
labour force is employed in trade, 19%
in finance, 11% in construction and 8%
in agriculture. The main agricultural
activities are dairy farming (milk, butter),
livestock raising (cattle) and horticulture
(tomatoes and other vegetables, fruit,
plants, flowers); potatoes are the main
crop grown. Fishing is also important.
There are no significant mineral resources.
The main industries are electrical goods
and electronics (esp. radios and televisions), pharmaceuticals, printing and
food processing. Tourism and banking
and other financial services are the mainstays of the economy; tourism contributes
11% of GNP. The main energy sources
are imported fossil fuels. The main
exports are foodstuffs (tomatoes and
other vegetables, potatoes) and electrical
equipment (esp. radios and televisions).
The main imports are fuels, foodstuffs
and basic and miscellaneous manufactures. The main trading partner is the
United Kingdom. (Detailed foreign-trade
figures n.a.) Net invisible earnings
(tourism receipts, income from financial
services, investment income) account for
a major share of GNP.

There is no central bank. Employers'
associations and trade unions are integrated into British structures.

Political structure. Guernsey is an internally self-governing dependency of the
British crown (i.e. the monarch) on the
basis of constitutional practice, statute
law and common law; there is no written
constitution. The British government is
responsible for defence and foreign affairs
and also effectively for discharging the
crown's extensive powers of appointment
etc. Executive power is formally vested
in the British monarch, represented by a
lieutenant-governor; it is exercised by the
bailiff and other government officials, all
of whom are appointed by the crown, and
by committees elected by the legislature
from among its members. The bailiff is
head of government, president of the
legislature and head of the judiciary.
Legislative power is vested in the 60-
member States of Deliberation (33 of its
members are directly elected for a three-
year term, 22 are indirectly elected for a
six-year term, two represent the island
of Alderney, and three belong ex officio).
All citizens over the age of 18 are entitled
to vote; resident Commonwealth and
Irish citizens normally also have voting
rights. Judicial power is vested in the 13-
member Royal Court, composed of the
bailiff and 12 indirectly elected judges
[jurat, pl. -s]; appeal courts are the three-
member Court of Appeal and, in some
cases, the Judicial Committee of the Privy
Council, a body composed of senior
judges in the British House of Lords.
Guernsey is divided into 10 parishes
[douzaine, pl. -s], which have few
administrative or political functions;
the islands of Alderney and Sark have
extensive internal autonomy.

There are no political parties. The
bailiff is Graham Dorey, the deputy
bailiff is de Vic G. Carey. The head of
state is Queen Elizabeth II, represented
by John Coward as lieutenant-governor;
the heir is Prince Charles.

Security and international affiliations.
Defence and foreign affairs are the respon-
sibility of the British government. The
Guernsey government is usually consulted

in matters of immediate concern to the islands. Guernsey is treated as part of the European Union (EU) for the purpose of free trade of goods, but it is not a member of the organization.

History. During the early Middle Ages Guernsey formed part of the Duchy of Normandy, a French fief. (*For earlier developments, see* FRANCE: HISTORY.) After William of Normandy conquered England in 1066 it became a possession of the English crown. When France regained control over Normandy proper in 1204, Guernsey, along with the other Channel Islands, remained in English hands. It has been attached to the English, later British, crown ever since. Existing Norman law and customs were largely retained, and over the years the island secured a large degree of self-government through royal charters. These granted an independent judiciary, tax sovereignty, tariff-free access to the English/British market and a range of other privileges. The bailiff, the sovereign's representative, was eventually given control over justice and civil affairs as president of what became the Royal Court. From the 17th century the judicial and legislative branches of government were gradually separated (a process only formally completed in 1948). In the 18th and 19th centuries Guernsey prospered from fishing, privateering and smuggling. During the Second World War (1939–45) it was occupied, like the other Channel Islands, by German troops from 1940–44.

Since the 1950s tourism has developed into a major economic activity.

See also entries on specific institutions, terms etc.

Guerra, Alfonso (1940–) Spanish politician. A qualified engineer, he joined the then illegal Spanish Socialist Workers' Party (PSOE) in 1962. He was elected to parliament in 1977 and became PSOE's deputy leader in September 1979. After the party's victory in the 1982 election he also became deputy prime minister. He was forced to resign his government post in January 1991 following allegations that his brother Juan had relied on his influence to promote business ventures (*see*

GUERRA AFFAIR). Considered the leader of the party's left wing, he has been sharply critical of the economic policies pursued by the PSOE government.

Guerra affair Business and political scandal involving Juan Guerra, the brother of Alfonso, deputy leader of the Spanish Socialist Workers' Party (PSOE) and deputy prime minister. In January 1990 it was alleged in media reports that Juan Guerra had amassed a personal fortune by using his brother's influence to buy property and obtain loans, and that he had run a private business from a government office in Seville, the capital of Andalusia. (The PSOE had been in power in Andalusia and at national level since May and October 1982 respectively.) Alfonso, said to have known about his brother's activities, resigned as deputy prime minister in January 1991. In December 1992 Juan was convicted of fraud and sentenced to one year's imprisonment and a heavy fine, and in June 1994 he was convicted on other charges and barred from public office for 6½ years.

guest workers In several countries, a collective name for foreign immigrant workers. Coined in Germany, the term 'guest worker' [Gastarbeiter] or its local equivalent is also used in Austria, Belgium, Denmark, Netherlands, Switzerland etc. From the 1950s onwards workers mainly from Italy and later also from Spain, Portugal, Turkey and Yugoslavia were invited into these countries to alleviate acute labour shortages in manufacturing industry and other sectors of the economy. Many put down roots in their adoptive countries. In most cases they and their descendants have retained their original citizenship, not least because the host countries have generally not allowed naturalization.

guilder [gulden, pl. -] Currency of the Netherlands. Common abbreviations are *f*, fl, Dfl, Hfl – all taken from 'florin' [florijn], an old name for the guilder – and NLG (the international standard in banking etc). It is divided into 100 cent or cents.

Guildford Four case *See* BIRMINGHAM SIX AND ....

gulden *See* GUILDER.

Gummer, John (1939–) British politician. He worked in publishing until his election to parliament for the Conservative Party in 1970. He was party chairman, in charge of the party organization, from 1983–85. After holding several junior ministerial posts he was appointed minister of agriculture, fisheries and food in 1989. In May 1993 he became environment secretary, a portfolio which includes housing and local government affairs. He is also a prominent lay member of the Church of England.

Guterres, António (1949–) Portuguese electrical engineer, businessman and politician. He has worked in the private sector and served as director of the Institute of Investment and State Participation. Elected to parliament for the Socialist Party (PS) in 1976, he was elected party leader in February 1992.

Gutiérrez Vergara, Antonio (1951–) Spanish trade-union official. He studied physics and worked for several companies before joining the Workers' Commissions (CCOO), one of the country's two main trade-union federations, as a full-time official in 1976. He was elected leader in November 1987.

Guyau, Luc (1948–) French farmer and trade-union official. He was president of the National Centre of Young Farmers (CNJA) from 1982–84. He became general secretary of the influential National Federation of Farmers' Unions (FNSEA) in 1986, and was elected its president in June 1992.

GWU *See* GENERAL WORKERS' UNION (Malta).

Gylys, Povilas (1948–) Lithuanian teacher and politician. He taught economics from 1969 and was briefly head of the Department of International Economic Relations at Vilnius University in 1992. A member of the Democratic Labour Party (LDDP), he was appointed foreign minister in December 1992.

Gymnich meeting In the European Union (EU), an informal gathering of foreign ministers usually held once during a member state's six-month presidency of the Council of Ministers. The term derives from Gymnich Castle in Germany, where the first such meeting took place in 1974.

Gypsies *See* GIPSIES.

Gysi, Gregor (1948–) German lawyer and politician. Although a member of the ruling communist Socialist Unity Party (SED) in East Germany, he defended many dissidents in the 1980s. He was elected leader of the relaunched SED, now the Democratic Socialist Party (PDS), in December 1989, a month after the collapse of communist rule. He was elected to parliament in the all-German election of December 1990. He resigned as party leader in January 1993.

293

H Abbreviation for Hungary, used for international vehicle registrations, postal addresses etc.

H (Norway) *See* CONSERVATIVE PARTY.

Haavisto, Heikki (1935–) Finnish farmer, lawyer and politician. He became general secretary of the influential Central Union of Agricultural Producers and Forest Owners (MTK) in 1966 and was its president from 1975–93. A member of the Centre Party (KESK), he was appointed foreign minister in May 1993.

Haddiema *See* LABOUR PARTY (Malta).

HADEP *See* PEOPLE'S DEMOCRACY PARTY *and* DEMOCRATIC PARTY (Turkey).

Hækkerup, Hans (1945–) Danish politician. An economics graduate, he was elected to parliament for the Social Democratic Party (SD) in 1976. A specialist in foreign- and security-policy issues, he became minister of defence in the centre-left coalition which took office in January 1993.

Hagen, Carl (1944–) Norwegian businessman and politician. A marketing specialist, he was director of the Norwegian subsidiary of the Tate & Lyle foodstuffs concern from 1970–74. He was secretary of the right-wing populist Anders Lange Party from 1973–74 and became leader of the renamed Progress Party (FrP) in February 1978. Under his leadership it has become the country's main protest party. He was elected to parliament in 1981.

Hågensen, Yngve (1938–) Norwegian trade-union official. He worked for the Musical Heritage Society from 1955. In 1969 he became a district official of the Norwegian Trade Union Confederation (LO). He was elected an LO secretary in 1977 and president in October 1989.

Haider, Jörg (1950–) Austrian lawyer and politician. Elected to parliament for the Freedom Party (FPÖ) in 1979, he became party leader in September 1986. Under his leadership the FPÖ has shifted sharply to the right, with considerable electoral success. He was elected chief minister of Carinthia in 1989, but was forced to resign in June 1991 after praising the employment policies of the nazi regime in the 1930s. In March 1992

he also became leader of the FPÖ parliamentary party.

Hajredini, Dzhevdet (1939–) Macedonian economist and politician. An ethnic Albanian, he has worked in the finance department of a major hydroelectric plant and has been president of several government boards in the electrical-industry and insurance fields. Elected to parliament for the Party for Democratic Prosperity - National Democratic Party (PPD-PND) in 1990, he was appointed finance minister in September 1992.

half-canton Federal division of Switzerland. The six half-cantons (Appenzell Ausser-Rhoden and Appenzell Inner-Rhoden, Basle-City and Basel-Country, and Nidwalden and Obwalden) are equivalent to full CANTONS in virtually all respects. The one major exception is that each elects only one member of the Council of States, the upper house of parliament, while the full cantons elect two members.

Halili, Nevzat (1945–) Macedonian teacher and politician. An English teacher, he was elected leader of the new Party for Democratic Prosperity - National Democratic Party (PPD-PND), the main representative of the Albanian community, in October 1990. When the party divided into two wings in February 1994, he was elected honorary chairman of the more moderate one.

Hall, Aleksander (1953–) Polish teacher, journalist and politician. A prominent member of the Solidarity movement in the 1980s, he spent nearly three years in hiding after the communist regime imposed martial law in 1981. He became a minister without portfolio in the Solidarity-led government of 1989–90. He was elected leader of the Democratic Right Forum (FPD) in November 1990, and leader of the Conservative Party (PK), formed by the FPD and two other right-wing parties, in December 1992.

Hamburg Federal state [Land] of Germany. Situated in the north and comprising the city of Hamburg, the state has an area of 755 sq km and a population of 1,689,000. Hamburg is Germany's second city, its largest port and a major industrial centre.

Political power is exercised by the Citizens' Assembly [Bürgerschaft], with 121 members elected for a four-year term, and an executive Senate [Senat] headed by a president. The administration combines the functions of a municipality and a state. The dominant party is the Social Democratic Party (SPD), and other major parties are the Christian Democratic Union (CDU) and the Greens. At the election in September 1993 the SPD gained 40.8% of the vote and 61 seats, the CDU 25.1% and 44 seats, the Greens 13.5% and nine seats, and the centre-right Instead Party (Statt), a local breakaway from the CDU, 5.6% and seven seats. The government is formed by the SPD, with external support from Statt, with Henning Voscherau as president. Hamburg was a founding member of the Hanseatic League in the Middle Ages. It became a free city of the Holy Roman Empire in 1510 – its official name is still the Free and Hanse City of Hamburg – and a state of the German Empire in 1871.

Hamilton inquiry *See* BEEF INDUSTRY AFFAIR.

Hanley, Jeremy (1945–) British accountant and politician. Elected to parliament for the Conservative Party in 1983, he became a junior minister in the Northern Ireland Office in 1990 and a junior defence minister in 1993. In July 1994 he was appointed party chairman (in charge of organization and campaigning) and minister without portfolio.

Hänni, Liia (1946–) Estonian physicist and politician. From 1970–90 she worked as a laboratory assistant and then as a researcher at the Physics Institute of the Estonian Academy of Sciences. Elected to parliament on the reformist People's Front (Rahvarinne) ticket in 1990, she later joined the new Estonian Rural Centre Party (EMKE). She was appointed minister without portfolio, with responsibility for reform issues, in the centre-right government which took office in October 1992.

Hannibalsson, Jón Baldvin (1939–) Icelandic teacher, journalist and politician. He has worked as a primary-school teacher and a headmaster, and was editor of a daily newspaper until his election to parliament for the Social Democratic Party in 1982. He became the party's leader in September 1984. He was minister of finance in 1987–88 and has been minister of foreign affairs and foreign trade since September 1988.

Hans-Adam II (1945–) Prince of Liechtenstein. An economics graduate with experience in banking, he was named regent in August 1984 when his father, Franz-Josef II, chose to retire from office. He succeeded to the throne on his father's death in November 1989. Under the constitution he has considerable executive powers. He married an Austrian countess, now Princess Marie, in 1967. They have four children.

Hänsch, Klaus (1938–) German journalist, civil servant, academic and politician. He was spokesman for the ministry of science and research from 1970–76 and then served as a ministerial adviser. He has also lectured in politics, history and sociology at the University of Duisburg since 1976. He was elected to the European Parliament for the Social Democratic Party (SPD) in 1979. In July 1994 he was elected president of the parliament for a $2\frac{1}{2}$ year term.

Hanzel, Milan (1947–) Slovakian lawyer and politician. He worked at the district military courts from 1972–92, serving as a judge from 1989. He then became a state secretary at the ministry of justice and was appointed minister of justice in the centrist coalition which took office in March 1994. He is a member of the Democratic Left Party (SDL', the successor to the Communist Party of Slovakia, KSS).

Harald V (1937–) King of Norway. A politics and economics graduate, he succeeded to the throne on the death of his father, Olav V, in January 1991. He married Sonja Haraldsen, now Queen Sonja, a language and art history graduate, in 1968. They have two children.

hard core (European Union) *See* INNER CORE *and* MULTI-TRACK EUROPE.

hard ecu plan Proposal for the creation of a common currency within the European Union (EU) alongside the existing national currencies. The ecu is the EU's notional currency, made up of the currencies of the member states. The hard ecu plan was put forward by the British government in June 1990 as an alternative to the single currency being considered within the context of ECONOMIC AND MONETARY UNION (EMU). It provided for the conversion of the ecu into a true currency (by the issue of banknotes for general circulation) managed by a European monetary fund and used in parallel with existing currencies. To ensure that it would retain its value – be a 'hard' currency, in other words – it would never be devalued against the national currencies. Although aspects of the plan were welcomed by several other governments, it was ultimately rejected in favour of a single currency. But after the currency crises of 1992 and 1993 (*see* ERM CRISES) cast doubt on its feasibility, the idea of a common currency was revived.

Harkis Ethnic group in France. The Harkis are Arabs and Berbers who fought on the French side during the Algerian war of independence (1954–62) and their descendants. After the war they were granted French citizenship and settled mainly in the south of France. Numbering around 450,000 today, they have retained a strong identity. They are distinguished from the North African immigrant communities in France.

Harlem Brundtland, Gro *See* BRUNDTLAND, ...

harmonization In the European Union (EU), the adaptation and standardization of member states' laws, rules and regulations on products, services, taxation etc. Harmonization is intended to remove trade barriers between member states and create equal conditions for the free movement of goods, services, capital and labour or people, the basic principle of the single internal market. It is usually effected by means of 'directives', decisions adopted by the Council of Ministers which give an outline of the required legislation but leave the details of implementation to the member states. *See also* APPROXIMATION *and* MUTUAL RECOGNITION.

Harmony for Latvia *See* NATIONAL HARMONY PARTY.

Harney, Mary (1953–) Irish academic and politician. She was appointed a professor of law in 1977. Elected to parliament for the centre-right Fianna Fáil in 1981, she joined the breakaway Progressive Democrats (PDs) in 1985. She was a junior environment minister from 1989–92. She was elected party leader in October 1993.

Haughey, Charles (1925–) Irish lawyer and politician. The founder and director of a leading accountancy firm, he was elected to parliament for the centre-right Fianna Fáil in 1957. In the 1960s he was successively minister of justice (1961– 64), agriculture (1964–66) and finance (1966–70). He was forced to resign in 1970 after being accused of having links with the Irish Republican Army (IRA) guerrilla group, a charge of which he was subsequently acquitted. He returned to government in 1977 as minister of health and social welfare. In 1979 he was elected party leader and prime minister. Ireland's dominant political figure of the 1980s, he was prime minister until the party lost the 1981 election, for nine months in 1982 and from 1987 until February 1992, when he resigned after being implicated in a telephone-tapping scandal.

Haute-Normandie *See* UPPER NORMANDY.

Havel, Václav (1936–) Czech playwright and politician. He became one of the country's best-known playwrights and theatre directors after the publication of his first play, *The Garden Party*, in 1963. An active supporter of the short-lived Prague Spring reform movement in 1968, he was barred from public life after the Soviet-led invasion which brought it to an end. He then worked at a brewery and in various other menial jobs. A founding member of the Charter 77 dissident movement and its spokesman from 1977–79, he was imprisoned on several occasions in the late 1970s and 1980s. He was a leading member of the Civic Forum (OF) movement which spearheaded the opposition to communist rule in 1989. After the collapse of the regime, parliament elected him president of Czechoslovakia in

December 1989. A strong advocate of the federation, he resigned in July 1992 when it became clear that it would be dissolved. In January 1993 he was elected president of the new Czech Republic (a largely non-executive post) for a five-year term.

Hawks *See* SERBIAN FALCONS.

HB *See* PEOPLE'S UNITY.

HCA *See* HELSINKI CITIZENS' ASSEMBLY.

HDUR *See* HUNGARIAN DEMOCRATIC UNION OF ROMANIA.

HDZ *See* CROATIAN DEMOCRATIC UNION.

HDZ-BiH *See* CROATIAN DEMOCRATIC UNION OF BOSNIA-HERZEGOVINA.

Heerma, Enneüs (1944–) Dutch politician. Elected to Amsterdam council for the Christian Democratic Appeal (CDA) in 1971, he was the city's alderman for economic affairs from 1978–86. In 1986 he was appointed junior minister for economic affairs, switching to housing later in the year. Elected to parliament in May 1994, he became the CDA's parliamentary leader – effectively leader of the opposition – in August.

HELCOM *See* BALTIC MARINE ENVIRONMENT PROTECTION COMMISSION.

Hellas Anglicized version of Ellás, the Greek name for Greece.

Hellenes and **Hellenic** Alternative, more literary, names for Greeks and Greek. They are taken from Hellas, the anglicized version of the native name for Greece.

Hellenic Republic [Ellinikí Dimokratía] Official name of Greece. 'Hellenic' is taken from Hellas, the anglicized form of the Greek name for Greece.

Hellsvik, Gun (1943–) Swedish lawyer, academic and politician. She has lectured in commercial law at Lund University and has been active in local politics in Lund for the centre-right Moderate Coalition Party (MS). She was appointed minister of justice in the centre-right coalition which took office in October 1991.

Helsingfors Swedish name for Helsinki, the Finnish capital. Swedish is Finland's second official language.

Helsinki Shorthand for the Finnish government. Helsinki is the capital of Finland.

Helsinki Citizens' Assembly (HCA) International political organization. The HCA was set up in 1990 as an independent network of civic initiatives, social and political groups and individuals in the 'Helsinki region', i.e. Europe, the former Soviet Union, Canada and the United States. It takes as its inspiration the Helsinki Final Act adopted by the Conference on Security and Cooperation in Europe (CSCE) in 1975 and the Prague Appeal, a call for Europe-wide respect for human rights adopted by Czech opposition intellectuals in 1985. It aims to provide a forum for citizens to express their views independently of governments, promote free and democratic development in the region, play an active role in the peaceful resolution of conflicts, and promote European integration. It monitors general economic, social and political developments and has organized a number of projects focusing on specific issues, such as nationalism, arms conversion, privatization and minority rights. National HCA committees have been set up in about half the CSCE countries. The secretariat is based in Prague (Czech Republic).

Helsinki Commission Shorthand for the BALTIC MARINE ENVIRONMENT PROTECTION COMMISSION.

Helsinki Committee In many countries, the national representative of the Europe-wide INTERNATIONAL HELSINKI FEDERATION FOR HUMAN RIGHTS (IHF).

Helsinki Convention Shorthand for the CONVENTION ON THE PROTECTION OF THE MARINE ENVIRONMENT OF THE BALTIC SEA AREA.

Helsinki Document International agreement adopted by the member states of the Conference on Security and Cooperation in Europe (CSCE). It was adopted on 10 July 1992, at the end of a two-day summit of heads of state and government in Helsinki, the Finnish capital. Subtitled 'The Challenges of Change', it follows on from the 1990 Charter of Paris – which marked the formal end of the Cold War and the division of Europe – and elaborates the CSCE's role in an emerging continent-wide security structure. It says the organization's tasks are to 'manage change' and 'prevent, manage and settle conflicts peacefully', and sets out a number of steps to make it more operational and effective. They involve strengthening existing institutions, creating new instruments of early warning, conflict prevention and crisis management, and establishing a framework for peace-keeping operations. Specifically it: (i) declares the CSCE a 'regional arrangement' under Chapter VIII of the United Nations Charter (which states that such groupings should 'make every attempt to achieve peaceful settlement of local disputes ... before referring them to the Security Council'); (ii) confirms the Council of Foreign Ministers as the CSCE's main decision-making body and strengthens the role of the Committee of Senior Officials (CSO) in managing and coordinating activities; (iii) provides for fact-finding and monitoring missions to areas of tension or conflict and for the appointment of a high commissioner on national minorities; (iv) declares that CSCE peace-keeping operations will conform to 'United Nations practice' (i.e. they will only be undertaken with the full consent of the parties concerned and only when an effective ceasefire is in place); and (v) establishes that the CSCE will in principle draw on the resources of the North Atlantic Treaty Organization (NATO), Western European Union (WEU), Commonwealth of Independent States (CIS) and other organizations to provide military forces for CSCE-sponsored peace-keeping operations.

Helsinki Final Act International agreement adopted by the states participating in the Conference on Security and Cooperation in Europe (CSCE). The Helsinki Final Act was signed by 33 European countries (all the sovereign states except Albania), Canada and the United States on 1 August 1975. A non-binding declaration covering security, economic, scientific, technological, environmental and human-rights matters, it was the first concrete result of the 'CSCE process', initiated three years earlier, which aimed at providing a framework for East-West relations and reducing tension between the two blocs in Europe. The significance of the docu-

ment was essentially twofold: the signatories committed themselves to a set of guidelines and principles concerning their multilateral and bilateral relations, and – at a time when the communist regimes of Eastern Europe were firmly entrenched – to respect individual human rights and collective self-determination. The Act has been signed by Albania and all the Soviet and Yugoslav successor states which have joined the CSCE since 1991. The Act consists of four sections or 'baskets', dealing with (i) security, (ii) cooperation in the fields of economics, science, technology and the environment, (iii) cooperation in humanitarian and other fields, and (iv) follow-up activities.

Specifically, the Declaration on Principles Guiding Relations between Participating States contained in basket 1 enshrines sovereign equality and respect for the rights inherent in sovereignty, refraining from the threat or use of force, inviolability of frontiers, territorial integrity of states, peaceful settlement of disputes, non-intervention in internal affairs, respect for human rights and fundamental freedoms (including the freedom of thought, conscience, religion or belief), equal rights and self-determination of peoples, cooperation among states, and fulfilment in good faith of obligations under international law. Basket 2 provides for cooperation (through exchanges, international conferences, joint programmes etc) in a wide range of fields, including commerce, research, environmental protection, transport, tourism and training. Basket 3 provides for improvements in human contacts (by facilitating reunification of families, travel, tourism, sporting links, cultural exchanges etc) and improvement in exchange of information (by facilitating the circulation of and access to publications, better working conditions for journalists etc). Basket 4 provides for the continuation of the CSCE process through follow-up meetings, meetings of experts etc.

Helsinki process Shorthand for the Europe-wide negotiations on cooperation in security, economic, scientific, technological, environmental and human-rights matters

initiated by the CONFERENCE ON SECU-
RITY AND COOPERATION IN EUROPE
(CSCE) in 1972 and leading to the
adoption of the Helsinki Final Act two
years later and a number of subsequent
agreements. The term 'CSCE process' is
also widely used. The term 'Helsinki
process' is sometimes used informally
to denote a process of negotiating confi-
dence- and security building measures
in other regions of conflict, such as the
Balkans or the Mediterranean.

Helsinki Protocol Shorthand for an addi-
tion to the CONVENTION ON LONG-RANGE
TRANSBOUNDARY AIR POLLUTION or
Geneva Convention.

Helsinki region Shorthand for Europe, the
former Soviet republics, Canada and the
United States, i.e. those countries whose
governments have signed the Helsinki
Final Act, the first document of the CON-
FERENCE ON SECURITY AND COOPERATION
IN EUROPE (CSCE) adopted in 1975.

Helsinki Watch International human-rights
organization. Helsinki Watch is the European arm of Human Rights Watch, a US-
based network founded in 1987 to monitor and promote observance of human
rights worldwide. It issues general annual
reports and detailed reports on individual
countries. It works closely with Amnesty
International, but generally takes a
broader view of the human-rights situation in a country. It takes its name from
the Helsinki Final Act, a document containing detailed commitments on human
rights adopted by virtually all European
countries, the former Soviet Union,
Canada and the United States in 1975.

Helveg Petersen, Niels *See* PETERSEN, ...

Helvetia Shorthand for Switzerland, used
on postage stamps and in other contexts
instead of the country's name in the four
official languages (German, French,
Italian and Romansh). It is the Latin name
for Switzerland, taken from a Celtic tribe
which lived in the region at the time of
the Roman Empire.

Hemiciclo ('Hemicycle' or 'Semicircle')
Shorthand for the CONGRESS OF DEPUTIES,
the lower house of the Spanish parliament. The name is taken from the shape
of the debating chamber.

Hemicycle Shorthand for the EUROPEAN
PARLIAMENT, the parliament of the European Union (EU). The name is taken from
the shape of the debating chamber.

HEP *See* DEMOCRATIC PARTY (Turkey).

Her Majesty's Government (HMG)
Formal name of the British government.

Her Majesty's Loyal Opposition Formal
name of the OFFICIAL OPPOSITION, the
largest opposition party in the United
Kingdom.

Herceg-Bosna Croat shorthand for the
CROATIAN REPUBLIC OF HERZEG-BOSNIA,
a self-proclaimed state within Bosnia-
Herzegovina.

Hercegovina *See* HERZEGOVINA.

hereditary peer (United Kingdom) *See* PEER.

Herløv Andersen, Yvonne (1942–)
Danish social worker and politician. A
qualified care assistant, she has been a
social-education teacher (1970–81), head
of department at a children's hospital
(1975–81), head of department at a
correctional institution (1981–87) and
director of a hostel for the homeless
(1987–94). A member of the Centre
Democrats (CD), she was elected to parliament in 1977 and was appointed minister of social affairs in February 1994.

Hermannsson, Steingrímur (1928–)
Icelandic electrical engineer and politician. Elected to parliament for the centrist
Progressive Party (F) in 1971, he became
its leader in April 1979. He has been
minister of justice, religious affairs and
agriculture (1978–79), fisheries and communications (1980–83) and foreign affairs
(1987–88). He was prime minister of a
centre-right coalition from 1983–87 and
of a centre-left coalition from 1988–91.

Herri Batasuna *See* PEOPLE'S UNITY.

Herzeg-Bosnia Shorthand for the
CROATIAN REPUBLIC OF HERZEG-BOSNIA,
a self-proclaimed state within Bosnia-
Herzegovina.

Herzegovina [Hercegovina] Historical
region of Bosnia-Herzegovina. Covering
the southern third of the country, Herzegovina is a geographical description and
has no administrative status or distinct
ethnic or historical identity. Like the rest
of the country, its population has been
very mixed since the late Middle Ages,

with Croats, Muslims, Serbs and other groups represented. The western half is predominantly Croat.

Herzog, Roman (1934–) German academic and politician. He lectured in constitutional law until he entered politics. A member of the Christian Democratic Union (CDU) since 1970, he was minister of education and internal affairs in the state of Baden-Württemberg from 1978–80 and 1980–83 respectively. He was then appointed to the Federal Constitutional Court and became its president in 1987. He was elected federal president (a non-executive post) in May 1994 and was sworn in for a five-year term in July.

Heseltine, Michael (1933–) British publisher and politician. Director of two major publishing groups from 1961–70, he was elected to Parliament for the Conservative Party in 1966. He held several junior ministerial posts from 1970–74 and was appointed environment secretary (also responsible for housing and local government affairs) when the Conservatives returned to power in 1979. He was made defence secretary in 1983. He resigned in 1986 over what he saw as the decline of collective Cabinet government under Margaret Thatcher. He challenged her for the party leadership in 1990: the contest led to her resignation, but he was defeated in the second round by John Major. He then returned to the government as environment secretary. In April 1992 he took on the trade and industry portfolio and also became president of the Board of Trade.

Hesoun, Josef (1930–) Austrian car mechanic, trade-union official and politician. He became a full-time official with the Construction Workers' and Woodworkers' Union (GBH) in 1961 and has been its president since April 1986. He also became vice-president of the Austrian Trade Union Federation (ÖGB) in October 1987. A member of the Social Democratic Party (SPÖ), he was elected to parliament in 1979 and was appointed minister of employment and social affairs in December 1990.

Hesse [Hessen] Federal state [Land] of Germany. Situated in the centre, Hessen has an area of 21,114 sq km and a population of 5,923,000. The capital is Wiesbaden, but the main city is Frankfurt, Germany's financial centre; other major cities are Kassel and Darmstadt. The economy is based on manufacturing (chemicals, motor vehicles, electronics, engineering), financial and other services, agriculture and forestry. Hesse is one of Germany's most productive and affluent states. Political power is exercised by the State Assembly [Landtag], with 110 members elected for a four-year term, and a government headed by a minister-president. The main parties are the Social Democratic Party (SPD), the Christian Democratic Union (CDU), the Greens and the centrist Free Democratic Party (FDP). At the election in January 1991 the SPD gained 40.8% of the vote and 46 seats, the CDU 40.2% and 46 seats, the Greens 8.8% and 10 seats and the FDP 7.4% and eight seats. The government is formed by an SPD-Green coalition headed by Hans Eichel. Historically divided into a number of small states but with a strong regional identity, Hesse was established as a federal state after the Second World War.

Hessen *See* HESSE.

Hexagonal Group *See* CENTRAL EUROPEAN INITIATIVE.

Hezbollah [Hizballah] Turkish guerrilla group. Hezbollah is one of several Islamic fundamentalist groups that emerged in the late 1980s. It has been responsible for assassinations of prominent advocates of secularist views, including human-rights campaigners, academics, lawyers and journalists. It is strongly influenced by the Lebanese Hezbollah [Ḥizb Allāh] ('Party of God') and shares its strongly anti-US and anti-European stance. Like its namesake it also has close links with Iranian groups.

Hfl Abbreviation for the gulden or GUILDER, the Dutch currency. It is taken from Holland, the informal name for the Netherlands, and florin [florijn], an old name for the guilder.

Hibernia Literary name for Ireland. Hibernia was the Roman name for the island.

hidden government [sottogoverno] In Italy, a common name for the perceived informal coalition of elements in the government, political parties, civil service, police, intelligence agencies, armed forces, business and organized crime aimed at controlling the reins of power outside the constitutional order. The existence, extent and influence of the *sottogoverno* have been a major issue of debate in Italy for many years. At its broadest it can be said to include the traditional workings of the informal economy and the deep-rooted system of patronage known as 'clientism' [clientelismo]. Although much criticized, this was also widely seen as a necessary lubricant of economic and social life and operated with the consent of the millions of people who benefited from it. Since the late 1970s, however, a succession of events, scandals and revelations has suggested the existence of a web of collusion, corruption and illegality not merely underlying but institutionalized at the heart of public life, which constitutes, critics claim, a fundamental threat to Italian democracy. Elements of the *sottogoverno* were revealed, in some cases many years after the events in question, in the kidnapping and murder of Aldo Moro, a former prime minister, in 1978; the bombing of Bologna railway station by far-right extremists in 1980; the P-2 affair, involving the activities of a secret society composed of influential people with right-wing sympathies, exposed in 1981; the Banco Ambrosiano affair, involving the collapse of a major bank in 1982; the Gladio affair, involving the activities of a secret paramilitary force, exposed in 1990; the assassination and bombings carried out by the Armed Phalange group in 1992 and 1993; and above all the illegal party-funding and other scandals which broke in 1992 and 1993, which revealed endemic corruption, bribery, embezzlement and criminal association. *See also* ITALIAN CORRUPTION SCANDALS, MAFIA *and specific entries on affairs etc.*

high commissioner [ríkisumboðsmaður (Faroese), rigsombudsmand (Danish)] Senior officer of state in the Faroe Islands, a Danish dependency. The representative of the Danish crown and government,

s/he advises the Faroese parliament and government and is responsible for defence, foreign affairs and other matters not delegated to the territory.

high commissioner on national minorities Official of the Conference on Security and Cooperation in Europe (CSCE). This post was established in July 1992 as part of a package of measures aimed at improving the CSCE's conflict-prevention and crisis-management mechanisms. The high commissioner is charged with identifying potential ethnic conflicts at an early stage and initiating 'good offices' missions to the countries concerned. S/he submits regular reports to the Committee of Senior Officials (CSO) and the Council of Foreign Ministers.

High Court of Justice or **High Court** [Haute Cour de Justice] French judicial body. Set up under the 1958 constitution, the High Court is composed of an equal number of members of the National Assembly and the Senate, the two houses of parliament. Its sole power is to try the president of the republic for high treason. An indictment must be backed by a majority of members of both houses. The High Court was originally also responsible for trying government ministers for offences allegedly committed while in office, but this power was transferred to the new Court of Justice in July 1993.

Hillsborough Agreement *See* ANGLO-IRISH AGREEMENT.

Hintze, Peter (1950–) German clergyman and politician. He studied theology and then practised as a Lutheran Protestant vicar, pastor and then priest from 1977–83. From 1984–90 he was the federal commissioner for alternative national service. He was elected to parliament for the Christian Democratic Union (CDU) in 1990. Briefly a junior minister from 1991–92, he was elected the party's general secretary in April 1992.

Hirš, Pavel (1942–) Czech biologist and politician. Before he entered politics in 1989 he worked at the Technical University of Prague and the Czechoslovak Academy of Sciences as a researcher, specializing in medical technology. Elected to parliament for the Czechoslovak

Socialist Party (ČSS) in 1992, he was elected leader of the renamed Liberal National Social Party (LSNS) in May 1993.

historical party In the former communist countries, a political party with roots in the pre-communist era. Most of these played important roles in their respective countries until they were either banned or subordinated by the communist regimes which held power from the mid 1940s until 1989/91. Examples are the Radical Democratic Party (RDP) and Bulgarian Agrarian National Union (BZNS) in Bulgaria, the Liberal National Social Party (LSNS) in the Czech Republic, the Independent Smallholders' Party (FKgP) in Hungary, the Farmer's Union of Latvia (LZS), the Social Democratic Party of Lithuania (LSDP) and the Christian Democratic National Peasants' Party (PNT-CD) in Romania.

historical regions [región histórica, pl. regiones -s] In Spain, a collective name for the autonomous communities or regions whose historical, linguistic and cultural characteristics set them apart from the rest of the country. Traditionally three such regions are recognized, the Basque Country, Catalonia and Galicia. They were the first to be granted autonomy in the early 1980s and have wider powers of self-government than the other regions. The term is often extended to include other regions with a strong identity, such as Andalusia and Navarre.

hitlerism Political outlook based on the values and policies of Adolf Hitler, who ruled Germany from 1933 until his death in 1945. *See* NAZISM.

HIV-infected blood affair Medical scandal and political controversy in France surrounding the distribution for transfusions of blood contaminated by HIV, the virus that causes AIDS. During 1984–85 the National Blood Transfusion Centre (CNTS) processed unscreened blood even though the technique for identifying and destroying the virus was known. As a result around 1,500 hemophiliacs were infected with HIV and by mid 1994 around 400 had died from aids and aids-related diseases. In October 1992 the

director of the CNTS and his deputy were found guilty of knowingly distributing the contaminated blood. Reacting to calls for the responsible ministers to be made accountable for failing to stop the distribution, parliament in December 1992 called for the indictment of Edmond Hervé (health), Georgina Dufoix (social affairs) and Laurent Fabius, prime minister from 1984–86 and at the time leader of the Socialist Party (PS). The motion was in fact tabled by the PS to give the former ministers an opportunity to clear their names.

Hizballah *See* HEZBOLLAH.

HMG Abbreviation for Her Majesty's Government, the formal name of the British government.

HND *See* CROATIAN INDEPENDENT DEMOCRATS.

HNS *See* CROATIAN PEOPLE'S PARTY.

Holland Informal name for the Netherlands, widely used, especially abroad. It properly refers only to the historical region of Holland in the west, now divided into the provinces of North Holland and South Holland.

Holocaust Common name for the mass persecution and murder of Jews, and by extension other minorities, perpetrated by the German nazi regime. As soon as it came to power in 1933, the far-right National Socialist (Nazi) Party under Adolf Hitler began to implement the racial-purity policies at the core of its ideology. Members of 'inferior', 'deviant' or 'unfit' groups – Jews, Gipsies, homosexuals – were stripped of their civil rights and property and confined to ghettos or labour and concentration camps. After the outbreak of the Second World War in 1939 the policy was extended to the occupied territories. Many thousands of people were killed or died as a result. The 'final solution' programme adopted in 1942 provided for the systematic genocide of the Jewish people in Europe. Between 4 and 5 million Jews were killed in extermination camps (Auschwitz-Birkenau, Belzec, Majdanek, Sobibor, Treblinka etc) until 1945. The total number of Jews killed during the nazi period is estimated at 6 million. Around

500,000 Gipsies were also killed. From the 1950s West Germany paid compensation to survivors of the camps and other victims of nazi persecution. Communist East Germany refused to do so on the grounds that it was not a successor state to the Third Reich.

Holst, Johan Jørgen (1937–94) Norwegian politician. He worked as a researcher at the Norwegian Institute of International Affairs (NUPI) from 1969–76 and was its director from 1981–88 and in 1989–90. A member of the Norwegian Labour Party (DNA), he was a junior minister for defence and then foreign affairs from 1976–81 and defence minister from 1986–89. When Labour formed another government in 1990, he returned as defence minister. In April 1993 he was appointed foreign minister. He played a key role in the secret negotiations leading to the peace agreement between Israel and the Palestine Liberation Organization (PLO) in September 1993. He died in January 1994 after suffering a stroke the previous month.

Holy Crown *See* SACRA CORONA.

Holy Mountain [Ágion Óros] or **Mount Athos** [Áthos] Autonomous district of Greece. A peninsula situated on the northeastern coast, Holy Mountain or Mount Athos has an area of 336 sq km and a population of 1,500. It is a Greek Orthodox religious community (belonging to the order of Saint Basil) consisting of 20 monasteries. Under a constitution drawn up in 1927 and recognized by the Greek government, Mount Athos is described as a 'self-governing republic'. Legislative power is vested in the 20-member Holy Council [Ierá Sínaxis], in which each monastery is represented; executive power is vested in the Board [Epistasía], composed of four members appointed by annual rotation; the Greek government is represented by a governor appointed by the foreign minister. The first monastery on Mount Athos was founded in 963. The monasteries were granted a charter by a Byzantine emperor later in the 10th century and also enjoyed autonomous status under Ottoman rule (1430–1913). The territory's special status was confirmed in 1927 and in the Greek constitution adopted in 1975. Women and female animals are barred from the territory.

Holy See [Sancta Sedes (Latin)] Formal name of the Papacy, the governing body of the worldwide Roman Catholic Church, based in the VATICAN CITY. The Holy See is the bishopric or see of Rome, the Church's primary see because its incumbent is also head of the Church or pope. (According to Catholic teaching the pope's authority is ultimately derived from his position as successor to the apostle Peter as bishop of Rome.) The pope is also the Vatican's head of state. 'Holy See' and 'Vatican' are often used interchangeably, but the two are distinct legal entities. Properly the Vatican is merely the territorial base for the Holy See. It is a sovereign state, but relations with other governments are the responsibility of the Holy See.

home counties In the United Kingdom, a collective name for counties bordering London or, more generally, those near London. These days the term often includes the whole of the SOUTHEAST region outside Greater London (i.e. Berkshire, Buckinghamshire, Essex, Hertfordshire, Hampshire, Kent, Oxfordshire, Surrey and Sussex).

home rule (United Kingdom) *See* DEVOLUTION.

Home Rule Party *See* SELF-GOVERNMENT PARTY.

Homeland [Ojczyzna], in full **Catholic Election Committee 'Homeland'** [Katolicky Komitet Wyborczy 'Ojczyzna'] (KKW'O') Polish political organization. Ojczyzna was formed prior to the September 1993 election as an alliance of four right-wing parties, the Christian National Union (ZChN), Conservative Party (PK), Peasant Christian Party (SLCh) and Christian Democratic Party (PChD). It gained 6.4% of the vote but no seats, having failed to reach the 8% alliances needed to secure for representation. *See also individual party entries and* ALLIANCE FOR POLAND.

Homeland Accord [Tėvynės Santara] Lithuanian political organization. The

Accord is a loose alliance of centre-right and right-wing opposition parties formed after the victory of the left-wing Democratic Labour Party (LDDP) in the October/November 1992 election. It includes the Homeland Union (TS, the successor to the Reform Movement, Sąjūdis), Christian Democratic Party (KDP), Citizens' Charter (PCh), Political Prisoners' and Exiles' Union (PKTLS) and four smaller parties. It holds 52/141 seats in parliament. The leader is Vytautas Landsbergis, who is also the TS's leader.

Homeland Union [Tėvynės Sąjunga] (TS) Lithuanian political party. The TS was founded in May 1993 as the successor to the Reform Movement or Movement (Sąjūdis). Founded in 1988 as a broad-based alliance aimed at the reform of communist society and 'sovereignty' for Lithuania, then still part of the Soviet Union, Sąjūdis spearheaded the independence campaign. It gained an overwhelming majority in the multiparty election in February/March 1990. It formed a government when independence was achieved in the wake of the abortive Soviet coup in August 1991 and initiated a programme of rapid economic reform. The more narrowly based alliance it led in the October/November 1992 election incurred heavy losses, gaining 19.8% of the vote and 30/141 seats. The Sąjūdis parliamentary group consists of 16 deputies, who have joined the Homeland Accord (Tėvynės Santara) alliance. The TS has adopted a right-wing programme. The leader is Vytautas Landsbergis, Sąjūdis's leader since its foundation.

homes-for-votes affair Controversy in the United Kingdom surrounding the alleged attempts by Westminster local council to use housing policy to manipulate local election outcomes. Situated in central London, Westminster is the country's richest and most prestigious local authority, and during the 1980s it was also a flagship of the Conservative government. In July 1989 a television documentary made detailed allegations that it had operated a 'designated sales' programme between 1987 and 1989, under which thousands of council tenants in marginal electoral wards were induced to move elsewhere and the vacated homes were sold at discount prices to private purchasers considered more likely to vote Conservative. Many properties were also reportedly left empty even though the district had a large number of homeless. (The Conservatives substantially increased their overall majority on the council in the 1990 local election.) The district auditor, an independent official supervising local government, who had launched an investigation into the allegations, published a provisional report in January 1993. He described the designated sales programme as 'unlawful' and 'unauthorized' and assessed its cost to council funds at 21.3 million pounds (27.1 million ecus). He accused the council leader, Shirley Porter (Lady Porter), and nine other council members and officials of 'wilful misconduct'. Under English law they will be personally liable for the monies lost if convicted of wrongdoing. (One of them has committed suicide.) In March 1994 the district auditor launched a second inquiry into other council policies allegedly aimed at gerrymandering.

Honecker, Erich (1912–94) German politician. A member of the Communist Party of Germany (KPD) from 1929, he was imprisoned by the nazi regime from 1935–45. He was leader of the youth wing of the renamed Socialist Unity Party (SED) in East Germany from 1946–55, became a member of the politburo in 1958 and party leader in 1971. In 1976 he also became head of state of East Germany. The country's dominant political figure in the 1970s and 80s, he was forced to resign in October 1989 in the face of widespread popular protests. After German reunification in October 1990, moves were initiated to arrest him, but while under treatment for liver cancer in a Soviet military hospital in former East Germany he fled to Moscow in March 1991 and took refuge in the Chilean embassy. He was extradited to Germany in July 1992 to face trial on specimen charges of manslaughter (of 13 people killed while trying to flee to West Germany in the 1960s and 70s) and mis-appropriation of state funds. His trial opened in November 1992 but he was released the following January on health grounds. He joined his wife in Chile, where one of his daughters lived, and died in May 1994.

Horn, Gyula (1932–) Hungarian economist, civil servant and politician. He worked in the finance ministry from 1954–59, in the foreign ministry from 1959–61, as a diplomat from 1961–69 and then in the influential international department of the communist Hungarian Socialist Workers' Party (MSzMP), which he headed from 1983–85. He became a junior foreign minister in 1985 and was made foreign minister in 1989, a post he held until the reconstituted Hungarian Socialist Party (MSzP) lost power after the multiparty election the following year. A supporter of economic and political reform, he was elected party leader in May 1990. After the MSzP won the May 1994 election, he became prime minister of a centre-left coalition with the Alliance of Free Democrats (SzDSz) in July.

Hörnlund, Börje (1935–) Swedish forestry engineer and politician. He has been a forestry inspector and manager. He was active in local government for the Centre Party (Cp) for many years, and served as chairman of the Swedish Federation of County Councils from 1977–80. Elected to parliament in 1976, he was appointed minister of labour in the centre-right coalition which took office in October 1991.

Hory, Jean-François (1949–) French civil servant and politician. A specialist in public law, he worked in the administration of the French dependency of Mayotte and was also its representative in the National Assembly from 1981–86. He then returned to domestic politics and was elected leader of the Left Radical Movement (MRG) in June 1992. He was also elected to the European Parliament in 1994 and became leader of the European Radical Alliance (ERA) group in July.

HOS *See* CROATIAN DEFENCE ASSOCIATION.

Hospitallers *See* SOVEREIGN MILITARY ORDER OF MALTA.

Hôtel Matignon or **Matignon** Shorthand for the French prime minister's office. The Matignon in Paris is the official residence of the prime minister.

House of Assembly Parliament of Gibraltar. It has 15 elected members and two ex-officio members, the attorney-general and the financial and development secretary (who is responsible for economic affairs). Members are elected for a four-year term by a system under which voters may vote for a maximum of eight candidates and a party is restricted to a maximum of eight seats regardless of its popular vote.

House of Bernadotte [Släkt Bernadotte] Royal dynasty of Sweden. The name is taken from the French marshal Jean-Baptiste Bernadotte, who was named crown prince by parliament in 1810 and ruled as King Carl XIV Johan from 1818–44.

House of Bourbon [Casa de Borbón] Royal dynasty of Spain. One of the major ruling houses of Europe since the 16th century, the Bourbons are descended from Louis (1270–1342), grandson of King Louis IX of France and duke of Bourbon. They have ruled in Spain intermittently since 1700.

House of Commons Lower house of the British Parliament. The Commons has 651 members elected for a five-year term by a system of simple majority voting in single-member constituencies. *See also* HOUSE OF LORDS.

House of Counties [Županijski Dom] Upper house of the Croatian parliament, the Sabor. It has 68 members, 63 elected for a four-year term on a regional basis, three from each of the 21 *županije*, and five appointed by the president. Essentially a revising chamber, its decisions can in most cases be overruled by the lower house, the House of Representatives, by a simple majority.

House of Keys *See* TYNWALD.

House of Lords Upper house of the British Parliament and supreme court of the United Kingdom. The Lords has around 1,200 members, known as 'peers': around 775 hereditary nobles; around 380 'life peers', ennobled by the sovereign, on the advice of the prime minister and nominally for public service; the lord chancellor, who is also ex officio the speaker or president; around 20 lords of appeal or law lords, former senior judges; and two archbishops and 24 bishops of the Church of England. Only a small number of members, mostly life peers, regularly attend sessions. The Lords has the power to amend legislation passed by the lower house, the House of Commons, but ultimately it can only delay and not veto bills. As a judicial body the House of Lords consists of the lord chancellor and the lords of appeal. As a body the latter are commonly known as the Law Lords. It is the ultimate court of appeal for the United Kingdom (with the exception of criminal cases in Scotland, in which the High Court of Justiciary is the appeal court) and the crown dependencies of Guernsey, Jersey and Man.

House of Oldenburg [Oldenborgerne] Common name for the royal dynasties of Denmark and Norway. Count Christian of Oldenburg (in Germany) was elected king of Denmark and Norway in 1448 and 1450 respectively. His line ruled in Norway until 1814 and in Denmark until 1863, when a member of a collateral branch of the family (Schleswig-Holstein-Sonderburg-Glücksburg) ascended the throne as Christian IX. In 1905 one of his grandsons was elected king of Norway and took the name Haakon VII.

House of Orange-Nassau or **House of Orange** [Huis van Oranje-Nassau] Royal dynasty of the Netherlands. The name derives from the principality of Orange in southern France, inherited by William of Nassau (1533–84), a German-Dutch nobleman who was the most prominent leader of the Dutch revolt against Spain. Princes of Orange subsequently held senior posts in the Dutch Republic, and in 1815 a member of the dynasty became king of the Netherlands as William I.

House of Provinces *See* HOUSE OF COUNTIES.

House of Representatives [Zastupnički Dom] Lower house of the Croatian parliament, the Sabor. It has 138 members: 60 are elected by simple majority in single-member constituencies; 60 are elected by proportional representation, with parties requiring at least 3% of the popular vote to qualify for seats; and 13 seats are reserved for the Serb minority and five for other ethnic minorities.

House of Representatives [Voulí Antiprósopon] Parliament of Cyprus. It has 56 members elected for a five-year term by proportional representation. An additional 24 seats reserved for the Turkish Cypriot community have been vacant since 1963, when the Turkish Cypriot parties withdrew from the republic's political institutions.

House of Representatives [Abgeordnetenhaus] Parliament of Berlin, a federal state of Germany.

House of Representatives [Il-Kamra tad-Deputadi] Parliament of Malta. It has 65 members elected for a five-year term by proportional representation (using the single-transferable-vote system) in multi-member constituencies. When a party gains a majority of votes but through anomalies in the electoral system fails to gain a majority of seats (as happened in 1987), it will be allocated additional seats until it has a majority of one.

House of Windsor Royal dynasty of the United Kingdom. The name is taken from Windsor Castle, one of the royal residences. It was adopted in 1917, during the First World War, because of the German connotations of the existing name of Saxe-Coburg-Gotha.

Howard, Michael (1941–) British lawyer and politician. Elected to Parliament for the Conservative Party in 1983, he held several junior ministerial posts from 1985. He was secretary of state for employment from 1990–92 and of environment (which includes local government affairs and housing) from 1992–93. He was appointed home secretary in May 1993.

Hoxha, Nexhmije (1920–) Albanian politician. The wife of Enver Hoxha, the country's leader from 1944 until his death in 1985, she held a series of senior posts in the communist Party of Labour (PPSh) and affiliated organizations for many years. A strong opponent of reform, she was removed from all her posts in 1990. She was expelled from the party and arrested on corruption charges the following year. In January 1993 she was convicted of misuse of public funds between 1985–90 and sentenced to nine years' imprisonment, later extended to 11 years'.

Höynck, Wilhelm (1933–) German diplomat. A law graduate, he entered the diplomatic service in 1964. He held a series of senior posts in the foreign ministry from 1975, becoming its deputy political director in 1990. Appointed German ambassador to the Conference on Security and Cooperation in Europe (CSCE) in 1991, he became the CSCE's first general secretary in May 1993.

Høyre *See* CONSERVATIVE PARTY (Norway).

HR Abbreviation for Croatia, used for international vehicle registrations, postal addresses etc. It is taken from Hrvatska, the Croat name for Croatia.

Hradčany Shorthand for the Czech presidency. The Hradčany or Prague Castle in Prague is the official residence of the president.

HRK Abbreviation for the KUNA, the Croatian currency, used in banking etc.

HRU *See* PARTY FOR THE DEFENCE OF HUMAN RIGHTS.

Hrvatska Croat name for Croatia.

HSDMS *See* CZECHOMORAVIAN CENTRE PARTY.

HSLS *See* CROATIAN SOCIAL LIBERAL PARTY.

HSP *See* CROATIAN PARTY OF RIGHTS.

HSP *See* HUNGARIAN SOCIALIST PARTY.

HSS *See* CROATIAN PEASANT PARTY.

Hue, Robert (1946–) French nurse and politician. He has been active in local government for the French Communist Party (PCF) since the mid 1960s. He was elected mayor of the Paris suburb of Montigny-lès-Cormeilles in 1977 and became a member of the Île-de-France regional council in 1982. He subsequently became president of the association of PCF deputies and regional and local councillors. He was elected to the party central committee in 1987 and the politburo in 1990. A supporter of long-time party leader Georges Marchais, he succeeded him in January 1994.

HUF Abbreviation for the FORINT, the Hungarian currency, used in banking etc.

human dimension In the Conference on Security and Cooperation in Europe (CSCE), an umbrella term for human-rights and humanitarian issues. The 1975 Helsinki Final Act, the CSCE's founding document, sets out a number of principles and provides for cooperation on human rights in the broadest sense, from reuniting families to circulation of information and cultural exchanges. But progress in these fields was minimal until the improvement in East-West relations in the late 1980s and the subsequent end of the Cold War and collapse of communist rule. Three human-rights conferences were held at this time, in Paris (May–June 1989), Copenhagen (June 1990) and Moscow (September 1991). The second conference approved the COPENHAGEN DOCUMENT guaranteeing the rights of citizens and committing governments to pluralist democracy and the rule of law. Since then a number of specialist meetings and seminars have been organized under the rubric of the 'human dimension' on such issues as tolerance, migration, minority rights, media freedom and citizenship rights.

Human Rights Prize *See* COUNCIL OF EUROPE ....

Human Rights Union *See* PARTY FOR THE DEFENCE OF HUMAN RIGHTS.

Hume, John (1937–) British politician. He studied politics and international relations and was president of the Credit Union League of Ireland from 1964–68. A Northern Irish Catholic, he became a prominent civil-rights campaigner in the 1960s. He was a founding member of the Social Democratic and Labour Party (SDLP) in 1970, becoming its deputy leader. In November 1979 he was elected party leader. He has been a member of the European Parliament since 1979 and a member of the House of Commons since 1983.

hung parliament In the United Kingdom, the situation in which no party has an overall majority of seats in the House of Commons, the lower house of Parliament. Since the country's simple-majority voting system (known as 'first-past-the-post') tends to reward the largest party with a disproportionate number of seats, this is a rare occurrence. No party has gained more than half the popular vote in the 14 elections since 1945, but only one election (February 1974) produced a hung parliament.

Hungarian Christian Democratic Movement [Mad'arské Krest'ansko-Demokratické Hnutie (Slovak), Magyar Kereszténydemokrata Mozgalom (Hungarian)] (MKDH or MKDM) Slovakian political party. Founded in 1989, the MKDM is one of the parties representing the ethnic Hungarian community in the south. It contested the June 1992 election jointly with Coexistence: the alliance gained 7.4% of the vote and the party 5/150 seats. The leader is Béla Bugár.

Hungarian Democratic Forum [Magyar Demokrata Fórum] (MDF) Hungarian political party. Founded in 1987, the MDF is a centre-right party favouring a relatively gradual transition to the market economy. At the March/April 1990 election it became the largest group in parliament, gaining 24.7% of the vote and 165/386 seats. It then formed a coalition with two other parties. In 1992 and 1993 around 30 deputies left the parliamentary group to sit as independents or join other groups. It was heavily defeated in the May 1994 election, gaining 11.7% and 37 seats. The party was led by József Antall until his death in December 1993. The current leader is Lajos Für.

Hungarian Democratic Union of Romania [Uniunea Democrată Maghiară din România (Romanian), Romániai Magyar Demokraták Szövetsége (Hungarian)] (UDMR or RMDSz) Romanian political party. Formed in 1990 after the collapse of the communist regime, the RMDSz is the main representative of the ethnic Hungarian community in Transylvania. It campaigns for the rights of the Hungarian and other minorities and for 'self-administration' for the majority-Hungarian districts within Romania. At the September 1992 election it gained 7.5% of the vote and 27/341 seats, making it the fifth-largest party in parliament. The leader is Béla Markó.

Hungarian Justice and Life Party [Magyar Igazság és Élet Párt] (MIÉP) Hungarian political party. Initially called the Hungarian Justice Party, the MIÉP was formed in June 1993 by right-wing members of the Hungarian Democratic Forum (MDF). It stands for 'Hungarian and Christian ideals' and has close links with the Hungarian Way (Magyar Ut) movement founded in 1992 by István Csurka, a former MDF member. It gained 1.6% of the vote but no seats at the May 1994 election. The joint leaders are Csurka and Lajos Horváth.

Hungarian Justice Party *See* HUNGARIAN JUSTICE AND LIFE PARTY.

Hungarian Path *See* HUNGARIAN WAY.

Hungarian Socialist Party [Magyar Szocialista Párt] (MSzP) Hungarian political party. The MSzP is the successor to the Hungarian Socialist Workers' Party (MSzMP), which was formed in 1948 by the merger of the Hungarian Communist Party (MKP) and the Hungarian Social Democratic Party (MSzDP) and held power as the sole legal party until the introduction of a multiparty system in October 1989. That month it was renamed and adopted a mainstream left-wing programme. At the March/April 1990 election the MSzP gained 10.9% of the vote and 33/386 seats. Campaigning on a platform of market reforms and social justice, it won the May 1994 election, gaining 33.0% and 209 seats. It then formed a coalition with the centrist Alliance of Free Democrats (SzDSz). The leader and prime minister is Gyula Horn, the party president is Iván Vitány.

Hungarian Truth and Life Party *See* HUNGARIAN JUSTICE AND ....

Hungarian Way [Magyar Ut] Hungarian cultural and political organization. Founded in September 1992 by István Csurka, then a leading member of the Hungarian Democratic Forum (MDF), Magyar Ut is a strongly nationalistic mass movement. It accuses 'communists, liberals and Jews' of conspiring against the Hungarian people and calls for the creation of a 'new Hungarian living space' (i.e. the annexation of Hungarian-speaking regions in neighbouring countries). It has close links with the Hungarian Justice and Life Party (MIÉP), a far-right breakaway from the MDF.

Hungarian Workers' Party [Magyar Munkáspárt] (MMP) Hungarian political party. The MMP has its roots in the communist Hungarian Socialist Workers' Party (MSzMP). When the MSzMP majority voted to relaunch the party as the Hungarian Socialist Party (MSzP) in 1989, a year before it lost power, a minority formed a new party. It initially took the old name, but this was changed in December 1992. Campaigning on a broadly reformist communist platform, it gained 3.2% of the vote at the May 1994 election but no seats, having failed to pass the 4% threshold for parliamentary representation. The leader is Gyula Thürmer.

Hungary [Magyarország] Country in central Europe.

Official data. Name: Hungarian Republic [Magyar Köztársaság]; capital: Budapest; form of government: parliamentary republic; head of state: president; head of government: prime minister; flag: three horizontal stripes, red, white and green; national holiday: 20 August (Saint Stephen's Day); language: Hungarian; religion: none; currency: forint (Ft) = 100 fillér; abbreviation: H.

Geography. Hungary has an area of 93,033 sq km. Land-locked, it is bordered by Slovakia in the north, Ukraine and Romania in the east, Yugoslavia and Croatia in the south, and Slovenia and Austria in the west. The dominant physical feature is the Great Hungarian Plain [Nagy Magyar Alföld], which covers the eastern half of the country. The land to the west of the Danube [Duna] river consists of rolling plains, hill lands and low mountains. The mountains in the northeast form part of the Carpathians. Some 57% of the land is arable, another 14% is covered by pastures and 18% is forested. The main rivers are the Danube and Tisza. The climate is humid continental, with hot summers and cold winters; rainfall is moderate, lower in the east.

Demography. Hungary has a population of 10,296,000. Population density is 111 per sq km (land area). Some 62% of the

people live in urban areas, and around a quarter lives in Budapest and its suburbs (population 2.5 million, city 2.0 million). Other major cities are Debrecen, Miskolc, Szeged, Pécs and Győr. In ethnic terms 91.2% of the people are Hungarians. Minorities include Gipsies (5.8% of the total population), Germans (1.6%), Slovaks (1.1%), Croats, Romanians and Poles. The German community is declining in numbers as a result of emigration to Germany. Hungary has also taken in around 30,000 refugees from former Yugoslavia. There are very large ethnic Hungarian communities in the neighbouring countries, numbering 1.62 million in Romania, 580,000 in Slovakia, 380,000 in Yugoslavia and 180,000 in Ukraine. The main language is Hungarian. In religious terms 64.1% of the population is nominally Roman Catholic, 19.2% Calvinist Protestant, 4.1% Lutheran Protestant, 0.9% Jewish, 0.5% Hungarian Orthodox; most of the remainder is not religious.

Sociography. Hungary scores 0.863 on the United Nations human development index (HDI), ranking 31st in the world and 23rd among 32 European countries. There are 33 doctors and 101 hospital beds for every 10,000 people. Education is compulsory between the ages of six and 16. There is one teacher for every 14 students. Enrolment is 75% at the secondary level and 15% at the tertiary level. The literacy rate is 97%. Real annual income per head (in terms of purchasing power) is US$ 6,080.

Infrastructure and communications. Hungary's transport and communications network is developed but in need of modernization; the telecommunications system in particular is relatively limited. There are 61,340 km of paved roads and 1.91 million passenger cars (185 per 1,000 people), 7,770 km of railways and 1,622 km of navigable waterways. The main (inland) port is Budapest. The main airport is at Budapest (Ferihegy); there are no other airports with scheduled services. There are 31 daily newspapers, with a combined circulation of 2.51 million (237 per 1,000 people). There are 6.25 million radio receivers, 4.22 million television sets and 1.87 million telephones in use (respectively 605, 408 and 181 per 1,000 people).

Economic structure. The Hungarian economy is based on manufacturing, agriculture and food processing. Although essentially developed, diversified and trade-oriented, it is in need of major investment and restructuring. The transition from a command to a market-based economy initiated in 1989 is causing great dislocation and has led to steep falls in industrial and agricultural production in particular. Between 1990 and 1993 GDP contracted by 13%, inflation averaged 27% per year, the currency lost a third of its value, and unemployment rose to 13%. The current account moved into surplus during this period and growth resumed in 1993. The foreign debt stands at around US$ 22 billion (80% of GDP).

Services contribute 49% of GDP, industry contributes 39% (manufacturing 26%), and agriculture and forestry 12%. Some 30% of the labour force is employed in manufacturing, 14% in farming and 13% in trade. The main crops grown are cereals (maize, wheat), potatoes and sugarbeets; horticulture (fruit and vegetables, esp. apples and grapes), livestock raising (pigs, cattle, poultry) and dairy farming (eggs) are other important agricultural activities. Forestry is of regional importance. The main mineral resources are lignite, coal and bauxite. The main industries are engineering, electrical goods, chemicals, food processing, textiles, petrochemicals and iron and steel. Tourism is an important source of foreign exchange, contributing 2% of GNP. The main energy sources are domestic lignite and nuclear power and imported fossil fuels; 10% of export earnings are required to cover net fuel imports. The main exports are textiles and clothing (11% of the total), electrical equipment (9%), meat and meat products (9%), fruit and vegetables (6%), motor vehicles (5%), pharmaceuticals (5%) and iron and steel; foodstuffs account for 23% of the total, machinery and transport equipment for 22%. The main imports are machinery and transport equipment, basic manufactures, fuels and chemicals. The main trading partners are: exports: Germany (28%), Russia, Ukraine and other members of the Commonwealth of Independent States (CIS) (12%), Austria (11%), Italy, France; imports: Germany (22%), Russia, Ukraine and other CIS members (19%), Austria (16%), Italy (7%), Czech Republic, Switzerland; two-fifths of all trade is with European Union (EU) countries.

The Hungarian National Bank [Magyar Nemzeti Bank] is the central bank. The main employers' association is the National Federation of Entrepreneurs (VOSz); the main labour organization is the National Confederation of Hungarian Trade Unions (MSzOSz).

Political structure. Hungary is a parliamentary republic on the basis of a transitional constitution adopted in 1989, replacing the communist constitution last amended in 1983. The head of state is the president, who is elected for a four-year term by the legislature; s/he is nominally commander of the armed forces but has few real powers. Executive power is vested in the prime minister and the council of ministers. Legislative power is vested in the 394-member National Assembly [Országgyűlés] elected for a four-year term by a mixed system of proportional representation and majority voting (with a 4% threshold for gaining seats); eight seats are allocated to ethnic minorities. All citizens over the age of 18 are entitled to vote. Judicial power is ultimately vested in the five-member Supreme Court [Legfelsőbb Bíróság], whose president is elected by the legislature and whose other members are appointed by the president of the republic; the Constitutional Court [Alkotmányos Bíróság] adjudicates on constitutional matters. Administratively the country is divided into 19 counties [megye, pl. megyék], five county-level cities and the city of Budapest; the counties are subdivided into around 1,500 municipalities.

The main political parties are the Hungarian Socialist Party (MSzP), Alliance of Free Democrats (SzDSz), Hungarian Democratic Forum (MDF), Independent Smallholders' Party (FKgP),

Christian Democratic People's Party (KDNP), Alliance of Young Democrats (FIDESz) and Hungarian Workers' Party (MMP). At the general election in May 1994 the MSzP gained 33.0% of the vote and 209/386 seats, the SzDSz 19.8% and 70 seats, the MDF 11.7% and 37 seats, the FKgP 8.9% and 26 seats, the KDNP 7.1% and 22 seats, FIDESz 7.0% and 20 seats, the MMP 3.2% and no seats, and others two seats. The government is formed by a centre-left coalition of the MSzP and SzDSz, with Gyula Horn as prime minister. Other senior ministers are Gábor Kuncze (deputy prime minister, interior), László Kovács (foreign affairs), László Békesi (finance), Pál Vastagh (justice) and György Keleti (defence). The head of state is President Árpád Göncz, who was elected in August 1990.

Security and international affiliations. The Hungarian armed forces number 78,000 (army 60,500, airforce 17,500). There is also a 15,900-strong paramilitary border guard. Military service is compulsory and consists of 12 months' basic training.

Hungary is a member of the Central European Initiative (CEI), Conference on Security and Cooperation in Europe (CSCE), Council of Europe and Visegrad Group, as well as the United Nations and its specialized agencies. It has applied for membership of the European Union (EU).

History. The area of modern Hungary was inhabited by Celtic tribes when the Romans conquered the area to the south and west of the Danube river in 14 BC. During the Europe-wide migrations that helped trigger the collapse of the Roman Empire in the 5th century it was occupied by Germanic and Slavic peoples. The wider Carpathian basin became the base for nomadic peoples from the Eurasian steppes to the east: the Huns in the 5th century, the Avars from the 6th century until their defeat by the Franks in the 790s, and the Magyars in the 10th century subjugated the local population and invaded and plundered the prosperous regions to the west and south. The Magyars originated in the upper Volga region and were based on the lower Don in the 9th cen-

tury, when they were forced further west by the Pechenegs. They were organized as a federation of ten hordes or tribes. (These were known to the neighbouring Turkic peoples as the On Ogur, 'Ten Arrows', from which the name 'Hungary' is derived.) Led by Árpád, the Magyars crossed the Carpathian Mountains around 896 and gained control of the whole basin after defeating Great Moravia in 906. Their raids into the Holy Roman or German Empire ended after a heavy defeat at the Battle of the Lechfeld in 955. Their ruler, Géza, accepted Christianity in 975. In 1001 his son István was crowned the first king of Hungary as Stephen I. The Kingdom of Hungary, which remained in existence until 1918, included not only modern Hungary but also Slovakia, Ruthenia (now part of Ukraine), Transylvania (Romania), Vojvodina (Yugoslavia) and Croatia. Over the next two centuries a state administration was established, Christianity became the dominant religion, the Magyar elite became a land-owning upper class, Magyars settled in border areas such as Transylvania, and the population in the core territory was magyarized. In 1241–42 the country was devastated by a Mongol invasion, during which around half the total population died. The last king of the Árpád line died in 1301. From then until 1918 Hungary was ruled, with one exception, by foreign kings (French Angevins, a Luxemburger, Polish Jagellonians and Austrian Habsburgs), although the Hungarian nobility retained a large measure of political control until 1526. In the 15th century, and especially under Matthias Corvinus (1458–90), Hungary was the dominant regional power and one of Europe's most prosperous countries. After defeat by the Ottoman Turks and the death of King Louis II at the Battle of Mohács in 1526, Hungary was partitioned: the bulk became part of the Ottoman Empire, the western fringe fell to the Habsburgs, and Transylvania was made a principality under Turkish suzerainty (in 1566).

Between 1683 and 1699 the Habsburgs reconquered historical Hungary. They imposed a centralized Austrian-dominated administration and restored the primacy of Roman Catholicism over Lutheran and Calvinist Protestantism, which had taken root the previous century. The Hungarian nobility thwarted Austrian attempts at economic and social reform in the 1790s. Other reforms did grant more rights to Hungarians; this in turn led to demands for equality from Romanians, Croats, Serbs and Slovaks, who constituted a majority of the population. Inspired by nationalist and democratic uprisings elsewhere in Europe, including Austria, the Hungarians secured a series of political and social reforms in 1848 and, led by Lajos Kossuth, declared their independence the following year. The Austrians suppressed the rebellion with the help of a Russian army. Renewed demands for self-determination from 1861 led to the establishment of the 'dual monarchy' of Austria-Hungary in 1867, with separate parliaments and administrations for the two states. The magyarization policies introduced by successive conservative governments antagonized the other nationalities. As the Habsburg Empire disintegrated at the end of the First World War (1914–18), the Croats and Slovaks declared their independence, Romanian troops occupied Transylvania, and the Hungarian Republic was proclaimed. In 1919 communist revolutionaries led by Béla Kun established a 'soviet republic', but this was overthrown after five months. The borders of rump Hungary were established under the 1920 Treaty of Trianon. It left 3.2 million ethnic Hungarians in neighbouring countries, many of them living immediately across the borders. Centre-right governments sought to introduce some reforms in the 1920s but were unable to deal with a worsening economic situation. In 1932 Miklós Horthy, who had been made regent in 1920 after the formal restoration of the monarchy, appointed a far-right government under Gyula Gömbös. When Gömbös died in 1936 Horthy took power himself. Intent on regaining territories lost after 1918, he formed an alliance with Germany during the Second World War (1939–45). Extensive border corrections

were imposed on Slovakia and Romania, also German allies. After Horthy tried to end the alliance in 1944, German troops invaded and he was forced to abdicate.

In 1945 Hungary was occupied by Soviet troops. The right-wing Independent Smallholders' Party (FKgP) won a general election, but over the next four years the communists, led by Mátyás Rákosi, established control by neutralizing other political forces. The Hungarian Workers' Party (MMP) formally took power after a manipulated election in 1948. A 'people's republic' was proclaimed in 1949. The new regime suppressed political dissent, nationalized the economy, introduced central planning and allied itself closely with the Soviet Union. In 1953 Rákosi was replaced by Imre Nagy, under whose leadership some economic reforms were introduced and political repression was reduced. Nagy was replaced by Rákosi in 1955, but after a popular uprising in 1956 he was reinstated. When the reform movement restored multiparty democracy and proclaimed Hungary's neutrality, it was crushed by Soviet troops at a cost of around 25,000 lives. Nagy and others were executed for treason in 1958. Repression was relaxed in the 1960s, and during the 1970s and 80s Hungary's was among the more liberal communist regimes. János Kádár, who had been party leader since 1956, was replaced in May 1988. The new leadership introduced political and economic reforms. A democratic constitution was adopted in October 1989. The Hungarian Democratic Forum (MDF) under József Antall won the multiparty election in March/April 1990 and formed a centre-right coalition. Weakened by splits and held responsible for the dislocation associated with the economic transformation, the MDF was heavily defeated in the May 1994 election. The Hungarian Socialist Party (MSzP), the relaunched communist party, gained an absolute majority of seats and formed a coalition with the Alliance of Free Democrats (SzDSz) in July.

See also entries on specific institutions, organizations, parties, people, terms etc.

Hunt, David (1942–) British lawyer and politician. Elected to Parliament for the Conservative Party in 1976, he held several junior ministerial posts from 1984. Although not a Welshman, he was made secretary of state (= minister) for Wales in 1990. In May 1993 he became secretary of state for employment. In July 1994 he was appointed chancellor of the Duchy of Lancaster (= minister without portfolio), with responsibility for the civil service, science and open government; he was also made chairman of several key Cabinet committees, thus taking on a coordinating role within the government.

Hurd, Douglas (1930–) British diplomat, writer and politician. He worked in the diplomatic service from 1952–66, with senior postings in China, the United Nations and Italy. He then joined the Conservative Party's research department. He was elected to Parliament in 1974. After holding several junior ministerial posts from 1979, he was appointed secretary of state for Northern Ireland in 1984, home secretary in 1985 and foreign secretary in October 1989. He has also written a number of thriller novels.

HV Abbreviation for Hrvatska Vojska ('Croatian Army'), the armed forces of Croatia. It should not be confused with the Croatian Defence Council (HVO), the army of the Croatian Republic of Herzeg-Bosnia, a self-proclaimed state within Bosnia-Herzegovina. The two forces generally work closely together.

HVA Abbreviation for Hauptverwaltungs-aufklärung ('Central Administrative Intelligence'), the external intelligence agency of former East Germany. A department of the Ministry for State Security (MfS) and the State Security Service (SSD), it ran an extensive espionage network in West Germany and other countries. *See also* STASI.

HVO *See* CROATIAN DEFENCE COUNCIL.

HZDS *See* MOVEMENT FOR A DEMOCRATIC SLOVAKIA.

I Abbreviation for Italy, used for international vehicle registrations, postal addresses etc.

I Progressisti *See* PROGRESSIVE ALLIANCE.

I Verdi *See* GREEN FEDERATION.

IBEC *See* IRISH BUSINESS AND EMPLOYERS' CONFEDERATION.

Ibercorp affair Controversy in Spain surrounding the activities of Ibercorp, a financial-services group handling the personal investments of leading members of the ruling Spanish Socialist Workers' Party (PSOE). The Madrid-based company's clients have included Miguel Boyer and Carlos Solchaga, both former finance ministers, and Mariano Rubio and Luis Angel Rojo, the former and current governor of the Bank of Spain, the central bank; its director, Mario de la Concha, has been a close associate of Rubio in particular. In 1991 and 1992 media reports alleged that Ibercorp concealed the identity of its clients, helped them to evade taxation, relied on insider-trading practices, and received privileged treatment from the Bank of Spain. They cited the rescue of Ibercorp's struggling merchant-banking subsidiary in March 1992 as an example of the latter, and also offered evidence that (contrary to correct practice) Rubio and de la Concha had exchanged confidential information. The allegations also raised the issue of the central bank's impartiality as the regulator of the financial sector and, given the close links between Ibercorp and senior ministers, its autonomy from the government. In May 1994 Rubio and de la Concha were arrested on charges of fraud, misappropriation of public funds and tax evasion (*see* RUBIO AFFAIR). This prompted Solchaga to resign his parliamentary seat. The agriculture minister, Vicente Albero, also resigned after admitting that he had failed to pay tax on income derived from investments handled by Ibercorp.

Iberian countries or **Iberia** Collective name for Portugal and Spain. The two countries form the Iberian Peninsula, named after the people who inhabited eastern Spain during Roman times.

IC *See* INITIATIVE FOR CATALONIA.

Iceland [Ísland] Country in northwestern Europe.

Official data. Name: Republic of Iceland [Lyðveldið Ísland]; capital: Reykjavík; form of government: parliamentary republic; head of state: president; head of government: prime minister; flag: blue with a red white-edged Scandinavian cross; national holiday: 17 June (National Day); language: Icelandic; religion: Evangelical Lutheranism; currency: króna (kr) (pl. krónur) = 100 aurar; abbreviation: ÍS.

Geography. Situated in the North Atlantic Ocean on the edge of the Arctic Circle, 800 km northwest of Great Britain, 900 km west of Norway and 300 km southeast of Greenland, Iceland consists of a main island and many islets. The total area is 102,819 sq km. The country consists of plateaus dissected by steep valleys, low-lying coastal plains (in the southwest in particular), volcanic mountains and ice fields (including the Vatnajokull glacier in the southeast). It has a heavily indented coastline. Only 1% of the land is arable, another 23% is covered by pastures and 1% is forested. The climate is generally subarctic, moderated by temperate marine influences; summers are short and cool and winters cold to very cold; rainfall is moderate to heavy; temperatures and rainfall are lower in the north.

Demography. Iceland has a population of 264,000. Population density is 3 per sq km (glacier-free land area), the lowest by far in Europe. Some 91% of the people live in urban areas, and around three-fifths live in Reykjavík and its suburbs. In ethnic, linguistic and religious terms Iceland is very homogeneous. Some 96.2% of the population is Icelandic and 92.6% Evangelical Lutheran. Foreign nationals account for 3.8% of the population, and include citizens of Denmark, the United States, Sweden and Germany.

Sociography. Iceland scores 0.914 on the United Nations human development index (HDI), ranking 14th in the world and 10th among 32 European countries. There are 27 doctors and 100 hospital beds for every 10,000 people. Education is compulsory between the ages of seven and 15. There is one teacher for every 18 students. Enrolment is 95% at the secondary level and 25% at the tertiary level. The literacy rate is virtually 100%. Real annual income per head (in terms of purchasing power) is US$ 17,480. Income differentials are small.

Infrastructure and communications. Iceland has a highly developed but limited transport and communications network, with local air services linking all the centres of population and coastal shipping particularly important for freight transport. There are 2,280 km of paved roads and 120,000 passenger cars (464 per 1,000 people). There are no railways or navigable waterways. The main port is Reykjavík. The main airports are at Reykjavík and Keflavík, and there are 19 other airports with scheduled services. There are six daily newspapers, with a combined circulation of 131,000 (518 per 1,000 people, among the highest rates in the world). There are 155,000 radio receivers, 76,000 television sets and 130,000 telephones in use (respectively 601, 295 and 504 per 1,000 people).

Economic structure. The Icelandic economy is highly developed but heavily dependent on the fishing industry, which employs an eighth of the labour force, contributes around a fifth of GDP and generates three-quarters of export earnings; it is consequently vulnerable to changes in world prices and demand for fish. After a period of high growth in the second half of the 1980s, economic performance in the 1990s has been characterized by negligible growth, large current-account deficits (averaging over 3% of GDP per year), large public deficits (up to 4% of GDP), high but falling inflation (from 26% to below 4%) and low unemployment (around 2%).

Services contribute 60% of GDP, industry contributes 28% (manufacturing 14%, fish processing 5%), and agriculture and fishing 12% (fishing 9%). Some 18% of the labour force is employed in public services, 14% in trade, 12% in manufacturing and 12% in fishing and fish processing. The fishing industry (cod, shrimp etc) is the third-largest in Europe. The main crops grown are potatoes and vegetables; livestock raising (sheep) is also an important agricultural activity. There are no significant mineral resources. The main industries are fish processing and metalworking (aluminium). The main energy sources are domestic hydroelectric and geothermal power and imported fossil fuels; some 10% of export earnings are required to cover net fuel imports. The main exports are fish and fish products (79% of the total) and aluminium (9%). The main imports are machinery and transport equipment, basic manufactures, other manufactured goods and fuels. The main trading partners are: exports: United Kingdom (24%), Germany (12%), United States (11%), France (10%), Japan (7%), Spain (5%); imports: Germany (13%), United States (13%), Netherlands (10%), Norway (10%), Denmark (9%), United Kingdom (8%), Sweden (8%), Japan (7%).

The Central Bank of Iceland [Seðlabanki Íslands] is the central bank. The main employers' associations are the Employers' Federation of Iceland (VSÍ) and the Industrial Alliance (SI); there are also several associations of the fishing industry; the main labour organization is the Labour Federation of Iceland (ASÍ).

Political structure. Iceland is a parliamentary republic on the basis of a constitution adopted in 1944. The head of state is the president, who is directly elected for a four-year term; s/he has no real powers. Executive power is effectively vested in the prime minister and the cabinet. Legislative power is vested in the Parliament [Alþing or Althing], whose 63 members are elected for a four-year term by a system of proportional representation. All citizens over the age of 18 are entitled to vote. Judicial power is ultimately vested in the Supreme Court [Hæstiréttur], whose eight members are appointed by the president. Administratively the country is divided into 27 counties [sýsla, pl. sýslur], which are subdivided into 29 towns and 188 communes.

The main political parties are the Independence Party (Sj), Progressive Party (F), Social Democratic Party (A), People's Alliance (Ab) and Women's Alliance (K). At the general election in

April 1991 the Independents gained 38.6% of the vote and 26/63 seats, the Progressives 18.9% and 13 seats, the Social Democrats 15.5% and 10 seats, the People's Alliance 14.4% and nine seats, and the Women's Alliance 8.3% and five seats. The government is formed by a centrist coalition of Independents and Social Democrats, with Davíd Oddsson as prime minister. Other senior ministers are Jón Baldvin Hannibalsson (foreign affairs and foreign trade), Fridrik Sophusson (finance) and Thorsteinn Pálsson (fisheries, justice, ecclesiastical affairs). The head of state is President Vigdís Finnbogadóttir, who was first elected in 1980.

Security and international affiliations. Iceland has no standing army, only a small paramilitary coastguard. Defence needs are met by American troops based at the Keflavík airbase within the framework of the North Atlantic Treaty Organization (NATO); currently numbering 3,000 (navy 1,800, airforce 1,200), they are due to be reduced to 1,400.

Iceland is a member of the Conference on Security and Cooperation in Europe (CSCE), Council of Europe, European Economic Area (EEA), European Free Trade Association (EFTA), North Atlantic Treaty Organization (NATO), Nordic Council and Western European Union (WEU), as well as the Organization for Economic Cooperation and Development (OECD) and the United Nations and its specialized agencies.

History. Iceland's first settlers were Irish monks, who arrived in the early 9th century but left soon afterwards following the arrival of Norwegian Vikings. The first permanent Viking settlement was established in 874 on the site of modern Reykjavík. The number of settlers, most of Norwegian origin, increased toward the end of the century. An independent commonwealth was established in 930. Its legislature, the Althing, lays claim to being the oldest in the world. By the 11th century the people had converted to Christianity. Weakened by a civil war, the commonwealth accepted Norwegian sovereignty in 1262. Like Norway, Iceland came under Danish rule in 1380. An

economic decline set in, the climate deteriorated, and epidemics depleted the population. When Norway was transferred to Sweden in 1814, Iceland remained part of Denmark.

The 19th century saw a revival of cultural and national consciousness. Growing demands for independence resulted in the restoration of the Althing (initially as a consultative body) in 1845, limited self-government in 1874, full internal government in 1903, and the establishment of Iceland as a separate state under the Danish crown (with the Danish government retaining responsibility for foreign policy and defence) in 1918. Universal suffrage was introduced in 1915. During the Second World War (1939–45), with Denmark occupied by Germany, Iceland was occupied by British troops in 1940 and American troops in 1941.

In 1944 the Althing declared Iceland a sovereign republic, thus severing all remaining links with Denmark. Iceland was a founding member of the North Atlantic Treaty Organization (NATO) in 1949. It signed a defence agreement with NATO in 1951 providing for the deployment of US troops at the Keflavík base. (Iceland has no armed forces.) Iceland joined the Nordic Council in 1953 and the European Free Trade Association (EFTA) in 1970. In an attempt to protect the country's fishing industry, the mainstay of the economy, territorial waters were extended from a four- to a 200-mile zone between 1958 and 1975. This led to tension with other countries, in particular Britain, and sparked three naval skirmishes, dubbed the 'cod wars', in 1975–76. Since 1918 Iceland's political scene has been dominated by four parties: the right-wing Independence Party, the centrist Progressive Party, the left-wing People's Alliance and the centre-left Social Democratic Party. The Independents led centre-right or centrist coalitions from 1944–56, 1959–71, 1974–78 and 1983–88; centre-left coalitions held power from 1956–59, 1971–74, 1978–79 and 1988–91; and a centrist coalition held power from 1979–83. The Progressives and Social Democrats formed a government in September

1988. This was succeeded in April 1991 by a coalition of the Independents and Social Democrats. From the mid 1970s to the late 1980s the economy was plagued by high inflation, caused by budget and current-account deficits, and low fish prices.

See also entries on specific institutions, organizations, parties, people, terms etc.

ICPRP *See* INTERNATIONAL COMMISSION FOR THE PROTECTION OF THE RHINE AGAINST POLLUTION.

ICRC Abbreviation for International Committee of the Red Cross, a humanitarian relief agency based in Geneva (Switzerland). It has been active in Bosnia-Herzegovina and the other Yugoslav successor states since the federation's disintegration and the outbreak of civil wars in 1991/92.

ICTU *See* IRISH CONGRESS OF TRADE UNIONS.

Idealists *See* GREY WOLVES.

IDS *See* ISTRIAN DEMOCRATIC ASSEMBLY.

IEP Abbreviation for the PUNT, the Irish currency, used in banking etc.

IEPG *See* INDEPENDENT EUROPEAN PROGRAMME GROUP.

IG Metall *See* METALWORKERS' UNION.

IGC *See* INTERGOVERNMENTAL CONFERENCE.

IHF *See* INTERNATIONAL HELSINKI FEDERATION FOR HUMAN RIGHTS.

Ikurriña ('Flag' in Basque) Flag of the Basque Country, an autonomous community or region of Spain. It combines a white cross and a green diagonal cross on a red background. Its display was banned during the Franco regime (1939–75).

I£ Abbreviation for the PUNT, the Irish currency.

il (pl. iller) Turkish administrative division, usually translated as 'province' or 'vilayet'. Each of the 76 *iller* is administered by a governor [vali] representing the central government and a council elected for a four-year term. The lower-level districts and communes have their own elected councils. The *iller* are grouped in eight geographical regions, which have no political functions.

il-Haddiema *See* LABOUR PARTY (Malta).

Île-de-France Region of France. Situated in the north and centred on Paris, the national and regional capital, Île-de-France has an area of 12,012 sq km and a population of 10,836,000. By far the country's most populous region, it is also its economic, social and cultural heartland. The economy is based on manufacturing (motor vehicles, electronics, textiles, chemicals), public and other services, agriculture and tourism.

Iliadhis, Konstantinos *See* ELIADES, ...

Iliescu, Ion (1930–) Romanian politician. He joined the Romanian Communist Party (PCR) youth wing in 1944 and was its leader from 1956–60. Trained as a hydraulic engineer, he held a series of senior party and government posts in the 1960s, culminating in his election to the central committee in 1968. He lost influence after he criticized the growing personality cult around President Ceauşescu. He held a series of middle-ranking posts in the 1970s and 80s. During the revolution that overthrew Ceauşescu in December 1989 he emerged as the leader of the National Salvation Front (FSN) and became interim president. He was confirmed as head of state in a direct election in May 1991 and again in October 1992 as the candidate of the Democratic National Salvation Front (FSND), now the Social Democracy Party (PDSR). As required by the consitution, he has relinquished all party offices.

illegal party-funding scandals (Italy) *See* ITALIAN CORRUPTION SCANDALS.

iller Plural of IL, the main Turkish administrative division.

Illes Balears *See* BALEARIC ISLANDS.

IMRO *See* INTERNAL MACEDONIAN REVOLUTIONARY ORGANIZATION - DEMOCRATIC PARTY FOR MACEDONIAN NATIONAL UNITY.

Independence [Neodvisnost], in full **Confederation of New Trade Unions of Slovenia 'Independence'** [Konfederacija Novih Sindikatov Slovenije 'Neodvisnost'] (Neodvisnost or KNSS) Slovenian trade-union federation. Neodvisnost, founded in 1990, has 14 affiliated unions with a total membership of around 135,000 (a sixth of the labour force). The president is France Tomšič.

Independence [Nezavisnost], in full **Independent Trade Unions of Serbia** [Nezavisni Sindikati Srbije] (Nezavisnost)

Yugoslav trade-union federation. Nezavisnost was set up in 1991 by members of the Serbian branch of the Trade Union Federation (SSJ, now the Autonomous Trade Union Federation, SSSJ)) who rejected its close links with the ruling Socialist Party (SPS). It subsequently allied itself with the opposition Democratic Movement of Serbia (DEPOS). It has a membership of 200,000 (5% of the labour force), including influential journalists, academics and teachers. The leader is Branislav Čanak.

Independence Party [Sjálfstæðisflokkurinn] (Sj) Icelandic political party. Founded in 1929 by a merger of conservative and liberal groups, the Independence Party is right-wing in orientation. Traditionally the country's largest party, it has led or participated in most coalition governments since 1946. At the April 1991 election it gained 38.6% of the vote and 26/63 seats. The leader is Davíd Oddsson.

Independent European Programme Group (IEPG) Intergovernmental organization. Established in 1976, the IEPG is an informal group of the European members of the North Atlantic Treaty Organization (NATO) aimed at improving cooperation in arms procurement and strengthening their arms industries. The 13 members are Belgium, Denmark, France, Germany, Greece, Italy, Luxemburg, Netherlands, Norway, Portugal, Spain, Turkey and the United Kingdom. (Iceland, the remaining European NATO state, does not have an army.) The IEPG's work is organized through three 'panels', which identify opportunities for collaboration, arrange specific projects, and determine common procedures. Meetings are held biannually at the level of national armaments directors and annually at the level of defence ministers. The secretariat is based in Lisbon (Portugal). In 1989 the IEPG set up the EUCLID programme to promote cooperation in research and development among European defence contractors. In December 1992 ministers decided to incorporate the IEPG into the WESTERN EUROPEAN UNION (WEU).

independent nuclear deterrent Common term for the United Kingdom's strategic nuclear force. Constituted in the early 1960s and nominally independent, it has always been seen, in effect, as a key component of the collective defence of Western Europe within the framework of the North Atlantic Treaty Organization (NATO). It is based on Polaris submarine-launched missiles, which are due to be replaced by TRIDENT missiles in the mid 1990s. Both systems are American-made.

Independent Self-Governing Trade Union *See* SOLIDARITY.

Independent Smallholders', Farmworkers' and Citizens' Party or **Independent Smallholders' Party** [Független Kisgazda, Földmunkás és Polgari Párt] (FKgP) Hungarian political party. Founded in 1930, the FKgP became the country's largest party at the 1945 election but was dissolved after the communist takeover in 1948. It was relaunched in 1988. It advocates a rapid transition to a market economy (including the reprivatization of all land and full compensation for expropriated owners) and has conservative views on social issues, stressing its commitment to Christian values. It joined the centre-right coalition after the 1990 multiparty election. The party split in June 1992 when the majority of the parliamentary group refused to support the leadership's decision to leave the government over the issue of land privatization. At the May 1994 election it gained 8.9% and 26 seats. The leader is József Torgyán.

Independent Trade Union Confederation - Luxemburg [Onofhängege Gewerkschaftsbond - Lëtzebuerg] (OGB-L) Luxemburg trade-union federation. Founded in 1979, the OGB-L is the country's largest labour organization. It has 14 affiliated unions with a total membership of 36,000 (around a fifth of the labour force). It is the dominant partner in the General Confederation of Labour (CGT-L). John Castegnaro is president of both organizations.

Independent Trade Union Federation *See* SUPPORT.

Independent Trade Unions of Serbia *See* INDEPENDENCE (Yugoslavia).

Industrial Reconstruction Institute [Istituto di Ricostruzione Industriale] (IRI) Italian industrial conglomerate. IRI is the holding company for the bulk of Italy's state-owned sector, which is by far the largest in Western Europe. Founded in 1933, it had grown to the world's sixth-largest conglomerate by the early 1990s. Among the 500-odd companies under its umbrella are the SIP telephone network and several other utilities, the ANAS road-building company, the STET telecommunications group, the ILVA steel group, the SME food group, the Finmeccanica engineering group, the Iritecnica construction group, the INA insurance group, the Alitalia airline, the RAI broadcasting company, several major banks and a range of other industrial undertakings. Many IRI companies have been loss-making for years. The conglomerate's aggregate debts totalled 70.7 trillion lire (36.2 billion ecus) at the end of 1993; losses in that year totalled 10.2 trillion lire (5.2 million ecus). In January 1992 parliament approved the privatization of state companies in principle, and in March 1993 it approved an extensive restructuring programme providing for the eventual privatization of most IRI subsidiaries.

INF Abbreviation for 'intermediate-range nuclear forces'. *See* EUROSTRATEGIC MISSILES.

INF Treaty *See* INTERMEDIATE-RANGE NUCLEAR FORCES TREATY.

informateur In Belgium and the Netherlands, a senior political figure asked by the king or queen to investigate options for forming a coalition government. An *informateur* is usually a respected figure retired from party politics or without ambitions for high office. On the basis of informal talks with party leaders s/he will recommend a particular course of action to the monarch, who will then appoint a *formateur* to form a government.

Information and Democratic Security Service [Servizio per l'Informazione e la Sicurezza Democratica] (SISDE) Former Italian intelligence agency. Until its incorporation into the NATIONAL AGENCY FOR INFORMATION AND STATE SECURITY

(ANISS) in January 1994, SISDE was a civilian intelligence agency nominally responsible to the interior minister. In the late 1970s senior SISDE officers came under suspicion of involvement in a far-right campaign of violence and destabilization, the so-called 'strategy of tension'. Since 1990 senior SISDE officers have been accused of political corruption, embezzlement (specifically, diverting funds allocated for covert operations to politicians, soldiers and police officers and for personal gain) and association with organized crime and the Armed Phalange, a group which claimed responsibility for a number of bombings and assassinations. SISDE was reorganized after concrete evidence of the agency's illegal activities emerged in 1993 in the course of the investigations into political corruption (*see* ITALIAN CORRUPTION SCANDALS). *See also* HIDDEN GOVERNMENT.

Information and Military Security Service [Servizio per l'Informazione e la Sicurezza Militare] (SISMI) Former Italian intelligence agency. Until its incorporation into the NATIONAL AGENCY FOR INFORMATION AND STATE SECURITY (ANISS) in January 1994, SISMI was a military intelligence agency nominally responsible to the defence minister. In the late 1970s senior SISMI officers came under suspicion of involvement in a far-right campaign of violence and destabilization, the so-called 'strategy of tension'. Since 1990 elements within the agency have also been linked to the Armed Phalange, a group which has claimed responsibility for a number of bombings and assassinations. SISMI was reorganized after concrete evidence of the agency's illegal activities emerged in 1993 in the course of the investigations into political corruption (*see* ITALIAN CORRUPTION SCANDALS). *See also* HIDDEN GOVERNMENT.

INI *See* NATIONAL INDUSTRY INSTITUTE.

initiative (Switzerland) *See* POPULAR INITIATIVE.

Initiative for Catalonia [Iniciativa per Catalunya] (IC) Spanish political organization. Founded in 1987, the IC is a left-wing electoral alliance active in Catalonia. It comprises the United Socialist Party [Partit Socialista Unificat de Catalunya] (PSUC), the Communist Party [Partit dels Comunistes de Catalunya] (PCC) and the Left Nationalist Accord [Entesa dels Nacionalistes d'Esquerra] (ENE). At the March 1992 regional election it gained 6.4% of the vote and 7/135 seats. Nationally it is affiliated to the UNITED LEFT (IU). The leader is Rafael Ribó Massó.

INLA *See* IRISH NATIONAL LIBERATION ARMY.

inner core In the European Union (EU), an informal name for the six members of the original European Economic Community (EEC), i.e. Belgium, France, Germany Italy, Luxemburg and the Netherlands. Broadly speaking they are also the most committed to closer integration. The term is also used in relation to the planned economic and monetary union (EMU). In this context Italy is usually not considered part of the 'inner core' or 'hard core' because of its problems in meeting the criteria for participation. *See also* MULTI-TRACK EUROPE *and* EUROPE OF CONCENTRIC CIRCLES.

İnönü, Erdal (1926–) Turkish physicist, academic and politician. He lectured in nuclear physics at the Middle East Technical University in Ankara and the Bosporus University in İstanbul from 1960–83. The son of a former president, İsmet İnönü, he was elected leader of the new Social Democratic Party (SODEP) in 1983. When the party merged with the People's Party (HP) to form the Social Democratic People's Party (SHP), he became its deputy leader. He was elected SHP leader in June 1986 and elected to parliament later in the year. In November 1991 he became deputy prime minister in a coalition led by the centre-right True Path Party (DYP). He retired as party leader and deputy prime minister in September 1993.

Institute of Directors (IoD) British employers' association. The IoD was founded in 1903. Its membership includes around 33,000 British-based company directors and 15,000 from overseas. The president is Peter Walters, the director-general Tim Melville-Ross.

institutional government [governo istituzionale] or **technical government** [governo tecnico] In Italy, a government led by in eminent figure and composed primarily of technical experts who may or may not be members of a political party. Such governments are usually formed to serve in a caretaker capacity at times of political deadlock or crisis. They are traditionally headed by the president of the Senate or the Chamber of Deputies, the two houses of parliament, and their ministers are usually drawn from the legal, academic or business world.

intergovernmental conference (IGC) In the European Union (EU), a conference of the member states convened to debate and decide on amendments to the basic treaties of the Union or to draft new ones. An IGC can be convened with the support of a majority of member states, but its conclusions must be agreed unanimously and ratified by all. The two most recent IGCs, on economic and monetary union and political union, were held concurrently in 1990–91 and resulted in the Maastricht Treaty establishing the EU.

intergovernmental cooperation In the European Union (EU), cooperation among the member states outside the 'supranational' structures of the European Community (EC), the core of the organization. Intergovernmental forms of cooperation have been a feature of the European integration process since the establishment of the European Economic Community (EEC, now the EC) in 1958. They were gradually introduced in non-economic policy areas, either as a prelude to incorporation within the EC decision-making process (e.g. research and technology, environment) or because perceived national interests and sensitivities precluded the transfer of powers from national governments to the supranational structure (e.g. foreign policy, immigration). The Maastricht Treaty, which entered into force in November 1993, formalized intergovernmental cooperation in two 'pillars', the Common Foreign and Security Policy (CFSP) and Cooperation on Justice and Home Affairs (CJHA).

intermediate nuclear forces (INF) and
intermediate-range nuclear forces *See*
EUROSTRATEGIC MISSILES.

**Intermediate-Range Nuclear Forces
Treaty** or **INF Treaty** Bilateral agreement between the Soviet Union and the
United States. Signed on 8 December
1987, the INF Treaty provided for the
elimination over a three-year period of all
land-based intermediate-range nuclear
weapons deployed or due to be deployed
by the two countries. It affected only 4%
of the superpowers' nuclear arsenals,
but represented a major breakthrough
in East-West relations as the first true
disarmament rather than arms-control
agreement. The dismantling and
destruction of the around 2,000 warheads
covered by the treaty, virtually all of
them located in Europe, was completed
in 1991. They included the Tomahawk
cruise and Pershing II missiles deployed
by the United States in Western Europe,
and the Soviet SS-4s, SS-5s and SS-20s
deployed in the Soviet Union and Eastern
Europe. The treaty provides for extensive
verification procedures, including base
inspections and satellite surveillance,
over a 13-year period.

**Internal Macedonian Revolutionary
Organization - Democratic Party for
Macedonian National Unity** [Vnatrešna
Makedonska Revolucionerna Organiza-
cija - Demokratska Partija za Makedon-
sko Nacionalno Edinstvo] (VMRO-
DPMNE) Macedonian political party.
Founded in 1990, it has the same name
but has no direct link with a nationalist
organization which fought for Macedonian independence from Turkey in the
late 19th century. It is strongly nationalistic (rejecting guaranteed rights for the
Albanian and other ethnic minorities),
calls for a rapid transition to a market-
based economy, and has conservative
views on social issues. At the December
1990 election (when Macedonia was still
part of Yugoslavia) it gained 38/120
seats. The leader is Ljupčo Georgievski.

internal market In the European Union
(EU) and the European Economic Area
(EEA), a shorthand for the SINGLE INTER-
NAL MARKET.

**International Commission for the Pro-
tection of the Rhine against Pollution**
or **Rhine Commission** (ICPRP) Intergovernmental organization. The Commission was established in 1963 to carry out
research on the pollution of the Rhine,
one of Europe's major waterways, and to
propose measures to protect and rehabili-
tate the river. The six members are France,
Germany, Luxemburg, Netherlands,
Switzerland and the European Commission (representing the European Union,
EU). The secretariat is based in Koblenz,
Germany.

**International Conference on Former
Yugoslavia** International conference
sponsored by the European Union (EU)
and the United Nations (UN) aimed at
finding solutions to the interrelated conflicts in former Yugoslavia. Also referred
to as the Geneva Conference, since many
of its negotiating sessions are held in that
Swiss city, it was set up in August 1992
as a more broadly based successor to a
conference convened by the European
Community (EC, now the European
Union, EU) a year earlier and to unite
the UN and EC peace efforts. The Conference has at various stages dealt with all
the conflicts arising from the disintegration of the Yugoslav federation and has
sought to establish basic principles for
negotiated settlements, such as guarantees
for the rights of minorities. It has concentrated on settling the conflicts in Bosnia-
Herzegovina and Croatia and preventing
an escalation of fighting to the Kosovo
region of Yugoslavia and Macedonia.
Representatives of all national and
regional governments and of the various
ethnic communities (such as the Bosnian
Serbs, Bosnian Croats and Croatian
Serbs) in former Yugoslavia are involved
in the negotiating process. The chief
mediators have been, on behalf of the
EC/EU, first Peter Carrington and since
August 1992 David Owen, both former
British foreign ministers; and on behalf
of the UN, first Cyrus Vance and since
May 1993 Thorvald Stoltenberg, former
US and Norwegian foreign ministers
respectively. The mediators have put
forward several plans to resolve the civil

war between Muslims, Serbs and Croats in Bosnia-Herzegovina, such as the VANCE-OWEN PLAN in October 1992 and the OWEN-STOLTENBERG PLAN in July 1993. *See also* BOSNIAN CIVIL WAR.

International Conference on the Protection of the North Sea or **North Sea Conference** Intergovernmental organization. This is a loose grouping of the eight North Sea littoral states – Belgium, Denmark, France, Germany, Netherlands, Norway, Sweden and the United Kingdom – and several other interested states and intergovernmental organizations. Its aim is to improve the marine environment of the North Sea, traditionally a crossroads of trade routes, a rich source of fish and since the 1970s a major source of oil and gas. Three international conferences on the protection of the North Sea have been held. At the first conference in Bremen (Germany) in October/November 1984 the eight states adopted a basic declaration and agreed a range of specific anti-pollution and surveillance measures. At the second conference in London (United Kingdom) in November 1987 they agreed to reduce and in some cases end the dumping of pollutants and to declare the North Sea a 'special protection area' under international maritime law. At the third conference in The Hague (Netherlands) in March 1990 they agreed further cuts in the permitted levels of major pollutants such as lead, mercury, cadmium and dioxin.

International Contact Group *See* CONTACT GROUP.

International Helsinki Federation for Human Rights (IHF) International human-rights and political organization. The IHF was set up in 1982 to promote compliance with the human-rights provisions of the HELSINKI FINAL ACT and other agreements adopted within the framework of the Conference on Security and Cooperation in Europe (CSCE). It gathers and disseminates information on the human-rights situation in the CSCE countries – now comprising all the states of Europe and the former Soviet Union – and seeks to exert pressure on governments to meet their obligations in the field of human rights. National committees, often called 'Helsinki committees', have been set up in most CSCE countries. The secretariat is based in Vienna (Austria).

International War Crimes Tribunal for Former Yugoslavia or **Yugoslav War Crimes Tribunal** International judicial body set up under the auspices of the International Court of Justice (ICJ), part of the United Nations system. The Tribunal – the first of its kind since the trials of German and Japanese leaders after the Second World War – was set up by the UN Security Council in May 1993 and began gathering evidence in November. Composed of 11 judges appointed by the UN General Assembly, its brief is 'to prosecute persons alleged to have committed or ordered the commission of grave breaches of the Geneva Convention of 1949, violations of law or customs of war, crimes against humanity and the crime of genocide' since the beginning of 1991 in the various conflicts in former Yugoslavia, i.e. Bosnia-Herzegovina, Croatia, Macedonia, Slovenia and rump Yugoslavia. It works in tandem with the UNITED NATIONS WAR CRIMES COMMISSION FOR FORMER YUGOSLAVIA. It is based in The Hague (Netherlands), where the ICJ is also based.

internment without trial or **internment** In the United Kingdom, the imprisonment of suspected members of terrorist organizations without trial. The measure was last in force in Northern Ireland from 1971–75, at the height of the campaign of political violence waged by the Irish Republican Army (IRA) and other guerrilla groups (*see* NORTHERN IRELAND QUESTION). It aroused strong resentment in the Catholic community and was criticized by human-rights groups. Its reintroduction as a means of combating terrorism was a key demand of the Protestant unionist parties until the IRA declared a ceasefire in September 1994.

Intervention Group of the National Gendarmerie or **Intervention Group** [Groupe d'Intervention de la Gendarmerie Nationale] (GIGN) French paramilitary police force. The GIGN is an elite unit of the NATIONAL GENDARMERIE specializing in crowd and riot control and certain undercover security activities.

intervention stocks (European Union) *See* FOOD MOUNTAINS.

IoD *See* INSTITUTE OF DIRECTORS.

IOM or **IoM** Abbreviation for Isle of Man, the official name of Man.

IOM£ or **IoM£** Abbreviation for the POUND, the currency of the Isle of Man.

Ionescu-Quintus, Mircea (1917–) Romanian lawyer, writer and politician. He practised law in Prahova county from 1940–87. He became a member of the National Liberal Party (NLP) in 1945, two years before it was banned by the communists. At the party's relaunch in 1990, several months after the overthrow of the Ceauşescu regime, he was elected deputy leader. He was a member of parliament in 1990–91 and justice minister in the Stolojan government in 1991–92. In February 1993 he was elected party leader. He has published several collections of epigrams and other literary works.

IP *See* INDEPENDENCE PARTY.

Iparretarak *See* NORTHERNERS.

IPLO *See* IRISH PEOPLE'S LIBERATION ORGANIZATION.

IRA *See* IRISH REPUBLICAN ARMY.

Iraqgate *See* ARMS-TO-IRAQ AFFAIR.

Iraultza *See* REVOLUTION.

Ireland [Éire] Country in western Europe, also referred to as the Irish Republic or Éire.

Official data. Name: Republic of Ireland [Poblacht na hÉireann]; capital: Dublin [Baile Átha Cliath]; form of government: parliamentary republic; head of state: president; head of government: prime minister; flag: three vertical stripes, green, white and orange; national holiday: 17 March (Saint Patrick's Day); languages: Irish and English; religion: none; currency: punt (£) = 100 pence [pingin]; abbreviation: IRL.

Geography. The smaller of the two main British Isles, Ireland is situated 80 km west of Great Britain. The Republic of Ireland occupies all but the northeast of the island (five-sixths of the total area) and has an area of 70,285 sq km. The Atlantic Ocean is to the west and south,

and the Irish Sea to the east; the only land border is with Northern Ireland, which is part of the United Kingdom. The centre consists of low-lying rolling plains and hill lands. These lowlands are surrounded by mountain ranges along the coasts (including Macgillicuddy's Reeks in the southwest and the Wicklow Mountains in the east). Some 14% of the land is arable, another 71% is covered by pastures and 5% is forested. The main river is the Shannon. The climate is temperate marine, with cool to mild summers and cool winters; rainfall is heavy in the west, moderate to heavy in the east.

Demography. Ireland has a population of 3,516,000. Population density is 51 per sq km (land area). Some 57% of the people live in urban areas, and just under a third lives in Dublin and its suburbs (population 1.0 million). Other major cities are Cork [Corcaigh], Limerick [Luimneach], Galway [An Gaillimh] and Waterford [Port Láirge]. The rural areas are sparsely populated. Around 94% of the population is Irish. Foreign nationals, mainly citizens of the United Kingdom (including Irish from Northern Ireland), account for the remaining 6%. English and Irish are the main languages. Irish is the first language of around 70,000 people in the west and northwest; in total around a quarter of the population is said to be proficient in Irish. There is a large Irish community in the United Kingdom. In religious terms 93.2% of the population is nominally Roman Catholic, 3.2% Anglican (Church of Ireland), 0.8% Jewish and 0.5% Presbyterian Protestant.

Sociography. Ireland scores 0.892 on the United Nations human development index (HDI), ranking 21st in the world and 14th among 32 European countries. There are 15 doctors and 39 hospital beds for every 10,000 people, among the lowest figures in Europe. Education is compulsory between the ages of six and 15. There is one teacher for every 23 students. Enrolment is 78% at the secondary level and 26% at the tertiary level. The literacy rate is virtually 100%. Real annual income per head (in terms of purchasing power) is US$ 11,430.

Infrastructure and communications.
Ireland has a developed transport and
communications network, although the
telecommunications system is relatively
limited in some rural areas. There are
86,770 km of paved roads and 796,000
passenger cars (228 per 1,000 people),
2,810 km of railways and virtually no
navigable waterways. The main ports are
Dublin, Cork, Foynes/Shannon and
Waterford. The main airports are at
Dublin and Shannon, and there are nine
other airports with scheduled services.
There are seven daily newspapers, with
a combined circulation of 669,000 (191
per 1,000 people). There are 2.15 million
radio receivers, 991,000 television sets
and 916,000 telephones in use (respectively 615, 284 and 262 per 1,000 people).

Economic structure. The Irish economy
is developed, diversified and one of the
most trade-oriented in Europe (exports
account for two-thirds of national income).
It is based on manufacturing (esp. electrical goods), agriculture and tourism.
The agricultural sector is more important
than in most other Western European
countries, and many rural areas are
strongly dependent on it. After a period
of fluctuating growth from 1980–86
(averaging 2.2% per year), economic
performance since then has been marked
by high growth (averaging 5.6% until
1990 and 2.3% until 1993), current-
account surpluses and low inflation
(around 3%), but also by persistent very
high unemployment (around 18%).

Services contribute 53% of GDP,
industry contributes 37% (manufacturing
around 27%), and agriculture and fisheries 10%. Some 17% of the labour force
is employed in manufacturing, 14% in
trade and 13% in farming. The main
agricultural activities are livestock raising
(cattle, poultry) and dairy farming (milk,
butter); the main crops grown are cereals
(barley, wheat), potatoes and sugarbeets.
Fishing is of regional importance. The
main mineral resources are lead, zinc,
natural gas and peat. The main industries
are food processing and electrical and
electronic goods (esp. data-processing
equipment); other important branches are

pharmaceuticals and chemicals, building
materials, precision engineering, textiles
and glass. Tourism is a major source of
foreign exchange, contributing 4% of
GNP (1% net). The main energy sources
are imported fossil fuels and domestic
natural gas and peat; 4% of export earnings are required to cover net fuel imports.
The main exports are electrical equipment
(26% of the total, incl. office and data-
processing equipment 19%), foodstuffs
(24%, incl. beef and other meat and meat
products 7%), chemicals and pharmaceuticals (16%), textiles and clothing, and
professional instruments; machinery and
transport equipment account for 31% of
the total, foodstuffs for 24%. The main
imports are machinery and transport
equipment, basic manufactures and
chemicals. The main trading partners
are: exports: United Kingdom (33%),
Germany (13%), France (11%), United
States (8%), Netherlands (6%), Italy,
Belgium; imports: United Kingdom
(42%), United States (15%), Germany
(8%), France (5%), Japan, Netherlands;
three-quarters of all trade is with other
European Union (EU) countries.

The Central Bank of Ireland [Bank
Ceannais na hÉireann] is the central
bank. The main employers' association
is the Irish Business and Employers'
Confederation (IBEC); the main labour
organization is the Irish Congress of
Trade Unions (ICTU).

Political structure. Ireland is a parliamentary republic on the basis of a constitution adopted in 1937. The head of state
is the president [uachtaran], who is directly elected for a seven-year term; s/he has
certain limited powers but normally acts
on the advice of the government. Executive power is vested in the prime minister
[taoiseach] and the council of ministers.
Legislative power is vested in the bicameral Parliament [Oireachtas], composed
of the 166-member Assembly of Ireland
[Dáil Éireann], elected for a five-year term
by a system of proportional representation, and the 60-member Senate [Seanad
Éireann], partly indirectly elected by
panels representing social and economic
groups and partly appointed by the prime

minister. All citizens over the age of 18 are entitled to vote. Judicial power is ultimately vested in the five-member Supreme Court [Cúirt Uachtarach] appointed by the president on the advice of the government. Administratively the country is divided into 29 counties [contae, pl. contha] and five county boroughs [contaebuirg, pl. -í]; the counties are subdivided into three non-county boroughs, 49 urban districts and 28 towns; they are grouped in eight regions [réigiún, pl. réigiúin], which have coordinating functions; the historical provinces of Connaught, Leinster, Munster and the three counties of Ulster within the Republic have no administrative or political functions.

The main political parties are Fianna Fáil (FF), Fine Gael (FG), Labour Party, Progressive Democrats (PDs), Democratic Left Party (DLP) and Green Alliance / Comhaoltás Glas. At the general election in November 1992 Fianna Fáil gained 39.1% of the vote and 68/166 seats, Fine Gael 24.5% and 45 seats, Labour 19.3% and 33 seats, the PDs 4.7% and 10 seats, the DLP 2.8% and four seats, and the Greens 1.4% and one seat. The government is formed by a centrist coalition of Fianna Fáil and Labour, with Albert Reynolds as prime minister. Other senior ministers are Dick Spring (deputy prime minister, foreign affairs), Bertie Ahern (finance), Máire Geoghegan-Quinn (justice) and David Andrews (defence). The head of state is President Mary Robinson, who was elected in November 1990 and took office the following month.

Security and international affiliations. The Irish armed forces number 13,000 (army 11,200, navy 1,000, airforce 800). There is no conscription.

Ireland is a member of the Conference on Security and Cooperation in Europe (CSCE), Council of Europe, European Economic Area (EEA), European Union (EU) and Western European Union (WEU), as well as the Organization for Economic Cooperation and Development (OECD) and the United Nations and its specialized agencies.

History. Celtic tribes settled in Ireland in the 4th century BC. By the 1st century AD the island was divided into numerous small states which owed allegiance to five main kingdoms, Ulster, Connaught, Meath, Leinster and Munster. One of their rulers was usually recognized as 'high king', but the title was often disputed. Christianity was introduced in the 5th century. The monasteries subsequently played an important role as centres of learning, more so than in other European countries. From the late 8th century the Vikings raided coastal areas and established a number of settlements (including Dublin) and trading posts. The Irish kingdoms were briefly united in the early 11th century, when the Vikings were decisively defeated at the Battle of Clontarf in 1014. The English became involved in Irish affairs in the 12th century. In 1171 King Henry II declared himself lord of Ireland, a claim recognized by the Irish high king in 1175. English control was limited to the region centred on Dublin, called the Pale, while an increasingly assimilated Anglo-Irish aristocracy and native Irish rulers held sway in the rest of the country. In the 16th century the English sought to break the power of the feudal lords and establish control. In 1541 King Henry VIII was proclaimed king of Ireland. A new source of conflict emerged when the English crown broke with the Catholic Church and insisted on the supremacy of the new Anglican Church in Ireland as well. Between 1559 and 1603 there were three uprisings against English rule. From 1607 the authorities distributed confiscated Irish Catholic lands among Scottish and English Protestant settlers in Ulster (modern Northern Ireland). There were further uprisings against English rule in the 1640s and from 1688–91.

During the 18th century the Protestants, who accounted for a tenth of the population, owned nine-tenths of the land and had a monopoly of political power. There was a further rebellion in 1798, led by Wolf Tone (a Protestant) and the United Irishmen, a predominantly Protestant organization. In 1801 the Irish parliament was abolished and the country was united with Great Britain. This dented Protestant dominance, especially after the emancipation of the Catholics in 1829, and brought some social and economic reforms. The failure of the potato crop in 1845 and 1846 caused a devastating five-year famine, during which a million people died and another million were forced to emigrate. Mass emigration to the United States and Britain and its colonies continued for the rest of the century. (The population of the whole of Ireland fell from 8.1 million to 6.3 million between 1845 and 1851, and to 4.5 million by the turn of the century.) At this time English also replaced Gaelic or Irish as the dominant spoken language. From the 1840s nationalist agitation concentrated on alleviating poverty through land reform as well as securing 'home rule' or independence. British governments sponsored home-rule bills in 1886, 1893 and 1914, which were strongly resisted by Irish Protestants. The first two were defeated in Parliament; the third was passed but its implementation was deferred on the outbreak of the First World War (1914–18). In 1916 there was a brief but politically significant rebellion in Dublin, the Easter Rising. In the 1918 election the Sinn Féin movement, campaigning on a platform of full independence, gained two-thirds of the Irish seats in the House of Commons. It formed an unofficial parliament and constituted a provisional government under Éamon de Valera. Sinn Féin's military wing, the Irish Republican Army (IRA), launched a guerrilla war in 1919. In 1920 Parliament set up two Irish parliaments, one for the six northern counties with a Protestant majority and one for the other 26 counties. An agreement between the British government and Irish representatives, signed in 1921 and in effect from 1922, established the Irish Free State in the southern counties as a self-governing dominion within the British Commonwealth; Northern Ireland remained within the United Kingdom. The partition of Ireland and limited independence were rejected by many nationalists, including de Valera. They were defeated in a short civil war. A new constitution adopted in 1937 severed all links with the United Kingdom.

Since independence domestic politics has been dominated by Fianna Fáil and Fine Gael, two broadly centre-right parties whose origins lie in the civil war: Fianna Fáil was founded in 1926 by opponents of the Anglo-Irish treaty, while Fine Gael was formed in 1932 from the merger of Cumann na nGaedhael and other parties which had accepted it. Since the 1970s their traditionally opposed views on Irish reunification and the Northern Ireland question – a defining issue of Irish politics – have converged, while their economic and social policies have become more distinct. Fianna Fáil was in power for 35 out of 41 years between 1932 and 1973. De Valera was the country's dominant political figure during this period, as prime minister until 1959 and then as president (a non-executive post) until his death in 1973. Ireland's agricultural and underdeveloped economy became more industrialized from the late 1950s. Living standards, then among the lowest in Europe, rose sharply in the 1960s and 80s, although unemployment and emigration remained high especially in the latter period. Ireland was a founding member of the European Free Trade Association (EFTA) in 1960 and joined the European Community (EC), now the European Union (EU), in 1973. Fine Gael and the Labour Party held power for 10 out of the 16 years from 1973. The dominant political leaders of the 1970s and 80s were Garret FitzGerald (Fine Gael) and Charles Haughey (Fianna Fáil). The 1980s saw a growing reaction to the traditionally strong influence of the Catholic Church, but efforts to legalize abortion and divorce proved highly controversial and failed. From the early 1980s successive governments cooperated with their British counterparts to contain and find a solution to the violent conflict in Northern Ireland. The Anglo-Irish Agreement signed in November 1985 gave the Irish government a consultative role in Northern Ireland affairs. In July 1989 Fianna Fáil formed a coalition with the

Progressive Democrats, who had broken away from it four years earlier. In January 1993 it formed a coalition with Labour.

See also entries on specific institutions, organizations, parties, people, terms etc.

IRI *See* INDUSTRIAL RECONSTRUCTION INSTITUTE.

Irish [Gaeilge] One of the two official languages of Ireland, also called Gaelic. Irish is the island's original Celtic language. For historical and cultural reasons it was made the 'first' official language (and English the 'second') when Ireland gained its independence from the United Kingdom in 1922, even though it was spoken by only a small section of the population. Its use has been strongly promoted by successive governments both as a first and a second language. Around a quarter of Ireland's people claim to have an adequate passive command of the language. It is spoken as a first language by around 70,000 people in the far west and northwest of the country, in districts known as the Gaeltacht ('Irish-speaking areas').

Irish beef industry affair *See* BEEF INDUSTRY AFFAIR.

Irish Business and Employers' Confederation (IBEC) Irish employers' association. The IBEC was formed in January 1993 from the merger of the Federation of Irish Employers (FIE) and the Confederation of Irish Industry (CII). It has around 3,700 members from all sectors of the economy. The president is Tom Jago, the director-general John Dunne.

Irish Congress of Trade Unions (ICTU) Irish trade-union federation. Founded in 1894, the ICTU has 70 affiliated unions representing around 450,000 workers in Ireland and 230,000 in Northern Ireland (a quarter of the combined labour forces of the two territories). The general secretary is Peter Cassells.

Irish Gaelic Alternative name for IRISH or Gaelic, one of the official languages of Ireland. The longer form is used to distinguish it from the related Scots Gaelic spoken in neighbouring Scotland.

Irish National Liberation Army (INLA) British and Irish guerrilla group. The INLA emerged in 1975 as the armed wing of the Irish Republican Socialist Party (IRSP), which had split from Sinn Féin after its decision to take part in the electoral process. Its aims are the withdrawal of British troops from Northern Ireland and the reunification of Ireland as a 'revolutionary communist state'. It has carried out bombings and shootings in Northern Ireland, mainland Britain and mainland Europe, targeting soldiers, police officers, government officials and political activists. It was apparently riven by internal divisions in the late 1980s. By that time the IRSP had also become virtually defunct.

Irish People's Liberation Organization (IPLO) British and Irish guerrilla group. IPLO was formed in 1987 as a breakaway from the Irish Republican Army (IRA), the main guerrilla group fighting for an end to British rule in Northern Ireland and the reunification of Ireland. It has claimed responsibility for a number of bombings and assassinations over the years. It was involved in violent clashes with the IRA in 1992 and was reportedly disbanded in November that year.

Irish Republic Alternative name for Ireland. It is often used in Britain to distinguish the independent Republic of Ireland from Northern Ireland, which is part of the United Kingdom.

Irish Republican Army (IRA) British and Irish guerrilla group. The IRA aims to secure an end to British rule in Northern Ireland and the reunification of Ireland. Founded in 1919, before Irish independence, it split in 1921 over acceptance of partition and the creation of the independent Irish Free State in the south. From the 1930s it became increasingly marginalized. This changed in the late 1960s, when demands by the Catholic minority in Northern Ireland for an end to discrimination was met by violence from Protestants. In 1970 the organization split into an 'official' wing, which wanted to achieve a united socialist republic in Ireland through electoral politics, and a 'provisional' wing, which advocated guerrilla action to force the withdrawal of British troops (which had been introduced

327

in Northern Ireland in 1969) as a prelude to reunification. Organized in small cells, the IRA – the longer form 'Provisional IRA' is common but now redundant – took up arms in 1969. Its attacks were concentrated on what it considered 'legitimate targets': army and police officers, judges, politicians and members of rival Protestant or unionist guerrilla groups as well as police stations and military installations. Its operations in mainland Britain were initially aimed at similar targets but subsequently also at economic targets and civilians. It also attacked British military personnel and installations in mainland Europe, and was also active in the Republic of Ireland in the 1970s. Some of its most devastating attacks were mounted in mainland Britain, including the bombings of four public houses in 1974, causing the deaths of 28 people, and the bombings of London's financial district in April 1992 and April 1993, which caused few casualties but extensive property damage. In August 1994 the IRA announced a 'complete cessation of military operations' from September. The ceasefire was declared because of the 'new situation' which had arisen since the British and Irish governments' Downing Street Declaration of December 1993, the latest initiative to resolve the Northern Ireland conflict. The IRA has been responsible for around 1,500 deaths in Northern Ireland since 1969. The organization has close links with Sinn Féin, the party which is widely considered its political wing.

IRL Abbreviation for Ireland, used for international vehicle registrations, postal addresses etc.

IR£ Abbreviation for the PUNT, the Irish currency.

Iron Curtain The perceived barrier created by the Soviet Union and its Eastern European allies after the Second World War (1939–45) in order to cut themselves off from contact with Western Europe. Although the restrictions on the movement of people and information were relaxed from the mid 1950s onwards, the term continued to be used in the context of the East-West divide until the collapse of communist rule in Eastern Europe in

1989. Coined (in a different context) in the early part of the century, the term gained wide currency after Winston Churchill, Britain's prime minister during the Second World War, used it in a speech in 1946.

ÍS Abbreviation for Iceland, used for international vehicle registrations, postal addresses etc.

Isamaa *See* FATHERLAND.

ISK Abbreviation for the KRÓNA, the Icelandic currency, used in banking etc.

İslâmi Hareket *See* ISLAMIC MOVEMENT.

Islamic Movement [İslâmi Hareket] Turkish guerrilla group. Like similar fundamentalist groups, the Islamic Movement emerged in the late 1980s. It has been responsible for assassinations of prominent advocates of secularist views, including human-rights activists, academics, lawyers and journalists.

Ísland Icelandic name for Iceland.

island area British administrative division. Covering the peripheral island groups of Scotland, each of the three island areas (Orkney Islands, Shetland Islands, Western Isles) has a council elected for a four-year term and headed by a convener. The councils are responsible for all local services, including housing, education and social services. They thus combine the powers and responsibilities of the regional and district councils in the rest of Scotland.

Islas Baleares *See* BALEARIC ISLANDS.

Islas Canarias *See* CANARY ISLANDS.

Isle of Man Official name of Man.

ISP *See* INDEPENDENT SMALLHOLDERS' ... PARTY.

Istituto di Ricostruzione Industriale *See* INDUSTRIAL RECONSTRUCTION INSTITUTE.

Istria question Controversy over formerly Italian territories now divided between Slovenia and Croatia. The historical region of Istria, a peninsula at the head of the Adriatic Sea and including districts to the north, was divided between Austria and the Venetian Republic from the early Middle Ages until Austria gained control over the whole territory in 1797. Inhabited by Italians, Slovenes and Croats, it became part of Italy in 1919. Most of the region was occupied by Yugoslav forces at the end of the Second World War in 1945. Up to 200,000 Italians fled or were expelled across the border to Italy. A new border was agreed in 1947, further adjustments were made in 1954, the border issue was settled in 1975, and an agreement on compensation for lost property etc was signed in 1983 (but not implemented). In recent years Istrian exiles and their descendants have raised demands for compensation or restitution of their property, and leading members of the far-right Italian Social Movement (MSI) have called for the region's reincorporation into Italy. A small number of ethnic Italians still lives in Istria.

Istrian Democratic Assembly [Istarski Demokratski Sabor] (IDS) Croatian political party. The IDS calls for greater autonomy for the Istrian peninsula in the northwest, a distinctive historical region. It gained the region's three directly elected seats in the August 1992 general election and gained 66.6% of the vote in the regional elections in February 1993. The leader is Ivan Jakovčić.

Italian bribery scandals *See* ITALIAN CORRUPTION SCANDALS.

Italian Communist Party *See* DEMOCRATIC LEFT PARTY.

Italian Confederation of Workers' Unions [Confederazione Italiana dei Sindacati dei Lavoratori] (CISL) Italian trade-union federation. Founded in 1950, the CISL has 17 affiliated federations with a total membership of around 3.1 million (an eighth of the labour force). Traditionally close to the Christian Democratic Party (DC, now the Italian People's Party, PPI), it has adopted a more independent stance in recent years. The general secretary is Sergio D'Antoni.

Italian corruption scandals Series of interlocking political scandals in Italy involving corruption, bribery, embezzlement and criminal association which broke in 1992 and 1993, throwing the country into its worst political crisis since the Second World War and eventually bringing down much of the country's political and business establishment. The revelations completely discredited the five parties which had ruled the country

since the 1950s, in particular the Christian Democratic Party (DC) and Italian Socialist Party (PSI). They also provided telling evidence of what has been called Italy's *sottogoverno* ('hidden government'), an informal coalition of elements in the government, political parties, civil service, police, intelligence agencies, armed forces, business and organized crime aimed at controlling the reins of power outside the constitutional order. The scandals were sparked by an investigation into illegal party funding involving Italian Socialist Party (PSI) officials. A Milan-based team of magistrates uncovered cases of corruption in Milan, a PSI stronghold, Venice, Florence and other cities. By early 1993 it became clear that the corruption was not confined to the PSI. The investigations – codenamed Operation Clean Hands [Mani Pulite] – were exposing a system of administrative and political corruption whereby the ruling parties extracted billions of lire in bribes and kickbacks, known as *tangenti* ('tangents'), from private and state-owned companies in exchange for public-sector contracts and other favours. By February 1994, the second anniversary of the first arrest, 338 out of 630 deputies, 100 out of 315 senators, 873 businesspeople as well as hundreds of senior civil servants and local-government officials were under investigation or under arrest. Since then many more businesspeople in particular have come under investigation. These included several senior executives of Fininvest, the conglomerate owned by Silvio Berlusconi, who became prime minister in May 1994 after his right-wing Freedom Alliance had won a general election on a platform of 'renewal'. The Bank of Italy (= central bank) has estimated that around 150 trillion lire (77 billion ecus) were paid out in bribes and kickbacks over a ten-year period.

In detail, in February 1992 a junior PSI official based in Milan, Mario Chiesa, was arrested for accepting bribes while in charge of an old people's home. In July a senior PSI member, Gianni De Michelis, was placed under investigation. In December the PSI leader, Bettino Craxi, was placed under investigation. In February 1993 the first two party leaders, Craxi and Giorgio La Malfa of the Italian Republican Party (PRI), were forced to resign; the first three ministers, Claudio Martelli, Giovanni Goria (who had briefly been prime minister in 1987–88) and Francisco De Lorenzo, resigned; the mayors of Rome and Milan resigned; and several senior industrial managers were arrested. In March, in a dramatic twist, a number of DC leaders, including Giulio Andreotti, seven times prime minister and perhaps the country's most influential politician of the 1970s and 80s, Antonio Gava and Paolo Cirino Pomicino, were placed under investigation for association with the Mafia and Camorra, the Sicily- and Naples-based crime syndicates; two more ministers and the leader of the Italian Liberal Party (PLI), Renato Altissimo, resigned; the former president of the state-owned energy concern ENI, Gabriele Cagliari, was arrested. In April another former prime minister, Arnaldo Forlani, came under investigation; and a Senate committee revealed claims by two Mafia informers that Andreotti had been closely associated with the Mafia for years and was implicated in at least two murders. In May Ciriaco De Mita became the fourth former prime minister to come under investigation; the president of the huge state-owned conglomerate IRI was arrested; the first allegations of corruption were made against Democratic Left Party (PDS) officials; and the Chamber of Deputies abolished the right of parliamentary immunity in cases of corruption. In June Andreotti's immunity was lifted in connection with the investigation into the murder of a journalist in 1979; and a number of industrial managers, ministers and former ministers were arrested. In July Cagliari and another prominent businessman, Raul Gardini, a former chief executive of the Ferruzzi conglomerate, committed suicide; their deaths came amid allegations that around 150 billion lire (77 million ecus) – the largest single bribe revealed thus far – had been paid to politicians of the five ruling parties in 1989–90 in connection with the liqui-dation of the Enimont chemicals consortium. In September the first member of the judiciary was arrested on charges of corruption and abuse of power; and Andreotti admitted that he had received a bribe from a businessman (the key allegation the murdered journalist was about to publish). In October a number of Sicilian magistrates came under investigation for association with the Mafia; Craxi agreed to cooperate with investigations (he subsequently admitted that the PSI had secured more than 200 billion lire, 103 million ecus, in illegal funds between 1987 and 1990); and the trial opened of Sergio Cusani, the financier at the centre of the Enimont affair. In November Carlo De Benedetti, chairman of the Olivetti electronics concern and one of the country's most prominent industrialists, was arrested; and members of the secret services accused four former interior ministers of receiving monthly payments from secret funds (these allegations, primarily aimed at President Scalfaro, who had held the post from 1983–87, were widely regarded as an attempt to undermine his pivotal role in the process of political reform which had been set in motion by the corruption revelations). In December concrete evidence emerged of Andreotti's dealings with the Mafia; and an official of the Northern League (Lega Nord), one of the new parties, was arrested. In January 1994 the president of CARIPLO, the country's largest savings bank, Roberto Mazzotta, came under investigation. In February 1994 Craxi repeated allegations that the PDS and its predecessor, the Italian Communist Party (PCI), had also been involved in illegal party funding; and the trial of Goria opened. In March the old ruling parties were swept aside in an early general election; most of the members of parliament under investigation thus lost their immunity; and Craxi and 12 others went on trial for accepting bribes from an insurance company. In April the Enimont trial ended with Cusani's conviction. In May three senior executives of Fininvest, the conglomerate owned by the new prime minister, Silvio Berlusconi, were arrested for false accounting; and Goria died. In June Craxi, two senior executives of the Fiat car company and 27 others were indicted on charges in connection with contracts for Milan's transport network. In July the largest corruption trial to date – described by the prosecuting magistrate as the 'father of all corruption trials' – opened in Milan, with Craxi, Forlani, De Michelis and Cirino Pomicino (and Northern League leader Umberto Bossi) among the 32 accused politicians, senior civil servants and businesspeople; Andreotti was charged not just with association with the Mafia but with actual membership; the government issued an emergency decree abolishing the system of pre-trial detention, which it claimed was being abused by the magistrates investigating the corruption cases; it was forced to rescind it after a public outcry; Fininvest's construction arm, run by Paolo Berlusconi, the prime minister's brother, was implicated in paying bribes to the Revenue Guard (GdF), the finance police; six high-ranking GdF officials were accused of covering up fraud and tax evasion in return for bribes; Paolo Berlusconi was charged with paying a kickback on land bought by CARIPLO; and Craxi and Martelli were convicted of corruption in connection with the Banco Ambrosiano affair and sentenced to 8$^1/_2$ years' imprisonment.

See also CLIENTISM, HIDDEN GOVERN-MENT, PARTYOCRACY *and entries on specific affairs, people etc.*

Italian Democratic Socialist Party [Partito Socialista Democratico Italiano] (PSDI) Italian political party. Founded in 1947 as a breakaway from the Italian Socialist Party (PSI), the PSDI is centrist in orientation and participated in most coalitions formed between 1946 and 1993. At the April 1992 election it gained 2.7% of the vote and 16/630 seats. Like the other government parties, it was deeply implicated in the illegal party-funding and other scandals which broke in 1992 and 1993 (*see* ITALIAN CORRUP-TION SCANDALS). It lost virtually all its support in local and regional elections in 1993 and did not contest the March 1994

general election. The leader is Enrico Ferri.

Italian General Confederation of Labour [Confederazione Generale Italiana del Lavoro] (CGIL) Italian trade-union federation. Founded in 1944, the CGIL is Italy's largest labour organization, with a total membership of around 4.6 million (a fifth of the labour force) organized in 17 unions. It is most strongly represented in the agricultural and manufacturing sectors. Traditionally close to the Italian Communist Party (PCI), it has followed a more independent course in recent years. The general secretary is Bruno Trentin.

Italian kickback scandals *See* ITALIAN CORRUPTION SCANDALS.

Italian Liberal Party [Partito Liberale Italiano] (PLI) Italian political party. Founded in 1848, the PLI participated in most coalitions formed between 1946 and 1993. At the April 1992 election it gained 2.8% of the vote and 17/630 seats. Like the other government parties, it was deeply implicated in the illegal party-funding and other scandals which broke in 1992 and 1993 (*see* ITALIAN CORRUPTION SCAN-DALS). It lost virtually all its support in local and regional elections in 1993 and did not contest the March 1994 general election. Many of its members have joined the new CENTRE UNION (UDC). The leader is Raffaele Costa.

Italian People's Party [Partito Populare Italiano] (PPI) Italian political party. The PPI was founded in January 1994 as the successor to the Christian Democratic Party (DC), the country's dominant politi-cal force since the late 1940s, which had been discredited by a series of corruption and other scandals breaking in 1992 and 1993 (*see* ITALIAN CORRUPTION SCANDALS). The DC was founded in 1943 as the successor to a party also called the PPI. Backed by the Roman Catholic Church and seen as the main bulwark against the Italian Communist Party (PCI), it estab-lished itself as the country's largest party in the 1946 election and led all coalition governments over the next 48 years. More a coalition of interest groups than a tight-ly knit political party, it consisted of a number of factions [corrente, pl. correnti] with stances ranging from centre-left to right-wing and led by powerful leaders. The DC-led governments of the 1950s and 60s were committed to rapid industrialization and extensive state participation in the economy. The party's support declined steadily from a peak of 48.7% in the 1948 election to 29.7% in April 1992, when it gained 206/630 seats. Later that year it was thrown into deep crisis as evidence emerged first of its involvement in corruption (primarily bribes and kickbacks) and then of association with orgnized crime. Investigations revealed long-standing links between senior party leaders and the Mafia and Camorra, the main crime syndicates in the south, the party's traditional power base. Most of its long-time leaders (including Giulio Andreotti, Arnaldo Forlani and Ciriaco De Mita) were forced to resign their posts in March 1993. In local and regional elections later in 1993 the DC lost heavily in the north and centre, but less so in the south. Following the party's relaunch as the PPI a minority of rightwingers broke away to form the Christian Democratic Centre (CCD). The PPI contested the March 1994 general election in a centrist alliance and gained 11.1% and 33 seats. The party leader is Rocco Buttiglione, the party president Rosa Russo Jervolino, and the parliamentary leader Nino Andreatta.

Italian Republican Party [Partito Repubblicano Italiano] (PRI) Italian political party. Founded in 1894, the PRI is a centre-right party which participated in most coalitions formed between 1946 and 1993. It was influential over the years as a voice of the country's business and industrial interests. At the April 1992 election it gained 4.4% of the vote and 27/630 seats. It had previously left the government because of the lack of progress on political and economic reforms. Like the other coalition parties, it was deeply implicated in the illegal party-funding and other scandals which broke in 1992 and 1993 (*see* ITALIAN CORRUPTION SCANDALS). It lost virtually all its support in local and regional elections in 1993 and did not contest the March 1994 general election. Many of its members have

joined the new DEMOCRATIC ALLIANCE (AD). The leader is Giorgio La Malfa.

Italian Social Movement - National Right [Movimento Sociale Italiano - Destra Nazionale] (MSI-DN or MSI) Italian political party. The MSI was founded in 1946 as the successor to the outlawed National Fascist Party (PNF), which had been in power from 1922–43 under Benito Mussolini. It merged with another far-right party in 1973 to form the MSI-DN. At the April 1992 election it gained 5.4% of the vote and 34/630 seats. After the government parties were discredited by a series of corruption scandals, it increased its support in local and regional elections in 1992 and 1993, particularly in its traditional strongholds in the south. It sought to broaden its support base by launching the NATIONAL ALLIANCE (AN) in January 1994. Rejecting the 'neo-fascist' label and now describing itself as 'post-fascist', the party advocates strong central government, is very conservative on social issues, and takes a strongly nationalistic line in foreign policy. The leader is Gianfranco Fini.

Italian Socialist Party [Partito Socialista Italiano] (PSI) Italian political party. Founded in 1892, the PSI established itself as the country's third political force behind the Christian Democrats and the Communists in the 1950s. Initially strongly left-wing, it shifted to the centre-left in the 1960s. From 1963 it took part in most coalition governments. Although it never challenged the two main parties in terms of popular support, it gained considerable influence as the second government party. Party leader Bettino Craxi led a five-party coalition in 1983–87. At the April 1992 election the PSI gained 13.6% of the vote and 92/630 seats. As the party's prominent role in a web of illegal party financing and corruption came to light (*see* ITALIAN CORRUPTION SCANDALS), Craxi was forced to resign as leader in February 1993 and its support in local and regional elections collapsed, particularly in its traditional powerbase of Milan and Lombardy. A left-wing faction broke away to form Socialist Renewal (RS) in May 1993 and

Craxi supporters formed the Socialist Federation (FS) in January 1994. The PSI contested the March 1994 election within the Progressive Alliance and gained 2.2% of the vote and 15 seats. The leader is Ottaviano Del Turco. (In 1990 the slogan 'Socialist Unity' [Unità Socialista] was added to the party logo, and since then the party has sometimes been referred to as the Socialist Unity Party, PUS or US.)

Italian Swiss Collective name for the Italian-speaking people of Switzerland. Most live in the southern canton of Ticino and in adjoining parts of Grisons. They number around 250,000 (4.5% of Swiss citizens and 3.7% of the total population). They should not be confused with Italian citizens who live and work in the country.

Italian Union of Labour [Unione Italiana del Lavoro] (UIL) Italian trade-union federation. Founded in 1950, the UIL has 35 affiliated federations with a total membership of around 1.5 million (6% of the labour force). Until recently it had close links with the Italian Socialist Party (PSI). The general secretary is Pietro Larizza.

Italy [Italia] Country in southern Europe.

Official data. Name: Italian Republic [Repubblica Italiana]; capital: Rome [Roma]; form of government: parliamentary republic; head of state: president; head of government: prime minister; flag: three vertical stripes, green, white and red; national holiday: Republic Day (first Sunday in June); language: Italian; religion: none; currency: lira (L) (pl. lire) = 100 centesimi; abbreviation: I.

Geography. Italy consists of a peninsula covering around five sixths of the total area of 301,277 sq km, the two large Mediterranean islands of Sardinia and Sicily, and around 70 small islands. It is bordered by Switzerland and Austria in the north, Slovenia and the Adriatic Sea in the east, the Mediterranean Sea in the south, and France in the west; neighbouring countries across the various seas are Croatia, Albania, Malta and Tunisia. Much of the country is mountainous. The main ranges are the Alps along the northern borders and the Apennine chain [Appennino], which runs along the penin-

sula. The main low-lying areas are the large fertile Po Valley in the north, the Arno and Tiber [Tevere] basins (in Tuscany and around Rome respectively), the southeast (the 'heel' of Italy) and the coastal strips. Some 42% of the land is arable, another 17% is covered by pastures and 22% is forested. The main rivers are the Po and its tributaries, Tiber and Arno. The climate is generally mediterranean, with hot summers and mild winters. Temperatures are lower in upland areas, and higher in the south; rainfall is moderate, heavier in the mountains and lighter in the south.

Demography. Italy has a population of 57,235,000. Population density is 195 per sq km (land area). Some 67% of the people live in urban areas. The most densely populated regions are the northern plains and the coastal areas. The main urban centres are Rome (metropolitan population 3.8 million, city 2.7 million), Milan [Milano] (3.9 million, 1.4 million), Naples [Napoli] (2.7 million, 1.1 million) and Turin [Torino] (1.7 million, 1.0 million). Other major cities are Palermo, Genoa [Genova], Bologna, Florence [Firenze], Catania, Bari, Venice [Venezia], Messina, Verona, Taranto, Trieste, Padua [Padova] and Cagliari. The overwhelming majority of the people are ethnic Italians and speak Italian, although regional identification is strong and regional dialects are pronounced. The Sardinian dialects, spoken by 1.5 million Sardinians (2.6% of the total population), are usually considered a separate language. Ethnic minorities include Friulians and Ladins in the northeast (550,000 or 1.0% of the total), German-speaking South Tyroleans (300,000) in the north, French- or Franco-Provençal-speaking Aostans (200,000) in the northwest, Albanians (90,000) in the south, Gipsies (80,000), Slovenes (53,000) in the northeast, Greeks (15,000) in the southeast, and Catalans (12,000) in Sardinia. Foreign nationals officially account for 0.8% of the population, but there are also thought to be around 1.5 million illegal immigrants, mainly from African countries. In religious terms nearly four-fifths of the people are nominally Roman

Catholics; there are also 50,000 Protestants and 40,000 Jews; most of the remainder are not religious.

Sociography. Italy scores 0.891 on the United Nations human development index (HDI), ranking 22nd in the world and 15th among 32 European countries. There are 44 doctors and 69 hospital beds for every 10,000 people. Education is compulsory between the ages of six and 13. There is one teacher for every 19 students. Enrolment is 78% at the secondary level and 29% at the tertiary level. The literacy rate is 97%. Real annual income per head (in terms of purchasing power) is US$ 17,040. Income levels in the south are roughly half of those in the north and centre (around $ 13,000 compared to $ 23,000).

Infrastructure and communications. The transport and communications network in northern and central Italy is highly developed; in the south and on the islands the road, rail and telecommunications systems are more limited, particularly in the rural areas, and the electronic media have a wider reach than the press. There are 302,400 km of paved roads and 27.3 million passenger cars (474 per 1,000 people), 19,560 km of railways and 2,400 km of navigable waterways. The main ports are Genoa, Trieste, Taranto, Venice, Savona, Livorno, Ravenna, Palermo and Naples. The main airports are at Rome (Leonardo da Vinci - Fiumicino) and Milan (Linate and Malpensa), and there are 27 other airports with scheduled services. There are 73 daily newspapers, with a combined circulation of 6.01 million (105 per 1,000 people). There are around 30 million radio receivers, 17.0 million television sets and 32.1 million telephones in use (respectively 521, 295 and 556 per 1,000 people).

Economic structure. The Italian economy is highly developed, diversified and trade-oriented, with traditionally a substantial state-owned sector. It is the third-largest economy in Europe and the fifth-largest in the world as well as the world's sixth-largest trading power. It is based on engineering and other manufacturing, agriculture, trade and tourism. The

south, known as the Mezzogiorno, is more dependent on agriculture and far less industrialized than the north and centre. After a period of sustained growth from 1984–89 (averaging 3.3% per year), economic performance in the 1990s has been marked by growth declining to -0.1% in 1993, current-account deficits (averaging 0.9% of GDP), relatively high inflation (averaging 5.6%, falling below 4% in 1993), and persistent high unemployment (around 11% nationwide, around 18% in the south). The national debt stands at around 115% of GDP, one of the highest levels in the European Union (EU). The unofficial economy is estimated to be equivalent to a sixth of official GDP.

Services contribute 64% of GDP, industry contributes 33% (manufacturing 22%), and agriculture, forestry and fisheries 3%. Some 20% of the labour force is employed in manufacturing, 19% in trade, 8% in farming and 8% in construction. The main crops grown are cereals (wheat, maize, barley, rice), potatoes, sugarbeets, olives, oilseeds, soybeans, pulses and tobacco; other important agricultural activities are horticulture (fruit and vegetables, esp. tomatoes, grapes, apples, citrus fruit), livestock raising (cattle for meat and hides, pigs, sheep, chickens) and dairy farming (cheese, milk); Italy is the largest producer of fruit and vegetables in Europe. Forestry and fishing are of regional importance. The main mineral resources are oil, lignite, pyrites, fluorspar, marble, zinc, lead, mercury and sulphur. The main industries are engineering (esp. motor vehicles, industrial machinery), electrical goods and electronics; other important branches are textiles and clothing (incl. footwear), chemicals, food processing (esp. meat and dairy products and wine), iron and steel and other metalworking, petrochemicals, wood processing and glass and ceramics; the manufacturing industry is the second-largest in Europe and the fourth-largest in the world. Tourism is a major source of foreign exchange, contributing 2.0% of GNP (0.6% net); the tourism industry is the second-largest in Europe and third-largest in the world. The main energy sources are domestic and imported fossil fuels; 9% of export earnings are required to cover net fuel imports. The main exports are industrial machinery (17% of the total), textiles and clothing (incl. footwear) (16%), electrical equipment (incl. office equipment) (14%), transport equipment (11%, incl. cars 7%), chemicals (10%), foodstuffs (esp. fruit and vegetables) (5%), wood and wood products, iron and steel; machinery and transport equipment account for 42% of the total, miscellaneous manufactures for 25% and basic manufactures for 21%. The main imports are machinery and transport equipment, basic manufactures, chemicals, fuels and foodstuffs. The main trading partners are: exports: Germany (21%), France (15%), United States (7%), United Kingdom (7%), Switzerland, Belgium and Luxemburg, Netherlands, Japan, Spain; imports: Germany (21%), France (14%), United States (6%), Netherlands (5%), United Kingdom (5%), Belgium and Luxemburg (5%), Switzerland, Japan; nearly three-fifths of all trade is with other European Union (EU) countries.

The Bank of Italy [Banca d'Italia] is the central bank. The main employers' association is the General Confederation of Italian Industry (CONFINDUSTRIA); the main labour organizations are the Italian General Confederation of Labour (CGIL), Italian Confederation of Workers' Unions (CISL) and Italian Union of Labour (UIL).

Political structure. Italy is a parliamentary republic on the basis of a constitution adopted in 1948. The head of state is the president, who is elected for a seven-year term by an electoral college composed of members of the legislature and regional delegates; s/he appoints the prime minister and may dissolve parliament but has few other powers. Executive power is vested in the prime minister [presidente del consiglio] and the council of ministers. Legislative power is vested in the bicameral Parliament [Parlamento], composed of the Chamber of Deputies [Camera dei Deputati], whose 630 members are elected for a five-year term by a mixed system of simple majority voting and proportional representation, and the Senate [Senato], with 315 members elected by a similar system and around 10 members appointed for life. The two houses have equal powers. All citizens over the age of 18 are entitled to vote; the minimum voting age for Senate elections is 25. Judicial power is ultimately vested in the Supreme Court of Appeal [Corte Suprema di Cassazione]; the 15-member Constitutional Court [Corte Costituzionale] adjudicates on constitutional matters. Italy is divided into 20 autonomous regions [regione autonoma, pl. regioni autonome]. They are Abruzzi, Aosta Valley [Valle d'Aosta / Val d'Aoste], Apulia [Puglia], Basilicata, Calabria, Campania, Emilia-Romagna, Friuli - Venezia Giulia, Lazio, Liguria, Lombardy [Lombardia], Marches [Marche], Molise, Piedmont [Piemonte], Sardinia [Sardegna], Sicily [Sicilia], Trentino - Alto Adige, Tuscany [Toscana], Umbria and Veneto. Aosta Valley, Friuli - Venezia Giulia, Sardinia, Sicily and Trentino - Alto Adige have more extensive powers of self-government than the other regions. Administratively the regions are divided into 95 provinces [provincia, pl. province], which are subdivided into around 8,100 communes.

The main political parties are Come On Italy (Forza Italia, FI), the Democratic Left Party (PDS, a successor to the Italian Communist Party, PCI), National Alliance (AN, based on the Italian Social Movement - National Right, MSI-DN), Italian People's Party (PPI, a successor to the Christian Democratic Party, DC), Communist Refoundation Party (RC, a successor to the PCI), Pact for Italy, Radical Party (PR), Green Federation or Greens (Verdi), Italian Socialist Party (PSI), Network (La Rete), Democratic Alliance (AD), Christian Democratic Centre (CCD, a successor to the DC), Social Christian Party (PCS, a successor to the DC) and Centre Union (UDC); the main regional parties are the Northern League (Lega Nord, LN), South Tyrol People's Party (SVP), Aosta Valley

Union (UV) and Sardinian Action Party (PSdA). At the election in March 1994 Forza Italia gained 21.0% of the vote and 102/630 seats, the PDS 20.4% and 117 seats, the AN 13.5% and 109 seats, the PPI 11.1% and 33 seats, the Northern League 8.4% and 117 seats, the RC 6.0% and 39 seats, the Pact for Italy 4.6% and 13 seats, the Pannella List (dominated by the PR) 3.5% and six seats, the Greens 2.7% and 11 seats, the PSI 2.2% and 15 seats, the Network 1.9% and nine seats, the AD 1.2% and 17 seats, the CCD 27 seats, the PCS six seats, the UDC four seats, the SVP three seats, the UV one seat, and an independent one seat. (At the April 1992 election the DC had gained 29.7% and 206 seats, the PDS 16.1% and 107 seats, the PSI 13.6% and 92 seats, the Northern League 8.7% and 55 seats, the RC 5.6% and 35 seats, the MSI-DN 5.4% and 34 seats, the Italian Republican Party, PRI, 4.4% and 27 seats, the Italian Liberal Party, PLI, 2.8% and 17 seats, the Greens 2.8% and 16 seats, the Italian Democratic Socialist Party, PSDI, 2.7% and 16 seats, the Pannella List 1.2% and seven seats, the Network 1.0% and 12 seats, the SVP three seats, the UV one seat, and the Federation of Pensioners, FPU, one seat.) The government is formed by the right-wing Freedom Alliance, with Silvio Berlusconi as prime minister. Other senior ministers are Roberto Maroni (deputy prime minister, interior), Giuseppe Tatarella (deputy prime minister, posts and telecommunications), Gianni Letta (cabinet secretary), Antonio Martino (foreign affairs), Alfredo Biondi (justice), Giulio Tremonti (finance), Giancarlo Pagliarini (budget), Lamberto Dini (treasury), Cesare Previti (defence), Clemente Mastella (labour), Adriana Poli Bortone (agriculture) and Altero Matteoli (environment). The head of state is President Oscar Scalfaro, who was elected in May 1992.

Security and international affiliations. The Italian armed forces number 344,600 (army 223,300, navy 43,600, airforce 77,700); they are due to be reduced to 287,000. There are also three major paramilitary forces: the 111,800-strong Corps of Carabinieri [Corpo dei Carabinieri], the 80,400-strong Public Security Guard [Guardia di Pubblica Sicurezza] (PS), and the 64,100-strong Finance Guard [Guardia di Finanza] (GdF). Military service is compulsory and consists of 12 months' basic training. Some 13,000 American troops are stationed in Italy.

Italy is a member of the Central European Initiative (CEI), Conference on Security and Cooperation in Europe (CSCE), Council of Europe, European Economic Area (EEA), European Union (EU), North Atlantic Treaty Organization (NATO) and Western European Union (WEU), as well as the Group of Seven (G-7), the Organization for Economic Cooperation and Development (OECD) and the United Nations and its specialized agencies.

History. In the 6th century BC the main peoples in the centre of the Italian peninsula were the Etruscans, Latins and Sabines; the Greeks had established a number of colonies in the south; and Celts or Gauls inhabited the north. Over the next two centuries the Latin city of Rome conquered its neighbours, and by 264 all of central and southern Italy was under its rule. The Romans then fought three wars with the Carthaginians, based on the North African coast. After destroying Carthage in 146, the Romans went on to conquer the whole Mediterranean region. The institutions of the Roman Republic, which had evolved from the late 6th century, were undermined by a series of civil wars and effectively replaced by absolute imperial rule under Augustus (27 BC – AD 14). Under Emperor Hadrian (117–38) the Roman Empire reached its greatest extent: it comprised all of continental Europe south of the Rhine and Danube rivers, Britannia (England and Wales), Dacia (modern Romania), Asia Minor (Turkey), Syria (including Israel/Palestine), Egypt and North Africa. Christianity quickly took root throughout the Empire, especially in the eastern cities and Rome itself. Christians were persecuted between the 1st and 3rd centuries, but Emperor Constantine granted freedom of religion in 313. Rome was confirmed as the seat of the Papacy, the government of the Catholic Church.

The Europe-wide migrations during the 5th century precipitated the collapse of the Western Roman Empire in 476. Northern Italy was ruled by the Germanic Ostrogoths (until 553) and then the Lombards, while the Eastern Roman or Byzantine Empire retained control of most of the south. Roman civilization, including its Greek and hellenistic antecedents and mediated by Christianity, exercised a powerful influence on European law, politics and culture throughout the Middle Ages and beyond, not least through the continued use of Latin as the language of administration, education etc. In 754 the Papacy became a temporal power when King Pepin of the Franks granted it conquered territory in central Italy; the Papal States would remain an major political force for the next 11 centuries. In 774 the Lombard kingdom was conquered by the Franks. When King Charlemagne (768–814) was crowned 'Roman emperor' in Rome in 800, the Frankish Empire extended across most of Western Europe. The various partitions after his death resulted in the creation of the Kingdom of Italy within the Holy Roman or German Empire. Feudal fragmentation from the 10th century onwards led to the emergence of autonomous states, which were increasingly able to resist attempts to impose imperial authority. Southern Italy remained in Byzantine hands throughout this period, with the exception of Sicily, which came under Muslim Arab rule in the 820s. During the 11th–13th centuries political events in northern Italy were moulded by the struggle for supremacy between the Papacy and the Empire, mirrored locally in struggles between Guelfs and Ghibellines. The Normans (descendants of the Vikings) conquered southern Italy in the late 11th century and in 1130 established the Kingdom of Sicily, also called Naples or the Two Sicilies in later centuries. In the absence of a strong central authority after the withdrawal of the German emperors in the 13th century, northern and central Italy fragmented into a number of small

but increasingly powerful city states, notably the republics of Venice, Florence and Genoa and the duchy of Milan. These cities were among the most important commercial and industrial centres of Europe. They were also the cradle of the 14th- and 15th-century cultural revival called the Renaissance, which was marked by renewed interest in Greco-Roman learning and values, a flowering of the arts and scientific advances. Between 1494 and 1525 France and the Habsburgs (rulers of the Holy Roman Empire, Austria and, from 1516, Spain and its Italian possessions), each supported by local allies, vied for supremacy in the peninsula. The city states suffered major devastation during the wars, which ended in defeat for France. Their decline was accelerated by the cutting of traditional trade routes to the East (by the Ottoman Turks) and the opening of the new Atlantic and Cape routes, which shifted the balance of economic power to northwestern Europe. After the War of the Spanish Succession (1701–13/14) Austria replaced Spain as the dominant power in Italy. France conquered or controlled all of Italy after 1796 and the country's political map was extensively redrawn. The Venetian Republic was dissolved in 1797.

Following the post-Napoleonic reorganization of Europe carried out by the Congress of Vienna in 1814/15, there were nine Italian states: Piedmont-Sardinia and Austrian-ruled Lombardy and Venetia in the north; Parma, Modena, Lucca, Tuscany and the Papal States in the centre; and Naples/Sicily in the south. A national movement seeking the unification of all the Italian states, called the Risorgimento ('Revival'), inspired by Giuseppe Mazzini, Giuseppe Garibaldi and others and spearheaded by Piedmont-Sardinia, gained ground from the 1830s. National uprisings were suppressed in 1848–49. Unification was achieved between 1859 and 1870, culminating in the occupation of Rome and its proclamation as the national capital. King Victor Emmanuel II of Piedmont-Sardinia was proclaimed king of Italy in 1861. The liberal constitution in force in Piedmont-

Sardinia was extended to the incorporated states. Between 1889 and 1912 Italy established a colonial empire by conquering Eritrea, Somalia and Libya, but was defeated by Abyssinia (now Ethiopia) in 1896. Italy entered the First World War (1914–18) in 1915 on the side of France and the United Kingdom. It was awarded the Austrian territories of South Tyrol (with a large German-speaking population) and the port of Trieste in 1919. The far-right National Fascist Party (PNF) led by Benito Mussolini, exploiting widespread resentment at the meagre war gains, political disenchantment and economic problems, rapidly rose to prominence after 1918. Mussolini was asked to form a government in 1922. After the PNF won a manipulated election in 1924, Mussolini disbanded all other parties in 1925 and ruled as dictator. Italian troops conquered Abyssinia in 1935–36. An ally of Germany from 1936, Italy entered the Second World War (1939–45) in 1940. After the invasion by Allied forces in 1943, Mussolini was dismissed and the new government declared war on Germany. Mussolini was able to retain control in the north under German protection until his execution by resistance fighters in 1945.

The monarchy was abolished and a republic established after a referendum in 1946. The 1947 peace treaty deprived Italy of all its colonies except Somalia (which became independent in 1960). The Christian Democratic Party (DC) emerged as the largest party at the 1948 election, with the Italian Communist Party (PCI) second and the Italian Socialist Party (PSI) third. This pattern of electoral support remained largely unchanged until the early 1990s, as did the pattern of short-lived four- and five-party centrist coalitions headed by the DC, with the PSI becoming the key junior partner in the 1970s. Although 52 governments held office between 1946 and 1994, the changes were more like cabinet reshuffles and none signalled a major departure in terms of policy or personnel. Apparent political instability thus masked an underlying continuity unmatched in any other

major Western European country. Italy became a founding member of the North Atlantic Treaty Organization (NATO) in 1949 and of the European Economic Community (EEC), now the European Union (EU), in 1958. From the 1950s the country was rapidly transformed from a predominantly agricultural economy into one of the world's major industrial powers. A key feature of Italy's economic and social structure is the divide between the industrialized and affluent north and centre and the more agricultural and poorer south (Mezzogiorno). Despite massive investment over the years the gap has not been narrowed. From the 1950s the Mafia and other crime syndicates strengthened their influence in Sicily and other southern regions, and in the 1970s they became major players in worldwide drug trafficking. From the mid 1970s to the early 1980s terrorist violence by various far-right and -left groups, such as the Red Brigades, presented a major security problem and threatened political stability.

In an indication of growing popular dissatisfaction with the political establishment and the influence of organized crime, several new parties, in particular the federalist Northern League (Lega Nord) and the anti-Mafia Network (La Rete), gained significant support at the April 1992 election, producing a more fragmented parliament. The DC, PSI and the PCI's successor, the Democratic Left Party (PDS), all lost votes. Oscar Luigi Scalfaro was elected president of the republic in May. The assassination of two senior judges in May and July by the Mafia strengthened calls for change. This coincided with growing evidence, uncovered by a team of Milan-based magistrates, that the PSI was involved in systematic violations of the party-funding laws. Later in the year it became clear that the corruption was not limited to Milan or the PSI, but involved all the government parties. The investigations exposed a system of political corruption whereby the ruling parties extracted trillions of lire from businesses in exchange for public-sector contracts and other favours. In April 1993 voters overwhelmingly approved several referendums on constitutional changes, including the partial abolition of the system of proportional representation in elections, which was widely seen as a major contributory factor to the ossification of the political system. A transitional government under Carlo Azeglio Ciampi was appointed to put the electoral reform in place and take urgent measures to improve the state of public finances. (High budget deficits have been a major economic problem since the 1970s.) By this time Italy had been thrown into its worst political crisis since the Second World War, as revelations mounted of illegal activities involving senior politicians and business-people, members of the secret services and organized crime, providing evidence of what has been called the 'hidden government' [sottogoverno]. By the end of the year the leaders of the five ruling parties had resigned, most ministers had resigned or been replaced, hundreds of politicians and industrialists were either under investigation or arrest, and the government parties had been thoroughly discredited. Their electoral support collapsed in local and regional elections in May/June and November/December. The main beneficiaries were the PDS, Northern League, Greens and the far-right Italian Social Movement (MSI, the intellectual heir of the Fascist Party). The sense of national crisis was heightened by four bomb attacks in May and July carried out by the Armed Phalange, a group widely thought to have links with far-right elements in the secret services and the Mafia. The transformation of the country's political system was confirmed in the March 1994 election, which was won by a right-wing alliance comprising Come On Italy (Forza Italia), set up by the businessman Silvio Berlusconi two months earlier, the Northern League, and the National Alliance (AN), a more broadly based grouping founded by the MSI. More than two-thirds of the elected deputies and senators were newcomers to parliament. Berlusconi formed a government in May.

See also entries on specific institutions, organizations, parties, people, terms etc.

ITL Abbreviation for the LIRA, the Italian currency, used in banking etc.

IU *See* UNITED LEFT.

Ivanov, Risto (1960–) Macedonian economist and politician. He worked for a civil-engineering firm from 1982–86 and then for the communist Socialist Youth Union of Yugoslavia until 1990. He was director of a clothing firm from 1991–93. Now a member of the Reform Forces of Macedonia - Liberal Party (RSM-LP), he was appointed a deputy prime minister in July 1993.

Izetbegović, Alija (1925–) Bosnian lawyer, writer and politician. A Slav Muslim, he was a prominent opponent of the communist regime from the late 1940s until its collapse in the late 1980s. He was imprisoned for 'pan-Islamic activities' from 1946–49 and for 'counterrevolutionary acts' from 1983–88. In between he published several works on the role of Islam in a modern and multicultural world. In May 1990 he was elected leader of the new Democratic Action Party (SDA). When the SDA was returned as the largest single party in the election the following December, he was elected president of the republic's collective presidency. He was confirmed in the post when Bosnia-Herzegovina declared its independence from the Yugoslav federation in March 1992 and has held it throughout the civil war which broke out later that month.

Jaanilinn question Border dispute between Estonia and Russia. In 1945, five years after Estonia's annexation by the Soviet Union, a strip of land to the east of the Narva river was incorporated into Russia (as was the Petseri district in the southeast). The main town is Ivangorod, whose Estonian name is Jaanilinn. Its population is almost entirely Russian.

Jagland, Thorbjørn (1950–) Norwegian politician. Leader of the Norwegian Labour Party (DNA) youth wing from 1977–81, he became the party's research secretary in 1981 and its general secretary in 1986. In November 1992 he was elected party leader after Gro Harlem Brundtland stood down to concentrate on her duties as prime minister. After his election to parliament in September 1993 he also became leader of the parliamentary group.

Jakobsen, Mimi (1948–) Danish linguist, academic and politician. She lectured in German philology from 1977. Elected to parliament for the Centre Democrats (CD) in 1979, she was minister of culture from 1982–86 and minister of social affairs from 1986–88. She was elected party leader in November 1989. In January 1993 she became minister for industrial coordination in the centre-left coalition, and in January 1994 she took over the industry portfolio.

Jan Mayen Dependency of Norway. A small island in the Arctic Ocean situated 500 km east of Greenland and 550 km northeast of Iceland, Jan Mayen has around 25 temporary inhabitants, the staff of a radio and navigation station. Annexed by Norway in 1929, the island, or rather its surrounding fishing and whaling grounds, has been the source of territorial disputes between Denmark, Iceland and Norway since the 1970s. At that time each country declared a 200-mile economic zone – Norway around Jan Mayen, Denmark off the coast of its dependency Greenland, and Iceland around its territory – which overlapped at various points. Norway and Iceland resolved their differences in 1980. Denmark and Norway submitted their claims to the International Court of Justice (ICJ), which ruled in June 1993 that the disputed waters should be divided roughly equally between the two countries.

Janičina, Milan (1948–) Slovakian lawyer and politician. He worked for Slovak television and the Institute of Geodesy and Cartography (ÚGK) during the 1980s. From 1990–92 he held a senior post in the ministry of privatization, set up after the collapse of communist rule in 1989. A member of parliament for the Slovak National Party (SNS) since 1993, he joined the breakaway National Democratic Party (NDS) in February 1994 and was appointed to the key post of minister of privatization in the centrist coalition which took office the following month.

Janša, Janez (1958–) Slovenian politician. A specialist on defence and security issues, he was expelled from the Slovenian League of Communists (ZKS) in 1989 for his reformist views. He was elected to parliament for the Slovenian Democratic Alliance (SDZ) in April 1990 and was appointed defence minister in May of that year. He joined the Social Democratic Party (SDSS) in 1992 and was elected its leader in May 1993. He was dismissed from the government in March 1994 after being held responsible for instances of unethical behaviour by military-police officers.

Janssens, François (1943–) Belgian lawyer and trade-union official. He was a legal adviser to the General Labour Federation (ABVV/FGTB) from 1968–72. He then became national secretary and from 1977 president of the Union of Employees, Technicians and Administrative Workers (BBTK/SETCa). He was elected president of the General Labour Federation in September 1989.

Jarnjak, Ivan (1941–) Croatian administrator and politician. He worked for an engineering company before entering politics. A member of the right-wing Croatian Democratic Union (HDZ), he was appointed junior interior minister in 1991 and became interior minister in April 1992.

Jaruzelski, Wojciech (1923–) Polish soldier and politician. A career soldier in the Polish army since 1943, he rose to the rank of general. He was appointed minister of defence in 1968, became prime minister and leader of the ruling communist Polish United Workers' Party (PZPR) in 1981, and also head of state in 1985. In December 1981 he declared martial law to curtail the activities of the Solidarity movement. He remained head of state when communist rule crumbled in 1989, but the following year he agreed to stand down, doing so formally in December. In April 1993 he was indicted over his role in the suppression of workers' protests in Gdynia in 1970 (when he was defence minister), which had resulted in the deaths of at least 44 people.

Jaurlaritza ('Government') Basque name for the government of the Basque Country, an autonomous community or region of Spain.

Jean (1921–) Grand Duke of Luxemburg. He took over the duties of head of state from his ailing mother, Charlotte, in 1961 and succeeded to the throne on her abdication in November 1964. He married Princess Joséphine-Charlotte of Belgium in 1953. They have five children.

Jedenastego Listopada and **Jedenasty Listopad** *See* ELEVENTH OF NOVEMBER ALLIANCE.

Jelinčič, Zmago (1948–) Slovenian soldier and politician. He served in the French Foreign Legion before entering politics. He was elected leader of the far-right Slovenian National Party (SNS) in October 1991 and was elected to parliament in December 1992.

Jelved, Marianne (1943–) Danish teacher and politician. She was elected to parliament for the Radical Liberals (RV) in 1987 and was their parliamentary leader from 1988–93. She became minister of economic affairs in the centre-left coalition which took office in January 1993.

Jensen, Ole Vig (1936–) Danish teacher and politician. He was active in local government for the centrist Radical Liberal Party (RV) for many years before his first election to parliament in 1971. He was minister of cultural affairs from 1988–90 and was appointed education minister in the centre-left government which took office in January 1993.

Jersey Territory in western Europe, a dependency of the United Kingdom.

Official data. Name: Bailiwick of Jersey; capital: Saint Helier; form of government: internally self-governing dependency of the British crown; head of state: British monarch, represented by a lieutenant-governor; head of government: bailiff; flag: white with a diagonal red cross and the state emblem in the centre; national holidays: Queen's Official Birthday (second Saturday in June), 9 May (Liberation Day); languages: French and English; religion: Anglicanism (Church of England in Jersey); currencies: pound (£) = 100 pence, British pound; abbreviation: GBJ.

Geography. The largest of the Channel Islands situated between France and Britain, Jersey has an area of 116 sq km. The terrain is generally low-lying, with hills rising to a low plateau in the north. Around three-fifths of the land is arable and around a fifth is covered by pastures. The climate is temperate marine, with mild summers and cool winters; rainfall is moderate.

Demography. Jersey has a population of 85,900. Population density is 741 per sq km. The main town is Saint Helier. Most people are native Channel Islanders, but there is also a substantial number of immigrants from Britain. The main language is English; Norman French (a dialect of French) is also spoken in the rural areas; French is used for some official purposes. In religious terms most of the people are Anglicans; there are also small groups of Roman Catholics and other Christians.

Sociography. The standard of living in Jersey is very high. There are 11 doctors and 89 hospital beds for every 10,000 people. Education is compulsory between the ages of five and 16. There is one teacher for every 16 students. Enrolment is 76% at the secondary level; there is one college of higher education, but most students study in Britain. The literacy rate is virtually 100%. GNP per head (unadjusted for purchasing power) is US$ 34,200, among the highest in Europe.

Infrastructure and communications.
Jersey has a highly developed but limited transport and communications network closely integrated with that of Britain; ferry and air links are particularly important. There are around 340 km of paved roads and 60,700 passenger cars (721 per 1,000 people). There are no railways or navigable waterways. The main port is Saint Helier. There is an airport at Saint Peter (States of Jersey). There is one daily newspaper, with a circulation of 24,000 (300 per 1,000 people); British papers are also widely read. There are around 100,000 radio receivers, around 50,000 television sets and 90,000 telephones in use (respectively around 1,200, around 600 and 1,068 per 1,000 people).

Economic structure. The Jersey economy is highly developed, relatively diversified and closely linked to the British economy. Jersey maintains a customs and monetary union with the United Kingdom and Guernsey. Taxation is low. The economy is based on financial services, tourism and agriculture. Since the late 1980s economic performance has been marked by relatively high growth, relatively low inflation and very low unemployment (detailed figures n.a.).

Services contribute 93% of GDP (financial services 42%), industry contributes 2%, and agriculture and fisheries around 5%. Some 16% of the labour force is employed in finance, 14% in trade and 9% in construction. The main agricultural activities are dairy farming (milk, butter) and horticulture (tomatoes and other vegetables, fruit, plants, flowers); potatoes are the main crop grown. Fishing is also important. There are no significant mineral resources. The main industries are electronics, textiles and food processing. Banking and other financial services and tourism are mainstays of the economy, contributing 42% and 20% of GNP respectively. The main energy sources are imported fossil fuels. The main exports are electrical goods, foodstuffs (tomatoes and other vegetables, potatoes) and textiles and clothing. The main imports are fuels and basic and miscellaneous manufactures. The main trading partner is the United Kingdom (exports 67% of the total, imports 85%). Net invisible earnings (income from financial services, tourism receipts, investment income) account for around half of GNP.

There is no central bank. Employers' associations and trade unions are integrated into British structures.

Political structure. Jersey is an internally self-governing dependency of the British crown (i.e. the monarch) on the basis of constitutional practice, statute law and common law; there is no written constitution. The British government is responsible for defence and foreign affairs and also effectively for discharging the crown's extensive powers of appointment etc. Executive power is formally vested in the British monarch, represented by a lieutenant-governor; it is exercised by the bailiff and other government officials, all of whom are appointed by the crown, and by committees elected by the legislature from among its members. The bailiff is head of government, president of the legislature and head of the judiciary. Legislative power is vested in the 58-member States of Deliberation, composed of directly and indirectly elected members elected for various terms and five ex-officio members. All citizens over the age of 18 are entitled to vote; resident Commonwealth and Irish citizens normally also have voting rights. Judicial power is vested in the 13-member Royal Court composed of the bailiff and 12 indirectly elected judges [jurat, pl. -s]; appeal courts are the three-member Court of Appeal and, in some cases, the Judicial Committee of the Privy Council, a body composed of senior judges in the British House of Lords. Jersey is divided into 12 parishes [douzaine, pl. -s], which have few administrative or political functions.

There are no political parties. The bailiff is Peter Crill, the deputy bailiff is Philip Martin Bailhache. The head of state is Queen Elizabeth II, represented by John Sutton as lieutenant-governor; the heir is Prince Charles.

Security and international affiliations. Defence and foreign affairs are the responsibility of the British government.

The Jersey government is usually consulted in matters of immediate concern to the island. Jersey is treated as part of the European Union (EU) for the purpose of free trade of goods, but it is not a member of the organization.

History. During the early Middle Ages Jersey formed part of the Duchy of Normandy, a French fief. (*For earlier developments, see* FRANCE: HISTORY.) After William of Normandy conquered England in 1066 it became a possession of the English crown. When France regained control over Normandy proper in 1204, Jersey, along with the other Channel Islands, remained in English hands. It has been attached to the English, later British, crown ever since. Existing Norman law and customs were largely retained, and over the years the island secured a large degree of self-government through royal charters. These granted an independent judiciary, tax sovereignty, tariff-free access to the English/British market and a range of other privileges. In 1617 the bailiff, the sovereign's representative, was given control over justice and civil affairs as president of what became the Royal Court. In 1771 the judicial and legislative branches of government were separated when the States assumed the Court's powers of legislation. In the 18th and 19th centuries the island prospered from fishing, privateering and smuggling. During the Second World War (1939–45) Jersey, like the other Channel Islands, was occupied by German troops from 1940–44.

Tourism has developed into a major economic activity since the 1950s, and financial services since the 1970s.

See also entries on specific institutions, terms etc.

Jeszenszky, Géza (1941–) Hungarian historian, academic and politician. A lecturer in international relations from 1976, he was elected to parliament for the centre-right Hungarian Democratic Forum (MDF) in 1990. He was appointed minister of foreign affairs in May, a post he held until the MDF-led coalition lost power in July 1994.

Jews Religious and ethnic group in Europe. Originating from Israel/Palestine, Jews settled throughout the Eastern Mediterranean region from the 2nd century BC. During the early Middle Ages there were substantial Jewish communities in Muslim-ruled Spain and in a number of Western European cities (e.g. Cologne, Frankfurt, Augsburg, Bordeaux, Venice). From this period dates the broad cultural division into two branches of Jewry and Judaism, the Sephardi (rooted in Spain) and Ashkenazi (rooted in Germany and France). At this time Jews often enjoyed state protection and certain privileges. A Christian religious revival in the late 11th century, sparked and fuelled by the Crusades, marked the beginning of centuries of institutionalized discrimination and persecution. Jewish settlement in Poland, Lithuania, Belorussia and Ukraine began in the mid 12th century. Jews were expelled from England and France in the 13th century. Persecution intensified in Germany and elsewhere during the Europe-wide plague epidemic known as the 'black death' (1347–54), for which Jews were often made scapegoats. Many thousands fled east during this period. The substantial Jewish communities in Spain and Portugal were expelled in 1492 and 1496 respectively. Because Jews were prohibited from owning or working land and restricted in other ways, they almost invariably lived in towns and cities and worked as craftspeople, traders and moneylenders and later also as merchants, bankers, administrators, scholars and artists. Jews gained full civil and political rights in France in 1791 and during the 19th century elsewhere in Europe. During the 19th century religious 'anti-semitism' (which had for long allowed conversion to Christianity as a way out of formal discrimination) gave way to racial anti-semitism. Discrimination, persecution and poverty induced many Eastern European Jews to emigrate to America, Britain, France and elsewhere from the 1880s onwards. The emergence of European national movements inspired 'zionism', which aimed to reestablish the ancient Jewish homeland in Palestine.

During the nazi regime in Germany (1933–45) Jews were stripped of their civil rights and property and confined to ghettos or labour camps. After the outbreak of the Second World War in 1939 this policy was extended to the occupied territories. In 1942 the nazis adopted the 'final solution' programme providing for the systematic extermination of the Jewish people in Europe. Around 6 million Jews were killed during what became known as the HOLOCAUST. Emigration to Israel, the United States and elsewhere after the Second World War further reduced their numbers. Today there are around 1.4 million Jews in Europe (excluding Russia and the other members of the Commonwealth of Independent States and Turkey), equivalent to around 0.3% of the continent's total population. The largest communities are in France (660,000, 1.2% of the total population), Britain (330,000, 0.6%), Hungary (80,000, 0.8%), Germany (40,000), Belgium (35,000), Italy (35,000), Ireland (28,000), Netherlands (28,000), Switzerland (20,000), Sweden (20,000) and Romania (18,000). The various branches of religious Judaism are broadly divided into 'orthodox', 'conservative', 'reform' and 'liberal'. Many Jews are not religious but most retain a strong cultural and historical identity. Yiddish, the German-based language of Eastern Europe's Jews and their descendants, is still spoken by a small number of people.

J£ Abbreviation for the POUND, the Jersey currency.

JNA Abbreviation for Jugoslovenska Narodna Armija ('Yugoslav National Army'), the armed forces of the Yugoslav federation until its disintegration in 1991/92 and now the armed forces of rump Yugoslavia. The Serbocroat word *narodna* can be translated as both 'people's' and 'national', and during communist rule the JNA was commonly referred to in English as the Yugoslav People's Army.

Joden (sing. Jood/Jodin) Dutch name for JEWS.

Johansson, Olof (1937–) Swedish politician. He worked as a farmer, journalist, teacher and farmers' representative until 1966, when he became secretary of the Centre Party (Cp) parliamentary group. Elected to parliament in 1970, he held two junior ministerial posts from 1976–82 and was elected party leader in February 1987. He became environment minister in the centre-right coalition which took office in October 1991. He resigned from the government in June 1994 after it approved a controversial bridge and tunnel link across the Sound [Öresund] to Denmark.

John Bull Personification of England or the United Kingdom. John Bull first appeared as a character in an allegory published in 1712. Usually represented as a bulldog, he has been widely used since then in caricatures, satirical writings etc.

John Paul II (until 1978 **Karol Wojtyła**) (1920–) Polish clergyman, pope or head of the Roman Catholic Church and head of state of the Vatican City State. Ordained a Roman Catholic priest in 1946, he lectured in ethics and theology from 1953–58 and was archbishop of Kraków from 1963–78. He was made a cardinal in 1967. In October 1978 the College of Cardinals elected him pope, supreme head of the Catholic Church worldwide (and ex officio the Vatican's head of state). The first Pole to hold the office and the first non-Italian since 1523, he took the name John Paul II. He played an influential role in Polish politics in the 1980s, expressing support for opponents of the communist regime.

Johnsen, Sigbjørn (1950–) Norwegian accountant and politician. He was deputy chairman of the Equal Status Council from 1976–83. Elected to parliament for the Norwegian Labour Party (DNA) in 1976, he was appointed finance minister in November 1990.

Joint Commission on Wages and Prices or **Parity Commission** [Paritätische Lohn- und Preiskommission] Austrian advisory body. Formed in 1957, the Parity Commission is the pivot in the country's system of 'social partnership', i.e. the tripartite cooperation between employers, trade unions and government. It brings together the two national employers' associations, the Association of Austrian Industrialists (VÖI) and Federal Economic Chamber (BWK), the two labour organizations, Austrian Trade Union Federation (ÖGB) and Federal Chamber of Labour (ÖAKT), representatives from the agricultural sector, the federal chancellor (= prime minister) and the ministers of agriculture, economic affairs and labour and social affairs. It serves as a forum for discussion and negotiation not only on wages and prices but also on other aspects of economic and social policy and on general macroeconomic issues. The Commission's decisions and recommendations are based on consensus. They have no legal force but carry great weight.

Joint Committee of the European Economic Area or **EEA Joint Committee** Institution of the European Economic Area (EEA), the intergovernmental organization of the European Union (EU) states and six of the seven members of the European Free Trade Association (EFTA) established to create a single market across the 18 countries. Composed of government representatives and officials of the European Commission, the EU's administrative and executive arm, the Committee is the EEA's decision-making body. It is primarily responsible for (i) administering the Agreement on the European Economic Area (EEA Agreement), (ii) resolving any disputes concerning its interpretation and application, and (iii) implementing the general guidelines laid down by the Council, the EEA's senior body. Decisions must be unanimous. If the Committee cannot reach agreement on a particular matter, it may request binding arbitration from an outside body or put the matter before the EU's Court of Justice, which has ultimate authority in the interpretation of EU laws and the terms of the EEA Agreement. The Committee chair alternates between an EU and an EFTA member every six months.

Jonsson, Bertil (1940–) Swedish forestry worker and trade-union official. He worked at a sawmill from 1955–71. He then became a full-time official of the Swedish Timberworkers' Union (STF) and was elected its leader in 1978. He was elected deputy leader of the Swedish Trade Union Confederation (LO) in 1990 and leader in December 1993.

Jovanović, Vladislav (1933–) Yugoslav lawyer, diplomat and politician. He joined the diplomatic service in 1957, serving in Belgium, Turkey and the United Kingdom. A member of the Socialist Party of Serbia (SPS), the successor to the League of Communists, he was appointed foreign minister of Serbia in August 1991. He also became federal foreign minister in July 1992, but resigned in September in protest against the 'anti-Serbian' policies of the prime minister, Milan Panić. He was reappointed after Panić's removal from office in March 1993.

Juan Carlos I (1938–) King of Spain. In 1969 Francisco Franco formally designated him his successor as head of state, and he was sworn in as king on the dictator's death in November 1975. Initially endowed with considerable executive powers, he played a key role in the restoration of democratic rule. Under the 1978 constitution he became a constitutional monarch. As commander-in-chief of the armed forces he was instrumental in thwarting an attempted military coup in 1981. He married Princess Sofia of Greece, now Queen Sofia, in 1962. They have three children.

Juden (sing. Jude/Jüdin) German name for JEWS.

judeţ (pl. -e) Romanian administrative division, usually translated as 'county'. Each of the 40 *judeţe* has a prefect appointed by the government and an elected council with limited powers. Bucharest, the national capital and considered a county for administrative purposes, has a slightly different structure.

Jugoskandić affair *See* DAFIMENT AND ....

Jugoslavija Serb name for Yugoslavia.

Juifs (sing. Juif/Juive) French name for JEWS.

JUJEM Abbreviation for Junta de Jefes de Estado Mayor ('Council of Chiefs of Staff'), the senior body of the Spanish armed forces.

Juncker, Jean-Claude (1954–) Luxemburg politician. Trained as a lawyer, he was leader of the youth wing of the Christian Social People's Party (CSV) from 1979–85. Elected to parliament in 1984, he was appointed minister of finance in July 1984, minister of finance, labour and the budget in June 1989, and minister of finance and labour in July 1994. He has also been president of the CSV since March 1990.

Junta ('Council') Government of Andalusia, an autonomous community or region of Spain. The name is also used in several other regions.

Juppé, Alain (1945–) French civil servant and politician. He was an inspector of finance from 1972–76. He then became an adviser to Jacques Chirac, leader of the Rally for the Republic (RPR), when he was prime minister (1976–78) and mayor of Paris. He held several posts in the Paris local government in the early 1980s. He was elected to parliament for the RPR in 1986 and became spokesman of the second Chirac administration (1986–88). He was elected RPR general secretary in July 1988 and became foreign minister in the centre-right government formed in March 1993.

Jura question Controversy in Switzerland over the status of French-speaking districts in the predominantly German-speaking canton of Bern. After years of agitation, including sporadic political violence, the new canton of Jura was created in 1979 from the French Swiss and Roman Catholic districts in Bern's far northwest. Districts to the south with a majority of Protestant French Swiss and a substantial minority of (Protestant) German Swiss opted to remain within Bern. The status of these districts is still in dispute, with many French Swiss demanding the unification of the whole Jura region in a single canton.

Jürgenson, Toivo (1957–) Estonian civil servant, businessman and politician. He worked for the Tallinn city council from 1980, becoming head of its housing department in 1987. He was deputy director of a construction company from 1989 until his election to parliament for the Fatherland (Isamaa) alliance in 1992. He was appointed economy minister in January 1994.

Jurkāns, Jānis (1946–) Latvian linguist, teacher and politician. He is a specialist in English language and literature. Barred from teaching for political reasons, he worked as a house painter and rescue seaman in the 1980s. He joined the reformist and later pro-independence People's Front (LTF) in 1989 and became its foreign-affairs spokesman. After its election victory in 1990 he was appointed minister in charge of external relations, and when Latvia regained its independence from the Soviet Union in September 1991 he became foreign minister. He resigned in October 1992. He headed the centre-left Concord for Latvia - Economic Rebirth (SLAT) list in the June 1993 election, and was elected leader of the reconstituted National Harmony Party (TSP) in February 1994.

Justice and Home Affairs Council Institution of the European Union (EU), a specialist meeting of responsible ministers within the framework of COOPERATION ON JUSTICE AND HOME AFFAIRS (CJHA).

Jvfl *See* SOCIAL DEMOCRATIC PARTY (Faroe Islands).

K Abbreviation for the KUNA, the Croatian currency.

K or **k** Abbreviation for the KORUNA, the Czech currency.

K *See* CENTRE (Estonia).

K Abbreviation for the KROON, the Estonian currency.

K *See* CENTRE PARTY (Finland).

K or **k** Abbreviation for the KORUNA, the Slovakian currency.

Kääriäinen, Seppo (1948–) Finnish politician. He worked in the Centre Party (KESK) head office from 1980–90. Elected to parliament in 1987, he was appointed minister of trade and industry in August 1993.

Kacin, Jelko (1955–) Slovenian civil servant and politician. He was made responsible for civil defence in 1985 and became deputy defence minister in 1991. He was information minister in 1991–92, during the period when Slovenia secured its independence from Yugoslavia. He then worked in private business until his appointment as defence minister in March 1994. He is a member of the Liberal Democratic Party (LDS).

Kaczmarek, Wiesław (1958–) Polish mechanical engineer, banker and politician. He researched and lectured in precision mechanics at the Technical University of Warsaw from 1981–89. He then worked for a foreign-investment agency and became a bank director in 1991. He was elected to parliament on the communist Polish United Workers' Party (PZPR) ticket in 1989 and subsequently joined its successor, the Social Democratic Party (SdRP). He became minister for privatization in the left-wing government which took office in October 1993.

Kaczyński, Jarosław (1949–) Polish lawyer, academic and politician. He was a prominent member of the Solidarity movement, which spearheaded the opposition to communist rule in the 1980s. In 1989 he was elected to the Senate, the upper house of parliament, on the Solidarity ticket. In May 1990 he became leader of the new centre-right Centre Alliance (POC). From 1990–91 he was head of President Wałęsa's office, but he clashed with him over policy issues and his lead-

ership style. He was a member of the Sejm, the lower house, from 1991–93.

Kalderash Alternative name for GIPSIES or Romanies, sometimes used in Eastern Europe. The Kalderash are one of the traditional major regional and occupational subdivisions of Gipsies.

Kaliningrad Region [oblast] of Russia, an enclave surrounded by Lithuania to the north and Poland to the south. Centred on the city of Kaliningrad, formerly Königsberg and renamed after a Soviet president, the region was formed at the end of the Second World War (1939–45) from the northern half of East Prussia, German territory allocated to the Soviet Union. The German population, which had fled or been expelled, was replaced by Russian settlers. The site of an important Soviet naval base and several other military establishments, the whole region was closed to outsiders for many years. It was declared a 'special economic zone' in 1990 in an effort to encourage investment from abroad. Following the disintegration of the Soviet Union in 1991 it became geographically separated from the rest of Russia. It is highly dependent on Lithuania for food and energy supplies. There are plans to rename the city and the region.

Kalvoda, Jan (1953–) Czech lawyer and politician. In 1990 he was elected to parliament for the broad-based Civic Forum (OF), which had spearheaded the opposition to communist rule. When the Forum split in 1991 he joined the right-wing Civic Democratic Alliance (ODA). He was elected its leader in March 1992. In July he was appointed a deputy prime minister, with responsibility for legislative affairs.

kancleris ('chancellor') President or speaker of the Seimas, the Lithuanian parliament.

Kanis, Pavol (1948–) Slovakian sociologist, academic and politician. A philosophy graduate, he taught at the Vyškov military academy and did research from 1972–89. A member of the Democratic Left Party (SDĽ, the successor to the Communist Party of Slovakia, KSS), he was elected to the Czechoslovak federal parliament in 1990 and to the Slovakian parliament in 1992. He was appointed minister of defence in the centrist coalition formed in March 1994.

Kanther, Manfred (1939–) German lawyer and politician. He was elected to the Hesse state legislature for the Christian Democratic Union (CDU) in 1974. He became state finance minister in 1987 and party leader in the state in 1991. He was appointed federal interior minister in July 1993.

Kanton *See* CANTON (Switzerland).

Kanzler Shorthand for Bundeskanzler ('federal chancellor'), the head of government or prime minister of Austria or Germany.

Kanzlerkandidat ('chancellor candidate') In Germany, the person chosen by a party to lead it in a general election and to become federal chancellor or prime minister if it is victorious.

Karadjordjević, Aleksandar (1945–) Yugoslav businessman and claimant to the throne. His father, Petar or Peter II, was king of Yugoslavia from 1934 until the monarchy was abolished by the communists in 1945. He was born in exile in London and has worked as a businessman in Britain and the United States. He continues to live in exile but visited Yugoslavia in June 1992. (Several political parties have called for the restoration of the monarchy.)

Karadžić, Radovan (1945–) Bosnian doctor, writer and politician. A qualified psychiatrist specializing in the treatment of neuroses and depression, he worked in several state hospitals in the 1970s and 80s. In July 1990 he was elected leader of the new Serbian Democratic Party (SDS), which established itself as the main representative of the Serb community in the election later that year. In December 1992, nine months after the civil war broke out, he was elected president of the self-proclaimed Serbian Republic. He has published five anthologies of poetry.

Karamanlis, Konstantinos (1907–) Greek lawyer and politician. He first entered parliament in 1935 for the right-wing Populist Party, which eventually became the National Radical Union (ERE). He was appointed prime minister in 1955. After a dispute with the then king and a general election defeat in 1963 he went into self-imposed exile in France. He was the leading conservative opponent of the military dictatorship which ruled from 1967–74. After its collapse he returned to Greece to head a civilian government. He led the newly formed New Democratic Party (ND) to victory in the election later that year. In 1980 he was elected president of the republic for a five-year term. He failed to gain sufficient support for his reelection. In May 1990 he was again elected president (a largely non-executive post since constitutional changes introduced in 1986).

Karayalçın, Murat (1943–) Turkish economist and politician. In the 1970s he worked for the State Planning Organization (DPT) and was briefly a junior government minister. In 1981 he founded a housing cooperative, Kentkoop, of which he remained director until 1992. A member of the Social Democratic People's Party (SHP), he was elected mayor of Ankara, the capital, in 1989. In September 1993 he succeeded Erdal İnönü as party leader and deputy prime minister.

Karazija, Rimantas (1936–) Lithuanian veterinarian and politician. He taught at the Academy of Veterinary Sciences from 1959, becoming its director in 1976. A member of the Democratic Labour Party (LDDP), he was appointed minister of agriculture in December 1992.

Karelia question Controversy over the status of a formerly Finnish territory now part of Russia. Situated at the head of the Gulf of Finland to the north and west of Saint Petersburg (formerly Leningrad), Finnish Karelia was ceded to the then Soviet Union after Finland's defeat in the 1939–40 Winter War. Most of the local Karelian and Finnish population, around 415,000 people, fled to Finland at the time. After the collapse of communist rule and the disintegration of the Soviet Union in 1991, Karelian exiles and their descendants began to call for the restitution of their land and property, other forms of compensation and/or the return of the territory to Finland. None of the major parties supports these demands.

Karlsruhe Shorthand for the FEDERAL CONSTITUTIONAL COURT in Germany. The Court sits in the city of Karlsruhe, in the southwestern state of Baden-Württemberg.

Kärnten *See* CARINTHIA.

Katharevusa [Katharévousa] ('pure language') Form of the Greek language. Katharevusa was developed in the 19th century as a result of efforts to rid the language of foreign elements and systematize it by reintroducing ancient Greek vocabulary and grammar. It was the official language until 1976, when it was replaced by Demotic, the standard spoken language. It is still used in legal and technical writing and in higher education.

Katyn massacre Execution of around 4,500 Polish army officers by the Soviet secret police during the Second World War. The officers belonged to a 15,000-strong force captured by the Soviet army following the German-Soviet partition of Poland in 1939. Apparently shot in April/May 1940, their mass graves were discovered by German troops in the Katyn forest near Smolensk, Russia, in April 1943. For years the Soviet authorities blamed the Germans for the massacre. During communist rule the Polish authorities accepted this version of events. Already a potent reminder of long-standing Polish-Russian antagonism, Katyn thus also became a symbol of the reality behind the slogan of 'fraternal solidarity' among communist countries. In April 1990 the Soviets officially admitted responsibility for the massacre. In July and September 1991 more mass graves of Polish officers were found near Kharkov and Ivano-Frankovsk in Ukraine. In September 1993 the Polish government set up an official inquiry into the Katyn massacre.

KBH Abbreviation for Katonai Biztonsági Hivatal ('Military Security Office'), the Hungarian military intelligence service, responsible to the defence minister.

Kč Abbreviation for the KORUNA, the Czech currency.

Kčs Abbreviation for the koruna, the currency of former Czechoslovakia. The most common equivalent abbreviations for the new Czech and Slovakian koruna are Kč and Sk respectively.

KDH *See* CHRISTIAN DEMOCRATIC MOVEMENT.

KDNP *See* CHRISTIAN DEMOCRATIC PEOPLE'S PARTY.

KDP *See* CHRISTIAN DEMOCRATIC PARTY (Lithuania).

KdR *See* MOVEMENT FOR THE REPUBLIC.

KDS (Czech Republic) *See* CHRISTIAN DEMOCRATIC PARTY.

KdS (Sweden) *See* CHRISTIAN DEMOCRATIC COMMUNITY PARTY.

KDU-ČSL *See* CHRISTIAN DEMOCRATIC UNION - CZECHOSLOVAK PEOPLE'S PARTY.

keeper of the seals [garde des sceaux] Honorary title held by the French justice minister. S/he is formally responsible for the official seals of the French state.

Kelam, Tunne (1936–) Estonian historian, writer and politician. He worked at the Central State Archive in Tartu from 1959–65 and was a senior editor of the Estonian Encyclopaedia from 1965–75. Strongly critical of Soviet policy and an advocate of Estonian independence, he was dismissed from his job in 1975 and worked as a nightwatchman on a farm until 1988. He was a founding member of the Estonian National Independence Party (ERSP) in 1988 and led the Congress of Estonia, an unofficial pro-independence assembly, from its formation in 1990 until its dissolution after independence from the Soviet Union had been achieved in August 1991. He was elected to parliament for the ERSP in 1990 and became the party's leader in November 1993.

Keleti, György (1946–) Hungarian soldier, civil servant and politician. He qualified as a signal officer in 1969, studied at the Military Academy from 1974–77 and later worked for the defence ministry. He served as its spokesman from 1989–92. A member of the communist Hungarian Socialist Workers' Party (MSzMP) until 1989, he joined the Hungarian Socialist Party (MSzP), its successor, in 1992 and was elected to parliament. He was appointed defence minister in the

MSzP-led coalition which took office in July 1994.

Kelly, Petra (1947–92) German civil servant and politician. She worked for the European Community (EC) from 1972–80, eventually becoming responsible for social policy within the consultative Economic and Social Committee (ECOSOC). A founding member of the Greens in 1972, she was the party's spokeswoman from 1980–82 and a member of parliament from 1983–90. In the 1980s she was one of the country's best-known campaigners on environmental, disarmament and human-rights issues. She was killed by her partner, Gert Bastian, a prominent disarmament campaigner, in October 1992 in what may have been a suicide pact.

KEPU *See* CENTRE PARTY (Finland).

Kernow Cornish name for Cornwall, a county in the southwest of England (United Kingdom). The Cornish people have a strong identity, although the local Celtic language is now virtually extinct.

KESK *See* CENTRE PARTY (Finland).

Keskus *See* CENTRE (Estonia).

Keskusta *See* CENTRE PARTY (Finland).

KF *See* CONSERVATIVE PEOPLE'S PARTY.

KGB Abbreviation for Komitet Gosudarstvennoy Bezopasnosti ('State Security Committee'), the main intelligence agency of the former Soviet Union. Responsible for internal security, the surveillance of dissidents, foreign intelligence gathering and border control, it was active in these spheres in Estonia, Latvia and Lithuania until they regained their independence in August 1991.

Kıbrıs Turkish name for Cyprus.

kickback scandals (Italy) *See* ITALIAN CORRUPTION SCANDALS.

Kinkel, Klaus (1936–) German lawyer, civil servant and politician. He worked in a senior post at the interior ministry from 1965–74 and at the foreign office from 1974–79. He was director of the Federal Intelligence Service (BND) from 1979–82. He became a junior justice minister in 1982 and was appointed justice minister in 1991. Previously unaffiliated, he joined the centrist Free Democratic Party (FDP) later that year and became foreign

minister in succession to Hans-Dietrich Genscher in May 1992. In June 1993 he was also elected leader of the FDP.

Kinnock, Neil (1942–) British politician. He taught in the Workers' Education Association (WEA) from 1966 until his election to Parliament for the Labour Party in 1970. He became education spokesman in 1979. He was elected party leader in October 1983, after Labour's heavy election defeat earlier that year. He initiated a series of policy and organizational reforms aimed at modernizing the party. Labour improved its support in the 1987 and 1992 elections but failed to dislodge the Conservatives. He resigned as leader in July 1992. In July 1994 he was nominated as one of the United Kingdom's members of the European Commission, the administrative and executive arm of the European Union (EU), to serve from January 1995.

Kipriakí Dimokratía ('Republic of Cyprus') Official name of Cyprus in Greek.

Kípros Greek name for Cyprus.

Kjærsgaard, Pia (1947–) Danish administrator, social worker and politician. She has worked for an insurance company, an advertising agency and as a home help. A member of parliament for the far-right anti-tax Progress Party (FP) since 1984, she became its leader in November 1985.

KKE *See* COMMUNIST PARTY OF GREECE.

KKTC Abbreviation for Kuzey Kıbrıs Türk Cumhuriyeti ('Turkish Republic of Northern Cyprus'), the official name of Northern Cyprus in Turkish.

KKW Ojczyzna and **KKWO** or **KKW'O'** *See* HOMELAND.

Klaus, Václav (1941–) Czech economist and politician. He worked in the Economic Institute of the Czechoslovak Academy of Sciences in the 1960s, but was dismissed in 1970 for his reformist views. He then worked at the Czechoslovak State Bank. He was a prominent member of the opposition Civic Forum (OF) movement in 1989, and after the collapse of the communist regime was appointed finance minister in the federal government. He was elected leader of the new right-wing Civic Democratic Party (ODS) in April

1991. When the party came first in the June 1992 elections, he formed a coalition government in the Czech Republic which took office in July on a programme of rapid economic reform. It also negotiated the dissolution of the Czechoslovak federation.

KLD *See* LIBERAL DEMOCRATIC CONGRESS *and* FREEDOM UNION.

klein rechts *See* SMALL RIGHT.

Klerides, Glavkos (1919–) Cypriot lawyer and politician. He was closely involved in the independence negotiations and was minister of justice in a transitional government in 1959–60. On independence in 1960 he was elected to the House of Representatives and became its president (a post he held until 1976). During the 1960s and 70s he was head of the Greek-Cypriot delegation in successive rounds of negotiations with Turkish Cypriot representatives aimed at finding a settlement to the country's ethnic problems. He also served as acting head of state during this time, particularly for five months in 1974 after the abortive coup and the intervention by Turkey which led to the island's division. He founded and became leader of the United Party (EK) in 1969 and of the Democratic Rally (DISI), its more broadly based successor, in 1976. After two unsuccessful attempts in 1983 and 1988, he was elected president of the republic in the second round in February 1993. He subsequently resigned all party offices.

Klestil, Thomas (1932–) Austrian civil servant, diplomat and politician. An economics graduate, he worked at the Federal Chancellery (= prime minister's office) and then at the foreign ministry. He has been Austria's ambassador to the United Nations (1978–82), ambassador to the United States (1982–87) and general secretary at the foreign ministry (1987–92). A member of the centre-right Austrian People's Party (ÖVP), he was elected federal president (a non-executive post) in May 1992.

Klikovac, Uroš (1948–) Yugoslav lawyer and politician. He has been a member of the republican assembly of his native Montenegro and of the federal parliament for the League of Communists and its successor, the Democratic Socialist Party (DPSCG), since the late 1980s. He was appointed a deputy prime minister at federal level in March 1994.

Kliridhis, Glavkos *See* KLERIDES, ...

Klose, Hans-Ulrich (1937–) German lawyer and politician. A member of the Social Democratic Party (SPD), he was mayor of Hamburg from 1974–81 and party treasurer from 1987–91. He was elected to the federal parliament in 1983, and became leader of the SPD parliamentary group in November 1991.

Kn Abbreviation for the KROON, the Estonian currency.

Kňažko, Milan (1945–) Slovakian actor and politician. He was attached to the Slovak National Theatre from 1985–89. In 1990–91, after the collapse of communist rule, he served as minister of international relations of the Slovak Republic, then still part of the Czechoslovak federation. Elected to parliament for the Movement for a Democratic Slovakia (HZDS) in 1992, he was appointed deputy prime minister and again minister of international relations. He became foreign minister of independent Slovakia in January 1993. Dismissed in March, he left the HZDS and founded the Alliance of Democrats (ADSR) in June. When the ADSR joined the new Democratic Union (DEÚS) in April 1994, he was elected its deputy leader.

Knights Hospitaller, Knights of Malta and **Knights of Saint John** *See* SOVEREIGN MILITARY ORDER OF MALTA.

KNSB *See* CONFEDERATION OF INDEPENDENT TRADE UNIONS IN BULGARIA.

KNSS and **KNSS Neodvisnost** *See* INDEPENDENCE (Slovenia).

Knudsen, Grete (1940–) Norwegian teacher and politician. She has taught at secondary level, held the post of principal at several schools and has also been a schools inspector. Elected to parliament for the Norwegian Labour Party (DNA) in 1981, she was appointed minister of social affairs in September 1992. She became minister of trade and shipping in January 1994.

København Danish name for Copenhagen, the Danish capital.

Kočárník, Ivan (1944–) Czech economist and politician. He was director of the research department of the Czechoslovak finance ministry from 1985–89 and was appointed deputy finance minister in 1990. A founding member of the right-wing Civic Democratic Party (ODS), he became a deputy prime minister and finance minister of the Czech Republic in July 1992.

Kohl, Helmut (1930–) German politician. He studied law, politics and history and then worked for a chemical concern during the 1960s. He was elected to the legislature of his home state of Rhineland-Palatinate for the Christian Democratic Union (CDU) in 1959. In 1963 he became leader of the CDU parliamentary party and from 1969–76 was the state's prime minister. He was elected CDU chairman at federal level in April 1973. He was elected to the federal parliament and became leader of the CDU parliamentary party in 1976. He became federal chancellor in October 1982 when the centrist Free Democratic Party (FDP) switched coalition partners. Germany's dominant political figure ever since, he led the CDU to election victories in 1983 and 1987. After the collapse of East Germany's communist regime in 1989 he was a strong advocate of rapid reunification, which was achieved in October 1990. He led the CDU to victory in the all-German election in December of that year.

Koivisto, Mauno (1923–) Finnish economist and politician. He was a director of a major bank from 1959–67. He was briefly finance minister before becoming prime minister of a coalition led by his Social Democratic Party (SDP) in 1968. From 1972–79 he was again finance minister and from 1979–81 again prime minister. In September 1981 he was elected interim president in succession to the ailing Urho Kekkonen. (Following precedent, he resigned from all party posts at this time.) He was elected president in January 1982 and reelected in 1988. He retired in March 1994.

KOK *See* NATIONAL COALITION PARTY.

Kok, Wim (1938–) Dutch trade-union official and politician. A graduate in business studies, he joined the trade-union movement. He was leader of the Dutch Trade Union Federation (NVV) from 1973–75 and of the Dutch Trade Union Confederation (FNV), its successor, from 1975–85. Elected to parliament for the Labour Party (PvdA) in May 1986, he was elected party leader the following July. In November 1989 he became deputy prime minister and finance minister in a centre-left coalition. In August 1994 he became prime minister at the head of a left-right coalition with the People's Party for Freedom and Democracy (VVD) and Democrats 66 (D'66).

Kokoomus *See* NATIONAL COALITION PARTY.

Koller, Arnold (1933–) Swiss lawyer, academic and politician. A native of Appenzell, he lectured in commercial law from 1971. He was a member of parliament for the Christian Democratic People's Party from 1971–86 and leader of the parliamentary party from 1980–84. He became a member of the Federal Council (= government) in 1987, taking responsibility for defence until February 1989 and then for justice and police.

Kołodko, Grzegorz (1949–) Polish economist, academic and politician. He lectured at the Warsaw School of Economics from 1976–94, also serving as director of its Finance Institute from 1989. He was a member of the communist Polish United Workers' Party (PZPR) from 1969–90. A supporter of its successor, the Democratic Left Alliance (SLD), he was appointed deputy prime minister in charge of the economy and finance minister in April 1994.

Kołodziejczyk, Piotr (1939–) Polish soldier and politician. A career navy officer, with the rank of vice-admiral, he was commander of the navy from 1984–89. He was defence minister in 1990–91 and was reappointed to the post, on the recommendation of President Wałęsa, in the left-wing coalition which took office in October 1993. He was a member of the communist Polish United Workers' Party (PZPR) until its dissolution in 1990.

Koncijančič, Janez (1941–) Slovenian businessman and politician. A graduate in law, he was president of the communist youth movement in Slovenia and in Yugoslavia between 1966 and 1971. He was a member of the Slovenian republican government from 1971–73. He then worked in business, serving as managing director of the airline Inex Adria, later Adria Airways, from 1982–93. He was elected to parliament for the Social Democratic Reform Party (SDP), the successor to the League of Communists (ZKS), in 1992. In May 1993 he was elected leader of the Associated List of Social Democrats (ZLSD), formed by the merger of the SDP and two smaller parties.

Kongeriget Danmark ('Kingdom of Denmark') Official name of Denmark.

Kongeriket Norge ('Kingdom of Norway') Official name of Norway.

Koninkrijk België ('Kingdom of Belgium') Official name of Belgium in Dutch.

Koninkrijk der Nederlanden ('Kingdom of the Netherlands') Official name of the Netherlands in Dutch.

Konstantinos or **Constantine of Glücksburg** (from 1964–73 **King Konstantinos II**) (1940–) Former king of Greece. He succeeded to the throne on the death of his father, Pavlos or Paul II, in 1964. He dismissed the prime minister, Georgios Papandreou, in 1965 in a clash over control of the armed forces. The election planned to resolve the ensuing constitutional crisis was preempted by a rightwing military coup in April 1967. After a countercoup against the 'colonels' regime' failed in December that year, he fled into exile with his family. He has lived in Britain ever since. He did not accept the abolition of the monarchy in 1973, but did accept the outcome of a referendum on the issue held in December 1974, after the restoration of democratic rule. When he declared in 1993 that he would be willing to 'resume his duties' if asked to, he was criticized by left-wing parties for refusing to recognize the country's republican constitution. In April 1994 parliament voted to strip him of his citizenship and confiscate his remaining property in the country.

Kontić, Radoje (1937–) Yugoslav metallurgical engineer and politician. He worked at the Nikšić ironworks in his native Montenegro from 1961–78, eventually becoming its technical and financial manager. He has also been a part-time lecturer in metallurgy. A member of the League of Communists, he has been minister without portfolio at federal level (1978–82 and 1986–89) and deputy prime minister and prime minister of Montenegro (1982–86 and 1989–91 respectively). Elected to the republican and federal parliaments for the renamed Democratic Socialist Party (DPSCG) in 1990, he was appointed deputy prime minister at federal level in 1992 and prime minister in February 1993.

Konungariket Sverige ('Kingdom of Sweden') Official name of Sweden.

Kooijmans, Peter (1933–) Dutch lawyer, academic, diplomat and politician. He lectured in international and European Community law from 1965–72 and 1978–93. A specialist in human-rights issues, he was a United Nations rapporteur on torture in the 1980s. He was deputy foreign minister from 1973–77 and foreign minister from January 1993 until the party lost power in August 1994. He is a member of the Christian Democratic Appeal (CDA).

Kopliku, Bashkim (1943–) Albanian electronic engineer and politician. He was chief engineer at a television production plant before entering politics. Elected to parliament for the Democratic Party (PDSh) in 1991, he was appointed a deputy prime minister in April 1992, with responsibility for the key portfolios of internal affairs until April 1993 and economic reform since then.

Kornazhev, Petŭr (1930–) Bulgarian lawyer and politician. He has practised law since 1954 and written a number of books on legal issues. He was elected president of the Bulgarian Union of Lawyers when it was reconstituted in 1990 after the collapse of communist rule. He was appointed justice minister in the non-party government in June 1993. He is a member of the Bulgarian Social Democratic Party (BSDP).

koruna (pl. koruny) Currency of the Czech Republic. Common abbreviations are K, k, Kč, Čk and CZK (the international standard in banking etc). It is divided into 100 haléřů. It was introduced in January 1993 to replace the koruna of the former Czechoslovak federation. The anglicized forms 'crown' and 'hellers' are also used.

koruna (pl. koruny) Currency of Slovakia. Common abbreviations are K, k, Sk and SKK (the international standard in banking etc). It is divided into 100 halierov. It was introduced in January 1993 to replace the koruna of the former Czechoslovak federation. The anglicized forms 'crown' and 'hellers' are also used.

koruny Plural of KORUNA, the Czech and Slovakian currencies.

Koschnick, Hans (1929–) German civil servant and politician. He worked as an administrator in his native Bremen from 1954–63. Elected to the Citizens' Assembly (= parliament) for the Social Democratic Party (SPD) in 1955, he joined the Senate (= government) in 1963, taking responsibility for internal affairs. He was Senate president and mayor of Bremen from 1967–85. (Bremen is a 'city state', in which the administrative and political functions of a federal state and municipality are combined.) He was elected to the federal parliament in 1987. In July 1994 he was appointed administrator of Mostar, the Bosnian city disputed by Muslims and Croats which they had agreed to place under European Union (EU) administration for a two-year period.

Kosmet Shorthand for KOSOVO-METOHIJA, a province of Serbia, a constituent republic of Yugoslavia. The province is widely referred to as Kosovo, which was its official name from 1971–90.

Kosmo, Jørgen (1947–) Norwegian construction worker, trade-union official and politician. He was active in local government for the Norwegian Labour Party (DNA) from 1976 and worked for the Building Industry Union from 1979–83. Elected to parliament in 1985, he was appointed defence minister in April 1993.

Kosova Albanian name for KOSOVO-METOHIJA or Kosovo, a province of Serbia, a constituent republic of Yugoslavia.

Nearly four-fifths of the province's people are ethnic Albanians. *See also* REPUBLIC OF KOSOVO.

Kosovo Shorthand for KOSOVO-METOHIJA, a province of Serbia, a constituent republic of Yugoslavia. It was the province's official name from 1971–90.

Kosovo i Metohija *See* KOSOVO-METOHIJA.

Kosovo-Metohija [Kosovo i Metohija] Province [pokrajina] of Serbia, a constituent republic of Yugoslavia, widely referred to as Kosovo. Situated in the southwest, Kosovo has an area of 10,887 sq km and a population of 1,955,000. In ethnic terms 77.4% of the people are Albanians, 13.2% Serbs, 3.7% Slav Muslims (recognized as an ethnic group in Yugoslavia) and 1.7% Montenegrins; there are also small groups of Gipsies, Turks and others. Since 1990 more than 250,000 Albanians have emigrated, mainly to Germany and the United States. Albanian and Serb are the main languages. Most Albanians are nominally Muslims, while the Serbs are Orthodox Christians. The capital is Priština [Prishtinë (Albanian)]. The economy is based on agriculture (cereals, fruit and vegetables, sheep farming), forestry and mining (lead, zinc etc). Kosovo is the least developed and poorest region of Yugoslavia. The main political party is the Democratic League of Kosovo (DSK or LDK), the main representative of the Albanian community. Kosovo formed the heartland of the medieval Serbian kingdom from the 11th century. It became part of the Ottoman Empire after the Battle of Kosovo in 1389. The region and the battle remain key symbols of Serb national identity and history, and for this reason the incorporation of Kosovo was a primary aim of Serbian policy when the country regained its independence in the 19th century. This was achieved in 1913, against the wishes of the Albanian majority. When Yugoslavia was reconstituted under communist control after the Second World War, Kosovo was made a region [oblast] within Serbia. Growing Albanian demands for autonomy led to violent demonstrations in 1968. Kosovo was made an autonomous province in 1971, and from 1974 effectively enjoyed the same powers as the federation's full republics. There were more demonstrations against Serb domination in March–May 1981. In July 1990 the Serbian government abolished the provincial assembly and government. The republic's new constitution adopted in September formally revoked the province's autonomy (and also restored the official name of Kosovo-Metohija). Since then the rights of the Albanian community have been eroded under a policy of 'serbianization'. The teaching of Albanian was banned and many Albanians were dismissed from public-sector jobs, the main source of employment. The Albanian opposition organized an unofficial referendum on sovereignty in September 1991, which gained overwhelming approval. On this basis a government in exile was formed in October, the REPUBLIC OF KOSOVO was proclaimed in December, and an election to a 'constituent assembly' was held in May 1992. In the face of Serbia's unwillingness to restore autonomy, many Kosovans have become radicalized and are now calling for the region's constitution as a separate republic within Yugoslavia, for full independence or for unification with Albania.

Kostović, Ivica (1943–) Croatian doctor, civil servant and politician. A specialist in neurobiology, he has taught at the Zagreb Medical School and served as its dean. From 1991 he worked for the health and foreign ministries on human-rights and humanitarian issues. In October 1993 he was appointed a deputy prime minister, with responsibility for humanitarian affairs.

Kouchner, Bernard (1939–) French doctor and politician. He founded Médecins sans Frontières in 1971 and Médecins du Monde in 1980, serving as director for both organizations, which aim to help victims of famine and disasters worldwide. He was brought into the centre-left government in 1988 as junior minister for humanitarian aid. In April 1992 he became minister for health and humanitarian aid, a post he held until the Socialist Party (PS) lost power in March 1993. He was elected to the European Parliament on the PS ticket in June 1994. He is not a party member.

Kouvelakis, Giorgos (1936–) Greek lawyer and politician. He began working for the Council of State, a government advisory body, in 1963. In 1969 he was forced to resign his post by the right-wing military regime which had seized power two years earlier. He lived in exile in Switzerland and France until the restoration of democracy in 1974. He then returned to the Council and became a senior counsellor in 1981. In October 1993 he was appointed justice minister in the Pan-Hellenic Socialist Movement (PASOK) government.

Kováč, Michal (1930–) Slovakian economist and politician. He held senior posts in banking in the 1960s. He was expelled from the Communist Party in 1969 because of his reformist views. He worked as a bank clerk in the 1970s and as a researcher and lecturer in the 1980s. After the collapse of the communist regime in 1989 he was appointed finance minister of the Slovak Republic in 1990. He was elected to parliament for the Movement for a Democratic Slovakia (HZDS) the same year and was briefly president of the Federal Assembly in 1992. After the dissolution of the Czechoslovak federation he was elected president of Slovakia (a post with limited powers) in February 1993.

Kováč, Roman (1940–) Slovakian doctor, trade-union official and politician. He worked as a researcher and lecturer at several medical institutes from 1966–90, becoming director of the Research Institute of Medical Bionics in 1990. From 1990–92 he was also president of the Czech and Slovak Trade Union Confederation (ČSKOS). In June 1992 he was elected to parliament for the Movement for a Democratic Slovakia (HZDS) and was appointed a deputy prime minister and minister of control (= economic affairs). He resigned his post in February 1994 and joined the Democratic Union (DEÚS), a breakaway from the HZDS, in March. He was appointed a deputy prime minister in the centrist coalition formed later in the month.

Kovács, László (1939–) Hungarian economist and politician. He worked in the influential international department of the communist Hungarian Socialist Workers' Party (MSzMP) from 1975–86. He then became a deputy foreign minister and was appointed senior deputy foreign minister in 1989, a post he held until the relaunched Hungarian Socialist Party (MSzP) lost power in the 1990 multiparty election. He was elected to parliament at the time. He was appointed foreign minister in the MSzP-led coalition formed in July 1994.

Kovács Kósa, Magda (1940–) Hungarian teacher, trade-union official and politician. She has taught Hungarian and French and served as a school principal. From 1985–90 she was a secretary of the Central Council of Trade Unions (SzOT). A long-standing member of the communist Hungarian Socialist Workers' Party (MSzMP), she joined its reformist successor, the Hungarian Socialist Party (MSzP), in 1989. Elected to parliament in the May 1994 election, she was appointed minister of labour in the MSzP-led coalition which took office in July.

KOZ See TRADE UNION CONFEDERATION OF THE SLOVAK REPUBLIC.

Kozinc, Miha (1952–) Slovenian lawyer and politician. He practised law until his appointment as minister of justice and administration in May 1992. He resigned in June 1994 after media reports linked him to irregularities in the granting of state housing loans. He is a member of the centre-left Liberal Democratic Party (LDS).

Kozlík, Sergej (1950–) Slovakian economist, civil servant and politician. He worked for various state economic agencies and the finance ministry from 1974, serving as director of the Anti-Monopoly Office from 1990–92 and the government's economic policy department from 1992–93. A member of the Movement for a Democratic Slovakia (HZDS), he was a deputy prime minister from November 1993 until the HZDS lost power in March 1994.

KOZSR See TRADE UNION CONFEDERATION OF THE SLOVAK REPUBLIC.

KPN See CONFEDERATION FOR AN INDEPENDENT POLAND.

kr Abbreviation for the KRÓNA, KRONA and KRONE, the currencies of the Faroe Islands and Iceland, Sweden, and Denmark and Norway respectively.

Kračun, Davorin (1950–) Slovenian economist, academic and politician. He taught economics until his appointment as planning minister in 1992. He was elected to parliament for the centre-left Liberal Democratic Party (LDS) in December of that year. In January 1993 he was made minister of economic relations and development, with primary responsibility for the introduction of a market-based economy.

kraj (pl. -e) Czech administrative division, usually translated as 'region'. There are eight *kraje*, one of which is the city of Prague, the national capital. They are administered by a committee elected for a five-year term. A reorganization of the regional and local government structure is under consideration.

kraj (pl. -a) Slovakian administrative division, usually translated as 'region'. There are four *kraja*, one of which is the city of Bratislava, the national capital. They are administered by a committee elected for a five-year term. A reorganization of the regional and local government structure is under consideration.

Krajina Historical region of Croatia. The Krajina takes its name from the Military Frontier [Militärgrenze (German), Vojna Krajina (Serbocroat)] of the Austro-Hungarian Empire. This was a belt of land along the border with the Ottoman Empire, stretching from the Dalmatian coast along both banks of the Sava river (now the border with Bosnia-Herzegovina) to the Banat (modern Vojvodina, part of Serbia). It was settled from the late 16th century onwards by Serbs fleeing Turkish rule. They were given land and special rights in return for providing military service to the Austrian emperor. The Military Frontier was abolished in 1881, the Ottoman threat having long since passed, and the region was incorporated into Croatia. During the Second World War (1939–45) its Serb population suffered greatly from the policy of genocide pursued by the German-sponsored Croatian state. As the Yugoslav federation disintegrated in 1990/91, the Serbs in Croatia grew increasingly concerned at the Croat nationalist rhetoric of the Croatian Democratic Union (HDZ), which had won the multiparty election in April/May 1990. After Croatia declared its independence in June 1991, local Serb forces backed by the Yugoslav federal army were able to secure control over most Serb-majority areas, comprising nearly a third of Croatian territory and an eighth of its population, in a six-month civil war which left 6,000 people dead and 400,000 homeless (*see* CROATIAN CIVIL WAR). In December two breakaway regions, Krajina proper in the southwest and Western Slavonia in the centre, joined to form the REPUBLIC OF SERBIAN KRAJINA (RSK); the region of Slavonia, Baranja and Western Srem in the east joined the following April.

Kreis Shorthand for LANDKREIS, an intermediate-tier administrative division in Germany.

KrF *See* CHRISTIAN PEOPLE'S PARTY (Denmark, Norway).

Kristovskis, Ģirts-Valdis (1962–) Latvian civil engineer and politician. He worked for a farm-equipment company from 1984–89. He was elected to parliament for the pro-independence People's Front (LTS) in 1990, when Latvia was still part of the Soviet Union, and for the new centre-right Latvian Way (LC) in June 1993. He was appointed interior minister the following August.

króna (pl. krónur) Currency of the Faroe Islands. Common abbreviations are kr, FKr and FOK (the international standard in banking etc). It is divided into 100 oyru. It has parity with the Danish krone, which is also legal tender in the Faroes. The anglicized form 'crown' is also used.

króna (pl. krónur) Currency of Iceland. Common abbreviations are kr and ISK (the international standard in banking etc). It is divided into 100 aurar. The anglicized form 'crown' is also used.

krona (pl. kronor) Currency of Sweden. Common abbreviations are kr, SKr and SEK (the international standard in banking etc). It is divided into 100 öre. The anglicized form 'crown' is also used.

krone (pl. -r) Currency of Denmark. Common abbreviations are kr, DKr and DKK (the international standard in banking etc). It is divided into 100 øre. The anglicized form 'crown' is also used.

krone (pl. -r) Currency of Norway. Common abbreviation are kr, NKr and NOK (the international standard in banking etc). It is divided into 100 øre. The anglicized form 'crown' is also used.

kroner Plural of KRONE, the Danish and Norwegian currencies.

kronor Plural of KRONA, the Swedish currency.

krónur Plural of KRÓNA, the Faroese and Icelandic currencies.

kroon (pl. -) Currency of Estonia. Common abbreviations are K, Kn, EK and EEK (the international standard in banking etc). It is divided into 100 sent. The kroon was introduced in June 1992 to replace the rouble, previously the Soviet rouble. The anglicized form 'crown' is also used.

Krzaklewski, Marian (1949–) Polish electronics engineer, academic and trade-union official. He lectured at the Silesian Technical University in Wrocław and was active in the opposition Solidarity trade union from the early 1980s. (The communist regime was replaced by a Solidarity-led government in September 1989.) In February 1991 he was elected Solidarity's leader in succession to Lech Wałęsa, who had been elected president of the republic.

KSČM *See* COMMUNIST PARTY OF BOHEMIA AND MORAVIA.

KSSh *See* TRADE UNION CONFEDERATION OF ALBANIA.

KTUM *See* CONFEDERATION OF MALTA TRADE UNIONS.

Kučan, Milan (1941–) Slovenian politician. A member of the Slovenian League of Communists (ZKS, then part of the Yugoslav League of Communists) from 1958, he held a series of senior posts in the party and the Slovenian government from 1969 onwards, including president of the republic's parliament (1978–82) and president of the party central committee (1986–89). A reformer, he was elected president of the republic in the multiparty election of April 1990. He then left the relaunched Social Democratic Reform Party (SDP). Standing as an independent, he was reelected to the presidency, a largely non-executive but influential post under the new Slovenian constitution, in December 1992.

Kukan, Eduard (1939–) Slovakian diplomat and politician. He joined the Czechoslovak foreign service in 1964. He served in Zambia (1968–73), United States (1977–81) and other countries and was ambassador to Ethiopia from 1985–88. He was appointed Czechoslovakia's ambassador to the United Nations in 1990 and was confirmed as Slovakia's ambassador following the federation's dissolution at the end of 1992. In March 1994 he was appointed foreign minister. He does not belong to a political party.

Kullmann Five, Kaci *See* FIVE, ….

kuna [pl. kune] Currency of Croatia. Common abbreviations are K and HRK (the international standard in banking etc). It is divided into 100 lipe. It was introduced in May 1994 to replace the dinar.

Kuncze, Gábor (1950–) Hungarian economist and politician. He is a specialist in production engineering. He was elected to parliament in 1990 with the support of the centrist Alliance of Free Democrats (SzDSz). He joined the party in 1992, became its parliamentary leader in 1993, and was its candidate for prime minister at the May 1994 election. He became deputy prime minister and minister of the interior in the centre-left coalition which took office in July.

kune Plural of KUNA, the Croatian currency.

Kurdistan Workers' Party [Partîya Karkerên Kurdistan (Kurdish)] (PKK) Turkish guerrilla group. Rooted in far-left groups formed in the late 1960s, the PKK was first organized in 1974 and formally established in 1978. It advocates an independent and socialist Kurdistan including all traditionally Kurdish areas in the Middle East; a minority wing is said to be willing to accept regional autonomy within Turkey rather than full independence. (The Kurds form a majo-

rity in contiguous regions in southeastern Turkey, northern Iraq, northwestern Iran and northeastern Syria. They number around 12 million in Turkey alone.) The PKK launched an insurrection in 1984. Initially operating from bases in Lebanon and northern Iraq, it increased its strength to around 10,000 (it claims 30,000) and was able to extend its activities in the early 1990s. It has also abducted foreign tourists and journalists in the southeast (mainly for publicity purposes) and carried out bombings in cities and tourist resorts in other parts of the country. According to official figures, more than 12,000 civilians, soldiers, police officers and guerrillas have died in the fighting since 1984. The PKK has support within emigrant Kurdish communities in Germany, France and Britain and has attacked Turkish embassies, banks and other establishments in those countries. Along with several front organizations it was banned in France and Germany in November 1993. Abdullah Öcalan, known as 'Apo', has led the PKK since its foundation.

Kuvend Popullor *See* PEOPLE'S ASSEMBLY.

Kuzey Kıbrıs Turkish name for Northern Cyprus.

Kvederavičius, Algirdas (1938–) Lithuanian mechanical engineer and trade-union official. He held several senior posts in the union movement in the 1980s (when Lithuania was still part of the Soviet Union) and was elected president of the National Consumers' Association in 1990. In March 1993 he was elected chairman of the Trade Union Centre (LPSC), the country's main trade-union federation.

Kwaśniewski, Aleksander (1954–) Polish journalist and politician. He held senior posts in the youth wing of the communist United Polish Workers' Party (PZPR) until 1985, when he was appointed youth minister. He held several other ministerial posts until the PZPR lost power to the Solidarity movement in 1989. He was elected leader of the relaunched Social Democratic Party (SdRP) in January 1990. He is also leader of the SdRP-led Democratic Left Alliance (SLD).

Kyprianou, Spyros (1932–) Cypriot lawyer and politician. In the 1950s he represented Archbishop Makarios and the Greek Cypriot community in London and New York. On independence in 1960 he was appointed foreign minister, a post he held until 1972. He then practised law and in May 1976 became leader of the new centre-right Democratic Party (DIKO). He led the party to an absolute majority in the election of that year. As speaker of parliament he assumed the duties of president of the republic on Makarios's death in 1977. He was elected president in 1978 and 1983, but lost to Georgios Vassiliou in 1988.

Kypros Alternative transcription of Kípros, the Greek name for Cyprus.

L Abbreviation for the LEK, the Albanian currency.

£ Abbreviation for the POUND, the currencies of Gibraltar, Guernsey, Jersey, Man and the United Kingdom. It is also used in Cyprus, Ireland and Malta as abbreviations for the líra, punt and lira respectively. It is taken from the *libra*, an ancient Roman unit of weight.

L Abbreviation for the LIRA, the currencies of Italy, San Marino and the Vatican.

L Abbreviation for the LITAS, the Lithuanian currency.

L Abbreviation for Luxemburg, used for international vehicle registrations, postal addresses etc.

L Abbreviation for the LEU, the Romanian currency.

L'Autre Europe *See* ANOTHER EUROPE.

La Malfa, Giorgio (1939–) Italian journalist, academic and politician. He has worked for *La Stampa*, a major daily newspaper, and has taught politics at various universities. Elected to parliament for the centre-right Italian Republican Party (PRI) in 1972, he was budget minister from 1980–82. The son of a former PRI leader, he was elected party leader in September 1987. He resigned in February 1993 after being implicated in illegal party funding. He was reinstated as leader in January 1994. He did not stand in the March general election, but was elected to the European Parliament in June.

La Rete *See* NETWORK.

La Rioja *See* RIOJA.

lääni (pl. -t) Finnish administrative division, usually translated as 'province'. Eleven of the *läänit* are administered by a govern.or [mauherra] appointed by the president. The twelfth, the autonomous Swedish-speaking *län* of Åland Islands, has an elected council and extensive autonomy. The main unit of local government in the rest of Finland is the municipality, which has a council elected for a four year-term.

Laar, Mart (1960–) Estonian teacher, historian and politician. From 1987–90 he was director of the Department for the Protection of Cultural Heritage. He joined the new Christian Democratic Union (KDL) in 1989 and was elected to parliament in 1990. Leader of the Fatherland

(Isamaa) alliance which won the September 1992 election, he became prime minister of a centre-right coalition in October.

Lab *See* LABOUR PARTY (Ireland, United Kingdom).

Laborinho Lúcio, Álvaro (1941–) Portuguese lawyer and politician. He worked as a public prosecutor and judge until he joined the Centre for Judicial Studies (CEJ) in 1979. He was head of this organization from 1981–90. He joined the centre-right Social Democratic Party (PSD) government as a junior justice minister in January 1990 and was appointed justice minister two months later.

Labour Federation of Iceland [Alþýdusamband Íslands] (ASÍ) Icelandic trade-union federation. The ASÍ represents around 65,000 workers (nearly half the labour force). Founded in 1916, it was originally linked to the Social Democratic Party but has been politically unaffiliated since 1950. The president is Benedikt Davídsson, the general secretary is Lára Júliúsdóttir.

Labour Market Board [Arbetsmarknadsstyrelsen] (AMS) Swedish advisory and executive body. The AMS is an autonomous public agency set up in 1948 to administer the country's labour market. Its brief is to balance the interests of workers and employers, ease structural change in the economy, and maintain full employment. Its executive board is composed of representatives of the government, employers' associations and trade unions.

Labour Party (Labour or Lab) British political party. Founded in 1900 as the political wing of the Trades' Union Congress (TUC) and taking its current name in 1906, Labour formed its first government in 1924. It joined a national-unity coalition during the Second World War, won the 1945 election and remained in power until 1951. It held power again from 1964–70 and 1974–79 (during the latter period as a minority government). It became sharply divided between left and right wings after its defeat by the Conservative Party in 1979, and a section of the party left in 1981 to form the Social

Democratic Party (SDP, which later merged with the Liberals). In 1983 the party gained 28.6% of the vote, its worst result since 1918. At the April 1992 election it gained 34.4% and 271/651 seats. The leader is Tony Blair, the deputy leader John Prescott, and the general secretary Tom Sawyer.

Labour Party (Iceland) *See* SOCIAL DEMO-CRATIC PARTY.

Labour Party [Páirtí an Lucht Oibre] Irish political party. Founded in 1912 as the political wing of the trade-union movement, Labour became a separate entity in 1930. Traditionally the country's third-largest party, it was the junior partner in several coalitions with the centre-right Fine Gael between 1948 and 1987, most recently from 1982–87. At the November 1992 election it gathered substantial support outside its Dublin base for the first time and more than doubled its share of the vote, gaining 19.3% and 33/166 seats. In January 1993 it formed a coalition with the centre-right Fianna Fáil. The leader is Dick Spring.

Labour Party [Partit tal-Ħaddiema] Maltese political party. Founded in 1921, the Labour Party was in power from 1949–50, 1955–58 and 1971–87. In the 1970s it pursued left-wing economic policies and a non-aligned foreign policy under its long-time leader Dom Mintoff. At the February 1992 election it gained 46.5% of the vote and 31/65 seats. The leader is Alfred Sant.

Labour Party [Partij van de Arbeid] (PvdA) Dutch political party. Founded in 1946 as the successor to the Social Democratic Workers' Party (SDAP) founded in 1894, the PvdA is the country's main left-wing party, traditionally securing between a quarter and a third of the vote. It has participated in a number of coalition governments, most recently in 1973–77, 1981–82 and since 1989. It gained 31.9% of the vote and 49/150 seats at the September 1989 election, but only 24.0% and 37 seats in May 1994. In August it formed a left-right coalition with the right-wing People's Party for Freedom and Democracy (VVD) and the centre-left Democrats 66 (D'66). Wim

Kok is the party leader and prime minister, Felix Rottenberg is the party president, and Jacques Wallage is the parliamentary leader.

Labour Party (Norway) *See* NORWEGIAN LABOUR PARTY.

Labour Union [Unia Pracy] (UP) Polish political party. The UP has its roots in the Citizens' Parliamentary Club (OKP), the political wing of the Solidarity movement that led the opposition to communist rule in the 1980s and won the partially free election of 1989. It was formed in June 1992 by the merger of Labour Solidarity (SP), the Democratic Social Movement (RDS), the Polish Social Democratic Union (PUSD) and a wing of the Polish Socialist Party (PPS). It has adopted a mainstream left-wing programme and argues for a slowdown in the transition to a market economy and for greater regard for its social costs. At the September 1993 election it gained 7.3% of the vote and 41/460 seats. The leader is Ryszard Bugaj.

Lacina, Ferdinand (1942–) Austrian economist and politician. A member of the Social Democratic Party (SPÖ), he worked for the Vienna chamber of labour and for the holding company of Austria's nationalized industries in the 1970s. He entered the government as junior minister in 1980, became transport minister in 1984 and was also given responsibility for the public sector in 1985. He was appointed finance minister in June 1986.

Ladins Ethnic group in Italy. The 30,000 Ladins live dispersed in the mountain valleys of the northeastern region of Trentino - Alto Adige. Their Romance language – not to be confused with Ladino, a Spanish-based language once common among Sephardic Jews in the Eastern Mediterranean region – is related to Friulian and Romansh. It is officially recognized. The Ladins have traditionally allied themselves with the region's German-speaking South Tyroleans.

lady In the United Kingdom, the title of a woman who has inherited or received a peerage. In both cases she is entitled to a seat in the House of Lords, the upper house of Parliament. The title is also used for the wives of men who hold a peerage or a knighthood. The male equivalent is 'lord'.

Laermann, Karl-Hans (1929–) German civil engineer, academic and politician. He has lectured in civil and structural engineering since 1970 and 1974 respectively. Elected to parliament for the centrist Free Democratic Party (FDP) in 1976, he was appointed minister of education and science in February 1994.

Lafontaine, Oskar (1943–) German politician. A member of the Social Democratic Party (SPD), he worked in local government in his home state of Saarland until his election as mayor of Saarbrücken in 1976. In January 1985 he became the state's prime minister, a post he has held ever since. Deputy leader of the SPD at national level from 1987–91, he was the party's candidate for federal chancellor (= prime minister) in the all-German election of 1990. During the campaign he was seriously injured by a mentally disturbed woman, but made a full recovery.

lagmand See LØGMAÐUR.

Lagting (Faroe Islands) See LØGTING.

Lagting (Norway) See STORTING.

Lahnstein, Anne Enger (1950–) Norwegian nurse and politician. She became secretary of the Centre Party (Sp) parliamentary group in 1980 and was elected to parliament in 1985. A specialist on social and foreign affairs, she led the parliamentary group from 1989–91 and was elected party leader in April 1991.

Lajoinie, André (1929–) French politician. A member of the French Communist Party (PCF) since 1948, he eventually became its spokesman on agricultural issues. He was elected to parliament in 1978 and became leader of the PCF group in the National Assembly in 1981. He was the party's presidential candidate in 1988.

Lakos, László (1945–) Hungarian veterinarian, administrator and politician. He was manager of a cooperative farm from 1968–90. He was elected to parliament for the Hungarian Socialist Party (MSzP), the successor to the communist Hungarian Socialist Workers' Party (MSzMP), in 1990. He was appointed agriculture minister in the MSzP-led coalition which took office in July 1994.

Laliotis, Konstantinos or **Kostas** (1951–) Greek dentist, journalist and politician. He was editor of the magazine *Agonistís* from 1975–77 and publisher of the newspaper *Exórmisi* from 1977–85. A founding member of the Pan-Hellenic Socialist Movement (PASOK) in 1974, he served as deputy minister for youth and sport from 1982–85 and as deputy minister for the press and government spokesman from 1985–86. He became a member of parliament in 1992 and was appointed minister for the environment, town planning and public works when PASOK returned to power in October 1993.

Lalonde, Brice (1946–) French journalist and politician. He rose to national prominence in the 1970s as a campaigner on environmental issues. In December 1990 he was a co-founder and became leader of Ecology Generation (GE). From 1988–92 he was minister for the environment (initially a junior post, but given full cabinet rank in 1991) in the centre-left government.

Lalumière, Catherine (1936–) French lawyer, academic and politician. She is a specialist in public law. From 1981–86 she held several junior ministerial posts in the Socialist Party (PS) government, including minister for consumer affairs from 1981–83. She was a member of parliament for the PS from 1986–89. She served as secretary-general of the Council of Europe for a five-year term from June 1989 to May 1994. In June 1994 she was elected to the European Parliament on the centre-left Radical Energy list.

Lamassoure, Alain (1944–) French civil servant and politician. In the 1970s he worked at the Court of Accounts and was an adviser to President Giscard d'Estaing. He was elected to parliament for the centre-right Republican Party (PR) in 1986. When the right returned to power in March 1993 he was appointed a junior foreign minister, with responsibility for European affairs.

Lambergs, Aristids (1933–) Latvian businessman and politician. He fled Latvia with his parents in 1945, after Soviet

362

troops had occupied the country, and eventually settled in the United States. He was managing director of a construction company and was active in the American Latvian community. He returned to Latvia when it regained its independence in August 1991. Elected to parliament for the right-wing National Independence Movement (LNNK) in June 1993, he was elected leader of the reconstituted National Conservative Party (LNNK) in June 1994.

Lamfalussy, Alexandre (from 1992 **Baron Lamfalussy**) (1929–) Belgian economist and academic. Born in Hungary, he left with his family when the communists took power after the Second World War (1939–45). He began working for the Banque de Bruxelles in 1955 and was its managing director from 1965–75. At the same time he lectured part-time in economics at the University of Louvain. He joined the Bank for International Settlements (BIS) in 1976 and was its director-general from 1985–93. In January 1994 he became president of the new European Monetary Institute (EMI), an institution of the European Union (EU) conceived as the forerunner of an EU-wide central bank. He was ennobled in 1992.

Lamont, Norman (1942–) British politician. He worked in banking and journalism until his election to Parliament for the Conservative Party in 1972. He served as a junior minister from 1979 and became chief secretary to the Treasury, a post of Cabinet rank with responsibility for public spending, in 1989. He was chancellor of the exchequer (= finance minister) from November 1990 until May 1993, when he was replaced in a government reshuffle.

län (Finland) *See* LÄÄNI.

län (pl. -) Swedish administrative division, usually translated as 'county'. Each of the 24 *län* is administered by an elected council [landsting], an executive board [länsstyrelse], and a governor [landshövding] appointed by the central government. The counties deal primarily with strategic and health matters. The lower-level municipalities, the main units of local government, deal with housing, education and most other matters.

Land Shorthand for *Bundesland* ('federal province' or 'federal state'), the federal divisions of Austria and Germany respectively. *See* BUNDESLAND.

Land of the Eagles Literary name for Albania. It is a literal translation of 'Shqipëria', the native name for Albania.

Länder Shorthand for *Bundesländer* ('federal provinces' or 'federal states'), the federal divisions of Austria and Germany respectively. *See* BUNDESLAND.

Landeshaupt (pl. -häupter) Head of government in a federal province of Austria, usually translated as 'provincial governor' or 'governor'.

Landkreis or **Kreis** (pl. -e) German administrative division, usually translated as 'district' or 'county'. In 13 of the 16 states, the *Kreis* is the intermediate-level unit between the state [Land] and the municipality [Gemeinde] outside the large cities. Each has a council [Kreisrat] elected for a four-year term. Their responsibilities are largely administrative, with political power primarily exercised at state and municipal level. Most large cities are 'district-free' [kreisfrei] and combine the functions of *Kreis* and municipality. The city states of Berlin, Bremen and Hamburg do not have a *Kreis* structure.

Landsbergis, Vytautas (1932–) Lithuanian musician, academic, writer and politician. He lectured in music at the Lithuanian Conservatory and the Vilnius Pedagogical Institute until 1990, and also published several biographies of Lithuanian composers. In October 1988 he was elected leader of the new Reform Movement (Sajūdis), which sought to secure Lithuania's independence from the Soviet Union. After Sajūdis gained a majority in the multiparty election in March 1990 he was elected president of the parliament. When Lithuania regained its independence in August 1991 he effectively became head of state, a post he held until Sajūdis was defeated in the October/November 1992 election. Later in November he was elected leader of the Homeland Accord opposition alliance, and in May 1993 he was confirmed as leader of the Homeland Union (TS), Sajūdis's successor.

Landsgemeinde (pl. -n) Parliament of the Swiss half-cantons of Appenzell Ausser-Rhoden, Appenzell Inner-Rhoden, Nidwalden and Obwalden and the canton of Glarus. The *Landsgemeinde* is an annual open-air assembly of all adult citizens. It debates important issues, adopts cantonal laws and taxation measures, and elects all senior administrative and judicial officials. Voting is by a show of hands. In the past such assemblies were held in many other cantons as well.

Landsmål *See* NYNORSK.

Landsstýri ('Territorial Government') Government of the Faroe Islands.

Landtag (pl. -e) ('Provincial Assembly') Parliament in the federal provinces of Austria.

Landtag (pl. -e) ('State Assembly') Parliament in most federal states of Germany. In Berlin the legislature is called the House of Representatives [Abgeordnetenhaus], and in Bremen and Hamburg it is called the Citizens' Assembly [Bürgerschaft].

Landtag Parliament of Liechtenstein. It has 25 members elected for a four-year term by proportional representation in two multi-member constituencies. Parties must obtain at least 8% of the popular vote to qualify for representation.

Lang, Ian (1940–) British politician. He worked in insurance and banking until his election to Parliament for the Conservative Party in 1979. He became a junior minister in the Scottish Office in 1986 and was promoted to secretary of state for Scotland in November 1990.

Lang, Jack (1939–) French lawyer, academic and politician. From 1963–72 he was a theatre director in Nancy, and from 1976 he lectured in international law. A member of the Socialist Party (PS), he was appointed minister of culture in 1981. With the exception of the period of right-wing government in 1986–88, he held this post until the party lost power in the March 1993 election. He also served as government spokesman and minister of education in 1992–93. In December 1993 he was stripped of his parliamentary seat for spending more than the legal limit on his election campaign. He was elected to the European Parliament in June 1994.

language community (Belgium) *See* COMMUNITY.

language question (Belgium) *See* BELGIAN LANGUAGE QUESTION.

Languedoc-Roussillon Region of France. Situated in the south along the Mediterranean Sea, Languedoc-Roussillon has an area of 27,376 sq km and a population of 2,163,000. Dialects of Occitan are widely spoken throughout the region, and Catalan is spoken by around 210,000 people in the south; these languages do not have official status but are allowed to be taught in schools. The capital is Montpellier, and the other main cities are Perpignan and Nîmes. The economy is based on agriculture (wine, fruit and vegetables), tourism and manufacturing. Traditionally agricultural and poor, Languedoc's economy has become more diversified since the 1970s. The region has a strong historical and cultural identity.

Lapland Geographical region of northern Europe, extending across northern Norway, Sweden, Finland and the Kola Peninsula of Russia. It is named after the LAPPS or Sami, its indigenous people. The region's environment and economy were profoundly affected by radioactive fallout from the Chernobyl nuclear accident in 1986, which caused the contamination of grasslands and reindeer.

Lapps Ethnic group in northern Europe, also known as Sami, Saami, Saame etc. The Lapps live in Lapland, a region within the Arctic Circle stretching across northern Norway, Sweden, Finland and the Kola Peninsula of Russia. They number around 70,000 and form a small minority in their traditional homeland. Lapp or Lappish, related to Finnish, is the first language of around half of them. The Lapps were traditionally nomadic and engaged in hunting, fishing and reindeer herding. Most are now settled and engaged in farming. Since the 1970s official consultative Lapp assemblies have been set up in Finland, Norway and Sweden. They have limited decision-making powers in the spheres of education, language and culture. The Nordic

Sami Council is the main representative body of Lapps from the whole region.

large privatization (former communist countries) *See* MASS PRIVATIZATION.

Larizza, Pietro (1934–) Italian economist and trade-unionist. He began working for the Cassa del Mezzogiorno, the state bank promoting development in southern Italy, and joined the Italian Union of Labour (UIL), one of the main trade-union federations, in 1962. He became a full-time UIL official in 1976. He was elected an organization secretary in 1981 and general secretary in February 1993.

lat and **lati** Anglicized form and plural respectively of LATS, the Latvian currency.

lats (pl. lati) Currency of Latvia. Common abbreviations are Ls and LVL (the international standard in banking etc). It is divided into 100 santimi. It was introduced alongside the rouble [rūblis] in March 1993 and became the sole legal tender three months later. The anglicized forms 'lat' and plural 'lats' are also used.

Latvia [Latvija] Country in northeastern Europe, formerly part of the Soviet Union.

Official data. Name: Republic of Latvia [Latvijas Republika]; capital: Rīga; form of government: parliamentary republic; head of state: president; head of government: prime minister; flag: three horizontal stripes (proportion 2:1:2), maroon, white and maroon; national holiday: 18 November (Independence Day); language: Latvian; religion: none; currency: lats (Ls) (pl. lati) = 100 santimi; abbreviation: LV.

Geography. The middle of the three Baltic countries, Latvia has an area of 64,589 sq km. It is bordered by Estonia in the north, Russia and Belorussia in the east, Lithuania in the south, and the Baltic Sea in the west; a neighbouring country across the sea is Sweden. The country consists almost entirely of low-lying rolling plains, studded with around 4,000 lakes. Some 27% of the land is arable, another 13% is covered by pastures and 39% is forested. The main river is the Daugava. The climate is humid continental, with mild summers and cold winters; rainfall is moderate.

Demography. Latvia has a population of 2,596,000. Population density is 40 per sq km (land area), among the lowest in Europe. Some 71% of the people live in urban areas, and around a third lives in Rīga. Other major cities are Daugavpils, Liepāja, Jelgava, Jūrmala and Ventspils. In ethnic terms 52.0% of the people are Latvians, 34.0% Russians, 4.5% Belorussians, 3.5% Ukrainians, 2.3% Poles and 1.3% Lithuanians. Most Russians live in the cities. Under legislation adopted since independence in 1991, most non-Latvians are not eligible for citizenship. The main languages are Latvian and Russian. In religious terms most Latvians are nominally Lutheran Protestant and most Russians are nominally Russian Orthodox; there are also small groups of Roman Catholics and other Christians.

Sociography. Latvia scores 0.865 on the United Nations human development index (HDI), ranking 30th in the world and 22nd among 32 European countries. There are 40 doctors and 147 hospital beds for every 10,000 people, among the highest figures in Europe. Education is compulsory between the ages of six and 15. There is one teacher for every 11 students. Enrolment is around 90% at the secondary level and around 20% at the tertiary level. The literacy rate is 96%. Real annual income per head (in terms of purchasing power) is US$ 7,540.

Infrastructure and communications. Latvia's transport and communications network is relatively developed but in need of modernization and extension; the telecommunications system in particular is limited. There are 38,760 km of paved roads and 242,000 passenger cars (90 per 1,000 people), 2,400 km of railways and 300 km of navigable waterways. The main ports are Rīga, Liepāja and Ventspils. The main airport is at Rīga (Spilve). There are five daily newspapers, with a combined circulation of 331,000 (122 per 1,000 people). There are 1.33 million radio receivers, 1.13 million television sets and 836,000 telephones in use (respectively 493, 418 and 310 per 1,000 people).

Economic structure. The Latvian economy is based on manufacturing and agriculture. Although essentially developed and diversified, it is in need of major investment and restructuring. The gradual transition from a command to a market-based economy initiated in the early 1990s is causing severe dislocation and has led to steep falls in industrial and agricultural production as well as food and energy shortages. Between 1990 and 1993 GDP contracted by around half, inflation averaged around 190% per year, and unemployment rose to around 20% (unofficial estimate). There were some signs of recovery in 1994.

Services contribute 23% of GDP, industry contributes 52% (manufacturing 39%), and agriculture, forestry and fisheries 25%. Some 24% of the labour force is employed in manufacturing, 18% in agriculture, forestry and fishing, 13% in trade and 9% in construction. The main agricultural activities are dairy farming (milk, eggs) and livestock raising (pigs, cattle, chickens); horticulture (vegetables) is also important. The main crops grown are cereals (barley, oats), potatoes, sugarbeets and animal fodder. Forestry and fishing are also important. The main mineral resources are peat, dolomite, clay, gypsum, gravel and sand. The main industries are engineering (esp. transport equipment, industrial machinery, electrical goods) and food processing (esp. meat products and beverages); other important branches are textiles (incl. footwear), wood processing, chemicals (fertilizer), pharmaceuticals, building materials (cement, bricks) and metalworking. The main energy sources are hydroelectric power and imported fossil fuels; 30% of export earnings are required to cover net fuel imports. The main exports are foodstuffs (16% of the total, esp. dairy, meat and fish products), textiles and clothing (13%), transport equipment (13%, esp. railway vehicles), iron and steel (8%), chemicals (7%), industrial machinery (7%) and electrical equipment (6%); machinery and transport equipment, miscellaneous manufactures and foodstuffs each account for about a fifth of the total. The main imports are machinery and transport equipment, fuels and

chemicals. The main trading partners are: exports: Russia (28%), Netherlands (8%), Germany (6%), Sweden (6%), Ukraine (6%), Belorussia, United Kingdom; imports: Russia (28%), Germany (10%), Lithuania (9%), Sweden (5%), Finland, Estonia, Belorussia; trade with Russia and the other members of the Commonwealth of Independent States (CIS) is declining rapidly, that with Western European countries is growing.

The Bank of Latvia [Latvijas Banka] is the central bank. There are several employers' and business associations; the main labour organization is the Association of Free Trade Unions of Latvia (LBAS).

Political structure. Latvia is a parliamentary republic on the basis of a constitution adopted in 1922 and restored in 1991. The head of state is the president, who is elected by the legislature for a three-year term. S/he nominally commands the armed forces and has the right of legislative initiative and several other powers. Executive power is vested in the prime minister and the council of ministers. Legislative power is vested in the Parliament [Saeima], whose 100 members are elected for a three-year term by a system of proportional representation (with a 4% threshold for gaining seats). All citizens over the age of 18, including those living abroad, are entitled to vote; citizenship is generally restricted to those who were Latvian citizens at the time of the Soviet annexation in 1940 and their descendants. Judicial power is ultimately vested in the Supreme Court [Augstākā Tiesa]. Administratively the country is divided into 26 districts [rajons, pl. rajoni] and seven district-level cities; the districts are subdivided into 567 municipalities.

The main political parties are the Latvian Way (LC), National Conservative Party of Latvia (LNNK, the successor to the National Independence Movement of Latvia, LNNK), National Harmony Party (TSP, the successor to Harmony for Latvia - Economic Rebirth, SLAT), Farmers' Union of Latvia (LZS), Equal Rights (Līdztiesība/Ravnopraviye), Christian Democratic Union of Latvia

(LKDS), Democratic Party (DP, the successor to the Democratic Centre Party, DCP) and Economists' Political Union (TPA, a breakaway from the SLAT); For Fatherland and Freedom (TUB) is an electoral alliance. At the general election in June 1993 the LC gained 32.4% of the vote and 36/100 seats, the LNNK 13.4% and 15 seats, SLAT 12.0% and 13 seats, the LZS 10.6% and 12 seats, Equal Rights 5.8% and seven seats, the TUB 5.4% and six seats, the LKDS 5.0% and six seats, and the DCP 4.8% and five seats. The government is formed by the centre-right LC, with Māris Gailis as prime minister. Other senior ministers are Valdis Birkavs (deputy prime minister, foreign affairs), Andris Piebalgs (deputy prime minister, finance), Jānis Vaivads (deputy prime minister, education and science), Jānis Zvanītājs (economy), Girts-Valdis Kristovskis (internal affairs), Romāns Apsītis (justice) and Jānis Arveds Trapāns (defence). The head of state is President Guntis Ulmanis, who was elected in July 1993.

Security and international affiliations. The Latvian armed forces number 5,000; they are in the process of formation. There is also a paramilitary border guard. Military service is compulsory and consists of 18 months' basic training.

Latvia is a member of the Baltic Council, Conference on Security and Cooperation in Europe (CSCE) and Council of Baltic Sea States (CBSS), as well as the United Nations and its specialized agencies. It has applied for membership of the Council of Europe.

History. Originating further east, the ancestors of the Latvians (related to the Lithuanians and other Baltic peoples) settled in modern Latvia during the 1st millennium BC. Vikings from across the Baltic Sea raided the coastal areas and established trading posts from the 8th century AD onwards. At this time the country consisted of various tribal states and was divided into Viking and Kievan (Russian) spheres of influence. Later it consisted of four distinct regions, Courland (in the west), Livonia (also including southern Estonia), Zemgallia and Latgallia. All were conquered by the Teutonic Knights, a German Christian military order, in the 13th century. Society was organized on feudal lines, and there developed a sharp division between a German elite and the Latvian peasantry. Following a Russian invasion in 1558 the rulers sought protection from neighbouring powers. Poland-Lithuania took control of the Latvian states in 1561; Livonia fell to Sweden in 1629. The Swedes introduced a number of reforms aimed at improving the condition of the peasantry. Russia occupied all territories during the Great Northern War (1700–21), fulfilling a long-standing ambition to acquire a 'window to the seas'. Rīga became an important Russian port.

A Latvian cultural and national movement emerged in the 19th century. The Russian authorities introduced reforms from the 1860s but reverted to a policy of russification in the 1880s. Latvia suffered heavily from fighting between the German and Russian armies during the First World War (1914–18). The country was granted autonomy after the overthrow of the tsar in 1917 and declared its independence in 1918. This was recognized by the Soviet Union in 1920. A constitution was adopted in 1922. Many economic and social reforms were implemented in the 1920s, including the division of the large German-owned agricultural estates among landless peasants. Government coalitions were short-lived. Growing polarization between left and right induced President Kārlis Ulmanis to declare a state of emergency in 1934 and suspend parliament. During the Second World War (1939–45) the country was invaded and annexed by the Soviet Union in 1940 and occupied by German troops from 1941–44.

During the Soviet period Latvia was integrated into the communist economic system and suffered political repression, most harshly in the 1940s, 50s and 60s. There was also substantial Russian immigration and extensive industrialization. Latvia was one of the most prosperous Soviet republics. The greater freedom of expression allowed under the policy of

glasnost ('openness'), introduced after Mikhail Gorbachev became the Soviet leader in 1985, gave rise to an increasingly vociferous reform movement. Initially focused on human-rights, environmental and cultural issues, it became overtly economic and political with the establishment of the broad-based People's Front (LTF) in October 1988. After the LTF's victory in the March/April 1990 multiparty election the republican parliament reaffirmed Latvia's nominal independence and assumed a range of autonomous powers, in name as well as in practice. Full independence was regained after the abortive Soviet coup by communist hardliners in August 1991 and recognized by the Soviet Union the following month. The government initiated a range of market reforms in 1992. Anatolijs Gorbunovs, the country's effective leader since May 1990, led the new centre-right Latvian Way (LC) to a relative victory in the June 1993 election. (The LTF had fragmented after the restoration of independence.) The transformation of the economy has been accompanied by disruption and social dislocation. Relations with Russia have been tense since independence, primarily because of related disputes over the citizenship status and treatment of the large ethnic Russian minority and the slow pace of the Russian troop withdrawal from Latvia. The latter was completed in August 1994.
See also entries on specific institutions, organizations, parties, people, terms etc.

Latvian Farmers' Union and **Latvian Peasants' Union** *See* FARMERS' UNION OF LATVIA.

Latvian Way [Latvijas Ceļš] (LC) Latvian political party. The LC was founded in February 1993 by members of the People's Front (LTF), the broadly based reform and pro-independence movement which had won the multiparty election in 1990, when Latvia was still part of the Soviet Union. It adopted a centre-right programme. Led by Anatolijs Gorbunovs, a former Communist Party official and at the time effectively head of state, it gained 32.4% of the vote and 36/100 seats at the June 1993 election, becoming the largest party in parliament. It formed a coalition with the Farmers' Union (LZS) in August 1993, and formed a minority government after the LZS' withdrawal in July 1994.

Latvijas Ceļš *See* LATVIAN WAY.

Lauristin, Marju (1940–) Estonian journalist, academic and politician. She worked for Estonian Radio from 1962–66 and lectured in journalism from 1972–89. She was a leading member of the Estonian People's Front, formed in 1988 to secure Estonia's independence from the Soviet Union (achieved after the abortive coup in August 1991). In September 1990 she was elected leader of the newly formed Estonian Social Democratic Party (ESDP). She was appointed minister for social affairs in the centre-right coalition which took office in October 1992.

Lausanne Shorthand for the Federal Supreme Court in Switzerland. The Court sits in the city of Lausanne, in the western canton of Vaud.

law lord In the United Kingdom, the common name for a lord of appeal, a member of the House of Lords qualified to deal with judicial matters. As a body they are commonly known as the LAW LORDS.

Law Lords Common name for the House of Lords, the upper house of the British Parliament, in its function as the country's supreme judicial body. The Law Lords comprises the lord chancellor and those members of the House of Lords who are former senior judges. The latter are called 'lords of appeal in ordinary' and commonly known as 'law lords'.

law officers In the United Kingdom, the collective name for the government's senior advisers on legal matters. There are four law officers: the attorney-general in England, Wales and Northern Ireland and the lord advocate in Scotland, each assisted by a solicitor-general. All four are usually members of Parliament and invariably members of the ruling party. The attorney-general advises ministers and government departments on legal matters, superintends the work of the Crown Prosecution Service (CPS) and the Serious Fraud Office (SFO), is head of the barristers' profession (the 'Bar') and has a range of other responsibilities. The lord advocate advises the Scottish Office and other government departments on Scottish matters and is responsible for drafting legislation pertaining to Scotland.

Lazio Autonomous region of Italy. Situated in the centre along the Tyrrhenian Sea, Lazio has an area of 17,203 sq km and a population of 5,146,000. The region is dominated by Rome [Roma], the regional and national capital. The economy is based on agriculture (cereals, wine, fruit and vegetables), manufacturing (chemicals, textiles, metalworking), public and other services and tourism. Lazio formed the core of the Papal States from the 8th century until their incorporation into unified Italy in 1870.

LB *See* LEFT BLOC.

LBAS *See* ASSOCIATION OF FREE TRADE UNIONS OF LATVIA.

£C Abbreviation for the LÍRA or pound, the Cypriot currency.

LC *See* LATVIAN WAY.

LCGB *See* LUXEMBURG CHRISTIAN TRADE UNION CONFEDERATION.

LCV Abbreviation for the LIRA, the Vatican currency.

LD *See* LIBERAL DEMOCRATS.

LDDP *See* DEMOCRATIC LABOUR PARTY OF LITHUANIA.

LDK *See* DEMOCRATIC LEAGUE OF KOSOVO.

LDP *See* LIBERAL DEMOCRATIC PARTY (Estonia).

LDR *See* FEDERATION OF LIBERAL, DEMOCRATIC AND REFORM PARTIES OF THE EUROPEAN UNION.

LDS *See* LIBERAL DEMOCRATIC PARTY *and* LIBERAL DEMOCRATIC PARTY OF SLOVENIA.

LDs *See* LIBERAL DEMOCRATS.

LdU *See* ALLIANCE OF INDEPENDENTS.

Le Pen, Jean-Marie (1928–) French soldier and politician. He served as a paratrooper in Indochina and Algeria in the 1950s. He was a member of parliament from 1956–62 as a supporter of the right-wing populist Pierre Poujade. In October 1972 he founded the far-right National Front (FN). Under his leadership the party became an important political force in the 1980s. He stood in the 1974 and 1988 presidential elections, gaining

14.4% of the vote in the latter. He was a member of parliament from 1986–88 and has been a member of the European Parliament since 1984.

leader of the council or **council leader** British local government official. 'Leader of the council' is the usual title for the executive head of a district, metropolitan district, London borough or county council in England and Wales and a district council in Scotland. S/he is usually the leader of the largest party on the council. (Many councils appoint a 'chief executive', who is responsible for day-to-day administration and implementation of policy but is nominally non-political.)

leader of the House of Commons British government minister. S/he is primarily responsible for arranging government business in the House of Commons, the lower house of Parliament, and for supervising the passage of its legislative programme.

leader of the opposition In the United Kingdom, the official title of the parliamentary leader of the largest opposition party. As such s/he enjoys various rights and privileges within the parliamentary process and is entitled to financial support. The office also exists in countries and territories whose parliamentary systems are based on or influenced by the British model, e.g., in Europe, Ireland, Malta and Gibraltar.

league [lega, pl. leghe] In Italy, a shorthand for regional league, one of the regional parties now organized in the NORTHERN LEAGUE (Lega Nord).

Leetsar, Jaan (1946–) Estonian agronomist and politician. A specialist in soil-improvement techniques, he has worked as a researcher and was director-general of the Estonian Central Farmers' Union until his appointment as agriculture minister in October 1992. He is a member of the Estonian Rural Centre Party (EMKE).

Lefkoşa Turkish name for Nicosia, the capital of Cyprus and the Turkish Republic of Northern Cyprus.

Left Bloc [Levý Blok] (LB) Czech political organization. The LB was formed prior to the June 1992 election as an alliance of the Communist Party of Bohemia and

Moravia (KSČM), the Democratic Left (DL) movement and several small left-wing groups. It gained 14.1% of the vote and 35/200 seats in the Czech parliament. It was dissolved after a split within the KSČM in June 1993, but was later reconstituted as an alliance of the new Democratic Left Party (SDL) and other left-wing deputies. The leader is Marie Stiborová.

Left Party [Vänsterpartiet] (Vp or V) Swedish political party. Founded in 1917, the Left Party – the most recent of its various names – followed an independent communist line until it redefined itself as left-socialist in 1990. It has adopted a programme which focuses on environmental issues and equal rights for men and women. It has given external support to minority Social Democratic governments on several occasions, most recently from 1982–91. At the September 1991 election it gained 4.5% of the vote and 16/349 seats. The leader is Gudrun Schyman.

Left Radical Movement [Mouvement des Radicaux de Gauche] (MRG) French political party. Founded in 1973 as a breakaway from the Radical Party, the centre-left MRG has formed an electoral alliance with the Socialist Party (PS) since 1981. At the March 1993 election it gained 0.9% of the vote and 6/577 seats. The leader is Jean-François Hory.

Left-Wing Alliance [Vasemmistoliitto] (VL or Vas) Finnish political party. The VL was formed in 1990 by the merger of several orthodox and reformist communist groups, in particular the Finnish People's Democratic League (SKDL) dominated by the Finnish Communist Party (SKP) and the Democratic Alternative (DEVA). The SKDL had gained around a fifth of the vote in the 1950s and 60s but lost support in the 1980s. Campaigning on a left-socialist programme, the new party gained 10.1% of the vote and 19/200 seats at the March 1991 election. The party leader is Claes Andersson, the parliamentary leader is Esko Helle.

lega, Lega Lombarda, Lega Nord and **lega regionale** See LOMBARD LEAGUE and NORTHERN LEAGUE.

legal instrument In the European Union (EU), one of the mechanisms at the disposal of the Council and the Commission to implement their decisions. They are the 'DIRECTIVE', the 'REGULATION' and the 'DECISION'.

Legebiltzarre ('Legislature') Basque name for the parliament of the Basque Country, an autonomous community or region of Spain.

leghe and **leghe regionali** See REGIONAL LEAGUE and NORTHERN LEAGUE.

Legislative Chambers [Wetgevende Kamers (Dutch), Chambres Législatives (French)] Parliament of Belgium, composed of the CHAMBER OF DEPUTIES and the SENATE.

Legislative Council See TYNWALD.

lehendakari See LENDAKARI.

lei Plural of LEU, the Romanian currency.

Leinster House Shorthand for the Irish parliament or specifically the DÁIL ÉIREANN, the lower house. Leinster House in Dublin is the seat of the Dáil as well as the SEANAD ÉIREANN, the upper house.

lek (pl. -ë) Currency of Albania. Common abbreviations are L and ALL (the international standard in banking etc). It is divided into 100 qindarka or qindars. The anglicized plural 'leks' and the simple form 'lek' are also used.

lekë Plural of LEK, the Albanian currency.

lendakari ('president' in Basque) Head of government or chief minister of the Basque Country, an autonomous community or region of Spain. The Basque title is also used by Spanish speakers.

Léotard, François (1942–) French civil servant and politician. He worked in central and local government until his election to parliament for the centre-right Republican Party (PR) in 1978. He has been its general secretary (1982–88) and leader (1988–90) and is now honorary president. He was also minister of culture and communications from 1986–88 and has been mayor of Fréjus since 1977. He resigned all his political posts in June 1992 after being accused of corruption. He was cleared of all charges in February 1993 and was reelected to parliament the following month.

Les Verts *See* GREENS (France).

Let's Go Italy *See* COME ON ITALY.

Letta, Gianni (1935–) Italian lawyer, journalist and politician. He began working for the daily newspaper *Il Tempo* in 1959 and eventually served as its managing director and editor from 1973–87. In 1987 he became a vice-president of Fininvest Comunicazione, a subsidiary of the conglomerate owned by Silvio Berlusconi. Having joined Berlusconi's new Come On Italy (Forza Italia), which became the largest party in the March election, he was appointed to the key post of cabinet secretary in the right-wing coalition formed in May.

Lettish and **Letts** Alternative names for the Latvian language and Latvians. *See* LATVIA.

Lëtzebuerg Letzeburgish name for Luxemburg.

Letzeburgish [Lëtzebuergesch] One of the official languages of Luxemburg, also called Luxemburgish. A dialect of German, Letzeburgish was declared an official language, alongside French and German, in 1984. It is increasingly used in public life.

leu (pl. lei) Currency of Romania. Common abbreviations are L and ROL (the international standard in banking etc). It is divided into 100 bani.

Leutheusser-Schnarrenberger, Sabine (1951–) German lawyer, civil servant and politician. She worked at the German Patent Office (DPA) from 1979 until her election to parliament for the centrist Free Democratic Party (FDP) in 1990. In May 1992 she was appointed justice minister.

lev (pl. -a) Currency of Bulgaria. Common abbreviations are Lv and BGL (the international standard in banking etc). It is divided into 100 stotinki.

leva Plural of LEV, the Bulgarian currency.

Levkosía Greek name for Nicosia, the Cypriot capital.

LF (Austria) *See* LIBERAL FORUM.

LF and **LFr** Abbreviations for the FRANC, the Luxemburg currency.

Lib Dem and **Lib Dems** *See* LIBERAL DEMOCRATS.

Liberal Alliance of Montenegro [Liberalni Savez Crne Gore] (LSCG or LS) Yugoslav political party. Founded in 1990 and active in Montenegro, the LS is a centrist party advocating the introduction of a fully market-based economy. At the December 1992 election it gained 12.4% of the vote and 13/85 seats in the republic's parliament. The leader is Slavko Perović.

Liberal, Democratic and Reformist Group (European Union) *See* FEDERATION OF LIBERAL, DEMOCRATIC AND REFORM PARTIES OF THE EUROPEAN UNION.

Liberal Democratic Congress [Kongres Liberalno-Demokratyczny] (KLD) Former Polish political party. Founded in 1988, the KLD advocated a rapid transition to a market economy and was influential in determining government economic policy in the first four years after the end of communist rule in 1989. At the September 1993 election it gained 4.0% of the vote but no seats, having failed to reach the 5% required for representation. It merged with the Democratic Union (UD) to form the FREEDOM UNION (UW) in April 1994.

Liberal Democratic Party [Liberaaldemokraatlik Partei] (LDP) Estonian political party. The centre-right LDP was founded in 1990, when Estonia was still part of the Soviet Union. It contested the September 1992 election within the Fatherland (Isamaa) alliance, gaining 6/101 seats. It withdrew from the Isamaa parliamentary group in June 1994. The party leader is Paul-Eerik Rummo.

Liberal Democratic Party [Liberalna Demokratična Stranka] (LDS) Former Slovenian political party. Founded in 1990, the LDS emerged from the communist youth movement, which had advocated reformist views since the early 1980s. Centre-left in orientation, it formed a coalition government in May 1992. At the election the following December it consolidated its position as the country's largest party, gaining 23.7% of the vote and 22/90 seats. In March 1994 it absorbed several smaller parties and was renamed the LIBERAL DEMOCRATIC PARTY OF SLOVENIA (LDS).

Liberal Democratic Party of Slovenia [Liberalna Demokracija Slovenije] (LDS)

Slovenian political party. The centre-left LDS was formed in March 1994 by the merger of the LIBERAL DEMOCRATIC PARTY (LDS), the Socialist Party (SSS) and sections of the Democratic Party (DSS) and the Greens (Zeleni, ZS). It is the largest party in parliament, with 30/90 seats. The leader is Janez Drnovšek, the prime minister, who was also leader of the old LDS.

Liberal Democrats (Lib Dem or Lib Dems) British political party. The Liberal Democrats were formed in 1988 by the merger of the Liberal Party and the bulk of the Social Democratic Party (SDP). The Liberals dominated British politics in the 19th and early 20th centuries, holding office for 52 of the 83 years between 1839 – when the name 'Liberal Party' was first used – and 1914. It was subsequently replaced as the main alternative to the Conservatives by Labour, but its fortunes revived in the 1970s. In 1983 it formed an electoral alliance with the SDP, which had broken away from the Labour Party in 1981. After the 1987 election the two parties agreed on a formal merger. The Liberal Democrats' programme is centrist in economic terms and liberal on social issues. It also calls for wide-ranging constitutional reform and the introduction of proportional representation in elections. At the April 1992 election the party gained 17.9% of the vote and 20/651 seats. The leader is Paddy Ashdown, the party president Robert Maclellan. (The party was formally called the Social and Liberal Democratic Party, SLD, for a year after its foundation.)

Liberal Forum [Liberales Forum] (LF) Austrian political party. The Liberal Forum was set up in February 1993 by members of the Freedom Party (FPÖ) who objected to the increasingly right-wing populist line promoted by the party leader, Jörg Haider. Advocating traditional right-leaning liberal policies, the LF holds 5/183 seats in parliament. The leader is Heide Schmidt, the former FPÖ deputy leader.

Liberal Group (European Union) *See* FEDERATION OF LIBERAL, DEMOCRATIC AND REFORM PARTIES OF THE EUROPEAN UNION.

Liberal National Social Party [Liberální Strana Národně Sociální] (LSNS) Czech political party. Founded in 1897 as the National Socialist Party (NSS) and later renamed the Czechoslovak Socialist Party (ČSS), the party was allowed to function within the communist-dominated National Front from 1948–89. It was relaunched in 1990 and adopted a broadly centrist platform. It gained 2.8% of the vote at the June 1990 election and contested the June 1992 election within the Liberal Social Union (LSU) alliance, which gained 6.5% of the vote and 16/200 seats in the Czech parliament. The party was renamed and left the LSU in June 1993. It holds five seats. The leader is Pavel Hirš.

Liberal Party [Venstre] (V) Danish political party. Founded in 1870, the Venstre ('Left') has participated in a number of coalitions since 1945, most recently as a junior partner in successive centre-right coalitions from 1982–93. At the December 1990 election it gained 15.8% of the vote and 29/175 seats. Uffe Ellemann-Jensen has been the leader since 1984.

Liberal Party (Faroe Islands) *See* UNION PARTY.

Liberal Party [Venstre] (V) Norwegian political party. Founded in 1884, the Venstre ('Left') gained around a tenth of the vote in the 1950s and 60s and joined several centre-right coalitions. The party split in 1972 over Norway's proposed entry into then European Community (EC) and subsequently lost most of its support, failing to win any seats in the 1985 and 1989 elections. It retained considerable strength at local level, and returned to parliament with 3.6% of the vote and one seat (out of 165) at the September 1993 general election. The leader is Odd Einar Dørum.

Liberal Party (Sweden) *See* PEOPLE'S PARTY - THE LIBERALS.

Liberal Party 1993 [Partidul Liberal 1993] (PL'93 or PL) Romanian political party. The PL'93 was formed in June 1993 from the merger of two factions of the NATIONAL LIBERAL PARTY (PNL), known as the Youth Wing and the Democratic Convention wing, which had split from it in 1990. Both contested the September 1992 election within the opposition Democratic Convention (DCR) and gained 13/341 seats between them. A wing of the Civic Alliance Party (PAC) joined the new party in July 1993. The leader is Dinu Patriciu.

Liberal Party of Switzerland [Liberale Partei der Schweiz (German), Parti Libéral Suisse (French)] (LPS or PLS) Swiss political party. The Liberals are active in the four western cantons of Basel-City, Geneva, Neuchâtel and Vaud. At the October 1991 election the party gained 3.0% of the vote and 10/200 seats. The party president is François Jeanneret, the parliamentary leader is Jean-François Leuba.

Liberal Reform Party [Parti Réformateur Libéral] (PRL) Belgian political party. A successor to the Liberal Party founded in 1846, the PRL became the Walloon wing of the renamed Freedom and Progress Party (PLP) in 1961. A separate organization from 1974, it merged with a French-speaking liberal group in Brussels and adopted its present name in 1979. The party has participated in a number of coalitions since 1945. Like its counterpart, the Flemish Liberals and Democrats (VLD), it has a right-wing economic programme and liberal views on social issues. At the November 1991 election it gained 8.2% of the vote and 20/212 seats. The leader is Jean Gol.

Liberal Social Union [Liberální Sociální Unie] (LSU) Czech political organization. The LSU was formed in 1991 as a electoral alliance of the Czechoslovak Socialist Party (ČSS, now the Liberal National Social Party, LSNS), the Green Party (SZ) and the Agrarian Party (ZS). It contested the June 1992 election on a centrist programme of economic reform with safeguards for the vulnerable in society, the agricultural sector and the environment, and gained 6.5% of the vote and 16/200 seats in the Czech parliament. The LSNS left the alliance in June 1993.

Līdztiesība *See* EQUAL RIGHTS.

Liechtenstein Country in central Europe.

Official data. Name: Principality of Liechtenstein [Fürstentum Liechtenstein]; capital: Vaduz; form of government: parliamentary monarchy; head of state: prince; head of government: chief of government; flag: two horizontal stripes, blue and red, with a gold crown in the canton; national holiday: 15 August (National Day); language: German; religion: none; currency: Swiss franc; abbreviation: FL.

Geography. Situated in the Alps, Liechtenstein has an area of 160 sq km. It is bordered by Austria in the east and Switzerland in the south and west. The terrain is mountainous with the exception of the river plain of the Rhine [Rhein], which forms the border with Switzerland. Some 25% of the land is arable, another 38% is covered by pastures and 19% is forested. The climate is alpine, with hot summers and cold winters. Temperatures are lower in the mountains; rainfall is moderate in the lowland areas and heavy in the mountains.

Demography. Liechtenstein has a population of 30,100. Population density is 188 per sq km. The main towns are Vaduz and Schaan. Some 63.6% of the people are Liechtenstein citizens. Foreign nationals account for the remaining 36.4%, and include citizens of Switzerland (15.7% of the total), Austria (7.7%), Germany (3.7%), Italy, Turkey, Spain and Greece. The main language is German. In religious terms 87.0% of the population is nominally Roman Catholic and 7.9% Protestant; most of the remainder are not religious.

Sociography. The standard of living in Liechtenstein is very high. There are 14 doctors and 37 hospital beds for every 10,000 people. Education is compulsory between the ages of seven and 16. There is one teacher for every 12 students. Enrolment is 79% at the secondary level; there are no local institutions of higher education, and most students study in Switzerland, Austria and Germany. The literacy rate is virtually 100%. GNP per head (unadjusted for purchasing power) is US$ 32,790, among the highest in Europe.

Infrastructure and communications.
Liechtenstein has a highly developed but
limited transport and communications
network fully integrated into that of its
neighbours; there is no locally based
radio or television service. There are 320
km of paved roads and 16,900 passenger
cars (582 per 1,000 people), 19 km of
railways and no navigable waterways.
The nearest major (inland) port is Basel
in Switzerland. The nearest major international airport is at Zürich (Switzerland).
There are two daily newspapers, with a
combined circulation of 16,000 (577 per
1,000 people); Swiss, Austrian and
German papers are also widely read.
There are 19,000 radio receivers, 9,000
television sets and around 25,000 telephones in use (respectively 655, 310 and
876 per 1,000 people).

Economic structure. The Liechtenstein
economy is highly developed, diversified,
trade-oriented and closely linked to that
of Switzerland. Liechtenstein maintains
a customs and monetary union with
Switzerland. The economy is based on
light industry, financial services and
tourism. Since the late 1980s economic
performance has been marked by low
but steady growth, substantial current-
account surpluses, low inflation (averaging 3.8% per year) and very low unemployment (1.3% in 1993).

Services contribute around 53% of
GDP, industry contributes around 45%,
and agriculture and forestry around 2%
(detailed figures n.a.). Some 33% of the
labour force is employed in manufacturing, 11% in trade, 8% in construction
and 7% in financial services; immigrant
workers (from Austria, Switzerland etc),
either resident locally or in the neighbouring countries, make up three-fifths of the
total. The main agricultural activities are
livestock raising (cattle, pigs, sheep),
dairy farming and horticulture (grapes
and other fruit); the main crops grown are
cereals (maize) and potatoes. Forestry is
also important. The only mineral resource
is stone. The main industries are precision
and other engineering; other important
branches are pharmaceuticals, electrical
goods, ceramics, furniture, building

materials and printing (postage stamps).
Tourism and banking and other financial
services are mainstays of the economy
and major sources of foreign exchange.
The main energy sources are imported
fossil fuels and electricity (from Switzerland). The main exports are machinery
and transport equipment (46% of the
total, incl. electrical and electronic equipment), metal products (19%), precision
instruments (esp. dentistry and other
medical equipment) (12%), pharmaceuticals (8%) and building materials
(8%). The main imports are miscellaneous
manufactures, machinery and transport
equipment, basic manufactures and
chemicals. The main trading partners are
Switzerland (15% of exports), Germany
and Austria; nearly half of all trade is
with European Union (EU) countries
(detailed figures n.a.). Net invisible
earnings (tourism receipts, income from
financial services) account for a significant share of GNP.

There is no central bank. There are
several employers' associations and trade
unions, including the Liechtenstein
Employees' Association (LANV).

Political structure. Liechtenstein is a
parliamentary monarchy on the basis of a
constitution adopted in 1921. Executive
power is vested in the prince, who retains
substantial powers, and in the prime
minister [Regierungschef] and the government; the latter are elected by the legislature. Legislative power is vested in the
prince and the Parliament [Landtag],
whose 25 members are elected for a four-
year term by a system of proportional
representation (with an 8% threshold for
gaining seats). Voting is compulsory for
all citizens over the age of 20. Judicial
power is ultimately vested in the five-
member Supreme Court [Oberster
Gerichtshof]; the five-member State
Court [Staatsgerichtshof] adjudicates on
administrative matters. Administratively
the country is divided into 11 municipalities [Gemeinde, pl. -n].

The main political parties are the
Fatherland Union (VU), Progressive
Citizens' Party (FBP) and Free List (FL).
At the general election in October 1993

the VU gained 50.1% of the vote and 13/25 seats, the FBP 41.3% and 11 seats, and the FL 8.5% and one seat. The government is formed by a centre-right coalition of the VU and FBP, with Mario Frick as prime minister (also responsible for finance and justice). Other senior ministers are Thomas Büchel (deputy prime minister, internal affairs, agriculture and forestry, education, environment), Andrea Willi (foreign affairs, culture, youth and sport) and Michael Ritter (economy, welfare, health, family). The head of state is Prince Hans-Adam II, who succeeded to the throne in November 1989; the heir is Prince Alois.

Security and international affiliations. Liechtenstein has no standing army, but general conscription may be imposed in an emergency. Responsibility for defence and some foreign affairs is delegated to Switzerland.

Liechtenstein is a member of the Conference on Security and Cooperation in Europe (CSCE), Council of Europe, European Economic Area (EEA) and European Free Trade Association (EFTA), as well as the United Nations and some of its specialized agencies.

History. From the early Middle Ages the area of modern Liechtenstein was divided between two lordships within the Holy Roman or German Empire, Vaduz and Schellenberg. (*For earlier developments, see* SWITZERLAND: HISTORY.) Both were ruled by the Brandis family from 1434–1608. Schellenberg then passed to the Liechtenstein family. It purchased Vaduz in 1712. In 1719 the two lordships were united as the Principality of Liechtenstein. It declared itself independent in 1806 and achieved full sovereignty later that year following the dissolution of the Holy Roman Empire. It was a member of the Rhine Confederation (1806–15) and the German Confederation (1815–66). From 1852–1918 it formed a customs and currency union with Austria. The standing army was abolished in 1868. A customs and currency union with Switzerland was signed in 1923 and came into effect the following year. In 1938 the two main parties, the right-wing

Progressive Citizens' Party (FBP) and the centre-right Fatherland Union (VU), formed a coalition which has remained in power ever since.

From the 1950s Liechtenstein was transformed from a relatively poor agricultural economy into a very prosperous one based on light industry and financial services. After two failed referendums in the 1970s, women gained the vote in July 1984. (Liechtenstein was the last European country to introduce universal adult suffrage.) Prince Franz-Josef II retired in August 1984 and was succeeded by his son, Hans-Adam II. Adopting a higher profile in foreign policy, Liechtenstein joined the United Nations in September 1990 and became a full member of the European Free Trade Association (EFTA) in May 1991. Membership of the European Economic Area (EEA), the new Western-Europe-wide single market, was approved in a referendum in December 1992, but participation had to be delayed because of problems arising from Switzerland's decision not to join.

See also entries on specific institutions, organizations, parties, people, terms etc.

Lietuva Lithuanian name for Lithuania.

Lietuvos Respublika ('Republic of Lithuania') Official name of Lithuania.

lieutenant-governor Senior officer of state in Guernsey, Jersey and Man. Appointed by the British crown, i.e. the government, the lieutenant-governor is the personal representative of the sovereign in each of the territories and the official channel of communication between the islands' legislatures and the British government.

life peer In the United Kingdom, a member of the nobility (baron or baroness) ennobled for life by the sovereign on the advice of the prime minister. Life peers' titles lapse on their deaths. All are entitled to sit in the House of Lords, the upper house of Parliament.

life senator [senatore a vita] In Italy, a member of the Senate, the upper house of parliament, appointed for life. The honour is usually reserved for influential and respected political figures, academics and industrialists. Former presidents of the republic are life senators by right, and five senators are appointed by the president of the day.

Liguria Autonomous region of Italy. Situated in the northwest between the Mediterranean Sea and the Ligurian Alps, Liguria has an area of 5,418 sq km and a population of 1,702,000. The region is dominated by Genoa [Genova], the capital; other major cities are La Spezia and San Remo. The economy is based on manufacturing (chemicals, textiles, food processing, shipbuilding), tourism and agriculture (fruit and vegetables, flowers). Liguria was the heartland of the Genoese Republic from the 11th century. The republic was dissolved in 1797 and later annexed by France. In 1815 Liguria became part of the Kingdom of Sardinia, the nucleus of unified Italy.

Lilić, Zoran (1953–) Yugoslav mechanical engineer and politician. From 1978–90 he worked for the Rekord engineering company in Belgrade, becoming its managing director in 1989. He was elected to the Serbian parliament for the Socialist Party of Serbia (SPS) in 1990 and became its speaker in January 1993. He was elected federal president of Yugoslavia (a non-executive post) in June that year.

Lilley, Peter (1943–) British economist and politician. He worked as a development consultant and investment adviser until his election to Parliament for the Conservative Party in 1983. He held junior ministerial posts in the Treasury (= finance ministry) from 1987. He was appointed secretary of state for trade and industry in 1990 and became secretary of state for social security in April 1992.

Limousin Region of France. Situated in the centre, Limousin has an area of 16,942 sq km and a population of 719,000. Dialects of Occitan are widely spoken throughout the region, but the language has no official status. The capital is Limoges. The economy is based on agriculture (cattle and sheep farming) and light industry (leather, ceramics). Limousin is one of France's poorest regions, and emigration has been heavy throughout the 20th century. Like other parts of southern France, Limousin has a strong regional identity.

Linkevičius, Linas (1961–) Lithuanian electrical engineer, journalist and politician. In the 1980s he worked for the Komsomol, the Soviet youth organization, and became involved in the communist reform movement. In 1992 he was elected to parliament for the Democratic Labour Party (LDDP), the successor to the Communist Party. He was appointed defence minister in October 1993.

Lipponen, Paavo (1941–) Finnish politician. He worked briefly as a journalist before joining the Finnish Social Democratic Party (SDP) as research and international secretary in 1967. He subsequently became head of its political department, and from 1979–82 was secretary to the prime minister. Elected to parliament in 1983, he became party leader in June 1993.

Lipstok, Andres (1957–) Estonian economist, civil servant and politician. He began working in local government, specializing in finance matters, in 1982 and later also served as an elected town and county councillor. He was briefly deputy finance minister in 1988–89 (when Estonia was still part of the Soviet Union). A member of the rightwing Liberal Democratic Party (LDP), he was appointed finance minister in June 1994.

líra (pl. líres) Currency of Cyprus. Common abbreviations are £, C£, £C and CYP (the international standard in banking etc). It is divided into 100 sént. The anglicized versions 'pound' and 'cents' are also widely used.

lira (pl. lire) Currency of Italy. Common abbreviations are L, LIT, Lit and ITL (the international standard in banking etc). It is divided into 100 centesimi. The Italian lira is also legal tender in San Marino and the Vatican.

lira (pl. liri) Currency of Malta. Common abbreviations are LM, Lm, M£ and MTP (the international standard in banking etc). It is divided into 100 centeżmu and 1,000 milleżmi. The anglicized versions 'pound', 'cents' and 'mils' are also widely used.

lira (Northern Cyprus) *See* LIRA (Turkey).

376

lira (pl. lire) Currency of San Marino. Common abbreviations are L, LSM and SML (the international standard in banking etc). It is divided into 100 centesimi. It has parity with the Italian lira, which is also legal tender in San Marino.

lira (pl. -) Currency of Turkey and Northern Cyprus. Common abbreviations are TL and TRL (the international standard in banking etc). It is divided into 100 kuruş. The anglicized version 'pound' is also used.

lira (pl. lire) Currency of the Vatican City State. Common abbreviations are L, LCV and VCL (the international standard in banking etc). It is divided into 100 centesimi. It has parity with the Italian lira, which is also legal tender in the Vatican.

lire Plural of lira, the currencies of Italy, San Marino and the Vatican.

líres Plural of LÍRA or pound, the Cypriot currency.

liri Plural of LIRA or pound, the Maltese currency.

Lisbon Shorthand for the Portuguese government. Lisbon is the capital of Portugal.

Lista Pannella *See* RADICAL PARTY (Italy).

Lista Verde *See* GREEN FEDERATION.

Liste Campora *See* CAMPORA LIST.

Liste Médecin *See* MÉDECIN LIST.

Listopad 11 *See* ELEVENTH OF NOVEMBER ALLIANCE.

LIT or **Lit** Abbreviation for the LIRA, the Italian currency.

litai Plural of LITAS, the Lithuanian currency.

litas (pl. litai) Currency of Lithuania. Common abbreviations are L and LTL (the international standard in banking etc). It is divided into 100 centai. It was introduced in June 1993 to replace the talonas ('coupon'). This had been introduced in May 1992 as a temporary currency alongside the former Soviet rouble, which ceased to be legal tender the following October. The anglicized plural 'litas' is also used.

Lithuania [Lietuva] Country in northeastern Europe, formerly part of the Soviet Union.

Official data. Name: Republic of Lithuania [Lietuvos Respublika]; capital: Vilnius; form of government: parliamentary republic; head of state: president; head of government: prime minister; flag: three horizontal stripes, yellow, green and red; national holiday: 16 February (Restoration of Independence Day); language: Lithuanian; religion: none; currency: litas (L) (pl. litai) = 100 centai; abbreviation: LT.

Geography. The southernmost and largest of the three Baltic countries, Lithuania has an area of 65,301 sq km. It is bordered by Latvia in the north, Belorussia in the east and southeast, Poland and Russia (the Kaliningrad region) in the southwest, and the Baltic Sea in the west. It consists almost entirely of low-lying rolling plains studded with lakes. Some 49% of the land is arable, another 22% is covered by pastures and 16% is forested. The main river is the Nemunas. The climate is humid continental, with mild summers and cold winters; rainfall is moderate.

Demography. Lithuania has a population of 3,798,000. Population density is 58 per sq km (land area). Around 69% of the people live in urban areas, and around a fifth lives in Vilnius. Other major cities are Kaunas, Klaipėda, Šiauliai and Panevėžys. In ethnic terms 80.2% of the people are Lithuanians, 8.9% Russians, 7.0% Poles, 1.6% Belorussians and 1.1% Ukrainians; there are also small groups of Tatars, Latvians and Germans. Most Russians live in the cities, most Poles in the southeast. The main languages are Lithuanian, Russian and Polish. In religious terms most Lithuanians and Poles are nominally Roman Catholic, and most Russians, Belorussians and Ukrainians are nominally Orthodox.

Sociography. Lithuania scores 0.868 on the United Nations human development index (HDI), ranking 28th in the world and 20th among 32 European countries. There are 49 doctors and 123 hospital beds for every 10,000 people, among the highest figures in Europe. Education is compulsory between the ages of seven and 15. There is one teacher for every 12 students. Enrolment is around 90% at the secondary level and around 20% at the tertiary level. The literacy rate is 96%. Real annual income per head (in terms of purchasing power) is US$ 5,410.

Infrastructure and communications. Lithuania's transport and communications network is relatively developed but in need of modernization and extension; the telecommunications system in particular is limited. There are 55,040 km of paved roads and 534,000 passenger cars (142 per 1,000 people). There are 2,010 km of railways and 600 km of navigable waterways. The main port is Klaipėda. The main airport is at Vilnius and there are two other airports with scheduled services. There are six daily newspapers, with a combined circulation of 467,000 (123 per 1,000 people). There are 1.34 million radio receivers, 1.43 million television sets and 838,000 telephones in use (respectively 357, 382 and 223 per 1,000 people).

Economic structure. The Lithuanian economy is based on manufacturing and agriculture. Although essentially developed and diversified, it is in need of major investment and restructuring. The transition from a command to a market-based economy initiated in the late 1980s is causing severe dislocation and has led to steep falls in industrial and agricultural production as well as food and energy shortages. Between 1990 and 1993 GDP contracted by around half, inflation averaged around 200% per year, and unemployment rose to around 15% (unofficial estimate). There were some signs of recovery in 1994.

Services contribute 26% of GDP, industry contributes 53% (manufacturing around 45%), and agriculture, forestry and fisheries 21%. Some 29% of the labour force is employed in manufacturing, 19% in farming, forestry and fishing, 12% in trade and 9% in construction. The main agricultural activities are livestock raising (cattle, pigs, poultry) and dairy farming (milk, eggs); horticulture (fruit and vegetables) is also important; the main crops grown are cereals (barley), sugarbeets, potatoes and flax. Forestry and fishing are of regional importance. The main mineral resources are peat, limestone, gravel, clay and sand. The

main industries are food processing (esp. dairy and meat products), textiles and engineering (esp. industrial machinery, electrical goods); other important branches are petrochemicals, chemicals, wood processing (paper, furniture), metalworking, shipbuilding and building materials (bricks). The main energy sources are nuclear and geothermal power and imported fossil fuels; 4% of export earnings are required to cover net fuel imports. The main exports are foodstuffs (31% of the total, esp. meat and dairy products), textiles and clothing (28%), industrial machinery (10%), electrical equipment (10%), chemicals (5%) and petrochemicals (5%); foodstuffs account for 31% of the total, miscellaneous manufactures for 28% and machinery and transport equipment for 20%. The main imports are foodstuffs, fuels and basic and miscellaneous manufactures. The main trading partners are: exports: Russia (32%), Ukraine (15%), Germany (5%), Belorussia, Poland, Latvia; imports: Russia (58%), Ukraine (8%), Germany (5%), Italy, Poland; trade with Russia and the other members of the Commonwealth of Independent States (CIS) is declining rapidly, that with Western European countries is growing.

The Bank of Lithuania [Lietuvos Bankas] is the central bank. There are several employers' and business associations; the main labour organizations are the Trade Union Centre of Lithuania (LPSC), Workers' Union of Lithuania (LDS) and Trade Union Federation of Lithuania (LPSS).

Political structure. Lithuania is a parliamentary republic on the basis of a constitution adopted in 1990; it formally severed all links with the Soviet Union and came into force when the country regained its independence in August 1991. The head of state is the president, who is directly elected for a five-year term. S/he appoints the prime minister and the commander of the armed forces and has extensive powers in the foreign-policy sphere. Executive power is also vested in the prime minister and the council of ministers. Legislative power is vested in the Parliament [Seimas], whose 141 members are elected for a four-year term by a mixed system of proportional representation and majority voting (with a 4% threshold for gaining seats and special provisions for ethnic minorities). All citizens over the age of 18, including those living abroad, are entitled to vote. Judicial power is ultimately vested in the Supreme Court [Aukščiausiasis Teismas] elected by the legislature for a 10-year term. Administratively the country is divided into 44 districts [rajonas, pl. rajonai] and 11 district-level cities; the districts are subdivided into 81 municipalities.

The main political parties are the Democratic Labour Party of Lithuania (LDDP), Homeland Union (Tėvynės Sąjunga, TS, the successor to the Reform Movement, Sąjūdis), Christian Democratic Party of Lithuania (KDP), Citizens' Charter (PCh), Social Democratic Party of Lithuania (LSDP), Political Prisoners' and Exiles' Union (PKTLS) and Polish Union of Lithuania (LLS); the Homeland Accord is an alliance of the TS, KDP, PCh, PKTLS and four other parties. At the general election in October/November 1992 the LDDP gained 44.7% of the vote and 72/141 seats, Sąjūdis, the PCh and PKTLS 19.8% and 30 seats, the KDP and two smaller parties 11.6% and 16 seats, the LSDP 6.0% and eight seats, and the LLS 2.3% and four seats. The government is formed by the left-wing LDDP, with Adolfas Šleževičius as prime minister. Other senior ministers are Aleksandras Vasiliauskas (economy), Eduardas Vilkelis (finance), Povilas Gylys (foreign affairs), Romasis Vaitekūnas (interior), Jonas Prapiestis (justice) and Linas Linkevičius (defence). The head of state is President Algirdas Brazauskas, who was elected in February 1993.

Security and international affiliations. The Lithuanian armed forces number 4,900 (army 4,300, navy 300, airforce 300); they are in the process of formation. There is also a 5,000-strong paramilitary border guard. Military service is compulsory and consists of 12 months' basic training.

Lithuania is a member of the Baltic Council, Conference on Security and Cooperation in Europe (CSCE), Council of Baltic Sea States (CBSS) and Council of Europe, as well as the United Nations and its specialized agencies. It has applied for membership of the North Atlantic Treaty Organization (NATO).

History. Originating further east, the ancestors of the Lithuanians (related to the Latvians and other Baltic peoples) settled in modern Lithuania during the 1st millennium BC. In the 13th century the Lithuanian states and their neighbours joined forces to resist the Teutonic Knights. But by 1290 this German Christian military order had conquered all territories to the north and west of Lithuania. The country was united for the first time under Mindaugas (1236–63), who was crowned king in 1253, and permanently from 1290. Exploiting a power vacuum created by the Mongols' destruction of the Kievan (Russian) principalities in the 1240s, Lithuania extended its borders eastward and southward under Gediminas (1316–41) and his successors. The army and nobility were able to maintain control over a vast region (including modern Belorussia and northwestern Ukraine) by granting the subject states autonomy and relying on their Orthodox Christian elites for administration. To counter the threat of the Teutonic Knights, Lithuania concluded an alliance with Poland in 1385 based on the personal union of their crowns. In 1386 Grand Prince Jogaila converted to Roman Catholicism, married Queen Jadwiga and ruled in Poland as Władysław II Jagiełło. Most of the Lithuanian nobles and peasants were baptized the following year. (Lithuania was the last European country to adopt Christianity.) In 1569 the Polish-Lithuanian union was completed with the establishment of a single administration.

In the 17th and 18th centuries the centre of power shifted west to Poland and the Lithuanian and Belorussian nobilities became polonized. Weakened by political and ethnic tension, Poland was partitioned among its neighbours (Prussia, Austria and Russia) in three stages between 1772 and 1795. Under the final partition rump Lithuania became part of the Russian Empire. There were uprisings against Russian rule in 1830–31 and 1863. The policy of russification was intensified in the 1880s. The country was occupied by German troops during the First World War (1914–18). Lithuania declared its independence in 1918. It was able to repel invasions by Soviet and Polish forces, and independence was recognized in 1920. Poland's occupation of the region around Vilnius, Lithuania's traditional capital, remained a major source of tension. In 1923 Polish sovereignty was recognized internationally but not by Lithuania. The dispute was effectively resolved in 1939 when the region was allocated to Lithuania under the German-Soviet pact dividing Poland. A constitution establishing a parliamentary democracy was adopted in 1922. Many economic and social reforms were implemented in the 1920s, in particular a radical land reform. Government coalitions were short-lived. Antanas Smetona, the dominant political leader of the period, seized power in a military coup in 1926 and established a right-wing dictatorship. During the Second World War (1939–45) the country was invaded and annexed by the Soviet Union in 1940 and occupied by German troops from 1941–44.

During the Soviet period Lithuania was integrated into the communist economic system and suffered political repression, most harshly in the 1940s, 50s and 60s. There was also extensive industrialization. The greater freedom of expression allowed under the policy of *glasnost* ('openness'), introduced after Mikhail Gorbachev became the Soviet leader in 1985, gave rise to an increasingly vociferous reform movement. Initially focused on human-rights, environmental and cultural issues, it became overtly economic and political with the establishment of the broad-based Reform Movement (Sąjūdis) in June 1988. Led by Vytautas Landsbergis, Sąjūdis won the multiparty election in February/March 1990. In March parliament proclaimed the restoration of Lithuanian indepen-

dence. This was a symbolic declaration, but highly significant in the context of crumbling central authority across the Soviet Union. The Soviet authorities responded by imposing an economic blockade (until June) and briefly resorted to force in January 1991. Independence became a fact after the abortive Soviet coup by communist hardliners in August. It was recognized by the Soviet Union the following month. The government initiated a range of market reforms in 1991 and 1992. Weakened by splits and held responsible for the dislocation associated with the economic transformation, Sąjūdis lost the October/November 1992 election to the Democratic Labour Party (LDDP), the successor to the Communist Party. The new government stressed its commitment to economic reform. LDDP leader Algirdas Brazauskas was elected president in February 1993. Lithuania was admitted to the Council of Europe in May. The last Russian troops left the country in August.

See also entries on specific institutions, organizations, parties, people, terms etc.

little constitution (Poland) *See* SMALL CONSTITUTION.

little Yugoslavia *See* RUMP YUGOSLAVIA.

Live Differently [Anders Gaan Leven] (AGALEV) Belgian political party. Founded in 1982, AGALEV is a left-alternative and environmentalist party in Flanders. At the November 1991 election it gained 4.9% of the vote and 7/212 seats. This made it, together with its Walloon counterpart, the Ecology Party (ÉCOLO), one of the most successful environmentalist movements in Europe. The leader is Johan Malcorps.

Ljubijankić, Irfan (1947–) Bosnian doctor and politician. He is an ear, nose and throat specialist. He was leader of the Bihać branch of the Muslim Democratic Action Party (SDA) and president of the regional assembly from 1991 until March 1993. He was appointed foreign minister the following October.

Ljubljana Shorthand for the Slovenian government. Ljubljana is the capital of Slovenia.

LKDS *See* CHRISTIAN DEMOCRATIC UNION OF LATVIA.

Lloyd's crisis Financial crisis and political controversy in the United Kingdom concerning the losses incurred by the Lloyd's insurance market and the implications for the ruling Conservative Party. Lloyd's of London specializes in insuring perceived high risks worldwide. It consists of nearly 300 syndicates, which in effect operate as small insurance companies and are represented by underwriting agents who assess risks. Lloyd's' underwriting capital is provided by around 17,000 'names', wealthy individuals who accept unlimited personal liability in case their syndicate makes a loss but otherwise gain substantial profits and tax advantages. Losses had been very rare in the corporation's 300-year history, but between 1991 and 1994 it reported shortfalls totalling 6.7 billion pounds (8.5 billion ecus) for the years 1988–91 (results are announced three years in arrears). The losses were due to a succession of natural disasters and massive pollution-related claims. Many names now face large demands for payment and possibly personal bankruptcy if they are unable to pay. The issue has a specific political dimension in that the affected names include up to 50 Conservative members of the House of Commons, the lower house of Parliament, who if declared bankrupt would have to resign their seats. Lloyd's operates several schemes and options which enable names to ease the burden by spreading payments over a period of time.

LM or **Lm** Abbreviation for the LIRA, the Maltese currency.

LN *See* NORTHERN LEAGUE.

LNNK *See* NATIONAL CONSERVATIVE PARTY OF LATVIA.

LO *See* DANISH TRADE UNION CONFEDERATION.

LO *See* NORWEGIAN TRADE UNION CONFEDERATION.

LO *See* SWEDISH TRADE UNION CONFEDERATION.

løgmaður [lagmand (Danish)] ('lawman') Head of government or chief minister of the Faroe Islands.

Løgting [Lagting (Danish)] Parliament of the Faroe Islands. It has 32 members elected for a four-year term by proportional representation in seven multimember constituencies.

Loire Country [Pays de la Loire] Region of France. Situated in the west along the Atlantic Ocean, the Loire Country has an area of 32,082 sq km and a population of 3,087,000. The capital is Nantes, and the other main cities are Angers, Le Mans and Saint-Nazaire. The economy is based on agriculture (cattle and pig farming, wine) and manufacturing (food processing, engineering, chemicals).

Lombard League [Lega Lombarda] Italian political party. Founded in 1979 and named after a medieval alliance, the League's main demand initially was for full autonomy for Lombardy, Italy's wealthiest region centred on Milan. It also called for an end to political corruption and the repatriation of foreigners. At the May 1990 local elections it gained 19% of the vote and became the second largest party in the region. In February 1991 it joined forces with other regional parties to form the NORTHERN LEAGUE. The leader is Umberto Bossi.

Lombardia *See* LOMBARDY.

Lombardy [Lombardia] Autonomous region of Italy. Situated in the north between the Alps and the Po river, Lombardy has an area of 23,857 sq km and a population of 8,941,000. It is Italy's most populous and leading industrial and commercial region, dominated by Milan [Milano], the capital and the country's second city and financial centre. Other major cities are Brescia and Bergamo. The economy is based on manufacturing (chemicals, metalworking, engineering, textiles), agriculture (cereals, fruit and vegetables), tourism, and financial and other services. The Duchy of Milan, broadly coextensive with Lombardy, was one of Italy's leading powers during the Middle Ages. It lost its independence in the 16th century and came successively under Spanish, Austrian, French and Austrian control. It became part of unified Italy in 1859.

Lomé Convention International agreement providing the framework for development assistance granted by the European Union (EU) to 70 developing countries organized in the Africa, Caribbean and Pacific Group of States (ACP Group). The first such convention was signed in Lomé, Togo, in 1975. It was renewed for the third time in December 1989. Lomé IV, similar in scope to previous agreements, allocates 12 billion ecus in financial aid (primarily loans and grants) to the ACP countries over a five-year period. It provides specifically for development projects, tax benefits, guaranteed prices for certain exports, preferential access to EU markets, environmental-protection measures, economic restructuring and other forms of assistance. Nearly all the ACP countries are former colonies of EU member states.

Lomé IV *See* LOMÉ CONVENTION.

London Shorthand for the British government. London is the capital of the United Kingdom.

London borough or **borough** British administrative division. The boroughs, 32 in number, are the constituent units of Greater London. Each has a council elected for a four-year term. It is formally headed by a mayor, elected for a one-year term; the executive leader is called the leader of the council. Borough councils are responsible for local services, such as housing, education and social services. The counterparts of the metropolitan boroughs in the other major conurbations of England, they combine the functions divided between county and district councils in the rest of the country. They inherited many of the powers and responsibilities of the Greater London Council, which was abolished in 1986. In recent years many of their powers have been transferred to bodies appointed by central government. The City of London, covering the historical centre of London, has a special administrative structure.

London Declaration *See* DOWNING STREET DECLARATION.

Longuet, Gérard (1946–) French civil servant and politician. He worked in local government and briefly in the prime minister's office in the 1970s. A member of parliament for the centre-right Republican Party (PR) from 1978–81 and since 1986, he held several junior ministerial posts in the Chirac government of 1986–88. He was elected general secretary of the PR in 1989 and leader in November 1990. He became minister of industry, posts and telecommunications and foreign trade in the centre-right government which took office in March 1993.

lord In the United Kingdom, the title of a man who has inherited or received a peerage. In both cases he is entitled to sit in the House of Lords, the upper house of Parliament. The female equivalent is 'lady'.

lord advocate (United Kingdom) *See* LAW OFFICERS.

lord chancellor British government minister. Nominally the most senior member of the government behind the prime minister, the lord chancellor is responsible for the administration of the justice system, is formally head of the judiciary, and also presides over the House of Lords, the upper house of Parliament.

Lord Chancellor's Department British government department. It is in charge of the administration of the judicial system in England and Wales. Its responsibilities are broadly similar to those of the justice ministry in other countries. It is headed by the lord chancellor.

lord high chancellor Formal title of the LORD CHANCELLOR.

lord-lieutenant British local government official. The lord-lieutenant is the sovereign's permanent representative in the counties of England and Wales and regions of Scotland. The incumbent is nominally the chief executive authority and head of the magistracy, but the office is representative and has no effective powers.

lord mayor British local government official. The lord mayor is the formal head of the council in a district in England and Wales that is designated a city. The post, usually rotated on an annual basis, has no executive powers.

lord of appeal in ordinary or **lord of appeal** In the United Kingdom, a member of the British House of Lords who is qualified to deal with judicial matters. Lords of appeal, commonly known as 'law lords', are former senior judges who effectively carry out the functions of the House of Lords as the final court of appeal. As a body they are commonly known as the Law Lords.

lord of Mann Head of state of Man. The title has been held by the king or queen of England, later Great Britain, since 1405. 'Mann' is an older form of 'Man'.

lord president of the Council British government minister. An office usually combined with that of leader of the House of Commons or another senior ministerial post, the lord president is responsible for administering the affairs of the Privy Council, which has a range of advisory, legislative and supervisory powers.

lord privy seal British government minister. The honorary office of lord privy seal is usually combined with that of leader of the House of Lords. The incumbent is the government's senior representative in the upper house and responsible for planning and supervising the passage of its legislative programme through the chamber. The privy seal is one of the seals of state.

lord provost British local government official. The lord provost is the formal head of the council in the four cities of Scotland (Glasgow, Edinburgh, Aberdeen and Dundee). The post carries no executive powers.

Lords Shorthand for the HOUSE OF LORDS, the upper house of the British Parliament.

Lorraine Region of France. Situated in the northeast and bordering on Germany and Luxemburg, Lorraine has an area of 23,547 sq km and a population of 2,299,000. German is spoken in some eastern rural areas. The capital is Metz, and the other main cities are Nancy and Thionville. The economy is based on manufacturing (electronics, steel) and agriculture. Lorraine has suffered considerable problems because of the decline of heavy industry and coal mining, and structural unemployment is high. Historically part of the Holy Roman Empire, Lorraine became part of France in stages between 1648 and 1766. It was ceded to Germany in 1871 after the Franco-Prussian War, returned to France in 1919 after the First World War, annexed by Germany during the Second World War, and again returned to France in 1945.

Löschnak, Franz (1940–) Austrian lawyer and politician. He worked for the Vienna city council until 1977, when he was appointed to a senior post in the Federal Chancellery (= prime minister's office), heading it from 1985–87. A member of the Social Democratic Party (SPÖ), he was appointed minister of health and the civil service in 1987 and became interior minister in February 1989.

lottizzazione ('allocation') In Italy, a system of patronage whereby senior posts in the public sector are shared out among members or appointees of political parties broadly in accordance with the latter's electoral strengths. A specific elaboration of the 'PARTYOCRACY' [partitocrazia] developed by the Christian Democratic Party (DC), Italian Socialist Party (PSI) and three smaller parties, the practice flourished from the 1950s until the exposure of the nationwide web of political corruption in 1992 and 1993 and the discrediting of the five ruling parties. It extended to all spheres of public life, from the civil service and local government to the state-owned utilities, banks, industrial concerns and broadcasting organizations. (Italy's public sector is the largest in Western Europe.) The main beneficiaries were the DC and PSI, but the largest opposition party, the Italian Communist Party (PCI, now the Democratic Left Party, PDS), also accepted the principle of *lottizzazione* in some spheres. Thus, senior posts in the two main state holding companies were 'allocated' to the DC and PSI respectively, and those in the three state television channels were 'allocated' to the DC, PSI and PCI/PDS respectively. *See also* CLIENTISM.

Low Countries Collective name for Belgium, Luxemburg and the Netherlands. It is generally used only as a geographical term; the more common usage in current affairs is 'Benelux countries' or 'Benelux', after the Benelux Economic Union.

Lower Austria [Niederösterreich] Federal province [Land] of Austria. Situated in the northeast around Vienna, but not including it, Lower Austria has an area of 19,172 sq km and a population of 1,472,000. The capital was transferred from Vienna, a province in its own right, to Sankt Pölten in 1986. The economy is based on agriculture (wheat, sugarbeets, wine) and manufacturing. The Provincial Assembly [Landtag] has 56 members elected for a five-year term. The main political parties are the centre-right Austrian People's Party (ÖVP), the Social Democratic Party (SPÖ), the far-right Freedom Party (FPÖ) and the right-wing Liberal Forum (LF). At the provincial election in May 1993 the ÖVP gained 26 seats, the SPÖ 20, the FPÖ seven and the LF three. The chief minister is Erwin Pröll.

Lower Normandy [Basse-Normandie] Region of France. Situated in the northwest along the Channel, Lower Normandy has an area of 17,589 sq km and a population of 1,398,000. The capital is Caen. The economy is based on agriculture (dairy farming), manufacturing (food processing) and tourism.

Lower Saxony [Niedersachsen] Federal state [Land] of Germany. Situated in the northwest, Lower Saxony has an area of 47,349 sq km and a population of 7,578,000. There is a small ethnic minority of 60,000 Frisians in the northwest. The capital is Hannover, and other main cities are Braunschweig, Osnabrück, Oldenburg and Göttingen. The economy is based on manufacturing (motor vehicles, chemicals, engineering) and agriculture (cereals, dairy and meat farming). Traditionally agricultural and relatively poor, the state has become highly industrialized since the 1950s. Political power is exercised by the State Assembly [Landtag], with 151 members elected for a four-year term, and a government headed by a minister-president. The main parties are the Social Democratic Party (SPD), the Christian Democratic Union (CDU), the Greens and the centrist Free Democratic Party (FDP). At the election in March 1994 the SPD gained 44.3% of the vote and 81 seats, the CDU 36.4% and 67 seats, the Greens 7.4% and 13 seats, and the FDP 4.4% and no seats. The minister-president is Gerhard Schröder. Historically divided into the Duchy, later Kingdom, of Hannover and several other states, Lower Saxony was established as a federal state in 1946.

loyalism In Northern Ireland (United Kingdom), an alternative term for 'UNIONISM', i.e. support for the territory's status as part of the United Kingdom and rejection of reunification with Ireland. The term 'loyalist' is usually reserved for the Protestant guerrilla groups active in the province, such as the Ulster Freedom Fighters (UFF) and Ulster Volunteer Force (UVF). (They declared a ceasefire in October 1994.)

LPS *See* LIBERAL PARTY OF SWITZERLAND.

LPSC *See* TRADE UNION CENTRE OF LITHUANIA.

Ls Abbreviation for the LATS, the Latvian currency.

LS (Yugoslavia) *See* LIBERAL ALLIANCE OF MONTENEGRO.

LSAP *See* LUXEMBURG SOCIALIST WORKERS' PARTY.

LSCG *See* LIBERAL ALLIANCE OF MONTENEGRO.

LSDP *See* SOCIAL DEMOCRATIC PARTY OF LITHUANIA.

LSM Abbreviation for the LIRA, the San Marino currency.

LSNS *See* LIBERAL NATIONAL SOCIAL PARTY.

LSU *See* LIBERAL SOCIAL UNION.

LT Abbreviation for Lithuania, used for international vehicle registrations, postal addresses etc.

LTL Abbreviation for the LITAS, the Lithuanian currency, used in banking etc.

Lubbers, Ruud (1939–) Dutch economist and politician. He was a director of the family engineering firm, Hollandia Kloos, from 1963–77. He served as minister of economic affairs from 1973–77. Elected to parliament for the Christian Democratic Appeal (CDA) in 1977, he became its parliamentary leader in 1978. He became prime minister in November 1982, heading a centre-right coalition until

1989 and then a centre-left coalition with the Labour Party (PvdA). He became the Netherlands' longest-serving prime minister in 1991. He did not stand for parliament in the May 1994 election, but remained in office in a caretaker capacity during the three-month coalition negotiations.

Lucona affair Political and business scandal in Austria which implicated two senior members of the Social Democratic Party of Austria (SPÖ). The *Lucona* was a cargo ship which exploded and sank in the Indian Ocean in 1977. It subsequently emerged that it had been carrying scrap metal rather than the valuable uranium-processing equipment for which it had been insured. It later also emerged that several leading politicians had obstructed investigations into the affair to protect the owner, Udo Proksch, a close friend of theirs. Karl Blecha, the interior minister, and Leopold Gratz, president of the National Council (= lower house of parliament) and a former foreign minister, resigned in January 1989. Proksch was arrested in October 1989 after 19 months on the run. A report by a parliamentary commission of inquiry published in June 1990 was highly critical of the two ministers' roles in the affair. In March 1991 Proksch was convicted of the murder of the six *Lucona* crew members and attempted fraud, and sentenced to 20 years' imprisonment, later increased on appeal to life. Gratz was convicted of false testimony and fined in October 1993. The case against Blecha was abandoned because he had already been convicted of similar charges in relation to the Noricum affair, involving illegal arms exports.

Łuczak, Aleksander (1943–) Polish historian, academic and politician. A specialist in the history of farmers' movements, he worked as a researcher for the United Peasant Party (ZSL) from 1966 and was appointed a lecturer at Warsaw University in 1976 and professor in 1991. He was a deputy education minister from 1987–88. He has held several senior posts in the ZSL and its successor, the Polish Peasant Party (PSL). Elected to parliament in 1989, he was appointed a deputy prime minister

in charge of state administration and education minister in the left-wing coalition which took office in October 1993.

LUF Abbreviation for the FRANC, the Luxemburg currency, used in banking etc.

Luftwaffe ('Airforce') German name for the German airforce.

Luik, Jüri (1966–) Estonian journalist and politician. After working for the weekly magazine *Vikerkaar* from 1988–90 and then for the Estonian Institute in 1990–91, he was appointed to a senior post in the foreign ministry when Estonia regained its independence in September 1991. He was elected to parliament for the right-wing Fatherland (Isamaa) alliance in 1992. He was appointed a minister without portfolio in charge of relations with Russia, became defence minister in August 1993, and foreign minister in January 1994.

Lusatians *See* SORBS.

Lusitania Literary name for Portugal. Lusitania was a province of the Roman Empire broadly coextensive with modern Portugal.

lustrace *See* LUSTRATION.

lustration [lustrace] In the Czech Republic, the process of exposing people who collaborated with the security agencies during communist rule (1948–89). The term – taken from the Latin *lustratio*, 'purifying sacrifice' – has also been adopted in other former communist countries. *See* DECOMMUNIZATION *and* SCREENING.

Lux, Josef (1956–) Czech agronomist and politician. He worked in a agricultural cooperative in the 1980s. Elected to parliament for the Christian Democratic Union - Czechoslovak People's Party (KDU-ČSL) in June 1990, he was elected party leader the following September. In July 1992 he was appointed a deputy prime minister and agriculture minister of the Czech Republic.

Luxembourg and **Luxembourg ...** *See* LUXEMBURG *and* LUXEMBURG ....

Luxemburg [Lëtzebuerg (Letzeburgish), Luxembourg (French), Luxemburg (German)] Country in western Europe. *Official data.* Name: Grand Duchy of Luxembourg [Grousherzogdem Lëtzebuerg / Grand Duché de Luxembourg / Grossherzogtum Luxemburg]; capital: Luxemburg [Lëtzebuerg/ Luxembourg/Luxemburg]; form of government: parliamentary monarchy; head of state: grand duke/duchess; head of government: prime minister; flag: three horizontal stripes, red, white and light blue; national holiday: 23 June (National Day); languages: Letzeburgish, French and German; religion: none; currencies: franc (F) = 100 centimes, Belgian franc; abbreviation: L.

Geography. The smallest of the three Benelux countries, Luxemburg has an area of 2,585 sq km. Land-locked, it is bordered by Germany in the east, France in the south, and Belgium in the west and north. The northern third of the country consists of low mountains, an extension of the Ardennes range; the southern two-thirds consists of a low plateau and hill lands. Some 25% of the land is arable, another 20% is covered by pastures and 21% is forested. The main rivers are the Moselle [Mosel], Sûre and Our. The climate is humid continental, moderated by temperate marine influences; summers are mild, winters cold; rainfall is moderate.

Demography. Luxemburg has a population of 392,000. Population density is 152 per sq km. Some 84% of the people live in urban areas, mainly the city of Luxemburg (home to around a fifth of the total population) and in the south. Some 72.5% of the population are Luxemburgers. Foreign nationals account for the remaining 27.5%, and include citizens of Portugal (9.0% of the total), Italy (5.4%), France (3.4%), Belgium (2.5%) and Germany (2.4%). The main languages are Letzeburgish (a form of German), French and German; the latter two are the dominant written languages of administration and commerce respectively. In religious terms nearly all the people are nominally Roman Catholics.

Sociography. Luxemburg scores 0.908 on the United Nations human development index (HDI), ranking 17th in the world and 13th among 32 European countries. There are 20 doctors and 117 hospital beds for every 10,000 people.

Education is compulsory between the ages of six and 15. There is one teacher for every 12 students. Enrolment is 82% at the secondary level and 21% at the tertiary level. The literacy rate is virtually 100%. Real annual income per head (in terms of purchasing power) is US$ 20,800.

Infrastructure and communications. Luxemburg has a highly developed transport and communications network. There are 5,040 km of paved roads and 183,000 passenger cars (481 per 1,000 people), 270 km of railways and 37 km of navigable waterways. There is an inland port at Mertert. The main airport is at Luxemburg (Findel). There are five daily newspapers, with a combined circulation of 144,000 (380 per 1,000 people). There are 230,000 radio receivers, 100,000 television sets and 230,000 telephones in use (respectively 604, 262 and 604 per 1,000 people, among the highest in Europe).

Economic structure. The Luxemburg economy is highly developed and one of the most trade-oriented in the world (exports account for three-quarters of national income), with close links to its neighbours. Luxemburg maintains a customs and monetary union with Belgium. The economy is based on iron and steel production, the traditional mainstay, and increasingly also on financial services and electronics. Since the late 1980s economic performance has been marked by sustained growth (averaging around 3% per year), low inflation (around 3%) and low unemployment (below 2%); on these criteria the Luxemburg economy is among the most successful in Europe.

Services contribute 63% of GDP (finance 13%), industry contributes 35% (manufacturing 26%) and agriculture 2%. Some 20% of the labour force is employed in trade, 19% in manufacturing, 12% in financial services and 9% in construction; immigrant workers (from Portugal, Italy, France, Germany and Belgium), either resident locally or in the neighbouring countries, make up a third of the total. The main crops grown are cereals (barley, oats, wheat) and potatoes; horticulture (grapes and other fruit) and

livestock raising (cattle) are also important agricultural activities. There are no
significant mineral resources. The main
industry is iron and steel production and
other metalworking (aluminium); other
important branches are chemicals, rubber
(tyres), engineering, electronics, textiles
and food processing. Banking, insurance
and other financial services are an important source of foreign exchange, as
is tourism. The main energy sources
are hydroelectric power and imported
fossil fuels; 13% of export earnings are
required to cover net fuel imports. The
main exports are iron and steel (38% of
the total), plastic and rubber products
(13%), machinery and transport equipment (12%), textiles (6%) and chemicals
(5%); basic manufactures account for
around two-thirds of the total. The main
imports are basic manufactures, machinery and transport equipment, fuels and
chemicals. The main trading partners are:
exports: Germany (29%), France (17%),
Belgium (17%), Netherlands, United
Kingdom; imports: Belgium (39%),
Germany (31%), France (12%); five-
sixths of all trade is with other European
Union (EU) countries.

The Luxemburg Monetary Institute
[Institut Monétaire Luxembourgeois]
discharges some of the responsibilities
of a central bank. The main employers'
association is the Federation of Luxemburg Industrialists (FÉDIL); the main
labour organizations are the General
Confederation of Labour - Luxemburg
(CGT-L), Independent Trade Union
Confederation - Luxemburg (OGB-L)
and Luxemburg Christian Trade Union
Confederation (LCBG).

Political structure. Luxemburg is a
parliamentary monarchy on the basis of
a constitution adopted in 1868 and last
amended in 1956. Executive power is
formally vested in the grand duke/
duchess, who may intervene in legislative
questions and has certain judicial powers;
effectively it is exercised by the prime
minister and the council of ministers.
Legislative power is vested in the
Chamber of Deputies [Chambre des
Députés], whose 60 members are elected

for a five-year term by a system of
proportional representation. The Council
of State [Conseil d'État], whose 21 members are appointed for life by the grand
duke/duchess, has advisory and some
legislative powers. Voting is compulsory
for all citizens over the age of 18. Judicial
power is ultimately vested in the High
Court of Justice [Haute Cour de la
Justice]. Administratively the country is
divided into 25 communes [commune,
pl. -s]; the higher-level 12 cantons and
three districts have no administrative or
political functions.

The main political parties are the
Christian Social People's Party (CSV),
Luxemburg Socialist Workers' Party
(LSAP), Democratic Party (DP), Action
Committee for Democracy and Pension
Justice (ADR), Green List Ecological
Initiative (GLEI) and Green Alternative
Party (GAP). At the general election in
June 1994 the CSV gained 31.5% of the
vote and 21/60 seats, the LSAP 24.8%
and 17 seats, the DP 18.8% and 12 seats,
the Greens (GLEI and GAP) 10.9% and
five seats, the ADR 7.0% and five seats.
The government is formed by a centrist
coalition of the CSV and LSAP, with
Jacques Santer as prime minister (also
responsible for budget, culture). Other
senior ministers are Jacques Poos (deputy
prime minister, foreign affairs, foreign
trade, development cooperation), Jean
Spautz (interior, housing), Jean-Claude
Juncker (finance, labour), Robert Goebbels
(economy, public works, energy) and
Marc Fischbach (justice, education,
scientific research). The head of state is
Grand Duke Jean, who succeeded to the
throne in November 1964; the heir is
Prince Henri.

Security and international affiliations.
The Luxemburg armed forces number
800 (all army). There is no conscription.
Luxemburg is a member of the Benelux
Economic Union, Conference on Security
and Cooperation in Europe (CSCE),
Council of Europe, European Economic
Area (EEA), European Union (EU), North
Atlantic Treaty Organization (NATO)
and Western European Union (WEU),
as well as the Francophone Community

and Organization for Economic Cooperation and Development (OECD) and the United Nations and its specialized agencies.

History. The area of modern Luxemburg was conquered by the Romans in 51 BC and by the Germanic Franks in the late 5th century AD. The various partitions of the Frankish Empire after the death of Emperor Charlemagne in 814 eventually left the region within the East Frankish Kingdom, later the Holy Roman or German Empire. Historical Luxemburg – including the modern Belgian province of the same name – was established as a separate fief in 963, became a county in 1060 and a duchy in 1354. In the 13th and 14th centuries the House of Luxemburg was a major force in imperial politics: its members were elected to the imperial crown on four occasions between 1308 and 1437, and also held the royal crown of Bohemia, one of the most prestigious fiefs and prosperous states, on several occasions after 1346. Luxemburg was ceded to Burgundy in 1443 and, along with the other Burgundian possessions in the Low Countries, passed to the Habsburgs in 1482. From 1579–1795 it formed part of the Southern Netherlands (broadly coextensive with modern Belgium and Luxemburg), which was ruled by Spain until 1713 and then by Austria. It was annexed by France in 1795.

As part of the post-Napoleonic reorganization of Europe, the Congress of Vienna in 1815 established Luxemburg as a nominally independent grand duchy within the German Confederation, but it was effectively a Dutch dependency since the Dutch king was made the grand duke. Most of French-speaking western Luxemburg joined the anti-Dutch revolt in 1830. The grand duchy was divided the following year, the west becoming part of the new state of Belgium. The independent status of the remaining grand duchy was reaffirmed in 1839. (This is the traditional date for full independence.) The formal link with Germany was broken with the dissolution of the German Confederation in 1866. The following year the Prussian garrison was withdrawn and the major

powers guaranteed the country's neutrality. The personal union with the Dutch royal house was dissolved in 1890. During the First World War (1914–18) Luxemburg was occupied by German troops. Universal adult suffrage was introduced in 1918. In 1922 Belgium and Luxemburg established a customs and monetary union. During the Second World War (1939–45) the country was again occupied by the German army from 1940–44 and formally annexed by Germany in 1942.

Abandoning its policy of neutrality, Luxemburg became a founding member of the North Atlantic Treaty Organization (NATO) in 1949. The previous year it had joined Belgium and the Netherlands in the Benelux Economic Union and in 1958 it became a founding member of the European Economic Community (EEC), now the European Union (EU). Since 1945 political life has been dominated by the Christian Social People's Party (CSV), the Luxemburg Socialist Workers' Party (LSAP) and the right-wing Democratic Party (DP). All governments since 1947 have been coalitions of any two of these parties, with the CSV the senior partner except for a period of opposition from 1974–79. A CSV-DP coalition in power since July 1979 under Pierre Werner was replaced by a CSV-LSAP coalition in July 1984 under his party colleague Jacques Santer. In the 1960s and 70s the economy was successfully diversified to compensate for the decline of the steel industry, the mainstay since the late 19th century.

See also entries on specific institutions, organizations, parties, people, terms etc.

Luxemburg Shorthand for the Luxemburg government. The city of Luxemburg is the national capital.

Luxemburg Shorthand for the European Court of Justice (ECJ), an institution of the European Union (EU). The Court sits in Luxemburg. The city is also the seat of several other EU institutions and bodies, including the Court of Auditors and the secretariat of the European Parliament.

Luxemburg Christian Trade Union Confederation [Lëtzebuerger Chrëschtleche Gewerkschaftsbond] (LCGB) Luxemburg trade-union federation. Founded in 1921, the LCGB has a total membership of 23,000 (an eighth of the labour force). It has close links with the Christian Social People's Party (CSV). The president is Marcel Glesener, the general secretary Robert Weber.

Luxemburg compromise In the European Union (EU), the principle that a member state may veto a piece of legislation subject to majority voting if it deems a 'vital' national interest to be at stake. It is based on an informal agreement – with no status in EU law – from January 1966, which ended a six-month crisis in the then European Economic Community (EEC) triggered by the French government's rejection of the extension of majority voting. In the following years most decisions continued to be taken by unanimity rather than majority, so that the 'Luxemburg compromise' was rarely invoked. Under the 1986 Single European Act and the Maastricht Treaty establishing European Union (in force since November 1993) QUALIFIED MAJORITY VOTING, i.e. broadly two-thirds, was extended to a wide range of policy areas.

Luxemburg Palace [Palais de Luxembourg] Shorthand for the French SENATE, the upper house of parliament. The Palais de Luxembourg in Paris is the seat of the Senate.

Luxemburg Socialist Workers' Party [Lëtzebuerger Sozialistesch Aarbechterpartei (Letzeburgish), Parti Ouvrier Socialiste Luxembourgeois (French)] (LSAP or POSL) Luxemburg political party. Founded in 1902 and renamed in 1945, the LSAP is a mainstream democratic socialist party. Traditionally the country's second-largest party, it has participated in a number of coalition governments since 1945, most recently from 1974–79 and since 1984. At the June 1994 election it gained 24.8% of the vote and 17/60 seats. The leader is Jacques Poos, the party president is Ben Fayot.

Luxemburgish *See* LETZEBURGISH.

Lv Abbreviation for the LEV, the Bulgarian currency.

LV Abbreviation for Latvia, used for international vehicle registrations, postal addresses etc.

LVL Abbreviation for the LATS, the Latvian currency, used in banking etc.

Lyðveldid Ísland ('Republic of Iceland') Official name of Iceland.

Lykketoft, Mogens (1946–) Danish economist and politician. He worked for the Danish Trade Union Confederation (LO) from 1975 until his election to parliament for the Social Democratic Party (SD) in 1981. He was minister of taxation in 1981–82 and became minister of finance in the centre-left coalition formed in January 1993.

Lyssarides, Vassos (1920–) Cypriot doctor and politician. He has been a member of parliament since 1960 and leader of the Unified Democratic Union - Socialist Party (EDEK-SK) since its foundation in February 1969.

LZS *See* FARMERS' UNION OF LATVIA.

M (Estonia) *See* MODERATES.

M Abbreviation for Malta, used for international vehicle registrations, postal addresses etc.

M (Sweden) *See* MODERATE COALITION PARTY.

M-4 Codename for a French submarine-launched ballistic missile system, the main component of the country's strategic nuclear forces. Introduced in 1985 and deployed on five submarines, the 80 M-4 missiles have a range of 5,000 km and carry six multiple reentry warheads each.

maakond (pl. -ed) Estonian administrative division, usually translated as 'district' or 'county'. Each of the 15 *maakonded* is governed by a council [volikogu] elected for a three-year term. They are responsible for most local services. Tallinn, Tartu and four other cities are administered separately and have similar powers.

Maastricht Treaty Shorthand for the TREATY ON EUROPEAN UNION, agreed by the member states of the European Community (EC) at a summit in the Dutch city of Maastricht in December 1991 and signed there in February 1992.

Macedonia [Makedonija] Country in southeastern Europe, formerly part of Yugoslavia.

Official data. Name: Republic of Macedonia [Republika Makedonija]; capital: Skopje; form of government: parliamentary republic; head of state: president; head of government: prime minister; flag: red with a 16-pointed yellow star ('Star of Vergina') in the centre; national holiday: 8 September (Independence Day); language: Macedonian; religion: none; currency: denar (pl. -i) (Den) = 100 deni; abbreviation: MAK.

Geography. Macedonia has an area of 25,713 sq km. Land-locked, it is bordered by Yugoslavia in the north, Bulgaria in the east, Greece in the south, and Albania in the west. Most of the terrain consists of uplands and mountains, including the Jakupica, Plačkovica, Kožuf and Nidže ranges. These are interspersed with deep basins and valleys, the most important of which is the Vardar valley, which runs north-south through the country. Some 16% of the land is arable, another 26% is covered by pastures and 37% is forested. The climate is mediterranean in the Vardar valley (with hot summers and mild winters) and humid continental in the mountains (with hot summers and cold winters); rainfall is moderate.

Demography. Macedonia has a population of 2,063,000. Population density is 82 per sq km (land area). Most people live in the Vardar valley and western half of the country, 54% live in urban areas, and around a quarter in Skopje and its suburbs. Important regional centres are Tetovo, Kumanovo and Bitolj. In ethnic terms 64.6% of the people are Macedonians, 21.0% Albanians, 4.8% Turks, 2.7% Gipsies, 2.2% Serbs, and 1.7% Slav Muslims (considered an ethnic group in former Yugoslavia). Most Albanians live in the northwest; they are thought to be considerably underrepresented in the official figures and may account for up to a third of the total population. Gipsies are also underrepresented in the figures and are thought to number around 80,000. Macedonia has also taken in around 40,000 refugees from Bosnia-Herzegovina, Croatia and Serbia. There are substantial ethnic Macedonian communities in neighbouring Bulgaria (225,000) and Greece (150,000) and in Germany. In religious terms most Macedonians are nominally Macedonian Orthodox Christians, and the Albanians and Turks are Sunni Muslims.

Sociography. Macedonia was the least developed republic in former Yugoslavia, which scored 0.857 on the United Nations human development index (HDI) in 1990, ranking 37th in the world and 23rd among 27 European countries. There are 22 doctors and 55 hospital beds for every 10,000 people. Education is compulsory between the ages of seven and 15. There is one teacher for every 20 students. Enrolment is 28% at the secondary level and 10% at the tertiary level. The literacy rate is 89%. GNP per head (unadjusted for purchasing power) was around US$ 1,400 in 1990 and around US$ 750 in 1993.

Infrastructure and communications. Macedonia's transport and communications network is one of the least˙developed in Europe; the electronic media have a much wider reach than the press. There are 5,090 km of paved roads and 231,000 passenger cars (114 per 1,000 people), 690 km of railways and no navigable waterways. The nearest major port is Salonika in Greece. The main airport is at Skopje. There are five daily newspapers, with a combined circulation of around 80,000 (40 per 1,000 people). There are 365,000 radio receivers, 331,000 television sets and 357,000 telephones in use (respectively 179, 163 and 176 per 1,000 people).

Economic structure. The Macedonian economy is based on manufacturing, agriculture, mining and tourism. Although essentially developed and diversified, it is in need of major investment and restructuring. The transition from a command to a market-based economy initiated in the early 1990s, the disruption of traditional economic links following the disintegration of the Yugoslav federation in 1991/92 and the difficulties resulting from the tense relations with Greece and Yugoslavia are causing severe dislocation and have led to falls in industrial and agricultural production and the collapse of the tourism industry in particular. Between 1990 and 1993 GDP contracted by around a third, inflation averaged around 625% per year, and unemployment rose to around 40%. There were some signs of recovery in 1993 and 1994.

Services contribute 33% of GDP, industry contributes 53% (manufacturing around 43%), and agriculture, forestry and fisheries 14%. Some 39% of the labour force is employed in manufacturing, 13% in trade, 9% in construction and 8% in farming and forestry. Dairy farming (cheese, milk) and livestock raising (sheep, cattle) are the main agricultural activities; horticulture (fruit and vegetables) is also important; the main crops grown are cereals (wheat, barley, maize, rice), tobacco, cotton, oilseeds and sugarbeets. Forestry is also important, as was tourism until 1991. The main mineral resources are coal, iron, lead, zinc, nickel, copper, chromium and manganese. The main industry is textiles (incl. footwear); other important branches are food processing, electrical goods, metalworking, engineering, tobacco processing, chemicals, building materials (cement), wood processing and ceramics. The main energy sources are hydroelectric power and imported fossil fuels; 37% of export earnings are required to cover net fuel imports. The main exports are textiles and clothing (22% of the total), machinery (12%), foodstuffs (esp. fruit, cotton, meat) (6%), chemicals (5%) and tobacco and tobacco products (5%). The main imports are fuels, machinery and transport equipment and foodstuffs. The main trading partners are Germany, Bulgaria, Albania, Greece, Slovenia, Croatia and Yugoslavia (detailed figures n.a.). Net invisible earnings (remittances from Macedonians living and working abroad, development assistance, tourism receipts) traditionally account for a significant share of GNP.

The National Bank of Macedonia [Narodna Banka na Makedonija] is the central bank. There are several employers' and business associations and labour organizations.

Political structure. Macedonia is a parliamentary republic on the basis of a constitution adopted in November 1991, replacing one defining it as part of the Yugoslav federation. The head of state is the president, who is elected for a five-year term; if no candidate gains an absolute majority of votes, a run-off is held between the top two candidates. The president is commander of the armed forces, appoints the prime minister and has several other powers. Executive power is vested in the prime minister and the council of ministers, who are elected by the legislature. Legislative power is vested in the Assembly of the Republic [Sobranie na Republika], whose 120 members are elected for a four-year term by a system of majority voting. All citizens over the age of 18 are entitled to vote. Judicial power is ultimately vested in the Supreme Court [Vrhoven Sud]; the Constitutional Court [Ustaven Sud] adjudicates on constitutional matters. Administratively the country is divided into 30 districts [opština, pl. opštini].

The main political parties are the Internal Macedonian Revolutionary Organization - Democratic Party for Macedonian National Unity (VMRO-DPMNE), Social Democratic Alliance of Macedonia (SDSM, the successor to the League of Communists of Macedonia - Democratic Reform Party, SKM-PDP), Party for Democratic Prosperity - National Democratic Party (PDP-NDP or PPD-PND), Reform Forces of Macedonia - Liberal Party (RSM-LP, the successor to the Alliance of Reform Forces of Yugoslavia, SRSJ) and Socialist Party of Macedonia (SPM). At the general election in December 1990 the VMRO-DPMNE gained 37/120 seats, the SKM-PDP 31 seats, the PPD and PND (then separate parties) 25 seats, the SRSJ 19 seats, and the SPM four seats. The government is formed by a centre-left coalition of the SDSM, PPD-PND and RSM-LP, with Branko Crvenkovski as prime minister. Other senior ministers are Stevo Crvenkovski (deputy prime minister, foreign affairs), Bekir Zhuta (deputy prime minister), Risto Ivanov (deputy prime minister), Ljubomir Frčkovski (interior), Vlado Popovski (defence), Dzhevdet Hajredini (finance), Petruš Stefanov (economy) and Tuše Gošev (justice). The head of state is President Kiro Gligorov, who was elected in January 1991.

Security and international affiliations. The Macedonian armed forces number 10,400 (all army); they are in the process of formation. Military service is compulsory and consists of nine months' basic training. Some 1,000 United Nations troops of the UN Protection Force - Macedonia Command (UNPROFOR-M) are stationed in Macedonia.

Macedonia is a member of the Central European Initiative (CEI) and Conference on Security and Cooperation in Europe (CSCE), as well as the United Nations and its specialized agencies. It has applied for membership of the Council of Europe.

History. The Greek kingdom of Macedonia, centred on the Axiós river plain at the head of the Thermaic Gulf, was established in the 7th century BC. Under Philip II (359–36) it became the dominant power in Greece. At the end of his reign it included what became the historical region of Macedonia – northern Greece, the current Republic of Macedonia and modern southwestern Bulgaria – as well as the Greek region of Thessaly to the south and Thrace to the east. The conquest of the Persian Empire by Philip's son Alexander the Great (336–23) paved the way for the spread of Greek culture throughout the Eastern Mediterranean region. After Alexander's death his empire was partitioned. Rump Macedonia remained the dominant power in the region, but the Greek city states eventually regained their independence with the help of the Romans. The Roman Republic annexed Macedonia in 148 BC. Christianity became the dominant religion in the 4th century AD. In 395 the region was allocated to the Eastern Roman Empire, which became the Greek-dominated Byzantine Empire. During the Europe-wide migrations it was invaded by Goths, Huns and Avars. In the 6th century Slavic peoples, migrating from the north, settled in the region and converted to Orthodox Christianity. Most of historical Macedonia formed part of Bulgaria from 681 until its subjugation by Byzantium in 1118, became part of the second Bulgarian state in 1185, was regained by Byzantium in 1246 and fell to Serbia in 1330; Salonika and the coastal areas remained Byzantine throughout this period. The whole region was conquered by the Ottoman Turks in 1371. During the five centuries of Ottoman rule the peasants were reduced to serfs of Turkish landowners, but there were no attempts to turkify or islamicize the population. Central authority was generally weak in the later period, so that local governors had considerable powers, which they frequently exercised arbitrarily.

In the 19th century Macedonia, a strategic crossroads at the heart of the Balkan peninsula, ethnically mixed and historically disputed, became the subject of rival claims by the emerging post-Ottoman states – Greece, Serbia, Bulgaria and later Albania – and the 'Macedonian question' became a major international issue. A national movement also emerged at this time. After the Russo-Turkish War of 1877–78 Macedonia was allocated to newly independent Bulgaria under the Treaty of San Stefano. But at the Congress of Berlin later in the year the major powers, fearful of growing Russian influence in the Balkan region, forced its return to the Ottoman Empire. In 1903 there was a major uprising against Ottoman rule. At the end of the Second Balkan War (1913) historical Macedonia was partitioned between Greece, Bulgaria and Serbia, the latter gaining the area comprising the present republic. During the First World War (1914–18) the region was again occupied by Bulgaria. As part of Serbia, Macedonia joined the new Kingdom of Serbs, Croats and Slovenes in 1918, renamed Yugoslavia in 1929. During the Second World War (1939–45) it was overrun by the German, Italian and Bulgarian armies in 1941 and again allocated to Bulgaria.

On liberation in 1945 the Communists, led by Josip Broz Tito, took power throughout Yugoslavia. The Macedonians were recognized as a 'nation' in the new federation, Macedonia was established as a separate republic, and the Macedonian language was given official status. The regime suppressed political opposition and implemented orthodox communist economic policies. After breaking with the Soviet Union in 1948, it pursued more pragmatic and liberal policies. The independent Macedonian Orthodox Church was established in 1967. Like the other republics, Macedonia was given greater autonomy in 1974. It was by far the poorest republic during the communist period, and there was substantial emigration to the northern republics and other European countries. As Communist authority crumbled in the late 1980s, new nationalist and ethnic parties emerged. In the multiparty election in November/ December 1990 the Internal Macedonian Revolutionary Organization - Democratic Party for Macedonian National Unity (VMRO-DPMNE), the reform-minded League of Communists (later renamed the Social Democratic Alliance, SDSM) and two formations representing the ethnic Albanian community emerged as the largest parties. Kiro Gligorov, a prominent leader in the 1970s, was elected president in January 1991. The all-party coalition collapsed in October and the VMRO-DPMNE went into opposition. As the Yugoslav federation disintegrated, Macedonia initially favoured its continuation in a looser form, but in November 1991 parliament declared independence and adopted a new constitution. For historical reasons Greece objected to the new state's use of the name 'Macedonia' and refused to recognize it. Many countries thereupon also withheld diplomatic recognition. The international isolation exacerbated an already deep economic crisis caused by the transition to a market-based economy and the disruption of traditional links with the other former Yugoslav republics. In April 1993 the country was admitted to the United Nations under the temporary name of Former Yugoslav Republic of Macedonia (FYROM). The member states of the European Union (EU) except Greece recognized it under this name in December, as did Russia and the United States in February 1994. That month Greece closed the border between the two countries and imposed a trade blockade. Domestic tensions were heightened by growing Albanian complaints of discrimination.

See also entries on specific institutions, organizations, parties, people, terms etc.

Macedonia name question Dispute between Greece and Macedonia about the use of the name 'Macedonia'. When the former Yugoslav republic of Macedonia declared its independence in November 1991, Greece refused to recognize it on the grounds that its name implied a territorial claim on the neighbouring northern Greek region of the same name. (Since the creation of the republic within Yugoslavia in 1944, Greece has always referred to it by the name of its capital, Skopje.) The Greek government also objected to certain 'expansionist' passages in the new Macedonian constitution and the incorporation of what it considered an ancient Greek symbol, the 'Star of Vergina', into the new flag. Because of the controversy the European Community (EC, now the European Union, EU) and the United States initially withheld diplomatic recognition from the new state. It was admitted, with Greek agreement, to the United Nations under the temporary name of Former Yugoslav Republic of Macedonia (FYROM) in April 1993. The EU states except Greece recognized it under this name in December. In February 1994 Greece closed the border between the two countries and imposed a trade blockade on all goods except food and medicine. (Most of land-locked Macedonia's foreign trade passed through the Greek port of Salonika.) The move was strongly criticized by the other EU states and the European Commission, the EU's administrative and executive arm, which initiated legal proceedings against Greece. The name dispute is the latest manifestation of the long-standing controversy over the historical region of Macedonia (*see* MACEDONIA: HISTORY).

Mackay, James (from 1979 **Lord Mackay**) (1927–) British lawyer and politician. He lectured briefly in mathematics, qualified as a lawyer in 1955 and practised in his native Scotland. Ennobled in 1979, he was appointed lord advocate of Scotland, the country's senior law officer. In 1985 he was appointed a law lord, a member of the House of Lords qualified to deal with judicial matters. In June 1987 he was appointed lord chancellor (= justice minister) in the Conservative government.

Madama Palace [Palazzo Madama] Shorthand for the Italian SENATE, the upper house of parliament. The Palazzo Madama in Rome is the seat of the Senate.

Madeira Autonomous region of Portugal. Situated in the North Atlantic Ocean 900 km southwest of the mainland off the coast of North Africa, the Madeira archipelago consists of two inhabited islands and five uninhabited islets, with a total area of 794 sq km and a population of 253,000. The capital is Funchal. The economy is based on agriculture (sugar, wine, bananas), tourism and fishing. The dominant political parties are the centre-

right Social Democratic Party (PSD) and the Socialist Party (PS). At the election in October 1992, the PSD gained 39/55 seats in the regional legislature. Madeira was uninhabited when it became a Portuguese possession in 1420. Wide-ranging autonomy was granted in 1976.

Madrid Shorthand for the MADRID COMMUNITY, an autonomous region of Spain. The full name is commonly used to distinguish the region from the city and the province of Madrid.

Madrid Shorthand for the Spanish government. Madrid is the capital of Spain.

Madrid Community [Comunidad de Madrid] Autonomous community or region of Spain. Situated in the centre around Madrid, the national capital and Spain's largest city, the region has an area of 7,995 sq km and a population of 4,910,000. The economy is based on manufacturing (motor vehicles, engineering), public and other services, agriculture (cattle farming, cereals) and tourism. The main political parties are the centre-right People's Party (PP), the Spanish Socialist Workers' Party (PSOE) and the United Left (IU). At the May 1991 election the PP gained 47 seats in the 101-member legislature, the PSOE 41 and the IU 13. Historically part of New Castile, the province of Madrid was established as an autonomous region in 1983.

MAE Abbreviation for Ministero degli Affari Esteri ('Ministry of Foreign Affairs'), the Italian foreign ministry.

Mafia Italian crime syndicate. Based in Sicily but active throughout the country and internationally, the Mafia is not so much a single structured organization as a network of groups, known as 'clans' and 'families', who generally recognize each other's spheres of influence and accept a specific hierarchy among themselves. With roots going back to a 13th-century secret society opposed to foreign rule, the *mafie* were originally small private armies protecting the property of absentee landlords. During the 18th century they became powerful enough to control estates and exact money from landlords in return for protection of their crops. From the late 19th century the

Mafia became involved in criminal activities and expanded to other parts of Italy and the United States, where it called itself the Cosa Nostra ('Our Affair'). Its strength lay in a code of conduct based on family and personal loyalty, secrecy (the vow of silence, *omertà*, obliged members never to assist the authorities), and summary death for any transgressors. In Sicily the Mafia also benefited from local people's traditional antipathy to the authorities and acceptance of its alternative system of patronage (by granting protection in return for payments). Through extortion, intimidation, corruption, smuggling, kidnapping and assassination the Mafia extended its influence into all levels of society in Sicily and beyond. It controlled the construction sector in particular and had close links with local politicians. In the 1970s it also became involved in drug trafficking worldwide. In 1983–84 the clans fought an internal war for control over the huge profits from this trade. Unprecedented testimony from Mafia informers, known as *pentiti* ('repenters'), resulted in the conviction of 338 leading members of the organization, including Michele Greco, a key clan leader, in a 'maxi-trial' in December 1987. Further trials relying mainly on the evidence of informers followed. Greco and others were released on appeal in February 1991 but rearrested on the basis of a government decree. In August 1992, following the assassination of two senior magistrates, Giovanni Falcone and Paolo Borsellino, parliament adopted a range of special measures to combat organized crime. They included the establishment of the Anti-Mafia Investigation Directorate (DIA), which was granted wide-ranging powers. In October a magistrate's report linked one of the country's leading politicians, Giulio Andreotti, to the Mafia, and in November three members of parliament were accused of association with the Mafia. Salvatore ('Toto') Riina, head of the Corleone clan and allegedly the 'boss of bosses', was arrested in January 1993 after 25 years on the run. The investigations leading to Riina's arrest and the

exposure of endemic political corruption in 1993 also revealed the close links between the Mafia and the then ruling Christian Democratic Party (DC) at all levels of government, as well as the extent to which Mafia activities and bosses had been protected by the authorities, including members of the judiciary, over the years. The Mafia was thus shown to be a key player in Italy's perceived 'HIDDEN GOVERNMENT' [sottogoverno]. Riina, Greco and 13 other Mafia leaders went on trial for murder and other crimes in November 1993. *See also* MAFIAS.

mafias Collective name for the criminal organizations active in southern Italy and beyond. They include the Sicilian Mafia, the oldest and largest syndicate; the Camorra, based in Naples and the Campania region; the 'Ndrangheta, based in Calabria; the Sacra Corona, based in Apulia; and others. They are involved in extortion, corruption, kidnapping and other criminal activities throughout the region. The political corruption scandals that broke in 1993 also revealed extensive links between the mafias and leading politicians, businesspeople and some members of the judiciary. Over the years a range of measures has been adopted to combat the mafias, most recently the creation of the Anti-Mafia Investigation Directorate (DIA), the granting of special powers to the police and the judiciary and the deployment of troops in 1992. The term 'mafia' is now also applied to crime syndicates in other countries, such as those that have emerged in Eastern Europe and the former Soviet Union since the collapse of communist rule. *See also* MAFIA *and* ITALIAN CORRUPTION SCANDALS.

mafioso (pl. mafiosi) Member of the Mafia, the crime syndicate based on the Italian island of Sicily. The name is also applied generically to anyone involved in organized crime in other regions of southern Italy and beyond.

Maghrébins In France, a collective name for ethnic Arabs. Virtually all the country's 2.5 million Arabs have their roots in Algeria, Morocco and Tunisia, former French possessions across the Mediterranean Sea. These countries, and usually

Libya, are known collectively as the Maghreb countries (from the Arabic *maghrib*, 'west', i.e. of the Arab world).

magic formula [Zauberformel (German), formule magique (French)] In Switzerland, a common name for the arrangement whereby the four largest parties in parliament have formed a coalition at federal level since 1959.

Maguire Seven case Judicial scandal and political controversy in the United Kingdom involving the false conviction of seven Irish people for terrorist offences. The seven, the Maguires and their two sons, two relations and a family friend, were arrested in 1974 shortly after the bombing of public houses in Guildford and Woolwich (London) by the Irish Republican Army (IRA), the guerrilla group fighting for the withdrawal of British troops from Northern Ireland and the reunification of Ireland. They were convicted of possession of explosives and sentenced to between five and 14 years' imprisonment on the strength of confessions by two of the alleged bombers (one of whom was related to the Maguires) and forensic evidence. Subsequently it emerged that the confessions had been obtained under duress, and the forensic evidence was discredited. Even so, the seven were not granted leave to appeal and served their sentences in full. The convictions were finally overturned in June 1990. Like related miscarriages of justice, such as the BIRMINGHAM SIX AND GUILDFORD FOUR CASES, the Maguire Seven case cast doubt on the integrity of the criminal justice system and soured relations between Ireland and Britain.

Magvaši, Peter (1945–) Slovakian metallurgist, business manager, administrator and politician. In the 1980s and early 90s he served as technical, financial and general director in a number of state-owned companies. In 1993–94 he was managing director of the National Insurance Agency (RNP). He was appointed economy minister in the centrist coalition which took office in March 1994. He does not belong to a political party.

Magyar Köztársaság ('Hungarian Republic') Official name of Hungary.

Magyar Ut *See* HUNGARIAN WAY.

Magyarország Hungarian name for Hungary.

Magyars Alternative, more literary, name for Hungarians. It is taken from the native name for Hungarians.

maire French local government official, usually translated as 'mayor'. The *maire* is the chief executive of the commune or municipality, the main tier of local government, and is also the representative of the central government. S/he is elected by the municipal council.

Major, John (1943–) British politician. He worked in banking and was active in local politics until his election to Parliament for the Conservative Party in 1979. After holding several junior ministerial posts, he was appointed chief secretary to the Treasury, a post with Cabinet rank with responsibility for public spending, in 1987. In 1989 he was briefly foreign secretary and was appointed chancellor of the exchequer (= finance minister). In November 1990 he was elected leader of the Conservative Party and prime minister in succession to Margaret Thatcher, who had resigned after losing the confidence of the parliamentary party.

majorité, majorité présidentielle and **majority** (France) *See* PRESIDENTIAL MAJORITY.

majority voting (European Union) *See* QUALIFIED MAJORITY VOTING.

MAK Abbreviation for Macedonia, used for international vehicle registrations, postal addresses etc.

Makedonija Macedonian name for Macedonia.

mała konstytucja *See* SMALL CONSTITUTION.

Malcorps, Johan (1957–) Belgian politician. A graduate in philosophy and German philology, he was director of the Institute of Political Ecology from 1987–89. Elected to parliament for the Flemish environmentalist party Live Differently (AGALEV), he was elected its leader in January 1989.

Malesa affair *See* FILESA, MALESA AND ....

Malm, Stig (1942–) Swedish toolmaker and trade-union official. He began working full-time for the Swedish Metalworkers' Union (SMF) in 1967. In 1981

396

he was elected vice-president of the Swedish Trade Union Confederation (LO) and in May 1983 he took over as president. He resigned in December 1993 after media reports claimed he had granted himself large pay rises and benefits and had used his various positions (on the boards of government agencies and private companies) to secure financial and other favours for family members and friends.

Malta Country in southern Europe.

Official data. Name: Republic of Malta [Repubblika ta' Malta]; capital: Valletta; form of government: parliamentary republic; head of state: president; head of government: prime minister; flag: two horizontal stripes, white and red, with a red-edged George Cross medal in the canton; national holiday: 21 September (Independence Day); languages: Maltese and English; religion: Roman Catholicism; currency: lira (LM) (pl. liri) = 100 centeżmu = 1,000 milleżmi; abbreviation: M.

Geography. Situated in the central Mediterranean Sea 100 km south of Sicily (Italy), Malta consists of the main island of Malta itself, the small islands of Gozo [Għawdex] and Comino [Kemmuna] and three islets. The total area is 316 sq km. Neighbouring countries across the sea are Italy to the north, Tunisia to the west, and Libya to the south. The islands consist mostly of low plateaus. Some 41% of the land is arable, virtually none is covered by pastures or forested. The climate is mediterranean, with hot summers and cool winters; rainfall is light.

Demography. Malta has a population of 363,000. Population density is 1,149 per sq km. Some 85% of the people live in urban areas, around two-thirds in Valletta and its suburbs. In ethnic and religious terms Malta is very homogeneous. Some 95.7% of the population is Maltese and 97.3% is nominally Roman Catholic. There are small numbers of British nationals (2.1%) and Anglicans (1.2%). The main languages are Maltese (related to Arabic and strongly influenced by Italian), English and Italian, all three of which are widely spoken; English is the most widely used in public administration and education.

Sociography. Malta scores 0.842 on the United Nations human development index (HDI), ranking 41st in the world and 26th among 32 European countries. There are 23 doctors and 93 hospital beds for every 10,000 people. Education is compulsory between the ages of five and 16. There is one teacher for every 18 students. Enrolment is 78% at the secondary level and 11% at the tertiary level. The literacy rate is 87%. Real annual income per head (in terms of purchasing power) is US$ 7,580.

Infrastructure and communications. Malta has a developed transport and communications network. There are 1,450 km of paved roads and 105,000 passenger cars (294 per 1,000 people). There are no railways or navigable waterways. The main port is Valletta. There is an airport at Luqa. There are three daily newspapers, with a combined circulation of 67,000 (192 per 1,000 people). There are 150,000 radio receivers, 132,000 television sets and 179,000 telephones in use (respectively 420, 370 and 501 per 1,000 people).

Economic structure. The Maltese economy is developed, relatively diversified, and one of the most trade-oriented in the world (exports account for four-fifths of national income). It is based on light industry and tourism. The reliance on trade and tourism makes it vulnerable to changes in world economic conditions. Since the late 1980s economic performance has been marked by high but declining growth (averaging 6.4% per year), fluctuating current-account balances, low inflation (averaging 2.1%) and relatively low unemployment (around 4%). The unofficial economy is estimated to be equivalent to a third of official GDP.

Services contribute 60% of GDP, industry contributes 37% (manufacturing 27%), and agriculture and fisheries 3%. Some 27% of the labour force is employed in manufacturing, 10% in trade and 7% in transport and communications. The main agricultural activity is horticulture (tomatoes and other fruit and vegetables, flowers); dairy farming (milk, eggs) and livestock raising (pigs, poultry) are also important; the main crops grown are cereals (wheat, barley) and potatoes. The main mineral resource is stone. The main industries are textiles (incl. footwear), food processing and electrical goods (esp. audiovisual equipment); other important branches are ship repairing and printing. Financial services provide an important source of foreign exchange. Tourism is a mainstay of the economy, contributing 21% of GNP (15% net). The main energy source is imported fossil fuels; 9% of export earnings are required to cover net fuel imports. The main exports are electrical equipment (42% of the total), textiles and clothing (16%), precision instruments, building materials and foodstuffs; machinery and transport equipment account for 45% of the total, miscellaneous manufactures for 33%. The main imports are machinery and transport equipment, basic manufactures, foodstuffs, chemicals and fuels. The main trading partners are: exports: Italy (38%), Germany (19%), United Kingdom (7%), France (6%), Libya (5%), United States, Netherlands; imports: Italy (35%), United Kingdom (15%), Germany (12%), France (7%), Japan, United States; three-quarters of all trade is with European Union (EU) countries. Net invisible earnings (tourism receipts, shipping charges, income from financial services, development assistance) account for 18% of GNP, one of the highest shares in Europe.

The Central Bank of Malta [Il-Bank Central ta' Malta] is the central bank. The main employers' association is the Malta Employers' Association (MEA); the main labour organizations are the General Workers' Union (GWU) and the Confederation of Malta Trade Unions (KTUM).

Political structure. Malta is a parliamentary republic on the basis of a constitution adopted in 1974. The head of state is the president, who is elected by the legislature for a five-year term; s/he appoints the prime minister and has several other powers, but normally acts on the advice of the government. Executive power is vested in the prime minister and the cabinet. Legislative power is vested in the House of Representatives [il-Kamra tad-Deputadi], whose 65 members are elected for a five-year term by a system of proportional representation. If a party gains a majority of the popular vote but not of the seats, it is awarded additional seats until it has a parliamentary majority. All citizens over the age of 18 are entitled to vote. Judicial power is ultimately vested in the Court of Appeal [il-Qorti ta'l-Appell] and the Constitutional Court [il-Qorti Kostituzzjonali]. With the exception of a local council for the island of Gozo, there is no local government structure.

The main political parties are the Nationalist Party (PN), Labour Party (MLP or il-Haddiema) and Democratic Alternative (AD). At the general election in February 1992 the Nationalists gained 51.8% of the vote and 34/65 seats, Labour 46.5% and 31 seats, and the AD 1.7% and no seats. The government is formed by the centre-right Nationalists, with Eddie Fenech-Adami as prime minister. Other senior ministers are Guido De Marco (deputy prime minister, foreign affairs), Louis Galea (internal affairs, social development), John Dalli (finance), George Bonello Du Puis (economy) and Joseph Fenech (justice). The head of state is President Ugo Mifsud Bonnici, who was elected in April 1994.

Security and international affiliations. The Maltese armed forces number 1,700. There is no conscription.

Malta is a member of the Conference on Security and Cooperation in Europe (CSCE) and Council of Europe, as well as the Commonwealth, Non-Aligned Movement (NAM) and the United Nations and its specialized agencies. It has applied for membership of the European Union (EU).

History. The island of Malta came under the control of Carthage (across the sea in modern Tunisia) in the 5th century BC and was conquered by the Romans in 218 BC. It was allocated to the Eastern Roman Empire, later Byzantium, in 395 AD. It was conquered by Muslim Arabs in 870 and ruled successively by the Aghlabid, Fatimid and Almoravid dynasties based in North Africa. In 1090 it was conquered by Sicily, then ruled by the Normans. Like Sicily, it passed to the German Hohenstaufens in 1194, the French Anjous in 1266, Aragón in 1282 and (on the unification of Aragón and Castile) to Spain in 1479. In 1530 King Charles I (Charles V as Holy Roman emperor) conferred Malta on the Knights Hospitaller or Knights of Saint John, a Roman Catholic religious and military order which had been dispossessed of its previous base, the Greek island of Rhodes, by the Ottoman Turks eight years earlier. (The order is now commonly called the Knights of Malta.)

The Hospitallers' rule ended when French troops occupied the island in 1798. Two years later it was occupied by the British. As part of the post-Napoleonic reorganization of Europe in 1814/15 the Congress of Vienna confirmed British possession of Malta. It became a major British naval base, especially after the opening of the Suez Canal in 1869, and the naval docks became the mainstay of the economy. The colony was given limited internal self-government in 1921. As relations between the British authorities and the Maltese grew increasingly tense, the constitution was suspended in 1930, restored in 1933 and withdrawn in 1936. Malta suffered heavy German bombing during the Second World War (1939–45).

Self-government was restored in 1947. Malta gained independence in 1964 and became a republic in 1974. Since the establishment of representative government, power has alternated between the centre-right Nationalist Party and the Labour Party. The latter held power from 1947–50, 1955–62 and 1971–87, under the leadership of Dom Mintoff from 1955–84; the former held power from 1950–55 and 1962–71. Parliament proclaimed Malta's neutrality and non-alignment following the termination of the defence alliance with the United Kingdom in 1979. Since the closure of the British military base and naval docks at the same time, all governments have pursued policies aimed at restructuring and diversifying the economy. The Nationalist Party, led by Eddie Fenech-Adami, won the May 1987 election on a platform of economic liberalization and seeking membership of the European Community (EC, now the European Union, EU); an application was lodged in July 1990. The Nationalists were returned to office in February 1992 with an increased majority.

See also entries on specific institutions, organizations, parties, people, terms etc.

Malta Labour Party *See* LABOUR PARTY.

Man Territory in western Europe, a dependency of the United Kingdom, widely referred as the Isle of Man, its full name.

Official data. Name: Isle of Man; capital: Douglas; form of government: internally self-governing dependency of the British crown; head of state: lord, by right the British monarch, represented by a lieutenant-governor; head of government: chief minister; flag: red with the state emblem (three steel-coloured joined armoured legs or 'triskelion') in the centre; national holidays: Queen's Official Birthday (second Saturday in June), 5 July (Tynwald Day); language: English; religion: Anglicanism (Church of England); currencies: pound (£) = 100 pence, British pound; abbreviations: IOM and GBM.

Geography. Situated in the Irish Sea between Great Britain and Ireland, the Isle of Man has a total area of 572 sq km. It consists of a range of mountains and hill lands in the centre and low-lying coastal strips in the north and south. Around a fifth of the land is arable, half is covered by pastures, and a twentieth is forested. The climate is temperate marine, with mild summers and cool winters; rainfall is heavy.

Demography. Man has a population of 70,700. Population density is 124 per sq km. The main town is Douglas. Around half the people are native Manx and half are immigrants from Britain. The main language is English; Manx, the ancient Celtic language, is virtually extinct. In religious terms most people are nominally Anglicans; there are small groups of other Christians.

Sociography. The standard of living on Man is high. There are 13 doctors and 109 hospital beds for every 10,000 people. Education is compulsory between the ages of five and 16. There is one teacher for every 16 students. Enrolment is 90% at the secondary level; there is one college of further education, but most students study in Britain. The literacy rate is virtually 100%. GNP per head (unadjusted for purchasing power) is around US$ 10,000.

Infrastructure and communications. Man has a highly developed but limited transport and communications network closely integrated with that of Britain; ferry and air links are particularly important; there is no locally based television service. There are 330 km of paved roads and 39,400 passenger cars (616 per 1,000 people). There are 59 km of railways and no navigable waterways. The main port is Douglas. There is an airport at Ronaldsway. There is no daily, but one biweekly newspaper, with a circulation of 25,000 (179 per 1,000 people); British papers are also widely read. There are around 50,000 radio receivers, 20,000 television sets and 37,000 telephones in use (respectively around 750, 319 and 579 per 1,000 people).

Economic structure. The Manx economy is highly developed, diversified and closely linked to the British economy. Man maintains a customs and monetary union with the United Kingdom. Taxation is low. The economy is based on financial services, manufacturing and tourism. Since the late 1980s economic performance has been marked by low growth, falling inflation (from 10% to below 3%) and low but rising unemployment (up to 5%).

Services contribute 66% of GDP (financial services 20%), industry contributes 31% (manufacturing 16%), and agriculture, forestry and fisheries 3%. Some 18% of the labour force is employed in trade, 14% in finance, 11% in manufacturing and 10% in construction. The main agricultural activities are dairy farming and livestock raising (cattle, sheep); the main crops grown are cereals (barley) and potatoes. Fishing is also important. There are no significant mineral resources. The main industries are engineering (esp.

precision instruments), electronic and electrical goods, textiles and food processing. Banking and other financial services and tourism are mainstays of the economy, contributing 27% and 9% of GNP respectively. The main energy sources are imported fossil fuels. The main exports are electrical goods, textiles and clothing. The main imports are fuels, foodstuffs and basic and miscellaneous manufactures. The main trading partner is the United Kingdom. (Detailed foreign-trade figures n.a.) Net invisible earnings (income from financial services, tourism receipts) account for around a quarter of GNP.

The Financial Supervision Commission discharges some of the responsibilities of a central bank. Employers' associations and trade unions are generally integrated into British structures.

Political structure. Man is an internally self-governing dependency of the British crown (i.e. the monarch) on the basis of constitutional practice, statute law (including the 1961 Isle of Man Constitution Act) and common law. The British government is responsible for defence and foreign affairs, and also effectively for discharging the crown's powers of appointment etc. Executive power is formally vested in the British monarch, who is represented by a lieutenant-governor, but exercised by the chief minister and the council of ministers. The lieutenant-governor usually acts on the advice of the 10-member Executive Council, a consultative body composed of the government ministers. Legislative power is vested in the bicameral Tynwald, composed of the 24-member House of Keys elected for a four-year term by a system of majority voting, and the 10-member Legislative Council, eight of whom are elected by the House of Keys and two are members ex officio. The two houses function as separate bodies but sit together for certain matters. All citizens over the age of 21 are entitled to vote; resident Commonwealth and Irish citizens normally also have voting rights. Judicial power is vested in the High Court of Justice; the appeal court is the Judicial

Committee of the Privy Council, a body composed primarily of senior judges in the British House of Lords. Administratively the island is divided into four towns, five village districts and 15 parish districts.

There are no political parties. The chief minister is Miles Walker. The head of state is Queen Elizabeth II, Lord of Mann, represented by Laurence Jones as lieutenant-governor; the heir is Prince Charles.

Security and international affiliations. Defence and foreign affairs are the responsibility of the British government. The Manx government is usually consulted in matters of immediate concern to the island. Man is treated as part of the European Union (EU) for the purpose of free trade of goods, but it is not a member of the organization.

History. Originally inhabited by a Celtic people, the Isle of Man was raided and then invaded by the Vikings in the 9th century and became a dependency of Norway. The local legislative assembly, Tynwald, was established in 979. The island was ceded to Scotland in 1266. The Scots and English disputed control until 1405, when English sovereignty was recognized. Henceforward it was a fief of the English crown. The lordship was held by the Stanley family, later the earls of Derby, and then by the dukes of Atholl. In the 17th and 18th centuries the island became a centre of smuggling into England. In 1765 the then lord was pressured into selling Man to the United Kingdom. Man was administered directly by the British government (although not incorporated into the United Kingdom) until 1866, when a number of powers, including tax sovereignty, were restored. At the same time the House of Keys, the lower house of Tynwald, became a popularly elected body. Since then the island parliament and government have acquired virtual autonomy in internal affairs.

Since the 1950s financial services and light manufacturing have supplanted agriculture and fishing as the mainstays of the economy.

See also entries on specific institutions, organizations, terms, people etc.

Mancino, Nicola (1931–) Italian lawyer and politician. He worked in local government until his election to parliament for the Christian Democratic Party (DC), now the Italian People's Party (PPI), in 1976. He was the leader of the DC parliamentary party from 1984–89 and interior minister from June 1992 until May 1994.

mandarins In the United Kingdom, an informal name for high-ranking civil servants, who often play a key role in the formulation of government policy.

Mani Pulite ('Clean Hands') Codename for the investigations into illegal party funding by a Milan-based team of magistrates, which in 1992 first exposed the web of political corruption in Italian public life. *See* ITALIAN CORRUPTION SCANDALS.

Manolescu, Nicolae (1939–) Romanian journalist, historian, academic and politician. Most widely known as a literary critic, he was elected leader of the centrist Civic Alliance Party (PAC) in May 1991. He was also president of the opposition Democratic Convention (CDR) alliance from 1991–92.

Manouches and **Manush** Alternative names for GIPSIES or Romanies, widely used in France. The Manush or Sinti are one of the traditional major regional and occupational subdivisions among Gipsies.

Manx People and language of the Isle of Man. A Celtic language, Manx is now virtually extinct.

MAP *See* MEDITERRANEAN ACTION PLAN.

Marcha Real ('Royal March') National anthem of Spain.

Marchais, Georges (1920–) French steelworker, trade-union official and politician. Elected to the central committee of the French Communist Party (PCF) in 1956, he became its deputy general secretary in 1970 and general secretary in December 1972. He was first elected to parliament in 1973 and stood in the 1981 presidential election. He retired as party leader in January 1994, but retained a seat on the national committee (formerly the central committee).

Marches [Marche] Autonomous region of Italy. Situated in the centre on the Adriatic Sea, the region has an area of

9,693 sq km and a population of 1,447,000. The capital is Ancona. The economy is based on agriculture (cereals, olives, wine, dairy farming), fishing and light industry. Nominally part of the Papal States from the 8th century, the region was divided into four border provinces of the Holy Roman Empire – known as 'marches' – in the 10th century and later into several city states and principalities. Papal control was firmly established in the 16th century. The Marches became part of unified Italy in 1860.

Margrethe II (1940–) Queen of Denmark. She succeeded to the throne on the death of her father, Frederik IX, in January 1972. She married a French count, now Prince Henrik, in 1967. They have two children. She has worked (under various pseudonyms) as a translator, illustrator and designer.

Marianne Personification of the French Republic or France. The name was used pejoratively in the early 19th century for a pro-republican secret society. After the restoration of the republic in 1870 the figure of Marianne, usually represented wearing a Jacobin hat popular during the French Revolution, came to symbolize freedom.

Maribor arms-smuggling affair Controversy in Slovenia surrounding the smuggling of arms to Bosnia-Herzegovina and Croatia in violation of a United Nations embargo. A consignment of 120 tons of arms was discovered at Maribor airport in July 1993. According to press reports it had originated in Saudi Arabia and was destined for Bosnian government forces. In October the weekly *Mladina* claimed that such arms shipments – violating a UN embargo on arms exports to all the former Yugoslav republics – had been approved at the highest level in 1992, and that President Kučan, the then defence minister, Janez Janša, and the then interior minister, Igor Bavčar, had all been directly involved in the decision. All three denied the allegations. In December four people, including a Maribor-based intelligence officer and the director of Maribor airport, were charged with abuse of mandate. In testimony during the trial

Bavčar and intelligence officers confirmed that senior Slovenian officials had authorized the transit of arms shipments. In April 1994 President Kučan accepted that arms had been supplied to Bosnia-Herzegovina and Croatia in defiance of the UN embargo, but again denied his own involvement and called for a government investigation into the affair.

Marín, Manuel (1949–) Spanish politician. Active in the anti-Franco student movement, he was elected to parliament for the Spanish Socialist Workers' Party (PSOE) after the restoration of democracy in 1977. In the mid 1980s he was chief negotiator on Spain's membership of the European Community (EC, now the European Union, EU). In January 1986 he was appointed an EC commissioner, taking responsibility for social affairs and employment (1986–89), cooperation, development and fisheries (1989–93) and cooperation and development (since January 1993). He is also a vice-president of the Commission.

Marjanović, Mirko (1937–) Yugoslav businessman and politician. He has spent most of his working life in the foreign-trade field and was managing director of the state-owned firm Progres until he entered politics. He was elected to the Serbian republican parliament for the Socialist Party (SPS) in 1990. A close associate of President Milošević, he was appointed Serbia's prime minister in February 1994.

mark Anglicized form of the MARKKA, the Finnish currency.

mark Currency of Germany, also called 'deutschmark'. Common abbreviations are DM, D-Mark and DEM (the international standard in banking etc). It is divided into 100 pfennigs [Pfennige].

markka (pl. -a) Currency of Finland. Common abbreviations are Mk, FM, FMk, and FIM (the international standard in banking etc). It is divided into 100 penniä. The anglicized forms 'finnmark' and 'mark' and the simple plural 'markka' are also used.

Markó, Béla (1951–) Romanian writer, teacher and politician. He has taught French, been editor of several literary magazines and published several volumes of poetry and essays. An ethnic Hungarian, he was elected to parliament for the Hungarian Democratic Union of Romania (RMDSz) in 1990. He was elected party leader in January 1993.

Maroni, Roberto (1955–) Italian lawyer and politician. He worked for Avon Cosmetics until his election to parliament for the federalist Northern League (Lega Nord) in 1992. He has been a leading member of its main constituent, the Lombard League (Lega Lombarda), since its foundation in 1979. He was appointed a deputy prime minister and interior minister in the right-wing coalition formed in May 1994.

Marseillaise National anthem of France. Composed in 1792 during the French Revolution, it acquired its name because of its popularity with volunteer army units from Marseille. Adopted as the national anthem in 1795, it was banned for two periods in the 19th century because of its associations with the Revolution, but reinstated in 1879.

marshal [marszałek] President or speaker of the Sejm, the lower house of the Polish parliament. The title is also used for the president of the Senate, the upper house.

marszałek *See* MARSHAL.

Martelli, Claudio (1943–) Italian academic and politician. He lectured in philosophy until his election to parliament for the Italian Socialist Party (PSI) in 1979. He was the party's deputy leader from 1981–89 and was appointed justice minister in July 1989. He resigned in February 1993 following allegations that he had broken the party-financing laws. In July 1994 he was convicted of corruption in connection with the BANCO AMBROSIANO AFFAIR and sentenced to 8¹/₂ years' imprisonment. At the time he was also on trial in two major cases involving illegal party funding.

Martens, Wilfried (1936–) Belgian lawyer and politician. An adviser to several ministers in the 1960s and leader of the youth wing of the Flemish Christian People's Party (CVP) from 1965, he was elected party leader in 1972. He was first appointed prime minister in April 1979.

Except for a break between March and December 1981, he remained in power at the head of several centre-right coalitions until 1987 and of centre-left coalitions until March 1992, establishing himself as the country's dominant political figure of the 1980s. In May 1990 he was elected president of both the European People's Party, the umbrella organization of christian democratic parties in the European Union (EU), and the European Christian Democratic Union (ECDU). He was elected to the European Parliament in June 1994.

Martić, Milan (1954–) Croatian lawyer and politician. In 1990 he joined the new Serbian Democratic Party (SDS, subsequently renamed the SDS of Krajina, SDSK), the main representative of ethnic Serbs in Croatia. He fought in the civil war in 1991–92. In January 1994 he was elected president of the breakaway Republic of Serbian Krajina (RSK), defeating Milan Babić in the second round.

Martinazzoli, Mino (1931–) Italian lawyer and politician. He was active in local government for the Christian Democratic Party (DC) in his native Brescia until his election to parliament in 1972. He has been minister of justice (1983–86), defence (1989–90) and regional affairs and institutional reform (1991–92). In October 1992, when the DC's involvement in political corruption was coming to light and most of its senior leaders were discredited, he was elected general secretary (= leader). He was confirmed in this post when the DC was relaunched as the Italian People's Party (PPI) in January 1994. He resigned in March after the party's disappointing performance in the general election.

Martino, Antonio (1943–) Italian economist, academic and politician. He has studied, researched and lectured at the University of Chicago in the United States, the Free International University of Social Studies (LUISS) in Rome and elsewhere. A strong advocate of free-market economic policies, he has written three books on monetary theory. Previously a member of the Italian Liberal Party (PLI), he joined the new Come On Italy

(Forza Italia) in January 1994 and was instrumental in drafting its economic programme. He was elected to parliament in March and was appointed foreign minister in the right-wing coalition formed in May.

mass privatization or **large privatization** In the former communist countries, the sale of large state-owned industrial enterprises. During the communist period virtually all enterprises were state-owned. Their 'denationalization' or 'privatization' was a central element in the transition to a market-based economy planned by all the Eastern European governments which took over from the communists between 1989 and 1991. In most countries an early start was made with the dissolution of collective farms and the allocation of agricultural land to farmers or its return to previous owners or their heirs. Thousands of small businesses, primarily in the service sector, were also put up for auction, handed over to their staff or returned to former owners or their heirs in what were dubbed 'small privatizations'. The privatization of large industrial enterprises – more ambitious and more contentious – has proceeded more slowly, and very slowly in some countries (e.g. Slovakia). The means employed have also differed from country to country. Broadly speaking, Hungary has relied on general share issues (along the lines used in the 1980s for the privatization of British utilities, for instance), while Bulgaria, the Czech Republic, Poland and Romania have all initiated broad-based schemes under which adult citizens are issued with 'vouchers' or 'coupons' entitling them to buy shares in companies of their choice or invest in specially constituted share-holding funds. All privatization schemes allow for equity holdings by employees of the companies concerned, many for continued state control of utilities and strategic industries (e.g. mining, arms manufacturing) and residual state participation in key companies, and most for a large degree of foreign ownership.

In detail, in Hungary a stock exchange was reestablished in June 1990, a privatization programme was approved by parliament in September, and the first companies were put up for sale the same month; the intention was to reduce the state's stake in the economy to less than half by the end of 1994. In Czechoslovakia detailed legislation was adopted in February 1991; subsequently large enterprises were put up for sale to foreign and domestic investors and vouchers were distributed to millions of citizens in several stages; after the federation's dissolution at the end of 1992 the privatization programme was effectively suspended in Slovakia. In Poland plans for mass privatization were announced in June 1991, but political instability delayed adoption of the relevant legislation until April 1993; under the scheme, which was backed by the former communist parties, the equity of 460 large enterprises was divided among 19 foreign-managed 'national investment funds' and their shares were sold to Polish citizens at a nominal price, with 15% reserved for employees and 30% retained by the state; the funds would be dissolved after 10 years and the proceeds distributed among shareholders. In Romania legislation covering all 6,200 state enterprises except utilities was adopted in August 1991; under the scheme five 'private ownership funds' would manage 30% of the equity allocated to the public through the distribution of vouchers, while the remaining 70% would be held in a 'state ownership fund' and sold off in 10% tranches over a seven-year period, with advantageous terms for employees; the various funds came into operation in August 1992. In Bulgaria the government approved a privatization programme for medium-size and large enterprises in May 1993; a voucher scheme was agreed in June 1994, and privatization vouchers for 340 major companies went on sale in September. In former East Germany state-owned companies were sold off by a government agency set up after German reunification in October 1990, the TRUST AGENCY or Treuhandanstalt.

Mastella, Clemente (1947–) Italian journalist and politician. In the 1970s he worked for Italian Radio and Television

(RAI) and for the Christian Democratic Party (DC) as head of information and publications. He was elected to parliament in 1979 and was a junior defence minister from 1989–92. After the party was discredited because of its involvement in the corruption scandals which broke in 1993, he rejected the need for a relaunch. When this did happen, he joined the breakaway Christian Democratic Centre (CCD). He was appointed minister of labour in the right-wing coalition formed in May 1994.

Matica Hrvatska *See* MOTHER CROATIA.

Matica Slovenská *See* MOTHER SLOVAKIA.

Matignon Shorthand for the French prime minister's office. The Hôtel Matignon in Paris is the official residence of the prime minister.

Matinchev, Evgeni (1939–) Bulgarian economist, civil servant and politician. He has worked for the finance ministry and for a state construction company. In 1991 he was elected to parliament on the Movement for Rights and Freedoms (DPS) ticket, but he is not a member of the party. He was appointed a deputy prime minister and minister of social affairs in the non-party government formed in December 1992.

Matrix Churchill affair *See* ARMS-TO-IRAQ AFFAIR.

Matsis, Ioannis or **Yannakis** (1933–) Cypriot lawyer and politician. He became general secretary of the centre-right Democratic Rally (DISI) in 1976 and was elected to parliament in 1981. In June 1993 he was elected party leader in succession to Glavkos Klerides, who had been elected president of the republic.

Matteoli, Altero (1940–) Italian businessman and politician. He has been active in local politics in his native Tuscany for the far-right Italian Social Movement (MSI), now the core of the National Alliance (AN), since the 1960s. He was elected to parliament in 1983. He was appointed environment minister in the right-wing coalition formed in May 1994.

Matutes, Abel (1941–) Spanish businessman and politician. Before entering politics he built up a group of companies with interests in banking, property, hotels and other leisure interests on the island of Ibiza. Elected to parliament for the forerunner of the centre-right People's Party (PP) in 1977, he became its deputy leader in 1979. In January 1986 he was appointed a commissioner of the European Community (EC). He has been responsible for credit, investments and small and medium-size enterprises (1986–89), Mediterranean affairs and North-South relations (1989–93) and energy and transport (1993–94). He resigned in April 1994 to head his party's list in the elections to the European Parliament, to which he was elected in June.

Mauroy, Pierre (1928–) French teacher, trade-union official and politician. A deputy leader of the predecessor of the Socialist Party (PS) from 1966, he effectively held the same post in the PS from its foundation in 1971. He was elected to parliament and became mayor of Lille in 1973. When the left gained power in 1981 President Mitterrand appointed him prime minister. Economic problems and electoral setbacks led to his replacement in 1984. From May 1988 until January 1992 he was first secretary (= leader) of the PS. The following September he was elected president of the Socialist International, the umbrella organization of the world's democratic socialist parties.

Mawhinney, Brian (1940–) British academic and politician. He lectured in ethical issues at a major London hospital from 1970–84. Elected to Parliament for the Conservative Party in 1979, he was appointed a junior minister in the Northern Ireland Office – he is a native of the province – in 1986. He was switched to the health ministry in 1992 and joined the Cabinet as minister of transport in July 1994.

Maxwell affair Business scandal and political controversy in the United Kingdom surrounding the collapse of the media group run by Robert Maxwell. From the 1950s Maxwell built up a publishing and media group which by the mid 1980s included Mirror Group Newspapers (MGN) and a range of publishing and broadcasting interests in the United Kingdom, United States, France and other

European countries. He also served as a member of Parliament for the Labour Party from 1964–70. His death in November 1991, probably by suicide, was followed by the collapse of his business empire with debts totalling 1.76 billion pounds (2.24 billion ecus). It also emerged that around 450 million pounds had gone missing from the MGN pension fund, which meant it was unable to maintain payments to former employees. (The government subsequently announced emergency assistance for those affected.) In June 1992 three former executives of Maxwell-controlled companies, including his sons Kevin and Ian, were arrested on fraud charges in relation to the pension funds and other operations. In July 1993 they and three others were charged with additional offences involving frauds of over 300 million pounds. The affair led to calls for closer supervision of pension funds, stronger regulation of the financial sector, and relaxation of the libel laws (which Maxwell had frequently used to stop journalistic investigations into his business activities).

Mayhew, Peter (1929–) British lawyer and politician. Elected to Parliament for the Conservative Party in 1974, he held several junior ministerial posts until his appointment as attorney-general, the government's senior law officer, in 1987. In April 1992 he was appointed secretary of state for Northern Ireland.

mayor British local government official. The mayor is the formal head of the council in those districts in England and Wales designated as boroughs (usually medium-size towns) and in the London boroughs. The post usually rotates annually and carries no executive powers.

Maystadt, Philippe (1948–) Belgian politician. Elected to parliament for the Walloon Christian Social Party (PSC) in 1977, he entered the government in 1980. He has been minister for the budget and scientific policy (1981–85) and economic affairs (1985–88), and in May 1988 he became finance minister.

Mazowiecki, Tadeusz (1927–) Polish journalist and politician. He edited several Catholic magazines from 1948–81, includ-ing the influential *Więź* from 1958. A prominent opponent of the communist regime, he was closely associated with the Solidarity movement from its emergence in 1980. He was interned by the authorities in 1981–82. He was elected to parliament on the Solidarity ticket in the partly free election of June 1989 and became prime minister of the Solidarity-led government formed in September. He resigned in November 1990 after losing in the first round of the presidential election to Lech Wałęsa, the Solidarity leader and a former ally. In December 1990 he was elected chairman of one of Solidarity's successor parties, the centre-left Democratic Union (UD). In August 1992 the UN Human Rights Commission also appointed him a special rapporteur charged with investigating human-rights abuses in former Yugoslavia. In April 1994 he was confirmed as leader of the new Freedom Union (UW), formed by the merger of the UD and the Liberal Democratic Congress (KLD).

MC Abbreviation for Monaco, used for international vehicle registrations, postal addresses etc.

MC (European Union) *See* MONETARY COMMITTEE.

MC (North Atlantic Treaty Organization) *See* MILITARY COMMITTEE.

MCAs Abbreviation for 'monetary compensation amounts', an instrument of the European Union's COMMON AGRICULTURAL POLICY (CAP).

MÇP *See* NATIONAL ACTION PARTY.

MD (Italy) *See* NETWORK.

MD (San Marino) *See* DEMOCRATIC MOVEMENT.

MdB Abbreviation for Mitglied des Bundestages ('Member of the Federal Assembly'), a member of the Bundestag, the lower house of the German parliament.

MdC *See* CITIZENS' MOVEMENT.

MDF *See* HUNGARIAN DEMOCRATIC FORUM.

MdL Abbreviation for Mitglied des Landtages ('Member of the State Legislature'), a member of the legislature in one of Germany's federal states.

MDS (Bosnia-Herzegovina) *See* MUSLIM DEMOCRATIC PARTY.

MDS *See* MOVEMENT FOR A DEMOCRATIC SLOVAKIA.

Mečiar, Vladimír (1942–) Slovakian lawyer and politician. A leading member of the Communist Party youth movement, he was expelled from the party for his reformist views in 1970. He then worked as a welder and a company lawyer. After the collapse of the communist regime in 1989 he was appointed interior and environment minister of the Slovak Republic, then still part of the Czechoslovak federation. He became the republic's prime minister in 1990, but was dismissed by parliament the following year after being accused of abusing his power of access to secret-police files. In March 1991 he became leader of the new Movement for a Democratic Slovakia (HZDS). He returned as the republic's prime minister when the HZDS won the June 1992 election on a platform of sovereignty for Slovakia. In January 1993 he became prime minister of independent Slovakia. He was forced to resign in March 1994 after his government lost a vote of confidence in parliament.

Mecklenburg-Vorpommern *See* MECKLENBURG - WEST POMERANIA.

Mecklenburg - West Pomerania [Mecklenburg-Vorpommern] Federal state [Land] of Germany, formerly part of East Germany. Situated in the northeast on the Baltic Sea, the state has an area of 28,835 sq km and a population of 1,865,000. The economy is based on agriculture (cereals, cattle farming), manufacturing (shipbuilding, food processing) and tourism. Like the other eastern states, Mecklenburg - West Pomerania is experiencing major economic restructuring and high unemployment. The capital is Schwerin, but the main city is Rostock, a major port. Political power is exercised by the State Assembly [Landtag], with 66 members elected for a four-year term, and a government headed by a minister-president. The main parties are the Christian Democratic Union (CDU), Social Democratic Party (SPD), Democratic Socialist Party (PDS), the successor to the communist Socialist Unity Party, SED) and the centrist Free Democratic Party (FDP). At the election

in October 1990 the CDU gained 38.3% of the vote and 29 seats, the SPD 27.0% and 20 seats, the PDS 15.7% and 12 seats, the FDP 5.5% and four seats, and an independent one seat. The government is formed by a CDU-FDP coalition headed by Berndt Seite. Historically divided into several states within the Holy Roman Empire and then unified Germany but with a strong regional identity, Mecklenburg - West Pomerania was established as a state after the Second World War. It was divided into three districts by the East German authorities in 1952 and restored in 1990 prior to German reunification.

Meclisi Shorthand for Cumhuriyet Meclisi ('ASSEMBLY OF THE REPUBLIC'), the Northern Cypriot parliament.

Meclisi Shorthand for Türkiye Büyük Millet Meclisi ('GRAND NATIONAL ASSEMBLY OF TURKEY'), the Turkish parliament.

Médecin affair Political scandal in France surrounding Jacques Médecin, a prominent right-wing politician. He was forced to resign as mayor of Nice in September 1990 after he had been convicted of tax evasion and evidence had been uncovered of irregular payments from the city budget amounting to 13 million francs (2.0 million ecus). He was abroad on an official visit at the time and did not return to France, settling instead in Uruguay. In January 1992 he was found guilty of misusing public funds and was sentenced in absentia to one year's imprisonment and a heavy fine. He faces two other major charges of misusing public funds and business fraud.

Médecin List [Liste Médecin] Monaco political organization. Headed by Jean-Louis Médecin, mayor of Monaco-Ville from 1971–91, this alliance won 2/18 seats at the election in January 1993. Its members are broadly centrist in outlook and oppose some of the policies of Prince Rainier and the government appointed by him. (There are no political parties in Monaco.)

media ban (Ireland, United Kingdom) *See* BROADCASTING BAN.

médiateur *See* MEDIATOR.

mediator [médiateur] In France, the formal title of the ombudsperson, the independent official charged with investigating citizens' complaints of maladministration in government. S/he is appointed by the National Assembly, the lower house of parliament. *See also* OMBUDSMAN ....

Mediterranean Action Plan (MAP) Intergovernmental organization. The MAP was established in 1980 under the auspices of the United Nations Environment Programme (UNEP) to administer the CONVENTION FOR THE PROTECTION OF THE MEDITERRANEAN SEA AGAINST POLLUTION (Barcelona Convention), monitor pollution levels, and coordinate several practical programmes aimed at improving the marine environment. All 20 states with a coastline on the Mediterranean participate in the MAP. The secretariat is based in Athens (Greece).

Mediterranean countries Collective name used loosely for all those countries in Europe, the Middle East and North Africa bordering on the Mediterranean Sea. In the context of the European Union (EU), the term is used for Greece, Italy, Portugal (which does not actually border on the Mediterranean) and Spain.

megye (pl. megyék) Hungarian administrative division, usually translated as 'county'. Each of the *megyék* has a general assembly elected by the lower-level municipal councils, which are the main units of local government. There are also five county-level cities (Debrecen, Győr, Miskolc, Pécs, Szeged), which have a directly elected general assembly headed by a mayor. Budapest, the national capital and effectively also a county-level city, has a different structure, with an elected bicameral general assembly headed by a chief mayor.

Méhaignerie, Pierre (1939–) French agronomist and politician. He worked as a rural engineer and civil servant until his election to parliament in 1973 for a forerunner of the Social Democratic Centre (CDS). He has been leader of the CDS since June 1982. He was minister of agriculture from 1977–81 and minister of infrastructure, housing, regional planning and transport from 1986–88, and was appointed justice minister when the right returned to power in March 1993.

Meibion Glyndŵr *See* SONS OF GLENDOWER.

Meksi, Aleksandër (1939–) Albanian civil engineer, historian and politician. He has worked as an engineer and a restorer of medieval architecture. A founding member of the Democratic Party (PDSh) in 1990, he was elected to parliament in 1991. Following the PDSh's victory over the former communists in the March 1992 election, he was appointed prime minister in April.

Meleşcanu, Teodor Viorel (1941–) Romanian diplomat and politician. He worked for the foreign ministry from 1966, initially as a diplomatic attaché and later as an ambassador. Politically unaffiliated, he was appointed a minister of state (= deputy prime minister) and foreign minister in November 1992. He does not belong to a political party.

Melilla Dependency of Spain. Situated on the coast of Morocco and separated from Spain by the Mediterranean Sea, the town of Melilla has an area of 12.5 sq km and a population of 56,400. It is one of the 'sovereign territories' [plazas de soberanía] known collectively as Spanish North Africa. Around two-thirds of the people are Spanish, and a third are Arabs from Morocco. The economy is based on the duty-free port and the military base; fishing and tourism are also important. Melilla is administered as an integral part of Spain, as part of Málaga province and Andalusia region. Attached to it are Peñón de Vélez de la Gomera, a small fort on the coast, and the Peñón de Alhucemas and Chafarinas islands. The territory's special status is recognized in certain provisions of the local government structure. There is considerable support for greater autonomy. Melilla came under Spanish control in 1497. Its hinterland was transferred to Morocco when that country became independent in 1956, but Spain retained control of the town and the strategic port. Spanish sovereignty over Melilla and neighbouring Ceuta is disputed by Morocco.

Melkert, Ad (1956–) Dutch politician. He was secretary of the European Community's Youth Forum from 1981–84 and then took up a senior post with the Dutch Organization for International Relations (NOVIB), a development agency. He was elected to parliament for the Labour Party (PvdA) in 1986. He was appointed minister of social affairs and employment in the left-right coalition formed in August 1994.

Melville-Ross, Tim (1944–) British businessman and employers' representative. He worked for British Petroleum from 1963–73 and briefly as a stockbroker before joining the Nationwide Building Society. He was its managing director from 1985 and became managing director of the merged Nationwide Anglia in 1987. He was appointed director-general of the Institute of Directors (IoD), one of the main employers' associations, in August 1994.

Méndez, Cándido (1952–) Spanish chemical engineer, trade-union official and politician. He joined the General Workers' Union (UGT) in 1970, when the organization was still proscribed under the Franco regime, and became a full-time official after the restoration of democracy in the late 1970s. He was elected leader of the Andalusia regional branch in 1986 and leader of the national union in April 1994. He was also a member of parliament for the Spanish Socialist Workers' Party (PSOE) from 1980–87, but resigned his seat in protest against the PSOE government's economic policies.

Menteşe, Nahit (1932–) Turkish lawyer and politician. He was a member of parliament for the centre-right Justice Party (AP) from 1965 until the military coup in 1980. In the 1970s he served successively as minister of customs, transport, energy and natural resources. In 1991 he was reelected to parliament for the AP's successor, the True Path Party (DYP). He was appointed education minister in June 1993 and then interior minister in November.

MEP Abbreviation for Member of the European Parliament, the parliament of the European Union (EU).

Mercouri, Melina *See* MERKOURI, ...

Meri, Lennart (1929–) Estonian teacher, historian, writer and politician. From the 1950s until the 1970s he worked as a teacher, as an editor at Estonian Radio and at the Tallinnfilm film studio. He has written several works on the history of the Finno-Ugric peoples. A prominent pro-independence campaigner, he was appointed foreign minister in 1990 (when Estonia was still part of the Soviet Union) and was appointed ambassador to neighbouring Finland in 1992. Backed by the right-wing Fatherland (Isamaa) alliance, he came second in the first round of the presidential election in September 1992. In the run-off parliamentary vote (held because no candidate had gained an overall majority of the popular vote) in October he secured election with the support of other groups on the centre and right. He took office later that month for a five-year term.

Merkel, Angela (1954–) German physicist and politician. She worked at the Academy of Sciences in East Berlin until 1989. She became active in the opposition against communist rule, and in 1990 was a deputy spokeswoman in the last East German government. On German reunification in October 1990 she joined the Christian Democratic Union (CDU). She was appointed federal minister for women and youth in January 1991 and a became deputy leader of the CDU in September.

Merkouri, Melina (1925–94) Greek actress and politician. She appeared in numerous films in the 1950s, 60s and 70s, including *Never on Sunday*, released in 1960. Elected to parliament for the Pan-Hellenic Socialist Movement (PASOK) in 1977, she was culture minister from 1981–89. During this time she championed in particular the return to Greece of a collection of ancient sculptures known as the Elgin Marbles, held by the British Museum in London. She returned as minister of culture after PASOK regained power in October 1993. She died of lung cancer in March 1994.

Mesić, Stjepan or **Stipe** (1934–) Croatian lawyer and politician. He was expelled from the League of Communists of Yugoslavia in 1971 and imprisoned for his Croatian nationalist views from 1972–74. Elected to parliament for the right-wing Croatian Democratic Union (HDZ) in the multiparty election in April 1990, he was appointed prime minister and later that year became Croatia's representative in Yugoslavia's collective presidency. He became president of Yugoslavia in June 1991 but resigned the following December in the wake of Croatia's declaration of independence. He was elected president of the Sabor (= parliament) in September 1992. Critical of the HDZ's rightward drift, he left the party in May 1994 and was elected leader of the new Croatian Independent Democrats (HND). The following month he lost the Sabor presidency.

Metalworkers' Union [Industriegewerkschaft Metall] (IG Metall) German trade union. The IG Metall was founded in 1949 as the union for the metalworking and engineering industry within the German Trade Union Confederation (DGB). It has around 3.4 million members in the steel, car, engineering and electronics industries, equivalent to nearly half of those employed in these sectors. When it absorbed the engineering union of former East Germany in 1990 it became the largest union in the industrialized world. The president is Klaus Zwickel.

metropolitan county British administrative division. The six metropolitan counties (Greater Manchester, Merseyside, South Yorkshire, Tyne and Wear, West Midlands and West Yorkshire) cover the major conurbations in England outside London. Their elected councils were abolished in 1986 and their powers and responsibilities were transferred to the lower-level METROPOLITAN DISTRICTS or boroughs and a range of appointed bodies.

metropolitan district, metropolitan borough or **borough** British administrative division. The 36 metropolitan districts, many of which have either borough or city status, are the constituent units of the six metropolitan counties covering the main conurbations of England outside London. Each has a council elected for a four-year term. It is formally headed by a chair, mayor (in a borough) or lord mayor (city); the executive leader is called the leader of the council. Metropolitan district councils are responsible for local services, such as housing, education and social services. They inherited many of the powers and responsibilities of the metropolitan county councils after their abolition in 1986, so that, like the London boroughs, they combine the functions divided between county and district councils in the rest of the country. In recent years many of their powers have been transferred to bodies appointed by central government.

Meyer, Heinz-Werner (1932–94) German miner, economist, trade-union official and politician. He began working fulltime for the Mining and Energy Union (IG Bergbau und Energie) in 1957. He joined the executive in 1969 and was the union's leader from 1985–90. In May 1990 he was elected president of the German Trade Union Federation (DGB). A member of the Social Democratic Party (SPD), he represented it in the North Rhine - Westphalia state assembly from 1975–85 and in the federal parliament from 1987. He died of a heart attack in May 1994.

Mezzogiorno Geographical region of Italy. The Mezzogiorno – the 'land of the midday sun', *mezzogiorno* meaning 'midday' – comprises the country's eight southern regions: Abruzzi, Apulia [Puglia], Basilicata, Calabria, Campania, Molise, Sardinia and Sicily. Broadly coextensive with the historical Kingdom of Naples, it accounts for two-fifths of Italy's land area and just over a third of its population. The region's defining feature is that it lags sharply behind the north and centre in terms of economic development. It is more dependent on agriculture and less industrialized than the rest of the country, its GDP per head is roughly half, its level of structural unemployment is more than twice as high, and its infrastructure is vastly inferior. (There are also substantial variations within the Mezzogiorno, with Basilicata, Calabria, Campania and Sicily the least prosperous regions.) Among the interrelated geographical, historical, social, economic and political factors which have hampered the Mezzogiorno's development are a lack of fertile agricultural land, earthquakes, the persistence of feudal structures in Naples until well into the 19th century, heavy emigration, traditional antipathy to state authorities, the influence of criminal organizations (such as the Mafia and Camorra), and widespread corruption. Over the years successive governments have invested heavily in infrastructure, industrial ventures and other projects to develop the region, mainly through the Bank for the Mezzogiorno and later the Mezzogiorno Development Agency (APSM). These efforts have been quite successful in absolute terms but less so in relative terms, since the gap in living standards between north and south has been widening again in recent years. The transfer of resources to the south is also increasingly resented in the north.

MFDS *See* MOVEMENT FOR A DEMOCRATIC SLOVAKIA.

MfS Abbreviation for Ministerium für Staatssicherheit ('Ministry for State Security'), the government department in former East Germany responsible for internal security, surveillance of dissidents and espionage. Its operational arm was commonly known as the STASI.

MHP *See* NATIONAL ACTION PARTY.

MI-5 Common name for the SECURITY SERVICE, the British counterintelligence agency. The term first appeared in the 1910s and has remained in widespread use ever since. It stands for Military Intelligence, Section Five.

MI-6 Common name for the SECRET INTELLIGENCE SERVICE (SIS), the British intelligence agency. The term first appeared in the 1920s and has remained in widespread use ever since. It stands for Military Intelligence, Section Six.

Michael of Hohenzollern *See* MIHAI ....

Michaelides, Alexandros or **Alekos** (1933–) Cypriot businessman and politician. An economics graduate, he worked as a manager until 1972 and then became a prominent entrepreneur in the country's tourist industry. He formed the New Democratic Order Party (NEDIPA) in 1981, which failed to have an impact and merged with the right-wing Democratic Rally (DISI) in 1987. In February 1993 he was appointed foreign minister.

Michaelides, Konstantinos or **Dinos** (1937–) Cypriot lawyer, civil servant and politician. A member of the diplomatic service from 1961, he served in the Cypriot embassies in Greece and Egypt and was a senior adviser to President Kyprianou on diplomatic issues from 1978–80. He was minister to the presidency from 1982–85 and interior minister from 1985–88. Elected to parliament for the centre-right Democratic Party (DIKO) in 1991, he returned as interior minister in February 1993.

Michalek, Nikolaus (1940–) Austrian lawyer, notary and politician. He was appointed minister of justice in December 1990. He does not belong to a political party.

Midi-Pyrénées Region of France. Situated in the south, Midi-Pyrénées has an area of 45,348 sq km and a population of 2,461,000. The capital is Toulouse. The economy is based on agriculture (cereals, wine), manufacturing (engineering, electronics) and tourism. While Toulouse is a major industrial centre, most of the region is largely agricultural and relatively poor.

Mielke, Erich (1907–) German politician. A shipping clerk, he joined the Communist Party of Germany (KPD) in 1925. He lived in exile in the Soviet Union during the Second World War (1939–45). In 1950 he was elected to the central committee of the communist Socialist Unity Party (SED) of East Germany and also became a junior minister in the state security ministry. He headed this ministry, colloquially known as the Stasi, from 1957 until the collapse of the regime in 1989. In this capacity he was responsible for the surveillance of dissidents as well as foreign intelligence. He was arrested soon after German reunification in October 1990 and charged with manslaughter, espionage, embezzlement and other crimes. A court ruled in November 1992 that he was too ill to stand trial. In October 1993 he was found guilty, in a separate case, of participating in the murder of two police officers in 1931.

MIÉP *See* HUNGARIAN JUSTICE AND LIFE PARTY.

Mifsud Bonnici, Ugo (1932–) Maltese journalist, lawyer and politician. He edited the magazine *Malta Letterarja* from 1952–62 and practised law from 1955. Elected to parliament for the centre-right Nationalist Party (PN) in 1966, he has been minister of education (1987–90), internal affairs and education (1990–92) and education and human resources (1992–94). In April 1994 he was elected president of the republic (a non-executive post) for a five-year term.

Mihai or **Michael of Hohenzollern** (from 1927–30 and 1940–47 **King Mihai I**) (1921–) Former king of Romania and stockbroker. He was proclaimed king in 1927, under a regency, and again in 1940 after the abdication of his father, Carol II. He played a major role in the overthrow of the right-wing Antonescu dictatorship in 1944. Opposed to the communists' usurpation of power, he was forced to abdicate in December 1947. He went to live in exile in Switzerland, where he worked as an executive for an American brokerage firm. (Several political parties have called for the restoration of the monarchy.)

Mikhailov, Viktor (1944–) Bulgarian lawyer and politician. From 1967 he worked in the police force and the interior ministry, becoming director of the national police force in 1990. He was appointed interior minister in the non-party 'government of experts' formed in December 1992.

Milczanowski, Andrzej (1939–) Polish lawyer and politician. He was a state prosecutor from 1962–68 and then worked as a company lawyer. He joined the opposition Solidarity movement in 1980. He worked as a casual labourer until 1989 and was imprisoned in 1983–84 for organizing a strike. He headed the newly established State Protection Office (UOP) from 1990–92. He became a junior interior minister in June 1992 and interior minister the following month. He retained the post, on the recommendation of

President Wałęsa, after the change of government in October 1993. He does not belong to a political party.

Military Committee (MC) Institution of the North Atlantic Treaty Organization (NATO). The MC is NATO's senior military body. It is composed of the chiefs-of-staff of the member states or their permanent representatives (The exceptions are France, which is represented by a military mission, and Iceland, which, having no armed forces, is represented by a civilian.) It advises the political institutions, in particular the North Atlantic Council (NAC) and the Defence Planning Committee (DPC), on measures it considers necessary for the common defence of the NATO area. It is also responsible for the overall conduct of military affairs.

military sport group [Wehrsportgruppe, pl. -n] In Austria and Germany, a far-right group engaged in violence and propaganda activities. *Wehrsportgruppen* trace their roots to 19th-century nationalist university fraternities and similar groups. They have emerged in recent years as advocates of nazi ideology, in particular its racist elements. (Led by Adolf Hitler, the National Socialist or Nazi Party held power in Germany from 1933 and in Austria from 1938 until the end of the Second World War in 1945.) They have been involved in attacks on immigrants and refugees, including fire-bombings of their homes. They are usually named after respected figures within the far right, e.g. Wehrsportgruppe Hoffmann and Wehrsportgruppe Trenck.

milk lake (European Union) *See* FOOD MOUNTAINS.

Millan, Bruce (1927–) British accountant and politician. A member of Parliament for the Labour Party from 1953–88, he held several junior ministerial posts from 1964–70 and 1974–76. He was secretary of state for Scotland from 1976–79 and the party's spokesman on Scottish affairs until 1983. In January 1989 he was appointed a commissioner of the European Community (EC), taking responsibility for regional affairs.

Miller, Leszek (1946–) Polish electrician and politician. He worked for a linen factory in Żyrardów and was a trade-union representative until the mid 1970s. He graduated in political sciences in 1977. He then held several posts in the ruling communist Polish United Workers' Party (PZPR), becoming a member of the central committee in 1988. He was elected general secretary of the Social Democratic Party (SdRP), the PZPR's successor, in 1990 and became one of its deputy leaders in March 1993. Elected to parliament in 1991, he was appointed minister of labour and social policy in the left-wing coalition which took office in October 1993.

Millet Meclisi Shorthand for Türkiye Büyük Millet Meclisi ('GRAND NATIONAL ASSEMBLY OF TURKEY'), the Turkish parliament.

Milošević, Slobodan (1941–) Yugoslav politician. He worked in local government until 1969, joined and then managed a gas company, and was president of Serbia's largest bank from 1978–86. In September 1987 he was elected leader of the League of Communists of Serbia (SKS). In May 1989 he also became president of the Serbian republic. He was confirmed as leader of the renamed Socialist Party (SPS) in July 1990 but resigned the post after his reelection as president in December (under a new constitution). Reelected in an early election in December 1992, he has become the dominant political leader in rump Yugoslavia.

mini-Yugoslavia See RUMP YUGOSLAVIA.

minister In the United Kingdom, a junior member of the government. The exception is the minister of agriculture, fisheries and food, who is a senior member of the government. As in other countries, the term is also used generally for any member of the government.

minister-delegate [ministre-délégué] In France, a junior member of the government.

minister for the Gaeltacht Irish government minister. S/he is responsible for Irish-language affairs. The Gaeltacht is the region in the far west of the country where Irish is the first language.

minister of state or **state minister** [stats-minister] Head of government or prime minister of Denmark. The government's

formal name is State Council [Statsråd].

minister of state [ministre d'état] In France, a senior member of the government. This honorary title is conferred on several senior ministers, who also have departmental responsibilities.

minister of state [ministre d'état] Head of government of Monaco. Under the 1962 constitution which amended the terms of France's protection of Monaco, the minister of state is a French civil servant chosen by the prince (= head of state) from a list of three candidates presented by the French government. S/he heads the four-member Council of Government [Conseil de Gouvernement].

minister of state or **state minister** [stats-minister] Head of government or prime minister of Norway. The government's formal name is State Council [Statsråd].

minister of state [ministru de stat] In Romania, a senior member of the government or deputy prime minister. This honorary title is conferred on several senior ministers, who generally also have departmental responsibilities.

minister of state (Turkey) See STATE MINISTER.

minister of state In the United Kingdom, a junior member of the government.

minister-president [minister-president (Dutch), ministre-président (French)] Head of government in Flanders and Wallonia, the two main regions of Belgium.

minister-president [Ministerpräsident] Head of government in most federal states of Germany. In Berlin the equivalent title is 'governing mayor', and in Bremen and Hamburg it is 'president of the Senate'.

Ministry of Ownership Transformations [Ministerstwo Przekstałceń Własnościowych] Polish government department. Bringing together various government departments, agencies and committees, this ministry was set up in January 1991 to oversee the privatization of the state-owned companies which had dominated the economy under communist rule. See also MASS PRIVATIZATION.

Mitsotakis, Konstantinos (1918–) Greek lawyer and politician. A prominent resistance fighter in Crete during the Second

World War, he was first elected to parliament in 1946. From 1952–67 he held ministerial posts in successive centrist and centre-right governments, notably as finance minister (1963–67). He was forced into exile during the military dictatorship (1967–74). On his return he founded a political party, but in 1978 joined the right-wing New Democratic Party (ND). He again held ministerial office from 1978–81, latterly as foreign minister. He was elected party leader in September 1984. He became prime minister after the ND's narrow victory in the April 1990 election. In 1991 and 1992 he also briefly held the economy and foreign-affairs portfolios, and in August 1992 he also took responsibility for Aegean affairs. He resigned as party leader after the ND lost the September 1993 election to the Pan-Hellenic Socialist Movement (PASOK). In June 1994 parliament lifted his immunity and ordered him to stand trial in a special court on charges of abuse of power and perverting the course of justice in connection with a telephone-tapping affair. He is specifically accused of organizing the wiretapping of dozens of political opponents and journalists between 1988 and 1991, a period which included three general elections. In September 1994 he was also charged with accepting a bribe in connection with the sale in 1992 of a state-owned cement company, AGET Iraklis. The PASOK government also claims that much of his extensive collection of ancient Minoan art consists of stolen items.

Mitteleuropa ('Central Europe' in German) Concept used by those who wish to stress the historical, cultural and economic links among the countries and peoples of Central Europe, in particular Austria and Germany and their immediate eastern neighbours, Poland, the Czech Republic, Slovakia, Hungary and Slovenia. The concept of *Mitteleuropa* – the German term is normally used in this context – was coined in the German-speaking parts of the Austro-Hungarian Empire in the 19th century to denote an identity perceived to be distinct from both Prussian (German) and Russian (Slav) traditions.

Later *Mitteleuropa* was used in some circles to describe a 'natural' area of German political and economic hegemony. Because of its associations with German expansionism and racism the concept fell into disuse after 1945. It was revived in the Soviet-dominated countries of Eastern Europe in the 1980s in its original cultural sense, as a way of forging an identity distinct from the western and eastern blocs.

Mitterrand, François (1916–) French lawyer, writer and politician. He was decorated for his resistance activities during the Second World War. During the Fourth Republic (1946–58) he was a member of parliament and held ministerial posts in eleven governments, notably as interior minister from 1954–55 and justice minister from 1956–57. Originally more centrist in his views, he shifted to the left and became a prominent opposition leader during the first presidency of Charles de Gaulle (1958–65). He stood as the left's presidential candidate in 1965, losing to de Gaulle in the second round. In 1971 he became leader of the reconstituted Socialist Party (PS), which in due course became the dominant party of the left. He narrowly lost the 1974 presidential election to Valéry Giscard d'Estaing, but defeated him in May 1981. He resigned all party posts on becoming president of the republic, but remained the PS's dominant figure. He was reelected for a second seven-year term in 1988. He has published several books of essays on politics and other subjects.

Mixed Group [Gruppo Misto] Italian political organization. This is a centrist parliamentary group formed after the March 1994 election. Its main components are the Democratic Alliance (AD) and Italian Socialist Party (PSI). It has 50/630 seats. *See also individual party entries.*

Mk Abbreviation for the MARKKA, the Finnish currency.

MKD Abbreviation for the DENAR, the Macedonian currency, used in banking etc.

MKDH and **MKDM** *See* HUNGARIAN CHRISTIAN DEMOCRATIC MOVEMENT.

M£ Abbreviation for the LIRA or pound, the Maltese currency.

Mladić, Ratko (1943–) Bosnian soldier. He rose to the rank of lieutenant-colonel in the armed forces of the old Yugoslav federation, the Yugoslav People's Army (JNA). As commander in the Krajina region he gave strong support to the local Serb forces during the six-month civil war triggered by Croatia's declaration of independence in July 1991. In May 1992, two months after the outbreak of the civil war between Muslims, Serbs and Croats in neighbouring Bosnia-Herzegovina, he was promoted to general and appointed commander of the Bosnian Serb forces. He is a strong advocate of a 'Greater Serbia'.

MLP *See* LABOUR PARTY (Malta).

MM Abbreviation for Marina Militare ('Military Navy'), the Italian navy.

MMP *See* HUNGARIAN WORKERS' PARTY.

Mock, Alois (1934–) Austrian civil servant and politician. Trained as a lawyer, he held several senior posts in the education and foreign ministries from 1958. He was briefly education minister in 1969–70 and was elected to parliament for the centre-right Austrian People's Party (ÖVP) in 1970. He was leader of the Austrian Workers' and Employees' Federation (ÖAAB), the ÖVP's trade-union arm, from 1971–78 and party leader from 1979–89. When the party returned to government in a grand coalition with the Socialist Party (SPÖ, now the Social Democratic Party, SPÖ) in January 1987, he became foreign minister. He is also president of the European Democratic Union (EDU) and the International Democratic Union (IDU), two umbrella organizations of centre-right and right-wing parties.

Moczulski, Leszek (1930–) Polish historian, journalist and politician. He wrote for a number of daily and weekly newspapers in the 1960s and 70s. In September 1979 he became leader of the Confederation for an Independent Poland (KPN), a new right-wing nationalist formation. He was imprisoned by the communist authorities on two occasions between 1982 and 1986 for heading an illegal organization and 'conspiring to overthrow the government'. He stood in the November 1990 presidential election.

Moderate Coalition Party or **Moderate Party** [Moderata Samlingspartiet] (MS or M) Swedish political party. Founded in 1904 as the Conservative Party and renamed in 1970, the centre-right Moderates participated in several coalition governments from 1976–82. The party became the second-largest in parliament in 1979. At the September 1991 election the party gained 22.0% of the vote and 80/349 seats and then formed a four-party centre-right coalition. Carl Bildt has been party leader since 1986; the general secretary is Gunnar Hökmark.

Moderate Unity Party *See* MODERATE COALITION PARTY.

Moderates [Mõõdukad] (M) Estonian political organization. The Moderates are a centrist alliance of the Estonian Rural Centre Party (EMKE) and Estonian Social Democratic Party (ESDP) formed prior to the September 1992 election. The two parties gained 12/101 seats and formed a joint parliamentary group. *See also individual party entries.*

Modrow, Hans (1928–) German politician. Trained as a machine fitter, he held senior functions in the communist Free German Youth (FDJ) movement of East Germany and then in the ruling Socialist Unity Party (SED) from the 1950s. He was head of the party's Dresden branch from 1973–89 and was briefly prime minister of a reformist government from November 1989 – April 1990. (Germany was reunited in October 1990.) In December 1990 he was elected honorary chairman of the relaunched Democratic Socialist Party (PDS). In February 1993 he was charged with electoral fraud in the May 1989 local elections, and in January 1994 he was charged with perjury in connection with anti-communist demonstrations in October and November 1989.

Moǧultay, Mehmet (1945–) Turkish lawyer and politician. Elected to parliament for the Social Democratic People's Party (SHP) in 1987, he was appointed minister of labour and social security in 1991 and became minister of justice in July 1994.

Moldavia [Moldova] Historical region of Romania. The principality of Moldavia was founded in the 14th century. It became a vassal state of the Ottoman Empire in the 16th century. The eastern half, Bessarabia, was ceded to Russia in 1812 and the western half joined Wallachia to form Romania in 1859. Bessarabia became part of Romania after the First World War, but was ceded to the Soviet Union in 1940. Most of the territory was constituted as the Moldavian Soviet Socialist Republic. It became an independent country after the disintegration of the Soviet Union in 1991. Several nationalist groups in Romania are calling for the unification of the two countries. The majority of the population of independent Moldavia is ethnically Romanian, but there is only limited support for reunification.

Moldova Romanian name for MOLDAVIA, one of the country's historical regions. It is also widely used for the neighbouring Republic of Moldavia [Republica Moldova], a former Soviet republic.

Molise Autonomous region of Italy. Situated in the southeast on the Adriatic Sea, Molise is Italy's second-smallest region, with an area of 4,438 sq km and a population of 321,000. The capital is Campobasso. The economy is based on agriculture (cereals, livestock farming) and some light industry. Part of the MEZZOGIORNO, the region is one of the country's poorest; there has been substantial emigration since the 19th century. Molise became part of the Kingdom of Naples in the 12th century and was incorporated into unified Italy in 1860.

Mölln and Solingen cases Murders of ethnic Turks in Germany in arson attacks by far-right sympathizers. In October 1992 two girls and their grandmother were killed in an attack on their home in Mölln, Schleswig-Holstein. And in May 1993 five Turkish women and girls were killed and three were seriously injured in an attack on their home in Solingen, near Cologne. The Solingen case was the worst racial attack in Germany since the upsurge of such attacks in the early 1990s. In both cases young men with far-right and anti-foreigner views were arrested and charged with murder and arson. After the Mölln attack a number of small but high-profile far-right groups were banned. The main political parties also agreed on constitutional changes to stem the influx of refugees and immigrants since 1989, which was seen as one of the main reasons for the rise in attacks on foreigners. An amendment to the constitution restricting the hitherto very liberal right of asylum was adopted in May 1993. Germany has a substantial Turkish immigrant community, which settled in the country in the 1960s and 70s.

Moluccans *See* SOUTH MOLUCCANS.

Molyneaux, James or **Jim** (1920–) British businessman and politician. A partner in the family printing firm in Northern Ireland for many years, he was elected to Parliament for the Ulster Unionist Party (UUP) in 1970. He was elected parliamentary leader in 1974 and party leader in September 1979.

Monaco Country in southern Europe.

Official data. Name: Principality of Monaco [Principauté de Monaco]; capital: Monaco; form of government: parliamentary monarchy; head of state: prince; head of government: minister of state; flag: two horizontal stripes, red and white; national holiday: 19 November (National Day); language: French; religion: Roman Catholicism; currency: French franc; abbreviation: MC.

Geography. With a total area of 1.95 sq km, Monaco is the second smallest independent state in the world (after the Vatican). It consists of a rocky peninsula and a narrow stretch of coast on the Mediterranean Sea. It is surrounded by France. None of the land is arable, covered by pastures or forested. The climate is mediterranean, with hot summers and cool winters; rainfall is moderate.

Demography. Monaco has a population of 30,300. The whole territory is built up. Only around 15% of the population are Monegasque citizens. Foreign nationals account for the remaining 85%, and include citizens of France (47% of the total) and Italy (17%). The main language is French; Monegasque, a dialect of

Occitan or Provençal, is widely used among locals, while English and Italian are also widely spoken. In religious terms nearly all the people are nominally Roman Catholics.

Sociography. The standard of living in Monaco is very high. There are 27 doctors and 180 hospital beds for every 10,000 people. Education is compulsory between the ages of six and 16. There is one teacher for every eight students. Enrolment is around 90% at the secondary level; there are no local institutions of higher education, and most students study in France. The literacy rate is virtually 100%. GNP per head (unadjusted for purchasing power) is around US$ 16,000.

Infrastructure and communications. Monaco has a highly developed transport and communications network fully integrated into that of France. There are 50 km of paved roads and 17,000 passenger cars (563 per 1,000 people), 2 km of railways and no navigable waterways. Monaco is a port and has a heliport; the nearest international airport is at Nice (France). There is one daily newspaper, a local edition of a regional French newspaper; other French papers are also widely read. There are 11,000 radio receivers, 18,000 television sets and 53,000 telephones in use (respectively 364, 596 and 1,755 per 1,000 people).

Economic structure. The Monaco economy is highly developed and closely linked to the French economy. Monaco maintains a customs and monetary union with France. Taxation is very low. The economy is based on financial services, tourism and light industry. Since the late 1980s economic performance has been marked by steady growth, low inflation and negligible unemployment (detailed figures n.a.).

Services contribute 72% of GDP (financial services 18%), industry contributes 27% (manufacturing around 20%), and fisheries 1%. Some 22% of the labour force is employed in manufacturing, 20% in trade and 8% in financial services; immigrant workers (from France and Italy) make up a sixth of the total. Fishing is the only agricultural activity. There are no mineral resources. The main industries are cosmetics, pharmaceuticals, electronics, wood processing (paper) and textiles. Banking and other financial services and tourism are the mainstays of the economy. The main energy sources are imported fossil fuels and electricity (from France). The main exports are cosmetics, pharmaceuticals, electronic goods and foodstuffs (anchovies). The main imports are manufactured goods, foodstuffs and fuels. The main trading partner is France. (Detailed foreign-trade figures n.a.) Net invisible earnings (income from financial services, tourism and gambling receipts) account for about half of GNP.

There is no central bank. The main employers' association is the Monegasque Employers' Federation (FPM); the main labour organization is the Federation of Monaco Trade Unions (USM).

Political structure. Monaco is a monarchy on the basis of a constitution adopted in 1962. Under an agreement signed in 1861 Monaco is under the protection of France. Responsibility for defence, foreign affairs and some other spheres are delegated to the French government. Executive power is vested in the prince, who retains considerable powers, and is exercised jointly with the minister of state [ministre d'état], a French senior civil servant appointed by the prince, and the four-member Council of Government [Conseil de Gouvernement]. Legislative power is vested in the prince and the National Council [Conseil National], whose 18 members are elected for a five-year term by a system of proportional representation. All citizens over the age of 21 are entitled to vote. Judicial power is formally vested in the prince but effectively in the seven-member Supreme Tribunal [Tribunal Suprême]. Administratively the country is divided into four quarters [quartier, pl. -s].

There are no political parties, although at elections candidates usually form lists. At the general election in January 1993 the Campora List gained 15 seats, the Médecin List two seats and an independent one seat. The head of government is Jacques Dupont, and other senior

417

ministers are Denis Ravera (chief of cabinet), Michel Éon (internal affairs) and Jean Pastorelli (finance and economy). The head of state is Prince Rainier III; the heir is Prince Albert.

Security and international affiliations. Monaco has no standing army. Responsibility for defence and general foreign affairs is delegated to France. Monaco is a member of the Francophone Community and the United Nations and several of its specialized agencies.

History. Monaco was part of the Frankish Empire and then the Holy Roman Empire in the early Middle Ages. (*For earlier developments, see* FRANCE: HISTORY.) It was ceded to the Genoese Republic in 1191. The Grimaldi family established control over Monaco in 1297 after their expulsion from Genoa by a rival group. They allied themselves with France, which formally recognized Monaco's independence in 1489. Monaco accepted Spanish protection in 1524, became a principality in 1616, and accepted French protection in 1641. It was annexed by France in 1793. As part of the post-Napoleonic reorganization of Europe in 1814/15, it was restored as an independent principality under the protection of Piedmont-Sardinia. In 1861 Monaco again accepted French protection, and in 1865 the two countries established a customs union. The opening of the casino in 1861 established Monaco as an exclusive tourist resort. A measure of constitutional government was introduced in 1911. During the Second World War (1939–45) Monaco was occupied by Italian troops in 1940 and by German troops after Italy's surrender in 1943.

Prince Rainier III ascended the throne in 1949. Faced with demands from the National Council (= parliament) for wider powers, he suspended the Council in 1959. A new constitution restoring representative government and restricting the prince's executive and legislative powers was adopted in 1962. At this time Monaco's roles as a tax haven – it levies neither income nor corporation tax – led to a major dispute with France. This was resolved in 1963 by an agreement under which some foreign residents and some Monaco-based companies, most of them French-owned or operating in France, would be taxed at French rates. Monaco joined the United Nations in May 1993.

See also entries on specific institutions, organizations, people, terms etc.

Moncloa Palace or **Moncloa** [Palacio de la Moncloa] Shorthand for the Spanish prime minister's office. The Moncloa Palace in Madrid is the official residence of the prime minister and houses several government departments.

Monegasques Citizens or people of Monaco.

Monetary Committee (MC) Institution of the European Union (EU), part of the EUROPEAN MONETARY SYSTEM (EMS). The Committee is composed of officials from the member states' finance ministries, the deputy governors of the central banks, representatives of the European Commission (the EU's administrative and executive arm) and several independent experts. Its aim is to coordinate the monetary policies of the member states. It advises the Council of Ministers and the Commission on monetary and balance-of-payments issues, carries out tasks assigned to it by these bodies, and plays a key role in the operation of the EMS and the Exchange Rate Mechanism (ERM).

monetary compensation amounts (MCAs) (European Union) *See* COMMON AGRICULTURAL POLICY.

monetary union (European Union) *See* ECONOMIC AND ....

Monks, John (1945–) British trade-union official. An economics graduate, he joined the staff of the Trades' Union Congress (TUC) in 1969. He became head of its organization and industrial relations department in 1977 and deputy general secretary in 1987. He was elected general secretary in September 1993.

Monory, René (1923–) French businessman and politician. He has been managing director of an agricultural-machinery and an oil company. First elected to the Senate in 1968 for the Centrist Union (UC), a precursor of the Social Democratic Centre (CDS), he has been minister of industry (1977–78), economy (1978) and

education (1986–88). He was again
elected to the Senate in 1988, and was
elected its president in October 1992.

Montecitorio Shorthand for the Italian
CHAMBER OF DEPUTIES, the lower house
of parliament. The Montecitorio building
in Rome is the seat of the Chamber.

Monteiro, Manuel (1962–) Portuguese
lawyer and politician. He worked for the
Confederation of Portuguese Industry
(CIP) from 1988–90 and then for a major
bank. He was elected leader of the right-
wing Democratic Social Centre - People's
Party (CDS-PP) in March 1992.

Montenegro [Crna Gora] Republic of
Yugoslavia. Situated to the southwest of
Serbia, the other republic in the federation,
Montenegro has an area of 13,812 sq km
and a population of 616,000. In ethnic
terms 61.8% of the people are Montenegrins, 14.6% Slav Muslims (recognized
as an ethnic group in Yugoslavia), 9.3%
Serbs, 6.6% Albanians, 4.2% Yugoslavs
(self-description). The main language is
Serb or Serbocroat. Nearly all Montenegrins and Serbs are nominally Orthodox Christians, and most Albanians
are Muslims. The capital is Podgorića
(formerly Titograd), and the other major
city is Cetinje. The economy is based
on agriculture (sheep and goat farming,
cereals, tobacco), manufacturing (metalworking) and forestry. Legislative power
is exercised by the 85-member Assembly
[Skupština] elected for a four-year term;
executive power is exercised by a president, also elected for a four-year term,
and a government headed by a prime
minister. The dominant political party is
the Democratic Socialist Party (DPSCG
or DPS), the successor to the League of
Communists; the other main parties are
the right-wing National Party (NSCG or
NS), the centrist Liberal Alliance (LSCG
or LS), the far-right Serbian Radical Party
(SRS) and the Social Democratic Reform
Party (SDRP). At the republican election
in December 1992 the DPS gained 44.0%
of the vote and 46 seats, the NS 13.1%
and 14 seats, the LS 12.4% and 13 seats,
the SRS 7.8% and eight seats, and the
SDRP 4.5% and four seats. The president
is Momir Bulatović, the prime minister

Milo Djukanović. The region of Montenegro was settled by Serbs in the 7th
century. Geographically isolated, it
became independent after Serbia's defeat
by the Ottoman Empire in 1389 and
successfully resisted Turkish attempts
to gain control. From 1516–1852 it was
ruled by prince-bishops [vladika, pl.
vladike]. These were popularly elected
until 1697, when the hereditary principle
was introduced (the succession generally
passing from uncle to nephew). The theocratic structure was abolished in 1852.
In 1918 Montenegro joined the new state
of Yugoslavia. The Montenegro League
of Communists (SKCG) was relaunched
as the DPS in June 1991. In 1991/92 the
republican government supported Serbia
– Montenegro's traditional ally – in resist-
ing the dissolution of the Yugoslav federation. In March 1992 voters expressed
overwhelming support for continued close
links with Serbia. The following month
the two republics adopted a new federal
constitution.

Mõõdukad *See* MODERATES.

Moraitis, Georgios (1942–) Greek lawyer
and politician. Elected to parliament for
the Pan-Hellenic Socialist Movement
(PASOK) in 1977, he has been minister
of commerce (1982–84) and deputy
minister of agriculture (1984–86) and
defence (1988–89). He was appointed
minister of agriculture when PASOK
returned to power in October 1993.

moral question [questione morale] In Italy,
the issue of how to restore ethical values
in a political system whose credibility
has been shaken by endemic corruption
exposed in 1992 and 1993 (*see* ITALIAN
CORRUPTION SCANDALS). During the
March 1994 election campaign the left-
wing Progressive Alliance defined it as
the need to 'construct a new, modern
Italy based on efficiency, solidarity and
transparency in government'.

Morava *See* MORAVIA.

Moravčík, Jozef (1945–) Slovakian lawyer and politician. Between 1969 and
1985 he worked as a teacher, legal
adviser to a state-owned company and
as a lecturer at the Bratislava law school.
From 1985–90 he was head of the

economic law department at the Charles University in Prague. Elected to the Czechoslovak federal parliament in 1990 for Public Against Violence (VPN), the Slovak arm of the movement which had brought about the collapse of the communist regime the previous year, he later joined one of its successors, the Movement for a Democratic Slovakia (HZDS). He was foreign minister from June 1992 until the federation's dissolution at the end of the year. In March 1993 he was appointed foreign minister of Slovakia. He resigned his post in February 1994 and became leader of the Democratic Union (DEÚS), a breakaway from the HZDS, in March. Later in the month he was appointed prime minister of a centrist coalition.

Moravia [Morava] Historical region of the Czech Republic. Comprising the eastern half of the country, Moravia was established as an independent kingdom in the late 9th century. It became part of Bohemia in 1029, part of Austria in 1526, and a province of the new state of Czechoslovakia in 1918. In 1927 the small Czech-speaking part of Silesia was joined to it to form Moravia-Silesia. The province was dissolved in 1949. Since the collapse of communist rule in 1989 there have been demands for its restoration and (following the dissolution of the Czechoslovak federation at the end of 1992) for the creation of a 'Czechomoravian' federal republic.

Moravia-Silesia *See* MORAVIA *and* SILESIA.

Moro case Murder of Aldo Moro, one of Italy's leading politicians, by a far-left guerrilla group in 1978. Moro was a leading member of the Christian Democratic Party (DC) and had been prime minister on five occasions between 1963 and 1976. In the most sensational attack at a time of widespread political violence, he was kidnapped by the Red Brigades (BR) in March 1978 and shot two months later. The case has remained politically controversial largely because of Moro's allegation, contained in a diary he kept while in captivity, that he had been betrayed by members of his own party for reasons of personal ambition and to thwart his attempt to forge a 'historic compromise' with the Italian Communist Party (PCI). (He was kidnapped while on his way to a special session of parliament in which he was expected to announce an accommodation with the PCI.) The strongest opponent of any attempts to negotiate with the BR for Moro's release was his fellow party member but political rival Giulio Andreotti. In 1993 Andreotti, the country's most powerful politician in the 1980s, was implicated in corruption, association with the Sicilian Mafia and complicity in murder. In relation to the Moro case it was alleged that he had requested the Mafia to kill a journalist and a senior general who were said to have known about the political manoeuvres aimed at preventing Moro's release. *See also* HIDDEN GOVERNMENT.

MOS *See* MUSLIM ARMED FORCES.

Moslem ... *See* MUSLIM ....

Mosso d'Esquadra ('Youth Guard' in Catalan) Spanish police force. The Mosso d'Esquadra is the autonomous police force of Catalonia. The name is also used by Spanish speakers. A member of the force is called a *mosso d'esquadra* (pl. -s -).

Mother Croatia [Matica Hrvatska] Croatian cultural and political organization. Founded in 1842, Matica Hrvatska played a key role in the Croat national movement in the 19th century and after the creation of Yugoslavia in 1918. It was banned by the communist authorities in 1971. Several leading members were subsequently convicted and imprisoned for espionage, separatist agitation and other offences. The organization resumed its activities in 1990. It has close links with the ruling right-wing Croatian Democratic Union (HDZ). The president is Vlado Gotovac.

Mother Slovakia [Matica Slovenská] Slovakian cultural and political organization. Dating back to the 1860s, Matica Slovenská has played a key role in the development of Slovak national consciousness. It was banned during communist rule in Czechoslovakia, but since 1989 its membership has grown sharply. Strongly nationalistic, it is opposed to special rights for the substantial Hungarian minority in the south of the country. It has close links with the right-wing Slovak National Party (SNS). The president is Jozef Markus.

Motherland Party [Anatavan Partisi] (ANAP) Turkish political party. The centre-right ANAP was founded in 1983, after the military regime of the day again allowed some political activity (after disbanding all parties on taking power in 1980). Led by Turgut Özal, it won the restricted election in 1983 and the 1987 election. Özal relinquished the party leadership on becoming president of the republic in 1989, but remained ANAP's dominant figure until his death in 1993. At the October 1991 election the party gained 24.0% of the vote and 115/450 seats, coming second to its main rival on the right, the True Path Party (DYP). Since then more than 20 deputies have left the parliamentary group. The leader is Mesut Yılmaz.

motor regions (European Union) *See* FOUR MOTORS.

Mount Athos *See* HOLY MOUNTAIN.

Movement (Lithuania) *See* HOMELAND UNION.

Movement for a Democratic Slovakia [Hnutie za Demokratické Slovensko] (HZDS) Slovakian political party. The HZDS was formed in 1991 as a successor to Public Against Violence (VPN), the Slovak arm of the broadly based movement which had spearheaded the overthrow of communist rule in Czechoslovakia in 1989 and won the multiparty election held in 1990. The HZDS called for Slovak sovereignty and for a gradual transition to a market economy. At the June 1992 election it became the largest party in the Slovakian parliament, gaining 37.3% of the vote and 74/150 seats. It then formed a government which negotiated the dissolution of the Czechoslovak federation. Weakened by internal divisions and the defection of 19 deputies, it lost power in March 1994. The leader is Vladimír Mečiar.

Movement for Democracy *See* NETWORK.

Movement for Rights and Freedoms [Dvizhenie za Prava i Svobodi] (DPS) Bulgarian political party. The DPS has its roots in the resistance of ethnic Turks to the communist regime's 'bulgarianization' campaign of the mid 1980s. Formally constituted as a party in 1990, it has established itself as the main representative of the Turkish community. It calls for equal treatment of all citizens and rejects all forms of separatism and segregation. At the October 1991 election it gained 7.6% of the vote and 24/200 seats. The leader is Ahmed Doğan.

Movement for Self-Governing Democracy of Moravia and Silesia *See* CZECHOMORAVIAN CENTRE PARTY.

Movement for the Republic [Ruch dla Rzeczpospolitej] (RdR) Polish political party. Originally called the Christian Democratic Forum (FChD), the RdR was founded in 1992 by members of the Centre Alliance (POC) and Peasant Christian Party (SLCh) opposed to what they considered their parties' rightward drift. Its policies are broadly centre-right; it has close links with Pax, a liberal Catholic organization. For the September 1993 election it joined forces with several smaller parties in the Coalition for the Republic (KdR), which gained 2.8% of the vote but no seats (having failed to reach the 8% alliances required for representation). The party split into rival wings in December 1993, led by Stanisław Weglowski and Romuald Szeremietiew respectively. The latter joined the Alliance for Poland (PdP) in May 1994.

MP Abbreviation for Member of Parliament, used specifically for a member of the House of Commons, the lower house of the British parliament.

MpG *See* ECOLOGY PARTY - THE GREENS.

MRG *See* LEFT RADICAL MOVEMENT.

MS *See* MODERATE COALITION PARTY.

MSI and **MSI-DN** *See* ITALIAN SOCIAL MOVEMENT - NATIONAL RIGHT *and* NATIONAL ALLIANCE.

MSzOSz *See* NATIONAL CONFEDERATION OF HUNGARIAN TRADE UNIONS.

MSzP *See* HUNGARIAN SOCIALIST PARTY.

MTP Abbreviation for the LIRA or pound, the Maltese currency, used in banking etc.

multi-layered Europe *See* MULTI-TRACK EUROPE.

multi-track Europe or **variable geometry** In the European Union (EU), two terms associated with those who argue that the integration process should allow member states to participate in common policies and programmes according to their requirements or preferences. From the launch of the original European Economic Community (EEC) the member states had operated on the principle that they would proceed at the same speed and in step. This began to cause problems in the 1970s, not least because of the accession of three new members, Denmark, Ireland and the United Kingdom. Several suggestions for a more flexible approach to further integration were put forward (*see* EUROPE À LA CARTE *and* TWO-SPEED EUROPE), but they found little support at this time. They began to gain ground in the early 1990s especially in the United Kingdom and Denmark, where proposals for economic, monetary and political union contained in the Maastricht Treaty (agreed in December 1991 and in force since November 1993) were highly controversial. Although 'multi-track Europe' and 'variable geometry' are of recent coinage, they describe a situation which has been evolving for some time, with various combinations of states cooperating in specific fields either within or formally outside the EU framework. For instance, participation in the Exchange Rate Mechanism (ERM), set up in 1979, has always been incomplete (the Greek drachma has never been a member, the British pound was only a member from 1990–92 and the Italian lira left in 1992); Denmark, Ireland and the United Kingdom have not signed the 1985 and 1990 Schengen Accords on eliminating border controls; the United Kingdom has not participated in aspects of the emerging common social policy since 1989; Denmark and the United Kingdom have expressed reservations about eventual participation in the final stage of economic and monetary union (EMU); Denmark has opted out of the planned common defence policy and several other policies; and Denmark and Ireland are not full members of the Western European Union (WEU), the EU's projected 'defence component'. Moreover, the Community has a long tradition of transitional arrangements for new members and temporary exemptions or 'derogations' in the implementation of new laws. *See also* OPT-OUT *and* EUROPE OF CONCENTRIC CIRCLES.

Mumcu case Murder of Ugur Mumcu, a leading Turkish journalist and writer. Mumcu worked for the centre-left newspaper *Cumhuriyet* and was a prominent advocate of secularism and opponent of religious fundamentalism. He was killed by a car bomb in İstanbul in January 1993. His funeral turned into a mass demonstration in support of secular values. Three Islamic fundamentalist guerrilla groups claimed responsibility for the assassination. Although a number of people were detained for questioning, including Iranians and nationals from neighbouring Arab countries, no one has yet been charged.

municipality [municipio] Spanish administrative division. The smallest unit of local government, each municipality has a council [ayuntamiento] elected for a four-year term and headed by a mayor [alcalde] elected from among its members. The municipalities are responsible for most local services and have autonomy in their own spheres of competence.

Murcia Autonomous community or region of Spain. Situated in the southeast, Murcia has an area of 11,317 sq km and a population of 1,038,000. The capital is Murcia, and the other major city is Cartagena. The economy is based on agriculture (fruit and vegetables, cereals), manufacturing (food processing, petrochemicals), tourism and mining (lead, zinc). The main political parties are the Spanish Socialist Workers' Party (PSOE), the centre-right People's Party (PP) and the United Left (IU). At the May 1991 election the PSOE gained 24 seats in the 45-member legislature, the PP 17 and the IU four. An independent Muslim kingdom from the 11th century, Murcia was incorporated into Castile in 1243. It was established as an autonomous region in 1982.

Murmann, Klaus (1932–) German lawyer, businessman and employers' representative. He worked for and eventually became managing director of the Sauer-Sundstrand engineering firm. He was elected president of the Federal Association of German Employers (BDA) in November 1986. He is a member of the Christian Democratic Union (CDU).

Musaraj, Agron (1950–) Albanian teacher and politician. He taught mathematics before entering politics. A member of the Democratic Party (PDSh), he was appointed minister of the interior and public order in April 1993.

Muslim Armed Forces [Muslimanske Oružane Snage] (MOS) Bosnian paramilitary group. The MOS is a volunteer force nominally under the command of the Bosnian national army, but in practice it is a largely autonomous unit. It is committed to defending the interests of the Muslim community against the rival claims of Serbs and Croats.

Muslim-Croat Federation *See* FEDERATION OF BOSNIA-HERZEGOVINA.

Muslim-Croat war and **Muslim-Serb war** (Bosnia-Herzegovina) *See* BOSNIAN CIVIL WAR.

Muslim Democratic Party [Muslimanska Demokratska Stranka] (MDS) Bosnian political party. The MDS was formed in October 1993 by dissident members of the ruling Democratic Action Party (SDA) in the Bihać region after they had severed links with the central government and proclaimed the Autonomous Province of Western Bosnia. The leader is Fikret Abdić. (The rebellion was defeated in August 1994.)

Muslims Shorthand for SLAV MUSLIMS, a recognized 'nation' in former Yugoslavia and ethnic group in the successor states, in particular Bosnia-Herzegovina.

mutual recognition In the European Union (EU), the principle that member states recognize each other's rules, regulations and standards on such matters as the production of goods, delivery of services and granting of qualifications, in order to facilitate the functioning of the single internal market. 'Mutual recognition' was initially defined as the principle that goods lawfully manufactured in one member state should be allowed free entry into other member states. During the implementation of the single-market programme between 1987 and 1992 it was extended to a number of other areas, such as technical standards, health and safety requirements, financial services and educational and professional qualifications. It was widely used instead of the more cumbersome 'harmonization' or standardization of legislation. Mutual recognition also implies that member states accept the validity of each other's rules in situations where EU-wide rules have not yet been agreed. *See also* APPROXIMATION.

N Abbreviation for Norway, used for international vehicle registrations, postal addresses etc.

N-17 *See* SEVENTEENTH OF NOVEMBER REVOLUTIONARY ORGANIZATION.

NAA *See* NORTH ATLANTIC ASSEMBLY.

NAC *See* NORTH ATLANTIC COUNCIL.

NACC *See* NORTH ATLANTIC COOPERATION COUNCIL.

Nadir affair *See* POLLY PECK AFFAIR.

Nagy, Sándor (1946–) Hungarian economist and trade-union official. He held several senior posts in the communist youth movement in the 1970s. In 1984 he joined the then Central Council of Trade Unions (SzOT), and was elected its general secretary in 1988. When the SzOT was reconstituted as the independent National Confederation of Hungarian Trade Unions (MSzOSz) in March 1990, he was elected its president.

name question (Macedonia) *See* MACEDONIA ....

NAMMCO *See* NORTH ATLANTIC MARINE MAMMALS COMMISSION.

Nano, Fatos (1952–) Albanian economist and politician. He was brought into the government in 1990 when the communist Party of Labour (PPSh) came under pressure to introduce economic and political reforms. He was briefly prime minister in February–June 1991 but was forced to resign after a general strike. In June 1991 he was elected leader of the relaunched Socialist Party (PSSh). In July 1993 he was charged with misappropriating state funds, dereliction of duty and falsification of documents in connection with the disappearance in 1991 of Italian food aid worth US\$ 8 million. He was convicted and sentenced to 12 years' imprisonment in April 1994. The PSSh considers the case against him to be politically motivated and has confirmed him as leader.

NAR *See* NATIONAL LABOUR COUNCIL.

narod ('people' or 'nation' in Serbocroat) In Bosnia-Herzegovina, Croatia and Yugoslavia, the term used by Croat and Serb nationalists to stress their distinctiveness in terms of ethnicity, history, religion and language. The notion of separate Croat and Serb *narodi* has traditionally been disputed by many Croats and Serbs, who prefer to stress the common heritage. A complicating factor is the status of Slav Muslims, who have a distinct religion but otherwise have much in common with either Croats or Serbs or both and hence do not fit into the rigid *narod* pattern. The concept is also used in other Balkan countries, in effect to imply the primacy of rights derived from ethnic identity over rights held by virtue of citizenship. This distinction is used by some groups in effect to justify discrimination against minorities.

Národná Rada *See* NATIONAL COUNCIL OF THE SLOVAK REPUBLIC.

narrow band (European Union) *See* EXCHANGE RATE MECHANISM.

Narva question *See* JAANILINN QUESTION.

Naštase, Adrian (1950–) Romanian lawyer, academic and politician. A specialist in international law, he joined the National Salvation Front (FSN) during the overthrow of the Ceauşescu regime in December 1989. He was foreign minister from 1990–92. When the FSN split in April 1992 he joined the Democratic National Salvation Front (FSND). In November 1992 he was elected president of the Assembly of Deputies, the lower house of parliament. In July 1993 he was also elected leader of the renamed Social Democracy Party (PDSR).

National Action *See* SWISS DEMOCRATS.

National Action Party [Milliyetçi Hareket Partisi] (MHP) Turkish political party. The far-right MHP has been active under a range of names since its foundation as the National Party (MP) in 1948. The party was dissolved in 1953 after its programme, in particular the call for the creation of an Islamic state, had been declared unconstitutional. It was reformed the following year, split in the early 1960s and was again dissolved (like all political parties) by the military regime which took power in 1980. It was relaunched in 1983 as the Conservative Party (TP) and was called the National Labour Party (MÇP) from 1985–92. It contested the October 1991 election in an alliance with the Welfare Party (RP), which gained 16.9% of the vote. Six of its deputies have left the party and it now has 13/450 seats in parliament. The leader is Alparslan Türkeş.

National Agency for Information and State Security [Agenzia Nazionale per l'Informazione e la Sicurezza dello Stato] (ANISS) Italian intelligence agency. The ANISS was formed in January 1994 by the reorganization and merger of the Information and Democratic Security Service (SISDE) and the Information and Military Security Service (SISMI). Both had been thoroughly discredited by evidence that senior officers had been involved in right-wing terrorist activities, political corruption, embezzlement, coup plots and association with organized crime over many years. The ANISS is divided into an intelligence and counterintelligence branch. Unlike its predecessors, it is directly accountable to a three-member committee comprising the prime minister and the interior and defence ministers.

National Alliance [Alleanza Nazionale] (AN) Italian political organization. The AN was founded in January 1994 by the far-right Italian Social Movement - National Right (MSI-DN) and several small groups, including monarchists' and pensioners' organizations, and some independent right-wing politicians. The move was widely seen as an attempt by the MSI, the intellectual heir of the National Fascist Party (PNF, in power from 1922–43 under Benito Mussolini) to blur its links with fascism and attract support from the disintegrating Christian Democratic Party (DC), which had been discredited by a series of corruption scandals. The AN contested the March 1994 election within the right-wing Freedom Alliance, gained 13.5% of the vote and 109 seats, and joined the government formed by Silvio Berlusconi. The leader is Gianfranco Fini, who is also leader of the MSI.

National Assembly [Narodno Sobranie] Parliament of Bulgaria. The Sobranie has 240 members elected for a four-year term by a system of proportional representation. Parties must obtain at least 4% of the popular vote to qualify for seats.

National Assembly [Riigikogu] Parliament of Estonia. The Riigikogu has 101 members elected for a four-year term by a system of proportional representation involving individual, party-list and compensation mandates. It elects the president of the republic.

National Assembly [Assemblée Nationale] Lower house of the French parliament. The Assembly has 577 members elected for a five-year term by absolute majority in single-member constituencies. If no candidate wins a majority in the first round, a second round is of voting is held with normally the top two candidates standing. All overseas dependencies of France are also represented in the Assembly. *See also* SENATE.

National Assembly [Országgyűlés] Parliament of Hungary. The Assembly has 394 members elected for a four-year term: 176 by absolute majority in single-member constituencies, with a second round of voting if required; 210 by proportional representation (152 from regional lists and 58 from national lists); and eight seats are reserved for ethnic minorities. It elects the president of the republic.

National Assembly [Zgromadzenie Narodowe] Parliament of Poland, composed of the SEJM and the SENATE.

National Assembly [Državni Zbor] Lower house of the Slovenian parliament. It has 90 members elected for a four-year term: 38 by simple majority in single-member constituencies and 50 by proportional representation (with parties required to obtain at least 3% of the popular vote), and two seats are reserved for the Hungarian and Italian minorities. *See also* NATIONAL COUNCIL.

National Coalition Party (Estonia) *See* FATHERLAND.

National Coalition Party [Kansallinen Kokoomus] (Kokoomus or KOK) Finnish political party. Founded in 1918, Kokoomus is the country's main right-wing party. It remained in opposition for most years from 1945 until 1987, when it joined a four-party coalition. At the March 1991 election it gained 19.3% of the vote and 40/200 seats. The party leader is Sauli Niinisto, the parliamentary leader Ben Zyskowicz, and the general secretary Pekka Kivela.

National Confederation of Free Trade Unions of Romania - Brotherhood [Confederaţia Naţională a Sindicatelor Libere din România - Frăţia] (CNSLR-Frăţia) Romanian trade-union federation. The CNSLR-Frăţia was formed in June 1993 by the merger of two federations which succeeded the official communist organization in 1990, the National Confederation of Free Trade Unions of Romania (CNSLR) and Brotherhood (Frăţia). It has a total membership of around 850,000 (a twelfth of the labour force), mainly employed in the manufacturing sector. It generally works closely with the Alpha Cartel (Alfa) and the National Trade Union Bloc (BNS), two other major federations. The joint leaders are Victor Ciorbea and Miron Mitrea.

National Confederation of Hungarian Trade Unions [Magyar Szakservezetek Országos Szövetsége] (MSzOSz) Hungarian trade-union federation. The MSzOSz was founded in 1990 as the successor to the Central Council of Trade Unions (SzOT), which had been an arm of the communist People's Front. It has 65 affiliated unions with a total membership of around 1.3 million (nearly a third of the labour force). The leader is Sándor Nagy.

National Conservative Party of Latvia [Latvijas Nacionālā Konservatīvā Partija] (LNNK) Latvian political party. Founded in June 1994, the LNNK is the successor to the National Independence Movement (LNNK), which had been launched in 1988, when Latvia was still part of the Soviet Union. It champions the rights of ethnic Latvians, who are outnumbered by Russians in the major cities, advocates centre-right economic policies and has conservative views on social issues. At the June 1993 election the old LNNK gained 13.4% of the vote and 15/100 seats. The leader is Aristids Lambergs.

National Council [Nationalrat] Lower house of the Austrian parliament. It has 183 members elected for a four-year term by a system of proportional representation. Parties must obtain at least 4% of the vote to qualify for seats. *See also* FEDERAL COUNCIL.

National Council [Conseil National] Parliament of Monaco. It has 18 members elected for a five-year term by proportional representation. It has only limited legislative powers.

National Council (Slovakia) *See* ... OF THE SLOVAK REPUBLIC.

National Council [Državni Svet] Upper house of the Slovenian parliament. It has 40 members serving a five-year term: 22 are directly elected for a five-year term and 18 are appointed by an electoral college representing local, professional, industrial and other interest groups. It has limited veto powers over legislation passed by the lower house, the National Assembly [Državni Zbor], which may override its decisions by simple majority.

National Council [Nationalrat (German), Conseil National (French), Consiglio Nazionale (Italian)] Lower house of the Swiss parliament, the Federal Assembly. It has 200 members elected for a four-year term by proportional representation in multi-member constituencies based on the cantons or federal states. Unlike most other European legislatures, it cannot be dissolved normally before the end of its term. The National Council has equal powers with the upper house, the Council of States. The two houses elect the members of the Federal Council (= government) in joint session.

National Council of French Employers [Conseil National du Patronat Français] (CNPF or Patronat) French employers' association. Founded in 1946, the Patronat has around 900,000 member companies from all industrial and service sectors, organized on a branch and regional basis. The president is François Périgot, the secretary-general Yves Monier.

National Council of the Slovak Republic or **National Council** [Národná Rada Slovenskej Republiky] Parliament of Slovakia. It has 150 members elected for a five-year term by proportional representation. Parties must obtain at least 5% of the popular vote to qualify for seats. It elects the president of the republic.

National Democratic Association [Agrupament Nacional Democràtic] (AND) Andorran political party. The centre-right

AND was formed after the new constitution promulgated in May 1993 formally legalized political parties. It has its roots in the Andorran Democratic Association (ADA) and Andorran Democratic Party (PDA), the country's main political groupings during the 1970s and 80s. At the December 1993 election the AND gained 8/28 seats and became the largest single party in parliament. It subsequently formed a minority government. The leader is Oscar Ribas Reig.

National Democratic Party [Národno-Demokratická Strana] (NDS) Slovakian political party. The NDS was formed in March 1994 by a minority wing of the SLOVAK NATIONAL PARTY (SNS) which objected to the party's drift to the right. Describing itself as centre-right, it holds 6/150 seats in parliament The leader is Ľudovít Černák, the former SNS leader.

National Democratic Party of Germany [Nationaldemokratische Partei Deutschlands] (NPD) German political party. Founded in 1964, the NPD is the oldest of the far-right formations taking their inspiration from the National Socialists (Nazis) and Adolf Hitler, who ruled Germany from 1933–45. Although it has a relatively high profile, its electoral impact has been minimal, especially in recent years: at the December 1990 federal election it gained 0.3% of the vote. The leader is Günter Deckert.

National Environmental Policy Plan or **National Environment Plan** [Nationaal Milieubeleidsplan] (NMP) Dutch government programme. Adopted in 1990 and at the time considered the most comprehensive environmental project of its kind, its aim is to reduce pollution by at least 70% by the year 2010. It doubles the outlay on clean-up efforts to 15 billion guilders (7.0 billion ecus) over the twenty-year period and sets out concrete measures to reduce air, water and soil pollution and carbon emissions, improve energy conservation and waste disposal, and increase public transport provision. The costs are borne primarily by polluters, i.e. industry, agriculture and consumers as appropriate. The plan was a response to a series of government-commissioned reports which showed that the Netherlands, one of the world's most densely populated countries, was also one of the most polluted. Disagreements over an earlier version of the plan had brought down the centre-right coalition in 1989. A more detailed supplementary programme, NMP-2, was tabled in December 1993.

National Federation of Farmers' Unions [Fédération Nationale des Syndicats d'Exploitants Agricoles] (FNSEA) French trade union. The FNSEA is the main organization of France's farmers and as such wields considerable influence. Its affiliated departmental and local unions have a total membership of 700,000, nearly two-thirds of those employed in the agriculture sector. The president is Luc Guyau, the general secretary is Étienne Lapèze.

National Federation of Green Lists *See* GREEN FEDERATION.

National Front [Front National] (FN) French political party. Founded in 1972, the far-right FN has a strongly nationalistic and anti-foreigner programme, explicitly favouring white French (and European) citizens over non-white immigrants and their descendants with regard to employment, housing and social provision. In its economic policies it calls for a third way between capitalism and socialism. It made little impression at the polls until 1984, when it gained 10.9% of the vote in the election for the European Parliament. It scored similar successes in subsequent elections, attracting support from disenchanted voters from both the middle and working class. At the March 1993 election it gained 12.4% of the vote, but owing to France's majority voting system, no seats in parliament. Jean-Marie Le Pen has been the party's leader since its foundation.

National Front for the Liberation of Corsica *See* CORSICAN NATIONAL LIBERATION FRONT.

National Gendarmerie [Gendarmerie Nationale] French paramilitary police force. The Gendarmerie is a separate branch of the armed forces, and as such ultimately answerable to the defence minister and the president. Numbering around 96,300 (including a small number of conscripts), it is essentially a general police force charged with providing public security and maintaining law and order. The Intervention Group (GIGN), a specialist unit, is trained in crowd and riot control.

National Harmony Party [Tautas Saskaņas Partija] (TSP) Latvian political party. The TSP was founded in February 1994 as the successor to the Harmony for Latvia - Economic Rebirth (SLAT). This alliance had gained 12.0% of the vote and 13/100 seats at the June 1993 election. A centre-left party, the TSP advocates the gradual introduction of a market economy and the granting of citizenship rights to the large Russian community. The leader is Jānis Jurkāns.

National Heritage Department *See* DEPARTMENT OF NATIONAL HERITAGE.

National Independence Movement of Latvia *See* NATIONAL CONSERVATIVE PARTY OF LATVIA.

National Industry Institute [Instituto Nacional de Industria] (INI) Spanish industrial conglomerate. Founded in 1941, INI is the holding company for the bulk of Spain's state-owned sector, which is one of the largest in Western Europe and accounts for around 8% of the country's GDP. The more than 200 companies under its umbrella are active in all major industrial sectors, ranging from power generation to electronics, and in a number of service industries, ranging from sea transport to financial services. The INI has been loss-making for years. In 1992/93 47 companies earmarked for eventual privatization, including the Endesa power-supply company, the Inespal aluminium company and the Iberia airline, were grouped in a new holding company, Teneo. It made a profit of 3 billion pesetas (19 million ecus) in 1993, while Grupo INI, comprising the remaining INI companies, made a record loss of 125 billion pesetas (787 million ecus).

National Labour Council [Nationale Arbeidsraad (Dutch), Conseil National du Travail (French)] (NAR or CNT) Belgian advisory body. The Council was set up in 1949 to advise the government on major economic and social issues. Its members include representatives from trade unions and employers' associations and independent experts appointed by the government.

National Labour Party *See* NATIONAL ACTION PARTY.

National Liberal Party [Partidul Naţional Liberal] (PNL) Romanian political party. The PNL was founded in 1869, banned by the communists in 1947 and relaunched in 1990. It is a centre-right party which advocates a rapid transition to a market economy. Having gained 6.4% of the vote at the May 1990 election, it was then weakened by several splits and gained 2.7% of the vote in the September 1992 election, failing to pass the 3% threshold required for representation. One offshoot, the New Liberal Party (which had gained 0.5% at the 1992 election), rejoined the PNL in February 1993. The party split again in February 1994 after Radu Câmpeanu, who had lost the leadership to Mircea Ionescu-Quintus a year earlier, was reinstated by a minority wing.

National Party of Montenegro [Narodna Stranka Crne Gore] (NSCG or NS) Yugoslav political party. Founded in 1990, the NS is a far-right party advocating closer links between the federation's two republics, Montenegro and Serbia, i.e. a more centralized state structure. It is supported by both Serbs and Montenegrins. It became Montenegro's second-largest party at the December 1992 elections, gaining 13.1% of the vote and 14/85 seats in the republican parliament as well as 4/138 seats in the Federal Assembly. The leader is Novak Kilibarda.

National Salvation Front *See* DEMOCRATIC PARTY (Romania).

national secretary [secrétaire national] In France, the official title of the leader of the French Communist Party (PCF).

national socialism [Nationalsozialismus] Formal name of NAZISM.

National Trade Union Bloc [Blocul Naţional Sindical] (BNS) Romanian trade-union federation. Founded in 1991, the BNS represents a total of around 500,000 workers (a twentieth of the labour force). It is most strongly represented in the manufacturing sector. It generally works closely with the National Confederation of Free Trade Unions of Romania - Brotherhood (CNSLR-Frăția) and the Alpha Cartel (Alfa), two other major federations. The leader is Dumitru Costin.

National Unity Party [Ulusal Birlik Partisi] (UBP) Northern Cypriot political party. Founded in 1975, UBP has been the dominant party in the Turkish Cypriot state since its proclamation. It advocates broadly centre-right economic policies and has conservative views on social issues. Under the leadership of Rauf Denktaş, now president of the republic, it favoured a confederal solution to the island's division between the Greek and Turkish communities (*see* CYPRUS QUESTION). It now argues for a formal separation into two states. The party split over the issue in 1992, with supporters of the Denktaş line forming the Democratic Party (DP). After gaining 29.9% of the vote and 17/50 seats at the December 1993 election, the UBP went into opposition for the first time. The leader is Derviş Eroğlu.

nationalism In Northern Ireland (United Kingdom), support for the territory's eventual unification with the Republic of Ireland. The reunification of Ireland is supported by the great majority of the Catholic community, although Catholics are sharply divided between those who accept it can only be achieved with the consent of the majority Protestant community and those who reject the legitimacy of British rule in Northern Ireland and have supported or tolerated political violence by the Irish Republican Army (IRA) and others to end it. The former are usually called 'nationalists' and the latter 'republicans'. Their main representative political organizations are the Social Democratic and Labour Party (SDLP) and Sinn Féin respectively. (In August 1994 the IRA declared a ceasefire from September.) *See also* UNIONISM.

Nationalist Action Party *See* NATIONAL ACTION PARTY.

Nationalist Council [Cuncolta Nazionalista (Corsican)] (A Cuncolta) French political organization. The Cuncolta is the successor to the Corsican Self-Determination Movement (MCA), which was banned in 1987 after police investigations revealed that it maintained links with the illegal Corsican National Liberation Front (FLNC). (The MCA was itself the successor to the Confederation of Nationalist Committees, CCN, which had been banned in 1983 for its links with the FLNC.) It calls for the 'recognition of the national rights of the Corsican people' and advocates 'public struggles, including electoral ones' to achieve this aim. It is widely considered the political wing of the FLNC's hard-line 'historical' wing. The leader is Jean-Guy Talamoni.

Nationalist Labour Party *See* NATIONAL ACTION PARTY.

Nationalist Party [Partit Nazzjonalista] (PN or NP) Maltese political party. Founded in 1880, the Nationalist Party holds mainstream christian democratic views. It formed the government on several occasions before independence and from 1962–71. It narrowly defeated the Labour Party in 1987 to return to power. At the February 1992 election it gained 51.8% of the vote and 34/65 seats. Edward Fenech-Adami has been the leader since 1977; the general secretary is Austin Gatt.

Nationalrat *See* NATIONAL COUNCIL (Austria, Switzerland).

NATO *See* NORTH ATLANTIC TREATY ORGANIZATION.

NATO Council Shorthand for the NORTH ATLANTIC COUNCIL (NAC), the highest decision-making body of the North Atlantic Treaty Organization (NATO).

Navarra *See* NAVARRE.

Navarre [Navarra] Autonomous community or region of Spain. Situated in the north, on the southern slopes of the Pyrenees, Navarre has an area of 10,421 sq km and a population of 522,000. Basques account for around a quarter of the population. The capital is Pamplona. The economy is based on agriculture (dairy farming, vegetables, cereals), manufacturing (food processing, engineering, textiles, footwear) and forestry. The main political parties are the centre-right Navarre People's Union (UPN), allied to the People's Party (PP); the Socialist Party of Navarre (PSN), the regional branch of the Spanish Socialist Workers' Party (PSOE); People's Unity (Herri Batasuna, HB), which advocates the inclusion of Navarre in an independent Basque Country and supports violent action to achieve this aim; and Basque Solidarity (EA), which also considers Navarre part of the historical Basque Country but rejects violence. At the May 1991 election the UPN gained 20 seats in the 50-member legislature, the PSN 19, Herri Batasuna six and the EA three. Throughout the Middle Ages Navarre was an independent kingdom straddling the Pyrenees. The territory south of the mountains was annexed by Spain in 1512. It retained a degree of autonomy until the 18th century. It was established as an autonomous region in 1982.

nazism [Nazismus], in full **national socialism** [Nationalsozialismus] Political outlook in Germany and Austria based on the values and policies of the far-right National Socialist German Workers' Party (NSDAP) or Nazi Party, which under the leadership of Adolf Hitler (1889–1945) ruled Germany from 1933 and Austria from 1938 until Germany's defeat in the Second World War. An amalgam of various 19th-century political, social and racial theories, nazism was essentially based on nationalism, corporatism and authoritarianism, elements it shared with Italian FASCISM. It also asserted the superiority of the 'Aryan race', of which the Germans were the purest example, and the consequent inferiority of other 'races' such as Slavs, Gipsies and especially Jews. The Nazi Party was organized on the charismatic leadership principle, with Hitler recognized as the all-powerful *Führer* ('leader'). It gained substantial electoral support in the early 1930s, thriving on voters' anger at the economic depression, the traditional political parties and the terms of the 1919 Treaty of Versailles (imposed after Germany's defeat in the First World War). It became the largest party in 1932, and Hitler was asked to form a government in 1933. Once in power the nazis suppressed all opposition, introduced measures reflecting its economic, social and racial priorities, established a structure of party organizations that usurped state functions, and pursued a foreign policy aimed at incorporating all ethnic Germans within the 'Third Reich'. In the Second World War (1939–45), sparked by Germany's attack on Poland, the nazis were responsible for innumerable atrocities across Europe, including the use of slave labour, summary executions and random acts of violence, and the genocide of Jews and Gipsies (*see* HOLOCAUST). After 1945 the propagation of nazi ideology and the display of nazi symbols (flags, uniforms, salutes etc) were banned in Germany and Austria. For this reason established far-right political parties such as the National Democratic Party (NPD) and Republicans (REP) in Germany disclaim any links with the nazi past. In recent years other organizations and groups have openly declared their sympathies with nazi ideology, and fringe groups have evoked its racial elements to justify attacks on immigrants and refugees. Some of these have been banned.

NBH Abbreviation for Nemzet Biztonsági Hivatal ('National Security Office'), the Hungarian civilian intelligence service, responsible to the interior minister.

NCC *See* RED BRIGADES.

NCW *See* DUTCH CHRISTIAN EMPLOYERS' FEDERATION.

ND *See* NEW DEMOCRATIC PARTY.

'Ndrangheta Italian crime syndicate. Based in the southern region of Calabria but also active in the northern cities, the 'Ndrangheta developed into a major organization in the 1980s. It is involved in particular in kidnapping (for ransom), extortion (mainly in the construction sector) and money laundering. Since 1991 it has played a major role in arms-smuggling operations across the Adriatic Sea to supply protagonists in the Bosnian and Croatian civil wars. It generally cooperates with the MAFIA, its longer-established counterpart in neighbouring Sicily.

NDS *See* NATIONAL DEMOCRATIC PARTY.

Neapolitian Mafia *See* CAMORRA.

near abroad [blizheye zarubezhe] In Russia, a collective name for the former Soviet republics. Many of them have substantial ethnic Russian and/or Russian-speaking minorities. They include, to the west of Russia, Belorussia, Estonia, Latvia, Lithuania, Moldavia and Ukraine. The term was coined after the disintegration of the Soviet Union in 1991. Some nationalist groups argue that the 'near abroad' should be recognized as a Russian 'sphere of influence', and some extreme groups even call for its reincorporation into a reconstituted Soviet Union or Russian Empire (depending on their ideological stance).

Necker, Tyll (1930–) German businessman and employers' representative. An economics graduate, he joined and eventually became managing director of the Hako-Werke, a company manufacturing special industrial machinery and household appliances. He was president of the Confederation of German Industry (BDI) from 1987–90 and returned to the same post in August 1992.

Nederland Dutch name for the Netherlands.

Neman question Border dispute between Lithuania and Russia. The Neman [Nemunas] river forms the border between Lithuania and the Kaliningrad region of Russia. In the 1940s, when both territories were incorporated into the Soviet Union, the border was drawn on the Lithuanian bank. This is now disputed by Lithuania, which argues that under international law it should be in mid-river. The Neman is navigable and hence economically important.

Németh, Miklós (1948–) Hungarian economist, academic and politician. He lectured in political economy from 1971–77, worked at the National Planning Office from 1977–81 and then at the communist Hungarian Socialist Workers' Party (MSzMP). A reformist, he was prime minister from 1988 until the relaunched Hungarian Socialist Party (MSzP) lost the multiparty election in 1990. In June 1991 he was appointed a vice-president of the European Bank for Reconstruction and Development (EBRD).

Nemunas question *See* NEMAN QUESTION.
neo-communist party *See* POST-....
neo-fascism *See* FASCISM.
neo-gaullism *See* GAULLISM.
neo-nazism *See* NAZISM.
Neodvisnost *See* INDEPENDENCE (Slovenia).
Netherlands [Nederland] Country in western Europe, often referred to informally as Holland.

Official data. Name: Kingdom of the Netherlands [Koninkrijk der Nederlanden]; capital: Amsterdam; seat of government: The Hague [Den Haag]; form of government: parliamentary monarchy; head of state: king/queen; head of government: prime minister; flag: three horizontal stripes, red, white and blue; national holiday: 30 April (Queen's Official Birthday); language: Dutch; religion: none; currency: gulden (f) = 100 cent; abbreviation: NL.

Geography. The largest of the Benelux countries, the Netherlands has an area of 41,863 sq km. It is bordered by the North Sea in the west and north, Germany in the east and Belgium in the south. Most of the country is a low-lying coastal and river plain. Around a quarter of the land is below sea level, and in the west much of it is reclaimed. The only hilly areas are in the east and far southeast. Some 27% of the land is arable, another 32% is covered by pastures and 9% is forested. The main rivers are the Rhine [Rijn] and its branches the Waal and Lek, Meuse [Maas] and Scheldt [Schelde]. The climate is temperate marine, with mild summers and cool winters; rainfall is moderate.

Demography. The Netherlands has a population of 15,302,000. Population density is 451 per sq km (land area), among the highest in the world. Some 89% of the people live in urban areas and nearly a third lives in the Randstad Holland (population 4.8 million), a conurbation comprising the country's four main cities, Amsterdam, Rotterdam, The Hague and Utrecht. Other major cities are Eindhoven, Groningen, Tilburg, Nijmegen, Enschede and Arnhem. In ethnic terms 90.8% of the people are Dutch, 3.5% Frisians and 1.0% Surinamese and Antilleans; there are also small groups of

South Moluccans (36,000) and others of Indonesian descent. Foreign nationals account for 4.7% of the population, and include citizens of Turkey (210,000 or 1.4% of the total), Morocco (170,000 or 1.1%), Germany, Belgium and Spain. The Netherlands has also taken in around 40,000 refugees from former Yugoslavia. The main language is Dutch; Frisian is the main language in the northern province of Friesland. In religious terms 36.0% of the population is Roman Catholic, 17.5% Lutheran Protestant, 8.4% Calvinist, 2.2% Muslim, and 2.3% belongs to other faiths; 34.6%, one of the highest percentages in Europe, describes itself as unaffiliated or non-religious.

Sociography. The Netherlands scores 0.923 on the United Nations human development index (HDI), ranking ninth in the world and fifth among 32 European countries. There are 25 doctors and 60 hospital beds for every 10,000 people. Education is compulsory between the ages of five and 16. There is one teacher for every 14 students. Enrolment is 81% at the secondary level and 34% at the tertiary level. The literacy rate is virtually 100%. Real annual income per head (in terms of purchasing power) is US$ 16,820. Income differentials are small.

Infrastructure and communications. The Netherlands has a highly developed transport and communications network, with the road network among the densest in the world and rivers and canals particularly important for freight transport; the ports and airports serve as a major conduit for goods to and from Germany and other European countries. There are 102,350 km of paved roads and 5.51 million passenger cars (366 per 1,000 people), 2,830 km of railways and 6,340 km of navigable waterways. The main port is Rotterdam, the world's busiest; other major ports are Amsterdam, IJmuiden, Terneuzen, Vlissingen and Delfzijl. The main airport is at Amsterdam (Schiphol), and there are four other airports with scheduled services. There are 46 daily newspapers, with a combined circulation of 4.61 million (313 per 1,000 people). There are 12.15 million radio receivers,

5.01 million television sets and 9.75 million telephones in use (respectively 807, 333 and 648 per 1,000 people).

Economic structure. The Dutch economy is highly developed, diversified, trade-oriented (exports account for over half of national income) and closely linked to its neighbours. It is the sixth-largest economy in Europe and the world's seventh-largest trading power. It is based on a highly specialized agricultural sector and food-processing industry, manufacturing, trade and transport. Since the late 1980s economic performance has been marked by steady growth (averaging 3.2% per year) until 1991 and low growth since then, large current-account surpluses (over 3% of GDP) and low inflation (averaging around 2%), but also by relatively high unemployment (up to 9%).

Services contribute 62% of GDP, industry contributes 33% (manufacturing 22%), and agriculture 5%. Some 17% of the labour force is employed in manufacturing, 16% in trade and 9% in finance. The main agricultural activities are dairy farming (milk, butter, cheese, eggs), horticulture (fruit and vegetables, plants, flowers, bulbs) and livestock raising (cattle, pigs, chickens); the main crops grown are potatoes, sugarbeets and wheat. Fishing is of regional importance. The main mineral resources are natural gas, oil and salt; the Netherlands is the world's fourth-largest producer of natural gas. The main industries are food processing (including beverages and tobacco products), engineering, chemicals and petrochemicals; other important branches are electronics, metalworking, printing and textiles. Trade, transport, banking and other financial services and tourism are important sources of foreign exchange. The main energy sources are natural gas and imported oil; the Netherlands is a net exporter of fuels. The main exports are foodstuffs (20% of the total, esp. dairy products, meat), chemicals (16%), industrial machinery (12%), oil products (6%), electrical equipment (6%), natural gas and textiles and clothing; machinery and transport equipment account for 24% of the total. The main imports are machinery and transport equipment, basic manufactures, foodstuffs, chemicals and fuels. The main trading partners are: exports: Germany (29%), Belgium and Luxemburg (14%), France (11%), United Kingdom (10%), Italy (6%), United States, Spain; imports: Germany (26%), Belgium and Luxemburg (14%), United Kingdom (9%), United States (8%), France (8%), Italy, Japan; two-thirds of all trade is with other European Union (EU) countries.

The Netherlands Bank [Nederlandsche Bank] (DNB) is the central bank. The main employers' associations are the Federation of Dutch Industry (VNO) and the Dutch Christian Employers' Federation (NCW); the main labour organizations are the Dutch Trade Union Confederation (FNV), Christian National Trade Union Federation (CNV) and Federation of Managerial Staff (MHP).

Political structure. The Netherlands is a parliamentary monarchy on the basis of a constitution adopted in 1983. Executive power is formally vested in the king/queen but exercised by the prime minister and the cabinet. Legislative power is vested in the bicameral States-General [Staten-Generaal], composed of the Second Chamber [Tweede Kamer], whose 150 members are elected for a four-year term by a system of proportional representation, and the First Chamber [Eerste Kamer], whose 75 members are indirectly elected by the provincial legislatures for a four-year term. All citizens over the age of 18, including those living abroad, are entitled to vote. Judicial power is ultimately vested in the three-member Supreme Court [Hoge Raad] appointed by the legislature. The advisory Council of State [Raad van State], composed of senior political figures, has a range of consultative and judicial powers. Administratively the country is divided into 12 provinces [provincie, pl. -s], which are subdivided into 702 municipalities.

The main political parties are the Labour Party (PvdA), Christian Democratic Appeal (CDA), People's Party for Freedom and Democracy (VVD), Democrats 66 (D'66), General Elderly People's Union (AOV), Green Left (Groen Links),

Reformational Political Federation (RPF), Political Reformed Party (SGP), Reformed Political Union (GPV), Centre Democrats (CD), Socialist Party (SP) and Union 55+ (Unie 55+). At the general election in May 1994 the PvdA gained 24.% of the vote and 37/150 seats, CDA 22.2% and 34 seats, the VVD 19.9% and 31 seats, D'66 15.5% and 24 seats, the AOV 3.6% and six seats, Groen Links 3.5% and five seats, the CD 2.5% and three seats, the RPF 1.8% and three seats, the SGP 1.7% and two seats, the GPV 1.3% and two seats, the SP 1.3% and one seat, and Unie 55+ 0.9% and one seat. The government is formed by a left-right coalition of the PvdA, VVD and D'66, with Wim Kok as prime minister. Other senior ministers are Hans Dijkstal (first deputy prime minister, internal affairs), Hans van Mierlo (second deputy prime minister, foreign affairs), Gerrit Zalm (finance), Hans Wijers (economic affairs), Winnie Sorgdrager (justice) and Joris Voorhoeve (defence). The head of state is Queen Beatrix, who succeeded to the throne in April 1980; the heir is Prince Willem Alexander.

The Netherlands has two overseas dependencies, Aruba and the Dutch Antilles in the Caribbean, which are internally self-governing integral parts of the kingdom.

Security and international affiliations. The Dutch armed forces number 71,000 (army 43,300, navy 14,900, airforce 12,000, central staff 800). There is also a 3,600-strong paramilitary force, the Royal Military Constabulary [Koninklijke Marechaussee]. Military service is compulsory and consists of 9–12 months' basic training; conscription is due to be phased out by 1998.

The Netherlands is a member of the Benelux Economic Union, Council of Europe, European Economic Area (EEA), European Union (EU), North Atlantic Treaty Organization (NATO) and Western European Union (WEU), as well as the Organization for Economic Cooperation and Development (OECD) and the United Nations (UN) and its specialized agencies.

History. The area of the modern Netherlands was inhabited by Germanic tribes when the Romans conquered the southern half in the 1st century BC. After the collapse of the Roman Empire in the 5th century the Franks controlled the south, the Frisians the coastal areas and the Saxons the east. The whole region came under Frankish control during the reign of Charlemagne (768–814). The various partitions of the Frankish Empire after his death eventually left the region within the East Frankish Kingdom, later the Holy Roman or German Empire. During the 9th and 10th centuries the Vikings raided the coastal areas and established some trading posts. Feudal fragmentation from the 10th century onwards led to the emergence of autonomous states, including Holland in the west, Zeeland in the southwest, Utrecht (a bishopric) in the centre, Gelre in the east, and Friesland in the north. From the 11th century extensive dike building (on the coast and along the rivers) and land reclamation made new land available for agriculture. This in turn made possible the rise of a free peasantry (i.e. free of feudal bonds) and of the towns that would dominate Dutch history in the following centuries. The County of Holland became the dominant local power in the 14th century. In 1433 Philip of Burgundy, who already ruled Flanders, Brabant and other states to the south, inherited Holland and Zeeland. The Burgundian possessions passed to the Habsburgs in 1482. The other states came under Habsburg control during the reign of Emperor Charles V (1519–56). The historical Low Countries or Netherlands (i.e. including Belgium and Luxemburg) were thus united for the first time. On Charles's abdication the Habsburg Empire was divided into Austrian and Spanish branches, with the Low Countries allocated to the latter. A rebellion against Spanish rule, led by the powerful merchant class and sections of the nobility, including William of Orange, and fuelled in large measure by the rise of Protestantism, broke out in the 1560s. The seven northern provinces, broadly coextensive with the modern Netherlands, formed the Union of Utrecht in 1579 and declared their independence in 1581. Fighting continued until 1609, when Spain recognized the Dutch Republic; a final peace was signed in 1648, when the Republic was also formally detached from the Holy Roman Empire. The Republic was a confederation in which the provinces retained full sovereignty but cooperated in defence and foreign policy. It was dominated by Holland and its cities, above all Amsterdam, and the House of Orange, whose members served as 'stadholder' or 'governor' [stadhouder] in the seven provinces. In the 17th century the Dutch Republic became a major commercial and maritime power, acquiring great wealth through trade and conquests in the East and West Indies in particular. It lost its maritime supremacy after three naval wars with England between 1652 and 1674, and the War of the Spanish Succession (1701–13/14) ended its status as a major European power. In the first half of the 18th century domestic politics was dominated by a conflict between the urban oligarchies on the one side and the princes of Orange supported by the urban poor on the other; and in the second half, by the emergence of a reform movement. The country was occupied by French troops in 1795, and the reformist 'patriots' proclaimed the Batavian Republic. This became the Kingdom of Holland in 1806 and was annexed by France in 1810.

As part of the post-Napoleonic reorganization of Europe in 1814/15 the Congress of Vienna united the Low Countries as the Kingdom of the Netherlands under the House of Orange. In 1830 the southern provinces, overwhelmingly Catholic and dominated by French speakers, rebelled against Dutch rule and became independent as Belgium the following year. A liberal constitution was adopted in 1848. A constitutional settlement established full parliamentary democracy in 1917, completed with the extension of the franchise to women in 1922. This period marked the beginning of the characteristic 'pillarization' [verzuiling] of Dutch society into various denominational and other groups (in particular

Catholic, Protestant, socialist and unaffiliated). This segmentation, which extended to all aspects of public life, from party politics to the broadcasting system, remained entrenched until the 1960s. The Netherlands was hard-hit by the worldwide economic depression of the 1930s. During the Second World War (1939–45) the country was under German occupation from 1940–44/45.

The Netherlands joined Belgium and Luxemburg in the Benelux Economic Union in 1948, became a founding member of the North Atlantic Treaty Organization (NATO) in 1949 and of the European Economic Community (EEC), now the European Union (EU), in 1958. After four years of fighting, the Dutch East Indies became independent as Indonesia in 1949. Under a new constitution adopted in 1954, the remaining overseas possessions, the Dutch Antilles and Surinam, became internally self-governing. (Surinam became independent in 1975.) Since 1945 domestic politics has been dominated by three confessional parties (one Catholic, two Protestant) which merged into the Christian Democratic Appeal (CDA) in 1980, the Labour Party (PvdA) and the right-wing People's Party for Freedom and Democracy (VVD). Coalition governments and a large degree of consensus have been the norm. Centre-left coalitions held power from 1948–58, 1973–77, 1981–82 and 1989–94, centre-right coalitions from 1958–65, 1966–73, 1977–81 and 1982–89, and a centrist coalition in 1965–66. The CDA and its predecessors were the dominant coalition partners throughout this period. Under Ruud Lubbers the CDA formed a coalition with the VVD in November 1982 and with the PvdA in November 1989. Since the early 1980s successive governments have sought to reduce the public borrowing requirement and the cost of the generous welfare system. The CDA and PvdA suffered heavy losses in the May 1994 election. The PvdA, VVD and Democrats 66 (D'66) formed a left-right coalition in August.

See also entries on specific institutions, organizations, parties, people, terms etc.

Network [La Rete], in full **Movement for Democracy 'The Network'** [Movimento per la Democrazia - La Rete] (La Rete) Italian political party. The Network was founded in Sicily in 1991 to mobilize 'civil society' (i.e. the people) against political corruption and organized crime. Its foundation was precipitated by the dismissal of the mayor of Palermo, Leoluca Orlando, who had sought to take action against the Mafia but had been thwarted by his own Christian Democratic Party (DC). The new party gained 7.8% of the vote at the June 1991 regional election in Sicily. Supported by liberal sections of the Catholic Church and other reformist forces, it also attracted support in other parts of the country at the April 1992 general election, gaining 1.0% of the vote and 12/360 seats. It enjoyed considerable support in local elections in 1992 and 1993 as the established parties became discredited by a series of corruption scandals, and in the case of the DC also by association with organized crime. The Network contested the March 1994 election within the Progressive Alliance and gained 1.9% and nine seats. Orlando is the party leader.

neutrality (Switzerland) *See* PERMANENT NEUTRALITY.

new Bundesland (Germany) *See* NEW FEDERAL STATE.

New Democracy (Greece) *See* NEW DEMOCRATIC PARTY.

New Democracy [Ny Demokrati] (NYD) Swedish political party. Founded by two businessmen, Ian Wachtmeister and Bert Karlsson, in 1991 as a joke on the political establishment, New Democracy is a right-wing protest party advocating tax cuts, restrictions on foreigners and a range of other populist measures, including a sharp reduction in the price of alcohol. It achieved instant success at the September 1991 election, gaining 6.7% of the vote and 25/349 seats. Wachtmeister resigned as party leader in April 1994 and was succeeded by Harriet Colliander.

New Democratic Party [Néa Dimokratía] (ND) Greek political party. Founded as the successor to the centre-right National Radical Union (ERE) in 1974, after the collapse of the military dictatorship, the ND won the election held that year. It was in opposition from 1981–89, participated in two interim coalitions in 1989–90, and formed a government on its own after the April 1990 election, when it gained 46.9% of the vote and 152/300 seats. Traditionally centre-right, its economic programme became considerably more free-market and right-wing at this time. The party lost its parliamentary majority in September 1993 after the formation of the breakaway Political Spring (POLA). It lost power in the early election held the following month, gaining 39.3% and 110 seats. Konstantinos Mitsotakis, party leader since 1984, then tendered his resignation and was succeeded by Miltiades Evert.

new dinar (Yugoslavia) *See* SUPER DINAR.

new federal state or **new state** [neues Bundesland, pl. neue Bundesländer] In Germany, one of the five federal states on the territory of former East Germany. They are Brandenburg, Mecklenburg - West Pomerania, Saxony, Saxony-Anhalt and Thuringia. They were dissolved by the communist regime in 1952 but were reconstituted prior to German reunification in October 1990.

new independent states (NIS) Collective name for the successor states of the Soviet Union. They include, to the west of Russia, Estonia, Latvia, Lithuania, Belorussia, Ukraine and Moldavia.

new Land, **new Länder** and **new state** (Germany) *See* NEW FEDERAL STATE.

new strategic concept (North Atlantic Treaty Organization) *See* STRATEGIC CONCEPT.

new Yugoslavia *See* RUMP YUGOSLAVIA.

Newton, Tony (1937–) British politician. He worked in the Conservative Party research department from 1961–74, serving as its assistant director from 1970. Elected to Parliament in 1974, he held several junior ministerial posts from 1981, mostly in the health and social-security departments. He became secretary of state for social security in 1989 and leader of the House of Commons, with responsibility for organizing government business, in April 1992.

Nezavisnost *See* INDEPENDENCE (Yugoslavia).

NFT and **NFT Podkrepa** *See* SUPPORT.

NHO *See* CONFEDERATION OF BUSINESS AND INDUSTRY.

NHS Abbreviation for National Health Service, the system of state healthcare in the United Kingdom introduced in 1948. Its basic principles, free diagnosis and treatment of illness and funding from general taxation, have been much eroded in recent years.

Nicosia Shorthand for the Cypriot government. Nicosia is the capital of Cyprus. Since the division of the island in 1974, the north of the city has been part of the Turkish Cypriot sector and has functioned as the capital of Northern Cyprus.

Niederösterreich *See* LOWER AUSTRIA.

Niedersachsen *See* LOWER SAXONY.

Nielsen, Holger K. (1950–) Danish civil servant and politician. A graduate in political science, he has worked in the European Parliament and in the energy ministry. He was a member of parliament for the Socialist People's Party (SF) from 1981–84 and regained a seat in 1987. He was elected party leader in May 1991.

Niinisto, Sauli (1946–) Finnish lawyer and politician. He practised law from 1978–88. He was elected to the Salo town council for the right-wing National Coalition Party (KOK) in 1977 and became its chairman in March 1989. Elected to parliament in 1987, he was elected party leader in August 1994.

1992 and **1993** In the European Union (EU), shorthands for the process of establishing a SINGLE INTERNAL MARKET for goods, services, capital and labour. This had been a long-standing aim, and in 1986 the member states set themselves a deadline of the end of 1992 for its completion. This involved reaching agreement on and implementing 282 specific 'harmonizing' measures. In some countries the programme and the target became known as '1992', in others as '1993'.

NIS Abbreviation for 'new independent states', a collective name for the successor states of the Soviet Union. They include, to the west of Russia, Estonia, Latvia,

Lithuania, Belorussia, Ukraine and Moldavia.

NKr Abbreviation for the KRONE, the Norwegian currency.

NL Abbreviation for the Netherlands, used for international vehicle registrations, postal addresses etc.

NLG Abbreviation for the gulden or GUILDER, the Dutch currency, used in banking etc.

NMP *See* NATIONAL ENVIRONMENTAL POLICY PLAN.

NMR Danish, Norwegian and Swedish abbreviation for Nordens Ministerråd ('NORDIC COUNCIL OF MINISTERS').

no-fly zone (Bosnia-Herzegovina) *See* AIR-EXCLUSION ZONE.

Nogueira, Joaquim Fernando (1950–) Portuguese lawyer, civil servant and politician. He lectured in law from 1977–80 and held a senior post in a government regional office from 1980–83. Elected to parliament for the centre-right Social Democratic Party (PSD) in 1983, he was appointed minister of justice in 1987. In October 1991 he became minister of defence and minister of the presidency.

Noir, Michel (1944–) French businessman and politician. Before entering politics he worked as a product manager and sales director for an engineering company and as an independent marketing consultant. He was elected to parliament for the right-wing Rally for the Republic (RPR) in 1978. In the 1980s he served in several senior party posts and as a junior trade minister (1986–88). He was elected mayor of Lyon, France's second city, in March 1989. Increasingly at odds with the RPR leadership, he resigned from the party and from parliament in December 1990 and was reelected to the latter as an independent. In March and April 1994 he was charged with embezzling public funds and diverting campaign funds for personal use.

NOK Abbreviation for the KRONE, the Norwegian currency, used in banking etc.

nomenklatura ('nomenclature' in Russian) In the former communist countries, a common name for the ruling elite during the communist period. The term originated in the Soviet Union from the practice of filling posts in the party and state hierarchies from a list of names or *nomenklatura* of people approved by the Communist Party as politically reliable and qualified. Appointments were decided by the appropriate party organs from the national down to the local level. The system, whose operation was not officially acknowledged, was a key element in maintaining the party's hold on power. It was carried into the Eastern European satellite states after the Second World War and was greatly extended over the years. The *nomenklatura* gradually took on the character of a distinct social stratum: a dominant 'class' of appointees and their immediate dependants (numbering perhaps 0.5% of the total population) enjoying substantial material and other benefits. Following the collapse of communist rule in 1989 many senior members of the widely resented *nomenklatura* were removed from positions of authority. *See also* DECOMMUNIZATION *and* SCREENING.

nomós (pl. nomói) Greek administrative division, usually translated as 'prefecture' or 'department'. Each of the 51 *nomói* is administered by a prefect [nomárchis] appointed by the central government. Greater Athens, centred on the capital, is divided into four subprefectures. The main function of this tier is supervision of the activities of the municipalities, which are the main units of local government and have elected councils. Some of its functions are also being transferred to 13 higher-level regions created in 1987.

Non-Party Bloc in Support of Reforms or **Non-Party Reform Bloc** [Bezpartyjny Blok Wspierania Reform] (BBWR) Polish political organization. The BBWR was founded in June 1993 as an umbrella organization for supporters of President Wałęsa's programme of continued economic and political reforms and a strong presidency. The BBWR – the initials echo a similar 'presidential' movement formed by supporters of Józef Piłsudski in 1928 – gained 5.4% of the vote and 16/460 seats at the September 1993 election. The party president is Zbigniew Religa, the parliamentary leader is Andrzej Gąsienica-Makowski.

Nord-Pas-de-Calais Region of France. Situated in the north and bordering on Belgium, the region has an area of 12,414 sq km and a population of 3,969,000. Dutch or Flemish is spoken by around 100,000 people in the northwest; it has no official status but is allowed to be taught in schools. The capital is Lille, and the other main cities are Valenciennes, Lens, Béthune, Douai, Dunkirk [Dunkerque] and Calais. The economy is based on manufacturing (textiles, steel, electronics, engineering, food processing). One of France's major industrial centres, the region has suffered considerable problems because of the decline of heavy industry and coal mining, and structural unemployment is high.

Norden Danish, Norwegian and Swedish name for the Nordic area or the NORDIC COUNTRIES.

Nordic area *See* NORDIC COUNTRIES.

Nordic Cooperation Formal name of the intergovernmental cooperation among the Nordic countries – Denmark (and its dependencies Faroe Islands and Greenland), Finland, Iceland, Norway, Sweden – organized through the consultative NORDIC COUNCIL and the executive NORDIC COUNCIL OF MINISTERS. 'Nordic Council' is often used interchangeably to cover both aspects of the cooperation.

Nordic Council Interparliamentary assembly, a consultative body of what is formally called Nordic Cooperation. Set up in 1953, the Council has 87 members, elected annually by and from the parliaments of the five Nordic countries: 20 from Denmark (including two from the Faroe Islands and two from Greenland), 20 from Finland (including two from the Åland Islands), seven from Iceland, and 20 each from Norway and Sweden; the respective autonomous territories of the Åland Islands, Faroe Islands and Greenland have separate status within their respective delegations. The Council meets annually and is based in Stockholm (Sweden). It advises the Nordic Council of Ministers and governments on legislative matters, in particular concerning economic, cultural, legal, social, environmental and communications issues. Its

recommendations are not binding, but since they reflect the views of the Nordic parliaments they generally result in measures being taken by the respective governments through the Council of Ministers. Work between council sessions is delegated to a 10-member presidium, which has its own secretariat.

Nordic Council of Ministers Intergovernmental organization, commonly known as the Nordic Council. The Nordic Council of Ministers is the executive arm of what is formally called Nordic Cooperation. It was set up 1971 on the basis of the 1962 Helsinki Convention, which formalized the already extensive cooperation among the five Nordic countries.

Aims and objectives. The Nordic Council of Ministers aims to coordinate policy and legislation among member states on such matters as economic development, the labour market, finance, trade, social issues, education, culture, environment, legal affairs, communications, energy, regional development, and food and nutrition.

Membership. The Nordic Council of Ministers has five members: Denmark, Finland, Iceland, Norway and Sweden. All are founding members.

Structure and activities. The organization's governing body is the Council of Ministers, which holds formal and informal meetings throughout the year. Meetings are attended by the member states' ministers with responsibility for the subject under discussion. Decisions must be unanimous on all substantive issues. They are binding unless parliamentary approval is required under a member state's constitution. The Council is assisted by a secretariat, the Office of the Secretary-General. There are also around 650 committees dealing with specific aspects of Nordic cooperation. The numerous institutions set up under the auspices of the Council include the Nordic Investment Bank (NIB), Nordic Industrial Fund (NIF) and Nordic Cultural Fund (NKF). The secretariat is based in Copenhagen, the Danish capital. The secretary-general is Fridtjof Clemet (Norway).

History. Cooperation among the Nordic countries has traditionally been close for historical and cultural reasons. It began to take on more concrete forms in the early 1950s. In 1953 the Nordic Council, an interparliamentary assembly, was set up. In the same year the governments of Denmark, Iceland, Norway and Sweden set up joint committees to deal with economic, cultural, social, legal and communications matters. Among the first measures adopted was the relaxation and eventual abolition of all passport and currency controls and the creation of a single labour market (which came into force in 1954). A convention on social security was also adopted in 1954. In March 1962 the five Nordic governments initialled the Treaty of Nordic Cooperation, also known as the Helsinki Convention, which set up the Nordic Council of Ministers and formalized the structure of cooperation as it had developed over the previous decade. This agreement and a number of subsequent agreements formed the basis for Nordic Cooperation, at the time the most extensive form of regional cooperation in the world. The one sphere in which cooperation was limited and informal was foreign policy and defence issues, because Denmark, Iceland and Norway were members of the North Atlantic Treaty Organization (NATO) while Finland and Sweden followed a policy of neutrality during the 'cold war' between NATO and the Warsaw Pact. Since the late 1980s the Council's work has focused on the coordination of members' participation in the European integration process (initially through the establishment of the European Economic Area, EEA), and on providing assistance to the neighbouring Baltic republics.

Nordic countries or **Nordic area** Collective name for Denmark, Finland, Iceland, Norway and Sweden and the Danish dependencies of the Faroe Islands and Greenland. They are also called the Scandinavian countries. This term is less accurate, however, since it properly refers only to Denmark, Norway and Sweden. Greenland is geographically part of the North American continent.

Nordic model *See* SWEDISH MODEL.

Nordrhein-Westfalen *See* NORTH RHINE - WESTPHALIA.

Norge Norwegian name for Norway.

Norrback, Johan Ole or **Ole** (1941–) Finnish teacher and politician. An ethnic Swede, he was first elected to parliament for the Swedish People's Party (SFP) in 1979. He was its parliamentary leader from 1983–87 and became its leader in May 1990. He has been minister of defence (1987–90) and education and science (1990–91) and became minister of transport and communications and for Nordic cooperation in April 1991.

North Standard region of the United Kingdom. The North of England comprises the counties of Cleveland, Durham, Northumberland and Tyne & Wear, known collectively as the Northeast, and Cumbria. The region has an area of 15,401 sq km and a population of 3,084,000. The main cities are Newcastle-on-Tyne, Middlesbrough, Sunderland and Carlisle. The economy is based on manufacturing in the Northeast and on agriculture and tourism in Cumbria. The Northeast has suffered considerable problems because of the decline of the traditional heavy industries, shipbuilding and mining, and structural unemployment is high. The region is considered a unit principally for statistical purposes and has no administrative or political functions.

North Atlantic Assembly (NAA) Interparliamentary assembly, a consultative body of the North Atlantic Treaty Organization (NATO). Created in 1955 and given its present name in 1966, the North Atlantic Assembly brings together parliamentarians from NATO's 16 member states. It acts as a link between the national parliaments and NATO, but is wholly independent of the organization. It has 188 members nominated by the national parliaments and meets twice a year in Brussels (Belgium), NATO's headquarters. Since 1990 parliamentarians from the former communist countries of Eastern Europe and the Soviet Union have been taking part in the Assembly's activities as 'associate delegates'.

North Atlantic Cooperation Council
(NACC) Intergovernmental organization.
An initiative of the North Atlantic Treaty
Organization (NATO), the NACC – not
to be confused with the North Atlantic
Council (NAC), a NATO institution –
was founded in December 1991 with the
aim of building greater security in Europe
and to provide a practical basis for
'dialogue, partnership and consultation'
between NATO and the former communist countries of Eastern Europe and the
Soviet Union. The organization has 38
members, namely the 16 NATO countries, the former members of the Warsaw
Pact in Eastern Europe, the 15 former
Soviet republics, and Albania; Finland
has observer status. NACC meetings,
held at foreign-minister level, have
focused on general security issues, arms-
control measures and means of resolving
regional conflicts. Under the NACC's
auspices NATO is also extending expertise to the former communist countries
on such matters as training military
personnel, creating the structures for
'democratic control' of the armed forces,
and converting arms industries to civilian
use. *See also* PARTNERSHIP FOR PEACE.

North Atlantic Council or **NATO Council**
(NAC) Institution of the North Atlantic
Treaty Organization (NATO). The NAC
– not to be confused with the North
Atlantic Cooperation Council (NACC),
an independent organization – is the
highest decision-making body of NATO.
It is composed of representatives of member governments, either the permanent
representatives (ambassadors accredited
to NATO), foreign ministers or, at summit
meetings, heads of government. It generally meets at permanent-representative
level once a week and at foreign-minister
level twice a year. Meetings are chaired
by the NATO secretary-general. The
presidency rotates annually among the
foreign ministers of the member states.
The Council is assisted by a large number
of committees, whose areas of responsibility include political affairs, economic
affairs, information, infrastructure, budget,
force planning, nuclear planning, verification (of compliance with arms-control

agreements), scientific issues, environmental issues, civil emergency planning,
logistical support, communications
and information systems, armaments
cooperation, defence research, standardization, security, and air defence. It
also has control over several civilian
agencies concerned with such matters as
the production of weapons systems and
other equipment.

**North Atlantic Marine Mammals
Commission** (NAMMCO) Intergovernmental organization. The NAMMCO was
founded in April 1992 by four countries
which opposed the decision of the International Whaling Commission (IWC),
taken the previous year, to maintain the
ban on commercial whaling introduced
in 1985. The Faroe Islands, Greenland,
Iceland and Norway, all with major
whaling industries, argue that the IWC is
being undermined by interests wishing to
outlaw whaling on ethical grounds rather
than manage stocks. Iceland had formally
withdrawn from the IWC in June 1991
and Norway resumed commercial hunting
of minke whales in 1993. NAMMCO's
secretariat is based in Tromsö, Norway.

North Atlantic Treaty or **Washington
Treaty** International agreement setting
up the NORTH ATLANTIC TREATY ORGANI-
ZATION (NATO). It was signed in Washington (United States) on 4 April 1949 and
came into force on 24 August 1949.

North Atlantic Treaty Organization
(NATO) Intergovernmental organization.
NATO was founded in 1949 as a military
and political alliance of Western European countries, the United States and
Canada as a counterweight to the Soviet
Union and its Eastern European allies,
which formed the Warsaw Pact in 1955.
Providing for the collective defence of its
member states, it operates an integrated
military structure under centralized
control and command. After the collapse
of communism in 1989 and the dissolution of the Warsaw Pact in 1991 profoundly altered the face of Europe, NATO
redefined its tasks and policies and undertook a major restructuring of its military
wing. NATO now also sees itself as –
and is widely seen as – a key player in

the construction of a new pan-European security system. To this end it is strengthening ties with other intergovernmental organizations such as the Conference on Security and Cooperation in Europe (CSCE) and the Western European Union (WEU), and developing cooperation with its former adversaries.

Aims and objectives. NATO was set up under the North Atlantic Treaty, signed in Washington (United States) on 4 April 1949 and in force from 24 August 1949. The primary aim of collective defence is set out in article 5, which states: 'The parties agree that an armed attack against one or more of them in Europe or North America shall be considered an attack against them all, and consequently agree that, if such an armed attack occurs, each of them, in exercise of the right of individual or collective self-defence recognized by Article 51 of the United Nations Charter, will assist the party or parties so attacked by taking forthwith, individually and in concert with the other parties, such action as it deems necessary, including the use of armed force, to restore and maintain the security of the North Atlantic area.' The signatories also commit themselves to: (i) settling international disputes they may be involved in by peaceful means and refraining from the threat or use of force in any manner inconsistent with the purposes of the United Nations (article 1); (ii) developing their 'free institutions' and encouraging economic collaboration between them (article 2); (iii) maintaining and developing their individual and collective capacity to resist armed attack (article 3); and (iv) consulting together whenever the territorial integrity, political independence or security of any member state is threatened (article 4). The Treaty applies to the territories of all signatories and the area of the North Atlantic Ocean north of the Tropic of Cancer, including the signatories' vessels or aircraft operating in this area. In the Rome Declaration on Peace and Cooperation, adopted on 8 November 1991, the member states undertake to: (i) adapt their defences in light of the changes that have transformed Europe;

(ii) cooperate and consult with 'our new partners', i.e. the former Warsaw Pact members; (iii) help consolidate a now undivided Europe; and (iv) contribute to 'a new age of confidence, stability and peace'.

Membership: NATO has 16 members: Belgium, Canada, Denmark, France, Germany, Greece, Iceland, Italy, Luxemburg, Netherlands, Norway, Portugal, Spain, Turkey, United Kingdom and United States. All but four are founding members. Greece and Turkey joined in February 1952, West Germany in May 1955, and Spain in May 1982. Iceland (which has no armed forces) and Spain do not participate in the integrated military command structure. France withdrew from it in 1966, as did Greece on several occasions in the 1970s and 80s.

Structure and activities. NATO is organized around the following institutions: (i) the North Atlantic Council (NAC), the highest decision-making body, composed of either the permanent representatives (ambassadors accredited to NATO), foreign ministers or, at summit meetings, heads of government; at foreign-minister level it generally meets twice a year; (ii) the Defence Planning Committee (DPC) and Nuclear Planning Group (NPG), counterparts to the Council in defence matters, composed of the permanent representatives or defence ministers, who meet at least twice a year; (iii) the Office of the Secretary-General, the administrative and executive arm, headed by the secretary-general, who is elected for a five-year term by the Council, chairs the Council, DPC and NPG meetings, and is responsible for coordinating decision making; and (iv) the advisory Military Committee (MC), the highest military authority, composed of the chiefs-of-staff of the member states or permanent military representatives appointed by them. Decisions are taken by consensus. The presidency of the main institutions and their subsidiary bodies rotates annually among member states in order of their names in English. The Council and other bodies are assisted by a large number of committees dealing with political affairs, economic affairs, military planning, armaments cooperation, defence research etc. There are also several civilian agencies concerned with the production of weapons systems and other equipment.

NATO's key military arm is the Allied Command Europe (ACE), whose commander is directly answerable to the Military Committee. Its headquarters, the Supreme Headquarters Allied Powers Europe (SHAPE), is located near Mons in Belgium. It is responsible for the Allied Rapid Reaction Corps (ARRC), the core of the new defence structure.

Several independent organizations have very close links with NATO and effectively form part of its structure. The consultative North Atlantic Assembly is composed of 188 members delegated by the parliaments of the member states. The Eurogroup and the Independent European Programme Group (IEPG) are informal groupings aimed at coordinating policy and improving practical cooperation among the European member states. The North Atlantic Cooperation Council (NACC) brings together the NATO member states and the former Warsaw Pact members and successor states, as does the Partnership for Peace (PFP) programme.

NATO's headquarters is in Brussels (Belgium). The official languages are English and French. The secretary-general-designate is Willy Claes, the Belgian foreign minister. (The previous secretary-general, Manfred Wörner, died in August 1994.)

History. In response to the Soviet military presence in Eastern Europe from the end of the Second World War (1939–45) and its perceived threat to Western Europe, Belgium, France, Luxemburg, the Netherlands and the United Kingdom signed the Brussels Treaty for 'collective self-defence' in 1948. Efforts to secure the participation of the United States in the alliance, considered essential to counterbalance Soviet military power, bore fruit the following year. The North Atlantic Treaty was signed in 1949 by the five Brussels Treaty signatories, Canada, Denmark, Iceland, Norway, Portugal and the United States. (The Soviet Union

and its allies set up the Warsaw Pact in 1955.) The military structures put in place in the 1950s, providing for an integrated command, unified defence planning and coordination of arms procurement, remained virtually unchanged until the late 1980s. Greece and Turkey became NATO members in 1952 and West Germany in 1955. In 1956 it was agreed to improve and extend non-military cooperation among member states. Intermediate-range nuclear missiles were first deployed in Western Europe in the late 1950s, and in 1963 it was decided to establish a multinational nuclear taskforce. In 1966 France, acting on a pledge first made by President de Gaulle in 1959, withdrew from the integrated military structure on the grounds that it could not support a defence system that deprived it of sovereignty over its own armed forces. All NATO institutions were removed from French soil and the headquarters was moved from Paris to Brussels. In 1967 the North Atlantic Council approved the Harmel Report (named after Pierre Harmel, the Belgian defence minister), which defined NATO's future 'complementary' tasks as both guaranteeing military security and pursuing a policy of detente with the Warsaw Pact. In the early 1970s several developments reduced tension between the two military blocs, in particular the normalization of relations between West Germany and its eastern neighbours and the adoption of the Helsinki Final Act (1975) within the framework of the Conference on Security and Cooperation in Europe (CSCE). NATO's activities were nevertheless focused on counteracting the Warsaw Pact's growing military capability and the threat it was thought to pose to the West. Most member states approved substantial increases in defence spending and military contributions to NATO. In 1972 the Council endorsed the principle that NATO's overall military capability should not be reduced 'except as part of a pattern of mutual force reductions, balanced in scope and timing'. Greece withdrew from NATO's military structure in 1974 in protest at Turkey's invasion of

Cyprus (following an attempted coup by Greek Cypriots); it remained outside the structure for most of the 1970s and 80s. When the Warsaw Pact began to deploy a new generation of intermediate-range nuclear missiles, the SS-20s (which could reach all of Western Europe even when launched from well within the Soviet Union), NATO in December 1979 decided to introduce similar 'euromissiles' in Western Europe. At the same time it called for negotiations between the United States and the Soviet Union to reduce their numbers. This became known as the 'twin-' or 'double-track' approach. Against a background of serious deterioration in East-West relations and increased insecurity, the proposed deployment of cruise missiles and Pershing-IIs proved highly controversial in the European member states and gave rise to mass 'peace movements' in particular in Germany, Britain, the Netherlands and Belgium. Spain joined NATO in May 1982; its membership, under special conditions to meet domestic objections, was confirmed in a referendum in March 1986. With the bilateral US-Soviet arms-control negotiations deadlocked, deployment of cruise missiles and Pershing-IIs began as planned in November 1983. In March 1984 NATO endorsed a US proposal known as the 'zero option', under which NATO's deployment would be cancelled if the Soviet Union eliminated its intermediate-range missiles. The changes in Soviet foreign policy initiated under Mikhail Gorbachev (who came to power in March 1985) brought a rapid improvement in East-West relations in the late 1980s. The Stockholm Document, containing 'confidence- and security-building measures' aimed at reducing the risk of military confrontation, was agreed within the context of the CSCE in September 1986. In December 1987 the United States and the Soviet Union signed the Intermediate Nuclear Forces Treaty, which provided for the total elimination of this type of nuclear missile (not just in Europe but worldwide). Negotiations between NATO and the Warsaw Pact on reducing conventional forces in Europe, which had been dead-locked since they opened in 1973, also made some progress in early 1989.

The period between the collapse of communist rule in Eastern Europe later in the year and the formal dissolution of the Warsaw Pact and disintegration of the Soviet Union in 1991 marked the end of the Cold War and transformed the political and security situation in Europe. In December 1989 the Council resolved to strengthen NATO's 'political role' so as to contribute to a 'new architecture for Europe'. In November 1990 NATO and the Warsaw Pact declared that they no longer regarded each other as adversaries. The first section of the Treaty on Conventional Forces in Europe (CFE Treaty), providing for sharp reductions in weapons systems, was signed by the NATO and Warsaw Pact states in November 1990. The Open Skies Treaty, providing for reconnaissance flights to monitor compliance with arms-control agreements, was signed by the NATO states and the former Warsaw Pact members in March 1992. The second section of the CFE Treaty, providing for sharp reductions in troop levels, was signed in July 1992. (This had been held up primarily by the disintegration of the Soviet Union in 1991 and consequent disagreements among the successor states.) Throughout this time debate within NATO was dominated by the need to redefine the organization's role in the light of the new realities emerging in Europe. The rapid changes caused some tensions within the organization, particularly concerning the role of nuclear weapons, the nature of the US commitment (after the withdrawal of two-thirds of its European-based forces), 'burden sharing' among the member states, and the role of the 'European pillar'. At a summit in Rome (Italy) in November 1991 NATO unveiled its new Strategic Concept, replacing the reliance on 'forward defence' and 'flexible response' with a strategy based on smaller, more mobile forces and an emphasis on crisis management and preventive diplomacy. The accompanying Rome Declaration on Peace and Cooperation set out the context for the new strategy, in particular the development of a stronger 'European security identity' through cooperation with the CSCE and the Western European Union (WEU) and the creation of a new partnership with the former communist countries. In line with the new strategy the military command structure was streamlined and the Allied Rapid Reaction Corps (ARRC) set up. The North Atlantic Cooperation Council (NACC), bringing together the NATO states and the former Warsaw Pact members and successor states, held its first meeting in December 1991. The North Atlantic Council decided in June 1992 that NATO forces could be used in peace-keeping activities under the auspices of the CSCE (which does not have a military capability of its own). This decision marked a major departure for the organization in that it sanctioned in principle 'out-of-area' operations, i.e. operations outside the member states' territories. In January 1994 NATO issued an invitation to other European states to join a new cooperation structure, the Partnership for Peace (PFP), which was intended in part as a response to the wish expressed by several Eastern European countries to join NATO. Within six months nearly all of the countries invited, including Russia, had signed up to the programme.

See also entries on specific institutions, organizations, agreements, terms etc.

North Rhine - Westphalia [Nordrhein-Westfalen] Federal state [Land] of Germany. Situated in the west, North Rhine - Westphalia has an area of 34,068 sq km and a population of 17,679,000. By far the country's most populous state, it is centred on the Ruhr conurbation, the country's leading industrial region. The capital is Düsseldorf, and other major cities are Cologne [Köln], Essen, Dortmund, Duisburg, Bochum, Bielefeld, Gelsenkirchen, Bonn, Mönchengladbach and Münster. The economy is based on manufacturing (engineering, petrochemicals, chemicals, metalworking, textiles, food processing, motor vehicles), services, agriculture and mining (coal). Owing to

restructuring of the old heavy industries, unemployment is among the highest in western Germany. Political power is exercised by the State Assembly [Landtag], with 237 members elected for a five-year term, and a government headed by a minister-president. The dominant party is the Social Democratic Party (SPD), and the other main parties are the Christian Democratic Union (CDU), the centrist Free Democratic Party (FDP) and the Greens. At the election in May 1990 the SPD gained 50.0% of the vote and 122 seats, the CDU 36.7% and 89 seats, the FDP 5.8% and 14 seats, and the Greens 5.0% and 12 seats. The minister-president is Johannes Rau. Historically divided into many states within the Holy Roman Empire, most of the region became part of Prussia in the early 19th century. It was established as a separate state after the dissolution of Prussia (then a state of Germany) after the Second World War.

North Sea Conference Shorthand for the INTERNATIONAL CONFERENCE ON THE PROTECTION OF THE NORTH SEA.

north-south divide [divario Nord-Sud] In Italy, the perceived economic and social gap between the affluent and industrialized north and centre and the poorer and more agricultural south. *See* MEZZOGIORNO.

north-south divide In the United Kingdom, the perceived political, economic and social gap between Scotland and the north of England on the one hand and the south of England on the other. During the 1980s much of the north suffered disproportionately from deindustrialization, unemployment, relative poverty and social deprivation. The gap between the two regions was reinforced politically in that almost all parliamentary seats in the south outside London were held by the ruling Conservatives, while the overwhelming majority of urban seats in the north were held by Labour. Since a recession hit the south of England in the early 1990s the north-south divide has become more blurred, but it remains a potent symbol of regional dissatisfaction in England and national aspirations in Scotland.

Northern Bukovina or **Bukovina question** Controversy over the status of a formerly Romanian territory now part of Ukraine. Situated to the east of the Carpathian mountains, Bukovina formed part of the principality of Moldavia from the 14th century, came under Ottoman rule in 1512, was ceded to Austria in 1775 and became part of Romania in 1918. Romania was forced to cede Northern Bukovina to the Soviet Union in 1940. Just under three-quarters of the people of the region – now called Chernovtsy – is Ukrainian and around a fifth is Romanian. Nationalist groups in Romania are calling for the return of Northern Bukovina.

Northern Cyprus [Kuzey Kıbrıs] Territory in southeastern Europe or southwestern Asia.

Note: The information below refers to the territory controlled by the self-proclaimed Turkish Republic of Northern Cyprus (TRNC). Provision of a separate entry and information for the TRNC does not imply equal status with the internationally recognized Republic of Cyprus but reflects the island's de facto division since 1974.

Official data. Name: Turkish Republic of Northern Cyprus [Kuzey Kıbrıs Türk Cumhuriyeti]; capital: Nicosia [Levkoşa]; form of government: presidential republic; head of state: president; head of government: prime minister; flag: white with a red crescent and five-pointed star in the centre and two red horizontal bands near the top and bottom; national holiday: 15 November (Independence Day); language: Turkish; religion: none; currency: Turkish lira; abbreviation: KKTC.

Geography. Northern Cyprus has an area of 3,355 sq km. It occupies the northern third of the island of Cyprus, which is situated in the eastern Mediterranean Sea 80 km south of Turkey and 100 km west of Syria. The Kyrenia [Girne] mountain chain runs east-west across the centre. To the north is a narrow coastal plain, to the southeast a fertile plain. Around half the land is arable, a tenth is covered by pastures and a fifth is forested. The climate is mediterranean, with hot summers and mild winters; rainfall is light.

Demography. Northern Cyprus has a population of 178,000. Population density is 53 per sq km. Most people live in the plains. The main city is Nicosia; other major centres are Kyrenia [Girne], Morphou [Güzelyurt] and Famagusta [Gazimağusa]. In ethnic, linguistic and religious terms the population of Northern Cyprus is very homogeneous. Nearly all the people are Turkish Cypriots or Turks and nominally Sunni Muslims. The Turkish immigrants and their descendants are thought to number around 50,000.

Sociography. The standard of living in Northern Cyprus is relatively high. There are 15 doctors and 61 hospital beds for every 10,000 people. Education is compulsory between the ages of seven and 15. There is one teacher for every 25 students. Enrolment is 50% at the secondary level and 19% at the tertiary level. The literacy rate is around 90%. GNP per head (unadjusted for purchasing power) is around US$ 4,000.

Infrastructure and communications. Northern Cyprus has a relatively developed transport and communications network. There are 6,930 km of paved roads and 30,800 passenger cars (177 per 1,000 people). There are no railways or navigable waterways. The main ports are Famagusta, Kacelik and Kyrenia. There are airports at Ercan and Geçitkale. There are eight daily newspapers, with a combined circulation of 25,000 (140 per 1,000 people). There are around 50,000 radio receivers, 75,000 television sets and around 25,000 telephones in use (respectively around 300, 432 and around 150 per 1,000 people).

Economic structure. The Northern Cypriot economy is relatively developed, relatively undiversified, and closely linked to the Turkish economy. Northern Cyprus maintains a monetary union with Turkey and is strongly dependent on aid and loans from that country. The economy is based on agriculture, food processing and tourism. Since the late 1980s economic performance has been marked by high growth (averaging around 7% per year) and low unemployment (around 2%), but also by high current-account deficits and very high inflation (averaging 68% per year).

Services contribute 68% of GDP (trade 22%), industry contributes 22% (manufacturing 13%), and agriculture, forestry and fisheries 10%. Some 26% of the labour force is employed in farming, 10% in trade, 10% in construction and 10% in manufacturing. The main agricultural activity is horticulture (olives, fruit and vegetables, esp. citrus fruit); the main crops grown are potatoes, cereals (wheat and barley) and tobacco; livestock raising (sheep, goats, chickens) is also important. Fishing is of regional importance. The main mineral resources are copper and pyrites. The main industries are food processing and textiles. Tourism is a mainstay of the economy, contributing around 25% of GNP. The main energy sources are imported fossil fuels; 38% of export earnings are required to cover net fuel imports. The main exports are citrus fruit (43% of the total), potatoes and tobacco; foodstuffs account for 67% of the total. The main imports are basic manufactures, machinery and transport equipment, foodstuffs and fuels. The main trading partners are: exports: United Kingdom (67%), Turkey (14%); imports: Turkey (48%), United Kingdom (15%); a third of all trade is with European Union (EU) countries. Net invisible earnings (tourism receipts, development and other assistance from Turkey) are thought to account for about half of GNP.

The Central Bank of the Turkish Republic of Northern Cyprus [Kuzey Kıbrıs Türk Cumhuriyeti Merkez Bankası] (KKTC MB) discharges some of the responsibilities of a central bank. The main employers' association is the Turkish Cypriot Employers' Association (KTİS); the main labour organizations are the Turkish Cypriot Trade Union Federation (Türk-Sen) and Revolutionary Trade Union Federation (Dev-İş).

Political structure. Northern Cyprus is a presidential republic on the basis of a constitution adopted in 1985. Executive power is vested in the president, who is elected for a five-year term, and the prime minister and council of ministers, who are appointed by the president. Legislative power is vested in the Assembly of the Republic [Cumhuriyet Meclisi], whose 50 members are elected for a five-year term by a system of proportional representation (with a 5% threshold for gaining seats). All citizens over the age of 18 are entitled to vote. Judicial power is ultimately vested in the eight-member Supreme Court [Yüksek Mahkeme]. Administratively Northern Cyprus is divided into three districts [ilçe, pl. ilçeler], which are subdivided into 28 municipalities and 186 villages.

The main political parties are the National Unity Party (UBP), Democratic Party (DP), Republican Turkish Party (CTP) and Communal Liberation Party (TKP). At the December 1993 election the UBP gained 29.9% of the vote and 17/50 seats, the DP 29.2% and 15 seats, the CTP 24.2% and 13 seats, and the TKP 13.3% and five seats. The government is formed by a centrist coalition of the DP and CTP, with Hakkı Atun as prime minister. Other senior ministers are Özker Özgür (deputy prime minister), Atay Ahmet Raşit (foreign affairs and defence), Taner Etkin (interior) and Onur Borman (economy and finance). The head of state is President Rauf Denktaş, who was first elected in June 1976.

Security and international affiliations. The Northern Cypriot armed forces number 4,000 (all army). Military service is compulsory and consists of two years' basic training. Some 30,000 Turkish troops are stationed in Northern Cyprus. Some 1,400 United Nations troops of the UN Peace-Keeping Force in Cyprus (UNFICYP) are stationed in the buffer zone separating the Turkish and Greek Cypriot parts of the island.

Northern Cyprus has not been recognized diplomatically by any country except Turkey. It has observer status at the Economic Cooperation Organization and the Islamic Conference Organization.

History. When the island of Cyprus gained its independence from the United Kingdom in 1960, around four-fifths of its people were Greek-speaking Orthodox Christians and one-fifth were Turkish-speaking Muslims. (*For earlier developments, see* CYPRUS: HISTORY.) In 1963 the

Turkish Cypriot political parties withdrew from the power-sharing structures after thousands of Turkish Cypriots had been killed in intercommunal violence. The following year the United Nations Peace-Keeping Force in Cyprus (UNFI-CYP) was deployed throughout the island. In the mid 1960s the Turkish Cypriots set up separate administrative structures. In 1974 Greek Cypriot supporters of *énosis* or union with Greece, backed by the military regime in power in Greece at the time, staged a coup. Turkish troops thereupon invaded and occupied the north of the island, an area equivalent to 37% of its total area. All the Greeks in the region fled or were expelled from their homes during the four weeks of fighting. The Turkish Cypriots established a functioning government in the north and unilaterally proclaimed the Turkish Federated State of Cyprus in February 1975 and the Turkish Republic of Northern Cyprus in November 1983. (These were recognized only by Turkey.) There was also substantial immigration from Turkey during this period. The dominant political leader since the mid 1970s has been Rauf Denktaş. He was elected president of the self-proclaimed state in 1976 and has been reelected on three occasions. In 1992 he broke with the National Unity Party (UBP), the ruling party he founded, because it increasingly favoured *taksim* or partition of the island, and joined the breakaway Democratic Party (DP). The UBP remained the largest party at the December 1993 election but was forced to give way to a coalition of the DP and the Republican Turkish Party (CTP).

See also CYPRUS QUESTION *and entries on specific institutions, organizations, parties, people, terms etc.*

Northern Epirus question Controversy over the status of parts of southern Albania with an ethnic Greek majority. The existence of a Greek community was officially denied until the collapse of communist rule in 1990/91. Thought to number around 125,000 (no reliable figures are available), it has since sought to assert its identity. Greece has expressed concern about alleged human-rights

violations by the Albanian authorities. Greece does not dispute the border between the two countries, established in 1925, but the majority-Greek area is widely referred to as 'Northern Epirus' [Vóreios Ípiros], implying that it should be regarded as part of the Greek region of Epirus. This usage is also common internationally but is not recognized by Albania.

Northern European countries Collective name for Denmark, Finland, Iceland, Norway and Sweden and the Danish dependency of the Faroe Islands. They are also called the Nordic or Scandinavian countries. The latter term is less accurate, since it properly refers only to Denmark, Norway and Sweden.

Northern Ireland Constituent country of the United Kingdom, also referred to as Ulster. Situated in the northeastern quarter of the island of Ireland, across the Irish Sea from Great Britain, Northern Ireland has an area of 14,120 sq km and a population of 1,594,000. The population is sharply divided between Protestant and Roman Catholic communities; just under three-fifths has its roots in the former, just over two-fifths in the latter. The division transcends religion and has strong ethnic, historical and cultural dimensions. In stricter religious terms, 50.6% of the people describe themselves as Protestants (including Presbyterians 21.4%, Anglicans 17.7% and Methodists 3.8%) and 38.4% as Roman Catholics; 11.0% profess other faiths or describe themselves as non-religious. The capital is Belfast, and the other major city is Derry or Londonderry. The economy is based on manufacturing (engineering, textiles, electronics) and agriculture (cattle and dairy farming). Northern Ireland is the UK's poorest region, and structural unemployment is high, in part owing to the decline of the shipbuilding and textile industries in the 1970s and 80s. Northern Ireland has its own legal and educational systems and administration and local government structure, but no separate legislature or local executive. All laws pertaining to the region are adopted by the UK-wide House of Commons. Executive power is exercised by the Northern Ireland Office, a central government department headed by a senior minister. Local government is based on 26 district councils; the traditional six counties no longer have any administrative or political functions. The main political parties are the Ulster Unionist Party (UUP, also called the Official Unionist Party, OUP), Social Democratic and Labour Party (SDLP), Ulster Democratic Unionist Party (DUP), Sinn Féin (SF) and Alliance Party (AP). With the exception of the latter, political parties divide along communal lines, with the UUP and DUP supported by Protestants and the SDLP and Sinn Féin by Catholics. At the local elections in May 1993 the UUP gained 29.0% of the vote, the SDLP 21.9%, the DUP 17.2%, Sinn Féin 12.5% and the AP 7.7%. The historical region of Ulster, broadly coextensive with present-day Northern Ireland, came under English influence from the late 12th century onwards and was annexed in 1461. In an attempt to break resistance to English rule, the authorities began to encourage Scottish and English immigration to Ulster in the early 17th century. The Protestant settlers' descendants eventually outnumbered the local Catholic population and enjoyed a monopoly on political power and controlled the economy. The strong enmity between the two communities stems from this time. (The Battle of the Boyne, fought in 1690, became a symbol of the Protestant ascendancy.) Ireland-wide agitation for independence was strongly resisted by most Ulster Protestants. In 1920 two parliaments were set up, one for the six northern counties and one for the rest of Ireland. In 1922 the island was formally partitioned and the south became independent. Since then the clashing aspirations of the Protestant or unionist majority and the Catholic or nationalist minority have dominated Northern Ireland life. In 1969 economic and social tensions erupted in intercommunal violence, troops were introduced to maintain order, and the Irish Republican Army (IRA) and other guerrilla groups became active. In 1972 the British government abolished the Northern Ireland parliament and instituted direct rule from London. Since then several attempts have been made to reintroduce devolved government, settle the constitutional issue (i.e. the territory's relationship with Ireland) and end the political violence (*see* NORTHERN IRELAND QUESTION). The IRA declared a ceasefire in September 1994; the Protestant guerrilla groups did so in October. The conflict in Northern Ireland, the most violent in Western Europe, has claimed over 3,400 lives since 1969. *See also* GREAT BRITAIN AND NORTHERN IRELAND.

Northern Ireland Office British government department. Based in Belfast, the Northern Ireland Office is responsible for the administration of Northern Ireland. It is directly responsible for constitutional matters and internal security, and also carries out a range of functions fulfilled by separate departments in England and Wales. The Office is headed by the secretary of state for Northern Ireland, a minister with Cabinet rank.

Northern Ireland question Controversy over the status of NORTHERN IRELAND, a component of the United Kingdom. The conflict in Northern Ireland or Ulster is rooted in the troubled relationship between its two communities, Protestants and Catholics. Most Ulster Protestants were strongly opposed to the demands for Irish autonomy or independence in the 19th and early 20th centuries. (The island had been formally incorporated into the United Kingdom in 1801.) In 1920 two parliaments were set up, one for the six northern counties with a Protestant majority and one for the rest of Ireland. When the island was partitioned in 1922, following several years of fighting between the British army and auxiliary units and the Irish Republican Army (IRA), the south became independent while the north remained within the United Kingdom. In the late 1960s Catholic agitation for an end to discrimination in jobs and housing led to serious intercommunal violence. Army troops were introduced in 1969 to help maintain order. This time also saw a resurgence of the IRA and the emergence of other guerrilla groups on both sides.

In an effort to force reforms the British government abolished the Northern Ireland parliament and instituted direct rule from London in 1972. Since then several attempts have been made to end the violence and reintroduce devolved government based on 'power sharing' between the two communities (including the Sunningdale proposals of 1973–74, the Constitutional Convention of 1975–76 and the Northern Ireland Assembly of 1982–86), but they foundered on the resistance of one side or the other. Although the Republic of Ireland effectively lays claim to the territory under articles 2 and 3 of its constitution, the British and Irish governments have cooperated increasingly closely both on security issues and on finding a political settlement. In November 1985 they signed the Anglo-Irish Agreement, which gave the Irish government a consultative role in the affairs of Northern Ireland. This was rejected by the unionists as well as hard-line nationalists. Another three-stage initiative involving negotiations among the 'constitutional parties' (i.e. those opposed to political violence) and the British and Irish governments was launched in June 1991 (*see* BROOKE INITIATIVE). In the DOWNING STREET DECLARATION adopted in December 1993 the British and Irish governments indicated their willingness to broaden negotiations to include Sinn Féin if the IRA, regarded as its military wing, abandoned its campaign of violence. The IRA declared a ceasefire in September 1994; the Protestant guerrilla groups did so in October.

Northern League [Lega Nord] (LN) Italian political organization. The Northern League was founded in 1991 as an electoral alliance of the LOMBARD LEAGUE and the leagues [leghe] of Veneto, Piedmont and other northern regions. These regional parties adopted a programme calling for autonomy for the north, institutional reform, an end to government corruption and 'waste' (i.e. the transfer of resources from the rich north to the poorer south), controls on immigration and selective repatriation of foreigners. At the April 1992 election the League became a major force in national politics, gaining 21.1% of the vote in the north or 8.7% nationally and 55/630 seats. As the government parties became discredited by a series of corruption scandals, it increased its support in local and regional elections in 1992 and 1993. It also moderated its populist stance and concentrated on demands for political reform and the introduction of a federal system of government. It contested the March 1994 election in alliance with the right-wing Come On Italy (Forza Italia) and gained 19.0% in the north or 8.4% nationally and 117 seats (under a new electoral system). The leader is Umberto Bossi.

Northerners [Iparretarak] French guerrilla group. Formed in 1973 and banned in 1987, Iparretarak is a separatist group active in the French Basque Country. It has been responsible for a series of attacks on police officers, public buildings and property firms (which it accuses of encouraging the sale of land and property to non-Basques). It has close links with Basque Homeland and Liberty (ETA), the main Basque guerrilla group across the border in Spain.

Northwest Standard region of the United Kingdom. Centred on Manchester and Liverpool, the Northwest of England comprises the counties of Cheshire, Greater Manchester, Lancashire and Merseyside. It has an area of 7,332 sq km and a population of 6,377,000. The economy is based on manufacturing (engineering) and services. It has suffered considerable problems because of the decline of the traditional heavy and textile industries. The region and its main cities have strong identities. It is considered a unit principally for statistical purposes and has no administrative or political functions.

Norway [Norge] Country in northern Europe.

Official data. Name: Kingdom of Norway [Kongeriket Norge]; capital: Oslo; form of government: parliamentary monarchy; head of state: king/queen; head of government: prime minister; flag: red with a blue white-edged Scandinavian cross; national holiday: 17 May

(Independence Day); language: Norwegian; religion: Evangelical Lutheranism; currency: krone (kr) (pl. -r) = 100 øre; abbreviation: N.

Geography. One of the Nordic countries, occupying the western part of the Scandinavian peninsula, Norway has a total area of 323,878 sq km. It is bordered by the North Sea, the Norwegian Sea and Barents Sea (part of the Arctic Ocean) in the west, Russia, Finland and Sweden in the east, and the Skagerrak (an arm of the North Sea) in the south. Most of the country consists of mountains and plateaus; the coastline is deeply indented. The only low-lying areas are along the southern coast. Some 3% of the land is arable, another 1% is covered by pastures and 27% is forested. The climate is temperate marine along the coast and in the south (with mild summers and cold winters), subarctic inland (with cool summers and cold winters), and arctic in the far north (with short, cool summers and very cold winters); rainfall is very heavy in the southwest, and heavy to moderate in the rest of the country.

Demography. Norway has a population of 4,308,000. Population density is 14 per sq km, one of the lowest in Europe. Some 75% of the people live in urban areas, and around a quarter lives in Oslo and its suburbs. Other major cities are Bergen, Trondheim and Stavanger. In ethnic, linguistic and religious terms Norway is very homogeneous. Some 94.5% of the population is Norwegian and 87.9% nominally Lutheran Protestant. Norwegian is spoken and written in two recognized forms, Bokmål, used by around four-fifths of the population and the main written language, and Nynorsk. The two ethnic minorities are Lapps or Sami (numbering around 30,000) and Finns (12,000) in the far north. Foreign nationals account for 4.3% of the population, and include citizens of Denmark, Sweden, United Kingdom, Pakistan, United States and Vietnam.

Sociography. Norway scores 0.928 on the United Nations human development index (HDI), ranking fifth in the world and third among 32 European countries.

There are 32 doctors and 59 hospital beds for every 10,000 people. Education is compulsory between the ages of seven and 15. There is one teacher for every 13 students. Enrolment is 85% at the secondary level and 39% at the tertiary level. The literacy rate is virtually 100%. Real annual income per head (in terms of purchasing power) is US$ 17,170. Income differentials are small.

Infrastructure and communications. Norway has a highly developed transport and communications network; because of the difficult terrain, local air services and fjord ferries are particularly important in linking centres of population. There are 61,360 km of paved roads and 1.61 million passenger cars (379 per 1,000 people), 4,180 km of railways and 1,580 km of navigable waterways. The main ports are Bergen, Stavanger, Kristiansand, Oslo, Narvik and Trondheim. The main airports are at Oslo (Fornebu), Bergen (Flesland) and Stavanger (Sola), and there are 44 other airports with scheduled services. There are 61 daily newspapers, with a combined circulation of 2.16 million (510 per 1,000 people). There are 3.30 million radio receivers, 1.50 million television sets and 3.10 million telephones in use (respectively 775, 351 and 728 per 1,000 people).

Economic structure. The Norwegian economy is highly developed and trade-oriented (exports account for two-fifths of national income). It is based on the exploitation of the country's extensive natural resources, i.e. oil, natural gas, forests, hydroelectric power and fish; the manufacturing sector is relatively small and largely based on these resources. Since oil and gas account for nearly half of exports, the economy is vulnerable to changes in world prices and demand for these products. After a recession in the mid 1980s caused by a fall in oil prices, economic performance has been marked by steady growth (averaging 1.7% per year), growing current-account surpluses, falling inflation (from around 10% to 2%), but also by rising unemployment (from around 1% to 6%).

Services contribute 60% of GDP, industry contributes 37% (mining 15%, manufacturing 14%), and agriculture, forestry and fisheries 3%. Some 17% of the labour force is employed in trade, 14% in manufacturing, 8% in transport and communications, 7% in finance and 6% in construction. The main agricultural activity is livestock raising (cattle, sheep); the main crops grown are cereals (barley, oats, wheat) and potatoes. The fishing industry (cod, shellfish etc) is the largest in Europe. Forestry is also important. The main mineral resources are oil and natural gas (in the North Sea) and magnesium; Norway is Europe's largest oil producer and the world's tenth-largest. The main industries are food and fish processing, wood processing and metal-working (esp. aluminium); other important branches are engineering, ship-building, chemicals and petrochemicals. Shipping is a major source of foreign exchange; the Norwegian merchant fleet is the second-largest in Europe and the fifth-largest in the world. The main energy sources are hydroelectric power and fossil fuels; Norway is a substantial net exporter of fuels. The main exports are oil (38% of the total), natural gas (7%), chemicals (7%), ships (6%), fish and fish products (6%), aluminium (5%), wood products, machinery and iron and steel; mineral fuels account for 48% of the total, basic manufactures for 18%, machinery and transport equipment for 14%. The main imports are machinery and transport equipment and basic manufactures. The main trading partners are: exports: United Kingdom (26%), Germany (11%), Sweden (11%), Netherlands (8%), France (8%), United States (6%), Denmark (5%); imports: Sweden (15%), Germany (14%), United Kingdom (9%), United States (7%), Denmark (7%), Japan, Netherlands, France, Finland; two-thirds of all trade is with European Union (EU) countries.

The Bank of Norway [Norges Bank] is the central bank. The main employers' association is the Confederation of Business and Industry (NHO); the main labour organization is the Norwegian Trade Union Confederation (LO).

Political structure. Norway is a parliamentary monarchy on the basis of a constitution adopted in 1814 and amended on a number of occasions since then. Executive power is formally vested in the king/queen but is exercised by the State Council [Statsråd] or council of ministers headed by the prime minister [statsminister]. Legislative power is vested in the Parliament [Storting], whose 165 members are elected for a four-year term by a system of proportional representation. When dealing with legislative matters it divides into the 126-member Lower House [Odelsting] and the 39-member Upper House [Lagting]. The Storting cannot be dissolved before the expiry of its term. All citizens over the age of 18 are entitled to vote. Judicial power is ultimately vested in the Supreme Court [Høyersterett], whose 19 members are appointed by the monarch on the advice of the government. Administratively the country is divided into 19 counties [fylke, pl. -r], which are subdivided into 451 municipalities.

The main political parties are the Norwegian Labour Party (DNA or A), Centre Party (Sp), Conservative Party (Høyre, H), Christian People's Party (KrF), Socialist Left Party (SV), Progress Party (Frp), Liberal Party (Venstre, V) and Red Electoral Alliance (RV). At the general election in September 1993 the DNA gained 37.0% of the vote and 67/165 seats, the Sp 16.8% and 32 seats, Høyre 16.9% and 28 seats, the KrF 7.9% and 13 seats, the SV 7.9% and 13 seats, the Frp 6.3% and 10 seats, Venstre 3.6% and one seat, and the RV 1.1% and one seat. The government is formed by the DNA, with Gro Harlem Brundtland as prime minister. Other senior ministers are Bjørn Tore Godal (foreign affairs), Jens Stoltenberg (industry, petroleum and energy), Jørgen Kosmo (defence), Gunnar Berge (local government and labour) and Grete Faremo (justice). The head of state is King Harald V, who succeeded to the throne in January 1991; the heir is Prince Haakon Magnus.

Norway has several overseas dependencies: the Svalbard or Spitsbergen archipelago in the Arctic Ocean, the island of Jan Mayen in the Norwegian Sea, and Bouvet Island and Peter I Island in the Antarctic region; of these only Svalbard is permanently inhabited. Norway also lays claim to part of Antarctica.

Security and international affiliations. The Norwegian armed forces number 29,400 (army 12,900, navy 8,300, airforce 8,200). There is also a small paramilitary coast guard. Military service is compulsory and consists of 12–15 months' basic training.

Norway is a member of the Conference on Security and Cooperation in Europe (CSCE), Council of Baltic Sea States (CBSS), Council of Europe, European Economic Area (EEA), European Free Trade Association (EFTA), North Atlantic Treaty Organization (NATO), Nordic Council and Western European Union (WEU), as well as the Organization for Economic Cooperation and Development (OECD) and the United Nations and its specialized agencies. It has negotiated membership of the European Union (EU), and is due to join the organization at the start of 1995 pending the outcome of a referendum in November 1994.

History. From the 9th–11th centuries Norwegians joined other Viking groups in sea-borne raids, conquests and migrations across Europe and westward to Iceland, Greenland and North America. At this time the country was divided into numerous small kingdoms. The major ones in the south were united by Harald Hårfager ('Fairhair') around 900. Christianity was introduced in the early 11th century and quickly became the dominant religion. The 11th and 12th centuries were marked by civil wars and conflicts with Denmark and Sweden. King Haakon IV (1217–63) introduced reforms which regulated the succession and established a central administration. At this time Norwegian rule extended to the Faroe, Orkney and Shetland islands, Iceland and Greenland. The country was particularly hard-hit by the Europe-wide plague epidemic known as the 'black death', which killed up to two-thirds of the population in 1349–50. A prolonged economic decline followed.

The Union of Kalmar brought Norway under the Danish crown in 1397. It became a province of Denmark in 1536, but was allowed to retain some of its traditional political and legal institutions. The Protestant Reformation had been readily accepted, and the Evangelical Lutheran Church became the established church in the same year. In 1814 Norway was transferred to the Swedish crown. Following a rebellion, the Swedish government accepted a constitution for Norway which provided for a large measure of internal self-government.

The 19th century saw the emergence of a Norwegian cultural and national movement. As tension with Sweden grew, the Storting (= parliament) declared a plebiscite in 1905 and obtained overwhelming support for full independence. Sweden then agreed to dissolve the union. Universal suffrage for men was introduced in 1905 and extended to women in 1913. The 1920s saw rapid economic growth, in particular in the industries exploiting the country's natural resources. The Norwegian Labour Party (DNA) formed its second government in 1935 and remained in power for the next thirty years (apart from the war years and a brief period in 1963). It introduced a range of reforms establishing a comprehensive welfare state. During the Second World War (1939–45) Norway was occupied by Germany in 1940. The leader of a small far-right party, Vidkun Quisling, was installed as the head of government.

Abandoning its traditional policy of neutrality, Norway became a founding member of the North Atlantic Treaty Organization (NATO) in 1949. It set up the Nordic Council with its northern neighbours in 1953 and became a founding member of the European Free Trade Association (EFTA) in 1960. Einar Gerhardsen was prime minister for all but four years between 1945 and 1965. In the early 1970s the country was deeply divided over proposed membership of the then European Community (EC), which was finally rejected in a referendum in 1972 (by 53.5% to 46.5%). From the late 1970s the exploitation of offshore oil and gas deposits, the largest in Western Europe, transformed the economy. Since 1965 power has alternated between centre-right coalitions and minority Labour administrations. The former were in office from 1965–71, 1972–73, 1981–86 and 1989–90, and Labour was in office from 1971–72, 1973–81 and 1986–89. Gro Harlem Brundtland, who first became prime minister in February 1981, formed another Labour administration in November 1990 after the previous government had resigned over the EC membership issue. Another application to join what is now the European Union (EU) was made in November 1991; accession negotiations were concluded in March 1994, and a referendum on the issue was due to be held in November.

See also entries on specific institutions, organizations, parties, people, terms etc.

Norwegian Labour Party [Det Norske Arbeiderparti] (DNA or A) Norwegian political party. Founded in 1887, the DNA has been the country's dominant political force since 1933. It held power alone until 1963 (except for the German occupation from 1940–45) and since then repeatedly as a minority government, most recently from 1986–89 and since November 1990. At the September 1993 election it gained 37.0% of the vote and 67/165 seats. Gro Harlem Brundtland, party leader since 1981, resigned the post in 1992 to concentrate on her work as prime minister. The party chairman is Thorbjørn Jagland.

Norwegian Polar Research Institute [Norsk Polarinstitut] Norwegian scientific and advisory body. Founded in 1928 and reorganized under its present name in 1948, this independent institute sponsors and carries out research and monitors environmental and other developments in Norway's dependent territories. These comprise Svalbard and Jan Mayen in the Arctic Ocean and two small islands in the Antarctic region, none of which has any permanent inhabitants. The Institute is also responsible for advising the national government (and in the case of Svalbard, the local administration) on matters concerning the territories.

Norwegian Trade Union Confederation [Landsorganisasjonen i Norge ('National Organization in Norway')] (LO) Norwegian trade-union federation. Founded in 1899, the LO has 28 affiliated unions with a total membership of 780,000 (more than a third of the labour force). It has traditionally close links with the Norwegian Labour Party (DNA). The president is Yngve Hågensen.

Notat, Nicole (1947–) French teacher and trade-union official. She taught children with special needs until she became a full-time official for the teachers' union affiliated to the Democratic French Confederation of Labour (CFDT), one of the main trade-union federations. She was elected deputy general secretary of the CFDT in 1988 and general secretary in October 1992.

Novák, Jiří (1950–) Czech lawyer and politician. A member of the right-wing Civic Democratic Party (ODS), he was appointed justice minister of the Czech Republic in January 1992.

November 11 *See* ELEVENTH OF NOVEMBER ALLIANCE.

November 17 *See* SEVENTEENTH OF NOVEMBER REVOLUTIONARY ORGANIZATION.

Noviks affair Controversy in Latvia surrounding Alfons Noviks, accused of crimes against humanity committed during the 1940s and 50s. Noviks joined the predecessor of the State Security Committee (KGB) after the Soviet Union's annexation of Latvia in 1940 and rose from the ranks to become head of the secret police in Latvia before retiring in the mid 1950s. Calls for his prosecution grew after Latvia regained its independence in 1991. He was accused of involvement in the deportation of 14,000 Latvians to Siberia in 1941 and of personally ordering the torture and execution of hundreds of political prisoners. (More than 100,000 Latvians were deported to Siberia in the years after the Soviet takeover.) He was arrested in March 1994. The public prosecution service declared at the time that his advanced age – he was 86 – would not dissuade it from pressing charges.

NP *See* NATIONALIST PARTY.

NPD *See* NATIONAL DEMOCRATIC PARTY OF GERMANY.

NPG *See* NUCLEAR PLANNING GROUP.

NR Danish, Norwegian and Swedish abbreviation for Nordisk Råd ('NORDIC COUNCIL').

NRS Abbreviation for Natsionalna Razuznavatelna Sluzhba ('National Intelligence Service'), the Bulgarian intelligence agency.

NRW Abbreviation for Nordrhein-Westfalen or NORTH RHINE - WESTPHALIA, a federal state [Land] of Germany.

NS (Bulgaria) and **NS Edinstvo** *See* UNITY.

NS (Yugoslavia) and **NSCG** *See* NATIONAL PARTY OF MONTENEGRO.

NSS *See* INDEPENDENCE (Yugoslavia).

NSZZ Solidarność and **NSZZ'S'** *See* SOLIDARITY.

Nuclear Planning Group (NPG) Institution of the North Atlantic Treaty Organization (NATO). The NPG deals with all matters related to the role of nuclear forces in NATO's collective defence policy. In this field it has the same competence as the Defence Planning Committee (DPC) and the North Atlantic Council (NAC), the organization's other key decision-making bodies. Like the DPC it is composed of the defence ministers of the member states or their permanent representatives accredited to NATO. As France is not part of NATO's integrated military structure, it is not represented on the NPG.

Number 10 Shorthand for the British prime minister's office. Number 10 Downing Street in London is the official residence of the prime minister.

NVA Abbreviation for Nationale Volksarmee ('National People's Army'), the armed forces of former East Germany. On German reunification in October 1990 a small section of the NVA's officer corps but virtually none of its equipment and munitions was absorbed into the Bundeswehr, hitherto the West German army.

Ny Demokrati and **NYD** *See* NEW DEMOCRACY.

Nynorsk ('New Norwegian') Form of the Norwegian language, formerly also called Landsmål. It is based on the dialects of the western rural districts and was standardized in the mid 19th century. It is used by around a fifth of the population, mainly in the west. It has equal status with the more common form of the language, Bokmål.

Nyrup Rasmussen, Poul *See* RASMUSSEN, ...

O'Malley, Desmond or **Des** (1939–) Irish lawyer and politician. Elected to parliament for the centre-right Fianna Fáil in 1968, he was justice minister from 1970–73 and industry minister from 1977–81 and in 1982. He was expelled from the party in 1985 because of disagreements with the then leader Charles Haughey. In December that year he founded and became leader of the Progressive Democrats (PDs). He returned to government in 1989 as deputy prime minister and minister of industry and commerce in a coalition with Fianna Fáil. In November 1992 he and the other PD ministers resigned their posts, precipitating an early election. He resigned the party leadership in October 1993.

ÖAKT *See* FEDERAL CHAMBER OF LABOUR.

občina (pl. občine) Administrative division of Slovenia, usually translated as 'district'. Each of the 62 *občine* has an assembly elected for a four-year term. They are responsible for a range of local services and may enter into cooperation agreements with other assemblies to provide certain services jointly. The creation of intermediate-tier regions is under consideration.

Oberbürgermeister (pl. -) German local government official, usually translated as 'senior mayor' or 'mayor'. The title *Oberbürgermeister* is used in most large cities for the senior executive officer, who is called the *Bürgermeister* in towns and municipalities.

Oberösterreich *See* UPPER AUSTRIA.

objective one, objective two etc (European Union) *See* STRUCTURAL FUND.

oblast (pl. -i) Bulgarian administrative division, usually translated as 'region'. Each of the nine *oblasti* has a council elected for a 2 1/2 year term, a permanent committee responsible for day-to-day administration, and a governor appointed by the central government. Sofia, the national capital, combines the functions of a region and a lower-tier municipality. A reorganization of the regional government structure is under consideration.

Occhetto, Achille (1936–) Italian politician. Leader of the Italian Communist Party (PCI) youth wing from 1962–69,

he was elected to parliament in 1976. He became the party's deputy leader in 1987 and was elected leader in June 1988 in succession to the ailing Alessandro Natta. He initiated a major review of policy and structure, resulting in the PCI's relaunch as the Democratic Left Party (PDS) in February 1991. He resigned in June 1994 after the party's disappointing performance in the European elections.

Occitan Language in France. Occitan is the modern name given to the dialects spoken across the whole of southern France and the written language based on the *langue d'oc*, which flourished during the Middle Ages. It is a Romance language related to French and Catalan. Since the mid 19th century a literary movement has sought to revive it as a written language. The movement has also been a focus for regionalist sentiment. Around 1.6 million people are thought to have a good grasp of Occitan, and perhaps as many as 10 million people speak Occitan dialects while using French in formal contexts. The language has no official status, but it is allowed to be taught in schools. In the region of Provence it is usually called Provençal.

Occitania Slogan used by those who advocate the recognition of the OCCITAN language in southern France and call for more wide-ranging autonomy for the regions in which it is spoken.

OCTs *See* OVERSEAS COUNTRIES AND TERRITORIES.

ODA *See* CIVIC DEMOCRATIC ALLIANCE.

Oddsson, Davíđ (1948–) Icelandic broadcaster, administrator, writer and politician. He worked as a producer at Icelandic Radio, was the director of a health insurance fund, and published a number of plays before becoming mayor of Reykjavík, the national capital, in 1982. He was elected to parliament for the right-wing Independence Party in 1991. He became the party's deputy leader in 1989 and was elected leader in March 1991. He became prime minister of a centre-right coalition after the election in April of that year.

Odelsting *See* STORTING.

Oder-Neisse Line Common name for the border between Poland and Germany since 1945. At the end of the Second World War the victorious powers placed most German territory to the east of the Oder and Neisse rivers under Polish administration. The redrawn border was recognized by East Germany in 1950, and by West Germany de facto in 1970, in the context of a normalization of relations with Poland, but not de jure, on the grounds that the issue could only be finally settled when Germany was reunited. Shortly after this occurred in 1990, the two countries signed a treaty confirming the status quo.

ODIHR *See* OFFICE FOR DEMOCRATIC INSTITUTIONS AND HUMAN RIGHTS.

ODS *See* CIVIC DEMOCRATIC PARTY.

OFE *See* OFFICE FOR DEMOCRATIC INSTITUTIONS AND HUMAN RIGHTS.

Office for Democratic Institutions and Human Rights (ODIHR) Institution of the Conference on Security and Cooperation in Europe (CSCE). Originally called the Office for Free Elections (OFE), this body was set up in 1991 under the Paris Charter signed the previous year. Conceived as part of a system of confidence-building measures in Europe, its main function is to promote the CSCE's 'human dimension', i.e. human-rights and humanitarian issues. It also assists the high commissioner for national minorities and acts as a clearing house for information on national elections, population censuses and other developments in member states. It is based in Warsaw (Poland).

Office for Free Elections *See* OFFICE FOR DEMOCRATIC INSTITUTIONS AND HUMAN RIGHTS.

Office for the Protection of the Constitution *See* FEDERAL ....

Office of the High Commissioner on National Minorities Institution of the Conference on Security and Cooperation in Europe (CSCE). The post of high commissioner on national minorities was established in July 1992 as part of a set of measures to improve the CSCE's conflict-prevention and crisis-management mechanisms. S/he is charged with identifying potential ethnic conflicts at an early stage and initiating 'good offices' missions to the countries concerned, and submits regular reports to the Committee of Senior Officials (CSO) and the Council of Foreign Ministers.

official opposition or **the opposition** In the United Kingdom, the largest opposition party. Formally called Her Majesty's Loyal Opposition, it enjoys various rights and privileges in terms of the parliamentary process and the 'leader of the opposition' is entitled to financial support. The terms 'official opposition' and 'leader of the opposition' are also used in countries and territories whose parliamentary systems are based on or influenced by the British model, e.g., in Europe, Ireland, Malta and Gibraltar.

Official Unionist Party (OUP) Informal name for the ULSTER UNIONIST PARTY (UUP), the main party of the Protestant community in Northern Ireland, a component of the United Kingdom. The name dates from the period around 1970, when several groups broke away from the party.

ÖGB *See* AUSTRIAN TRADE UNION FEDERATION.

OGB-L *See* INDEPENDENT TRADE UNION CONFEDERATION - LUXEMBURG.

Ogi, Adolf (1942–) Swiss economist, administrator and politician. He worked for the Swiss Ski Federation from 1964–83, serving as its vice-president from 1971. He was a member of parliament for the right-wing Swiss People's Party from 1979–87 and party president from 1984–87. In January 1988 he became a member of the Federal Council (= government), taking responsibility for transport, communications and energy.

Ognjanović, Vuk (1939–) Yugoslav economist, academic and politician. He worked in business and local government and lectured in his native Montenegro in the 1960s and early 70s. He has been finance minister of Montenegro (1975–79), governor of the republic's central bank (1979–85), deputy finance minister at federal level (1985–90), deputy prime minister of Montenegro (1990–92) and governor of the Bank of Yugoslavia (= central bank) (1992–93). He was appointed minister of finance at federal level in August 1993. He is a member of the Democratic Socialist Party of Montenegro (DPSCG).

OH *See* FREE DEMOCRATS.

Oikonomides, Faidros (1945–) Cypriot economist and politician. He has been a member of the Labour Advisory Board and managing director of the Cyprus Import Corporation, and was chairman of the Employers' and Industrialists' Federation (OEV) from 1988–92. A member of the centre-right Democratic Rally (DISI), he was appointed finance minister in February 1993.

Oireachtas Parliament of Ireland, composed of the DÁIL ÉIREANN and the SEANAD ÉIREANN.

Ojczyzna *See* HOMELAND.

Økonomiske Råd *See* ECONOMIC COUNCIL.

old Bundesland (Germany) *See* OLD FEDERAL STATE.

old federal state or **old state** [altes Bundesland, pl. alte Bundesländer] In Germany, a federal state on the territory of former West Germany. They are Baden-Württemberg, Bavaria, Bremen, Hamburg, Hesse, Lower Saxony, North Rhine - Westphalia, Rhineland-Palatinate, Saarland and Schleswig-Holstein. West Berlin was also effectively part of West Germany but had a special status. It was reunited with East Berlin on the country's reunification in October 1990.

old Land and **old state** (Germany) *See* OLD FEDERAL STATE.

old Yugoslavia *See* FORMER YUGOSLAVIA.

Oldenburg Common name for the royal dynasties of Denmark and Norway. *See* HOUSE OF ....

Olechowski, Andrzej (1947–) Polish economist and politician. A specialist on international trade issues, he has worked for the UN Conference on Trade and Development (UNCTAD) (1974–78 and 1982–84), the Foreign Trade Research Institute in Warsaw (1978–82), the World Bank (1985–87) and the European Bank for Reconstruction and Development (EBRD) (1992–93). Between 1987 and 1992 he held several senior posts at the National Bank of Poland, the central bank, and in the ministry of foreign economic

relations. He was briefly finance minister in February–May 1992 and became an economic adviser to President Wałęsa later that year. He led the Non-Party Bloc in Support of Reforms (BBWR), sponsored by Wałęsa, in the September 1993 election. On the president's recommendation he was appointed foreign minister in the left-wing coalition which took office the following month.

Olsen, Erling Heymann (1927–) Danish economist, academic and politician. He was a researcher and from 1970 a lecturer at the Economic Institute of Copenhagen University, specializing in economic history. Elected to parliament for the Social Democratic Party (SD) in 1964, he was minister of housing in 1978–79 and 1981–82. When the party returned to government in March 1993, he was appointed justice minister.

Olsen, Jan Henry (1956–) Norwegian journalist, administrator and politician. He has worked for several local newspapers, the Norwegian Broadcasting Corporation (NRK), the Norsk Hydro-electricity company, and for several fisheries organizations. A member of the Norwegian Labour Party (DNA), he was appointed minister of fisheries in September 1992.

Olsson, Karl Erik (1938–) Swedish farmer and politician. A member of parliament for the Centre Party (Cp) from 1976–79 and since 1985, he was appointed minister of agriculture in the centre-right coalition which took office in October 1991.

Olszewski, Jan (1930–) Polish lawyer and politician. He defended many political activists in the 1960s and 70s. In the 1980s he was a senior adviser to the opposition Solidarity movement. After the collapse of communist rule in 1989 he joined the Centre Alliance (POC). He was appointed prime minister by President Wałęsa in December 1990 and formed a coalition of post-Solidarity parties which remained in office until June 1992. He then joined the Christian Democratic Forum (FChD), later renamed the Movement for the Republic (RdR), and was elected its honorary chairman.

ombudsman, -person or **-woman** In the
European Union (EU), the public official
charged with investigating citizens' complaints of maladministration in or by any
of the organization's institutions (except
the Court of Justice). The ombudsperson is
appointed by the European Parliament for
a five-year term. S/he deals with specific
complaints from individuals, companies
and organizations, may conduct inquiries
on his/her initiative, reports to the Parliament, and may propose changes to EU
law. The position of ombudsperson was
set up under the Maastricht Treaty, which
came into force in November 1993.
The practice of charging an independent
official with investigating citizens'
complaints against abuses by government
originated in Sweden, where the first
ombudsman – the term means 'representative' in Swedish – was appointed in
1809. From the 1950s onwards the office
was introduced in other Nordic countries,
other Western European countries and
elsewhere.

OMON Abbreviation for Otryad Militsii
Osobogo Naznacheniya ('Special Purpose
Police Squad'), an elite armed unit of the
interior ministry in the former Soviet
Union. Established in 1987, the 'black
berets', as they became known, were
originally charged with investigating
crimes but were increasingly used to
maintain order and specifically to break
up anti-government demonstrations and
intimidate reform and independence
movements. As such they were active in
Estonia, Latvia and Lithuania until these
countries regained their independence in
August 1991.

Omonia and **Omónoia** *See* CONCORD.

Onkelinx, Laurette (1958–) Belgian lawyer and politician. Elected to parliament
for the Walloon Socialist Party (PS) in
1989, she was appointed minister for
social integration, public health and the
environment in 1992. In May 1993 she
became chief executive of the French
Community, the body in Belgium's federal
structure primarily responsible for French-
language education and cultural matters.

open barracks Policy under which governments agree to exchange information on

troop levels and deployments and allow
inspection of army bases in each other's
countries. Analogous to the principle of
'OPEN SKIES', it has been adopted by the
Czech Republic, Hungary, Poland and
Slovakia, and is being considered by
other Eastern European countries as a
means of reducing tension and building
confidence between them.

open skies Policy under which unarmed
reconnaissance aircraft from one country
are allowed to fly over the territory of
another for military surveillance purposes.
The idea of 'open skies' was first proposed by President Eisenhower of the
United States in 1955, at the height of the
'cold war' between the North Atlantic
Treaty Organization (NATO) and the
Warsaw Pact, as a means of reducing
tension and building confidence between
the two military blocs. It was revived by
the Bush administration in 1989. The
OPEN SKIES TREATY, covering Europe,
much of the former Soviet Union and
North America, was signed in March
1992. The term 'open skies' is also used
in the context of the liberalization of air
transport, as proposed within the European Union (EU) for instance.

Open Skies Treaty International agreement
providing for unarmed reconnaissance
flights for the purpose of monitoring
compliance with arms-control agreements
and building confidence among countries.
The Open Skies Treaty was signed by the
16 member states of the North Atlantic
Treaty Organization (NATO) and nine
members of the former Warsaw Pact on
24 March 1992. Negotiations on the
treaty had begun in early 1990, when both
the Warsaw Pact and the Soviet Union
were still in existence and confidence-
building measures were still considered
essential in reducing tension between East
and West. The treaty regulates surveillance flights by any signatory country
over the territory of another. These can be
requested at 72 hours' notice but must
conform to a complex system of quotas
and agreed technologies (including video
cameras, infra-red scanning equipment
and all-weather radar). Any information
gained from such flights must be made

available to other signatories on request. The Open Skies Consultative Commission (OSCC), based in Vienna (Austria), will monitor compliance with the treaty once it comes into force. It is also charged with refining procedures and resolving technical problems.

opening of the Berlin Wall *See* BERLIN WALL.

openness (European Union) *See* TRANSPARENCY.

Operation Clean Hands [Operazione Mani Pulite] Codename for the investigations into illegal party funding by a Milan-based team of magistrates, which in 1992 first exposed the web of political corruption in Italian public life. *See* ITALIAN CORRUPTION SCANDALS.

Operation Deny Flight Codename for the monitoring of the AIR-EXCLUSION ZONE or no-fly zone over Bosnian airspace. North Atlantic Treaty Organization (NATO) forces are responsible for ensuring compliance with the ban, which was imposed by the United Nations in October 1992.

opposition, the Shorthand for the OFFICIAL OPPOSITION, the formal title of the largest opposition party in the United Kingdom.

opština (pl. opštini) Administrative division of Macedonia, usually translated as 'district'. Each of the 30 *opštini* has a council elected for a four-year term. They are responsible for a range of local services and may enter into cooperation agreements with other councils to provide certain services jointly.

opština (pl. opštine) Administrative division of Yugoslavia, usually translated as 'district'. The 240 *opštine* are responsible for local services as delegated to them by the authorities of the country's two constituent republics, Serbia and Montenegro. Each is run by a council elected for a four-year term.

opt-out In the European Union (EU), a special dispensation under which a member state is not bound by certain provisions of the founding treaties and their amendments. The first opt-outs were negotiated in the context of the Maastricht Treaty on European Union, which was agreed in December 1991. (Until then the major agreements had been accepted in full by all member states.) The British government negotiated opt-outs from the provisions on social policy and the automatic introduction of a single currency as part of 'stage three' of the planned economic and monetary union. After the Treaty's initial rejection in a referendum, the Danish government also negotiated opt-outs on the single currency, defence policy, immigration policy and EU citizenship. An exemption from a 'directive' or 'regulation', the EU's main legal instruments, is called a 'derogation'. *See also* VARIABLE GEOMETRY.

OPZZ *See* ALL-POLAND TRADE UNIONS ALLIANCE.

ØR *See* ECONOMIC COUNCIL.

orange or **yellow** In some countries, the colour associated with liberal parties. Examples are the Free Democratic Party (FDP) in Germany and the Liberal Democrats in Britain.

Orange [Oranje] Royal dynasty of the Netherlands. *See* HOUSE OF ORANGE-NASSAU.

orange In Northern Ireland (United Kingdom), the colour associated with the unionist or loyalist movement supporting the province's status as part of the United Kingdom. *See* UNIONISM.

Orange-Nassau [Oranje-Nassau] Royal dynasty of the Netherlands. *See* HOUSE OF ORANGE-NASSAU.

Orange Order British political and cultural organization. Active in Northern Ireland (and parts of Scotland), the Orange Order was formed in 1795 as a secret society with the aim of maintaining Protestant domination in Ireland and specifically in the province of Ulster, where Protestants were most strongly represented. Originally called the Orange Society, it was named after William of Orange, who as King William III of England had defeated his Catholic predecessor, James II, at the Battle of the Boyne in 1690. It was a leading force in the Protestant resistance to plans for Irish autonomy during the 19th century. Since the partition of Ireland in 1922 it has been a bastion of hard-line Protestant and unionist opinion in Northern Ireland.

Orbán, Viktor (1963–) Hungarian lawyer and politician. In March 1988 he became a spokesman of the new centre-left Alliance of Young Democrats (FIDESz), the first opposition group formed under communist rule. He has been the party's effective leader ever since, becoming parliamentary leader in May 1990 and, after an internal reorganization, party president in April 1993.

orbiting (European Union) *See* CONVENTION ON THE RIGHT TO ASYLUM.

Oreja, Marcelino (1935–) Spanish diplomat and politician. He entered the diplomatic service in 1958 and served mostly in intergovernmental organizations. He held a senior post at the Bank of Spain, the central bank, from 1971–74, was a junior foreign minister from 1974–76 and foreign minister from 1976–80, during the transition to democratic rule after the death of Francisco Franco. He was first elected to parliament for the centre-right People's Alliance (AP), now the People's Party (PP), in 1979. He served as secretary-general of the Council of Europe from 1984–89. He was appointed a commissioner of the European Union (EU) in April 1994, taking responsibility for energy and transport.

Øresund or **Öresund question** *See* SOUND QUESTION.

Orlando, Leoluca (1947–) Italian lawyer and politician. He practised and taught public law in the 1970s. From 1980 he held several senior positions in the city government of Palermo, the capital of his native Sicily, and in 1985 he became its mayor as the candidate of the Christian Democratic Party (DC). He left the DC in 1990 after the party hierarchy refused to support his strong measures against corruption and organized crime. In March 1991 he founded and became leader of a new reform movement, the Network (La Rete). In November 1993 he was elected mayor of Palermo with more than three-quarters of the popular vote. He was also elected to parliament in March 1994 and to the European Parliament in June.

ORs *See* OUTERMOST REGIONS.

Országgyűlés *See* NATIONAL ASSEMBLY (Hungary).

ÖS Abbreviation for the SCHILLING, the Austrian currency.

OSCOM *See* OSLO COMMISSION.

Oslo Shorthand for the Norwegian government. Oslo is the capital of Norway.

Oslo Commission (OSCOM) Intergovernmental organization. OSCOM is responsible for administering and implementing the CONVENTION FOR THE PREVENTION OF MARINE POLLUTION BY DUMPING FROM SHIPS AND AIRCRAFT (Oslo Convention). It operates a joint secretariat with the Paris Commission (PARCOM), which is responsible for a companion treaty, the CONVENTION FOR THE PREVENTION OF MARINE POLLUTION FROM LAND-BASED SOURCES. The secretariat, based in London (United Kingdom), is also responsible for administering the intergovernmental Agreement for Cooperation in Dealing with Pollution of the North Sea by Oil or Bonn Agreement concluded in 1969.

Oslo Convention Shorthand for the CONVENTION FOR THE PREVENTION OF MARINE POLLUTION BY DUMPING FROM SHIPS AND AIRCRAFT.

Ost-West-Gefälle (Germany) *See* EAST-WEST DIVIDE.

Österreich German name for Austria.

ostmark Common name for the mark, the currency of former East Germany. It was replaced with the West German mark when the two countries formed an economic and monetary union in July 1990 as a prelude to full reunification the following October.

Ostpolitik ('eastern policy') In Germany, the sphere of foreign policy concerned with relations with the eastern neighbours. The term gained wide currency – also abroad – during the late 1960s to describe the policy of rapprochement initiated by the West German government led by Willy Brandt. This led to the normalization of relations and treaties of reconciliation with East Germany, Poland, Czechoslovakia and the Soviet Union in the early 1970s. It involved the renunciation of German territorial claims, the resolution of other contentious issues dating from the Second World War (1939–45) and the abandonment of the so-called Hallstein Doctrine, under which

460

West Germany had refused to have diplomatic relations with any country that recognized East Germany. The term 'ostpolitik' is also used more generally for any Western European country's policy towards the former communist countries of Eastern Europe.

OTAN French abbreviation for the NORTH ATLANTIC TREATY ORGANIZATION (NATO).

Other Europe *See* ANOTHER EUROPE.

ÖTV *See* PUBLIC SERVICES AND TRANSPORT UNION.

OUP *See* ULSTER UNIONIST PARTY.

Ourselves Alone *See* SINN FÉIN.

out-of-area operations In the North Atlantic Treaty Organization (NATO), military operations carried out outside the member states' territories. NATO was founded in 1949 on the principle of 'collective defence' of a clearly designated area covering the members' territories and the North Atlantic Ocean north of the Tropic of Cancer. The geopolitical changes of the late 1980s and early 1990s, in particular the disintegration of the Warsaw Pact and the Soviet Union, gave rise to proposals that NATO forces might be used in international peace-keeping operations outside the NATO area. This suggestion was initially highly controversial, particularly in Germany and France, but a consensus in favour gradually emerged. In June 1992 it was decided in principle that NATO resources, expertise and forces could be used 'on a case-by-case basis' to undertake peace-keeping activities on behalf of the United Nations (UN) and the Conference on Security and Cooperation in Europe (CSCE), which does not have a military capability of its own; missions would have to be approved unanimously and any member state would be allowed to opt out of participation. Since then NATO forces have been deployed on behalf of the UN in former Yugoslavia.

outermost regions (ORs) In the European Union (EU), the collective name for the territories situated well beyond the European continent. They are the French overseas departments of French Guyana, Guadeloupe and Martinique (in the Caribbean) and Reunion (in the Indian Ocean), the Portuguese autonomous regions of the Azores and Madeira, and the Spanish autonomous community of the Canary Islands (in the North Atlantic Ocean). All are integral parts of the Union. In recognition of their geographical locations and economic characteristics, they are covered by a range of measures aimed at promoting their economic and social development.

overseas countries and territories (OCTs) In the European Union (EU), the collective name for the member states' non-European dependencies. These territories are not part of the Union but are covered by a range of special arrangements, such as preferential access to the EU market, development programmes etc.

overseas department [département d'outre-mer, pl. -s -] (DOM) French administrative division. The four overseas departments (French Guyana, Guadeloupe, Martinique, Reunion) are integral parts of the republic and hence of the European Union (EU). *See also* OUTERMOST REGIONS.

ÖVP *See* AUSTRIAN PEOPLE'S PARTY.

Owen, David (from 1992 **Lord Owen**) (1938–) British doctor and politician. First elected to Parliament for the Labour Party in 1966, he held several junior ministerial posts from 1967–70 and 1974–77 and was foreign secretary from 1977 until Labour lost power two years later. He left the party in 1981 and became a founding member of the Social Democratic Party (SDP). He was elected its leader in 1983. In 1987 he rejected the merger with the Liberal Party approved by a large majority of the membership, and he remained leader of a rump SDP until the party was disbanded in 1991. He did not stand in the 1992 election and later that year received a life peerage (entitling him to a seat in the House of Lords, the upper house of Parliament). In August 1992 he was appointed the European Community's special envoy on former Yugoslavia. As such he has been working in conjunction with the United Nations envoys, initially Cyrus Vance and then Thorvald Stoltenberg, on finding a settlement to the Bosnian civil war and other conflicts in the region.

Owen-Stoltenberg plan Proposal for a settlement to the civil war in Bosnia-Herzegovina, unveiled by the European Community (EC) and United Nations (UN) mediators, David Owen and Thorvald Stoltenberg, in July 1993. The successor to the VANCE-OWEN PLAN, it broadly revived the earlier EC-sponsored 'cantonization' plan calling for the country's three-way division along ethnic lines and also incorporated elements of a joint Yugoslav-Croatian partition plan. It provided for: (i) the creation of a 'union' of three 'republics', Muslim, Serb and Croat; (ii) a constitution based on self-government for the republics, with the union government responsible only for foreign affairs, foreign trade and safeguarding human rights; and (iii) ceasefire and demilitarization arrangements monitored by a UN force. The principle of partition was accepted by all three sides but negotiations eventually broke down on details. Initially the Muslim, Serb and Croat republics were allocated 31%, 52% and 17% of the territory respectively. The Muslim-led Bosnian government considered this unacceptable and demanded at least another 4% of Serb- and Croat-held areas which had been predominantly Muslim before the war. The Bosnian parliament rejected the 31% option in September 1993. Negotiations continued intermittently, but the plan was effectively abandoned by the end of year. Its successor was the CONTACT GROUP PLAN, tabled in July 1994.

Owen-Vance plan *See* VANCE-OWEN PLAN.

own resources In the European Union (EU), the collective term for the four sources of revenue that account for virtually all income. The organization's budget was originally financed by contributions from member states. Under a new system agreed in 1970 and fully implemented by 1980, the EU now has its own budgetary resources. They are: (i) agricultural levies on food imports from third countries and on sugar and isoglucose production; (ii) customs duties imposed on imports from third countries; (iii) a proportion of value added tax (VAT) receipts collected by the member states, currently 1.4% of the total; and (iv) a proportion of the gross domestic product of each member state, currently a maximum of 1.2%, to be increased to 1.27% by 1999. The latter, commonly known as the 'fourth resource', was agreed in June 1988 to meet the growing demands on the budget. The revenue generated by the four resources varies widely: in 1993 VAT payments accounted for 51.8% of total income, the GDP-related contribution for 21.4%, customs duties for 22.2%, agricultural levies for 3.8%, and other income for 0.8%.

Özal, Turgut (1927–93) Turkish economist and politician. Having gained a degree in electrical engineering, he studied economics and then worked in several government agencies, becoming director of the State Planning Organization (DPT) in 1967. From 1971–73 he worked for the World Bank. After a stint in private business in Turkey he became chief economic adviser to the Demirel government and then to the military regime which took power in 1980. In 1983 he became leader of the Motherland Party (ANAP), a new right-wing party formed with the approval of the military. He became prime minister after the ANAP won the restricted election in November of that year. A strong advocate of economic liberalization and a pro-western foreign policy, he established himself as the country's dominant political figure of the 1980s. In November 1989 he was elected president of the republic. He died of a heart attack in April 1993.

Özgür, Özker (1940–) Northern Cypriot teacher and politician. He taught English before entering politics. He has been leader of the left-wing Republican Turkish Party (CTP) since September 1976. He was a member of parliament from 1976–79, and was reelected in 1990 (but like many opposition members boycotted the proceedings until 1993). He became deputy prime minister in the centrist coalition which took office in January 1994.

462

P Abbreviation for Portugal, used for international vehicle registrations, postal addresses etc.

P-2 affair Political scandal in Italy surrounding the activities of Propaganda Two [Propaganda Due], a secret business and political organization. Bringing together around 1,000 senior politicians (including government ministers), military and secret-service officers, businesspeople and other influential people with right-wing sympathies, P-2 was formed in the early 1970s and operated as a highly influential 'masonic lodge' behind the scenes of Italian politics. Its existence was revealed in March 1981 following a police raid on the home of its 'grandmaster', Licio Gelli. Documents seized at the time showed that P-2 was involved in a wide range of criminal and seditious activities, including tax evasion, fraud, criminal association and far-right terrorism. The investigating magistrate's report described P-2 as a 'secret sect which has combined business and politics with the intention of destroying the constitutional order'. The disclosures brought down the government of the day, prompted a major reorganization of the armed forces, and led to a legal ban on secret societies. In July 1984 a parliamentary commission concluded that the list of P-2 members found at Gelli's home was authentic except in a few cases. In October 1992, after an 11-year investigation, Gelli and 15 others went on trial on charges including conspiracy, espionage, revealing state secrets and threatening the constitutional order. Although P-2 was supposedly disbanded soon after its discovery, the network it established – part of what has become known as the 'HIDDEN GOVERNMENT' [sottogoverno] – is widely thought to have remained influential in Italian politics throughout the 1980s and at least until the revelation of endemic corruption that brought down much of the country's political and business elite in 1993. In April 1994 an appeal court ruled that P-2 had not been guilty of conspiring against the state.

paarse coalitie *See* PURPLE COALITION.

PAC *See* CIVIC ALLIANCE PARTY.

PACA Abbreviation for PROVENCE-ALPES-COTE-D'AZUR, a region of France.

Pact for Italy [Patto per l'Italia] Italian political organization. The Pact was formed in January 1994 as a loose alliance of centre-right and centrist parties and groups supporting the policies of Mario Segni, a prominent advocate of political and economic reform. Commonly called the Segni Pact [Patto Segni], it includes reformist wings of the Christian Democratic Party (DC), the Italian Socialist Party (PSI) and other government parties discredited by the corruption scandals that broke in 1992 and 1993. It supports free-market economic policies and has liberal views on social issues. It contested the March 1994 election in alliance with the Italian People's Party (PPI), the reformist successor to the DC, and gained 4.6% of the vote and 13/630 seats. Segni is the leader.

Pacto de Ajuria Enea *See* AJURIA ENEA PACT.

Padania Slogan used by the Northern League (Lega Nord) and other regional groupings in Italy advocating the country's transformation into a federal state. The League nominally calls for the establishment of three semi-independent republics in the north, centre and south, although its more pragmatic objective is wide-ranging autonomy for the country's existing 20 regions. The northern republic has been dubbed 'Padania', after the Po river valley that dominates the region.

PADS and **PADSh** *See* DEMOCRATIC ALLIANCE PARTY OF ALBANIA.

Pagliarini, Giancarlo (1942–) Italian accountant, lecturer and politician. He started his own accountancy firm in the 1970s and taught at the University of Parma from 1980–86. Elected to parliament for the federalist Northern League (Lega Nord) in 1992, he was appointed budget minister in the right-wing coalition formed in May 1994.

País Vasco *See* BASQUE COUNTRY.

Paisley, Ian (1926–) British clergyman and politician. He was ordained a minister of the Free Presbyterian Church of Ulster in 1946. He has been a prominent leader of the Protestant community in

Northern Ireland since the late 1960s, defending the province's status as part of the United Kingdom and rejecting closer links with Ireland. First elected to Parliament in 1970, he founded and became leader of the Ulster Democratic Unionist Party (DUP) in September 1971. He has also been a member of the European Parliament since 1979.

Paisos Catalans *See* CATALAN LANDS.

Pál, László (1942–) Hungarian electrical engineer and politician. A specialist in industrial policy, he held several senior posts at the National Committee for Technological Development from 1969–89. He was a junior industry minister in 1989–90. Elected to parliament for the Hungarian Socialist Party (MSzP, the successor to the communist Hungarian Socialist Workers' Party, MSzMP) in 1990, he was appointed minister of industry and trade in the MSzP-led coalition formed in July 1994.

Pale Shorthand for the government of the Serbian Republic (SR), the state proclaimed by Serbs in Bosnia-Herzegovina. The town of Pale, southeast of Sarajevo, the Bosnian capital, is the seat of the SR government and assembly.

Paleokrassas, Ioannis (1934–) Greek economist, businessman and politician. He worked for the economy ministry and then held senior management posts with several commercial firms. He was general manager of the Ergobank from 1975–77. He was appointed a junior minister in 1977, was elected to parliament for the right-wing New Democratic Party (ND) in 1978, and was briefly minister of coordination in 1981. After the party returned to power in 1989 he served as minister of finance (1990–92) and commerce (1992). In January 1993 he was appointed a commissioner of the European Community (EC), taking responsibility for the environment, fisheries and nuclear safety.

Palme case Murder of Olof Palme, the Swedish prime minister, in 1986. Palme had been leader of the Social Democratic Party (SAP) since 1969 and prime minister from 1969–76 and since 1982. He was particularly active in international affairs during his time in office. He was shot and killed in Stockholm in February 1986 while walking home from the cinema with his wife. The assassin escaped. (Palme generally refused to have bodyguards.) The murder caused great shock in a country with no history of political violence. The subsequent police investigation proved highly controversial and gave rise to allegations of incompetence and malpractice. A petty criminal was convicted of the murder on circumstantial evidence but was acquitted on appeal. Another was later charged but then released for lack of evidence. Kurdish exile groups, arms dealers, organized crime and the US and Soviet secret services have all been linked to the murder, while the belief that it was the act of a single man with a grudge against Palme is also widely held. Another special parliamentary inquiry into the case was opened in November 1993.

Pálsson, Thorsteinn (1947–) Icelandic journalist and politician. Elected to parliament for the right-wing Independence Party in 1983, he became its leader the following November. He was minister of finance from 1985–87 and prime minister – the country's youngest-ever – in 1987–88. He lost the party leadership to Davíd Oddsson in March 1991. He was appointed to the key ministry of fisheries in the coalition formed by Oddsson after the April election.

Pan-Hellenic Socialist Movement [Panellínion Sosialistikón Kínima] (PASOK) Greek political party. Founded in 1974 after the collapse of the military regime, PASOK won the 1981 election and held power until 1989. Originally left-socialist and opposed to Greek membership of the then European Community (EC) and the North Atlantic Treaty Organization (NATO), it moved towards the mainstream European left in the 1980s. It returned to power after winning the early election in October 1993, gaining 46.9% of the vote and 170/300 seats. Andreas Papandreou has been party leader since its foundation.

Pangalos, Theodoros (1938–) Greek lawyer, economist and politician. A student in France when the military took power in

1967, he remained in exile until the regime's collapse in 1974. He was elected to parliament for the Pan-Hellenic Socialist Movement (PASOK) in 1981. He was deputy foreign minister with responsibility for European affairs from 1984–89, and was appointed to the same post after the party returned to power in October 1993. He became minister of transport and communications in July 1994. He resigned two months later to run for mayor of Athens in the October local elections.

Panić, Milan (1929–) Yugoslav and American businessman and politician. He claimed political asylum in the Netherlands while competing in a cycling championship in 1956. He then emigrated to the United States and founded a chemical company in 1960, which eventually became the ICN pharmaceutical concern. At the request of President Cosić he formed a non-party administration in Yugoslavia in July 1992. He sought to end Yugoslavia's international isolation caused by its involvement in the Bosnian civil war. He stood for the presidency of Serbia in December 1992, but lost to the incumbent, Slobodan Milošević. He lost a confidence vote in the federal parliament later that month and formally resigned in February 1993. He then returned to his business in the United States, but has remained active in opposition politics.

Pannella, Marco (1930–) Italian journalist and politician. He was a founding member of the Radical Party (PR) in 1955 and served as its secretary (= leader) from 1962–67. Since that time he has been one of the country's leading advocates of social and political reform, agitating for changes in the divorce, abortion, drugs and electoral laws and against political corruption (occasionally using hunger strikes and civil disobedience to promote his cause). In recent years he has concentrated on human-rights and environmental issues at a European level. At the March 1994 election he controversially allied himself with Silvio Berlusconi's new Come On Italy (Forza Italia) movement. He has been a member of parliament on

several occasions between 1976 and 1994 and has been a member of the European Parliament since 1979.

Pannella List *See* RADICAL PARTY (Italy).

Papadopoulos, Alexandros (1950–) Greek lawyer and politician. He was an adviser to the interior minister during the 1980s. Elected to parliament for the Pan-Hellenic Socialist Movement (PASOK) in 1989, he was appointed junior finance minister when PASOK returned to power in October 1993 and became finance minister in February 1994.

Papal Commission [Commissione Pontificale] Government of the Vatican City. The Commission is composed of six Roman Catholic cardinals and a lay special delegate appointed by the pope, in his capacity as the Vatican's head of state. It is responsible for all secular legislative, executive and administrative matters. It should not be confused with the separate government structures of the Holy See, including the Roman Curia, which administer the affairs of the worldwide Roman Catholic Church.

Papandreou, Andreas (1919–) Greek economist, academic and politician. He lived in exile in the United States for 20 years from 1939, lecturing in economics there from 1947–63. His father, Georgios, became prime minister in 1963 and brought him into the government. After the military coup in April 1967 he was arrested, but subsequently allowed to leave the country. He founded an opposition movement in exile, the precursor of the Pan-Hellenic Socialist Movement (PASOK) launched on the restoration of democratic rule in 1974. He became prime minister when the party won the 1981 election and was returned to office in 1985. He resigned after it lost its majority in 1989. At this time he was accused of abusing public trust and accepting bribes in the BANK OF CRETE AFFAIR, but was cleared of all charges in January 1992. He returned as prime minister after PASOK won an early election in October 1993.

Papandreou, Giorgos (1952–) Greek sociologist and politician. He left Greece in 1967 when his father, Andreas

Papandreou, the current prime minister, was forced into exile by the new military regime. He studied in the United States and Sweden in the early 1970s. (Democracy was restored in 1974.) Elected to parliament for the Pan-Hellenic Socialist Movement (PASOK) in 1981, he served as a junior culture minister from 1985–87 and as education minister in 1988–89. When PASOK returned to power in October 1993 he was appointed a junior foreign minister. In July 1994 he became minister of education and religious affairs.

Papantoniou, Ioannis or **Yannis** (1949–) Greek economist and politician. A student abroad when the military took over in 1967, he remained in exile until the regime's collapse in 1974. He worked for the Organization for Economic Cooperation and Development (OECD) from 1978–81. He then represented the Pan-Hellenic Socialist Movement (PASOK) in the European Parliament, served as junior economy minister from 1985–89 and was briefly minister of commerce in 1989. Elected to parliament the same year, he returned as junior economy minister when PASOK returned to power in October 1993 and took over as economy minister in May 1994.

Papariga, Alexandra or **Aleka** (1945–) Greek archeologist, accountant and politician. A member of the Communist Party (KKE) since 1968, she was barred from taking up an appointment as an archeology lecturer during the right-wing military dictatorship (1967–74). Initially active for the party mainly in Athens, she was elected to the politburo (= executive) in 1986. She was elected party leader with the support of the orthodox wing in February 1991. She was elected to parliament in 1993.

Papathelemis, Stelios (1938–) Greek lawyer and politician. Elected to parliament for the Democratic Centre Union (EDIK) in 1981 and for the Pan-Hellenic Socialist Movement (PASOK) in 1985, he was minister with responsibility for the north from 1987–89. He was appointed minister of public order when PASOK returned to power in October 1993.

Papon affair Controversy in France concerning Maurice Papon, a former government minister accused of involvement in war crimes during the Second World War. Papon participated in the resistance during the latter stages of the German occupation (1940–44). After liberation he held a range of senior posts in the civil service, served as chief of police in Paris, and then entered politics, serving as budget minister from 1978–81 in a centre-right coalition. In 1981 a news magazine first accused him of helping to organize the detention and deportation of 1,690 Jews, including 223 children, between 1942 and 1944, when he was a middle-ranking civil servant in Bordeaux. He denied the allegations and successfully sued the magazine for libel. In 1993 he also sued a writer who had repeated the allegations in a book, but in June 1994 the civil court ruled that only a criminal trial could determine whether the allegations were true or false. This intensified calls for Papon, aged 83, to be tried for crimes against humanity. *See also* TOUVIER AFFAIR.

Papoulias, Karolos (1929–) Greek lawyer and politician. A student in Germany when the military took power in 1967, he remained in exile until the regime's collapse in 1974. He was elected to parliament for the Pan-Hellenic Socialist Movement (PASOK) in 1977. He was deputy foreign minister from 1981–85 and foreign minister from 1985–89. He was reappointed to the latter post when the party returned to power in October 1993.

PAR *See* ARAGONESE PARTY.

Paraga, Dobroslav (1960–) Croatian politician. A theology and law student, he was imprisoned by the communist regime in 1981 for 'discrediting the image of Yugoslavia' after calling for an amnesty for political prisoners. He was released in 1984 but rearrested on several occasions over the next five years. He became leader of the relaunched far-right Croatian Party of Rights (HSP) in February 1990. A strong supporter of Croatian independence (declared in June 1991) but critical of President Tudjman, he was arrested on three occasions between November 1991 and April 1993. He was eventually tried for attempting to overthrow the government and organizing terrorist actions, but was cleared of all charges in November 1993.

PARCOM *See* PARIS COMMISSION.

Parek, Lagle (1941–) Estonian architect and politician. She worked at the Estonian Architectural Memorials Institute from 1972–83. In 1983 she was imprisoned for four years on charges of 'anti-Soviet agitation'. She was leader of the centre-right Estonian National Independence Party (ERSP) from 1989–93. Appointed interior minister in October 1992, she resigned in November 1993 following allegations of friction between the police (her responsibility) and the army.

Paris Shorthand for the French government. Paris is the capital of France. It is also the seat of a number of intergovernmental organizations, including the Organization for Economic Cooperation and Development (OECD) and the United Nations Educational, Scientific and Cultural Organization (UNESCO).

Paris Charter Shorthand for the CHARTER OF PARIS FOR A NEW EUROPE.

Paris Commission (PARCOM) Intergovernmental organization. The Paris Commission is responsible for administering and implementing the CONVENTION FOR THE PREVENTION OF MARINE POLLUTION FROM LAND-BASED SOURCES or Paris Convention. It operates a joint secretariat with the Oslo Commission (OSCOM), which is responsible for a companion treaty on the prevention of dumping from ships and aircraft. The secretariat, based in London (United Kingdom), is also responsible for administering the intergovernmental Agreement for Cooperation in Dealing with Pollution of the North Sea by Oil (Bonn Agreement) concluded in 1969.

Paris Convention Shorthand for the CONVENTION FOR THE PREVENTION OF MARINE POLLUTION FROM LAND-BASED SOURCES.

parish British administrative division. A subdivision of the district, the parish is the smallest unit of local government in the non-metropolitan counties of England. Around four-fifths of the around 10,000

parishes have councils, which are elected for four-year terms. They have limited powers in some matters of local concern.

Parity Commission *See* JOINT COMMISSION ON WAGES AND PRICES.

Parliament [Parlament] Parliament of Austria, composed of the NATIONAL COUNCIL and the FEDERAL COUNCIL.

Parliament *See* ... OF THE CZECH REPUBLIC.

Parliament [Parlement] Parliament of France, composed of the NATIONAL ASSEMBLY and the SENATE.

Parliament [Parlament] Parliament of Germany, composed of the FEDERAL ASSEMBLY (Bundestag) and the FEDERAL COUNCIL (Bundesrat).

Parliament [Parlamento] Parliament of Italy, composed of the CHAMBER OF DEPUTIES and the SENATE.

Parliament *See* ... OF ROMANIA.

Parliament Parliament of the United Kingdom, composed of the HOUSE OF COMMONS and HOUSE OF LORDS.

Parliament of Romania or **Parliament** [Parlamentul României] Parliament of Romania, composed of the ASSEMBLY OF DEPUTIES and the SENATE.

Parliament of the Czech Republic or **Parliament** [Parlament České Republiky] Parliament of Czech Republic, composed of the CHAMBER OF DEPUTIES and the SENATE.

Parliamentary Assembly Interparliamentary assembly, a consultative body of the Conference on Security and Cooperation in Europe (CSCE), also called the Assembly of Europe. Modelled on similar bodies such as the Parliamentary Assembly of the Council of Europe and the North Atlantic Assembly, the Assembly was established in April 1991 and held its first session in July 1992. It has 312 members drawn from the national parliaments of the member states. They meet once a year to discuss topical issues and make recommendations to the Council of Foreign Ministers, the CSCE's main decision-making body, and to national parliaments and governments.

Parliamentary Assembly Interparliamentary assembly, a consultative body of the Council of Europe. Composed of 234 members drawn from the national parliaments of the member states, the Assembly meets three times a year to discuss topical international issues and make recommendations to the Committee of Ministers, the Council's main decision-making body. It organizes its work through 16 ordinary committees dealing with specific policy areas. When the Assembly is not in session it is represented by the Standing Committee, composed of the president, vice-presidents and committee chairs. The president is Miguel Angel Martínez (Spain). Since 1990 'special guest' parliamentary delegations from Eastern European countries have been admitted to the plenary sessions.

Parliamentary Assizes or **Assizes** Informal name for the CONFERENCE OF THE PARLIAMENTS, an advisory body of the European Union (EU).

parliamentary commissioner for administration In the United Kingdom, the formal title of the ombudsperson, the independent official charged with investigating citizens' complaints of maladministration by government departments and certain public bodies. S/he is appointed by Parliament. *See also* OMBUDSMAN ....

partido regionalista *See* REGIONAL PARTY.

partitocrazia *See* PARTYOCRACY.

Partnership for Peace (PFP) Programme of the North Atlantic Treaty Organization (NATO). Based on an American proposal and launched in January 1994, the PFP provides for military cooperation between NATO and the communist countries of Central and Eastern Europe, including Russia and the other Soviet successor states. Its aim is to enhance security and stability in Europe by deepening the emerging 'partnership' between NATO and its former adversaries that was initiated with the launch of the North Atlantic Cooperation Council (NACC) in December 1991. It is seen as a compromise between the desire of several Eastern European countries, fearful of a revival of Russian expansionism, to join NATO, and NATO's reluctance to consider this in the short term, in part so as not to fuel Russian worries about becoming marginalized. The invitation to join the PFP did not extend security guarantees

or offer full membership, but did declare that participation would 'play an important role in the evolutionary process of the expansion of NATO'. Under the PFP the participating states accept certain basic principles, such as respect for fundamental freedoms and human rights and, more specifically, democratic control of the armed forces and transparency in defence planning. NATO and each participating state will then develop, on a bilateral basis, a detailed programme of activities, including joint training and military exercises and cooperation in peacekeeping and humanitarian operations. By the end of June 1994 19 of the 22 non-NATO NACC members had joined the PFP, including Russia. Finland and Sweden, two countries which had remained neutral during the Cold War, had also joined.

Party for Democratic Prosperity - National Democratic Party [Partija za Demokratski Prosperitet - Nacionalna Demokratska Partija (Macedonian), Partia e Prosperitet Demokratik - Partia Nacional Demokratike (Albanian)] (PDP-NDP or PPD-PND) Macedonian political party. Representing the Albanian community and supporting a rapid transition to a market economy, the PPD and PND were founded prior to the December 1990 election, when they gained 25/120 seats between them. They merged in 1991. The party split in February 1994, with one wing, including the deputies and ministers, favouring continued participation in the coalition government, while a more radical wing called for withdrawal and full autonomy and recognition of the Albanians as a 'nation'. The former is led by Abdurahman Aliti and Nevzat Halili (the former party leader and now honorary chairman), the latter by Arben Xhaferi. In July 1994 the deputies announced a boycott of parliament in protest at the conviction of 10 Albanians accused of conspiring to overthrow the government by setting up paramilitary units. Among the convicted is the party's former general secretary, Mithat Emini, a supporter of the 'continuity' wing.

Party for the Defence of Human Rights
[Partia për Mbrojtjen e të Drejtave të
Njeriut (Albanian)] or **Human Rights
Union** [Énosi Anthrópikon Dikaiomáton
(Greek)] (PMDN or EAD) Albanian
political party. The EAD was set up in
1992 as the political wing of the Concord
[Omónoia] movement, which represents
the interests of the Greek community in
the south. It is the successor to the Democratic Union (BD/ED), which had participated in the multiparty election in March/
April 1991 but was barred from standing
in the March 1992 election under a new
electoral law which effectively banned
ethnically based parties. The new party
gained 2.9% of the vote and 2/140 seats.
The leader is Vasil Mele.

party-funding scandals (Italy) *See* ITALIAN
CORRUPTION SCANDALS.

Party of Democratic Action *See* DEMO-
CRATIC ACTION PARTY.

Party of Democratic Socialism *See* DEMO-
CRATIC SOCIALIST PARTY.

Party of European Socialists (PES or PSE)
European Union (EU) political organization. The PES was founded in November
1992 as the successor to the looser
Confederation of Socialist Parties of the
European Community (CSPEC). It brings
together the 17 leading democratic socialist, social democratic and labour parties
in the 12 member states and Austria,
including the Socialist Party (PS) in
France, the Social Democratic Party
(SPD) in Germany, the Labour Party in
Britain, the Democratic Left Party (PDS)
in Italy, and the Spanish Socialist
Workers' Party (PSOE). There are also
10 observer and associate parties from
other European countries. The PES group
in the European Parliament, also called
the Socialist Group, is the largest, with
198/567 seats, and includes representatives from all member states. The PES
president is Willy Claes (Belgium), the
leader of the parliamentary group is
Pauline Green (United Kingdom).

Party of Labour *See* SOCIALIST PARTY OF
ALBANIA.

Party of Social Democracy *See* SOCIAL
DEMOCRACY PARTY OF ROMANIA.

Party of Wales *See* PLAID CYMRU.

Party X [Partia X] Polish political party.
The right-wing populist Party X – the X
reputedly symbolizes '10', as in the Ten
Commandments and 10 centuries of
Polish history, and the cross on the
ballot paper – was founded in 1990 by
Stanisław Tymiński, who came second in
the presidential election later that year.
The party's main plank is the creation of
a market economy from Poland's own
resources. At the September 1993 election
it gained 2.7% of the vote but no seats.

partyocracy [partitocrazia] In Italy, the
system of political control exercised by
the Christian Democratic Party (DC),
Italian Socialist Party (PSI) and the three
smaller ruling parties from the 1950s until
they lost power after the exposure in 1992
and 1993 of the endemic corruption of
which it formed a key element. Rooted
in the long-established system of 'CLIENT-
ISM' [clientelismo], the partyocracy was
developed by the DC and adapted and
extended by the PSI from the 1970s
onwards. It relied on the appointment of
party members to key posts, patronage,
personal recommendation and bribery. It
operated at every level of society, from
the installation of telephone lines to the
awarding of public-sector jobs and the
allocation of major infrastructure contracts. The system was most entrenched
in the south, where the DC in particular
also distributed public funds (in the form
of contracts, jobs, pensions etc) to companies and individuals in exchange for
votes. Large blocks of votes were also
secured through cooperation with criminal
organizations such as the Sicilian Mafia
and the Neapolitan Camorra.

Pashko, Gramoz (1955–) Albanian
economist, academic and politician. He
lectured at Tirana University from 1978–
91. He was a founding member in 1990
of the Democratic Party (PDSh), the
first opposition party allowed under
communist rule. From June–December
1991 he was a deputy prime minister and
economy minister in a coalition government. An advocate of a rapid transition to
a market economy, he joined the breakaway Democratic Alliance Party (PADSh)
in 1992.

PASOK *See* PAN-HELLENIC SOCIALIST MOVEMENT.

Pasqua, Charles (1927–) French businessman and politician. He worked for the Ricard drinks company from 1947–67 and then set up his own management consultancy. First elected to parliament in 1968, he was general secretary of the right-wing Rally for the Republic (RPR) from 1974–76. A member of the Senate from 1977–86 and since 1988, he became leader of the RPR group in the upper house in 1981. He was interior minister in the centre-right government of 1986–88 and was appointed to the same post when the right returned to power in March 1993.

Patriotic Union *See* FATHERLAND UNION.

Patronat *See* NATIONAL COUNCIL OF FRENCH EMPLOYERS.

Patto per l'Italia and **Patto Segni** *See* PACT FOR ITALY.

Pawlak, Waldemar (1959–) Polish agronomist, farmer and politician. He was elected leader of the Polish Peasant Party (PSL) in June 1991. In June 1992 he was appointed prime minister but was unable to form a government. In October 1993, after the left had won the previous month's early election, he became prime minister of a coalition comprising the PSL and the Democratic Left Alliance (SLD).

Pays de la Loire *See* LOIRE COUNTRY.

PC (Poland) *See* CENTRE ALLIANCE.

PC (United Kingdom) *See* PLAID CYMRU.

PCC *See* RED BRIGADES.

PCE *See* COMMUNIST PARTY OF SPAIN.

PCF *See* FRENCH COMMUNIST PARTY.

PCh *See* CITIZENS' CHARTER (Lithuania).

PCI *See* DEMOCRATIC LEFT PARTY (Italy).

PCP *See* PORTUGUESE COMMUNIST PARTY.

PCS (Italy) *See* SOCIAL CHRISTIAN PARTY.

PCS (Luxemburg) *See* CHRISTIAN SOCIAL PEOPLE'S PARTY.

PD (Ireland) *See* PROGRESSIVE DEMOCRATS.

PD (Luxemburg) *See* DEMOCRATIC PARTY.

PD (Romania) *See* DEMOCRATIC PARTY.

PDAR *See* AGRARIAN DEMOCRATIC PARTY OF ROMANIA.

PDC *See* CHRISTIAN DEMOCRATIC PEOPLE'S PARTY OF SWITZERLAND.

PDCS *See* SAN MARINO CHRISTIAN DEMOCRATIC PARTY.

PDP (Macedonia) *See* PARTY FOR DEMOCRATIC PROSPERITY - NATIONAL DEMOCRATIC PARTY.

PdP *See* ALLIANCE FOR POLAND.

PDP (San Marino) *See* DEMOCRATIC PROGRESSIVE PARTY.

PDP-NDP *See* PARTY FOR DEMOCRATIC PROSPERITY - NATIONAL DEMOCRATIC PARTY.

PDS *See* DEMOCRATIC PARTY OF ALBANIA.

PDS (Germany) *See* DEMOCRATIC SOCIALIST PARTY.

PDs (Ireland) *See* PROGRESSIVE DEMOCRATS.

PDS (Italy) *See* DEMOCRATIC LEFT PARTY.

PDSh *See* DEMOCRATIC PARTY OF ALBANIA.

PDSR *See* SOCIAL DEMOCRACY PARTY OF ROMANIA.

peace dividend The perceived financial and other benefits to be derived from the end of the Cold War, the military and political confrontation between East and West. The transformation brought about by the collapse of the communist regimes in Eastern Europe and the Soviet Union and the dissolution of the Warsaw Pact between 1989 and 1991 created prospects for substantial cuts in defence spending, conversion of military to civilian production, and additional investment in domestic projects and development cooperation. While defence spending was cut significantly in nearly all European countries, the benefits of the 'peace dividend' did not materialize to the extent expected, largely because post-cold-war restructuring proved costly and the economic downturn in Western Europe stretched government budgets (owing to falling tax revenues and rising social spending).

Peasant Alliance [Porozumienie Ludowe] (PL) Polish political party. The PL has its roots in Solidarity, the movement that spearheaded the opposition to communist rule in the 1980s. It favours substantial state subsidies for the agriculture sector and has strong links with Rural Solidarity, a farmers' union. At the September 1993 election it gained 2.3% of the vote but no seats, having failed to obtain the 5% required for representation. It joined the right-wing Alliance for Poland (PdP) in May 1994. The leader is Gabriel Janowski.

Peasants' Union of Latvia *See* FARMERS' UNION OF ....

Pechory question *See* PETSERI QUESTION.

peer In the United Kingdom, a member of the nobility (duke, marquess, earl, viscount or baron and their female equivalents). Hereditary peers have inherited their titles. Life peers have been ennobled by the sovereign on the advice of the prime minister, and their titles lapse on their deaths. All peers are entitled to sit in the House of Lords, the upper house of Parliament.

Peirens, Willy (1936–) Belgian trade-union official. He was national secretary and then campaigning officer of the Catholic Labour Youth from 1968–77. He then became national secretary of the Confederation of Christian Trade Unions (ACV/CSC), and was elected its president in November 1986, taking office in August 1987. He is from Flanders.

Pekkarinen, Mauri (1947–) Finnish politician. He worked in local and then national government until his election to parliament for the Centre Party (KESK) in 1979. He was chairman of the board of directors of the Finnish Broadcasting Company (Yleisradio) from 1987–91. In April 1991 he was appointed minister of internal affairs.

penny (pl. pence) British monetary unit, equivalent to 1/100th of a pound. The common abbreviation is p.

Pentagonal Group *See* CENTRAL EUROPEAN INITIATIVE.

pentapartito ('five parties') In Italy, the five-party centrist coalition that held power from the early 1970s until May 1994. The *pentapartito* was dominated by the Christian Democratic Party (DC) and the Italian Socialist Party (PSI), and included the smaller Italian Republican Party (PRI), Italian Liberal Party (PLI) and Italian Democratic Socialist Party (PSDI). (The PRI chose to remain outside the coalition on several occasions.) All five parties were discredited by the web of illegal party funding and other corruption exposed in 1992 and 1993 (*see* ITALIAN CORRUPTION SCANDALS). They subsequently suffered numerous splits and by the time of the March 1994 general election had lost most of their electoral support.

pentito (pl. pentiti) ('repenter') In Italy, a former member of the Mafia or another crime syndicate who agrees to give evidence against the organization. Testimony from *pentiti*, informers or 'supergrasses', led to the conviction of 338 leading Mafia members in 1987 and to nearly 300 arrests in 1992, and implicated leading members of the then ruling Christian Democratic Party (DC) in criminal activities in 1993. For years previously the Mafia's code of silence, *omertà*, had frustrated efforts to secure convictions. The authorities have sought to encourage informers by offering them protection, reduced sentences and/or new identities abroad.

PEO *See* ALL-CYPRUS FEDERATION OF LABOUR.

People's Alliance [Alþýðubandalag] (Ab) Icelandic political party. Founded as an electoral alliance of communists and left-wing socialists in 1956 and constituted as a single party in 1968, the People's Alliance followed an independent communist line until December 1991, when it redefined itself as a left-socialist party. It has participated in several governments, most recently in 1971–74, 1978–83 and 1988–91. At the April 1991 election it gained 14.4% of the vote and 9/63 seats. The leader is Ólafur Ragnar Grímsson.

People's Assembly [Kuvend Popullor] Parliament of Albania. It has 140 members elected for a four-year term: 100 are elected by absolute majority in single-member constituencies, with a second round of voting if required; the remaining 40 seats are allocated on a proportional basis to parties which have obtained at least 4% of the popular vote. The Assembly elects the president of the republic (by a two-thirds majority of the votes cast).

People's Democracy Party [Halkın Demokrasi Partisi] (HADEP) Turkish political party. The HADEP was founded in May 1994 to replace the DEMOCRATIC PARTY (DEP), which was banned by the Constitutional Court the following month for advocating Kurdish separatism. The leader is Murat Bözlak.

People's Europe *See* CITIZENS' EUROPE.

People's Front [Rahvarinne] Estonian
political organization. It has its roots in
the Estonian People's Front, a reformist
and eventually pro-independence alliance
set up in 1988, when Estonia was still
part of the Soviet Union. Its remnants,
the ESTONIAN PEOPLE'S CENTRE PARTY
(ERKE) and two other groups, contested
the September 1992 election as a centre-
left alliance under the name People's
Front. They gained 15/101 seats and
formed a joint parliamentary group under
the name Centre [Keskus] (K).

People's Harmony Party *See* NATIONAL
HARMONY PARTY.

People's Labour Party *See* DEMOCRATIC
PARTY (Turkey).

People's Party [Fólkaflokkurin] (Fkfl)
Faroese political party. Founded in 1940,
the People's Party advocates greater
autonomy for the Faroes within Denmark
and is right-wing in its economic policies.
It has led or participated in many coalition governments, most recently from
1974–85 and from 1991 until April 1993.
At the July 1994 election it gained 6/32
seats. The leader is Anfinn Kallsberg.

People's Party [Partido Popular] (PP)
Spanish political party. Founded in 1976
as the People's Alliance (AP) and renamed
in 1989, the PP was originally a right-
wing party but has shifted towards the
christian-democratic mainstream in the
1980s, a move formalized at the 1989
congress. It subsequently absorbed
several small centre-right parties, including the Christian Democratic Party (DC)
and the Liberal Party (PL). It became the
second-largest party in parliament at the
1986 election, and has steadily increased
its electoral support since then. At the
June 1993 election it gained 34.8% of the
vote and 141/350 seats. The leader is
José María Aznar, the general secretary
Javier Arenas.

**People's Party for Freedom and Demo-
cracy** [Volkspartij voor Vrijheid en
Democratie] (VVD) Dutch political party.
Founded in 1948 as the successor to
the Liberal Union, the right-wing VVD
supports free-market economic policies
but has liberal views on social issues.

The country's third-largest party, it has
participated in a number of coalition
governments, most recently from 1977–
81 and 1982–89 and since August 1994,
when it joined a left-right administration
with the Labour Party (PvdA) and Democrats 66 (D'66). At the May general
election it had gained 19.9% of the vote
and 31/150 seats. The leader is Frits
Bolkestein, the party president is Dian
van Leeuwen-Schut.

People's Party of Montenegro *See*
NATIONAL PARTY OF ....

People's Party - The Liberals or **People's
Party** [Folkpartiet-Liberalerna] (Fp or F)
Swedish political party. Founded in its
present form in 1934, the People's Party
has its roots in the Liberal Party organized
in the late 19th century; it is still often
referred to by its old name. A member of
successive centre-right coalitions between
1976 and 1982, it joined a similar coalition in October 1991. It gained 9.2% of
the vote and 33/349 seats at the September 1991 election. Bengt Westerberg has
been party leader since 1983.

People's Trade Union *See* UNITY.

People's Union [Volksunie] (VU) Belgian
political party. Founded in 1954 by
several Flemish nationalist groups, the
Volksunie advocates full autonomy for
Flanders within a federal Belgium, is
centrist in its economic policies and has
conservative views on social issues. It
has participated in coalition governments
in 1977–78 and 1988–91. At the November 1991 election it gained 5.9% of the
vote and 10/212 seats. The party leader
is Bert Anciaux.

People's Unity [Herri Batasuna] (HB)
Spanish political party. Formed in 1978
from the merger of four left-wing Basque
nationalist parties, Herri Batasuna – the
Spanish equivalent is rarely used – advocates Basque independence and generally
supports the campaign of violence waged
by Basque Homeland and Liberty (ETA).
It has participated in regional and national
elections since 1979 but has generally
refused to take its seats. At the October
1990 regional election in the Basque
Country it gained 17.3% of the vote and
13/75 seats, and at the June 1993 general

election it gained the equivalent of 0.9% nationwide and 2/350 seats. The party is also active in the Navarre region, which it considers part of the Basque homeland. The leaders are Iñaki Esnaola and Jon Idigoras.

Peponis, Anastasios or **Sakis** (1938–) Greek lawyer and politician. Elected to parliament for the Pan-Hellenic Socialist Movement (PASOK) in 1977, he has been minister of industry, energy and technology (1981–82 and 1986–89), radio and television (1984) and the presidency (1989). When the party returned to power in October 1993 he was appointed to the key post of minister to the prime minister.

PER *See* ROMANIAN ECOLOGY PARTY.

Pereira Lopes, José (1939–) Portuguese bank employee, trade-union official and politician. He has held senior posts in the trade-union movement since the late 1970s and was elected president of the General Workers' Union of Portugal (UGTP) in April 1984. He has also been a member of parliament for the centre-right Social Democratic Party (PSD) since 1985.

Pérez Rubalcaba, Alfredo (1951–) Spanish chemist, academic and politician. He has lectured in organic chemistry. A member of the Spanish Socialist Workers' Party (PSOE), he was a junior education minister from 1988–92 and minister of education and science from 1992–93. In July 1993 he was appointed to the new post of minister of the presidency (= head of the prime minister's office) and parliamentary affairs.

Périgot, François (1926–) French businessman and employers' representative. He joined the Unilever concern in 1955, becoming managing director of its Spanish subsidiary in 1971 and head of Unilever France in 1976. In December 1986 he was elected president of the National Council of French Employers (Patronat). In June 1994 he also became president of the Union of Industrial and Employers' Confederations of Europe (UNICE).

Permanent Council Institution of the Western European Union (WEU). The Permanent Council is the standing body of the Council, the organization's decision-making body composed of foreign and defence ministers. It meets at ambassadorial level, usually every two weeks, and is chaired by the secretary-general. Its brief is to discuss in greater detail the views expressed by the Council and follow up its decisions. It also supervises two key working groups, the Special Working Group and Defence Representatives Group, which deal with political and military aspects of European security respectively.

permanent neutrality or **neutrality** In Switzerland, the principle under which the country does not join military or political alliances and does not take sides in any conflict. Dating from the 16th century and first formally recognized by its neighbours in 1815, neutrality is the overriding principle of Swiss foreign policy. It differs from other countries' non-alignment policies in that, on current interpretation, it does not allow Switzerland to comply with, say, a United Nations (UN) resolution imposing sanctions on an aggressor country as this would imply taking sides. For this reason Switzerland is not a member of the United Nations, although it does participate in UN agencies and other organizations providing humanitarian and development assistance. (UN membership was last rejected in a referendum in March 1986.) Because of its traditional neutrality, Switzerland is host to numerous international organizations and conferences and is often asked to represent a country's interests in another country when they do not have bilateral diplomatic relations.

PES *See* GREEN PARTY OF SWITZERLAND.

PES (European Union) *See* PARTY OF EUROPEAN SOCIALISTS.

peseta Currency of Spain. Common abbreviations are Pta, Ptas and ESP (the international standard in banking etc). It is divided into 100 céntimos. The Spanish peseta is also legal tender in Andorra.

PET Abbreviation for Politiets Efterretningstjeneste ('Police Intelligence Service'), the Danish intelligence agency.

Peterle, Alojz or **Lojze** (1948–) Slovenian economist and politician. In the 1970s and 80s he worked at the Institute of Urban Planning and the Institute of Social

Planning. He became leader of the newly formed Slovenian Christian Democrats (SKD) in September 1989. He was prime minister of a centre-right coalition from 1990–92, during which time Slovenia declared and secured its independence from Yugoslavia. In January 1993 he became deputy prime minister and foreign minister in a centre-left coalition.

Petersen, Niels Helveg (1939–) Danish politician. First elected to parliament for the centrist Radical Liberals (RV) in 1966, he worked at the European Commission from 1974–77. He was party leader from 1978–88 and minister of economic affairs in a centre-right coalition from 1988–90. He became foreign minister in the centre-left coalition formed in January 1993.

Petkov, Krŭstyo (1943–) Bulgarian economist, academic and trade-union official. Since 1973 he has held several senior research and academic posts, including director of the Georgi Dimitrov Research Institute for Trade Union Studies (1982–88), director of the Institute of Sociology of the Bulgarian Academy of Sciences (1988–90) and professor of sociology at Sofia University (since 1988). From 1982–89 he was a member of the executive of the official Central Council of Trade Unions (TsSPS). He became its president in December 1989, and president of the relaunched Confederation of Independent Trade Unions in Bulgaria (KNSB) in February 1990.

Petö, Iván (1946–) Hungarian historian and politician. He worked at the New Hungarian Central Archives before his election to parliament for the centrist Alliance of Free Democrats (SzDSz) in 1990. He was its parliamentary leader in 1990–91 and was elected party leader in November 1992.

Petrides, Konstantinos or **Kostas** (1949–) Cypriot economist, academic and politician. A specialist in operational research and management information systems, he worked in Canada in the late 1970s. He returned to Cyprus in 1981 to become head of research at the Industrial Training Authority and worked for the cooperative movement from 1985. He was appointed minister of agriculture and natural resources in the centre-right administration appointed by President Klerides in February 1993. He does not belong to a political party.

Petsamo question Controversy over the status of a formerly Finnish territory now part of Russia. The sparsely populated but strategically important Petsamo region, including the port of that name on the Arctic Ocean, was ceded to the then Soviet Union after Finland's defeat in the 1939–40 Winter War. After the collapse of communist rule and the disintegration of the Soviet Union in 1991, several far-right nationalist groups in Finland began to call for the return of Petsamo. None of the major parties supports their demands. *See also* KARELIA QUESTION.

Petseri question Border dispute between Estonia and Russia. Like a strip of land to the east of the Narva river, the south-eastern district of Petseri or Petserimaa [Pechory or Pechorsky rayon in Russian] was ceded to Russia in 1945, five years after Estonia's annexation by the Soviet Union.

pfennig [Pfennig, pl. -e] German monetary unit, equivalent to 1/100th of a mark. Common abbreviations are Pf or pf.

P4P and **PFP** *See* PARTNERSHIP FOR PEACE.

PHARE countries Collective name for the former communist countries of Eastern Europe covered by the European Union's PHARE PROGRAMME.

PHARE programme European Union (EU) programme aimed at providing financial and technical assistance to formerly communist countries in Eastern Europe. Established in 1989 as the Poland and Hungary Action for Restructuring of the Economy (hence PHARE), it has been extended to most other countries of the region seeking to restructure their economies along market-based lines. To be eligible for aid, a country is expected to commit itself to the rule of law, respect for human rights, a pluralist political system, free and fair elections, and economic liberalization. Projects are geared to modernizing the transport network, industry and the financial system, developing the private sector, establishing new social structures (training programmes etc) and rehabilitating the environment. A subsidiary programme, PHARE Democracy, was launched in July 1992 with the aim of supporting political reform. *See also* CENTRE FOR COOPERATION WITH EUROPEAN ECONOMIES IN TRANSITION (CCEET) *and* GROUP OF TWENTY-FOUR.

Piat case Murder of Yann Piat, a French member of parliament, in 1994. Piat was elected to the National Assembly for the centre-right Republican Party (PR) in March 1993, representing Hyères on the Côte d'Azur. (She had previously been a deputy for the far-right National Front, FN, but had been expelled from the party in 1988.) She was shot from a passing motorcycle in February 1994 in what was regarded as a contract killing. Two men were subsequently charged with her murder. She had campaigned against political corruption, drug trafficking and the influence of organized crime in the region. Her private papers showed she was about to accuse several local politicians of taking bribes from criminal organizations.

Picardie *See* PICARDY.

Picardy [Picardie] Region of France. Situated in the north, Picardy has an area of 19,400 sq km and a population of 1,827,000. The capital is Amiens. The economy is based on agriculture (cereals) and manufacturing (food processing, chemicals, engineering).

Piebalgs, Andris (1957–) Latvian teacher and politician. He taught physics in a secondary school from 1980 and was its headmaster from 1984. He was elected to parliament for the pro-independence People's Front (LTF) in 1990, when Latvia was still part of the Soviet Union, and for the centre-right Latvian Way (LC) in 1993. Education minister from 1990–93, he was appointed a deputy prime minister and minister of finance in September 1994.

Piedmont [Piemonte] Autonomous region of Italy. Situated in the northwest, Piedmont has an area of 25,399 sq km and a population of 4,338,000. One of Italy's leading industrial, commercial and agricultural regions, it is dominated by Turin [Torino], the capital. Other impor-

tant cities are Novara and Alessandria. The economy is based on manufacturing (engineering, motor vehicles, textiles, food processing) and agriculture (cereals, fruit and vegetables, livestock and dairy farming). The House of Savoy held extensive lands in Piedmont by the 12th century, and gained control of virtually the whole region in the 15th. Piedmont-Savoy became the Kingdom of Sardinia in 1720 when it acquired the island. In the 19th century it led the movement to unify Italy, completed in 1870.

pieds noirs (sing. pied noir) ('black feet') In France, a collective name for settlers in Algeria who returned to France when the colony became independent. The *pieds noirs* are descendants of French people as well as some Italians and Spaniards who settled across the Mediterranean Sea after the territory's annexation by France in 1830. Numbering around 1 million, they left Algeria en masse when it became independent in 1962. Most settled in the south of France. Many have sought to preserve a distinct identity – they see themselves as 'exiles' and reject their official status as 'repatriates' – and have traditionally supported far-right parties, most recently the National Front (FN). The name *pieds noirs* originated from the North African Arab population's nickname for French soldiers, who wore black boots.

Piemonte *See* PIEDMONT.

Pilip, Ivan (1963–) Czech economist and politician. He worked at the Czechoslovak Academy of Sciences and the Economic University in the late 1980s, specializing in foreign-trade issues. He then managed the family medical-products firm (which had been returned as part of the restitution of private property following the collapse of communist rule). A member of the Christian Democratic Party (KDS), he was appointed junior education minister in 1992 and became education minister in April 1994. He was also elected the KDS's leader in December 1993.

pillar In the European Union (EU), the common name for one of the organization's main components, as established under the Maastricht Treaty (in force since November 1993). There are three 'pillars': the European Community (EC), the Common Foreign and Security Policy (CFSP) and Cooperation on Justice and Home Affairs (CJHA). The first is based on 'SUPRANATIONAL COOPERATION', the other two on 'INTERGOVERNMENTAL COOPERATION'.

Pinheiro, João de Deus (1919–) Portuguese lawyer and politician. A judge, he was appointed minister of justice and attorney-general after the 1974 revolution, holding these posts until 1976 and 1977 respectively. He was minister of education and culture in the centre-right Social Democratic Party (PSD) government from 1985–87 and foreign minister from 1987–92. In January 1993 he became a European commissioner, responsible for information, relations with the European Parliament, culture and promoting the image of the European Union (EU).

pink zone In Croatia, a Serb-populated district outside the United Nations Protected Areas (UNPAs) but still patrolled by the United Nations Protection Force I (UNPROFOR I). The 'special status' of the 'pink zones' was recognized in UN Security Council Resolution 762, adopted in June 1992, five months after the UNPAs were established as part of a ceasefire agreement in the civil war. They are effectively part of the UNPAs and the breakaway Republic of Serbian Krajina. *See also* CROATIAN CIVIL WAR.

Pinto Basto Gouveia, Teresa (1946–) Portuguese politician. A member of the centre-right Social Democratic Party (PSD), she was elected to parliament in 1987 and was a junior culture minister from 1985–90 and a junior environment minister from 1991. In June 1993 she was appointed minister of the environment.

Pittner, Ladislav (1934–) Slovakian economist and politician. He was arrested by the communist authorities for 'subversive activities' in 1950 and sentenced to three years' imprisonment. From 1953–67 he worked as a labourer and then as a manager for a state-owned construction company. He was allowed to resume his education in 1965 and graduated in economics in 1970. From 1967–90 he

worked as a systems analyst and later senior researcher at the Institute of Economy and Management Organization in the Building Trade (ÚEOS). A member of the Christian Democratic Movement (KDH), he was interior minister of Slovakia, then still part of the Czechoslovak federation, from 1990–92 and was elected to the Slovakian parliament in 1992. He returned as interior minister in the centrist coalition which took office in March 1994.

Pivetti, Irene (1963–) Italian journalist and politician. She worked for a conservative Roman Catholic organization until she entered politics. A member of the federalist Northern League (Lega Nord), she was elected to the Chamber of Deputies, the lower house of parliament, in 1992. She was elected its president in May 1994.

PK *See* CONSERVATIVE PARTY (Poland).

PKK *See* KURDISTAN WORKERS' PARTY.

PKTLS *See* POLITICAL PRISONERS' AND EXILES' UNION.

PL (Poland) *See* PEASANT ALLIANCE.

PL Abbreviation for Poland, used for international vehicle registrations, postal addresses etc.

PL (Romania) and **PL'93** *See* LIBERAL PARTY 1993.

Plaid Cymru ('Party of Wales') (PC) British political party. Founded in 1925, Plaid Cymru – the Welsh name is commonly used – advocates independence for Wales within the European Union (EU) and the restoration of Welsh culture and the Welsh language. It is centre-left in its economic policies and broadly conservative on social issues. At the April 1992 general election it gained 9.0% of the vote in Wales (equivalent to 0.5% nationwide) and four of the 32 Welsh seats in the House of Commons. The leader is Dafydd Wigley.

plaza de soberanía (pl. -s de -) Spanish administrative division, usually left untranslated or translated as 'sovereign territory'. The *plazas de soberanía* comprise the dependencies of Ceuta, Melilla and Peñón de Vélez de la Gomera on the Moroccan coast and several islands off it. Collectively known as Spanish

North Africa, they are administered as integral parts of Spain, but their special status is recognized in certain provisions of the local government structure. They are also called *presidios* ('fortresses' or 'garrisons'), reflecting their traditional function as military bases after coming under Spanish control in the 15th and 16th centuries. *See also individual territory entries.*

PLI *See* ITALIAN LIBERAL PARTY.

PLS *See* LIBERAL PARTY OF SWITZERLAND.

PLZ Abbreviation for the ZŁOTY, the Polish currency, used in banking etc.

PM Abbreviation for 'prime minister', used in the United Kingdom and Ireland in particular.

PMDN *See* PARTY FOR THE DEFENCE OF HUMAN RIGHTS.

PN *See* NATIONALIST PARTY.

PNL *See* NATIONAL LIBERAL PARTY.

PNT-CD *See* CHRISTIAN DEMOCRATIC NATIONAL PEASANTS' PARTY.

PNV *See* BASQUE NATIONALIST PARTY.

Poblacht na hÉireann ('Republic of Ireland') Official name of Ireland in Irish. Éire is the Irish name for the country.

POC *See* CENTRE ALLIANCE.

PoCo Abbreviation for Political Cooperation, the former name of the COMMON FOREIGN AND SECURITY POLICY (CFSP), an intergovernmental 'pillar' of the European Union (EU).

Poder Andaluz *See* ANDALUSIAN POWER.

Podkański, Lesław (1956–) Polish mechanical engineer, civil servant and politician. In the 1980s he worked for a leather factory in Lublin and was active at local and then national level for the United Peasant Party (ZSL), now the Polish Peasant Party (PSL). From 1990–92 he worked as a commercial director in two manufacturing companies. He then became a junior minister in the foreign-trade ministry. He was put in charge of the department when the left-wing coalition took office in October 1993.

Podkrepa *See* SUPPORT.

Poitou-Charentes Region of France. Situated in the west, Poitou-Charentes has an area of 25,809 sq km and a population of 1,602,000. The capital is Poitiers, and the other main cities are Angoulême

and La Rochelle. The economy is based on agriculture (cattle farming, wine), manufacturing (food processing, engineering) and tourism.

Pokka, Hannele (1952–) Finnish lawyer and politician. She worked for the Central Union of Agricultural Producers (MTK) from 1976 until her election to parliament for the Centre Party (KESK) in 1979. In April 1991 she was appointed justice minister.

pokrajina (pl. pokrajine) Administrative division of Yugoslavia, usually translated as 'autonomous province' or 'province'. In the old Yugoslav federation, particularly from the 1970s, the two *pokrajine* within the Serbian republic (Kosovo-Metohija and Vojvodina) enjoyed the same powers as the constituent republics in all but name. Under the new Serbian constitution adopted in September 1990 they retained their status but effectively lost the autonomy associated with it. The Kosovo assembly had been suspended the previous July.

Pol, Marek (1953–) Polish economist and politician. He held several senior positions at the Polmo agricultural-machinery factory in Poznań in the 1980s. He was a member of parliament from 1989–91, first for the communist Polish United Workers' Party (PZPR) and after its dissolution for one of its successors, the Polish Social Democratic Union (PUSD). In September 1993 he was reelected to parliament for the Labour Union (UP), which had been formed the previous year by the merger of the PUSD and two other parties. He was appointed minister of industry and trade in the left-wing coalition formed in October 1993. (He joined the government in an individual capacity, not as a representative of the UP, which did not sign the coalition agreement.)

POLA *See* POLITICAL SPRING.

Poland [Polska] Country in central Europe.
Official data. Name: Republic of Poland [Polska Rzeczpospolita]; capital: Warsaw [Warszawa]; form of government: parliamentary republic; head of state: president; head of government: prime minister; flag: two horizontal stripes, white and red;

national holiday: 3 May (National Day); language: Polish; religion: none; currency: złoty (Zł) (pl. -ch) = 100 groszy; abbreviation: PL.

Geography. Poland has a total area of 312,663 sq km. It is bordered by the Baltic Sea and Russia (Kaliningrad region) in the north, Lithuania, Belorussia and Ukraine in the east, Slovakia and the Czech Republic in the south, and Germany in the west. Most of the country consists of low-lying plains, studded with lakes in the northeast and rising to hills and a low plateau in the southeast. The Sudeten Mountains [Sudety] and Carpathian Mountains [Karpaty] form the southern border. Some 47% of the land is arable, another 13% is covered by pastures and 28% is forested. The main rivers are the Vistula [Wisła] and Oder [Odra]. The climate is humid continental, with hot summers and cold winters; rainfall is moderate.

Demography. Poland has a population of 38,521,000. Population density is 127 per sq km (land area). Some 61% of the people live in urban areas. The main conurbations are Warsaw (population 2.4 million, city 1.7 million) and the Upper Silesia region centred on Katowice and including Sosnowiec, Bytom and Gliwice (2.8 million). Other major cities are Łódź, Cracow [Kraków], Wrocław, Poznań, Gdańsk, Szczecin, Bydgoszcz, Lublin, Białystok, Częstochowa and Gdynia. In ethnic, linguistic and religious terms Poland is very homogeneous. Some 97.4% of the population is Polish and 95.0% is nominally Roman Catholic. Ethnic minorities include Germans in the southwest (around 500,000 or 1.3% of the total), Ukrainians (180,000) and Belorussians (170,000) in the east, and small numbers of Slovaks, Russians and Gipsies. Religious minorities include Orthodox (2.3% of the total), Protestant and other Christians.

Sociography. Poland scores 0.815 on the United Nations human development index (HDI), ranking 49th in the world and 30th among 32 European countries. There are 21 doctors and 70 hospital beds for every 10,000 people. Education is compulsory between the ages of seven and 14. There is one teacher for every 17 students. Enrolment is 76% at the secondary level and 22% at the tertiary level. The literacy rate is 96%. Real annual income per head (in terms of purchasing power) is US$ 4,500.

Infrastructure and communications. Poland's transport and communications network is relatively well developed but in need of modernization and extension; the railways are particularly important for freight transport, and the telecommunications system is limited. There are 225,130 km of paved roads and 6.50 million passenger cars (170 per 1,000 people), 26,230 km of railways and 4,000 km of navigable waterways. The main ports are Gdańsk, Gdynia and Szczecin. The main airport is at Warsaw (Okecie), and there are 11 other airports with scheduled services. There are 48 daily newspapers, with a combined circulation of 6.72 million (185 per 1,000 people). There are 10.94 million radio receivers, 9.91 million television sets and 5.48 million telephones in use (respectively 286, 259 and 144 per 1,000 people).

Economic structure. The Polish economy is based on manufacturing, mining and agriculture. Although essentially developed and diversified, it is in need of major investment and restructuring and has a relatively unproductive agricultural sector. The transition from a command to a market-based economy initiated in 1989 is causing severe dislocation and has led to steep falls in industrial and agricultural production. GDP contracted by 18% in 1991–92, but grew again by 6% in 1992–93. Over the whole period inflation averaged 119% per year, the currency lost half its value, the current-account deficit averaged just over 1% of GDP per year, and unemployment rose to 16%. Growth reached 5% and inflation fell to 35% in 1993. The foreign debt stands at around US$ 46 billion (65% of GDP).

Services contribute 46% of GDP, industry contributes 47% (manufacturing around 38%, mining around 4%), and agriculture, forestry and fisheries 7%. Some 30% of the labour force is employed in farming, forestry and fishing (one of the highest shares in Europe), 24% in manufacturing and 9% in trade. The main crops grown are potatoes, cereals (wheat, rye, barley, oats), sugarbeets and oilseeds; horticulture (fruit and vegetables, esp. apples and cabbages), livestock raising (pigs, cattle, poultry) and dairy farming (milk, eggs) are also important agricultural activities. Forestry is also important and fishing is of regional importance. The main mineral resources are coal, lignite, silver, copper, zinc and sulphur; Poland is Europe's second-largest coal producer and the world's fifth-largest; the mining industry is a major source of foreign exchange. The main industries are engineering (esp. industrial machinery, electrical goods and cars), food processing and textiles; other important branches are iron and steel and other metalworking, petrochemicals, chemicals, wood processing and ceramics. The main energy sources are coal and lignite and imported fossil fuels; 10% of export earnings are required to cover net fuel imports. The main exports are foodstuffs (16% of the total, esp. cereals, meat products), chemicals (incl. fertilizer) (12%), textiles and clothing (9%), industrial machinery (8%), electrical equipment (8%), transport equipment (8%), wood and wood products (8%), coal (7%), non-ferrous metals (6%) and iron and steel (5%); basic manufactures account for 25% of the total, machinery and transport equipment for 24%, foodstuffs for 16%. The main imports are machinery and transport equipment, fuels, chemicals and foodstuffs. The main trading partners are: exports: Germany (31%), Netherlands (6%), Russia (6%), Italy (6%), United Kingdom, France; imports: Germany (24%), Russia (9%), Italy (8%), Netherlands (6%), United Kingdom (6%), Austria (5%), France (5%). The National Bank of Poland [Narodowy Bank Polski] (NBP) is the central bank. The main employers' association is the Confederation of Polish Employers (KPP); the main labour organizations are the All-Poland Trade Unions Alliance (OPZZ) and Solidarity (Solidarność).

Political structure. Poland is a parliamentary republic on the basis of a constitution adopted in 1952 and substantially amended in 1989, 1990 and 1992; a new constitution is being drafted. The head of state is the president, who is elected for a five-year term; s/he is commander of the armed forces, nominates the prime minister and has certain other powers. Most executive powers are vested in the prime minister and the council of ministers. Legislative power is vested in the bicameral National Assembly [Zgromadzenie Narodowe], composed of the 460-member Assembly [Sejm] elected for a four-year term by a system of proportional representation (with thresholds for gaining seats of 5% for parties and 8% for alliances), and the 100-member Senate [Senat] elected for a four-year term on a provincial basis. All citizens over the age of 18 are entitled to vote. Judicial power is ultimately vested in the Supreme Court [Sąd Najwyzsy] appointed by the president; the Constitutional Tribunal [Trybunał Konstytucyjny] adjudicates on constitutional matters. Administratively the country is divided into 49 provinces or voivodships [województwo, pl. województwa], which are subdivided into 822 towns and 2,121 communes.

The main political parties are the Social Democratic Party of the Republic of Poland (SdRP, the successor to the communist Polish United Workers' Party, PZPR), Polish Peasant Party (PSL), Freedom Union (UW, formed by the merger of the Democratic Union, UD, and Liberal Democratic Congress, KLD), Labour Union (UP), Confederation for an Independent Poland (KPN), Non-Party Bloc in Support of Reforms (BBWR), Christian National Union (ZChN), Centre Alliance (POC), Conservative Party (PK), Real Politics Union (UPR), Movement for the Republic (RdR), Peasant Alliance (PL) and Conservative Coalition (KK, a breakaway from the PK); the Democratic Left Alliance (SLD) is an alliance dominated by the SdRP; the Alliance for Poland (PdP) includes ZChN, POC, PL, KK and part of the RdR; the Eleventh of November Alliance includes the UPR, PK and three other parties; Solidarity (Solidarność or NSZZ'S') and Self-Defence (Samoobrona) are trade unions; Homeland (Ojczyzna or KKW'O') was an electoral alliance of the ZChN, PK and two other parties; the Coalition for the Republic (KdR) was an electoral alliance dominated by the RdR. At the general election in September 1993 the SLD gained 20.4% of the vote and 171/460 seats, the PSL 15.4% and 132 seats, the UD 10.6% and 74 seats, the UP 7.3% and 41 seats, the KPN 5.8% and 22 seats, the BBWR 5.4% and 16 seats, and German ethnic-minority organizations four seats; among the parties and alliances which failed to secure representation, the KKW'O' gained 6.4% of the vote, Solidarity 4.9%, the POC 4.4%, the KLD 4.0%, the URP 3.2%, Self-Defence 2.8%, Party X 2.7%, the KdR 2.7% and the PL 2.3%. The government is a left-wing coalition of the SLD and PSL, with Waldemar Pawlak of the PSL as prime minister. Other senior ministers are Grzegorz Kołodko (deputy prime minister with responsibility for the economy, finance), Aleksander Łuczak (deputy prime minister with responsibility for state administration, education), Włodzimierz Cimoszewicz (deputy prime minister with responsibility for social policy, justice), Andrzej Olechowski (foreign affairs), Andrzej Milczanowski (internal affairs), Piotr Kołodziejczyk (defence), Andrzej Śmietanko (agriculture) and Wiesław Kaczmarek (privatization). The head of state is President Lech Wałęsa, who was elected in November/December 1990.

Security and international affiliations. The Polish armed forces number 287,500 (army 188,500, navy 19,200, airforce 79,800). There is also a 16,000-strong paramilitary border guard. Military service is compulsory and consists of 18 months' basic training.

Poland is a member of the Central European Initiative (CEI), Conference on Security and Cooperation in Europe (CSCE), Council of Baltic Sea States (CBSS), Council of Europe and Visegrad Group, as well as the United Nations and its specialized agencies. It has applied for membership of the European Union (EU).

History. Celtic, Germanic, Slavic and Baltic tribes passed through and settled in the Polish plain from the 5th century BC onwards. From the 6th century AD related Slav groups arrived from the east. In the 9th and 10th centuries the area was divided into around 20 small states. Those of the Polanians – from which Poland derives its name – in the west were united as Great Poland under the Piast dynasty. King Mieszko I converted to Christianity in 966, the traditional date of the foundation of the Polish state. Over the next hundred years the other Polish states, including Little Poland, Mazovia, Silesia and Pomerania, recognized the Piasts as kings of Poland. In the 12th and 13th centuries the country was divided into powerful duchies, all ruled by Piasts, and central authority was weak. German immigration was encouraged at this time, and by the end of the 13th century Pomerania and Silesia had become germanized and been incorporated into the Holy Roman or German Empire. National unity was restored in 1320 with the coronation of King Władysław I. In 1374 the nobles secured a range of privileges from King Louis of Hungary, who had inherited the Polish throne in 1370. These laid the foundations of their power and the relative weakness of royal power that characterized the Polish state from the 16th century onwards. In 1386 the Polish and Lithuanian crowns were joined when Queen Jadwiga married Lithuania's grand prince, who then ruled in Poland as King Władysław II (1386–1434). In the 16th century the Polish-Lithuanian dual monarchy was a major power. It was Europe's largest state, stretching from the Baltic Sea to the Black Sea and incorporating many ethnic and religious groups. In 1569 Poland and Lithuania were united under a single administration. The Union of Lublin also confirmed a constitutional arrangement whereby a parliament representing the nobility shared power with an elected monarch. Internal division and intermittent wars with Russia, Sweden and the Ottoman Empire weakened Poland during the 17th and 18th centuries. It lost extensive territories to Russia, was a principal battleground during the Great Northern War (1700–21), and became virtually a Russian protectorate in 1714. It lost over a quarter of its territory to Russia, Prussia and Austria in 1772. A liberal constitution, reducing the powers of the nobility, was adopted in 1791. In 1793 and 1795 two further partitions extinguished the Polish state.

In 1807 the Grand Duchy of Warsaw, comprising central Poland, was established under French protection. It was annexed by Russia in 1813. As part of the post-Napoleonic reorganization of Europe in 1814/15, the Congress of Vienna established the Kingdom of Poland as an autonomous state within the Russian Empire, and Cracow, the country's ancient capital, as a 'free city'. There were uprisings against Russian rule in 1830–31, 1846 and 1863–64. 'Congress Poland' was dissolved in 1864 and a policy of russification was introduced. Similar policies of germanization were pursued in the territories held by Prussia/ Germany. Cracow was annexed by Austria in 1846. Poland declared its independence at the end of the First World War (1914–18). The country's new borders were confirmed in the 1919 Treaty of Versailles and after a short war with the Soviet Union (1920–21). Ukrainians, Belorussians, Jews and other ethnic and religious groups accounted for just under a third of the total population. A parliamentary constitution was adopted in 1921. Józef Piłsudski, who had been commander of the armed forces and the country's effective leader from 1918–23, seized power in a military coup in 1926. The authoritarian regime he established was continued after his death in 1935. In 1939, after Germany and the Soviet Union had signed a secret pact dividing Poland between them, the country was invaded by German forces – the start of the Second World War – and Soviet forces. Over the next six years Poland suffered more than any other European country (with the exception of the Soviet Union): around 5.8 million people were killed, all but 125,000 of them civilians and 3.2 million of them Jewish (victims of the nazi regime's extermination policy); in the Soviet-occupied territories hundreds of thousands of people were deported. The Soviet army, including many Polish units, drove the Germans from Polish soil in 1944/45.

In 1945 Poland's borders were redrawn, 'moving' it westward: the east was allocated to the Soviet Union and the German provinces of Pomerania and Silesia and around half of East Prussia became Polish. Around 3 million Poles from the east were resettled in the west. (The German population had fled or been expelled in 1944/45.) The new communist-dominated government secured international recognition (over the wartime government in exile) and allied itself closely with the Soviet Union. The forerunner of the United Polish Workers' Party (PZPR) and its allies won the 1947 election and a 'people's republic' was declared in 1952. The regime suppressed political dissent, nationalized the economy and introduced central planning. Strikes and mass demonstrations in 1956, 1970 and 1976 were suppressed, but the first two did prompt leadership changes. In 1980 widespread strikes forced the government to recognize independent trade unions, and the Solidarity movement, led by Lech Wałęsa, became the focus of opposition to communist rule over the next decade. To quash growing agitation for reform, the government declared martial law in December 1981. Solidarity was banned and went underground. (Martial law was lifted in December 1982.) Opposition grew in the late 1980s. The government conceded a range of political and economic reforms in April 1989. Partly free elections in June brought an overwhelming victory for Solidarity. The formation of a Solidarity-led government in September marked the first step in the collapse of communist rule throughout Eastern Europe over the next three months. A reform programme aimed at a rapid transition to a market-based economy,

dubbed 'controlled shock' or 'big bang', was implemented at the start of 1990. In 1990/91 Solidarity split into a number of parties. Wałęsa
was elected president of the republic in December 1990. The reform process, accepted in principle by all main parties, was hampered by frequent changes of government and ministers within the post-Solidarity coalition and by political fragmentation. Some 29 parties and groups gained seats at the October 1991 election. Poland was admitted to the Council of Europe in November. A revised constitution, commonly known as the 'small constitution', came into force in December 1992. In 1992 and 1993 Poland became the first post-communist country to show signs of economic recovery. An early election in September 1993, called after the Suchocka government had lost a vote of confidence, was won by the Democratic Left Alliance (SLD) and the Polish Peasant Party (PSL), both of which had their roots in the communist period.

See also entries on specific institutions, organizations, parties, people, terms etc.

Polaris Codename for a British submarine-launched ballistic missile system, the main component of the country's strategic nuclear forces. A modified version of a US model introduced in 1967, the 48 Polaris missiles are deployed on three submarines, have a range of 4,600 km and carry three multiple reentry warheads each. Polaris is due to be replaced by the TRIDENT system in the mid 1990s.

Poli Bortone, Adriana (1943–) Italian classicist, academic and politician. She lectured in Latin literature from 1972. She was elected to parliament for the far-right Italian Social Movement (MSI), now the core of the National Alliance (AN), in 1983. She was appointed minister of agriculture in the right-wing coalition formed in May 1994.

Polish Peasant Party [Polskie Stronnictwo Ludowe] (PSL) Polish political party. The PSL was formed in 1990 from the merger of several successors to the United Peasant Party (ZSL), one of the parties which had been allowed to function under communist rule. It has a traditional left-

wing economic and social programme aimed at advancing farmers' interests, including strong state support for the agricultural sector. At the September 1993 election it gained 15.4% of the vote and 132/460 seats, becoming the second-largest party in parliament. The following month it formed a coalition with the Democratic Left Alliance (SDL), and party leader Waldemar Pawlak became prime minister.

political acquis *See* ACQUIS POLITIQUE.

Political Association of Economists *See* ECONOMISTS' POLITICAL ASSOCIATION.

Political Cooperation Former name of the COMMON FOREIGN AND SECURITY POLICY (CFSP), an intergovernmental 'pillar' of the European Union (EU).

Political Prisoners' and Exiles' Union [Politinių Kalinių ir Tremtinių Laisvės Sąjunga] (PKTLS) Lithuanian political organization. The PKTLS was formed in 1989 to defend the interests of Lithuanian people persecuted, imprisoned and/or sent into internal exile by the Soviet authorities for their political views. Since the restoration of independence in 1991 its main objectives have been to gain compensation for its members and to bring those guilty of crimes during the communist era to justice. It contested the October/November 1992 election in alliance with the Reform Movement (Sąjūdis) but then formed a separate parliamentary group. It has 6/141 seats. The leader is Balys Gajauskas.

Political Reformed Party [Staatkundig Gereformeerde Partij] (SGP) Dutch political party. Founded in 1918, the SGP is one of the country's three small Christian fundamentalist parties known as the 'small right'. At the May 1994 election it gained 1.7% of the vote and 2/150 seats. The leader is Bas van der Vlies, the party president is D. Slagboom.

Political Spring [Politikí Ánoixi] (POLA) Greek political party. POLA was founded in June 1993 by Antonis Samaras, a former member of the right-wing New Democratic Party (ND). Its declared aim is to put issues above personalities and thereby to break the mould of established politics. Broadly right-wing populist, it gained 4.9% of the vote and 10/300 seats at the October 1993 election.

political union In the European Union (EU), a policy objective aimed at the integration of member states' policies in a range of non-economic fields, such as foreign affairs, security, defence, home affairs and justice. The realization of political union in general and cooperation on foreign affairs in particular has been a long-standing aspiration within the European Community (EC) and now the EU. But progress in this field has proved more elusive than in the economic field. This is primarily because member states have been unwilling to put political cooperation on the same footing as economic cooperation by developing a supranational structure involving the transfer of sovereign powers. All political cooperation has thus been on an 'intergovernmental' basis, with member states retaining full decision-making powers and acting by consensus. After several failed attempts, the then six-member Community in October 1970 endorsed a plan calling for political union by 1980 and set up European Political Cooperation (EPC) as its precursor. The interior and justice ministers set up the informal Trevi Group in 1975. The 1986 Single European Act defined a set of principles governing cooperation on foreign policy. The Maastricht Treaty, concluded in December 1991 and in force since November 1993, gave a significant boost to political integration by establishing the COMMON FOREIGN AND SECURITY POLICY (CFSP) and COOPERATION ON JUSTICE AND HOME AFFAIRS (CJHA) as the EU's two intergovernmental 'pillars'.

Political Union of Economists *See* ECONOMISTS' POLITICAL ASSOCIATION.

Polly Peck affair Controversy in the United Kingdom and Northern Cyprus surrounding the collapse of the Polly Peck International (PPI) conglomerate. Polly Peck, a small British clothing company, was bought by the Turkish Cypriot businessman Asil Nadir in 1979. With headquarters in London, PPI rapidly expanded into a major concern based on fruit-growing and -processing and leisure and other interests in Northern Cyprus, the self-proclaimed Turkish Cypriot state on the island. By the end of the 1980s PPI was said to employ around a tenth of the Northern Cypriot labour force and control around a third of the territory's economy. It had also acquired the US-based Del Monte group (making it the world's third-largest fruit business) and the Japanese electronics concern Sansui. It collapsed in October 1990 with substantial debts. The London-based operation was placed in the hands of administrators, while the Northern Cypriot government took over the assets in its jurisdiction. Nadir was arrested in London in December 1990 on charges of fraud and false accounting involving 150 million pounds (191 million ecus). Released on bail while awaiting trial, he fled to Northern Cyprus in May 1993. The affair was further complicated in Britain by allegations of judicial irregularities and revelations that Nadir had made substantial donations to the ruling Conservative Party.

Polo del Buon Governo *See* GOOD GOVERNMENT ALLIANCE.

Polo della Libertà *See* FREEDOM ALLIANCE.

Polska Polish name for Poland.

Polska Rzeczpospolita ('Republic of Poland') Official name of Poland.

Pomaks Religious and ethnic group in Bulgaria. The Pomaks are Bulgarian-speaking Muslims. They are the descendants of people who converted to Islam between the 15th and 19th centuries, when the Balkan region was part of the Ottoman Empire. They number around 300,000 and live mainly in the south and southwest. During the 1970s the communist regime launched a campaign of 'bulgarianization', forcing Pomaks to adopt 'Bulgarian' (i.e. non-Muslim) names and discouraging them from practising Islam and observing their customs. There are also small groups of Pomaks in neighbouring Macedonia and Greece.

Pompidou Group Shorthand for the COOPERATION GROUP TO COMBAT DRUG ABUSE AND ILLICIT TRAFFICKING IN DRUGS.

Pons, Bernard (1926–) French doctor and politician. First elected to parliament in 1967, he was a junior agriculture minister from 1969–73, served as general secretary of the right-wing Rally for the Republic (RPR) from 1979–84, and was elected the RPR's parliamentary leader in June 1988.

Pontifical Commission See PAPAL COMMISSION.

Poos, Jacques (1935–) Luxemburg economist and politician. He has worked in the finance ministry and at the national statistical office and was managing director of the daily newspaper *Tagblatt* from 1964–76. Elected to parliament for the Luxemburg Socialist Workers' Party (LSAP) in 1974, he became its deputy leader in 1982. He was minister of finance from 1976–79 and became deputy prime minister and foreign minister in 1984. He is also responsible for foreign trade and development cooperation.

Popescu, Dan Mircea (1950–) Romanian lawyer, academic and politician. From 1975 he worked as a legal adviser and then researcher with the Bucharest Political Science Institute and lectured in international relations. He was appointed a minister of state (= deputy prime minister) with responsibility for quality of life and social security in April 1991 and became minister of employment and social security in October 1991. He was again appointed a minister of state in November 1992. He is a member of the Social Democracy Party (PDSR), the successor to the Democratic National Salvation Front (FSND).

Popiełuszko case Murder of Jerzy Popiełuszko, a Polish priest and anti-communist activist, in 1984 and the subsequent trials related to it. A prominent advocate of Solidarity, the then illegal movement spearheading opposition to the communist regime, Popiełuszko was kidnapped and killed in October 1984. Four members of the Security Service (SB) were convicted of his murder in February 1985. The case was reopened in July 1990 after it was revealed that one of them had claimed that senior government officials had been involved in this and other murders. The following October Władysław Ciaston and Zenon Płatek,

two former generals and in the mid 1980s head of the SB and head of the interior ministry's religious-affairs department respectively, were arrested and charged with planning Popiełuszko's murder. They were acquitted in August 1994 after a 26-month trial.

Popovski, Vlado (1941–) Macedonian academic and politician. He has researched and lectured in political science and has been an adviser to President Gligorov. A member of the Social Democratic Alliance (SDSM), he was appointed defence minister in September 1992.

Popular Front (Estonia) See PEOPLE'S FRONT.

popular initiative or **initiative** In Switzerland, the means by which citizens can secure a national referendum on an amendment to the constitution. The right of initiative is a key element in the country's system of semi-direct democracy. If a petition setting out a particular proposal is signed by 100,000 voters (around 2.5% of the electorate), it must be put to a popular vote. Its adoption requires a 'double majority', i.e. the consent of a majority of voters and of the 26 cantons and half-cantons. Most initiatives are concerned with specific legislative proposals, in some cases relatively minor, but they have to be framed as constitutional amendments since only they can be the subject of an initiative-led referendum. The initiative is used by pressure groups to bring about changes in government policy or, less ambitiously, to generate political debate on a particular issue. In several cantons, initiatives can be used to propose specific legislation as well as amend the cantonal constitution. See also REFERENDUM.

Popular Party See PEOPLE'S PARTY (Spain).

Portillo, Michael (1953–) British politician. He worked for the Conservative Party research department and as an adviser to several ministers from 1976 until his election to Parliament in 1984. He held several junior ministerial posts from 1987 and was appointed chief secretary to the Treasury, a post with Cabinet rank with responsibility for public spending, in April 1992. He became secretary of state for employment in July 1994.

Portugal Country in southwestern Europe.

Official data. Name: Portuguese Republic [República Portuguesa]; capital: Lisbon [Lisboa]; form of government: parliamentary republic; head of state: president; head of government: prime minister; flag: two vertical stripes, green and red (in proportion 2:3), with the state emblem on the dividing line; national holiday: 10 June (Portugal Day); language: Portuguese; religion: none; currency: escudo (Esc or $) = 100 centavos; abbreviation: P.

Geography. The smaller of the two Iberian countries, Portugal has a total area of 92,389 sq km. This includes the islands of the Azores [Açores], 1,200 km to the west of the mainland, and Madeira, 1,000 km to the southwest. It is bordered by Spain in the north and east, and the Atlantic Ocean in the south and west. The north consists of mountains and plateaus and a narrow coastal plain, the south of rolling plains and hill lands. The islands are largely mountainous. Some 38% of the land is arable, another 6% is covered by pastures and 40% is forested. The main rivers are the Tagus [Tejo] and Douro. The climate is mediterranean, moderated by temperate marine influences; summers are mild to hot and winters cool; rainfall is heavy in the north and moderate in the centre and south.

Demography. Portugal has a population of 9,823,000. Population density is 107 per sq km (land area). Some 61% of the people live in urban areas. The main cities are Lisbon (metropolitan population 2.2 million) and Porto (1.2 million). Other important cities are Setúbal and Coimbra. In ethnic, linguistic and religious terms Portugal is very homogeneous. Some 99.0% of the population is Portuguese (including around 100,000 people of African descent) and 94.5% is nominally Roman Catholic. Foreign nationals account for 1.0% of the population. There are also thought to be around 100,000 illegal immigrants, mainly from Cape Verde and the other former African colonies. Around 1.0 million Portuguese

citizens live and work abroad, mainly in France, Switzerland and Germany.

Sociography. Portugal scores 0.838 on the United Nations human development index (HDI), ranking 42nd in the world and 27th among 32 European countries. There are 27 doctors and 46 hospital beds for every 10,000 people. Education is compulsory between the ages of six and 15. There is one teacher for every 14 students. Enrolment is 37% at the secondary level and 18% at the tertiary level. The literacy rate is 85%, the lowest in Western Europe. Real annual income per head (in terms of purchasing power) is US$ 9,450.

Infrastructure and communications. Portugal's transport and communications network is relatively well developed; the road and telecommunications systems are limited in some rural areas, and the electronic media have a much wider reach than the press. There are 61,600 km of paved roads and 1.61 million passenger cars (154 per 1,000 people), 3,590 km of railways and 820 km of navigable waterways. The main ports are Lisbon, Porto-Leixões and Setúbal. The main airports are at Lisbon and Faro, and there are 15 other airports with scheduled services. There are 34 daily newspapers, with a combined circulation of around 550,000 (around 55 per 1,000 people). There are 2.48 million radio receivers, 1.79 million television sets and 3.56 million telephones in use (respectively 238, 172 and 342 per 1,000 people).

Economic structure. The Portuguese economy is developed, diversified and trade-oriented (exports accounting for nearly two-fifths of national income). It is based on light industry, tourism and agriculture. Compared to other Western European countries, the agricultural sector is relatively unproductive, the industrial sector less advanced, and several regions are relatively undeveloped and highly dependent on agriculture. After a period of high growth from 1985–90 (averaging 4.4% per year), economic performance in the 1990s has been marked by lower growth (averaging 1.5%), current-account deficits, high but falling inflation (from

13% to below 6%), and relatively high unemployment (around 6%).

Services contribute 54% of GDP, industry contributes 40% (manufacturing 29%), and agriculture, forestry and fisheries 6%. Some 23% of the labour force is employed in manufacturing, 16% in farming, 15% in trade and 8% in construction. The main crops grown are cereals (wheat, maize) and potatoes; horticulture (grapes, olives, tomatoes, figs etc), livestock raising (sheep, cattle, goats) and dairy farming are also important agricultural activities. Fishing (sardines, cod, tuna, anchovies) and forestry (esp. cork) are also important. The main mineral resources are stone, granite, marble, pyrites, tungsten and uranium. The main industries are textiles and clothing (incl. footwear), food processing (incl. wine and other beverages) and wood processing (cork products, pulp); other important branches are chemicals, building materials, metal-working, electrical goods and engineering. Tourism is a major source of foreign exchange, contributing around 7% of GNP (5% net). The main energy sources are imported fossil fuels and hydroelectric power; 13% of export earnings are required to cover net fuel imports. The main exports are textiles and clothing (42% of the total, incl. clothing 22%, textiles 8%, footwear 5%), wood and wood products (9%, incl. cork 5%), electrical equipment (9%), foodstuffs (7%), transport equipment (6%) and chemicals (5%); miscellaneous manufactures account for 34% of the total, basic manufactures for 23%, machinery and transport equipment for 20%. The main imports are machinery and transport equipment, fuels, foodstuffs and chemicals. The main trading partners are: exports: Germany (19%), Spain (15%), France (14%), United Kingdom (10%), Netherlands (6%), Italy; imports: Spain (17%), Germany (15%), France (13%), Italy (10%), United Kingdom (7%), Netherlands (7%), Belgium; three-quarters of all trade is with other European Union (EU) countries. Net invisible earnings (remittances from workers abroad, tourism receipts, funds from EU programmes) account for 15% of GNP, one of the highest shares in Europe.

The Bank of Portugal [Banco de Portugal] is the central bank. The main employers' association is the Confederation of Portuguese Industry (CIP); the main labour organizations are the General Confederation of Portuguese Workers - National Union Federation (CGTP-IN) and the General Workers' Union (UGTP).

Political structure. Portugal is a parliamentary republic on the basis of a constitution adopted in 1976 and last amended in 1989. The head of state is the president, who is directly elected for a five-year term; if no candidate gains an absolute majority of the votes, a run-off is held between the top two candidates. The president is commander of the armed forces, appoints the prime minister, has certain other powers, and is advised by the Council of State [Conselho de Estado], composed of senior political figures. Executive power is vested in the prime minister and the council of ministers. Legislative power is vested in the Assembly of the Republic [Assembleia da República], whose 230 members are elected for a four-year term by a system of proportional representation. All citizens over the age of 18, including those living abroad, are entitled to vote. Judicial power is ultimately vested in the 30-member Supreme Court of Justice [Supremo Tribunal de Justiça]; the 13-member Constitutional Court [Tribunal Constitucional] adjudicates on constitutional matters, and the 38-member Supreme Administrative Court [Supremo Tribunal Administrativo] on administrative matters. Administratively the country is divided into 18 districts [distrito, pl. -s] and two autonomous regions [região autónoma, pl. regiões -s] (Azores [Açores] and Madeira); the districts and regions are subdivided into 305 local councils.

The main political parties are the Social Democratic Party (PSD), Socialist Party (PS), Portuguese Communist Party (PCP), Democratic Social Centre - People's Party (CDS-PP) and National Solidarity Party (PSN); the United Democratic Coalition (CDU) is an alliance dominated by the

PCP. At the general election in October 1991 the PSD gained 50.6% of the vote and 135/230 seats, the PS 29.1% and 72 seats, the CDU 8.8% and 17 seats, the CDS-PP 4.4% and five seats, and the PSN 1.7% and one seat. The government is formed by the centre-right PSD, with Aníbal Cavaco Silva as prime minister. Other senior ministers are José Manuel Durão Barroso (foreign affairs), José Manuel Dias Loureiro (internal affairs), Eduardo Catroga (finance), Alvaro Laborinho Lúcio (justice) and Joaquim Fernando Nogueira (defence). The head of state is President Mário Soares, who was first elected in February 1986.

Portugal has one overseas dependency, Macau on the south coast of China, a 'special territory' with extensive internal self-government; it is due to be returned to Chinese sovereignty in 1999. Portugal has not recognized the annexation of East Timor by Indonesia in 1976.

Security and international affiliations. The Portuguese armed forces number 50,700 (army 27,200, navy 12,500, airforce 11,000). There are also three paramilitary forces: the 20,900-strong National Republican Guard [Guarda Nacional Republicana] (GNR), the 20,000-strong Public Security Police [Polícia de Segurança Pública] (PSP) and an 8,900-strong border guard. Military service is compulsory and consists of 4–18 months' basic training.

Portugal is a member of the Conference on Security and Cooperation in Europe (CSCE), Council of Europe, European Economic Area (EEA), European Union (EU), North Atlantic Treaty Organization (NATO) and Western European Union (WEU), as well as the Organization for Economic Cooperation and Development (OECD) and the United Nations and its specialized agencies.

History. The Celtic Lusitanians, who dominated the western third of the Iberian peninsula and had formed a federation, were defeated by the Romans in 139 BC. In the wake of the Europe-wide migrations that helped trigger the collapse of the Roman Empire in the early 5th century AD the Germanic Suevi (Swabians)

and Visigoths established states in the peninsula and ruled over its romanized population. Christianity became the dominant religion in the 6th century. The Suevi kingdom, based in the northwest and west, was conquered by the Visigoths in 575. Muslim Arab invaders crossed from North Africa in 711 and conquered all but the far north of the peninsula within a few decades. In the northwest, only the territory north of the Douro river remained in Christian hands. Initially part of Asturias and then León, this region became the County of Portugal in the 10th century. It became virtually independent in 1095. After a victory over the Muslims in 1139 Count Afonso proclaimed the Kingdom of Portugal, which was recognized internationally in 1179. The reconquest of the Muslim-held lands was completed in 1270, when the borders of modern Portugal were established. Under the Aviz dynasty (1383–1580) Portugal became one of Europe's first centralized states. Its rulers, especially King Manuel I (1495–1521), also promoted conquests in North Africa and maritime exploration further afield. The uninhabited Azores archipelago and Madeira were discovered in the 1420s and settled in the 1430s. Portuguese voyagers circumnavigated Africa to reach India, Indonesia and China and sailed westwards to South America. By the end of the 16th century Portugal was one of the world's major trading powers and had established an extensive colonial empire.

In 1580 King Philip II of Spain successfully claimed the Portuguese throne, and Portugal effectively lost its independence. It was restored in 1640 under the Bragança dynasty, but in the meantime the economy had gone into sharp decline and many of the colonies had been lost. During the Napoleonic period French troops invaded the country in 1807 but were expelled four years later in the course of the Peninsular War (1808–14). The fighting caused great devastation and sparked a social and political upheaval. The royal family had fled to Brazil in 1807, and on his return the new king was forced to grant a liberal constitution in 1822. (Brazil declared its independence in the same year.) The 19th century was dominated by the struggle between liberals and conservatives, later polarized into republicans and monarchists. The monarchy was overthrown and a republic proclaimed in 1910. During the First World War (1914–18) Portugal reaffirmed its traditional alliance with the United Kingdom and fought on the side of the Allies. The First Republic, which had been marked by weak governments and political violence from left and right, ended in 1926 when the military took power. A measure of stability returned after António Salazar was appointed finance minister in 1928. He was given effective control over much of the government and became prime minister in 1932. The 1933 constitution established a corporate state, with a limited franchise and the far-right National Union as the only legal political party. Under the New State [Estado Novo] programme, some social reforms were implemented and development projects carried out, but all political dissent was suppressed.

Portugal became a founding member of the North Atlantic Treaty Organization (NATO) in 1949. Already the least developed and poorest country in Western Europe, Portugal fell further behind economically during the Salazar dictatorship. From the mid 1960s the wars against independence movements in the African colonies (Angola, Cape Verde, Guinea-Bissau, Mozambique, Sao Tome and Principe) became an additional drain on national resources. Salazar was succeeded by Marcelo Caetano in 1968. The regime was overthrown in a bloodless coup in 1974. The colonies were granted independence, and at home radical left-wing officers were briefly in the ascendant in 1975. The new constitution that took effect in 1976 established democratic rule. The Socialist Party (PS) became the largest party in the election held that year and formed a minority administration. There were frequent changes of government between 1978 and June 1983, when the PS formed a coalition with the centre-right Social Democratic Party (PSD). The PSD formed a minority government

under Aníbal Cavaco Silva in June 1985. Mário Soares, the PS leader, was elected president of the republic in February 1986. After its victory in the April 1987 election the PSD formed the first majority government since the 1974 revolution. Portugal joined the European Community (EC), now the European Union (EU), in January 1986. This and greater political stability initiated a period of rapid economic growth, with a high level of foreign investment, and rising living standards. Constitutional amendments adopted in June 1989 removed references to socialism and the commitment to a state-dominated economy, thus paving the way for an extensive privatization programme and liberalization measures.

See also entries on specific institutions, organizations, parties, people, terms etc.

Portuguese Communist Party [Partido Comunista Português] (PCP) Portuguese political party. The PCP was founded in 1921 and banned from 1926 until the revolution which overthrew the Caetano regime in 1974. It participated in several interim governments from 1974–76. It has followed a strictly orthodox communist line throughout its history. Since 1987 it has been the dominant partner in the United Democratic Coalition (CDU). The alliance gained 8.8% of the vote and 17/230 seats at the October 1991 election. The leader is Carlos Carvalhas. Alvaro Cunhal, who led the party from 1960 until his retirement in 1992, retains considerable influence.

POSL *See* LUXEMBURG SOCIALIST WORKERS' PARTY.

post-communist countries Collective name for the Eastern European states whose communist regimes collapsed or were overthrown between 1989 and 1991. They now comprise, outside the Commonwealth of Independent States (CIS), Albania, Bosnia-Herzegovina, Bulgaria, Croatia, Czech Republic, Estonia, Hungary, Latvia, Lithuania, Macedonia, Poland, Romania, Slovakia, Slovenia and (rump) Yugoslavia.

post-communist party In the former communist countries, a political party which held power during communist rule (from the late 1940s until 1989) and subsequently relaunched itself as a mainstream left-wing or centre-left party. Examples of 'post-communist' parties are the Bulgarian Socialist Party (BSP), the Hungarian Socialist Party (MSzP), the Democratic Labour Party of Lithuania (LDDP), the Social Democratic Party (SdRP) in Poland, the Social Democracy Party of Romania (PDSR), the Democratic Left Party (SDL') in Slovakia, and the Socialist Party of Serbia (SPS) and Democratic Socialist Party of Montenegro (DPSCG or DPS) in Yugoslavia. All have abandoned communist principles and policies. In some there have been extensive changes in leadership but in others the old leaders have remained in place. All have continued to enjoy substantial electoral support. In Romania and Yugoslavia they have retained power, and in Lithuania, Poland and Hungary they have returned to power after a period in opposition. *See also individual party entries.*

post-fascism *See* FASCISM.

post-Solidarity party In Poland, a political party with roots in SOLIDARITY, the broadly based movement that spearheaded the opposition to communist rule in the 1980s and won the partially free election of June 1989. The orientations of its offshoots range from right-wing to mainstream left-wing, the latter reflecting Solidarity's origins as an independent trade union. The main ones are the Democratic Union (UD) and Liberal Democratic Congress (KLD), which have merged to form the Freedom Union (UW), the Labour Union (UP) and the Centre Alliance (POC). *See also individual party entries.*

post-Yugoslav (civil) wars *See* BOSNIAN CIVIL WAR *and* CROATIAN CIVIL WAR.

pound Anglicized version of various currencies, namely the líra (Cyprus), lira (Malta and Turkey) and punt (Ireland). *See individual currency entries.*

pound Currency of Gibraltar. Common abbreviations are £, G£ and GIP (the international standard in banking etc). It is divided into 100 pence. It has parity with the British pound sterling, which is also legal tender in Gibraltar.

pound Currency of Guernsey. Common abbreviations are £ and G£. It is divided into 100 pence. It has parity with the British and Jersey pounds, which are also legal tender in Guernsey.

pound (Ireland) *See* PUNT.

pound Currency of Jersey. Common abbreviations are £ and J£. It is divided into 100 pence. It has parity with the British and Guernsey pounds, which are also legal tender in Jersey.

pound Currency of Man. Common abbreviations are £ and IoM£. It is divided into 100 pence. It has parity with the British pound sterling, which is also legal tender in Man.

pound sterling or **pound** Currency of the United Kingdom. Common abbreviations are £ and GBP (the international standard in banking). It is divided into 100 pence. The British pound is also legal tender in Gibraltar, Guernsey, Jersey and Man.

PP (Iceland) *See* PROGRESSIVE PARTY.

PP (Spain) *See* PEOPLE'S PARTY.

PPD and **PPD-PND** *See* PARTY FOR DEMOCRATIC PROSPERITY - NATIONAL DEMOCRATIC PARTY.

PPE *See* EUROPEAN PEOPLE'S PARTY.

PPI *See* ITALIAN PEOPLE'S PARTY.

PR (France) *See* REPUBLICAN PARTY.

PR (Italy) *See* RADICAL PARTY.

Prague Shorthand for the Czech government. Prague is the capital of the Czech Republic.

Prague Castle [Hradčany] Shorthand for the Czech presidency. The Hradčany in Prague is the official residence of the president.

Praha Czech name for Prague, the Czech capital.

Prandini, Giovanni or **Gianni** (1940–) Italian politician. He worked as an insurance agent before his election to parliament for the Christian Democratic Party (DC) in 1972. He has held the ministerial portfolios of merchant navy (1987–88) and public works (1989–92). In September 1993 he was accused of extorting, on behalf of his party, a total of 20.5 billion lire (10.5 million ecus) from private companies in exchange for road-building contracts while he was minister of public works.

Prapiestis, Jonas (1952–) Lithuanian lawyer, academic and politician. He lectured in law at Vilnius University from 1975 and was also assistant dean of the law faculty from 1982–90. A member of parliament for the Democratic Labour Party (LDDP) from 1990–92, he was appointed minister of justice in December 1992.

PRC *See* COMMUNIST REFOUNDATION PARTY.

PRD *See* RADICAL DEMOCRATIC PARTY.

prefect [préfet] In France, common name for the COMMISSIONER OF THE REPUBLIC, the representative of central government at department level. 'Prefect' was in official use until 1982.

préfet *See* PREFECT.

Prescott, John (1938–) British ship steward and politician. He worked as a trainee chef and steward on the Cunard shipping line for 10 years before studying economics and politics from 1963–68. He was briefly a full-time official of the National Union of Seamen (NUS) until his election to Parliament for the Labour Party in 1970. Since 1983 he has been a party spokesman on transport (1983–84 and 1988–92), employment (1984–87 and 1992–94) and energy (1987–88). He was elected the party's deputy leader in July 1994.

presidency of the Council or **presidency** In the European Union (EU), shorthands for the presidency of the COUNCIL OF THE EUROPEAN UNION or Council of Ministers, the main decision-making body. It is held in turn by each member state for six months.

president In Spain, shorthand for the president of the government [presidente del gobierno], i.e. the prime minister.

president of the Council or **president** In the European Union (EU), shorthand for the president of the COUNCIL OF THE EUROPEAN UNION or Council of Ministers, the main decision-making body. S/he is the foreign minister of the member state holding the six-month presidency.

president of the Council of Ministers or **president of the Council** [presidente del Consiglio dei Ministri] Head of government or prime minister of Italy. The shorter version is widely used in Italy, but it is generally not reduced to 'president',

to avoid confusion with the shorthand for 'president of the republic', i.e. the head of state.

president of the government or **president** [presidente del gobierno] Head of government or prime minister of Spain.

president of the Senate [Präsident des Senats or Senatspräsident] Head of government in Bremen and Hamburg, two federal states of Germany. In both states the government is called the Senate [Senat].

presidential majority or **majority** [majorité présidentielle] In France, members of parliament who support the policies of the president of the republic (who has wide-ranging executive powers), specifically those not affiliated to a particular party. Throughout the Fifth Republic the president has usually enjoyed majority support in parliament. But since presidential and general elections do not coincide, this is not invariably the case (e.g. 1986–88 and since 1993). In those circumstances the term is not used. *See also* COHABITATION.

presidential ministry [ministerstwo prezydjalne] In Poland, one of the government appointments in which the president of the republic has a say. The three 'presidential' ministries are the key portfolios of foreign affairs, internal affairs and defence. Article 61 of the 1992 Constitutional Act (a partial revision of the constitution) states that the ministers in question shall be appointed 'after consultation with the president'. Other ministers are proposed by the prime minister without consideration of the president's views. All ministers are formally appointed by the president.

presidio *See* PLAZA DE SOBERANÍA.

Previti, Cesare (1934–) Italian lawyer and politician. He has been a close associate of the businessman Silvio Berlusconi since the late 1960s, acting as his personal lawyer and serving in several senior posts in his Fininvest conglomerate. When Berlusconi formed Come On Italy (Forza Italia) in January 1994, he joined the new movement and was elected to parliament in the March election. He was appointed minister of defence in the right-wing coalition formed in May.

PRI *See* ITALIAN REPUBLICAN PARTY.

Priebke affair Controversy in Italy surrounding Erich Priebke, a German officer accused of involvement in the country's worst war crime committed during the Second World War (1939–45). Some 335 people were executed at the Ardeatine Caves [Fosse Ardeatine] outside Rome in March 1944 in reprisal for a bomb attack by Italian resistance fighters which had killed 33 German soldiers. At the time Priebke was a captain in the elite SS corps and deputy to Herbert Kappel, who ordered the massacre. He escaped from a prison camp in 1946 and after two years in hiding fled to Argentina (helped, he claims, by Vatican officials). He lived there openly for 46 years until he was traced by the US television network ABC. In May 1994 an Italian court issued a warrant for his arrest and an Argentine judge placed him under house arrest pending a formal extradition request. In a newspaper interview at this time Priebke, aged 81, admitted his involvement in the massacre but claimed he was merely obeying orders.

Primacialny Palace [Primaciálny Palác] Shorthand for the Slovakian presidency. The Primacialny Palace in Bratislava is the president's official residence.

prince of Asturias Title conferred on the heir to the Spanish throne.

prince of Wales Title conferred on the heir to the British throne.

Principality, the Shorthand for Andorra, Liechtenstein, Monaco or Wales (United Kingdom). All four have been principalities since the Middle Ages.

Privy Council British advisory, legislative and judicial body. The Privy Council has around 300 members appointed for life, including eminent persons appointed by the sovereign on the recommendation of the prime minister and virtually all present and past members of the Cabinet (who are normally appointed on taking office) and senior opposition leaders. Meetings are chaired by the sovereign, while the administrative work is carried out under the direction of the lord president of the Council, invariably a senior government minister. The Privy Council was the main executive body before the emergence of Cabinet government in the late 18th century. Today the Council's main formal function is to advise the sovereign on 'orders in Council': these are either (i) decisions made under the 'royal prerogative', the sovereign's residual powers now exercised by the government in his/her name (e.g. regarding public appointments), or (ii) those authorized by acts of Parliament, in effect a form of delegated legislation. (Since the sovereign has no executive powers, his/her acceptance of the government's 'advice' is a formality.) In addition to other advisory functions, the Council has supervisory powers over various professional and church bodies. Its Judicial Committee, composed of 'law lords', i.e. members of the House of Lords (= upper house of parliament) who have held high judiciary office, is the final court of appeal from the courts of Guernsey, Jersey and Man as well as other British dependencies and a number of independent Commonwealth countries.

PRL *See* LIBERAL REFORM PARTY.

Pro Patria *See* FATHERLAND.

professional ban (Germany) *See* BERUFSVERBOT.

Progress Party [Fremskridtspartiet] (FP) Danish political party. Founded in 1972, the FP is a far-right protest party which advocates sharp reductions in the level of income tax, the size of the public sector and the number of immigrants. Recently it has also called for the deportation of all refugees. At the December 1990 election it gained 6.4% of the vote and 12/179 seats. The party was dominated for many years by its founder, Mogens Glistrup. He lost the leadership in 1985 after serving a two-year sentence for tax fraud, and was expelled from the party in 1990. The current leader is Pia Kjærsgaard.

Progress Party [Fremskrittspartiet] (Frp) Norwegian political party. Founded in 1973, the Frp advocates radical free-market economic policies and drastic cuts in taxation and welfare provisions. Since the late 1980s it has also called for restrictions on immigration and the repatriation of foreigners. The country's main protest party, its electoral support has fluctuated widely: it gained 13.0% of the vote and 22/165 seats at the September 1989 election but 6.3% and 10 seats at the September 1993 election. The leader is Carl Hagen.

Progressisti *See* PROGRESSIVE ALLIANCE *and* ALLIED PROGRESSIVE GROUP.

Progressive Alliance [Alleanza Progressista] Italian political organization. The Alliance was formed in February 1994 by eight parties from the centre to the communist left of the political spectrum to contest the general election held the following month. It was dominated by the Democratic Left Party (PDS) and also included the Communist Refoundation Party (RC), the Greens (Verdi), the Italian Socialist Party (PSI), the centre-left Network (La Rete), the centrist Democratic Alliance (AD), the centre-left Social Christian Party (PCS) and the left-wing Socialist Renewal (RS). Its manifesto called for investment in job-creation programmes, improvements in social welfare and tax equality, privatization of state-owned industries, and the achievement of sound public finances. It gained 34.4% of the vote and 213/630 seats at the election. The PDS, Greens, Network and PCS formed a single parliamentary group, the Allied Progressives, with Luigi Berlinguer as leader. *See also individual party entries.*

Progressive Citizens' Party [Fortschrittliche Bürgerpartei] (FBP) Liechtenstein political party. Founded in 1918, the right-wing FBP has ruled the country in coalition with the other main party, the centre-right Fatherland Union (VU), since 1938. At the February 1993 election it gained 44.2% of the vote and 12/25 seats. The FBP-led government fell the following September after the FBP parliamentary party tabled a motion of no confidence in its own leader and prime minister, Markus Büchel, over his allegedly autocratic leadership style. In a fresh election held in October, the party gained 41.3% and 11 seats. The current leader is Thomas Büchel, the party president is Otmar Hasler.

Progressive Democrats (PD or PDs) Irish political party. The PDs broke away from the centre-right Fianna Fáil in 1985. They present themselves as a break from the traditional parties, which have their roots in the civil war of the 1920s. They advocate right-wing economic policies and have liberal views on social issues. The party was in government from 1989–92 as Fianna Fáil's junior coalition partner. At the November 1992 election it gained 4.7% of the vote and 10/166 seats. Des O'Malley was the leader until October 1993, when he was succeeded by Mary Harney.

Progressive Left Alliance [Sinaspismós tis Aristerás kai tis Próodou] (Sinaspismós, SIN or SAP) Greek political party. Sinaspismós was formed in 1989 as an electoral alliance of 10 parties dominated by the orthodox Communist Party of Greece (KKE) and the Greek Left (EAR). Describing itself as a left-wing alternative to the ruling Pan-Hellenic Socialist Movement (PASOK), it held the balance of power after the June 1989 election and joined the right-wing New Democratic Party (ND) in a seven-month interim coalition. In June 1991 the KKE withdrew from the alliance, although a reformist wing stayed within it. The following month Sinaspismós constituted itself as a party and adopted a traditional left-wing economic programme. At the October 1993 election it gained 2.9% of the vote, narrowly failing to pass the 3% required for parliamentary representation. The leader is Nikolaos Konstantinopoulos.

Progressive Party [Framsóknarflokkurinn] (F) Icelandic political party. Founded in 1916, the Progressive Party is centrist in orientation. The country's second-largest party, it has participated in most coalition governments since 1946, most recently from 1980–91. At the April 1991 election it gained 18.9% of the vote and 13/63 seats. The leader is Steingrímur Hermannsson.

Progressive Party of Working People [Anorthotikó Kómma Ergazómenou Laoú] (AKEL) Cypriot political party. Founded in 1941 as the successor to the Communist Party, which had been banned by the British colonial authorities in 1931, AKEL is the country's main left-wing party, with strong support in the trade unions. It calls for a federal solution to the island's division; among the major parties it has traditionally been the most willing to take account of Turkish Cypriot concerns (*see* CYPRIOT QUESTION). At the May 1991 election it gained 30.6% of the vote and 18/56 seats. The leader is Dimitrios Christofias.

Progressive Trade Union Confederation of Turkey [Türkiye Devrimci İşçi Sendikaları Konfederasyonu] (DİSK) Turkish trade-union federation. DİSK was founded in 1967 as a left-wing breakaway from the Trade Union Confederation (Türk-İş). It has 30 affiliated unions with a total membership of 700,000 (3.5% of the labour force). It is most strongly represented in the manufacturing sector. The president is Kemal Nebioğlu, the general secretary Süleyman Çelebi.

Progressives (Italy) *See* PROGRESSIVE ALLIANCE *and* ALLIED PROGRESSIVE GROUP.

Prokeš, Jozef (1950–) Slovakian physicist and politician. He worked as a researcher at the Slovak Academy of Sciences from 1986–90. He was coopted and then elected to the Slovak parliament for the Slovak National Party (SNS) in 1990. He was chairman of the parliament in 1991–92, deputy chairman in 1992–93, and a deputy prime minister from November 1993 until March 1994.

Propaganda Due or **Propaganda Two affair** *See* P-2 AFFAIR.

proportionality [Proporz] In Austria, the system whereby the electoral strengths of the two main parties, the Social Democratic Party (SPÖ) and the Austrian People's Party (ÖVP), are reflected in the composition of the governing bodies of all public institutions, including nationalized industries, banks, chambers of commerce, media organizations, universities etc. The practice operates at national, provincial and local level. It evolved after 1945 as part of the wide-ranging 'social partnership' between government, employers and trade unions aimed at ensuring steady economic growth and full employment.

proportionality In the European Union (EU), the principle that EU or member-state authorities should use appropriate means to achieve particular ends. Measures that are deemed to go beyond what is strictly necessary have been declared illegal by the European Court of Justice on several occasions. An example is a government agency insisting on excessive administrative formalities in a particular sphere that have the effect of discriminating against nationals from other member states.

Proporz *See* PROPORTIONALITY (Austria).

Protestant Action Force *See* ULSTER VOLUNTEER FORCE.

Protestants Religious and ethnic group in NORTHERN IRELAND, a component of the United Kingdom. The religious label is often used interchangeably with 'unionists' and 'loyalists'.

Protocol on Social Policy or **Social Protocol** International agreement within the framework of the European Community (EC), now the European Union (EU). An annex to the Maastricht Treaty agreed in December 1991 and in force since November 1993, the Social Protocol regulates the operation of the AGREEMENT ON SOCIAL POLICY adopted by all member states except the United Kingdom.

Protopapas, Christos (1956–) Greek economist and trade-union official. He joined the National Bank of Greece, a major commercial bank, in 1978. He was elected general secretary of the Bank Employees' Federation (OTOE) in 1984 and became the union's president in 1989. In October 1993 he was elected president of the General Confederation of Greek Workers (GSEE). He is a member of the Pan-Hellenic Socialist Movement (PASOK) and sits on the party's executive.

Provençal Alternative name for OCCITAN, a language spoken in southern France. 'Provençal' is widely used in the region of Provence in preference to 'Occitan'.

Provence-Alpes-Côte-d'Azur Region of France. Situated in the southeast on the Mediterranean Sea and bordering on Italy, the region has an area of 31,400 sq km and a population of 4,349,000. The population has grown rapidly since the

1950s, particularly along the coast. Dialects of Occitan and Italian are widely spoken in the region; these languages have no official status but are allowed to be taught in schools. The capital is Marseille, the country's third-largest city; the other main cities are Nice, Toulon, Cannes, Avignon and Aix-en-Provence. The economy is based on manufacturing (petrochemicals, chemicals, food processing), tourism and agriculture (wine, fruit and vegetables). Like the other regions of southern France, Provence has a strong regional identity. It was a separate state within the Holy Roman Empire during the Middle Ages and became part of France in 1481.

province [provincie (Dutch), province (French)] Belgian administrative division. Each province has a directly elected council, a governor appointed by the monarch, and an executive committee elected by the council. The role of the provinces is largely restricted to supervising the activities of the communes, the main units of local government. Most powers are held by the geographical regions and language-based cultural communities on the one hand and the communes on the other.

province [provincia, pl. province] Italian administrative division. All but one of the 95 provinces have a council [consiglio provinciale] elected for a five-year term and an executive council [giunta provinciale] headed by a president. (The exception is Aosta Valley province, which is coextensive with the autonomous region of the same name.) The provinces generally have only administrative and little political significance, with most powers held by the regions and communes.

province [provincie] Dutch administrative division. Each of the 12 provinces has an assembly [provinciale staten] elected for a four-year term, an executive committee [gedeputeerde staten], and a commissioner [commissaris] appointed by the crown on the advice of the central government. The assemblies elect the members of the First Chamber, the upper house of parliament. The provinces have several powers and strong regional identities, but the main units of local government are the municipalities.

province [provincia] Spanish administrative division. The intermediate unit between the autonomous communities or regions and the municipalities, most of the 50 provinces are administered by a delegation [diputación provincial], elected by and from the municipal councils. The seven provinces which are also autonomous communities have no such structures. The provinces are primarily used for administrative and statistical purposes and have little political significance.

province (Yugoslavia) *See* POKRAJINA.

Province, the In Ireland and the United Kingdom, a shorthand for Northern Ireland, a component of the United Kingdom. The territory is broadly coextensive with the historical province of Ulster.

provincial governor or **governor** [Landeshaupt, pl. -häupter] Head of government in a federal province of Austria.

Provisional IRA or **Provisionals** Informal name for the IRISH REPUBLICAN ARMY (IRA), the main guerrilla group seeking the withdrawal of British troops from Northern Ireland and the reunification of Ireland. (It declared a ceasefire in September 1994.) Known colloquially as the Provos, the Provisional IRA emerged in 1970 from a split within the IRA. Since the 'official' wing abandoned violence and the IRA label and formed a political party, the adjective 'provisional' is now redundant. It is still commonly used by its opponents.

Provisional Sinn Féin Informal name for SINN FÉIN, the British and Irish political party. The party split into 'official' and 'provisional' wings in 1970. When the former adopted a new name (Workers' Party), the longer form for the latter became redundant. It is still commonly used by its opponents.

provost British local government official. The provost is the formal head of the council in many districts in Scotland. S/he has no executive powers.

PRSh *See* REPUBLICAN PARTY OF ALBANIA.

PS (Belgium) *See* SOCIALIST PARTY.

PS (France) *See* SOCIALIST PARTY.
PS (Italy) *See* PUBLIC SECURITY GUARD.
PS (Portugal) *See* SOCIALIST PARTY.
PS *See* SOCIAL DEMOCRATIC PARTY OF SWITZERLAND.
PSA *See* FREEDOM PARTY OF SWITZERLAND.
PSC (Belgium) *See* CHRISTIAN SOCIAL PARTY.
PSC (Spain) *See* SOCIALIST PARTY OF CATALONIA.
PSD (France) *See* SOCIAL DEMOCRATIC PARTY.
PSD (Portugal) *See* SOCIAL DEMOCRATIC PARTY.
PSdA *See* SARDINIAN ACTION PARTY.
PSdG *See* SOCIALIST PARTY OF GALICIA.
PSDI *See* ITALIAN DEMOCRATIC SOCIALIST PARTY.
PSDR *See* ROMANIAN SOCIAL DEMOCRATIC PARTY.
PSDS and **PSDSh** *See* SOCIAL DEMOCRATIC PARTY OF ALBANIA.
PSE (Spain) and **PSE-EE** *See* BASQUE SOCIALIST PARTY - BASQUE LEFT.
PSE (European Union) *See* PARTY OF EUROPEAN SOCIALISTS.
PSI *See* ITALIAN SOCIALIST PARTY.
PSL *See* POLISH PEASANT PARTY.
PSL *See* FREEDOM PARTY OF SWITZERLAND.
PSM *See* SOCIALIST LABOUR PARTY.
PSOE *See* SPANISH SOCIALIST WORKERS' PARTY.
PSOE-A *See* SPANISH SOCIALIST WORKERS' PARTY OF ANDALUSIA.
PSS *See* SOCIALIST PARTY OF ALBANIA.
PSS *See* SAN MARINO SOCIALIST PARTY.
PSS *See* SOCIAL DEMOCRATIC PARTY OF SWITZERLAND.
PSSh *See* SOCIALIST PARTY OF ALBANIA.
Pta and **Ptas** Abbreviations for the PESETA, the Spanish currency.
PTE Abbreviation for the ESCUDO, the Portuguese currency, used in banking etc.
Public Security Guard [Guardia di Pubblica Sicurezza] (PS) Italian paramilitary police force. Numbering 80,400, the PS carries out general police duties, including maintaining public order and investigating crimes. It is a branch of the armed forces but is answerable to the interior minister. Its activities overlap with those of the other main national police force, the Corps of Carabinieri.

Public Services and Transport Union [Gewerkschaft Öffentliche Dienste, Transport und Verkehr] (ÖTV) German trade union. Founded in 1949 as the union for much of the public sector within the GERMAN TRADE UNION FEDERATION (DGB), the ÖTV is Germany's second-largest union, with 2.0 million members. The chairwoman is Monika Wulf-Mathies.
Puech, Jean (1942–) French teacher, civil servant and politician. Active in local government in his native Aveyron since the 1960s, he became president of the department's council in 1976 and represented it in the Senate (= the upper house of parliament) from 1989–93. At this time he was also president of the Association of Departmental Councils (ACGF). He was appointed minister of agriculture and fisheries in the centre-right government formed in March 1993. He is a member of the Republican Party (PR).
Puglia *See* APULIA.
Pujol, Jordi (1930–) Spanish banker and politician. A committed Catalan nationalist, he was imprisoned for two years by the Franco regime in the 1950s for his political activities. During the transition to democracy in the late 1970s he became leader of the newly founded centre-right Convergence and Union (CiU) alliance. In March 1980 he led it to victory in the Catalan election and became the region's head of government. He has been the dominant leader in Catalan politics ever since, being returned to office in 1984, 1988 and 1992.
PUNR *See* ROMANIAN NATIONAL UNITY PARTY.
punt (pl. -aí or -) Currency of Ireland. Common abbreviations are £, I£, IR£ and IEP (the international standard in banking etc). It is divided into 100 pence/pingin. The anglicized form 'pound' was widely used when the punt had parity with the British pound, until 1979, but 'punt' is now more common to avoid confusion between the two currencies.
purple coalition [paarse coalitie] In the Netherlands, a broad coalition of right- and left-wing parties excluding the centre-right Christian Democratic Appeal (CDA). The idea of a 'purple coalition' was first

put forward in the early 1990s as a more liberal (on social issues) and fresh alternative to the CDA, which along with its precursors had dominated all coalitions since 1918. Given the broad consensus on economic policy in the Netherlands, differences between right and left were seen as less of an obstacle to cooperation than in other countries. After the May 1994 election negotiations were opened between the Labour Party (PvdA), the right-wing People's Party for Freedom and Democracy (VVD) and the centre-left Democrats 66 (D'66), leading to the formation of a 'purple coalition' in August. The term is taken from the colours traditionally associated with the left and right, red and blue.

PvdA *See* LABOUR PARTY (Netherlands).

QM and **QMV** *See* QUALIFIED MAJORITY VOTING.

quaestor In the European Union (EU), a member of the European Parliament elected to supervise administrative and financial matters affecting his/her colleagues, specifically to scrutinize their interests and expenses. The five quaestors are elected for $2\frac{1}{2}$ year terms. (The *quaestor* was the custodian of the public treasury in the ancient Roman Republic.)

Quai d'Orsay Shorthand for the French foreign ministry. The ministry's main building is on the Quai d'Orsay, on the left bank of the Seine river in Paris. Several other government buildings are also located there.

qualified majority voting or **qualified majority** (QMV or QM) In the European Union (EU), a method of voting based on weighted votes per member state. QMV is used in the Council of Ministers, the EU's main decision-making body, in specified policy areas. Each member state is allocated a number of votes broadly in line with its population, although smaller states are given relatively greater weight. France, Germany, Italy and the United Kingdom have 10 votes each, Spain eight, Belgium, Greece, the Netherlands and Portugal five each, Denmark and Ireland three each, and Luxemburg two. A qualified majority is defined as 54 votes out of 76 from at least eight member states. A 'blocking minority' is therefore 23 votes or 30% of the total. The weighting of votes and setting of the majority threshold are intended to strike a balance between the influence of larger and smaller states. In the first three decades of the then European Community most decisions were taken by unanimity, and QMV was rarely used. It was introduced in 1987 for measures related to the completion of the single internal market and extended to health, education, culture, energy, transport, environment, tourism, technology, social and industrial policy and consumer rights under the Maastricht Treaty, which came into force in November 1993. Most important decisions still require unanimity.

queen of England Informal title for the sovereign of the United Kingdom of Great Britain and Northern Ireland. The United Kingdom was established with the union of England and Scotland in 1707.

questione del Sud ('southern question') *See* MEZZOGIORNO.

questione morale *See* MORAL QUESTION.

quiet revolution [rivoluzione quieta] In Italy, a common name for the transformation of the political system that took place after the exposure of endemic corruption and other scandals in 1992 and 1993, which discredited the Christian Democratic Party (DC) and the other ruling parties and swept them from power in the March 1994 election. *See also* ITALIAN CORRUPTION SCANDALS.

Quinn, Ruairi (1946–) Irish architect and politician. A member of parliament for the Labour Party since 1977, he was minister of labour from 1984–87 and became minister of employment and enterprise when the party returned to government in January 1993.

Quirinale Palace [Palazzo del Quirinale] Shorthand for the Italian presidency. The Palazzo del Quirinale in Rome is the official residence of the president.

497

R *See* RESISTANCE.

Raad van State *See* COUNCIL OF STATE (Netherlands).

Račan, Ivica (1944–) Croatian sociologist and politician. He was elected to the central committee of the League of Communists of Croatia (SKH) in 1972 and held senior posts in the League of Communists of Yugoslavia (SKJ) from 1982. In December 1989 he was elected leader of the SKH, which soon afterwards relaunched itself as the Social Democratic Party - Party of Democratic Changes (SDP). He was elected to parliament in 1990. In April 1994 he was confirmed as leader of the Social Democratic Party of Croatia (SDPH), formed by the merger of the SDP and a small centre-left party.

Rad *See* RADICAL PARTY (France).

Radical Democratic Party [Radikalna Demokraticheska Partiya] (RDP) Bulgarian political party. The RDP is the successor to the centre-right party founded in 1902 and suppressed by the communist regime in 1948. Relaunched in 1989, it is a leading member of the UNION OF DEMOCRATIC FORCES (SDS) alliance. The leader is Aleksandŭr Yordanov.

Radical Democratic Party [Freisinnig-Demokratische Partei der Schweiz (German), Parti Radical-Démocratique Suisse (French)] (FDP or PRD) Swiss political party. Founded in 1894, this centre-right party has been one of the country's dominant political forces for many years and is a member of the four-party coalition which has been in power since 1959. It traditionally articulates the views of big business, industry and the banking sector. At the October 1991 election it gained 20.9% of the vote and 44/200 seats. The party president is Franz Steinegger, the parliamentary leader is Pascal Couchepin.

Radical Energy [Énergie Radicale] French political organization. Radical Energy was formed to contest the June 1994 election to the European Parliament, the parliament of the European Union (EU), on a populist left-wing platform stressing the need to combat unemployment and social injustice on a Europe-wide scale. Headed by the businessman and former minister Bernard Tapie, the list attracted considerable support from disaffected Socialist Party (PS) supporters and gained 12.0% of the vote and 13/87 seats. Together with deputies from four other countries it formed the European Radical Alliance (ERA) parliamentary group.

Radical Liberal Party or **Social Liberal Party** [Det Radikale Venstre] (RV) Danish political party. Founded in 1905 by left-wing members of the Liberal Party (Venstre), the centrist Radical Liberals have participated in several coalition governments, most recently in 1988–90 and since January 1993. The party has also given external support to centre-right coalitions, particularly on economic issues. At the December 1990 election it gained 3.5% of the vote and 7/179 seats. The leader is Marianne Jelved, the party president is Grethe Erichsen, the parliamentary leader is Jens Bilgrav-Nielsen.

Radical Party [Parti Radical] (Rad) French political party. Founded in 1901, the Radicals played a prominent role in French politics until the 1960s. Traditionally a party without rigid structures, it suffered numerous splits and has shifted its ideological stance between left and centre on several occasions. It has also been known under several other names, including the Radical Socialist Party. Its programme has been broadly centrist since the 1970s. It joined the centre-right UNION FOR FRENCH DEMOCRACY (UDF) in 1978, and has contested successive elections under its banner. At the March 1993 election it gained 13/577 seats. The leader is Yves Galland.

Radical Party [Partito Radicale] (PR) Italian political party. Founded in 1955, the PR is an independent centre-left party which sees itself as a vehicle for raising controversial issues. It has championed civil rights and environmental issues in particular and has also consistently attacked the 'autocracy' of the leading political parties. Its influence in Italian politics has been much greater than its electoral support, which reached a peak of 3.4% in 1979. The party has not formally participated in elections since 1987 and has instead put forward candidates on a list headed by Marco Pannella, a former party leader. At the March 1994 election the Pannella List [Lista Pannella] gained 3.5% of the vote and 6/630 seats. The current leader is Emma Bonino.

Radicals' Decree *See* BERUFSVERBOT.

Radice, Roberto (1938–) Italian businessman and politician. He owns a boatbuilding firm and another that produces refuse containers. He entered politics with the new Come On Italy (Forza Italia) movement in January 1994, was elected to parliament in March, and was appointed minister of public works in the rightwing coalition formed in May.

Radikalenerlass *See* BERUFSVERBOT.

RAF (Germany) *See* RED ARMY FACTION.

RAF Abbreviation for the Royal Air Force, the British airforce.

Rahvarinne *See* PEOPLE'S FRONT.

RAID *See* SEARCH, AID, INTERVENTION AND DISSUASION.

Rainier III (1923–) Prince of Monaco. He became head of state on the death of his grandfather, Prince Louis II, in May 1949. He is the 26th ruler of the Grimaldi dynasty, which has reigned in Monaco since 1297. Under the constitution he retains considerable executive powers. He married the American film star Grace Kelly in 1956; she died in a car accident in 1982. He has three children.

rajonas (pl. rajonai) Lithuanian administrative division, usually translated as 'district'. Each of the 44 *rajonai* has a council elected for a five-year term. They are responsible for most local services. Vilnius, Kaunas and nine other cities are administered separately and have similar powers.

rajons (pl. rajoni) Latvian administrative division, usually translated as 'district'. Each of the 26 *rajoni* is administered by a council elected for a three-year term. They are responsible for most local services. Rīga Daugavpils, Liepāja and four other cities are administered separately and have similar powers.

Rally for the Republic [Rassemblement pour la République] (RPR) French political party. Founded in 1976, the right-wing RPR is the successor to the Rally of the French People (RPF) founded by Charles

de Gaulle in 1947. While it continues to stress the tenets of GAULLISM, the party has abandoned much of its statist economic policies in favour of support for deregulation and privatization. (In recognition of this change it is now sometimes called 'neo-gaullist'.) It formed an electoral alliance with the Union for French Democracy (UDF) in 1985, which won the 1986 election and formed a government with RPR leader Jacques Chirac as prime minister. In 1988 Chirac stood against François Mitterrand in the presidential election, but the latter was reelected and an early general election brought the Socialist Party back to power. The alliance with the UDF was renewed in 1990 as the Union for France (UPF). This scored an overwhelming victory at the general election in March 1993, with the RPR gaining 20.3% of the vote and 247/577 seats and becoming the largest single party in parliament. One of its senior members, Édouard Balladur, was appointed prime minister and formed a centre-right government. Chirac has been party leader since 1976. The leader of the parliamentary group is Bernard Pons.

Rapid Intervention Force [Forza di Intervento Rapido] (FIR) Italian military force. The FIR is an elite commando unit of the armed forces, ultimately answerable to the defence minister. It is trained to deal with cases of hostage taking and other specialist assignments and has also been involved in anti-terrorist operations.

Rapid Reaction Corps or **Force** *See* ALLIED COMMAND EUROPE RAPID REACTION CORPS.

rapporteur In the European Union (EU), the spokesperson of a committee of the European Parliament. S/he drafts its report on a legislative proposal put before the Parliament (by the European Commission or the Council of Ministers) and guides it through all its stages in the parliamentary process.

RARA or **RaRa** *See* REVOLUTIONARY ANTI-RACIST ACTION.

Raşit, Atay Ahmet (1943–) Northern Cypriot economist and politician. Elected to parliament for the centre-right National

Unity Party (UBP) in 1985, he was trade and industry minister from 1990 until the party split and he joined the Democratic Party (DP) in 1992. He was appointed minister of foreign affairs and defence in the DP-led coalition which took office in January 1994.

Rasmussen, Poul Nyrup (1943–) Danish economist and politician. He worked for the Danish Trade Union Confederation (LO) from 1971–86, serving as its chief economist from 1980–86, and was managing director of a pension fund from 1986–88. Elected to parliament for the Social Democratic Party (SD) in 1988, he was elected party leader in April 1992. In January 1993 he became prime minister of a centre-left coalition.

Rau, Johannes (1931–) German businessman and politician. He managed a publishing company from 1954–67. In 1958 he was elected to the parliament of North Rhine - Westphalia for the Social Democratic Party (SPD). He was the state's science and research minister from 1970–78. He was elected party leader at state level in 1977 and became prime minister of Germany's largest state in May 1978. He has been an SPD deputy leader at federal level since 1982 and was the party's candidate for federal chancellor (= prime minister) in the 1987 general election.

Rauch-Kallat, Maria (1949–) Austrian teacher, social worker and politician. She taught at a secondary school in Vienna until 1983 and then worked for a social charity. A specialist on the integration of disabled people and children's welfare, she was also an adviser to the ministry of education and the arts in the 1980s. A member of the centre-right Austrian People's Party (ÖVP), she was appointed minister of the environment, youth and family affairs in November 1992.

Ravnopraviye *See* EQUAL RIGHTS.

Raznjatović, Zeljko (1951–) Yugoslav businessman and politician. Nicknamed 'Arkan' and nominally the owner of a sweet shop, he was involved in a range of criminal activities before he entered politics. He lived in several Western European countries in the 1970s, and is wanted for armed robbery in the Netherlands and Sweden and for murder in Italy. In the 1980s he was implicated in several shootings in Yugoslavia, but was never charged, allegedly because of his connections with the communist secret service, for which he is also said to have been a hitman. In 1991 he formed the Serbian National Guard (SNG) or Tigers, a paramilitary group which has fought alongside local Serb forces in the Bosnian and Croatian civil wars. He has been accused of murdering hundreds of civilians. Particularly active in the government-sponsored 'serbianization' campaign in the Kosovo region, which has an Albanian majority, he was elected to the Serbian parliament with the support of Kosovan Serbs in 1992. He formed the Serbian Unity Party (SSJ) in September 1993.

RC *See* COMMUNIST REFOUNDATION PARTY.

RDD *See* RUSSIAN DEMOCRATIC MOVEMENT.

RDE *See* EUROPEAN DEMOCRATIC ALLIANCE.

RDP *See* RADICAL DEMOCRATIC PARTY (Bulgaria).

RdR *See* MOVEMENT FOR THE REPUBLIC.

Real Politics Union [Unia Polityki Realnej] (UPR) Polish political party. Founded in 1987 and registered as a party in 1989, the UPR is a right-wing populist formation advocating radical free-market policies. At the September 1993 election it gained 3.2% of the vote but no seats, having failed to obtain the 5% required for representation. It joined the Eleventh of November Alliance in December 1993. The leader is Janusz Korwin-Mikke.

realignment (European Union) *See* EXCHANGE RATE MECHANISM.

recommendation In the European Union (EU), a non-binding decision by the Council of Ministers or the Commission. A 'recommendation' usually expresses a view on an aspect of policy for which binding decisions (such as 'directives' and 'regulations') have not yet been agreed. Member states usually abide by them.

recommunization In the former communist countries, the perceived preferment of public officials and others closely associated with the previous communist regimes in the civil service, armed forces, media etc. Allegations that 'recommunization' is taking place are most often heard in those countries where post-communist parties have regained power (e.g. Hungary, Lithuania and Poland), or where many senior and middle-ranking officials were not replaced after the 1989 upheavals (e.g. Romania). In most countries low-ranking public officials retained their posts but switched their allegiance to new political parties and interest groups. *See also* DECOMMUNIZATION *and* SCREENING.

red In most countries, the colour associated with left-wing political parties, ranging from social democrats to hard-line communists. Red as a symbol of the left and revolution has its roots in the Jacobin tradition of the French Revolution, and it has been explicitly associated with socialism and communism since the 1840s.

Red Army Faction [Rote Armee Fraktion] (RAF) German guerrilla group. The RAF has its roots in the far-left students' movement of the late 1960s. Its aims are to destroy 'western capitalism' by violent action and thus to bring about a worldwide 'marxist revolution'. To this end it has carried out arson attacks, bombings, armed robberies, kidnappings and assassinations since 1968; it has been responsible for more than 30 deaths. Its primary targets have been military facilities (including American bases in Germany), army and police officers and leading business and political figures. It kidnapped and murdered the president of the Confederation of German Employers' Associations (BDA), Hanns-Martin Schleyer, in 1977; bombed the airforce headquarters of the North Atlantic Treaty Organization (NATO) in Ramstein in 1981; killed the head of the Deutsche Bank, Alfred Herrenhausen, in November 1989; launched an attack on the US embassy in Bonn in January 1991; and killed Detlev Rohwedder, the head of the Trust Agency (Treuhandanstalt), the organization in charge of the privatization of East German industry after reunification, in April 1991. In the 1970s the RAF was commonly known as the Baader-Meinhof Group, after its two most prominent leaders at the time, Andreas Baader and Ulrike Meinhof. Arrested in 1976 and

1972 respectively, they committed suicide in prison in 1977 and 1976. At this time the RAF was known to have extensive links with similar groups active in other countries, such as the Red Brigades in Italy and Direct Action in France, and with Palestinian guerrilla groups. After the collapse of communist rule in East Germany in 1989 it was revealed that the regime had trained and sheltered RAF members since the late 1970s. Several former activists living in East Germany were subsequently arrested.

red belt [ceinture rouge] In France, a traditional stronghold of the French Communist Party (PCF) in the working-class suburbs of Paris, the national capital. Although this support base was much eroded in the 1970s and 80s, it remains sufficiently solid for the PCF to win more parliamentary seats under France's single-member constituency electoral system than parties with more substantial but more thinly spread popular support.

red belt [cintura rossa] In Italy, a traditional stronghold of the Italian Communist Party (PCI) and now of its two successors, the Democratic Left Party (PDS) and Communist Refoundation Party (RC). It comprises the central regions of Emilia-Romagna, Marches, Tuscany and Umbria. The strength of support for communist and left-wing parties in the 'red belt' is not so much based on socio-economic factors – the regions are among Italy's most affluent – as on a combination of traditions of anticlericalism (most of the area belonged to the Papal States until Italian unification in the mid 19th century), local autonomy and civic action and the prominent role played by the PCI in the resistance movement during the Second World War (1939–45).

red-black coalition [rotschwarze Koalition] In Germany, a coalition between the Social Democratic Party (SPD) and Christian Democratic Union (CDU), the two largest parties. Such coalitions have been formed at state level on several occasions, and a 'black-red' coalition (with the CDU as the senior partner) held power at federal level from 1966–69. They are also called 'grand coalitions'.

501

Red Brigades [Brigate Rosse] Italian guerrilla group and a common name for a number of its offshoots. The far-left Red Brigades were responsible for a series of murders of police officers, judges, politicians and businesspeople – people it considered 'enemies of the working class' – in the 1970s. Their aim was to undermine the Italian state and spark a marxist revolution. The group's most spectacular act was the kidnapping of a former prime minister, Aldo Moro, in March 1978 and his murder two months later. By 1983 most of its members had been arrested and convicted and the organization appeared to be broken. Several Red Brigades offshoots have emerged since the mid 1980s to claim responsibility for a number of bombings and murders. Thus the Union of Fighting Communists [Unione dei Comunisti Combattenti] (UCC) murdered an airforce general, Licio Giorgeri, in March 1987. The Fighting Communist Party [Partito Comunista Combattente] (PCC) murdered a leading member of the then ruling Christian Democratic Party (DC), Roberto Ruffili, in April 1988. And the Fighting Communist Nuclei [Nuclei Comunisti Combattenti] (NCC) bombed premises belonging to the national employers' association in October 1992.

red-green coalition [rotgrüne Koalition] In Germany, a coalition between the Social Democratic Party (SPD) and the Greens. The first such coalition was formed in the state of Hesse in 1985.

Red Hand Commando British guerrilla group. The Red Hand Commando is the smallest of the groups claiming to defend the interests of the majority Protestant community in Northern Ireland and its wish to remain part of the United Kingdom. It has been responsible for the deaths of members of the rival Irish Republican Army (IRA) as well as Catholic civilians. The group's name is taken from the Red Hand of Ulster, a traditional symbol of the province's Protestants.

red-yellow coalition [rotgelbe Koalition] In Germany, a centre-left coalition between the Social Democratic Party (SPD) and the Free Democratic Party (FDP). The two parties shared power at the federal level from 1969–82. Red-yellow coalitions have been formed in several states since then.

Redondo, Nicolás (1927–) Spanish metalworker and trade-union official. During the Franco regime (1939–75) he was active in the then proscribed General Workers' Union (UGT) and Spanish Socialist Workers' Party (PSOE). He was elected leader of the UGT in April 1976. He was also elected to parliament for the PSOE in 1977, but resigned his seat in 1987 in protest against the PSOE government's economic policies. He retired as UGT leader in April 1994.

Redwood, John (1951–) British banker and politician. He worked as an investment adviser for the Rothschild merchant bank until his election to Parliament for the Conservative Party in 1987. He held several junior ministerial posts from 1989, and, although not a Welshman, was appointed secretary of state for Wales in May 1993.

referendum In Switzerland, a popular vote on proposals for constitutional and major legislative changes. The key element in the country's system of semi-direct democracy, referendums are held at all levels of government, federal, cantonal and municipal. At the federal level, all amendments to the constitution, emergency legislation and proposals for the country to join international organizations (because they affect the long-standing policy of 'permanent neutrality') must be submitted to a referendum. Their adoption requires a 'double majority', i.e. the consent of a majority of voters and of the 26 cantons and half-cantons. In addition, laws passed by parliament have to be put to a referendum if requested by a petition of 50,000 voters (just over 1% of the electorate) or eight cantons or half-cantons within 90 days of their adoption. At the cantonal and municipal level, rules on referendums vary. In some cantons all legislation must be submitted to a popular vote. *See also* POPULAR INITIATIVE.

reflection group (European Union) *See* GROUP OF WISE PEOPLE.

502

Reform Forces of Macedonia - Liberal Party [Reformski Sili na Makedonija - Liberalna Partija] (RSM-LP) Macedonian political party. The party was originally the Macedonian branch of the Alliance of Reform Forces of Yugoslavia (SRSJ) set up in 1990 by the then federal prime minister, Ante Marković. Centre-left in orientation, it gained 19/120 seats at the December 1990 election in the republic. The leader is Stojan Andov.

Reform Movement (Lithuania) *See* HOMELAND UNION.

Reformational Political Federation [Reformatorische Politieke Federatie] (RPF) Dutch political party. Founded in 1975, the RPF is one of the country's three small Christian fundamentalist parties known as the 'small right'. At the May 1994 election it gained 1.8% of the vote and 3/150 seats. The leader is Leen van Dijke, the party president is H. Visser.

Reformed Political Association [Gereformeerd Politiek Verbond] (GPV) Dutch political party. Founded in 1948, the GPV is one of the country's three small Christian fundamentalist parties known as the 'small right'. At the May 1994 election it gained 1.3% of the vote and 2/150 seats. The leader is Gert Schutte, the party president is J. Blokland.

Regierender Bürgermeister ('governing mayor') Head of government in Berlin, a federal state of Germany. Since Berlin is a city state, its government structure combines the functions of a municipality and a state.

Regierungsbezirk (pl. -e) German administrative division, usually translated as 'administrative district'. In six of the larger states (Baden-Württemberg, Bavaria, Hesse, Lower Saxony, North Rhine - Westphalia and Rhineland-Palatinate) the administrative districts are subdivisions used for administrative and statistical purposes. They have no political significance.

Regierungschef ('head of government') Head of government or prime minister of Liechtenstein.

region [gewest (Dutch), région (French), pl. -en, -s] One of the two federal divisions of Belgium. Under the constitutional reforms agreed in principle in 1970 and finalized in July 1993, the country's new federal structure is based on overlapping geographical regions and language-based cultural communities. Each of the three regions – Brussels-Capital, Flanders and Wallonia – has a parliament elected for a five-year term and a government headed by a minister-president or president. They are responsible for a wide range of economic and social matters, including planning, housing, economic development, employment, energy, environment, public works, transport and foreign trade. The separately constituted communities are responsible for education, culture, language issues and a range of other matters.

region [région] French administrative division. Each of the 22 regions has a regional council [conseil régional] elected for a six-year term and headed by a president. They have responsibilities in the spheres of planning, economic development, transport, education and culture. Created in 1982 as part of a decentralization programme, the regions in many cases are broadly coextensive with historical regions. Direct elections for the assemblies were first held in 1986. *See also* DEPARTMENT.

region British administrative division. In Scotland outside the island areas, the nine regions are the first tier of local government. Each has a council elected for a four-year term and headed by a convener. The regional councils are primarily responsible for land-use planning, transport, education and social services. In recent years many of their powers have been transferred to bodies appointed by central government. A reorganization of the structure of regions and lower-level districts, under which single-tier or 'unitary' local authorities would be established, is under consideration.

region [réigiún, pl. réigiúin] Irish administrative division. The eight regions were set up at the beginning of 1994 to promote and coordinate public services provided by the national government and the local counties and county boroughs. Each has a council, with members drawn from the elected county and borough councils.

region Shorthand for AUTONOMOUS REGION, the first-tier administrative division in Italy.

region [região, pl. regiões] Portuguese administrative division. There are currently two regions, the archipelagos of the Azores and Madeira. Each has an assembly [assembleia] elected for a four-year term and a government [governo] headed by a president [presidente]. The regions enjoy extensive autonomy in local affairs. The establishment of a regional structure on the Portuguese mainland, replacing the 18 districts, is under consideration.

región histórica See HISTORICAL REGIONS.

Regional Development Fund and **Regional Fund** See EUROPEAN ....

regional league or **league** [lega regionale, pl. leghe regionali] In Italy, a regional party based in Lombardy, Veneto, Piedmont and other northern regions. Advocating regional autonomy, controls on immigration and other right-wing populist policies, the 'leagues' came to prominence in the late 1980s. They are now organized in the NORTHERN LEAGUE (Lega Nord).

regional party [partido regionalista] In Spain, a political party based in an autonomous community or region. All regional parties support greater autonomy for their region and most are centre-right in their economic policies and conservative on social issues. The most important are Convergence and Union (CiU) in Catalonia and the Basque Nationalist Party (EAJ/PNV), which have considerable influence at national level through their representation in parliament. Others are the Aragonese Regional Party (PAR), Navarre People's Union (UPN) and Valencian Union (UV). The more radical separatist parties of the Basque Country, Catalonia and Galicia are usually not included in this umbrella term.

regiones históricas See HISTORICAL REGIONS.

regulation In the European Union (EU), one of three binding legal instruments for implementing policy or decisions (the others being the 'directive' and the

'decision'). Adopted by the Council or in some cases the Commission, a 'regulation' is generally and directly applicable in all member states and is thus similar to a national law. Many aspects of the common policies on agriculture, external trade and fisheries are covered by regulations.

Rehn, Elisabeth (1935–) Finnish administrator and politician. She worked as an office manager from 1960. She was elected to parliament for the Swedish People's Party (SFP) in 1979 and was leader of its parliamentary group from 1987–90. She was appointed defence minister in June 1990. (She is the first woman in Europe to hold the defence portfolio, and the second in the world after the Sri Lankan prime minister Sirimavo Bandaranaike in the 1960s and 70s.) She came second in the January/February 1994 presidential election.

Reichstagsgebäude or **Reichstag** Former and future seat of the German parliament. The Reichstag building in Berlin was the seat of parliament, the Reichstag ('National Assembly'), until its suspension by the nazi regime in 1933. As part of the post-reunification decision to transfer the seat of government from Bonn to Berlin, it will in due course house the Bundestag, the lower house of parliament.

réigiún See REGION (Ireland).

Reino de España ('Kingdom of Spain') Official name of Spain.

reinserción See REINSERTION.

reinsertion [reinserción] In Spain, the policy by which prisoners convicted of terrorist offences who renounce violence are offered special privileges or reduced sentences and are gradually reintroduced or 'reinserted' into society. Introduced in the early 1990s, it is aimed primarily at members of the separatist Basque Homeland and Liberty (ETA). By the end of August 1994 25 of the around 600 ETA prisoners had renounced violence, and many more were reportedly considering doing so.

Reisch, Georg (1930–) Austrian civil servant, diplomat and politician. Trained as an agronomist, he worked for the agriculture ministry and then the foreign ministry in the 1950s and 60s. He was ambassador to Kenya from 1970–76, and Austria's permanent representative to the United Nations and other international organizations based in Geneva from 1983–88. In April 1988 he was appointed general secretary of the European Free Trade Association (EFTA).

REP *See* REPUBLICANS (Germany).

Repubblica del Nord *See* REPUBLIC OF THE NORTH.

republic [republika, pl. republike] Federal division of Yugoslavia. The two republics – Serbia and Montenegro – have their own constitutions, legislatures, presidents and governments. They have sovereignty over all matters which are not specified in the federal constitution.

Republic, the In the United Kingdom, a shorthand for the Republic of Ireland. It is often used to distinguish it from Northern Ireland, which is a component of the United Kingdom.

Republic of Cyprus [Kipriakí Dimokratía] Official name of Cyprus. The Republic is the internationally recognized state on the island. (The Turkish Republic of Northern Cyprus, TRNC, is only recognized by Turkey.)

Republic of Kosovo [Republika e Kosovës] State proclaimed in the KOSOVO-METOHIJA or Kosovo province of Serbia, a constituent republic of Yugoslavia, by representatives of the majority Albanian community. When the Serbian authorities suspended the provincial assembly in July 1990 as part of their policy of 'serbianization', its Albanian members organized a campaign of non-violent resistance and began to organize an alternative political structure inside as well as outside the province. In September 1991 a referendum on sovereignty organized among the Albanian community, which outnumbers the Serb population by an estimated 6-to-1, was approved virtually unanimously. The following month a provisional government headed by Bujar Bukoshi was formed in exile in Germany. (It has been recognized by Albania.) The Republic of Kosovo was proclaimed in December. In May 1992 the Democratic League of Kosovo (LDK) gained 96/130 seats in the election for a 'constituent assembly' and LDK leader Ibrahim Rugova was elected president of the republic. The unofficial government called for 'passive resistance' to the Serb authorities and set up a system of 'parallel' public services. It is also thought to have organized a 40,000-strong paramilitary force.

Republic of Serbian Krajina [Republika Srpska Krajina] (RSK) State proclaimed within Croatia by the local Serb community. The RSK was formed in December 1991 by the merger of two breakaway autonomous regions in the historical KRAJINA region, Krajina proper in the southwest and Western Slavonia in the centre; the eastern region of Slavonia, Baranja and Western Srem joined in April 1992. The three units, which do not have a common border, cover nearly a third of Croatian territory and have a combined population of around 400,000. The RSK's borders were in effect demarcated by the establishment of the Serb-populated United Nations Protected Areas (UNPAs) in January 1992 in the context of the ceasefire that ended the six-month civil war precipitated by Croatia's declaration of independence. The RSK has an 84-member assembly and an executive council, based in Knin, and a 40–50,000-strong army. The main party is the Serbian Democratic Party of Krajina (SDSK), whose declared aim is unification with Serbia. The president is Milan Martić. In September 1992 the assemblies of the RSK and the Serbian Republic (SR), its counterpart across the border in Bosnia-Herzegovina, approved plans for close political and economic cooperation between the two republics. *See also* CROATIAN CIVIL WAR.

Republic of Skopje or **Skopje** Name for Macedonia used in Greece since the region's establishment as a Yugoslav republic in 1944. Greece objects to the use of 'Macedonia' on the grounds that it implies a territorial claim on the northern Greek region of the same name. *See* MACEDONIA NAME QUESTION.

Republic of the North [Repubblica del Nord] Slogan used by the Northern League (Lega Nord) and other regional groupings advocating the transformation of Italy into a federal state. The League nominally calls for the establishment of three semi-independent republics in the north, centre and south. (Its more pragmatic objective is wide-ranging autonomy for the country's existing 20 regions.) The northern republic has also been dubbed 'Padania', after the Po river valley that dominates the region.

Republican Assembly *See* RALLY FOR THE REPUBLIC.

Republican Left of Catalonia [Esquerra Republicana de Catalunya (Catalan)] (ERC) Spanish political party. The ERC was founded in 1931, banned during the Franco regime (1939–75) and relegalized in 1977. Active in Catalonia, it advocates full independence for the region within the European Union (EU), is left-wing in its economic policies, and has liberal views on social issues. It gained 8.0% of the vote and 11/135 seats at the regional election in March 1992, and one seat (out of 350) at the general election in June 1993. The leader is Angel Colom, the party president is Heribert Barrera.

Republican Party [Tjóðveldisflokkurin] (Tvfl) Faroese political party. Founded in 1948, the Republican Party advocates full independence for the Faroes from Denmark. It has participated in several coalition governments, most recently in 1985–90 and from April 1993 – September 1994. At the July 1994 election it gained 4/32 seats. The leader is Finnbogi Ísakson.

Republican Party [Parti Républicain] (PR) French political party. The PR was formed in 1977 from the National Federation of Republican Independents (FNRI) and several other groups which had supported Valéry Giscard d'Estaing's election to the presidency in 1974. Centre-right in orientation, it has been the largest member of the UNION FOR FRENCH DEMOCRACY (UDF) alliance since its foundation in 1978 and has fought successive general elections under its banner. At the March 1993 election it gained 104/577 seats. The leader is Gérard Longuet; François Léotard, the previous leader and now honorary chairman, remains influential.

Republican Party (Ireland) *See* FIANNA FÁIL.

Republican Party of Albania [Partia Republikana të Shqipërisë] (PRSh) Albanian political party. Founded in 1991, the PRSh is a centre-right party with support among the small urban middle class. At the March 1992 election it gained 3.1% of the vote and one seat (out of 140). The leader is Sabri Godo.

Republican People's Party [Cumhuriyet Halk Partisi] (CHP) Turkish political party. The original CHP was founded in 1923 by Kemal Atatürk, the first president of the Republic of Turkey. It was the country's dominant modernizing and secularizing force and sole political party until 1946. It became a mainstream left-wing party in the 1970s. Disbanded after the military coup in 1980, the party was relaunched in 1992. It gained seats in parliament when 21 deputies from the Social Democratic People's Party (SHP) decided to join it. The leader is Deniz Baykal.

Republican Rally *See* RALLY FOR THE REPUBLIC.

Republican Security Companies [Compagnies Républicaines de Sécurité] (CRS) French paramilitary police force. The CRS is a branch of the national police force and directly answerable to the interior minister. It is used as a rapid-intervention force to quell civil disorder.

Republican Turkish Party [Cumhuriyetçi Türk Partisi] (CTP) Northern Cypriot political party. Founded in 1970, the CTP is a centre-left party. It favours a federal solution to the division of Cyprus between Greek and Turkish communities (*see* CYPRUS QUESTION). It boycotted parliament from 1991–93 in protest against the provisions of a new electoral law. At the December 1993 election it gained 24.2% of the vote and 13/50 seats. It then joined a coalition with the Democratic Party (DP). The leader is Özker Özgür.

republicanism In Northern Ireland (United Kingdom), an alternative term for NATIONALISM, support for the territory's unification with the Republic of Ireland. The term 'republican' is usually reserved for those who reject the legitimacy of

REPUBLICANS — RESOLUTION 781

British rule in Northern Ireland and have supported or tolerated political violence to end it. The main republican party is Sinn Féin, which has close links with the Irish Republican Army (IRA).

Republicans (Czech Republic) *See* ASSO-CIATION FOR THE REPUBLIC - REPUBLICAN PARTY OF CZECHOSLOVAKIA.

Republicans [Die Republikaner] (REP) German political party. Founded in 1983 by right-wing members of the Christian Social Union (CSU), the Republicans are a far-right party with a strongly national-istic and anti-immigration platform. At the all-German election in December 1990 it gained 2.1% of the vote (2.3% in the west and 1.3% in the east) but, having failed to pass the 5% threshold for repre-sentation, no seats. Since then it has established itself as the most popular of the new far-right parties, gaining seats in regional and local elections in several states, notably Bavaria and Baden-Würt-temberg. Most of its support comes from first-time voters and the over-60s age group. The leader is Franz Schönhuber.

Republik Österreich ('Republic of Aus-tria') Official name of Austria in German.

Republika e Shqipërisë ('Republic of Alba-nia') Official name of Albania. Shqipëria is the native name for the country.

Republika Hrvatska ('Republic of Croatia') Official name of Croatia.

Republikaner *See* REPUBLICANS (Germany).

Republikány *See* ASSOCIATION FOR THE REPUBLIC - REPUBLICAN PARTY OF CZECHOSLOVAKIA.

Resistance [Resistenza (Corsican)] (R) French guerrilla group. Resistance is one of the separatist movements in Corsica opposed to the island's 'colonization' by France. It is a breakaway from the CORSICAN NATIONAL LIBERATION FRONT (FLNC).

Resistenza *See* RESISTANCE.

Resolution 713 Decision of the United Nations Security Council calling for an ARMS EMBARGO on Yugoslavia, i.e. the six-republic federation before its disinte-gration. It was adopted on 25 September 1991, during the civil war precipitated by the Croatian and Slovenian declarations of independence.

Resolution 716 Decision of the United Nations Security Council outlining its position on ending the effective division of Cyprus into Greek Cypriot and Turkish Cypriot states (*see* CYPRUS QUESTION). Adopted on 11 October 1991, Resolution 716 essentially reaffirms and refines earlier resolutions on the issue. It states that the 'fundamental principles' of a Cyprus settlement are 'the sovereignty, independence, territorial integrity and non-alignment of the Republic of Cyprus; the exclusion of union in whole or in part with any other country and any form of partition or secession; and the establish-ment of a new constitutional arrangement for Cyprus that would ensure the well-being and security of the Greek Cypriot and Turkish Cypriot communities in a bicommunal and bizonal federation'. It also states that this position is based on 'one State of Cyprus comprising two politically equal communities'. It also endorses UN-sponsored talks between the two sides in Cyprus and Greece and Turkey 'to complete the set of ideas on an overall framework agreement'. It has provided the basis for negotiations on a 'set of ideas' put forward by the UN secretary-general, Boutros Boutros-Ghali, in April 1992.

Resolution 757 Decision of the United Nations Security Council imposing comprehensive sanctions on 'Serbia and Montenegro', i.e. rump Yugoslavia, for supporting the breakaway Serb republics in the Croatian and Bosnian civil wars. Approved on 30 May 1992, it obliges all UN members to sever trade links, freeze Yugoslav government assets in their countries, impose an oil embargo, cut air links, and ban all sporting and cultural contacts.

Resolution 781 Decision of the United Nations Security Council declaring a ban on military flights in the airspace over Bosnia-Herzegovina and calling on the United Nations Protection Force (UN-PROFOR) to monitor compliance with it. Adopted on 9 October 1992, it was intended as part of the international effort to end the Bosnian civil war. *See* AIR-EXCLUSION ZONE.

Resolution 824 Decision of the United Nations Security Council placing six mainly Muslim cities and towns in Bosnia-Herzegovina under UN protection, calling on local Serb forces to cease attacking them, and authorizing UN military observers to monitor their security. Adopted on 6 May 1993, it was intended as part of the international effort to end the Bosnian civil war. *See* SAFE AREA.

Rete *See* NETWORK.

retornados ('returnees') In Portugal, a collective name for settlers in Africa who returned to Portugal when the colonies became independent in the mid 1970s. Most *retornados* were from Angola and Mozambique. Many had been born there and had not previously set foot in Portugal. They numbered around 700,000, equivalent to 7% of the total population, and their integration posed major economic and social problems at the time.

Revenue Guard [Guardia di Finanza] (GdF) Italian paramilitary police force. Numbering 64,100, the GdF is responsible for investigating crimes involving tax evasion, customs violations, fraud, corruption etc. It is a branch of the armed forces but is answerable to the finance minister. Its activities overlap to some extent with those of the main paramilitary force, the Corps of Carabinieri. In July 1994 senior GdF officials were accused of accepting bribes from businesses under investigation for tax evasion and fraud (*see* ITALIAN CORRUPTION SCANDALS).

Reviglio, Franco (1935–) Italian economist and politician. He lectured in finance at Turin University until his election to parliament for the Italian Socialist Party (PSI) in 1979. He was immediately appointed minister of finance, a post he held until 1981. He was managing director of the state energy holding company ENI from 1983–89. He returned to government in 1992 as minister for the budget, planning and the Mezzogiorno (= southern regions). He was appointed finance minister in February 1993, but resigned the following month after being accused of directing ENI funds to political parties.

Revolution [Iraultza (Basque)] Spanish guerrilla group. Iraultza advocates the creation of an independent, marxist state in the Basque Country and an end to foreign investment in the region. Since 1982 it has carried out a series of bombings intended to cause damage to property. Its main targets have been local, American and French banks and business interests.

Revolutionary Anti-Racist Action [Revolutionaire Antiracistische Actie] (RARA or RaRa) Dutch guerrilla group. Since 1985 the far-left RARA has carried out around 30 arson attacks and bombings against the property of organizations it considers guilty of racial discrimination. It has concentrated on public buildings, to protest against the government's 'criminal' policy on asylum seekers, and, in the past, on premises of Shell and other companies with links to apartheid South Africa. In 1992 the group announced it would broaden its range of targets.

Revolutionary Left [Devrimci Sol] (Dev-Sol) Turkish guerrilla group. An offshoot of the far-left Revolutionary Youth (Dev Genç), Dev-Sol espouses a marxist ideology, seeking 'to unify the proletariat to stage a national revolution', and is also strongly nationalist, opposing Turkish membership of the North Atlantic Treaty Organization (NATO) and the US military presence in the country. From the late 1970s it carried out a number of attacks on government, NATO and US targets. Most of its members were either killed or arrested in the early 1980s. A seven-year mass trial of 723 Dev-Sol members ended in 1989 with death sentences for seven leaders and long prison sentences for most others. The group resurfaced in the late 1980s. It concentrates its attacks on 'local and foreign representatives who serve the imperialists and their political, economic and military bases', in particular serving and retired police and military officers, government officials, and American military personnel, diplomats and businesspeople. In both 1991 and 1992 it claimed responsibility for nearly 30 assassinations; many of its members were also killed in confrontations with the security forces.

Revolutionary People's Struggle
[Epanastatikó Laïkó Agónas] (ELA)
Greek guerrilla group. Opposed to
capitalism, Greek membership of the
North Atlantic Treaty Organization
(NATO) and the European Union (EU),
ELA has taken responsibility for a series
of bombings of government and economic targets since its emergence in 1976.
Intended to be symbolic, the attacks
generally cause material damage but no
casualties. The organization is thought to
have close links with the Seventeenth of
November Revolutionary Organization,
another guerrilla group, and appears to
have absorbed the First of May group
active in the 1980s.

Rexrodt, Günter (1941–) German economist and politician. He worked in private
business and at a bank before joining the
Berlin Chamber of Commerce. A member
of the centrist Free Democratic Party
(FDP), he was finance senator (= minister)
in the Berlin state government from
1985–89. He then joined the board of
Citibank in Frankfurt and later became its
chairman. In 1991 he became an executive
director of the Treuhandanstalt, the
agency responsible for the privatization
of state assets in former East Germany. In
January 1993 he was appointed economy
minister in the federal government.

Reykjavík Shorthand for the Icelandic
government. Reykjavík is the capital of
Iceland.

Reynolds, Albert (1932–) Irish businessman and politician. In the 1960s and 70s
he was owner and managing director of
a petfood company and a chain of leisure
centres. Elected to parliament for the
centre-right Fianna Fáil in 1977, he has
held the ministerial portfolios of posts
and transport (1979–82), industry and
commerce (1987–88) and finance (1988–
91). He was dismissed in November 1991
for tabling a no-confidence motion in the
prime minister, Charles Haughey. The
following February he was elected to
succeed Haughey as leader and prime
minister. In January 1993 he formed a
centrist coalition with the Labour Party.

RG *See* GENERAL INFORMATION BRANCH.

Rhaetians and **Rhaetoromans** *See*
ROMANSH.

Rheinland-Pfalz *See* RHINELAND-
PALATINATE.

Rhine Commission Shorthand for the
INTERNATIONAL COMMISSION FOR THE
PROTECTION OF THE RHINE AGAINST
POLLUTION.

Rhineland-Palatinate [Rheinland-Pfalz]
Federal state [Land] of Germany. Situated
in the southwest, Rhineland-Palatinate
has an area of 19,849 sq km and a population of 3,881,000. The capital is Mainz,
and the other major cities are Ludwigs-
hafen, Koblenz, Kaiserslautern and Trier.
The economy is based on manufacturing
(engineering, chemicals, footwear),
agriculture (wine, cereals) and tourism.
Traditionally agricultural and poor, the
state has become increasingly industrialized since 1945. Political power is exercised by the State Assembly [Landtag],
with 101 members elected for a four-year
term, and a government headed by a
minister-president. The main parties are
the Social Democratic Party (SPD), the
Christian Democratic Union (CDU), the
centrist Free Democratic Party (FDP) and
the Greens. At the April 1991 election
the SPD gained 44.8% of the vote and 47
seats, the CDU 38.7% and 40 seats, the
FDP 6.9% and seven seats, and the Greens
6.4% and seven seats. The government
is formed by an SPD-FDP coalition
headed by Rudolf Scharping. The state
was formed in 1946 from the Rhenish
Palatinate (part of Bavaria) and parts of
Hesse, Hesse-Nassau, Oldenburg and the
Rhine province of Prussia.

Rhône-Alpes Region of France. Situated
in the southeast, Rhône-Alpes is the
country's second-largest region, with an
area of 43,698 sq km and a population of
5,441,000. The capital is Lyon, France's
second city, and the other main cities are
Grenoble, Saint-Étienne and Valence.
The economy is based on manufacturing
(engineering, electronics, machinery,
chemicals, food processing, textiles),
agriculture, tourism and services.

Ribas Reig, Oscar (1935–) Andorran lawyer and politician. He worked in business
and banking before entering politics. The

509

effective leader of the country's reformist groups (in the absence of a formal party structure), he became the country's first representative head of government in January 1982. He resigned in 1984 after conservatives blocked proposals for constitutional and political reform. He returned as prime minister in 1990 but left office again, for the same reasons as before, in January 1992. He was reelected in May after a general election brought victory for his supporters. After the promulgation in May 1993 of a constitution which established Andorra as a fully sovereign country and, among other reforms, legalized political parties, he also became leader of the centre-right National Democratic Association (AND). He formed a new centre-right government in February 1994.

Rifkind, Malcolm (1946–) British lawyer and politician. Elected to Parliament for the Conservative Party in 1974, he held several junior ministerial posts from 1979. He was secretary of state for Scotland from 1986–90 and then became minister for transport. In April 1992 he was appointed defence secretary.

Rifondazione Comunista *See* COMMUNIST REFOUNDATION PARTY.

Rīga Shorthand for the Latvian government. Rīga is the capital of Latvia.

rigsombudsmand *See* RÍKISUMBOÐSMAÐUR.

Riigikogu *See* NATIONAL ASSEMBLY (Estonia).

ríkisumboðsmaður Senior officer of state of the Faroe Islands, usually translated as 'high commissioner' or 'chief administrator'. The representative of the Danish crown and government, s/he advises the Faroese parliament and government and is responsible for defence, foreign affairs and other matters not delegated to the territory.

Riksdag Swedish name for the EDUSKUNTA, the Finnish parliament. Swedish is Finland's second official language.

Riksdag Parliament of Sweden. It has 349 members elected for a three-year term, 310 by proportional representation in 28 multi-member constituencies and 39 seats allocated to achieve a nationally proportional result. Parties must gain at least 4% of the popular vote to qualify for representation.

Riksmål *See* BOKMÅL.

Rioja [La Rioja] Autonomous community or region of Spain. Situated in the north, Rioja is Spain's smallest region, with an area of 5,034 sq km and a population of 260,000. The capital is Logroño. The economy is based on agriculture (wine, fruit and vegetables) and some light industry (food processing). The main political parties are the Spanish Socialist Workers' Party (PSOE), the centre-right People's Party (PP) and the Rioja Progressive Party (PRP). At the election in May 1991 the PSOE gained 16 seats in the 33-member legislature, the PP 15 and the PRP two. Historically part of Old Castile, the province of Rioja was made into a separate autonomous region in 1982 in recognition of its geographical separation from the Castilian heartland and of its distinctive economic and social structure.

Ripa di Meana, Carlo (1929–) Italian journalist, publisher and politician. He worked on and edited several left-wing publications in the 1950s, worked in publishing in the 1960s, and held several senior posts in the Italian Socialist Party (PSI) and served as a regional councillor in Lombardy in the 1970s. He was appointed a commissioner of the European Community (EC) in 1985, taking responsibility for culture and tourism (1985–88) and then environment (1989–92). In 1992 he returned to domestic politics as environment minister. He resigned from the government and the PSI in March 1993 in protest against political corruption and joined the Greens (Verdi), becoming their national spokesman. He was elected to the European Parliament in June 1994.

RIR *See* ROYAL IRISH REGIMENT.

Ritter, Michael (1957–) Liechtenstein lawyer, civil servant and politician. A specialist in international law, he joined the government's legal staff in 1984. From 1986–89 he chaired the Advice and Complaints Office, which examines citizens' complaints of maladministration. A member of the centre-right Fatherland Union (VU), he was appointed minister for the economy, welfare, health and family issues in December 1993.

Ritzen, Jo (1945–) Dutch educationalist, economist, academic and politician. He lectured in education economics and public-sector economics in the 1970s and 80s and advised the government on employment policy in the 1980s. A member of the Labour Party (PvdA), he was appointed minister of education and science in November 1989. In August 1994 he was also given the culture portfolio.

rivoluzione quieta *See* QUIET REVOLUTION.

RKP *See* SWEDISH PEOPLE'S PARTY.

RMDSz *See* HUNGARIAN DEMOCRATIC UNION OF ROMANIA.

RN Abbreviation for Royal Navy, the British navy.

RO Abbreviation for Romania, used for international vehicle registrations, postal addresses etc.

Robinson, Mary (1944–) Irish lawyer and politician. A prominent civil-rights lawyer and campaigner on social issues (such as the rights of illegitimate children and homosexuals and the right to obtain information on abortion), she twice stood unsuccessfully for the Labour Party in parliamentary elections. She left the party in 1985 over its support for the Anglo-Irish Agreement on Northern Ireland, which she felt took insufficient account of the views of the Protestant community in the province. Standing as an independent and supported by the Labour Party and the Workers' Party, she was elected president of the republic (a non-executive post) in November 1990.

ROC Abbreviation for Republic of Cyprus, the official name of the internationally recognized state on the island. (The Turkish Republic of Northern Cyprus, TRNC, is only recognized by Turkey.)

Rocard, Michel (1930–) French civil servant and politician. He was secretary of the Socialist Students' Association (AÉS) from 1953–55 and became an inspector of finance in 1958. He led the small Unified Socialist Party (PSU) from 1967 until its merger with the Socialist Party (PS) in 1973. When the PS gained power in 1981 he became minister for

planning and then agriculture (1983–85). He resigned over the introduction of proportional representation. President Mitterrand appointed him prime minister in 1988 and he formed a centre-left government. He was replaced in 1991 after the government had failed to secure parliamentary majorities for several major bills and amid growing disunity within the PS. He became party leader after its heavy defeat in the March 1993 general election, but resigned in June 1994 after a disappointing performance in the European elections. He himself was elected to the European Parliament.

Rock, the Informal name for Gibraltar. It refers to the ridge which is the dominant physical feature of the Gibraltar peninsula.

Rockall question Border dispute between the United Kingdom, Denmark (representing the Faroe Islands), Iceland and Ireland. Rockall is an uninhabited small island in the North Atlantic Ocean, 380 km west of Scotland, 400 km northwest of the Faroe Islands, 560 km southwest of the Faroe Islands and 720 km south of Iceland. It was annexed by the United Kingdom in 1955, but the other countries also lay claim to it and surrounding sea and sea-bed, which are rich in fish and mineral resources. The dispute centres around whether Rockall is part of the continental shelf and whether it is an island or merely a rock or cliff. In international law both issues affect the rights to claim territorial and economic jurisdiction over the surrounding waters. Ireland and the United Kingdom signed a partial boundary agreement in 1988.

ROL Abbreviation for the LEU, the Romanian currency, used in banking etc.

Roldán affair Controversy in Spain surrounding Luis Roldán, a senior police officer accused of embezzlement, and his allegations of abuse of power and corruption against senior government ministers. Roldán headed the paramilitary Civil Guard [Guardia Civil] from 1986 until December 1993, when he was replaced as part of a restructuring of the organization, which had been tainted by corruption and incompetence. At this time media reports alleged that Roldán had amassed a personal fortune during his tenure by accepting kickbacks on government contracts and buying property with public funds meant for covert operations. (His personal wealth was estimated at around 400 million pesetas, 2.5 million ecus, while his nominal earnings over the seven years had amounted to around 50 million pesetas.) A parliamentary commission of inquiry was set up in March 1994. In April Roldán was summonsed in a separate judicial inquiry. When he failed to appear in court, a warrant for his arrest was issued on charges of misappropriation of public funds and tax evasion. His disappearance – he was believed to have fled abroad – prompted the resignation of the interior minister, Antoni Asunción, and the attorney-general, Eligio Hernández. In May José Luis Corcuera, interior minister from 1988–93 and as such Roldán's immediate superior, resigned his parliamentary seat. In June three deputy commanders of the Civil Guard and the commander and five high-ranking officials of the national police, all considered close to Roldán, were dismissed. In interviews and letters published in May and June Roldán alleged that the prime minister, Felipe González, had ordered secret investigations into political opponents, and that many government ministers had enriched themselves by diverting public funds. He also admitted he had profited from 'the system'. The political impact of the affair was heightened by its concurrence with another corruption affair involving a senior government appointee, the governor of the central bank (*see* RUBIO AFFAIR). In April and June parliament approved a series of anti-corruption measures, including greater powers for the independent auditors of public-sector accounts, the establishment of a special prosecutor's office, and tougher penalties for offenders.

Roma (sing. Rom) Ethnic group dispersed throughout Europe, more commonly known as GIPSIES. 'Roma' is the Gipsies' generic name for themselves. Together with 'Romanies' and 'Romany people' it is increasingly used by outsiders in preference to 'Gipsies' and its equivalents in other languages and other names considered derogatory.

Roman, Petre (1946–) Romanian engineer, academic and politician. A professor of fluid mechanics and head of the hydraulics department at Bucharest Polytechnic, he supported the National Salvation Front (FSN) which emerged during the revolution that overthrew the Ceauşescu regime in 1989. He was appointed prime minister, but resigned after anti-government demonstrations in September 1991. When the Front's majority wing broke away to form the Democratic National Salvation Front (FSND, now the Social Democracy Party, PDSR) in March 1992, he was confirmed as leader of the reformist FSN, now the Democratic Party (PD).

Roman Catholics or **Catholics** Religious and ethnic group in NORTHERN IRELAND, a component of the United Kingdom. The religious label is often used interchangeably with 'nationalists' and 'republicans'.

Romani *See* ROMANY *and* GIPSIES.

Romania [România] Country in southeastern Europe.

Official data. Name: Romania [România]; capital: Bucharest [Bucureşti]; form of government: presidential republic; head of state: president; head of government: prime minister; flag: three vertical stripes, blue, yellow and red; national holiday: 1 December (National Day); language: Romanian; religion: none; currency: leu (L) (pl. lei) = 100 bani; abbreviation: RO.

Geography. One of the Balkan countries, Romania has a total area of 237,500 sq km. It is bordered by Ukraine in the north, Moldavia or Moldova, Ukraine and the Black Sea in the east, Bulgaria in the south, and Yugoslavia and Hungary in the west. The Carpathian Mountains [Carpaţii] are the dominant physical feature, running sickle-shaped through the north, east and centre of the country. To the west of the mountains lie hill lands and low mountains (Transylvania), to the east hill lands and plains (Moldavia), to the southeast the Black Sea coastal plain (Dobruja), and to the south hill lands and river plains (Wallachia). Some 46% of the land is arable, another 19% is covered by pastures and 28% is forested. The main rivers are the Danube [Dunărea], Mureş and Prut. The climate is humid continental, with hot summers and cold winters; rainfall is moderate. Temperatures are lower and rainfall is heavier in the mountains.

Demography. Romania has a population of 22,789,000. Population density is 99 per sq km. Some 53% of the people live in urban areas. The main city is Bucharest (metropolitan population 2.3 million, city 2.1 million). Other major cities are Braşov, Constanţa, Timişoara, Cluj-Napoca, Iaşi, Galaţi, Craiova, Brăila, Ploieşti and Oradea. In ethnic terms 89.4% of the people are Romanians, 7.1% Hungarians, 1.8% Gipsies and 0.5% Germans; there are also small groups of Ukrainians, Armenians, Turks, Tatars, Serbs and others. The 1.62 million ethnic Hungarians live mainly in eastern and western Transylvania and form the majority in several districts. Gipsies are considerably underrepresented in official figures; they are thought to number around 750,000 (3.3% of the total population). Since 1990 most of the 200,000 ethnic Germans have emigrated to Germany. The majority of the population of neighbouring Moldavia is ethnically Romanian, and there is a substantial Romanian community in Ukraine. The main languages are Romanian and Hungarian. In religious terms most Romanians are nominally Romanian Orthodox and the Hungarians are either Roman Catholics or Protestants; there are also small groups of other Orthodox Christians, Muslims and 18,000 Jews.

Sociography. Romania scores 0.729 on the United Nations human development index (HDI), ranking 72nd in the world and 31st among 32 European countries. There are 16 doctors and 93 hospital beds for every 10,000 people. Education is compulsory between the ages of six and 16. There is one teacher for every 23 students, among the worst ratios in Europe. Enrolment is 75% at the secondary level and 11% at the tertiary level. The literacy rate is 95%. Real annual income per head (in terms of purchasing power) is around US$ 3,500, among the lowest in Europe.

Infrastructure and communications. Romania's transport and communications network is one of the least developed in Europe; the railways are particularly important for freight and passenger transport. There are 78,040 km of paved roads and 1.29 million passenger cars (56 per 1,000 people, among the lowest rates in Europe), 11,080 km of railways and 1,720 km of navigable waterways. The main ports are Constanţa, Sulina, Galaţi and Brăila. The main airport is at Bucharest (Otopeni), and there are 13 other airports with scheduled services. There are 36 daily newspapers, with a combined circulation of 3.12 million (134 per 1,000 people). There are 3.26 million radio receivers, around 4 million television sets and 3.02 million telephones in use (respectively 140, around 170 and 130 per 1,000 people).

Economic structure. The Romanian economy is based on manufacturing and agriculture. Although essentially developed and diversified, it is in need of major investment and restructuring, and has a relatively unproductive agricultural sector and inefficient distribution system. The gradual transition from a command to a market-based economy is causing severe dislocation and has led to steep falls in industrial and agricultural production as well as food and energy shortages. Between 1990 and 1993 GDP contracted by 33%, inflation averaged 137% per year, the currency lost 97% of its value, the current-account deficit averaged 4.1% of GDP per year, and unemployment rose to 10%. There were some signs of recovery in 1994.

Services contribute 32% of GDP, industry contributes 49% (manufacturing around 40%), and agriculture, forestry and fisheries 19%. Some 30% of the labour force is employed in manufacturing, 29% in farming, forestry and fishing, 15% in public services and 8% in trade. The main crops grown are cereals (maize, wheat, barley), sugarbeets, potatoes and oilseeds; horticulture (fruit and vegetables, esp. grapes, apples, plums), dairy farming (milk, eggs) and livestock raising (sheep, pigs, poultry, cattle) are also important agricultural activities. Forestry and fishing (incl. fish farming) are also important. The main mineral resources are lignite, coal, oil, iron, salt and methane gas. The main industries are textiles, food processing (incl. wine) and engineering; other important branches are wood processing, iron and steel and other metalworking, building materials (cement), oil refining and chemicals. Tourism is of regional importance (Black Sea coast). The main energy sources are domestic and imported fossil fuels and hydroelectric power; 17% of exports are required to cover net fuel imports. The main exports are industrial machinery (12% of the total), petrochemicals (11%), iron and steel (11%), chemicals (7%), furniture (7%) and textiles (6%). The main imports are fuels, machinery and transport equipment and basic manufactures. The main trading partners are: exports: Germany (13%), Russia (9%), Italy (8%), France (6%), Iran (6%), United Kingdom (6%), Austria (5%), United States; imports: Germany (11%), Russia (10%), Italy (6%), France (5%), United Kingdom, China; a third of all trade is with European Union (EU) countries.

The National Bank [Banca Naţională] is the central bank. There are several employers' organizations; the main labour organizations are the National Confederation of Free Trade Unions of Romania - Brotherhood (CNSLR-Frăţia), the Alpha Cartel (Alfa) and the National Trade Union Bloc (BNS).

Political structure. Romania is a republic on the basis of a constitution adopted in 1991, replacing the communist constitution of 1965. Executive power is shared between the president and the government. The president is directly elected for a five-year term. Barred from holding party office, s/he is the head of state and commander of the armed forces, appoints the prime minister and has extensive executive powers. The prime minister and the government are responsible for the administration of the country. Legislative power is vested in the bicameral Parliament of Romania [Parlamentul României], composed of the 341-member Assembly of Deputies [Adunarea Deputaţilor] and the 143-member Senate [Senat], both elected for four-year terms by systems of proportional representation (with a 3% threshold for gaining seats); 13 members of the Assembly are appointed by the president to represent the smaller ethnic minorities. All citizens over the age of 18 are entitled to vote. Judicial power is ultimately vested in the Supreme Court of Justice [Curtea Supremă de Justiţie]; the Constitutional Court [Curtea Constituţională] adjudicates on constitutional matters. Administratively the country is divided into 41 counties [judeţ, pl. -e], including the county-level city of Bucharest; the counties are subdivided into 260 towns and 2,705 communes; the historical regions of Moldavia, Transylvania, Wallachia and others have no administrative or political functions.

The main political parties are the Social Democracy Party of Romania (PDSR, the successor to the Democratic National Salvation Front, FSND, and the National Salvation Front, FSN), Democratic Party (PD, a successor to the National Salvation Front, FSN), Christian Democratic National Peasants' Party (PNT-CD), Romanian National Unity Party (PUNR), Hungarian Democratic Union (UDMR or RMDSz), Greater Romania Party (România Măre), Civic Alliance Party (PAC), Liberal Party 1993 (PL'93, formed from the merger of two wings of the National Liberal Party, PNL), Socialist Labour Party (PSM), Romanian Social Democratic Party (PSDR), Romanian Ecology Party (PER) and Agrarian Democratic Party (PDAR); the Democratic Convention of Romania (CDR) is an opposition alliance. At the general election in September 1992 the FSND gained 27.7% of the vote and 117/328 seats, the CDR 20.2% and 82 seats (PNT-CD 42, PAC 13, PNL 13, PSDR 10, PER 4), the FSN 10.2% and 43 seats, the PUNR 7.7% and 30 seats, the RMDSz 7.5% and 27 seats, România Măre 3.9% and 16 seats, the PSM 3.0% and 13 seats, and the

PDAR 3.0% and no seats. The government is formed by the left-wing PDSR and independents, with Nicolae Văcăroiu as prime minister. Other senior ministers are Teodor Viorel Meleşcanu (deputy prime minister, foreign affairs), Mircea Coşea (deputy prime minister, economic reform), Florin Georgescu (deputy prime minister, finance), Dan Mircea Popescu (deputy prime minister, employment and social security), Ioan Doru Tărăcilă (interior), Gheorghe Tinca (defence) and Iosif Gavril Chiuzbaian (justice). The head of state is President Ion Iliescu, who assumed power in December 1989 and was first elected in May 1990.

Security and international affiliations. The Romanian armed forces number 203,100 (army 161,000, navy 19,000, airforce 23,100). There are also two paramilitary forces, a 12,000-strong border guard and the 10,000-strong Gendarmerie. Military service is compulsory and consists of 12–18 months' basic training.

Romania is a member of the Black Sea Economic Cooperation Organization (BSECO), Conference on Security and Cooperation in Europe (CSCE) and Council of Europe, and works closely with the Visegrad Group; it is also a member of the United Nations and its specialized agencies.

History. During the 1st millennium BC the area of modern Romania was settled by the related Thracians and Getae, peoples tracing their origins to the Eurasian steppes. The Dacians, a westerly branch of the Getae, established a powerful unified state around 70 BC. The Romans conquered most of Dacia in 106 AD. Thriving in economic terms and culturally relatively advanced, the region attracted many Roman settlers and became extensively romanized. Military pressures forced the Romans to abandon Dacia and withdraw south of the Danube in 270. From then until the 13th century the region was overrun by a series of invaders from the north and east, including the Goths, Huns, Gepids, Avars, Slavs, Bulgars, Magyars, Pechenegs and Cumans. They exercised political control but the local romanized communities retained

their identity (many appear to have sought refuge in the Carpathian Mountains). The Slavs in particular, who settled in large numbers in the 6th and 7th centuries, were assimilated. The Romanians, who had become christianized in the 4th century, adopted Orthodox Christianity during the period of Bulgar domination in the 9th century. By the turn of the millennium the region was divided into a number of small feudal states: those in the northwest, modern Transylvania, were under Hungarian control and those in the south and east were under Pecheneg and then Cuman control until their state was destroyed by the Mongols in 1241. Romanian princes from Transylvania established the independent principalities of Wallachia in the south and Moldavia in the east in the late 13th and early 14th century respectively. Both states soon clashed with the Ottoman Turks. They were forced to recognize the suzerainty of the Ottoman Empire in 1417 and 1513 respectively, but, unlike conquered states to the south, retained considerable autonomy and continued to struggle against Turkish domination. Prince Michael of Wallachia (1593–1601) was able to unite the three Romanian states (Wallachia, Moldavia and Transylvania) briefly in 1600–01. Transylvania, ruled by a Hungarian nobility retaining considerable autonomy under Hungarian and Turkish suzerainty, came under Austrian Habsburg control in 1711. The Ottomans imposed semi-direct rule in Moldavia and Wallachia from 1711 and 1714 respectively, through appointed Greek governors from the influential Phanariote families. As Ottoman power waned, Russia occupied the two principalities in 1769, 1787–91 and 1828–34. In 1812 eastern Moldavia, called Bessarabia, and Bukovina to the north were ceded to Russia. A national Romanian uprising against the Phanariote regimes in 1821 was suppressed after Russian and Turkish intervention, but led to the restoration of native rule in both principalities.

Wallachia and Moldavia regained their independence following the Crimean War (1853–56). Unification was achieved in several stages: both states elected a single prince in 1859, declared their legal union in 1861 and secured international recognition of their independence in 1878. A constitution establishing parliamentary government was adopted in 1866. The Kingdom of Romania was proclaimed in 1881. Romania entered the First World War (1914–18) on the side of the Allies in 1916. Around 250,000 Romanian soldiers were killed during the fighting (this was a third of the total mobilized forces, in relative terms among the highest losses for any belligerent). The incorporation of all Romanian-majority regions was achieved when Bessarabia and Bukovina were ceded by Russia in 1918 and Transylvania by Hungary in 1920. The 1920s and 30s were dominated by the National Liberal Party (PNL) and National Peasants' Party (PNT). Democratic rule was marred by election rigging, royal interference, corruption and violence by the far-right Iron Guard (which became a potent force in the mid 1930s). In 1938 King Carol II established a personal dictatorship. In 1940 Romania was forced to cede two-fifths of its territory to its neighbours: Bessarabia and Bukovina to the Soviet Union and most of Transylvania to Hungary. Carol II abdicated and Ion Antonescu established a far-right military dictatorship. Romania entered the Second World War (1939–45) on the side of Germany in 1941. In 1944 Antonescu was deposed, King Michael took power and ended the alliance with Germany. This could not prevent the country's occupation by the Soviet army, however. Transylvania was restored to Romania in 1945.

In 1946 the national government was replaced by a left-wing coalition, and a communist-dominated alliance won the election that year. In 1947 all opposition parties were banned, the monarchy was abolished and a 'people's republic' was proclaimed. In 1948 the Romanian Communist Party (PCR) became the sole legal party. The new regime nationalized the economy, introduced central planning and became a firm ally of the Soviet Union. Under Nicolae Ceauşescu, who became the country's leader in 1965, it

pursued a more independent foreign policy in the 1970s and 80s and adopted increasingly repressive policies at home. Misguided economic policies depressed living standards in the 1980s. In the wake of the collapse of communist rule in neighbouring countries, Ceauşescu was overthrown and killed in a bloody revolution in December 1989. The National Salvation Front (FSN), dominated by former PCR members and led by Ion Iliescu, took power. The FSN won the multiparty election in May 1990 and Iliescu was confirmed as president. A new constitution was approved in December 1991. The FSN split in April 1992 over economic policy. After the September 1992 election the Democratic National Salvation Front (FSND), now the Social Democracy Party (PDSR), formed a minority administration supported informally by various left-wing and far-right nationalist parties. Growing dissatisfaction with the slow pace of reform and the deteriorating economic situation led to several major demonstrations and strikes in 1993 and 1994. Since 1990 there has been considerable tension between ethnic Romanians and Hungarians in Transylvania, straining relations between Romania and Hungary. Romania was admitted to the Council of Europe in November 1993.

See also entries on specific institutions, organizations, parties, people, terms etc.

România Măre *See* GREATER ROMANIA *or* GREATER ROMANIA PARTY.

Romanian Cradle *See* ROMANIAN HEARTH.

Romanian Ecology Party [Partidul Ecologist Român] (PER) Romanian political party. Founded in 1989, the PER contested the September 1992 election within the DEMOCRATIC CONVENTION (CDR) alliance, and gained 4/341 seats. The leader is Otto Weber.

Romanian Hearth [Vatră Românească] (VR) Romanian cultural and political organization. Romanian Hearth was set up in 1990 primarily to defend the rights of ethnic Romanians in Transylvania. Strongly nationalistic, it effectively seeks to restrict the social, cultural and political rights of the region's substantial Hungarian minority, which it accuses of wanting to reunite Transylvania with Hungary. It has close links with the Romanian National Unity Party (PUNR).

Romanian National Unity Party [Partidul Unităţii Naţionale Române] (PUNR) Romanian political party. The PUNR was founded in 1990 as the electoral wing of Romanian Hearth [Vatră Românească], the far-right nationalist organization mainly active in Transylvania (which has a substantial ethnic Hungarian community). At the September 1992 election the party gained 7.7% of the vote and 30/341 seats. The leader is Gheorghe Funar.

Romanian Social Democracy Party *See* SOCIAL DEMOCRACY PARTY OF ROMANIA.

Romanian Social Democratic Party [Partidul Social-Democrat Român] (PSDR) Romanian political party. The PSDR – not to be confused with the Social Democracy Party (PDSR) – was founded in 1893 and was one of the country's main parties in the 1920s and 30s. It was forced to merge with the Romanian Communist Party in 1948. It was relaunched after the collapse of the Ceauşescu regime in 1989. It contested the September 1992 election within the opposition DEMOCRATIC CONVENTION (CDR) alliance, and gained 10/341 seats. The leader is Sergiu Cunescu.

Romanies Alternative name for GIPSIES, an ethnic group dispersed throughout Europe. It is taken from Roma, the Gipsies' name for themselves. It is increasingly used in preference to 'Gipsies'.

Romansh Ethnic group in Switzerland, also known as Romantsch, Rumantsch, Rhaetians, Rhaetoromans etc. The Romansh live in the eastern canton of Grisons [Grischun in Romansh] and number around 40,000. Their language is related to Friulian and Ladin (both spoken further to the east in the Italian Alps) and Italian. It was recognized as Switzerland's fourth national language in 1938 and has official status in Grisons.

Romany [Romani] Language of the GIPSIES or Romanies, an ethnic group dispersed throughout Europe. Romany is derived from Sanskrit and related to the languages of northern India, the Gipsies' ancestral

home. It has a rich oral tradition but is rarely written down. It is usually divided into around 15 mutually intelligible regional dialects, which are differentiated according to features they have incorporated from the languages spoken in the areas where Gipsies have lived over the centuries. Most of Europe's estimated 5 million Gipsies speak Romany as well as the language of the country they live in. 'Romany' is also used as an alternative to 'Gipsy'.

Romany Parliament *See* EUROPEAN ....

Rome Shorthand for the Italian government. Rome is the capital of Italy.

Rome Declaration on Peace and Cooperation International agreement by the members of the North Atlantic Treaty Organization (NATO). Adopted at a summit meeting in Rome (Italy) on 8 November 1991, this declaration effectively amended the alliance's aims and objectives to take account of the transformation of the political and military situation in Europe since the end of the Cold War and the dissolution of the Warsaw Pact. It defined future tasks and policies in relation to the emerging Europe-wide security structures and the evolving 'partnership' with the former communist countries of Central and Eastern Europe. Specifically it: (i) reaffirms the consensus among the member states on the development of a 'European security identity' and defence role; (ii) invites the former communist countries to participate in a new forum, the North Atlantic Cooperation Council (NACC); (iii) extends to them NATO's expertise in political, military, economic and scientific consultation and cooperation; and (iv) reaffirms the NATO members' commitment to strengthening the role of the Conference on Security and Cooperation in Europe (CSCE) and makes specific suggestions for achieving this. It concludes by declaring that 'in a world where the values we uphold are shared ever more widely we gladly seize the opportunity to adapt our defences accordingly; to cooperate and consult with our new partners; to help consolidate a now undivided continent of Europe; and to make our Alliance's contribution to a new age of confidence, stability and peace'. *See also* STRATEGIC CONCEPT.

Rome Treaty *See* TREATY OF ROME.

Rönsch, Hannelore (1942–) German administrator and politician. Between 1960 and 1983 she worked at the Federal Criminal Investigation Office (BKA) and for a housing association. Elected to parliament for the Christian Democratic Union (CDU) in 1983, she was appointed minister for families and senior citizens in January 1991.

Rosenmöller, Paul (1956–) Dutch trade-union official and politician. Originally a far-left activist, he studied sociology before taking a manual job in the port of Rotterdam and becoming a trade-union representative. He was elected to parliament for the Green Left (Groen Links) in 1989 and became the party's leader in May 1994.

Rossem Belgian political party. Named after Jean-Pierre van Rossem, its founder and leader until October 1992, Rossem was founded in 1991 as a protest party. Describing itself as 'ultra-liberal', its aims include the privatization of the social-security system and the abolition of marriage. At the October 1991 election it gained 3.2% of the vote and 3/212 seats.

rotgelbe Koalition *See* RED-YELLOW COALITION.

rotgrüne Koalition *See* RED-GREEN COALITION.

rotschwarze Koalition *See* RED-BLACK COALITION.

rouble [rubla] Former currency of Estonia. *See* KROON.

rouble [rūblis] Former currency of Latvia. *See* LATS.

rouble [rublis] Former currency of Lithuania. *See* LITAS.

Roumania and **Roumanian** ... *See* ROMANIA *and* ROMANIAN ....

Royal Air Force (RAF) Formal name of the British airforce.

royal assent In the parliamentary monarchies (e.g. Belgium, Denmark, Luxemburg, Netherlands, Norway, Spain, Sweden and the United Kingdom), the signing into law by the monarch of an act passed by parliament. Since s/he has few

or no real powers under the constitution, this is almost invariably a formality. (A notable recent exception was King Baudouin of Belgium's refusal in 1990 to sign, on moral grounds, a law liberalizing abortion; he effectively abdicated for several days during which time the law was promulgated by parliament under another provision of the constitution.)

Royal Irish Regiment (RIR) British military force. A branch of the army, the RIR is involved in security work in Northern Ireland and in policing the border with Ireland. It was formed in July 1992 by the merger of the Royal Irish Rangers and the Ulster Defence Regiment (UDR). The latter had been set up in 1970 as a part-time locally recruited force to carry out security work in the region. Its role was controversial because its officers were almost exclusively drawn from the Protestant community, and it was accused of directing its efforts primarily at Catholic extremist groups (such as the Irish Republican Army, IRA) to the exclusion of Protestant groups.

royal prerogative or **crown prerogative** In the parliamentary monarchies (e.g. Belgium, Denmark, Luxemburg, Netherlands, Norway, Spain, Sweden and the United Kingdom), the powers and privileges invested in the monarch, the 'crown', now almost invariably exercised by the prime minister and government in his/her name. In some countries (e.g. Belgium, Netherlands) the monarch's only real power lies in the appointment of a prospective prime minister, while in Sweden s/he has no powers at all. In the United Kingdom the exercise of the royal prerogative is controversial, not because the king/queen has significant real powers but because it gives the government wide-ranging executive powers not subject to parliamentary scrutiny or approval. These include the declaration of war, ratification of international treaties and numerous appointments (ambassadors, judges, peers, bishops, members of public bodies etc). This situation has arisen in part because there is no written constitution and hence no formal separation of executive, legislative and judicial powers.

Royal Ulster Constabulary (RUC) British police force. The RUC is the police force of Northern Ireland. It had a paramilitary character until the 1970s, when it was reorganized along the lines of other police forces in the United Kingdom. Its role in maintaining law and order in the region is controversial because its officers are overwhelmingly drawn from the Protestant community, and it has often been accused of mistreating Catholic suspects and prisoners.

Royaume de Belgique ('Kingdom of Belgium') Official name of Belgium in French.

RP *See* WELFARE PARTY.

RPF *See* REFORMATIONAL POLITICAL FEDERATION.

RPR *See* RALLY FOR THE REPUBLIC.

RRC *See* ALLIED COMMAND EUROPE RAPID REACTION CORPS.

rreth (pl. -ët) Albanian administrative division, usually translated as 'district'. Each of the 26 *rrethët* is administered by a council elected for a three-year term.

RRF *See* ALLIED COMMAND EUROPE RAPID REACTION CORPS.

RSK *See* REPUBLIC OF SERBIAN KRAJINA.

RSM Abbreviation for San Marino, used for international vehicle registrations, postal addresses etc. It is taken from Repubblica di San Marino ('Republic of San Marino').

RSM-LP *See* REFORM FORCES OF MACEDONIA - LIBERAL PARTY.

Ruberti, Antonio (1927–) Italian civil engineer, academic and politician. He lectured in engineering at La Sapienza University in Rome until 1987. A member of the Italian Socialist Party (PSI), he was minister of research and higher education in 1988 and from 1989–92. He became a commissioner of the European Community (EC) in January 1993, taking responsibility for science, research and training.

Rubiks, Alfrēds (1935–) Latvian politician. An engineer by training, he held a series of senior posts in the Latvian Communist Party (LKP) from the 1960s. He was appointed mayor of Rīga, the capital, in 1984. When the party split in 1990, he was elected leader of the orthodox wing.

That year he was also elected to the central committee of the Soviet Communist Party. After the abortive Soviet coup in August 1991 – which enabled Latvia to regain its independence – he was charged with attempting to overthrow the legitimate government. Although under arrest, he was elected to parliament for the Equal Rights (Ravnopraviye) movement in June 1993.

Rubio affair Controversy in Spain surrounding Mariano Rubio, accused of abuse of power and tax evasion while serving as governor of the central bank. Rubio was governor of the Bank of Spain for two terms from 1984–92. In April 1994 the daily newspaper *El Mundo* alleged that while in office he had used privileged information to make gains on the stockmarket – a practice known as 'insider dealing' – and channelled the profits into a secret bank account. (Some aspects of the alleged misconduct were technically not illegal but widely considered unethical for a person in Rubio's position.) A parliamentary commission of inquiry was set up soon afterwards. In May he was detained on charges of fraud, misappropriation of public funds and tax evasion. This prompted Carlos Solchaga, economy and finance minister during most of Rubio's tenure and as such his immediate superior, to resign his current post as leader of the Spanish Socialist Workers' Party (PSOE) parliamentary group. The agriculture minister, Vicente Albero, also resigned after admitting he had been 'negligent' in not paying tax on income derived from investments handled by Ibercorp, the company which had also handled Rubio's investments. The political impact of the affair was heightened by its concurrence with another corruption affair involving a senior government appointee (*see* ROLDÁN AFFAIR). In April and June parliament approved a series of anti-corruption measures, including greater powers for the independent auditors of public-sector accounts, the establishment of a special prosecutor's office, and tougher penalties for offenders. *See also* IBERCORP AFFAIR.

rubla ('rouble') Former currency of Estonia. *See* KROON.

rūblis ('rouble') Former currency of Latvia. *See* LATS.

rublis ('rouble') Former currency of Lithuania. *See* LITAS.

RUC *See* ROYAL ULSTER CONSTABULARY.

Rugova, Ibrahim (1944–) Yugoslav writer and politician. An ethnic Albanian, he graduated in philosophy and literature and began work as a researcher at the Institute of Albanian Studies in 1972. A prominent human-rights activist, he was elected leader of the new Democratic League of Kosovo (LDK) in December 1989. This made him effectively the leader of the Albanian majority in the Kosovo region. In May 1992 he and the party gained overwhelming majorities in unofficial elections, and he was declared president of the self-proclaimed Republic of Kosovo.

Rühe, Volker (1942–) German teacher and politician. He was a member of the Hamburg state parliament for the Christian Democratic Union (CDU) from 1970 until his election to the federal parliament in 1976. He became a senior party spokesman on foreign and security issues and a deputy leader of the parliamentary party. He was CDU general secretary from 1989–92. He was appointed defence minister in April 1992.

Rumania and **Rumanian ...** *See* ROMANIA *and* ROMANIAN ....

Rumantsch *See* ROMANSH.

Ruml, Jan (1953–) Czech politician. Refused a place at university by the communist authorities because of his political views, he worked as a boilerman and courier and in several other menial jobs. He was active in various dissident organizations in the 1970s and 80s, including Charter 77. In 1990, following the collapse of communist rule, he was appointed deputy interior minister in the Czechoslovak government. Elected to the Czech parliament for the right-wing Civic Democratic Party (ODS) in June 1992, he became interior minister of the Czech Republic in July.

Rummo, Paul-Eerik (1942–) Estonian writer and politician. One of the country's best-known poets, he was secretary of the Estonian Writers' Union from 1968–89. From 1989–92 he was an adviser to the government on cultural affairs. He was elected leader of the new Liberal Democratic Party (LDP) in October 1990. In October 1992 he also became minister of education and culture, a post he held until June 1994, when the LDP left the centre-right coalition.

rump Yugoslavia Shorthand for Yugoslavia. It is used to distinguish the current Yugoslav federation, formed by Serbia and Montenegro in April 1992, from the Socialist Federal Republic of Yugoslavia or FORMER YUGOSLAVIA, the federation of six republics which collapsed in 1991/92 as Croatia, Slovenia, Macedonia and Bosnia-Herzegovina declared their independence. Other informal names like 'little Yugoslavia', 'mini-Yugoslavia' and 'new Yugoslavia' are also used.

Rural Coordination [Coordination Rurale] (CR) French trade union. CR is a loose association founded in 1991 by farmers unhappy with what they saw as the increasingly complaisant stance of the National Federation of Farmers' Unions (FNSEA). It is strongly opposed to the reform of the European Union's Common Agricultural Policy (CAP) agreed in May 1992 and the terms of the worldwide General Agreement on Tariffs and Trade (GATT) agreed in December 1993, both of which aim to deregulate the agricultural sector. The leader is Philippe Arnaud.

Rural Solidarity *See* SOLIDARITY.

Russian Democratic Movement [Vene Demokraatlik Liikumine (Estonian), Rossiyskoye Demokratskoye Dvizheniye (Russian)] (VDL or RDD) Estonian political organization. Founded in 1990 (when Estonia was still part of the Soviet Union) to protect the interests of the substantial ethnic Russian minority, the RDD was officially registered in 1992. It demands equal rights for Russian speakers, most of whom have not been granted citizenship of independent Estonia. The RDD did not take part in the September 1992 election. The leader is Aleksandr Khmorov.

Russo Jervolino, Rosa (1936–) Italian economist and politician. She worked for the National Council of Economy and Labour (CNEL) as a researcher and manager from 1961–68 and for the Italian Women's Centre (FIM) from 1969–78. Elected to parliament for the Christian Democratic Party (DC) in 1979, she has been minister of special affairs (1987–89), social affairs (1989–92) and education (1992 until May 1994). In October 1992, when the DC's involvement in political corruption was coming to light and most of its senior leaders were discredited, she was elected party president. She was confirmed in this post when the DC was relaunched as the Italian People's Party (PPI) in January 1994.

Ruthenia question *See* SUBCARPATHIA QUESTION.

Ruthenians Ethnic group in Yugoslavia and Croatia. The Ruthenians are descendants of Ukrainian immigrants from Ruthenia, on the western slopes of the Carpathian Mountains. From the 17th century onwards they were encouraged to settle in Vojvodina and Slavonia, then strategically important regions of Hungary on the border with the Ottoman Empire.

There are around 30,000 Ruthenians in Vojvodina, now part of Yugoslavia, and around 25,000 in Slavonia, now part of Croatia.

Rüütel, Arnold (1928–) Estonian agronomist and politician. A specialist in livestock breeding, he worked as a teacher, researcher and administrator in the agricultural sector until 1977. In that year he was elected to the central committee of the Estonian Communist Party. He was chairman of the presidium of the Supreme Council (= parliament) from 1983–90. Broadly supportive of greater autonomy for the republic, which was then still part of the Soviet Union, he left the party in 1990. Standing as an independent, he was elected chairman of the Supreme Council, a new post with wider powers, after the multiparty election in February. In September 1992 he was the candidate of several centre-left parties for the new post of president of the republic. He gained a plurality of the popular vote but not the required absolute majority, and lost to Lennart Meri in the parliamentary run-off.

RV *See* RADICAL LIBERAL PARTY.

S Abbreviation for the SCHILLING, the Austrian currency.

S (Denmark) *See* SOCIAL DEMOCRATIC PARTY.

$ Abbreviation for the ESCUDO, the Portuguese currency.

S *See* SOCIAL DEMOCRATIC LABOUR PARTY OF SWEDEN.

S Abbreviation for Sweden, used for international vehicle registrations, postal addresses etc.

's-Gravenhage Formal Dutch name of The Hague, the seat of government of the Netherlands, usually called Den Haag.

Saame and **Saami** Alternative spellings of Sami, the self-description of the LAPPS, an ethnic group in Northern Europe. 'Sami' is now also widely used by outsiders in preference to 'Lapps'.

Saarland Federal state [Land] of Germany. Situated in the southwest and bordering on France and Luxemburg, Saarland has an area of 2,570 sq km and a population of 1,084,000. The capital is Saarbrücken. The economy is based on manufacturing (metalworking, engineering) and mining (coal). The traditional coal- and steel-based heavy industries are being restructured, and unemployment is among the highest in the western states. Political power is exercised by the State Assembly [Landtag], with 51 members elected for a five-year term, and a government headed by a minister-president. The dominant party is the Social Democratic Party (SPD), and the other main parties are the Christian Democratic Union (CDU) and the centrist Free Democratic Party (FDP). At the election in January 1990 the SPD gained 54.4% of the vote and 30 seats, the CDU 33.4% and 18 seats, and the FDP 5.6% and three seats. The minister-president is Oskar Lafontaine. Historically part of Holy Roman Empire, the Saar region has been a bone of contention between France and Prussia and later Germany since the late 18th century, particularly after the development of its heavy industries. It was under French administration from 1919–35 and from 1945–57. It was returned to Germany after a plebiscite.

Saavedra, Jerónimo (1936–) Spanish academic and politician. A specialist in labour relations, he lectured in business studies at Las Palmas University from 1976. A member of the Spanish Socialist Workers' Party (PSOE), he was president of the Canary Islands regional government from 1983–87 and 1990–93 and has been a member of the national parliament since 1986. In July 1993 he was appointed minister of public administration, which includes responsibility for relations with the 17 autonomous communities or regions.

Sabor Parliament of Croatia, composed of the HOUSE OF REPRESENTATIVES and the HOUSE OF COUNTIES.

SACEUR Abbreviation for Supreme Allied Commander Europe, the commander of the ALLIED COMMAND EUROPE (ACE), a military arm of the North Atlantic Treaty Organization (NATO).

Sachsen *See* SAXONY.

Sachsen-Anhalt *See* SAXONY-ANHALT.

Sacirbey, Muhamed (1956–) Bosnian and American lawyer and diplomat. He was 11 when his family emigrated to the United States. During the 1980s and early 90s he worked as a lawyer and investment banker. After Bosnia-Herzegovina declared its independence in March 1992 he became an adviser to the new government. He was appointed Bosnia's ambassador to the United Nations when the country was admitted to the organization the following May.

Sacra Corona ('Holy Crown') Italian crime syndicate. Active in the southeastern region of Apulia since the late 1980s, the Sacra Corona is engaged in extortion, drug trafficking, arms smuggling and other criminal activities. It is relatively unstructured and consists of groups aligned to and cooperating with either the Mafia, Camorra or 'Ndrangheta, the more established organizations in nearby Sicily, Naples and Calabria respectively.

Saeima ('Assembly') Parliament of Latvia. It has 100 members elected for a three-year term by a system of proportional representation, with parties requiring at least 4% of the popular vote to qualify for seats.

SAF *See* SWEDISH EMPLOYERS' CONFEDERATION.

safe area In Bosnia-Herzegovina, one of the six largely Muslim cities and towns which are under the protection of the United Nations. In the course of the BOSNIAN CIVIL WAR, which broke out in March 1992, Serb forces besieged the eastern towns of Srebrenica, Goražde and Žepa. When it seemed they were about to be overrun, in May 1993, the UN Security Council adopted Resolution 824, which declared them and the cities of Sarajevo, Tuzla and Bihać 'safe areas' and called on 'all parties' (i.e. the Serb forces) to halt their attacks on them. The United Nations Protection Force II (UNPROFOR II) was reinforced by a further 7,600 troops to monitor their security and patrol the 'total exclusion zones' around them. Modelled on the 'safe havens' declared in northern Iraq to protect the Kurds at the end of the 1991 Gulf War, the UN decision was intended to contain the fighting and provide relief to the large numbers of Muslim refugees who had fled to the three eastern towns in particular. In February 1994 Serb forces agreed to lift the siege of Sarajevo, which they had imposed soon after the start of the civil war in March 1992. In March 1994 Serb forces launched an attack on Goražde. They occupied the town in April after heavy fighting and despite air strikes by North Atlantic Treaty Organization (NATO) forces acting on behalf of the United Nations, but agreed to pull back later in the month.

safe haven (Bosnia-Herzegovina) *See* SAFE AREA.

Safe Home *See* SECURE HOME.

Sahlin, Mona (1957–) Swedish administrator, trade-union official and politician. Elected to parliament for the Social Democratic Labour Party (SAP) in 1982, she was minister of labour from 1990 until the party lost power in October 1991. She was elected SAP general secretary in February 1992.

Šainović, Nikola (1948–) Yugoslav mining engineer and politician. He has researched and lectured in metallurgy and mining engineering. A member of the

Socialist Party of Serbia (SPS), he was appointed a deputy prime minister and minister of mining and energy in the Serbian government in 1991. From July–November 1992 he was also federal minister of economic affairs. He was appointed prime minister of Serbia in February 1993, and a deputy prime minister at federal level, with overall responsibility for economic and financial reform, in February 1994.

Saint Patrick's Day National holiday of Ireland. It is celebrated on 17 March, the feast day of Saint Patrick, the country's patron saint.

Saint Stephen's Day National holiday of Hungary. It is celebrated on 20 August in honour of King István or Stephen I, the first king of Hungary. He ruled from 997–1038 and was canonized in 1083.

Sąjūdis *See* HOMELAND UNION.

SAK *See* CENTRAL ORGANIZATION OF FINNISH TRADE UNIONS.

Sakharov Prize for Human Rights Award made annually by the European Parliament, the parliament of the European Union (EU), to a European individual, group or organization in recognition of an outstanding contribution to international understanding or in defence of freedom of expression. It was instituted in 1988 in honour of the Soviet scientist and human-rights campaigner Andrei Sakharov (1921–89). Winners have included the Czechoslovak politician Alexander Dubček (1989), the Yugoslav Albanian writer Adem Demaci (1991) and the Bosnian newspaper *Oslobodjenje* (1993).

Salmond, Alex (1954–) British economist and politician. He worked in the civil service and for the Royal Bank of Scotland until 1987, when he was elected to parliament for the Scottish National Party (SNP). He was elected party leader in September 1990.

Salolainen, Pertti (1940–) Finnish journalist and politician. He has worked in television, as a foreign correspondent, and, from 1969–75, for the Finnish Employers' Confederation (STK). He was elected to parliament for the right-wing National Coalition Party (Kokoomus) in 1970. When the party joined a left-right coalition in April 1987 he was appointed minister of foreign trade. In April 1991 he also became deputy prime minister in a centre-right coalition. He was leader of Kokoomus from June 1991 – August 1994.

Salzburg Federal province [Land] of Austria. Situated in the centre and bordering on Germany, Salzburg has an area of 7,155 sq km and a population of 493,000. The capital is Salzburg. The economy is based on tourism, manufacturing (textiles, metalworking), agriculture and forestry. The Provincial Assembly [Landtag] has 36 members elected for a five-year term. The main political parties are the centre-right Austrian People's Party (ÖVP), the Social Democratic Party (SPÖ), the far-right Freedom Party (FPÖ) and the Citizens' List (BL), the local branch of the Green Alternative (GA). At the election in March 1994 the ÖVP gained 14 seats, the SPÖ 11, the FPÖ eight and the BL three. The government is formed by the three largest parties and headed by Hans Katschthaler (ÖVP). Historically an autonomous archbishopric within the Holy Roman Empire, Salzburg became part of Austria in 1816.

Samaras, Antonis (1951–) Greek economist and politician. Elected to parliament for the right-wing New Democratic Party (ND) in 1977, he was finance minister from 1989–90 and foreign minister from 1990–92. He was dismissed in April 1992 for criticizing the prime minister's stance on the dispute over the name of the former Yugoslav republic of Macedonia as too conciliatory. In June 1993 he founded a new party, Political Spring (POLA).

sametová revoluce and **sametová rodvod** *See* VELVET REVOLUTION *and* VELVET DIVORCE.

Sami (sing. -) Self-description of LAPPS, an ethnic group in northern Europe, also spelled Saame, Saami etc. The name is now also widely used by outsiders in preference to 'Lapps'.

Sammarinese Citizens or people of San Marino.

San Marino Country in southern Europe. *Official data.* Name: Most Serene Republic of San Marino [Serenissima Repubblica di San Marino]; capital: San Marino; form of government: parliamentary republic; heads of state and government: two captains-regent; flag: two horizontal stripes, white and light blue, with the state emblem in the centre; national holiday: 3 September (Republic Day); language: Italian; religion: none; currencies: lira (pl. lire) = 100 centesimi, Italian lira; abbreviation: RSM.

Geography. Situated in the Apennine Mountains [Appennino], San Marino is surrounded by Italy and has an area of 61 sq km. The terrain is mountainous, with several narrow river valleys. Some 35% of the land is arable, another 22% is covered by pastures and 8% forested. The climate is mediterranean, moderated by alpine influences; summers are hot and winters cool; rainfall is moderate.

Demography. San Marino has a population of 24,100. Population density is 395 per sq km. Some 90% of the people live in urban areas. Some 83.8% are Sammarinese. Foreign nationals, almost all from Italy, account for the remaining 16.2%. Around 20,000 San Marino citizens are resident abroad, mainly in Italy. The main language is Italian. In religious terms nearly all the people are nominally Roman Catholics.

Sociography. The standard of living in San Marino is high. There are 27 doctors and 66 hospital beds for every 10,000 people. Education is compulsory between the ages of six and 14. There is one teacher for every seven students. Enrolment is 70% at the secondary level and 28% at the tertiary level (including students studying abroad). The literacy rate is 98%. GNP per head (unadjusted for purchasing power) is US$ 17,000.

Infrastructure and communications. San Marino has a highly developed but limited transport and communications network fully integrated into that of Italy. There are 100 km of paved roads and 19,400 passenger cars (831 per 1,000 people). There are no railways or navigable waterways. The nearest major port is Ravenna, and the nearest international airport is at Bologna (both in Italy). There are no daily newspapers; Italian papers are widely read. There are 13,000 radio receivers, 7,000 television sets and 16,000 telephones in use (respectively 558, 300 and 687 per 1,000 people).

Economic structure. The San Marino economy is highly developed and closely linked to the Italian economy. San Marino maintains a customs and monetary union with Italy. The economy is based on tourism, which contributes about three-fifths of national income, and on light industry. Since the late 1980s economic performance has been marked by steady growth, relatively high inflation (averaging around 6% per year), and low but rising unemployment (from 1% to 5%).

Services contribute 75% of GDP, industry contributes 21% (manufacturing around 15%), and agriculture and forestry 4%. Some 33% of the labour force is employed in manufacturing and mining, 17% in trade and 8% in construction. The main agricultural activities are dairy farming (cheese), livestock raising (meat, hides, wool) and horticulture (grapes, olives); the main crops grown are cereals (wheat, maize). Forestry is also important. The main mineral resource is stone. The main industries are engineering, printing (stamps), handicrafts (ceramics), building materials (stone, cement), wood processing (furniture), textiles and food processing (wine, olive oil). The tourism industry is the mainstay of the economy and provides most of the country's foreign exchange. The main energy sources are imported natural gas and electricity (from Italy). The main exports are postage stamps, wine, textiles, furniture, handicrafts and building stone. The main trading partner is Italy. (Detailed foreign-trade figures n.a.) Net invisible earnings (tourism receipts) account for a major share of GNP.

There is no central bank. The main employers' association is the National Industry Association of San Marino (ANIS); the main labour organization is the United Trade Union Centre (CSU), comprising the Democratic Confederation of San Marino Workers (CDLS) and San Marino Confederation of Labour (CSdL).

Political structure. San Marino is a parliamentary republic on the basis of a constitution adopted in 1600 and supplementary legislation, in particular an electoral law of 1926. Legislative power is vested in the Grand and General Council [Consiglio Grande e Generale], whose 60 members are elected for a five-year term by a system of proportional representation. The Council elects two of its members for a six-month term as captains-regent [capitano reggento, pl. capitani reggenti], who act as joint heads of state and government and presidents of the Council. Executive power is vested in the 10-member Congress of State [Congresso di Stato], also elected by the legislature. All citizens over the age of 18, including those living abroad, are entitled to vote. Judicial power is ultimately vested in the Council of Twelve [Consiglio dei Dodici], elected by the legislature. Administratively the country is divided into nine municipalities or castles [castello, pl. castelli].

The main political parties are the San Marino Christian Democratic Party (PDCS), Democratic Progressive Party (PDP, the successor to the San Marino Communist Party, PCS), San Marino Socialist Party (PSS), People's Alliance (AP), Democratic Movement (MD) and Communist Refoundation Party (RC). At the general election in May 1993 the PDCS gained 41.4% and 26/60 seats, the PSS 23.7% and 14 seats, the PDP 18.6% and 11 seats, the AP 7.7% and four seats, the MD 5.3% and three seats, and the RC 3.4% and two seats. The government is formed by a centrist coalition of the PDCS and PSS. Senior ministers include Gabriele Gatti (foreign and political affairs), Clelio Galassi (finance and budget) and Antonio Lazzaro Voltinari (internal affairs, civil protection and justice).

Security and international affiliations. San Marino has no standing army, but general conscription may be imposed in an emergency. Responsibility for defence and general foreign affairs is delegated to Italy. San Marino is a member of the Conference on Security and Cooperation in Europe (CSCE) and Council of Europe, as well as the United Nations and some of its specialized agencies.

History. By tradition the Republic of San Marino was established in 301 by Saint Marinus and a group of Christians who settled there to escape persecution. By the 12th century it had developed into a commune with its own statutes and by the mid 15th century it was a republic ruled by an oligarchy. (*For earlier developments, see* ITALY: HISTORY.) A statute adopted in 1600 established many of the principles of parliamentary government still in force today. In 1631 San Marino's independence was recognized by the Papal States, the region's dominant power. As the Italian states became united in the mid 19th century, San Marino chose to remain independent. In 1862 it signed a friendship treaty with Italy that also set up a customs union. In 1923 Italy's fascist regime gained control in San Marino. During the Second World War (1939–45) the country was occupied by German troops after Italy's surrender in 1943.

Since 1945 politics has been dominated by the San Marino Christian Democratic Party (PDCS), the San Marino Communist Party (PCS) and its successor, the Democratic Progressive Party (PDP), and the San Marino Socialist Party (PSS) and several breakaways. A PCS-PSS coalition was in power until 1957, several PDCS-led coalitions until 1978, a PCS-led coalition until July 1986, a PDCS-PCS coalition until March 1992, and a PDCS-PSS coalition since then. Since the 1950s tourism has replaced agriculture, forestry and stone quarrying as the mainstay of the economy. San Marino joined the United Nations in March 1992.

See also entries on specific institutions, organizations, parties, terms etc.

San Marino Christian Democratic Party [Partito Democratico Sammarinese] (PDCS) San Marino political party. Founded in 1948, the PDCS has participated in coalition governments from 1957–78 and since 1986. The country's largest party since the 1970s, it gained 41.4% of the vote and 26/60 seats at the May 1993 election. The leader is Cesare Antonio Gasperoni.

San Marino Confederation of Labour *See* UNITED TRADE UNION CENTRE.

San Marino Socialist Party [Partito Socialista Sammarinese] (PSS) San Marino political party. The PSS was formed in 1990 from the merger of the party of the same name and the Unitarian Socialist Party (PSU). Both parties have participated in a number of coalition governments since 1945, and the PSS became the junior partner in a centrist coalition in March 1992. At the May 1993 election it gained 23.7% of the vote and 14/60 seats. The leader is Emma Rossi.

Sandžak *See* SANJAK.

Sanjak [Sandžak] Historical region of Yugoslavia. Sanjak spans the border of Serbia and Montenegro, Yugoslavia's two constituent republics. Just over half of its 400,000 inhabitants are Serbs and Montenegrins and just under half are Slav Muslims. The region became part of the Ottoman Empire in the 15th century and was constituted as the district or *sancak* – hence the current name – of Novi Pazar in 1856. Occupied by Austria from 1878–1912, it was divided between Serbia and Montenegro after the First Balkan War (1912–13). Since the late 1980s the Muslims have accused the Serbian authorities of human-rights violations, and they are now demanding autonomy for the region.

Sant, Alfred (1948–) Maltese economist and politician. He has been deputy chairman of the Malta Development Corporation, head of the Labour Party's information department (1982–84) and party president (1984–87). He was elected to parliament in 1987 and became party leader in March 1992.

Santer, Jacques (1937–) Luxemburg lawyer and politician. He became a full-time official with the Christian Social People's Party (CSV) in 1966 and was its general secretary from 1972–74 and president from 1974–82. Elected to parliament in 1974, he was appointed minister of finance, labour and social security in 1979 and became prime minister of a centre-left coalition in July 1984. In July 1994 he was designated president of the European Commission, the administrative and executive arm of the European Union (EU), to serve from January 1995.

Santkin, Jacques (1948–) Belgian civil servant and politician. He was an inspector of social laws from 1973–79 and then served as an adviser to several ministers. A member of the Walloon Socialist Party (PS), he was active in local government in his native Luxemburg province in the 1970s and 80s and was elected to parliament in 1984. He was appointed minister of health, environment and social integration in January 1994.

São Bento Palace [Palácio de São Bento] Shorthand for the Portuguese parliament. The São Bento in Lisbon is the seat of the Assembly of the Republic.

SAP (Greece) *See* PROGRESSIVE LEFT ALLIANCE.

SAP *See* SOCIAL DEMOCRATIC LABOUR PARTY OF SWEDEN.

SÄPO Abbreviation for Säkerhetspolis ('Security Police'), the Swedish intelligence agency.

Saraiva de Carvalho, Otelo (1936–) Portuguese soldier and politician. He was the operational commander of the army coup which overthrew the right-wing Caetano dictatorship in 1974 and paved the way for the establishment of democratic rule. He became head of the military police, but was dismissed in 1975 after an attempted left-wing coup. He was arrested in 1984 on suspicion of leading a far-left urban guerrilla group, the People's Forces of 25 April (FP-25, named after the date of the 1974 coup). He was found guilty of organizing a terrorist group and sentenced to 15 years' imprisonment in 1987. He was released on a technicality in 1989 pending an appeal. He also remains under investigation on other charges.

Sarajevo Shorthand for the Bosnian government. Sarajevo is the capital of Bosnia-Herzegovina.

Sard Alternative name for Sardinian, the language of Sardinia, an autonomous region of Italy. Closely related to Italian, it is widely spoken but rarely written.

Sardegna *See* SARDINIA.

Sardinia [Sardegna] Special autonomous region of Italy. The second-largest island in the Mediterranean Sea, Sardinia has an area of 24,090 sq km and a population of 1,645,000. Italian is the official language, but most people speak dialects of Sardinian, generally considered a separate Romance language; there is also a 12,000-strong Catalan-speaking community in the north. The capital is Cagliari, and the other main city is Sassari. The economy is based on agriculture (cereals, wine, fruit and vegetables, sheep and goat farming), fishing, mining (zinc, lead), manufacturing (metalworking, petrochemicals) and tourism. The island is one of Italy's poorest regions, and emigration has been heavy since the 19th century. Political power is exercised by the Regional Assembly [Consiglio Regionale], with 80 members elected for a five-year term, and an executive council headed by a president. The main parties are the right-wing Come On Italy (Forza Italia), the Democratic Left Party (PDS), the far-right National Alliance (AN, based on the Italian Social Movement, MSI), the Italian People's Party (PPI, the successor to the Christian Democratic Party, DC), the centre-left Sardinia List (Lista Sardegna, an alliance including the Italian Socialist Party, PSI), the centrist Pact for Italy or Segni Pact, the Communist Refoundation Party (RC), and the Sardinian Action Party (PSdA), which advocates greater autonomy. At the election in June 1994 Forza Italia gained 18 seats, the PDS 16, the PPI 13, the AN 10, the Sardinia List seven, the Segni Pact six, the RC four, the PSdA four and others two. An Aragonese possession from 1326–1708 and then briefly under Austrian control, Sardinia was united with Piedmont-Savoy to form the Kingdom of Sardinia in 1720. Sardinia-Piedmont took the leading role in the movement to unify Italy, completed in 1870. In recognition of its strong regional identity and position as an island, Sardinia was made an autonomous region with special statute in 1947.

Sardinian Action Party [Partito Sardo d'Azione] (PSdA) Italian political party. Founded in 1921, the PSdA advocates greater autonomy for Sardinia, is centre-left in its economic policies and has relatively liberal views on social issues. It has participated in several coalition governments in the region. It gained 10/80 seats at the June 1991 regional election and four seats at the June 1994 election. The leader is Michele Colombu.

Sardo and **Sardu** Italian and native names for Sardinian, the language of Sardinia, an autonomous region of Italy. Closely related to Italian, it is widely spoken but rarely written.

Sark Dependency of Guernsey, which in turn is a dependency of the United Kingdom. The fourth-largest of the Channel Islands, Sark has an area of 5.5 sq km and a population of 400. The economy is based on dairy farming and market gardening. The island has some autonomy over local affairs. Administration is in the hands of the seigneur, the hereditary lord of the island, the seneschal (the chief executive and judicial officer) and the 12-member Chief Pleas. Guernsey is responsible for police, health, education and other matters.

Sarkozy, Nicolas (1955–) French politician. Trained as a lawyer, he was elected mayor of Neuilly-sur-Seine in 1983 and elected to parliament for the right-wing Rally for the Republic (RPR) in 1988. He was appointed minister for the budget and government spokesman in the centre-right coalition formed in March 1993.

SAS *See* SPECIAL AIR SERVICE.

Savezna Skupština ('Federal Assembly') Parliament of Yugoslavia, composed of the CHAMBER OF CITIZENS and CHAMBER OF REPUBLICS.

Savisaar, Edgar (1949–) Estonian economist and politician. He became leader of the broadly based People's Front (Rahvarinne) in 1988, when Estonia was still part of the Soviet Union. In 1989 he was appointed a deputy prime minister and chairman of the State Planning Committee. He left the Communist Party in 1990. He was appointed prime minister after the Front won the February/March 1990 election. In October 1991 he became leader of the new centre-left Estonian People's Centre Party (ERKE). He resigned as prime minister in January 1992.

Savov, Stefan (1924–) Bulgarian lawyer, translator and politician. After completing his law degree he was interned for his anti-communist views and later worked as a construction worker and translator. When the right-wing Democratic Party (DP) was relaunched in January 1990, he was elected its leader. Elected to parliament in 1990, he was its president from 1991–92. In March 1993 he became parliamentary leader of the Union of Democratic Forces (SDS), the alliance of which the DP is a member.

Saxony [Sachsen] Federal state [Land] of Germany, formerly part of East Germany. Situated in the east and bordering on the Czech Republic and Poland, Saxony has an area of 18,338 sq km and a population of 4,641,000. There is a small Sorb-speaking minority of 30,000 people in the northeast. The capital is Dresden, and the other main cities are Leipzig, Chemnitz (formerly Karl-Marx-Stadt) and Zwickau. The economy is based on manufacturing (engineering, textiles, chemicals), mining (lignite, uranium, zinc etc) and agriculture. Traditionally one of Germany's leading industrial regions, Saxony, like the other eastern states, is experiencing extensive economic restructuring and high unemployment. Political power is exercised by the State Assembly [Landtag], with 120 members elected for a four-year term, and a government headed by a minister-president. The dominant party is the Christian Democratic Union (CDU); the other major parties are the Social Democratic Party (SPD), Democratic Socialist Party (PDS, the successor to the communist Socialist Unity Party, SED), Alliance 90 / Greens (B'90) and the centrist Free Democratic Party (FDP). At the election in September 1994 the CDU gained 58.1% of the vote and 77 seats, the SPD 16.8% and 22 seats, the PDS 16.5% and 21 seats, B'90 4.1% and no seats, and the FDP 1.8% and no seats. The minister-president is Kurt Biedenkopf. Unlike most German states, Saxony has existed as a distinct political entity since the early Middle Ages and has a strongly developed regional identity. Under the House of Wettin it emerged as one of the major powers within the Holy Roman Empire. It became a duchy in 1423, a kingdom in

1806 and a state of unified Germany in 1871. It was divided into three districts by the East German authorities in 1952 but restored in 1990 prior to German reunification.

Saxony-Anhalt [Sachsen-Anhalt] Federal state [Land] of Germany, formerly part of East Germany. Situated in the centre, Saxony-Anhalt has an area of 20,444 sq km and a population of 2,797,000. The capital is Magdeburg, and the other main city is Halle. The economy is based on agriculture (cereals, vegetables, dairy farming) and manufacturing (chemicals, engineering). Like the other eastern states, Saxony-Anhalt is experiencing extensive economic restructuring and high unemployment. Political power is exercised by the State Assembly [Landtag], with 99 members elected for a four-year term, and a government headed by a minister-president. The main parties are the Christian Democratic Union (CDU), the Social Democratic Party (SPD), Democratic Socialist Party (PDS, the successor to the communist Socialist Unity Party, SED) and the Greens. At the election in June 1994 the CDU gained 34.4% of the vote and 37 seats, the SPD 34.0% and 36 seats, the PDS 20.0% and 21 seats, and the Greens 5.1% and five seats. The government is formed by a coalition of the SPD and the Greens, with Reinhard Höppner as minister-president. Historically divided into many states, most of the region became part of Prussia in the 17th and 18th centuries. Saxony-Anhalt was established as a state after the dissolution of Prussia in 1947, divided into two districts by the East German authorities in 1952 and restored in 1990 prior to reunification.

Sb (Faroe Islands) *See* UNION PARTY.

SB Abbreviation for Służba Bezpieczeństwa ('Security Service'), one of the Polish agencies responsible for internal security and the surveillance of dissidents during communist rule. It was a department of the interior ministry.

Scalfaro, Oscar Luigi (1918–) Italian lawyer and politician. First elected to parliament for the Christian Democratic Party (DC) in 1946, he held several junior ministerial posts from 1954. He has been minister of transport (1966–68), education (1972–73) and internal affairs (1983–87). He was deputy speaker of the Chamber of Deputies from 1976–83 and was elected speaker in April 1992. The following month he was elected president of the republic, a largely non-executive but influential post, for a seven-year term.

Scandinavian countries or **Scandinavia** Collective name for Denmark, Norway, Sweden and, more loosely, Finland and Iceland. The Scandinavian Peninsula properly comprises only Norway and Sweden. These two countries have close linguistic and historical ties with Denmark, while Finland has close historical and economic ties with Sweden. A more accurate and increasingly common name for the whole region is 'Nordic countries' or 'Nordic area'.

Sch Abbreviation for the SCHILLING, the Austrian currency.

Scharping, Rudolf (1947–) German politician. He studied law, politics and sociology. He was elected to the Rhineland-Palatinate state assembly for the Social Democratic Party (SPD) in 1975 and became the SPD group leader in 1985. In May 1991 he became minister-president at the head of a centre-left coalition. In June 1993 he was also elected leader of the SPD at federal level.

Schäuble, Wolfgang (1942–) German lawyer, civil servant and politician. He was elected to parliament for the Christian Democratic Union (CDU) in 1972. After serving as a party whip for several years he was appointed head of the Federal Chancellery (= prime minister's office) in 1984. In 1989 he was appointed interior minister. In November 1991 he became leader of the CDU parliamentary party. He has been confined to a wheelchair since he was shot and paralysed by a mentally unstable assailant in October 1990.

Schengen Accords Two international agreements adopted by nine of the twelve member states of the European Union (EU) providing for the abolition of passport controls on their common or internal borders, the strengthening of controls on their external borders, and cooperation on immigration and police matters. The Accords – named after the Luxemburg village on the Moselle river which the negotiators were passing by boat as they finalized terms on the first agreement – consist of an outline agreement signed on 14 June 1985 and a supplementary agreement signed on 19 June 1990. They allow for completely free and unchecked movement of people within the signatories' territories. To prevent criminals and illegal immigrants from exploiting this freedom, the Accords contain a series of 'compensatory measures', such as stronger external border controls, harmonization of visa regulations, common criteria for granting political asylum, compilation of a central computer database with information on wanted persons, illegal immigrants and stolen property (called the Schengen Information System, SIS), cooperation to restrict the illegal movement of guns and explosives, and acceptance of 'hot pursuit' of suspects across borders. The Accords were meant to take effect in 1991, but political complications and practical problems with the SIS software have delayed their implementation. *See also* SCHENGEN GROUP.

Schengen Group Intergovernmental organization. The Schengen Group is an informal grouping of nine of the twelve member states of the European Union (EU) which have signed the SCHENGEN ACCORDS on removing border controls. Its members are Belgium, France, Greece, Germany, Italy, Luxemburg, Netherlands, Portugal and Spain. Its day-to-day activities are organized through monthly meetings of the Central Group, comprising government officials from each member state. Overall political direction is provided by a twice-yearly meeting of the justice and foreign ministers. The removal of border controls was first discussed by the French and German governments in the early 1980s. France, Germany and the three Benelux countries adopted the Schengen Accords in June 1985 and June 1990. Italy joined the Group later in 1990, Portugal and Spain in 1991 and Greece in 1992. These states regarded the Schengen initiative as a key adjunct to the single-

market programme (implemented between 1987 and 1992), but Denmark, Ireland and the United Kingdom maintained that it did not oblige them to eliminate passport controls on people travelling within the EU. Subsequent disagreements among the signatories and technical problems with the central computer system, the Schengen Information System (SIS), have delayed implementation of the Accords.

Schengen Information System (SIS) *See* SCHENGEN ACCORDS.

schilling [Schilling, pl. -e] Currency of Austria. Common abbreviations are S, Sch, ÖS, AS and ATS (the international standard in banking etc). It is divided into 100 Groschen or groschen.

Schleswig-Holstein Federal state [Land] of Germany. Situated in the north between the North Sea and the Baltic Sea and bordering on Denmark, Schleswig-Holstein has an area of 15,730 sq km and a population of 2,680,000. There are two small ethnic minorities, 30,000 Danish speakers in the north and 10,000 Frisian speakers on the west coast. The capital is Kiel, and the other main cities are Lübeck and Flensburg. The economy is based on manufacturing (engineering, food processing, shipbuilding), agriculture (dairy farming, cattle and pig farming, cereals) and tourism. Traditionally agricultural, the state has undergone extensive industrialization since the 1950s. Political power is exercised by the State Assembly [Landtag], with 89 members elected for a four-year term, and a government headed by a minister-president. The main parties are the Social Democratic Party (SPD), the Christian Democratic Union (CDU), the far-right German People's Union (DVU), the centrist Free Democratic Party (FDP), and the South Schleswig Voters' Association (SSW), which represents the interests of the Danish community. At the election in April 1992 the SPD gained 46.2% of the vote and 45 seats, the CDU 33.8% and 32 seats, the DVU 6.3% and six seats, the FDP 5.6% and five seats, and the SSW 1.9% and one seat. The minister-president is Heide Simonis. The two duchies of Schleswig and Holstein, for centuries disputed between Denmark and the Holy Roman Empire, and the city of Lübeck became part of the German Empire in 1871. After a plebiscite in Schleswig in 1920 the border with Denmark was redrawn broadly in line with ethnic divisions. The state of Schleswig-Holstein was established after the Second World War.

Schlüter, Poul (1929–) Danish lawyer and politician. Elected to parliament for the Conservative People's Party (KF) in 1964, he became party leader in 1974. In September 1982 he formed a minority centre-right coalition, becoming the first Conservative prime minister for 81 years. He formed similar coalitions after the elections of 1984, 1987 and 1990. He resigned as prime minister in January 1993 when a judicial inquiry accused him of misleading parliament over the TAMILGATE AFFAIR. In September 1993 he also resigned as party leader.

Schmidhuber, Peter (1931–) German lawyer and politician. He worked for the Bavarian government until his election to parliament for the right-wing Christian Social Union (CSU) in 1965. From 1978–87 he was a minister in the Bavarian government and the Bavarian representative to the federal government. In September 1987 he was appointed a commissioner of the European Community (EC), taking responsibility for regional policy until January 1989 and for the budget since then.

Schmidt, Heide (1948–) Austrian lawyer, civil servant and politician. She worked for the education and arts ministry from 1972–77 and for two legal firms from 1977–88. She became general secretary of the then right-wing Freedom Party (FPÖ) in 1988, was elected to parliament in 1990 and became the party's deputy leader in 1991. In February 1993 she left the FPÖ in protest at its drift to the far right and became leader of the newly formed Liberal Forum (LF).

Schmögnerová, Brigita (1947–) Slovakian economist and politician. She worked as a researcher in mathematical methods and microeconomic issues at the Economic Institute of the Slovak Academy of Sciences from 1976. After the collapse of communist rule in 1989 she also served as an adviser to several government departments. A member of the Democratic Left Party (SDL', the successor to the Communist Party of Slovakia, KSS), she was appointed a deputy prime minister, with responsibility for economic reforms, in the centrist coalition which took office in March 1994.

Schönhuber, Franz (1923–) German journalist and politician. He worked for a Munich newspaper in the 1960s and joined Bavarian Radio (BR) in 1972, becoming head of regional television programmes in 1975. He was dismissed in 1982 after publishing what was considered a positive account of his time in the Waffen-SS, the elite military corps of the nazi movement, for which he had volunteered in 1942. In November 1983 he became joint leader of the newly founded far-right Republicans (REP). In May 1985 he was elected the party's sole leader.

Schulte, Dieter (1940–) German metal-worker and trade-union official. He began working for the Thyssen concern in 1959. He was elected to its works council in 1983, became the council's president in 1990 and was elected to the concern's supervisory board in 1991. The same year he was elected to the executive of the Metalworkers' Union (IG Metall). In June 1994 he was elected president of the German Trade Union Federation (DGB). He is a member of the Social Democratic Party (SPD).

Schüssel, Wolfgang (1945–) Austrian politician. In 1975 he became secretary of the centre-right Austrian People's Party (ÖVP) parliamentary group and general secretary of the Austrian Economic Federation, an ÖVP affiliate. In 1979 he was elected to parliament for the ÖVP. He was appointed minister of economic affairs in April 1989.

schwarzrote Koalition *See* BLACK-RED COALITION.

Schweiz German name for Switzerland.

Schweizerische Eidgenossenschaft ('Swiss Confederation') Official name of Switzerland in German.

Schyman, Gudrun (1948–) Swedish social worker, film maker and politician.

531

She worked for the Stockholm local government from 1971, made documentary films from 1976, and again worked in local government from 1981. A member of parliament for the Left Party (Vp) since 1988, she was elected party leader in January 1993.

Scognamiglio, Carlo (1944–) Italian economist, academic, businessman and politician. He has lectured in finance, industrial economy and political economy since 1973. During the 1980s he held senior posts in the Rizzoli and Mondadori publishing groups and the state-owned STET telecommunications group. He was elected to the Senate, the upper house of parliament, for the Italian Liberal Party (PLI) in 1992 and for the new right-wing Come On Italy (Forza Italia) in March 1994. He was elected president of the Senate, an influential post in the Italian political system, in April.

Scotland Constituent country of the United Kingdom. Situated in the northern third of Great Britain and surrounded by the North Sea in the east and the Atlantic Ocean in the west, Scotland has an area of 78,783 sq km and a population of 5,100,000. Almost all people consider themselves Scots, and regional identification is strong. Gaelic, the original Celtic language of the region, is spoken by around 65,000 people in the northwest. The capital is Edinburgh and the largest city is Glasgow; other major cities are Aberdeen and Dundee. The economy is based on manufacturing (engineering, electronics, textiles), mining (oil), agriculture (cattle and dairy farming), fisheries and forestry. Until the growth of the North Sea oil industry in the 1970s Scotland's economic development lagged behind that of the country as a whole; structural unemployment remains high largely as a result of the decline of the heavy industries in the 1970s and 80s. Scotland has its own legal and educational systems, administration and local government structure, but no separate legislature. All laws pertaining to Scotland are adopted by the UK-wide House of Commons, which has certain structures and procedures to take account of the country's distinctive position. The Scottish Office is the main government department dealing with Scottish affairs. The main political parties are the Labour Party, which has been dominant since the 1920s, the Conservative Party, the Scottish National Party (SNP), which advocates independence, and the Liberal Democrats. At the April 1992 general election Labour gained 39.0% of the vote, the Conservatives 25.7%, the SNP 21.5% and the Liberal Democrats 13.1%. Most of Scotland was united in 843 when Kenneth I MacAlpin, king of the Scots, also became king of the Picts; the kingdom of Strathclyde was absorbed under Malcolm II (1005–34). From the late 11th century the country came under English influence, but its independence was restored after the Battle of Bannockburn in 1314. In 1603 King James VI also became king of England on the death of Queen Elizabeth I. In 1707 the English and Scottish parliaments were formally merged and the two countries were united as the United Kingdom of Great Britain. The union, under which Scotland effectively lost much of its autonomy, led to rebellions in 1715 and 1745–46. In the 19th century the Strathclyde region around Glasgow became a major centre of coal mining and the textile, steel and shipbuilding industries. Growing discontent with perceived English dominance led to the rise of nationalist sentiment from the 1960s onwards, in particular following discovery of oil off the Scottish coast. In 1979 a proposal to establish an elected Scottish assembly gained the support of a majority of voters in a referendum but not of the required 40% of the total electorate. Support for greater autonomy or outright independence has increased since then, and some form of devolution of power is now backed by all major parties except the Conservatives. *See also* GREAT BRITAIN AND NORTHERN IRELAND.

Scots Gaelic Alternative name for Gaelic, a language spoken by around 65,000 people in northwestern Scotland (United Kingdom). It is used to distinguish it from the related Irish Gaelic or Irish.

Scott inquiry *See* ARMS-TO-IRAQ AFFAIR.

Scottish Constitutional Convention British political movement. The Convention was set up in 1988 to draft proposals and campaign for a separate Scottish parliament and more generally for a degree of internal self-government for the country within the United Kingdom. It brings together representatives of local councils, churches, trade unions and business organizations and the Labour and Liberal Democratic parties. Its work has been boycotted by Scotland's two other political parties, the Scottish National Party (SNP), which advocates independence, and the Conservative Party, which rejects the need for constitutional change.

Scottish Grand Committee British advisory body. A standing committee of the House of Commons, the lower house of Parliament, the Scottish Grand Committee is composed of the 72 members elected for Scottish seats. Its two main functions are to scrutinize draft legislation pertaining to Scotland and to question ministers at the Scottish Office, the government department responsible for Scottish affairs. Its scope was widened in March 1993, but its role remains purely consultative.

Scottish Labour Party British political party, the Scottish branch of the LABOUR PARTY.

Scottish National Party (SNP) British political party. Founded in 1934, the SNP advocates independence for Scotland within the European Community. It is broadly left-wing in its economic policies and has relatively liberal views on social issues. At the April 1992 general election it gained 21.5% of the vote in Scotland (equivalent to 1.9% nationally) and three of the 72 Scottish seats. The leader is Alex Salmond, the party chairwoman is Winifred Ewing.

Scottish Office British government department. Based in Edinburgh, the Scottish Office is responsible for a wide range of functions in Scotland which in England are carried out by separate ministries. It deals with home affairs, health, education and culture, agriculture, industry, training and development. The Office is headed by the secretary of state for Scotland, a government minister with Cabinet rank.

Scottish Trades' Union Congress (STUC) British trade-union federation. Founded in 1897, the STUC is a separate organization within the national Trades' Union Congress (TUC). It has 57 affiliated unions representing a total of 850,000 workers in Scotland (a third of the labour force). It has close links with the Scottish Labour Party. The general secretary is Campbell Christie.

SČP *See* SERBIAN CHETNIK MOVEMENT.

screening or **vetting** In the former communist countries, the process of investigating high-ranking officials and others to determine in particular whether they collaborated with the security police during the communist period. The former security agencies played a major role in suppressing dissent during communist rule (from the late 1940s until 1989) and operated extensive networks of informants to this end. Screening legislation was adopted in Czechoslovakia in October 1991, in Bulgaria in March 1992, in Poland in July 1992 and in Hungary in March 1994; in East Germany screening was carried out after German reunification in October 1990 on the basis of legislation already in force in West Germany. Similar measures have been implemented in Albania, Croatia and other countries, but not, notably, in Romania and Yugoslavia, where relaunched communist parties have remained in power. Members of parliament, civil servants, diplomats, army and police officers, local government officials, judges, state prosecutors, journalists, academics, teachers and others have been subjected to screening. In most cases those found to have been deeply involved with the security agencies have been dismissed from their posts and/or barred from holding public office for life or for set periods. Some have also been charged with specific criminal offences. Screening has been criticized by human-rights organizations and others on the grounds that it encourages witchhunts, can be manipulated for ulterior political purposes, leads to false accusations (because of the unreliability of documentary evidence) and amounts to retrospective legislation. Certain aspects of the process have been declared unconstitutional in some countries. *See also* DECOMMUNIZATION.

Scrivener, Christiane (1925–) French economist and politician. She worked in business from 1958, specializing in international technical cooperation. A member of the centre-right Union for French Democracy (UDF), she was a junior minister responsible for consumer affairs in 1976–78 and a member of the European Parliament from 1979–88. In January 1989 she became a commissioner of the European Community (EC), with responsibility for taxation issues and since January 1993 also for consumer affairs.

SCV Abbreviation for the Vatican City, used for international vehicle registrations etc. It is taken from Stato della Città del Vaticano ('Vatican City State'), the state's official name in Italian.

SD (Czech Republic) *See* FREE DEMOCRATS.

SD (Denmark) *See* SOCIAL DEMOCRATIC PARTY.

SD *See* SWISS DEMOCRATS.

SDA *See* DEMOCRATIC ACTION PARTY.

SDL (Czech Republic) *See* DEMOCRATIC LEFT PARTY.

SDL' (Slovakia) *See* DEMOCRATIC LEFT PARTY.

SDLP *See* SOCIAL DEMOCRATIC AND LABOUR PARTY.

SDP (Bulgaria) *See* SOCIAL DEMOCRATIC PARTY.

SDP *See* SOCIAL DEMOCRATIC PARTY OF CROATIA.

SDP *See* FINNISH SOCIAL DEMOCRATIC PARTY.

SDP (Iceland) *See* SOCIAL DEMOCRATIC PARTY.

SDP (Slovenia) *See* ASSOCIATED LIST OF SOCIAL DEMOCRATS.

SDPH *See* SOCIAL DEMOCRATIC PARTY OF CROATIA.

SDPR *See* SOCIAL DEMOCRACY PARTY OF ROMANIA.

SdRP *See* SOCIAL DEMOCRATIC PARTY OF THE REPUBLIC OF POLAND.

SDS (Bosnia-Herzegovina) *See* SERBIAN DEMOCRATIC PARTY.

SDS (Bulgaria) *See* UNION OF DEMOCRATIC FORCES.

SDS (Croatia), **SDS Krajine, SDS of Krajina** and **SDSK** *See* SERBIAN DEMOCRATIC PARTY OF KRAJINA.

SDSM *See* SOCIAL DEMOCRATIC ALLIANCE OF MACEDONIA.

SDSS *See* SOCIAL DEMOCRATIC PARTY OF SLOVAKIA.

SDSS *See* SOCIAL DEMOCRATIC PARTY OF SLOVENIA.

SEA *See* SINGLE EUROPEAN ACT.

Seanad Éireann or **Seanad** ('Senate of Ireland') Upper house of the Irish parliament, the Oireachtas. The Senate has 60 members: 49 are indirectly elected (six by the universities and 43 by panels representing language, culture and education, agriculture, labour, industry and commerce, engineering and architecture, and public administration and social services) and 11 are appointed by the prime minister. All serve a five-year term. The lower house, the Dáil, may override its decisions by a simple majority.

Search, Aid, Intervention and Dissuasion [Recherche, Aide, Intervention et Dissuasion] (RAID) French paramilitary police force. RAID is an elite commando unit of the national police service trained to deal with cases of hostage taking and other specialist assignments. It has also been involved in anti-terrorist operations.

seat question In the European Union (EU), a controversy over the permanent siting of the European Parliament. At the moment most plenary sessions are held in Strasbourg (France), committee and political-group meetings are held in Brussels, the EU's headquarters, and the secretariat is based in Luxemburg. The Parliament has repeatedly expressed a preference for concentrating its activities in Brussels. The arrangements can only be changed by a unanimous decision of the Council of Ministers.

Second Chamber [Tweede Kamer] Lower house of the Dutch parliament, the States-General. It has 150 members elected for a four-year term by proportional representation. *See also* FIRST CHAMBER.

second pillar In the European Union (EU), an informal name for the COMMON FOREIGN AND SECURITY POLICY (CFSP), one of the EU's two intergovernmental components alongside the supranational European Community (EC).

Second Republic [Seconda Repubblica] Common name for the current system of government in Italy. It is usually dated from the March 1994 election, which swept away a political establishment discredited by revelations of endemic corruption and other scandals (*see* ITALIAN CORRUPTION SCANDALS). The new parliament is considering constitutional reforms and the adoption of a new constitution. The First Republic dated from the abolition of the monarchy in 1946.

second stage (European Union) *See* ECONOMIC AND MONETARY UNION.

secret files affair or **state snooping affair** Controversy in Switzerland concerning the activities of the state security agencies. In November 1989 a parliamentary commission disclosed that the federal prosecutor's office held 900,000 secret files on 200,000 Swiss citizens and foreign residents deemed to be threats to state security. It emerged that these included, besides terrorist suspects, members of parliament, anti-nuclear campaigners, leading feminists and others, and that the files contained information unrelated to any security considerations, such as foreign travel. (The commission had been investigating the allegation that the justice minister, Elisabeth Kopp, had violated official secrecy and abused her position by warning her husband that a company in which he was a senior director would be named in a confidential report on money laundering.) The revelations of the extent of surveillance of citizens caused an outcry and sparked a wide-ranging debate on the role of the state in a democratic society. The files were entrusted to an independent body and people were allowed access to them. In June 1993 a commission set up by the government concluded that since 1945 the security agencies had directed their activities exclusively against the political left and that they had at times been overzealous and unprofessional.

Secret Intelligence Service (SIS) British intelligence agency. Commonly known as MI-6 (from its original name, Military Intelligence, Section Six), the SIS is engaged in information gathering and espionage abroad. It is answerable to the foreign secretary and ultimately to the prime minister. Its existence was not officially acknowledged until May 1992.

secretary [segretario] In Italy, the official title of the leader in most political parties.

secretary of state [secrétaire d'état] In France, a junior member or minister of the government.

secretary of state or **state secretary** [Staatssekretär] In Germany, a junior member or minister of the federal government.

secretary of state [segretario dello stato] In San Marino, a member of the government. The latter's formal name is the Congress of State [Congresso dello Stato].

secretary of state In the United Kingdom, a senior member of the government. The title is held by most ministers of Cabinet rank.

Secure Home [Kindel Kogu] Estonian political organization. Comprising three centre-left groups, the Estonian Coalition Party (EKE) and Estonian Rural Union (EML), and the Estonian Democratic Justice Union - Estonian Pensioners' League (EDÕL-EPÜ), Kindel Kogu was formed to contest the September 1992 legislative election and support the presidential candidacy of Arnold Rüütel, who had effectively been president of the republic since 1990. The alliance gained 17/101 seats and Rüütel gained 42.2% of the popular vote, but lost to Lennart Meri in the parliamentary run-off. *See also individual party entries.*

Securitate ('Security') Shorthand for the Department of State Security (DSS), the security police in Romania during communist rule. The 26,000 Securitate agents were feared for their ruthless suppression of political dissent during the Ceauşescu regime (1965–89). The department was disbanded after the revolution which overthrew him in December 1989. Several senior officers were subsequently convicted of serious crimes but many lower-ranking members were absorbed into the new Romanian Intelligence Service (SRI), the armed forces and the police.

Security Council Resolution ... *See* RESOLUTION ....

Security Service British intelligence agency. Commonly known as MI-5 (from its original name, Military Intelligence, Section Five), the Security Service is responsible for internal security and counterintelligence activities. It is directly answerable to the home secretary and ultimately to the prime minister. In June 1992 it was given overall control over anti-terrorist operations in mainland Britain (such as those directed against the Irish Republican Army, IRA).

Seehofer, Horst (1949–) German politician. Trained in public administration, he was elected to parliament for the right-wing Christian Social Union (CSU) in 1980. He was appointed a junior minister of labour and social affairs in 1989 and became minister of health in May 1992.

Segni, Mario or **Mariotto** (1939–) Italian lawyer, academic and politician. He has taught law at various universities. Elected to parliament for the Christian Democratic Party (DC) in 1976, he held several junior ministerial posts in the 1980s. He then established himself as one of the country's leading champions of political and social reform. As part of his campaign against graft in politics, he sponsored a referendum on electoral reform in April 1993; its adoption was widely seen as a symbol of voters' disapproval of the endemic corruption within the political and business elite. He left the discredited DC in March 1993. After a brief period as leader of the new Democratic Alliance (AD), he formed the Pact for Italy in January 1994. He failed to win a parliamentary seat in the March election, but was elected to the European Parliament in June 1994.

Segni Pact *See* PACT FOR ITALY.

Séguin, Philippe (1943–) French academic, civil servant and politician. He lectured at the Institute of Political Studies from 1971–77 and also worked for several government departments. He was a senior adviser to the then prime minister, Raymond Barre, in 1977–78. Elected to parliament for the right-wing Rally for the Republic (RPR) in 1978, he was

minister of social affairs and employment in the Chirac administration (1986–88). After the right lost power in 1988 he became increasingly critical of the RPR leadership but remained within the party. In April 1993 he was elected president of the National Assembly, the lower house of parliament.

Seimas ('Assembly') Parliament of Lithuania. It has 141 members elected for a five-year term: 71 by absolute majority in single-member constituencies, with a second round of voting if required, and 70 by proportional representation. Parties must gain at least 4% of the popular vote to qualify for seats; there are special provisions for parties representing ethnic minorities.

Seiters, Rudolf (1937–) German politician. He studied law and worked in local government in Lower Saxony until his election to parliament in 1969 for the Christian Democratic Union (CDU). A senior party whip for many years, he was appointed head of the Federal Chancellery (= prime minister's office) in 1989 and became interior minister in November 1991. He resigned in July 1993 after taking political responsibility for an incident in June in which an officer of the GSG-9 anti-terrorist unit and a suspected member of the Red Army Faction (RAF) were killed.

Sejm ('Assembly') Lower house of the Polish parliament, the National Assembly. The Sejm has 460 members elected for a four-year term by a system of proportional representation. Under changes in the electoral law adopted in May 1993, 391 seats are divided among parties who obtain at least 5% of the popular vote and electoral alliances who obtain at least 8%, and 69 seats are divided among those parties with more than 7% of the vote. *See also* SENATE.

SEK *See* CYPRUS WORKERS' CONFEDERATION.

SEK Abbreviation for the KRONA, the Swedish currency, used in banking etc.

Šeks, Vladimir (1943–) Croatian lawyer and politician. He was a prominent human-rights activist during the communist regime. Elected to parliament for the right-wing Croatian Democratic Union

(HDZ) in the 1990 multiparty election, he was elected its deputy speaker and chaired its constitutional committee until August 1992, when he was appointed a deputy prime minister.

Selami, Eduard (1961-) Albanian philosopher, academic and politician. He lectured in philosophy and ethics from 1985–90. He was a founding member of the Democratic Party (PDSh), the first opposition party under communist rule, in 1990. In April 1992 he was elected party leader in succession to Sali Berisha, who had been elected president of the republic.

Self-Government Party or **Home Rule Party** [Sjálvstýrisflokkurin] (Sjfl) Faroese political party. Founded in 1906, the Self-Government Party advocates independence for the Faroes within Denmark, is centrist in its economic policies, and has liberal views on social issues. It has participated in many coalition governments, most recently from 1981–85, 1989–90 and since April 1993. At the July 1994 election it gained 2/32 seats. The leader is Lassi Klein.

Sellafield question *See* THORP QUESTION.

semi-canton *See* HALF-CANTON *and* CANTON (Switzerland).

Sén Abbreviation for Sénateur ('Senator'), a member of the Senate, the upper house of the French parliament.

Sen Abbreviation for Senatore ('Senator'), a member of the Senate, the upper house of the Italian parliament.

Senate [Senaat (Dutch), Sénat (French)] Upper house of the Belgian parliament, the Legislative Chambers. The Senate currently has 182 members: 106 directly elected by proportional representation, 50 indirectly elected by the provincial legislatures, and 25 coopted, all serving a four-year term; the heir to the throne is a member as of right. Under the constitutional changes that transformed Belgium into a federal state, finalized in July 1993, it will in future have 72 members: 40 directly elected by proportional representation, 21 indirectly elected by the legislatures of the three language-based cultural communities (Flemish, French and German-Speaking), and 10 coopted, all serving a four-year term; the heir to the

throne will continue to be a member as of right. The Senate's main function in the new structure will be to regulate disputes between the regions and communities. It will also have equal powers with the lower house, the Chamber of Deputies, in matters concerning the rights of the linguistic and cultural groups at federal level and in amending the constitution.

Senate [Senát] Upper house of the Czech parliament. It has 81 members elected for a six-year term in single-member constituencies, with a third of the seats renewed every two years. Its decisions may be overruled by the lower house, the Chamber of Deputies, by a simple majority.

Senate [Sénat] Upper house of the French parliament. The Senate has 321 members indirectly elected for a nine-year term, 309 by members of the communal, departmental and regional councils and 12 by the Superior Council of French Citizens Abroad (CSFÉ). A third of the seats are renewed every three years. Legislation adopted by the lower house, the National Assembly, requires the approval of the Senate. If it refuses to endorse a decision by the Assembly, a joint committee is set up to work out a compromise; if it cannot do so, the view of the Assembly prevails. The president of the Senate becomes acting president of the republic in the event of the president's death or resignation.

Senate [Senat] Government of Berlin, Bremen and Hamburg, three federal states of Germany.

Senate (Ireland) *See* SEANAD ÉIREANN.

Senate [Senato] Upper house of the Italian parliament. The Senate has 315 seats elected for a five-year term. Under reforms adopted in 1993, 232 members are elected by simple majority in single-member constituencies and the remaining 83 seats are allocated on a proportional basis among parties which have gained at least 4% of the popular vote. Previously it was elected by proportional representation on a regional basis. The Senate also has a variable number of life members (usually around 10), including all former presidents of the republic and five appointed by the president of the day.

It has equal powers with the lower house, the Chamber of Deputies.

Senate [Senat] Upper house of the Polish parliament, the National Assembly. It has 100 members elected for a four-year term by majority voting on a provincial basis. Each province elects two members, except for Warsaw and Katowice, which elect three. The Senate has limited veto powers over legislation passed by the lower house, the Sejm, which can in turn override its decisions by a two-thirds majority.

Senate [Senat] Upper house of the Romanian parliament. It has 143 members, elected for a four-year term by a system of proportional representation. Parties must obtain 3% of the popular vote to qualify for seats. Legislation adopted by the lower house, the Assembly of Deputies, in principle requires the approval of the Senate. If it rejects an Assembly draft, a joint committee is convened to work out a compromise; if it cannot do so, the view of the Assembly prevails.

Senate [Senado] Upper house of the Spanish parliament, the Cortes. The Senate has 254 members: 208, four from each of the 52 provinces, directly elected for a four-year term, and 46 indirectly elected by the legislatures of the 17 autonomous regions. Legislation adopted by the lower house, the Congress of Deputies, requires the approval of the Senate. If it refuses to endorse a decision by the Congress, a joint committee is set up to work out a compromise; if it cannot do so, the view of the Congress prevails.

senator [Senator] In Bremen, Berlin and Hamburg (Germany), a member of the state government. The government is called the Senate [Senat] in all three states.

senatore a vita See LIFE SENATOR.

Senyera ('Banner' in Catalan) Flag of Catalonia, an autonomous community or region of Spain. It consists of nine alternating yellow and red horizontal stripes. Its display was banned during the Franco regime (1939–75).

SER See SOCIAL AND ECONOMIC COUNCIL.

Serb [Srpski] Official language of Yugoslavia. See SERBOCROAT.

Serb-Croat war (Croatia) See CROATIAN CIVIL WAR.

Serb Krajina See KRAJINA and REPUBLIC OF SERBIAN KRAJINA.

Serb Lands [Srpske Zemlje] Collective name for the regions inhabited by Serbs and Serb Orthodox Christians. They include Serbia proper, the main republic of Yugoslavia, most of northwestern and much of eastern Bosnia-Herzegovina and much of southern and southeastern Croatia. Serb settlement outside Serbia largely dates from the 16th and 17th centuries, when the Austrians gave land and special rights to Serbs fleeing Turkish rule in return for military service in what were then border regions with the Ottoman Empire (*see* KRAJINA). Serb nationalists advocating a 'GREATER SERBIA' also regard Montenegro and Macedonia as 'Serb lands'. The Kosovo and Vojvodina regions within Serbia have large non-Serb populations.

Serb-Muslim war (Bosnia-Herzegovina) *See* BOSNIAN CIVIL WAR.

Serb National Party See SERB PEOPLE'S PARTY.

Serb People's Party [Srpska Narodna Stranka] (SNS) Croatian political party. Founded in 1991, the SNS seeks to promote the cultural and individual rights of ethnic Serbs in Croatia. Its support is largely based in Zagreb and the other main cities. It did not back the uprising by Serb forces in the Krajina region in 1991 (*see* CROATIAN CIVIL WAR). At the August 1992 election it gained 1.1% of the vote and 3/138 seats. The leader is Milan Dukić.

Serb Republic See SERBIAN REPUBLIC.

Serbia [Srbija] Republic of Yugoslavia. Serbia has an area of 88,361 sq km and a population of 9,781,000. It accounts for 86% of the area and 94% of the population of the federation, dwarfing the other republic, Montenegro. In ethnic terms 65.7% of the people are Serbs, 17.2% Albanians (concentrated in the southwestern region of Kosovo), 3.5% Hungarians (in the northern region of Vojvodina), 3.2% Yugoslavs (self-description), 2.4% Slav Muslims (recognized as an ethnic group in Yugoslavia), 1.4% Montenegrins and 1.1% Croats; there are also small numbers of Slovaks, Gipsies, Bulgarians,

Romanians, Vlachs and others. The main languages are Serb, Albanian and Hungarian. Most Serbs are nominally Serbian Orthodox Christians, the Albanians are Muslims, and the Hungarians Roman Catholics. The capital is Belgrade [Beograd], and the other major cities are Novi Sad, Niš, Priština and Subotica. The economy is based on agriculture (cereals, fruit and vegetables, pig farming), manufacturing (metalworking, engineering, textiles, chemicals) and mining. The economy has virtually collapsed as a result of market-led restructuring, the loss of trade with other former Yugoslav republics and above all the imposition of international sanctions because of Serbia's involvement in the Bosnian civil war. Legislative power is exercised by the 250-member Assembly [Skupština] elected for a four-year term; executive power is exercised by the president, also elected for a four-year term, and a government headed by a prime minister. The dominant party is the Socialist Party of Serbia (SPS), the successor to the League of Communists; the other major parties are the far-right Serbian Renewal Movement (SPO), the far-right Serbian Radical Party (SRS), the centrist Democratic Party (DS), the centrist Democratic Movement of Serbia (DEPOS), the right-wing Democratic Party of Serbia (DSS), the Democratic Union of Vojvodina Hungarians (DZVM or VMDK) and the Democratic League of Kosovo (DSK or LDK). At the republican election in December 1993 the SPS gained 35.1% of the vote and 123/250 seats, DEPOS (then an alliance including the SPO) 17.4% and 45 seats, the SRS 13.7% and 39 seats, the DS 12.1% and 29 seats, the DSS 2.8% and seven seats, and the VMDK 2.0% and five seats; the LDK boycotted the poll. The president is Slobodan Milošević, the prime minister Mirko Marjanović. Serbia was united as a kingdom in 1169. It came under Turkish domination after the Battle of Kosovo in 1389 and was annexed by the Ottoman Empire in 1459. There were major uprisings against Turkish rule in the 1680s, 1780s, 1804–13 and 1815–17. Serbia secured a degree of autonomy in 1829 and regained its independence in 1878, becoming a kingdom in 1882. The new state initially comprised only northern Serbia proper, but its territory was greatly enlarged after the Balkan Wars (1912–13 and 1913) to include all of Serbia proper and Macedonia. The policy of seeking to bring the ethnic Serbs of Vojvodina, Bosnia-Herzegovina and Croatia into the Serbian state led to friction with Austria-Hungary, which was one of the causes of the First World War (1914–18). In 1918 Serbia became the nucleus of the newly created Kingdom of Serbs, Croats and Slovenes, renamed Yugoslavia in 1929. When Yugoslavia was reconstituted under communist control at the end of the Second World War (1939–45), Serbia became one of its six republics, with Kosovo and Vojvodina becoming autonomous provinces within its borders. As communist authority crumbled in the late 1980s, the Serbian government strongly opposed demands from the other republics for a looser federation. In 1989/90 the autonomous provinces were effectively abolished. The League of Communists (SKS) was relaunched as the SPS in July 1990. As the four other republics declared their independence in 1991/92, the Serbian government supported the uprisings of the Serb minorities in Croatia and then Bosnia-Herzegovina. In April 1992 Serbia and Montenegro adopted a new federal constitution. *See also* KOSOVO-METOHIJA, VOJVODINA *and* YUGOSLAVIA.

Serbia and Montenegro and **Serbia-Montenegro** Alternative names for Yugoslavia used by those, including the United Nations and the European Union (EU), who do not recognize the current state as the legal or sole successor to the old federation or former Yugoslavia. Serbia and Montenegro are the two republics which formed a new federation in April 1992.

Serbian Chetnik Movement [Srpski Četnicki Pokret] (SČP) or **Chetniks** [Četnici] Yugoslav, Bosnian and Croatian paramilitary group. The SČP is the armed wing of the far-right Serbian Radical Party (SRS), which advocates the creation of a 'Greater Serbia'. It takes its name and inspiration from the Chetniks [Četnici], the Serb nationalist movement active in the 19th century and the guerrilla army which fought against the Germans, Croats and communist resistance fighters during the Second World War (1939–45). It is the largest of the country's paramilitary groups, with a strength of 8,000. It has fought alongside local Serb forces in the Bosnian and Croatian civil wars and has been linked to a number of massacres of Muslims and Croats. The leader is Vojislav Šešelj, who also heads the SRS. (In April 1994 the SRS announced that the SČP had been dissolved 'to avoid accusations of covert activity in neighbouring states'.)

Serbian Democratic Party [Srpska Demokratska Stranka] (SDS) Bosnian political party. Founded in 1990 and closely linked to the party of the same name in Croatia and the Socialist Party of Serbia (SPS), the SDS is the main representative of the Serb community. At the December 1990 election in the republic it gained 72/240 seats. It calls for the unification of the Serb-populated areas with Serbia and is the moving force behind the breakaway Serbian Republic. The leader is Radovan Karadžić.

Serbian Democratic Party of Krajina [Srpska Demokratska Stranka Krajine] (SDS Krajine or SDSK) Croatian political party. Founded in 1990 and closely linked to the party of the same name in Bosnia-Herzegovina and the Socialist Party of Serbia (SPS), the SDSK is the main representative of the Serb community. It calls for the unification of the Serb-populated areas with Serbia and is the moving force behind the breakaway Republic of Serbian Krajina. The leaders are Milan Martić and Milan Babić.

Serbian Falcons [Srpski Sokolovi] Yugoslav, Bosnian and Croatian paramilitary group. Like similar Serb groups, the Falcons take their inspiration from the Chetniks [Četnici], the Serb nationalist movement active in the 19th century and the guerrilla army which fought against the Germans, Croats and communist resistance fighters during the Second World War (1939–45). They are the armed wing of the far-right Serbian Royalist Movement (SRP), which advocates the restoration of the monarchy in a 'Greater Serbia'. The leader is Sinisa Vučinić, who also heads the SRP.

Serbian Guard *See* SERBIAN NATIONAL GUARD.

Serbian Hawks *See* SERBIAN FALCONS.

Serbian Krajina *See* KRAJINA *and* REPUBLIC OF SERBIAN KRAJINA.

Serbian National Guard [Srpska Narodna Garda] (SNG) or **Tigers** [Tigari] Yugoslav, Bosnian and Croatian paramilitary group. Formed in 1991, the Tigers advocate the creation of a 'Greater Serbia' and have fought alongside local Serb forces in the Bosnian and Croatian civil wars. They have also been active – effectively with the approval of the Serbian authorities – in intimidating and controlling the Albanian majority in the Kosovo region. They have been accused of murdering thousands of Muslim, Croat and Albanian civilians, and are also said to be involved in organized crime. The leader is Zeljko Raznjatović, nicknamed 'Arkan'.

Serbian Radical Party [Srpska Radikalna Stranka] (SRS) Yugoslav political party. Founded in 1990, the SRS is one of the most extreme Serb nationalist parties advocating the incorporation of all 'Serb lands' into a 'Greater Serbia'. It has a large paramilitary wing, the Serbian Chetnik Movement (SČP), which actively supports local Serb forces in Bosnia-Herzegovina and Croatia. Modelled on the fascist parties of the 1930s, it stresses the importance of the *vodj* ('leader'), who is Vojislav Šešelj. At the elections in December 1992 it became the country's second-largest party, gaining 22.6% of the vote and 73/250 seats in the Serbian parliament, 7.8% and 8/85 seats in the Montenegrin parliament, and 34/138 seats in the Federal Assembly. After breaking off its alliance with the ruling Socialist Party of Serbia (SPS), it lost some ground at the early election in Serbia in December 1993, gaining 13.7% and 39 seats.

Serbian Renewal Movement [Srpski Pokret Obnove] (SPO) Yugoslav political party. Founded in 1989, the SPO is a far-right Serb nationalist party advocating the incorporation of all 'Serb lands' into a single state of 'Greater Serbia' and the restoration of the monarchy. It is strongly opposed to the ruling Socialist Party of Serbia (SPS). It contested the December 1992 and December 1993 elections within the opposition DEMOCRATIC MOVEMENT OF SERBIA (DEPOS). The leader is Vuk Drašković.

Serbian Republic [Srpska Republika] (SR) State proclaimed within Bosnia-Herzegovina by representatives of the Serb community. Most Bosnian Serbs, who number around a third of the population, opposed the dismemberment of the Yugoslav federation in 1991. In September four 'autonomous regions' were proclaimed in Serb-populated areas, and in October most Serb members of parliament set up a separate assembly. Its call for a boycott of the referendum on independence held in February/March 1992 was widely heeded by Serbs. In March it proclaimed the Serbian Republic of Bosnia-Herzegovina (SRBiH). (The 'of Bosnia-Herzegovina' was later dropped in line with a decision to delete all references to the country.) The SR has an assembly and a government, based in Pale, and an 80,000-strong army. The dominant party is the Serbian Democratic Party (SDS), which holds 70/83 seats in the assembly. The president is Radovan Karadžić, leader of the SDS. In the first few months of the civil war which broke out in March 1992 Serb forces were able to gain control of around two-thirds of Bosnian territory, including all Serb-majority districts, mainly in the northwest, and some ethnically mixed areas in the east. By the end of the year most non-Serbs had fled or been expelled from these territories. In September 1992 the SR assembly formally declared its support for the republic's eventual unification with Serbia. Later that month it approved plans for close political and economic cooperation with the Republic of Serbian Krajina (RSK), its counterpart across the border in Croatia. *See also* BOSNIAN CIVIL WAR.

Serbian Republic of Krajina *See* REPUBLIC OF SERBIAN KRAJINA.

serbianization [srbizacija] In Serbia (Yugoslavia), the policy of asserting Serb dominance in all spheres of society and public life and circumscribing the rights of ethnic minorities. Since 1990 it has been implemented, formally and informally, in the Kosovo region, which has a large Albanian majority, and to a lesser extent in Vojvodina, which has a substantial Hungarian minority. In Kosovo it has involved the introduction of Serbs into positions of political and economic power (local government officers, company managers etc), the dissolution of local political institutions, a ban on teaching Albanian and on its use in the official media, the dismissal of Albanians from public-sector jobs, and intimidation by the armed forces, police and paramilitary groups (operating effectively with the approval of the authorities).

Serbocroat [Srpskohrvatski] Official language of former Yugoslavia and still the official language of one of its successor states, Bosnia-Herzegovina. The term 'Serbocroat' was coined in the 19th century to stress the underlying unity of the South Slav dialects and languages spoken in Serbia, Croatia, Bosnia-Herzegovina and Montenegro. A standardized version was adopted as the official language of the new Yugoslav state established in 1918. The established written forms, Serb and Croat, share the same grammar, but the former is written in the cyrillic script and the latter in the latin script and there are some differences in vocabulary, syntax, accent and stress. (Many linguists compare these to the differences between British and American English or between Portuguese and Brazilian Portuguese.) Serb and Croat nationalists have always sought to exaggerate the differences, however, and following the disintegration of the old Yugoslav federation in 1991/92 Croat [Hrvatski] was declared the official language of Croatia and Serb [Srpski] became the official language of rump Yugoslavia, comprising Serbia and Montenegro. In Bosnia-Herzegovina the name 'Bosnian' is gaining currency.

Serenissima Repubblica di San Marino ('Most Serene Republic of San Marino') Official name of San Marino in Italian.

Serpent's Island question *See* BESSARABIA QUESTION.

Serra, Jaume (1959–) Andorran businessman and politician. An economics graduate, he has worked in industry, commerce and tourism. He was appointed minister for the economy in January 1994. He is close to the centre-right National Democratic Association (AND).

Serra, Narcís (1943–) Spanish economist, academic and politician. He taught economics at several universities from 1965–77. A member of the Catalan Socialist Party (PSC), the regional branch of the Spanish Socialist Workers' Party (PSOE), he was elected mayor of his native Barcelona in 1979. When the PSOE came to power in 1982, he was appointed defence minister, a key post in view of the prominent role played by the military during the Franco regime (1939–75). He was made deputy prime minister in March 1991, and was also given responsibility for coordinating economic policy in July 1993.

Serreqi, Alfred (1938–) Albanian doctor and politician. He was elected to parliament for the new Democratic Party (PDSh) in 1991. He was a deputy health minister in 1991–92 and then briefly headed the party's international department. In April 1992 he was appointed foreign minister in the coalition formed by the PDSh after its defeat of the former communists in the previous month's early election.

Šešelj, Vojislav (1954–) Yugoslav philosopher, academic and politician. He has lectured in philosophy and political science at the University of Sarajevo (now in Bosnia-Herzegovina). From 1984–86 he was imprisoned by the communist authorities for his Serb nationalist views. He founded the far-right Serbian Radical Party (SRS) in January 1990. In 1991 he also set up a paramilitary force, the Serbian Chetnik Movement (SČP), which has fought alongside local Serb forces in Bosnia-Herzegovina and Croatia. He has been accused of organizing massacres of Muslims and Croats. He was elected to parliament in 1990.

set aside (European Union) *See* COMMON AGRICULTURAL POLICY.

set of ideas (Cyprus) *See* CYPRUS QUESTION *and* RESOLUTION 716.

SEV *See* FEDERATION OF GREEK INDUSTRIES.

seven wise people (United Kingdom) *See* GROUP OF WISE PEOPLE.

Seventeenth of November Revolutionary Organization [Dekaeptá Noémvris Epanastatikó Orgánosi] (N-17) Greek guerrilla group. This far-left group emerged in 1975, when it claimed responsibility for the murder of an American intelligence officer. It is opposed to capitalism, Greek membership of the North Atlantic Treaty Organization (NATO) and the European Union (EU), the existence of US military bases in Greece, and the Turkish military presence in Cyprus. It has been responsible for 20 assassinations of politicians, state prosecutors, businesspeople and foreign diplomats. It is thought to have close links with the Revolutionary People's Struggle (ELA), another guerrilla group. The organization is named after the day in 1973 when Athens students staged an uprising against the military dictatorship in power at the time.

Seveso accident Environmental disaster caused by an explosion at a chemical factory in Seveso, Italy, in 1976. The explosion resulted in the discharge of a cloud of dioxin gas, a highly toxic by-product in the manufacture of herbicides. Crops and other vegetation were contaminated, the town had to be evacuated and domestic animals destroyed. The dioxin did not cause any human deaths but many people exposed to it subsequently developed chloracne, a serious skin disorder. Probably the worst industrial accident in Europe since 1945, it prompted national governments and the European Community (EC, now the European Union, EU) to review regulations on the use of hazardous chemicals. The EC's 'Seveso Directive', adopted in June 1982, sets out a procedure for identifying and reducing the risks of major industrial accidents.

SF (Denmark) *See* SOCIALIST PEOPLE'S PARTY.

SF Abbreviation for Finland, used for international vehicle registrations, postal addresses etc. It is taken from Suomi and

Finland, the country's names in Finnish and Swedish, the two official languages.

SF (Ireland, United Kingdom) *See* SINN FÉIN.

SFP *See* SWEDISH PEOPLE'S PARTY.

SFr Abbreviation for the FRANC, the Swiss currency.

SFRJ and **SFRY** Abbreviations, in Serbo-croat and English respectively, for the Socialist Federal Republic of Yugoslavia, the official name of the Yugoslav federation from 1963 until April 1992, when it was reconstituted as the Federal Republic of Yugoslavia (FRJ or FRY), comprising two of the formerly six republics (Serbia and Montenegro). *See also* FORMER YUGOSLAVIA.

SGB *See* SWISS TRADE UNION FEDERATION.

SGP *See* POLITICAL REFORMED PARTY.

shadow cabinet In the United Kingdom, the parliamentary leadership of the largest opposition party. Its members are responsible for portfolios which correspond to or 'shadow' those of government ministers. In the Labour Party the shadow cabinet members are elected by the parliamentary group and the party leader allocates portfolios. In the Conservative Party the leader appoints the shadow cabinet.

shadow government (Italy) *See* HIDDEN GOVERNMENT.

SHAPE Abbreviation for Supreme Headquarters Allied Powers Europe, the headquarters of the ALLIED COMMAND EUROPE (ACE), a military arm of the North Atlantic Treaty Organization (NATO).

Shephard, Gillian (1940–) British civil servant and politician. She worked as an education officer and schools inspector from 1963–75. In the 1980s she chaired several health authorities and was a county councillor for the Conservative Party in Norfolk. Elected to Parliament in 1987, she became a junior minister in 1990, joined the Cabinet as secretary of state for employment in 1992 and was made minister of agriculture, food and fisheries in May 1993. She became secretary of state for education in July 1994.

sherpas In the European Union (EU), an informal name for the civil servants who prepare meetings of the Council of Ministers and the European Council (the summit of heads of government). They are usually attached to the European Commission, the EU's administrative and executive arm, or represent national governments. (The Sherpa are a Himalayan people renowned as guides and porters in mountaineering expeditions.)

ShIK Abbreviation for Shërbimi Informativ Kombëtar ('National Information Services'), the Albanian intelligence agency.

shire counties In the United Kingdom, the non-metropolitan counties of England. *See* COUNTY (United Kingdom).

shock therapy (Poland) *See* CONTROLLED SHOCK.

SHP *See* SOCIAL DEMOCRATIC PEOPLE'S PARTY.

Shqipëria Albanian name for Albania.

Shqipëria e Madhë *See* GREATER ALBANIA.

Sicilia *See* SICILY.

Sicilian Mafia *See* MAFIA.

Sicily [Sicilia] Special autonomous region of Italy. The largest island in the Mediterranean Sea, situated off the southern coast of Italy, Sicily has an area of 25,709 sq km and a population of 4,990,000. The capital is Palermo, and the other main cities are Catania, Messina and Syracuse [Siracusa]. The economy is based on agriculture (fruit and vegetables, wine, cereals, sheep and goat farming), manufacturing (petrochemicals, chemicals, food processing), mining (natural gas), fishing and tourism. The island is one of Italy's poorest regions, and emigration has been heavy since the 19th century. Political power is exercised by the Regional Assembly [Consiglio Regionale], with 90 members elected for a five-year term, and an executive council headed by a president. The main political parties are the Italian People's Party (PPI, the successor to the Christian Democratic Party, DC), the Italian Socialist Party (PSI), the Democratic Left Party (PDS) and the centre-left Network (La Rete). At the election in June 1991 the DC gained 42.0% of the vote and 39 seats, the PSI 14.0% and 13 seats, the PDS 10.8% and 13 seats, and the Network 7.8% and six seats. As in the rest of Italy, the party-political scene has been transformed by the corruption scandals which have come to light since 1992. From the 6th century Sicily was ruled successively by Byzantines, Arabs, Normans, Germans (Hohenstaufens), French (Angevins), Aragonese, Spanish Habsburgs, Austrian Habsburgs and Spanish Bourbons. During the centuries of foreign rule the local nobility retained many privileges but also staged numerous revolts. In 1816 the island was merged with Naples to form the Kingdom of the Two Sicilies. It became part of unified Italy in 1861. In recognition of its strong regional identity and position as an island, Sicily was made an autonomous region with special statute in 1947. A feature of the island's political and social life is the role played by organized crime: it is the home base of the Mafia.

Siculi Romanian name for Szeklers, ethnic Hungarians living in eastern Transylvania, a historical region of Romania.

Sigurimi ('Security') Common name for the State Security Service, the Albanian security police during communist rule. The Sigurimi was feared for its ruthless suppression of dissent. At the time of its dissolution in 1991 it was said to employ around 30,000 people, nearly 1% of the country's total population.

SIK Abbreviation for Shërbimi Informativ Kombëtar ('National Information Services'), the Albanian intelligence agency. The more accurate abbreviation is 'ShIK'.

Silajdžić, Haris (1945–) Bosnian historian, academic and politician. A Slav Muslim, he was elected to parliament for the Democratic Action Party (SDA) in 1990. When Bosnia-Herzegovina declared its independence from Yugoslavia in March 1992, he was appointed foreign minister. In the early stages of the civil war he was a strong advocate of a multiethnic and unitary Bosnian state. He was appointed prime minister in October 1993. In May 1994 he also became prime minister of the new Muslim-Croat Federation.

Silesia [Slezsko] Historical region of the Czech Republic. Czech Silesia corresponds to the small part of the Polish historical region of Silesia not ceded by Austria to Prussia in 1742. It became a province of Czechoslovakia in 1918 and was joined to Moravia in 1927. Moravia-Silesia was dissolved in 1949. Since the collapse of communist rule in 1989, there have been growing demands for the creation of an autonomous region of Silesia or a wider Moravia-Silesia.

Silesia [Śląsk] Historical region of Poland. Situated in the southwest, Silesia was part of the Polish kingdom established in the late 10th century. Immigration of German settlers was encouraged, and by the 14th century the region had become predominantly German and been incorporated into the Holy Roman Empire. It passed to the Austrian Habsburgs in 1526, was conquered by Prussia in 1742, and became part of unified Germany in 1871. After the First World War (1914–18) Poland acquired the key industrial centres of Upper Silesia. Most of the German population fled or was expelled towards the end of the Second World War (1939–45), and the whole region was allocated to Poland in 1945. The rights of the remaining German minority, estimated today at around 500,000 or 5% of the region's population, were suppressed under communist rule.

Silesian Germans [Silesiendeutsche] Collective name for ethnic Germans who fled or were expelled from Silesia, now part of Poland, at the end of the Second World War (1939–45). Since the collapse of Poland's communist regime in 1989 Silesian German organizations have reaffirmed their demands for compensation, restitution of their property and/or the right to resettle. *See also* Silesia (Poland).

Siliņš, Andris (1945–) Latvian toolmaker, economist and trade-union official. Between 1978 and 1990 he held several senior posts in the trade-union movement in Latvia and in the Soviet All-Union Central Council of Trade Unions (VTsPS). When most of the republic's unions withdrew from the Soviet structure in May 1990 to form the Association of Free Trade Unions of Latvia (LBAS), he was elected its chairman.

Silva, Aníbal Cavaco *See* Cavaco Silva, ….

Simeon of Saxe-Coburg-Gotha (from 1943–46 **King Simeon II**) (1937–) Former king [tsar] of Bulgaria. He succeeded to the throne (at the age of seven) on the death of his father, Boris III. When the new communist government abolished the monarchy in 1946 he went into exile, eventually settling in Spain. He never formally abdicated. (Since the collapse of communist rule in 1989/90 several parties have called for the restoration of the monarchy.)

Simić, Željko (1958–) Yugoslav journalist, writer and politician. He has written for newspapers and magazines and published several books on cultural and other issues. A close adviser of President Milošević of Serbia since the late 1980s, he was appointed a federal deputy prime minister in July 1993. He is a member of the Socialist Party of Serbia (SPS).

Simitis, Konstantinos or **Kostas** (1936–) Greek lawyer, academic and politician. He practised and taught law until his appointment as minister of agriculture in the Pan-Hellenic Socialist Movement (PASOK) government formed in 1981. Elected to parliament in 1985, he has served as minister of economic affairs (1985–87) and education and religion (1989–90) and became minister of industry, commerce, energy and technology when PASOK returned to power in October 1993.

Šimko, Ivan (1955–) Slovakian economist and politician. During the 1980s he worked at the Institute of Regional Planning (VÚOP) and in the Bratislava chief architect's office. He was a member of the Czechoslovak federal parliament for the Christian Democratic Movement (KDH) from 1990 until the federation's dissolution at the end of 1992. He was briefly Slovakia's justice minister in 1992. He was appointed a deputy prime minister, with responsibility for legislative affairs, in the centrist coalition which took office in March 1994.

Simović, Tomislav (1948–) Yugoslav mechanical engineer and politician. He worked for a railway-carriage factory in his home town of Kraljevo from 1976 until 1993, becoming its managing director in 1990. He was appointed economy minister in March 1993. He is a member of the Socialist Party of Serbia (SPS).

SIN and **Sinaspismós** *See* PROGRESSIVE LEFT ALLIANCE.

sindaco (pl. sindaci) Italian local government official, usually translated as 'mayor'. S/he is the chief executive of the commune [comune] or municipality, the main tier of local government, and the representative of the central government. The *sindaco* was formerly elected by the municipal council, but following reforms introduced in 1993, s/he is now directly elected. The office's powers have also been significantly increased.

síndic general ('syndic-general') President or speaker of the General Council, the Andorran parliament.

Single Act *See* SINGLE EUROPEAN ACT.

single currency In the European Union (EU), a policy objective aimed at establishing permanently fixed exchange rates and/or replacing existing currencies with a new currency. It is considered a key prerequisite of ECONOMIC AND MONETARY UNION (EMU). The term 'common currency' is also used, although this causes some confusion because it is also used in the context of an alternative proposal for a currency that would circulate alongside existing currencies (*see* HARD ECU PLAN).

Single European Act (SEA) International agreement adopted by the member states of the European Community (EC), now the European Union (EU). Signed on 17 February 1986 and effective from 1 July 1987, it represented the first comprehensive revision of the basic treaties of the Community, in particular the TREATY OF ROME establishing the European Economic Community (EEC, now the EC). It provided for the completion of the single internal market, extended cooperation in several policy areas, formalized the status of several Community bodies and structures, and streamlined decision making within the organization. Some of its provisions were superseded by the TREATY ON EUROPEAN UNION, which came into force in November 1993.

Specifically, the Act comprises four titles and 34 articles. Title I sets out the

basic objective of 'making concrete progress towards European unity'. Title II consists of a series of amendments to the basic treaties as regards both policies and institutions. It outlines the means for achieving the internal market, an 'area without internal frontiers, in which the free movement of goods, persons, services and capital is ensured', by the end of 1992, establishes economic and monetary union as an objective, gives formal status to the European Monetary System (EMS), and extends cooperation in monetary, social, regional, environmental, research and technology policy. It also extends the scope for qualified majority voting (to matters which had previously required unanimity) in the Council of Ministers, increases the powers of the European Parliament to delay and amend legislation, and formalizes the status of the European Council, the biannual summit meeting of member states' heads of government. Title III contains an intergovernmental agreement (i.e. formally outside the EC framework) on closer cooperation in foreign-policy matters through European Political Cooperation (EPC).
See also entries on specific treaties, institutions, policies, terms etc.

single internal market, single market or **internal market** In the European Union (EU) and the European Economic Area (EEA), the guarantee of free movement of goods, services, capital and people – as within a single country – throughout the participating states. The creation of a 'common market' was a key objective set out in the Treaty of Rome establishing the European Economic Community (EEC) in 1958. A major barrier to the free movement of goods was removed in 1968 with the completion of the customs union, which abolished internal tariffs. Further progress proved slow until 1985, when the Commission published a white paper identifying the remaining barriers, proposing 282 measures to remove them and setting out a timetable for doing so by the end of 1992. The project was considered a key precondition for an eventual ECONOMIC AND MONETARY UNION (EMU) and was approved by the heads of govern-

ment in June 1985. The Single European Act, a revision of the Treaty of Rome agreed in February 1986, defined the single market as an 'area without internal frontiers, in which the free movment of goods, persons, services and capital is ensured'. The single market was established on schedule on 1 January 1993. A year later it was extended, with some exceptions, to five of the seven member states of the European Free Trade Association (EFTA) (*see* AGREEMENT ON THE EUROPEAN ECONOMIC AREA). The single-market programme – dubbed '1992' in some countries and '1993' in others – in principle removed physical barriers (border controls and formalities etc), technical barriers (different national standards and regulations etc) and fiscal barriers (differential rates of value-added tax, excise duties and other indirect taxes etc). This was done mainly by 'harmonization' and 'approximation' of member states' laws and 'mutual recognition' of standards. A number of exceptions still remained, however, such as wide variations in some indirect taxes and, in some states, passport controls at internal borders for immigration and security purposes. The programme was also to be complemented by a range of 'flanking measures' concerned with workers' rights, regional assistance, immigration, competition and tendering rules etc. *See also* ECONOMIC AND SOCIAL COHESION.

single market In the European Union (EU) and the European Economic Area (EEA), shorthand for the SINGLE INTERNAL MARKET.

Sinn Féin ('We Ourselves' or 'Ourselves Alone') (SF) British and Irish political party. Sinn Féin – the Irish name is commonly used – has its roots in the struggle for Irish independence. Founded in 1905, it opposed the creation of the Irish Free State in 1922 which ended British rule in the south of the island but left Northern Ireland within the United Kingdom. A dominant force until then, it subsequently became marginalized in (southern) Ireland while maintaining support within the Catholic community in Northern Ireland. It was banned there from 1956–

73. When the party split in 1969 into an 'official' wing and a 'provisional' wing, the latter retained the name Sinn Féin and is still sometimes called Provisional Sinn Féin. It advocates the reunification of Ireland as a 'democratic socialist' republic. It has generally been supportive of the violent campaign waged by the Irish Republican Army (IRA) – it is widely seen as its political wing – but is also believed to have been instrumental in the IRA's decision to declare a ceasefire from September 1994. Since the 1970s it has had the support of around a third of Catholic voters in Northern Ireland. At the British general election in April 1992 it gained 10.0% of the vote in Northern Ireland but no seats; at the local elections in May 1993 it gained 12.5%. At the Irish election in November 1992 it gained 1.6% of the vote and no seats. Gerry Adams has been party leader since 1983.

Sinti Alternative name for GIPSIES or Romanies, widely used in Germany. The Sinti or Manush are one of the traditional major regional and occupational subdivisions among Gipsies.

SIS Abbreviation for Serviço de Informações e Segurança ('Information and Security Service'), the Portuguese intelligence agency.

SIS Abbreviation for Slovenská Informátičná Služba ('Slovakian Information Service'), the Slovakian intelligence agency.

SIS (United Kingdom) *See* SECRET INTELLIGENCE SERVICE.

SIS Abbreviation for Schengen Information System, the central computer database on wanted persons, illegal immigrants and stolen property set up under the SCHENGEN ACCORDS.

SISDE *See* INFORMATION AND DEMOCRATIC SECURITY SERVICE.

SISMI *See* INFORMATION AND MILITARY SECURITY SERVICE.

sistemizaţie *See* SYSTEMIZATION.

SIT Abbreviation for the TOLAR, the Slovenian currency, used in banking etc.

siva ekonomija *See* GREY ECONOMY.

Six, the Shorthand for the founding member states of the European Union (EU), i.e. Belgium, France, Italy, Luxemburg, the Netherlands and West Germany. The term has no relevance today, except that it is sometimes used to describe the 'inner core' of EU members generally most committed to further integration.

Six Counties Informal name for Northern Ireland, a component of the United Kingdom. When Ireland was partitioned in 1922, six of the island's 32 counties remained within the United Kingdom as Northern Ireland. They no longer have any administrative or political functions.

Sj *See* INDEPENDENCE PARTY.

Sjfl *See* SELF-GOVERNMENT PARTY.

Sk Abbreviation for the KORUNA, the Slovakian currency.

SK Abbreviation for Slovakia, used for postal addresses etc.

Skandalidis, Konstantinos or **Kostas** (1938–) Greek electrical engineer and politician. He joined the Pan-Hellenic Socialist Movement (PASOK) as a full-time official in 1984. Elected to parliament in 1989, he was appointed minister for Aegean affairs in October 1993 and became interior minister in July 1994.

SKD *See* SLOVENIAN CHRISTIAN DEMOCRATS.

Škegro, Borislav (1955–) Croatian economist and politician. He has worked at the Zagreb Economic Institute and been an economic adviser to President Tudjman. A member of the right-wing Croatian Democratic Union (HDZ), he was appointed a deputy prime minister in April 1993.

SKK Abbreviation for the KORUNA, the Slovakian currency, used in banking etc.

SKL *See* FINNISH CHRISTIAN UNION.

Skopje Name for Macedonia used in Greece since the region's establishment as a Yugoslav republic in 1944. Greece objects to the use of 'Macedonia' on the grounds that it implies a territorial claim on the northern Greek region of the same name. *See* MACEDONIA NAME QUESTION.

Skopje Shorthand for the Macedonian government. Skopje is the capital of Macedonia.

Skoularikis, Giannis (1929–) Greek lawyer and politician. A specialist in labour law, he worked for the Council of State, a government advisory body, until the military seized power in 1967. Following the restoration of democracy in 1974 he was elected to parliament for the Pan-Hellenic Socialist Movement (PASOK). He served as minister of public order from 1981–85 and briefly as deputy interior minister in 1988 and justice minister in 1989. In July 1994 he was appointed minister of labour.

SKr Abbreviation for the KRONA, the Swedish currency.

Skubiszewski, Krzysztof (1926–) Polish lawyer and diplomat. A specialist in international law, he taught at the Academy of Sciences from 1973–89. He was appointed foreign minister in the government formed by the anti-communist Solidarity movement in September 1989. He retained the post in successive governments of different complexions until October 1993. He is not a member of a political party.

Skupština ('Assembly') Parliament of Bosnia-Herzegovina. It is composed of the 130-member Chamber of Citizens [Vijeće Gradjanstvo] and the 110-member Chamber of Municipalities [Vijeće Općina]. Elections to the Skupština were last held in December 1990. It effectively ceased to function as a national parliament when most Serb and Croat representatives withdrew from it and set up their own assemblies in the run-up to the civil war that broke out in March 1992.

Skupština ('Assembly') Parliament in Montenegro and Serbia, the two constituent republics of Yugoslavia.

Skupština Shorthand for Savezna Skupština ('Federal Assembly'), the Yugoslav parliament, composed of the CHAMBER OF CITIZENS and CHAMBER OF REPUBLICS.

Sládek, Miroslav (1950–) Czech mathematician and politician. A specialist in information processing, he worked at various research institutes before entering politics. After the collapse of communist rule in December 1989 he founded and became leader of the new far-right Association for the Republic - Republican Party of Czechoslovakia (SPR-RSČ) or Republicans.

Śląsk *See* SILESIA (Poland).

SLAT *See* NATIONAL HARMONY PARTY.

Slav Macedonians Alternative name for Macedonian-speaking people in Greece. The Greek authorities do not recognize the existence of a distinct Macedonian ethnic group in the northern region of Macedonia, although they accept that a number of people in the region speak a 'Slavic dialect', i.e. Macedonian. *See also* MACEDONIA NAME QUESTION.

Slav Muslims or **Muslims** Ethnic group in Bosnia-Herzegovina and neighbouring countries. Slav Muslims are the descendants of local Slavs who converted to Islam during the five centuries of Ottoman rule which ended in the late 19th century. (In the Balkan region religion has historically been one of the key differentiators between ethnic groups.) The largest single group in Bosnia-Herzegovina, they were recognized as a 'nationality' following the reconstitution of Yugoslavia in 1945 and as a 'nation' in 1967. According to the 1991 census in the old Yugoslav federation, there were 1.91 million Slav Muslims in Bosnia-Herzegovina (43.7% of the republic's population), 320,000 in Serbia and Montenegro (present-day Yugoslavia) (3.1%), 48,000 in Croatia (1.0%), and 35,000 in Macedonia (2.1%). Their status as a distinct group is denied by many Croat and Serb nationalists, who consider them Croats or Serbs of Muslim faith respectively. In recent years, and especially since the outbreak of the Bosnian civil war in March 1992, the country's Slav Muslims have increasingly begun to call themselves 'Bosnians' [Bosniaki].

SLD (Poland) *See* DEMOCRATIC LEFT ALLIANCE.

SLD (United Kingdom) *See* LIBERAL DEMOCRATS.

Šleževičius, Adolfas (1948–) Lithuanian mechanical engineer and politician. He worked for several dairy companies and held several junior ministerial posts in the agriculture ministry when the republic was still part of the Soviet Union. A member of the Democratic Labour Party (LDDP), the successor to the Communist Party, he was appointed prime minister in March 1993. He was also elected party leader the following month, succeeding Algirdas Brazauskas, who had been elected president of the republic.

Slezsko *See* SILESIA (Czech Republic).

SLO Abbreviation for Slovenia, used for international vehicle registrations, postal addresses etc.

Slota, Ján (1953–) Slovakian mining engineer and politician. A member of the Slovak National Party (SNS), he was a member of the Czechoslovak federal assembly from 1990 until the federation's dissolution at the end of 1992. He became mayor of Žilina in November 1990 and was elected to the Slovak parliament in June 1992. He was elected party leader in February 1994.

Slovak National Party [Slovenská Národná Strana] (SNS) Slovakian political party. Founded in 1990, the SNS was the first major party to advocate independence for the republic. It advocates a rapid transition to a market-based economy, has a conservative stance on social issues, and has close links with the Matica Slovenská ('Mother Slovakia') cultural organization. At the June 1992 election it gained 7.9% of the vote and 15/150 seats in the Slovakian parliament. The party split in February 1994, with a minority wing (including six deputies) forming the National Democratic Party (NDS) and the majority shifting to the right. The leader is Ján Slota.

Slovak Republic [Slovenská Republika] Official name of Slovakia.

Slovakia [Slovensko] Country in central Europe, formerly part of Czechoslovakia.

Official data. Name: Slovak Republic [Slovenská Republika]; capital: Bratislava; form of government: parliamentary republic; head of state: president; head of government: prime minister; flag: three horizontal stripes, white, blue and red, with the state emblem left of centre; national holiday: 1 January (Independence Day); language: Slovak; religion: none; currency: koruna (Sk) (pl. koruny) = 100 halierov; abbreviations: SR and SQ.

Geography. Slovakia has an area of 49,030 sq km. Land-locked, it is bordered by Poland in the north, Ukraine in the east, Hungary in the south, and Austria and the Czech Republic in the west. Slovakia is dominated by the Carpathian Mountains, including the High Tatra [Vysoké Tatry] range on the border with Poland. There are rolling plains in the southwest and southeast. The main rivers are the Danube [Dunaj], Morava, Váh and Hron. Some 33% of the land is arable, another 17% is covered by pastures and 41% is forested. The climate is humid continental, with hot summers and cold winters; temperatures are lower in the mountains; rainfall is moderate, heavier in the mountains.

Demography. Slovakia has a population of 5,329,000. Population density is 111 per sq km (land area). Some 71% of the people live in urban areas. The main cities are Bratislava and Košice; other important regional centres are Nitra, Prešov, Banská Bystrica and Žilina. In ethnic terms 85.7% of the people are Slovaks, 10.8% Hungarians, 1.4% Gipsies and 1.1% Czechs; there are also small groups of Ukrainians, Ruthenians and Poles. Most Hungarians live in the south along the Hungarian border. Gipsies are considerably underrepresented in the official figures; they are thought to number around 400,000 (7.6% of the total population). There are also small communities of Slovaks in the Czech Republic, Hungary and Yugoslavia. The main languages are Slovak and Hungarian. In religious terms 60.4% of the population is nominally Roman Catholic, 6.2% Lutheran Protestant and 3.4% Slovak Uniate (Orthodox affiliated to the Roman Catholic Church); most of the remainder describes itself as unaffiliated or non-religious.

Sociography. Former Czechoslovakia scored 0.872 on the United Nations human development index (HDI) in 1992, ranking 27th in the world and 19th among 32 European countries. In Slovakia there are 36 doctors and 74 hospital beds for every 10,000 people. Education is compulsory between the ages of six and 14. There is one teacher for every 18 students. Enrolment is 43% at the secondary level and 18% at the tertiary level. The literacy rate is 96%. Real annual income per head in Czechoslovakia (in terms of purchasing power) was US$ 6,570 in 1992.

Infrastructure and communications. Slovakia's transport and communications network is relatively developed but in need of modernization and extension; the telecommunications system in particular is limited. There are around 13,000 km of paved roads and 906,000 passenger cars (172 per 1,000 people), 3,661 km of railways and 170 km of navigable waterways. The main (inland) ports are Bratislava and Komárno. The main airport is at Bratislava (Ivanka), and there are five other airports with scheduled services. There are 19 daily newspapers, with a combined circulation of 1.27 million (240 per 1,000 people). There are 2.48 million radio receivers, 1.61 million television sets and 1.28 million telephones in use (respectively 470, 305 and 276 per 1,000 people).

Economic structure. The Slovakian economy is based on manufacturing and agriculture. Although essentially developed, diversified and trade-oriented, it is in need of major investment and restructuring. The gradual transition from a command to a market-based economy initiated in 1990 and the loss of traditional markets in the Czech Republic since the dissolution of the Czechoslovak federation is causing dislocation and has led to steep falls in industrial and agricultural production. Between 1990 and 1993 GDP contracted by 29%, inflation averaged 25% per year, and unemployment rose to 14%. There were some signs of recovery in 1994.

Services contribute 33% of GDP, industry contributes 60% (manufacturing around 50%), and agriculture and forestry 7%. Some 32% of the labour force is employed in manufacturing, 11% in farming, 10% in construction and 8% in trade. The main crops grown are cereals (wheat, barley), potatoes, sugarbeets and oilseeds; other important agricultural activities are livestock raising (pigs, cattle, sheep), dairy farming and horticulture (fruit and vegetables, incl. grapes). Forestry is also important. The main mineral resources are lignite, magnesite, zinc, lead, copper and iron. The main industries are engineering, chemicals and food processing; other important branches are metalworking (esp. iron and steel), electrical goods, textiles, petrochemicals, wood

processing, building materials and armaments. The main energy sources are nuclear and hydroelectric power and imported fossil fuels; 28% of export earnings are required to cover net fuel imports. The main exports are machinery (18% of the total), iron and steel (12%), textiles and clothing (12%), chemicals (12%), foodstuffs (7%), transport equipment (5%), electrical equipment, wood products and oil products; basic manufactures account for 36% of the total, machinery and transport equipment for 23%. The main imports are fuels and machinery and transport equipment. The main trading partners are: exports: Germany (24%), Russia, Ukraine and other members of the Commonwealth of Independent States (CIS) (17%), Austria (8%), Hungary (7%), Italy (6%), Poland, France; imports: Russia, Ukraine and other CIS members (36%), Austria (10%), Italy (5%), Poland; a third of all trade is with European Union (EU) countries. (Foreign-trade figures refer to 1992 and exclude trade with the Czech Republic.)

The National Bank of Slovakia [Národná Banka Slovenská] is the central bank. The main employers' association is the Association of Slovak Entrepreneurs (ZPS); the main labour organizations are the Trade Union Confederation of the Slovak Republic (KOZSR or KOZ) and the Independent Slovak Trade Unions (NSO).

Political structure. Slovakia is a parliamentary republic on the basis of a constitution which took effect when it became an independent state in January 1993. The head of state is the president, who is elected for a five-year term by the legislature by a three-fifths majority; s/he is commander-in-chief of the armed forces, appoints the prime minister, may veto ministerial appointments and dismiss ministers, and has certain other powers. Executive power is vested in the prime minister and the council of ministers. Legislative power is vested in the National Council of the Slovak Republic [Národná Rada Slovensky Republiky], whose 150 members are elected for a four-year term by a system of proportional representation (with a 5% threshold for gaining seats). All citizens over the age of 18 are entitled to vote. Judicial power is ultimately vested in the 12-member Supreme Court [Najvyšší Súd] appointed by the legislature for a four-year term; the 10-member Constitutional Court [Ústavný Súd], appointed by the president for a seven-year term from a list of 20 nominees proposed by parliament, adjudicates on constitutional matters. Administratively the country is divided into four regions [kraj, pl. -a], including the region-level city of Bratislava; the regions are subdivided into 38 districts [okres, pl. -y] and municipalities.

The main political parties are the Movement for a Democratic Slovakia (HZDS), Democratic Left Party (SDL', the successor to the Communist Party of Slovakia, KSS), Christian Democratic Movement (KDH), Democratic Union of Slovakia (DEÚS or DÚ, a breakaway from the HZDS), Slovak National Party (SNS), Coexistence (ESWS), Hungarian Christian Democratic Movement (MKDH or MKDM), National Democratic Party (NDS, a breakaway from the SNS) and Social Democratic Party of Slovakia (SDSS). At the election in June 1992 the HZDS gained 37.3% of the vote and 74/150 seats, the SDL' 14.7% and 29 seats, the KDH 8.9% and 18 seats, the SNS 7.9% and 15 seats, Coexistence and the MKDM 7.4% and nine and five seats respectively, and the SDSS 4.0% and no seats. The government is formed by a four-party centrist coalition of the SDL', DEÚS, KDH and NDS, with Jozef Moravčík as prime minister. Other senior ministers are Roman Kováč (deputy prime minister with responsibility for non-economic issues), Ivan Šimko (deputy prime minister with responsibility for legislative affairs), Brigita Schmögnerová (deputy prime minister with responsibility for economic transformation), Eduard Kukan (foreign affairs), Pavol Kanis (defence), Rudolf Filkus (finance), Ladislav Pittner (interior), Peter Magvaši (economy) and Milan Hanzel (justice). The head of state is President Michal Kováč, who was elected in February 1993.

Security and international affiliations. The Slovakian armed forces number around 47,000 (army 33,000, airforce 14,000). There is also a small paramilitary border guard. Military service is compulsory and consists of 12 months' basic training.

Slovakia is a member of the Central European Initiative (CEI), Conference on Security and Cooperation in Europe (CSCE), Council of Europe and Visegrad Group, as well as the United Nations and its specialized agencies.

History. Previously dominated by Celtic and then Germanic tribes, modern Slovakia was settled by Slavs migrating from the east in the 6th and 7th centuries, towards the end of the Europe-wide migrations. The Avars, a nomadic Asian people, held political sway until their defeat by the Frankish Kingdom in the 790s. The region then became part of Great Moravia (which also included Bohemia and parts of modern Poland and Hungary). Christianity became the dominant religion around this time. After Great Moravia's defeat by the Magyars in 906, the region became part of the new Hungarian state. Slovakia formally became a crown land of the Kingdom of Hungary in the early 11th century. Hungarian rule, in various forms, lasted until 1918. After King Louis II was killed in battle against the Ottoman Turks in 1526, Ferdinand of Austria was elected king and Hungary thus passed to the Habsburgs. During the time when most of the kingdom was under Turkish control (1526–1699), Bratislava [Pozsony in Hungarian], the Slovak capital, became the royal capital, a status it retained until 1784; the Hungarian parliament continued to meet there until 1848. Hussite ideas gained ground in Slovakia in the 15th century and Lutheran and Calvinist ideas in the 16th century. After two religious wars in 1603 and 1669–71 the Habsburgs were able to restore the dominance of Roman Catholicism. A number of social and economic reforms were introduced in the second half of the 18th century.

The 19th century saw the emergence of a Slovak cultural and national movement.

In the years after the abortive Hungarian uprising of 1848–49, the Austrian-dominated central government encouraged Slovak national aspirations as a counterweight to Hungarian power. The Hungarians regained control of Slovakia with the establishment of the Austro-Hungarian 'dual monarchy' in 1867 and implemented a policy of magyarization. There was substantial emigration during this period. As the Habsburg Empire disintegrated at the end of the First World War (1914–18) Slovakia joined the Czech lands of Bohemia and Moravia to the west to form the new state of Czechoslovakia. A democratic constitution was adopted in 1920. Coalition governments including the main Czech and Slovak parties were the norm in the 1920s and 30s. The Slovaks became increasingly disaffected by the centralized structure and perceived Czech domination. In 1938 Czechoslovakia, under pressure from the major European powers, was forced to accept the Munich Agreement (under which the German-majority areas in the Czech lands were ceded to Germany) and the Vienna Agreement, under which the Hungarian-populated regions of southern Slovakia were ceded to Hungary. Slovakia was granted autonomy at this time. It declared its independence in 1939, the day before German troops occupied the Czech lands. During the Second World War (1939–45) Slovakia, under the leadership of Josef Tiso, was effectively a German protectorate. A two-month uprising against German rule took place in 1944.

In 1945 all of Czechoslovakia was occupied by Soviet troops and the pre-1938 borders were restored (with the exception of Ruthenia, which was ceded to the Soviet Union). A measure of autonomy was granted to Slovakia, but this was rescinded when the Czechoslovak Communist Party took power in 1948 and proclaimed a 'people's republic'. The new regime suppressed political dissent, nationalized the economy, introduced central planning and allied itself closely with the Soviet Union. Slovakia, hitherto largely agricultural, underwent extensive industrialization from the 1950s. In 1968 a new national leadership headed by Alexander Dubček (a Slovak) introduced far-reaching political and economic reforms. The Prague Spring was crushed after seven months when Soviet and other Warsaw Pact troops invaded the country. In the only surviving measure from the reform programme, the unitary state was reconstituted as a federation of the Czech and Slovak republics in 1969. Growing calls for political reform in 1989 culminated in what was dubbed the 'velvet revolution' in November, when the communists relinquished power. In February 1990 the Soviet Union agreed to withdraw its troops. The anti-communist Public Against Violence (VPN) and Civic Forum (OF), its Czech counterpart, won the multiparty election in June. Czechoslovakia was admitted to the Council of Europe in January 1991. At a new election in June 1992 the Movement for a Democratic Slovakia (HZDS), committed to self-determination, became the largest party in Slovakia and formed a government under Vladimír Mečiar. (The VPN had fragmented in 1991.) Parliament declared Slovakia a sovereign state in July and adopted a new constitution in September. The terms of the latter and other government policies were criticized by the ethnic Hungarian minority. The two republican governments negotiated the federation's dissolution, and Slovakia became an independent state at the start of 1993. Michal Kováč was elected president in February. Internal divisions within the HZDS and growing criticism of the slow pace of economic reform forced the resignation of the Mečiar government in March 1994.

See also entries on specific institutions, organizations, parties, people, terms etc.

Slovenia [Slovenija] Country in southeastern Europe, formerly part of Yugoslavia.

Official data. Name: Republic of Slovenia [Republika Slovenija]; capital: Ljubljana; form of government: parliamentary republic; head of state: president; head of government: prime minister; flag: three horizontal stripes, white, blue and red, with the state emblem in the canton; national holiday: 25 June (National Day); language: Slovene; religion: none;

currency: tolar (T) = 100 stotin; abbreviation: SLO.

Geography. Slovenia has an area of 20,256 sq km. It is bordered by the Adriatic Sea and Italy in the west, Austria in the north, Hungary in the east, and Croatia in the south. The northern border region is very mountainous, consisting of the Julian Alps [Julijske Alpe] and the Karavanke range. The southwest consists of a high plateau, an extension of the Dinaric Alps. The east and southeast is hilly or low-lying. Some 12% of the land is arable, another 20% is covered by pastures and 45% is forested. The climate is alpine in the mountains (with mild summers and cold winters), mediterranean in the southwest (with hot summers and mild winters) and humid continental in the east (with hot summers and cold winters); rainfall is moderate to heavy.

Demography. Slovenia has a population of 1,997,000. Population density is 99 per sq km. Some 51% of the people live in urban areas. The main cities are Ljubljana and Maribor; regional centres are Celje, Kranj, Velenje, Koper and Novo Mesto. In ethnic terms 87.8% of the people are Slovenes, 2.8% Croats, 2.4% Serbs and 1.4% Slav Muslims (considered an ethnic group in former Yugoslavia); there are also small groups of Hungarians, Italians and Gipsies. Slovenia has taken in around 40,000 refugees from the Bosnian and Croatian civil wars (around 100,000 according to unofficial estimates). The main language is Slovene. In religious terms nearly all the people are nominally Roman Catholics; there are also small groups of Old Catholics, Protestants, Orthodox, Muslims and Jews.

Sociography. Slovenia was the most developed republic in former Yugoslavia, which scored 0.857 on the United Nations human development index (HDI) in 1990, ranking 37th in the world and 23rd among 27 European countries. There are 21 doctors and 72 hospital beds for every 10,000 people. Education is compulsory between the ages of seven and 15. There is one teacher for every 17 students. Enrolment is 46% at the secondary level and 16% at the tertiary level. The literacy rate is 98%. GNP per head (unadjusted for purchasing power) is US$ 6,330, the highest of the former communist countries.

Infrastructure and communications. Slovenia's transport and communications network is relatively well developed but in need of modernization and extension. There are 10,530 km of paved roads and 584,000 passenger cars (296 per 1,000 people). There are 1,370 km of railways and virtually no navigable waterways. The main port is Koper. The main airports are at Ljubljana (Brnik) and Maribor, and there is one other airport with scheduled services. There are four daily newspapers, with a combined circulation of 322,000 (163 per 1,000 people). There are 601,000 radio receivers, 445,000 television sets and 657,000 telephones in use (respectively 304, 225 and 333 per 1,000 people).

Economic structure. The Slovenian economy is based on manufacturing, agriculture and tourism. Although essentially developed, diversified and trade-oriented, it is in need of investment and restructuring. The transition from a command to a market-based economy initiated in the late 1980s and the loss of traditional markets since the disintegration of the Yugoslav federation in 1991/92 is causing severe dislocation and has led to falls in industrial and agricultural production in particular. Between 1990 and 1993 GDP contracted by 20%, inflation averaged over 200% per year, and unemployment rose to 15%. Inflation fell to 31% in 1993 and growth resumed in 1994.

Services contribute 52% of GDP, industry contributes 42% (manufacturing 33%), and agriculture and forestry 6%. Some 30% of the labour force is employed in manufacturing, 13% in farming and forestry and 11% in trade. The main agricultural activities are livestock raising (cattle, pigs) and dairy farming (milk, eggs); the main crops grown are cereals (maize, wheat), potatoes, sugarbeets and hops; horticulture (fruit and vegetables, esp. apples and grapes) is also important. Forestry provides a major source of foreign exchange. The main mineral resources are coal, lead and zinc. The main industry is engineering (incl. cars); other important branches are textiles (incl. footwear), food processing (incl. beer and wine), electrical goods, wood processing (paper, furniture), metalworking (incl. aluminium and other non-ferrous metals) and chemicals. Tourism is an important source of foreign exchange, contributing around 10% of GNP. The main energy sources are nuclear and hydroelectric power and domestic and imported fossil fuels; 9% of export earnings are required to cover net fuel imports. The main exports are wood and wood products (16% of the total, incl. furniture 6%), transport equipment (13%, incl. cars 7%), industrial machinery (13%), electrical equipment (12%), metal products (10%), textiles and clothing (8%), foodstuffs and chemicals; machinery and transport equipment account for 38% of the total, basic manufactures for 28%. The main imports are machinery and transport equipment, basic manufactures and chemicals. The main trading partners are: exports: Germany (28%), Croatia (13%), Italy (13%), France (9%), Austria (5%); imports: Germany (23%), Italy (14%), Croatia (13%), Austria (8%), France (8%); half of all trade is with European Union (EU) countries.

The Bank of Slovenia [Banka Slovenije] is the central bank. There are several employers' and business associations; the main labour organizations are the Confederation of Free Trade Unions of Slovenia (ZSSS) and Independence - Confederation of New Trade Unions of Slovenia (Neodvisnost or KNSS).

Political structure. Slovenia is a parliamentary republic on the basis of a constitution adopted in December 1991, replacing one defining it as part of the Yugoslav federation. The head of state is the president, who is directly elected for a four-year term; if no candidate gains an absolute majority of votes, a run-off is held between the top two candidates. The president nominates the prime minister and has several other powers. Executive power is vested in the prime minister and the council of ministers, whose appointments require parliamentary approval. Legislative power is vested in a bicameral

parliament composed of the 90-member National Assembly [Državni Zbor], elected for a four-year term by a mixed system of proportional representation and majority voting (with a 3% threshold for gaining seats), and the 40-member National Council [Državni Svet] elected partly directly and partly indirectly for a five-year term; two seats in the Zbor are reserved for representatives of the Hungarian and Italian minorities. All citizens over the age of 18 are entitled to vote. Judicial power is ultimately vested in the seven-member Supreme Court [Vrhovno Sodišče], elected for a nine-year term by the legislature; the nine-member Constitutional Court [Ustavno Sodišče], also elected for a nine-year term, adjudicates on constitutional matters. Administratively the country is divided into 62 districts [občina, pl. občine].

The main political parties are the Liberal Democratic Party of Slovenia (LDS, formed by the merger of the Liberal Democratic Party, LDS, the SSS and sections of the DSS and ZS), Slovenian Christian Democrats (SKD), Associated List of Social Democrats (ZLSD, the successor to the Social Democratic Reform Party, SDP, and Associated List, ZL), Slovenian National Party (SNS), Slovenian People's Party (SLS), Democratic Party of Slovenia (DSS), Greens of Slovenia (ZS), Social Democratic Party of Slovenia (SDSS) and Socialist Party of Slovenia (SSS). At the December 1992 general election the (old) LDS gained 23.7% of the vote and 22/90 seats, the SKD 14.5% and 15 seats, the ZL 13.6% and 14 seats, the SNS 9.9% and 12 seats, the SLS 8.8% and 10 seats, the DSS 5.0% and six seats, the ZS 3.7% and five seats, the SDSS 3.3% and four seats, and the SSS 2.8% and no seats. The government is formed by a centrist coalition of the LDS, SKD and ZLSD, with Janez Drnovšek as prime minister. Other senior ministers are Lojze Peterle (deputy prime minister, foreign affairs), Mitja Gaspari (finance), Davorin Kračun (economic relations and development), Maks Tajnikar (economic affairs), Andrej Ster (internal affairs), Jelko Kacin (defence) and Meta

Zupančič (justice). The head of state is President Milan Kučan, who was first elected in April 1990 and reelected in December 1992.

Security and international affiliations. The Slovenian armed forces number 15,000 (army 13,000, navy and airforce 2,000); they are due to be expanded to around 20,000. There is also a 4,500-strong paramilitary police force. Military service is compulsory and consists of six or seven months' basic training.

Slovenia is a member of the Central European Initiative (CEI), Conference on Security and Cooperation in Europe (CSCE) and Council of Europe, as well as the United Nations and its specialized agencies.

History. Settled by Illyrians and (from the 3rd century BC) Celtic tribes, the area of modern Slovenia was conquered by the Romans in 35 BC. During the Europe-wide migrations that helped trigger the collapse of the Roman Empire in the early 5th century AD the Germanic Ostrogoths briefly controlled the region. In the 6th century the Slavic Slovenes, migrating from the northeast, began to settle in Slovenia and lands to the north and east. To escape domination by the Avars, a nomadic Asian people, they allied themselves with the Bavarians and Franks in the 8th century. The region was incorporated into the Frankish Kingdom in 745 and divided into several border provinces or marches, including Carniola, Carinthia and Styria. Christianity became the dominant religion around this time. Slovenes to the east rebelled against Avar rule in 869 and briefly formed an independent state under Prince Kocelj until 874. When the Frankish Empire was partitioned in the early 9th century, the region became part of the East Frankish Kingdom, later the Holy Roman or German Empire. From the 10th century the marches developed into autonomous duchies, the districts north of the Drava river were germanized, and the Slovene peasants became serfs of German landowners. Between the late 13th and late 15th centuries the Habsburgs gained control of all Slovene lands. They would remain part of the Austrian Empire

until 1918, but were never united into a single unit. There were several peasant rebellions during the 15th and 16th centuries. Lutheran and Calvinist ideas also gained ground in the 16th century, but the Habsburgs were able to restore the dominance of Roman Catholicism by 1620.

Social and economic reforms introduced in the second half of the 18th century and the region's incorporation into the Illyrian Provinces of the French Empire from 1809–14 contributed to the emergence of a Slovene cultural and national movement in the 19th century. As the Habsburg Empire disintegrated at the end of the First World War (1914–18) the Slovenes joined the other South Slav peoples to establish the Kingdom of Serbs, Croats and Slovenes, renamed Yugoslavia in 1929. The new state was destabilized from the outset by rivalry between Serbs and Croats in particular, while in Slovenia (and elsewhere) there was growing dissatisfaction with the centralized administration. In 1929 King Alexander II imposed a personal dictatorship. During the Second World War (1939–45) Yugoslavia was overrun by the German and Italian armies in 1941, and Slovenia was partitioned between Italy, Germany and Hungary. The strongest resistance movement was the communist-led Liberation Front (OF).

On liberation in 1945 the Communists, led by Josip Broz Tito, took power throughout Yugoslavia. The monarchy was abolished and Slovenia became a constituent republic of the new federation. The regime suppressed political opposition and implemented orthodox communist economic policies. After breaking with the Soviet Union in 1948, it pursued more pragmatic and liberal policies. Slovenia was by far Yugoslavia's most prosperous republic during the communist period. A long-running border dispute with Italy was settled in 1954, when most of the Istrian peninsula and districts to the north (inhabited by Slovenes and Croats) became part of Yugoslavia while the port of Trieste remained part of Italy. Like the other republics, Slovenia was given greater autonomy under a new federal constitution adopted in 1974. In the 1980s, as central authority weakened, the Slovene League of Communists (ZKS) responded to growing calls for economic and political reforms. The multiparty election in April 1990 was won by the broad-based anti-communist Democratic Movement (DEPOS), while the former ZKS leader Milan Kučan, a supporter of reform, was elected president. All coalition governments formed since then have been strongly committed to establishing a market-based economy. Slovenia's and Croatia's declarations of independence in June 1991 set in train the disintegration of the Yugoslav federation. After ten days of fighting between Slovene forces and the federal army the latter agreed to withdraw (in July). A new constitution was adopted in December 1991. Independence was recognized internationally in January 1992, and the country was admitted to the United Nations in May 1992 and to the Council of Europe in May 1993. After the December 1992 election a broad coalition was formed under Janez Drnovšek. The restructuring and reorientation of the economy began to bear fruit in 1993, and economic growth resumed in 1994.

See also entries on specific institutions, organizations, parties, people, terms etc.

Slovenian Christian Democrats
[Slovenska Krščanski Demokrati] (SKD) Slovenian political party. Founded in 1989, the SKD was the largest member of the Democratic Opposition (DEMOS) alliance which defeated the former communists in the April 1990 election. (DEMOS was dissolved in 1991.) The party led a coalition which remained in power until May 1992, and joined another coalition in January 1993. At the December 1992 election it gained 14.5% of the vote and 15/90 seats. The party leader is Lojze Peterle, the parliamentary leader Ignac Polajnar.

Slovenian National Party [Slovenska Nacionalna Stranka] (SNS) Slovenian political party. The SNS was founded in 1991 by the right wing of the Slovenian Democratic Alliance (SDZ) and adopted its present name in 1992. It has moved sharply to the right, and now advocates the deportation of foreign refugees and the annexation of parts of Croatia. At the December 1992 election it gained 9.9% of the vote and 12/90 seats. The leader is Zmago Jelinčič.

Slovenian People's Party [Slovenska Ljudska Stranka] (SLS) Slovenian political party. The SLS was founded as a farmers' pressure group in 1988 and registered as a political party, the Slovenian Farmers' Alliance (SKZ), in 1990. It was renamed in 1991. Generally right-wing in orientation, the party's concerns reflect its strong support among farmers and in the rural areas. At the December 1992 election it gained 8.8% of the vote and 10/90 seats. The leader is Marjan Podobnik.

Slovenská Republika ('Slovak Republic') Official name of Slovakia.

Slovensko Slovak name for Slovakia.

slow track (European Union) *See* ECONOMIC AND MONETARY UNION *and* MULTI-TRACK EUROPE.

SLS *See* SLOVENIAN PEOPLE'S PARTY.

small constitution [mała konstytucja] Common name for the Constitutional Act, a series of amendments to Poland's 1952 communist constitution. Signed into law on 17 November 1992 and effective from 8 December, the Act aims to streamline the workings of the political institutions. It redefines the powers of the executive and legislative branches, i.e. presidency, government and parliament, and relations between them. The division of power was left vague in the 1952 constitution – devised for what was effectively a one-party state – and became the cause of intense controversy after the collapse of communist rule in 1989. This was widely felt to be hampering the progress of political and economic reforms. Work on a completely new constitution, dubbed the 'large constitution', began in 1989.

small privatization In the former communist countries, the transfer of small state-owned businesses into private ownership. During the communist period virtually all enterprises were state-owned. As part of the transition to a market-based economy initiated by all the Eastern European governments which took over from the communists between 1989 and 1991, thousands of shops, restaurants, workshops and other small businesses were privatized from 1991 onwards. This was done by putting them up for auction, handing them over to managers and staff, or returning them to former owners or their heirs who had been expropriated by the communists. *See also* MASS PRIVATIZATION.

small right [klein rechts] In the Netherlands, a collective name for the political parties with a fundamentalist Calvinist Protestant programme. They are the Reformational Political Federation (RPF), Political Reformed Party (SGP) and Reformed Political Union (GPV). They consistently gain around 4–5% of the vote between them.

SMEs Abbreviation for 'small and medium-sized enterprises', an umbrella term widely used in the European Union (EU).

Śmietanko, Andrzej (1955–) Polish agronomist and politician. He worked on a state farm from 1982–85 and for an agricultural-machinery collective from 1985–92. He then became deputy director of the Agricultural Market Agency (ARR). Elected to parliament for the Polish Peasant Party (PSL) in September 1993, he was appointed agriculture minister in the new left-wing coalition which took office the following month.

Smith, John (1938–94) British lawyer and politician. He practised law in his native Scotland until his election to parliament for the Labour Party in 1970. He held several junior ministerial posts from 1974 and was secretary of state (= minister) for trade from 1978 until Labour lost power in 1979. He became the party's chief spokesman on financial and economic matters in 1987 and was elected leader in July 1992. He died of a heart attack in May 1994.

SML Abbreviation of the LIRA, the San Marino currency, used in banking etc.

SMP *See* FINNISH RURAL PARTY.

SNG *See* SERBIAN NATIONAL GUARD.

SNG *See* COMMONWEALTH OF INDEPENDENT STATES.

SNP *See* SCOTTISH NATIONAL PARTY.

SNS (Croatia) *See* SERB PEOPLE'S PARTY.

SNS *See* SLOVAK NATIONAL PARTY.

SNS *See* SLOVENIAN NATIONAL PARTY.

Soares, Mário (1924–) Portuguese lawyer and politician. He was arrested several times for his political activities during the Salazar regime and spent four years in exile from 1970. He was a founding member of the Socialist Party (PS) in 1973 and became its first leader. He returned home after the 1974 revolution. He was foreign minister in 1974–75 and prime minister of PS-led coalitions in 1976–78 and 1983–85. In February 1986 he was elected president of the republic, a largely non-executive post, and thereupon resigned from the PS. In January 1991 he was elected for a further five-year term.

Sobranie Shorthand for Narodno Sobranie ('NATIONAL ASSEMBLY'), the Bulgarian parliament.

Sobranie Shorthand for Sobranie na Republika ('ASSEMBLY OF THE REPUBLIC'), the Macedonian parliament.

Social Agreement Shorthand for the AGREEMENT ON SOCIAL POLICY, an international agreement signed by all European Union (EU) states except the United Kingdom. It is also known informally as the Social Chapter or Social Protocol.

Social and Economic Council [Sociaal-Economische Raad] (SER) Dutch advisory body. The SER was set up in 1950 to advise the government on major economic and social issues. Its 45 members include representatives of employers' associations, trade unions and independent experts appointed by the government.

Social and Liberal Democratic Party *See* LIBERAL DEMOCRATS.

Social Chapter Common name for the AGREEMENT ON SOCIAL POLICY or Social Agreement, an international agreement signed by all European Union (EU) states except the United Kingdom. A chapter on social policy was included in the draft Maastricht Treaty, but this was eventually taken out because its provisions were rejected by the British government.

Social Charter Shorthand for the CHARTER OF THE FUNDAMENTAL SOCIAL RIGHTS OF WORKERS, an international agreement signed by all European Union (EU) member states except the United Kingdom. It should not be confused with the European Social Charter, a separate agreement adopted within the framework of the Council of Europe.

Social Christian Party [Partito Cristiano Sociale] (PCS) Italian political party. The PCS was founded in October 1993 by centre-left members of the then ruling Christian Democratic Party (DC), which had become discredited by a series of corruption and other scandals breaking in 1992 and 1993. It contested the March 1994 election within the Progressive Alliance and gained 6/630 seats; it has joined the Allied Progressive parliamentary group. The leader is Pierre Carniti.

social cohesion (European Union) *See* ECONOMIC AND ....

Social Democracy *See* CZECH SOCIAL DEMOCRATIC PARTY.

Social Democracy (Denmark) *See* SOCIAL DEMOCRATIC PARTY.

Social Democracy of the Republic of Poland *See* SOCIAL DEMOCRATIC PARTY OF ....

Social Democracy Party of Romania [Partidul din Democraţie Socială din România] (PDSR) Romanian political party. The PDSR – not to be confused with the Romanian Social Democratic Party (PSDR) – was founded in July 1993 as the successor to the Democratic National Salvation Front (FSND), which in turn had its roots in the National Salvation Front (FSN), the movement which emerged during the revolution that overthrew the communist regime of Nicolae Ceauşescu in December 1989. The FSN formed a provisional government and assumed legislative authority. Having converted itself into a political party with a broadly centre-left orientation, it gained two-thirds of the vote at the May 1990 election; its leader, Ion Iliescu, was elected president by an even larger majority. Tension then grew between a reformist wing calling for rapid economic transformation and a more conservative wing dominated by former communists and led by Iliescu. The latter broke away in April 1992 and set up the FSND. At the September 1992 election the FSND gained 27.7% of the vote and 117/341

seats. It then formed a minority government. The leader is Adrian Naştase, the party president is Oliviu Gherman. As president of the republic Iliescu is no longer a party member, but he retains considerable influence.

Social Democratic Alliance of Macedonia [Socijal-Demokratski Sojuz na Makedonija] (SDSM) Macedonian political party. The SDSM was founded in 1989 as the successor to the League of Communists of Macedonia (SKM). It now has a mainstream left-wing programme. At the December 1990 election in the republic it gained 31/120 seats. SDSM members have held senior ministerial posts in broadbased coalition governments since then. Branko Crvenkovski is the party leader. Kiro Gligorov, the former leader and now president of the republic, retains considerable influence.

Social Democratic and Labour Party (SDLP) British political party. Founded in 1970, the SDLP is a centre-left party active in Northern Ireland. It draws its support from the Catholic community, and around two-thirds of Catholics vote for it. The party is opposed to all forms of discrimination and political violence, and calls for the eventual reunification of Ireland by consent (i.e. with the approval of the Protestant majority). At the April 1992 general election it gained 23.5% of the vote in Northern Ireland and four of the 17 seats; at the May 1993 local elections it gained 21.9%. John Hume has been the leader since 1979; the deputy leader is Seamus Mallon.

Social Democratic Centre [Centre des Démocrates Sociaux] (CDS) French political party. A christian democratic party formed in 1976, the CDS joined the UNION FOR FRENCH DEMOCRACY (UDF) alliance in 1978 and has fought successive elections under its banner. From 1988–93 it formed a separate group in parliament, the Centre Union (UDC). At the March 1993 election it gained 57/577 seats. The leader is Pierre Méhaignerie, the party president is Dominique Baudis, and the general secretary is Bernard Bosson.

Social Democratic Labour Party of Sweden [Sveriges Socialdemokratiska Arbetarepartiet] (SAP, S or A) Swedish political party. Founded in 1889, the SAP has been the country's dominant political force since the 1930s. It governed alone or in coalition from 1932–76 (except for a brief period in 1936) and from 1982–91. During this time it erected what is widely regarded as the prototype of the social democratic welfare state. At the September 1991 election the party scored its worst result since the 1910s, gaining 37.6% of the vote and 138/349 seats. It remained by far the largest group in parliament, but the four centre-right parties formed a coalition. The leader is Ingvar Carlsson, the general secretary Mona Sahlin.

Social Democratic Party *See* ... OF AUSTRIA.

Social Democratic Party *See* DEMOCRATIC SOCIALIST PARTY OF BOSNIA-HERZEGOVINA

Social Democratic Party [Sotsialnodemo-kraticheska Partiya] (SDP) Bulgarian political party. The SDP has its roots in the BULGARIAN SOCIAL DEMOCRATIC PARTY (BSDP). This split in 1991 over its continued participation in the broad-based Union of Democratic Forces (SDS). The wing which remained within the SDS was renamed the SDP in April 1992. It has 3/240 seats in parliament. The leader is Ivan Kurtev.

Social Democratic Party [Socialdemo-kratiet] (SD or S) Danish political party. Founded in 1871, the Social Democrats have been the country's largest party since 1924. They governed either alone or in coalition for most years from then until 1982, and returned to power at the head of a four-party centre-left coalition in January 1993. At the December 1990 election the party gained 37.4% of the vote and 69/179 seats. The leader is Poul Nyrup Rasmussen.

Social Democratic Party or **Equality Party** [Javnaðarflokkurin] (Jvfl) Faroese political party. Founded in 1948, it has headed or participated in a number of coalition governments, most recently from 1985–89 and since 1991. At the November 1990 election it gained 10/32 seats, but in July 1994 its representation was halved. The leader is Jóannes Eidesgaard.

Social Democratic Party [Parti Social-Démocrate] (PSD) French political party. The PSD was founded in 1973 as the Movement of Socialist Democrats (MDS) by right-leaning members of the Socialist Party (PS). It was renamed in 1982. It joined the centre-right UNION FOR FRENCH DEMOCRACY (UDF) alliance in 1978 and has fought successive elections under its banner. At the March 1993 election it gained 7/577 seats. The general secretary is André Santini.

Social Democratic Party *See* ... OF GERMANY.

Social Democratic Party or **Labour Party** [Alþýðuflokkurinn] (A) Icelandic political party. Founded in 1916, the party has participated in a number of coalition governments since 1945, most recently from 1978–79 and since 1987. At the April 1991 election it gained 15.5% of the vote and 10/63 seats. The leader is Jón Baldvin Hannibalsson.

Social Democratic Party *See* ... OF THE REPUBLIC OF POLAND.

Social Democratic Party [Partido Social Democrata] (PSD) Portuguese political party. Founded in 1974 as the Popular Democratic Party (PDP) and renamed in 1976, the PSD is a centre-right party. It participated in several coalitions until 1985, when it formed a minority government. It secured an absolute majority in the 1987 election. At the October 1991 election it gained 50.4% of the vote and 135/230 seats. Aníbal Cavaco Silva has been the party leader since 1985; the general secretary is Alfredo Falcão Cunha.

Social Democratic Party *See* ROMANIAN SOCIAL DEMOCRATIC PARTY *or* SOCIAL DEMOCRACY PARTY OF ROMANIA.

Social Democratic Party *See* SOCIAL DEMOCRATIC LABOUR PARTY OF SWEDEN.

Social Democratic Party *See* ... OF SWITZERLAND.

Social Democratic Party of Albania [Partia Socialdemokratike e Shqipërisë] (PSDSh) Albanian political party. Founded in 1991, the PSDSh came third in the March 1992 election, gaining 4.3% of the vote and 7/140 seats. It favours a gradual rather than a rapid transition to a market economy. The leader is Skendër Gjinushi.

Social Democratic Party of Austria

[Sozialdemokratische Partei Österreichs] (SPÖ) Austrian political party. Founded as the Socialist Democratic Workers' Party in 1889 and subsequently renamed the Socialist Party, the SPÖ briefly formed a government in 1919–20. Banned by the Dollfuss regime in 1934, it was relaunched in 1945, at the end of the Second World War. It was the junior partner in a grand coalition with the Austrian People's Party (ÖVP) until 1966. It has formed the government either alone or as the senior coalition partner since 1970, under Bruno Kreisky until 1983. At the October 1990 election it gained 43.1% of the vote and 80/183 seats. The party's name was changed in 1991. The leader is Franz Vranitzky, the parliamentary leader is Heinz Fischer.

Social Democratic Party of Croatia

[Socijaldemokratska Partija Hrvatske] (SDPH or SDP) Croatian political party. The SDP was founded in 1990 as the Party of Democratic Changes (SDP), the main successor to the League of Communists of Croatia (SKH). Its programme is now mainstream left-wing. It gained 5.5% of the vote and 11/138 seats at the August 1992 election. It merged with the small Social Democratic Party (SDH) and adopted its current name in April 1994. The leader is Ivica Račan.

Social Democratic Party of Germany

[Sozialdemokratische Partei Deutschlands] (SPD) German political party. The SPD traces its origins to the General German Workers' Association (ADAV) founded in 1863, one of the earliest socialist political organizations. It adopted its present name in 1891. It became the largest single party in 1912 and formed its first government in 1918. It was banned during the Hitler regime (1933–45). It held power in several states in West Germany from 1949, shed its remaining formal marxist ideology in 1959, and came to power at federal level in 1966, when it joined a grand coalition with the Christian Democratic Union (CDU). It led a coalition with the centrist Free Democratic Party (FDP) from 1969–82. The party has been in opposition at federal level since then, but has continued to hold or share power in many states, in particular North Rhine - Westphalia (the most populous), Hesse and the city states of Bremen and Hamburg. In September 1990 the Social Democratic Party (SDP) in East Germany, which had been reestablished after the collapse of communist rule, merged with the SPD in the west. At the all-German election in December 1990 the party gained 33.5% of the vote (35.7% in the west, 24.3% in the east) and 239/662 seats. The leader is Rudolf Scharping, the parliamentary leader is Hans-Ulrich Klose, and the general secretary is Günter Verheugen.

Social Democratic Party of Lithuania

[Lietuvos Socialdemoktratų Partija] (LSDP) Lithuanian political party. Founded in 1896, the LSDP has been banned and/or exiled for most of its existence. It was relaunched in Lithuania, then still part of the Soviet Union, in 1989. At the October/November 1992 election it gained 6.0% of the vote and 8/141 seats. The leader is Aloyzas Sakalas.

Social Democratic Party of Slovakia

[Sociálnodemokratická Strana Slovenska] (SDSS) Slovakian political party. Founded in 1990, the SDSS gained 4.0% of the vote in the June 1992 election for the Slovak parliament but no seats, having failed to obtain the 5% required for representation. The leader is Jaroslav Volf.

Social Democratic Party of Slovenia

[Socialdemokratična Stranka Slovenije] (SDSS) Slovenian political party. The SDSS was founded in 1989 as the first opposition party under communist rule. At the December 1992 election it gained 3.3% of the vote and 4/90 seats. The leader is Janez Janša.

Social Democratic Party of Switzerland

[Sozialdemokratische Partei der Schweiz (German), Parti Socialiste Suisse (French)] (SP, SPS, PS or PSS) Swiss political party. Founded in 1888, the Social Democratic Party has been one of the country's dominant parties for many years and is a member of the four-party coalition which has been in power since 1959. At the October 1991 election it gained 19.0% of the vote and 43/200 seats. The party president is Peter Bodenmann, the parliamentary leader Ursula Mauch.

Social Democratic Party of the Republic of Poland [Socjaldemokracja Rzeczpospolitej Polskiej] (SdRP) Polish political party. The SdRP was founded in 1990 as the successor to the communist Polish United Workers' Party (PZPR). It has adopted a mainstream left-wing economic and social programme. It is the dominant partner in the DEMOCRATIC LEFT ALLIANCE (SLD), formed in 1991 with the All-Poland Trade Unions Alliance (OPZZ) and several smaller groups. The leader is Aleksander Kwaśniewski.

Social Democratic People's Party [Sosyal Demokratik Halkçı Parti] (SHP) Turkish political party. The SHP was formed in 1985 from the merger of the People's Party (HP) and the Social Democratic Party (SODEP). Both had been founded in 1983 as successors to the Republican People's Party (CHP), which had been disbanded after the 1980 military coup. It established itself as the second-largest party in parliament in 1987. It contested the October 1991 election in an alliance with the Kurdish-based People's Labour Party (HEP), which gained 20.8% of the vote; the party gained 66/450 seats. It then joined the centre-right True Path Party (DYP) in a coalition government. In 1992, 21 of the SHP's 66 deputies joined the relaunched CHP. The party leader is Murat Karayalçın, the general secretary is Cevdet Selvi.

Social Democratic Reform Party *See* ASSOCIATED LIST OF SOCIAL DEMOCRATS.

Social Development Fund Council of Europe programme. Originally called the Resettlement Fund, it was set up in 1956 to help member states to resettle refugees. Its scope has broadened considerably since then. It now also makes financial contributions to projects aimed at (i) providing training and jobs for the unemployed and low-cost housing for the homeless, and (ii) promoting education, public health and regional and rural development. It may contribute up to 40% of a project's total cost.

social dimension In the European Union (EU), an umbrella term for the non-economic aspects of the single internal market established at the start of 1993. In 1988 the European Commission published proposals to promote individual and collective rights of workers in such fields as health and safety, working conditions, information and consultation etc. They were formalized in the CHARTER OF THE FUNDAMENTAL SOCIAL RIGHTS OF WORKERS (Social Charter) and in the AGREEMENT ON SOCIAL POLICY (widely known as the Social Chapter) appended to the Maastricht Treaty, which came into force in November 1993. The British government has rejected both agreements.

social dumping In the European Union (EU), the transfer of production capacity and thus jobs from one member state to another with lower wages and other labour costs and/or lower standards in job protection and health and safety. Since the establishment of the single internal market at the start of 1993 there are no barriers to companies moving from one country to another for these or any other reasons. The issue of 'social dumping' is highly contentious within the EU, with critics arguing that it constitutes unfair competition and that it will lead to an erosion of welfare provisions and workers' rights.

Social Fund *See* EUROPEAN ....

Social Liberal Party *See* RADICAL LIBERAL PARTY.

social partners In many countries and the European Union (EU), the collective name for employers' associations and trade unions. In some countries they participate and cooperate with the government or other interest groups in joint bodies. Examples are the Joint Council on Prices and Wages in Austria, the National Labour Council (NAR/CNT) in Belgium, the Economic Council (ØR) in Denmark, the Social and Economic Council (SER) in the Netherlands and the Economic and Social Committee (ECOSOC) in the EU. *See also individual body entries.*

social partnership [soziale Partnerschaft] In Austria, the system whereby the government, employers' associations and trade unions work together with the aim of securing steady economic growth and full employment. It has operated since 1945 and covers all spheres of economic and social policy. *See also* JOINT COMMISSION ON WAGES AND PRICES.

Social Protocol Shorthand for the Protocol on Social Policy, an annex to the 1991 Maastricht Treaty establishing the European Union (EU) which regulates the operation of the AGREEMENT ON SOCIAL POLICY. This was signed by all EU member states except the United Kingdom.

Socialist Group (European Union) *See* PARTY OF EUROPEAN SOCIALISTS.

Socialist Labour Party [Partidul Socialist de Muncă] (PSM) Romanian political party. The PSM was founded in 1990 by former members of the banned Romanian Communist Party (PCR) and two small left-wing parties. It sees itself as the PCR's intellectual heir and is committed to the 'revival of socialism'. At the September 1992 election it gained 3.0% of the vote and 13/341 seats. The leader is Ilie Verdeţ.

Socialist Left Party [Sosialistisk Venstreparti] (SV) Norwegian political party. The SV was formed as an electoral alliance of various left-wing groups in 1973 and constituted as a single party in 1975. Its orientation is to the left of the Labour Party (DNA). At the September 1993 election it gained 7.9% of the vote and 13/165 seats. The leader is Erik Solheim, the parliamentary leader is Kjellbørg Lunde.

Socialist Party *See ...* OF ALBANIA.

Socialist Party [Parti Socialiste] (PS) Belgian political party. The PS has its roots in the Belgian Workers' Party founded in 1885. It formed the Walloon wing of the Belgian Socialist Party (PSB) from 1945 until 1978, when it became a separate organization. Generally more left-leaning than its Flemish counterpart, the PS has participated in many coalition governments since 1945, most recently since 1988. The largest party in Wallonia, it gained 13.6% of the vote and 35/212 seats at the November 1991 election. In January 1994 three senior party members were implicated in corruption (*see* AGUSTA AFFAIR). The leader is Philippe Busquin.

Socialist Party [Socialistische Partij] (SP) Belgian political party. The SP has its roots in the Belgian Workers' Party founded in 1885. It formed the Flemish wing of the Belgian Socialist Party (BSP) from 1945 until 1978, when it became a separate organization. Generally more right-leaning than its Walloon counterpart, the SP has participated in many coalition governments since 1945, most recently since 1988. Traditionally the second-largest party in Flanders, it gained 12.0% of the vote and 28/212 seats at the November 1991 election. The party president is Frank Vandenbroucke, the secretary is Linda Blomme.

Socialist Party *See* UNIFIED DEMOCRATIC UNION OF CYPRUS - SOCIALIST PARTY.

Socialist Party [Parti Socialiste] (PS) French political party. Established in its current form in 1971, the PS traces its roots to the French Section of the Workers' International (SFIO) founded in 1905. The SFIO led a left-wing coalition in 1936–38 and it participated in many governments during the Fourth Republic (1946–58). Its electoral support declined sharply in the 1950s, and in the 1960s it formed several alliances with other parties in an effort to consolidate the vote of the non-communist left. This led to the formation of the PS as a broadly based party, under the leadership of François Mitterrand, in 1971. After Mitterrand was elected president of the republic in 1981, he called early elections, which the PS won. It then formed the first majority left-wing government in France since the Second World War. The party lost power in 1986, but in the early election called after Mitterrand's reelection as president in 1988 it gained sufficient seats to form a centre-left coalition. Policy and personal differences among the three major factions (which had a quasi-formal status within the party) deepened from 1990 onwards. At the March 1993 election the PS lost half its popular vote and three-quarters of its seats, securing 17.6% and 54/577 seats. Michel Rocard, a former prime minister, was subsequently elected leader. He resigned after the party's disappointing performance in the European elections in June 1994 and was succeeded by Henri Emmanuelli. The parliamentary leader is Martin Malvy.

Socialist Party [Socialistische Partij] (SP) Dutch political party. Founded in 1971 as the Communist Party of the Netherlands - Marxist-Leninist (CPN-ML), the SP initially advocated far-left policies based on orthodox marxist, leninist and maoist principles. It has since changed its name and stance, advocating a planned economy coupled with workers' self-management. At the May 1994 election it gained 1.3% of the vote and 2/150 seats, entering parliament for the first time. The leader is Jan Marijnissen.

Socialist Party [Partido Socialista] (PS) Portuguese political party. The PS has its roots in the Portuguese Socialist Workers' Party (PSOP), which was founded in 1875 and banned by the Salazar regime in 1928. The party was established in its current form in exile in 1973. Legalized after the 1974 revolution, it led or participated in most coalition governments until 1985. At the October 1991 election it gained 20.0% of the vote and 72/230 seats. Mário Soares was the party leader from 1973 until his election as president of the republic in 1986. The current leader is António Guterres.

Socialist Party (Yugoslavia) *See ...* OF SERBIA.

Socialist Party of Albania [Partia Socialiste e Shqipërisë] (PSSh) Albanian political party. The Socialist Party is the successor to the ultra-orthodox communist Party of Labour (PPSh), which was the country's only legal party from 1944 until 1990. Having adopted a reformist programme, it won the 1991 multiparty election but was forced to relinquish its absolute hold on power. It was then renamed and its orientation was further shifted towards the mainstream left. It lost the March 1992 election to the Democratic Party (PDSh), gaining 25.7% of the vote and 38/140 seats. The leader is Fatos Nano. After his conviction for misappropriating public funds – a charge the party considers to be politically motivated – in April 1994, Servet Pellumbi, the deputy leader, became acting leader.

Socialist Party of Austria *See* SOCIAL DEMOCRATIC PARTY OF AUSTRIA.

Socialist Party of Catalonia [Partit dels Socialistes de Catalunya] (PSC) Spanish political party. Founded in 1978, the PSC is the Catalan branch of the SPANISH SOCIALIST WORKERS' PARTY (PSOE). The second-largest party in Catalonia since the introduction of autonomy in 1980, it gained 27.3% of the vote and 39/135 seats at the March 1992 regional election. The leader is Raimon Obiols.

Socialist Party of Cyprus *See* UNIFIED DEMOCRATIC UNION OF CYPRUS - SOCIALIST PARTY.

Socialist Party of Galicia [Partido Socialista de Galicia] (PSdG) Spanish political party. Founded in 1978, the PSdG is the Galician branch of the SPANISH SOCIALIST WORKERS' PARTY (PSOE). It has led or participated in several regional governments since the introduction of autonomy in 1981. At the October 1993 election in Galicia it gained 23.5% of the vote and 19/75 seats. The leader is Antolín Sánchez Presedo.

Socialist Party of Serbia [Socijalistička Partija Srbije] (SPS) Yugoslav political party. The SPS was founded in 1990 as the successor to the League of Communists of Serbia (SKS) and the associated Socialist Alliance. The party has adopted a 'democratic socialist' programme, but the leadership is identical with that of the old SKS and it has retained control of most levers of power in the republic and in Yugoslavia as a whole. At the December 1992 elections it gained 30.6% of the vote and 101/250 seats in the republican election and 47/138 seats in the Federal Assembly; at the early election for the former in December 1993 it gained 35.1% and 123 seats. Slobodan Milošević has been the leader since 1986 and president of Serbia since 1990. Milomir Minić, the general secretary, is also acting party leader because Milošević is barred by the constitution from holding party office.

Socialist People's Party [Socialistisk Folkeparti] (SF) Danish political party. Founded in 1957 by independent communists, the SF's orientation is to the left of the Social Democratic Party (SD). In the past it was strongly opposed to Denmark's membership of the European

563

Community (EC) and the North Atlantic Treaty Organization (NATO). At the December 1990 election it gained 8.3% of the vote and 15/179 seats. The leader is Holger K. Nielsen.

Socialist Unity [Unità Socialista] (US) Additional name adopted by the ITALIAN SOCIALIST PARTY (PSI) in 1990.

Sofia Shorthand for the Bulgarian government. Sofia is the capital of Bulgaria.

Soisson, Jean-Pierre (1934–) French civil servant and politician. He was first elected to parliament in 1968 for the Independent Republicans, a predecessor of the centrist Republican Party (PR). He was minister of youth, sport and leisure from 1978–81. He was then active in regional politics in his native Burgundy. He joined the centre-left government in 1988, serving as minister of labour (1988–91), the civil service and administrative modernization (1991–92) and agriculture and rural development (1992–93). He has also been involved in several centrist reform movements.

Sokolovi *See* SERBIAN FALCONS.

Solana, Javier (1942–) Spanish physicist and politician. He worked as a researcher and lecturer in the 1970s. A member of the Spanish Socialist Workers' Party (PSOE) since 1964, he was elected to parliament following its relegalization in 1977. Since the party gained power in 1982, he has been minister of culture (1982–88), government spokesman (1985–88) and minister of education and science (1988–92). He became foreign minister in June 1992.

Solberg, Hill-Marta (1951–) Norwegian teacher and politician. She has been active in local government in her native Nordland county for the Norwegian Labour Party (DNA) since the mid 1980s. She was elected the party's deputy leader and elected to parliament in 1993. In January 1994 she was appointed minister of social affairs.

Solbes, Pedro (1942–) Spanish civil servant and politician. A specialist in European economic relations, he was a commercial counsellor at the Spanish embassy to the European Community (EC) from 1973–78 and then held a

series of senior advisory posts in several ministries. He was appointed a junior minister with responsibility for relations with the EC in 1985 and minister of agriculture, fisheries and food in 1991. In July 1993 he was appointed minister of economy and finance in the minority Spanish Socialist Workers' Party (PSOE) government. He is not a party member.

Solchaga, Carlos (1944–) Spanish economist and politician. In the 1970s he held several senior positions at the Bank of Spain, the central bank, and worked as a researcher in various other institutions. In 1974 he joined the then still illegal Spanish Socialist Workers' Party (PSOE). He was appointed industry minister when the PSOE took office in 1982. From 1985–93 he held the key post of minister of economy and finance. Elected leader of the PSOE parliamentary group in June 1993, he resigned in May 1994 in connection with the RUBIO AFFAIR.

Solheim, Erik (1955–) Norwegian politician. A history and sociology graduate, he was elected leader of the youth wing of the Socialist Left Party (SV) in 1977, general secretary in 1981 and party leader in April 1987. He was elected to parliament in 1989.

solicitor-general (United Kingdom) *See* LAW OFFICERS.

Solidarity [Solidarność], in full **Independent Self-Governing Trade Union 'Solidarity'** [Niezależny Samorządny Związek Zawodówy 'Solidarność'] (NSZZ Solidarność or NSZZ'S') Polish trade union. Solidarity has its roots in anti-government agitation in the 1970s and was founded in 1980 in the wake of strikes centred in Gdańsk. It quickly gained around 10 million members and became a powerful force demanding economic and political reform of the communist system. It was banned after the imposition of martial law in December 1981; its leader, Lech Wałęsa, and other prominent members were detained and barred from public life. The union remained active underground throughout the 1980s. It was relegalized in April 1989 after the government and opposition groups agreed on a 'new social contract'.

The political wing of Solidarity won an overwhelming majority in the partly free election of June 1989 and formed a government under Tadeusz Mazowiecki. During 1990 the movement began to split along union/parliamentary and right/left lines and over the pace and direction of reform, intensified by personal rivalries culminating in Wałęsa and Mazowiecki both running for president of the republic. Wałęsa resigned as Solidarity leader after he became president in December. In September 1993 Solidarity's political wing gained 4.9% of the vote in the election for the Sejm (= lower house), narrowly failing to pass the 5% threshold for representation, and 9/100 seats in the Senate. The union's membership now stands at around 1.3 million (a tenth of the labour force). The leader is Marian Krzaklewski.

Solidarity Pact [Solidarpakt] Agreement in Germany on the medium-term financing of the cost of reunification. When the transfer of resources to eastern Germany required for economic restructuring, infrastructure improvements and environmental rehabilitation proved to be much greater than initially anticipated, the federal government floated the idea of establishing a national consensus on how to finance it. The final terms of the Solidarity Pact were agreed by the main political parties, state and local governments, employers' associations and trade unions in March 1993. It provides for the extension of the temporary 'solidarity surcharge' of 7.5% on income tax, reductions in federal expenditure, increased borrowing by the public sector, and the allocation of additional financial resources to the federal states to help them pay for transfers to eastern Germany. These measures will raise 55 billion marks (28.7 billion ecus) annually over a five-year period.

Solidarność *See* SOLIDARITY.

Solidarpakt *See* SOLIDARITY PACT.

Solingen case *See* MÖLLN AND ....

Sons of Glendower [Meibion Glyndŵr] British guerrilla group. Named after Owain Glyndŵr or Owen Glendower, a Welsh prince who led a rebellion against English rule at the start of the 15th cen-

tury, the group advocates full independence for Wales. It emerged in 1979 and initially specialized in arson attacks on holiday homes owned by non-Welsh people. In the late 1980s it also attacked targets outside Wales and the homes of several government ministers.

Sophusson, Fridrik (1943–) Icelandic teacher and politician. Elected to parliament for the right-wing Independence Party in 1978, he was minister of industry and energy from 1987–88 and became finance minister in April 1991.

Sorbs Ethnic group in Germany, also known as Lusatians and, informally, Wends. Numbering around 120,000, the Sorbs live in two neighbouring regions in the east, around the city of Bautzen in northeast Saxony and around Cottbus in southeast Brandenburg. Around half still speak High Sorb and Low Sorb respectively, two forms of a Slavic language related to Polish. Both are recognized and taught in schools.

Sorgdrager, Winnie (1948–) Dutch lawyer, civil servant and politician. She worked as an administrator for Twente Polytechnic from 1971–79. She then became a public prosecutor, latterly practising at the Arnhem and The Hague regional courts. A member of the centre-left Democrats 66 (D'66), she was appointed minister of justice in the left-right coalition formed in August 1994.

sottogoverno *See* HIDDEN GOVERNMENT.

Sound question Controversy over a fixed link between Denmark and Sweden across the Sound [Øresund/Öresund] strait. The two governments signed an agreement in August 1991 on the construction of a 17-kilometre road-and-rail link between the cities of Copenhagen and Malmö consisting of two bridges and a tunnel. The project is opposed by environmentalists, who predict that the partial blocking of the Sound will hamper the flow of relatively clean salt water into the polluted Baltic Sea and thus upset its vulnerable ecosystem. In 1993 the Swedish Centre Party (Cp), which shares this view, threatened to withdraw from the coalition if the project went ahead. When the government gave its formal

---

approval in June 1994, the environment minister, Olof Johansson, the Cp leader, resigned his post but his party colleagues remained in office. In 1973 a similar project had foundered on Danish opposition.

South Moluccans or **Moluccans** Ethnic group in the Netherlands, also known informally as Ambonese. The South Moluccans are the descendants of soldiers and civil servants who served in the Dutch East Indies army and administration and came to the Netherlands after the colony became independent as Indonesia in 1949. Most of them were from Ambon and other islands in the Moluccas archipelago – the famed 'Spice Islands'. These had been subject to strong Portuguese and then Dutch influences from the 16th century. The Ambonese refused to join independent Indonesia and proclaimed the Republic of the South Moluccas (RMS). The rebellion was defeated within a year and around 15,000 RMS supporters then left for the Netherlands. In the 1970s the Free South Moluccan Organization carried out several guerrilla actions in the Netherlands, including a train hijacking. Today the South Moluccans number around 36,000. They retain a strong identity, distinct from the small group of other Indonesians who settled in the Netherlands in the 1950s.

South Tyrol [Südtirol (German), Alto Adige (Italian)] Province of Italy, part of the TRENTINO - ALTO ADIGE autonomous region. Also known as Bozen/Bolzano, after its capital, South Tyrol is situated in the Alps and Dolomites in the northeast and borders on Austria. It has an area of 7,400 sq km and a population of 479,000. Just under three-quarters of the people are German-speaking South Tyroleans, around a fifth are ethnic Italians (concentrated in the main towns), and there are also 30,000 speakers of Ladin (a Romance language related to Friulian and Romansh); German is a full official language alongside Italian. The economy is based on agriculture and tourism. The province enjoys extensive autonomy in the economic, social, educational and cultural spheres. The main political party is the South Tyrol People's Party (SVP), which gained 52.0% of the

vote and 19/35 seats at the provincial election in November 1993. Part of the Holy Roman Empire during the Middle Ages, the region eventually became part of the Austrian Habsburg territory of Tyrol. Together with the predominantly Italian-speaking region of Trentino it was ceded to Italy in 1919. Agitation by German speakers for self-government, supported by Austria, led to the creation of the special autonomous region of Trentino - Alto Adige in 1948. More extensive autonomy was granted to the province of South Tyrol in principle in 1969 and specific measures were implemented in the 1970s and 80s. The controversy over South Tyrol's status was formally resolved when a further package of autonomy measures was approved by the Italian and Austrian parliaments and the regional and provincial assemblies in June 1992.

South Tyrol People's Party [Südtiroler Volkspartei (German)] (SVP) Italian political party. Founded in 1945, the SVP is the main representative of the German-speaking community in South Tyrol, a province within the Trentino - Alto Adige region. It defines itself as a christian democratic party, but is more conservative on social issues than its counterparts in other countries. It has been the largest party in South Tyrol since its foundation. At the November 1993 provincial election it gained 52.0% of the vote and 19/35 seats; at the April 1992 and March 1994 general elections it gained 3/630 seats. The leader is Siegfried Brugger, the party president is Roland Riz.

Southeast Standard region of the United Kingdom. Centred on London, the Southeast is Britain's most populous and wealthiest region. Comprising the counties of Bedfordshire, Berkshire, Buckinghamshire, East Sussex, Essex, Greater London, Hampshire, Hertfordshire, Kent, Oxfordshire, Surrey, West Sussex and the Isle of Wight, it has an area of 24,614 sq km and a population of 16,978,000. The economy is based on services (concentrated in London), manufacturing, agriculture and tourism. Other important cities besides London are Southampton,

Portsmouth, Brighton and Oxford. The region is considered a unit primarily for statistical purposes and has no administrative or political functions; Greater London is sometimes treated separately.

southern question [questione del Sud]
In Italy, the problems and controversies surrounding the wide gap between the industrialized and rich north and centre and the less developed and far poorer south. *See* MEZZOGIORNO.

Southwest Standard region of the United Kingdom. The Southwest comprises the English counties of Avon, Cornwall, Devon, Dorset, Gloucestershire, Somerset and Wiltshire. It has an area of 26,457 sq km and a population of 5,303,000. The main cities are Bristol, Plymouth and Bournemouth. The economy is based on manufacturing, agriculture and tourism. Several counties, Cornwall in particular, have a strong local identity. The region is considered a unit principally for statistical purposes and has no administrative or political functions.

Sovereign Military Order of Malta or **Knights of Malta** Roman Catholic monastic order with the status of a sovereign state, also known as the Knights Hospitaller of Saint John of Jerusalem, Knights Hospitaller, Knights of Saint John and Hospitallers. The order has its roots in a hospital founded in the 11th century to care for sick Christian pilgrims visiting Jerusalem. During the Crusades – the intermittent attempts by European Christians to wrest Palestine, the 'Holy Land', from Muslim control – it developed into an international organization with a powerful military arm. After the fall of the last Christian-held city in Palestine, Acre, in 1291 it transferred its headquarters to Cyprus and then to Rhodes. The order ruled the latter island as an independent state from 1309 until its defeat by the Ottoman Turks in 1522. In compensation King Charles I of Spain gave it possession of Malta in 1530. It was expelled from the island by French troops in 1798. The order was reconstituted in 1834 as a monastic community engaged solely in charitable work. Granted sovereign status, it has many of the trappings of a state and is recognized as such by over 40 countries. Its 'territory', however, consists of its headquarters and another building in Rome (Italy). In 1991 the Maltese government gave it the use of a fortress, a palace and a church on the island. The head of the order, whose title is 'prince and grand master', is Andrew Bertie (United Kingdom), who was elected in April 1988.

sovereignty of Parliament In the United Kingdom, the constitutional principle that supreme political authority resides in Parliament, comprising the sovereign (in effect the Cabinet or government acting in his/her name), the House of Lords and, crucially, the House of Commons. The key implication of the principle is that any law passed by Parliament is by definition constitutional and cannot be challenged. A 'judicial review' can be requested, but the courts can only rule on whether there has been an irregularity in the implementation of a law, not on its 'constitutionality'. The British political system thus differs markedly from that of most other European countries, where sovereignty is nominally vested in the people and divided among legislative, executive and judicial bodies at national, regional or even local level, the power of the legislature is circumscribed by the constitution, and laws must conform to its provisions as interpreted by a constitutional court or similar body.

Soviet successor states Collective name for the 15 constituent republics of the Soviet Union which became independent after its disintegration in 1991. They include, to the west of Russia, Estonia, Latvia and Lithuania (collectively called the Baltic states), Belorussia, Ukraine and Moldavia. All except the Baltic states joined the loose Commonwealth of Independent States (CIS).

Soysal, Mümtaz (1929–) Turkish lawyer, academic and politician. A lecturer in constitutional law at Ankara University, he came to prominence in the 1960s as a human-rights activist and was imprisoned for 18 months after the 1971 military coup. He was a deputy chairman of the human-rights organization Amnesty

International in the 1970s. In the mid
1980s he became a regular contributor to
Milliyet, one of the country's major daily
newspapers. Elected to parliament for the
Social Democratic People's Party (SHP)
in 1991, he was appointed foreign minister in July 1994.

soziale Partnerschaft (Austria) *See* SOCIAL
PARTNERSHIP.

SP (Belgium) *See* SOCIALIST PARTY.

SP Abbreviation for Suojelupoliisi ('Protection Police'), the Finnish intelligence
agency.

SP (Netherlands) *See* SOCIALIST PARTY.

Sp (Norway) *See* CENTRE PARTY.

SP *See* SOCIAL DEMOCRATIC PARTY OF
SWITZERLAND.

Spadolini, Giovanni (1925–94) Italian
journalist, historian, academic and politician. He was editor of two major newspapers, the *Resto del Carlino* (1955–68)
and *Corriere della Sera* (1968–72), and
lectured in modern history at Florence
University. He was elected to the Senate,
the upper house of parliament, for the
centre-right Italian Republican Party
(PRI) in 1972. He was party leader from
1979–87. He also served as minister for
the environment (1974–76), education
(1979) and defence (1983–85) and was
briefly prime minister of a five-party
coalition in 1981–82. From July 1987
until April 1994 he was president of the
Senate (an influential post in the Italian
political system). He died in August 1994.

Spain [España] Country in southwestern
Europe.

Official data. Name: Kingdom of Spain
[Reino de España]; capital: Madrid; form
of government: parliamentary monarchy;
head of state: king/queen; head of government: president; flag: three horizontal
stripes, red, yellow and red (in proportions 1:2:1), with the state emblem in the
centre; national holidays: 24 June (King
Juan Carlos's Saint's Day), 12 October
(National Day), 6 December (Constitution Day); language: Spanish; religion:
none; currency: peseta (Pta, Ptas) = 100
céntimos; abbreviation: E.

Geography. The larger of the two
Iberian countries, Spain has a total area
of 504,783 sq km. This includes the

Balearic Islands [Islas Baleares] in the
Mediterranean Sea, the Canary Islands
[Islas Canarias] in the Atlantic Ocean
100 km off the coast of Morocco and
1,200 km to the southwest of Spain, and
the enclaves of Ceuta and Melilla on the
north Moroccan coast. Spain is bordered
by the Bay of Biscay (part of the Atlantic
Ocean), France and Andorra in the north,
the Mediterranean Sea in the east and
south, Gibraltar and (across the Strait of
Gibraltar) Morocco in the south, and
Portugal and the Atlantic Ocean in the
west. The dominant physical feature is
the central plateau (Meseta). It is surrounded by the Cantabrian Mountains
[Cordillera Cantábrica] to the north, the
Iberic ranges [Sistema Ibérico] to the east
and the Sierra Morena to the south. Other
major mountain ranges are the Pyrenees
[Pirineos] on the northern border with
France, the Sistema Central in the centre
and the Sierra Nevada in the south. The
main low-lying areas are the Ebro valley
in the northeast, the coastal plain around
Valencia in the east, and the Guadalquivir
valley in Andalusia in the south. Some
41% of the land is arable, another 21% is
covered by pastures and 31% is forested.
The main rivers are the Ebro, Guadalquivir, Tagus [Tajo] and Douro [Duero].
The climate is temperate marine in the
north and northwest (with mild summers
and cool winters), semi-arid in the centre
(hot summers and cold winters), and
mediterranean in the rest of the country
(hot summers and cool winters); rainfall
is heavy in the northwest, moderate in the
mountains and the southwest, and light
in the centre, east and southeast.

Demography. Spain has a population
of 39,141,000. Population density is 79
per sq km (land area). Some 78% of the
people live in urban areas. The main cities
are Madrid (metropolitan population 4.6
million, city 3.1 million), Barcelona
(4.1 million, 1.7 million), Valencia (1.3
million, 750,000) Seville [Sevilla] and
Zaragoza. Other major cities are Málaga,
Bilbao [Bilbo (Basque)], Las Palmas,
Valladolid, Palma de Mallorca, Murcia,
Córdoba, Hospitalet, Vigo, Gijón, Granada
and Alicante [Alacant (Valencian)]. Some

76% of the people live in urban areas. In ethnic and linguistic terms 72.3% of the people are Castilian Spaniards, 16.3% Catalans and Valencians (mainly in Catalonia, the Balearic Islands and Valencia in the east), 8.1% Galicians (in Galicia in the northwest) and 2.3% Basques (in the Basque Country and Navarre in the north); these totals include around 500,000 Gipsies (1.3% of the total population). Many Castilian speakers in the Basque Country and Navarre consider themselves ethnic Basques. Foreign nationals account for 0.9% of the population, and include citizens of the United Kingdom, Germany, Portugal and France. There are also thought to be around 150,000 illegal immigrants, mainly from North Africa and Latin America. Around 3.5 million Spanish citizens live and work abroad, mainly in the United States, France, Germany and Switzerland. In religious terms nearly all the people are nominally Roman Catholics; there are around 250,000 other Christians and 300,000 Muslims.

Sociography. Spain scores 0.888 on the United Nations human development index (HDI), ranking 23rd in the world and 16th among 32 European countries. There are 38 doctors and 44 hospital beds for every 10,000 people. Education is compulsory between the ages of six and 16. There is one teacher for every 21 students. Enrolment is 74% at the secondary level and 32% at the tertiary level. The literacy rate is 97%. Real annual income per head (in terms of purchasing power) is US$ 12,670.

Infrastructure and communications. Spain has a developed transport and communications network, highly developed in the main cities; the railway system is relatively limited, as are the road and telecommunications systems in some rural areas, and the electronic media have a much wider reach than the press. There are 239,880 km of paved roads and 12.1 million passenger cars (317 per 1,000 people), 12,560 km of railways and 1,045 km of navigable waterways. The main ports are Bilbao, Tarragona, Algeciras / La Línea, Barcelona and Cartagena. The main airports are at Madrid (Barajas) and Barcelona, and there are 29 other airports with scheduled services. There are 81 daily newspapers, with a combined circulation of around 3.3 million (around 85 per 1,000 people). There are 12.6 million radio receivers, 17.2 million television sets and around 17 million telephones in use (respectively 330, 452 and 445 per 1,000 people).

Economic structure. The Spanish economy is generally highly developed and diversified, although some regions are relatively undeveloped and highly dependent on agriculture. It is the fifth-largest economy in Europe and the eighth-largest in the world. It is based on manufacturing, agriculture and food processing, and tourism, with traditionally a substantial state-owned sector. After a period of high growth from 1985–90 (averaging 4.1% per year), economic performance in the 1990s has been marked by negligible growth, substantial current-account deficits (above 3% of GDP), and relatively high but falling inflation (averaging 7%); since the mid 1980s unemployment has remained above 20%, the highest level in Western Europe.

Services contribute 64% of GDP, industry contributes 32% (manufacturing 21%), and agriculture, forestry and fisheries 4%. Some 20% of the labour force is employed in manufacturing, 19% in trade, 10% in construction and 10% in farming and fishing. The main agricultural activities are horticulture (olives, grapes, citrus and other fruit, vegetables), livestock raising (sheep, goats, cattle, pigs, poultry) and dairy farming; the main crops grown are cereals (wheat, barley, maize), potatoes and sugarbeets; Spain is Europe's second-largest producer of fruit and vegetables. Forestry (paper, cork, charcoal) and fishing (sardines, anchovies, tuna, shrimp) are of regional importance. The main mineral resources are coal, lignite, zinc, natural gas, precious stones, potash and sulphur; Spain is Europe's largest producer of zinc. The main industries are engineering (esp. cars) and food processing (incl. wine, olive oil); other important branches are chemicals, textiles (incl. footwear), petrochemicals, electrical goods, metalworking, iron and steel, wood processing and shipbuilding. The tourism industry is a major source of foreign exchange, contributing 4% of GNP (3% net); it is the third-largest in Europe and the fourth-largest in the world. The main energy sources are imported and domestic fossil fuels and nuclear power; 13% of export earnings are required to cover net fuel imports. The main exports are transport equipment (20% of the total, incl. cars and other motor vehicles 17%), foodstuffs (14%, incl. citrus and other fruit 5%), iron and steel (9%), industrial machinery (9%), textiles and clothing (7%), chemicals (7%), foodstuffs, wood products, oil products and electrical equipment; machinery and transport equipment account for 39% of the total, basic manufactures for 24%. The main imports are machinery and transport equipment, basic manufactures, fuels and chemicals. The main trading partners are: exports: France (20%), Germany (14%), Italy (11%), United Kingdom (8%), Netherlands (8%), Portugal (7%), United States (6%); imports: Germany (16%), France (15%), Italy (10%), United Kingdom (8%), Japan (5%), United States, Netherlands; two-thirds of all trade is with other European Union (EU) countries. Net invisible earnings (remittances from workers abroad, tourism receipts) account for 3% of GNP.

The Bank of Spain [Banco de España] is the central bank. The main employers' association is the Spanish Confederation of Employers' Organizations (CEOE); the main labour organizations are the Workers' Commissions (CCOO) and the General Workers' Union (UGT).

Political structure. Spain is a parliamentary monarchy on the basis of a constitution adopted in 1978. The king/queen is head of state and commander of the armed forces. Executive power is vested in the president of the government [presidente del gobierno] or prime minister and the council of ministers. Legislative power is vested in the bicameral Parliament [Cortes Generales], composed of the 350-member Congress of Deputies [Congreso de los Diputados] elected for a four-year term by a system of proportional representa-

tion, and the 254-member Senate [Senado] elected for a four-year term on a provincial and regional basis. All citizens over the age of 18 are entitled to vote. Judicial power is ultimately vested in the 20-member Supreme Court [Tribunal Supremo] elected for a five-year term by the legislature; the 12-member Constitutional Court [Tribunal Constitucional], elected for a nine-year term by the legislature, adjudicates on constitutional matters. Spain is composed of 17 autonomous communities or regions [comunidad autónoma, pl. -es - s], which have their own elected legislatures and governments. They are Andalusia [Andalucía], Aragón, Asturias, Balearic Islands [Illes Balears / Islas Baleares], Basque Country [País Vasco / Euskadi], Canary Islands [Canarias], Cantabria, Castile-León [Castilla-León], Castile - La Mancha [Castilla - La Mancha], Catalonia [Catalunya/Cataluña], Extremadura, Galicia [Galicia/Galiza], Madrid Community [Comunidad de Madrid], Murcia, Navarre [Navarra], Rioja [La Rioja] and Valencian Community [Comunidad Valenciana / Comunitat Valenciana]. Andalusia, the Basque Country, Catalonia and Galicia have more extensive powers of self-government than the other regions. Administratively the regions are divided into 50 provinces [provincia, pl. -s], which are subdivided into 8,047 municipalities.

The main national political parties are the Spanish Socialist Workers' Party (PSOE), People's Party (PP) and United Left (IU). Regional parties include Andalusian Power (Poder Andaluz, PA), the Aragonese Party (PAR), the Mallorcan Union (UM) in the Balearic Islands, the Basque Nationalist Party (PNV/EAJ), Basque Solidarity (EA) and People's Unity (Herri Batasuna, HB) in the Basque Country, the Canary Coalition (CC), Convergence and Union (CiU) and the Republican Left (ERC) in Catalonia, the Galician Nationalist Bloc (BNG), and the Valencian Union (UV). At the general election in June 1993 the PSOE gained 39.6% of the vote and 159/350 seats, the PP 34.8% and 141 seats, the IU 9.6% and 18 seats, the CiU 17 seats, the PNV/EAJ five seats, the CC four seats, Herri Bata-suna two seats, and the PAR, EA and UV one seat each. The government is formed by the PSOE, with Felipe González as prime minister. Other senior ministers are Narcís Serra (deputy prime minister), Juan Alberto Belloch (interior and justice), Pedro Solbes (economy and finance), Javier Solana (foreign affairs) and Julián García Vargas (defence). The head of state is King Juan Carlos I, who succeeded to the throne in November 1975; the heir is Prince Felipe.

Security and international affiliations. The Spanish armed forces number 200,700 (army 138,900, navy 32,000, airforce 29,800). There is also a 66,000-strong paramilitary force, the Civil Guard [Guardia Civil]. Military service is com-pulsory and consists of nine months' basic training.

Spain is a member of the Conference on Security and Cooperation in Europe (CSCE), Council of Europe, European Economic Area (EEA), European Union (EU), North Atlantic Treaty Organization (NATO) and Western European Union (WEU), as well as the Organization for Economic Cooperation and Development (OECD) and the United Nations and its specialized agencies.

History. Celtic peoples migrated into the Iberian peninsula from the north from the 10th century BC onwards. The Phoenicians, Greeks and then Carthagini-ans established trading settlements along the eastern and southern coasts, and the latter extended their influence further inland in the 230s. They lost their posses-sions to the Romans after the Second Punic War (218–01). The Romans sub-jugated most of the inland Celtic states in the 2nd century and completed the conquest of the peninsula in 27 BC. The region became thoroughly romanized during four centuries of Roman rule. Christianity was introduced in the early 2nd century AD. During the Europe-wide migrations that helped trigger the collapse of the Roman Empire in the early 5th century the Germanic Visigoths estab-lished a kingdom in Spain in 419. Chris-tianity became the dominant religion in

the 6th century. Muslim Arab invaders crossed from North Africa in 711 and conquered all but the far north of the peninsula within a few decades. The Caliphate of Córdoba (755–1031) was one of Europe's most advanced states, benefiting from the fusion of Muslim, Christian and Jewish traditions. It frag-mented into rival states in the early 11th century. The Christian reconquest of Spain began at this time. It was conducted by the feudal states of Asturias/León, Castile, Navarre, Aragón and Catalonia (and Portugal). The Muslims were deci-sively defeated at the Battle of Navas Tolosa in 1212, after which their control was restricted to the Kingdom of Granada (modern southern Andalusia). By this time Castile and Aragón had absorbed the other states except Navarre. Aragón, which had been united with Catalonia in 1137, also became a major Mediterranean power in the 14th century after acquiring the Balearic Islands, Sicily and Sardinia. In 1479 Aragón and Castile were united as a result of the marriage of King Ferdinand II and Queen Isabella I. Under their rule (they died in 1516 and 1504 respectively) the administration was centralized, Granada and Navarre were conquered in 1492 and 1512, all of south-ern Italy came under Spanish control, and Christopher Columbus, who sought to reach Asia by sailing westwards, began the exploration of the Americas on behalf of the Spanish crown. In 1516 Charles of Habsburg, Ferdinand and Isabella's grandson, who had already become ruler of much of the Low Countries and would become Holy Roman emperor in 1519, ascended the Spanish throne as King Charles I. In the following decades the Spanish conquered the Aztec and Inca states and other territories in the Americas, and Spain became a world power. Charles divided his possessions on his abdication in 1555/56. His son Philip II inherited Spain, the Low Countries and the colonial empire. The Low Countries rebelled in the 1560s, and the north declared its independence as the Dutch Republic in 1581. Over the next century Spain lost its position as the dominant European power to France and its position as the world's leading maritime power to England and the Dutch Republic. The death of the last Spanish Habsburg in 1700 and the accession of a French Bourbon led to the War of the Spanish Succession (1701–13/14). Under the 1713 Treaty of Utrecht Spain lost the Southern Netherlands and Gibraltar, and the Italian possessions temporarily. A range of social and economic reforms were introduced during the reign of King Charles III (1759–88).

In 1808 Emperor Napoleon of France installed his brother Joseph as king of Spain, but Spanish forces, assisted by the British, defeated the French in the Peninsular War (1808–14) and the Bourbon monarchy was restored. The fighting caused great devastation and sparked a social and political upheaval, both at home and abroad. In the 1810s and 20s the American colonies rebelled and became independent. (The exceptions were Cuba and Puerto Rico, which were lost to the United States in 1898.) The 19th century and early 20th century were dominated by power struggles between liberals and conservatives, overlaid by a dynastic dispute (over the succession by Queen Isabella II in 1834), demands for autonomy in Catalonia and the Basque Country, and, increasingly, republican agitation and the rise of workers' organizations. The army overthrew liberal governments in 1823, 1868 and at the end of the short-lived First Republic (1873–74). Growing social tensions, disillusionment with parliamentary government and a military setback in Morocco led to a military coup by Miguel Primo de Rivera in 1923. His right-wing dictatorship collapsed in 1930 after King Alfonso XIII withdrew his support, but he himself was forced to abdicate the following year after election results revealed overwhelming support for the abolition of the monarchy. Many reforms were introduced during the Second Republic (1931–39), including universal adult suffrage and regional autonomy. Victory for the left-wing parties in the 1936 election sparked a revolt by 'nationalist' army officers led by Francisco Franco. The 'republican'

forces were defeated in a three-year civil war that cost an estimated 750,000 lives. Franco became chief of state and established a far-right dictatorship.

During the 1960s and early 70s the country enjoyed sustained economic growth and industrial expansion, buoyed by foreign investment, remittances from abroad (by emigrant workers) and a tourism boom. The monarchy was restored in 1975, when Juan Carlos, the grandson of the last king, became head of state on Franco's death. He signalled his intention to restore democratic rule by appointing a moderate conservative, Adolfo Suárez, as prime minister in 1976. Political parties and trade unions were legalized later that year, elections for a constituent assembly were held in 1977, a new constitution was adopted in 1978, and autonomy was extended to the Basque Country, Catalonia and the other regions. Spain was admitted to the Council of Europe in 1977. In February 1981 King Juan Carlos and senior army officers played a key role in foiling an attempted far-right coup. Spain joined the North Atlantic Treaty Organization (NATO) in May 1982. The October 1982 election was won by the Spanish Socialist Workers' Party (PSOE) led by Felipe González. Spain became a member of the European Community (EC), now the European Union (EU), in January 1986. This gave another boost to economic development, although unemployment also remained high. The PSOE was reelected in June 1986 and October 1989 with reduced majorities; it lost its absolute majority in the June 1993 election but remained in office as a minority administration.

See also entries on specific institutions, organizations, parties, people, terms etc.

Spanish Confederation of Employers' Organizations [Confederación Española de Organizaciones Empresariales] (CEOE) Spanish employers' association. Founded in 1977, the CEOE has 165 affiliated organizations from all sectors of the economy. The president is José María Cuevas, the secretary-general is Juan Jiménez Aguilar.

572

Spanish North Africa Collective name for the Spanish dependencies of Ceuta and Melilla (including Peñón de Vélez de la Gomera and several islands) on the coast of Morocco. Called *plazas de soberanía* ('sovereign territories'), they have been Spanish possessions since the 15th and 16th centuries. They are claimed by Morocco. *See also individual territory entries.*

Spanish Socialist Workers' Party [Partido Socialista Obrero Español] (PSOE) Spanish political party. Founded in 1879, the PSOE is one of Europe's oldest socialist parties and one of the country's main parties since the 1930s. It was banned under the Franco dictatorship (1939–75). It gained just under a third of the vote in the 1977 and 1979 elections and came to power in 1982 with an absolute majority of seats. It was returned to office in 1986 and 1989. The party's main support is in the poorer southern regions, in particular Andalusia, and in the industrialized north. Since the late 1980s there has been a significant minority within the party which opposes the government's centrist economic policies. It is led by Alfonso Guerra and is known as the *guerrista* wing; the majority is often called the *felipista* wing, after Felipe González, the party leader and prime minister, or as the *renovadores* ('reformers'). At the June 1993 election the party lost its absolute majority, gaining 38.7% of the vote and 159/350 seats. It then formed a minority government. González has been party leader since 1974; Guerra is the deputy leader, Joaquín Almunia the parliamentary leader, and Ciprià Ciscar the organization secretary.

Spanish Socialist Workers' Party of Andalusia [Partido Socialista Obrero Español de Andalucía] (PSOE-A) Spanish political party. The PSOE-A is the Andalusian branch of the SPANISH SOCIALIST WORKERS' PARTY (PSOE). It is the region's largest party and has formed the government since the introduction of autonomy in 1982. At the June 1990 regional election it gained 49.6% of the vote and 61/109 seats, but its support fell to 38.6% and 45 seats in

June 1994. The leader Manuel Chaves, the party president is Carlos Sanjuan de la Rocha.

Spautz, Jean (1930–) Luxemburg steel-worker, trade-union official and politician. He worked as a rolling mill operator until his election to parliament for the Christian Social People's Party (CSV) in 1959. He was chairman of the party's youth wing from 1960–66, leader of the Luxemburg Christian Trade Union Federation (LCGB) from 1967–80, chairman of the CSV from 1982–90, and has been honorary chairman since then. He was appointed minister of the interior, family affairs, housing and social security in July 1984, minister of the interior and housing and urban affairs in June 1989, and minister of the interior and housing in July 1994.

SPD *See* SOCIAL DEMOCRATIC PARTY OF GERMANY.

speaker In many countries, the president of the parliament or one of its chambers. In most cases this is a largely ceremonial office, but in some countries (e.g. Bulgaria, France, Italy, Poland, United Kingdom) the speaker or president has considerable formal powers and informal influence. In Estonia, Latvia and Lithuania the president of the parliament was effectively the head of state from the restoration of independence in 1991 until the adoption of new constitutional arrangements in 1992 and 1993.

Special Air Service (SAS) British military force. Set up in its present form in 1947, the SAS is an elite commando unit of the armed forces which specializes in undercover military and counterinsurgency operations. It is trained specifically to cause disruption and gather information behind enemy lines. Domestically it has been involved in security work in Northern Ireland. It has served as a model for similar units set up in other countries.

special autonomous region Shorthand for AUTONOMOUS REGION WITH SPECIAL STATUTE, the status granted to five of Italy's 20 autonomous regions.

Special Branch British police force. The Special Branch deals with political matters, including anti-terrorist operations. It also serves as the executive arm of the Security

Service (MI-5), and the activities of the two agencies are increasingly overlapping.

Special Intervention Group [Gruppo Intervento Speciale] (GIS) Italian military force. The GIS is an elite commando unit of the armed forces specializing in anti-terrorist and undercover operations.

Special Operations Groups [Grupos Especiales de Operaciones] (GEO) Spanish military force. The GEO is an elite commando unit of the armed forces specializing in anti-terrorist and under-cover operations.

special relationship In the United Kingdom, a term used to indicate the country's traditionally close ties with the United States. It is based on linguistic, historical, cultural and political affinities. The two countries became allies during the Second World War (1939–45) and subsequently played a leading role in the North Atlantic Treaty Organization (NATO), set up to counter the perceived Soviet threat.

Speroni, Francesco (1946–) Italian flight technician and politician. A graduate in political science, he worked for Alitalia, the national airline, before he entered politics. He was elected to the European Parliament for the autonomist Lombard League (Lega Lombarda) in 1989 and to the Italian parliament for the more broadly based Northern League (Lega Nord) in 1992. He was appointed to the key post of minister for institutional reform in the right-wing coalition formed in May 1994.

Spiroiu, Constantin Nicolae (1936–) Romanian soldier and politician. A career army officer, now with the rank of lieutenant-general, he played a prominent role in the overthrow of the Ceauşescu regime in December 1989. He was defence minister from June 1990 until March 1994. He is a member of the Social Democracy Party (PDSR, the successor to the Democratic National Salvation Front, FSND).

Spitaels, Guy (1931–) Belgian lawyer, academic and politician. He taught law at Brussels University until his election to parliament for the Walloon Socialist Party (PS) in 1977. For the next four years he held several ministerial posts, including that of deputy prime minister (1979–81). He was leader of the PS from 1981–92.

In January 1992 he became chief minister of the Wallonian regional government. He resigned in January 1994 after being implicated in the AGUSTA AFFAIR.

Spitsbergen Informal name for Svalbard, the dependency of Norway in the Arctic Ocean. It properly refers to the main island of the archipelago.

SPÖ *See* SOCIAL DEMOCRATIC PARTY OF AUSTRIA.

SPO *See* SERBIAN RENEWAL MOVEMENT.

Spolužitie *See* COEXISTENCE.

SPR-RSČ *See* ASSOCIATION FOR THE REPUBLIC - REPUBLICAN PARTY OF CZECHOSLOVAKIA.

Spring, Dick (1950–) Irish lawyer and politician. He briefly practised law before being elected to parliament for the Labour Party in 1981. He became the party's leader in November 1982. From 1982–87 he was deputy prime minister and minister for the environment (1982–83) and energy (1983–87) in a coalition led by Fine Gael. When Labour – having doubled its share of the vote in the November 1992 election – returned to government in January 1993 in a coalition led by Fianna Fáil, he became deputy prime minister and foreign minister.

SPS *See* SOCIAL DEMOCRATIC PARTY OF SWITZERLAND.

SPS (Yugoslavia) *See* SOCIALIST PARTY OF SERBIA.

Spychalska, Ewa (1949–) Polish teacher, trade-union official and politician. She was secretary of the Building Workers' Union from 1987–90. She then became deputy leader of the All-Poland Trade Unions Alliance (OPZZ), the country's largest federation, and was elected its leader in December 1991. She was also elected to parliament for the left-wing Democratic Left Alliance (SLD) in 1991.

SQ Abbreviation for Slovakia, used for international vehicle registrations etc. When Slovakia became independent in 1993 this letter combination was adopted because more obvious ones were already allocated to other countries.

SR (Bosnia-Herzegovina) *See* SERBIAN REPUBLIC.

SR Abbreviation for Slovakia. It is taken from Slovenská Republika ('Slovak

Republic'), the country's official name in Slovak.

SRBH and **SRBiH** *See* SERBIAN REPUBLIC.

Srbija *See* SERBIA.

srbizacija *See* SERBIANIZATION.

SRI Abbreviation for Serviciul Român de Informaţii ('Romanian Information Service'), the Romanian intelligence agency. *See also* SECURITATE.

Srpska Garda *See* SERBIAN NATIONAL GUARD.

Srpska Krajina *See* KRAJINA *and* REPUBLIC OF SERBIAN KRAJINA.

Srpska Narodna Garda *See* SERBIAN NATIONAL GUARD.

Srpska Republika *See* SERBIAN REPUBLIC.

Srpske Zemlje *See* SERB LANDS.

Srpski Sokolovi *See* SERBIAN FALCONS.

SRS *See* SERBIAN RADICAL PARTY.

SSD Abbreviation for Staatssicherheitsdienst ('State Security Service'), the security police of former East Germany. It was commonly known as the STASI.

SSDP *See* FINNISH SOCIAL DEMOCRATIC PARTY.

SSSJ *See* AUTONOMOUS TRADE UNION FEDERATION OF YUGOSLAVIA.

stability pacts (former communist countries) *See* BALLADUR PLAN.

Stadtstaat *See* CITY STATE.

stage two and **stage three** (European Union) *See* ECONOMIC AND MONETARY UNION.

standard region British administrative division. The eight standard regions of England (East Anglia, East Midlands, North, Northwest, Southeast, Southwest, West Midlands, Yorkshire and Humberside) are delimited principally for statistical and administrative purposes. They have no political functions.

Ständerat *See* COUNCIL OF STATES.

Standing Conference of Local and Regional Authorities of Europe (CLRAE) Interparliamentary assembly at regional and local level, a consultative body of the Council of Europe. Set up in 1957, the Conference brings together 312 representatives appointed or elected by local and regional assemblies in the member states. It meets annually and discusses topics of mutual interest in such fields as local autonomy, planning, social issues and environmental protection. It

has consultative powers and submits opinions and resolutions to the Committee of Ministers, the Council's main decision-making body.

Standing Council (Western European Union) *See* PERMANENT COUNCIL.

STAPO or **Stapo** Abbreviation for Staatspolizei ('State Police'), the Austrian intelligence agency.

Star of Vergina State emblem of Macedonia. The Star of Vergina – a disc representing the sun framed by 16 rays – was the emblem of the dynasty founded by Philip II of Macedonia, the father of Alexander the Great, who gained control over the Greek peninsula in 338 BC. Its adoption by the former Yugoslav republic of Macedonia and incorporation into its new flag in August 1992 was strongly criticized in Greece, where it is regarded as a symbol of Greek culture and history. *See also* MACEDONIA NAME QUESTION.

Stasi Abbreviation for Staatssicherheitsdienst ('State Security Service') (SSD), the security police in the former East Germany. The operational arm of the Ministry for State Security (MfS), the Stasi was responsible for intelligence gathering abroad (particularly in West Germany), domestic security and surveillance of dissidents. It employed around 86,000 full-time staff and at least 100,000 part-time informers known as 'informal staff'. By the time of its dissolution in December 1989, two months after the collapse of the orthodox communist regime, it had collected information on six million East Germans, more than a third of the population, and two million West Germans. On German reunification in October 1990 the files were entrusted to a special agency headed by an East German pastor, Joachim Gauck. Individuals were given the right of access to their files and an opportunity to clear their names. Subsequent revelations led to a series of resignations of senior East German politicians accused of having been Stasi informers, and to arrests of senior West German officials accused of spying for the Stasi.

State Council [Statsråd] Government of Denmark. The official title of the prime minister is 'state minister' [statsminister].

State Council [Valtioneuvusto (Finnish) / Statsråd (Swedish)] Government of Finland.

State Council [Statsråd] Government of Norway. The official title of the prime minister is 'state minister' [statsminister], and the title of the other ministers is 'state councillor' [statsråd].

State Council (Slovenia) *See* NATIONAL COUNCIL.

state councillor or **councillor of state** [statsråd] In Norway, a member or minister of the government. The latter's formal name is State Council [Statsråd].

state minister or **minister of state** [statsminister] Head of government or prime minister in Denmark and Norway. In both countries the government's formal name is State Council [Statsråd].

state minister or **minister of state** [ministru de stat] In Romania, a senior member of the government. This honorary title is conferred on several senior ministers, who generally also have departmental responsibilities.

state minister [devlet bakanı] In Turkey, a senior minister without portfolio. State ministers may be given general responsibilities (e.g. coordinating economic policy), more specific briefs (e.g. implementing measures to strengthen human rights) or, most commonly, specific responsibilities (e.g. managing or supervising state bodies, organizations or companies). In recent cabinets nearly half of all ministers have been state ministers.

State Presidency [Državno Predsjedništvo] Supreme executive body of Bosnia-Herzegovina. The collective Presidency acts as commander-in-chief of the armed forces, directs foreign policy and appoints the prime minister. Its seven members are elected for a four-year term by the legislature and should reflect the country's ethnic diversity. From their number they elect a president for a one-year term; s/he is effectively the head of state. (The principles of rotating leadership and balanced ethnic representation reflect the constitutional arrangements of the old Yugoslav federation.) Under the state of emergency imposed at the outbreak of civil war in March 1992, the prime minister, the president of the Skupština (= parliament) and the commander of the armed forces have been coopted onto the presidency and the mandate of the president has been extended indefinitely.

state secretary or **secretary of state** [Staatssekretär] In Germany, a junior member or minister of the federal government.

state snooping affair (Switzerland) *See* SECRET FILES AFFAIR.

State Tribunal *See* TRIBUNAL OF STATE.

States Shorthand for the STATES OF DELIBERATION or the STATES OF JERSEY, the parliaments of Guernsey and Jersey respectively.

States-General [Staten Generaal] Parliament of the Netherlands, composed of the SECOND CHAMBER and FIRST CHAMBER.

States of Deliberation Parliament of Guernsey. The States has 58 voting and two non-voting members. The former comprise the bailiff, the head of government; 12 councillors [conseillers] elected for six-year terms by the States of Election (an electoral college composed of representatives of lower-level bodies and members of the States), with half retiring every three years; 33 people's deputies directly elected for six-year terms; 10 representatives of the local parishes; two representatives of the island of Alderney (elected by the local legislature). The two senior law officers, the attorney-general [procureur] and solicitor-general [comptroller], are members ex-officio; they may speak but are not entitled to vote. Members of the States form a number of committees which act as the executive arm of government.

States of Jersey Parliament of Jersey. The States has 53 voting and five non-voting ex-officio members. The former comprise 12 senators elected for six-year terms, half retiring every three years; 12 constables [connetables] representing the local parishes; and 29 deputies elected for three-year terms. The latter comprise the lieutenant-governor, the representative of the sovereign; the bailiff, the head of government; the dean of Jersey, the senior religious leader; and the attorney-general and solicitor-general, the senior law officers. Members of the States form a number of committees which act as the executive arm of government.

STB Abbreviation for Statní Tajná Bezpeč-nost ('State Security'), the security police of former Czechoslovakia during communist rule. A branch of the national police force, the National Security Corps (SNB), and responsible to the interior minister, the STB carried out surveillance of political dissidents. It was disbanded in February 1990, two months after the fall of the regime. A number of newly elected politicians and newly appointed government officials were subsequently accused of having collaborated with the STB, leading to resignations and some arrests.

Steel, David (1938–) British journalist, broadcaster and politician. Elected to Parliament for the Liberals in 1965, he was party leader from 1976–88. In 1981 he was instrumental in establishing an electoral alliance with the new Social Democratic Party (SDP, a breakaway from the Labour Party). He announced his resignation after the alliance's relatively disappointing performance in the 1987 election. After the two parties merged the following year to form the Liberal Democrats, he became the spokesman on foreign affairs. He held this post until July 1994 and took over as president of the Liberal International in September.

Stefanov, Petruš (1945–) Macedonian chemist and politician. He worked as a researcher and then as managing director at a chemical company before entering politics. A member of the Reform Forces of Macedonia - Liberal Party (RSM-LP), he was appointed minister for the economy in September 1992.

Steichen, René (1942–) Luxemburg notary, solicitor and politician. He was elected to parliament for the Christian Social People's Party (CSV) in 1979. He was appointed minister for agriculture and viticulture in July 1984, and was also given the rural development, culture and research portfolios in June 1989. In Janu-

ary 1993 he became a commissioner of the European Community (EC), taking responsibility for agriculture and rural development.

Steiermark See STYRIA.

Stekelenburg, Johan (1941–) Dutch trade-union official. He has been a full-time union representative all his working life, first with the Metalworkers' Union and then the Industrial Union. He was elected vice-president of the Dutch Trade Union Confederation (FNV) in 1985 and president in April 1988.

Ster, Andrej (1958–) Slovenian lawyer and politician. From 1983 he worked as a finance inspector and then as a local government officer in his home town of Kranj. He was a member of parliament from 1990–92, initially for the Slovenian Democratic Union (SDZ) and for the breakaway National Democratic Party (NDS) from 1991. He joined the Slovenian Christian Democrats (SKD) in 1993. He was appointed interior minister in June 1994.

sterling Shorthand for the POUND STERLING, the British currency.

Stich, Otto (1927–) Swiss teacher, administrator and politician. An economics graduate, he taught business studies at secondary level until 1971 and then joined the Cooperative Movement. He was a deputy managing director and head of personnel from 1980–83. He was a member of parliament for the Social Democratic Party from 1963–83 and was also active in local government in his home canton of Solothurn. In January 1984 he was elected to the Federal Council (= government), taking responsibility for finance. He was Switzerland's president (a non-executive post) in 1988 and 1994.

STK See CONFEDERATION OF INDUSTRY AND EMPLOYERS.

Stockholm Shorthand for the Swedish government. Stockholm is the capital of Sweden.

Stockholm Document International agreement adopted by the states participating in the Conference on Security and Cooperation in Europe (CSCE). Signed on 19 September 1986, the Stockholm Document contains the conclusions of the Conference on Confidence and Security Building Measures in Europe, held in Stockholm (Sweden) from 1984–86. It sets out a series of mandatory measures for the notification, observation and inspection of military manoeuvres. Specifically, the signatory countries undertake to give notice of major manoeuvres, invite observers from other countries to them, and accept on-site inspections during the exercises. At the time the agreement signalled a significant improvement in East-West relations in Europe.

Stoiber, Edmund (1941–) German lawyer and politician. He worked for the Bavarian government from 1967 and was elected to the state legislature for the right-wing Christian Social Union (CSU) in 1974. He was the party's general secretary from 1978–83, head of the State Chancellery (= prime minister's office) from 1982–88, and interior minister from 1988–93. He became minister-president (= prime minister) of Bavaria in May 1993.

Stoica, Ion Aurel (1943–) Romanian mechanical engineer, academic and politician. A specialist in tribology, he has lectured in mechanics at the Cluj-Napoca Polytechnic Institute. He became chairman of the steering committee of the National Salvation Front (FSN), now the Democratic Party (PD), in March 1991. He was a government minister from 1990–92, in charge of living standards and social welfare until 1991 and then of relations with parliament.

Stojanović, Zoran (1947–) Yugoslav lawyer, academic and politician. He lectured in law at the University of Novi Sad until 1992, when he was appointed a member of the Federal Constitutional Court. He became justice minister in March 1993. He is a member of the Socialist Party of Serbia (SPS).

Stoltenberg, Jens (1959–) Norwegian politician. An economics graduate, he was executive secretary of the Labour Youth Association (AUF) from 1985–89 and leader of the Oslo branch of the Norwegian Labour Party (DNA) and a junior environment minister from 1990–92. He was elected a DNA deputy leader in

November 1992. In October 1993 he was appointed minister of industry and energy. He is the son of Thorvald Stoltenberg, a former defence and foreign minister.

Stoltenberg, Thorvald (1931–) Norwegian diplomat and politician. He joined the foreign service in 1959, held several junior posts in Labour governments in the 1970s and was minister of defence from 1979 until the party lost power in 1981. He was foreign minister from 1987–89 and served briefly as the United Nations' high commissioner for refugees before returning as foreign minister in a new Labour government formed in November 1991. In May 1993 he took over from Cyrus Vance as the UN's special envoy on former Yugoslavia.

Stormont Castle or **Stormont** Shorthand for the government of Northern Ireland, a component of the United Kingdom. Stormont Castle in Belfast is the seat of the Northern Ireland Office, the British government department which has been responsible for administering the province since the imposition of direct rule in 1972 (*see* NORTHERN IRELAND QUESTION). Stormont Castle had until then been the official residence of the Northern Ireland prime minister. Parliament House, the seat of the former parliament, is nearby.

Storting Parliament of Norway. The Storting has 165 members elected for a four-year term by proportional representation in 19 multi-member constituencies. When dealing with legislative matters it divides into the 126-member Lower House [Odelsting] and the 39-member Upper House [Lagting]. The Lagting must approve legislation passed by the Odelsting. Its decisions may be overridden by the lower house by a two-thirds majority. Unlike most other legislatures in Europe, the Storting cannot be dissolved before the expiry of its term.

Strasbourg Shorthand for the Council of Europe and one of its key institutions, the European Court of Human Rights. The city of Strasbourg, on the border between France and Germany in the historically disputed region of Alsace, was chosen in 1949 as the headquarters for the Council – the first major pan-

European intergovernmental organization – to symbolize the new spirit of reconciliation and cooperation (in the aftermath of the Second World War).

Strasbourg Shorthand for the European Parliament, the parliament of the European Union (EU). Its plenary sessions are held in this French city, while committee meetings are held in Brussels and the secretariat is based in Luxemburg. *See* SEAT QUESTION *and previous entry.*

Strategic Concept International agreement by the member states of the North Atlantic Treaty Organization (NATO). Adopted at a summit meeting in Rome (Italy) in November 1991, this document sets out the alliance's new defence strategy, developed to take account of the transformation of the political and military situation in Europe since the end of the Cold War, the collapse of the communist regimes and the dissolution of the Warsaw Pact, and hence the disappearance of the Soviet-led threat. The new strategy replaces 'forward defence' and 'flexible response', which had relied on a potentially massive use of conventional and nuclear forces to deter aggression. The Strategic Concept reaffirms NATO's fundamental principles: that its purpose is 'purely defensive', that 'security is indivisible' (i.e. an attack on one member is regarded as an attack on all), and that collective defence is based on an integrated military structure and requires an 'appropriate mix' of nuclear and conventional forces. In recognition of the 'new instabilities' arising from the radically changed situation in Europe, it also postulates a second dimension to security based on dialogue, cooperation, preventive diplomacy and crisis management. The strategy thus aims to integrate political and military elements and sees cooperation and partnership with the former communist countries as essential to its success. Practical implications of the new strategy are a reduced reliance on nuclear weapons, major changes in the alliance's military structure, substantial reductions in military forces, improvements in their mobility and adaptability to different contingencies, and greater use of multinational units. The key com-

ponent of the new military structure, the Rapid Reaction Corps (RRC), was set up in October 1992. *See also* ROME DECLARATION ON PEACE AND COOPERATION.

strike force (France) *See* FORCE DE FRAPPE.

strong franc [franc fort] In France, the policy of seeking to maintain the franc's parity against the German mark. It has been pursued by left- as well as right-wing governments since the early 1980s as an alternative to regular devaluations. It brought down inflation, but, because interest rates had to be kept relatively high, also depressed economic growth and increased unemployment. The franc/mark rate remained broadly stable from 1987 until the turmoil within the Exchange Rate Mechanism (ERM) in September 1992 and July–August 1993 (*see* ERM CRISES).

structural fund In the European Union (EU), one of the programmes aimed at eliminating structural and regional disparities between and within the member states. There are three such funds, the guidance section of the European Agricultural Guidance and Guarantee Fund (EAGGF), the European Regional Development Fund (ERDF) and the European Social Fund (ESF). They provide funding of up to half the total cost of projects in the spheres of social, regional, infrastructure, technology, energy and environmental policy. They were reformed in 1989 to concentrate action on five priority objectives: (i) promoting regions whose development is lagging behind, (ii) converting regions seriously affected by industrial decline, (iii) combating long-term unemployment, (iv) improving training opportunities for young people, and (v) diversifying the agricultural structure of rural areas. Regions and programmes covered under these headings are often referred to as 'objective one', 'objective two' etc. In 1989 it was agreed to double the size of the structural funds by 1993. Their total commitments have been set at 141.5 billion ecus for the period 1994–99. Around two-thirds of this sum is allocated to 'objective one' regions, defined as those areas where income per head is less than 75% of the

EU's average. They include the island of Corsica in France, Greece, Ireland, southern Italy, Portugal, most of Spain, and Merseyside and Northern Ireland in the United Kingdom. *See also individual fund entries and* ECONOMIC AND SOCIAL COHESION.

STUC *See* SCOTTISH TRADES' UNION CONGRESS.

STV *See* BASQUE WORKERS' SOLIDARITY.

Styria [Steiermark] Federal province [Land] of Austria. Situated in the southeast, Styria has an area of 16,387 sq km and a population of 1,199,000. The capital is Graz, Austria's second city, and the other major city is Leoben. The economy is based on manufacturing (cars, engineering), mining (iron, magnesite), forestry and agriculture. The Provincial Assembly [Landtag] has 54 members elected for a five-year term. The main political parties are the centre-right Austrian People's Party (ÖVP), the Social Democratic Party (SPÖ) and the far-right Freedom Party (FPÖ). At the election in September 1991 the ÖVP gained 26 seats, the SPÖ 19 and the FPÖ nine. The government is formed by an ÖVP-SPÖ coalition, and the chief minister is Josef Krainer.

Suárez Pertierra, Gustavo (1949–) Spanish lawyer, academic, civil servant and politician. He lectured in canon law at the Complutense University of Madrid from 1978–82. He then joined the justice ministry as director of religious affairs and held several senior posts within the defence ministry from 1984–93. In July 1993 he was appointed minister of education and science in the minority Spanish Socialist Workers' Party (PSOE) government. He is not a member of the party.

Subcarpathia question Controversy over the status of a district of Ukraine with ethnic Hungarian, Slovak and Romanian minorities. Officially called Transcarpathia [Zakarpatiya] and also known by several other names, including Carpatho-Ruthenia and Carpatho-Ukraine, the district in question is situated in the northeastern Carpathian Mountains and bordered in the west and south by Poland, Slovakia, Hungary and Romania. It was part of the Hungarian province of Ruthenia from the 10th century until the First World War, incorporated into Czechoslovakia in 1920, annexed by Hungary in 1938 and ceded to the Soviet Union in 1945. Around two-thirds of the people are Ukrainians or Ruthenians, a sixth are Hungarians, and there are smaller numbers of Slovaks, Romanians and Russians. None of the neighbouring counties has any formal claim on the territory, but some nationalist groups in Hungary, Czechoslovakia and now Slovakia are calling for its reincorporation into their respective countries.

subgovernment (Italy) *See* HIDDEN GOVERNMENT.

submerged economy [economia sommersa] In Italy, the unofficial or black economy. It is thought to be equivalent to around a sixth of the official gross domestic product.

subsidiarity In the European Union (EU), the principle that decisions should be taken at the most appropriate level of government (i.e. local, regional, national or supranational) and specifically at the lowest practicable level and as closely as possible to the citizen. The idea of 'subsidiarity' gained currency in the 1980s in the context of the single-market programme, under which regulations were drafted on the basis that decisions should be taken and implemented as appropriate by individual businesses, local authorities, national governments etc. It was generalized in the 1991 Maastricht Treaty. Article 3b states: '... the Community shall take action, in accordance with the principle of subsidiarity, only if and in so far as the objectives of the proposed action cannot be sufficiently achieved by the member states and can therefore, by reason of the scale or effects of the proposed action, be better achieved by the Community. Any action by the Community shall not go beyond what is necessary to achieve the objectives of this Treaty.' In December 1992 the European Council, the summit of heads of government, sought to clarify the principle – which had become a subject of major argument – by declaring that subsidiarity 'contributes to the respect for the national identities of member states and safeguards their powers' and 'aims at decisions within the European Union being taken as closely as possible to the citizen'. The British government in particular has invoked 'subsidiarity' to argue that a growing number of issues decided at Community level should properly be left to national governments and parliaments. Others, such as proponents of a 'Europe of the regions', invoke it to argue that more powers should be devolved from national to regional and local levels. (The term 'subsidiarity' was coined in the Roman Catholic Church. A papal encyclical of 1931 set out the doctrine that decisions affecting people's lives should be taken as far down the chain of command as possible, the lowest level of responsibility being the individual.)

Suchocka, Hanna (1946–) Polish lawyer, academic and politician. A lecturer in constitutional law, she was a member of parliament for the Democratic Party (SD), an ally of the ruling communists, in the late 1970s. She left the party over the imposition of martial law in 1981. Returning to parliament on the Solidarity ticket in the partly free election of 1989, she joined the new centre-left Democratic Union (UD, now the Freedom Union, UW) in 1991. She was prime minister of a centrist coalition from July 1992 until October 1993, in a caretaker capacity after it lost a confidence vote in May.

Sudeten Germans [Sudetendeutsche] Collective name for ethnic Germans expelled from Czechoslovakia after the Second World War. Sudetenland was the predominantly German-speaking region on the northern and western rim of Bohemia and Moravia. Both provinces became Austrian possessions in 1526 and were incorporated into the new state of Czechoslovakia in 1918. After strong agitation by local people Sudetenland was ceded to Germany in 1938 under the Munich Agreement. It was returned to Czechoslovakia at the end of the Second World War in 1945. An estimated 2.5 million Sudeten Germans were expelled or fled across the border to Germany at this time. After the collapse of the communist regime in Czechoslovakia in 1989 Sudeten German organizations reaffirmed their demands for compensation, restitu-

tion of their property and/or the right to resettle. This was rejected by the new Czechoslovak authorities.

Südtirol *See* SOUTH TYROL.

Suisse French name for Switzerland.

Suomen Tasavalta ('Republic of Finland') Official name of Finland in Finnish.

Suomi Finnish name for Finland.

super dinar or **new dinar** Informal name for the DINAR, the Yugoslav currency. The 'super' dinar was introduced in January 1994 in an attempt to halt hyperinflation, which had reached 60% per day by the end of 1993. It was made fully convertible and linked to the German mark. At the same time tight controls were imposed on the money supply and government spending was cut. The measures eliminated price inflation almost overnight and triggered a modest economic upturn.

supergrass In Northern Ireland (United Kingdom), a common name for a former member of one of the province's guerrilla groups who agrees to give evidence against it. Testimony from 'supergrasses' led to the conviction of a number of Irish Republican Army (IRA) and Irish National Liberation Army (INLA) activists during the 1980s. Such evidence has been used less since then because of problems surrounding its admissibility in court.

supergun affair *See* ARMS-TO-IRAQ AFFAIR.

superprocuratore *See* SUPERPROSECUTOR.

superprosecutor [superprocuratore] In Italy, the common name for a senior public prosecutor investigating the activities of the Sicilian Mafia and other crime syndicates. Superprosecutors work within the Anti-Mafia Investigation Directorate (DIA), an elite law-enforcement agency with special powers to coordinate the fight against organized crime.

Support [Podkrepa], in full **Independent Trade Union Federation 'Support'** [Nezavisima Federatsiya na Truda 'Podkrepa'] (Podkrepa) Bulgarian trade-union federation. Founded in 1989, Podkrepa initially operated underground. It was a driving force behind the general strike in November 1990 which brought down the Lukanov government and led to the formation of a national-unity administration, marking the end of communist rule. The federation is a founding member of the UNION OF DEMOCRATIC FORCES (SDS) alliance. It has 33 affiliated unions with a total membership of around 475,000 (a tenth of the labour force). The president is Konstantin Trenchev, the secretary is Svilen Marinov.

supranational cooperation In the European Union (EU), cooperation and decision making within the structures of the European Community (EC), the core of the organization. An intergovernmental organization is considered 'supranational' when the member states transfer specified legislative and executive powers to it and its decisions are binding on them and their citizens. The EC has operated on a supranational basis from its beginnings as the European Economic Community (EEC) in 1958, with the Council of Ministers as the main decision-making body. Over the years more and more non-economic policy areas have been incorporated into the EC framework. The EU's two other 'pillars' alongside the EC, the Common Foreign and Security Policy (CFSP) and Cooperation on Justice and Home Affairs (CJHA), are based on INTERGOVERNMENTAL COOPERATION.

Sûreté Nationale or **Sûreté** ('National Security') Common name for the criminal investigation department of the French police. It was renamed the National Police [Police Nationale] in 1986, but the old name is still widely used.

Surján, László (1941–) Hungarian doctor, lecturer and politician. He has researched and lectured in pathology. He was elected leader of the relaunched Christian Democratic People's Party (KDNP) in March 1989 and became a member of parliament in 1990. From May 1990 until July 1994 he was minister of social welfare.

Surveillance Authority of the European Free Trade Association or **EFTA Surveillance Authority** (ESA) Institution of the European Free Trade Association (EFTA). The Authority was set up at the start of 1994 with the launch of the European Economic Area (EEA), the Western-Europe-wide internal market also covering the European Union (EU) countries. It is responsible for ensuring that (i) member states correctly implement, apply and interpret the rules governing the EEA and (ii) commercial enterprises abide by competition rules. It has the power to initiate actions at the EFTA Court against offending parties. In matters affecting both EFTA and EU countries, it works closely with the European Commission, which is responsible for supervising the internal market in the EU. The Authority has five members and decisions are by majority.

Šušak, Gojko (1945–) Croatian businessman and politician. He has worked in catering, accounting, computing, communications and other businesses, mainly in Canada. He was elected to parliament for the right-wing Croatian Democratic Union (HDZ) in 1990 and appointed defence minister in August 1991.

Süssmuth, Rita (1937–) German educationalist, academic and politician. For many years a lecturer in education, she was elected to the Bundestag (= parliament) for the Christian Democratic Union (CDU) in 1983. She was minister for youth, family and health from 1985–88 and was also given the women's affairs portfolio in 1986. She was elected president of the Bundestag in November 1988.

SV *See* SOCIALIST LEFT PARTY.

Svalbard Dependency of Norway, often referred to informally as Spitsbergen. An archipelago in the Arctic Ocean situated around 660 km north of Norway and consisting of Spitsbergen proper, eight other islands and numerous islets, Svalbard has an area of 62,924 sq km and a population of 3,500. Around a quarter of the people are Norwegian citizens and most of the remainder are Russians. Longyearbyen is the administrative centre. The only economic activity of note is coal mining. There are other mineral deposits and oil and gas deposits offshore, but they are not exploited. Administration is in the hands of a governor appointed by the justice ministry. Svalbard was an important whaling station in the 17th century. It became the subject of conflicting claims to sovereignty after the discovery of coal deposits in the early 20th century. Under an international treaty signed by 41 countries in 1920, Norway was granted sovereignty. Economic rights were granted to all signatories, but only Norwegian and Soviet, and now Russian, companies have been active in Svalbard. In recent years interest has grown in the rich fishing grounds around the archipelago and the offshore oil and gas deposits.

Sverige Swedish name for Sweden.

Svizzera Italian name for Switzerland.

SVP (Italy) *See* SOUTH TYROL PEOPLE'S PARTY.

SVP *See* SWISS PEOPLE'S PARTY.

Sweden [Sverige] Country in northern Europe.

Official data. Name: Kingdom of Sweden [Konungariket Sverige]; capital: Stockholm; form of government: parliamentary monarchy; head of state: king/queen; head of government: prime minister; flag: blue with a yellow Scandinavian cross; national holiday: 6 June (Flag Day); language: Swedish; religion: Evangelical Lutheranism; currency: krona (kr) (pl. kronor) = 100 öre; abbreviation: S.

Geography. The largest of the Nordic countries, occupying the eastern part of the Scandinavian peninsula, Sweden has a total area of 449,964 sq km. It is bordered by Norway in the west and north, Finland, the Gulf of Bothnia and the Baltic Sea in the east and south, and Denmark (across the Sound Strait), the Skagerrak and Kattegat (arms of the North Sea) in the southwest. The country consists of mountains in the west and north, low mountains, hill lands and rolling plains in the northeast and centre, and low-lying plains in the south. There are around 96,000 lakes, the largest of which are Vänern, Vättern and Hjälmaren. One sixth of the total area lies north of the Arctic Circle. Some 7% of the land is arable, another 2% is covered by pastures and 64% is forested. The climate is humid continental in the centre (mild summers, cold winters), subarctic in the north (short, mild summers and very cold winters) and temperate marine in the south (mild summers and cool winters); rainfall is moderate, lighter in the north and heavier in the mountains.

Demography. Sweden has a population of 8,727,000. Population density is 21 per sq km (land area), among the lowest in Europe. More than four-fifths of the people live in the southern half of the country and 83% live in urban areas. The three major cities are Stockholm (metropolitan population 1.4 million), Göteborg and Malmö. Other major centres are Uppsala, Norrköping, Örebro, Västerås, Linköping, Jönköping, Helsingborg and Borås. In ethnic terms 90.8% of the people are Swedes and 2.5% Finns (mostly second-generation immigrants); there are also around 15,000 Lapps or Sami in the north. The main language is Swedish. Some 89.5% of the people are nominally Lutheran Protestant, and there are also groups of other Protestants and Roman Catholics. Foreign nationals account for 4.6% of the population, and include citizens of Finland (1.6% of the total), Croatia, Norway, Denmark, Turkey, Iran, Poland and Germany. Sweden has also taken in around 60,000 refugees from former Yugoslavia.

Sociography. Sweden scores 0.928 on the United Nations human development index (HDI), ranking fourth in the world and second among 32 European countries. There are 25 doctors and 63 hospital beds for every 10,000 people. Education is compulsory between the ages of seven and 16. There is one teacher for every nine students, among the best ratios in Europe. Enrolment is 86% at the secondary level and 33% at the tertiary level. The literacy rate is virtually 100%. Real annual income per head (in terms of purchasing power) is US$ 17,490. Income differentials are small.

Infrastructure and communications. Sweden has one of the most highly developed transport and communications networks in the world. There are 94,910 km of paved roads and 3.61 million passenger cars (419 per 1,000 people), 11,200 km of railways and 2,050 km of navigable waterways. The main ports are Gothenburg, Helsingborg, Trelleborg, Stockholm and Malmö. The main airports are at Stockholm (Arlanda) and Gothenburg (Landvetter), and there are 40 other airports with scheduled services. There are 179 daily newspapers, with a combined circulation of 4.97 million (565 per 1,000 people). There are 7.27 million radio receivers, 3.75 million television sets and 8.20 million telephones in use (respectively 845, 436 and 953 per 1,000 people).

Economic structure. The Swedish economy is highly developed, diversified and trade-oriented. It is based on engineering, metalworking and other manufacturing industries, and forestry. After many years of steady growth, economic performance since the late 1980s has been marked by declining growth and recession from 1991–93 (with GDP contracting by 4.5%), balanced current accounts, falling inflation (from 10% to 2%) and soaring unemployment (from 2% to more than 10%).

Services contribute 64% of GDP, industry contributes 33% (manufacturing 22%), and agriculture and forestry 3%. Some 18% of the labour force is employed in manufacturing, 14% in trade, 9% in finance, 7% in transport and communications and 6% in construction. The main agricultural activities are livestock raising and dairy farming; the main crops grown are cereals (barley, wheat, oats), potatoes and sugarbeets. The forestry industry is the second largest in Europe and a major source of foreign exchange. Fishing is of regional importance. The main mineral resources are iron, lead, zinc, uranium and silver; Sweden is Europe's largest producer of iron and lead. The main industries are engineering (esp. cars and industrial machinery) and wood processing; other important branches are food processing, chemicals, and iron and steel and other metalworking. The main energy sources are hydroelectric and nuclear power and imported fossil fuels; 6% of export earnings are required to cover net fuel imports. The main exports are wood and wood products (18% of the total, incl. paper 10%, wood and pulp 6%), transport equipment (12%, incl. cars 5%), electrical equipment (7%), iron and steel (6%), industrial machinery (5%); machinery and transport equipment account for 43% of the total, basic manufactures for 26%. The main imports are machinery and transport equipment, basic manufactures, chemicals and fuels. The main trading

partners are: exports: Germany (15%), United Kingdom (9%), Norway (8%), United States (8%), Denmark (7%), Finland (6%), France (6%), Netherlands (5%), Italy, Belgium; imports: Germany (19%), United States (9%), United Kingdom (8%), Denmark (8%), Norway (8%), Finland (7%), Japan (5%), France, Netherlands, Italy; half of all trade is with European Union (EU) countries.

The National Bank of Sweden [Sveriges Riksbank] is the central bank. The main employers' associations are the Swedish Employers' Confederation (SAF) and the Federation of Swedish Industry (SIF); the main labour organizations are the Swedish Trade Union Confederation (LO) and the Central Organization of Salaried Employees (TCO).

Political structure. Sweden is a parliamentary monarchy on the basis of a constitution adopted in 1975. The head of state is the king/queen, who has no powers. Executive power is vested in the prime minister and the council of ministers. Legislative power is vested in the Parliament [Riksdag], whose 349 members are elected for a three-year term by a system of proportional representation (with a 4% threshold for gaining seats). All citizens over the age of 18 are entitled to vote. Judicial power is ultimately vested in the 24-member Supreme Court [Högsta Domstolen]. Administratively the country is divided into 24 counties [län, pl. -], which are subdivided into 286 municipalities.

The main political parties are the Social Democratic Labour Party of Sweden (SAP, S or A), Moderate Coalition Party (MS or M), People's Party - The Liberals (Fp or F), Centre Party (Cp or C), Christian Democratic Community Party (KdS), New Democracy (Ny Demokrati, NYD), Left Party (Vp or V) and Ecology Party - The Greens (MpG). At the general election in September 1991 the SAP gained 37.7% of the vote and 138/349 seats, the MS 21.9% and 80 seats, the Fp 9.1% and 33 seats, the Cp 8.5% and 31 seats, the KdS 7.1% and 26 seats, Ny Demokrati 6.7% and 25 seats, the Vp 4.5% and 16 seats, and the MpG 3.4% and no seats. The government is formed by a centre-right coalition of the MS, Cp, Fp and KdS, with Carl Bildt as prime minister. Other senior ministers are Bengt Westerberg (deputy prime minister, health and social affairs), Margaretha af Ugglas (foreign affairs), Anne Wibble (finance), Gun Hellsvik (justice) and Anders Björck (defence). The head of state is King Carl XVI Gustaf, who succeeded to the throne in September 1973; the heir is Princess Victoria.

Security and international affiliations. The Swedish armed forces number 64,800 (army 43,500, navy 9,800, airforce 11,500); they are due to be reduced to around 37,500. There is also a small paramilitary coast guard. Military service is compulsory and consists of 7–15 months' basic training.

Sweden is a member of the Conference on Security and Cooperation in Europe (CSCE), Council of Baltic Sea States (CBSS), Council of Europe, European Economic Area (EEA), European Free Trade Association (EFTA) and Nordic Council, as well as the Organization for Economic Cooperation and Development (OECD) and the United Nations and its specialized agencies. It has negotiated membership of the European Union (EU), and is due to join the organization at the start of 1995 pending the outcome of a referendum in November 1994.

History. In the 7th century the Svear – from whom Sweden derives its name – gained control over most of central Sweden, while the Göta or Goths dominated the south. Both played prominent roles in the Viking raids, conquests and migrations across Europe from the 9th–11th centuries. Christianity became the dominant religion in the late 12th century. In 1167 Knut of Svealand was also accepted as king of Götaland. Civil wars between the rival royal families lasted for another century. A stable monarchy was established in the early 14th century. In 1397 Sweden was loosely united with Denmark and Norway in the Union of Kalmar. As tension with Denmark, the dominant regional power, grew, the Swedish estates dissolved the Union in 1523 by electing a local noble, Gustav

Vasa, as king. The Protestant Reformation was readily accepted, and the Evangelical Lutheran Church became the established church in 1527. Under Gustav II Adolf (Gustavus Adolphus, 1611–32) and his successors Sweden became the dominant regional power and a major European power. At this time Sweden ruled over Finland, Estonia and other Baltic regions and several German states. In 1679 King Carl XI Gustav established an absolute monarchy with the support of the Riksdag (= parliament), thus breaking the power of the nobility. Defeat in the Great Northern War (1700–21) ended the country's status as a major European power. Growing pressure for democratic government led to the adoption of a constitution in 1723 in which the crown was subordinated to parliament. After a partial restoration of absolute rule under Gustav III (1771–92), parliamentary government was entrenched in a new constitution adopted in 1809. Sweden was forced to cede Finland to Russia in the same year. As part of the post-Napoleonic reorganization of Europe, it was given control over Norway in 1814. Sweden's traditional commitment to neutrality and non-alignment also dates from this period.

The 19th century was marked by widespread poverty and mass emigration. Social reforms (including compulsory education) and economic liberalization measures were introduced from the 1850s. The union between Sweden and Norway was dissolved in 1905. Universal adult suffrage was introduced in 1921. The country was hard hit by the worldwide economic depression of the 1930s. The Social Democratic Labour Party (SAP) scored major gains in the 1932 election. It held power, alone or in coalition, for the next 44 years (except for a short break in 1936), during which time it established one of the world's most comprehensive welfare states (giving rise to the term 'Swedish model'). An agreement between government, employers and trade unions in 1938 ensured smooth industrial relations for the next forty years, providing the basis for strong economic growth in the 1950s and 60s and the country's transformation into a highly industrialized economy. An all-party administration held power during the Second World War (1939–45), when Sweden was able to preserve its neutrality.

Sweden became a founding member of the Nordic Council in 1953 and of the European Free Trade Association (EFTA) in 1960. Tage Erlander, who had been prime minister since 1946, was succeeded by Olof Palme in 1969. The SAP lost power to a centre-right coalition in 1976, but returned to office as a minority administration in September 1982. Palme was assassinated in February 1986 and succeeded by Ingvar Carlsson. Within a context of general prosperity and low unemployment, the economy was plagued in the 1980s by high labour costs and consequent high inflation, high taxation, high budget deficits and balance-of-payments deficits. A series of cuts in public spending and taxation have been introduced since February 1990, both by the SAP government and the centre-right coalition that succeeded it in October 1991. In December 1990 parliament approved plans to apply for membership of the European Community (EC), now the European Union (EU). An application was submitted in July 1991, negotiations were concluded in March 1994, and a referendum on the issue would be held in November.

See also entries on specific institutions, organizations, parties, people, terms etc.

Swedish Employers' Confederation [Svensk Arbetsgivareföreningen] (SAF) Swedish employers' association. Founded in 1902, the SAF has 34 affiliated associations with a total of around 42,000 member companies from all branches of manufacturing and the services. The chairman is Ulf Laurin, the director-general is Göran Tunhammar.

Swedish model Common name for the organization of the welfare state as evolved in Sweden and, by extension, the other Nordic countries. In 1938 the Social Democratic government sponsored an agreement between the trade-union federations and employers' associations providing for centralized bargaining on wages and conditions. This formed the basis for sustained economic growth over the next four decades, which in turn provided the resources for the creation of a comprehensive social-welfare system. (The Social Democrats remained in power throughout this period.) The consensus between employers and trade unions broke down in the 1970s and economic growth has stagnated since then. Despite being forced to curtail public spending in the 1980s and 90s, successive governments have retained a strong commitment to generous welfare provision and full employment.

Swedish People's Party [Svenska Folkpartiet (Swedish), Ruotsalainen Kansanpuolue (Finnish)] (SFP or RKP) Finnish political party. Founded in 1906, the SFP represents the interests of the Swedish-speaking community (around 6% of the total population). It is centrist in orientation and has participated in most coalition governments since 1945. At the March 1991 election it gained 5.4% of the vote and 12/200 seats. The leader is Ole Norrback, the parliamentary leader Boris Renlund, and the secretary Peter Stenlund.

Swedish Trade Union Confederation [Landsorganisationen i Sverige ('National Organization in Sweden')] (LO) Swedish trade-union federation. The LO was founded in 1898 by the Social Democratic Labour Party (SAP), with which it retains close links. It has 22 affiliated unions with a total membership of around 2.3 million (half the labour force). The president is Bertil Jonsson, the secretary is Margaretha Svensson.

Swiss Confederation Official name of Switzerland.

Swiss Democrats [Schweizer Demokraten (German), Démocrates Suisses (French)] (SD or DS) Swiss political party. Founded in 1961 as National Action, the Swiss Democrats advocate a range of far-right populist views, the main plank being the reduction of the number of foreign residents. At the October 1991 election the party gained 2.8% of the vote and 5/200 seats. The leader is Rudolf Keller.

Swiss Germans or **German Swiss** Collective name for the German-speaking

people of Switzerland. Most live in the
north and east, and they number around
4.2 million (73.5% of Swiss citizens and
61.3% of the total population). The Swiss
German dialects are widely used in public
life, but the written and official language
is standard German.

Swiss Guard [Guardia Svizzera] Vatican
police and military force. Consisting of
around 100 Swiss soldiers, this corps is
responsible for maintaining public order
and internal security within the Vatican
City and protecting the pope. It was set
up by Pope Julius II in the 16th century.

Swiss Liberal Party *See* LIBERAL PARTY OF
SWITZERLAND.

Swiss People's Party [Schweizerische
Volkspartei (German), Parti Suisse de
l'Union Démocratique du Centre (French)]
(SVP or UDC) Swiss political party. The
People's Party was formed in 1971 by
the merger of the Agrarian Party and the
Swiss Democratic Party. The former was
a member of the four-party coalition which
had been in power since 1959, and the
new party also became part of the government. Generally right-wing with strong
support in the small-business sector, it
gained 11.8% of the vote and 25/200 seats
at the October 1991 election. The party
president is Hans Uhlmann, the parliamentary leader Theo Fischer.

Swiss Romands or **French Swiss** Collective name for the French-speaking people
of Switzerland. Most live in the west of
the country, and they number around 1.2
million (20.1% of Swiss citizens and
17.2% of the total population).

Swiss Trade Union Federation [Schweiz-
erischer Gewerkschaftsbund (German),
Union Syndicale Suisse (French)] (SGB
or USS) Swiss trade-union federation.
Founded in 1880, the federation represents around 440,000 workers, an eighth
of the labour force. It has close links with
the Social Democratic Party. The president is Walter Renschler.

Switzerland [Schweiz (German), Suisse
(French), Svizzera (Italian)] Country in
central Europe.

Official data. Name: Swiss Confederation [Schweizerische Eidgenossenschaft /
Confédération Suisse / Confederazione

Svizzera]; capital: Bern; form of government: federal republic; head of state and
government: president of the Federal
Council; flag: red, with a white cross in
the centre; national holiday: 1 August
(National Day); languages: German,
French and Italian; religion: none;
currency: Franken/franc/franco (Fr) (pl. -,
-s, franchi) = 100 Rappen/centimes/
centesimi; abbreviation: CH.

Geography. Switzerland has an area of
41,293 sq km. Land-locked, it is bordered
by Germany in the north, Austria and
Liechtenstein in the east, Italy in the
south, and France in the west. The southern half of the country is dominated by
the Alps; the other major mountain range
is the Jura in the northwest. Between them
lies a central plateau, which covers around
a third of the country. Some 11% of the
land is arable, another 40% is covered by
pastures and 26% is forested. The main
rivers are the Rhine [Rhein], Rhône, Aare,
Inn and Ticino. The climate is alpine, with
mild summers and cold winters; temperatures are generally lower in the mountains;
rainfall is moderate to heavy, very heavy
in the mountains.

Demography. Switzerland has a population of 6,996,000. Population density is
176 per sq km (land area). The centre is
densely populated and the mountain areas
are very sparsely populated. Some 60%
of the people live in urban areas, and
around a third lives in the five main cities,
Zürich, Basel, Geneva [Genève], Bern and
Lausanne, and their suburbs. In ethnic,
linguistic and religious terms Switzerland
shows great diversity. German or Swiss
German dialects are spoken in the north
and east, French in the west, Italian in the
south, and Romansh in the eastern mountains. Swiss nationals account for 82.9%
of the population, and include German
Swiss or Swiss Germans (73.5% of Swiss
nationals, 61.3% of the total population),
French Swiss or Swiss Romands (20.1%,
17.2%), Italian Swiss (4.5%, 3.7%) and
Romansh Swiss (0.8%, 0.6%). Foreign
nationals account for 17.9% of the total
population, the highest percentage in any
major European country; they include
citizens of Italy (5.4% of the total), former

587

Yugoslavia (3.0%), Portugal (1.6%), Spain (1.6%), Germany (1.2%) and Turkey (1.1%). Switzerland has also taken in around 30,000 refugees from former Yugoslavia. In religious terms Switzerland is also extremely fragmented, in many cases along cantonal lines. Some 46.2% of the population is Roman Catholic, 44.0% Protestant, 2.2% Muslim and 0.3% Jewish.

Sociography. Switzerland scores 0.931 on the United Nations human development index (HDI), ranking second in the world and first among 32 European countries. There are 32 doctors and 85 hospital beds for every 10,000 people. Education is compulsory between the ages of seven and 15 or 16; it is the responsibility of the cantons. There is one teacher for every 12 students. Enrolment is 55% at the secondary level and 28% at the tertiary level. The literacy rate is virtually 100%. Real annual income per head (in terms of purchasing power) is US$ 21,780, the highest in Europe.

Infrastructure and communications. Switzerland has a highly developed transport and communications network, including several key north-south transit routes across the Alps. There are 62,150 km of paved roads and 3.01 million passenger cars (442 per 1,000 people), 5,020 km of railways and 65 km of navigable waterways. The main (inland) port is Basel. The main airports are at Zürich and Geneva, and there are four other airports with scheduled services. There are 104 daily newspapers, with a combined circulation of 3.19 million (471 per 1,000 people). There are 2.69 million radio receivers, 2.48 million television sets and 6.15 million telephones in use (respectively 394, 363 and 902 per 1,000 people).

Economic structure. The Swiss economy is highly developed, diversified and trade-oriented. It is the sixth-largest economy in Europe and the world's eleventh-largest trading power. It is based on manufacturing, financial services and tourism. After years of steady growth in the 1980s (averaging 2.3% per year), economic performance since 1991 has been marked by a slight contraction of GDP, large

current-account surpluses (up to 4% of GDP), relatively high but falling inflation (from 6% to 2%), and low but rising unemployment (from below 1% to 5%).

Services contribute 60% of GDP (finance 16%), industry contributes 36% (manufacturing 26%), and agriculture and forestry 4%. Some 24% of the labour force is employed in manufacturing, 21% in trade, 13% in finance, 10% in construction and 6% in transport and communications; immigrant workers (from Italy, Spain, former Yugoslavia, Portugal etc) make up a fifth of the total. The main agricultural activity is dairy farming (milk, butter, eggs); livestock raising and horticulture (fruit and vegetables) are also important; the main crops grown are cereals (wheat, rye, barley), potatoes and sugarbeets. Forestry is of regional importance. There are no significant mineral resources. The main industries are engineering, precision engineering (esp. clocks, watches and scientific instruments), pharmaceuticals and other chemicals, and food processing; other important branches are electrical goods, petrochemicals, textiles and wood processing. Banking, insurance and other financial services are an important source of foreign exchange, as is the tourism industry (which contributes 3% of GNP, 0% net). The main energy sources are hydroelectric and nuclear power and imported fossil fuels; 5% of export earnings are required to cover net fuel imports. The main exports are industrial machinery (21% of the total), chemicals (11%), pharmaceutical goods (9%), clocks and watches (8%), electrical equipment (6%), scientific instruments (5%) and textiles and clothing (5%). The main imports are machinery and transport equipment, fuels and chemicals. The main trading partners are: exports: Germany (23%), France (10%), Italy (9%), United States (8%), United Kingdom (7%), Japan, Austria; imports: Germany (34%), France (11%), Italy (10%), United States (6%), United Kingdom (5%), Japan, Netherlands, Austria; three-fifths of all trade is with European Union (EU) countries. Net invisible earnings (income from financial services, tourism receipts) account for 6% of GNP.

The Swiss National Bank [Schweizer-ische Nationalbank / Banque Nationale Suisse / Banca Nazionale Svizzera] is the central bank. The main employers' association is the Federation of Swiss Employers' Organizations; the main labour organizations are the Swiss Trade Union Federation and the Christian National Trade Union Federation.

Political structure. Switzerland is a federal republic composed of 23 cantons on the basis of a constitution adopted in 1874 and last amended in 1978. Executive power is vested in the Federal Council [Bundesrat / Conseil Fédéral / Consiglio Federale], whose seven members are elected for a four-year term by a joint session of the legislature; one of the members is elected federal president for a one-year term and acts as head of state and government. Legislative power is vested in the bicameral Federal Assembly [Bundesversammlung / Assemblée Fédé-rale / Assemblea Federale], composed of the 200-member National Council [Nationalrat / Conseil National / Consiglio Nazionale] elected for a four-year term by a system of proportional representation, and the 46-member Council of States [Ständerat / Conseil des États / Consiglio degli Stati] elected for a four-year term on a cantonal basis (two from each canton and one from each half-canton). Parliament cannot be dissolved before the expiry of its term. There is a strong element of direct democracy: constitutional amend-ments and most legislation require the electorate's approval through referendums. All citizens over the age of 18 are entitled to vote in federal elections; voting arrange-ments for cantons and municipalities are determined locally. Judicial power is ulti-mately vested in the 30-member Federal Court [Bundesgericht / Tribunal Fédéral / Tribunale Federale] elected for a five-year term by the legislature; the court sits in Lausanne. The cantons [Kanton/canton/cantone, pl. -e/-s /cantoni] have their own constitutions, legislatures and governments and have extensive autonomy. They are Aargau, Appenzell, Basel, Bern, Fribourg/Freiburg, Geneva [Genève], Glarus,

Grisons [Graubünden/Grigioni/Grischun (Romansh)], Jura, Lucerne [Luzern], Neuchâtel, Sankt Gallen, Schaffhausen, Schwyz, Solothurn, Thurgau, Ticino, Unterwalden, Uri, Valais/Wallis, Vaud, Zug and Zürich. Appenzell, Basel and Unterwalden are composed of the half-cantons of Appenzell Inner Rhodes [Appenzell-Innerrhoden] and Appenzell Outer Rhodes [Appenzell-Ausserrhoden], Basel-City [Basel-Stadt] and Basel-Country [Basel-Land], and Nidwalden and Obwalden respectively; they effectively function as full cantons. The cantons are divided into 2,915 communes, which have extensive local autonomy.

The main political parties are the Radical Democratic Party (FDP/PRD), Social Democratic Party (SPS/PSS), Christian Democratic People's Party (CVP/PDC), Swiss People's Party (SVP/UDC), Green Party (GPS/PÉS), Liberal Party (LPS/PLS), Alliance of Independents (LdU/AdI), Freedom Party (FPS/PSL, the successor to the Car Party, APS/PSA), Swiss Democrats (SD/DS) and the Evan-gelical People's Party (EVP/PPÉ). At the general election in October 1991 the Radical Democrats gained 20.9% of the vote and 44/200 seats, the Social Demo-crats 19.0% and 43 seats, the Christian Democrats 17.8% and 37 seats, the People's Party 11.8% and 25 seats, the Greens 6.4% and 14 seats, the Liberals 3.0% and 10 seats, the Car Party 5.1% and eight seats, the Democrats 2.8% and five seats, the Independents 2.7% and six seats, the Evangelical People's Party 1.9% and three seats, others five seats. The government is formed by a centre-right coalition of the four largest parties. The members of the Federal Council are Flavio Cotti (foreign affairs), Jean-Pierre Delamuraz (economic affairs), Ruth Dreifuss (internal affairs), Arnold Koller (justice), Adolf Ogi (transport, communi-cations and energy), Otto Stich (finance) and Kaspar Villiger (defence). Stich is the head of state for 1994, and Villiger is due to hold the office in 1995.

Security and international affiliations. The Swiss armed forces are organized on a militia basis: the regular forces number

1,800 and reserves number 625,000. Military service is compulsory and consists of 17 weeks' basic training followed by refresher courses of a total of 24 weeks over a 12-year period and then a total of 39 days over a 10-year period, until the age of 42.

Switzerland is a member of the Conference on Security and Cooperation in Europe (CSCE), Council of Europe and European Free Trade Association (EFTA), as well as the Francophone Community and Organization for Economic Cooperation and Development (OECD); it is a member of several specialized agencies of the United Nations, including the International Monetary Fund (IMF) and World Bank, but not of the organization itself.

History. The lands between the Rhine and the Alps were settled by the Celtic Helvetii – from which the Latin name for Switzerland, Helvetia, is derived – in the 3rd century BC. They were conquered by the Romans in 58 BC. During the Europe-wide migrations that helped trigger the collapse of the Roman Empire in the early 5th century the region came under the control of the Germanic Alemannians and Burgundians. It was incorporated into the Frankish Kingdom in the 530s. Christianity became the dominant religion in the 8th century. The various partitions of the Frankish Empire in the 9th century eventually left the region divided between the Kingdom of Burgundy and the East Frankish Kingdom. In 1033 the former was absorbed into what had become the Holy Roman or German Empire. Throughout this period, in fact throughout the Middle Ages, the region's relative geographical isolation meant that central authority was often nominal, local rulers enjoyed considerable autonomy, and peasant communities (particularly in the mountain valleys) could secure release from feudal obligations to their nominal lords. In the 12th and 13th centuries the Habsburg family – which later became one of Europe's most powerful dynasties – acquired extensive possessions in the north and east. In 1291 the central mountain districts of Schwyz, Unterwalden and Uri formed an 'eternal union' to resist Habsburg encroachment. They were joined by five others by 1353, including the urban-dominated cantons of Zürich, Lucerne and Bern. Over the next century the Swiss Confederation broke Habsburg power in the region and gained control over the strategic trans-Alpine passes. Under the Peace of Basel in 1499 Emperor Maximilian I (a Habsburg) recognized Switzerland's political independence. Another five cantons joined the Confederation by 1513. Together with a number of subject districts – which would be admitted as full cantons in the early 19th century – the territory of the 13-canton Confederation broadly corresponded to modern Switzerland. Swiss mercenaries were Europe's most sought after soldiers in the 15th and 16th centuries. During the 16th century Switzerland became a centre of the Protestant Reformation, providing a base for Huldrych Zwingli in Zürich and John Calvin in Geneva (which was not within the Confederation at the time). Cantons, which retained full sovereignty in all matters, divided along Roman Catholic and Protestant lines and fought several wars among themselves.

Switzerland was formally detached from the Holy Roman Empire under the 1648 Treaty of Westphalia (which ended the Thirty Years' War). The country was occupied by French troops in 1798, and local supporters of the French Revolution proclaimed a centralized state, the Helvetic Republic. Cantonal powers were restored in 1803. As part of the post-Napoleonic reorganization of Europe in 1814/15, the Congress of Vienna restored the Confederation and recognized its 'permanent neutrality'. The city of Geneva, which had been an independent republic since 1534, joined the Confederation at this time. In 1845 seven conservative Roman Catholic cantons established a 'separate federation' in reaction to growing calls for political and social reforms in the large cantons and main cities. They were defeated in a short civil war in 1847. The constitution adopted in 1848 strengthened the power of the federal government and parliament but also reaffirmed cantonal rights. The key elements of Switzerland's system of semi-direct democracy, the popular initiative and the referendum, were introduced in 1867 and 1874 respectively. The economy became increasingly industrialized from the 1870s. Switzerland's neutrality was respected during the First World War (1914–18) and the Second World War (1939–45). In 1920 Geneva was chosen as the headquarters of the new League of Nations.

From the 1950s until the late 1980s the economy was characterized by steady growth, harmonious labour relations, and a labour shortage (met by immigration of foreign workers from Italy and other countries). Political stability at federal level has been secured since 1959 through a coalition of the four largest parties in parliament. Switzerland became a founding member of the European Free Trade Association (EFTA) in 1960. Although it had been a member of the League of Nations, Switzerland decided not to join its successor, the United Nations (UN), on the grounds that it would compromise its neutral status. A referendum proposing membership was rejected in 1966. After years of campaigning, the franchise was extended to women in 1971 (at federal level). After three decades of agitation, the French-speaking part of Bern became the separate canton of Jura in 1979. Voters again rejected UN membership in March 1986. In December 1992 they also narrowly rejected (by 50.3% to 49.7%) Switzerland's participation in the European Economic Area (EEA), the Western-Europe-wide single market. (All the main parties, employers' associations and trade unions had recommended acceptance.) The UN and EEA referendums revealed a growing divergence of views between the German- and French-speaking cantons, with most of the former voting against Swiss participation and the latter overwhelmingly in favour.

See also entries on specific institutions, organizations, parties, people, terms etc.

SYN and **Synaspismos** *See* PROGRESSIVE LEFT ALLIANCE.

syndic-general [síndic general] President or speaker of the General Council, the Andorran parliament.

sýsla (pl. sýslur) Icelandic administrative division, usually translated as 'county' or 'district'. Since a reorganization completed in 1992, the 27 *sýslur* constitute the intermediate tier of government throughout the country. Each has a council [sýslunefndir] composed of one or more representatives of the towns and rural communes, the basic units of local government, and headed by a government-appointed prefect [sýslumaður]. They are responsible for most local services, in particular education and social welfare and (in the rural areas) matters related to farming. They also supervise the local councils.

systemization [sistemizaţie] In Romania, the policy of forced resettlement from the countryside pursued by the Ceauşescu regime in the 1980s. The programme involved the demolition of hundreds of villages and the resettlement of their inhabitants in new 'agro-industrial centres'. It was halted immediately after Ceauşescu's overthrow in 1989. Its effects, especially the destruction of established communities and disruption of traditional economic patterns, are still widely felt in the rural areas.

SZ *See* GREEN PARTY (Czech Republic).

SzDSz *See* ALLIANCE OF FREE DEMOCRATS.

Szeklers Ethnic group in Romania, also known as Szekels or Siculi. The Szeklers are the descendants of Hungarians who during the Middle Ages were encouraged to settle in eastern TRANSYLVANIA to protect what was then the eastern frontier of the Kingdom of Hungary – *székely* means 'frontier guard' in Hungarian. Today they number around 850,000 and form the majority in Covasna and Harghita counties and a substantial minority in Mureş. Most are Calvinist Protestants. They have a cultural identity distinct from ethnic Hungarians living to the west, nearer the Hungarian border.

szok kontrolowany *See* CONTROLLED SHOCK.

T Abbreviation for the TOLAR, the Slovenian currency.

Tabone, Vincent or **Ċensu** (1913–) Maltese doctor and politician. An ophthalmic surgeon and specialist in medical law, he was for many years president of the Medical Association. He was general secretary of the centre-right Nationalist Party from 1962–72, deputy leader from 1972–77 and president of the executive committee from 1978–85. Elected to parliament in 1966, he was minister of labour from 1966–71 and became foreign minister when the party returned to power in 1987. In April 1989 he was elected president of the republic (a non-executive post). He retired at the end of his term in April 1994.

TAC Abbreviation for 'total allowable catch', a key element of the European Union's COMMON FISHERIES POLICY (CFP).

Tajnikar, Maks (1951–) Slovenian economist, academic and politician. He lectured in economics at the Ljubljana University from 1974–92. He was appointed minister for small businesses in 1992 and minister of economic affairs in January 1993. He is a member of the Associated List of Social Democrats (ZLSD).

taksim ('partition' in Turkish) In Cyprus, a term associated with those who advocate the country's division into separate Greek Cypriot and Turkish Cypriot states. The island has been de facto divided since 1974, when an attempted coup by supporters of *énosis* or union with Greece sparked an invasion by Turkish troops. Today all the main political parties in the self-proclaimed Turkish Republic of Northern Cyprus essentially support a formalization of the status quo, either in a confederal framework or without any formal links between the two states. *See also* CYPRUS QUESTION.

Tallinn Shorthand for the Estonian government. Tallinn is the capital of Estonia.

talonas ('coupon') Former currency of Lithuania. *See* LITAS.

Tamilgate affair Controversy in Denmark over the handling of visa applications by Sri Lankan Tamil refugees which eventually led to the resignation of Poul Schlüter, prime minister from 1982–93. In 1987 the then justice minister, Erik Ninn-Hansen, ordered that the families of Sri Lankan Tamil refugees would no longer be granted entry visas to Denmark. The decision was in breach of Danish law and was later reversed. (One of the rejected applicants subsequently died in intercommunal violence in Sri Lanka.) Ninn- Hansen, who in the meantime had become speaker of parliament, resigned in October 1989. Public attention focused on Schlüter's role in the affair and in particular on whether he had misled parliament when declaring in 1989 that 'nothing has been swept under the carpet'. A senior judge charged with investigating the affair published a report in January 1993 criticizing the prime minister for not revealing the full circumstances to parliament. Schlüter then resigned, leading to the replacement of his centre-right coalition by a centre-left coalition. Ninn-Hansen, still a member of parliament, was impeached in March 1994. In June 1994 Grethe Fenger Møller, labour minister from 1982–86, was convicted of giving false testimony to the parliamentary inquiry into Tamilgate and sentenced to a 60-day suspended sentence.

tánaiste ('deputy') Deputy head of government or deputy prime minister of Ireland. The Irish title is also commonly used by English speakers. Historically it was conferred on a king's appointed successor.

Tanev, Georgi (1935–) Bulgarian agronomist and politician. He worked on a state farm and as a researcher in animal science until his appointment as deputy agriculture minister in 1991. He became minister of agriculture in the non-party government formed in December 1992.

tangenti scandals and **Tangentopoli scandals** Common names for the illegal party funding and other corruption scandals which broke in Italy in 1992 and 1993 (*see* ITALIAN CORRUPTION SCANDALS). They are taken from *tangente* (pl. *tangenti*), which literally means 'tangent' or 'curve' and is used by extension for a bribe or kickback paid in return for a favour, in this particular case usually payments made to the ruling political parties in return for public-sector contracts. 'Tangentopoli' ('Bribesville' or 'Kickback City') refers to Milan, where the first scandals broke.

taoiseach ('leader') Head of government or prime minister of Ireland. The Irish title is also commonly used by English speakers. Historically it was conferred on a king or chieftain.

Tapie, Bernard (1943–) French businessman and politician. Trained as an electronic engineer, he built up and bought companies in the electronic, media, sportswear and other industries in the 1980s, eventually grouped in the Bernard Tapie Finance holding company. Elected to parliament for the Left Radical Movement (MRG) in 1989, he was briefly a junior minister responsible for urban renewal in 1992–93. His business group has been in financial difficulties since 1992. Since December 1993 he has been charged on several counts of fraud, tax evasion and corruption in connection with his business interests. He is also under investigation in connection with a match-fixing scandal and other irregularities involving the football club he owns, Olympique de Marseille. His parliamentary immunity was lifted in December 1993 and June 1994. One of the country's most popular politicians, he was elected to the European Parliament on the Radical Energy list in June 1994. He regained his parliamentary immunity when he was sworn in as a new member the following month.

Tărăcilă, Ioan Doru (1951–) Romanian lawyer and politician. He practised law in Călăraşi from 1977. He was elected to parliament for the National Salvation Front (FSN), now the Social Democracy Party (PDSR), in 1990 and was appointed interior minister in March 1994.

Tarschys, Daniel (1944–) Swedish academic and politician. He lectured in Eastern European studies from 1983 and in political science from 1985 at the universities of Uppsala and Stockholm respectively. He was a member of parliament for the centrist People's Party (Fp) from 1976–82 and 1985–94, latterly heading the foreign-affairs committee. He was elected secretary-general of the Council of Europe in April 1994 and took up the post in July.

Tatarella, Giuseppe (1935–) Italian lawyer, journalist and politician. He has been active in local and regional politics for the far-right Italian Social Movement (MSI), now the core of the National Alliance (AN), in his native Apulia since the 1960s. He was elected to parliament in 1979. He was appointed a deputy prime minister and minister of posts and telecommunications in the right-wing coalition formed in May 1994.

TB *See* FOR FATHERLAND AND FREEDOM.

TBMM *See* GRAND NATIONAL ASSEMBLY OF TURKEY.

TC Abbreviation for Turkey. It is taken from Türkiye Cumhuriyeti ('Republic of Turkey'), the country's official name in Turkish.

TCO *See* CENTRAL ORGANIZATION OF SALARIED EMPLOYEES.

TD Abbreviation for Teachta Dala ('Member of the Dáil'), a member of the Dáil, the lower house of the Irish parliament.

technical government (Italy) *See* INSTITUTIONAL GOVERNMENT.

ten principles In the Conference on Security and Cooperation in Europe (CSCE), the basic tenets guiding relations between member states. Since all sovereign states of Europe belong to the CSCE, these principles are recognized – at least nominally – across the continent. First set out in the 1975 HELSINKI FINAL ACT and reiterated in the 1990 CHARTER OF PARIS FOR A NEW EUROPE (Paris Charter), they are: (i) sovereign equality and respect for the rights inherent in sovereignty, (ii) refraining from the threat or use of force, (iii) inviolability of frontiers, (iv) territorial integrity of states, (v) peaceful settlement of disputes, (vi) non-intervention in internal affairs, (vii) respect for human rights and fundamental freedoms, including the freedom of thought, conscience, religion or belief, (viii) equal rights and self-determination of peoples, (ix) cooperation among states, and (x) fulfilment in good faith of obligations under international law.

Teneo *See* NATIONAL INDUSTRY INSTITUTE.

TENs *See* TRANS-EUROPEAN NETWORKS.

ter Beek, Relus (1944–) Dutch politician. Elected to parliament for the Labour Party (PvdA) in 1971, he was its international secretary from 1971–75 and then became its defence spokesman. He was minister of defence in the centre-left coalition which was in office from November 1989 until August 1994.

terapia wstrząsowa ('shock therapy') *See* CONTROLLED SHOCK.

Tērauda, Vita Anda (1962–) Latvian economist and politician. The daughter of Latvian parents, she was born in the United States and lived there until Latvia regained its independence from the Soviet Union in 1991. A graduate in international politics and international economics, she held several senior posts at the foreign ministry from 1992 and was appointed to the key post of minister for state reform in September 1994. She is a member of the centre-right Latvian Way (LC).

Terceira República *See* THIRD REPUBLIC (Portugal).

territorial collectivity [collectivité territoriale] French administrative division. There are three territorial collectivities: Corsica, a region of France, and the overseas dependencies of Mayotte and Saint Pierre and Miquelon. A territorial collectivity has wider powers in specific areas than a department, but fewer than a territory.

Territorial Surveillance Directorate [Direction de la Surveillance de Territoire] (DST) French intelligence agency. The DST is a branch of the defence ministry. It is responsible for state security and counterintelligence operations. Its work overlaps with that of the General Information Branch (RG) of the national police force.

Teufel, Erwin (1949–) German politician. Elected mayor of Spaichingen in his native Baden-Württemberg in 1964, he was elected to the state legislature in 1972 for the Christian Democratic Union (CDU). He held several junior ministerial posts from 1972 and became leader of the CDU parliamentary group in 1978. He was elected the state's prime minister in January 1991.

Tėvynės Sąjunga *See* HOMELAND UNION.

Tėvynės Santara *See* HOMELAND ACCORD.

TEZ Abbreviation for 'total exclusion zone', as imposed around a 'SAFE AREA' declared by the United Nations in Bosnia-Herzegovina.

TGNA *See* GRAND NATIONAL ASSEMBLY OF TURKEY.

TGWU *See* TRANSPORT AND GENERAL WORKERS' UNION.

Thatcher, Margaret (from 1992 **Baroness** or **Lady Thatcher**) (1925–) British politician. Trained as a chemist and a lawyer, she was elected to Parliament for the Conservative Party in 1959. She was education minister from 1970 until the party lost power in 1974. The following year she was elected party leader. In 1979 she led the Conservatives to victory at the polls to become Britain's first woman prime minister. Returned to office in 1983 and 1987, her government was committed to implementing a radical free-market programme which became known as 'THATCHERISM'. From 1988 she found herself increasingly at odds with senior party colleagues over economic, local-taxation and European policy in particular. She was forced to resign as party leader and prime minister in November 1990. She was ennobled in 1992.

thatcherism Political outlook based on the values and policies of Margaret Thatcher, the British prime minister from 1979–90. After the Conservatives won the 1979 election they began to implement a radical economic programme inspired by 19th-century liberalism and 20th-century 'new right' ideas and essentially based on a preference for market forces over government action and self-help over communal provision. In practical terms this entailed selling state-owned industries and utilities ('privatization'), introducing market concepts into the public services, removing legal restraints on economic action and reducing the role of government at national and local level ('deregulation'), shifting the tax burden from direct to indirect taxation, and curbing the power and influence of trade unions. The tenets of privatization and deregulation have been influential in the former communist countries and in many Western European countries, particularly those where the state has traditionally played a major role in the economy (such as Greece, Italy, Portugal and Spain). Other elements of Thatcher's philosophy, such as her vision of the European Union (EU) as in essence a free-trade area with limited supranational structures, has been influential in the United Kingdom but less so abroad.

The Hague Shorthand for the Dutch government. The Hague is the seat of government of the Netherlands, but not the national capital, which is Amsterdam.

third pillar In the European Union (EU), an informal name for COOPERATION ON JUSTICE AND HOME AFFAIRS (CJHA), one of the EU's two intergovernmental components alongside the supranational European Community (EC).

Third Republic [Trzecia Rzeczpospolita] Common name for the current system of government in Poland. It is usually dated from June 1989, when the ruling communist party was defeated in partly free elections by the Solidarity movement, or from the following September, when a Solidarity-led government took office. Key sections of the 1952 communist constitution were abolished or amended in November 1992. The drafting of a new constitution has been under consideration since 1989.

Third Republic [Terceira República] Common name for the current system of government in Portugal. It is dated from the overthrow of the right-wing dictatorship in 1974 and the subsequent establishment of democratic rule. A new constitution replacing that of the Second Republic (1926–74) was adopted in 1976.

third stage (European Union) *See* ECONOMIC AND MONETARY UNION.

Thirty-Two Counties Informal name for the whole of Ireland, the Republic and Northern Ireland (a part of the United Kingdom), used particularly in the context of demands for the island's reunification. Ireland was divided into 32 counties when it came under English rule in the 16th century.

Thomas, Charles H. (1934–) American diplomat. He joined the Department of State in 1960 and served in a number of

foreign postings, including Honduras, Uruguay, Portugal (1974–77) and Belgium (1982–85). He was the Department's director of North Atlantic Treaty Organization (NATO) affairs from 1978–83 and deputy assistant secretary for European and Canadian affairs from 1985–89. He then served as ambassador to Hungary. In August 1994 he was appointed the US's special envoy to former Yugoslavia. As such he has been closely involved in the international effort to end the civil war in Bosnia-Herzegovina.

Thorgrimson, Finn (1935–) Danish economist and trade-union official. He joined the Danish Trade Union Confederation (LO) in 1970. He was elected its deputy leader in 1982 and became leader in November 1987.

THORP question Controversy in the United Kingdom and Ireland surrounding the environmental impact of a nuclear-reprocessing plant located in northwestern England. The Thermal Oxide Nuclear Reprocessing Plant (THORP) is designed to convert spent nuclear fuel from various sources into plutonium for reuse in nuclear-energy reactors. Its construction began at Sellafield in 1978 and was completed in March 1992. During this time environmental groups and local citizens' groups and political leaders waged a campaign to stop the plant becoming operational. They stressed in particular the environmental and health hazards associated with radioactive discharges, the inherent dangers of transporting nuclear materials, and the increased risk of nuclear proliferation. The Irish government, which had been critical for years of the level of radioactive emissions into the atmosphere and the Irish Sea from the existing nuclear-power plant at Sellafield, also made clear its opposition to THORP. The government agreed to hold two public consultations on environmental and health issues and on economic and political implications in 1992 and 1993, but did not accede to demands for a full public inquiry (which would have had a wider remit). In December 1993 the government formally approved the commencement of operations at THORP.

An application for a judicial review of the decision was rejected by the courts in March 1994.

Thrace [Trakya] Geographical region of Turkey. The southeastern corner of the historical region of Thrace extending into Greece and Bulgaria, Turkish Thrace is that part of the country situated on the European continent. It is separated from Asian Turkey, Anatolia, by the Bosporus Strait, Sea of Marmara and Dardanelles Strait. It accounts for around a thirtieth of Turkey's area and a tenth of its population. Together with the Marmara region to the south it is economically the most developed part of Turkey, centred on İstanbul, the country's largest city and leading industrial and commercial centre. İstanbul, the ancient Byzantium and medieval Constantinople, is home to small Greek Orthodox, other Christian and Jewish communities. Thrace is divided into four provinces, grouped into a region for administrative purposes.

three Guys affair *See* AGUSTA AFFAIR.

Thüringen *See* THURINGIA.

Thuringia [Thüringen] Federal state [Land] of Germany, formerly part of East Germany. Situated in the centre, Thuringia has an area of 16,251 sq km and a population of 2,546,000. The capital is Erfurt, and the other main cities are Gera, Jena and Weimar. The economy is based on manufacturing (engineering, ceramics, textiles), agriculture, tourism and forestry. Like the other eastern states, Thuringia is experiencing extensive economic restructuring and high unemployment. Political power is exercised by the State Assembly [Landtag], with 89 members elected for a four-year term, and a government headed by a minister-president. The main parties are the Christian Democratic Union (CDU), the Social Democratic Party (SPD), the Democratic Socialist Party (PDS, the successor to the communist Socialist Unity Party, SED), the centrist Free Democratic Party (FDP), and Alliance 90 (B'90) and the Greens. At the election in October 1990 the CDU gained 45.4% of the vote and 44 seats, the SPD 22.8% and 21 seats, the PDS 9.7% and nine seats, the FDP 9.3% and nine seats, B'90 and the Greens 6.5% and six seats. The government is formed by a CDU-FDP coalition, headed by Bernhard Vogel as minister-president. Historically divided into many small territories since the Middle Ages, Thuringia was constituted as a state in 1920. It was divided into three districts by the East German authorities in 1952 but restored in 1990 prior to German reunification.

Tietmeyer, Hans (1931–) German civil servant, politician and banker. He worked in the economy ministry from 1962–82, serving as head of the economic policy unit from 1973. He was a state secretary (= junior minister) in the finance ministry from 1982–89. He was appointed to the board of the German Federal Bank (Bundesbank), the central bank, in 1990 and became its vice-president in 1991. He took over as president in October 1993. He is a member of the Christian Democratic Union (CDU).

Țigani (sing. Țigan/că) Romanian name for GIPSIES or ROMANIES.

Tigari and **Tigers** *See* SERBIAN NATIONAL GUARD.

Time Export affair *See* FILESA, MALESA AND ....

Tinca, Gheorghe (1941–) Romanian diplomat and politician. He joined the diplomatic service in 1966 and served in Romania's permanent missions to the United Nations and various UN organizations, specializing in security, arms-control and disarmament issues. He held several senior posts in the foreign ministry from 1987–94. He was appointed defence minister in March 1994. He does not belong to a political party.

Tindemans, Leo (1922–) Belgian economist and politician. First elected to parliament for the Flemish Christian People's Party (CVP) in 1961, he was successively minister of community relations (1968–72), agriculture (1972–73) and the budget and institutional issues (1973–74), prime minister of two broad-based coalitions (1974–78), president of the CVP (1979–81) and foreign minister (1981–89). One of the country's dominant political leaders in the 1970s and 80s, he was also president of the European People's Party

(EPP) from 1976–85. Elected to the European Parliament for a second time in 1989, he was leader of the EPP parliamentary group from January 1992 until July 1994.

Tirana Shorthand for the Albanian government. Tirana is the capital of Albania.

Tirol *See* TYROL.

TİSK *See* CONFEDERATION OF EMPLOYERS' ASSOCIATIONS OF TURKEY.

titoism [titoizam] Political outlook in Yugoslavia and the successor states based on the values and policies of Josip Broz Tito (1892–1980), who ruled the country from 1945 until his death. Tito was leader of the communist resistance movement during the Second World War. In 1948 he rejected the Soviet model and advocated instead a national and more pragmatic form of communism. This was characterized by decentralization in the economic sphere (through 'self-management'), dilution of party control in the political sphere (through a federal structure and limited tolerance of dissent), and non-alignment in foreign policy. The federal political system was designed to balance the aspirations of the country's many ethnic groups. It came under growing strain after his death and eventually collapsed in the early 1990s, leading to the disintegration of the Yugoslav federation (*see* FORMER YUGOSLAVIA) and the outbreak of civil wars in several successor states.

TKP *See* COMMUNAL LIBERATION PARTY.

TL Abbreviation for the LIRA, the Turkish currency.

Tobback, Louis (1938–) Belgian teacher and politician. First elected to parliament for the Flemish Socialist Party (SP) in 1974, he was its parliamentary leader from 1978–88. In May 1988 he became interior minister in a centre-left coalition. He has also held several smaller portfolios since then.

Tőkes, László (1937–) Romanian clergyman and politician. An ethnic Hungarian, he followed his father into the ministry of the Calvinist Reformed Church. In the late 1980s he became an outspoken critic of the Ceauşescu regime. The authorities' attempt in December 1989 to remove him from his parish in Timişoara sparked the demonstrations which led to its overthrow. He was appointed bishop of Oradea in March 1990 and elected honorary president of the new Hungarian Democratic Union of Romania (RMDSz) in April 1990.

tolar Currency of Slovenia. Common abbreviations are T and SIT (the international standard in banking etc). It is divided into 100 stotin. It was introduced in October 1991 in place of the Yugoslav dinar. There are several plural forms of 'tolar' in Slovene; internationally the simple form 'tolar' and the anglicized 'tolars' are used.

Töpfer, Klaus (1938–) German economist, academic and politician. He worked for the Saarland and Rhineland-Palatinate governments and also held several university posts from 1970. A member of the Christian Democratic Union (CDU), he became environment and health minister in the Rhineland-Palatinate state government in 1985. He was appointed federal minister of environment, nature conservation and nuclear safety – a new portfolio – in May 1987.

Torgyán, József (1932–) Hungarian lawyer and politician. He practised law in Újpest from 1957–90, but was barred from taking cases 'of a political nature' because of his involvement in the 1956 anti-communist uprising. In the 1990 multiparty election he was elected to parliament for the right-wing Independent Smallholders' Party (FKgP). He was elected joint party leader in April 1991 and became its sole leader in June. In June 1994 he also took over as leader of the parliamentary group.

Tories and **Tory Party** Informal names for the British CONSERVATIVE PARTY. They were introduced as terms of abuse in the late 18th century to describe the political grouping which eventually became the Conservatives. It has now largely lost its pejorative connotation.

Toscana *See* TUSCANY.

Tosk [Toskë] Form of the Albanian language. Tosk is spoken in the south of the country. It has formed the basis for the written language since the 1940s, replacing Geg, the other main form of Albanian.

total allowable catch (TAC) (European Union) *See* COMMON FISHERIES POLICY.

total exclusion zone (TEZ) (Bosnia-Herzegovina) *See* SAFE AREA.

Tóth, Július (1935–) Slovakian mechanical engineer, administrator and politician. He worked for the East Slovakia Ironworks (VSŽ) in Košice from 1961–92, as head of the financial department from 1990. In 1970 he was expelled from the Communist Party for his reformist views. Politically unaffiliated, he was appointed finance minister in the Slovakian government in June 1992 and also became a deputy prime minister in November 1993. He held both posts until the Mečiar government lost a vote of confidence in March 1994.

Toubon, Jacques (1941–) French civil servant and politician. Between 1965 and 1976 he held several senior posts in the agriculture and the interior ministries and (from 1974) in the prime minister's office. He was deputy general secretary of the right-wing Rally for the Republic (RPR) from 1977–81 and general secretary from 1984–88. He was elected to parliament in 1981. He was appointed minister of culture in the centre-right coalition formed in March 1993.

Touvier affair Controversy in France surrounding Paul Touvier, convicted of war crimes committed during the Second World War. Touvier was head of the pro-German Militia [Milice] in Lyon during the German occupation in 1943–44. He escaped from police custody in 1947 and went into hiding with the assistance of several conservative Roman Catholic organizations. He was convicted of treason and sentenced to death in his absence in 1947 but was pardoned in 1971. After a long campaign by Jewish and wartime resistance groups he was arrested in 1989 on a charge of crimes against humanity (which is not subject to a statute of limitation). He was specifically accused of ordering the execution of seven Jewish hostages in retaliation for the murder of a senior member of the pro-German Vichy government (set up in southeastern France after the surrender in 1940). He was found guilty and sentenced to life imprisonment in April 1994. The Touvier case attracted widespread attention because it was the first time a French citizen had been charged with crimes against humanity and because it highlighted the authorities' reluctance hitherto to prosecute alleged collaborators.

TPA *See* ECONOMISTS' POLITICAL ASSOCIATION.

TR Abbreviation for Turkey, used for international vehicle registrations, postal addresses etc.

Trade Union Centre of Lithuania [Lietuvos Profesinių Sajungų Centras] (LPSC) Lithuanian trade-union federation. Formed in March 1993 by the merger of the Confederation of Free Trade Unions (LLPSK) and 13 other federations, the new organization has a total membership of around 260,000 (a sixth of the labour force). The president is Algirdas Kvederavičius.

Trade Union Confederation of Albania [Konfederata e Sindikatave të Shqipërisë] (KSSh) Albanian trade-union federation. The KSSh was founded in 1991 as the successor to the Central Council of Trade Unions (KQBPSh), which had been an arm of the communist Democratic Front. It has 17 affiliated federations. The leader is Kastriot Muço.

Trade Union Confederation of the Slovak Republic [Konfederácia Odborových Zväzov Slovenskej Republiky] (KOZSR or KOZ) Slovakian trade-union federation. The KOZ was founded in 1990 as the successor to the Slovak section of the Revolutionary Trade Union Movement (ROH) of Czechoslovakia, which had been an arm of the communist regime. Its affiliated unions represent a total of around 1.8 million workers (around two-thirds of the labour force). The president is Alojz Engliš.

Trade Union Confederation of Turkey [Türkiye İşçi Sendikaları Konfederasyonu] (Türk-İş) Turkish trade-union federation. Founded in 1952, Türk-İş has 32 affiliated unions and federations with a total membership of around 1.7 million (a twelfth of the labour force). It is most strongly represented in the manufacturing sector. The president is Bayram Meral, the general secretary is Şemsi Denizer.

Trade Union Confederation of Workers' Commissions [Confederación Sindical de Comisiones Obreras] or **Workers' Commissions** [Comisiones Obreras] (CCOO) Spanish trade-union federation. Founded in 1956, the Workers' Commissions were active underground until the end of the Franco dictatorship in 1975. They represent around 990,000 workers (8% of the labour force), and are most strongly represented in the manufacturing sector. They have had traditionally close links with the Communist Party of Spain (PCE), although only a minority of members votes for the party. The leader is Antonio Gutiérrez Vergara.

Trade Union Federation of Yugoslavia *See* AUTONOMOUS ....

Trades' Union Congress (TUC) British trade-union federation. Founded in 1868, the TUC is Europe's oldest labour federation. It has 73 affiliated unions with a total membership of around 7.5 million (just over a quarter of the labour force). It has close links with the Labour Party: most TUC member unions are affiliated to the party and as such have voting rights at party conferences. The general secretary is John Monks.

traffic-light coalition [Ampelkoalition] In Germany, a centre-left coalition government comprising the Social Democratic Party (SPD), the Free Democratic Party (FDP) and the Greens. The first such coalition was formed in the state of Brandenburg in October 1990. The term is taken from the colours associated with the three parties, red, yellow and green respectively.

Trakya *See* THRACE.

trans-European networks (TENs) In the European Union, a series of international infrastructure projects aimed at maximizing the benefit of the single internal market (established at the start of 1993) and improving the competitiveness of the EU economies. Trans-European networks in the areas of transport, telecommunications and energy – rail links, cabling networks, pipelines etc – should knit the different areas of the EU together more tightly, promote the interconnection, interoperability and accessibility of national networks, remove invisible barriers at national borders, and improve links between the centre and the periphery and other relatively inaccessible regions. The first TEN projects were approved in June 1994.

Transcarpathia question *See* SUBCARPATHIA QUESTION.

transparency or **openness** In the European Union (EU), the opening up of the decision-making process and the workings and proceedings of the institutions by giving the public and the media access to official documents, minutes of meetings, voting records etc. In response to calls for greater 'transparency', the Council of Ministers in December 1993 decided to prepare a code for the disclosure of documents, and in February 1994 the European Commission announced that all but a small number of its documents would be made available. The Council's proposals in particular have been criticized by media representatives and some member governments and national parliaments as too restrictive. The problem of lack of 'transparency' arises in part from the EU's unique evolution and structure: its primary legislative powers are held not by the European Parliament but by the Council of Ministers, whose meetings, like those of a national government, are closed. There have been suggestions that the Council's decision-making meetings should be open. The term 'transparency' is also used in other contexts, for instance in relation to financial dealings. *See also* DEMOCRATIC DEFICIT.

Transport and General Workers' Union (TGWU) Gibraltarian trade union. The Gibraltar district branch of the TGWU, one of Britain's largest unions, was founded in 1924 and has 5,500 members (two-fifths of the labour force). It has close links with the Gibraltar Socialist Labour Party (GSLP). The district officer is Jose Netto.

Transylvania Historical region of Romania. Situated to the north and west of the Carpathian Mountains and comprising over a third of the country's territory, Transylvania was conquered by the Magyars/Hungarians in the 10th century.

German and Hungarian immigration was encouraged by the local Hungarian nobility from the 13th century, but the majority of the population remained ethnically Romanian. The region enjoyed considerable autonomy within the Kingdom of Hungary and under Turkish suzerainty from 1566–1699. After the First World War (1914–18) most of Transylvania was awarded to Romania. During the Second World War (1939–45) it was forced to cede half back to Hungary. Today Hungarians account for about a third of Transylvania's population, and a distinct group, the Szeklers, form the majority in several counties. Most ethnic Germans have emigrated to Germany since 1990. Intercommunal tension has grown since the overthrow of the Ceauşescu regime in 1989 and has soured relations between Hungary and Romania. At issue are Hungarian language and education rights and demands for local autonomy.

Trapāns, Jānis Arveds (1938–) Latvian journalist and politician. His family left Latvia for the United States after the country's annexation by the Soviet Union in 1940. He joined the US Defence Department in 1962. From 1982–90 he was director of the Latvian language programme for Radio Free Europe (RFE), and from 1990–94 he was coordinator of RFE's Foreign Relations Unit and the Freedom Research Institute. In September 1994 he was appointed minister of defence in the centre-right Latvian Way (LC) government. He does not belong to a political party.

Trápeza Krítis affair *See* BANK OF CRETE AFFAIR.

Travellers Alternative name for GIPSIES or Romanies, widely used in the United Kingdom and Ireland.

Treasury [Trésor] French government department. Headed by a senior civil servant within the budget ministry, the Treasury is responsible for collecting government revenue, disbursing public funds and supervising expenditure by local authorities. Unlike its namesake in Britain, it is an administrative body and does not formulate policy.

Treasury British government department. The Treasury is responsible for fiscal policy, monetary policy, public spending and related matters. Its functions are broadly equivalent to those of the finance ministry in other countries. It is formally headed by the prime minister, who is 'first lord' of the Treasury, but in practice by the chancellor of the exchequer.

Treasury secretary Shorthand for CHIEF SECRETARY TO THE TREASURY, a senior government post in the United Kingdom.

Treaty of Guarantee International agreement under which Greece, Turkey and the United Kingdom undertake to protect the independence and territorial integrity of Cyprus. It was accepted in principle in 1959 and signed by the four countries on 16 August 1960, the day Cyprus became independent. Article 2 states that Greece, Turkey and the United Kingdom 'recognize and guarantee the independence, territorial integrity and security of the Republic of Cyprus' and 'undertake to prohibit, so far as concerns them, any activity aimed at promoting, directly or indirectly, either union of Cyprus with any other state or partition of the island'. The United Kingdom is the former colonial power, and Greece and Turkey have close links with the island's Greek Cypriot and Turkish Cypriot communities respectively. *See also* CYPRUS QUESTION.

Treaty of Maastricht or **Maastricht Treaty** Common name for the TREATY ON EUROPEAN UNION, agreed by the member states of the European Community (EC) at a summit in the Dutch city of Maastricht in December 1991 and signed there in February 1992. It came into force in November 1993.

Treaty of Rome or **Rome Treaty** International agreement by the six members of the European Coal and Steel Community (ECSC) – Belgium, France, Italy, Luxemburg, the Netherlands and West Germany – establishing the European Economic Community (EEC), now the European Community (EC). It was signed on 25 March 1957 and came into force on 1 January 1958. Since a second treaty establishing the European Atomic Energy Community (EURATOM) was signed at the same time, the two agreements are sometimes referred to as the 'Treaties of Rome'. Although it has been amended and supplemented by the 1986 Single European Act and the 1992 Maastricht Treaty establishing the European Union, the Treaty of Rome has remained the foundation for the EC and now the European Union (EU) and still provides the ultimate authority for most of the organization's decisions and activities.

Specifically, in the preamble the signatories declare their intention to 'lay the foundations of an ever closer union among the peoples of Europe'. Article 2 states that 'The Community shall have as its task, by establishing a common market and progressively approximating the economic policies of member states, to promote throughout the Community a harmonious development of economic activities, a continuous and balanced expansion, an increase in stability, and accelerated raising of the standard of living and closer relations between the states belonging to it'. Article 3 sets out the means by which these objectives are to be achieved: (a) the elimination of customs duties and similar restrictions between member states, (b) the establishment of a common customs tariff and a common commercial policy towards third countries, (c) the abolition of obstacles to freedom of movement for persons, services and capital, (d) the adoption of a common agricultural policy, (e) the adoption of a common transport policy, (f) the institution of a system to prevent distortion of competition in the common market, (g) the introduction of measures to coordinate the economic policies of the member states and remedy disequilibria in their balances of payments, (h) the approximation of national laws as required for the proper functioning of the common market, (i) the creation of the European Social Fund (ESF) to improve employment opportunities for workers, (j) the establishment of the European Investment Bank (EIB) to facilitate the economic expansion of the Community, and (k) the association of overseas countries and dependent territories to increase trade and promote economic and social development. Article 4 provides for the creation of the Community's institutions. Articles 5 to 248 deal more specifically with the activities and policies set out in article 3, the composition and powers of the Community institutions, financial provisions, the admission of new members and other aspects.

See also TREATY ON EUROPEAN UNION *and entries on specific institutions, policies, programmes, terms etc.*

Treaty on Conventional Forces in Europe or **CFE Treaty** International agreement providing for sharp reductions in conventional land-based weapons and troop levels in Europe. The CFE Treaty was originally signed on 19 November 1990 by the 16 member states of the North Atlantic Treaty Organization (NATO) and the then six Warsaw Pact countries. It was the outcome of 17 years of negotiations between the two military blocs, within the Mutual and Balanced Force Reductions (MBFR) talks from 1973 – which had made little progress at a time of heightened East-West tension – and within the wider Conventional Forces in Europe (CFE) framework from 1989. The collapse of communism and the end of the Cold War created the conditions for agreement on an arms-reduction treaty, the first of its kind. The CFE Treaty imposed equal ceilings on non-nuclear heavy weapons deployed by NATO and the Warsaw Pact between the Atlantic Ocean and the Ural Mountains. It restricted each side to 20,000 tanks, 20,000 artillery pieces, 30,000 armoured combat vehicles, 6,800 combat aircraft and 2,000 attack helicopters. Excess equipment – including around 40,000 tanks and other weapons, most of them belonging to the Soviet Union and the Warsaw Pact – would be destroyed over a 40-month period. The question of troop reductions was left to a new round of negotiations, known as CFE-1A. These were complicated primarily by the collapse of the Soviet Union in late 1991 and the consequent disagreements among the successor states over the division of the Soviet conventional arsenal and troops. The

CFE-1A Concluding Act was eventually signed by the now 29 states on 10 July 1992. It sets upper limits on the number of army and airforce troops for each participating country (naval and paramilitary forces are not covered). Specific limits include 325,000 for France, 345,000 for Germany, 1,450,000 for Russia, 450,000 for Ukraine, 260,000 for the United Kingdom and 250,000 for the US forces in Europe. Both parts of the treaty came into force on 17 July 1992. Further negotiations on conventional forces will be conducted within the Forum for Security Cooperation (FSC), an institution of the Conference on Security and Cooperation in Europe (CSCE), and will thus also encompass the other European countries.

Treaty on European Union or **Maastricht Treaty** International agreement among the member states of the European Community (EC) establishing the European Union (EU) and extending the scope of cooperation. The outcome of a year-long negotiating process at two parallel intergovernmental conferences on economic and monetary union and political union, it was finalized on 11 December 1991 at a summit meeting of the heads of government in the Dutch city of Maastricht and signed there on 7 February 1992. It came into force on 1 November 1993, 10 months after the projected date. The ratification process was delayed because the Treaty proved highly controversial in Denmark, where voters rejected it in a referendum in June 1992 and only approved it the following May after the government had negotiated several 'opt-outs' from its provisions; in the United Kingdom, where ratification was not completed until July 1993 because of divisions within the governing Conservative Party over its perceived centralizing or 'federalist' tendencies and opposition criticism of the government's decision to 'opt out' of the provisions on social policy; and in Germany, where its constitutionality was challenged on the grounds that it was undemocratic and infringed national sovereignty. The Treaty is due to be reviewed by an intergovernmental conference in 1996.

The Maastricht Treaty represents a comprehensive revision of the organization's founding treaties, in particular the 1957 Treaty of Rome establishing the European Economic Community (EEC) – now formally renamed the European Community to reflect the wider range of issues under its jurisdiction – and its amendments contained in the 1986 Single European Act. It establishes the European Union, composed of three 'pillars': (i) the European Communities, with the European Community (EC) at its core and including the European Coal and Steel Community (ECSC) and European Atomic Energy Community (EAEC or EURATOM); (ii) the Common Foreign and Security Policy (CFSP); and (iii) Cooperation on Justice and Home Affairs (CJHA). The latter two are forms of 'intergovernmental cooperation'. The incorporation of these policy spheres into the supranational EC framework was not acceptable to several member states because of the transfer of sovereignty this would have implied. The Treaty's main features are the following: it (i) defines the objectives of the Union; (ii) expands the Community's existing responsibilities and incorporates new policy areas or aspects thereof (e.g. education, culture, health, development cooperation, consumer protection, industry, research and technology, trans-European transport and telecommunications networks, environment); (iii) expands Community responsibilities in social policy (not applicable in the United Kingdom); (iv) lays down the structural framework and a timetable for economic and monetary union (EMU); (v) extends majority voting in the Council of Ministers to certain policy areas (e.g. health, aspects of social policy, energy, tourism); (vi) increases the legislative powers of the European Parliament in certain policy areas (e.g. internal-market matters, education, health, consumer protection, environment); (vii) establishes several new institutions (e.g. European Monetary Institute, Committee of the Regions) and programmes (e.g. Cohesion Fund) and restructures others (e.g. European Investment Bank); (viii) strengthens mechanisms of financial control; (ix) defines the limits of Community competence ('subsidiarity'); (x) introduces the concept of EU citizenship and strengthens citizens' rights; (xi) establishes a common foreign and security policy; (xii) establishes a common policy on judicial affairs (covering asylum, border controls, immigration, police cooperation etc); and (xiii) lays the foundations for an eventual common defence policy.

Specifically, the Treaty consists of seven titles, 18 protocols and 33 declarations. Title I contains 'common provisions' laying down the principles on which the Treaty is based: 'This Treaty marks a new stage in the process of creating an ever closer union among the peoples of Europe, in which decisions are taken as closely as possible to the citizen', and the EU 'shall be founded on the European Communities, supplemented by the policies and forms of cooperation established by this Treaty' (article A). The Union sets itself the following objectives: 'to promote economic and social progress which is balanced and sustainable, in particular through the creation of an area without internal frontiers, through the strengthening of economic and social cohesion and through the establishment of economic and monetary union, ultimately including a single currency', 'to assert its identity on the international scene, in particular through the implementation of a common foreign and security policy including the eventual framing of a common defence policy, which might in time lead to a common defence', 'to strengthen the protection of the rights and interests of the nationals of its member states through the introduction of a citizenship of the Union', 'to develop close cooperation on justice and home affairs', 'to maintain in full the *acquis communautaire* [= laws etc] and build on it', and the objectives of the Union 'shall be achieved ... while respecting the principle of subsidiarity' (article B). 'The Union shall be served by a single institutional framework' (article C). 'The Union shall respect the national identities of its member states, whose systems of government are founded on the principles of

democracy. The Union shall respect fundamental rights, as guaranteed by the European Convention for the Protection of Human Rights and Fundamental Freedoms ... and as they result from the constitutional principles common to the member states, as general principles of Community law' (article F). Title II contains the provisions amending the Treaty of Rome establishing the Community (i.e. the supranational 'pillar') as amended by the 1986 Single European Act. The amended article 2 states that 'The Community shall have as its task, by establishing a common market and an economic and monetary union and by implementing the common policies or activities referred to in articles 3 and 3a, to promote throughout the Community a harmonious and balanced development of economic activities, sustainable and non-inflationary growth respecting the environment, a high degree of convergence of economic performance, a high level of employment and of social protection, the raising of the standard of living and quality of life, and economic and social cohesion and solidarity among member states'. The amended article 3 states that the activities of the Community shall include '(a) the elimination of customs duties and similar restrictions between member states ..., (b) a common commercial policy, (c) an internal market based on the free movement of goods, persons, services and capital, (d) measures concerning the entry and movement of persons in the internal market ..., (e) a common policy in the sphere of agriculture and fisheries, (f) a common policy in the sphere of transport, (g) a system ensuring that competition in the internal market is not distorted, (h) the approximation of member states' laws to the extent required for the functioning of the common market, (i) a policy in the social sphere comprising the European Social Fund, (j) the strengthening of economic and social cohesion, (k) a policy in the sphere of the environment, (l) the strengthening of the competitiveness of industry, (m) the promotion of research and technological development, (n) encouragement for the establishment and development of trans-European networks, (o) a contribution to the attainment of a high level of health protection, (p) a contribution to education and training of quality and to the flowering of the cultures of the member states, (q) a policy in the sphere of development cooperation, (r) the association of the overseas countries and territories in order to increase trade and promote jointly economic and social development, (s) a contribution to the strengthening of consumer protection, and (t) measures in the spheres of energy, civil protection and tourism'. The new article 3a states that these activities shall include 'the adoption of an economic policy which is based on the close coordination of member states' economic policies, on the internal market and on the definition of common objectives' and 'the irrevocable fixing of exchange rates leading to the introduction of a single currency and the definition and conduct of a single monetary policy and exchange-rate policy, the primary objective of both of which shall be to maintain price stability'. The new article 3b states: 'In areas which do not fall within its exclusive competence, the Community shall take action, in accordance with the principle of subsidiarity, only if and in so far as the objectives of the proposed action cannot be sufficiently achieved by the member states and can therefore ... be better achieved by the Community'. The amended article 4 adds the Court of Auditors as one of the Community's main institutions. The remainder of the title lists the amendments, additions and deletions to articles 5 to 248 of the Treaty of Rome, which deal more specifically with the activities and policies set out in article 3, the composition and powers of the Community institutions, financial provisions and other aspects. Among these, article 8 establishes citizenship of the Union, articles 8a–8e set out the rights this entails, article 138d establishes the right of citizens to petition the European Parliament, article 138e establishes the post of ombudsperson (empowered to investigate instances of alleged maladministration by Community bodies), article 171 gives the Court of Justice the right to impose fines on member states that fail to comply with its rulings, article 189b outlines the 'co-decision procedure' (under which the European Parliament has equal legislative powers with the Council of Ministers in some policy areas), article 198a establishes the Committee of the Regions (COR), and article 198d gives the European Investment Bank (EIB) legal personality. Title III amends the treaty establishing the European Coal and Steel Community (ECSC). Title IV amends the treaty establishing the European Atomic Energy Community (EAEC or EURATOM). (These two organizations were integrated into the Community framework in 1967 but remain legally distinct.) Title V comprises the provisions on the Common Foreign and Security Policy (CFSP). Title VI comprises the provisions on Cooperation on Justice and Home Affairs (CJHA). Title VII contains the 'final provisions', dealing with technical matters such as ratification procedures. The protocols include the statutes of the EMI and the proposed European central bank, the terms of the British and Danish opt-outs and the Agreement on Social Policy signed by all members except the United Kingdom. The most important of the declarations deals with the Western European Union (WEU), which 'will be developed as the defence component of the European Union and as a means to strengthen the European pillar of the Atlantic Alliance'.

See also TREATY OF ROME *and entries on specific institutions, policies, programmes, terms etc.*

Treaty on Open Skies *See* OPEN SKIES TREATY.

Tremonti, Giulio (1949–) Italian economist, academic and politician. A specialist in taxation law, he began lecturing at the University of Pavia in 1975. He has also served on several key government advisory bodies, including the technical committee of the finance ministry. He was appointed finance minister in the right-wing coalition formed in May 1994. He does not belong to a political party.

Trentin, Bruno (1926–) Italian trade-union official. A law graduate, he joined the Italian General Confederation of Labour (CGIL), the largest trade-union federation, in 1949. He initially worked in its economic studies department, became an assistant secretary in 1958, national secretary in 1977, and was elected general secretary in October 1988. He was also a member of parliament for the Italian Communist Party (PCI) from 1960–72.

Trentino - Alto Adige [Trentino-Südtirol (German)] Special autonomous region of Italy. Situated in the northeast in the Alps and Dolomites and bordering on Austria, Trentino - Alto Adige has an area of 13,618 sq km and a population of 935,000. Around three-fifths of the people are ethnic Italians, just over a third are German-speaking South Tyroleans, and there are also small numbers of Ladins and Friulians; German speakers form the majority in the province of SOUTH TYROL [Südtirol] or Bolzano/Bozen; both Italian and German are official languages. The two capitals and main cities are Bolzano/Bozen and Trento/Trient. The economy is based on agriculture (cereals, fruit and vegetables, dairy farming), tourism, manufacturing and mining. The main political parties are the South Tyrol People's Party (SVP), the main representative of the German speakers, the centre-right Italian People's Party (PPI, the successor to the Christian Democratic Party, DC) and the far-right National Alliance (AN, based on the Italian Social Movement, MSI). As in the rest of Italy, the party-political scene has been transformed by the corruption scandals which have come to light since 1992. The region is unusual in that many powers have been devolved to the two provinces of South Tyrol and Trentino. Part of the Holy Roman Empire during the Middle Ages, the region was divided between the Austrian Habsburg territory of Tyrol and the Bishopric of Trent. In 1815 the latter became part of Tyrol. The whole region was ceded to Italy in 1919. Agitation by the German community for self-government, supported by Austria, led to the creation of the autonomous region 'with special statute' in 1948. More extensive autonomy has been granted to South Tyrol since the 1970s.

Treuhand and **Treuhandanstalt** *See* TRUST AGENCY.

Trevi Group Former name of COOPERATION ON JUSTICE AND HOME AFFAIRS (CJHA), an intergovernmental 'pillar' of the European Union (EU).

Tribunal of State [Trybunał Stanu] Polish judicial body. The Tribunal is responsible for trying senior office holders, such as the president of the republic and government ministers, who are accused of violations of the constitution and criminal offences committed while in office. It is chaired by the president of the Supreme Court; its members are elected by the Sejm (= lower house of parliament) for the duration of its term of office; they may not be members of parliament.

Trichet, Jean-Claude (1942–) French civil servant. He was an inspector of finance from 1971–76. He then moved to the Treasury, a government department. He served as president of the Paris Club of Experts (concerned with rescheduling Third World debt) in the early 1980s and as chief-of-staff at the ministry of economy and finance under Édouard Balladur (the current prime minister) from 1986–88. He became head of the Treasury in 1987. He was appointed governor of the Bank of France, the central bank, in September 1993.

Tricolore ('Tricolour') National flag of France. First used at the start of the French Revolution in 1789 and adopted by the First Republic in 1794, it consists of three vertical stripes, blue, white and red. The design has served as a model for the flags of Belgium, Ireland, Italy, Romania and other countries in Europe and beyond.

Tricolore ('Tricolour') National flag of Italy. Modelled on the flag of the French Revolution, it consists of three vertical stripes, green, white and red.

Trident Codename for the submarine-launched ballistic missile system due to be deployed as the main component of the British strategic nuclear forces from the mid 1990s onwards. With eight multiple reentry warheads and a range of 12,000 km, it is much more powerful than the

POLARIS system it will replace. It has been developed in the United States.

TRL Abbreviation for the LIRA, the Turkish currency, used in banking etc.

TRNC Abbreviation for the Turkish Republic of Northern Cyprus, the official name of Northern Cyprus.

troika In the European Union (EU), a three-member group composed of the foreign minister of the country holding the rotating presidency of the Council of Ministers and his/her counterparts from the previous and succeeding presidencies. The troika arrangement is intended to assist the presidency and ensure continuity of policy making and activities. The three ministers most commonly undertake formal or informal diplomatic missions on behalf of the Union. The arrangement has also been adopted by the Conference on Security and Cooperation in Europe (CSCE).

True Path Party [Doğru Yol Partisi] (DYP) Turkish political party. The DYP was founded in 1983 as the successor to the Justice Party (AP). This had been one of the country's two main parties in the 1960s and 70s but was disbanded by the military regime that took power in 1980; the AP itself had been the successor to the Democratic Party (DP), which had held power in the 1950s and was ousted by a coup in 1960. The DYP is centre-right in orientation, with a strong commitment to secularism. Having steadily increased its support in the 1980s, it supplanted its main rival, the Motherland Party (ANAP), as the largest single party in parliament at the October 1991 election, when it gained 27.0% of the vote and 178/450 seats. It then formed a coalition with the Social Democratic People's Party (SHP). Süleyman Demirel, the AP and DYP leader since 1965, was elected president of the republic in May 1993. He was succeeded as party leader and prime minister by Tansu Çiller.

Trust Agency [Treuhandanstalt or Treuhand] German government agency. The Treuhand was set up in 1990 by the post-communist government of East Germany to administer, restructure and privatize the around 13,000 state-owned enterprises (which employed around half the country's labour force). It was transformed into a federal government agency on German reunification later that year. It has wound up the majority of companies because they were deemed unviable in a free market, divided some into smaller units, guaranteed bank loans to those which it thought could be made viable through restructuring, and sold those for which it could find buyers (usually German or foreign companies and in some cases employees and managers). The closures and privatizations contributed to the sharp rise in unemployment in eastern Germany. The Treuhand's first chief executive, Detlev Rohwedder, was assassinated in April 1991 by the Red Army Faction (RAF) guerrilla group. The current head is Birgit Breuel. The agency is based in Berlin.

Trzecia Rzeczpospolita *See* THIRD REPUBLIC (Poland).

TS *See* HOMELAND UNION.

Tsiganes and **Tsigani** (sing. Tsigan/ka) French and Bulgarian name respectively for GIPSIES or Romanies.

Tsochatzopoulos, Apostolos or **Akis** (1939–) Greek civil engineer and politician. He lived in exile in Germany during the military dictatorship of 1967–74. He became a junior minister in the Pan-Hellenic Socialist Movement (PASOK) government in 1981 and was elected to parliament in 1985. He was minister to the prime minister in 1986–87 and minister of the interior in 1987–89. He was reappointed to the latter post after PASOK returned to power in October 1993. In July 1994 he became the party's general secretary.

Tsochev, Kiril (1947–) Bulgarian electrical engineer, administrator, businessman and politician. A specialist in foreign-trade issues, he served as director of two state-owned companies, Energoproekt and Elektroimpex, during the communist period. In 1992 he founded a private consultancy, Mikra. In June 1994 he was appointed a deputy prime minister and minister of trade in the Berov non-party government.

TSP *See* NATIONAL HARMONY PARTY.

TT *See* CONFEDERATION OF INDUSTRY AND EMPLOYERS.

TUB *See* FOR FATHERLAND AND FREEDOM.

TUC *See* TRADES' UNION CONGRESS.

Tuchyňa, Jozef (1941–) Slovakian soldier and politician. He became a divisional commander in the Czechoslovak army in 1984 and commander of a military district in 1990, with the rank of lieutenant-general. Politically unaffiliated but close to the Movement for a Democratic Slovakia (HZDS), he was appointed interior minister in the Slovak government in June 1992. He held the post until the HZDS-led government lost a vote of confidence in March 1994.

Tudjman, Franjo (1922–) Croatian soldier, historian and politician. He worked for the Yugoslav ministry of defence and the general staff, leaving the army in 1961 with the rank of major-general. He then worked as an academic historian. In 1967 he was dismissed from his post at Zagreb University and expelled from the League of Communists for his Croatian nationalist views, and in the 1970s and 80s he was imprisoned for a total of five years for 'counterrevolutionary activities'. In June 1989 he became leader of the newly founded right-wing Croatian Democratic Union (HDZ). He led the party to victory in the multiparty election in April 1990 and was elected president of the republic the following month. In August 1992 he was confirmed in the office, which had become an executive post under the new post-independence constitution.

Tuđman, Franjo *See* TUDJMAN, ...

Tudor, Corneliu Vadim (1950–) Romanian journalist, writer and politician. He was a leading member of the Communist Party during the Ceauşescu regime. After its overthrow in December 1989 he launched an extreme nationalist magazine, *România Măre*, which quickly became the country's best-selling publication. In June 1991 he became leader of the new Greater Romania Party (România Măre). He has published several anthologies of poetry.

Tupp, Enn (1941–) Estonian civil servant and politician. He is a graduate in physical education studies and a specialist in defence issues. He entered politics in the late 1980s, serving as a local councillor and member of parliament. He joined the defence ministry as an adviser in 1992 and became head of the defence policy department in January 1994. In June he was appointed defence minister. He is a member of the right-wing Fatherland (Isamaa) party.

Türk-İş *See* TRADE UNION CONFEDERATION OF TURKEY.

Türk-Sen *See* TURKISH CYPRIOT TRADE UNION FEDERATION.

Turkey [Türkiye] Country in southeastern Europe and southwestern Asia.

Official data. Name: Republic of Turkey [Türkiye Cumhuriyeti]; capital: Ankara; form of government: parliamentary republic; head of state: president; head of government: prime minister; flag: red with a white crescent and five-pointed star to the left of centre; national holiday: 29 October (Republic Day); language: Turkish; religion: none; currency: lira (TL) (pl. -) = 100 kuruş; abbreviation: TR.

Geography. Turkey has an area of 779,452 sq km. It is bordered by Bulgaria and the Black Sea in the north, Georgia, Armenia, Azerbaijan (Nakhichevan region) and Iran in the east, Iraq, Syria and the Mediterranean Sea in the south, and the Aegean Sea and Greece in the west. Turkey straddles the European and Asian continents. The smaller European part in the northwest, Thrace [Trakya], has an area of 23,764 sq km. It consists of rolling plains and a low plateau, with low mountains in the north and south. It is separated from the Asian part, Anatolia [Anadolu], by the Bosporus Strait, Sea of Marmara and Dardanelles Strait. Anatolia consists of a central plateau surrounded by the Pontic ranges in the north and the Taurus Mountains [Toros Dağları] in the south. The west and east are also dominated by high mountains and plateaus. With the exception of the region around the Gulf of İskenderun in the south-centre, the coastal strips are narrow. Some 34% of the land is arable, another 12% is covered by pastures and 26% is forested. The main rivers are the Euphrates [Fırat], Tigris [Dicle], Kızıl and Sakarya (all in Anatolia). The climate is mediterranean in Thrace and in the coastal regions (with hot summers and mild winters) and semi-arid in the centre (hot summers and cold winters); rainfall is heavy in the south-west, moderate in the northwest and the coastal regions, and light in the centre.

Demography. Turkey has a population of 59,869,000. Population density is 78 per sq km (land area). The northwest, western and northern coasts and the area around the Gulf of İskenderun are the most densely populated; the centre and east are sparsely populated. Some 61% of the people live in urban areas. The main cities are İstanbul (metropolitan population around 10 million, city 6.6 million), Ankara (2.8 million, 2.4 million) and İzmir (1.9 million, 1.7 million). Other major cities are Adana, Bursa, Gaziantep, Konya, Mersin, Kayseri, Eskişehir and Diyarbakır. In ethnic terms 85.7% of the people are Turks, 10.6% Kurds and 1.6% Arabs; these totals included around 500,000 Gipsies; there are also around 150,000 Circassians, 150,000 Turkmens, 100,000 Georgians, and smaller numbers of Armenians, Kazakhs, Greeks and others. Most Kurds live in the southeast; they are considerably underrepresented in official figures and are thought to number around 12 million. There is a large Turkish community in neighbouring Bulgaria (around 750,000) and smaller communities in Macedonia (100,000), Greece (90,000) and other Balkan countries. There are also large immigrant Turkish and Kurdish communities in Germany (numbering around 1.4 million and 450,000 respectively) and smaller communities in other Western European countries. Turkey has taken in around 30,000 refugees from former Yugoslavia. The main language is Turkish. In religious terms nearly all the people are nominally Muslims (around 80% Sunni and 20% Shia, mainly Alawi [Alevi]); there are around 100,000 Orthodox Christians.

Sociography. Turkey scores 0.739 on the United Nations human development index (HDI), ranking 68th in the world and 23rd out of 97 developing countries. There are nine doctors and 22 hospital beds for every 10,000 people. Education

is compulsory for five years between the ages of six and 14. There is one teacher for every 27 students. Enrolment is 40% at the secondary level and 13% at the tertiary level. The literacy rate is 81%. Real annual income per head (in terms of purchasing power) is US$ 4,840.

Infrastructure and communications. Turkey has a relatively developed transport and communications network; it is limited in the rural areas and the centre and east. Road transport (lorries, buses) is particularly important and the electronic media have a much wider reach than the press. There are 51,440 km of paved roads and 1.88 million passenger cars (33 per 1,000 people), 8,430 km of railways and around 1,200 km of navigable waterways. The main ports are İskenderun, İstanbul, Mersin and İzmir. The main airports are at İstanbul (Atatürk) and Ankara (Esenboğa), and there are 10 other airports with scheduled services. There are around 400 daily newspapers, with a combined circulation of 3.09 million (55 per 1,000 people). There are 8.80 million radio receivers, 10.53 million television sets and 8.20 million telephones in use (respectively 154, 184 and 141 per 1,000 people).

Economic structure. The Turkish economy is relatively developed and diversified. It is based on agriculture and manufacturing. Many parts of the country are undeveloped and highly dependent on agriculture. Since the late 1980s economic performance has been characterized by high but fluctuating growth (averaging 4.6% per year), fluctuating current-account balances (deteriorating to a deficit of 5% of GDP in 1993), very high inflation (around 70% per year), and high unemployment (around 8%) as well as high underemployment; the foreign debt stands at around US$ 55 billion (around 50% of GDP).

Services contribute 52% of GDP (trade 18%), industry contributes 31% (manufacturing 20%, mining 2%), and agriculture, forestry and fisheries 17%. Some 46% of the labour force is employed in farming, forestry and fishing, 15% in manufacturing and 11% in trade. The main crops grown are cereals (wheat, barley, maize), potatoes, pulses, sugar-beets, oilseeds, cotton, tobacco and tea; horticulture (tomatoes, citrus fruit, grapes, nuts, apples and other fruit and vegetables, olives), livestock raising (sheep, goats, cattle, poultry) and dairy farming (cheese) are also important agricultural activities; Turkey is a major producer of fruit and vegetables. Forestry and fishing are of regional importance. The main mineral resources are lignite, coal, oil, natural gas, iron, chromium and copper. The main industries are textiles, food processing, petrochemicals, chemicals and engineering; other important branches are iron and steel and other metalworking, building materials, ceramics, tobacco processing and wood processing. Tourism is a major source of foreign exchange, contributing 4% of GNP (3% net). The main energy sources are imported and domestic fossil fuels and hydroelectric power; 18% of export earnings are required to cover net fuel imports. The main exports are textiles and clothing (36% of the total, incl. clothing 25%), foodstuffs (15%, incl. dried fruit 5%), iron and steel (14%), tobacco and leather; foodstuffs, basic manufactures and miscellaneous manufactures each account for around a quarter of the total. The main imports are machinery and transport equipment, fuels and basic manufactures. The main trading partners are: exports: Germany (26%), Italy (13%), United States (6%), France (6%), United Kingdom (6%), Russia, Ukraine and other members of the Commonwealth of Independent States (CIS) (5%), Iran, Libya; imports: Germany (16%), United States (11%), Italy (8%), Saudi Arabia (7%), France (6%), Russia, Ukraine and other CIS members (5%), United Kingdom (5%), Japan (5%); two-fifths of all trade is with European Union (EU) countries. Net invisible earnings (tourism receipts, remittances from Turks working abroad, development assistance) account for 7% of GNP.

The Central Bank of the Republic of Turkey [Türkiye Cumhuriyeti Merkez Bankası] (TCMB) is the central bank. The main employers' associations are the Confederation of Employers' Asso-ciations of Turkey (TİSK) and the Turkish Industrialists' and Businesspeople's Association (TÜSİAD); the main labour organizations are the Trade Union Confederation of Turkey (Türk-İş) and the Progressive Trade Union Confederation of Turkey (DİSK).

Political structure. Turkey is a republic on the basis of a constitution adopted in 1982. Executive power is shared between the president and the government. The president is elected for a five-year term by a two-thirds majority of the legislature; s/he is head of state, appoints the prime minister and has extensive powers. The prime minister and the government are responsible for the administration of the country. Legislative power is vested in the Grand National Assembly of Turkey [Türkiye Büyük Millet Meclisi] (TBMM), whose 450 members are elected for a five-year term by a system of proportional representation (with a 7% threshold for gaining seats). All citizens over the age of 18 are entitled to vote. Judicial power is ultimately vested in the Court of Cassation [Yargıtay] for criminal and military cases, the Council of State [Danıştay] for administrative cases, and the Constitutional Court [Anayasa Mahkemesı] for constitutional matters. Administratively the country is divided into 76 provinces or vilayets [il, pl. iller], which are in turn divided into districts [ilçe, pl. ilçeler] and then communes.

The main political parties are the True Path Party (DYP), Motherland Party (ANAP), Social Democratic People's Party (SHP), Welfare Party (RP), Republican People's Party (CHP), People's Democracy Party (HADEP, the successor to the Democratic Party, DEP, and the People's Labour Party, HEP), National Action Party (MHP, the successor to the National Labour Party, MÇP) and Democratic Left Party (DSP). At the general election in October 1991 the DYP gained 27.0% of the vote and 178/450 seats, ANAP 24.0% and 115 seats, the SHP and HEP 20.8% and 66 and 22 seats respectively, the RP and MÇP 16.9% and 43 and 19 seats respectively, and the DSP 10.8% and seven seats. The government is formed by a centrist coalition of the DYP and SHP, with Tansu Çiller as prime minister. Other senior ministers are Murat Karayalçın (deputy prime minister), Mümtaz Soysal (foreign affairs), Nahit Menteşe (interior), İsmet Atilla (finance and customs), Mehmet Gölhan (defence) and Mehmet Moğultay (justice). The head of state is Süleyman Demirel, who was elected in May 1993.

Security and international affiliations. The Turkish armed forces number 480,000 (army 370,000, navy 50,000, airforce 60,000); they are due to be reduced to around 350,000. There are also two paramilitary forces, the 70,000-strong Gendarmerie [Jandarma] and a 1,100-strong coast guard. Military service is compulsory and consists of 15 months' basic training. Defence spending is equivalent to 4.7% of GDP. Around 30,000 Turkish troops are stationed in Northern Cyprus to support Turkish Cypriot forces.

Turkey is a member of the Black Sea Economic Cooperation Organization (BSECO), Conference on Security and Cooperation in Europe (CSCE), Council of Europe, North Atlantic Treaty Organization (NATO) and Western European Union (WEU), as well as the Economic Cooperation Organization (ECO), Islamic Conference Organization, Organization for Economic Cooperation and Development (OECD) and the United Nations and its specialized agencies. It has applied for membership of the European Union (EU).

History. Central Anatolia was the core territory of the Hittites, who formed a powerful state from the 18th to the 12th centuries BC. Greek colonists established a number of city states on the Aegean coast from the 10th century onwards. Phrygia and Lydia were major kingdoms in western Anatolia in the 8th–7th and 7th–6th centuries respectively. The whole region was conquered by the Persian Empire in 546. Thrace, across the Bosporus Strait in Europe, also fell to Persia in the 510s. The conquest of the Persian Empire by the Macedonians under Alexander the Great (336–23) paved the way for the spread of Greek culture throughout the Eastern Mediterranean region. The empire disin-

tegrated after Alexander's death, and several states were established in Anatolia. The Romans became the dominant force in the region in the 2nd century and annexed all the states over the next two centuries. In 330 AD Emperor Constantine established the city of Byzantium, renamed Constantinople (modern İstanbul), as the Empire's second capital. The whole region remained part of the Greek-dominated Byzantine Empire for the next seven centuries.

Muslim Turkic peoples from Central Asia entered Anatolia in the 11th century. After the Battle of Manzikert in 1071 the Oğuz and their ruling family, the Seljuks, established the first Turkish state in the region, the Sultanate of Rum or Iconium [Konya]. This also marked the beginning of the gradual turkification and islamicization of Greek and Armenian Christian populations in the region. The Seljuk sultanate was destroyed by the Mongols in 1243, and the power vacuum was filled by several small states. In 1301 one of the Seljuk generals, Osman, proclaimed himself sultan. Within two centuries the Ottoman dynasty – named after its founder – conquered extensive Byzantine territories in western Anatolia and southeastern Europe and subjugated the Turkish states in eastern Anatolia to become the dominant power in the Eastern Mediterranean. Constantinople, the last remnant of the Byzantine Empire, fell in 1453; it was renamed İstanbul and became the capital of the Ottoman Empire. At the height of its power and wealth, under Sultan Süleyman I (1520–66), the Empire stretched from Hungary to Iraq, Egypt and North Africa. The Ottomans' success was due to an effective army (relying in part on conscription among subject peoples), ruthless suppression of rebellions, autocratic powers held by the sultan, use of non-Turkish administrators (who often exercised considerable powers), and some recognition of the religions, customs and legal structures of the subject peoples (under the *millet* or 'nation' system). Some of the sources of Ottoman power also contributed to its erosion, however. A diffuse state structure, arbitrary and

TURKEY

corrupt administration, military rigidity, social stratification and lack of economic dynamism weakened the Empire from the 18th century onwards. For much of the 19th century central authority was only nominal in many peripheral regions. The central European possessions were lost after a war with Austria and Poland (1683–99). Reverses in a series of wars with Russia (1768–84, 1806–12, 1853–56 and 1877–78) led to further loss of territory and strengthened Russian influence in the Balkans. There, and elsewhere, the subject peoples began to agitate for independence in the early 19th century. Greece declared its independence in 1821, Serbia secured a degree of autonomy in 1829 and full independence in 1878, Wallachia and Moldavia regained their independence in 1856 (and later united to form Romania), Bulgaria became virtually independent in 1878 and formally so in 1908, and Albania declared its independence in 1912. At the end of the Second Balkan War (1913) Turkey lost all its remaining possessions in Europe except for the districts west of İstanbul, the modern region of Thrace [Trakya].

There were several attempts at internal reform during the 19th century. Initiated by Sultan Selim I (1789–1807) and his successors, they concentrated on modernizing the army, the administration (in particular through centralization), the public finances and the legal and education systems. The so-called Tanzimat reforms from 1839 onwards culminated in the adoption of a constitution providing for parliamentary government in 1876. It was suspended within a year by Sultan Abdül-hamid II (1876–1909), who reintroduced autocratic rule but also promoted certain social and economic reforms. The growing influence of foreign powers (United Kingdom, France, Russia, Italy) was strengthened in 1881, when administration of the public finances had to be placed in the hands of an international organization controlled by them. Pressure for reform and a rebellion by young officers, the Young Turks, forced the restoration of constitutional rule in 1908. Reformers and nationalists then dominated the govern-

ment. The Ottoman Empire was an ally of Germany and Austria during the First World War (1914–18). The 1920 Treaty of Sèvres provided for the loss of all Arab territories (Iraq, Syria, Palestine etc), extensive territorial concessions to Greece, the creation of independent Armenian and Kurdish states in the east, and the occupation of strategic coastal areas by Greek, French and Italian troops. Its terms were rejected by a provisional 'nationalist' government set up by Mustafa Kemal, a senior military officer. During a two-year war with Greece and offensives in the east the nationalists were able to expel all occupying troops and assert control throughout the country, at great human cost. The 1923 Treaty of Lausanne established the current borders of Turkey, with the exception of the southern district of İskenderun (a major port), which was regained from French-ruled Syria in 1939.

The sultanate was abolished in 1922 and a republic proclaimed in 1923; the caliphate was abolished in 1924, ending Islam's status as the state religion. Kemal Atatürk (as he became known after parliament gave him the name 'Father of the Turks' in 1933) was the country's undisputed leader until his death in 1938. Committed to a complete overhaul of Turkish society on the basis of republicanism, nationalism and secularism, he and his Republican People's Party (CHP) government embarked on a programme of 'modernization' and 'europeanization' (including the emancipation of women, the introduction of the latin alphabet and surnames, the development of industry and the promotion of European culture). The CHP was the sole legal party until 1946. It lost power to the centre-right Democratic Party (DP) in 1950. Turkey became a member of the Council of Europe in 1949 and of the North Atlantic Treaty Organization (NATO) in 1952. During the Cold War Turkey's position as a bridge between the Balkans, Caucasus and Middle East regions and as a neighbour of the Soviet Union gave it major strategic importance. The military, claiming that the DP was abandoning 'kemalism', seized power in 1960. DP leader Adnan Menderes was executed for treason in 1961. Civilian government was restored under a new constitution the same year. During the 1960s and 70s power alternated between the Justice Party (AP), the DP's successor, and centre-left coalitions led by the CHP. At this time Turkey's predominantly agricultural economy acquired a substantial manufacturing base. Economic growth has been high ever since, but so have inflation and structural under- and unemployment (due to the high birth rate and rapid urbanization). Escalating political violence by far-left and -right groups led to another military coup in 1971. Civilian government was restored in 1974. In the same year Turkish troops invaded Cyprus after Greek Cypriots supportive of the island's unification with Greece had staged a coup and thus threatened the position of the Turkish Cypriot minority. Political instability, mounting violence and economic problems induced the military to take power again in September 1980. Civilian government was restored after the new centre-right Motherland Party (ANAP) won the partly free elections in November 1983. Remaining restrictions on political activity were lifted over the following years. Turgut Özal, ANAP's leader and prime minister, was elected president in November 1989. After the October 1991 election the centre-right True Path Party (DYP), the successor to the DP and AP, formed a coalition with the Social Democratic People's Party (SHP). DYP leader Süleyman Demirel was elected president after Özal's death in April 1993.

See also entries on specific institutions, organizations, parties, people, terms etc.

Turkish Cypriot Trade Union Federation [Kıbrıs Türk İşçi Sendikaları Federasyonu] (Türk-Sen) Northern Cypriot trade-union federation. Founded in 1954, Türk-Sen has 15 affiliated unions with a total membership of 12,000 (a fifth of the labour force). It has close links with the Trade Union Confederation of Turkey (Türk-İş). The president is Hüseyin Curcioğlu.

Turkish Cypriots Ethnic group in Cyprus. They are the Turkish-speaking and Muslim people of the island. Numbering around 130,000, they were originally settled throughout the island but since its effective division in 1974 they live in the northern third, the self-proclaimed Turkish Republic of Northern Cyprus. There is a sizeable Turkish Cypriot community in the United Kingdom.

Turkish Cyprus Shorthand for the Turkish Republic of Northern Cyprus (TRNC) and alternative name for NORTHERN CYPRUS.

Turkish Grand National Assembly *See* GRAND NATIONAL ASSEMBLY OF TURKEY.

Turkish Republic of Northern Cyprus (TRNC) Official name of Northern Cyprus.

Türkiye Cumhuriyeti ('Republic of Turkey') Official name of Turkey.

Tuscany [Toscana] Autonomous region of Italy. Situated in the centre between the Tyrrhenian Sea and the Apennines, Tuscany has an area of 22,992 sq km and a population of 3,599,000. The capital is Florence [Firenze], and the other main cities are Livorno, Pisa and Siena. The economy is based on agriculture (cereals, olives, fruit and vegetables, wine, cattle and pig farming), manufacturing (metalworking, chemicals, textiles), tourism and mining (marble). The region is one of Italy's most productive and affluent. The prosperous cities of Tuscany were virtually independent from the 11th to the 15th centuries. Florence became the dominant regional power in the 14th century and a great centre of European culture in the 15th and 16th centuries. Tuscany was united with the annexation of the Republic of Siena in 1559. Under Austrian Habsburg rule from 1737, it was incorporated into unified Italy in 1860.

Tvfl *See* REPUBLICAN PARTY (Faroe Islands).

TVK *See* CONFEDERATION OF SALARIED EMPLOYEES.

Tweede Kamer *See* SECOND CHAMBER.

Twelve, the Shorthand for the European Union (EU). The organization has had twelve member states since the accession of Spain and Portugal in 1986.

Twenty-Six Counties Informal name for the Republic of Ireland, used particularly in the context of relations with Northern Ireland (part of the United Kingdom) and demands for the island's reunification. Following partition in 1922, 26 of Ireland's 32 counties became the independent Irish Free State, while six counties remained within the United Kingdom as Northern Ireland (hence the informal usage 'Six Counties' for the province). Following two reorganizations the Republic is now in fact divided into 29 counties.

twin-speed Europe and **twin-track Europe** *See* TWO-SPEED EUROPE.

two-speed Europe In the European Union (EU), a term associated with those who argue that the integration process should allow member states to participate in common policies and programmes according to their requirements or preferences. The idea was first raised in 1975 in a report on further integration by an ad hoc committee chaired by the Belgian politician Leo Tindemans. In the specific context of economic and monetary union it suggested that if member states with 'weaker' economies were unable to sign up they should allow the 'stronger' states to proceed and join them when their economies permitted; in this way the integration process would not be held back. The 'two-speed' idea initially found little support within the then European Community (EC), which had always operated on the principle that members proceed at the same speed and in step. But it was picked up in the late 1980s both by critics of further integration and advocates of more rapid economic integration (Tindemans among the latter). Terms and phrases like 'fast track' and 'slow track' in the context of the realization of EMU and 'MULTI-TRACK EUROPE', 'variable geometry' and 'Europe à la carte' in a wider context broadly cover the same ground. *See also* OPT-OUT *and* DEROGATION.

two-tier Europe and **two-track Europe** *See* TWO-SPEED EUROPE.

Tynwald Parliament of Man. Tynwald is composed of (i) the House of Keys, with 24 members elected for a five-year term by a system of proportional representation, and (ii) the 10-member Legislative Council, comprising the bishop of Sodor and Man and attorney-general ex-officio and eight members elected by the House of Keys. Both houses sit together but vote separately on most issues. The Legislative Council is a revising chamber and only has delaying powers. First convened in 979, Tynwald is one of Europe's oldest legislatures.

Tynwald Day National holiday of Man. Celebrated on 5 July, Tynwald Day marks the occasion when bills adopted during the sessions of Tynwald, the Manx parliament, are formally enacted and proclaimed to the people in a traditional open-air public ceremony.

Tyrol [Tirol] Federal province [Land] of Austria. Situated in the west and bordering on Germany in the north and Italy in the south, Tyrol has an area of 12,647 sq km and a population of 646,000. The capital is Innsbruck. The economy is based on tourism, manufacturing and agriculture. The Provincial Assembly [Landtag] has 36 members elected for a five-year term. The main political party is the centre-right Austrian People's Party (ÖVP). At the provincial election in March 1994 it gained 19 seats, the Social Democratic Party (SPÖ) seven, the far-right Freedom Party (FPÖ) six and the Green Alternative (GA) four. The government is formed by all four parties and headed by Alois Partl as chief minister. The southern third of the province was ceded to Italy in 1919 (*see* SOUTH TYROL).

Tyszkiewicz, Zygmunt (1934–) British businessman and employers' representative. Born in Poland, he was brought up in England from 1939. He joined the Shell oil concern in 1957, holding a series of senior management posts in Africa, Latin America and Europe from 1970. He became secretary-general of the Union of Industrial and Employers' Confederations of Europe (UNICE) in September 1985.

613

uachtaran ('president') Head of state or president of Ireland. The title is also used by English speakers.

UB Abbreviation for Urząd Bezpieczeństwa ('Security Office'), one of the Polish government agencies responsible for internal security and the surveillance of dissidents during the communist period.

Überhangmandat *See* EXCESS SEATS.

UBP *See* NATIONAL UNITY PARTY.

UCC *See* RED BRIGADES.

UD *See* DEMOCRATIC UNION *and* FREEDOM UNION.

UDA *See* ULSTER DEFENCE ASSOCIATION.

UDB *See* BRETON DEMOCRATIC UNION.

UDC (Italy) *See* CENTRE UNION.

UDC (Spain) *See* CONVERGENCE AND UNION.

UDC *See* SWISS PEOPLE'S PARTY.

UDF (Bulgaria) *See* UNION OF DEMOCRATIC FORCES.

UDF *See* UNION FOR FRENCH DEMOCRACY.

UDMR *See* HUNGARIAN DEMOCRATIC UNION OF ROMANIA.

UDR *See* ROYAL IRISH REGIMENT.

UE French, Italian, Portuguese and Spanish abbreviation for the European Union (EU).

UEBL *See* BELGIUM-LUXEMBURG ECONOMIC UNION.

UEDC *See* EUROPEAN CHRISTIAN DEMOCRATIC UNION.

UFF *See* ULSTER FREEDOM FIGHTERS.

Ugglas, Margaretha af *See* AF UGGLAS, ...

UGT *See* GENERAL WORKERS' UNION (Spain).

UGTP *See* GENERAL WORKERS' UNION OF PORTUGAL.

UIL *See* ITALIAN UNION OF LABOUR.

UITUA *See* UNION OF INDEPENDENT TRADE UNIONS OF ALBANIA.

UK Abbreviation for the United Kingdom, in full the United Kingdom of Great Britain and Northern Ireland.

Uka, Rexhep (1953–) Albanian agronomist and politician. A specialist in plant protection, he worked as a researcher and lecturer at the agriculture faculty of Tirana University from 1980–92. Elected to parliament for the Democratic Party (PDSh) in 1991, he was appointed a deputy prime minister and minister of agriculture and food in 1992, and minister without portfolio with responsibility for local government in April 1993.

Ülkü Ocakları and **Ülkücüler** *See* GREY WOLVES.

Ulmanis, Guntis (1939–) Latvian economist and politician. He has worked in several state institutions, including the Bank of Latvia, from the 1960s. He joined the relaunched Farmers' Union (LZS) in 1992 and was elected to parliament in June 1993. The following month he was elected president of Latvia, a nonexecutive post. He is the great-nephew of Kārlis Ulmanis, the last president of Latvia before the country's annexation by the Soviet Union in 1940.

Ulster Common name for NORTHERN IRELAND, a component of the United Kingdom. Six of the nine counties of the historical province of Ulster became Northern Ireland when Ireland was partitioned in 1922. Many unionists (i.e. supporters of the territory's status as part of the United Kingdom) prefer to use 'Ulster' to 'Northern Ireland' to accentuate its distinction from the Republic of Ireland.

Ulster Defence Association (UDA) British political organization and guerrilla group. The UDA was formed as an umbrella group for many Protestant 'defence associations' in Northern Ireland or Ulster in 1971, shortly after the Irish Republican Army (IRA) relaunched its violent campaign for Irish reunification. It is the largest organization of its kind in the province. It has always denied involvement in violence; but the Ulster Freedom Fighters (UFF), which is widely considered its military wing, has been responsible for the deaths of around 500 alleged IRA members and Catholic civilians. Because of its alleged violent activities the UDA was banned in August 1992 (the UFF had been banned in 1973). It has close links with the small Ulster Loyalist Democratic Party (ULDP), which advocates the creation of an independent Northern Ireland state. The UFF and the other Protestant guerrilla groups declared a ceasefire in October 1994, the IRA having done so the previous month.

Ulster Defence Regiment (UDR) Former British military force. Involved in security work in Northern Ireland, it was merged with another regiment to form the ROYAL IRISH REGIMENT (RIR) in 1992.

Ulster Democratic Unionist Party (DUP) British political party. The DUP has its roots in the Ulster Unionist Party (UUP), the main representative of the majority Protestant community in Northern Ireland which ruled the territory from its creation in 1922 until the imposition of direct rule from London in 1972. The DUP was founded in 1971 by hard-line members of the UUP and several other groups opposed to Catholic demands for a share of political power. It has centrist economic policies and conservative views on social issues. Its support is strongest among the urban working class within the Protestant community. The party contested the April 1992 general election in alliance with the UUP and gained three of the 17 Northern Irish seats in the House of Commons; at the May 1993 local elections it gained 17.2% of the vote. Ian Paisley has been the party's leader since its foundation.

Ulster Freedom Fighters (UFF) British guerrilla group. Formed in 1973 and banned the same year, the UFF claims to defend the Protestant community in Northern Ireland or Ulster against the violent campaign by the Irish Republican Army (IRA) and others seeking the re-unification of Ireland. It has been responsible for the deaths of more than 500 alleged IRA members and Catholic civilians. It is widely considered to be a front for the ULSTER DEFENCE ASSOCIATION (UDA), and also has links with the Ulster Volunteer Force (UVF), a smaller guerrilla group. The Protestant groups declared a ceasefire in October 1994, the IRA having done so the previous month.

Ulster Unionist Party (UUP) British political party. The UUP was founded in 1905 to articulate the wish of Ulster's majority Protestant community to remain within the United Kingdom and not to become part of an independent Ireland. It ruled Northern Ireland from its creation in 1922 until the imposition of direct rule from London in 1972. Since several party splits around 1970, with one wing eventually becoming the Ulster Democratic Unionist Party (DUP), the UUP has also been known as the Official Unionist Party (OUP). Generally right-wing in economic terms and conservative on social issues, it has the support of just under two-thirds of the Protestant community. It contested the April 1992 general election in alliance with the DUP and gained nine of the 17 Northern Irish seats in the House of Commons; at the May 1993 local elections it gained 29.0% of the vote. The leader is James Molyneaux.

Ulster Volunteer Force (UVF) British guerrilla group. Founded in 1966 and banned in 1975, the UVF takes its name from the organization set up in 1912 to resist the granting of autonomy for Ireland within the United Kingdom. It claims to defend the majority Protestant community in Northern Ireland or Ulster against the violent campaign by the Irish Republican Army (IRA) and others seeking the reunification of Ireland. Sometimes using the cover name Protestant Action Force, it has been responsible for the deaths of around 200 alleged IRA members and Catholic civilians. It has links with the Ulster Freedom Fighters (UFF), the largest Protestant guerrilla group in the province. The UFF and the other Protestant groups declared a ceasefire in October 1994, the IRA having done so the previous month.

Umbria Autonomous region of Italy. Situated in the centre, Umbria has an area of 8,456 sq km and a population of 823,000. The capital is Perugia, and the other main city is Terni. The economy is based on agriculture (cereals, wine, fruit and vegetables, sheep farming), manufacturing (chemicals, metalworking, textiles) and tourism. Umbria was nominally part of the Papal States from the 10th century, but papal control was not firmly established until the 16th century. It became part of unified Italy in 1860.

UN ... *See* UNITED NATIONS ....

Unckel, Per (1950–) Swedish politician. He was leader of the youth wing of the centre-right Moderate Coalition Party (MS) from 1971 until his election to parliament in 1976. He was the party's general secretary from 1986–91. He was appointed minister of education in the centre-right coalition which took office in October 1991.

UNECE *See* United Nations Economic Commission for Europe.

UNFICYP *See* United Nations Peace-Keeping Force in Cyprus.

UNHCR Abbreviation for the United Nations High Commission for Refugees, a specialized agency of the United Nations responsible for humanitarian relief work. It has been active in Bosnia-Herzegovina and the other Yugoslav successor states since the federation's disintegration and the outbreak of civil wars in 1991/92.

UNICE *See* Union of Industrial and Employers' Confederations of Europe.

Unified Democratic Union of Cyprus - Socialist Party [Eniéia Dimokratiká Énosi Kíprou - Sosialistikí Kómma] (EDEK-SK or EDEK) Cypriot political party. Founded as a political movement in 1960, EDEK was formally set up as a party in 1969. It is centre-left in orientation. Regarding a solution to the island's division, it is traditionally less willing to take account of Turkish Cypriot concerns than the main left-wing party, the Progressive Party of Working People (AKEL). At the May 1991 election it gained 10.9% of the vote and 7/56 seats. Vassos Lyssarides has been party leader since its foundation.

Union, the Shorthand for the European Union (EU) or the European Community (EC), its main component.

Union citizenship Shorthand for European Union citizenship.

Union for France [Union pour la France] (UPF) French political organization. The UPF is an electoral alliance formed in 1990 by the country's two main right-of-centre groups, the Rally for the Republic (RPR) and Union for French Democracy (UDF). They put forward joint candidates in the 1992 regional elections, agreed a joint government programme for the March 1993 legislative election, and also agreed in principle on a process of US-style 'primaries' for selecting a joint candidate for the next presidential election (due in 1995). UPF-backed candidates won four-fifths of the National Assembly seats at the 1993 general election.

Union for French Democracy [Union pour la Démocratie Française] (UDF) French political organization. Founded in 1978, the UDF is an umbrella organization of several centrist and centre-right parties, the most important of which are the Republican Party (PR), Social Democratic Centre (CDS), Social Democratic Party (PSD) and Radical Party (Rad). It has contested the last two general elections in alliance with the Rally for the Republic (RPR), gaining 18.5% of the vote and 129/577 seats in June 1988 and 19.1% and 213 seats in March 1993. (The difference in seat totals is due to the fact that the single-member-constituency voting system accentuated the decline in the Socialist Party's support.) The UDF parties then joined the new centre-right government formed by Édouard Balladur. Valéry Giscard d'Estaing has been the alliance's nominal leader since 1988; the parliamentary leader is Charles Millon. *See also individual party entries.*

Union for Real Politics *See* Real Politics Union.

Union Jack Common name for the flag of the United Kingdom. Officially called the Union Flag, it combines the crosses of Saint George (the traditional flag of England), Saint Andrew (Scotland) and Saint Patrick (Ireland).

Union of Democratic Forces [Sŭyuz na Demokratichni Sili] (SDS) Bulgarian political organization. The SDS was founded in 1989 as an umbrella organization of parties, groups and movements opposed to the ruling Communist Party and its successor, the Bulgarian Socialist Party (BSP). Membership has changed repeatedly since its foundation. At the general election in October 1991 the SDS comprised 12 parties, including the Bulgarian Social Democratic Party (BSDP), Democratic Party (DP) and Radical Democratic Party (RDP), the Support (Podkrepa) trade-union federation, a students' association and two human-rights groups. Campaigning for a rapid transition to a market economy, the SDS gained 34.4% of the vote and 110/240 seats, narrowly defeating the BSP. It formed a minority government from

November 1991 until December 1992. The chairman of the coordinating council is Filip Dimitrov, and the parliamentary leader is Stefan Savov. In March/April 1993 the BSDP and several smaller groups left the SDS to form the Bulgarian Social Democratic Union (BSDS). *See also individual party entries.*

Union of Fighting Communists *See* RED BRIGADES.

Union of Independent Trade Unions of Albania [Bashkimi i Sindikatave të Pavarura të Shqipërisë] (BSPSh) Albanian trade-union federation. The BSPSh was set up in 1991 as an umbrella group for the independent trade unions which emerged after the communist regime lifted the ban on their activities. It was the driving force behind the general strike in May–June 1991 which led to the collapse of communist rule. The union claims a membership of 350,000 (a third of the labour force). The leader is Valer Xheka.

Union of Industrial and Employers' Confederations of Europe (UNICE) International employers' association. Founded in 1958, UNICE seeks to represent the interests of business and industry at the level of the European institutions. It originally brought together the national employers' associations of European Community (EC) member states, but it now represents 32 organizations from 22 countries. The president is François Périgot (France), the secretary-general is Zygmunt Tyszkiewicz (United Kingdom).

Union Party [Sambandsflokkurin] (Sb) Faroese political party. Founded in 1906, the Union Party advocates continued close links between the Faroes and Denmark, is centrist in its economic policies and has liberal views on social issues. It has participated in several coalitions, most recently from 1981–85 and 1989–90, and has led a centre-left coalition since September 1994. At the July 1994 election it gained 8/32 seats. The leader is Edmund Joensen.

unionism In Northern Ireland (United Kingdom), support for the territory's status as part of the United Kingdom and rejection of its unification with the Republic of Ireland. Most unionists also reject any form of cooperation with the Republic (such as the 1985 Anglo-Irish Agreement) that implies it has a special interest in Northern Ireland affairs. The overwhelming majority of the Protestant community supports the union. The two main unionist parties are the Ulster Unionist Party (UUP) and the Ulster Democratic Unionist Party (DUP). The Protestant guerrilla groups active in the province are usually called 'loyalists'. *See also* NATIONALISM.

United Democratic Coalition [Coligação Democrático Unitário] (CDU) Portuguese political organization. The CDU is a left-wing electoral alliance founded in 1987 and dominated by the PORTUGUESE COMMUNIST PARTY (PCP). Other members include the Greens (Os Verdes) and two small left-wing parties. At the October 1991 election it gained 8.8% of the vote and 17/230 seats.

United Ireland Party *See* FINE GAEL.

United Kingdom (UK) Shorthand for the United Kingdom of Great Britain and Northern Ireland. It is used as the country's official name in diplomatic circles, international organizations etc. It is widely used interchangeably with 'Great Britain' and 'Britain' in the English-speaking world, but rarely so in European countries, where local forms of 'Great Britain' and the informal 'England' are more common. The Channel Islands, i.e. Guernsey and Jersey and their dependencies, and the Isle of Man are not part of the United Kingdom. They are formally 'crown dependencies' and largely internally self-governing. *For full country entry, see* GREAT BRITAIN AND NORTHERN IRELAND.

United Left [Izquierda Unida] (IU) Spanish political organization. The IU is an electoral alliance of communist and left-socialist parties formed in 1986. It is dominated by the COMMUNIST PARTY OF SPAIN (PCE), and also includes the Party of Socialist Action [Partido de Acción Socialista] (PASOC), Republican Left [Izquierda Republicana] (IR) and several regional parties. At the June 1993 election the alliance gained 9.6% of the vote and

18/350 seats, consolidating its position as the third-largest parliamentary group. The leader is Julio Anguita, who is also leader of the PCE.

United List *See* ASSOCIATED LIST OF SOCIAL DEMOCRATS.

United Nations Economic Commission for Europe (UNECE or ECE) Intergovernmental organization, a subsidiary body of the United Nations. Formed in 1947, the ECE is one of the five regional economic commissions set up by the United Nations Economic and Social Council (ECOSOC). Originally established with the intention of contributing to economic reconstruction after the Second World War, the ECE now aims to promote sustainable development in Europe and make recommendations on the economic, environmental and technological problems of the region. Its 53 members comprise all European members of the United Nations, the Soviet successor states, Canada, Israel, Switzerland and the United States. Its organs include the plenary session, which meets annually, committees of experts, and a secretariat. In recent years the Commission's activities have concentrated on environmental issues and transport, and since the collapse of communist rule in Eastern Europe also on macroeconomic analysis of developments in the region, preparation of statistical information and trade facilitation. Other fields of activity are agriculture, energy, industry and science and technology. The ECE secretariat also administers the Convention on Long-Range Transboundary Air Pollution. The secretariat is based in Geneva (Switzerland). The executive secretary is Gerald Hinteregger (Austria).

United Nations Peace-Keeping Force in Cyprus (UNFICYP) International military force. It was established in 1964 under a mandate from the UN Security Council to try to prevent the recurrence of intercommunal violence between Greek Cypriots and Turkish Cypriots and to contribute to the maintenance of law and order. Since the hostilities which led to the division of the island in 1974, its tasks include supervising the ceasefire

and patrolling the buffer zone between the Greek and Turkish forces. Its strength was reduced from 2,100 to 1,400 in 1993.

United Nations Protected Areas (UNPAs) Collective name for Serb-populated districts within Croatia under United Nations protection. The UNPAs were established in January 1992 as part of a ceasefire agreement in the civil war between local Serb forces (backed by the Yugoslav army) and the Croatian army. Covering nearly a third of Croatian territory, they are patrolled by the 18,000-strong United Nations Protection Force I (UNPROFOR I), whose brief is to provide security for the Serbs and demilitarize the region. *See also* CROATIAN CIVIL WAR *and* REPUBLIC OF SERBIAN KRAJINA.

United Nations Protection Force (UNPROFOR) Collective name for the international military forces established by the UN Security Council for peace-keeping purposes in former Yugoslavia. There are three separate UNPROFOR forces: (i) UNPROFOR I, deployed in the Serb-populated areas within Croatia designated as UN Protected Areas (UNPAs); (ii) UNPROFOR II, deployed in Bosnia-Herzegovina to protect humanitarian supply routes and the Muslim 'safe areas'; and (iii) the UNPROFOR Macedonia Command, deployed in Macedonia to prevent the regional conflict spreading to that country. *See also individual force entries.*

United Nations Protection Force I (UNPROFOR I) International military and police force deployed in Croatia. It was established by the UN Security Council under Resolution 743 in February 1992 as part of a peace plan for the Serb-populated areas which had sought to break away from Croatia after its secession from the Yugoslav federation in 1991. UNPROFOR's brief was to supervise the withdrawal of the Yugoslav and Croatian armies from the designated United Nations Protected Areas (UNPAs), demobilize the local Serb forces (which has not been achieved), monitor the ceasefire, and protect the local population. UNPROFOR I comprises 14,600 soldiers from around 30 countries. *See also* CROATIAN CIVIL WAR.

United Nations Protection Force II (UN-
PROFOR II) International military force
deployed in Bosnia-Herzegovina. It was
established by the UN Security Council
in June 1992 and deployed in October,
initially to ensure the security of Sarajevo
airport and the delivery of humanitarian
aid to the victims of the civil war. It was
subsequently also charged with safeguarding humanitarian supply routes and
distributing aid throughout the country
and, in June 1993, with protecting six
Muslim 'safe areas' declared by the
Security Council. By mid 1994 UNPRO-
FOR II's strength had been increased
from 2,100 to 14,400. French and British
soldiers form the largest contingents. *See
also* BOSNIAN CIVIL WAR.

**United Nations Protection Force Macedo-
nia Command** (UNPROFOR M) International military force deployed in Macedonia. UNPROFOR M was established
by the UN Security Council in December
1992 at the request of the Macedonian
government to monitor the country's
borders with Albania and Yugoslavia, to
act as a deterrent against attack, and to
prevent the civil war in Bosnia-Herzegovina and the potential civil war in Kosovo
(a province of Yugoslavia) spreading
south. The 1,250-strong force comprises
troops and military observers from four
Nordic countries and the United States.

**United Nations Security Council Resolu-
tion ...** *See* RESOLUTION ....

**United Nations War Crimes Commission
for Former Yugoslavia** or **Yugoslav
War Crimes Commission** International
judicial body. Set up by the UN Security
Council in October 1992, its brief is to
'examine and analyse information concerning possible breaches of international
humanitarian law and the Geneva conventions in the territory of former Yugoslavia' after 1 January 1991. (The Geneva
conventions govern the status of prisoners,
casualties and civilians in war.) It submits
relevant evidence to the INTERNATIONAL
WAR CRIMES TRIBUNAL FOR FORMER
YUGOSLAVIA.

United Trade Union Centre [Centrale
Sindacale Unitaria] (CSU) San Marino
trade-union federation. The CSU is an
umbrella organization for the Democratic
Confederation of Sammarinese Workers
[Confederazione Democratica dei Lavora-
tori Sammarinesi] (CDLS) and the San
Marino Confederation of Labour [Con-
federazione Sammarinese del Lavoro]
(CSdL). It has a total membership of
3,300 (a quarter of the labour force).
Marco Beccari leads the CDLS, Pio
Chiaruzzi the CSdL.

Unity [Edinstvo], in full **People's Trade
Union 'Unity'** [Narodna Sindikata
'Edinstvo'] (Edinstvo) Bulgarian trade-
union federation. Founded in 1990,
Edinstvo is the smallest of the three
national federations. It has 86 affiliated
unions organized in 14 regional groups,
with a total membership of around
375,000 (just under a tenth of the labour
force). The president is Ognyan Bonev.

UNMOs Abbreviation for United Nations
Military Observers. UNMOs are unarmed
soldiers deployed in areas of conflict who
report directly to United Nations officials
on military activities by the belligerents,
compliance with ceasefires and other
agreements etc. Around 500 UNMOs
have been deployed in Bosnia-Herzegovina and Croatia since the outbreak of
the civil wars in those countries. They are
distinct from UNITED NATIONS PROTECTION
FORCE (UNPROFOR) troops.

UNPAs *See* UNITED NATIONS PROTECTED
AREAS.

UNPROFOR (Bosnia-Herzegovina) *See*
UNITED NATIONS PROTECTION FORCE II.

UNPROFOR (Croatia) *See* UNITED
NATIONS PROTECTION FORCE I.

UNPROFOR (Macedonia) *See* UNITED
NATIONS PROTECTION FORCE MACEDONIA
COMMAND.

UNPROFOR I *See* UNITED NATIONS
PROTECTION FORCE I.

UNPROFOR II *See* UNITED NATIONS
PROTECTION FORCE II.

UNPROFOR M *See* UNITED NATIONS PRO-
TECTION FORCE MACEDONIA COMMAND.

UOP Abbreviation for Urząd Ochrony
Państwa ('State Protection Office'), the
Polish intelligence agency.

UP *See* LABOUR UNION.

UPF *See* UNION FOR FRANCE.

Upper Austria [Oberösterreich] Federal province [Land] of Austria. Situated in the northwest, Upper Austria has an area of 11,980 sq km and a population of 1,362,000. The capital is Linz, and the other main city is Wels. The economy is based on agriculture, manufacturing (engineering, motor vehicles, chemicals) and tourism. The Provincial Assembly [Landtag] has 56 members elected for a six-year term. The main political parties are the centre-right Austrian People's Party (ÖVP), the Social Democratic Party (SPÖ) and the far-right Freedom Party (FPÖ). At the provincial election in October 1991 the ÖVP gained 26 seats, the SPÖ 19 and the FPÖ 11. The chief minister is Josef Ratzenböck.

Upper Normandy [Haute-Normandie] Region of France. Situated in the northwest along the Channel, Upper Normandy has an area of 12,317 sq km and a population of 1,753,000. The capital is Rouen, and the other main city is Le Havre. The economy is based on manufacturing (petrochemicals, chemicals, cars, food processing) and agriculture (cattle and pig farming).

UPR *See* REAL POLITICS UNION.

Urba affair Political scandal in France concerning illegal funding of the Socialist Party (PS) and President Mitterrand's 1988 reelection campaign. A police inspector, Antoine Gaudino, published a book in October 1990 alleging that the consultancy firm Urba had channelled illegal donations to the PS in the 1980s. The money, totalling at least 25 million francs (3.8 million ecus), was raised by invoicing leading building companies for fictitious services. The payments were made in exchange for preferential treatment in public-works tenders. Several of the companies concerned were subsequently awarded contracts. In November 1991 Urba's former director and eight others went on trial for corruption. Twenty-seven PS members implicated by the investigating magistrate were protected from prosecution under a law, adopted in January 1990, which granted a retrospective amnesty for politicians involved in illegal party funding. In September 1992 Henri Emmanuelli, the PS's treasurer from 1988–92, was indicted on fraud charges in relation to donations made during his tenure. (The issue of party funding had been controversial in France for some time. The 1990 law effectively acknowledged that all political parties had received illegal corporate and other donations in the past. It also provided for public funding for political parties.)

US *See* ITALIAN SOCIALIST PARTY.

USS *See* SWISS TRADE UNION FEDERATION.

UUP *See* ULSTER UNIONIST PARTY.

UV *See* AOSTA VALLEY UNION.

UVF *See* ULSTER VOLUNTEER FORCE.

UW *See* FREEDOM UNION.

V (Denmark) *See* LIBERAL PARTY.

V (Norway) *See* LIBERAL PARTY.

V (Sweden) *See* LEFT PARTY.

V Abbreviation for the Vatican City.

V (European Union) *See* GREENS.

Văcăroiu, Nicolae (1943–) Romanian economist and politician. A specialist in finance and credit, he worked for the State Planning Committee from 1972. After the overthrow of the Ceauşescu regime in 1989 he was appointed a junior minister in the economy ministry and in 1991 he switched to the finance ministry, dealing with taxation issues. Politically unaffiliated, he was appointed prime minister by President Iliescu in November 1992 and formed a minority administration based on the Democratic National Salvation Front (FSND), now the Social Democracy Party (PDSR).

Vaduz Shorthand for the Liechtenstein government. Vaduz is the capital of Liechtenstein.

Vähi, Tiit (1947–) Estonian mechanical engineer and politician. Qualified in precision mechanics, he worked at a motor depot from 1972–89 and was its director from 1976. He was appointed minister of transport and communications in 1989. (Estonia regained its independence from the Soviet Union in August 1991.) He was prime minister of a non-party government from January–October 1992. Elected to parliament for the new centre-left Estonian Coalition Party (EKE) in September 1992, he was elected party leader in March 1993.

Vaitekūnas, Romasis (1943–) Lithuanian civil servant and politician. He worked as a police detective in Šiauliai from 1971 and became the city's chief of police in 1991. He was appointed interior minister in December 1992. He is a member of the Democratic Labour Party (LDDP), the successor to the Communist Party.

Vaivads, Jānis (1946–) Latvian teacher and politician. He has taught physics and mathematics. He was elected to parliament for the pro-independence People's Front (LTF) in 1990, when Latvia was still part of the Soviet Union, and for the centre-right Latvian Way (LC) in 1993. He was appointed a deputy prime minis-

ter and minister of education and science in September 1994.

Val d'Aoste *See* AOSTA VALLEY.

Valencia Shorthand for the VALENCIAN COMMUNITY, an autonomous region of Spain. The full name is commonly used to distinguish the region from the city and the province of Valencia.

Valencian Community [Comunidad Valenciana (Spanish), Comunitat Valenciana (Valencian)] Autonomous community or region of Spain, widely referred to as Valencia. Situated in the east along the Mediterranean Sea, Valencia has an area of 23,305 sq km and a population of 3,798,000. Valencian, closely related to Catalan, is spoken by around half the population; it has equal official status with Spanish. The capital is Valencia [València in Valencian], and the other main cities are Alicante [Alacant], Elche [Elx] and Castellón [Castelló]. The economy is based on agriculture (cereals, fruit and vegetables), manufacturing (food processing) and tourism. Valencia is the country's most productive agricultural region, and one of the Mediterranean region's leading producers of oranges, olives and grapes in particular. The main political parties are the Valencian Socialist Party (PSPV, the regional branch of the Spanish Socialist Workers' Party, PSOE), the centre-right People's Party (PP), the Valencian Union (UV), which favours greater autonomy, and the United Left (IU). At the election in May 1991 the PSPV gained 45 seats in the 89-member legislature, the PP 31, the UV seven and the IU six. An independent Muslim kingdom from 1021, Valencia was conquered by Aragón in 1245 and became part of unified Spain in 1479. It retained a measure of autonomy until 1707. It was established as an autonomous community in 1982.

Valentić, Nikica (1950–) Croatian lawyer and politician. In the 1980s he was managing director of an engineering consultancy he founded, and in 1990 he became managing director of the INA oil company, Croatia's largest state-owned enterprise. Elected to parliament for the right-wing Croatian Democratic Union

(HDZ) in 1992, he was appointed prime minister in March 1993 and formed a government the following month.

Valle d'Aosta *See* AOSTA VALLEY.

Valletta Shorthand for the Maltese government. Valletta is the capital of Malta.

value-added tax (VAT) In the European Union (EU), an indirect tax applicable in all member states, a proportion of which is allocated to the financing of EU activities. Levied on goods and services at each stage of production according to the increase in value or price, VAT was first introduced in the 1960s, replacing a variety of indirect taxes. The applicability and rates of VAT are decided by national governments. They range widely from country to country, from 0% on certain essential goods to more than 30% on luxury goods. Standard rates ranged from 12% in Spain to 22% in Denmark in 1992. In October 1992 finance ministers agreed that from 1993 a minimum standard rate of 15% would be applied in all countries. The proportion of VAT receipts passed on by the member states as a contribution to the EU budget was originally set at 1.0% and raised to 1.4% in 1986. This source provides around half the EU's revenue.

van Aartsen, Jozias (1947–) Dutch politician. He worked for the parliamentary group of the right-wing People's Party for Freedom and Democracy (VVD) from 1970 and was appointed director of the party's research institute in 1974. He joined the interior ministry in 1979, becoming its secretary-general in 1985. He was appointed minister of agriculture and fisheries in the left-right coalition formed in August 1994.

van den Brande, Luc (1945–) Belgian lawyer and politician. Elected to parliament for the Flemish Christian People's Party (CVP) in 1977, he became the party's parliamentary leader in 1984 and minister of employment and labour in 1988. In March 1992 he became chief minister of the Flemish regional government, also taking responsibility for the economy, external relations and several other portfolios.

van den Broek, Hans (1936–) Dutch lawyer and politician. He practised law,

worked for a major industrial company and was active in local government until his election to parliament in 1976 for the Christian Democratic Appeal (CDA). He was appointed a junior foreign minister in 1981 and was foreign minister from 1982–93. In January 1993 he became a European commissioner, with responsibility for external political relations, in particular for developing the European Union's common foreign and security policy and directing enlargement negotiations with applicant countries.

van der Stoel, Max (1924–) Dutch politician and diplomat. He was international secretary of the Labour Party (PvdA) from 1958–65 and was first elected to parliament in 1963. He was foreign minister from 1973–77 and 1981–82 and the Netherlands' permanent representative to the United Nations from 1983–86. In December 1992 the Conference on Security and Cooperation in Europe (CSCE) appointed him to the new post of high commissioner for national minorities.

van Eekelen, Willem or **Wim** (1931–) Dutch diplomat and politician. He worked in the diplomatic service from 1957. A member of the right-wing People's Party for Freedom and Democracy (VVD), he was a junior defence minister from 1978–81, a junior foreign minister from 1982–86 and defence minister from 1986–88. In April 1989 he was appointed secretary-general of the Western European Union (WEU).

van Mierlo, Hans (1931–) Dutch journalist and politician. A law graduate, he worked for the *Algemeen Handelsblad*, a major daily newspaper, from 1960–67, first as editor of domestic news and then of the opinion page. A founding member of the centre-left Democrats 66 (D'66), he was elected to parliament and became party leader in 1967. He held the post until 1974 and was again elected to it in June 1986. He was briefly defence minister in 1981–82. He became second deputy prime minister and minister of foreign affairs in the left-right coalition formed in August 1994.

van Miert, Karel (1942–) Belgian politician. He taught international relations and worked for the European Community (EC, now the European Union, EU) and the Belgian government in the 1970s. He became president of the Flemish Socialist Party (SP) in 1978, a member of the European parliament in 1979 and a member of the Belgian parliament in 1985. He resigned all three posts to take up his appointment as a European commissioner in January 1989. He was responsible for transport, credit and investments, financial instruments and consumer protection until January 1993, and is now in charge of competition policy and EU personnel.

van Rompuy, Herman (1947–) Belgian economist, civil servant, lecturer and politician. He was a senior adviser to the prime minister and then the finance minister from 1975–80. From 1980–88 he was director of the Centre for Political, Economic and Social Studies and lectured at various universities. He was elected president of the Flemish Christian People's Party (CVP) in September 1988. In September 1993 he also became a deputy prime minister and budget minister.

Vance-Owen plan Proposal for a settlement to the civil war in Bosnia-Herzegovina, put forward by the United Nations (UN) and European Community (EC) mediators, Cyrus Vance and David Owen, in October 1992 but eventually abandoned. In essence it constituted a compromise between the country's division along ethnic lines (Muslim, Serb and Croat) envisaged in an earlier EC-sponsored 'cantonization' plan and a recognition of the territorial gains made by the Serbs since the war broke out in March 1992. It provided for: (i) the creation of 10 provinces based largely on ethnicity but also taking into account aspects such as economic and transport links; (ii) a constitution based on extensive autonomy for the provinces within a decentralized state; and (iii) ceasefire and demilitarization arrangements monitored by a UN force. The plan was accepted by the Croats and the Muslim-led central government, but rejected by the Serbs in April 1993 and in a referendum among the Serb community in May. It was replaced by the OWEN-STOLTENBERG PLAN in July.

Vandenbroucke, Frank (1955–) Belgian economist and politician. He worked as a researcher from 1982–85. He was elected to parliament for the Flemish Socialist Party (SP) in 1985 and was briefly leader of the parliamentary group before being elected party president in January 1989.

Vanni d'Archirafi, Raniero (1931–) Italian diplomat, civil servant and politician. He joined the diplomatic service in 1956, becoming an ambassador in 1983. He was ambassador to Spain from 1984–87 and to West Germany from 1987–89 and was a director-general at the foreign ministry from 1989–93. In January 1993 he became a commissioner of the European Community (EC), with responsibility for internal-market issues, financial institutions, and small and medium-sized enterprises.

variable geometry (European Union) *See* MULTI-TRACK EUROPE.

Vas *See* LEFT-WING ALLIANCE.

Vassiliou, Georgios (1931–) Cypriot economist and politician. In 1962 he founded a marketing research bureau, which eventually became the largest consultancy of its kind in the region. He stood as an independent in the February 1988 presidential election and was elected with the support of the left-wing Progressive Party of Working People (AKEL). He stood for reelection in 1993 but lost to Glavkos Klerides in the second round. In April 1993 he formed a centrist political party, the Free Democratic Movement (KED).

Vastagh, Pál (1946–) Hungarian lawyer, academic and politician. A lecturer at the University of Szeged from 1971, he was dean of the law faculty in 1988–89. In 1990 he was elected to parliament for the Hungarian Socialist Party (MSzP), the successor to the communist Hungarian Socialist Workers' Party (MSzMP). He was appointed justice minister in the MSzP-led coalition which took office in July 1994.

VAT *See* VALUE-ADDED TAX.

Vatican City [Civitas Vaticanae (Latin), Città del Vaticano (Italian)] Country in southern Europe, often referred to as the Vatican or the Holy See.

Note: The information below refers to the Vatican City State, the territorial base for the Holy See or Papacy, the governing body of the worldwide Roman Catholic Church; it does not cover the Church and its institutions.

Official data. Name: Vatican City State [Status Civitatis Vaticanae / Stato della Città del Vaticano]; capital: n.a.; form of government: elective absolute monarchy; head of state and government: sovereign, ex officio the pope, the head of the Roman Catholic Church; flag: two vertical stripes, yellow and white, with the papal emblem on the white; national holiday: 22 October (Investiture of Pope John Paul II); languages: Latin and Italian; religion: Roman Catholicism; currencies: lira (L) (pl. lire) = 100 centesimi, Italian lira; abbreviations: V and SCV.

Geography. The Vatican is the world's smallest independent state, with a total area of 0.44 sq km. It consists of the Basilica of Saint Peter and adjacent buildings in the northwest of Rome, the Italian capital, and twelve churches and buildings in and outside the city. The land is fully built up. The climate is mediterranean, with hot summers and cool winters; rainfall is moderate.

Demography. The Vatican has a population of around 800. Around half are Vatican citizens and the other half are foreign nationals, mostly from Italy and Switzerland. The main language is Italian. In religious terms nearly all the people are Roman Catholics.

Sociography. The standard of living in the Vatican is very high (detailed figures n.a.).

Infrastructure and communications. The Vatican City has a highly developed transport and communications network fully integrated into that of Rome and Italy; the Holy See operates a book-publishing company, news agency, newspaper and radio station. The length of the road network and number of passenger cars n.a. There is 1 km of railway track and there are no navigable waterways. There is no nearby major port. The nearest international airport is at Rome (Leonardo da Vinci - Fiumicino).

There is one daily newspaper (circulation n.a.); Italian and other papers are also widely read. Number of radio receivers and television sets n.a.; there are around 1,500 telephones in use (1,875 per 1,000 people).

Economic structure. The Vatican economy is highly developed and closely linked to the Italian economy. The Vatican maintains a customs and monetary union with Italy. Taxes are very low. The economy is based on financial services and tourism.

Services contribute nearly all of GDP, with industry contributing a small proportion. Most of the labour force of 2,500 (three times the size of the resident population) is employed in services and a small number is employed in manufacturing; workers commuting from Italy make up two-thirds of the total. There is no agricultural activity and there are no mineral resources. The main industries are printing (postage stamps, books) and handicrafts (souvenirs). Banking and other financial activities (on behalf of the Roman Catholic Church) and tourism are the mainstays of the economy. The main energy sources are imported fossil fuels and electricity (from Italy). The main exports are postage stamps and books. The main imports are manufactured goods, foodstuffs and fuels. The main trading partner is Italy. Net invisible earnings (income from financial services, tourism receipts, donations from Roman Catholics worldwide) account for most of GNP. (Detailed figures on economic structure and performance, foreign trade etc n.a.)

The Institute of Religious Works [Istituto per le Opere di Religione] (IOR) discharges some of the responsibilities of a central bank. There is no employers' association; the only labour organization is the Association of Vatican Lay Workers (ADLV).

Political structure. The Vatican City is an elective absolute monarchy on the basis of a constitution adopted in 1967. The head of state is the pope, the bishop of Rome and the head of the Roman Catholic Church, who is elected for life by the Sacred College of Cardinals. All executive, legislative and judicial powers are vested in him. He delegates administration of the Vatican to a seven-member Papal Commission [Commissione Pontificale] headed by a president. Judicial powers are exercised by various tribunals or delegated to Italy. The Holy See, the governing body of the Roman Catholic Church worldwide, is a separate legal entity and has a separate structure.

The head of state is Pope John Paul II. The president of the Papal Commission is Rosalio José Castillo Lara.

Security and international affiliations. The Vatican has no standing army. Responsibility for defence is delegated to Italy. The 100-strong Swiss Guard performs certain defence-related duties. Foreign affairs are the responsibility of the Holy See, which is a member of the Conference on Security and Cooperation in Europe (CSCE) as well as several specialized agencies of the United Nations, but not of the organization itself. The Vatican City is a member of several UN subsidiary agencies in its own right.

History. In 754 King Pepin the Short of the Franks recognized the temporal – in addition to the spiritual – authority of the Papacy or Holy See in Rome and adjoining districts. (*For earlier developments, see* ITALY: HISTORY.) The Donation of Pepin was extended northwards in the next two years to Ravenna and the Pentapolis region. For the next 11 centuries the Papal States controlled much of central Italy. The seat of government was established on the Vatican hill in Rome in 1377. In 1860 the northern half of the Papal States was incorporated into the emerging unified Italian state. The occupation of Rome in 1870 and its proclamation as the national capital completed the process of unification. The Holy See refused to acknowledge the loss of its temporal powers (which it argued had been granted by a higher power). The dispute was resolved in 1929 with the signing of the Lateran Treaty, which established the Vatican City State as a neutral and inviolable territory under the sovereignty of the Holy See. Since then the Vatican has served as the territorial base for the Holy See.

The Polish cardinal Karol Wojtyła was elected pope in October 1978 and took the name John Paul II. Under a major reorganization of the administration of the Vatican and the Holy See, he delegated most of his temporal powers to the Papal Commission and the Secretariat of State respectively. The Concordat or treaty governing relations with Italy was renewed in February 1984.

See also entries on specific institutions, organizations, terms etc.

Vatră Românească *See* ROMANIAN HEARTH.

Väyrynen, Paavo (1946–) Finnish politician. Elected to parliament for the Centre Party (KESK) in 1970, he was party chairman from 1980–90. He has been minister of education (1975–76), labour (1976–77) and foreign affairs (1977–82, 1983–87 and 1991–93). In April 1993 he was nominated the party's candidate for the presidency of the republic and resigned as foreign minister to concentrate on his campaign. He came third in the vote in January 1994.

VB *See* FLEMISH BLOC.

VBO *See* BELGIAN BUSINESS FEDERATION.

VCL Abbreviation for the LIRA, the Vatican currency, used in banking etc.

VD *See* FREE DEMOCRATS (Estonia).

VDL *See* RUSSIAN DEMOCRATIC MOVEMENT.

veguer Andorran government official, usually left untranslated or translated as 'magistrate'. The two *veguers* are the personal representatives of the co-princes or joint heads of state. Until the adoption of a constitution in May 1993 the *veguer de França* (representing the president of France) and the *veguer episcopal* (representing the bishop of Urgell in Spain) had extensive legislative and judicial powers. The new constitution transferred sovereignty to the people of Andorra, so that the powers of the co-princes and *veguers* are now largely nominal.

Veil, Simone (1927–) French lawyer, civil servant and politician. A Jew, she survived deportation to a nazi concentration camp during the Second World War. She qualified as a judge in 1956. She worked for the justice ministry from 1957 and became general secretary of the High Council of the Judiciary (CSM) in 1970.

From 1974–79 she was health minister in successive centre-right governments. Elected to the European Parliament in 1979, she served as its president until 1982 and was leader of the Liberal, Democratic and Reformist Group (LDR) from 1984–92. She returned to domestic politics in March 1993, taking up the senior post of minister of social affairs, health and urban affairs in the new centre-right government.

Velika Hrvatska *See* GREATER CROATIA.

Velika Srbija *See* GREATER SERBIA.

velvet divorce [sametová rodvod (Czech), zamatová rodvod (Slovak)] In former Czechoslovakia, the common name for the process set in motion after the general election in June 1992 that resulted in the federation's dissolution – mutually agreed – at the end of the year and the creation of the two independent states of the Czech Republic and Slovakia on 1 January 1993. The term was derived from the 'VELVET REVOLUTION' of 1989.

velvet revolution [sametová revoluce (Czech), zamatová revolúcia (Slovak)] In former Czechoslovakia, the common name for the three-week period of largely peaceful mass demonstrations in November–December 1989 that culminated in the collapse of communist rule and the formation of a government of 'national understanding'.

Veneto Autonomous region of Italy. Situated in the northeast, Veneto has an area of 18,364 sq km and a population of 4,453,000. The capital is Venice [Venezia], and the other main cities are Padua [Padova], Verona and Vicenza. The economy is based on agriculture (cereals, wine, fruit and vegetables, cattle farming), manufacturing (textiles, food processing, metalworking, chemicals) and tourism. It is one of Italy's most productive and affluent regions. The Republic of Venice, one of Europe's primary trading powers during the Middle Ages, gained control over the whole of the Veneto region in the 15th century. It became an Austrian possession in 1815 and was incorporated into unified Italy in 1866.

Venizelos, Evangelos (1957–) Greek lawyer, academic and politician. He worked for the Council of State, a government advisory body, and the Supreme Court from 1978–84. He then lectured in constitutional law at Thessalonika University. Elected to parliament for the Pan-Hellenic Socialist Movement (PASOK) in September 1993, he became government spokesman in the PASOK government formed the following month, and was also appointed minister for the press and mass media (a new portfolio) in July 1994.

Venstre *See* LIBERAL PARTY (Denmark, Norway).

Verdeţ, Ilie (1925–) Romanian politician. He held a series of senior posts in the Romanian Communist Party (PCR) from 1948, including secretary of the central committee from 1974–78 and 1982–85. He was appointed a deputy prime minister in 1965 and was prime minister from 1979–82 and minister of mining from 1985–86. He lost his place on the party executive in 1986. He was made chairman of the Central Auditing Committee, a post he held until the overthrow of the Ceauşescu regime and the banning of the PCR in December 1989. In August 1991 he was elected leader of the new Socialist Labour Party (PSM), the PCR's intellectual heir.

Verdi *See* GREEN FEDERATION.

Verfassungsschutz *See* FEDERAL OFFICE FOR THE PROTECTION OF THE CONSTITUTION.

Vergina Star *See* STAR OF VERGINA.

Verheugen, Günter (1944–) German journalist, civil servant and politician. He was a senior official at the interior ministry from 1969–74 and at the foreign ministry from 1974–76. He became general secretary of the centrist Free Democratic Party (FDP) in 1977. After the FDP switched coalition partners in 1982 he joined the Social Democratic Party (SPD). He was elected to parliament the following year. In August 1993 he became the party's general secretary (responsible for organization and campaigning).

Verhofstadt, Guy (1953–) Belgian politician. He was active in local government for the right-wing Party for Progress and Democracy (PVV) of Flanders and served as political secretary to party leader Willy de Clercq from 1977–81. He was elected party president in 1982. Elected to parliament in 1985, he was a deputy prime minister and minister for the budget, science policy and planning from 1985–88. In June 1989 he again became leader of the PVV. The party was relaunched as the Flemish Liberals and Democrats (VLD) in 1992.

Verts *See* GREENS (France).

Verzetnitsch, Friedrich (1945–) Austrian plumber and trade-union official. He joined the staff of the Austrian Trade Union Federation (ÖGB) in 1970. He became head of its youth department in 1973, secretary of the organization department in 1982 and secretary of the executive committee in 1983. He was elected ÖGB president in October 1987.

vetting (former communist countries) *See* SCREENING.

Viannet, Louis (1933–) French postal worker and trade-union official. A full-time union representative from 1967, he was general secretary of the Federation of Post Office and Telecommunications Workers (FPTT) from 1979–82. He then became deputy leader of General Confederation of Labour (CGT), the largest trade-union federation. In January 1992 he was elected its leader.

Victoria Palace [Palatul Victoria] Shorthand for the Romanian government. The Victoria Palace in Bucharest is the official residence of the prime minister and also houses several government departments.

Videnov, Zhan (1959–) Bulgarian politician. A specialist in foreign economic relations, he was elected to parliament for the Bulgarian Socialist Party (BSP), the successor to the Bulgarian Communist Party (BKP), in June 1990. He was elected party leader in December 1991.

Vidošević, Nadan (1960–) Croatian economist and politician. He has worked as an accountant and manager in several companies in his native Split. Elected to parliament for the right-wing Croatian Democratic Union (HDZ) in 1992, he briefly served as prefect of Split-Dalmatia county in 1993 and was appointed minister of economic affairs in October 1993.

Vienna Shorthand for the Austrian government. Vienna is the capital of Austria. It is also the seat of several United Nations agencies and other intergovernmental organizations.

Vienna [Wien] Province [Land] of Austria. Situated in the northeast, it has an area of 415 sq km and a population of 1,573,000. The province is coextensive with the city of Vienna, the national capital, by far the country's largest city and its dominant economic and cultural centre. The economy is based on services and manufacturing. The Provincial Assembly [Landtag] has 100 members elected for a four-year term. The administration combines the functions of a municipality and a province. The Social Democratic Party (SPÖ) has been the city's dominant party since the late 1910s. At the November 1991 election it gained 52 seats; the far-right Freedom Party (FPÖ) gained 23 seats, the centre-right Austrian People's Party (ÖVP) 18 and the Green Alternative (GA) seven. The mayor is Helmut Zilk.

viguier French name for VEGUER, the personal representative of one of the co-princes or joint heads of state of Andorra.

Vihreät *See* GREEN ALLIANCE.

Viinanen, Iiro (1944–) Finnish businessman and politician. A qualified mechanical engineer, he was managing director of the Konevalmistamo engineering company from 1967–84. He was elected to parliament for the right-wing National Coalition Party (KOK) in 1983 and was appointed finance minister in April 1991.

Vila Amigo, Marc (1961–) Andorran lawyer, academic and politician. He has worked as a notary since 1986 and has lectured in law since 1987. He was appointed minister of foreign affairs in February 1994.

vilayet *See* İL.

Vilkelis, Eduardas (1953–) Lithuanian economist and politician. He worked for the finance ministry and other government departments from 1976. In 1991–92 he was a senior manager in a new private company. A member of the Democratic Labour Party (LDDP), he was appointed finance minister in December 1992.

Villiger, Kaspar (1941–) Swiss business-man and politician. He is joint owner and has been director of the family firm producing cigars and bicycles. He represented the centre-right Radical Democratic Party in the Lucerne cantonal parliament from 1972–82 and in the federal parliament from 1982–89. He was elected to the Federal Council (= government) in February 1989, taking responsibility for defence.

Vilnius Shorthand for the Lithuanian government. Vilnius is the capital of Lithuania.

Visegrad countries Collective name for the Czech Republic, Hungary, Poland and Slovakia. It has been in use since February 1991, when Czechoslovakia, Hungary and Poland agreed at a meeting at Visegrad Castle in Hungary to work together following the collapse of communist rule and the end of Soviet domination. The term is sometimes also used to cover Bulgaria and Romania, which work closely with the Visegrad Four.

Visegrad Four or **Visegrad Group** Inter-governmental organization. The Visegrad Group is an informal grouping compris-ing the Czech Republic, Hungary, Poland and Slovakia. It has its roots in a summit meeting of the Czechoslovak, Hungarian and Polish heads of state and government in Visegrad, Hungary, in February 1991. A treaty of cooperation was signed the following October. The Group's main aims are: (i) to achieve the members' full integration into the European economic, political and security order through eventual membership of the European Union (EU) and the North Atlantic Treaty Organization (NATO); (ii) to coordinate their relations with these two organiza-tions and act jointly to secure member-ship; and (iii) to cooperate on a range of economic, political and security issues. The first concrete result of the Visegrad Group's work was the Central European Free Trade Agreement (CEFTA) conclu-ded in December 1992. Cooperation is also being developed in security matters, defence research, arms procurement, labour and social-affairs policy, foreign-trade issues and other spheres.

VL See LEFT-WING ALLIANCE.

Vlaams Blok See FLEMISH BLOC.

Vlaanderen See FLANDERS.

Vlachs Ethnic group dispersed throughout the Balkan region, also known as Aroma-nians, Aromuns etc. From the early Middle Ages the name 'Vlach' was applied by the Slav peoples in the Balkans to the romanized communities who spoke Latin-based dialects. Their heartland was and is modern Romania, but Vlachs were settled throughout the region. Today they are scattered in mountain villages in Yugo-slavia, Greece, Albania and Bulgaria. They are thought to number around 300,000 in total. The Vlach language is usually considered a form of Romanian.

VLD See FLEMISH LIBERALS AND DEMOCRATS.

VMDK See DEMOCRATIC UNION OF VOJVODINA HUNGARIANS.

VMRO-DPMNE See INTERNAL MACEDO-NIAN REVOLUTIONARY ORGANIZATION - ....

VNO See FEDERATION OF DUTCH INDUSTRY.

Voeren question Controversy in Belgium over the status of the commune of Voeren [Fourons in French], which is part of Dutch-speaking Flanders but has a major-ity French-speaking population. Voeren has been a focus of the country's long-standing language dispute between Flemings and Walloons since 1962, when it was transferred from Liège to Limburg province because at that time a majority of the population was Dutch-speaking. Recurrent tension between Dutch and French speakers became a national issue in 1986, when the elected mayor, José Happart, was dismissed for refusing to take a required test of proficiency in Dutch. His subsequent reelection brought down the government of the day. The issue was defused in 1988 when Happart agreed not to press his appointment as mayor in return for concessions on the use of French in the commune. See also BELGIAN LANGUAGE QUESTION.

Voerstreek question See VOEREN QUESTION.

VÖI See ASSOCIATION OF AUSTRIAN INDUSTRIALISTS.

voivodship See WOJEWÓDZTWO.

Vojvodina Province [pokrajina] of Serbia, a constituent republic of Yugoslavia. Situated in the north and bordering on

Croatia, Hungary and Romania, Vojvodina has an area of 21,506 sq km and a population of 2,013,000. In ethnic terms the region is among the most heterogeneous in Europe: 54.4% of the people are Serbs, 18.9% Hungarians, 8.2% Yugoslavs (self-description), 5.4% Croats, 3.4% Slovaks, 2.3% Romanians, 2.1% Montenegrins and 0.9% Ruthenians, and there are also small groups of Gipsies, Germans, Turks and others; a total of 24 ethnic groups are officially recognized. The main languages are Serb (the official language) or Serbo-croat and Hungarian. Most Serbs are nominally Serbian Orthodox Christians, while most Hungarians and Croats are Roman Catholics. The capital is Novi Sad, and the other main cities are Subotica and Zrenjanin. The economy is based on agriculture (cereals, fruit and vegetables, cattle farming) and manufacturing (food processing). Vojvodina is the country's most productive agricultural region. The main political parties are the Socialist Party of Serbia (SPS), the far-right Serbian Radical Party (SRS) and the Democratic Union of Vojvodina Hungarians (DZVM or VMDK). At the May 1992 election the SPS gained 93/120 seats in the provincial assembly. The chief minister is Boško Perošević. Vojvodina was part of the Kingdom of Hungary from its foundation in the 10th century until 1526, when it became part of the Ottoman Empire. It was reconquered in two stages in 1699 and 1718. The Hungarian authorities encouraged settlement of this strategically important and fertile border area, and Serbs who had emigrated from Ottoman-ruled Serbia in the 17th century were joined by Hungarians, Slovaks, Germans, Ruthenians and others. In 1918 the region was incorporated into the new state of Yugoslavia. It became an autonomous province within Serbia in 1946. In the 1970s and 80s it enjoyed similar powers to the federation's full republics. In 1990, as central authority crumbled, the Serbian government effectively abolished the province's autonomous status and restricted the rights of the minorities, in particular the use of Hungarian as an official language.

Volksunie *See* PEOPLE'S UNION.

von Weizsäcker, Richard (1920–) German lawyer and politician. He served as president of the congress of the Lutheran Church from 1964–70. He was elected to parliament for the Christian Democratic Union (CDU) in 1969, held a range of senior party posts from 1971, including deputy leader of the parliamentary group from 1972–79, and was a deputy speaker of parliament from 1979–81. In 1981 he became governing mayor of West Berlin. In July 1984 he was elected federal president (a non-executive post) with the support of all the main parties, including the opposition Social Democrats. He was elected to a second term in 1989 and retired at the end of June 1994.

Voorhoeve, Joris (1945–) Dutch economist and politician. A specialist in development economics and international relations, he worked for the World Bank from 1973–77 and for the Scientific Council for Government Policy, a government advisory body, from 1977–79. He was director of the research institute linked to the right-wing People's Party for Freedom and Democracy (VVD) from 1979–82. He has also lectured at several universities. A member of parliament for the VVD from 1982–89, he was leader of the parliamentary group from 1986. From 1990–94 he was director of the Dutch Institute for International Relations (Clingendael). He was appointed defence minister in the left-right coalition formed in August 1994.

VOPO or **Vopo** Abbreviation for Volks-polizei ('People's Police'), the police force of former East Germany. It was disbanded on German reunification in 1990. Many of its officers were retrained and joined the new state police forces.

Vorarlberg Federal province [Land] of Austria. Situated in the far west and bordering on Germany, Switzerland and Liechtenstein, Vorarlberg has an area of 2,601 sq km and a population of 340,000. The capital is Bregenz. The economy is based on tourism, manufacturing (textiles) and agriculture. The Provincial Assembly [Landtag] has 36 members elected for a five-year term. The dominant political party is the centre-right Austrian People's Party (ÖVP), which has been in power since the 1950s; the other main parties are the Social Democratic Party (SPÖ), the far-right Freedom Party (FPÖ) and the Green Alternative (GA). At the September 1994 provincial election the ÖVP gained 20 seats, the FPÖ seven, the SPÖ six and the Greens three. The chief minister is Martin Purtscher.

voucher privatization (former communist countries) *See* MASS PRIVATIZATION.

Voulí Shorthand for Voulí Antiprósopon ('HOUSE OF REPRESENTATIVES'), the Cypriot parliament.

Voulí ('Assembly') Parliament of Greece. The Voulí has 300 members elected for a four-year term by proportional representation in multi-member constituencies. It elects the president of the republic. A presidential veto on legislation may be overturned by an absolute majority of members (i.e. 151).

Voynet, Dominique (1956–) French politician. She has studied medicine. Active for the Greens (Les Verts) in local government in the Franche Comté region since the early 1980s, she has been one of the party's four spokespeople and was elected senior spokeswoman in November 1993.

VP Abbreviation for Volkspolizei ('People's Police'), the police force of former East Germany. It was disbanded on German reunification in 1990. Many of its officers were retrained and joined the new state police forces.

Vp (Sweden) *See* LEFT PARTY.

VR *See* ROMANIAN HEARTH.

Vranitzky, Franz (1937–) Austrian economist and politician. A member of the Social Democratic Party (SPÖ), he worked for the finance ministry and held senior posts at several major banks before being appointed finance minister in 1984. In June 1986 he became federal chancellor (= prime minister) following the resignation of Fred Sinowatz. After the election later that year he formed a grand coalition with the centre-right Austrian People's Party (ÖVP). In May 1988 he was also elected SPÖ leader.

VSÍ *See* EMPLOYERS' FEDERATION OF ICELAND.

VU (Belgium) *See* PEOPLE'S UNION.

VU (Liechtenstein) *See* FATHERLAND UNION.

VVD *See* PEOPLE'S PARTY FOR FREEDOM AND DEMOCRACY.

Wachtmeister, Ian (1932–) Swedish businessman, writer and politician. He worked for two large metalworking firms until 1983 and then formed his own company, The Empire, producing aluminium and brass products. He also published two satires on Swedish life in the 1980s. Together with another businessman he founded New Democracy (NYD), a right-wing protest party, in February 1991. He resigned as leader in April 1994.

Waechter, Antoine (1949–) French ecologist and politician. One of France's foremost environmentalist campaigners since the 1970s, he became a spokesman for the Greens (Les Verts) in 1986 and stood as their presidential candidate in 1988. From 1989–94 he was a member of the European Parliament and co-leader of the European Greens group.

Waigel, Theo (1939–) German lawyer and politician. He worked for the Bavarian civil service until his election to the state parliament in 1972 for the right-wing Christian Social Union (CSU), the Bavarian counterpart of the Christian Democratic Union (CDU). He became the CSU's parliamentary leader in 1982 and party leader in October 1988 after the death of Franz-Josef Strauss. He was also appointed finance minister in the federal government in April 1989.

Waldegrave, William (1946–) British politician. He worked for the Conservative Party from 1971–75 and for the GEC engineering concern from 1975–81. Elected to Parliament in 1979, he held several junior ministerial posts from 1981 until his appointment as secretary of state for health in 1990. In 1992 he became chancellor of the Duchy of Lancaster (= minister without portfolio), with responsibility for the civil service, science and open government. In July 1994 he was appointed minister of agriculture, food and fisheries.

Waldheim, Kurt (1918–) Austrian diplomat and politician. After a twenty-year career in the diplomatic service, including a posting as Austria's permanent representative at the United Nations (1964–68), he was appointed foreign minister in 1968. When the centre-right Austrian People's Party (ÖVP) lost power two years later he returned to the UN. He served as the organization's secretary-general from 1972–81. After an academic appointment in the United States he returned to Austrian politics in 1986 as the ÖVP's candidate for federal president (a non-executive post). He won the election despite revelations that he had served as an intelligence officer in the German army during the Second World War (1939–45). An independent commission of historians cleared him of complicity in war crimes in the Balkans but said that he had known about them and that he had misrepresented his war record. He did not seek a second term in 1992.

Wales [Cymru] Constituent country of the United Kingdom. Situated in the west of mainland Britain and surrounded by the Irish Sea on three sides, Wales has an area of 20,768 sq km and a population of 2,886,000. Most people consider themselves Welsh, and regional identification is strong. Welsh, the original Celtic language of the region, is spoken by around a fifth of the people, mainly in the rural north and centre; it has official status. The capital is Cardiff, and the other main cities are Swansea, Newport and Wrexham. The economy is based on manufacturing (engineering, electronics, textiles), agriculture (sheep and dairy farming) and services. Structural unemployment was high in the 1970s and 80s due to the decline of the heavy industries and coal mining. In political terms Wales has no distinct status. It has no separate legislature or executive, but there is some decentralization of administration. The Welsh Office is the main government department dealing with Welsh affairs. The main political parties are the Labour Party, which has been dominant since the 1920s, the Conservative Party, the Liberal Democrats and Plaid Cymru (PC), which advocates independence. At the April 1992 general election Labour gained 49.5% of the vote, the Conservatives 28.6%, the Liberal Democrats 12.4% and Plaid Cymru 8.8%. In the early Middle Ages Wales was divided into several states, in particular Gwynedd, Powys and

Deheubarth. They were united in 1267 under Llywelyn ap Gruffydd, who was proclaimed prince of Wales. This failed to stop the English conquest of the country, however, which was completed by 1284. In 1536 Wales was formally incorporated into the Kingdom of England. In the 19th century South Wales became a major centre of coal mining and heavy industries. Growing discontent with perceived English dominance and the continuing decline of the Welsh language led to the rise of nationalist sentiment from the 1960s onwards, but proposals for an elected assembly with limited powers were rejected in a referendum in 1979. *See also* GREAT BRITAIN AND NORTHERN IRELAND.

Walęsa, Lech (1943–) Polish electrician, trade-union official and politician. He was involved in union activities throughout his employment at the Lenin shipyard in Gdańsk during the 1970s. He came to prominence as leader of the strike in August 1980 which gained concessions from the communist government and led to the founding of the independent trade union Solidarity. On the declaration of martial law in 1981 he was interned, but released 11 months later. He returned to work at the shipyard in 1983. By now one of Eastern Europe's best-known dissidents, he was awarded the 1983 Nobel Peace Prize. He returned to public life in 1988, leading the delegation which negotiated a 'new social contract' with the government in April 1989. This marked the beginning of the dismantling of the communist regime. He resumed the leadership of Solidarity, which had been relegalized as part of the reforms. The Solidarity movement became increasingly divided over economic policy and other matters. He defeated his erstwhile ally Tadeusz Mazowiecki in the first round of the presidential election in November 1990, and went on to win a landslide victory over Stanisław Tymiński in the second round in December. In office for a five-year term, he gave strong backing to the reform programmes of successive governments and has sought to increase the powers of the presidency.

Wall, the Shorthand for the BERLIN WALL, the barrier around West Berlin erected by the East German communist authorities in 1961 and maintained until the regime's collapse in 1989.

Wallage, Jacques (1946–) Dutch sociologist and politician. He was an executive member of Groningen city council for the Labour Party (PvdA) from 1972 until his election to parliament in 1981. He was appointed a junior education and science minister in 1989. He became the PvdA's parliamentary leader in August 1994.

Wallenberg case Controversy surrounding the disappearance of the Swedish businessman and diplomat Raoul Wallenberg at the end of the Second World War and his subsequent fate. As a special envoy to Hungary in 1944–45 Wallenberg saved, at great personal risk, up to 100,000 Jews from deportation to nazi death camps by issuing them with Swedish passports, establishing safe houses and taking other steps to help the inhabitants of the Budapest ghetto. He was arrested for espionage after the Soviet army occupied Budapest in January 1945. The Soviet authorities initially refused to disclose his fate and eventually declared he had died of a heart attack while in custody in Moscow in 1947. For years afterwards, however, freed Soviet prisoners claimed they had seen him alive in prison. (At the last unconfirmed sighting in 1975 he would have been aged 63.) Soviet documents released in 1991 and 1993 indicated that he had been shot on government orders in 1947, but the Wallenberg family and others do not regard the evidence as conclusive. Wallenberg is honoured in Israel as the most outstanding of 'righteous gentiles' who helped Jews during the nazi persecution.

Wallonia [Wallonie] Region of Belgium. Covering the southern half of the country, Wallonia has an area of 16,845 sq km and a population of 3,256,000. It comprises the French-speaking provinces of Belgium, namely Hainault [Hainaut], Namur, Luxemburg [Luxembourg], Liège and Walloon Brabant. There is a small community of 67,000 German speakers in the eastern districts bordering Germany.

The main cities are Liège, Charleroi, Mons and Namur. Brussels [Bruxelles], the country's largest city and political centre and overwhelmingly French-speaking, is not part of Wallonia but a region in its own right (Brussels-Capital). The economy is based on manufacturing (steel, engineering), agriculture and forestry. The traditional coal-mining and heavy industries have been in decline since the 1960s, and structural unemployment is high. Under the constitutional reforms transforming Belgium into a federal state, finalized in July 1993, legislative power in the region is exercised by the 75-member Wallonian Parliament [Parlement Wallon] elected for a five-year term, and executive power is exercised by a government headed by a president. Responsibility for education, culture, language issues and some other matters lies with two separately constituted language-based 'communities', the FRENCH COMMUNITY and the GERMAN-SPEAKING COMMUNITY. Government institutions are based in Namur and Brussels. The main political parties are the Socialist Party (PS), the right-wing Liberal Reform Party (PRL), the Christian Social Party (PSC), the Ecology Party (ÉCOLO) and the far-right National Front (FN). The government is formed by a coalition of the PS and PSC, headed by Robert Collignon. During the Middle Ages the area of modern Wallonia consisted of a number of autonomous territories within the Holy Roman Empire, in particular Hainault, Brabant, Namur, Liège and Luxemburg. Most were united under the dukes of Burgundy in the 14th and 15th centuries and, along with the rest of the Low Countries, became part of the Habsburg Empire and then Spain by inheritance. The region became an Austrian possession in 1713, was annexed by France in 1795, and became part of the Netherlands in 1815. Walloons spearheaded the revolution in 1830 which led to the creation of Belgium. In the early 19th century Wallonia was one of the first regions of continental Europe to become industrialized. It was economically dominant within Belgium until the

1960s. Escalating language and economic disputes with Dutch-speaking Flanders led to an agreement in principle in 1970 to create a federal structure. Its final terms were adopted in July 1993.

Wallonian or **Walloon** Collective name for the dialects of French spoken in Belgium, specifically the regions of Wallonia and Brussels-Capital. The formal spoken language and written language is virtually identical with French, and French is the official language of Wallonia. *See also* BELGIAN LANGUAGE QUESTION.

Wallonie *See* WALLONIA.

Walloon Socialist Party *See* SOCIALIST PARTY (PS) (Belgium).

Walloons People of WALLONIA, a region of Belgium, or, more generally, the French-speaking people of Belgium as a whole.

Walsh, Joe (1943–) Irish agronomist and politician. He has worked as a research scientist and manager of a dairy company. A member of parliament for the centre-right Fianna Fáil from 1977–81 and since 1982, he was appointed a junior minister for agriculture, food and forestry in 1987 and became minister of the department in February 1992.

Warsaw Shorthand for the Polish government. Warsaw is the capital of Poland.

Warsaw Pact *See* WARSAW TREATY ORGANIZATION.

Warsaw Treaty Organization or **Warsaw Pact** Former intergovernmental organization. The Warsaw Pact was founded in 1955 as a regional defence alliance of the Eastern European communist countries led by the Soviet Union. A counterweight to the North Atlantic Treaty Organization (NATO), it comprised Bulgaria, Czechoslovakia, East Germany, Hungary, Poland, Romania and the Soviet Union; Albania withdrew in 1968. Within the framework of the alliance Soviet troops were eventually stationed in East Germany, Poland, Hungary and Czechoslovakia. The changes in Soviet foreign policy initiated in the mid 1980s had a profound effect on the Warsaw Pact. At the annual summit in July 1989, members accepted the growing political, economic and ideological divergence between them. The following October they also renounced the so-called Brezhnev doctrine, under which Pact members were obliged to intervene militarily in any allied state where 'socialism' was perceived to be under threat. The Pact effectively disintegrated after the collapse of communist rule in Eastern Europe in 1989. It was formally disbanded as a military alliance in February 1991 and as a political alliance in July. All Soviet and Russian troops were withdrawn from Czechoslovakia and Hungary by June 1991, from Poland by September 1993 and from former East Germany by August 1994. (The last Russian troops were withdrawn from Lithuania by August 1993 and from Estonia and Latvia by August 1994.)

Washington Treaty Shorthand for the North Atlantic Treaty, the international agreement establishing the NORTH ATLANTIC TREATY ORGANIZATION (NATO). It was signed in Washington (United States) on 4 April 1949 and came into force on 24 August 1949.

Wathelet, Melchior (1949–) Belgian politician. A law and economics graduate, he was elected to parliament for the Christian Social Party (PSC) in 1977. From 1981 he held a number of posts in the Wallonian regional government and became its chief minister in 1985. In May 1988 he joined the national government as a deputy prime minister and minister of justice; in March 1992 he was also given the economic affairs portfolio.

Way of Latvia *See* LATVIAN WAY.

We Ourselves *See* SINN FÉIN.

weakening In the European Union (EU), a term associated with those who argue that the EU, in particular the supranational European Community (EC) at its core, has too many powers and that some of them should be returned to national governments. It is contrasted with 'DEEPENING', i.e. becoming more integrated. *See also* EUROPE OF NATIONS.

Wehrsportgruppe *See* MILITARY SPORT GROUP.

Weiss, Birte (1941–) Danish journalist and politician. She worked for several newspapers and Danish Radio (DR) until her election to parliament for the Social Democratic Party (SD) in 1971. She was

appointed minister of internal affairs in the centre-left coalition which took office in January 1993.

Weiss, Peter (1952–) Slovakian philosopher and politician. From 1978 he worked for a Communist Party research institute. In December 1989, after the collapse of communist rule, he was elected leader of the party's reformist wing, which subsequently organized itself as the Democratic Left Party (SDL').

Welfare Party [Refah Partisi] (RP) Turkish political party. The RP was founded in 1983 as the successor to the National Salvation Party (MSP), which had been disbanded after the 1980 military coup. It is the country's main Islamic fundamentalist party. It contested the October 1991 election in an alliance with the National Action Party (MHP), which gained 16.9% of the vote; the party gained 43/450 seats. The leader is Necmettin Erbakan, who had also been MSP leader since its foundation in 1972.

Welsh People and language of WALES, a constituent country of the United Kingdom.

Welsh Labour Party British political party, the Welsh branch of the LABOUR PARTY.

Welsh Office British government department. Based in Cardiff, the Welsh Office is responsible for planning, economic development, health, social services, housing, local government and other matters in Wales, functions that are carried out by separate departments in England. It is also responsible for promoting the Welsh language and culture. The Office is headed by the secretary of state for Wales, a government minister of Cabinet rank.

Welsh Party *See* PLAID CYMRU.

Wende, die ('the change' or 'the turning point') In Germany, a shorthand for the period which began with the collapse of the communist regime in East Germany in November 1989 and culminated in the country's reunification in October the following year.

Wends *See* SORBS.

West, the Shorthand for the member states of the North Atlantic Treaty Organization (NATO), the military alliance formed in 1949 as a counterweight to the Soviet

Union and its Eastern European allies. The term was commonly used during the Cold War, the political and military confrontation between NATO and the Warsaw Pact – the East – which lasted until the late 1980s.

West Germany Common name for the Federal Republic of Germany (FRG) until the reunification of Germany in October 1990.

West Midlands Standard region of the United Kingdom. Situated in central England and centred on Birmingham, the West Midlands comprises the counties of Hereford and Worcester, Shropshire, Staffordshire, Warwickshire and West Midlands. It has an area of 13,013 sq km and a population of 5,255,000. The economy is based on manufacturing (engineering, metalworking, motor vehicles) and agriculture. Other major cities apart from Birmingham are Coventry, Stoke-on-Trent and Wolverhampton. The region is considered a unit principally for statistical purposes and has no administrative or political functions.

Westendorp, Carlos (1937–) Spanish diplomat, civil servant and politician. During the 1960s and 70s he worked in the Spanish embassies in Brazil, the Netherlands and elsewhere and held several senior posts in the industry and foreign ministries. He was appointed a junior minister with responsibility for relations with the European Community (EC) in 1981, became Spain's ambassador to the EC in 1986, and was appointed secretary of state for European affairs (essentially his earlier government post) in March 1991.

Westerberg, Bengt (1943–) Swedish politician. He studied economics and then worked in Stockholm's local government for many years. He was elected leader of the People's Party (Fp, also known as the Liberal Party) in October 1983. He became a member of parliament the following year. He became deputy prime minister and minister of health and social affairs in the centre-right coalition which took office in October 1991.

Westerberg, Per (1951–) Swedish economist, accountant and politician. He worked as a controller for the Saab-Scania motor company from 1974–77 and part-time from 1979–90. Elected to parliament for the centre-right Moderate Coalition Party (MS) in 1979, he was appointed minister of industry and commerce in the centre-right coalition which took office in October 1991.

Western Bosnia *See* AUTONOMOUS PROVINCE OF ....

Western European countries Collective name for the European countries that have not been under communist rule. During the 'cold war' between the Warsaw Pact and the North Atlantic Treaty Organization (NATO) from the late 1940s until the late 1980s, they could be divided into NATO members and neutrals (e.g. Austria, Finland, Ireland, Sweden and Switzerland, which maintained a policy of non-alignment in defence and security matters). This distinction became redundant with the collapse of the communist regimes and the Warsaw Pact in 1989/90. Throughout the post-1945 period all Western European countries operated market-based economies (unlike the communist countries of Eastern Europe), but some did not have pluralist and democratic political systems. This distinction became redundant with the collapse of the dictatorships in Greece, Portugal and Spain in the mid 1970s.

Western European Union (WEU) Intergovernmental organization. The WEU was founded in 1955 by the Benelux countries, France, Italy, the United Kingdom and West Germany with wideranging ambitions of cooperation among its members. Economic, political and cultural aspects were soon effectively transferred to other Western European organizations (such as the Council of Europe and the European Community) and the WEU was reduced to a minor forum. The organization was reactivated in 1984 in response to a growing desire among Western European governments to cooperate more closely on defence policy and arms procurement. In recent years the WEU's role has been redefined as a 'bridge' between the European Union (EU) and the North Atlantic Treaty Organization (NATO) and an 'integral component' of the European integration process.

Aims and objectives. The meeting in Rome in October 1984 relaunching the WEU adopted a declaration that set out the objectives of strengthening the 'European pillar' of NATO and harmonizing members' views on defence issues, arms control and disarmament, East-West relations, and armaments production and procurement. The Maastricht Treaty establishing the European Union (EU), agreed in December 1991 and in force since November 1993, states that 'the objective is to build up the WEU as the defence component of the European Union' and 'to develop the WEU as a means to strengthen the European pillar of the Atlantic Alliance'.

Membership. The WEU has 15 members: Belgium, France, Germany, Greece, Italy, Luxemburg, Netherlands, Portugal, Spain and the United Kingdom are full members, Iceland, Norway and Turkey are associate members, and Denmark and Ireland are observer members.

Structure and activities. The WEU's governing body is the Council, composed of the foreign and defence ministers of the member states. It meets twice a year. The presidency of the Council is held by each member state for a one-year term. Decisions on substantive issues must be unanimous. The Permanent Council meets as required at ambassadorial level. The Council and Permanent Council are served by a secretariat. Three subsidiary agencies deal with arms-control and disarmament issues, security and defence issues, and cooperation in the field of armaments. Their functions are due to be taken over by the WEU Institute for Security Studies, founded in 1990. There is also a 115-member consultative Assembly, composed of parliamentarians from the member states. It usually meets twice a year and makes recommendations to the Council. The secretariat is based in Brussels (Belgium). The secretary-general is Wim van Eekelen, a former Dutch defence minister.

History. In the 1950s and 60s the WEU was mainly concerned with the question of West German rearmament (a controversial issue given Germany's role as the aggressor in the Second World War), and in the 1970s with political questions such as East-West relations and the implications of the restoration of democratic rule in Greece, Portugal and Spain. Efforts to reactivate the WEU were set in motion in June 1984 with a meeting of defence ministers – the first since 1973 – and formalized the following October. In the mid 1980s the main political focus was on strengthening the 'European pillar' of the North Atlantic Treaty Organization (NATO), while practical work was concerned with cooperation on arms manufacture (such as the development of a European fighter aircraft). Portugal and Spain joined the WEU in November 1988. The reduction in East-West tension, the collapse of communist rule in Eastern Europe and the US's decision to reduce its troop levels in Western Europe sparked a major debate within the WEU about the organization's future role. Broadly speaking, France, Germany and others favoured the WEU's eventual integration into the European Union (EU) as the operational arm of a future common defence policy, while the United Kingdom, the Netherlands and others favoured its strengthening as the European arm of NATO. The issue was partly resolved by a formulation agreed within the context of the Maastricht Treaty (agreed in December 1991) that the WEU would in due course become the 'defence component' of the EU. In recognition of the WEU's changing role, six new countries were admitted in November 1992 as full, associate or observer members, depending on their respective willingness to commit themselves to a common defence policy. At the same time it was decided to transfer the seats of the Council and secretariat from Paris and London to Brussels, headquarters of both the EU and NATO. In December 1992 the Independent European Programme Group (IEPG), an informal group aimed at practical cooperation in arms procurement to which all but two

WEU members belonged, decided to continue its activities within the WEU framework. In November 1993 it was agreed that EU member states would make troops available for future WEU peace-keeping operations. In May 1994 nine former communist states in Central and Eastern Europe signed cooperation agreements with the WEU and became 'associate partners'.

See also entries on specific institutions, organizations, agreements, terms etc.

Westh, Bjørn (1944–) Danish surveyor and politician. He worked as a land surveyor from 1969–81. Elected to parliament for the Social Democratic Party (SD) in 1977, he was agriculture minister in 1981–82. He returned to the same post in the centre-left coalition formed in January 1993, also taking responsibility for fisheries.

Westminster Shorthand for the British Parliament, composed of the HOUSE OF COMMONS and HOUSE OF LORDS. Both houses meet in the Palace of Westminster, situated in the City of Westminster, a borough of London. The name is also used to refer to the government, but in this sense the more common shorthand is Whitehall, taken from a nearby street and district with many government offices.

Westminster gerrymandering affair *See* HOMES-FOR-VOTES AFFAIR.

WEU *See* WESTERN EUROPEAN UNION.

WEU Assembly *See* ASSEMBLY OF THE WESTERN EUROPEAN UNION.

WEU Council *See* COUNCIL (Western European Union).

White Eagles [Beli Orlovi] Yugoslav, Bosnian and Croatian paramilitary group. Like similar Serb groups, the White Eagles advocate the creation of a 'Greater Serbia'. They have fought alongside local Serb forces in the Bosnian and Croatian civil wars. They have been linked to massacres of Muslims and Croats and are also said to be involved in organized crime in Serbia. The leader is Mirko Jović.

white paper In the European Union (EU), a document published by the European Commission setting out policy and legislative proposals on a particular issue. It is more specific than a consultative

'green paper'. The term 'white paper' or 'white book' is also used in many countries for a government document setting out legislative proposals for consideration by parliament.

Whitehall Shorthand for the British government and/or the civil service. Many government buildings are located in Whitehall, a street and district in London. *See also* WESTMINSTER.

Wibble, Anne (1943–) Swedish economist, academic and politician. She lectured at the Stockholm School of Economics from 1967–77 and then took up a senior post in the Stockholm city planning office. She began working full-time for the centrist People's Party (Fp) in 1980 and was elected to parliament in 1985. She was appointed finance minister in the centre-right coalition which took office in October 1991.

wide band (European Union) *See* EXCHANGE RATE MECHANISM.

widening (European Union) *See* BROADENING.

wielkie uderzenie ('big bang') *See* CONTROLLED SHOCK.

Wien *See* VIENNA.

Wiesenthal, Simon (1908–) Austrian architect and war-crimes investigator. He worked as an architect in Lvov (then in Poland, now in Ukraine) until 1941, when the city was occupied by German troops. A Jew, he was imprisoned in nazi labour and concentration camps for the next three years. Since the end of the Second World War he has been active in exposing nazi war criminals. From 1947–54 he headed the Linz-based Jewish Historical Documentation Centre and in 1961 he set up the Jewish Documentation Centre in Vienna. Over the years he and his associates have tracked down or identified over 1,000 war criminals. He has written several books on his work.

Wijers, Hans (1951–) Dutch economist and politician. A specialist in industrial policy, he worked for the social-affairs and economy ministries from 1982–84 and then as a management consultant. A member of the centre-left Democrats 66 (D'66), he was appointed minister of economic affairs in the left-right coalition formed in August 1994.

Willi, Andrea (1955–) Liechtenstein civil servant and politician. A graduate in politics and international law, she worked for a cultural foundation in Zürich (Switzerland) from 1982–87. She then joined the diplomatic service. In December 1993 she was appointed foreign minister and minister of culture, youth and sport. She is a member of the centre-right Fatherland Union (VU).

Windsor Royal dynasty of the United Kingdom. The name is taken from Windsor Castle, one of the royal residences. It was adopted in 1917, during the First World War, because of the German connotations of the existing name, Saxe-Coburg-Gotha.

wine lake (European Union) *See* FOOD MOUNTAINS.

wise people *See* GROUP OF ....

Wissmann, Matthias (1949–) German solicitor and politician. He was leader of the youth wing of the Christian Democratic Union (CDU) from 1973–83. Elected to parliament in 1983, he was briefly minister of scientific research and technology from January–May 1993 and was then appointed minister of transport.

województwo [pl. województwa] Polish administrative division, usually translated as 'province' or 'voivodship'. Each of the 49 *województwa* is administered by a governor [wojewod] appointed by the government and a council [rada] elected for a four-year term by the members of the local councils. The cities, towns and communes are the main units of local government and have considerable autonomy in their spheres of competence. A reorganization of the *województwo* structure into larger regions is under consideration.

Wojtyła, Karol *See* JOHN PAUL II.

Wolf, Markus or **Mischa** (1923–) German civil servant. He left Germany with his parents, both prominent communists, when the nazis came to power in 1933. The family settled in the Soviet Union the following year and he later studied at the Comintern training school in Moscow. At the end of the Second World War (1945) he returned to Soviet-occupied East Germany and held several posts in the administration. From 1953–87 he was in charge of the East German external intelligence service, which built up an extensive and effective spy network in West Germany and other western countries. He left for the Soviet Union shortly before German reunification in 1990, but returned the following year and was immediately arrested. In December 1993 he was sentenced to six years' imprisonment on several counts of treason and corruption.

Wolffensperger, Gerrit Jan (1944–) Dutch lawyer, academic and politician. He worked as a photographer and studied law from 1962–67 and lectured in private law at the University of Amsterdam from 1969–73. He wrote on legal issues for *De Volkskrant*, a leading daily newspaper, in the 1970s. A member of the centre-left Democrats 66 (D'66), he became an executive member of Amsterdam city council in 1978 and was elected to parliament in 1986. He was elected the party's parliamentary leader in August 1994.

Women's Alliance [Samtök um Kvennalista] (K) Icelandic political party. Founded in 1983, the Women's Alliance became the first women's party in the world to gain representation in a national parliament in the election of that year. Its main aim is to promote the interests of women and children; it also advocates decentralization of power. At the April 1991 election it gained 8.3% of the vote and 5/63 seats. The leadership is collective.

Workers' Commissions *See* TRADE UNION CONFEDERATION OF WORKERS' COMMISSIONS.

Workers' Power *See* GENERAL CONFEDERATION OF LABOUR – WORKERS' POWER.

Wörner, Manfred (1934–94) German lawyer and politician. Elected to parliament for the Christian Democratic Union (CDU) in 1965, he was the party's defence spokesman for most of the 1970s and was appointed defence minister when the CDU returned to power in 1982. He became secretary-general of the North Atlantic Treaty Organization (NATO) in July 1988. He was appointed for a second four-year term in 1992. He died ᴏᶠ cancer in August 1994.

WTO *See* WARSAW TREATY ORGANIZATION.

Xhulali, Safet *See* ZHULALI, ...

Xhuta, Bekir *See* ZHUTA, ...

Xunta ('Council') Galician name for the government of Galicia, an autonomous community or region of Spain. The term is also commonly used by Spanish speakers in preference to the Spanish equivalent, Junta.

yellow or **orange** In some countries, the colour associated with liberal parties. Examples are the Free Democratic Party (FDP) in Germany and the Liberal Democrats in Britain.

Yennimatas, Yiorgos *See* GENNIMATAS, GIORGOS.

Yiannopoulos, Evangelos *See* GIANNOPOULOS, ...

Yılmaz, Mesut (1947–) Turkish economist, businessman and politician. He set up and directed an export company and then a haulage firm before entering politics. Elected to parliament for the centre-right Motherland Party (ANAP) in 1983, he was minister of culture and tourism from 1986–87 and foreign minister from 1987–90. He was elected leader of ANAP in June 1991 and was then appointed prime minister, a post he held until the party's defeat in the election the following October.

Yordanov, Aleksandŭr (1952–) Bulgarian literary critic and politician. He was a research associate at the Institute of Literature at the Bulgarian Academy of Sciences from 1985 until his election to the Narodno Sobranie (= parliament) for the centre-right Radical Democratic Party (RDP) in 1991. He was elected president of the Sobranie in November 1992 and also leader of the RDP in June 1993.

Yorkshire and Humberside Standard region of the United Kingdom. Situated in eastern England, Yorkshire and Humberside comprises the counties of Humberside, North Yorkshire, South Yorkshire and West Yorkshire. It has an area of 15,420 sq km and a population of 4,954,000. The main cities are Leeds, Sheffield, Bradford, Hull and York. The economy is based on manufacturing (engineering, metalworking, chemicals, textiles), agriculture, tourism and fishing. The region has suffered considerable problems because of the decline of the traditional heavy and textile industries and coal mining, and structural unemployment is high. The region is considered a unit primarily for statistical purposes and has no administrative or political functions. Yorkshire, which before the administrative reorganization of 1974 also included the northern part of Humberside, has a strong regional identity.

Young Democrats (Hungary) *See* ALLIANCE OF ....

YU Abbreviation for Yugoslavia, used for international vehicle registrations, postal addresses etc.

YUD Abbreviation for the DINAR, the Yugoslav currency, used in banking etc.

Yugoslav Peace Conference *See* INTERNATIONAL CONFERENCE ON FORMER YUGOSLAVIA.

Yugoslav People's Army [Jugoslovenska Narodna Armija] (JNA) Alternative name for the Yugoslav National Army, the armed forces of the Yugoslav federation until its disintegration in 1991/92 and now the armed forces of rump Yugoslavia. The Serbocroat *narodna* can be translated as both 'people's' and 'national', and during communist rule the JNA was commonly referred to in English as the Yugoslav People's Army.

Yugoslav successor states Collective name for the five countries established after the disintegration of the Yugoslav federation in 1991/92. They are Bosnia-Herzegovina, Croatia, Macedonia, Slovenia and rump Yugoslavia (composed of the republics of Serbia and Montenegro). The latter considers itself the legal and sole successor to the old federation, but this claim has not been internationally recognized.

Yugoslav War Crimes Commission Shorthand for the UNITED NATIONS WAR CRIMES COMMISSION FOR FORMER YUGOSLAVIA.

Yugoslav War Crimes Tribunal Shorthand for the INTERNATIONAL WAR CRIMES TRIBUNAL FOR FORMER YUGOSLAVIA.

Yugoslavia [Jugoslavija] Country in south-eastern Europe, comprising Serbia and Montenegro, two republics of the former Yugoslav federation (which also included Bosnia-Herzegovina, Croatia, Macedonia and Slovenia).

Note: Some of the information below does not reflect the dislocation and disruption caused by the disintegration of the old Yugoslav federation and the economic sanctions imposed by the United Nations on the new federation because of its involvement in the Bosnian and Croatian civil wars.

Official data. Name: Federal Republic of Yugoslavia [Federativna Republika Jugoslavija]; capital: Belgrade [Beograd]; form of government: federal republic; head of state: president; head of government: prime minister; flag: three horizontal stripes, blue, white and red; national holiday: 29 November (Republic Day); language: Serb; religion: none; currency: dinar (Din) (pl. -i) = 100 para; abbreviations: FRJ and YU.

Geography. Yugoslavia has an area of 102,173 sq km. Virtually land-locked, it is bordered by the Adriatic Sea, Croatia and Bosnia-Herzegovina in the west, Hungary and Romania in the north, Bulgaria in the east, and Macedonia and Albania in the south. The northern third of the country forms part of the fertile Pannonian Basin drained by the Danube [Dunav], Tisa and Sava rivers. Most of the centre and south consists of hills and mountains, including the Dinaric Alps in the west and spurs of the Carpathian and Balkan chains in the east. The other main river is the Morava. Some 35% of the land is arable, another 20% is covered by pastures and 25% is forested. The climate is largely humid continental, with hot summers and cold winters; temperatures are higher in the plains, lower in the mountains; the coastal strip has a mediterranean climate, with hot summers and mild winters; rainfall is heavy in the west, moderate in the east.

Demography. Yugoslavia has a population of 10,561,000. Population density is 101 per sq km (land area). Around three-fifths of the people live in urban areas, and a sixth in Belgrade and its suburbs (metropolitan population 1.7 million). Other major cities are Novi Sad, Niš, Priština, Subotica and Podgorića (formerly Titograd). In ethnic terms 62.3% of the people are Serbs, 16.6% Albanians, 5.0% Montenegrins, 3.3% Hungarians, 3.3% Yugoslavs (self-description), 3.1% Slav Muslims (considered an ethnic group in former Yugoslavia), 1.3% Gipsies and 1.1% Croats; there are also smaller groups of Slovaks, Romanians, Bulgarians,

Vlachs and Ruthenians. Gipsies are considerably underrepresented in official figures; they are thought to number around 375,000 (3.7% of the total population). Most Albanians live in the Kosovo region in the southwest, most Hungarians in Vojvodina in the north, and most Montenegrins in Montenegro. Yugoslavia has taken in around 450,000 refugees from the Bosnian and Croatian civil wars. There are large ethnic Serb communities in those countries, numbering 1.37 million in the former and 582,000 in the latter (1991 census). The main languages are Serb or Serbocroat (written in the cyrillic script), Albanian and Hungarian. In religious terms most Serbs and Montenegrins are nominally Serbian and Montenegrin Orthodox Christians respectively, most Albanians are nominally Muslims or Roman Catholics, and most Hungarians are nominally Roman Catholics or Protestants.

Sociography. Former Yugoslavia scored 0.857 on the United Nations human development index (HDI) in 1990, ranking 37th in the world and 23rd among 27 European countries. There are 20 doctors and 61 hospital beds for every 10,000 people. Education is compulsory between the ages of seven and 15. There is one teacher for every 18 students. Enrolment is 33% at the secondary level and 13% at the tertiary level. The literacy rate is 89%. GNP per head (unadjusted for purchasing power) was around US$ 2,200 in 1990 and around US$ 1,000 in 1992.

Infrastructure and communications. Yugoslavia's transport and communications network is relatively developed but in need of repair, modernization and extension; it is limited in many rural areas in the south. There are 26,950 km of paved roads and 1.41 million passenger cars (136 per 1,000 people), 4,030 km of railways and around 1,500 km of navigable waterways. The main ports are Bar and (inland) Belgrade. The main airport is at Belgrade, and there are three other airports with scheduled services. There are 12 daily newspapers, with a combined circulation of 1.06 million (98 per 1,000 people). There are 1.91 million radio

receivers, 1.70 million television sets and 1.84 million telephones in use (respectively 184, 165 and 178 per 1,000 people).

Economic structure. The Yugoslav economy is based on manufacturing, agriculture and mining. Although essentially developed and diversified, it is in need of major investment and restructuring. The Kosovo region is considerably less developed and diversified than the rest of the country. The transition from a command to a market-based economy initiated in the early 1990s, the disruption of traditional economic links following the disintegration of the Yugoslav federation in 1991/92 and above all the United Nations sanctions imposed in 1992 have brought the economy to near-collapse. Only the agricultural sector remains relatively intact. GDP contracted by around half between 1990–93; inflation averaged nearly 300% in 1990–91 and then shot up to hyperinflationary levels, exceeding 2,000% per month by the end of 1993; and unemployment rose to around 50% (conservative unofficial estimate); a currency reform and accompanying financial measures ended hyperinflation in 1994. There is a substantial unofficial economy.

Services contribute 40% of GDP, industry contributes 48% (manufacturing around 40%, mining 3%), and agriculture and forestry 12%. Some 39% of the labour force is employed in manufacturing, 13% in trade, 8% in construction and 5% in farming and forestry. The main crops grown are cereals (maize, wheat), oilseeds, sugarbeets, animal fodder and tobacco; other important agricultural activities are horticulture (fruit and vegetables, esp. plums), livestock raising (pigs, cattle, sheep) and dairy farming. Forestry is of regional importance. The main mineral resources are coal, bauxite, lead, copper, zinc and limestone. The main industries are engineering (esp. industrial machinery, cars), food processing and textiles; other important branches are metalworking (incl. iron and steel), wood processing, electrical goods, chemicals, petrochemicals and armaments. The main energy sources are fossil fuels and hydroelectric power; 24% of export earnings are required to cover net fuel imports. The main exports are textiles and clothing (22% of the total, incl. clothing 14%, footwear), industrial machinery (13%), chemicals (9%), nonferrous metals (9%), transport equipment (7%), iron and steel (5%), fruit and vegetables; basic manufactures account for 27% of the total, miscellaneous manufactures for 23%, machinery and transport equipment for 20%. The main imports are machinery and transport equipment, fuels, basic manufactures and chemicals. The main trading partners are: exports: Germany (30%), Soviet Union / Russia, Ukraine and other members of the Commonwealth of Independent States (CIS) (18%), Italy (14%), Switzerland (8%), United States, Romania; imports: Germany (20%), Soviet Union / Russia, Ukraine and other CIS members (13%), Italy (11%), Libya (5%), United States, Austria, France; around two-fifths of all trade is with European Union (EU) countries. (Foreign-trade figures refer to 1991, i.e. before the imposition of sanctions.)

The National Bank of Yugoslavia [Narodna Banka Jugoslavije] is the central bank. There are several employers' and business associations, including the Yugoslav Chamber of Commerce and Industry (PKJ); the main labour organizations are the Autonomous Trade Union Federation of Yugoslavia (SSSJ) and Independence (Nezavisnost).

Political structure. Under the constitution adopted in April 1992 Yugoslavia is a federal republic comprising two republics [republika, pl. republike], Montenegro [Crna Gora] and Serbia [Srbija]. The head of state is the president, who is elected for a four-year term by a joint session of the legislature. S/he appoints the prime minister and has several other powers. Executive power is vested in the prime minister and the council of ministers. The president and prime minister should be from different republics. Legislative power is vested in the bicameral Federal Assembly [Savezna Skupština], composed of the Chamber of Citizens [Veće Gradjana] of 138 members (108 from Serbia, 30 from Montenegro) elected for a four-year

term by a system of proportional representation, and the Chamber of Republics [Republičko Veće] of 40 members (20 from each republic) indirectly elected for a four-year term by the two republican assemblies. The two houses have equal powers. All citizens over the age of 18 are entitled to vote. Judicial power is ultimately vested in the 11-member Federal Court [Savezni Sud] elected for a nine-year term by the legislature; the seven-member Federal Constitutional Court [Savezni Ustavni Sud], also elected for a nine-year term, adjudicates on constitutional matters. The two republics have their own constitutions, legislatures and governments, and have sovereignty over all issues not specified in the federal constitution. The provinces of Kosovo-Metohija and Vojvodina within Serbia have some local autonomy. Administratively both republics are divided into districts [opština, pl. opštine].

The main political parties are, in Serbia, the Socialist Party of Serbia (SPS), Serbian Renewal Movement (SPO), Democratic Party (DS), Democratic Party of Serbia (DSS), Democratic Movement of Serbia (DEPOS), Democratic Union of Vojvodina Hungarians (DZVM or VMDK) and Democratic League of Kosovo (DSK or LDK); in Montenegro, the Democratic Socialist Party of Montenegro (DPSCG or DPS), Socialist Party of Montenegro (SPCG or SP), National Party of Montenegro (NSCG or NS), Liberal Alliance of Montenegro (LSCG or LS) and Serbian Radical Party (SRS). At the federal election in December 1992 the SPS gained 47/138 seats, the SRS 34 seats, DEPOS (then an alliance including the SPO) 20 seats, the DPS 17 seats, the DS and SP five seats each, the NS four seats, and the VMDK three seats; the LDK boycotted the poll. The government is formed by a left-wing coalition of the SPS and DPS, with Radoje Kontić as prime minister. Other senior ministers are Jovan Zebić, Željko Simić, Nikola Šainović and Uroš Klikovac (deputy prime ministers), Vladislav Jovanović (foreign affairs), Djordje Blagojević (internal affairs), Pavle Bulatović (defence), Vuk Ognjanović (finance), Tomislav Simović (economy) and Zoran Stojanović (justice). The head of state is President Zoran Lilić, who was elected in June 1993. The president of Serbia is Slobodan Milošević, the president of Montenegro is Momir Bulatović.

Security and international affiliations. The Yugoslav armed forces number 136,500 (army 100,000, navy 7,500, airforce 29,000). Defence spending as a proportion of GDP is among the highest in Europe.

Yugoslavia is a member of the Central European Initiative (CEI) and Conference on Security and Cooperation in Europe (CSCE), but is suspended from both organizations; it is also a member of the Non-Aligned Movement (NAM). The United Nations has not recognized Yugoslavia's claim to membership as the successor state to the old Yugoslav federation.

History. Settled by Illyrians, the area of modern Yugoslavia south of the Danube river was conquered by the Romans in 29 BC. It was allocated to the Eastern Roman Empire, later Byzantium, in 395 AD. During the Europe-wide migrations from the late 4th century onwards it was invaded by Goths, Huns and Avars. In the 7th century the Slavic Serbs, migrating from the northeast, settled in the wider region. They converted to Orthodox Christianity in the late 9th century (while the related Croats to the west converted to Roman Catholicism). At this time control of the region was disputed between the Byzantine Empire and Bulgaria. The first united Serb state was established by Prince Stefan Vojislav of Zeta in 1036, but it collapsed after the death of his successor in 1101. In 1169 Stefan Nemanja reasserted Serbia's independence from Byzantium. The independent Serb Orthodox Church was established in 1219. Under the Nemanja dynasty Serbia became a major regional power. King Stefan Dušan (1331–55) ruled over historical Macedonia (i.e. including northern Greece), central Greece and Albania, but the empire disintegrated after his death. The Ottoman Turks first attacked Serbia in 1386 and inflicted a heavy defeat at the Battle of Kosovo Polje in 1389, at which the king and most of the nobles were killed. Serbia became an Ottoman vassal state in 1396 and was incorporated into the Empire in 1459. Many Serbs migrated north- and westwards to escape Turkish domination and settled in (largely depopulated) districts of the Banat (modern Vojvodina), Slavonia and Croatia, which were then part of Hungary. These came under Ottoman rule themselves in 1526. The geographically relatively isolated region of Montenegro was able to retain a large measure of independence throughout the Turkish period. There were major uprisings against Ottoman rule in the 1680s, 1780s, 1804–13 and 1815–17. The Austrian Habsburgs gained control of the Banat and the neighbouring regions in 1699 and held northern Serbia (including Belgrade) from 1718–39.

Serbia secured a degree of autonomy in 1829 and regained its independence in 1878, becoming a kingdom in 1882. The new state initially comprised only northern Serbia proper, but its territory was greatly enlarged after the Balkan Wars of 1912–13 and 1913 to include all of Serbia proper and Macedonia. The policy of seeking to bring the ethnic Serbs of Vojvodina, Bosnia-Herzegovina and Croatia into the Serbian state led to friction with Austria-Hungary. This was one of the causes of the First World War (1914–18). Serbia and Montenegro were invaded by the Austrian, German and Bulgarian armies in 1915. Around 350,000 Serbian soldiers were killed in the fighting (more than a third of the total mobilized forces, in relative terms the highest losses for any belligerent). In 1918 Serbia became the core of the new Kingdom of Serbs, Croats and Slovenes, which also included Montenegro. The new state was destabilized from the outset by dissatisfaction with the centralized administration and rivalry between Serbs and Croats in particular. In 1929 King Alexander II imposed a personal dictatorship. The name Yugoslavia – meaning 'country of the South Slavs' – was adopted at this time to symbolize the common heritage of the main ethnic groups. During the Second World War (1939–45) the German and Italian armies overran Yugoslavia in 1941. German-backed regimes were set up in Serbia and Montenegro, while Macedonia, Kosovo and parts of Vojvodina were allocated to Bulgaria, Albania and Hungary respectively. Thousands of people died in armed resistance to the occupying forces and in fighting between the two main resistance movements, the monarchist Chetniks and the communist-dominated Partisans. The latter were victorious in the civil war. (Around 1.5 million people, most of them civilians, were killed throughout Yugoslavia in the four war years.)

On liberation in 1945 the Communists, led by Josip Broz Tito, took power throughout Yugoslavia. The monarchy was abolished, Serbia and Montenegro became constituent republics of the new federation, Kosovo and Vojvodina became provinces within Serbia, and Macedonia became a separate republic. The regime suppressed political opposition and implemented orthodox communist economic policies. After breaking with the Soviet Union in 1948, it pursued more pragmatic and liberal policies. The republics and the provinces were given greater autonomy under a new federal constitution adopted in 1974. As Communist authority crumbled in the late 1980s, the Serbian government in particular strongly opposed demands from the other republics for a looser federation. The autonomous powers of Serbia's two provinces, Kosovo (which has a large Albanian majority) and Vojvodina (which has a substantial Hungarian minority), were effectively abolished under a new constitution adopted in September 1990. In December the successors to the League of Communists, the Socialist Party of Serbia (SPS) and Democratic Socialist Party of Montenegro (DPSCG), won the multiparty elections in the two republics. As the four other republics declared their independence in 1991/92, Serbia gave strong political and military support to Serb rebels in Croatia and then Bosnia-Herzegovina. In April 1992 Serbia and Montenegro adopted a new federal constitution. Slobodan Milošević, the president

of Serbia and SPS leader, became the dominant political leader in rump Yugoslavia. In May the United Nations (UN) imposed wide-ranging economic and diplomatic sanctions on Serbia and Montenegro for their involvement in the Bosnian and Croatian civil wars. Over the following months Yugoslavia was suspended from all major intergovernmental organizations (including the UN and the Conference on Security and Cooperation in Europe, CSCE). The combined effect of the sanctions, high military spending and the structural problems associated with the old command economy brought about the collapse of the country's economic and financial system. Loss of confidence in the currency led to hyperinflation and more than half the labour force became unemployed. Despite these problems, the SPS and DPSCG retained power in the federal election in December 1992 and the SPS retained control in Serbia after an early election in December 1993. Anti-inflation measures and government spending cuts introduced at the start of 1994 steadied the economy.

See also FORMER YUGOSLAVIA *and entries on specific institutions, organizations, parties, people, terms etc.*

Yugoslavs Ethnic group in the former Yugoslav federation and the successor states. From the 1950s the self-description 'Yugoslav' became increasingly popular among people born in mixed marriages, but also among those who did not identify with their parents' nationality, wanted to stress their commitment to a common Yugoslav identity or resented ethnically or nationally based classifications. The number of people defining themselves as Yugoslav fluctuated considerably after the category was first included in the 1961 census: it reached a peak of 5.4% of the total population in 1981 but, reflecting the rise of nationalist sentiment, fell to 3.0% in 1991. At this time 5.5% of the people of Bosnia-Herzegovina described themselves as Yugoslavs, 3.3% in Serbia and Montenegro (present-day Yugoslavia) and 2.2% in Croatia.

Z Abbreviation for the ZŁOTY, the Polish currency.

Zagreb Shorthand for the Croatian government. Zagreb is the capital of Croatia.

Zalm, Gerrit (1952–) Dutch economist, civil servant and politician. He held several senior posts in the ministries of finance and economic affairs from 1977. He joined the Central Planning Office (CPB), a government advisory body, in 1988 and became its director the following year. He was a member of the Labour Party (PvdA) in the 1970s but later joined the right-wing People's Party for Freedom and Democracy (VVD). He was appointed minister of finance in the left-right coalition formed in August 1994.

zamatová revolúcia and **zamatová rodvod** *See* VELVET REVOLUTION *and* VELVET DIVORCE.

Zapadna Bosna *See* AUTONOMOUS PROVINCE OF WESTERN BOSNIA.

Zastupnički Dom *See* HOUSE OF REPRESENTATIVES (Croatia).

Zauberformel *See* MAGIC FORMULA.

Zbor Shorthand for the Državni Zbor ('NATIONAL ASSEMBLY'), the lower house of the Slovenian parliament.

ZChN *See* CHRISTIAN NATIONAL UNION.

Zebić, Jovan (1939–) Yugoslav economist, civil servant and politician. He has worked for the agriculture ministry and the Belgrade local government and has been a deputy governor of the National Bank of Serbia. He was a deputy prime minister and finance minister of Serbia from 1991–93 and became a deputy prime minister at federal level in March 1993. He is a member of the Socialist Party of Serbia (SPS), the successor to the League of Communists.

zeleni bereti ('green berets') Informal name for soldiers of the Bosnian army.

Żelichowski, Stanisław (1944–) Polish forestry manager and politician. He has been active in local government for the United Peasant Party (ZSL), now the Polish Peasant Party (PSL), since the 1960s. He was elected to parliament in 1989. He was appointed minister for environmental protection, natural resources and forestry in the left-wing coalition formed in October 1993.

Zeman, Miloš (1944–) Czech economist and politician. Prevented from completing his studies because of his political views, he joined the Communist Party during the reformist Prague Spring of 1968. He was expelled two years later for criticizing the return to orthodoxy. During the 1970s and 80s he worked for several economic research institutes, losing his job twice for political reasons. He was a prominent member of the anti-communist Civic Forum (OF) in 1989 and was elected to parliament after the collapse of communist rule in 1990. He joined the Czechoslovak, now Czech, Social Democratic Party (ČSSD) in 1992 and was elected party leader in February 1993.

Zhelev, Zhelyu (1935–) Bulgarian philosopher, sociologist and politician. Having submitted a doctoral dissertation considered to be anti-communist (it disputed Lenin's theory of matter), he was expelled from the Communist Party in 1965. He was again allowed to work as a sociologist in 1972. In 1982 the authorities banned his book on the nature of totalitarianism. By now a prominent dissident, he became leader of the opposition Union of Democratic Forces (SDS) alliance in 1989. In August 1990 parliament elected him president of the republic. In January 1992 he was reelected for a five-year term in Bulgaria's first direct presidential election.

Zhivkov, Todor (1911–) Bulgarian politician. Trained as a printworker, he joined the Bulgarian Communist Party (BKP) in 1928. In 1948, four years after the party took power, he was elected to the central committee. He became party leader in 1954 and was the country's undisputed leader for the next 35 years, also holding the post of prime minister from 1962 and that of head of state from 1971. He was removed from office by reform-minded communists in October 1989. In February 1991 he was charged – the first of Eastern Europe's former communist rulers to be put on trial – with embezzlement of public funds and abuse of power. He was found guilty in September 1992 and sentenced to seven years' imprisonment. In the meantime he had also been charged with sponsoring terrorism, inciting ethnic hatred (against the Turkish community) and other crimes. In January 1994 he lost his appeal to the Supreme Court.

Zhulali, Safet (1944–) Albanian teacher and politician. He taught mathematics until he entered politics. Elected to parliament for the Democratic Party (PDSh) in March 1992, when the former communists were defeated, he was appointed defence minister the following month.

Zhuta, Bekir (1935–) Macedonian economist and politician. Between 1967 and 1986 he was a member of parliament for the League of Communists (SKM), a junior government minister and a judge on the constitutional court in Macedonia, which was then still part of the Yugoslav federation. From 1986–92 he was deputy governor of the National Bank of Macedonia. An ethnic Albanian, he joined the Party for Democratic Prosperity - National Democratic Party (PPD-PND) in 1990 and was appointed a deputy prime minister in March 1991.

Zieleniec, Josef (1946–) Czech economist and politician. He has worked as a researcher and lecturer at the Research Institute of Machine Technology and Economics (1973–86) and the Institute of Economics at the Czechoslovak Academy of Sciences (1986–90). He joined the right-wing Civic Democratic Party (ODS) in 1991. He was appointed minister of foreign relations in the Czech government in July 1992, and on the dissolution of the Czechoslovak federation at the end of the year he became foreign minister of the independent Czech Republic.

Zł Abbreviation for the ZŁOTY, the Polish currency.

ZL *See* ASSOCIATED LIST OF SOCIAL DEMOCRATS.

złoty (pl. -ch) Currency of Poland. Common abbreviations are Z, Zł and PLZ (the international standard in banking etc). It is divided into 100 groszy. The simple plural form 'złoty' and the anglicized 'zlotys' are also used.

ZLSD *See* ASSOCIATED LIST OF SOCIAL DEMOCRATS.

ZS (Czech Republic) *See* AGRARIAN PARTY.

ZS *See* GREENS OF SLOVENIA.

ZSAO *See* FEDERATION OF SWISS EMPLOYERS' ORGANIZATIONS.

Zsidók (sing. Zsidó/nő) Hungarian name for JEWS.

ZSSS *See* CONFEDERATION OF FREE TRADE UNIONS OF SLOVENIA.

Zubak, Kresimir (1947–) Bosnian lawyer and politician. He was elected to parliament for the Croatian Democratic Union (HDZ-BiH) in 1990. In July 1992 he joined the breakaway Croat assembly which proclaimed the Croatian Community (later Republic) of Herzeg-Bosnia. He fought in the civil war and was wounded. He was appointed Herzeg-Bosnia's justice minister in 1993. In February 1994 he was appointed head of a new 'presidential council' and thus effectively became the state's leader (replacing Mate Boban). In May 1994 he was elected president of the new Muslim-Croat Federation.

županija (pl. županije) Croatian administrative division, usually translated as 'county' or 'province'. The 21 *županije* were constituted in December 1992 as an intermediate tier of local government. Each has a council elected for a four-year term and a governor [župan]. They have some powers and a range of responsibilities, and also serve as regional arms of the central government.

Žuta, Bekir *See* ZHUTA, ….

Zvanītājs, Jānis (1957–) Latvian mechanical engineer, academic and politician. He became director of the Manufacturing and Business Institute of Rīga's Technical University in 1989. In September 1994 he was appointed economy minister in the centre-right Latvian Way (LC) government. He does not belong to a political party.

Zwickel, Klaus (1939–) German tradeunion official. A member of the Metalworkers' Union (IG Metall) since 1954, he became its executive secretary in 1986 and deputy leader in 1989. He took over the union leadership on his predecessor's resignation in May 1993 and was confirmed in the post the following October.